Twentieth-Century Literary Criticism

Topics Volume

Guide to Gale Literary Criticism Series

For criticism on	Consult these Gale series
Authors now living or who died after December 31, 1959	*CONTEMPORARY LITERARY CRITICISM (CLC)*
Authors who died between 1900 and 1959	*TWENTIETH-CENTURY LITERARY CRITICISM (TCLC)*
Authors who died between 1800 and 1899	*NINETEENTH-CENTURY LITERATURE CRITICISM (NCLC)*
Authors who died between 1400 and 1799	*LITERATURE CRITICISM FROM 1400 TO 1800 (LC)* *SHAKESPEAREAN CRITICISM (SC)*
Authors who died before 1400	*CLASSICAL AND MEDIEVAL LITERATURE CRITICISM (CMLC)*
Black writers of the past two hundred years	*BLACK LITERATURE CRITICISM (BLC)*
Authors of books for children and young adults	*CHILDREN'S LITERATURE REVIEW (CLR)*
Dramatists	*DRAMA CRITICISM (DC)*
Hispanic writers of the late nineteenth and twentieth centuries	*HISPANIC LITERATURE CRITICISM (HLC)*
Native North American writers and orators of the eighteenth, nineteenth, and twentieth centuries	*NATIVE NORTH AMERICAN LITERATURE (NNAL)*
Poets	*POETRY CRITICISM (PC)*
Short story writers	*SHORT STORY CRITICISM (SSC)*
Major authors from the Renaissance to the present	*WORLD LITERATURE CRITICISM, 1500 TO THE PRESENT (WLC)*

ISSN 0276-8178

Volume 58

Twentieth-Century Literary Criticism

Topics Volume

**Excerpts from Criticism of Various Topics
in Twentieth-Century Literature, including Literary
and Critical Movements, Prominent Themes and
Genres, Anniversary Celebrations, and Surveys
of National Literatures**

Jennifer Gariepy
Editor

**Pamela Willwerth Aue
Christine M. Bichler
Joann Cerrito
Laurie Di Mauro
Nancy Dziedzic
David M. Galens
Thomas Ligotti
Lynn M. Spampinato
Brandon Trenz**
Associate Editors

 *Gale Research Inc.*

An International Thomson Publishing Company

 I T P

NEW YORK • LONDON • BONN • BOSTON • DETROIT • MADRID
MELBOURNE • MEXICO CITY • PARIS • SINGAPORE • TOKYO
TORONTO • WASHINGTON • ALBANY NY • BELMONT CA • CINCINNATI OH

STAFF

Jennifer Gariepy, *Editor*

Pamela Willwerth Aue, Christine M. Bichler, Joann Cerrito, Laurie Di Mauro, Nancy Dziedzic, David M. Galens, Thomas Ligotti, Lynn M. Spampinato, Brandon Trenz, *Associate Editors*

Marlene H. Lasky, *Permissions Manager*
Margaret A. Chamberlain, Linda M. Pugliese, *Permissions Specialists*
Susan Brohman, Diane Cooper, Maria Franklin, Arlene Johnson, Josephine M. Keene,
Michele Lonoconus, Maureen Puhl, Shalice Shah, Kimberly F. Smilay, Barbara A. Wallace, *Permissions Associates*
Edna Hedblad, Tyra Y. Phillips, *Permissions Assistants*

Victoria B. Cariappa, *Research Manager*
Eva M. Felts, Mary Beth McElmeel, Donna Melnychenko, Tamara C. Nott, Tracie A. Richardson,
Norma Sawaya, *Research Associates*
Alicia Noel Biggers, Melissa Brown, Maria E. Bryson, Julie C. Daniel, Shirley Gates, Michele McRobert,
Amy Beth Wieczorek, *Research Assistants*

Mary Beth Trimper, *Production Director*
Mary Kelley, *Production Associate*

Barbara J. Yarrow, *Graphic Services Supervisor*
Sherrell Hobbs, *Macintosh Artist*
Willie F. Mathis, *Camera Operator*
Pamela A. Hayes, *Photography Coordinator*

Library of Congress Catalog Card Number 76-46132
ISBN 0-8103-2440-7
ISSN 0276-8178

Printed in the United States of America

10 9 8 7 6 5 4 3 2 1

I(T)P™ Gale Research Inc., an International Thomson Publishing Company.
ITP logo is a trademark under license.

Contents

Preface vii
Acknowledgments xi

Preface

Since its inception more than fifteen years ago, *Twentieth-Century Literary Criticism* has been purchased and used by nearly 10,000 school, public, and college or university libraries. *TCLC* has covered more than 500 authors, representing 58 nationalities, and over 25,000 titles. No other reference source has surveyed the critical response to twentieth-century authors and literature as thoroughly as *TCLC*. In the words of one reviewer, "there is nothing comparable available." *TCLC* "is a gold mine of information—dates, pseudonyms, biographical information, and criticism from books and periodicals—which many libraries would have difficulty assembling on their own."

Scope of the Series

TCLC is designed to serve as an introduction to authors who died between 1900 and 1960 and to the most significant interpretations of these author's works. The great poets, novelists, short story writers, playwrights, and philosophers of this period are frequently studied in high school and college literature courses. In organizing and excerpting the vast amount of critical material written on these authors, *TCLC* helps students develop valuable insight into literary history, promotes a better understanding of the texts, and sparks ideas for papers and assignments. Each entry in *TCLC* presents a comprehensive survey of an author's career or an individual work of literature and provides the user with a multiplicity of interpretations and assessments. Such variety allows students to pursue their own interests; furthermore, it fosters an awareness that literature is dynamic and responsive to many different opinions.

Every fourth volume of *TCLC* is devoted to literary topics that cannot be covered under the author approach used in the rest of the series. Such topics include literary movements, prominent themes in twentieth-century literature, literary reaction to political and historical events, significant eras in literary history, prominent literary anniversaries, and the literatures of cultures that are often overlooked by English-speaking readers.

TCLC is designed as a companion series to Gale's *Contemporary Literary Criticism,* which reprints commentary on authors now living or who have died since 1960. Because of the different periods under consideration, there is no duplication of material between *CLC* and *TCLC*. For additional information about *CLC* and Gale's other criticism titles, users should consult the Guide to Gale Literary Criticism Series preceding the title page in this volume.

Coverage

Each volume of *TCLC* is carefully compiled to present:

- criticism of authors, or literary topics, representing a variety of genres and nationalities

- both major and lesser-known writers and literary works of the period

- 8-15 authors or 4-6 topics per volume

- individual entries that survey critical response to each author's work or each topic in literary history, including early criticism to reflect initial reactions; later criticism to represent any rise or decline in reputation; and current retrospective analyses.

Organization of This Book

An author entry consists of the following elements: author heading, biographical and critical introduction, list of principal works, excerpts of criticism (each preceded by an annotation and followed by a bibliographic citation), and a bibliography of further reading.

- The **Author Heading** consists of the name under which the author most commonly wrote, followed by birth and death dates. If an author wrote consistently under a pseudonym, the pseudonym will be listed in the author heading and the real name given in parentheses on the first line of the biographical and critical introduction. Also located at the beginning of the introduction to the author entry are any name variations under which an author wrote, including transliterated forms for authors whose languages use nonroman alphabets.

- The **Biographical and Critical Introduction** outlines the author's life and career, as well as the critical issues surrounding his or her work. References to past volumes of *TCLC* are provided at the beginning of the introduction. Additional sources of information in other biographical and critical reference series published by Gale, including *Short Story Criticism, Children's Literature Review, Contemporary Authors, Dictionary of Literary Biography,* and *Something about the Author,* are listed in a box at the end of the entry.

- Most *TCLC* entries include **Portraits** of the author. Many entries also contain reproductions of materials pertinent to an author's career, including manuscript pages, title pages, dust jackets, letters, and drawings, as well as photographs of important people, places, and events in an author's life.

- The **List of Principal Works** is chronological by date of first book publication and identifies the genre of each work. In the case of foreign authors with both foreign-language publications and English translations, the title and date of the first English-language edition are given in brackets. Unless otherwise indicated, dramas are dated by first performance, not first publication.

- Critical excerpts are prefaced by **Annotations** providing the reader with information about both the critic and the criticism that follows. Included are the critic's reputation, individual approach to literary criticism, and particular expertise in an author's works. Also noted are the relative importance of a work of criticism, the scope of the excerpt, and the growth of critical controversy or changes in critical trends regarding an author. In some cases, these annotations cross-reference excerpts by critics who discuss each other's commentary.

- **Criticism** is arranged chronologically in each author entry to provide a perspective on changes in critical evaluation over the years. All titles of works by the author featured in the entry are printed in boldface type to enable the user to easily locate discussion of particular works. Also for purposes of easier identification, the critic's name and the publication date of the essay are given at the beginning of each piece of criticism. Unsigned criticism is preceded by the title of the journal in which it appeared. Some of the excerpts in *TCLC* also contain translated material. Unless otherwise noted, translations in brackets are by the editors; translations in parentheses or continuous with the text are by the critic. Publication information (such as footnotes or page and line references to specific editions of works) have been deleted at the editor's discretion to provide smoother reading of the text.

- A complete **Bibliographic Citation** designed to facilitate location of the original essay or book follows each piece of criticism.

- An annotated list of **Further Reading** appearing at the end of each author entry suggests secondary sources on the author. In some cases it includes essays for which the editors could not obtain reprint rights.

Cumulative Indexes

- Each volume of *TCLC* contains a cumulative **Author Index** listing all authors who have appeared in Gale's Literary Criticism Series, along with cross references to such biographical series as *Contemporary Authors* and *Dictionary of Literary Biography*. For readers' convenience, a complete list of Gale titles included appears on the first page of the author index. Useful for locating authors within the various series, this index is particularly valuable for those authors who are identified by a certain period but who, because of their death dates, are placed in another, or for those authors whose careers span two periods. For example, F. Scott Fitzgerald is found in *TCLC,* yet a writer often associated with him, Ernest Hemingway, is found in *CLC*.

- Each *TCLC* volume includes a cumulative **Nationality Index** which lists all authors who have appeared in *TCLC* volumes, arranged alphabetically under their respective nationalities, as well as Topics volume entries devoted to particular national literatures.

- Each new volume in Gale's Literary Criticism Series includes a cumulative **Topic Index,** which lists all literary topics treated in *NCLC, TCLC, LC 1400-1800,* and the *CLC* yearbook.

- Each new volume of *TCLC,* with the exception of the Topics volumes, includes a **Title Index** listing the titles of all literary works discussed in the volume. In response to numerous suggestions from librarians, Gale has also produced a **Special Paperbound Edition** of the *TCLC* title index. This annual cumulation lists all titles discussed in the series since its inception and is issued with the first volume of *TCLC* published each year. Additional copies of the index are available on request. Librarians and patrons will welcome this separate index; it saves shelf space, is easy to use, and is recyclable upon receipt of the following year's cumulation. Titles discussed in the Topics volume entries are not included *TCLC* cumulative index.

Citing *Twentieth-Century Literary Criticism*

When writing papers, students who quote directly from any volume in Gale's literary Criticism Series may use the following general forms to footnote reprinted criticism. The first example pertains to materials drawn from periodicals, the second to material reprinted from books.

[1]T. S. Eliot, "John Donne," *The Nation and the Athenaeum,* 33 (9 June 1923), 321-32; excerpted and reprinted in *Literature Criticism from 1400 to 1800,* Vol. 10, ed. James E. Person, Jr. (Detroit: Gale Research, 1989), pp. 28-9.

[2]Clara G. Stillman, *Samuel Butler: A Mid-Victorian Modern* (Viking Press, 1932); excerpted and reprinted in *Twentieth-Century Literary Criticism,* Vol. 33, ed. Paula Kepos (Detroit: Gale Research, 1989), pp. 43-5.

Suggestions Are Welcome

In response to suggestions, several features have been added to *TCLC* since the series began, including annotations to excerpted criticism, a cumulative index to authors in all Gale literary criticism series, entries devoted to criticism on a single work by a major author, more extensive illustrations, and a title index listing all literary works discussed in the series since its inception.

Readers who wish to suggest authors or topics to appear in future volumes, or who have other suggestions, are cordially invited to write the editors.

Acknowledgments

The editors wish to thank the copyright holders of the excerpted criticism included in this volume and the permissions managers of many book and magazine publishing companies for assisting us in securing reprint rights. We are also grateful to the staffs of the Detroit Public Library, the Library of Congress, the University of Detroit Mercy Library, Wayne State University Purdy/Kresge Library Complex, and the University of Michigan Libraries for making their resources available to us. Following is a list of the copyright holders who have granted us permission to reprint material in this volume of *TCLC*. Every effort has been made to trace copyright, but if omissions have been made, please let us know.

COPYRIGHTED EXCERPTS IN *TCLC,* VOLUME 58, WERE REPRINTED FROM THE FOLLOWING PERIODICALS:

The Antioch Review, v. 36, Spring, 1978. Copyright © 1978 by the Antioch Review Inc. Reprinted by permission of the Editors.—*Canadian Library Journal,* v. 48, October, 1991. © 1991 The Canadian Library Association. Reprinted by permission of the publisher.—*Columbia Journalism Review,* v. XXXI, March-April, 1993 for "Tina's 'New Yorker' " by Eric Utne. © 1993 Graduate School of Journalism, Columbia University. Reprinted by permission of the publisher and the author.—*Commentary,* v. 28, August, 1959 for "Harold Ross's 'New Yorker': Life as a Drawing-Room Comedy" by Hilton Kramer. Copyright © 1959, renewed 1987./ v. 70, December, 1980 for "Lies about the Holocaust" by Lucy S. Dawidowicz. by the American Jewish Committee. All rights reserved. Both by permission of the publisher and the author.—*Commonweal,* v. CII, July 4, 1978. Copyright © 1978 Commonweal Publishing Co., Inc. Reprinted by permission of Commonweal Foundation.—*The Denver Quarterly,* v. 8, Summer, 1973 for "Not for the Old Lady Dubuque" by George Weales. Reprinted by permission of the author.—*Dissent,* v. 28, Fall, 1981 for "The Denial of the Dead" translated by Audri Durchslag, by Nadine Fresco. © 1981, by Dissent Publishing Corporation. Reprinted by permission of the publisher and the author.—*German Studies Review,* v. I, October 1978. © copyright 1978 by the German Studies Association. All rights reserved. Reprinted by permission of the publisher.—*Harper's Magazine,* v. 207, October, 1953. Copyright 1953, renewed 1981 by *Harper's Magazine.* All rights reserved. Reprinted by special permission.—*Holocaust and Genocide Studies,* v. 4, 1989. Reprinted by permission of the publisher.—*The Humanist,* v. 53, September-October, 1993. Copyright 1993 by the American Humanist Association. Reprinted by permission of the author.—*Interchange,* vs. 14 & 15, 1983 & 1984. © The Ontario Institute for Studies in Education 1983. Reprinted by permission of the publisher.—*The Iowa Review,* v. 20, Spring-Summer, 1990 for "On Virginia Woolf on the Essay" by Carl H. Klaus. Copyright © 1990 by The University of Iowa. Reprinted by permission of the publisher and the author.—*Journalism Quarterly,* v. 23, December, 1946. Copyright 1946 by the Association for Education in Journalism. Reprinted by permission of the publisher.—*Midstream,* v. XXXIII, April, 1987 for "'Revisionism' The Roques Affair" by Henry H. Weinberg. Copyright © 1987 by The Theodor Herzl Foundation Inc. Reprinted by permission of the publisher and the author.—*The Nation,* New York, v. 232, February, 1981. Copyright 1981 *The Nation* magazine, The Nation Company, Inc. Reprinted by permission of the publisher.—*National Review,* New York, v. XXXVII, October 4, 1985. © 1985 by National Review Inc., 150 East 35th Street, New York, NY 10016. Reprinted with permission of the publisher.—*New German Critique,* v. 11, Spring-Summer, 1984. © New German Critique, Inc., 1984. All rights reserved. Reprinted by permission of the publisher.—*The New Leader,* v. LXXV, July 13-27, 1992. © 1992 by The American Labor Board Conference on International Affairs, Inc. Reprinted by permission of the publisher.—*The New Republic,* v. 140, June 29, 1959. © 1959, renewed 1987 The New Republic, Inc. Reprinted by permission of *The New Republic.*—*New Statesman,* v. 98, November 2, 1979. © 1979 The Statesman & Nation Publishing Co. Ltd. Reprinted by permission of the publisher.—*The New York Review of Books,* v. XXIV, May 26, 1977. Copyright © 1977 Nyrev, Inc. Reprinted with permission from *The New York Review of Books.*—*The New York Times Book Review,* November 18, 1984. Copyright © 1984 by The New York Times Company. Reprinted by permission of the publisher.—*New York* Magazine, v. 18, March 25, 1985, v. 25, July 20, 1992. Copyright © 1995 K-III Magazine Corporation. All rights reserved. Reprinted with the permission of *New York* Magazine.—*The New Yorker,* v. LXI, April 22, 1985. From the Notes and Comment section in "The Talk of the Town" by William Shawn. © 1985 by The New Yorker Magazine, Inc. v. LXX, June

27-July 4, 1994 for "Storyville" by Roger Angell. © 1994 by the author. Both reprinted by permission of the publisher.—*Newsweek,* v. LXXVI, October 12, 1970. © 1970, Newsweek, Inc. All rights reserved. Reprinted by permission of the publisher.—*Papers on Language & Literature.* v. 11, Summer, 1975. Copyright © 1975 by the Board of Trustees, Southern Illinois University at Edwardsville. Reprinted by permission of the publisher.—*Patterns of Prejudice,* v. 15, January, 1981; v. 20, July, 1986. Reprinted by permission of the publisher.—*Quadrant,* v. XXV, October, 1981 for "Chomsky and the Neo-Nazis" by W. D. Rubenstein. Reprinted by permission of *Quadrant,* Sydney, Australia and the author.—*The Saturday Review of Literature,* v. XXX, August 30, 1947. Copyright 1947, renewed 1975 *Saturday Review* magazine. Reprinted by permission of Saturday Review Publications, Ltd..—*The Sewanee Review,* v. LXXXVI, Winter, 1978 for "The Odor of Durability" by Spencer Brown; v. XCVI, Fall, 1988 for "Itinerant Passages: Recent American Essays" by William Howarth. © 1978, 1988 by The University of the South. Reprinted with the permission of the editor of *The Sewanee Review* and the authors.—*The Southern Review,* Louisiana State University, v. 21, Autumn, 1985 for "The Modernist Essay: The Case of T. S. Eliot—Poet as Critic" by J. P. Riquelme. Copyright, 1985, by the author. Reprinted by permission of the author.—*Studies in American Humor,* n.s. v. 3, Spring, 1984. Copyright © 1984 by Southwest Texas State University. Reprinted by permission of the publisher.—*Studies in Short Fiction,* v. 20, Fall, 1983. Copyright 1983 by Newberry College. Reprinted by permission of the publisher.—*The Sunday Times,* London, November 30, 1980. © Times Newspaper Limited 1980. Reproduced from *The Sunday Times,* London by permission.—*Time,* New York, v. 99, May 1, 1972. Copyright 1972 Time Warner Inc. All rights reserved. Reprinted by permission from *Time.—The University of Denver Quarterly,* v. 8, Summer, 1973. Reprinted by permission of the publisher.—*The Virginia Quarterly Review,* v. 61, Winter, 1985. Copyright, 1985, by *The Virginia Quarterly Review,* The University of Virginia. Reprinted by permission of the publisher.—*The Wall Street Journal,* June 30, 1958. © 1958, renewed 1986 Dow Jones & Company, Inc. All rights reserved Worldwide. Reprinted by permission of *The Wall Street Journal.—Yad Vashem Studies,* v. XIII, 1979. Reprinted by permission of the publisher.

COPYRIGHTED EXCERPTS IN *TCLC*, VOLUME 58, WERE REPRINTED FROM THE FOLLOWING BOOKS:

Andrade, Jorge Carrera. From *Reflections on Spanish-American Poetry.* Translated by Don C. Bliss and Gabriela de C. Bliss. State University of New York Press, 1973. Copyright © 1973 State University of New York. All rights reserved. Reprinted by permission of the publisher.—Barnouw, David. From "Attacks on the Authenticity of the Diary," in *The Diary of Anne Frank: The Critical Edition.* Edited by David Barnouw and Gerrold van der Stroom, translated by Arnold J. Pomerans and B. M. Mooyaart-Doubleday. Bantam Doubleday Dell Publishing Group, Inc., 1989. Copyright © 1986 by Anne Frank-Fonds, Basle/Switzerland. All rights reserved. Used by permission of Doubleday, a division of Bantam Doubleday Dell Publishing Group, Inc. In the British Commonwealth by Anne Frank-Fonds.—Brushwood, John S. From "The Spanish American Short Story from Quiroga to Borges," in *The Latin American Short Story: A Critical History.* Edited by Margaret Sayers Peden. Twayne, 1983. Copyright © 1983 by G. K. Hall & Co. All rights reserved. Reprinted with the permission of Twayne Publishers, an imprint of Macmillan Publishing Company.—Core, George. From "Stretching the Limits of the Essay," in *Essays on the Essay: Redefining the Genre.* Edited by Alexander J. Butrym. University of Georgia Press, 1989. © 1989 by the University of Georgia Press. All rights reserved. Reprinted by permission of the publisher.—Eatwell, Roger. From "The Holocaust Denial: A Study in Propaganda Technique," in *Neo-Facism in Europe.* Luciano Cheles, Ronnie Ferguson, Michalina Vaughan, eds. Longman, 1991. © Longman Group UK Limited, 1991. All rights reserved. Reprinted by permission of the publisher.—Ellison, Fred P. From "The Writer," in *Continuity and Change in Latin America.* Edited by John J. Johnson. Stanford University Press, 1964. Copyright © 1964, renewed 1992 by the Board of Trustees of Leland Stanford Junior University. Reprinted with the permission of the publishers, Stanford University Press.—Foster, David William. From *Gay and Lesbian Themes in Latin American Writing.* University of Texas Press, 1991. Copyright © 1991 by the University of Texas Press. All rights reserved. Reprinted by permission of the publisher and the author.—Haines, Helen E. From *What's in a Novel.* Columbia University Press, 1942. Copyright 1942, renewed 1970 Columbia University Press, New York. All rights reserved. Reprinted with permission of the publisher.—Holmes, Charles S. From *The Clocks of Columbus: The Literary Career of James Thurber.* Atheneum, 1972. Copyright © 1972 by Charles S. Holmes. All rights reserved. Reprinted with the permission of Atheneum Publishers, an imprint of Macmillan

Publishing Company.—Kostelanetz, Richard. From "Innovations in Essaying," in *Essaying Essays: Alternative Forms of Exposition.* Edited by Richard Kostelanetz. Out of London Press, 1975. All rights reserved. Reprinted by permission of the publisher.—Lipstadt, Deborah E. From *Denying the Holocaust: The Growing Assault on Truth and Memory.* The Free Press, 1993. Copyright © 1993 by The Vidal Sassoon International Center for the Study of Antisemitism, The Hebrew University of Jerusalem. All rights reserved. Reprinted with the permission of the Free Press, a division of Simon & Schuster, Inc..—Lipstadt, Deborah E. From "The Evolution of American Holocaust Revisionism," in *Remembering for the Future: Working Papers and Addenda, Vol. III.* Edited by Yehuda Bauer and others. Pergamon Press, 1989. Copyright © 1989 Pergamon Press plc. All rights reserved. Reprinted by permission of the publisher.—Lukács, Georg. From *Soul and Form.* Translated by Anna Bostock. Merlin Press, 1974. Translation copyright The Merlin Press Ltd. Reprinted by permission of the publisher.—Martin, Edward A. From " 'The New Yorker'," in *H. L. Mencken and the Debunkers.* University of Georgia Press, 1984. Copyright © 1984 by the University of Georgia Press. All rights reserved. Reprinted by permission of the publisher.—Martínez, José Luis. From "Unity and Diversity," in *Latin America in Its Literature.* Edited by César Fernádez Moreno, Julio Ortega, and Ivan A. Schulman, translated by Mary G. Berg. Holmes & Meier, 1980. Copyright © 1980 by Holmes & Meier Publishers, Inc. All rights reserved. Reprinted by permission of the publisher.—Meyer, Doris. From an introduction to *Lives on the Line: The Testimony of Contemporary Latin American Authors.* Edited by Doris Meyer. University of California Press, 1985. Copyright © 1988 by The Regents of the University of California. Reprinted by permission of the publisher and the author.—Muñoz, Braulio. From *Sons of the Wind: The Search for Identity in Spanish American Indian Literature.* Rutgers University Press, 1982. Copyright © 1982 by Rutgers, The State University of New Jersey. All rights reserved. Reprinted by permission of Rutgers, The State University.—O'Neill, Charles. From "The Essay as Aesthetic Ritual: W. B. Yeats and 'Ideas of Good and Evil'," in *Essays on the Essay: Redefining the Genre.* Edited by Alexander J. Butrym. University of Georgia Press, 1989. © 1989 by the University of Georgia Press. All rights reserved. Reprinted by permission of the publisher.—Peterson, Theodore. From *Magazines in the Twentieth Century.* Second edition. University of Illinois Press, 1964. © 1964, renewed 1992 by the Board of Trustees of the University of Illinois. Reprinted by permission of the publisher and the author.—Sanders, Scott Russell. From "The Singular First Person," in *The Secrets of the Universe.* Beacon Press, 1991. © 1991 by Beacon Press. Used by permission of the publisher.—Shawn, William. From an excerpt in *Here at the "New Yorker."* By Brendan Gill. Random House, 1975. Copyright © Brendan Gill 1975. All rights reserved. Reprinted by permission of Random House, Inc.—Taylor, Diana. From *Theatre of Crisis: Drama and Politics in Latin America.* University Press of Kentucky, 1991. Copyright © 1991 by The University Press of Kentucky. Reprinted by permission of the publisher.—Vidal-Naquet, Pierre. From *Assassins of Memory: Essays on the Denial of the Holocaust.* Translated by Jeffrey Mehlman. Columbia University Press, 1992. Copyright © 1992 Columbia University Press, New York. All rights reserved. Reprinted with the permission of the publisher.—Vidal-Naquet, Pierre. From *Assassins of Memory: Essays on the Denial of the Holocaust.* Translated by Jeffrey Mehlman. Columbia University Press, 1992. Copyright © 1992 Columbia University Press, New York. All rights reserved. Reprinted with the permission of the publisher.—Virgillo, Carmelo. From "Primitivism in Latin American Fiction," in *The Hero-American Enlightenment.* Edited by A. Owen Aldridge. University of Illinois Press, 1971. © 1971 by the Board of Trustees of the University of Illnois. Reprinted by permission of the publisher and the author.—Woolf, Virginia. From *The Common Reader.* Harcourt Brace and Company, 1925, L. & V. Woolf, 1925. Copyright 1925 by Harcourt Brace And company. Renewed 1953 by Leonard Woolf. Reprinted by permission of Harcourt Brace and Company, Inc.

PHOTOGRAPHS AND ILLUSTRATIONS APPEARING IN *TCLC,* VOLUME 58, WERE RECEIVED FROM THE FOLLOWING SOURCES:

©Jerry Bauer: **p. 116**; Photograph by Gil Jain: **p. 127**; Photograph by Sueiro: **p. 164**; Photograph by Jesse A. Fernandez: **p. 166**; Photograph by Berestein: **p. 168**; Photograph by Hans Beacham: **p. 172**; Photograph by David D. Clark: **p. 181**; Dust jacket for the 1964 translation by George D. Schade of *CONFABULARIO* by Juan Jose Arreola (1952) published by the University of Texas Press. The dust jacket, with illustration by Kelly Fearing, is reproduced by permission of the publisher: **p. 189**; William Mangold: **p. 291**; The Bettmann Archive: **p. 320**; Fairchild Publications, Inc.: **p. 344.**

Holocaust Denial Literature

INTRODUCTION

Holocaust denial literature is based on the premise that the treatment of Jews and members of other ethnic and social groups by the Nazi regime during World War II has been misrepresented by historians, journalists, and governments. Authors of Holocaust denial literature first contended that the wartime killings were implemented without Adolf Hitler's knowledge by the lesser officers of the SS who ran the concentration camps. These authors ultimately have come to maintain that there were no systematic killings at all and that the gas chambers in Nazi concentration camps were used only for delousing clothing, not killing human beings. As anti-Israel sentiment grew within certain political factions, the denial movement embraced the theory of a world-wide Jewish conspiracy to gain sympathy for Zionist ideals by propagating a Holocaust "story." In the 1970s and 1980s Holocaust denial gained public attention with the trial in France of Robert Faurisson, a University of Lyons professor who was prosecuted under French law for his Holocaust denial writings; the establishment in 1980 of the *Journal of Historical Review*, the periodical of the Institute of Historical Review, a group of revisionists who claimed to be legitimate historians; and the publication, beginning in 1987, of Holocaust denial advertisements in major American university newspapers. The latter engendered controversy when critics denounced the decision to run the advertisements as little more than insensitive attempts to falsify history. Newspaper editors countered that their actions were governed by the principle of freedom of expression rather than historical accuracy. Freedom of expression was also invoked in the case of Robert Faurisson when Noam Chomsky, a noted American linguistic theorist, argued that Faurisson and all scholars have the right to research and publish without fear of persecution. The debate continues over what place, if any, Holocaust denial literature has in universities and libraries.

REPRESENTATIVE WORKS

App, Austin J.
> *The Six Million Swindle: Blackmailing the German People for Hard Marks with Fabricated Corpses* 1974

Butz, Arthur R.
> *The Hoax of the Twentieth Century: The Case Against the Presumed Extermination of European Jewry* 1976

Faurisson, Robert
> *The "Problem of the Gas Chambers," or "The Rumor of Auschwitz"* 1979

> *Memoire en defense contre ceux qui m'accusent de falsifier l'histoire: la question des chambres à gaz* 1980
> *A Prominent False Witness: Elie Wiesel* 1990

Friedrich, Christof [pseudonym of Ernst Zundel] and Thomson, Eric
> *The Hitler We Loved and Why* 1980

Grimstad, William N.
> *The Six Million Reconsidered: Is the Nazi Holocaust Story a Zionist Propaganda Ploy?* 1979

Harwood, Richard [pseudonym of Richard Verrall]
> *Did Six Million Really Die? The Truth at Last* 1974

Hoggan, David L.
> *The Myth of the Six Million* 1969

Irving, David
> *Hitler's War* 1977

Journal of Historical Review 1980—

Leuchter, Fred
> *The Leuchter Report: The End of a Myth. An Engineering Report on the Alleged Execution Gas Chambers at Auschwitz, Birkenau and Majdanek, Poland* 1988

Rassinier, Paul
> *The Drama of the European Jews* 1975
> *Debunking the Genocide Myth* 1978 [Reprinted as *The Holocaust Story and the Lies of Ulysses*]
> *The Real Eichmann Trial, or, the Incorrigible Victors* 1979

Roques, Henri
> *The "Confessions" of Kurt Gerstein* 1989

Smith, Bradley R.
> *Confessions of a Holocaust Revisionist* 1988

The Spotlight 1975—

Worldwide Growth and Impact of "Holocaust" Revisionism: A Handbook of Revisionist Views and the Controversy Today 1985

OVERVIEWS

Roger Eatwell

SOURCE: "The Holocaust Denial: a Study in Propaganda Technique," in *Neo-Fascism in Europe*, Luciano Cheles, Ronnie Ferguson, Michalina Vaughan, eds., Longman Group Limited, 1991, pp. 120-46.

[*In the following essay, Eatwell analyzes propaganda techniques used in Holocaust denial literature*]

The Holocaust of Jews during the Second World War is part of modern collective memory. Images of the emaciated living, of rag-doll heaps of the dead, of gas chambers and ferocious SS guards, are vivid not just for survivors. Popular media, such as film and television, provide constant reminders of the twentieth century's potential for bestiality. Yet, during the 1970s and 1980s there was a notable growth of articles, pamphlets and books seeking to deny that there was a systematic Nazi policy of genocide. Such views might be considered the historical or political equivalent of the 'scientific' belief that the moon is made of green cheese. However, four opening points about the growth of this Holocaust-denial literature illustrate the dangers of dismissing its potential impact, especially at a time when there are signs that anti-Semitism may be reviving, and criticisms of Israel growing.

Firstly, such propaganda should not be seen solely within the context of the limited circulations achieved by most contemporary Fascist publications. Laws banning the publication of Nazi works have hampered German Fascists from focusing on these arguments. However, among notable Holocaust-denial works which have circulated is Thies Christophersen's pamphlet *Die Auschwitz Lüge,* first published in 1973 by Kritik-Verlag (Mohrkirch). By 1979 over 100,00 copies had allegedly been distributed. That year also saw the appearance of Wilhelm Stäglich's 498-page *Der Auschwitz-Mythos,* published by Grabert Verlag (Tübingen). This was quickly suppressed but, apparently, only after all but seven of its 10,000-copy run had been sold; subsequently, it has been republished in English and French, while German language editions are advertised for smuggling back to Germany.

This republication of works abroad illustrates a second important point: the international aspect of the Holocaust denial and, especially, the link between some of the groups and individuals involved. These international links can be seen most clearly through the activities of the American Institute for Historical Review (IHR), founded in 1978. Many leading European, American and Arab 'Historical Revisionists', as they prefer to be known, have attended IHR conferences and contributed to its *The Journal of Historical Review.* Among the most active have been Arthur Butz and Robert Faurisson. The former is an Associate Professor of Electrical Engineering and Computer Sciences at Northwestern University, Illinois. He is best known for his 315-page book *The Hoax of the Twentieth Century,* first published in 1976 by the Historical Review Press (Brighton). The latter has been a Senior Lecturer in Literary Criticism at the University of Lyon-2. His prolific works in the 1980s include the 304-page book *Mémoire en défense contre ceux qui m'accusent de falsifier l'histoire,* published by La Vieille Taupe (Paris). This contained a preface written by the left-wing American linguistician Noam Chomsky, a document which caused considerable outcry and surprise. These points illustrate a third factor which should be underlined at the outset: some Historical Revisionists are highly educated. Among earlier ones who were capable of sustaining a more sophisticated level of debate, it is important to note Maurice Bardèche, the brother-in-law of the literary Fascist Robert Brasillach. Bardèche wrote several books and articles which anticipated Historical Revisionist themes, and edited the neo-Fascist journal *Défense de l'Occident.*

In her book *The Holocaust Denial* (1986), Gill Seidel draws attention to a fourth point: the clear Fascist and/or racist motivation of this literature. It is interesting, here, to note Richard Harwood's widely-distributed pamphlet *Did Six Million Really Die?* (1974). On page 2, Harwood reveals his motivation when he writes:

> what happens if a man dares to speak of the race problem, of its biological and political implications? He is branded as that most heinous of creatures, a 'racialist'. And what is racialism, of course, but the very hallmark of the Nazi! They (so everyone is told, anyway) murdered Six Million Jews because of racialism, so it must be a very evil thing indeed. When Enoch Powell drew attention to the dangers posed by coloured immigration into Britain in one of his early speeches, a certain prominent Socialist raised the spectre of Dachau and Auschwitz to silence his presumption.

It is interesting to note that this is removed in the 1987(?) revised edition, which admits that a small number of errors crept into the original version. However, the revised edition includes a more esoteric reference to Fascism in relation to the former French distributor of the pamphlet, François Duprat, who was assassinated in 1978. The new introduction notes that Duprat's party, the *Front National,* was subsequently taken over by 'opportunists', a clear reference to the less overtly Fascist tone which emerged as support grew during the 1980s. If further evidence is sought about motivation, it should be noted that Harwood subsequently turned out to be Richard Verrall, a leading member of the British National Front during the 1970s. The apparently anodyne Historical Review Press, which published the pamphlet, has close links with British Fascist and racist organisations. It has been active in distributing a wide range of literature, including works by Butz, Christophersen, Faurisson and Stäglich, and it distributes IHR publications. The motivation of other publishers has not always been strictly Fascist. In America, anti-Semitism seems more to be the key. Some money has also come from Arab sources, clearly with the desire of delegitimising Israel. In France, Faurisson's works have been published by a left-wing collective called La Vieille Taupe, which includes Jewish supporters. Here again, anti-Israel sentiments, which are common in sections of both the Communist and non-Communist left, seem to be central (this position tends to be pro-Palestinian, seeing Israel as capitalist and imperialist—even racist—in the light of its policies towards the Palestinians).

The linking publishing theme is therefore political manipulation rather than a desire to engage in academic debate. In its more sophisticated form, this even involves a form of Gramsci-ism, the belief that the radical needs to fight at the level of ideas in order to undermine dominant cultural-political values. While such views are normally found on he left, the French *Nouvelle Droite* offers a notable example of 'Gramsci-ism of the right' (moreover, the extent to which contemporary Fascist tracts circulate at the international level means that this *Nouvelle Droite* position has been influential elsewhere). A leading member of La Vieille Taupe has even claimed that Louis Pauwels, the director of the French conservative newspaper *Le Figaro* and a leading figure in the *Nouvelle Droite,* met Faurisson in private and expressed support for Historical Revisionism. Pressure from advertisers, and the threat of legal action prevented Pauwels openly siding with Faurisson, but he later financed a trip to America for a 'revisionist' member of La Vieille Taupe. While such testimony must be treated with extreme caution, it underlines the possibility that Historical Revisionism is viewed as useful by more respectable members of the right (and left).

These diverse political motivations are a vital perspective, but unduly emphasising them can lead to the belief that all Historical Revisionists are frauds in the sense that they are consciously lying. Most undoubtedly are but Faurisson, in particular, appears to believe what he is arguing. Certainly, his earlier writings on French literature had a tendency to adopt the Messianic view that he had seen the true light, whereas countless others had been deceived, a markedly similar line to his one on the Holocaust. Emphasis on the Fascist and racist links also means that Holocaust-denial arguments tend to be ignored or parodied. Once the political associations of the individual have been established, substantive debate of the *issue* seems unnecessary. Such an approach leads to underestimating the potential appeal of some arguments. Evidence as to their potential can be seen by the fact that the author Colin Wilson wrote a review of Harwood's pamphlet which reveals that he was clearly impressed. The Henri Roques affair in France offers further evidence of the potential appeal of such arguments, even to academics (it also attracted considerable popular-media attention). In 1985, a student was awarded a doctorate at the University of Nantes for a Historical Revisionist critique of the Gerstein document (see below). The degree was subsequently revoked as a result of a series of irregularities involving the connivance of some academics. It is impossible to tell whether the individuals concerned were convinced by the arguments or saw them, more, as politically useful. Certainly, some had connections with various Fascist and racist groups. Nevertheless, there seems to be a strong case for analysing the appeal of Holocaust-denial arguments more systematically.

· · · · ·

An important question when approaching the Holocaust denial is whether it would be better to ignore the literature. It could be argued that discussing such claims could both give them legitimacy in the sense that they are seen as worthy of debate, and increase their familiarity among those who might otherwise have been unaware of their existence. This may have been the best policy when such works were rare, but their recent growth makes a more specific response vital, especially as ignoring them could be seen as confirming a conspiracy (a common Historical Revisionist allegation) of silence.

It has been argued that such a response should focus on legal suppression. Censorship raises a series of wide-ranging issues about democratic politics. However, even at the pragmatic level, it is possible to question whether legal proceedings can be deemed unequivocally useful. The threat of legal action (mainly under race relations laws) has probably served to deter the wider publication of Historical Revisionist arguments. On the other hand, there were various prosecutions against Faurisson in the

1980s, followed by appeals and counter-appeals. In the end, both sides claimed victory. The anti-racist groups stressed that Faurisson had to pay damages and was given a suspended sentence. He argued that the court had ultimately concluded that his work on the gas chambers was 'scientific', and that the charge that he had been deliberately negligent was not proven. This process almost certainly helped keep alive an issue which might otherwise have remained on the fringes. The prohibition of the public sale of the French journal *Annales d'histoire révisionniste* in 1987 may have harmed its sales (it was limited to subscription sales) but it is not clear that it will limit the impact of the ideas. Holocaust denial works have circulated fairly widely in Germany in spite of bans. Moreover, banning may even increase the appeal of such works by reinforcing the claim that there is a conspiracy to suppress them.

This still leaves the problem of *how* to study such literature. Many social scientists have sought to analyse Fascist propaganda within the framework of quantitative content analysis, which seeks to measure the recurrence of key terms. There have been a series of major objections to this approach. One concerns a failure to perceive that such terms, for example 'freedom', can have radically different meanings. There is also the problem of the selection of texts. This is a particularly significant issue in the context of the Holocaust denial because it is useful to distinguish between two types of text.

The first, and by far the largest group, is the sort which involves an overtly Fascist or racist content. This would include crude works such as the grossly-mistitled Committee for Truth in History's *The Six Million Reconsidered,* published in 1979 by the Historical Review Press. This is littered with references to Jewish power, Zionism's baneful consequences and other familiar themes. It is not necessary to move beyond the contents page to see the tone: 'Zion's Own "Six Million" Plans . . . The Tsarist Pogrom Myth . . . Jews and Organized Crime . . . Jews and Communism . . . Epilogue in Palestine'. It would also include Harwood's *Did Six Million Really Die?* (mentioned above), though the tone of this is far less crude. The second group includes texts like Faurisson's article 'The Mechanics of Gassing', published in *The Journal of Historical Review* (No. 1, 1980), or the Italian Carlo Mattogno's article 'Le Mythe de l'extermination des juifs', which appeared in the *Annales d'histoire révisionniste* (No. 1, 1987). Such texts are normally more 'academic', in the sense that they include extensive footnotes, and refer to major secondary works, e.g. Mattogno's forty-two page article has an average of almost two footnotes per page, including many leading works on the Holocaust and related areas.

Several objections could be made to this division. Firstly, it is not clear how to classify some works. Butz's *The Hoax of the Twentieth Century* is lengthy and has extensive footnotes, which might indicate that it should be classed as a type-2 work. On the other hand, it has limited references to Jewish influence and Zionism which place it in type-1. Secondly, it could be argued that the type-2 works are normally published by people with clear Fascist, racist or anti-Zionist intentions. Why, therefore, separate them out from type-1 works, which often have the same publishers? A third objection concerns the fact that an absence of crude Fascism or racism in a particular text does not mean that the author has not expressed such views in other texts, especially in those not intended for widespread circulation. A common distinction in analysing contemporary Fascist propaganda concerns the differences between its public ('exoteric') and private ('esoteric') appeals. This distinction is undoubtedly relevant to many Historical Revisionists. David McCalden, for example, when wearing his public hat as Director of the IHR, tried to present an academic facade (he left the IHR in 1982, mainly because of friction with its founder, Willis Carto). However, in a limited-circulation tract he referred to the sponsor of the 1988 Oxford conference on the Holocaust in the following terms: 'Typically, the wealthy [Robert] Maxwell has bought himself a Holocaust© Expert ® in the form of Prof. Yehuda Bauer, who cannot make up his mind these days whether to sell his services to the *nouveau riche* Slovakian-Jewish barrow-boy Maxwell, or to the *nouveau riche* Iraqi-Jewish barrow-boy Vidal Sassoon'. It is hardly necessary to be an expert in anti-Semitic stereotyping to recognise the old themes of the wandering, money-centred, scheming Jew.

However, distinguishing between two types of Holocaust denial text underlines a strategy delineated in a La Vieille Taupe samizdat circular of 1986 and seems to fit a more general Holocaust denial perspective on how to exert influence. The La Vieille Taupe tract advocated agit-prop developments for popular consumption, accompanied by a deepening of the historical and theoretical knowledge of the Holocaust for more educated audiences (this involves the classic Communist distinction between 'agitation' for the less educated and 'propaganda' for the educated, a terminology not mirrored in the West, where the term 'propaganda' tends to have more pejorative connotations). Such a division still leaves the problem of how to approach the texts. Quantitative content analysis could be used to analyse type-1 Historical Revisionism, though whether such an investigation would produce anything worth while is another matter. It seems far less suitable for the type-2 texts, which do not include the ideological framework of normal Fascist propaganda. Indeed, type-2 texts tend to read like academic history articles (the main exception is the currency of words such as 'myth', which more than hint at conspiracy theory). Thus, such an approach would not pick up the key *values* which are the focus of social science content studies of Fascist propaganda of the Hitler-speech type.

In the following description of Historical Revisionism, a form of qualitative content analysis is therefore used which seeks to create a general account of the major arguments. In constructing this model, it is important to note the following points. Firstly, such an approach risks sanitising the debate by making it seem more credible, and especially by underplaying the overt Fascist or racist aspects of type-1 arguments. This seems acceptable in the context of this chapter where such links are clearly stated, and where a major purpose is to seek to understand any potential appeal to educated audiences. Secondly, the order of

presentation of an argument can influence its force. For example, psychologists have debated the question of whether arguments are most powerful when presented in climatic, or anti-climatic manners. The order of the following model tries to reflect what have been qualitatively judged to be the most frequently-used Holocaust-denial claims. It begins with what have become the most common assertions, and ends with less frequent arguments (though an increasing Historical Revisionist perception of the possibilities of the last argument given below, the 'scientific' one, is changing the balance). Thirdly, the model begins with a series of brief quotations which set out what the more cogent Historical Revisionists do *not* claim. They frequently state that their position is travestied by critics, and there is some truth in this. For example, the Publisher's Preface to Seidel's *The Holocaust Denial* misleadingly claims that 'Now it is being argued that Jewry emerged unharmed' from the war. Another work claims that 'The Revisionist propaganda is a reiteration of the forgery . . . *The Protocols of the Elders of Zion*. Holocaust-denial arguments may share conspiracy theory as the basis of their appeal, but they are not based on forgery in the sense of creating documents (though the Hitler diaries, 'discovered' in 1983, conformed very much to the Historical Revisionist view of the world).

Historical Revisionists often argue that Jews ultimately benefited from the Holocaust because the 'myth' led to the establishment of Israel, reinforced group solidarity at a time of assimilation, and hindered a revival of anti-Semitism. However, they do *not* normally deny the following points (all the quotations are taken from the IHR's pamphlet *The Worldwide Growth and Impact of 'Holocaust' Revisionism*, published by the IHR in 1985 in Torrance):

> The existence of a vast network of concentration camps . . . The fact that Jewish, and other, practitioners of illegal behind-the-lines partisan warfare were executed by German *Einsatzgruppen* . . . And the fact that in these round-up operations *some innocent people* . . . were indeed killed . . . The fact that many Jews perished . . . and that their casualties from all causes—including natural attrition, disease, malnutrition, bombings, military actions, pogroms conducted by indigenous Eastern European populations, *Einsatzgruppen* actions, nameless ad-hoc atrocities and general wartime havoc—numbered unquestionably in the hundreds of thousands . . . The fact that some atrocities *did* occur . . . None of this is denied. *What is denied is that there was a deliberate German policy of systematic extermination of Jews.*

Historical Revisionist arguments can usefully be grouped under five main headings, though there tends to be some overlap. They will not be dissected until the following section as the object, here, is to reconstruct as accurate an account as possible of the more 'academic' type of Holocaust-denial case. However, it is important to note that it is not possible completely to divorce content from technique.

1. Documentary, trial and confessional evidence

Stäglich notes [in *The Auschwitz Myth*] that 'As a source material for historiography, documents of every kind are assigned pre-eminent rank'. Much play is, therefore, made of the assertion that, in spite of the Allies capturing vast quantities of German documents, no specific order can be found in which Hitler clearly orders the killing of the Jews, or in which key aspects of the Holocaust are set out. As Harwood argues [in *Did Six Million Really Die?*]: 'It should be emphasised straight away that there is not a single document in existence which proves that Germans intended to, or carried out, the deliberate murder of Jews.' This claim holds that many of the so-called key documents which are alleged to have been part of the planning of the Holocaust are open to different interpretations. For example, at the famous Wannee conference in January 1942, which saw the gathering of leading Nazi figures involved in the 'Final Solution', no reference was made to the experimental gassings which had allegedly been carried out during the preceding year, nor to future gassings. For Historical Revisionists, this constitutes evidence that it was simply a discussion of Jewish population numbers which is seen as perfectly understandable in view of Nazi plans to resettle them in camps.

Butz, in his book *The Hoax of the Twentieth Century,* has tried to show that the language about the Holocaust to be found in documents is open to different interpretations—a line which has been followed by others. The term 'Final Solution' (*Endlösung*), it is argued, can be found in contexts where it clearly refers to emigration, or resettlement in Jewish ghettos. The phrase 'Special Treatment' (*Sonderbehandlung*), normally seen as designating those to be gassed, can also be found in reference to prominent figures, such as the French Socialist leader Léon Blum, who survived the war. In these cases, 'Special Treatment' referred to providing better accommodation or rations. This argument holds that there is a paradox between occasional highly provocative Nazi speeches about the fate of the Jews, for example Hitler's speech in the Reichstag on 30 January 1939, and the alleged euphemisms of the documents. For Historical Revisionists this poses no fundamental problem. Rhetoric was part of the Nazis' style, part of their social control. Conventional accounts of the Holocaust, it is held, need a rationale based on an Orwellian double-think: they have to hold that the Nazis in public could be viciously anti-Semitic, but in private dealt only in euphemisms.

Evidence from the post-war trials, especially Nuremberg, is particularly attacked. In part, this involves an attack on the very legality of the victors trying the vanquished, for example charge number one (conspiracy to wage aggressive war) could be seen as applying to one of the judging nations, the Soviet Union, which had invaded both eastern Poland and Finland during 1939-40. More specifically, trial procedure is attacked on two counts. Firstly, much of what was admitted in evidence was not cross-checked. This is seen as hardly surprising in view not only of the presumption of guilt on the part of the accused, but also of the allegedly high percentage of of Jews working for the various prosecutors. Secondly, it is argued that much testimony derived from torture, the threat of being handed over to the Russians, or the promise of leniency in return

for a co-operative attitude. Thus Albert Speer, Hitler's architect, 'court' confidant, and Minister of Munitions during the war, was given the relatively light sentence of twenty years because he told the court what it wanted to hear: namely, that Hitler headed an evil empire (though he—Speer—knew nothing of the worst atrocities).

Faurisson, Roques and others have sought to prove, through internal textual criticism, that much of the court or interrogation information is worthless. Their use of the Gerstein document is a good example of this approach. Gerstein was an SS officer in charge of procuring Zyklon B crystals (which served both as a fumigator and as a source of lethal gas). He was interrogated in France at the end of the war, before committing suicide. Historical Revisionists look for internal contradictions in such testimony, or for patently ludicrous statements, for example the claim that hundreds of victims were packed into gas chambers of only a few square meters. They allege that such claims prove that the witness was simply saying what he believed his captors wanted him to say.

Finally, the controversial British historian David Irving wrote, in a letter which appeared in *The Spectator* on 25 November 1989, that the Auschwitz death books had been found in a Moscow archive. They revealed that 74,000 people had died in the camp, which he noted was 'of course, bad enough: nearly twice as many as died in the July 1943 RAF attack on Hamburg' (see below for further examples of this tendency to compare the Holocaust with Allied 'atrocities'). Irving added that his documentary research in the New York Yivo Institute revealed an order that deaths in Auschwitz should be carefully recorded; he thus argues that the documented 74,000 deaths can be treated as an accurate figure—a dramatic reduction on the accepted figure!

2. Jewish and other survivor testimony

Considerable attention is also paid to survivor testimony. It is frequently claimed that there are countless oral and written accounts about gas chambers existing in camps which are now accepted as not having been involved in the mass gassing campaign, for example Dachau or Ravensbrück. 'I-too-was-there' evidence has also been used to counter claims of gas chambers. Christophersen's pamphlet *Die Auschwitz Lüge* often figures prominently because the author worked as an army agricultural researcher in Auschwitz for eleven months. Great play is made of the fact that the Allies had aerial reconnaissance shots of Auschwitz, which was a major centre of war production. None of these, it is alleged, reveals evidence to support conventional Holocaust-survivor accounts, for example there were no groups waiting for 'selections', or to enter gas chambers; there were no crematoria with constantly burning chimneys.

It is worth concentrating on a single article. It clearly impresses the Historical Revisionists as it has appeared in both the *Journal of Historical Review,* and in the *Annales d'histoire révisionniste* (though the latter has generally seemed short of substantial new material). Its author is Howard F. Stein, an Associate Professor of Psychiatry at the University of Oklahoma. The editorial of the IHR journal notes:

> Dr Stein is himself of Jewish origin, and believes that forty of his relatives died in Europe during World War Two. His focus is not so much on history as meanings. He feels that it is wrong to label the Holocaust a 'hoax' or 'lie' because the people who are propagating it actually believe in it themselves. It is this phenomenon of self-deception which he addresses in his very fine article.

Or in Stein's own words:

> Whatever did happen in the Holocaust must be made to conform to the group-fantasy of what ought to have happened. For the Jews, the term 'Holocaust' does not simply denote a single catastrophic era in history, but is a grim metaphor for the meaning of Jewish history . . . One is either anxiously awaiting persecution, experiencing persecution, recovering from it, or living in a period that is a temporary reprieve from it.

Thus, Stein is arguing that the experiences of camp life were interpreted within a framework of a history of persecution. In camps where families were broken up, where the smells and sounds of industrial production were strong, even repellent, it was easy to imagine all forms of horror. This tendency was fuelled by the fact that some horrific acts did take place within the camps. Limited, non-systematic killings, were therefore incorporated into a collective picture of genocide because of the very nature of Jewish psychology when faced with incarceration in concentration camps.

3. Cui Bono?

A third form of argument is to pose the question: who benefits from the Holocaust 'myth'? Usually, the focus is upon the Jews and Israel. Harwood claims that belief in the Holocaust was not only important in leading to the creation of Israel but, by the early 1970s, had led to £6 billion compensation being paid by West Germany. A 1988 article by Mark Weber claims that, at the end of 1987, the West Germany government gave a figure of eighty billion marks as the total sum paid in compensation [' "Holocauste": réparations versées par l'Allemagne de l'Ouest', *Annales d'histoire révisionniste*, Winter 1988-89]. More generally, belief in the Holocaust is seen as useful both in fostering Jewish solidarity and limiting the revival of anti-Semitism. Faurisson, in a samizdat circular, has attacked the film *Shoah* partly along these lines, claiming that Menachem Begin approved an allocation of $850,000 towards the making of the film as it furthered Jewish national interests. The Holocaust is portrayed as a form of rite of passage; discovering the Holocaust, becoming immersed in the Holocaust, is part of the very process of becoming an adult Jew (it then continues as a way of bonding Jews together in a sense of shared past persecution and potential future threat).

The wartime Allies are also portrayed as beneficiaries of the Holocaust 'myth'. Belief in German atrocities helps deflect attention from alleged Allied war crimes, such as the fire-bombing of Dresden in the closing stages of the

war, or the Soviet killing of Polish officers at Katyn. The Soviet Union, in particular, benefits because the Holocaust deflects attention from the gulags and the Stalinist terror. Indeed, the Soviet Union is often portrayed as a major factor in the creation of the Holocaust myth. It is argued that all the main alleged extermination camps are in what was to become Communist Europe. It was many years before Western observers were allowed into these camps, by which time they had been heavily rebuilt. Faurisson, for example, argues that what is now shown as the main gas chamber at Auschwitz appears on plans as a series of small rooms. Butz adds that the creation of Israel and subsequent US support for Israel has fostered the USSR's interests in the Middle East by preventing the Americans lining up fully behind anti-Communist Arab states. The USSR, therefore, has a strong vested interest in keeping Holocaust memories alive.

4. Holocaust 'myths' and 'lies'

Another line of attack is to point to parallels with other myths and, especially, to attack the historiography of the Holocaust. It is often pointed out that the First World War saw a vast number of atrocity stories, including claims that the Germans boiled corpses into soap, or transfixed babies on bayonets. All the major stories later turned out to be fakes. Paradoxically, they featured prominently in First World War propaganda, whereas the Holocaust attracted little attention during the Second World War. Historical Revisionists argue that this points to the conclusion that much of the Holocaust is a post-war fabrication. It is often added that Allied intelligence services, and the Vatican, had considerable knowledge of what was happening in occupied Europe; thus, if there had been systematic genocide, these sources would have made more of it during the war.

It is noted that there are some fakes relating to the Holocaust which are even admitted by Jewish groups. Many photographs relating to the Holocaust are alleged to be faked, or presented in a misleading way. Perhaps the most common charge of all, in terms of forgery, is the claim that Anne Frank's diary was clearly written after the War, a claim that has found some echo among journalists and others beyond the confines of Historical Revisionism. The argument is based on the claim that parts are in ball-point pen, that the handwriting varies, and that the thoughts are beyond those of a young girl. In spite of the publication of a detailed defence of the validity of the work by a Dutch official organisation, Faurisson repeated the forgery claim in 1989. However, the argument is not always featured. Butz, while clearly agreeing with the charge, argues that it is irrelevant to proof about the Holocaust as the diary refers to a period of hiding in Amsterdam. Anne Frank subsequently died in a typhoid epidemic in Bergen-Belsen.

It is also frequently argued that the common images of rag-doll-emaciated dead are (when genuine) pictures of typhoid and other epidemic victims. These diseases took a heavy toll near the end of the war, when supplies of food and medicine broke down as Germany collapsed (Anne Frank died in March 1945). There were earlier major epidemics at Auschwitz and elsewhere. In these latter cases, large numbers of bodies had to be cremated quickly, or buried in pits. It is alleged that much of the Holocaust literature and, especially, imagery relate to these events. Such events, it is suggested, help explain the large number of crematoria in the camps; such crematoria were also needed simply because camps such as Auschwitz were large industrial-population centres.

Historians of the Holocaust are attacked for careless research, even deliberate disortion. Thus Faurisson, in a 1987 samizdat circular, claimed that the leading British historian Martin Gilbert had deliberately altered part of the Gerstein evidence for his book *The Holocaust,* enlarging the physical size of the gas chambers to make the evidence seem more plausible. He also claimed that Gilbert's books were full of manipulation and slipshod scholarship. For example, in *Auschwitz and the Allies* Gilbert writes that in 1942 'hundreds of thousands of Jews were being gassed every day at Belzec, Chelmno, Sobibor and Treblinka'. As the hundreds of thousands is in words, not numerals, this cannot be a typographical error. The four million Jews, normally considered to have been gassed (rather than shot, etc.), therefore met their end in a month, according to Gilbert. Gilbert is a leading historian, so the fact that such an error can creep into his work is used by the Historical Revisionists to cast doubt on all historical accounts.

Historical Revisionists have put considerable efforts into trying to use population statistics to show that six million Jews cannot possibly have died. Much of this is derived from the works of French socialist Paul Rassinier, who was imprisoned in Buchenwald for resistance activities. Harwood puts the argument concisely when he writes: '*The World Almanac* of 1938 gives the number of Jews in the world as 16,588,259. But after the war the *New York Times,* February 22nd 1948 placed the number of Jews in the world at a minimum of 15,600,000 and a maximum of 18,700,000'. These figures are used to estimate Jewish losses, through epidemics, random killings etc., as in the hundreds of thousands.

5. 'Scientific' arguments

A final set of arguments can be grouped under the heading 'scientific'. From his earliest writings, Faurisson tried to show the scientific impossibility of mass gassings, for example in his article 'The Mechanics of Gassing', he developed the remarkable claim that gassings, in the way alleged in Holocaust literature, were scientifically impossible. He used evidence from the gassing of single prisoners in US executions, and from the commercial use of Zyklon B. He noted that barracks which had been fumigated with Zyklon B were supposed to be left for twenty hours before special teams went to test them. In American executions, the problems of venting a single small room meant that the acidic vapours were turned into a salt, and then flushed out with water. Yet it is alleged that large gas chambers were quickly vented in camps which contained Germans as well as Jews. It is also claimed that teams, usually without masks, went into the chambers within minutes to remove bodies. A different scientific point was raised by the IHR's 1982 offer of $50,000 for evidence that a single Jew was gassed. It asked for forensic evidence—in particular,

an autopsy showing that a single person had been gassed. The IHR claims that no one came forward.

The controversial British right-wing historian David Irving has written: 'Unlike the writing of history, chemistry is an exact science. Old fashioned historians have always conducted endless learned debates about meanings and interpretations . . . Recently, however, the more daring modern historians have begun using the tools of forensic science'.

Before 1988, Irving's public line accepted that Jews had been systematically killed, but he claimed this was not ordered by Hitler. His conversion to the Holocaust denial position came, allegedly, as the result of evidence compiled by an American expert in gas chamber construction, Fred Leuchter, who visited Auschwitz, Birkenau and Majdanek in early 1988. From his study of the design of the installations, Leuchter concluded that they could not have been used for mass gassings. Forensic samples taken in the gas chambers were analysed in the USA, revealing no significant traces of hydrocyanic gas, though comparison samples taken in delousing chambers for clothes revealed significant levels. This evidence was collated in a report that Irving published in 1989, a document which, he claimed, marked 'the end of the line' for the Auschwitz myth. Irving clearly hoped that the report would exert an appeal even over academic audiences, for the cover states that free copies were being distributed to 'heads of the History, Chemistry, Physics and Engineering departments, the libraries and junior common rooms of every university in the United Kingdom' (though it is not clear how many, if any, were sent; certainly none appear to have arrived at Bath University).

. . . . .

Some books on propaganda list a small number of specific techniques which are seen as central to persuasion. This approach has been rightly criticised on the grounds that there are literally thousands of verbal and non-verbal forms of persuasion. Even in connection with Historical Revisionism, it is possible to delineate a substantial list of devices.

Some techniques are more common in type-1 arguments than in type-2. For example, type-1 texts tend to use a framework of keywords, repetition and stereotyping around the basic arguments. Thus, terms such as 'conspiracy', 'Zionist', 'International Capital/Capitalism' often figure prominently. *The Six Million Reconsidered* is a good example of this. Clearly, these terms, especially 'conspiracy', seek to play on anti-Semitic tendencies. They are not normally present in type-2 arguments, though it could be argued that the presence of words such as 'myth' reflects a more subtle awareness of propaganda technique. There is some evidence that educated audiences are more influenced by propaganda which allows them to make the last link for themselves. Thus, even if the often crude anti-Semitism of type-1 Historical Revisionism failed to alienate educated readers at the outset, it might lead to a lower level of retention of the basic message by too clearly stressing conclusions.

This discussion raises the possibility that it might be best to analyse such texts in terms of hidden messages. One structure which has been common in much propaganda is the story of the martyr as hero. The hidden message in the Holocaust denial could read as follows: Hitler is dead, but he helped warn the world of the dangers of conniving Jews and of expansionary world Communism (stressing the anti-Communist side of Fascism is a common form of rehabilitation). This raises a fascinating area, but it moves away from directly countering the model of Historical Revisionism set up in the previous section. It is, therefore, necessary to revert to a more overt content-based analysis. Limitations on length . . . make it impossible to consider all overt techniques, or to counter every argument put earlier. Nevertheless, four headings help to dismantle the basic technique.

1. Deception/lying

The whole of the Holocaust denial could be seen as deception, in the sense that it is hard to accept that most advocates believe the proposition that there was no systematic genocide. There is also clear lying within specific arguments. Two examples from Harwood's main pamphlet illustrate the point. (a) He claims that by 1938 most Jews had left Germany, all with a 'sizeable proportion of their assets'. In fact, most Jews who were lucky enough to leave Germany lost the majority of their assets. (b) He claims that the International Committee of the Red Cross found no evidence, in its wartime visits to Germany and the occupied territories, of 'a deliberate policy to exterminate the Jews' (changed in the 1987(?) edition to 'no evidence whatsoever of "gas chambers" '). Harwood omitted to point out that the report he referred to specifically stated that there was a Nazi policy of extermination.

2. Selection/suppression

Much of type-2 Historical Revisionism avoids easily-traceable specific deception, as does the better type-1 literature. It relies more on selection, or rather suppression, as all history inevitably involves selection.

An example of suppression would be Harwood's quotation from Colin Cross's book *Adolf Hitler*. Harwood writes: 'Cross . . . observes astutely that "The shuffling of millions of Jews around Europe and murdering them, in a time of desperate war emergency, was useless from any rational point of view" '. The clear implication is that Cross doubts the Holocaust, but reading his book shows, that, shortly afterwards, he uses this line of argument to demonstrate the fanatical anti-Semitism of the Nazis!

A more general example of suppression is a tendency to say little about the *Einsatzgruppen* period, or the euthanasia programme which helped set up the mechanics of gassing. There is also a focus on Auschwitz, which was an industrial complex of 100,000 people as well as a death camp. Little or nothing is said about other camps in Poland which had no such labour need and which operated for human destruction. Faurisson's 'scientific' discussion of gassing is particularly selective. It does not refer to the fact that Zyklon B was not the only form of gassing (carbon monoxide was also used in specially converted sealed lorry-backs, and in gas chambers). He fails to point out that the *Sonderkommando* who emptied the gas chambers

were young Jews, for whom the Nazis would hardly impose rigorous safety standards. Gas chambers, with their bare walls, clearly would not retain dangerous pockets of gas as long as barracks, which he claims were left for a day before being entered after delousing. Moreover, the very fact that Zyklon B was regularly used on an extensive scale to fumigate barracks in camps shows that the venting problem in a large open space was not critical. These same points apply to Leuchter's arguments about the dangers of using gas in the camps. Other aspects of selection in the Leuchter report include his claim that Zyklon B would only be effective in warm temperatures, but that his visit revealed the chambers to be damp and cold. As the camps were unoccupied and as he visited Poland in February, the low temperature is hardly surprising; he omits to mention that central Europe in the summer is relatively hot. He also glosses over the fact that his samples were taken surreptitiously—hardly under controlled scientific conditions. Moreover, there are hypotheses which could explain why there should be higher concentrations of hydrocyanic acid in the walls of delousing chambers than in those of gas chambers: for example, the human body would absorb far more gas than clothes.

Overall, the focus of Historical Revisionism has increasingly centred on the evidence about the existence of gas chambers. Why Jews should have been in concentration camps is glossed over. Historical Revisionists sometimes point out that the British used camps during the Boer War, or that the Americans interned aliens during the Second World War. However, the Nazis' first concentration camps, such as Dachau (which was not specifically for Jews), were set up shortly after they came to power in 1933—not during a war-emergency. Virulent anti-Semitic outpourings were a feature of the 'thought' of many Nazis, especially Hitler, well before the Second World War. It is true that there is a growing debate about the centrality of anti-Semitism to Nazism in general, but it is grossly disingenuous to portray the camps, with their concomitant degradation, torture and killings, as simply a response to the War.

3. Authority/status claims

In order to boost their arguments, academic credentials are stressed or invented. Thus: the Institute of Historical Review; its *Journal of Historical Review;* its annual conferences held in America; the Historical Review Press; the *Annales d'histoire révisionniste*—reminiscent, in its title, of the prestigious French history journal, *Annales*. The IHR managed to place an advertisement in the *London Review of Books,* and came close to placing a full-page one in *History Today*. The *Journal of Historical Review,* Winter 1980, listed seventeen members of its Editorial Advisory Board: nine were given as being current or retired academics. None were serious historians, but it is important to underline the fact that Historical Revisionism has attracted highly educated supporters.

In other cases, fraudulent academic or status credentials have been employed. The most notorious example is 'Richard Harwood', who not only used a pseudonym for *Did Six Million Really Die?*; he also found it necessary to state on the back cover that he was 'a writer and specialist in political and diplomatic aspects of the Second World War. At present he is with the University of London' (Harwood's name, and therefore this reference, is omitted from the 1987 (?) revised edition). Rassinier is frequently referred to as a 'Professor' or 'geographer'. In fact, he was an anti-Semitic writer and teacher. Harwood shows nothing if not nerve in referring to a book about Allied bombing and the post-war trials as being written by J. P. Veale, 'the distinguished English jurist' ('lawyer' in the revised edition). Veale was in fact an obscure solicitor.

4. Evidence/proof

Ultimately, the key to the Holocaust-denial technique can be seen in the Historical Revisionists' concept of evidence and proof. Many of them stress that, at one point, they believed in the Holocaust but that their eyes had been opened when they looked more closely at the evidence. Clearly, this raises the question of what is valid evidence and proof. Stäglich, a former magistrate, argues [in *The Auschwitz Myth*] that:

> According to the time-honored principle of Roman law *in dubio pro reo,* he [the accused] must be acquitted when the facts of the case leave room for doubt, even though his innocence cannot be definitely established . . . Thus the accused—the German people—are under no obligation to prove that 'gas chambers' did not exist. Rather it is up to our accusers to prove that they did.

There are, unquestionably, some valid legal problems which can be raised about the Nuremberg trials and about other aspects of evidence relating to the Holocaust. However, it is important not to confuse legal and historical practice, for example hearsay, or evidence obtained under duress, may be invalid in a court of law but they are not necessarily ignored by historians. Moreover, it is important to stress that hearsay evidence or evidence obtained under duress constitute only a small part of Holocaust evidence. The knowledge that the Nazi state practised systematic genocide is based on normal historical methodology which uses as many sources as possible to reach a conclusion which is *beyond reasonable doubt*. It is not necessary that every piece of evidence be without a flaw, simply that the whole case be based on careful weighing of all the evidence. As such, it is possible to question whether the number of Jews who died was six million. Indeed, respectable writers have done so: Gerald Reitlinger gives a figure of just over four million [*The Final Solution,* 1971]. Details of decision-making and of the process of genocide can also be questioned; again, there is a growing debate about these issues, especially whether the Holocaust was in some way inevitable. What cannot be doubted is that millions of Jews (and others) suffered appallingly, and that the Nazi state committed genocide.

The more sophisticated arguments stress the need for 'scientific' proof. There is a sleight of hand here in the sense that historical arguments cannot exhibit some features of 'paradigmatic' scientific arguments, for example repeatability. However, it is interesting to adapt the Popperian notion which holds that science can be demarcated from metaphysics because scientists are supposed to employ fal-

sifiable conjectures. (The fact that this view of science can be criticised is irrelevant here.) The whole basis of Historical Revisionism relies on the fact that it will not accept falsification. Even when Historical Revisionism appears to conform to this Popperian notion, there is a trick. The IHR's offer of a $50,000 reward for forensic evidence seems to require just one autopsy. However, the Nazis clearly did not carry out autopsies on their own gas victims, whose bodies were subsequently cremated or burned. (Autopsies were carried out on those who died during the horrifying medical experiments inflicted on some camp inmates.) In some cases, corpses were even exhumed in order to burn them. This request for forensic evidence plays on popular images of large piles of rag-doll dead found at the time of the liberation of the camps. It is true that there were many dead in camps such as Dachau and Bergen-Belsen, but these were the victims of typhoid and maltreatment rather than of gassing. In the extremely unlikely event that an autopsy was found, the IHR would probably still manage to avoid considering this as proof. Such an autopsy could be challenged as a forgery. Even if this tactic failed, it could be argued that the person was not gassed in a mass gas chamber, but as a result of the random killings which Historical Revisionists accept did happen. Moreover, to be on the safe side, the IHR insisted that such evidence be examined by its own panel of 'experts'! Thus, even after a claimant, Mel Mermelstein, took the IHR to court over the $50,000 reward, and a judge had taken 'judicial notice' of the fact of gassings, the IHR still maintained that gassings had not been proven (the IHR claimed that the court awarded Mermelstein damages rather than the reward).

More generally, the Holocaust denial relies on introducing an element of doubt into the argument, for example as some eyewitnesses may have remembered incorrectly, or even lied, it is held that all eyewitnesses cannot be believed. As there were myths of atrocities in the First World War, it is claimed that there are similar myths for the Second World War. However, as Descartes has shown, if we try to doubt everything, we find that there is nothing of which we can be certain except our own ability to doubt. Historical Revisionism relies on an unattainable conception of proof in which there is not the slightest doubt in any area.

. . . . .

In view of the above discussion, the potential attraction of Historical Revisionism could be seen within two main psychological frameworks. Firstly, it appeals to those who are already Fascist or racist, or who have personality traits which lend themselves to such views. Secondly, it is especially appealing to those with a predisposition to view the world in terms of conspiracy theory. Such individuals are thus able to discount what psychologists call 'dissonance' (conflicting evidence): evidence as to the existence of the Holocaust, for instance, can be dismissed as the product of Jewish manipulation. Michael Billig has argued [in 'The Extreme Right: Continuities in anti-Semitic Conspiracy Theory in post-war Europe', in *The Nature of the Right,* 1989] that 'psychological approaches to the study of conspiracy theory can basically be grouped around two themes: the study of cognitive and motivational factors'. In the former case, there is a tendency to argue that the search for explanations is natural. Conspiracy theory appeals precisely because it offers a simple explanation of complex and diverse political events. In the latter case, the emphasis is more on the psychological compensations to be gained from a belief in conspiracy theory. Thus, there could be a sense of superiority which comes from believing that one knows a hidden truth; or repressed emotions could be projected onto the alleged conspirators. However, while these approaches are important, they seem better at explaining why the Holocaust denial might appeal to less rather than more educated audiences. They also ignore important non-psychological aspects of the potential appeal of such arguments.

The French sociologist Jacques Ellul has argued that education is not necessarily a defence against propaganda. Indeed, he believes that there are three reasons why educated audiences might be susceptible to propaganda: they receive large amounts of unverifiable, unsystematic information; they believe themselves capable of judging; and they tend to think that they ought to have an opinion on matters. To this might be added the academic tendency to look for new arguments, to reject the 'conventional wisdom'.

Another way of considering the potential appeal involves looking at some epistemological problems in coming to terms with Historical Revisionist arguments. The difficulties can be seen most clearly by considering debates about the nature of scientific knowledge, a particularly appropriate analogy as some Historical Revisionists make great play of the scientific nature of their work. Harry Collins and Trevor Pinch have shown in their study of scientists' response to the paranormal that most reject such work outright because it does not fit existing theories. Proponents of paranormal views are usually seen as frauds. There seems to be a parallel with much of the literature on Historical Revisionism, where critics have often clearly read little of what they criticise, and quickly resort to attacks on individual motivations. It could be countered that this is a grossly misleading parallel. Scientists dismiss the paranormal because it does not fit existing *theories*; the Holocaust denial is rejected because it contradicts well established *facts*. However, a final point about the sociology of science illustrates the problem of frameworks in discussing Historical Revisionism. It has become commonplace to argue that what we observe depends largely upon what we know, or rather believe we know. Much of the literature on the Holocaust has clearly been produced within a framework of what has become known as the 'Intentionalist' view of Nazi anti-Semitism. This holds that anti-Semitism was fundamental to Nazism, and the Holocaust the inevitable, or almost inevitable, consequence. Radical supporters of what has become known as the 'Functionalist' or 'Structuralist' school see anti-Semitism as little more than a rhetorical prop of Nazi agitation. The functionalist interpretation makes it more difficult to understand the Holocaust, especially when added to facts such as that some Jews were allowed to leave Germany as late as 1940.

Academically, Historical Revisionism plays on the view that knowledge is ideologically structured, that the historian is not a totally impartial observer, however much he may try to follow the injunction to empathise. The editorial of the first *Annales d'histoire révisionniste,* published in 1987, specifically refers to the tradition of history, allegedly dating from Herodotus, which sees its main task as teaching lessons rather than discovering objective facts. As the early Judaeo-Christian historical tradition shared similar traits, Historical Revisionists seek to portray the history of the Holocaust as a latter-day version of the 'exemplar' rather than the Enlightenment philosophy of history. In other words, the goal is not the discovery of facts, even laws, in a neutral scientific spirit; the point is to teach morals, to defend the community's interest. The Holocaust is portrayed as a useful lesson to Jews to retain group solidarity; it is a means of combating anti-Semitism. It is important, in this context, to admit that there seem to be books on the Holocaust which have been written with the intention of stressing lessons rather than closely examining all facts (or with other non-historical motives in mind). And in drawing such lessons, style, often based on emotive appeals, has sometimes transcended the demands of strict historical scholarship.

The same issue of *Annales d'histoire révisionniste* also plays on the revisionism which is inherent in all history. Lucy Dawidowicz has pointed out, that, in the case of Nazi Germany, major academic revisionism goes back to the early 1960s with the publication of A. J. P. Taylor's *The Origins of the Second World War.* This viewed Hitler as a pragmatist in foreign policy, lacking a grand design. A notable contribution to late 1970s revisionism was David Irving's book *Hitler's War.* This claimed that no documentary evidence could be found which showed that Hitler either ordered, or knew about the Holocaust. Himmler and the SS were portrayed as the guilty parties. Irving went on to offer a $1000 reward, through his short-lived magazine *Focal Point,* to anyone who could produce a genuine document showing that Hitler clearly had knowledge of the Holocaust. The debates in the 1980s between the 'Intentionalists' and 'Functionalists' are therefore only a part of a growing revisionism of Nazi history. The drift of this has been to challenge the totalitarian model of the 1950s with its emphasis on features such as the dominant leader purveying a clearly defined ideology.

Historical Revisionists in the late 1980s took particular comfort from aspects of the bitter *Historikerstreit* debate in West Germany. This began with an attempt by the historian Ernst Nolte to 'relativise' the Holocaust, but soon spread to question central aspects of the 'conventional' wisdom on Nazi Germany. He claimed that the Holocaust was only one of many examples of terror and genocide in world history. Moreover, Nolte saw it as a reaction to fear born of the Russian revolution, and the ensuing terror and gulags. More specifically, he claimed that the World Zionist Organization had, in effect, declared war on Nazi Germany, and this gave grounds to treat Jews as prisoners of war! This argument is especially interesting for the questions it raises about the nature of history. For example, while Nolte does raise some important questions in comparative history, he seems motivated by a clear desire to rehabilitate aspects of Germany's past. At least, this seems the most charitable explanation of views such as his claim that there existed a Jewish declaration of war on Germany: how could diverse peoples, with no state, yet alone army, 'declare war'?

The French historian Pierre Vidal-Naquet has written [in *Les assassins de la mémoire,* 1987] in relation to Historical Revisionism that 'to deny history is not to revise it'. This glosses over the fact that it is not always easy to provide a neat philosophical definition of what is history and what is propaganda. In some ways, the distinction is one of intention: the historian should seek to provide as objective an account as possible; the propagandist seeks to serve an ulterior political motive. The vast majority of Historical Revisionist writings have a clear political motive, usually anti-Semitic and/or neo-Fascist. However, the distinction between history and propaganda cannot simply be one of intention. There are many works, which are usually seen as history, where there is a clear, overt, or at least implicit, political position; for example, are not most Western accounts of Fascism written from the perspective of the superiority of liberal democratic systems? And if intention is the sole key to propaganda, how should we view the writings of an Historical Revisionist who actually believed what he or she wrote?

Propaganda has, therefore, also to be understood in terms of the nature of the arguments. One such approach would be to claim that propaganda teaches us *what* to think, rather than *how* to think. The distinction opens up fruitful avenues for further thought, but fails fully to resolve the problem in the sense that much history surely tells us what to think. A more helpful one-liner is the view that propaganda serves to *narrow* thought, whereas history serves to *broaden* it. The legitimate historiography of the Holocaust raises a vast number of questions. These include detailed questions about the procurement of transport for the Jews. It encompasses more general questions about the Nazi regime, for instance whether the system was truly totalitarian, or whether it was more chaotic and fragmented than has generally been assumed. Holocaust historiography even raises sweeping issues, such as the question of human nature, or the concept of progress. On the other hand, Historical Revisionism concentrates on a small number of issues and, on many of these, it is misleading, downright wrong, even dishonest. Historical Revisionism ignores vast amounts of evidence which contradict its position. As such, it is hardly likely to influence the central views of the professional historian or serious student of the Holocaust. Unfortunately, the history of propaganda indicates that the 'big lie' or the repetition of a small number of points, can, all too easily influence the views of the less well informed. It is, ultimately, for this reason that the central arguments and the propaganda technique of the Historical Revisionists are worthy of an essay in specific analysis and refutation.

Brian Siano

SOURCE: "Dancing with the Fuhrer," in *The Humanist,* Vol. 53, No. 5, September-October, 1993, pp. 42-4.

[*In the following essay, Siano focuses on the writings of David Irving and Willis Carto, two major figures in the Holocaust denial movement.*]

There's a scene in the Mel Brooks movie *The Producers* where Gene Wilder and Zero Mostel visit a writer whose stage play could be the guaranteed flop they need to make a million dollars. (Rent the film if you need an explanation.) The writer is a deranged Nazi and his play, *Springtime for Hitler,* is subtitled "A Gay Romp with Adolf and Eva at Berchtesgarten." He invites Wilder and Mostel to celebrate and, while singing old German drinking songs over schnapps, says wistfully: "Not many people knew this, but the fuhrer was a *terrific* dancer."

"Really?" Mostel replies tentatively. "I never dreamed. . . . "

"Zat is becauss you were taken in!" shouts the playwright. "Zey told *lies.*"

That's sort of the experience I had reading David Irving, the historian-at-large of the neo-Nazi Institute for Historical Review. Irving is somewhat unique among this crowd, and not just because his last name's Irving; some of his books, unlike those of the other Holohoaxers, are actually available in otherwise respectable bookstores. The *Sunday Times* of London even enlisted his aid (albeit reluctantly) in obtaining the recently discovered Goebbels diaries from Moscow. And Irving's circulation in neo-Nazi circles does give him some unique career opportunities; in 1992, he announced that he'd recently obtained the original transcripts and some surviving tapes of Adolf Eichmann's memoirs, dictated throughout the late 1950s.

In 1989, Irving delivered a speech to a neo-Nazi rally held (big surprise) in a Munich beer cellar. Irving declared that Hitler had never ordered the mass murder of the Jews and that, apart from Jews being shot or used as slaves, there were no gas chambers—and therefore no mass murders. Defending himself in court three years later, Irving referred to the Holocaust as a "blood lie" that had been cruelly propagated against the people of Germany.

(Remember, these folks are a whole new realm of *extreme.* Other Holohoaxers maintain that the Jews died from food shortages, that they were merely well-cared-for slave laborers, and even that a swimming pool had been built for their personal recreational use at Auschwitz.)

Accepting Irving's contention that Hitler was out of the loop for the final solution would require ignoring the fact that Hitler had a phenomenal memory for logistics and military information. Very little went on in the Reich that he didn't know about or couldn't recall in detail. And to suppose that Hitler didn't sanction mass murder would require ignoring hundreds of hours of speeches calling for the extermination of European Jewry. The Goebbels diaries reveal Hitler's jubilation over the notorious 1938 *Kristallnacht,* in which he ordered the arrests of 20,000 to 30,000 Jews, saying that they would "pay dearly for their own mistakes." On the fifty-third anniversary of this event, Irving addressed a gathering of neo-Nazis in Halle, Germany. He hailed the resurgent nationalism that was driving the Nazi revivalist movement and assured his listeners that their numbers would double over the next few years.

Irving's take on Eichmann's memoirs is instructive. He claims that Eichmann thought the final solution meant merely exporting the Jews to Madagascar—which Irving feels "would have been an ideal solution to a perennial world tragedy."

But at one point in his memoirs, Eichmann himself stated that Reinhard Heydrich delivered the following message: "I've come from the Reichsfuhrer SS. The fuhrer has given the order for the physical destruction of the Jews." Irving promptly falls all over himself trying to explain this incriminating statement away—describing Eichmann as a scared fugitive grasping at any kind of extenuating circumstance, and reminding us that this is a *postwar* document and so we have to be cautious about taking it at face value, etc., etc. (Never mind all those documents written *during* the war about how well the gas chambers were working.)

Irving also dwells obsessively on how obsessive *Eichmann* was getting while in Argentina:

> He keeps coming back to the horrible thought. Did *they* manage to use *us?* Did the Zionists use the Nazis to further their own ends? Was the Holocaust something they themselves inflicted on their own body, in order to bring about their Zionist cause in the long run?

But rather than contest these ridiculous ravings, Irving relates an instructive little story: Eichmann claimed that a young girl had been removed from a camp-bound train because she wasn't Jewish, but at the waiting station where she was deposited, a Jewish man protested having a non-Jew left there. This story, Irving says, is an "ugly depiction of the way man behaves unto man." Amazing: Adolf Eichmann is a put-upon, persecuted bureaucrat and a man on his way to the concentration camps becomes a symbol of human evil. Welcome to David Irving's moral universe.

As you might have guessed by now, the IHR's *Journal of Historical Review* isn't exactly bursting with useful historical research. It's basically a hate-sheet, filled with diatribes about how the Jews have somehow strong-armed several continents' worth of scholars, historians, and journalists. Most of the Holohoaxers are fond of retelling stories about how they fearlessly stood fast to their principles in the face of intimidation and harassment from the Jews. They've also somehow convinced themselves that the Holocaust "myth" is essential in maintaining massive U.S. support for Israel every year.

The most powerful figure in the Holohoax movement is millionaire Willis Carto. Carto's financial largesse endows any number of anti-Semitic and neo-Nazi organizations, such as the Liberty Lobby, its newsletter the *Spotlight*, David Duke's misnamed Populist Party, the Noontide Press, and the IHR. Carto himself stays very much in the shadows; I ran a few searches on newspaper databases and found only a handful of passing references. But Carto is listed on IHR letterhead as its founder, and the business license for Noontide/IHR was filed by his wife Elisabeth.

Carto denies that he is either a Nazi or an anti-Semite. He characterizes himself as an "anti-Zionist," which (in his scheme of things) means belated support for the Nazis during World War II. During the late 1950s, his newsletter *Right* recommended that people join George Lincoln Rockwell's American Nazi Party. In a passage remarkably like the ravings in Eichmann's diaries, Carto wrote:

> Who is using who? Who is calling the shots? History supplies the answer to this. History tells us plainly who our Enemy is. Our Enemy today is the same Enemy of 50 years ago and before— and that was before Communism. The Communists are "using" the Jews we are told . . . who was "using" the Jews fifty years ago—one hundred or one thousand years ago? History supplies the answer. The Jews came first and remain Public Enemy No. 1.

Or, to put a finer point to it:

> In fact, no objective Scholar can deny today that the world would be a far better place to live if Germany had won—even if it had meant the defeat of American arms!

A lot of the other materials sold by Carto's enterprises are mainly for long-term fans of the Third Reich. One can obtain reprints of the *Protocols of the Learned Elders of Zion,* coffee-table books of Hitler's paintings, memoirs of Nazi high officials, and biographies of famous anti-Semites. For a splash of multiculturalism, there are books on race and IQ scores. And if that ain't enough, the *Spotlight* runs ads for books about Nikola Tesla's energy theories, quasi-survivalist tomes on military tactics and changing your identity, and regular columns on investing in silver, "the Gentile metal." Ernst Zundel has even reportedly written about a secret Nazi stash of UFOs at the South Pole, under the pen name of "Christof Friedrich." (I'd love to get hold of *that* one.)

And so we come full circle, back to the Harry Elmer Barnes isolationist crowd discussed last issue [in *The Humanist*]. The fascist movements in America in the 1930s were based upon an anti-Semitism that seems unbelievable today. Back then, Charles Coughlin was a Catholic priest whose radio broadcasts pushed a pro-Hitler, hate-the-Jews-and-free-the-silver-markets message; today, even a creep like David Duke has to smokescreen his agenda behind silky codewords. But that's beginning to change; the words regarding *mass extermination* are being minced less and less these days.

It's at this point that Holocaust revisionism cannot be seen as anything other than part of a global neo-Nazi movement. It encompasses skinheads in London and Berlin, armed-and-dangerous American groups like the Posse Comitatus and Christian Identity, former Nazis still alive and active in Europe, and even the Nation of Islam and the minions of Bo Gritz and Lyndon LaRouche.

One indication of the interrelatedness of these groups came from an investigation by the Simon Weisenthal Center this past year. A journalist posed as the representative of a fictitious Australian white supremacist magazine called the *Right Way* in order to gain the confidence of neo-Nazis operating in Germany. Several of the Nazis contacted claimed to be close friends with Willis Carto and IHR head Mark Weber. This claim was borne out by *Weber's* contacting the journalist—at a phone number known only to the Nazis he contacted—to obtain a copy of the *Right Way.* (When Weber met with the journalist, he bitched at length about how little Carto was paying him. There goes *his* promising career.)

The moral debates about the Holocaust are pretty much the only things the Reich produced that will last a thousand years. There's the question of whether such horrors can happen at any time, to any people, or whether it's a scar that Jews alone will collectively bear. People can argue over whether the Holocaust has been trivialized through its numerous dramatizations and reevaluations, or whether a less psychologically intriguing form of mass murder deserves to be compared with it. But frankly, the Holohoaxers just don't deserve such weighty treatment. In fact, it would be an insult to leap from them to such questions.

So instead, as promised last issue, I'd like to propose a simple test which the Holohoaxers can do to settle the matter once and for all. Fred Leuchter's arguments about the gas chambers being unworkable are the most oft-cited of the Holohoaxers' claims. Let's see them *prove* it—and put some of Willis Carto's money to good use for a change.

All they have to do is build another gas chamber, being sure to follow the specs for the ones found at the camps. Then they can climb right in and have the requisite amount of Zyklon-B introduced.

I don't see why the Holohoaxers have passed up this definitive, Evel Kneivel approach for so long. After all, if they're wrong, they can at least pride themselves on having stayed in the Fuhrerbunker until the very end, so to speak. They'd also avoid having to face the scorn and ridicule that is usually the lot of failed "heretics."

And if they *survive*—if any of them comes goose-stepping out after an hour or so—I promise to retract every rotten thing I've said about them in these columns. Scout's honor.

Pierre Vidal-Naquet

SOURCE: "Theses on Revisionism," in *Assassins of Memory: Essays on the Denial of the Holocaust,* translated by Jeffrey Mehlman, Columbia University Press, 1992, pp. 79-98.

[*In the following essay, originally published in French in 1985, Vidal-Naquet provides an analysis of the phenomenon of anti-Semitic historical revisionism.*]

I shall call "revisionism" the doctrine according to which the genocide practiced by Nazi Germany against Jews and Gypsies did not exist but is to be regarded as a myth, a fable, or a hoax. I shall speak of "revisionism" in the absolute sense of the word, but there are also relative revisionisms of which I shall say a few words.

The word itself has a history which is strange and would merit elaboration. The first modern "revisionists" were, in France, the partisans of a "revision" or judicial review of

---

On refutations of Holocaust denial literature:

I was the Israeli Consul-General in Chicago when the Nazis marched in Skokie. In the forefront of the legal defence of the Nazis' march was a liberal Jewish lawyer. Here, then, you had the spectacle of a band of people in Nazi uniforms marching through the heart of a Jewish suburb of Chicago where some 90 percent of the Jews had numbers tatooed on their arms—and the Nazi marchers are defended by a Jew.

Professor Arthur Butz appears at Northwestern University, in the same area of Chicago where 80,000 Jews now live who survived the crematoria, who had seen their children and their parents gassed and burned to death, and he explains to them that there never was a Holocaust. Professor Butz, a Jew, is brought to trial, and who defends him? A Jew. And who pays for his defence? Jews. Yes, we have a problem.

The problem has other aspects too. That of the youth, for example. The young generation does not want to believe that such a thing could have happened. And there are the youngsters—Jewish youngsters—who will echo Jesse Jackson's "I'm sick and tired of hearing about the Holocaust!"—or words to that effect. Then there is the aspect of the Third World. The historians of the future will not be only European or American historians. There is a Third World that knew not the Holocaust, and they hear this discussion and find themselves in a dilemma: Was there a Holocaust or not?

Moshe Gilboa, in Denying the Holocaust, *by Yisreal Gutman, Shazar Library, 1985.*

---

the trial of Alfred Dreyfus (1894), but the word was quickly turned around by their adversaries, and that reversal should be considered as symptomatic. The word has subsequently taken on a meaning that is at times positive, at times negative, always implying the critique of a dominant orthodoxy. Bernstein and his friends were revisionists in relation to orthodox Marxists, and the term has been transmitted to the Maoists who use it to characterize their Soviet enemies. In relation to traditional Zionism, the disciples of Vladimir Jabotinsky, currently in power in Israel, were also "revisionists," as are the American historians who contest the officially and traditionally received version of the origins of the Cold War.

The revisionists of Hitler's genocide, however, invoke as their predecessor, not without being partially justified, a different American historical school, which may be epitomized by the name of H. E. Barnes (1889-1968). A "radical" historian and sociologist (in the American sense of the term), at least at the beginning of his career, an anti-imperialist and anticolonialist, Barnes rose up against the historical orthodoxy that ascribed blame for World War I solely to the central European empires. Although not totalitarian, that orthodoxy was no less real in France and England than in the United States. The French "yellow book" of 1914 removed the most embarrassing episodes and occasionally resorted to out and out fraudulence, as in the case of its presentation of the Russian general mobilization (July 30, 1914) as following the Austro-Hungarian mobilization (July 31). During the war, for the first time, propaganda was employed in a massive way. In both camps, historians entered the fray. In 1919, for example, an American historian published a collection significantly and paradoxically entitled *Volleys from a Non-Combatant.* In the liberal world, the orthodoxy was not imposed as it was and had to be in the totalitarian world, but existed no less. In 1935, the French historian Jules Isaac, the author of well-known manuals for lycée students, chose to submit as a thesis topic to the Sorbonne the Poincaré ministry (January 1912-January 1913), which, in the historiographical context of the day, would have raised the problem of Poincaré's responsibility in the origin of the war. The Sorbonne requested that "for reasons of appropriateness," the name of Poincaré not be mentioned in the subject description. Isaac refused that compromise and wrote to the Dean of the Faculté des Lettress: "If, 'for reasons of appropriateness,' the Faculté forbids me from mentioning the name of Poincaré in the title, 'for reasons of appropriateness' the Faculté can also ask me not to bring into full relief, in the course of my work, the personal role of Poincaré." What was true after the First World War remained true after the second. On December 22, 1950, President Truman addressed a convention of the American Historical Society and asked it to help him in implementing a federal historical curriculum for the fight against communism. It was, to be sure, a matter of opposing lies with the truth, but is truth so easy to cast in federal terms?

H. E. Barnes unfortunately was not satisfied with destroying the orthodoxy of the Entente and their American allies. He reversed it. His book, *The Genesis of the World War,* discovered—or rather invented—a "Franco-Russian plot which caused the war." He did not hesitate to "reveal," for example, that Jaurés was assassinated "by instigation of the Russian secret police." Jules Isaac could say of him, with due moderation, that he was "audacious, and extremely capricious in his application of historical method."

Barnes's book still has a lesson for us. Addressing the French public, the patriarch of American revisionism invoked the Dreyfus Affair; by recalling the example of the Affair, he ends up whitewashing Germany entirely of any responsibility in the genesis of the world conflict—which is as absurd as the opposite thesis. The Affair was thus a reference, and as paradoxical as it may seem, it would remain so for a number of revisionists of the Nazi genocide.

It is in fact a valid point of reference, but in an entirely different sense. Hannah Arendt quite properly saw in it one of the first stages of the genesis of modern totalitarianism. Mutatis mutandis, the evidence for Dreyfus's guilt, despite the "proof" that flooded the case and which the anti-Dreyfusards strained to turn around, remains, for the anti-Dreyfusard core, as central a dogma as the innocence of Hitler, accused of genocide, is for the revisionist of today. The exculpation of Hitler in the name of Dreyfusard values, and with the obstinacy of the most narrow-minded nationalists, is a modern refinement worthy of interest.

The Dreyfus Affair, the struggle against the nationalist versions of the 1914-1918 war, the struggle against the "lies" of the Second World War, and against the greatest of all "lies," Hitler's genocide, that "hoax of the twentieth century": such are the three elements that allow one to grasp the "good conscience" of the revisionists and particularly of the "radical" or "*gauchiste*" revisionists, of Paul Rassinier and Jean-Gabriel Cohn-Bendit. Rassinier's case is quite remarkable: a socialist, a pacifist who was nonetheless in the Resistance, a deportee, he is the true father of contemporary revisionism.

> Rassinier, with a kind of obstinacy whose enigmatic character one is hard put to dispell, remained faithful within that absolute novelty, the world of the concentration camps, to the lesson of 1914. If he described his experience in all its details, worked to conceptualized and thematize it, it was not in order to convey it, but rather to reduce its experiential character, cleansing it of all that seemed repetitious in it. He did not magnify the SS out of fascination or by virtue of who knows what masochism. He banalized them with the sole aim of fitting *one war into the other,* and of crediting the behavior of all concerned— that of the victim and that of the executioner, that of the German soldiers and that of their adversaries—to the account of a common "unreasonable abjection." [A. Finkielkraut, *L' Avenir d'une négation: Réflexion sur la question du genocide,* 1982]

Denying—for a long time in isolation—the Hitlerian genocide, Rassinier took himself simultaneously for Romain Rolland "above the melee" in 1914 and Bernard Lazare, the solitary fighter for truth and justice in 1896. His example would influence H. E. Barnes and would contribute to the transition from the older revisionism to the modern variety. It was necessary to reconstitute this context, and we shall attempt to delineate it with greater precision. Need we, however, refute the "revisionist" theses, and specifically the most characteristic of them, the negation of the Hitlerian genocide and its preferred instrument, the gas chamber? At times it has seemed necessary to do so. Such will certainly not be my intention in these pages. In the final analysis, one does not refute a closed system, a total lie that is not refutable to the extent that its conclusion has preceded any evidence. It was once necessary to prove that the *Protocols of the Elders of Zion* was a fabrication. As Hannah Arendt has said, if so many believed the document to be authentic, "the historian's job is no longer [only] to detect the hoax. Nor is his task to invent explanations concealing the essential historical and political fact: a forgery was believed in. That fact is more important than the (historically speaking, secondary) fact that one was dealing with a forgery."

. . . . .

Propaganda, or, *bourrage de crâne,* "skull-cramming," as it was called during the war of 1914-1918; propaganda and *bourage de crâne* during the war of 1939-1945. The great Hitlerian slaughter is placed on the same level as the "children with their hands cut off" of 1914; we would quite simply be dealing with a maneuver of psychological warfare. That central theory of "revisionism" has the merit of recalling for us two fundamental elements of the world conflict. On the whole, Allied propaganda made very little use of the great massacre in its psychological war against Nazi Germany. In general, information about the genocide, when it began to filter through (which was quite early on), encountered huge obstacles, not the least of which was—precisely—the precedent of 1914-1918. In a sense it may be said that the first "revisionists," and there were a number of Jews among them, had been recruited during the war in the intelligence agencies of the Allied powers. All this, for example, has been established beyond refutation in a recent work by Walter Laqueur [*The Terrible Secret,* 1980].

In the flow of information coming from the occupied territories were to be found the true, the less true, and the false. The general meaning of what was occurring left no doubt, but as far as the modalities were concerned, there were frequently grounds for hesitating between one version and another. Concerning the camp at Auschwitz, for example, it was not until April 1944, following a number of escapes, that it became possible to establish a firsthand description—which proved remarkably precise—of the extermination process. Those "protocols of Auschwitz" were to be made public by the American War Refugee Board only in November 1944. Starting in May 1944, the deportation and massacre of Hungarian Jews constituted events announced by the Allied and neutral press virtually on a daily basis.

I spoke of the "true" and the "false." That simple opposition accounts rather inadequately for what occurred. From errors concerning architectural form to confusions about distances and numbers, all kinds of imprecision existed, as did a number of phantasms and myths. But they did not exist in isolation, like some creation sui generis or "rumor," a hoax hatched by a specific milieu, such as the New York Zionists. They existed as a shadow projected by—or prolonging—reality. Consider as well that the most direct and authentic reports, when they arrived at Allied intelligence services, needed to be deciphered, since they were written in the coded language of the totalitarian systems, a language that most often could not be fully interpreted until the end of the war.

We shall give an example of both these phenomena, starting with the second. British secret services had deciphered the codes used by the Germans for their internal communications. Among the police documents that came to be known in this manner there were statistics: entries and exits of human raw material for a certain number of camps, including Auschwitz, between the spring of 1942 and February 1943. One of the columns indicating "departures by any means" was interpreted to mean death. But there was no mention in such texts of gassings. Thanks to an official Polish publication, we are quite familiar with this kind of document. For instance, this statistic entered on October 18, 1944 in the women's camp at Birkenau, which adds up various "departures" diminishing the number of those enrolled in the camp: natural death, transit, and "special treatment," which was subsequently deciphered as meaning gassing.

One of the crucial documents discussed in Laqueur's book

is a telegram sent from Berne to London, on August 10, 1942, by G. Riegner, the secretary of the World Jewish Congress. That telegram, written on the basis of information conveyed by a German industrialist, announced that there were plans at Hitler's headquarters to assemble all of Europe's Jews "to be at one blow exterminated." Among the means studied: prussic acid. There is a remarkable share of error and myth in the document. The decision to proceed with exterminations had been taken months before; the use of prussic acid (Zyklon B), which was inaugurated in September 1941 for Soviet war prisoners, had been common at Auschwitz since the spring of 1942, and the utilization of gas obviously contradicts the notion of an extermination in a single blow, which would have required a nuclear weapon, and which did not exist at the time. In Freudian terms, we may say that there was a condensation and displacement of information.

But a condensation of what? One of the most remarkable debates provoked among historians by Hitler's extermination policy pitted Martin Broszat against Christopher Browning in the same German scholarly journal.

Refuting a semi-revisionist book by the British historian David Irving, which had exonerated Hitler—in favor of Himmler—of responsibility for the great slaughter, Broszat saw in the "final solution," which was indeed an extermination, something that was partially improvised and developed, as it were, on a case-by-case basis. To which Browning responded that the information communicated by Hoess (according to Himmler) and by Eichmann (according to Heydrich) had to be taken quite seriously: it was during the summer of 1941 that Hitler took the decision to exterminate the Jews. That such an order, communicated to a few individuals, and having begun in quick order to be executed, should become through condensation the "one blow" of Riegner's telegram is not at all implausible.

But how would one not also insist on the crucial role of different phases in a process developing in time, phases concerning which Broszat has contributed important clarifications? Various phases or stages included: the model ghetto at Theresienstadt and the "family camp" at Auschwitz; the ghettos with their privileged social strata, whose members believed they would escape, by virtue of those privileges, a common fate that they helped to implement; at the very sites of extermination, the situation of those who were not selected for the gas chamber. Only gradual phases or stages of every sort allowed the extermination policy to be pursued with relative smoothness. All these stages of a process, these phases of a murder serve as so many arguments for the revisionists. Because Jewish weddings were celebrate at Maidanek, near Lublin, it will be pretended that the camps were, if need be, places of rejoicing. But who does not perceive that such phases were the temporal and social conditions necessary for the proper functioning of the killing?

· · · · ·

Revisionism is to be found in multiple and various forms: tracts, "scholarly" volumes, common propaganda, mimeographed pamphlets, apparently distinguished journals, video cassettes. Examining a collection of such documents on the shelves of a library, noting the number of translations of a single text, reading the numerous scholarly references to newspapers or to obscure volumes, one has the impression of a single vast international enterprise. Such a conclusion may be excessive, although undeniably there exists in California the center of a revisionist International, which receives and distributes all this literature. There is nothing surprising about all this: it is simply the result of the planetary circulation of information and the dominant position of the United States in the world market. In point of fact, the "information" is often disseminated, on very different levels, by the same individuals. Take the case of Dietlieb Felderer, who was born at Innsbruck in 1942, moved to Sweden, is a Jehovah's Witness, and thus belongs, through conversion, to a group that was persecuted, but not exterminated, during the Hitler period. A collaborator of the *Journal of Historical Review,* a periodical with scientific pretentions, he also publishes—in Täby, Sweden—a truly obscene anti-Semitic mimeographed periodical, *Jewish Information,* distributes numerous tracts, and organizes (theoretically each summer) "revisionist" trips to Poland. Taking such new-style tourists to Auschwitz or the remains of Treblinka and explaining to them that nothing very serious happened there is, all the same, a rather unprecedented idea, and surely furnishes a number of exceptionally piquant sensations. Revisionism occurs at the intersection of various and occasionally contradictory ideologies: Nazi-style anti-Semitism, extreme right-wing anticommunism, anti-Zionism, German nationalism, the various nationalisms of the countries of eastern Europe, libertarian pacifism, ultra-left-wing Marxism. As may be easily anticipated, these doctrines at times appear in a pure state, and at others—and even most frequently—in alloyed form. Let us give a few rather unfamiliar examples. A Hungarian publishing firm in London has brought out, in addition to an English translation of the *Protocols of the Elders of Zion,* a book entitled *The World Conquerors,* in which, through a remarkable reversal, it is explained that the real war criminals of World War II were the Jews. The book is also violently anticommunist, accusing all Hungarian communists, and even all Spanish communists of being Jews. Such a reversal is characteristic of this ideology. In *The Jew Süss* (1940), it was the Jews who were the torturers.

Whereas traditional (Maurrassian) French anti-Semitism tends to be pro-Israeli, *all* revisionists are resolute anti-Zionists. Some make the transition from anti-Zionism to anti-Semitism, which is the case for a certain extreme left. Others follow the same path in the other direction. The absolute necessity of anti-Zionist discourse for revisionism is easy to explain. It is a matter of anticipating the creation of the state of Israel. Israel is a state that employs violent means of domination. That being the case, by proceeding as though such an entity already existed in 1943, it is possible to overlook the fact that the Jewish communities were unarmed. Pressing things to an extreme, one can even explain Nazism as a (no doubt phantasmatic) creation of Zionism.

Once that is established, German nationalism can very well be combined with the defense of Arab positions.

There is a Palestinian revisionism that has, moreover, a number of staunch adversaries. There are also, even in Israel, several Judeo-revisionists, though they appear to be quite few in number.

Generally speaking, the thematic of all these works, and particularly those inspired by (old- or new-style) German national socialism, is quite impoverished. One has the sense that all these volumes are pre-programmed, that their pages pile up without contributing anything new. The reader regularly relearns the same facts: that the Jews declared war on Hitler's Germany as of 1933, as is infallibly documented in some obscure journal or another from the Midwest; that the losses they endured during the war and which, moreover, were quite moderate, were solely due to the random effects of the partisan resistance effort; that there were no extermination facilities; that deaths in the camps were due almost exclusively to typhus. I shall limit myself here to observing a point of method and to pointing out several deviations.

It is a fundamental practice of revisionism to refuse to distinguish between words and reality. During the world war, there were declarations by Allied leaders directed at the Germans that were horrendous, as well as acts that were no less so and that constitute war crimes in every sense of the term. But it is striking to observe that the revisionists, although they mention these acts (the bombing of Dresden, the dramatic evacuation of Germans from regions becoming Polish or becoming Czechoslovakian again, etc.), always put the accent on rather hysterical texts, smacking of the crudest wartime racism and which never even began to be applied. Since one Theodore Kaufmann, who is baptized for the occasion a personal adviser to Roosevelt, published a wartime pamphlet entitled *Germany Must Perish,* predicting the sterilization of the Germans, that pamphlet is placed on the same level as the speeches of Hitler and Himmler, which had every chance of being implemented.

Nadine Fresco has suggestively compared the revisionist method with a well-known Freudian joke, that of the kettle: "A borrowed a copper kettle. Upon its return, B complains that the kettle has a big hole, making it unusable. Here is A's defense: '1. I never borrowed the kettle from B. 2. The kettle had a hole in it when I borrowed it from B. 3. I returned the kettle in perfect condition.' "

There are numerous examples. Concerning the "Wannsee agreement" (January 20 1942), which shows a number of functionaries at work on the "final solution," it will simultaneously be said—or suggested—that since it is unsigned, it is hardly a trustworthy document, and that it contains nothing very surprising. A kind of record is reached on the subject of Himmler's secret speeches, in which the theory and practice of mass murder are set forth with relatively little dissimulation. It will be claimed *simultaneously* that these texts, published under a title not agreed to by their author, have been tampered with, that words that are not present in the original have been interpolated (such as *umbringen,* "to kill," which no doubt has replaced some other term, such as "to evacuate") *and* that their meaning is in fact benign: the extermination of Judaism (*Austrottung des Judentums*) is not the extermination of the Jews. But the joke about the kettle may be extended beyond Freud. Why wouldn't A say: *I* was the one who loaned the kettle to B, and it was in perfect condition. There is an entire literature proving that the true murderers of the Jews and above all of the Germans were Jews: Jewish kapos, Jewish partisans, etc. The collective murder, which never took place, was thus fully justifiable and justified.

This is a transcending, through excess, of the revisionist norm. There are also transcendences through lack. The British historian David Irving believes that the final solution was elaborated by Himmler and kept secret from Hitler, despite a formal order, given by the German chancellor in November 1941, not to exterminate the Jews.

. . . . .

Let us return to the geography of revisionism and raise the question of its political and intellectual bearing. I do not dispose of all the necessary elements, and the few hypotheses I shall formulate are of necessity tentative and schematic. Several markers can nevertheless be established. Two countries dominate—by far—revisionist production: Germany and the United States. In the first, such books are numerous and enjoy a certain success if one may judge from the reprintings a number of them have gone through. They are tightly bound to a specific milieu: an extreme right-wing that sees itself as heir to Nazism and dreams of its rehabilitation.

Revisionism in the strict sense has not won any adepts in the extreme or ultra-left, or very few. Small terrorist groups, to be sure, have made the transition from anti-Zionism and aid to the Palestinian liberation movement to outright anti-Semitism, but without invoking the revisionist argument. The declaration of the German terrorist Ulrike Meinhof is often quoted: "Six million Jews were killed and thrown onto the dungheap of Europe because they were money-Jews (*Geldjuden*)." Reading that statement in context, one sees that it is but a variation on the theme of Bebel's formula: "Anti-Semitism is the socialism of fools." It remains that a transition is possible and has occasionally occurred.

In the United States, revisionism is above all the specialty of a Californian group, W. A. Carto's Liberty Lobby, which draws on venerable and solid anti-Semitic, anti-Zionist, and anti-black traditions and also draws—or attempts to—on the nationalism of Americans of Germanic origin. It does not appear that gestures toward libertarians, despite the patronage of H. E. Barnes, have met with much success. In academic and intellectual circles, a work like Arthur Butz's is almost completely unknown.

In several countries, on the contrary, revisionism is the specialty not of the racist and anti-Semitic extreme right, but of several groups of individuals coming from the extreme left. This is the case in Sweden following the intervention on Robert Faurisson's behalf of the extreme left-wing sociologist Jan Myrdal, whose intervention was on behalf not merely of the man but, in part, of his ideas; in Australia, following the action of the former secretary of the Victorian Council for Civil Liberties, John Bennett; and even in Italy, where a small Marxist libertarian group invokes its debt to Paul Rassinier.

And yet it is the French case that seems the most interesting and complex. Let us observe first of all this curious fact: to the extent that the international press has dealt with the revisionist problem, discussion, over the last three years, has centered on the case of Robert Faurisson. It was on his behalf that Noam Chomsky wrote a text that served as a preface to one of his books; and it was on the basis of his "theses" that newspapers the world over, in Germany as in America, published the most detailed analyses. This observation is all the more surprising in that in those two countries there were and still are revisionists of greater stature than Faurisson.

Not that his revisionism was of a particularly daunting sort. His originality has consisted in posing the problem on a strictly technical level. And even in that domain, he owes a lot to Butz. Certain of his formulations that provoked scandals were in reality mere translations or adaptations of German texts.

To be sure, Faurisson's social status, that of a university professor in a large city, in a country in which such credentials afford one access to the media more readily than elsewhere; his native talent for scandal, which is long-standing; the lawsuits brought against him; and the presentation of his work by an honorable sociologist, Serge Thion, have all played a role. It is equally remarkable that whereas in England, the country that invented freedom of the press, revisionists have not had access to the popular press, in France, in certain liberal or libertarian dailies (*Le Monde, Libération*), there have appeared the rudiments of a debate, with the reader occasionally being left with the impression that he is dealing with two equally valid positions between which one might very well hesitate.

Like other countries, France has always known—and still does know—a neo-Nazi tendency, symbolized by Maurice Bardèche and his journal, *Défense de l'Occident,* and recently revived by the New Right. Revisionist themes were featured in it very early on. With Paul Rassinier (1906-1967), a communist, then a socialist, a deportee to Buchenwald and to Dora, a life-long anticolonialist, but a friend of Bardèche and a writer for *Rivarol,* we are dealing with something else: the alliance of a pacifist and libertarian extremist left and an unabashedly Hitlerian extreme right. Anti-Semitism, intimately connected, in this case, with anti-Zionism, constitutes the bridge between the two. That alliance would be renewed in the next generation through the dissemination accorded revisionist positions in general and Faurisson's positions in particular by the Marxist group La Vieille Taupe and several adjacent ones (La Guerre Sociale, La Jeune Taupe, etc).

What is the political aim of this group, an aim in large part facilitated by the sacralization of the Jewish people over a period of several decades, by the belated remorse that gripped the West after the discovery of the great slaughter, and consequently by the protection the Israeli venture has enjoyed—even in its most debatable aspects? The central theme is perfectly clear: it is a matter of shattering the antifascist consensus resulting from the Second World War and sealed by the revelation of the extermination of the Jews. To the mind of the extreme left, the importance of Nazi crimes should be diminished and the guilt of the

West and of the communist world augmented in order to reveal a common oppression.

What would be needed, in brief, would be to change enemies. Is this completely unprecedented? Such ideologies have roots in France. At the end of the nineteenth century, the liberal consensus united peasants, workers, and bourgeois republicans in a common hostility to the "feudal" landholding aristocracy. Edouard Drumont, the author of *La France juive* [*Jewish France*], who was a great man and an important sociologist in the eyes of more than one socialist, also proposed a shift of enemies: no longer the lord's castle, with its torture chambers, but the mysterious lair where the Jew developed his riches with Christian blood. And he lashed out at official history: "The French historical school," wrote Drumont, "once again has passed by all this without seeing it, despite investigatory techniques it claims to have invented. It paused naively before dungeons that, according to Viollet-le-Duc himself, were latrines, before *in-pace* that were cellars; it did not enter the mysterious *sacrificarium,* the den more bloody than Bluebeard's, in which the childlike victims of Semitic superstition lie bloodless, their veins parched." A strange alliance indeed . . .

. . . . .

Just as the ancient city-states set up "treasures" at Delphi and Olympia that expressed their rivalry in the cult of Apollo and Zeus, the nations victimized by Hitler—or at least certain of them—have erected pavilions at Auschwitz recalling the misfortune befalling their citizens. Misfortunes also know competition. Among those pavilions, incongruously, there is a Jewish pavilion. For lack of an underwriting authority, it was erected by the Polish government and proclaims above all the martyrology of Poland.

A word should be said at this point about these "practices," specifically about those nations of eastern Europe from which the immense majority of the Jews who were murdered came and that currently constitute "socialist" Europe. It goes without saying that "revisionism" is totally banned there. But history? Let us simply say a few words—after a necessarily brief investigation—about historiography in three socialist countries: the U.S.S.R., because of the leading role it has within the system and because its armies liberated Auschwitz; the German Democratic Republic, in so much as it is heir to part of the territory and population of the national socialist state; and finally Poland, because it was on its territory that a majority of the exterminations took place.

To my knowledge, there is, in the strict sense, no Soviet historiography of the genocide of the Jews. A few books or booklets, either reports or propaganda, were published at the time of victory. The study of the German concentration camps appears to have been quite rudimentary—for reasons that seem obvious—and the only volume in Russian on Auschwitz I was able to locate was translated from the Polish and published in Warsaw.

To be sure, *The History of the Great Patriotic War (1941–1945)* by Boris Tepulchowski, which passes as being representative of post-Stalinist Soviet historiography, mentions the gas chambers and the extermination as it was practiced at Auschwitz, Maidanek, and Treblinka, but the victimized populations do not include the Jews, whereas the murder of six million Polish citizens is mentioned. Two lines explain that the entire Jewish population on occupied Soviet soil was exterminated. A Jewish nationality exists in the Soviet Union, but it is in some respects a negative nationality. Such is the situation reflected in Soviet historiography.

The case of the German Democratic Republic is rather different. According to official ideology, there has been an absolute break with the capitalist and Nazi period. Anti-Semitism and the exterminations are a legacy that must not be assumed in any manner whatsoever, neither by paying reparations to Israel, nor by sending a head of government to kneel at the site of the Warsaw ghetto. It is believed in East Berlin that the Federal Republic, on the contrary, should assume the heritage of Hitler's Germany, and for a long time, there was a pretense of believing that it was a continuation of it. The result is that studies of the extermination, although far from nonexistent as is sometimes erroneously claimed, are to a great degree instrumental and are a reaction less to the imperatives of knowledge and historical reflection than to the need to complete and rectify what is being written or done in the Federal Republic or to engage its leaders in polemics.

The revisionists appear not to have commented on a small but significant fact: although Poland, since the end of the war, has endured several political earthquakes, which have led to considerable emigration, including an emigration of militant nationalists not normally known for any excessive tenderness toward either the Jews or the communists (who, in revisionist ideology, were the first great fabricators of the "lie" of the extermination), there has not been a single Pole who has come forth to contribute anything to the revisionist cause.

In fact, the history of the death camps is in large part based on works published in Poland, through either documents reproduced in the Auschwitz Museum series, works of the Polish Commission on War Crimes, or volumes of the Jewish Historical Institute of Warsaw.

Obviously, such literature is in need of periodic correction. Polish nationalism, which is by tradition violently anti-Semitic, combined with Communist censorship, has intervened on numerous occasions. It is frequently the case that publications attach greater importance to the anti-Polish repression, which was ferocious, than to the extermination of the Jews. There is also frequently a posthumous naturalization as Poles of Jews, a naturalization that occurred only rarely during the period in question.

One nationalism can detect with relative ease the deformations due to another nationalism. The Polish historiography of the genocide and, in general, of the occupation period is taken quite seriously by Israeli historiographers, is debated, at times condemned, and that confrontation is a reflection of the great Judeo-Polish drama.

There is certainly not *an* Israeli historiography. A glance at the collection entitled *Yad Vashem Studies,* for example, reveals that it is shot through with tensions and is capable of integrating work from abroad; at times not without resistance. The great syntheses coming from the Diaspora, those of G. Reitlinger and R. Hilberg, and fundamental discussions such as Hannah Arendt's have been greeted with attacks of great violence. Among the more delicate points: the questions of Jewish "passivity," of Jewish collaboration (the collaboration of the rope and the hanged man), of the nationality of Hitler's Jewish victims, of the unique character of the slaughter, and finally that of the "banality of evil," which Hannah Arendt opposed to the demonization of Eichmann and his masters. These are genuine problems raised by the writing of history. Between a historiography that insists, to the point of absoluteness, on specificity, and one straining to integrate the great massacre into the movement and trends of history, which is not always a matter of course, the clash can only be violent. But, concerning Israel, can one limit the debate to history? The Shoah (Holocaust) exceeds it, first, by virtue of the dramatic role it played in the very origins of the state, then by what must indeed be called the daily use made of the great slaughter by the Israeli political class. The genocide of the Jews abruptly ceases being a historical reality, experienced existentially, and becomes a commonplace tool of political legitimation, brought to bear in obtaining political support within the country as well as in pressuring the Diaspora to follow unconditionally the inflections of Israeli policy. Such is the paradox of a use that makes of the genocide at once a sacred moment in history, a very secular argument, and even a pretext for tourism and commerce.

Need it be said that among the perverse effects of this instrumentalization of the genocide, there is a constant and adroitly fueled confusion of Nazi and Arab hatreds?

No one can expect the years 1939-1945 to fall into place in the (not always) peaceful realm of medieval charters and Greek inscriptions, but their permanent exploitation toward extremely pragmatic ends deprives them of their historical density, strips them of their reality, and thus offers the folly and lies of the revisionists their most fearsome and effective collaboration.

. . . . .

In concluding, can we attempt to state the test to which revisionism puts the historian? Meditating, after the war, on the theme of "negative dialectics," Adorno wondered [in *Dialectique négative,* 1978] to what extent it was possible to "think" after Auschwitz. What the Lisbon earthquake had been for Voltaire and the grave of theodicy for Leibniz, the genocide was—a hundredfold—for the generation that lived through it: "With the massacre by administrative means of millions of individuals, death became something which had never previously had to be feared in that form. . . . Genocide is the absolute integration, everywhere underway, in which men are leveled, trained, to use the military term, until, fused with the concept of their utter inanity, they are literally exterminated. . . . Absolute negativity is foreseeable; it no longer surprises anyone." Absolute negativity? Does such a concept have any meaning for a historian? Auschwitz has become a symbol, which it was not immediately after the war—the symbol of an enormous silence. But even that symbol can be chal-

lenged. Auschwitz juxtaposed an extermination camp (Birkenau), a work camp (Auschwitz I), and a factory-camp for the production of synthetic rubber (Auschwitz III Monowitz). The site of absolute negativity would rather be Treblinka or Belzec, although one can always conceive a crime more absolute than another. A historian, by definition, works in relative terms, and that is what makes any apprehension of revisionist discourse so difficult for him. The word itself has nothing shocking about it for a historian: he instinctively adopts the adjective as his own. If he is shown that there was no gas chamber functioning at Dachau, that *The Diary of Anne Frank,* as it has been published in various languages, raises problems of coherence if not of authenticity, or that Krema I, that of the Auschwitz camp, was reconstructed after the war by the Poles, he is prepared to yield.

Events are not things, even if reality possesses an irreducible opaqueness. A historical discourse is a web of explanations that may give way to an "other explanation," if the latter is deemed to account for diversity in a more satisfactory manner. A Marxist, for instance, will attempt to argue in terms of capitalist profitability, and will wonder whether simple destruction in gas chambers can or cannot be made to enter easily into such an interpretative framework. Depending on the case, he will either adapt the gas chambers to Marxism or suppress their existence in the name of the same doctrine. The revisionist enterprise, in its essence, does not, however, appear to me to partake of that quest for an "other explanation." What must be sought in it is rather that absolute negativity of which Adorno spoke, and that is precisely what the historian has such a hard time understanding. At stake is a gigantic effort not even to create a fictive world, but to eradicate from history an immense event.

In this order of thought, it must be admitted that two revisionist books, Arthur Butz's *The Hoax of the Twentieth Century* and Wilhelm Stäglich's *Der Auschwitz Mythos,* represent a rather remarkable success: that of the *appearance* of a historical narrative, better still, of a critical investigation, with all the external features defining a work of history, except for what makes it of any value: truth.

One can, to be sure, search out and find precedents for revisionism in the history of ideological movements. Under the Restoration, for pedagogical reasons, did not the Reverend Father Loriquet delete the Revolution and the Empire from the history he taught his pupils? But that was no more than "legitimate" deception, which, as we know from Plato on, is an inseparable part of education—an innocent game in relation to modern revisionisms.

To be sure, if I can speak at this point of absolutes, it is because we are dealing with pure discourse, not reality. Revisionism is an ancient practice, but the revisionist crisis occurred in the West only after the widespread broadcast of *Holocaust,* that is, after the turning of the genocide into a spectacle, its transformation into pure language and an object of mass consumption. There lies, I believe, the point of departure for considerations that will, I hope, be pursued by others than myself.

Lucy S. Dawidowicz

SOURCE: "Lies about the Holocaust," in *Commentary*, Vol. 70, No. 6, December, 1980, pp. 31-7.

[*An American educator and historian, Dawidowicz wrote and edited several studies of the Holocaust. In the following essay, she refutes the arguments of Holocaust denial writers.*]

Historians are always engaged in reinterpreting the past. They do so sometimes on the basis of newly found documentary sources, sometimes by reconsidering the known data from a different political position, or by taking into account a different time span, or by employing a new methodology. Every historical subject has undergone revision as each new generation rewrites the history of the past in the light of its own perspectives and values. But the *term* "revisionism" has applied specifically to dissident positions which are at variance with mainstream history on several subjects from the Civil War on. Three of these subjects have been politicized beyond the limits of historical truth—World War I, World War II, and the cold war (and there is a new subject, the war in Vietnam, now in the making).

In these three instances, revisionists, more ideological than academic in their approach, have tried to refute the prevailing views as to who was to blame for the outbreak of war. Using—and sometimes abusing—historical data, World War I revisionists have tried to prove that Germany was not to blame, or was less to blame than England. World War II revisionists have traveled the same route, picturing Franklin D. Roosevelt as the arch-villain. Cold-war revisionists have blamed the United States and absolved the Soviet Union for having initiated the cold war.

World War I revisionism was launched late in the 1920's with Sidney B. Fay's *The Origins of the World War,* which gave some historical dignity to what was more often a political and ideological issue. On the Right, conservatives and isolationists blamed England for the war and whitewashed Germany. On the Left, the Communists and their splinter groups attributed the origins of the war to the conspiratorial manipulations of the munitions-makers and the financiers. In Germany itself, the historical debate continued from the end of World War I until long past the end of World War II, but by now it would seem to have been put to rest by Fritz Fischer's definitive work, *Germany's War Aims in the First World War.*

As for World War II, the universal revulsion against the Third Reich and the open record of its belligerency did not create a hospitable climate for revisionism. Even in postwar Germany, where diehard Nazis continued to believe in the cause, they nevertheless did not dare to defend the Third Reich openly. The first—and still the only—revisionist work on World War II by a reputable historian was A. J. P. Taylor's mischievous book, *The Origins of the Second World War* (1961). There Taylor argued that Hitler had not planned a general war, and that the conflict, far from being premeditated, was "a mistake, the result on both sides of diplomatic blunders." Still, though Hitler was like other statesmen of his time in the conduct of his diplomatic affairs, Taylor explicitly declared that he outdid them all "in wicked deeds."

Historians everywhere roundly attacked Taylor for the book's conceptual perversity and its methodological flaws, but his book soon became the banner under which a swarm of Nazi apologists, cranks, and anti-Semites rallied. In twenty years' time, indeed, the allegations advanced by Taylor would come to appear mild and innocuous, for by 1980 one would find it being argued by so-called revisionists not only that Hitler's Germany was not to blame for World War II, but that the murder of six million European Jews by the Nazis had never taken place, that the Holocaust was a hoax invented by the Jews. Most shocking of all, these gross and malicious falsifications, far from being attacked and repudiated, have gained a respectful hearing in academic historical institutions in the United States.

In the same year that Taylor's book was published, 1961, a revisionist work appeared in Germany, written by an American, David L. Hoggan. The book had originated as a Harvard doctoral dissertation done in 1948, but it was revised, expanded, and Nazified in the ensuing years. Unable to find an American or a bona-fide German publisher, Hoggan gave his manuscript to a known Nazi publisher.

Hoggan's dissertation, according to one of his Harvard advisers, had been "no more than a solid, conscientious piece of work, critical of Polish and British policies in 1939, but not beyond what the evidence would tolerate." Thirteen years later, as published, it had turned into an apologia for Nazi Germany in which the English were portrayed as warmongers, the Poles as the real provokers of the war, and Hitler as the angel of peace. (The book also contained a short section on the Jews, arguing that from 1933 to 1938 the Third Reich treated its Jews more generously than Poland had.)

To support his outrageous claims, Hoggan tampered with sources, distorting and misreading those that did not fit his theories and prejudices, glossing over those that conflicted with them, and altogether ignoring those that actually confuted them. Nor, according to the president of the Association of German Historians, did he shrink from forgery. One noted German historian summed up Hoggan's work as follows: "Rarely have so many inane and unwarranted theses, allegations, and 'conclusions' . . . been crammed into a volume written under the guise of history."

How had a once "solid, conscientious piece of work" metamorphosed into this rubbish of Nazi apologetics? The credit for the reverse alchemy belongs to the late Harry Elmer Barnes, presumptive doyen of American isolationist historians, guru to fledgling libertarians, and patron saint of neo-Nazi cranks and crackpots in search of academic legitimacy.

Harry Elmer Barnes (1889-1968) was an American historian and sociologist of wide-ranging interests and knowledge, whose career as a professor and then as a journalist was aborted by his contentiousness and his cavalier disregard not only for accuracy but also for truth. He produced no original scholarly work, but synthesized information from his vast reading in a series of prolix and repetitious works on the history of Western civilization. By his own account, however, the "subject of war responsibility" occupied more of his time than any other theme.

In the 1920's Barnes became a World War I revisionist and was soon possessed by the idea that "vested political and historical interests" were behind the "official" accounts of Germany's responsibility for the outbreak of the war. The rabid energy which this notion provoked in him sustained Barnes as a revisionist into the period of World War II. As early as 1937, already a fanatical Roosevelt-hater, he described himself as a "noninterventionist." His rage against Roosevelt became still more intensified after Pearl Harbor—for which Barnes held Roosevelt responsible—and America's entry into the war in 1941.

Barnes's obsessions with warmongering conspiracies in government and in the historical profession held him in thrall until the end of his life. His writing grew ever more shrill, irresponsible, and irrational. (Finding few outlets to publish his polemical pieces, he felt compelled to have them privately printed.) People who had once held him in regard ceased to pay heed as he grew progressively paranoid, seeing sinister plots and powerful enemies everywhere. He began to write about the "historical blackout," that is, about a conspiracy to prevent him from publicizing his isolationist views. Here is a sample from one of the earlier articles:

> It is no exaggeration to say that the American Smearbund, operating through newspaper editors and columnists, "hatchet-men" book reviewers, radio commentators, pressure-group intrigue and espionage, and academic pressures and fears, has accomplished about as much in the way of intimidating honest intellectuals in this country as Hitler, Goebbels, Himmler, the Gestapo, and concentration camps were able to do in Nazi Germany.

By now a calcified isolationist, Barnes opposed America's involvement in Korea and soon found himself in the company not only of right-wing isolationists, ex-America Firsters, and Nazi apologists, but also of radical libertarians devoted to laissez-faire in the economy, noninterference by the state in domestic affairs, and isolationism (nonintervention) in foreign affairs. In this period Barnes became acquainted with one James J. Martin and wrote an introduction to Martin's oddball history of "individualist anarchism," published by the Libertarian Book Club in New York. It was at this time that Barnes became interested in Hoggan's dissertation and over the years guided him straight into Nazi apologetics.

As the years progressed, Barnes's hold on political reality continued to slip. He had begun his isolationist-revisionist career by whitewashing Kaiser Wilhelm's Germany and ended up by whitewashing Hitler's. In 1962 Barnes already doubted that the Third Reich had committed any atrocities or murder. In a privately printed pamphlet, *Blasting the Historical Blackout,* which praised A. J. P. Taylor's book, if with some reservations (he thought Hoggan's was better), Barnes alluded to what he called the "alleged wartime crimes of Germany": "Even

assuming that all the charges ever made against the Nazis by anybody of reasonable sanity and responsibility are true, the Allies do not come off much, if any, better." Then, with the shamelessness of a habitual liar, he charged that the sufferings of the Germans who had been expelled from Czech and Polish border areas after World War II and returned to Germany were "obviously far more hideous and prolonged than those of the Jews said to have been exterminated in great numbers by the Nazis."

Four years later, in 1966, in another rambling and paranoid piece, "Revisionism: A Key to Peace," published in a short-lived libertarian Journal, Barnes for all practical purposes denied that Hitler's Germany had committed mass murder. The following sentence is an elaboration of the one I quoted earlier:

> Even if one were to accept the most extreme and exaggerated indictment of Hitler and the National Socialists for their activities after 1939 made by anybody fit to remain outside a mental hospital, it is almost alarmingly easy to demonstrate that the atrocities of the Allies in the same period were more numerous as to victims and were carried out for the most part by methods more brutal and painful than alleged extermination in gas ovens.

In those days, even the neo-Nazis in Germany were circumspect in their journal, *Nation Europa* (which also published Barnes's articles), not daring to deny the facts of mass murder altogether but simply minimizing them. Only a certain Paul Rassinier in France was sufficiently divorced from reality to deny that the Third Reich had murdered the Jews.

Rassinier, once a Communist, then a socialist, had been interned in Buchenwald during the war, and afterward flipflopped into a rabid anti-Semite. In 1949 he published a book claiming the atrocities committed in the Nazi camps had been grossly exaggerated by the survivors. If any Jews had been murdered, Rassinier said, it was the Jewish *kapos* in the camps who had killed them. The book was widely denounced in France. Later Rassinier sued a newspaper editor for having called him a fascist; he was, he insisted, an anarchist. But the Paris court ruled against Rassinier on the ground that his book expressed ideas "identical with those proclaimed by the neo-Nazis."

In 1964 Rassinier wrote another book, *Le Drame des Juifs Européens,* an incoherent assemblage of arguments rehashed from the storehouse of anti-Semitic writings. Rassinier had one new wrinkle: arithmomania. He came up with the weird calculation that precisely 4,416,108 of the six million Jews said to have been murdered were actually alive and that the rest had probably not been killed by the Germans anyway. Around this time Barnes and Rassinier met, the rendezvous having been arranged by Mabel Narjes of Hamburg, co-translator of Hoggan's *Der erzwungene Krieg.*

Rassinier and Barnes obviously had much in common; Barnes undertook to translate Rassinier's book into English, and also reviewed Rassinier for the American public, or at least for those most likely to be interested—the readers of the *American Mercury.* (Founded as an iconoclastic journal in 1924 by H. L. Mencken, the *American Mercury* deteriorated after Mencken's resignation in 1933 and eventually became just an anti-Semitic rag.) Here is Barnes at his unpitiable worst:

> . . . the courageous author [Rassinier] lays the chief blame for misrepresentation on those whom we must call the swindlers of the crematoria, the Israeli politicians who derive billions of marks from nonexistent, mythical, and imaginary cadavers, whose numbers have been reckoned in an unusually distorted and dishonest manner.

Rassinier died in 1967 and Barnes a year later, but their fanaticism continued to inspire others in their quest for legitimacy. In 1969, a 119-page book, *The Myth of the Six Million,* by "Anonymous," appeared, with an introduction paying tribute to Barnes as "one of America's greatest historians." The introduction was written pseudonymously by Willis A. Carto, head of Liberty Lobby, the best financed anti-Semitic organization in the United States, which operates out of Washington, D.C. *The Myth of the Six Million* was published by a Liberty Lobby subsidary, Noontide Press. (*American Mercury* is also part of the interlocking network funded by Liberty Lobby.)

In his introduction, Carto explained that "Anonymous" was a collage professor who wished to protect his standing in the academic community by hiding his identity. It appears likely that the author was none other than David L. Hoggan, for in 1969 he sued Noontide Press for damages, claiming authorship of *The Myth of the Six Million.* The litigation dragged on until 1973, when the plaintiff withdrew his complaint. (Perhaps Carto settled out of court.) In 1974 a new edition of *The Myth of the Six Million* appeared, still authored by "Anonymous."

The Myth of the Six Million undertook to disprove all the evidence of the murder of the European Jews and to discredit all eyewitness testimony, including that of Rudolf Hoess, SS commandant at Auschwitz, and Kurt Gerstein, the SS officer who delivered the poison gas to Belzec and Treblinka. The author of *The Myth of the Six Million* did much the same thing that the author of *Der erzwungene Krieg* had done: distorting and faking some sources, suppressing others, and inventing still others. One example will suffice, as it is an item that turns up repeatedly in anti-Semitic tracts.

Benedikt Kautsky, an Austrian socialist, had been interned in Buchenwald and was later a slave laborer in Auschwitz. In his memoirs, *Teufel und Verdammte,* Kautsky wrote:

> I should now like briefly to refer to the gas chambers. Though I did not see them myself, they have been described to me by so many trustworthy people that I have no hesitation in reproducing their testimony.

The neo-Nazis cite Kautsky, with the appropriate bibliographical references including the correct page number, but falsify the passage so that he appears to corroborate their claim that there were no gas chambers.

We may not think much of Hoggan's anonymous scrib-

bling, but the booklet was well received in his circles. In England a pamphlet, *Did the Six Million Really Die?,* which drew heavily upon *The Myth of the Six Million,* was put forward as a historical work, published by a so-called Historical Review Press in Surrey; the author was advertised as one Richard E. Harwood, "a specialist in political and diplomatic aspects of the Second World War" who was "with the University of London." Actually he was Richard Verrall, editor of *Spearhead* magazine, unofficial organ of the National Front, an English racist group.

By now the neo-Nazis had regularly begun to exploit terms like "historical review" and "revisionism" in an effort to get attention in respectable circles. In New York a splinter group of the pro-Nazi German-American National Congress hit on the idea of a Revisionist Press to publish pseudoscholarly materials. They concealed their identity behind a post-office box number first in Brooklyn, then in Rochelle Park, New Jersey. In 1973 this Revisionist Press reprinted as a small book Barnes's paranoid essay, "Revisionism: A Key to Peace," from which I quoted earlier.

The neo-Nazi bid for academic reputability took a great leap forward when word got around that a professor at Northwestern University named Arthur R. Butz had published a book called *The Hoax of the Twentieth Century,* the hoax being the "Holocaust legend." Butz's book, published in 1976 by the Historical Review Press in Surrey—Harwood/Verrall's publisher—confidently argued that the Jews of Europe had not been "exterminated and that there was no German attempt to exterminate them." Butz—an associate professor of electrical engineering and computer sciences—was convinced that all the Jews said to have been murdered were still alive and he undertook to prove it, his expertise in computers no doubt standing him in good stead.

In his review of the assorted neo-Nazi writings on this subject, Butz gave good grades only to Rassinier, though he did not find him entirely accurate or reliable. Butz dismissed *The Myth of the Six Million* as "terrible," but considered Harwood's *Did the Six Million Really Die?* "quite good" (perhaps because the two authors shared the same publisher). As examples of "leading extermination mythologists," Butz lumped together Gerald Reitlinger (*The Final Solution*), Raul Hilberg (*The Destruction of the European Jews*), and me (*The War Against the Jews*).

The news of Butz's extracurricular career as an anti-Semitic scholar percolated from England back to Northwestern, and finally an account in the New York *Times* in late January 1977 raised Butz to national notoriety. His presence at Northwestern embarrassed the university, especially as its Jewish contributors threatened to withhold their financial support. The faculty, for its part, held firmly to the principle of academic freedom and the right of tenure. (Nowadays teaching at a university appears to be widely considered a fundamental civil right, like free speech or the right to bear arms.)

To demonstrate that Northwestern did not approve of Butz's views, the university administration prompted its history department to organize a series of lectures which would confirm that six million European Jews had indeed been murdered. These lectures, delivered by three Jews and a philo-Semite, were published in a booklet, *The Dimensions of the Holocaust* (1977), and distributed to show that the university stood foursquare on the side of honor and decency. As one of the four lecturers at Northwestern, I argued in private with some members of the faculty and the administration that the university's response was inadequate, for it seemed to me that they regarded the affair merely as an unfortunate incident affecting Jewish sensibilities. In fact, in their public statements the university's president and provost had treated the Butz scandal as a Jewish family sorrow, "a contemptible insult to the dead and the bereaved." No one at this great center of learning seemed to regard Butz's absurdities as an offense against historical truth, a matter supposedly of concern to an intellectual and academic community.

That same year, 1977, *Hitler's War* by David Irving came out. Irving, an English journalist with strong German sympathies and a record of disregard for verity or verification, argued in this book that the murder of the European Jews—whose historicity he did not deny—was Himmler's doing, and that Hitler was in fact innocent of those terrible deeds. Because Irving did not dispute the historical reality that the Jews were murdered, his work found no acceptance in the anti-Semitic canon.

Butz was the one who became a celebrity, even lecturing before an audience brought together by remnant supporters of the late Grand Mufti of Jerusalem (a Nazi collaborator). His book has been distributed in the United States by Carto's Noontide Press and by practically every other enterprising anti-Semitic group. One of Butz's "academic" sponsors has been Dr. Austin J. App, who used to teach English at LaSalle College in Philadelphia and claims to have been associated with Barnes. App's Nazi sympathies and anti-Semitic activities date back to the early 1940's; a prolific pamphleteer, he himself is the author of a 39-page effusion, *The Six Million Swindle,* which he has peddled along with the collected works of Butz, Harwood, and Hoggan.

In Germany, Udo Walendy, a Nazi in good standing from the old days, translated Butz (*Der Jahrhundert Betrug*) and published his version through a "revisionist" press which he operates. Walendy has his own wrinkle: he claims that the photographs of barely living camp inmates or of dead and rotted cadavers are "fake atrocity photographs."

France has had its equivalent of Butz in the person of Robert Faurisson, who until last year was an associate professor of French literature at the University of Lyon-2. In 1978 Faurisson began to write articles asserting that the "alleged gas chambers and the alleged genocide are one and the same lie . . . which is largely of Zionist origin." Furthermore, said Faurisson, "the participants in this lie . . . distort the purpose and nature of revisionist research." Faurisson's articles created such a furor that the university suspended him, a development which prompted all sorts of "civil libertarians" to come to his defense. Among them was Jean-Gabriel Cohn-Bendit, brother of Danny the Red of the 1968 Paris student riots. Cohn-

Bendit, according to Faurisson, wrote to express his support: "Let's fight to destroy those gas chambers which are shown to tourists in the camps where one knows now there hadn't been any at all." From this country, Noam Chomsky outdid even himself to sign an appeal in defense of Faurisson's civil rights.

In Australia Butz's book had a profound and unhinging effect on John Bennett, a Melbourne lawyer, for many years secretary of the regional Council for Civil Liberties. Converted by Butz, Bennett distributed about 200 copies of the book and thousands of copies of Faurisson's articles to persons in Australian public life. Early in 1979, Bennett began to speak of the murder of the European Jews as "a gigantic lie" created by "Zionist Holocaust propaganda" to make people support Israel. Several of his sensational letters-to-the-editor were published in leading Australian papers. The subsequent uproar soon brought about his dismissal from the Council for Civil Liberties. In the wake of this unfortunate episode, the Embassy of the Federal Republic of Germany, working together with Melbourne's Jewish community, mounted an exhibit on the Holocaust intended to remind those who had forgotten, or to inform those who never knew, that the Third Reich had undertaken to destroy the European Jews and by 1945 had indeed succeeded.

Meanwhile, back in the United States, the Revisionist Press in Brooklyn had published a small book called *The Revisionist Historians and German War Guilt*. Its author was Warren B. Morris, Jr., holder of a doctorate from Oklahoma State University for an undistinguished dissertation on a minor 19th-century German diplomat.

The idea for *The Revisionist Historians and German War Guilt,* Morris acknowledged in his preface, came from the Revisionist Press itself and Morris expressed his appreciation also to Austin J. App, author of *The Six Million Swindle.* Morris set himself the task of determining who was right—the "revisionists" or the "traditionalists"—on such matters as the destruction of the European Jews, aspects of Hitler's foreign policy, and the legitimacy of the Nuremberg trials. On the Jews his "revisionists" were Butz, Rassinier, App, and Harwood. (Hoggan was his "revisionist" on Hitler's foreign policy.) The "traditionalists" included Reitlinger, Hilberg, and me. Morris noticed that we were all Jewish, but thought it "only natural" for Jews "to have been in the forefront of Holocaust studies" because "they or their relatives suffered under Nazi persecution of the Jews."

After weighing the findings of Butz and company and comparing them with those of the "traditionalists," Morris reluctantly concluded that "Rassinier, Butz, App, Harwood, and other revisionists have failed to discredit the traditional accounts of the Nazi efforts to exterminate the Jews." *Ipse dixit.* Yet Morris still rendered their due to the Revisionist Press and his friend Dr. App. Even if the "revisionists" had failed "to prove their most important arguments," he wrote, "by forcing historians to reconsider their evaluation of Nazi policy toward the Jews," they have "indeed done a very valuable service to scholarship."

In one of the more astonishing episodes of the story being

unfolded here, the June 1980 issue of the *American Historical Review,* the journal of the American Historical Association, the preeminent professional organization of American historians, published a respectful review of Morris's book. How this sly attempt to give academic legitimacy to the outpourings of a variety of neo-Nazis and anti-Semites came to be offered for review in the first place, and how it came to be assigned for review two years after its publication, is a bit of a mystery. One might have thought that a knowledgeable book-review editor would promptly have seen its worthlessness and that a competent historian would have disdained to review it. (The book is a 141-page reproduction of a sloppy typescript, priced at $44.95.) As to the review itself, it was "agnostic" and impartial to the point of vacancy.

As the ranks of the pseudoscholars swelled, Willis Carto hit on the idea of creating an Institute of Historical Review, using the resources of Liberty Lobby and its network. In 1979 this Institute convoked a "Revisionist Convention" on the Northrup College campus in Los Angeles. Papers were read by Butz, Faurisson, App, and Walendy, arguing that there had been no Holocaust and no gas chambers; that all the camp photographs had been faked; that the Jews (alas) were still alive. The assemblage also heard speeches by Carto, John Bennett (who came all the way from Melbourne), and Devin Garrity, president of the right-wing publishing house, Devin-Adair.

The convention was dedicated to the memory of Harry Elmer Barnes; its opening speaker was none other than James J. Martin, Barnes's protege from the 1950's. In 1964 Martin had produced a two-volume, 1337-page compendium, published by Devin-Adair, which charged that between 1931 and 1941 American liberals had undergone a conspiratorial changeover from peace advocacy to war advocacy. (A reviewer summed up this "goulash of quotation, summary, and editorial comment" as "a scholarly disaster.") Now Martin has inherited Barnes's laurels and has been installed in the neo-Nazi pantheon as the "dean of historical revisionist scholars." He is the director of Ralph Myles Publishers, a firm which publishes revisionist books, some more fascist than academic. He also operates in the more rarefied atmosphere of the libertarians, where Right and Left sometimes bed together even if they don't always see eye to eye. Cato Institute, a libertarian outfit based in San Francisco, subsidized by the Koch Foundation (which supports the Libertarian party), recently published a collection of Barnes's more paranoid essays with a foreword by Martin.

At the 1979 revisionist convention, Carto announced that in 1980 the Institute of Historical Review would launch a quarterly, *Journal of Historical Review.* It was delivered as promised, with a lead article by Butz and other pieces by Faurisson, App, Walendy, and their ilk. A second issue followed, with similar contents, and a second convention was held last August at Pomona College, Claremont, California, this one dedicated to Rassinier's memory. Mabel Narjes, Hoggan's translator, who had brought Barnes and Rassinier together many years before, was flown over from Hamburg to speak about that historic encounter. Martin read a paper summarizing his forthcoming book

on genocide, the publication of which one can await only with anxiety.

Does any of this matter? Would any sensible and decent person be taken in by the absurd and malicious lie that Hitler's Germany never murdered six million Jews? Who would believe the monstrous falsehood that there were no gas chambers at Auschwitz? As it turns out, these are not just rhetorical questions.

While I was writing this article, a man associated with the Larry King radio show, a national network talk program, called to ask if I would debate with Faurisson. When I replied indignantly that Faurisson should not be provided with a platform for his monomania, the man mildly inquired why I was against discussing "controversial" matters on the radio. I in turn asked *him* if he thought the murder of the European Jews was a "controversial" matter. Had it not been established to his satisfaction as a historical fact? "I don't know," he answered. "I wasn't around at the time. I'm only thirty years old."

Perhaps it is not so hard after all to befuddle the ignorant, especially on Jewish matters, to which they are, at best, indifferent. Yet would Americans give a respectful hearing to someone who insisted that slavery had never existed in the United States, that blacks invented the story in order to get preferential treatment and federal aid, or that blacks had actually owned all the plantations? Somehow one doubts it.

Nor is it only the ignorant and the ill-informed who are involved here. The established academic and historical institutions of the United States, who should be the first to safeguard the truth of the past as it happened, have instead given respectful consideration to the most blatant falsifications of the recent past. The mindless review of Morris's tract in the *American Historical Review* is just one egregious example. Another is the response of the Organization of American Historians (OAH) to the *Journal of Historical Review,* the new quarterly of the "revisionists."

In the spring of 1980, each of the 12,000 members of the OAH received a complimentary copy of the inaugural issue of the *Journal.* A half-minute perusal should have sufficed to show that it was nothing more than a potpourri of anti-Semitic propaganda camouflaged to look like a learned journal. Some OAH members, in fact, protested the sale of the OAH membership list to neo-Nazis; others felt that, in the interests of intellectual freedom, the mailing list should be available to all. The OAH executive secretary responded to this division of opinion with irreproachable objectivity; he proposed to provide his Executive Board with "an analysis of the *JHR* as a historical publication," which analysis to "be developed by well-qualified historians," who would "focus on the credentials of the contributors and the use of evidence." Then, well-armed with a well-grounded analysis of this rubbish by well-qualified historians, the OAH's Executive Board would duly report to its members.

Report what, is not quite clear. Perhaps that the neo-Nazis did not have proper academic credentials, or that they failed to use primary sources? Again one wonders:

would the OAH have reacted the same way to a pseudoscholarly journal pushing KKK propaganda?

One turns with relief to the French historians. At the time of the Faurisson affair, thirty-four of France's leading historians issued a declaration attesting to the historical truth of the Holocaust and protesting the Nazi attempt to erase the past. The concluding paragraph of the declaration could well serve as a guide to American historians:

> Everyone is free to interpret a phenomenon like the Hitlerite genocide according to his own philosophy. Everyone is free to compare it with other enterprises of murder committed earlier, at the same time, later. Everyone is free to offer such or such kind of explanation; everyone is free, to the limit, to imagine or to dream that these monstrous deeds did not take place. Unfortunately they did take place and no one can deny their existence without committing an outrage on the truth. It is not necessary to ask how *technically* such mass murder was possible. It was technically possible, seeing that it took place.

On anti-Semitism and the alleged "Jewish Conspiracies":

Antisemitism frequently takes the form of a fear of international Jewish conspiracies. The 'theory' of the Holocaust as a Zionist lie is without doubt the greatest conspiracy theory of our time. The Zionists must deceive the whole world about events involving tens of millions of people—six million Jews to begin with, who have cooperatively kept their mouths shut about not being dead; plus thousands of other camp inmates who admit to having survived but lie in a perfectly synchronised manner about their experiences; plus any number of former Nazis who after the war made the fiendishly clever decision to back the Zionist lie by concocting perfectly coordinated stories about fictional acts of genocide; plus hundreds of thousands of random witnesses, judges, jurors and historians; plus an enormous army of scribes, clerks and typists who must have spent a busy year back in 1945 fabricating, doctoring, distorting, forging and systematically misinterpreting millions of pages of Nazi documents and war records. And all this centralised by the Zionist sages without a single slip-up.

Although the primary motivation of some of the 'historical revisionists' may be anti-Zionist, most of them, I think, are driven by a deeper and more encompassing animus. Most are antisemites, some of them avowed ones, who have found the Holocaust an inconvenient impediment to the expression of their views. If antisemitism has been generally less fashionable since the war, then this is largely the result of the widespread distaste provoked by the one programme of official antisemitism, the Nazi one, that was brought to its logical end. What better way of restoring antisemitism than by pronouncing the Holocaust a fraud?

Michael May, in his "Denying the Holocaust," in Index on Censorship, *December 1985.*

That is the required point of departure of every historical inquiry on this subject. This truth it behooves us to remember in simple terms: there is not and there cannot be a debate about the existence of the gas chambers.

About fifty years ago the great Dutch historian Johan Huizinga remarked that the critical historical faculty required three elements: "Common sense, practice, and above all a historical sense, a high form of that discrimination by which a connoisseur knows a true work of art from a false one." Huizinga believed that a higher level of historical discrimination now prevailed among educated persons than had in the past, and that trained historians had acquired greater sophistication in using historical evidence. Consequently, he concluded, "only the untrained are inclined now to accept flagrantly false versions." On the record presented here, his optimism about the historical profession was premature.

Gitta Sereny

SOURCE: "The Men Who Whitewash Hitler," in *New Statesman,* Vol. 98, No. 2537, November 2, 1979, pp. 670-73.

[*Sereny is an Austrian-born journalist and fiction writer whose works include* Into That Darkness: From Mercy Killing to Mass Murder *(1974) and* The True Story of the Hitler Diaries. *In the following essay, she attacks the logic and scholarship of neo-Nazi apologists.*]

There is a degree of indecency in entertaining a dialogue with individuals such as Richard Verrall and those of his persuasion. Nonetheless, it is necessary. We may despise them, but only at our peril do we mock or under-rate them, for the best—or worst—of them lack neither intelligence nor resources. According to the farmer and part-time publisher Robin Beauclerc (one of the original backers of the National Front), whose busy printing press produced not only Verrall's obnoxious pamphlet *Did Six Million Really Die?,* but also A. R. Butz's book *The Hoax of the Twentieth Century,* almost a million copies of the pamphlet have been distributed in 40 countries. I have seen them myself, as well as the Butz book, in schools, universities and libraries in Western Europe as well as the United States. Notoriously, both have arrived in Australia.

People who consider themselves generally well-informed say: 'But why go on with this ridiculous argument? If there is anything we know, surely, good God, we know about the horrible camps and the six million?' It is not only the World War II generation: an intelligent young person, glancing at the material on my desk, also said: 'But WHY does the *New Statesman* give him space? WHY take him seriously? Why spend precious time and space on refuting obvious lies?'

Time and space are indeed precious, and neither writers nor editors should squander them. There are two weighty reasons why one must pursue these debates with the Verralls, the Irvings, the Butzes and their like.

The first is that they are by no means motivated by an ethical or intellectual preoccupation with the historical truth, but rather by precise political aims for the future. As all political philosophies have needed their precursors, and parties their prophets, so they require a model, a hero, and it is of course Hitler whom they need to serve in that role. But, because people in general are good rather than evil, it must be a Hitler shown to have been not only powerful, but moral.

It does not matter that he created a police state—justification can be cobbled up for something which others have also done. It does not matter that he appropriated neighbouring lands and peoples. Ideological and demographic justifications can be devised. And it does not matter that he provoked and fought a bitter war, which cost the lives of millions. Wars have always been fought, they have always cost too many lives, and have always been 'justified'. None of these things, not even the ruthlessness with which he first pursued these aims, detract from Hitler's fitness to be the hero they seek and need.

There is one thing only for which there was no reason of war; no precedent; no justification. One thing of pure evil, and this they cannot afford to accept: the murderous gas-chambers in occupied Poland, the attempt to exterminate the Jews.

Time and again in their diatribes—here again in Verrall's letters [to the *New Statesman*]—regardless of the mountains of evidence, regardless of the living witness, they harp on their obsessional claim: there *was* no holocaust; there *were* no gas-chambers, not to speak of. And of course they return to their polemic about the six million figure, with which they perform degrading mental acrobatics.

The second reason why we must come to grips with both the substance and detail of the neo-Nazi claims is that sometimes mistakes have been made, have been given immense publicity, and become part of holocaust lore. At the risk of offence, we must correct and explain these mistakes, in order that they cannot be exploited again.

The likes of Verrall and Butz have shown a considerable talent for mixing truth with lies, by repetitive injecting of some truth into all lies, and lies into the truth. They make astute use of human errors (and of latent prejudice). So, they have succeeded to some extent in exploiting a terrible and astonishing fact, which is that after 35 years and billions of words, confusion still abounds on the subject of Hitler's genocide.

This has never shown up more plainly than in the case of the American television film *Holocaust*. As a member of a BBC panel of the night of its showing, I voiced misgivings about its factual errors, and tried to explain why these would be particularly difficult for the Germans to accept. Via satellite, the producer was more than impatient with my remarks. The film was highly successful, and useful in that it provided an emotional link, for millions of people, with events which many of them had rejected because they were impossible to visualise. But, after much expenditure on research, *Holocaust* could not lay the misunderstandings to rest.

The current argument with Mr Verrall, for example, deals with one main element in this confusion. He makes much

of what he calls the 'admission' by the Institute for Contemporary History in Munich that ' . . . no such things (as gas chambers) existed in . . . Belsen, Buchenwald and Dachau . . . etc etc'.

This so-called 'admission' stems from a letter which the historian Martin Broszat, now Director of the Institute, addressed in 1962 to the weekly *Die Zeit*. Professor Broszat remembers the letter well—'How could I forget it? Neo-Nazi and far-right publications have used it out of context ever since . . . '

The letter was written in yet another attempt—many have been made, by many people—to set the record straight. What Broszat was trying to do, he explains

> was to hammer home, once more, the persistently ignored or denied difference between concentration and extermination camps; the fundamental distinction between the methodical mass murder of millions of Jews in the *extermination* camps in occupied Poland on the one hand, and on the other the individual disposals of *concentration* camp inmates in Germany—not necessarily, or even primarily Jews—who were no longer useful as workers.

Most of the concentration camps in Germany proper had no gas chambers. Dachau had one which was never used. 'Mathausen, Natzweiler, had one. Sachsenhausen, too, I think', says Broszat. 'They used them towards the end, to replace the shootings and injections of small groups of prisoners, which had become so demoralizing for the staff.'

How is it then that the myth of gassing in the camps in Germany has been so universally accepted, thereby providing the neo-Nazis with their most treasured ammunition (the opportunity to refute what was never the case)? The explanation is both simple and infinitely complex.

German concentration camps, set up at first as SS-controlled detention centres for political, criminal and religious dissidents, and for sexual deviants and Jews, were neither then nor later *primarily* used for the imprisonment of Jews.

After 1940, as the need arose for an immense work-force for the war industries, the small penal camps, until then used only for Germans, Austrians and Czechs (including Jews from those countries) grew into huge installations with many hundreds of thousands of Russians, Poles and 'undesirables' from occupied Western Europe making up a vast slave-labour population.

Harshness of treatment varied between categories of prisoners. The German criminals were usually at the top of the camp hierarchy. 'Politicals' were in the middle, followed by religious and sexual deviants; with the Poles, the Russians and the Jews—in that order—at the bottom.

Millions of people died in these concentration-plus-labour camps: some—the most publicised—by torture, brutality or hideous medical experiments. But far more of them died from sickness and disease.

These were the camps that all Germans knew about and dreaded. *These* were the corpses found by the horrified Allied armies as they entered Germany. *These* made the photos and films we have principally seen. These emaciated skeletons, some still somehow upright, some lying on bunks in stupor, still others piled in naked, tumbled heaps ready for burning—these are the images that haunt us.

These people died by the million, but they were not 'exterminated' in the sense that the Nazis made uniquely their own. These camps had gas-oven crematoria, to dispose of the bodies. The chimneys belched out the smell of burning flesh, and the guards, in threat or mockery, told the prisoners: 'The only way you'll get out of here is through the chimneys'.

'Gassing' had been a part of the vocabulary in central Europe, and particularly in Germany proper, since the Nazis' destruction by gas of 80,000 physically and mentally handicapped people (children and adults) between 1939 and 1941. Thus, when sick or disabled prisoners in the German camps disappeared, when the chimneys smoked, and prisoner-workers reported that those missing had 'gone into the gas'—this was among men and women living in constant, deadly fear—it was not hard for 'gassing' to become a general term, used without much distinction.

The Allied troops who entered the camps had no idea what 'gassing' really was. All they knew was what they saw or heard about: the skeletons, some gaschambers, and hundreds of thousands of agonised tales and memories. As a welfare officer with UNRRA in 1945-6, I saw many of those sights, heard many of those tales, and tried to visualise those fearsome memories.

And then there was Auschwitz, and later Majdanek: the two, the *only* two, where the Nazis combined enormous labour installations and nearby facilities for extermination. Auschwitz, because so many people survived it, has added most to our knowledge, but also most to our confusion as between the two types of camps. What exactly was Auschwitz, which has become for many people the symbol-word for the whole Nazi horror?

It was, above all, by 1943 the largest slave-labour camp the Nazis had, with a population of 100,000 workers who were treated worse than animals, and whose expectation of life varied between ten days—if they were Jews or Russians—and a few weeks or months. Until spring 1942 it was just a small workcamp, with only the most rudimentary gassing installation. Then, I. G. Farben began to build a synthetic fuel and rubber factory—the 'Bunawerke'—on the adjacent marches, and ever-larger numbers of slave-labourers were dragged in, to build and then to operate it.

It was under the cover of constructing the Bunawerke that the Nazis made the slaves build the gaschambers at Birkenau, in a wooded area three miles from the main camp, called Camp II. It was here that, mainly in 1943, the 'selected'—mostly Jews, and some Russians—were brought from the railway sidings several miles away, and from the main camp. Also from Camp I, uniquely, came thousands of sick and feeble: not, for some mysterious reason, to die at once, but to be kept in utter squalor, virtually without rations, until they finally slipped away.

By the autumn of 1944, just over 700,000 Jews had died in the gaschambers at *Birkenau* (Camp II), and 20,000 Russians had been killed, but not gassed (that method was reserved for Jews). And by the time of liberation, 146,200 more Jews and several hundred thousand others had died of overwork and disease in Camp I.

Richard Verrall, busy with his vile numbers game, asserts that the confessions of Rudolf Höss, commandant of Auschwitz, were obtained 'under torture' in Poland, were 'nonsense' and are thus 'proof positive' of a hoax.

Whatever may be said about Höss, his role and his later manic pretensions, what really counts is that his statements to the American psychiatrist Dr G. M. Gilbert at Nuremberg were made *before* he was handed over to Poland, and that he said at Nuremberg almost exactly what he said in Poland—including two sets of estimates for the dead at Auschwitz. The second figure he cited each time, a total of about 1.3 million dead, comes very close to Gerald Reitlinger's most careful estimate: 700,000 Jews gassed in Camp II, and 500,000 prisoners (including 146,000 Jews) dead from exhaustion and disease in Camp I.

But this is in a sense beside the point, because Verrall and Butz, while trying to discredit Höss, cite him whenever they hope to make a point. As they totally deny the existence of the other extermination camps in occupied Poland, Auschwitz is something of a beam in their eye. But it is important for those of us interested in the truth to recall that Auschwitz, despite its emblematic name, was *not* primarily an extermination camp for Jews, and is not the central case through which to study extermination policy.

The first mass murders occurred while Auschwitz was still a penal labour-camp: they followed the 'Commissar Order' of March and July 1941, which commanded the liquidation of Soviet political commissars, gypsies, racial inferiors, 'asocials' and Jews. These killings—and none of the neo-Nazis have much to say about them—were presented as para-military operations. The hundreds of thousands of naked men, women and children who were shot on the edge of mass graves were described, even to their murderers the *Einsatzgruppen,* as 'partisans' and 'bandits'.

But the *Einsatzgruppen* actions showed the Nazis that this pseudo-military method could not work for the great masses of Jews yet to be dealt with. As we know from hundreds of statements by German witnesses in the *Einsatzgruppen* trials in West Germany, the killings put an intolerable strain on personnel—despite liberal supplies of alcohol and sex—and provoked protests from the Wehrmacht.

However, the Nazis had a tested solution at hand. Of the 80,000 unwanted people killed in the 'Euthanasia Programme' some (but only small children) had been killed by injections in special hospital wards. Most had died in gas chambers in the Euthanasia Institutes. Over 400 men and women—police, medical and administrative staff, under the direct authority of the Führer-Chancellery, in Department T-4—had done these murders.

Here was a technique, and a staff to operate it. The 'specialists' who had been prepared to kill helpless Germans and Austrians could safely be entrusted with the slaughter of millions of Jews and thousands of gypsies: eradicating, as Hitler put it, 'the bacilli on the body politic of the German race'.

Mr Verrall complains that among the vast documentation surviving 'there is not a single order . . . etc for a "gas chamber" '. Typically, neo-Nazi diatribes claim that there is no record of the vast transportation arrangements which would have been required to carry out an extermination programme.

Few of those who read this rubbish have an opportunity to examine the record themselves. But anyone who has actually worked in the archives is familiar with the hundreds of railway signals which survive, describing with horrible monotony the destination and contents of the trains to Sobibor and Treblinka.

And all researchers are only too familiar with the countless documents, 'orders, invoices, plans', and indeed 'blueprints' concerning precisely the construction of gas-chambers.

One of the documents (N. O. 365), the earliest I know of concerning gassing camps (and significantly linking them to T-4) is dated 25 October 1941, and states that 'Victor Brack (Chief of Section II of T-4) is ready to collaborate in the installation of the necessary buildings and gassing machinery . . . ' The longish letter, which concerns camps to be erected in Riga and Minsk, is quite explicit in the use the equipment is to be put to.

Thus between December 1941 and April 1942 ninety-six of Brack's T-4 men were posted to Occupied Poland and the 'Aktion Reinhard' (named after Reinhard Heydrich, killed in Czechoslovakia). They were assigned to the four specialised extermination camps, which were Chelmno, Belzec, Sobibor and Treblinka. These had been built under the command of the SS chief in Lublin, Odilo Globocnik.

These were not concentration or labour camps. The facilities provided housing for just a few German Waffen-SS, less than 100 Baltic or Ukrainian SS overseers, and a constantly-changing group of a few 'work-Jews'. Although millions arrived, no-one else lived long enough to eat, wash or sleep. These were meticulously-planned killing-plants. The official Polish estimates (which probably err on the conservative side) are that 2,000,000 Jews and 52,000 gypsies, at least one-third of them children, were killed in these four installations between December 1941 and October 1943. Of all those who reached them, 82 survived.

I am able to bear some witness to these events. My knowledge comes from research I did for my book *Into That Darkness,* the story of Franz Stangl, commandant of Treblinka. I talked with Stangl for weeks in prison; I talked to others who worked under him, and to their families. I talked to people who, otherwise uninvolved, witnessed these events in Poland. And I talked to a few of those very few who survived.

Butz claims in his *Hoax* that those (hundreds) who admitted taking part in extermination were doing so as plea-bargaining, in order to get lighter sentences. But those I talked to had been tried. Many had served their sentences,

and none of them had anything to gain—except shame—by what they told me. Stangl himself wanted only to talk, and then to die. And Stangl is dead. But if Verrall, Butz & Co were really interested in the truth, Stangl's wife, and many other witnesses are still able to testify.

The 'Aktion Reinhard' camps existed for one purpose only, totally unconnected with any requirement of war, and they were totally eradicated when their purpose was served. The buildings were pulled down, and trees were planted in the earth which had become so rich. Thirty-five years later they have grown tall. A letter from Globocnik to Himmler survives, dated Trieste 5 January 1944, and carefully phrased:

> For reasons of surveillance a small farm has been built on the site of each of the (former) camps, to be occupied by a farmer to whom an annuity must be assured in order to encourage him to maintain the farm . . .

In his own letter of commendation to Globocnik, dated 30 November 1943 Himler used his pet name for Globocnik:

> Dear Globus, I confirm your letter of 4.11.43 and your report on the completion of the Aktion Reinhardt (sic) . . . I want to express to you my gratitude and appreciation for the great and unique services you have rendered the whole of the German people by carrying through the Aktion Reinhardt. Heil Hitler! Cordially yours, H.H.

Here, then, is the truth for those who desire knowledge. Within one terrible universe of oppression and death—known to us through words like Belsen, Natthausen, Dachau—there was another universe, of methodically crazy slaughter of an unprecedented kind—the place-names being Chelmno, Belzec, Sobibor and Treblinka. Auschwitz, the most-cited, was a complex, transitional example. There are reasons why the worst names are least cited: one, complex in its roots, is that the Third Reich tried to present its (marginally) less hideous face towards the West, and the western armies never reached the territory of the death-camps. And well-run extermination camps leave few survivors to tell their stories.

The situation therefore presents some possibilities for confusion to pseudo-historians and neo-Nazi apologists. And they are assisted further by the fact that events of such magnitude lend themselves to dramatic 'use', are therefore used, and not-infrequently misused. In turn the Verralls and Butzes can allege that all such misuses are part of a 'Zionist' conspiracy.

It is vital for them to believe that anyone who is involved with this question must be Jewish, and thus unreliable. This to begin with, is nonsense: (a) many of the leading authorities on the Third Reich are not Jewish, and (b) many of those who are, are as objective as anyone can be. (In their anti-semitic outpourings, these individuals never refer to 'Jews', but almost invariably to 'Zionists'. They know that 35 years after Hitler many people will not accept the attack on 'Jews', but many be persuaded by the more 'political' label 'Zionist'. Of course, many Jews are not Zionists.)

But it *is* true that, along with many authentic works, there have been books or films which were only partly true, or even were partly faked. And unfortunately, even reputable historians often fail in their duty of care. For instance Martin Gilbert (biographer of Churchill) offers in *Final Journey* what is in many ways an admirably-presented resume of what happened to the European Jews.

But by quoting supposed 'eyewitnesses' who in fact are repeating hearsay, Gilbert perpetuates errors which—because they are so easily disproved—provide revisionists' opportunities. For instance, from his chapter 'The Treblinka Deathcamp': none of the 'Nazis in the camp . . . lived in the camp together' with their families; SS Hauptsturmführer von Eupen was never commandant of Treblinka, but of the nearby training-camp Trawniki; the 'cries of the victims and the weeping of the children' could *not* be heard in the neighbouring villages, for with good reason the murderers ensured there were no villages within miles; and the Germans did *not* bring 'the most famous musicians in the world from the Warsaw ghetto' to 'play when the transports arrived'. There *were* such orchestras, for instance at Auschwitz, which played when the slave-labourers marched to and from work. But there was no need for such a thing at any pure extermination camp.

David Irving's *Hitler's War* falls into the category of 'partly true'. It had some interesting historical material, but sold (admirably) both here and overseas because of its bold and spurious claim that Hitler himself was largely unaware of the 'Final Solution'. Such books do better than, for example, Helen Fein's scholarly socio-history *Accounting for Genocide,* which is surely essential for any serious researcher. But this is an area in which commercially-motivated rubbish can have terrible long-term consequences.

'Personal' accounts, such as the recently-published *Dora,* heavily-publicised in the *Guardian* are not rubbish in themselves. Jean Michel, no doubt at all, was a labourer at the terrible slave-camp in the Harz Mountains where the V-weapons were built. The problem with books like this is that they are 'ghosted' by professional word-smiths—the French are especially adept—who have neither interest in nor capacity for conveying truth with restraint. It is less the exaggerations than the false emphases and cheap humour which disqualify them.

Worse again are the partial or complete fakes, such as Jean Francois Steiner's *Treblinka* or Martin Gray's *For Those I Loved.* Steiner's book on the surface even seems right: he is a man of talent and conviction, and it is hard to know how he could go so wrong. But what he finally produced was a hodgepodge of truth and falsehood, libelling both the dead and the living. The original French book had to be withdrawn and reissued with all names changed. But it retained its format of imagined conversations and reactions—ie pure fiction—incredibly remaining, nonetheless, in serious bibliographies.

Gray's *For Those I Loved* was the work of Max Gallo the ghostwriter, who also produced *Papillon.* During the research for a *Sunday Times* inquiry into Gray's work, M. Gallo informed me coolly that he 'needed' a long chapter

on Treblinka because the book required something strong for pulling in readers. When I myself told Gray, the 'author', that he had manifestly never been to, nor escaped from Treblinka, he finally asked, despairingly: 'But does it matter?' Wasn't the only thing that Treblinka *did* happen, that it *should* be written about, and that some Jews should be shown to have been heroic?

It happened, and indeed many Jews were heroes. But untruth always matters, and not just because it is unnecessary to lie when so much terrible truth is available. Every falsification, every error, every slick re-write job is an advantage to the neo-Nazis.

One other thing assists the revisionists: many Jews, including survivors from the Warsaw Ghetto and Treblinka, are unwilling to bear witness and expose people like Gray for what they are. Understandably, they do not wish to bring back their fearsome experiences into the lives they have rebuilt. Tragically, they fear renewed anti-semitism.

To return to Britain, now sadly enough a kind of neo-Nazi centre: who are the 'growing number of academic and public figures' whom Richard Verrall cites (*NS* Letters 21 September) as moving towards his position? I think David Irving's silly claim has been adequately dealt with in the *Sunday Times,* and he at least did not deny that the murders occurred.

The Australian lawyer John Bennett has been dealt with adequately by Ken Buckley (*NS* 5 October) and may be left to his fellow Australians. Robert Faurisson, an associate professor of Literature at Lyons, author of some light literary guides (*As t'on lu Rimbaud etc*) is certainly a study: I had a long telephone conversation with him recently in which he sought an urgent meeting with me, on the grounds that the 'artistry' of my work *Into That Darkness* had produced 'final proof that the gas-chambers never existed'. The mechanism of double-think is admittedly fascinating.

A principal authority for Verrall is Paul Rassinier, whose work has been well-described by Raul Hilberg as 'a mixture of error, fantasy and fabrication'. Rassinier, now dead, *was* a historian and *was* for a while imprisoned at Buchenwald. But neither of those facts place him necessarily on the side of the angels: when he sued for defamation a writer who said that he had made common cause with neo-Nazis, the allegation was found proved.

And the 'respected German historian Helmut Diwald' is in fact just that. His field, however, is the period from Charlemagne to Wallenstein (the Thirty Years' War), and when his *Geschichte der Deutschen* (History of the Germans) appeared early this year, his chapter on the Third Reich was almost universally found to be defective and incomplete. The publishers withdrew the book: issuing jointly with Diwald an apology and a promise that a new edition would deal 'unequivocally . . . with the persecution and murder of the Jews in the Third Reich'.

Finally, A. R. Butz, who is an associate professor of engineering at Northwestern University, Illinois. His *Hoax of the Twentieth Century* makes, as Hugh Trevor-Roper observed 'a great parade of scholarship (but) . . . most of the book is irrelevant, and the central issue is evaded.' North-western's admirable response was to initiate, in the year Butz's tirade reached the US, first a course and then a summer school on their own campus, dealing with the facts of the holocaust. Always, the proper reply to these dishonourable men begins with knowledge.

ROBERT FAURISSON AND NOAM CHOMSKY

Pierre Vidal-Naquet

SOURCE: "On Faurisson and Chomsky," in *Assassins of Memory,* translated by Jeffrey Mehlman, Columbia University Press, 1992, pp. 65-73.

[*In the following essay, Vidal-Naquet impugns the motives of Robert Faurisson and Noam Chomsky in defending the authors of Holocaust denial literature.*]

Pursuing his crusade—whose theme may be summarized as follows: the gas chambers did not exist because they can not have existed; they can not have existed because they should not have existed; or better still: they did not exist because they did not exist—Robert Faurisson has just published a new book [*Mémoire en défense*].

This work is neither more nor less mendacious and dishonest than the preceding ones. I am not at the disposal of R. Faurisson, who, moreover, has not devoted a single line to attempting to respond to my dismantling of his lies in a text that he clearly is familiar with if we may judge from certain editorial details (such as the rectification of all too obvious cases of falsification). If every time a "revisionist" trotted out a new fable it were necessary to respond, all the forests of Canada would not suffice. I shall simply observe the following point: Faurisson's book is centered on the diary of the SS physician J. P. Kremer, a text I dealt with at length, showing that *not once* in the diary do the "special actions" in which the doctor participated have any relation with the struggle against typhus. Faurisson is unable, and for good reason, to supply a single argument, a single response on this subject. I have said as much, and will repeat it: his interpretation is a deliberate falsehood, in the full sense of the term. If one day it becomes necessary to analyze the rest of his lies and his falsifications, I shall do so, but such an operation seems to me to be of little interest and would be futile in the face of the sect whose prophet he has now become.

More troubling, because it comes from a man whose scientific stature, combined with the just and courageous fight he waged against the American war in Vietnam, have granted him great prestige, is the preface to Faurisson's book, which is by Noam Chomsky. An extraordinary windfall indeed: to maintain that the genocide of the Jews is a "historical lie" and to be prefaced by an illustrious linguist, the son of a professor of Hebrew, a libertarian and the enemy of every imperialism is surely even better than being supported by Jean-Gabriel Cohn-Bendit.

I read the text carefully and with an increasing sense of surprise. Epithets came to my pen, expressing, progressively, the extent of my surprise and my indignation. Finally, I decided to remove those adjectives from my text. Linguists, and even nonlinguists, will be able to restore them without difficulty. I shall proceed in order.

1. The preface in question partakes of a rather new genre in the republic of letters. Indeed, Noam Chomsky has read neither the book he prefaced, nor the previous works of the author, nor the criticisms addressed to them, and he is incompetent in the field they deal with: "I have nothing to say here about the work of Robert Faurisson or his critics, of which I know very little, or about the topics they address, concerning which I have no special knowledge." These are indeed remarkable qualifications. But since he needs to be able to affirm a proposition and its opposite, Chomsky nonetheless proclaims, a few pages further on, his competence. Faurisson is accused of being an anti-Semite: "As noted earlier, I do not know his work very well. But from what I have read—largely as a result of the nature of the attacks on him—I find no evidence to support [such conclusions]." He has also read his critics, specifically my article in *Esprit* (September 1980), and even the personal letters I sent to him on the subject, "a private correspondence which it would be inappropriate to cite in detail here." A fine case of scruples, and a fine example as well of double language, since Chomsky did not realize that the book he was prefacing contained unauthorized reproductions of a series of personal letters, and he himself does arrogate the right of summarizing (while falsifying) my own letters. I shall simply say to him: "Kindly publish—I give you my authorization—the entirety of that correspondence. It will then be possible to judge whether you are qualified to give me lessons in intellectual honesty."

2. Chomsky-the-Janus-faced has thus read Faurisson and not read him, read his critics and not read them. Let us consider the issues in logical order. What has he read of Faurisson which allows him to bestow so fine a certificate? For is he not "a relatively apolitical liberal of some sort"? Since Chomsky refers to *nothing* in support of this, it is impossible to know, and I shall simply say: Faurisson's *personal* anti-Semitism, in fact, interests me rather little. It exists and I can testify to it, but it is nothing compared with the anti-Semitism of his texts. Is it anti-Semitic to write with consummate calm that in requiring Jews to wear the yellow star starting at the age of six "Hitler was perhaps less concerned with the Jewish question than with ensuring the safety of German soldiers"? Certainly not, within Faurisson's logic, since in the final analysis there is no practical anti-Semitism possible. But within Chomsky's logic? Is the invention of an imaginary declaration of war against Hitler, in the name of the international Jewish community, by an imaginary president of the World Jewish Congress, a case of anti-Semitism or of deliberate falsification? Can Chomsky perhaps press linguistic imagination to the point of discovering that there are false anti-Semites?

Let us now pose the other side of the question. What does Noam Chomsky know of the "criticisms" that have been addressed to Faurisson, and specifically of the study that he refers to, which I published in *Esprit* and which attempts to analyze "historically" the "method" of Faurisson and of several others? The answer is simple. "Certain individuals have taken Faurisson's defense for reasons of principle. A petition with several hundred signatories, led by Noam Chomsky, protested against the treatment Faurisson has received by presenting his 'conclusions' as though they were in fact discoveries. That petition seems to me to be scandalous."

The content of those lines leaves no doubt about Chomsky's motives. It is not a question of the gas chambers; it is very little a question of Faurisson, and only secondarily of freedom of speech. It is above all a question of Noam Chomsky. It is as though, by anticipation, Jacques Prévert were speaking of him, and not of André Breton, when he wrote in 1930: "He was, then, quite thin-skinned. For a press clipping, he would not leave his room for eight days." Like many intellectuals, Chomsky is scarcely sensitive to the wounds he inflicts, but extremely attentive to whatever scratches he is forced to put up with.

But what is his argument? He signed, we are told, an innocent petition "in defense of Robert Faurisson's freedom of speech and expression." The petition said absolutely nothing about the character, quality, or validity of his research, but limited itself quite explicitly to defending elementary rights which are "taken for granted in democratic societies." My mistake, he contends, stems from my having made an error in English. I believed that the word "findings" meant "discoveries," whereas its meaning is "conclusions." I will not quibble on this last—insignificant—point, concerning which Chomsky's position is all the stronger in that he had received my own admission in a letter. But he forgot to specify that the error in question, which had appeared in my original manuscript, had been corrected prior to publication. The text that appeared in *Esprit* does not include it, and if Chomsky, rather bizarrely, reproaches me for it, it was because he was drawing on my correspondence with him. Moreover, the error was infinitesimal: *findings* is a scientific term, and it was legitimate for me to play on its etymological meaning, which is indeed "discoveries." Here, in addition, is what was written to me on this minuscule subject by a professor of Cambridge University, who is a native New Yorker, and who presumably knows the language spoken in Cambridge, Massachusetts: "Chomsky's bad faith in playing with words is alarming. To be sure, if one opens a dictionary to the word *findings* one will find, among other meanings, that of *conclusions*. And yet *no one,* and Chomsky knows this perfectly well, would ever make use of *findings,* or *discoveries,* or even *conclusions,* in this context, in the strictly neutral sense now invoked by Chomsky. Those words, and particularly the first two, imply absolutely that they be taken seriously as designating the truth. There are more than enough neutral words at the disposal of whoever needs them: one might, for example, use *views* or *opinions.*"

But let us return to the heart of the matter. Is the petition an innocent declaration in favor of a persecuted man that everyone, and first of all myself, could (or should) have signed?

Let us read:

> Dr. Faurisson has served as a respected professor of twentieth-century French literature and document criticism for over four years at the University of Lyon 2 in France. Since 1974 he has been conducting extensive independent historical research into the "Holocaust" question. Since he began making his findings public, Professor Faurisson has been subject to a vicious campaign of harassment, intimidation, slander, and physical violence in a crude attempt to silence him. Fearful officials have even tried to stop him from further research by denying him access to public libraries and archives.

Let us pass over what is excessive or even openly false in the petition. Faurisson has been forbidden from neither archives nor public libraries. Does the petition in fact present Robert Faurisson as a serious historian conducting genuine historical research? To ask that question is to supply an answer. The most droll aspect of it all is that one finds the following adage, which has become something of a motto, preceding works published by La Vieille Taupe: "What is terrible when one sets out after the truth is that one finds it." For my part, I maintain—and prove—that with the exception of the quite limited case of the *Diary of Anne Frank,* Faurisson does not set out after the truth but after falsehoods. Is that a "detail" which does not interest Chomsky? And if one is to understand that poorly informed, he signed on trust a genuinely "scandalous" text, how are we to accept his willingness to underwrite today the efforts of a falsifier?

3. But there is more still: regarding himself as untouchable, invulnerable to criticism, unaware of what Nazism in Europe was like, draped in an imperial pride and an American chauvinsim worthy of those "new mandarins" whom he used to denounce, Chomsky accuses all those who hold a different opinion from his own of being assassins of freedom.

That issue of *Esprit* (September 1980) must have driven him mad. Along with my five lines in which Chomsky's name was mentioned with reference to Faurisson, there were twelve pages by Paul Thibaud, who took the liberty of criticizing the inability of Chomsky (and Serge Thion) to gauge, in the case of Cambodia, the dimensions of the totalitarian phenomenon. Those pages are commented on as follows by Chomsky: "I omit discussion of an accompanying article by the editor that again merits no comment, at least among people who retain a commitment to elementary values of truth and honesty". But would not an "elementary respect for honesty and the truth" have obliged Chomsky to indicate the following fact, which is also elementary: Thibaud's article (of twelve pages) was a response to an article by Serge Thion, which was seventeen pages and entirely devoted to the defense and illustration of the theses of . . . Noam Chomsky? Is that how the editor of *Esprit* revealed his intolerance and dishonesty?

"I do not want to discuss individuals," Chomsky writes, and immediately thereafter, in accordance with the same double discourse with which we are beginning to be familiar, he attacks an imaginary "person" who "does indeed find the petition 'scandalous' [which was indeed the word I used], not on the basis of misreading, but because of what it actually says." An elegant way of not saying—and, at the same time, saying—that I assault the freedoms of my enemies. For Chomsky goes on to say: "We are obliged to conclude from this that the individual in question believes that the petition was scandalous because Faurisson *should* in fact be deprived of the normal right to self-expression, that he should be harassed and even subjected to acts of physical violence, etc." It happens that what I wrote was precisely the opposite, and that in the very page on which Chomsky did such a poor job of deciphering the five lines that so disturbed him. Was it really impossible to read that page through? The conditions under which Faurisson was brought to request leave of Lyon and enter the National Center of Broadcasted Instruction were certainly regrettable, and I have said as much, but his freedom of expression, subject to extant law, has not been threatened at all. He was able to be published on two occasions in *Le Monde.* Thion's book, in which his theses are vented, was not the subject of any lawsuit, and if Faurisson is the target of a civil suit, brought by various antiracist associations, which do not all have freedom as their primary goal, such lawsuits do not prevent him from writing or being published. Is not the book prefaced by Chomsky—with the exception of instances of libel toward specific individuals that it may contain—proof? Would he like a law passed by the republic requiring that Faurisson's works be read in public schools? Is he asking for all history books to be rewritten in accord with his discoveries—I mean, conclusions (*findings*)? Is he requesting at the very least that they be advertised and sold at the entrance to synagogues? Is every French intellectual required to assume in turn the roles of his exegete, like Serge Thion, his psychiatrist, like Pierre Guillaume, or his buffoon?

The simple truth, Noam Chomsky, is that you were unable to abide by the ethical maxim you had imposed. You had the right to say: my worst enemy has the right to be free, on condition that he not ask for my death or that of my brothers. You did not have the right to say: my worst enemy is a comrade, or a "relatively apolitical sort of liberal." You did not have the right to take a falsifier of history and to recast him in the colors of truth.

There was once, not so long ago, a man who uttered this simple and powerful principle: "It is the responsibility of intellectuals to speak the truth and to expose lies." But perhaps you know him?

POSTSCRIPT (1987)

This text, which was written six and a half years ago, could be prolonged indefinitely. Barely had I completed it when the affair took a rather droll turn, since, in a letter of December 6 addressed to Jean-Pierre Faye, Chomsky somehow disavowed not his text but the use that had been made of it with his agreement as a preface to Robert Faurisson's book. The book was nonetheless printed with the preface in question, which was dated October 11, 1980. On that same December 6, he wrote to Serge Thion concerning the same text: "If publication is not under

way, I strongly suggest that you not put it in a book by Faurisson," which did not prevent him from maintaining his fundamental position.

Let us restate the point with due calm: the principle he invokes is not what is at stake. If Chomsky had restricted himself to defending Faurisson's right to free speech, from my point of view there would not be any Chomsky problem. But that is not the issue. Nor is the issue for me one of responding to the innumerable proclamations, articles, and letters through which Chomsky, like some worn-out computer reprinting the same speech, has spewed forth his outrage at those who have been so bold as to criticize him, and specifically at the author of these pages.

It will suffice for me to observe: 1) that he went considerably further than was generally believed in his personal support of Faurisson, exchanging friendly letters with him, accepting event to be prefaced by the leader of the revisionist league Pierre Guillaume (while claiming—mendaciously—that he had not written a preface for Faurisson), characterizing Guillaume as "libertarian and antifascist on principle (which must have provoked some hilarity from the interested party, since he regards antifascism as fundamentally mendacious); 2) that he has not remained faithful to his own libertarian principles since he—whom the slightest legal action against Faurisson throws into a fit—went so far as to threaten a publisher

---

On Pierre Vidal-Naquet's *Assassins of Memory*:

Vidal-Naquet's concerns with preserving an accurate sense of both detail and scale about the Holocaust raise a difficult question: *is* it either possible or appropriate to protect "memory" of the Holocaust? It is that stance of *vigilance* which makes Vidal-Naquet's work, I think, both urgent and problematic. On the one hand, in continually reengaging the act of reading first-hand accounts of the Holocaust, Vidal-Naquet helps to keep such texts alive and, in doing so, to honor the memory of those who wrote them and to confirm the human integrity which they sought, against close to impossible odds, to preserve. On the other hand, responding at such length to "revisionist" historians who remain by virtually all accounts marginal in the profession does risk lending Holocaust deniers legitimacy. Even more, dramatizing the imperative of response to Holocaust denials may also elevate the imperatives of protection and preservation of "memory" to a level at which "the Holocaust" acquires a static quality—the parameters of its central events already set; its essential cast of characters already agreed upon; its meaning already assigned. Memory and history are without a doubt fragile—vulnerable, certainly, to the kinds of losses which Holocaust deniers seek to inflict—and yet perhaps guarding so vigilantly against such losses may actually exacerbate that vulnerability, by erecting a brittle wall around an event whose meaning to succeeding generations must, like that of any historical event, be subject to evolution.

Joanne Jacobson, in her "Denying The Holocaust," Michigan Quarterly Review, *Spring 1994.*

with a lawsuit over a biographical note concerning him in which several sentences had the misfortune of displeasing him. And in fact, he succeeded in having the biographical note in question assigned to a more loyal editor.

To be sure, it is not the case that Chomsky's theses in any way approximate those of the neo-Nazis. But why does he find so much energy and even tenderness in defending those who have become the publishers and defenders of the neo-Nazis, and so much rage against those who allow themselves to fight them? That is the simple question I shall raise. When logic has no other end than self-defense, it goes mad.

Henry H. Weinberg

SOURCE: " 'Revisionism': The Roques Affair," in *Midstream,* Vol. XXXIII, No. 4, April, 1987, pp. 11-13.

[*In the following essay, Weinberg studies the writings of French Holocaust deniers.*]

The pseudo-historians who have engaged in activities to exculpate the Nazis of their horrendous crimes, who have argued that the gas chambers never existed, have attempted to prove that all the evidence is false, and that all testimony can be challenged. There have also been those, the more esthetically oriented, who have expunged much of what had been earlier characterized as abominable. Some have absolved Nazism of responsibility by portraying the executioners as a small, isolated group of perverts; others have shown them as beings held in the grip of hidden, occult forces.

The French "school" of falsifiers of Holocaust history has shown particular predilection for pseudo-literary interpretation. What better way to blur historical information than through "interpretation"—"a rationalization that normalizes, smoothes, and neutralizes our vision of the past." [Saul Friedländer, *Reflections on Nazism, An Essay on Kitsch and Death,* 1984]. Such deception gains in apparent sophistication when it masquerades as academic research. The most recent scandal in France linked to the denial of Hitler's genocide against the Jews involves just such a scam.

On June 15, 1985, at the University of Nantes, a 65-year-old retired agronomist, Henri Roques, defended successfully a doctoral dissertation entitled innocuously: "The 'Confessions' of Kurt Gerstein. A comparative study of Different Versions. A Critical Edition." The scholarly title of the thesis concealed the true aim of its author. The use of the word "Confessions," and of quotation marks around it, was not innocent. At the time of the award of the doctorate only the four professors, who gave the thesis very high marks, and an audience composed of neo-Nazi sympathizers, were aware of its main thrust: the denial of the existence of Hitler's gas chambers. The fact that a respectable French university approved such a thesis did not come to public attention until a year later.

The minister in charge of universities ordered an investigation, and a group of University of Nantes faculty members signed a petition regretting that the "scientific reputation" of their university had been damaged. For French Jews, who had not hesitated to challenge previous attempts to deny the Holocaust, the Roques affair provided confirmation that the insidious lies about the tragedy had made further inroads and that the "revisionists" were aspiring to higher levels of respectability.

Unlike the cruder distortions of some of his mentors, Rassinier and Faurisson, Roques concentrated on destroying the validity of the testimony of a unique historical source: the SS officer Kurt Gerstein, who made six depositions concerning the gassing of 5000 Jews he witnessed in the Belzec extermination camp in 1942. Roques' thesis attempts to seek out contradictions between the six depositions, particularly in regard to the size of the gas chambers. He labels Gerstein a "mytho-maniac" who sold himself to the Zionists after the war, and whose testimony is "pure invention."

The use of "literary" interpretation (Roques' thesis was registered in the faculty of letters, not history), creates a displacement of meaning. What better way to trivialize the Holocaust than to classify its evidence as fiction, to use literary interpretation to falsify the text and to signify, through the use of classical tools of academic criticism, its irrelevance to reality and history. Projecting an aura of scholarly prudence, Roques said in response to a question about the existence of gas chambers: "I will not answer yes or no; I will tell you that there are legitimate reasons to deny their existence."

In a detailed analysis of his thesis, Georges Wellers showed Roques' bad faith and flawed methods of research. He also reconfirmed the validity of Gerstein's testimony. Moreover, a recording of the three-hour thesis defense, obtained by a Paris daily, leaves no doubt as to the intentions of the author. Throughout the session, the extermination of Jews in gas chambers is referred to as "rumors," "myths," and "legends." Among those in the invited audience were Robert Faurisson and a number of his supporters.

What is unusual about the Roques case is that for the first time a "revisionist historian" has sought and received the academic stamp of approval for his scandalous "interpretations." Although some of the most notorious pseudo-historians have taught in universities (Faurisson in France, Butz in the United States), they gained their academic credentials in other fields, such as French literature or chemistry. Roques, on the other hand, set out to obtain a doctorate on a thesis exculpating the Nazis. He has aspired to become the first "legitimate," academically sanctioned, expert, with a prestigious platform for the dissemination of the distortions. In the minds of French youth given to skepticism, the prestige of university sanctioned knowledge could indeed increase doubts about "controversial history."

How could the approval of such a thesis take place in a major French university, after repeated and highly publicized convictions of the notorious Professor Faurisson? Who were the members of Roques' doctoral committee? On learning, a year after the event, of the approval of Roques' thesis, the dean of the University of Nantes sheepishly attempted to exonerate his institution by stating: "The theories expressed in the thesis are the responsibility of its author, not of the university." The publicity about Roques' thesis brought into the limelight the background of the four academics who served on the doctoral committee.

It became apparent that they shared extreme, Right-wing views. The thesis director, Jean-Claude Rivière, a professor of medieval French literature at Nantes, was a leader in the "Nouvelle Droite," an influential Right-wing think tank. He has been listed as one of the most radical members of the militant extreme Right in France, as a proponent of eugenics, and of "biological realism."

The chairman of the doctoral "jury," Jean-Paul Allard, a professor of German at the University of Lyon, admitted that he was not competent to evaluate the thesis, yet commented that Roques' thesis was "excellent" and that he was going to recommend it to his students. Another member of the committee, Pierre Zind, a Marist priest, was a contributor to the journal *Eléments,* a "New Right" publication. During Roques' thesis defense Zind displayed his expertise in German military rankings, particularly those of the SS. Father Zind expressed admiration for the "dynamic persuasiveness" of the thesis. Thierry Buron, the fourth member of the committee, a junior lecturer in history at Nantes, was a follower of the Catholic fundamentalist bishop, Mgr. Lefèvre, who has expressed hostility to the Vatican's conciliatory moves toward the Jews.

Holocaust "revisionism" has brought to the surface the existence in France of a direct link between extreme Right-wingers and extreme Leftists who, for different ideological reasons, have claimed that the Holocaust is a hoax. Although none of the members of Roques' doctoral committee had direct links to Marxism, it is significant that the Leftist "revisionist," Pierre Guillaume, has used his publishing house, La Vieille Taupe—which had edited the writings of Rassinier, Faurisson and fellow Leftist Serge Thion—to distribute the introductory remarks Roques made at his thesis defense. It was Guillaume who prompted Noam Chomsky to write a preface to Faurisson's book, in the name of "freedom of speech." It is curious, as Shmuel Trigano has observed, that at the end of the 20th century, just as at the end of the 19th, anti-Semitism formed the only basis for a consensus between the extreme Left and the extreme Right in France.

It is noteworthy that there also exists in France a link between "revisionists" and prominent pro-Palestinian militants. The motivation is not difficult to detect. Hostility to Israel stimulates a rewriting of Jewish history, and vice versa. The Holocaust was allegedly invented by Jews to protect Israel's gains and to neutralize the effect of the injustice done to Palestinians. The perpetrators of today's genocide (Israel), deserve the one executed upon them, as well as the one that will fall upon them in the future. Their French supporters have also attempted to transfer to the Palestinians the emotionally charged vocabulary of the horrors of the Nazi era. Michael Marrus' argument that it is "inevitable" that Jews would be compared to Nazis because "every era operates in the shadow of its historical past," ["Is There a New Anti-Semitism?" *Middle East*

Focus, November 1983], fails to take into account the deliberate effort by Soviet and pro-Palestinian propagandists to fabricate such a transfer of rhetoric. The proliferation of Communist and Left-wing publications in France has facilitated this process.

In the midst of the controversy over Roques' thesis, the high-circulation Right-wing weekly, *Rivarol,* wrote that the goal of the uproar was to harm the National Front, the extreme Right-wing party which won 35 seats in the March, 1986 parliamentary elections. While the anti-immigration, ultra-nationalist platform of the party was aimed primarily at the three million migrant workers, many of them North African Arabs, several of its most prominent members had expressed anti-Semitic views. "The Jewish lobbies, opposed to the National Front," *Rivarol* added, "cannot accept a doubt to be thrown on the cornerstone of their legitimacy, the 'gas chambers.' "

Although Jean-Marie Le Pen, the leader of the National Front, denies that he is an anti-Semite, there is considerable doubt about his sincerity. Over the years, Le Pen has made comments about Jewish-French personalities that contained more than a tinge of anti-Semitism. In May, 1986, on a popular television program, he commented: "There exists a certain abnormality in the French political situation when everything turns around the Jewish question." Under the leadership of François Duprat, from 1972 to 1978, the National Front made a major contribution to the rehabilitation of Nazism. Duprat also distributed Richard Harwood's pamphlet "Did Six Million Really Die?"

Questioned about the Roques affair, Le Pen managed to remain equivocal, as he has on other controversial issues. He declared in the official organ of his party, *National Hebdo*: "Like most reasonable people, I admit that the massive death of Jews in Nazi camps took place. Not being an expert . . . I do not know how this figure (six million) was established. To cite the case of another genocide, in the Vendée (Brittany, in the post-Revolutionary period), I note that for 200 years the estimates varied from 50,000 to 500,000, and that only today, thanks to a more accurate counting method, the number of dead has been established as 117,000."

Le Pen has thus supported the arguments of the "revisionists" by placing the Holocaust in a perspective of *relativity*. The next best way to deprive the Jewish tragedy of its true dimension is to say that, while it may have occurred, it was not unique, as the Jews claim. If one suggests that the figure six million is an exaggeration, one can point to other exaggerated estimates in history, such as the killings in the Vendée, and remove the uniqueness from Hitler's genocide (the comparison to other mass killings—the outburst of violence against Armenians, the "regeneration" bloodbath of the Cambodian Communists, and Stalin's labor camps—leads to similar conclusions). The earliest of the notorious French "revisionists," Paul Rassinier, also argued that although there may well have been some extermination of Jews in gas chambers, there was nothing systematic about it, and that the number of deaths was much smaller than claimed. Thus, the "moderation" of Le Pen's position is deceptive, to say the least.

A more revealing reaction of the extreme Right came from the editor of the daily *Présent,* François Brigneau, a personal friend of Le Pen, who often expresses the ideology of the National Front. Brigneau wrote that there are grounds "to doubt the 'evidence,' the 'testimony,' and the 'admissions' about . . . Belzec, Sobibor, Treblinka, Majdanek, Auschwitz-Birkenau." He argued that no official document ordering the genocide has ever been found. Brigneau also reproduced Faurisson's statement, that "the so-called gas chambers and the so-called genocide of Jews are part of the same historical lie which has opened the gate to a gigantic political and financial swindle whose main beneficiaries are the State of Israel and international Zionism." Le Pen has not dissociated himself from his friend's article, just as he failed to denounce other anti-Semitic declarations of close political collaborators.

In July, 1986, Alain Devaquet, the Minister for Research and Higher Education, invalidated Roques' thesis defense (but not the thesis itself) and thus withdrew his title, "Doctor." Among the reasons given by the Minister were "irregularities in the examining process," including the falsification of the signature of one of the members of the doctoral committee. The Minister also ordered the suspension of the thesis director, Rivière. The investigation conducted by the government revealed a number of violations of procedure. Rivière agreed to "direct" Roques' work, although he had never met him three months before the thesis defense. He also violated regulations in letting Roques register after the deadline, exempting him from an examination and ordering a secretary to forge a signature.

To those familiar with the loosening of constraints on the expression of anti-Semitism in France in the last decade, and with the fact that former Nazi collaborators openly defended their past deeds, this new incident brought little surprise. A few years ago, a professor at the University of Paris publicly declared that he was proud of his service in the SS division "Charlemagne," and that he remained a Fascist. The prestigious Paris daily, *Le Monde,* offered Faurisson a forum.

As the government-ordered investigation would reveal, a number of faculty members at the University of Nantes knew that a pseudo-historical thesis had been approved by their colleagues, but preferred to remain silent. There are grounds for speculating that their silence was motivated by loyalty to a colleague and that in the predominantly Left-wing atmosphere of French university campuses, anti-Zionism may have created a dulling effect on efforts to combat "revisionism."

In a broader sense the reaction to Roques' thesis cannot be divorced from the attitudes prevailing in French society. Claude Lanzmann, creator of the film *Shoah,* referred to the fact that the newspapers, which devoted many pages to *Shoah,* also gave space to Roques' thesis. Lanzmann concluded, "there is a real anti-Semitic movement in France now." In a country where debates over the events of World War II have yet to be resolved, the presence of both Left and Right-wing anti-Semitism, which regularly finds an echo in the mass media, has allowed "revisionism" a place in public opinion as a somewhat eccentric, but nevertheless legitimate view.

"Scholarly" falsifiers of history are not a new phenomenon in France. Shortly after the end of the Dreyfus affair, an 800-page book, containing thousands of footnotes, tried to prove that all the facts presented on behalf of Dreyfus' exoneration showed, in fact, that he was guilty. The latest episode in a campaign charging the Jews with a betrayal of history made an abortive use of scholarship that was promptly unmasked. Although similar deceptions will no doubt be attempted again, the reaction of the government to the Roques case has given the Jewish community a measure of reassurance that distortions of Holocaust history, in spite of their recurrence, will be met with swift and vigorous condemnation.

Noam Chomsky

SOURCE: "His Right to Say It," in *The Nation,* New York, Vol. 232, No. 8, February, 1981, pp. 231-34.

[An American linguist, Chomsky is one of the major intellectual figures of the twentieth century. In addition to his seminal studies in the nature and function of human language, he has also published a number of works on social and political subjects. In the following essay, he defends his support of Holocaust deniers to disseminate their ideas.]

An article in *The New York Times* concerning my involvement in the "Faurisson affair" was headlined "French Storm in a Demitasse." If the intent was to imply that these events do not even merit being called "a tempest in a teapot," I am inclined to agree. Nevertheless, torrents of ink have been spilled in Europe, and some here. Perhaps, given the obfuscatory nature of the coverage, it would be useful for me to state the basic facts as I understand them and to say a few words about the principles that arise.

In the fall of 1979, I was asked by Serge Thion, a libertarian socialist scholar with a record of opposition to all forms of totalitarianism, to sign a petition calling on authorities to insure Robert Faurisson's "safety and the free exercise of his legal rights." The petition said nothing about his "holocaust studies" (he denies the existence of gas chambers or of a systematic plan to massacre the Jews and questions the authenticity of the Anne Frank diary, among other things), apart from noting that they were the cause of "efforts to deprive Professor Faurisson of his freedom of speech and expression." It did not specify the steps taken against him, which include suspension from his teaching position at the University of Lyons after the threat of violence, and a forthcoming court trial for falsification of history and damages to victims of Nazism.

The petition aroused considerable protest. In *Nouvel Observateur,* Claude Roy wrote that "the appeal launched by Chomsky" supported Faurisson's views. Roy explained my alleged stand as an attempt to show that the United States is indistinguishable from Nazi Germany. In *Esprit,* Pierre Vidal-Naquet found the petition "scandalous" on the ground that it "presented his 'conclusions' as if they were actually discoveries." Vidal-Naquet misunderstood a sentence in the petition that ran, "Since he began making his findings public, Professor Faurisson has been subject to. . . ." The term "findings" is quite neutral. One can say, without contradiction: "He made his findings public and they were judged worthless, irrelevant, falsified . . . ." The petition implied nothing about the quality of Faurisson's work, which was irrelevant to the issues raised.

Thion then asked me to write a brief statement on the purely civil libertarian aspects of this affair. I did so, telling him to use it as he wished. In this statement, I made it explicit that I would not discuss Faurisson's work, having only limited familiarity with it (and, frankly, little interest in it). Rather, I restricted myself to the civil-liberties issues and the implications of the fact that it was even necessary to recall Voltaire's famous words in a letter to M. le Riche: "I detest what you write, but I would give my life to make it possible for you to continue to write."

Faurisson's conclusions are diametrically opposed to views I hold and have frequently expressed in print (for example, in my book *Peace in the Middle East?,* where I describe the holocaust as "the most fantastic outburst of collective insanity in human history"). But it is elementary that freedom of expression (including academic freedom) is not to be restricted to views of which one approves, and that it is precisely in the case of views that are almost universally despised and condemned that this right must be most vigorously defended. It is easy enough to defend those who need no defense or to join in unanimous (and often justified) condemnation of a violation of civil rights by some official enemy.

I later learned that my statement was to appear in a book in which Faurisson defends himself against the charges soon to be brought against him in court. While this was not my intention, it was not contrary to my instructions. I received a letter from Jean-Pierre Faye, a well-known anti-Fascist writer and militant, who agreed with my position but urged me to withhold my statement because the climate of opinion in France was such that my defense of Faurisson's right to express his views would be interpreted as support for them. I wrote to him that I accepted his judgment, and requested that my statement not appear, but by then it was too late to stop publication.

Parts of my letter to Faye appeared in the French press and have been widely quoted and misquoted and subjected to fantastic interpretations. It was reported, for example, that I repudiated my comments after having learned that there is anti-Semitism in France, and that I was changing my views on the basis of clippings from the French press (in the same letter, I had asked Faye to send me clippings on another matter). My personal letter to Faye was incomprehensible to anyone who had not read Faye's original letter to me; a telephone call would quickly have clarified the facts.

The uproar that ensued is of some interest. In *Le Matin* (socialist), Jacques Baynac wrote that my fundamental error was to "defend, in the name of freedom of expression, the right to mock the facts"—"facts" determined, presumably, by some board of commissars or a reconstituted Inquisition. My lengthy discussion on the implications of this doctrine was excised from the occasionally recognizable version of the interview with me published

in *Le Matin.* In *Le Monde,* the editor of *Esprit,* Paul Thibaud, wrote that I had condemned "the entire French intelligentsia," launching a "general accusation" against *"les Français,"* without qualifications. Alberto Cavallari, Paris correspondent for the *Corriere della Sera,* went further still, claiming that I had condemned all of "French culture." The article is notable for a series of fabricated quotes designed to establish this and other allegations. What I had written was that though I would make some harsh comments about "certain segments of the French intelligentsia . . . certainly, what I say does not apply to many others, who maintain a firm commitment to intellectual integrity. . . . I would not want these comments to be misunderstood as applying beyond their specific scope." Similar qualifications are removed from the doctored "interview" in *Le Matin,* enabling the editors to allege that I describe France as "totalitarian."

Cavallari went on to explain that my rage against "French culture" derives from its refusal to accept the theory that linguistics proves that "the Gulag descends directly from Rousseau" and other imbecile ideas he chooses to attribute to me for reasons best known to himself. In *Nouvel Observateur,* Jean-Paul Enthoven offers a different explanation: I support Faurisson because my "instrumentalist theory of language, this 'generative grammar' . . . does not allow the means to think of the unimaginable, that is, the holocaust." He and Cavallari, among others, explain further that my defense of Faurisson is a case of the extreme left joining the extreme right, a phenomenon to which they devote many sage words. In *Le Matin,* Catherine Clement explains my odd behavior on the ground that I am a "perfect Bostonian," "a cold and distant man, without real social contacts, incapable of understanding Jewish-American humor, which relies heavily on Yiddish." Pierre Daix explains in *Le Quotidien de Paris* that I took up left-wing causes to "clear myself " of the reactionary implications of my "innatism." And so on, at about the same level.

To illustrate the caliber of discussion, after I had noted that Vidal-Naquet's comment cited above was based on a misunderstanding, he reprinted his article in a book (*Les Juifs,* F. Maspero), eliminating the passage I quoted and adding an appendix in which he claims falsely that "the error in question" had appeared only in an earlier draft, which I am accused of having illegitimately quoted. The example is, unfortunately, quite typical.

A number of critics (for example, Abraham Forman of the Anti-Defamation League in *Le Matin*) contend that the only issue is Faurisson's right to publish and that this has not been denied. The issue, however, is his suspension from the university because of threats of violence against him, and his court trial. It is of interest that his attorney, Yvon Chotard, who is defending him on grounds of freedom of expression and the right to an attorney of one's choice, has been threatened with expulsion from the anti-Fascist organization that is bringing Faurisson to trial.

As Faye predicted, many showed themselves incapable of distinguishing between defense of the right of free expression and defense of the views expressed—and not only in France. In *The New Republic,* Martin Peretz concluded from my expressed lack of interest in Faurisson's work that I am an "agnostic" about the holocaust and "a fool" about genocide. He claims further that I deny freedom of expression to my opponents, referring to my comment that one degrades oneself by entering into debate over certain issues. In short, if I refuse to debate you, I constrain your freedom. He is careful to conceal the example I cited: the holocaust.

Many writers find it scandalous that I should support the right of free expression for Faurisson without carefully analyzing his work, a strange doctrine which, if adopted, would effectively block defense of civil rights for unpopular views. Faurisson does not control the French press or scholarship. There is surely no lack of means or opportunity to refute or condemn his writings. My own views in sharp opposition to his are clearly on record, as I have said. No rational person will condemn a book, however outlandish its conclusions may seem, without at least reading it carefully; in this case, checking the documentation offered, and so on. One of the most bizarre criticisms has been that by refusing to undertake this task, I reveal that I have no interest in six million murdered Jews, a criticism which, if valid, applies to everyone who shares my lack of interest in examining Faurisson's work. One who defends the right of free expression incurs no special responsibility to study or even be acquainted with the views expressed. I have, for example, frequently gone well beyond signing petitions in support of East European dissidents subjected to repression or threats, often knowing little and caring less about their views (which in some cases I find obnoxious, a matter of complete irrelevance that I never mention in this connection). I recall no criticism of this stand.

The latter point merits further comment. I have taken far more controversial stands than this in support of civil liberties and academic freedom. At the height of the Vietnam War, I publicly took the stand that people I regard as authentic war criminals should not be denied the right to teach on political or ideological grounds, and I have always taken the same stand with regard to scientists who "prove" that blacks are genetically inferior, in a country where their history is hardly pleasant, and where such views will be used by racists and neo-Nazis. Whatever one thinks of Faurisson, no one has accused him of being the architect of major war crimes or claiming that Jews are genetically inferior (though it is irrelevant to the civil-liberties issue, he writes of the "heroic insurrection of the Warsaw ghetto" and praises those who "fought courageously against Nazism" in "the right cause"). I even wrote in 1969 that it would be wrong to bar counterinsurgency research in the universities, though it was being used to murder and destroy, a position that I am not sure I could defend. What is interesting is that these far more controversial stands never aroused a peep of protest, which shows that the refusal to accept the right of free expression without retaliation, and the horror when others defend this right, is rather selective.

The reaction of the PEN Club in Paris is also interesting. PEN denounces my statements on the ground that they have given publicity to Faurisson's writing at a time when there is a resurgence of anti-Semitism. It is odd that an organization devoted to freedom of expression for authors should be exercised solely because Faurisson's defense against the charges brought against him is publicly heard. Furthermore, if publicity is being accorded to Faurisson, it is because he is being brought to trial (presumably, with the purpose of airing the issues) and because the press has chosen to create a scandal about my defense of his civil rights. On many occasions, I have written actual prefaces and endorsements for books in France—books that are unread and unknown, as indeed is the case generally with my own writings. The latter fact is illustrated, for example, by Thibaud, who claims that I advocated "confiding Vietnamese freedom to the supposed good will of the leaders of the North." In fact, my writings on the war were overwhelmingly devoted to the U.S. attack on the peasant society of the South (and later Laos and Cambodia as well), which aimed to undermine the neutralization proposals of the National Liberation Front and others and to destroy the rural society in which the N.L.F. was based, and I precisely warned that success in this effort "will create a situation in which, indeed, North Vietnam will necessarily dominate Indochina, for no other viable society will remain."

Thibaud's ignorant falsifications point to one of the real factors that lie behind this affair. A number of these critics are ex-Stalinists, or people like Thibaud, who is capable of writing that prior to Solzhenitsyn, "every previous account" of "Sovietism" was within the Trotskyite framework (*Esprit*). Intellectuals who have recently awakened to the possibility of an anti-Leninist critique often systematically misunderstand a discussion of revolutionary movements and efforts to crush them that has never employed the assumptions they associate with the left. Thibaud, for example, cannot understand why I do not share his belief that Lenin, Stalin and Pol Pot demonstrate "the failure of socialism." Many left or ex-left intellectuals seem unaware that I never have regarded Leninist movements as having anything to do with "socialism" in any meaningful sense of the term; or that, having grown up in the libertarian anti-Leninist left, familiar since childhood with works that Thibaud has still never heard of, I am unimpressed with their recent conversions and unwilling to join in their new crusades, which often strike me as morally dubious and intellectually shallow. All of this has led to a great deal of bitterness on their part and not a little outright deceit.

As for the resurgence of anti-Semitism to which the PEN Club refers, or of racist atrocities, one may ask if the proper response to publication of material that may be used to enhance racist violence and oppression is to deny civil rights. Or is it, rather, to seek the causes of these vicious developments and work to eliminate them? To a person who upholds the basic ideas professed in the Western democracies, or who is seriously concerned with the real evils that confront us, the answer seems clear.

There are, in fact, far more dangerous manifestations of "revisionism" than Faurisson's. Consider the effort to show that the United States engaged in no crimes in Vietnam, that it was guilty only of "intellectual error." This "revisionism," in contrast to that of Faurisson, is supported by the major institutions and has always been the position of most of the intelligentsia, and has very direct and ugly policy consequences. Should we then argue that people advocating this position be suspended from teaching and brought to trial? The issue is, of course, academic. If the version of the Zhdanov doctrine now being put forth in the Faurisson affair were adopted by people with real power, it would not be the "Vietnam revisionists" who would be punished.

I do not want to leave the impression that the whole of the French press has been a theater of the absurd or committed to such views as those reviewed. There has been accurate commentary in *Le Monde* and *Libération,* for example, and a few people have taken a clear and honorable stand. Thus Alfred Grosser, who is critical of what he believes to be my position, writes in *Le Quotidien de Paris*: "I consider it shocking that Mr. Faurisson should be prevented from teaching French literature at the University of Lyons on the pretext that his security cannot be guaranteed."

In the Italian left-liberal journal *Repubblica,* Barbara Spinelli writes that the real scandal in this affair is the fact that even a few people publicly affirm their support of the right to express ideas that are almost universally reviled—and that happen to be diametrically opposed to their own. My own conclusion is different. It seems to me something of a scandal that it is even necessary to debate these issues two centuries after Voltaire defended the right of free expression for views he detested. It is a poor service to the memory of the victims of the holocaust to adopt a central doctrine of their murderers.

Nadine Fresco

SOURCE: "The Denial of the Dead," translated by Audri Durchslag, in *Dissent*, Vol. 28, No. 4, Fall, 1981, pp. 467-83.

[*In the following essay, which was originally published in French in 1980, Fresco offers an analysis of the Holocaust denial writings of Robert Faurisson.*]

Had he been able to attend the meeting of the First Civil Court on June 1, 1981, at the Palais de Justice in Paris, Hitler would undoubtedly have been overjoyed. Close to 40 years after the masterful—albeit incomplete—realization of his attempt to annihilate the life of the Jews, there were new zealots at work to annihilate the death of the Jews. In effect, the court was called upon to pass judgment on works of a new evangelist (literally, bearer of good news), Robert Faurisson. Faurisson had first been heard from two and a half years earlier with an article in *Le Monde* that concluded with the following words: "The nonexistence of 'gas chambers' is good news for poor humanity. Good news that it would be wrong to keep hidden any longer."

Who was this new evangelist? An associate professor at the University of Lyon when the affair began, Faurisson had previously been a teacher of literature at a girls' high school. At the time—we will return to it—the good news

with respect to the gas chambers was already waiting, as it were, in the anteroom of his mind. But his first article, published in 1961, was about literature. It caused a little stir when the journal *Bizarre* offered its readers an article, at first anonymous, entitled "Has One Read Rimbaud?" Writing about one of Rimbaud's sonnets, Faurisson demonstrated to a skeptical literary world that if Verlaine and François Coppée had already "gotten wind of a mystification" on the part of the adolescent poet, only he, Faurisson, had finally "arrived . . . at the simple and complete elucidation of an enigma that [now in 1961] has lasted 89 years." The sonnet, he affirmed, "has no sense if it is not an erotic one" and rests entirely on a "mystification."

Mystification. Let us keep the word in mind. I would not hesitate to say that it is the indispensable conceptual key for those wishing to understand Faurisson's thought.

It took another ten years for a repeat performance. 1972: the appearance of Faurisson's doctoral thesis, entitled "Has One Read Lautréamont?" There is a decided need of eyeglasses in France. The thesis begins with the following words:

> A hundred years. The mystification will have lasted a hundred years. In the space of one century, Isidore Ducasse [alias Lautréamont] succeeded in mystifying some of the greatest names in literature, criticism, and scholarship, both in France and beyond. There is no example, it seems, of a literary mystification so serious and long-lived.

Faurisson's obsession with demystification is his calling card. On page 13 of the catalog published in January 1978 by the Department of Literature and Classical and Modern Civilization of the University of Lyon-2, one finds the following: "Robert Faurisson, associate professor of 20th-century French literature. Specialization: criticism of texts and documents, investigation of meaning and counter-meaning, of the true and the false." This Mr. Faurisson is an expert in the investigation of truth and falsehood. What a noble enterprise has directed him these many years, over numerous and difficult paths. But literature was soon to appear too narrow a field for Faurisson's demystifying fever.

If I have taken this somewhat unusual detour, via Lautreamont and Rimbaud, enroute to the good news about the gas chambers, it is because there, already, we can see the two panels that form the theoretical diptych of Faurisson's thought. On the one hand, received ideas, prejudices, conformity, dupes, the establishment. But also mystifications and counterfeiters. On the other hand, simplicity and common sense. And also detection, scouring, demystification.

On December 28, 1978, *Le Monde* finally published the good news that the evangelist was burning to offer poor humanity. Two months earlier, Faurisson had addressed a circular to several newspapers that began with these words:

> I hope that some of the statements recently attributed to Louis Darquier de Pellepoix by the journalist Philippe Ganier-Raymond will finally

lead to the public's discovery that the alleged massacres in the "gas chambers" and the alleged "genocide" comprise one and the same lie, unfortunately endorsed until now by the official history (that of the victors) and by the colossal power of the communication media.

"I definitely find that they're talking about us too much at the moment," a friend said to me about that time, adding, "that's never a good thing." This "us," which included me, meant "us Jews." And in fact, in France, ever since October 1978, on the radio, in the newspapers, on television, everything seemed to be about us. All this had begun with the interview with Darquier published in *l'Express* [4 November 1978], to which Faurisson alluded.

Darquier had been general commissioner of Jewish Affairs from May 1942 to February 1944 and had personally overseen the successful operation tactfully called "Spring Breeze," better known as *"Rafle* [Roundup] *du Velodrome d'Hiver."* Despite his advanced age, Darquier had lost none of his anti-Semitic vitality. He explained that the only thing gassed in Auschwitz was the lice. "After the war, the Jews fabricated thousands of falsehoods," by which "they intoxicated the entire world."

This interview caused quite an uproar and, for some time, the French talked about the collaborators and those who were given amnesty, about Touvier, Leguay, Bousquet. They pitied, in retrospect, the fate of the unfortunate Jews handed over to the Nazis by a few bad men. And Pétain's ashes that were, it appears, finally to have been transferred to Douaumont, site of heavy combat during the First World War, remained discreetly piled in their little corner.

And when the three state-controlled TV channels refused to acquire the American series *Holocaust,* the unrest caused by the Darquier interview brought a reconsideration of this decision by the Second Channel. For the next 15 days, France lived with the biweekly tale of the genocide. The paradox was that this broadcast went a long way toward appeasing consciences. What was projected on French screens was indubitably sad, but it all happened, thank God, far from us. One could, thus, comfortably begin again to pity the Jews and condemn the Nazis. Neither of them was French. Everything was back in order.

It was during that period, some time between Darquier and the *Holocaust* series, that Faurisson entered the public scene. Rewarded for his perseverance, he saw his text finally published in *Le Monde* under the title " 'The Problem of the Gas Chambers' or 'The Rumor of Auschwitz.' " The readers of Maurice Bardèche's magazine *Défense de l'Occident* [Defense of the West] had already been privileged, as of June, to read the complete version of this document. Faurisson's defenders explain that he had no choice but to appear under the banner of Bardèche because no one else would publish the text. It seems to me that, on the contrary, there is always a choice between seeing oneself published by fascists and not being published at all. Conscious of the fact that the circulation of this extreme right-wing magazine was rather limited, Faurisson was careful to send his text to a number of important people, appending the following supplement:

Conclusions (from thirty years of research) of revisionist authors: (1) Hitler's "gas chambers" never existed. (2) The "genocide" (or the "attempted genocide") of the Jews never took place; clearly, Hitler never ordered (nor permitted) that someone be killed for racial or religious reasons. (3) The alleged "gas chambers" and the alleged "genocide" are one and the same lie. (4) This lie, essentially of Zionist origin, permitted a gigantic politico-financial swindle whose principal beneficiary is the State of Israel. (5) The principal victims of this lie and swindle are the Germans and Palestinians. (6) The tremendous power of the media has, until now, assured the success of the lie and prohibited the freedom of expression of those denouncing the lie. (7) The supporters of the lie now know that it is about to be uncovered; they distort the meaning and nature of revisionist research; they call "resurgence of nazism" or "falsification of history" what is only a just return to the concern for historical truth.

Circulars, articles, supplements. . . . Faurisson finally had an audience. But the reward had its flip side. Once public, such revelations could hardly avoid calling forth immediate reactions. At Lyons, there were displays of antipathy and Faurisson was lightly molested by Jewish students. Consequently, the president of the university chose to suspend his classes.

The reaction attested to a partisan sensibility that appeared unusual in a place traditionally devoted to the calm and respect that the evangelist thought he had every right to expect. Since that calm seemed decidedly difficult to regain, the unfortunate professor was compelled, in May 1979, to request of the secretary of education a transfer to teaching correspondence courses. The transfer was duly accorded, undoubtedly with the hope that such a measure would, little by little, help people forget the turmoil caused by the indelicacy and ingratitude with which the results of almost 20 years of work had been met.

With a moving sobriety, Robert Faurisson described those 20 years in a letter published in *Le Monde* on January 16, 1979:

> Up until 1960, I believed in the reality of these tremendous massacres in the "gas chambers." Then, upon reading Paul Rassinier, ex-deportee of the Resistance and author of *Le Mensonge d'Ulysse* [The Lie of Ulysses], I began to have doubts. After fourteen years of personal reflections, then four years of assiduous research, I became convinced, like twenty other revisionist authors, that I was confronting a historical lie. . . . In vain I searched for a single deportee capable of proving that he had actually seen, with his own eyes, a "gas chamber". . . . I would have been satisfied with even the slightest proof. That proof I never found. What I found instead were many false proofs, worthy of a witch trial.

May 1979: a tract circulates in Paris, entitled "Are the Gas Chambers Indispensable to Our Happiness?" and signed by "persons without qualities." In the middle of this tract, a sentence: "Professor Faurisson is a man alone." June 1979: a faction of the ultraleft, La Guerre Sociale [The Social War], prints a poster-tract with the headline "Who is the Jew?" One will have already guessed that the Jew today is none other than Robert Faurisson. April 1980: La Vieille Taupe [The Old Mole], a publishing house recently founded by another militant of the ultraleft, Pierre Guillaume, publishes a book by Serge Thion, *Vérité historique ou vérité politique? Le dossier de l'affaire Faurisson. La question des chambres à gaz* [Historical Truth or Political Truth? The File of the Faurisson Affair. The Question of the Gas Chambers]. On page 2 Thion writes,

> One can certainly say that Mr. Faurisson is a man of the right and, to be even more precise, a sort of right-wing anarchist. Nevertheless, one must also remember that until the beginning of this affair, many of his students and colleagues took him to be a man of the left. He is, by all standards, a man alone.

. . . . .

Robert Faurisson or the loneliness of the long-distance investigator. . . . In France, then—and the particularity is not without interest—it is a segment of the ultraleft that generously comes to the rescue of the solitary, oppressed new Jew. And since so generous a movement would hardly wish to be hindered by borders, a petition soon circulates in American universities that "claims for Faurisson the right to continue his research without impediment." Supporter of civil rights and free speech, and a friend of Serge Thion, Noam Chomsky signs this petition with, if I may say so, his eyes closed.

Poor Chomsky, innocent victim of a quasi-Pavlovian automatism. Someone mentions "rights"; he signs. Someone says "freedom of speech"; he signs. He goes even further with the famous preface (which is not really a preface, although it strangely resembles one) to Faurisson's book *Mémoire en défense* [A Memoir in Defense]. The press seized on the event, and I leave to others the delicate pleasure of pinpointing the ambiguities and contradictions that run through Chomsky's comments about the preface. But it is important to emphasize that the Faurisson affair is not an issue of legal rights. Faurisson's right to teach was not withdrawn. His books have not been the object of either seizure or censure. He has not been denied access to public libraries or archives. The suit against him is a private litigation.

If the Faurisson affair did not become a rights issue in France, it was for the simple reason that it wasn't one. And this explains how reviewers here could have seen Chomsky's defense of Faurisson's rights as irrelevant—or as implying that, in Chomsky's opinion, Faurisson's work had a legitimate claim on public and scholarly attention. Chomsky wrote in a style that is as classic as it is regrettable, attacking "the durable impact of Stalinism and doctrines of a Leninist variety, the strange Dadaist character of certain currents of intellectual life in post-war France," and describing the "hysteria and irrationality" of the "totalitarian involvements of the French intelligentsia," and "the contempt for facts" that characterizes "French intellectual discussions." There was a lamentable debate about

all this, a strangely chauvinistic exchange, as ridiculous on the one side as on the other, between Chomsky—who, breaking with his usual pattern, praised the traditions of American support for civil liberties—and some Gallic cocks defending their homeland!

Clearly unable to acknowledge that he has made a mistake, Chomsky chooses to confuse everything with such remarks as these: (1) "In one of my books, *Peace in the Middle East,* published in 1974, I wrote that it [the Holocaust] was the most fantastic explosion of insanity in human history." And (2) "I don't know enough about his [Faurisson's] work to determine if what he is claiming is accurate or not."

Recall that what Faurisson "claims" is very simply that the "explosion" did not occur. Chomsky, who does not *know* if what Faurisson says is the case, explains elsewhere "we don't want people to have religious or dogmatic *beliefs* about the existence of the Holocaust; we want them to know the *facts.* Personally I *believe* that the gas chambers existed." You, Noam Chomsky, *believe* in the existence of the gas chambers: but is this mere opinion or respect (the opposite of contempt) for facts? Imagine what someone like Chomsky, for example, would have to say about such . . . rationality.

Wishing to teach the intolerant French a lesson, Chomsky incessantly refers them to their own classics, specifically to Voltaire. I cannot help but be annoyed (in a manner entirely irrational) by the fact that in this Faurisson affair, which, admittedly, has a little something to do with anti-Semitism—except for those with the piercing eyes of old moles—Chomsky chooses as a model someone who in 1745 wrote about the Jews: "You will not find in them anything but an ignorant and barbarous people who have for a long time combined the most sordid avarice with the most detestable superstition." Of course, Voltaire added, "One should not, however, burn them." But this last suggestion "within such a context has the effect of a kind of stylistic coda" [L. Poliakov, *Histoire de l'antiséintisme, III: De Voltaire & Wagner, 1968*].

What appears absolute in Chomsky's political thinking is contempt. What is relative is the object of this contempt. 1980: in his preface to *Mémoire en défense,* Chomsky writes,

> I have frequently signed petitions that, in fact, were very extreme, in favor of Russian dissidents whose points of view were absolutely abhorrent, for instance, supporters of American slaughter exactly at the time it was ravaging Indochina, or of a politics favoring nuclear war, or of a religious chauvinism reminiscent of the Middle Ages. No one ever raised an objection. If someone had, I would have regarded him with the same *contempt* that those who denounce the petition in favor of Faurisson's civil rights deserve, and for the same reasons.

1972: in an article entitled "The Fallacy of Richard Herrnstein's IQ," Chomsky wrote,

> Imagine a psychologist in Hitler's Germany who thought he could show that Jews had a genetically determined tendency toward usury (like

squirrels bred to collect too many nuts) or a drive toward anti-social conspiracy and domination, and so on. If he were criticized for even undertaking these studies, could he merely respond that "a neutral commentator . . . would have to say that the case is simply not settled" and that the "fundamental issue" is "whether inquiry shall (again) be shut off because someone thinks society is best left in ignorance?" I think not. Rather, I think that such a response would have been met with justifiable *contempt*. At best he could claim that he is faced with a conflict of values. On the one hand, there is the alleged scientific importance of determining whether, in fact, Jews have a genetically determined tendency toward usury and domination (as might conceivably be the case). On the other, there is the likelihood that even opening this question and regarding it as a subject for scientific inquiry would provide ammunition for Goebbels and Rosenberg and their henchmen. Were this hypothetical psychologist to disregard the likely social consequences of his research (or even his undertaking of research) under existing social conditions, he would fully deserve the *contempt* of decent people. Of course, scientific curiosity should be encouraged (though fallacious argument and investigation of silly questions should not), but it is not an absolute value.

Replace the psychologist by Faurisson, the genetically determined tendency toward usury by the enormous politico-financial swindle that the lie about the alleged "gas chambers" represents. In your opinion, Noam Chomsky, who in the end deserves the contempt of decent people?

Poor Chomsky, blinded by the short-sightedness of others. So old and short-sighted the mole; so strangely short-sighted Serge Thion, Pierre Guillaume, *La Guerre Sociale*, & Co. that they were unable to see of what Robert Faurisson's alleged solitude really consisted.

June 1978: Robert Faurisson, on University of Lyon stationery and "in my position as Associate Professor at the University of Lyon-2," has an article published in German by the Deutscher Arbeitskreis [the German Work Group]—a neo-Nazi faction—an article entitled "There Were No Gas Chambers." By way of introduction, this group reminds its readers that this eminent university professor is to be numbered among the many revisionists who neutrally devote themselves to historical truth, while "German Zionists and Jews" (sic), panic-stricken before the inexorable march of the truth, attempt in vain to perpetuate the abominable myths of crimes imputed to the Nazis.

September 1979: at Northrup University, near Los Angeles, the first Revisionist Convention, sponsored by the Institute for Historical Review (IHR), is held. Speakers include some of the stars of revisionist science: Austin App (editor of *The Voice of German Americans*, and author of several pamphlets of high moral tone such as *Can Christianity survive when the Jews control the media and the money?*, also *Kosher Food Racket Exposed*, and *The Six Million Swindle*—all on the booklists of Liberty Bell Publications, publishers of Nazi books); Udo Walendy (who was a member of the Executive Committee of the NPD,

the German neo-Nazi party); Arthur Butz (author of the reference work of revisionist thought, *The Hoax of the Twentieth Century*, which was first published by the Historical Review Press in Richmond, England, the publishing house of the English fascist party, the National Front). And then, surprise of surprises, a man climbs to the rostrum to great applause to give a scientific lecture on "The Mechanics of Gassing." It is the new Jew, the lonely, flouted outsider, the hero of a segment of the French ultraleft: Robert Faurisson.

September 14, 1979: Before returning to his studies in France, Faurisson, whom Chomsky characterizes as a "relatively a political liberal," makes a short visit to the East Coast to give a lecture at the headquarters of the National Alliance (the American neo-Nazi party) outside of Washington. This visit is mentioned in the bulletin of the National Alliance, which usually is reserved for party members but, with a little wiliness, can be had. . . .

The National Alliance was founded and is directed by William Pierce, former member of the American Nazi party and translator into English of a brochure entitled *Bolshevism from Moses to Lenin*. The National Alliance publishes the monthly *National Vanguard*, whose "purpose is to propagate the fundamental truths of race and natural order," and which, in its booklist, refers to *Mein Kampf* as the "story of Germany's struggle for freedom and the philosophy behind it." Faurisson the outsider, Faurisson the apolitical man, now turns out to be a member of the Editorial Advisory Committee of the *Journal of Historical Review* and lecturer for the Nazis. But I have confidence that the rhetorical talents of Serge Thion (and of Chomsky?) will find novel ways of defending the solitude and apoliticism of the "respected professor of 20-century French literature and document criticism."

．．．．．

On the first page of *Spotlight* (a publication of the Liberty Lobby) of September 24, 1979, dedicated to the revisionist convention, an advertisement announces the book *Debunking the Genocide Myth* by Paul Rassinier. The advertisement goes on to describe the author as

> a socialist, pacifist, anti-Nazi, pro-Jewish [sic] historian and geographer [who] was captured in late 1943 and interned by the Nazis because of his activities with the French Resistance. After the war, however, Rassinier could not conscientiously justify by his own experience the horror stories of many of his fellow concentration camp inmates. So he set out on the thankless task of discovering what was true and what was false.

Rassinier's work is of primary importance for those who want to understand the functioning and subtleties of revisionist thinking. There is not an author in the pack who does not recognize and acknowledge him as a father.

Returning from Buchenwald and Dora where he had been interned for 19 months, Rassinier immediately set to work denouncing—in *Passage de la ligne* [Crossing the Line], *Le Mensonge d'Ulysse* [The Lie of Ulysses], *Ulysse trahi par les siens* [Ulysses Betrayed By His Own]—the behavior of the Communist prisoners, to whom the SS had delegated some power inside the camp. He concludes, with a rather dubious logic, that those responsible for the atrocities and deaths were not, therefore, the Nazis but the Communists. He severely criticizes certain inexact accounts by prisoners and deduces from these that, if there were exaggerations or even inventions with reference to the gas chambers at Dachau, the same might be true of other accounts. "My opinion about the gas chambers? There were some, although not so many as is thought. There were also exterminations by this method, although not so many as is claimed." In any case, there is no proof. And if some day the German archives were to reveal documents—

> ordering the construction of gas chambers for any other purpose than extermination—one never knows, with this terrible scientific genius of the Germans—one would have to admit that their utilization in certain cases was the result of one or two madmen among the SS. . . .

The welcome accorded Rassinier's ideas, at the end of the war, was not the warmest. Some, however, like Maurice Bardèche (already!), who became his publisher, were overjoyed. In the view of this confirmed fascist, the testimony of a member of the Resistance and a prisoner was of inestimable value. Bardeche published Rassinier's *Le véritable procès Eichmann ou les vainqueurs incorrigibles* [The Actual Eichmann Trial, or the Incorrigible Victors], in which the author wrote that "there is almost nothing [written about war crimes] except the two admirable books by Maurice Bardèche, *Nüremberg ou la Terre Promise* [Nuremberg or the Promised Land] and *Nuremberg II ou les Faux Monnayeurs* [Nuremberg II or the Counterfeiters]." Rassinier, renewing his confidence in his fascist publisher, gave him his new manuscript entitled *Le Drame des juifs europeens* [The Drama of the European Jews], which appeared in 1964. Here, Rassinier explains that

> they [the Jews] are not today a race so much as a type of life and of aspiration, and it is not a racial problem that they pose but—as the state of Israel proves only too well—an economic and social one . . . they intend to establish a commercial empire that, as was already indicated, would cover the entire world.

La Vieille Taupe, which had until then only published a few brochures, transformed itself into a publishing house in order to reprint Rassinier's works: *Le Mensonge d'Ulysse* [The Lie of Ulysses] in 1979 and *Ulysse trahi par les siens* [Ulysses Betrayed By His Own] in early 1980. Four months later, Thion's book *Vérité . . .* appeared.

The revisionists loudly call for "a debate about historical technique." They ask that efforts be made to "expand the sources" and "to publicize the results of studies, without, however, giving them a character of official truth." How respectably such things are said. . . . Serge Thion, who expresses himself in this way, indeed concludes his book most judiciously by reproducing an article about Faurisson by Georges Wellers, director of the Center for Contemporary Jewish Documentation (Paris), that had appeared in *Le Monde* on February 21, 1979. Thion generously characterizes this text, entitled "Un roman inspiré"

[An Inspired Fiction], as "a document of great importance." But let us not misunderstand this generosity. What wins Georges Wellers such critical honors is not what he says in the article but, rather, the fact that he "finally opens up a discussion of a scientific nature between two historical schools."

> For the first time [continues Thion] a specialist of the official school [read: "the exterminationists"] publicly confronts the arguments of the school called revisionist. . . . For the first time, a historian shows himself dissatisfied with a teleological argument ("where does this lead?"), a political argument ("an apology for nazism") or even a sentimental argument ("outrage to the memory of the dead"). The debate is raised to the level of a historical discussion.

One finally breathes the free and invigorating air of orderly battles, far from subterranean plots and subjectivities encumbered by affect. People confront each other with arms worthy of the highest demands of a faultless deontology. But I would wager that Georges Wellers was flabbergasted when he saw what Thion had made of his text. It was, in fact, explicitly and exclusively an analysis of the *methods* employed by Faurisson and a denunciation of the flagrant dishonesty that he represented. But, as we just witnessed, this categorical refutation of a method has miraculously been transformed, by the rigorously deontological pen of Thion, into a discussion of an argument. Hoping no doubt to have established the official recognition of the revisionist school, Thion adds, prophetically and somewhat menacingly perhaps, "Nothing and no one will be able to evade much longer the debate that we hope will be carried on with the greatest calm possible."

We are thus told of the existence of a revisionist school anxious to open discussions of a scientific nature. But the very expression "revisionist school" makes no sense. One cannot claim to be motivated solely by the need for a scientific deontology and at the same time devote oneself explicitly and entirely to the task of denunciation. One cannot pretend to establish a science whose only ethic is suspicion, where distrust is the only certitude. If one scans the list of books and articles published by the revisionist school, one discovers there one example after another of Faurisson's painful obsession with falsehood, masked by "that insistence on the love of truth that characterizes all the falsifiers"—*The Lie of Auschwitz, The Hoax of the Twentieth Century, The Six Million Swindle. The Actual Eichmann Trial, The Myth of Auschwitz, The Truth for Germany,* etc., etc., not to omit Thion's *Historical Truth or Political Truth,* which explicitly picks up the title that Rassinier had used in 1961 for a series of lectures.

. . . . .

Several revisionist authors preface their writings with autobiographical comments that are strangely similar. One certainty emerges: a person is not born a revisionist; he becomes one. On the first page of his *Hoax of the Twentieth Century,* Arthur Butz writes:

> In common with virtually all Americans who have had their opinions formed since the end of World War II, I had, until not very long ago, as-

sumed that Germany had given the world a particularly murderous outburst during World War II. This view has ruled Western opinion since 1945 and earlier, and I was no exception in accepting the essentials of it.

In his turn, Serge Thion writes about his escape from the herd of dupes: "The general populace undoubtedly believes as I believed for a long time that we possess a vast number of documents and verifiable information on the politics of Nazi extermination." Clearly, such is not the case. One, therefore, asks questions. And "all this converges toward a set of doubts that includes, yet goes beyond, the single question of the gas chambers."

How do these doubts work? In his letter to *Le Monde* on January 16, 1979, Faurisson cites the diary that Johann-Paul Kremer, SS doctor, kept during his tenure at Auschwitz. Kremer recounts, on October 18, 1942 that, for the eleventh time, he was present at a "special action" (Sonderaktion). Faurisson, who can't be had and who, like no one else, knows how to decipher a text, decides that this "special action," which the exterminationists insist on taking for a mass gassing, refers very simply to the executions of those condemned to death. Condemned by whom, when, why? It makes no difference. He writes, "Among the condemned are three women who arrived in a convoy from Holland; they are shot." This sentence is accompanied by a very impressive note that indicates the seriousness of Faurisson's work. The note consists of a biographical reference: " 'Auschwitz as Seen by the SS,' published by the Museum of Oswiecim [the Polish name for Auschwitz], 1974, p. 238, note 85."

Can one imagine a more scrupulous concern for reference, precision, and scientific rigor? But then perhaps Faurisson thinks it would be rather surprising if readers of *Le Monde* had access to such a book, published so far from France and behind the Iron Curtain. Unfortunately for Faurisson, I have the book. And note 85 on page 238, which reports the official transcript of Kremer's testimony in 1947, indeed indicates that three Dutch women were shot on that day. But the text of the note to which Faurisson refers reads: "At the time of the special action which I described in my diary on October 18, 1942, three Dutch women *refused to enter the gas chamber* [emphasis mine] and pleaded for their lives. They were young women, in good health, but despite this their prayer was not granted and the SS who participated in the action shot them on the spot." The times are decidedly difficult and it is surely with great reluctance that these evangelists find themselves compelled to tamper with facts in order to carry on their worldwide conversion.

The fundamental rule of revisionist argumentation is very simple: any evidence of massive extermination of the Jews in the gas chambers is unacceptable. First with respect to the Nazis. Faurisson announced some time ago what was to constitute the credo of his doctrine: "Hitler never ordered (nor permitted) that someone be killed because of race or religion." If this uncontestably audacious claim seems not to bother either American, English, or German revisionists, it did provoke grumblings among some of Faurisson's defenders in France. Pierre Guillaume, head of La Vieille Taupe Publishers, in a letter sent to the newspaper *Libération* and not printed—but, fortunately, included in Thion's book—discusses the torments that he as well as his friends experienced because of Faurisson's famous statement.

> I met Professor Faurisson at the end of November. I found a man desperate and on the verge of withdrawing into a paranoid delirium—a reaction that was, however, altogether understandable. I also found a man who thoroughly knew his subject (200 kilos of documents, representing the analysis of several tons of texts) and whose works were of the same general persuasion as, but went much further than, those of La Vieille Taupe. . . . As my own character was not strong enough for the task (I myself was on the verge of breaking)—it became vital for the development of the situation to gain support and, thus, to obtain everyone's agreement on a unified statement, with neither concessions nor second thoughts. This statement had, therefore, to integrate the famous sentence that seemed to render Faurisson indefensible: "Hitler never ordered the execution of a single Jew solely because of the fact that he was a Jew." [I would have the future archivists of revisionism note that the formulation, as Guillaume puts it, differs from the original credo; it specifically lacks the words "or permitted," which Faurisson seemed to insist upon.] The statement held that Faurisson's claim was, strictly speaking, true even though Hitler could not have cared less about what actually happened to the Jews. This done, I proved in practice that I was ready to follow Faurisson to the end. . . . Feeling thus supported, Faurisson began to eat normally and his paranoid symptoms disappeared completely.

Admit that it would have been a shame to lose such a text.

Why, then, did the Nazis build gas chambers? At Auschwitz, as Darquier explained, only lice had been gassed; it was a question of getting rid of the vermin. Himmler himself said as much when, on April 24, 1943, he explained to the SS officers that

> it is the same with anti-Semitism as with delousing. To remove lice has nothing to do with a world view. It is a question of cleanliness. In the same way exactly, anti-Semitism did not constitute for us a question of a world view. It is a question of cleanliness.

I do not know if Himmler would have understood Faurisson, but Faurisson understood Himmler. He demonstrates that

> it is utter dishonesty to present . . . as homicidal "gas chambers" sterilizers that were actually intended to disinfect clothing with gas. . . . Another form of gassing in fact existed in the German camps; it is the gassing of buildings to exterminate the vermin. There one used the famous Zyklon B about which such a fantastic myth has been constructed.

Unfortunately for the Nazis, the rumors about the treatment of the Jews deported to Poland were already circulating in Germany, clearly without foundation. An ordinance of November 9, 1942 announced by the Chancellery decreed that "in order to counter the development of rumors about this subject . . . the following commentaries are provided as information about the actual situation. . . . " The Nazis, it would seem, were already at this period worried about combating "the rumor of Auschwitz" that Faurisson so firmly denounces today. The ordinance continued:

> The total . . . elimination of millions of Jews established in the European economic area is a forced imperative in the struggle that is being waged by the German people to assure its very existence. Beginning with the territories of the Reich and moving on to the other European countries involved in the Final Solution, the Jews are transported to the East, to large camps—in part still to be built—where they are either assigned to work or sent farther East.

Faurisson, who has understood the Nazi mentality as well as that of the pseudo-victims, does not believe that the Germans felt any need to camouflage their language and has decided that for the Nazis, as for him, a spade is a spade. He certainly does not think that the expression "sent farther East" could be a euphemism of the *Amtssprache,* the administrative language used by the Nazis in their direction of the Final Solution. But what does Faurisson understand the exact meaning of "the Final Solution" to be? He most assuredly has a precise idea about this place "farther East" where the Jews disappeared. Armed with the "simple good sense" that he shares with Thion, Faurisson takes the texts "for what they are" and the Nazis at their very word. He knows that, different from Americans, Communists, Jews, etc., the Nazis did not lie. How does he know this? Never mind. The revisionists, who are experts in distinguishing the true from the false, do not believe for a moment that the Germans had recourse to an administrative language intended to camouflage their enterprise of extermination.

Contrary to Faurisson, Himmler believed that the Nazis needed to camouflage what they were doing. Thus, when the statistician Korherr, in his report to Himmler in the spring of 1943, uses the expression *Sonderbehandlung* (special treatment) to speak of the million and a half Jews already *durchgeschleust* (processed—literally: passed through the locks) in the camps, Himmler responds:

> I find this report very good as regards documentation for the future, that is to say, as camouflage. At present, it [the report] should be neither published nor communicated. The essential thing for me is, now as before, that . . . as many Jews as is humanly possible be transported to the East.

But Himmler states precisely that one should not speak of *Sonderbehandlung,* and that the term should be replaced by the word *Transportierung* (transport).

A few months later, it was this same Himmler's turn to learn a lesson in camouflage from General Pohl, chief of the WVHA (the central economic and administrative office of the SS), concerning the camp at Sobibor. Up to that point Sobibor had been referred to in the correspondence as a *Durchgangslager* (transit camp). Sobibor was located only 3 km. from the Bug River, which formed the farthest Eastern border of the territories occupied by the Nazis. To where, therefore, could the Jews coming from this camp "transit"? Himmler then writes to Pohl to propose that the camp at Sobibor be henceforth called a *Konzentrationslager* (concentration camp). But, in a letter dated July 15, 1943, the chief of the central office, on which all the Nazi camps were dependent, responds that they must continue to designate Sobibor a transit camp.

With the very words used by the Nazis themselves, let us now return to our Faurisson analysis of the texts. The *Endlösung der Judenfrage* (the Final Solution of the Jewish question) is therefore only a cleansing operation on a European scale. As many Jews as can be found in a region are put into railroad cars and transported Eastward for *Evakuierung* (evacuation), *Aussiedlung* (displacement), or *Umsiedlung* (resettlement). After which the region is declared *judenrein gemacht* (cleansed of Jews) or *judenfrei* (free of Jews)—a successful *"Bereinigung der Judenfrage"* (clean-up of the Jewish question). Since the vermin may offer some resistance to this salutary enterprise, the operation must be effected with *rücksichloser Härte* (relentless severity). The areas are, thereby, henceforth clean. But not yet the Jews. For it is known that, unfortunately, their transport to the East did not always occur under the most hygienic conditions. And so, from the moment of their arrival the majority among them were directed to the *Badanstalten* (bathhouses). The irrefutable proof that this was in order that they might take a shower, and not to asphyxiate them with gas, is that the areas intended for this action clearly displayed the signs *"Wasch u. Disinfektionsräume"* (wash & disinfection rooms). It was all simply a matter of getting rid of the vermin. Everything, then, accords perfectly: evacuation, cleansing, and transport farther East.

. . . . .

One can easily imagine, I think, that if documents dating from the war years reveal so little proof of the extermination of Jews by the Nazis, then documents originating after the German capitulation are hardly likely to reenforce the already tenuous position of the exterminationists. *Nüremberg ou la Terre Promise* [Nuremberg or the Promised Land] was written by Bardèche in 1948. Every revisionist owes it to himself to go back to this critical analysis and radical condemnation of an unjust trial— perpetrated on the vanquished by the victors—whose aim was the greatest profit for the *"amateurs* of the promised land."

The rumors of the alleged genocide of the Jews that circulated in Europe and the United States during the last years of the war constituted the principal evidence in the case for the prosecution. Nuremberg and the other war-crimes trials that have taken place since then are, therefore, according to Faurisson, in every way akin to the infamous witch trials of the Middle Ages. Once free of the so-called evidence extorted from the vanquished, only that advanced by the alleged victims remains. And it is unnecessary to say what one should think of that. When one is committed to the method routinely used by Faurisson, one sees quite easily what can be expected of the depositions of such people. It is without a doubt for this reason that Faurisson has, until now at least, neglected to examine the testimony of the survivors.

There are a great many things that Faurisson doesn't bother with. He never mentions, for example, the depositions taken during the various trials from the survivors of the *Sonderkommandos* (special commandos), who were responsible for emptying the gas chambers, transporting the corpses to the crematoria and burning them, and cleaning the gas chambers for the next operation. A former member of the Auschwitz *Sonderkommando,* among others, recounted how he had actually seen with his own eyes a gas chamber. His name: Dov Paisikovic. But (1) he was Jewish and thus had every interest in accusing the Nazis of imaginary crimes; (2) after the war, he emigrated to Israel, the country par excellence of the hoax of the 20th century; (3) he has since died and Faurisson is thus unable to meet with him; (4) the detailed description he gave of the functioning of the gas chambers was part of his deposition of October 17, 1963 at the Auschwitz trial—and we know what we should think of Nuremberg and subsequent trials.

The basic rule of revisionist argumentation is that all evidence of extermination is by definition inadmissible. A document dating from the war is inadmissible because it dates from the war. A document dating from immediately after the war is inadmissible because it dates from those years. The deposition of a Nazi at his trial is inadmissible because it is a deposition from a trial. This is a principle applicable to all the Nazis who were tried. If, as is the case, not one of them denied the existence of gas chambers, it is not because the gas chambers existed (a feeble exterminationist thought), but because the witnesses believed that if they assisted the victors, the judges would reward them with clemency. As for the testimonies and depositions of some hundreds of Jews who pretended to be survivors of the genocide, they are inadmissible because given by people who could only be instigators or, at best, accomplices in the rumor that led to the swindle from which they benefited.

. . . . .

In his *Wit and Its Relations to the Unconscious,* Freud recounts an old story: A borrows a copper caldron from B; when he returns it, B complains that the caldron has a large hole that renders it useless. A defends himself thus: first, I returned the caldron in good condition; second, it already had a hole when I borrowed it; third, I really never borrowed the caldron from B. Let us see how the genocide is nothing but a Talmudic story about a caldron. The story consists of these elements: First, it is the Jews who are the cause of the Second World War. They were, in fact, the first to declare war on Germany. How do I know this? First of all, from Hitler who always spoke the truth, whom I must understand literally, and who prophesied with great clairvoyance in his speech of January 30, 1939 that "If international Jewry succeeds in precipitating a world war, the result will hardly be a bolshevization of Europe

and a victory for Judaism but the extermination of the Jewish race in Europe."

But I also know it from Faurisson and Rassinier. Faurisson explains that "in the person of Chaim Weizmann, president of the World Jewish Congress, and future first president of the state of Israel, the international Jewish community declared war on Germany on September 5, 1939." Rassinier, undoubtedly more aware of the labyrinthine ways of politics, explains the entire affair at length in a book that appeared in 1967 entitled *Les responsables de la seconde guerre mondiale* [Those Responsible for the Second World War]. I am surprised that Serge Thion, who in his book is so quick to give moral lessons to professional historians, omitted mentioning this book by Rassinier in his bibliography of revisionist literature—which, he says, "is almost inaccessible in France for various reasons." Thion writes that "it will be necessary, one day, to rehabilitate Rassinier." It would be especially regrettable if, on that day, the books neglected by Thion were not included. Rassinier is an author unjustly "reduced to being published by the extreme right"—he, too, then—and who "wrote before his time." Here is a sample of what Rassinier wrote before the time was ripe. In *Les responsables de la seconde guerre mondiale,* he explains how the Jews organized the war against Germany:

> A Democrat, President Roosevelt was also a freemason and, consequently, his relations with the Jewish world were numerous and intimate. His entourage was Jewish, at least the greatest number of his most important advisers. Morgenthau, his Secretary of Treasury, was Jewish; his most influential advisers, Baruch and Weizmann, were too. Cordell Hull of the State Department is married to a Jew. . . . From the moment of his election, President Roosevelt accepted—first tacitly, then more openly—all the postulates of the Jewish policies. Perhaps this can be explained by the fact that he was very ill and that his sickness made him dependent on his wife who was, even more fiercely than he, devoted to the cause of the Jews. . . .

As for the Nazis,

> they found it entirely normal to view the Jews as foreigners in Germany since they behaved like foreigners. Noting that this doctrine [the Nazi doctrine] would help extricate a people of 70 million from their financial market, all the Jews of the world, instead of seeking a compromise, which was easily attainable given the fact that Hitler sought one, enflamed the argument by declaring themselves . . . in a state of war, not only with Nazi ideology—which would have been perfectly legitimate and would, at worst, have generated only an academic discussion— but with Germany, which implied a military intervention.

The Jews declared war on Hitler. What would you have done in his place? He was not, after all, going to turn the other cheek. And so he defended himself.

Second part of the caldron story: War is war, but nothing more. The Nazis are not guilty of the crime of which the pseudo-victims accuse them. As Butz explains, he dedicates his book (*The Hoax of the Twentieth Century*) to proving the hoax, that is, to a demonstration of what *did not* happen. This is the crux of the revisionist program: to prove that something *did not* take place, that a crime was not committed. The gas chambers were part of the propaganda of war. Proof: Himmler, according to Butz, sensing the wind change, had made contact a little before the end of the war with a representative of the World Jewish Congress. And Himmler explained to him that to stop the typhus epidemic in the camps, the Nazis had been obliged to burn a large number of corpses, for which reason they had constructed the crematoria. It was this that caused the confusion about the gas chambers. But Himmler committed "suicide" in a British prison. This was particularly unfortunate since, if he had been able to appear before the judges, he would clearly have told the truth—a Nazi, like a revisionist, always speaks the truth. Arthur R. Butz's book would then have been unnecessary; Himmler himself would have proven the hoax. But the demands of politics made it inconvenient that he be heard by the court. He therefore commited "suicide." Caldron or not, one will say what one wants; reasoning like that one does not find just anywhere.

The first two phases of the story of genocide in the image of a caldron are, then, (1) the Jews are responsible for the horrors they impute to the Nazis, and (2) these horrors never existed. But the punchline, the moment one laughs, is (3) the Jews, who pretend to be the victims, are actually the victors. On the basis of this colossal lie about "gas chambers" and "genocide," they succeeded in their incredible swindle, the greatest of all time. Make an accounting of the millions of marks paid by the Germans, in the name of reparations, for the millions of Jews who were *not* exterminated. As a swindle, it's not a bad one. But for the hoax to work, to hit pay dirt, so to speak, it is absolutely necessary that the true victors continue to pass for the victims. Hence the need for an organization of universal scope, propaganda . . . and so on.

The revisionists' real difficulty was to prove this void, this lie, this absence of the dead. The first of them, Rassinier, with a scholarly mixture of quotations, calculations, reasoning, deductions, cross-checking, collations, etc. challenged the estimate of the number of victims arrived at by the exterminationists. Instead, he offered figures that the reader is all the more easily able to accept for not having understood any of the scholarly mix that produced them. His conclusions: some industrial gassings plus the horrors of war—altogether around a million Jewish victims. Robert Faurisson, who has the obvious advantage of working at the end of a century that increasingly resembles a computer, arrives at more scientific conclusions:

> My view is the following: (1) the number of Jews exterminated by the Nazis (or victims of "genocide") is, happily, equal to zero. . . . I have rather good reasons to think that the number of deaths at Auschwitz (Jews and non-Jews) was around 50,000. . . . As for the number of deaths at all the concentration camps from 1933-34 to 1945, I think it had to be 200,000 or at most 360,000. Some day, I will cite my sources but I contend today that if we employed computers, we would

without a doubt soon know the real number of deaths.

In *La Drame des juifs européens,* Rassinier had denounced the dishonesty of Hilberg, Poliakov, and other Zionist agents who used all their Talmudic resources to arrive at the convenient and sacred number of six million. And now he quotes abundantly from an article in the journal *American Mercury*. (A curious documentary point: the address of this journal is the same as that of the Institute for Historical Review, organizing body of the Revisionist Congresses.)

> If it is true, as the *American Mercury* claims, that the international Zionist movement refuses to participate in a census of the world's Jewish population—what an admission!—thereby rendering it impossible, I can hardly see how else one could discover the truth.

The chapter immediately following these lines, very naturally, is entitled " 'The Jewish Migration' or 'The Wandering Jew' " and begins with these words: "To better understand the movement of the European Jewish population between 1933 and 1945, a rapid historical overview of Jewish migration on a worldwide scale seems to me indispensable: in short, the history of 'The Wandering Jew.' " To understand what happened to the alleged victims of the Second World War, one must go back, as Rassinier does, to the 18th century B.C. A wanderer, perhaps, but with "the agility of the merchant by calling"—and Rassinier goes on:

> Today [his book appeared in 1964] it is, to speak in metaphors, the gold in Fort Knox that is eyed. If the operation succeeded—it would suffice for the American arm of the international Zionist movement to exert pressure on Wall Street for it to be so—the Israeli port of registry of the Diaspora would become not only the commercial Center of the Atlantic world but, with oil being the energy source par excellence of its development and Jewish control of it being totally assured from the Middle East to Texas, also the command post of all its industry. . . . then . . . the appelation "the Chosen People" to which the Jews lay claim would take on all its significance

Is it the author of these lines that Thion hopes to rehabilitate?

Rassinier had understood everything: to find who profited from the crime that was *not* committed, one had clearly to search in the camp of the alleged victims and prove the gigantic plot that is at the base of such a swindle.

But how to prove this? These Jews who dare to pretend to be dead and demand reparation are in truth alive. But feigning to be dead, they are innumerable—that is, one cannot count them. They no longer wear the yellow star, thus it is difficult to spot them at a glance. Faurisson clearly explains that the Jews with the star

> were like paroled prisoners. Hitler was concerned perhaps less with the Jewish question than with ensuring the security of the German soldier. The German soldier would otherwise

have been unable to distinguish the Jews from the non-Jews. This sign designated them for him. . . . I know that sometimes one thinks that six- to fifteen-year-old children could not constitute a danger and that they should not have been subjected to wearing the star. But within the context of this military logic, there exist enough accounts and memoirs [how now? should one believe these?] where the Jews tell us that from earliest childhood they participated in all kinds of illicit activity or resistance against the Germans.

But after 1945, the wearing of the star was discontinued. How then to recognize the Jews? How count them? The proof that they are not dead, as the good sense of Rassinier, Faurisson, Thion, and Co. would have it, is that they are alive. But how demonstrate this? They move all the time, they are behind the Iron Curtain, they disguise themselves as common Americans, they change their names. Pages 327-28 of Thion's book provides the astounding and incontestable proof that the alleged dead are still alive.

Page 327: the little boy from the Warsaw ghetto, with his overly large cap, his frightened look, his arms raised before the German machine guns—how he caused the dupes to cry. . . . But rejoice; this little boy who, according to the exterminationist myth, was supposed to have died in a gas chamber in Treblinka, Faurisson explains, is today a very rich man living in the suburbs of London. Faurisson obtained this good news he is so eager to communicate to us from the *Jewish Chronicle* of August 11, 1978. There is nothing so striking to the imagination as to note at the end of a book on historical truth that a poor young Jew alleged to be dead is in fact alive and rich.

Page 328: same scenario. This time, the photograph is of Simone Veil. Faurisson writes,

> Let us take as an example convoy #71 which arrived at Auschwitz on April 16, 1944. All the women in this convoy, we are told, were gassed on the very day of their arrival. Among them figured the name of a certain Simone Jacob, born on June 13, 1927 in Nice. Now this young woman actually returned to France; by marriage she became Simone Veil and she today presides over the European Parliament.

Again one who was supposed to have been gassed is found to be alive—and rich too. That already makes two survivors. Draw your own conclusions.

. . . . .

In these troubled times, when one is no longer very clear about who is on the left (or right) of whom, a new pastime has emerged for the happy few who award themselves and others political marks whose common character the discerning reader will not fail to notice. Thus Thion about Faurisson: "a kind of anarchist of the right"; Chomsky about Thion: "a libertarian socialist scholar"; Jan Myrdal about Faurisson: "an anarchist of the liberal right"; Noam Chomsky about Noam Chomsky: "a kind of libertarian anarcho-syndicalist"; Chomsky about Faurisson: "a kind of relatively apolitical liberal"; and, finally, last but not least (too bad for the Dadaist-Stalinist amalgam that many will not fail to notice), David McCalden, alias Lewis Brandon, editor of the *Journal of Historical Review*: "I'm a detached cynic, a libertarian with a small 'l.'"

And then at the far end of the left—in France at least—there are the theoreticians, the hard and pure revolutionaries, the earthly representatives of a faultless rationalism: an ultraleft in the process of decomposition, abandoning for a time interfamilial anathemas and curiously trying to recompose itself on the basis of Faurisson's theories. During the demonstration that followed the bombing in front of the synagogue on the rue Copernic in Paris (October 3, 1980), a tract was distributed signed by diverse factions of this fragmented ultraleft—The Social War, The Young Mole (sic), The Friends of Potlach, The Commune Group of Kronstadt, and so forth. The following passages from the tract entitled "Our Kingdom is a Prison" speak for themselves:

> It is the constant need of our class societies to propose to the oppressed populations false enemies, fabricated horrors in place of the true ones. . . . Enough of anti-Semitism. Enough of anti-fascism. The one and the other are the "socialism of imbeciles". . . . The deportation and concentration of millions of people are not limited to an infernal idea of the Nazis; it has to do above all with the lack of manpower needed by the war machine that made it [war] a necessity. . . . The deportees who did not return are dead because of the war. . . . the only revolutionary attitude possible. . . . is the subversion of all war propaganda. . . . We will, perhaps, never possess "scientific" proof of the nonexistence of the Hitler "gas chambers."

The purists of the Communist Program, the French disciples of Amadeo Bordiga were the first to introduce in France the peculiar revolutionary idea of *Auschwitz ou le grand alibi* [Auschwitz or the Grand Alibi].

The demystifying madness of Faurisson could not, perhaps, find a better ally than the rationalist madness of these deep minds who take Marx at face value. Hegel is turned on his head; henceforth only the rational is real. A capitalist phenomenon among others, nazism—according to a strict Marxist theory—would hardly want to exterminate a human group that represents so much manpower. Marxism cannot account for extermination. To preserve Marxism, then, it is necessary that the extermination not have occurred; therefore, it did not. Q.E.D. The rest, the alleged gas chambers, are only "the keystone of a politico-religious fabrication," an "official and vengeful" delirium, composed of taboos and myths. And "the refusal of intellectual taboos" is sacred to Thion, Guillaume, and the others. Faced with the exterminationist Vulgate and the ensemble of traditional ideas that encumber contemporary thought, these people are skeptics just as others are believers. "Systematic doubt, pushed to its extreme, has become healthy and legitimate.

But we have not finished seeking the reasons that (in our world and in their minds) push certain people—among them a good number of Jews—to persist in this business of "demystification," in this need to claim that the millions who disappeared are alive, this need tirelessly to denounce the trickery of others, this need to dedicate themselves to the peculiar role of deniers of the dead.

W. D. Rubenstein

SOURCE: "Chomsky and the Neo-Nazis," in *Quadrant,* Vol. XXV, No. 10, October, 1981, pp. 8-14.

[Rubenstein is an American historian and educator. In the following essay, he discusses his correspondence with Noam Chomsky regarding the latter's defense of Robert Faurisson.]

The strange nexus between Noam Chomsky, the eminent linguist, and Robert Faurisson, an Associate Professor of Literature at the University of Lyon in France, who believes, in his own words that "there were no gas chambers at Auschwitz or anywhere else in wartime Europe," and who has described the Holocaust as "a historic lie", an "abominable lie", and a "politico-financial swindle" is by now fairly well known—at least in France and America, where it has received wide publicity in journals like the *New York Times, New Republic* and *Le Monde.* It is perhaps less well known in Australia, where, so far as I am aware, only one mainstream publication (*The Bulletin,* 3 February 1981) has reported on the matter. The purpose of this essay is to outline concisely the history of this affair, and to add what I believe is some interesting fresh information about it, particularly concerning Chomsky's attitudes and connections with Faurisson. This in turn leads on to a more basic discussion of Chomsky's view of the world and of history, and of the neo-Nazi view of these matters, which in my opinion are remarkably similar.

To the uninitiated, it is, of course, necessary to describe the *dramatis personae* and my own *locus standi* in this business. First, as to the neo–Nazis. Most Australians will be aware of the revival of Nazism, anti-semitism, and right-wing terrorism, especially in Europe. One of the central strands in this movement is the whitewashing of Hitler and his crimes, and central to this thrust are various attempts to prove that the Nazi mass murder of six million Jews never happened, and, moreover, that it was a legend concocted during and after the War by "Zionists" and "Marxists" in order to gain sympathy for the creation of Israel, to compel Germany to pay billions in retribution, and for various other diabolical ends stemming from the extreme wickedness of Jews and their allies. Although the centre of this revival is clearly West Germany, whose government recently confiscated literally tons of extremist hate literature of this type, it has devotees almost everywhere in the Western world: in England, through the British Movement, the National Front, and similar bodies, as well as in France, Australia, and the United States. Often the advocates of neo-Nazism have their origin in their own right-wing national traditions, although their basic view of politics is similar.

Those connected with the ultra-right fall into two distinct groups. One consists of Nazis pure and simple, purveyors of religious and racial hatred of a type which my generation hoped had perished in the Berlin bunker in 1945.

Far more important, and certainly more interesting, are the handful of intellectuals—if that is the right term—who have attached themselves to this movement. In an attempt to gain credibility in the English-speaking world, in 1979 an organisation with the misleading title of the "Institute of Historical Review" was founded in California by Willis A. Carto, who also finances other American lunatic fringe outfits, such as the "Liberty Lobby". It publishes a curious journal mistitled *Journal of Historical Review,* which purports to be a serious academic publication, but which in reality consists of neo-Nazi literature "disproving" the Holocaust, whitewashing the Nazis generally, attacking Roosevelt and Churchill (described in one issue as a "drunken chameleon") and the like. Some of the authors appear to have legitimate academic or professional standing—though they are never, of course, serious or respected historians—and to have little or no connection with the neo-Nazi right. One such man is Arthur Butz, Associate Professor of Electrical Engineering at Northwestern University, who wrote the current "Bible" of this movement, the notorious *Hoax of the Twentieth Century.* Another is Australia's best-known advocate of this position. There is also Robert Faurisson. (All three are members of the "Editorial Advisory Committee" of the *Journal of Historical Review.*)

One does not really know what to make of such men. Perhaps the best way of explaining them is to view them as the John Hinckley Juniors of the intelligentsia—lone-wolf malcontents, like Reagan's would-be assassin—who, unable to gain esteem by valid means, advocate the most outrageous, unbelievable thesis conceivable to win publicity for themselves. Many of the English-speaking among them claim to be dedicated "civil libertarians", mistrustful of "established authority" and of "establishment big lies", and the movement's intellectual component, at least in the English-speaking world, seems to have as much of what might be termed a libertarian-anarchist input as of a totalitarian one. This movement also advocates a consistent right-wing conspiracy theory of the world which is worthy of note, based upon a belief that "establishment big lies" emanate overwhelmingly from the United States, controller of the world's media.

Faurisson, who was born in England in 1929, holds a doctorate from the Sorbonne and teaches French literature at the University of Lyon. In his own words, he "specializes in the appraisal and evaluation of texts and documents". He has repeatedly claimed to be a liberal and an opponent of totalitarianism in all forms, although some Frenchmen have claimed otherwise. There can be no doubt that he is an active and committed member of the "Institute" and a vocal proponent of the notion that the Holocaust is a "Zionist hoax". Apart from his membership of the editorial committee of the *Journal,* Faurisson is the author of the leading article in its second issue, "The 'Problem of the Gas Chambers' "—the "problem" being that they did not exist—in which "after thirty years of research" he concludes that "the Hitler 'gas chambers' never existed . . . the 'genocide' . . . of the Jews never took place . . . This lie is largely of Zionist origin . . . whose chief beneficiary is the State of Israel. The principal victims of this fraud are the German people (but not the German rulers) and the entire Palestinian people." He has twice spoken at annual "conventions" organised by the "Institute" to denounce the Holocaust as a "Zionist hoax".

When Faurisson's activities became known in France, a considerable storm erupted, and he was the subject of great student hostility at his university. In early 1979 he was temporarily suspended from his teaching position, and his case has attracted great interest and notoriety in the French press. He has also been sued for defamation by Auschwitz survivors, a case which is proceeding as I write. Faurisson's case has also been taken up by ultra *left* French radicals, whose hatred of Israel exceeds their sense of shame, and another curious French *leftist* publishing house, La Vieille Taupe, has published two volumes by Faurisson. We shall return to these shortly.

I have devoted far more time to this verminous movement than it deserves. One other point, however, needs to be made clear: its effect on Jews. I have frequently heard the claim that the Holocaust was a "Zionist hoax" described by Jews as the "ultimate obscenity", and its impact upon many Jews, particularly those whose relatives were murdered by the Nazis, is certainly far in excess of its intrinsic importance. After reading one local outburst of this madness, a Melbourne Jew [Yehuda Svoray, "A Letter to the Age," *Australia-Israel Review,* March 28, 1979] wrote that "My grandmother, my aunt, my uncle and dozens of my friends and acquaintances were killed in Nazi extermination camps . . . I feel personally affronted, slapped in the face, spat upon . . . " and such reactions are common throughout the Jewish community. It seems difficult to believe that any Jew, or any sensitive human being, could react differently.

Let us turn now to Chomsky. To paraphrase what James Kenneth Stephen once wrote about Wordsworth

> Two voices are there: one is of the deep
> And one is of an old half-witted sheep
> Which bleats articulate inanity,
> And Chomsky both are thine!

Chomsky is, on the one hand, the "Einstein of linguistics", whose discoveries about the nature of language have made him one of the few social scientists to have become genuine celebrities, a man known and read throughout the world, from Cambridge, Massachusetts, where he holds the Ferrari Ward Professorship of Linguistics at M.I.T., to Paris and Australia. Chomsky is on the other hand a longstanding, comprehensive, and total opponent of American "imperialism" and militarism in all parts of the world. He was a major figure in the academic movement against the Vietnam War, and is a prolific writer on America's foreign policy, particularly in south-east Asia and Latin America.

Chomsky describes himself as a "libertarian socialist", or an "anarcho-socialist". He is a Jew, the son of a teacher of Hebrew at Jewish colleges in the United States. Indeed, Chomsky's M.A. thesis was on the linguistics of modern Hebrew, and he has many continuing contacts on the Israeli left. His knowledge of Israel and Zionism is extensive. In 1974 he published *Peace in the Middle East?* (in which he described the Nazi Holocaust as "the most fantastic outburst of collective insanity in human history"),

an extensive discussion of the Arab-Israeli dispute. Chomsky is, naturally, a committed anti-Zionist, but this is the least tendentious of his political works. Admittedly he does call for the destruction of Israel in its present form and its replacement by a utopian dream, a bi-national State in Palestine. But among anti-Zionists, whose writings are often thinly-disguised anti-semitism of the most vicious kind, Chomsky stands out as a critic of Israel of some sensitivity and perspicacity. Chomsky praises the Kibbutzim in glowing terms, for example, whereas many anti-Zionists condemn them out of hand as instruments of neo-colonialism.

Within the past three years Chomsky has attracted wide adverse publicity for his lengthy attack on the veracity of accounts of the Kampuchean auto-genocide. Much of the second volume of *The Political Economy of Human Rights* (1980) is devoted to this attack, which questions, at immense length, whether any of the sources upon which our knowledge of the Pol Pot atrocities is based are in fact reliable. Chomsky has had practice at the denial of genocide. But the evidence for genocide in Kampuchea had, by the time their volume neared publication, became so undeniable, that Chomsky and his co-author, after penning a hundred and sixty pages of text with forty pages of footnote references to prove that no massacres occurred in Kampuchea, added what must surely be one of the most blatant examples of intellectual dishonesty in the contemporary period. "When the facts are in, it may turn out that the more extreme condemnations were in fact correct". I do not often quote Albert Langer with approval, but he was surely right when he asked (of another leftist who denied that Pol Pot committed genocide and then was forced to admit that—in Langer's terms—the original reports were "by sheer coincidence" correct all along): "How did the malicious propagandists manage to fantasize the truth? By ESP?" Chomsky's attribution of supernatural powers to those who "were in fact correct" is patently designed for one purpose: to be quoted and requoted—*sans* his hundred and sixty page denial of Pol Pot genocide—to those who chastise him for his universally-discredited, and shameful, stance on Kampuchea.

Such tactics are typical of Chomsky's method of debate. The common feature of Chomsky's political writings is their tone of extreme self-righteousness. Chomsky's opponents are not merely mistaken. Nor are they even knaves and fools. They are, simultaneously, agents of Satan and complete imbeciles. Conversely, Chomsky and his handful of supporters are virtually alone among the Western intelligentsia in perceiving the truth: because of near-total "brainwashing under freedom", according to Chomsky, "what enters history in the United States (and, we believe, the West generally . . .) is a version of the facts that suits the ideological requirements of the dominant social groups", by which he means the Pentagon, the military-industrial complex, the multi-nationals, and the east coast media establishment. Enunciated most fully in his recent works, Chomsky's world-view has become extreme and complete with time, and extremely and completely self-righteous. Chomsky's world-view is not the usual one of Western left-liberals, nor even of Marxists, of whatever school. It combines a deep mistrust for all "established" and widely accepted sources of information with what might fairly be termed a left-wing conspiracy theory of history, albeit one of considerable subtlety.

What then, do neo-Nazis and Professor Chomsky have to do with each other? Just this: in 1980 Chomsky wrote an introduction to Faurisson's book, in which Faurisson defended himself "against those who accuse me of falsifying history". Chomsky had previously signed a petition protesting against Faurisson's suspension from his University, an action which aroused great controversy as well as surprise in France, and which had alerted a great many people to Chomsky's interest in the case. Chomsky here says little about Faurisson, but aggressively defends his right to publish, on civil libertarian grounds, and denounces the French intelligentsia which "loves to line up and march in step" because of its deep-seated guilt and inadequacy. It is not every week that a world-famous Jewish socialist intellectual writes an introduction to a work whitewashing the Nazis and their crimes; its publication led to a major storm which quickly spread to the English-speaking world.

Perhaps it is appropriate here to explain my own position in this matter. A group of five or six of us in Melbourne had been closely following the "no-Holocaust" movement for some time, especially in its Australian manifestation. Through the main progenitor of this line here, in mid-1980 we had obtained some unpublished letters addressed to the *New Statesman,* the left-wing English weekly, in reply to an article on this movement by Gitta Sereny (2 November 1979). One of these was dynamite. It was by Faurisson and began:

> Noam Chomsky . . . is aware of the research work I do on what (I) call the 'gas chambers and genocide hoax'. He informed me that Gitta Sereny had mentioned my name in an article in your journal. He told me I had been referred to 'in an extraordinarily unfair way'.

At this point, I had known nothing about Chomsky's connection with Faurisson; nor, I think, did anyone in the English-speaking world: certainly I had never seen it mentioned. Unless Faurisson was flatly lying, it seemed clear that Chomsky—against all *apparent* likelihood—was not only "aware" of this movement, but was in active and direct contact with one of its main spokesmen ("He told me . . ."), and furthermore had read Gitta Sereny's unusually informative and comprehensive article. Chomsky, furthermore, had evidently been in contact with Faurisson after reading Sereny's article. These are all important matters, as we shall see.

So extraordinary did this connection seem, that I wrote to Chomsky asking him whether this connection was true and what it signified. I did this with some misgiving, for I had been warned by several persons that Chomsky was, notoriously, a most vituperative correspondent, especially where he perceived a slight to himself, and that the self-righteous, self-destructive elements in Chomsky's published writings were in private magnified a dozen times. They certainly did not exaggerate, as I was to find out.

My correspondence with Chomsky lasted several months

in the middle of 1980. Because Chomsky is Chomsky, and the issues are serious, I have little hesitation in sharing his thoughts with a wider audience.

Chomsky's first reply to me restated his civil liberatarian belief in free speech, even for neo-Nazis. It did not go further and condemn Faurisson and the "no-Holocaust" school, nor did it comment upon the monstrous anti-semitic libel implicit or explicit in the claim that the Holocaust was a "Zionist hoax" invented for monetary and political gain.

> This [i.e. his previous reply] you find 'puzzling and unsatisfactory'. As I noted to you in my letter, it would indeed be 'puzzling and unsatisfactory' to someone with a deeply totalitarian mentality. To such people, it may seem incomprehensible, even immoral, to believe that those who disagree with one's convictions should have the right of free inquiry and expression. This is a standard view among Nazis and Stalinists, for example. On grounds of simple logic, your letter reveals that you share in these attitudes.

[In a footnote, the critic writes: "Needless to say, this is *not* the issue at all. No one, so far as I know, questions Faurisson's right to believe that the Holocaust was a hoax, or that the world is shaped like a pancake. The issue is whether Chomsky should write an introduction to a book claiming that my dead relatives in Warsaw are not only still alive, but are milking the German government of millions by fraud."]

Stalinist and Nazi that I am, more was to follow.

> You ask whether I believe that Faurisson's claims are valid or not. Which claims? You give exactly one example, namely Faurisson's claim that 'the Holocaust was a "historic lie" ' (Here quoting you, not him). Perhaps Faurisson holds this view, but it is interesting to see your basis for attributing it to him. Your source is the *Le Monde* article that you sent me, where Faurisson happens to say nothing of the kind. Rather, what he calls a 'historic lie' is the claim that there were 'wholesale massacres in gas chambers', or that there were gas chambers at all. Someone might well believe that there were no gas chambers but there was a Holocaust, obviously.

The learned linguist warms to the task, as William James put it.

> You find his [i.e. Faurisson's] assertions 'contrary to common sense, established history', etc.—again, an interesting reflection of the totalitarian mentality, or more properly in this case, the mentality of the religious fanatic.

Chomsky had never heard of me, my letter contained not one word about religion—but already I not only possess a totalitarian mentality but am a 'religious fanatic'! What, incidentally, is one to make of a world famous scholar and 'socialist' who in all seriousness claims that opposition to Nazism is religious fanaticism? But let us proceed.

> I see no anti-semitic implications in denial of the existence of gas chambers, or even denial of the holocaust. Nor would there be anti-semitic im-

plications, per se, in the claim that the holocaust (whether one believes it took place or not) is being exploited, viciously so, by apologists for Israeli repression and violence. I see no hint of anti-semitic implications in Faurisson's work, and find your argument to the contrary 'puzzling and unsatisfactory' to put it in mildest terms.

Chomsky's letters to me are each over 1500 words long, and became increasingly malevolent, truculent, and hostile. One final illustrative quote is perhaps in order. When I put it to him that his remark that "someone might well believe that there were no gas chambers but there was a Holocaust," was "absurd", I received the following reply:

> Again that reveals your complete incapacity to follow the most elementary logical reasoning—quite on a par, and a natural concomitant, of your gross falsification of documentary evidence, which I pointed out to you in my last letter . . . evidently taking falsification to be as much your privilege as gratuitous insult[!]. A person might well believe that there was a Holocaust—that, say, the Nazis followed a policy of slave labour under conditions so awful that millions of people died and were shovelled into crematoria—and yet believe that there were no gas chambers. If you cannot comprehend this, I suggest that you begin your education again at the kindergarten level.

And so forth, for many a paragraph. This matter had, evidently got deeply under Chomsky's skin. "At least", a friend remarked to me, "we ruined his summer holiday."

What, precisely, has Chomsky done wrong? His iniquity is serious for two main reasons. First, and most obviously, he had lent his reputation and name to an evil crew who are, plainly, happy to exploit it at every turn. It is difficult to believe that Chomsky (or anyone else) would be so naive as not to see that this would occur. Revealingly, Chomsky's introduction to Faurisson's book does not even state, as does his more recent discussion of this affair in *Nation,* that "Faurisson's views are diametrically opposed to views I hold and frequently expressed (on the reality of the Holocaust)"; it says nothing of the accuracy of Faurisson's claims, nor, of the movement to which Faurisson belongs. Chomsky ingenuously notes in his *Nation* article that parts of his introduction "appeared in the French press and have been widely quoted and misquoted", as if this should occasion the slightest surprise.

More revealingly still, Chomsky's petition, signature and introduction are diametrically opposed to his explicit statements on these matters in *The Political Economy of Human Rights* (Vol I), where he presents his reasons for *not* raising his voice on civil liberties violations in the Soviet Union, while concentrating exclusively on such violations in countries in the American orbit.

> Suppose that the purpose of protest is to relieve human suffering or defend human rights. Then more complex considerations arise. One must consider the plausible consequences for the victims of oppression . . . People with a genuine concern for human rights would . . . give serious consideration to the likely effects on the victims . . . Such persons will also consider how their finite energies can be distributed most efficaciously. It is a cheap and cynical evasion to plead that "we must raise our voices" whenever human rights are violated. Even a saint would not meet this demand. A serious person will try to concentrate protest efforts where they are most likely to ameliorate conditions for the victims of oppression. The emphasis should, in general, be close to home . . . for privileged Western intellectuals, the proper focus for their protest is at home.

For Chomsky, then, the standard seems to be: Faurisson, *si,* Sakharov, *non.*

So far as I am aware, Chomsky is the first intellectual of international stature to give the slightest support, explicit or implicit, to Faurisson and his allies. The normal reaction of decent people is, surely, to have absolutely no truck with Faurisson and his school, to ignore them or fight them. Chomsky has unquestionably given them far more publicity, at an international level, than they would otherwise have secured. He has also given them a patina of legitimacy, which they have willingly worn. If the movement thereby grows in significance, Chomsky must share part of the blame.

Chomsky's writings on the matter are not without a fair share of disingenuousness. Chomsky claims, for example, to know nothing about Faurisson's political connections, describing him in his introduction as "a sort of relatively apolitical liberal", although I and others had sent him evidence of Faurisson's right-wing connections months before his introduction was written. The same applies to Chomsky's much touted devotion to free speech. When Dr Kissinger was being considered for an appointment at Columbia University in 1977, according to Stephen Morris (*New Republic,* April 11, 1981) groups of left-wing extremists organised a campaign against the appointment on the grounds that Kissinger was a "war criminal". Chomsky was the principal speaker at one such meeting, held on April 26, 1977 at Columbia.

Is it any coincidence that Chomsky, ostensible first citizen of the left, should find something so attractive in Faurisson and his allies as to violate his own pious pronouncements on the duties of intellectuals to protest? I would suggest that the answer is no. I submit that the worldviews of Chomsky, and of Faurisson and his allies, are to a remarkable degree *identical.* From seemingly opposite perspectives, their visions of truth have converged. The views of Chomsky, as expressed in *The Political Economy of Human Rights* and elsewhere, and those of Faurisson and his allies in the "Institute of Historical Review" are manifestly similar in ways which go far beyond coincidence. I submit—and I am certain that any reader of both will confirm this—that both consider the following points as *basic* to a true understanding of the world:

1. The universally accepted sources of true knowledge, news, and history in the Western world are systematically and intentionally false. They are, instead, purveyors of deceit and distortion on so grand a scale that virtually no one in the Western world is aware of it.

2. These sources overwhelmingly emanate from the United States and a few like-minded European countries.

3. The ruling elite these sources plainly represent, and on whose behalf they continuously propagandise, are demonically evil and all-pervasively wicked. They are, in fact, the source of most of the evil in today's world. Mass murder, the systematic distortion of news and history, the enslavement of nations and peoples, are their everyday, routine activities, and they control most of the world. Their overthrow would usher in an era of peace and social justice.

4. The power of these sources largely derives from their alliance with the ruling economic interests of the United States and the American power structure. Apart from the direct economic influence which large corporations and the big banks hold over the mass media, there is an equally insidious process of self-censorship or quasi-censorship by the media whereby events or interpretations not acceptable to America's ruling elite are eliminated from the mass media and are restricted to fringe publications of limited circulation.

5. So universal is this process, that it is known only to a handful of *illuminati,* who, by virtue of their knowledge, are perceived by the ruling elite as extremely dangerous, and are tolerated only if they remain in obscurity. "This information" (the truth of the "criminal programs of the state", etc.), according to Chomsky (*Language and Responsibility*) "is accessible, but only for fanatics: in order to unearth it, you have to devote much of your life to the search . . . Everyone is led to think that what he knows represents a local exception. *But the overall pattern remains hidden . . .* What you face here is a very effective kind of ideological control, because one can remain under the impression that censorship does not exist . . . " (Original italics). According to Australia's best-known member of the "Institute of Historical Review", books advocating anti-establishment ideas are subject to "unofficial trade boycott" or openly suppressed.

6. The small group of *illuminati* to whom alone the truth is known form a kind of secular sainthood, well-entitled to moral outrage (and righteousness). Comparisons with the persecution of Galileo are commonly made by the "Institute", while Chomsky sees himself as fighting a brave lone battle. "The volume of the chorus proclaiming 'genocide' (in Cambodia)", according to Chomsky, " . . . made the occasional expression of scepticism appear pathological, as if someone were to proclaim that the earth is flat." (*The Political Economy of Human Rights*), a view echoed in almost identical terms by Arthur Butz in denying the Jewish Holocaust.

7. Both Chomsky and the ultra-right attach great, indeed central, importance to a non-existent holocaust which, in its alleged singular evil, serves the ruling elite by creating universal condemnation of regimes and ideologies which that elite wishes the masses to hate and fear. To the ultra-right the non-existent holocaust was, of course, that allegedly carried out by the Nazis against the Jews, (but invented by 'Zionists'); to Chomsky, it is the Cambodian "auto-genocide" which the Western media "have latched on

to . . . as a drowning man seizes a lifebuoy", in the absence of a Communist "bloodbath" in Vietnam. "If Cambodian terror did not exist, the Western propaganda systems would have to invent it, and in certain respects they did . . . ", Chomsky states, and then goes on to devote a hundred and sixty pages to showing how it was invented in *all* respects.

8. While fabricating these imaginary holocausts, the ruling elite carefully censors or ignores the true massacres which involved the "wrong" group of persons. To the ultra-right, this was the death of 8-10 million Germans during the war, "the people who suffered the most"; to Chomsky, these are what he describes as "benign" or even "constructive" massacres, with which the ruling elite is unconcerned or actively encourages.

To be sure, there are some differences between the two viewpoints. The position of the "Zionists", obviously central to the neo-Nazis, is not central to Chomsky, though his dislike of Israel is great. More generally, Chomsky's interest is mainly in East Asia, the "Institute's" in Europe.

At the basis of their identity of views is their common grounding, I believe, not in totalitarianism (though obviously this is the bottom line for most of the neo-Nazis) but in an exaggerated, utterly unrealistic notion of "civil liberties" bordering on anarchy and questioning any form of established authority over political power and history, no matter how well-established, and no matter to whom such doubt does harm. Like many others, I have always believed that the most evil men in the modern world were totalitarian system-builders, and especially the "terrible simplifiers", thereof, from Himmler to Pol Pot. I am no longer sure if that is true.

POSTSCRIPT

In July 1981 in a Paris court Faurisson was found guilty of libel against the eminent French historian Lev Poliakev (whose works on the Holocaust he had said, in effect, were untrue) and a number of Auschwitz survivors who had sued him. He was given a three-month suspended sentence and fined a substantial sum, to be donated to anti-racialist societies. "To claim the Holocaust is untrue is to kill its victims twice", the prosecutor declared. Chomsky's remarks on the verdict are not on record.

HOLOCAUST DENIAL LITERATURE IN AMERICA

Deborah E. Lipstadt

SOURCE: "The Evolution of American Holocaust Revisionism," in *Remembering for the Future: Working Papers and Addenda, Vol. III,* edited by Yehuda Bauer and others, Pergamon Press, 1989, pp. 2579-93.

[*Lipstadt is an American historian and educator whose writings focus on modern Jewish history. In the following essay, she traces the evolution of American Holocaust revisionism.*]

The roots of American Holocaust revisionism can be found in the work of an influential group of progressive American historians who were deeply disturbed by American involvement in World War I. Some of these historians were highly respected scholars who probably never dreamt that their historiographic approach and arguments would be utilized by a small but prolific group of individuals—most of whom are neither historians nor people of respected standing in the scholarly world—to place history on trial and to revise the truth.

In the aftermath of World War I a school of revisionist historians including prominent and respected figures such as Sidney B. Fay and Charles Beard sought to exonerate Germany from *sole* responsibility for the war. They were particularly distressed by the Allied use of German guilt in order to impose a severe peace and to extract what they considered to be unfair punishment. As a result in part of their attacks, criticism of the Versailles treaty was heard in a variety of circles in the United States. Despite widespread American disillusionment with the treaty, the most vociferous and fervent of these revisionists were relentless in their attacks on it and on Allied behavior in general. It was not until the first bombs were dropped on Pearl Harbor that some of these revisionists abandoned their battle to exonerate Germany. What had begun as a historical enterprise had become a battle to prevent the United States from becoming involved in any overseas conflagration. A scholarly enterprise had been turned into a political quest of major proportions.

These historians did not wage this battle alone. Their colleagues included prominent politicians, publishers, academics and other public figures. Among the better known members of this group were Charles Lindbergh, Colonel Robert McCormick, General R. E. Wood, Charles A. Beard, and Chester Bowles.

Despite the fact that there is but a limited personal link between these progressive/isolationist historians and the Holocaust revisionists the historiographic connection between them is crucial, for the former unwittingly provided the fertile soil in which the latter were nurtured. Even in their choice of the name revisionist, the Holocaust revisionists have have sought to associated themselves with what was a radical and controversial but generally legitimate school of thought, particularly as it pertained to World War I.

In the immediate aftermath of World War II a number of these isolationists once again took up the cudgels on behalf of Germany. They had varied objectives. Some, possibly prompted by their German American roots, wished to win more lenient economic and political conditions for a defeated Germany. Others may have been motivated by their middle-western Populist roots. In addition, there were those who were anti-communist and who believed that post-war Germany provided the best defense against the spread of communism. Many of them argued that Nazi Germany had also been an excellent defense but the Allies had been blind—or had been blinded—to this fact. There

were of course some among these critics who were simply and unambiguously fascist, xenophobic and openly antisemitic. (Best known among the latter were Gerald L. K. Smith, Gerald Winrod, and Upton Close.) Not all of those who were critical of Allied policy were associated with extremists and fringe elements. Some, particularly those who were closely identified with mainstream cultural and economic groups, were well respected individuals. They included Robert Taft, columnist Felix Morley, who had been editor of the Washington Post, Charles A. Beard and Robert Hutchins, the president of the University of Chicago.

Initially the World War II revisionist argument was focused on the Pacific conflict. Revisionists claimed that Roosevelt had sought a "back door" by which to maneuver America into World War II. In order to ensure American entry into the war, he had concealed the information which had reached him indicating that an attack on Pearl Harbor was forthcoming from the chiefs of the American armed forces. Convinced of Roosevelt's complicity in allowing the Pearl Harbor attack to occur, the *Chicago Tribune* accused him of deliberately sacrificing the lives of thousands of American soldiers. These isolationists generally shared a belief that a military and political conspiracy of major proportions had been perpetrated in order to drag this country into the war. In terms of their approach to the facts, it was this conviction that a conspiracy had existed that had the greatest impact on their findings.

But their critique was not limited to the Pacific theater. Led by journalists including John Flynn, George Morgenstern and William Henry Chamberlin, the critics turned their attention to the European arena and argued that Pearl Harbor was part of a bigger and more complex picture. They believed the Roosevelt administration had needed a war to divert public attention from the failures of the New Deal. John T. Flynn's *The Roosevelt Myth* accused Roosevelt of finding war a "glorious, magnificent escape from all the insoluble problems of America." Nothing had been accomplished by the war except to "put into Stalin's hands the means of seizing a great slab of the continent of Europe." The book, which was turned down by all major publishers because of its inflammatory rhetoric, was eventually published by what would become the leading revisionist publisher and reached the number two position on the *New York Times* best seller list.

Ignoring the uniqueness of Nazi atrocities, many of the World War II revisionists dismissed the notion the war could be defined as a moral struggle. All the sides, they argued, had been equally devious. George Morgenstern, an editor of the *Chicago Tribune,* offered one of the earliest American post-war examples of equalizing or "relativizing" wrong doings when he argued that none of the major powers involved in either Europe or Asia "could come to the United States with clean hands or represent itself as either a democracy or an exemplar of justice." While the Fascist "slave states" were "abhorrent to decent people," the British Empire which "rested upon the exploitation of hundreds of millions of natives," was equally abhorrent. Stalin's regime was "no more exemplary" than Hitler's.

Scholarly and historical works followed these apace. In

certain cases they were limited to severe attacks on Roosevelt and his domestic and foreign policy. In his two volumes on the topic, *American Foreign Policy in the Making* and *President Roosevelt and the Coming of the War,* Charles Beard was relentless in his critique of America's involvement in the war which, he claimed, left the country in greater danger than before and had enhanced the power of Stalin's ruthless regime.

There were those who, not satisfied with an attack on Roosevelt's policy, took their efforts a step further and sought to portray Germany as the much maligned victim of Allied aggression. It was this aggression, they claimed, which had forced the Germans to take the extreme steps for which they were now being castigated. Their arguments were important because they served as the intellectual model for those who would eventually seek not just to exculpate Germany for the Holocaust but to deny its existence all together.

The most obvious and direct link between the two generations of American isolationist historians and the Holocaust revisionists was Harry Elmer Barnes. During his long career Barnes occupied a prominent position in both the World War I and World War II isolationist camps. The war was hardly over when Barnes was attacking those who failed to acknowledge Allied responsibility for the war. But Barnes did not simply blame the Allies for having provoked the war, he claimed that a pervasive historical "blackout" had been created which was designed to prevent the truth about World War II from emerging. A vigorous conspiracy had been put in place by "court historians" to quash any information which might tarnish Roosevelt's image. Barnes argued that the blackout was necessary to silence critics such as himself who might try to question American "intervention" in World War II.

Barnes' diatribe about this "conspiracy" was contained in a lengthy pamphlet, "The Struggle Against Historical Blackout." It appeared in 1947 and by 1952 had undergone 9 printings. In this and subsequent pamphlets he issued after the war, Barnes contended that virtually all of Hitler's political and military moves including the occupation of Czechoslovakia were justified as a necessary means of "rectifying" the injustices of Versailles. In a letter to fellow revisionist historian Charles Tansill, Barnes described Hitler's demands in 1939 as the "most reasonable of all." In a letter to Harvard historian William Langer, who had authored a two volume defense of America's pre-war policies, Barnes wrote that he considered "the greatest public crime in human history" to be Roosevelt's foreign policy.

Charles C. Tansill's *Back Door to War* argued that Hitler had given Poland the opportunity of serving as "chief satellite in the Nazi orbit." The Poles' refusal, which was responsible for the outbreak of the war, was prompted— according to Tansill and many of his compatriots—by promises and guarantees the Poles had received from the British, promises Britain had made at America's urging. It was, therefore, American machinations which were ultimately responsible for World War II.

Many of these revisionists, irrespective of whether they came from the political, journalistic or academic world,

believed that sinister conspiratorial forces had been responsible for getting us into the war. They looked for and claimed to have found an interventionist "plot." This conviction about the existence of a conspiracy and their quest to find the conspirators prompted them to adopt hyperbolic rhetoric and proffer extreme arguments. As Nadine Fresco noted [in "The Denial of the Dead: On the Faurisson Affair," *Dissent,* Fall 1981], "one cannot establish a science whose only ethic is suspicion." Beyond the similarity in arguments made by the World War II revisionists and the Holocaust revisionists, it is this conspiracy theory which is one of the most compelling links between the two groups.

Some of the isolationist/revisionists were more sympathetic to Hitler than others. But irrespective of their differing views of Hitler virtually all of them were compelled to either totally eliminate or minimize the uniqueness of the Nazis' annihilation of the Jews and murder of millions of others from their evaluation of the war. While a few revisionists acknowledged it, e.g. William Henry Chamberlin, others simply ignored it. The more extreme among them took matters a step further and tried to neutralize German actions. It was the next generation, with Barnes at the helm, that took the ultimate step and tried to deny that they took place.

These isolationists/revisionists were engaged in an attempt to help Germany achieve a renewed moral standing in the world. They were almost unanimous in their belief that a strong revived Germany was the key to the future of Western Europe. They recognized that the Allies in general and Americans in particular were likely to balk at aiding a country which was perceived of as "cruel, if not genocidal." It was necessary, therefore, to lessen if not totally dissipate the unique qualities of German wartime behavior. They did so in two ways, by minimizing the severity of Germany's actions and by finding comparable Allied wrongs which would serve as immoral equivalents.

They severely assailed Allied policy towards Germany and Germans in the post-war period. Ignoring similar conditions in other parts of Europe, they riled against the food shortages in Germany and demanded special American immigration permits for Germans. Senator William Langer (Rep-North Dakota), who had vigorously opposed Roosevelt's foreign policy, spoke of a "savage and fanatical plot" to destroy fifteen million German women and children. (Extreme concern about the conditions of the German population did not always *ipso facto* indicate a lack of concern about what Jews had experienced. Langer was one of the outspoken Peter Bergson supporters in the Senate during the war. In 1943, he had publicly criticized the Bermuda Conference on the floor of the Senate and warned that "2,000,000 Jews in Europe have been killed off already and another 5,000,000 Jews are awaiting the same fate unless they are saved immediately. Every day, every hour, every minute that passes thousands of them are being exterminated." Langer's positions both during the war and after it are attributable in great measure to his opposition to the Democrats' foreign policy.)

Many of the isolationists/revisionists were particularly critical of a plan proposed by Secretary of the Treasury

Morgenthau which would have prevented the economic rehabilitation of Germany. Though the plan was never put into effect it was repeatedly cited by both World War II revisionists and Holocaust revisionists as an example of the Allies' diabolical attitude towards Germany. (Henry Regnery, an active revisionist publisher, published a book by a Stanford economist, Karl Brandt, who compared Morgenthau's proposal with the Nazi plan to destroy millions of Jews through starvation.)

The major thrusts of their attacks on Allied post-war action focused on the Nuremberg trials and the mass transfer of German citizens from Czechoslovakia and Poland in the immediate aftermath of the war. Senator Langer of North Dakota claimed that three million of the refugees had died en route. One prominent isolationist journalist, Freda Utley, described these population transfers as "crimes against humanity." Her choice of this particular phrase, which had already been given wide currency as a result of the Nuremberg indictments was telling. The *Chicago Tribune* accused the French of not permitting over half a million German prisoners of war to return home. According to the paper they were being kept as "slaves," denied food sufficient to allow them to work and beaten by "Moroccan savages."

These kind of charges would subsequently be used by "relativizers"—those who argue that while what the Nazis did was wrong other groups have behaved in a similar fashion—and "revisionists" alike in an attempt to free Germany of any unique burden of guilt. Many of these isolationist historians seemed, according to Justus Doenecke who has written a sympathetic portrait of them, to draw righteous justification from the fact that as a result of the population transfers, food shortages, Nuremberg trials, and the de-Nazification programs, they had found a way to portray Germany as the victim and America as the "malicious power." [*Not to the Swift: The Old Isolationists in the Cold War Era,* 1982]. This is not meant to suggest that Allied behavior in the immediate aftermath of the war was without fault. There had not been sufficient planning for this period and, consequently, there were many shortcomings in Allied post-war policies. The de-Nazification program, for example, was applied unequally and many inequities in punishment resulted from it. However, the vigor of the isolationists' attacks on the program did not abate even when it became clear that the Truman administration wished to change it.

Within months of the end of the war certain isolationist politicians and historians were engaged in an attempt to lessen any burden of responsibility or guilt which would be imposed on Germany as a whole. Lindbergh, in an interesting choice of phrases, opposed imposing punishment of an "eye for an eye." Some depicted the Germans as a people who themselves had been persecuted. Former Governor of Wisconsin, Philip La Follette, for example, described the Germans as the first victims of Nazi brutalities. But in order to free Germany of its particular burden of guilt those engaged in this struggle had to directly address the issue of the atrocities committed under the Nazis. Frederick Libby of the National Council for the Prevention of War, tried to mitigate Germany's burden by arguing that "no nation has a monopoly on atrocities. War itself is the supreme atrocity."

Others seemed inclined to try to create some doubt about the veracity of the various reports of Nazi horrors. They referred to them as "atrocity stories," a term which in the aftermath of World War I had begun to be commonly used as a synonym, particularly in the press, for something that was either totally untrue or *greatly* exaggerated. At the very least such a term had to conjure about doubts about the trustworthiness of the report. (General doubts about the reports of mass murder and other atrocities committed by the Germans had persisted as late as when the camps were liberated. In April 1945, the BBC had chosen not to broadcast its own reporter's account of the liberation of Buchenwald because it feared the public would not believe him. It waited a number of days until it received Edward R. Murrow's account. Because Murrow was held in such high esteem by the British, the BBC was convinced that his description of the horrors perpetrated by the Germans would be more likely to be accepted as accurate. Even Murrow worried that his report would be dismissed as exaggerated and in his famous broadcast he asked his listeners, "I pray you to believe what I have said.")

Robert Maynard Hutchins, president of the University of Chicago, a vigorous isolationist who had been an adviser to America First, wrote in 1945 that "the wildest atrocity stories" could not change the "simple truth" that "no men are beasts." (The implicit message in Hutchins' juxtaposition of the terms "wild atrocity story" with "simple truth" may have been unintended, but it must have had a subtle but important impact on readers.) An article in the *Progressive* by William B. Hesseltine, a historian at the University of Wisconsin, compared the *mythical* atrocity stories which had been circulated in the aftermath of the Civil War to those which emerged from Germany after the end of hostilities there. (A virtually identical argument would be made two decades later in an essay in the Holocaust revisionist publication, the *Journal of Historical Review.* By finding supposed historical parallels revisionists hoped to demonstrate that the case at hand was not the only time the public had been tricked.)

Many of these critics questioned the legality of the Nuremberg trials and accused the Allies of hypocrisy in holding them. They further "relativized" Germany's atrocities by arguing that the atrocities performed by the Allies were no different from those of the Nazis. William Neumann, whose pamphlet "Genesis of Pearl Harbor," had been one of the earliest publications attacking America's pre-war foreign policy, believed that Allied atrocities were the "point by point" equivalent of the Nazis. Stalin had invaded Poland in 1939, England and France had declared war on Germany and the United States had committed "acts of aggression" on Germany *before* Pearl Harbor. Had the outcome of the war been reversed the Allied leaders would have found themselves in the docket. Citing the Hitler-Stalin pact, Charles Beard questioned the validity of the trials.

Isolationist historians were not alone in criticizing the trial. Senator Taft argued that the trials were marked by a "spirit of vengeance" and the *Chicago Tribune* believed that Russia's participation transformed them into a "kangaroo court." Eventually Robert McCormick, the publisher of the *Chicago Tribune* and probably America's most important isolationist, refused to have dinner with former Attorney General Francis Biddle because he was a "murderer." The *New York Daily News* declared that the defendants' "real crime was that they did not win."

By the end of the 1950s the foundation had been set for those who would not simply relativize or seek to mitigate Germany's behavior. Many of the arguments which would form the foundation of Holocaust revisionism were well established within a decade of the end of the war. They included [the notion that] Hitler had only wanted peace and never planned to engage Europe in war; the Allies, bent on their own power quest, had forced Germany into war; the atrocities the Nazis were accused of committing were wildly exaggerated; a multitude of nations had committed similar wrongdoings but had never been called to account in the fashion similar to what had been done to Germany; and that Allied behavior during the war was as bad—if not worse—than Germany's.

With the exception of Harry Elmer Barnes, there was one thing that these critics of American involvement in the war and post-war Allied policy never suggested: that the atrocities had not happened. They may have claimed that they were not as bad as had been reported. They may have ignored their moral implications in order to argue that Allied and Axis behavior were virtually equal, but they did not deny that they were fact. Accusations to that effect would begin to be current in America in the 1950s.

Within a little over a decade after the liberation of Europe claims were being made in American that the death of the six million was not only greatly exaggerated but a total fabrication. (The earliest of these claims seem to have originated in Europe. In 1947 Maurice Bardeche, a leading French fascist, wrote two books attacking Allied war propaganda and claimed that a portion of the evidence regarding the concentration camps had been falsified. Shortly thereafter Rassinier's work appeared.) Most of these statements came from individuals with established antisemitic connections. They appear to have come to their Holocaust denial via their antisemitism.

From the very outset the deniers began by playing what one observer has called "a weird kind of numbers game." This became a persistent part of the revisionist argument. Attempts were and are made to demonstrate that it was statistically impossible for millions of Jews to have died. The arguments generally ignore established facts. In one of the early examples of American revisionism James Madole, who published the "National Renaissance Bulletin," ignored the fact that most of the Jewish victims had lived outside of Germany and wrote that "although the World Almanac attests to the fact that fewer than 600,000 Jews ever lived in Germany the Jews persisted in their monstrous lie that Nazi Germany had cremated six million of their co-racials." In subsequent years the numbers arguments would become slightly more sophisticated.

Benjamin H. Freedman who provided the financial support for the antisemitic publication "Common Sense" argued that there were many million more Jews in the United States than Jews were willing to admit. These were the 6,000,000 "allegedly put to death in furnaces and in gas chambers between 1939 and 1945." Offering an argument that would be echoed in the 1970s by a number of Holocaust revisionists, including Arthur Butz, Freedman contended that the reason the American Jewish community was opposed to a question about religious affiliation on the census was that it would reveal that the Jews who had "allegedly" died were actually in the United States.

The well-known American Nazi leader George Lincoln Rockwell called the Holocaust "a monstrous and profitable fraud." Rockwell agreed with Freedman's notion that the six million "later died happily and richly in the Bronx, New York."

In June 1959 Gerald L. K. Smith's "Cross and the Flag" informed its readers that the six million Jews were in the United States. The article was entitled "Into the Valley of Death Rode the Six Million. Or Did They?"

Though most of these claims of Holocaust denial were only printed in neo-fascist and antisemitic publications some gained wider circulation in more respectable and mainstream publications. A letter by Austin J. App in the Catholic paper "Brooklyn Tablet" offered proof that the figure of the six million was a "bloated libel." In the June 14, 1959 issue of the widely circulated Catholic weekly "Our Sunday Visitor" a letter writer claimed that "I was able to determine during six post-war years in Germany and Austria, there were a number of Jews killed, but the figure of a million was certainly never reached."

By the early 1960s more forceful exonerations of the Germans and explicit denials of the Holocaust began to appear. In France Paul Rassinier published a second work on the topic, the *Drama of the European Jews* which denied that millions of Jews had been killed by gas chambers. Rassinier, who had already published a book in 1949 claiming that the suffering of the Jews had been greatly exaggerated, had a major impact on Barnes. (In the 1970s Barnes translated *Drama of the European Jews* into English.)

In Germany *Der erzwungene Krieg: Die Ursachen und Urheber des 2 Weltkriegs [The Imposed War: The Origins and Originators of World War II]* written by an American, David Hoggan, was published by a house with known links to neo-Nazi groups. The book has been aptly described as an apology for Nazi Germany. According to Hoggan the English had to bear the responsibility for the war. Hitler had no desire to go to war and would not have done so if the Poles, encouraged by the British, had not pushed him into it. Hoggan's book, which voiced many of the arguments made by the World War II isolationists/revisionists, was attacked by German and American scholars as containing forgeries and unwarranted allegations and conclusions. It had started out as a Ph.D thesis at Harvard. In the intervening decade between the completion of this dissertation and its publication in Germany the book had transformed in part, it appears, through the influence of Barnes.

Barnes became one of Hoggan's vigorous defenders and often cited the book. His attack on the alleged conspiracy continued in 1962 when he published *Blasting the Historical Blackout*. In it he praised both A.J.P. Taylor's exoneration of Hitler's Germany and Hoggan's work. Barnes continued his diatribes about Allied wartime and post-war behavior in 1963 with the publication of "Revisionism and Brainwashing" which attacked the notion of German guilt for the two World Wars.

Apparently still somewhat reluctant to explicitly deny the existence of the Holocaust, he referred to the "alleged wartime crimes of Germany." Barnes praised Rassinier for questioning the existence of gas chambers in concentration camps in Germany and for shedding doubt on many of the "claims" made about the Holocaust. Although he did not specifically say that the Holocaust did not happen, his true intentions regarding the Holocaust were revealed in his reference to the death of six million Jews as a "theory" and his condemnation of historians and contemporary Germans for failing to admit that the "atrocities of the Allies were more brutal, painful, mortal and numerous than most extreme allegations made against the Germans." In a subsequent article *Revisionism: A Key to Peace* published in 1966 Barnes argued that it was "easy to demonstrate that the atrocities of the Allies . . . were more numerous as to victims and were carried out for the most part by methods more brutal and painful than alleged extermination in gas ovens."

In an article in *Rampart Journal* published in the summer of 1967 Barnes again expressed his doubts about the existence of a German plan to annihilate the Jews when he wrote of the "doings real or alleged at Auschwitz." He further rewrote the historical record by describing the assignment of the *Einsatzgruppen* as "battling guerilla warfare behind the lines." Ignoring the fact that information on gas chambers in various death camps had been publicized even before the war ended, he claimed that when it was "demonstrated that there had been no systematic extermination" in German concentration camps, those who wanted to maintain the evil image of the Nazi empire "moved [attention] on to Auschwitz, Treblinka, [and] Belzec" and claimed that there were gas chambers there.

He and other revisionists faced a fundamental challenge. They tried to exonerate Nazi Germany but the post-war German government accepted responsibility for the war and its atrocities. He severely castigated the government and academic community of the Federal Republic of Germany for not fighting this "unfair" verdict. He contrasted their behavior with the willingness of Weimar Germany to defend itself, contending that it was post-war Germany's behavior which was responsible for preventing "the restoration of Germany to its proper position of unity, power and respect among the nations of the world."

Barnes' standing as a historian is a matter of some dispute. There are those who argue that while Barnes' work was once respected it is now dismissed by scholars because of his obsession in his latter years with a conspiracy theory particularly as it related to World War II and the Holocaust. However, that Barnes' legacy is still at least somewhat in-tact was made clear by a 1975 edition of *History*

Teacher, a publication of the Society for History Education which is located at California State University at Long Beach. Entitled "Harry Elmer Barnes: Prophet of a 'Usable' Past" the publication identified Barnes as someone who practiced the "scholarship of commitment." *History Teacher* is designed to aid teachers in finding interesting and exciting ways of presenting historical information to their students.

According to the author Justus Doenecke, "the causes he [Barnes] heralded resemble our own and the dilemmas he faced are hauntingly familiar." Barnes' views regarding the Holocaust were never mentioned in this lengthy essay in which Barnes was portrayed as a useful model for those who believed in the relevance of history. His conviction that Allied atrocities overshadowed those of the Germans was also ignored. There was a passing reference to his tendency to present views which are only "partially digested." Any teacher who, having chosen to rely on Barnes' work, came upon his views about the Holocaust might well take them seriously—if they were not valid would *History Teacher* have suggested him as a role model for teachers?

Barnes was not the only American academic who attempted to exonerate Germany by denying the Holocaust. By the late 1950s Austin J. App, a professor of English, was not only writing to the Catholic *Brooklyn Tablet* offering "proof" that the figure of six million was "a bloated libel," but was appearing before varied audiences attacking Jews and accusing them of perpetrating a hoax. In the mid-1960s he wrote an article in *American Mercury* entitled "The Elusive Six Million." In this and subsequent articles he accused Zionists of wanting to "use the figure of six million vindictively as an eternal club for pressuring indemnities out of West Germany and for wringing financial contributions out of American Jews."

Even before issuing his explicit denials of the Holocaust, App had long been engaged in attacks on Jews and their supposed control of newspapers and radio. His articles and essays had appeared in various antisemitic publications. In the August 1948 issue of *Cross and Flag* he called for the re-education of Jews "away from their eye for an eyeism." In an article which appeared in *Conservative Viewpoint* in April 1970 he argued that the "most enormous massacre in history continues to be discreetly played down or ignored altogether because it was committed against German civilians by Anglo-Americans for the benefit of Soviet Russia."

In 1973 in a pamphlet entitled "The Six Million Swindle: Blackmailing the German People for Hard Marks with Fabricated Corpses," App reiterated his fully formulated argument that the accusation against Hitler that he wanted to exterminate all Jews was "a totally fabricated, brazen lie." He admitted that the Nazis wanted the Jews to emigrate but they had no intention to murder them. Relying on what has since become the standard method by which Holocaust revisionists dismiss evidence which contradicts their conclusions, he contended that the affidavits by Nazis admitting to the existence of a Final Solution are "often outright frauds" and that all testimony by Jews regarding mass murder was "in part or whole perjured, often well rewarded and altogether unreliable." This blanket denial of the validity of any evidence attesting to the Holocaust, including that by eyewitnesses, has become a centerpiece of the revisionists' methodology. Simply put, anything which disagrees with their foregone conclusion is dismissed.

In "The Six Million Swindle" App set out eight arguments about the Holocaust which were eventually adopted by the Institute for Historical Review as well as other revisionist groups and incorporated as the fundamentals of Holocaust revisionism. The eight assertions were:

> 1. The Reich wanted Jews to emigrate. Emigration, never annihilation, was its plan for the "solution" to Germany's Jewish "problem."
>
> 2. No Jews were gassed in any concentration camps. The Hitler gas chambers never existed.
>
> 3. The majority of Jews who disappeared and are still unaccounted for fell afoul in territories controlled by USSR.
>
> 4. Those Jews who did die at the hands of the Germans were subversives, spies and criminals.
>
> 5. The Jewish State has kept people from researching the topic for fear that the truth will emerge. Israel has been the principal beneficiary of this fraud.
>
> 6. The Jews have no evidence to prove a Holocaust occurred. They misquote Eichmann and other Nazis in order to try to substantiate their claims.
>
> 7. The burden of proof rests on the accusers not on the accused.
>
> 8. The main evidence that six million did not die is that Jewish researchers have discrepancies in their own research. Different Jewish historians offer different conclusions as to the number of victims who died at the hands of the Nazis. There are "ridiculous discrepancies in their calculations."

App seems to have missed a basic flaw in this last argument. If this were truly a fraud perpetrated by the Jews one would think that they would have seen to it that no discrepancies were allowed to creep into research by Jewish scholars. Yisrael Gutman has pointed out a similar flaw in another revisionist argument in relation to the "numbers game." Arthur Butz, in his attempt to prove that the Holocaust was a hoax, points out that Yad Vashem had only two and a half to three million sheets of testimony for the deceased. If Yad Vashem is really a deceitful and falsifying agency, as Butz claims it is, they should have had no trouble forging the additional sheets to fill their complement of six million.

The goal of Barnes, David Hoggan, Austin J. App and other revisionists both in the United States and in Europe was not simply to exonerate Germany but to de-demonize Hitler. Barnes argued that Hitler was unfairly portrayed in Western historical literature as a "pathological demon," a portrayal which was necessary in order to justify Allied "terrorism." In order to "make the thesis of diab-

olism sink in and stick," the Allies needed to find something "different and dramatic" with which to accuse Hitler. They did so by placing upon him the sole responsibility for starting the war and for committing unprecedented atrocities.

By the beginning of the 1970s the effort in the United States to exculpate Hitler and Germany of any unique inhumanity was in full swing.

Revisionism in the United States became a much more formidable obstacle to truth and a greater purveyor of hatred in the 1970s with the publication of a book by a professor at Northwestern University and with the founding of an institute to formally disseminate Holocaust revisionism and provide it with the veneer of academic respectability.

The publication of Arthur Butz's *The Hoax of the Twentieth Century* in 1976 won for the revisionists considerable media attention. Butz's position as a professor at one of the most prestigious universities in the country enhanced the sense of controversy. For many people it seemed hard to reconcile Holocaust revisionism with the pursuit of truth to which universities and their faculty are generally dedicated. The book was the subject of news articles in many of the nation's major papers. But Butz's contribution to this cause did not rest only in the fact that he was a professor at one of America's more important educational institutions. In his arguments and his methodology, he took a significantly different tack than his predecessors, one which revealed a far more subtle and sophisticated approach to this material than had been evidenced earlier.

What distinguished Arthur Butz from virtually all of the revisionists who preceded him was the veneer of scholarship and impression of seriousness and objectivity which he was able to convey. Well versed in academic etiquette, the format of his book immediately indicated that he understood the nuances of scholarly debate and would use them to his advantage. In contrast to many of the previous publications, particularly the poorly printed pamphlets which had typified much revisionist work, his book contained the requisite narrow margins, myriad of footnotes, and large bibliography. All these were items which generally distinguish serious scholarly works from popular ones. He quoted many of the prominent historians who worked in this field and thanked a number of legitimate research centers and archives. At first glance a reader had little reason to imagine the true import of his work.

More important than the form of the publication, however, was Butz's willingness to directly confront a host of issues. In an effort that was clearly designed to disarm an innocent reader, he did not shy from addressing issues which most revisionists had ignored. Not only did he cite the incriminating evidence offered at Nuremberg but he gave short shrift to the notion which had generally been offered by revisionists, that the Nuremberg defendants had been tortured into admitting their guilt. Rather, he argued, the defendants recognized that the world was so convinced that a Holocaust took place that they could not possibly deny it and hope to be believed.

The world has much more sympathy for the repentant sinner than for the unrepentant sinner. Even though the Germans had done no wrong, according to Butz, the world was so intent on seeing them as guilty that it was counterproductive for them to try to protest and maintain their innocence. They therefore used the next best means of defense: admit that it had occurred—even though they knew it had not—but argue that they had nothing to do with it. This approach provided Butz with the means to respond to one of the most oft-heard criticism of the revisionists: why do Germans not deny that the Holocaust happened? Because the "hoax" has been so widely accepted, if they did deny it they would only earn the enmity and contempt of the rest of the world.

His aura of scholarly objectivity was further enhanced by his willingness to find fault with other revisionist writers. He called *The Myth of the Six Million,* one of the earliest full length American revisionist publications, a "terrible" book. Of equal importance in establishing his scholarly veneer was his willingness to concede that as many as 1,000,000 Jews may have actually died. Moreover, he was willing to acknowledge that the *Einsatzgruppen* may have murdered civilians and that the Jews were "singled out for special persecution" by the Germans. These were things which many Holocaust revisionists found very hard to admit.

He did not try to totally "whitewash" German wartime behavior and, in contrast to Barnes, App, Rassinier and others, he did not try to justify the German persecution of the Jews by claiming that Jews were disloyal, that they could not be trusted or that they were interested in causing Germany's defeat. He gives the impression at times of being almost critical of Nazi antisemitism.

In this regard Butz even differs from some of the contemporary German historians. Ernst Nolte believes that once the war broke out the Nazis were justified in considering the Jews as a threat to their well being and security because Jewish leaders, e.g. Chaim Weizmann, had pledged loyalty to the Allies.

Among the more significant but subtle aspects of his tactics was that in the book and in articles published subsequently in the *Journal of Historical Review (JHR)* Butz addressed and acknowledged the validity of a number of the criticisms which were and are commonly used to shed doubt on the revisionists' methodology. One of the oft cited issues is that in the revisionists' ranks there are virtually no respected historians or individuals trained in this area of research. There are professors of engineering and physics but few historians. Butz bemoaned this and attributed it to the fact that respected scholars had been "frightened . . . away" from questioning something that is as "established as the Great Pyramid." It was because of this "sorry situation" that non-historians, such as himself, were left to investigate this area. If only others would fulfill their scholarly duties he could return to his electrical engineering.

He also acknowledged the validity of the criticism that this material did not not appear in the standard scholarly journals but was published in "ideological publications" such as the *Spotlight* and *National Zeitung.* Butz admitted that there should be a "distinction between the matters

treated by scholars and those treated in the popular press." In an optimal situation this material would appear in scholarly journals, but because of the conspiracy which exists to prevent its publication the normal channels of scholarly research had been blocked to those who would tell the truth. In the interest of exposing the "hoax," it was necessary for those who worked in this field to publish their findings in these ideological publications.

Butz's work appears to have been a major impetus for the founding of the Institute for Historical Review (IHR). Established in the late 1970s at the instigation and with the support of long time antisemite and Liberty Lobby leader, Willis Carto, the IHR was dedicated to "proving" that the Holocaust was a hoax perpetrated on the world by Zionists and other supporters of the State of Israel.

As was the case with Butz's book, the Institute was designed to win scholarly and academic acceptance for revisionism. Though the main thrust of its work was to expose the Holocaust as a "myth," its publications and conferences included discussion of other instances in which the "totems of 'history'" were "manipulat[ed]" by people with a "vested interest" in doing so.

The IHR quickly attracted to its midst a conglomeration of "cranks" as well as those who claimed to be the heirs to a genuine intellectual legacy. They drew on the work of those World War II isolationists/revisionists who had been so opposed to American involvement in foreign wars that they had rejected or ignored reports of Nazis wrong doings and were convinced that Allied military conspiracies had forced this country into war.

But all the IHR's efforts for academic respectability notwithstanding, it drew its major support and inspiration from Willis A. Carto, head of Liberty Lobby, a well established ultra-right antisemitic organization which publishes the antisemitic and anti-Zionist *Spotlight* and which maintains direct connections with other antisemitic publications including the *American Mercury, Washington Observer Newsletter,* and Noontide Press. Only the most superficial attempt has been made by either the IHR or any of these publications to camouflage the connection between them. In fact at one point the IHR, Noontide Press and the *American Mercury* all shared the same post office box. The publications which were part of this antisemitic network were known for their anti-Israel publications many of which contained alleged details of a "World Zionist Conspiracy." In some of them Israel was referred to as a "bastard state."

Carto had long been associated with the idea of Holocaust revisionism. In 1969 he wrote the introduction to one of the earliest American Holocaust revisionist publications, *The Myth of the Six Million.* (Its author was listed as "Anonymous." However, in all likelihood he was David Hoggan.) Carto blamed "international Jews" for the defeat of Hitler which "was the defeat of Europe. And America." How, he wondered, "could we have been so blind?" The Jews, it seemed, had conspired to achieve this goal and had the unique power to defeat Hitler, Europe and America. In September 1979 *Spotlight* described Carto as one of the "organizers of the convention."

Another individual with neo-Fascist and antisemitic connections who was associated with the Institute was William David McCalden, who until he was uncovered used the name Lewis Brandon. A former member of the National Front, McCalden edited antisemitic and racist publications in England prior to coming to the United States. He eventually had a falling out with Carto and left the Institute. He is currently still quite active in revisionist affairs, publishing his own materials and speaking at various gatherings.

The first IHR conference, which was held in late summer 1979 at the Northrop campus in Los Angeles, featured presentations by those whose names had already become associated with Holocaust revisionism. Though the IHR gatherings attracted their quota of eccentrics there were some people present who still had established reputations. One of these was James Martin, who was Barnes' protege and who eventually was seen by the revisionists as the leader of American Holocaust revisionism. Martin was a contributor to the 1970 edition of the Encyclopedia Britannica and had authored a number of works including one he co-wrote with a respected Libertarian scholar, Leonard Liggio. When Rassinier's book was translated into English it was dedicated to Barnes and Martin.

The convention passed a resolution calling on the Congress of the United States to "investigate, interalia, the truth of the alleged extermination of the six million Jews in Europe during World War II."

Though the IHR's main objective was to engage in Holocaust denial it occasionally included in its journals articles that have no connection with World War II or the Final Solution. This was obviously part of an attempt to demonstrate that the boundaries of the revisionist enterprise transcend the denial of the Holocaust. Lewis Brandon (David McCalden), in a letter which was distributed to students on various campuses, argued that history had long been manipulated by those who were "willing to parrot . . . just what the establishment wants them to," and that the IHR was dedicated to ending this. In the Spring 1982 edition of the journal an article by Barnes entitled "Revisionism and the Promotion of Peace" argued that revisionism was dedicated to the "honest search for historical truth and the discrediting of misleading myths that are a barrier to peace and goodwill among nations." It was, Barnes claimed, an "effort to correct the historical record in the light of a more complete collection of historical facts, a more calm political atmosphere and a more objective attitude."

The Holocaust, revisionists claimed, was not the only instance in which the historical record had been manipulated. Other events which demanded a revisionist examination were the American Revolution (the policies of the British were not that harsh), the War of 1812 (Madison was not pushed into war but made the decision based on his own convictions), the German invasion of Belgium in World War I (the British would have done the same thing if the Germans had not gotten there first) and Theodore Roosevelt's role in the Spanish American War (he ordered an attack on the Spanish fleet as part of his American imperialist and expansionist philosophy). As was often the

case with revisionist arguments, the issues they raised had a kernel of truth to them. By demonstrating that in each particular case popular impressions were not entirely accurate they apparently believed that they could lull the reader into accepting that a revisionist approach was needed in relation to the Holocaust.

This was the objective of Mark Weber's article on Civil War "concentration camps." Weber claimed that false reports about the suffering of Northern prisoners in Southern prisoner camps caused the North to order similar "special treatment" for prisoners in its camps. Exaggerations about conditions in the South multiplied with the passage of time as former prisoners wrote books supposedly documenting their experiences. The commander of Andersonville, the most notorious camp in the South, was executed because "in the imagination of inmates [he] became the cruel and inhuman author of all their sufferings." Weber described the proposal that Andersonville be maintained as a permanent reminder of the war as "shades of Dachau." Echoing Butz's approach to the conditions which faced Jews during World War II, Weber admitted that many prisoners on both sides had died but no one "deliberately killed prisoners." Rather "bad management, especially in the South, resulted in so much death and suffering."

The ultimate objective of Weber's work was revealed when he drew a direct parallel between the two wars and the world's reaction to them:

> In the Civil War as in the Second World War, the victorious side hysterically distorted the actual conditions in the camps . . . to brand the defeated adversary as intrinsically evil. . . . All the suffering and death in the camps of the side that lost the war was ascribed to a deliberate policy on the part of an inherently atrocious power. The victorious powers demanded "unconditional surrender" and arrested the defeated government leaders as "criminals."

There was one major difference, according to Weber, "in that the Civil War rendition of *Sonderbehandlung* never achieved the sinister notoriety of its Second World War counterpart." Nonetheless, Weber argued, in both wars

> the social-political system of the side that lost each war was deemed not merely different but morally depraved. The defeated side was judged ethically in terms of its readiness to atone for past sins and embrace the social systems of the conquerors.

But these momentary excursions into other issues are tangential to the true purpose of the IHR, the *JHR* and other North American revisionist enterprises. The objective was clearly stated in an IHR publication, *Dealing in Hate* by Michael F. Connors. "A final accounting must exculpate Germany of any unique inhumanity in the waging of World War II, just as revisionist scholarship has exonerated her of sole or even primary guilt for the war itself." Consequently the bulk of the articles which have thus far appeared in their journal and the various other publications the IHR issued concerned themselves with Germany's role in World War II in general and with the Holocaust specifically.

The World War II issue that is of prime importance to the revisionists is the question of Pearl Harbor. Continuing the battle which had been begun by the isolationists/revisionists in the months immediately after World War II ended, an entire issue of the *JHR* was devoted to this topic. Its explicit objective was to portray Roosevelt as the man who allowed the attack to take place so that America would be forced to enter the war. This obsession with Pearl Harbor has a dual objective: Firstly, to demonstrate Roosevelt's and, by association, the American government's duplicity.

Secondly it is designed to dispel the claim, supposedly made by the Allies and the "Court Historians" that World War II was a moral, as opposed to a power, struggle. The revisionists believe that if they can demonstrate that this was at its heart a conflagration like all others, then they can argue that any unique accusations of guilt or trials for special war crimes are invalid. In this case the revisionists have established a "straw man" in order to knock him down. America never claimed that it entered the war for moral reasons. But, as Josef Joffe has observed in relation to the historians' struggle currently raging in Germany, proving that the Allies were motivated by the "age-old quest for power and advantage" is far more subtle than trying to create an "immoral equivalence" of the gulag vs. the death camps or Auschwitz vs. Dresden.

In contrast to Nolte and his compatriots, the Holocaust revisionists do not accept the reality of Auschwitz or the other death camps. However, if they cannot achieve their aim of convincing the public that the Holocaust was a "hoax" then at the very least they want to convince it that all sides were equally evil. Any attempt to single one party out for special punishment and unique moral guilt is itself immoral. It is on this basis that the IHR has attracted "fellow travelers" such as David Irving and John Toland. This may well be the future direction that American revisionism will take. If it does it will, in all sad likelihood, acquire a far more receptive audience than it has through outright denial of the Holocaust. These are the kinds of arguments which find an attentive ear in contemporary America. This is a society which is peculiarly ahistorical and consequently, as the psychiatrist Walter Reich has observed, there is a current notion that "everything is debatable and that nothing should be accepted as true that was not personally seen and experienced." In light of recent developments in the Middle East such equivalencies have gained a particular currency.

Among the questions that remain to be assessed is the impact the Institute and its revisionist colleagues have had on North America beliefs regarding the Holocaust. What is clear is that Holocaust revisionism constitutes a major assault on truth. Revisionism, from its earliest manifestations to its most extreme form fosters an implicit distrust of historical assertions, particularly those that have an "official" imprimatur. Holocaust revisionism takes this assault on historical truth a step further and melds it with basic antisemitism. The result is a body of material that by all logical considerations should be accorded as much

weight as the "flat earth" school of thought. However, the long history of prejudice and the sustained life of antisemitism has taught that simply because a notion is bizarre and irrational does not mean it will not find those willing to enthusiastically espouse it.

Deborah E. Lipstadt

SOURCE: "The Battle for the Campus," in *Denying the Holocaust: The Growing Assault on Truth and Memory,* The Free Press, 1993, pp. 183-208.

[*In the following essay, Lipstadt investigates the controversy over the appearance of a Holocaust denial advertisement in various college newspapers in the United States.*]

In the early 1990s American college campuses became loci of intensive activity by a small group of Holocaust deniers. Relying on creative tactics and assisted by a fuzzy kind of reasoning often evident in academic circles, the deniers achieved millions of dollars of free publicity and significantly furthered their cause. Their strategy was profoundly simple. Bradley Smith, a Californian who has been involved in a variety of Holocaust denial activities since the early 1980s, attempted to place a full-page ad claiming that the Holocaust was a hoax in college newspapers throughout the United States. The ad was published by papers at some of the more prestigious institutions of higher learning in the United States.

Entitled "The Holocaust Story: How Much Is False? The Case for Open Debate," the ad provoked a fierce debate on many of the campuses approached by Smith. His strategy was quite straightforward: He generally called a paper's advertising department to ascertain the charge for publication of a full-page ad and then submitted camera-ready copy and a certified check in the proper amount. On occasion he inquired in advance whether a paper would be willing to run this particular ad. Even when he was rejected, the attempt to place the ad won him significant media attention. Campus newspapers began to use his name in headlines without identifying him, assuming readers would know who he was. Articles, letters, and op-ed pieces defended Holocaust denial's right to make its "views" known. But not all the results were necessarily what Smith would have wanted. On some campuses there was a backlash against him and Holocaust denial. Courses on the Holocaust that had languished on the back burner for an extended period materialized in the next semester's offerings. Campus administrators admitted that the ad constituted the final push necessary to move these courses from the planning stage to the schedule books. Professors from a wide variety of disciplines included discussion of the Holocaust in their courses. Movies, speakers, photographic exhibits, and other presentations relating to the Holocaust were brought to campus. Students participated in rallies, teach-ins, and protests.

This response prompted some observers to argue that the controversy had a positive impact. Students had become increasingly aware not only of the Holocaust but of the contemporary attempt to subvert history and spread antisemitism. While this may be a relatively accurate analysis of the immediate outcome of Smith's endeavor, there is another more sobering and pessimistic aspect to the matter. Analysis of the students', faculty's, and administration's responses reveals both a susceptibility to the worst form of historical revisionism and a failure to fully understand the implications of Holocaust denial, even among those who vigorously condemned it.

This was not Smith's first use of college newspapers to spread Holocaust denial. For a number of years Smith, along with other deniers, had been placing small ads containing the phone number and address of the Committee on Open Debate on the Holocaust (CODOH), an organization Smith had created with fellow denier Mark Weber in 1987. According to the ADL [Anti-Defamation League], CODOH was initially funded by the late William Curry, a Nebraska businessman known for his antisemitic activities. In 1986, he first attempted to place an ad denying the Holocaust in a campus newspaper. He sent one thousand dollars to the *Daily Nebraskan* for a full-page ad claiming the Holocaust was a hoax. The paper rejected the ad. Shortly thereafter Curry died, and Smith continued his work.

Smith claims that he has no connection to any other denial group and his only association is with CODOH. He has had a long-standing association with the IHR [Institute for Historical Review], serving as a contributing editor of its newsletter since June 1985. At the time he was placing the ads he still maintained a relationship with it. In 1986 he launched the IHR radio project, writing a regular column on the project for the IHR's newsletter, in which he touted his success in getting Holocaust denial onto the radio. Under the auspices of the IHR he planned to tour colleges and universities to speak about "Holocaust fraud and falsehood." Smith's objective was not to "plant seeds" for coming generations but to "take revisionist scholarship directly into our universities NOW!" In a letter to his followers he announced that the IHR had guaranteed to pay a portion of both his "start-up costs" and his "on-going expenses."

Before becoming involved with the IHR's radio project, Smith published *Prima Facie,* which he dedicated to "monitoring Holocaust Cultism, Censorship and Suppression of Free Inquiry." In it he attacked Mel Mermelstein, who had successfully challenged the IHR's demand for "proof" that the Holocaust happened. Smith's description of Mermelstein—as a "yokel" who had sued the institute because it refused to believe that "a hank of hair and a jar full of ashes proves" that Jews were "exterminated" in gas chambers—typified the tone of the newsletter. Mermelstein had developed a "tongue so twisted he could drill his own teeth."

Articles from *Prima Facie* have been reprinted in *Spearhead,* the publication of the right-wing extremist British National party. One such article referred to a wire service report of how a Gestapo officer watched with a smile as his German shepherd dog killed an elderly Jew in Poland in 1942. Smith's use of sarcasm in his attempt to cast doubt on the story was a hallmark of his style.

> Let's say the dog was an 80-pounder—hell let's say it was a 100-pounder! Now let's say the elderly Jew was frail and small, perhaps only a 100-pounder himself. Hell, let's say he was an 80-pounder! I do want to be fair about this. So one question to get straight about the German dog and the elderly Jew is this: How much of the one could the other really eat?

Smith's accomplice was Mark Weber, co-director of CODOH, one of the more active spokesmen for Holocaust denial, and a former member of the National Alliance, a pro-white organization. *Spotlight* described Weber as the "shining star" of defense witnesses at the Zundel trial. At the trial and in denial publications Weber has argued that the Jews who died were the "unifortunate victims" not of an extermination program but of "disease and malnutrition brought on by the complete collapse of Germany in the final months of the war." Repeating a denial argument that had first been voiced by Austin App, Weber contended that if the extermination program had actually existed, the Jews found alive by the Allied forces at the war's end "would have long since been killed."

Born in 1951, he was educated in a Jesuit high school in Portland, Oregon. In an interview in November 1989 with the *University of Nebraska Sower* he expressed his concern about the future of the white "race" in the United States and about the future of the country. Weber contended that the country was heading in one of two possible directions. Either it would become "a sort of Mexicanized, Puerto Ricanized country," a result of the failure of "white Americans" to reproduce themselves, or it would break up because of long-standing racial problems. He rejected the possibility of a unified American heritage or culture based on a multiplicity of races and groups. He did not think it desirable or feasible for "black Americans to be assimilated into white society." He seemed to yearn for a time when the United States was defined as a "white country" and nonwhites were "second-class citizens." This gave the country a "mooring, an anchor." He bemoaned the fact that "today we don't even have that." As the newspaper controversy became more public and Weber became more publicly involved in denial activities, his ideas on race were increasingly left unarticulated.

One of the first papers approached by CODOH, which for all intents and purposes consisted of Smith and Weber, was Pennsylvania State University's *Daily Collegian.* After running the small ad that contained CODOH's number for a few weeks it dropped it in response to campus criticism. Smith immediately sent a series of letters to local newspapers accusing the *Daily Collegian* of trying to "suppress and even censor radical scholarship." It may have been the *"Sturm und Drang"* he created with this small ad that persuaded him to expand his efforts.

Shortly after his failed attempt at Penn State he experienced the same problem with the *Stanford Daily,* which had been running a similar ad for a period of seven weeks. The editor cancelled it due to student protests. Smith, implying that Hillel, the Jewish student organization, controlled the *Daily*'s coverage of other issues, including American politics in the Middle East, urged the editor to take a stand for "free inquiry and open debate" by running the ad. He told Hillel students that it was in Jews' best interests to know the truth about the Holocaust.

In his publication *Revisionist Letters,* Smith tried to differentiate between antisemites who used Holocaust denial to attack Jews and his putative objective of uncovering the truth. He asserted that his editorial policy objective was to encourage "exposés of bigotry and antisemitism" in Holocaust "revisionism." An article in the magazine argued that the participation of "Nazi apologists" in Holocaust denial circles precluded the participation of other supporters, particularly the radical left. The author, Laird Wilcox, wondered how "revisionists" could argue that their speech was suppressed when there was a "substantial element in [their] own ranks that doesn't believe in it [free speech], except for themselves." Smith reiterated this idea in a column in his local newspaper, admitting that although the "search for truth" about the Holocaust was not antisemitic, there were "bigots" in the movement who were "self-avowedly anti-Jewish and who used revisionist scholarship as an attack on Jews." Smith seemed to be aware that any linkage of his efforts with extremist and racist groups would be a liability, particularly on campus.

His effort to distance himself from these overtly antisemitic groups was reflective of a shift by deniers to sever their overt ties to an array of neo-Nazi and extremist groups. Leonard Zeskind, the research director of the Center for Democratic Renewal in Kansas City, Missouri, and a respected specialist on extremism in America, categorized Smith's efforts as reflective of a general shift among "white supremacists" and extremists away from the political margins into the mainstream by avoiding any overt association with swastika-bedecked or white-sheeted fascist groups. David Duke's re-creation of his past during the presidential campaign was an example of this strategy, which confuses many people who can easily identify the objectives of the Klan, White Aryan Nation, and Posse Comitatus but who find it more difficult to recognize extremism when it is cloaked in a seemingly rational and familiar garb.

The ad Smith began to circulate in the spring of 1991 contained the deniers' familiar litany of claims. It declared the gas chambers a fraud, photographs doctored, eyewitness reports "ludicrously unreliable," the Nuremberg trials a sham, and camp internees well fed until Allied bombings destroyed the German infrastructure in the most "barbarous form of warfare in Europe since the Mongol invasions," preventing food from being delivered and causing the inmates to starve. According to Smith the notion of a Nazi attempt to destroy the Jews was the product of Allied efforts to produce "anti-German hate propaganda." Today that same propaganda was used by powerful forces to "scape-goat old enemies," "seek vengeance rather than reconciliation," and pursue a "not-so-secret political agenda."

He repeated the familiar protest that his sole objective was to uncover the truth through an open debate on the Holocaust—debate that had been suppressed by a powerful but secret group on campus as part of their larger political agenda. "Let's ask these people—what makes such behavior a social good? Who benefits?"

The ad contended that denial was forcing "mainline Holocaust historians" to admit the "more blatant examples" of Holocaust falsehoods. It was the deniers who had forced them to revise the "orthodox" Holocaust story. They had had to admit that the number of Jews killed at Auschwitz was far smaller than originally claimed, and had been made to confess that the Nazis did not use Jewish cadavers for the production of soap. It is correct that in recent years newly revealed documentation has allowed scholars to assess more precisely the number of Jews thought to have been murdered at Auschwitz. It is also accurate that scholars have long written that despite wartime rumors to the contrary, the Nazis apparently did not use Jewish cadavers for soap. There has been a wide array of other "revelations" by Holocaust historians, all part of the attempt to uncover the full details of one of the most horrifying acts of human destruction. Smith suggested to his readers that scholars and others who work in this field, all of whom vigorously repudiate Holocaust denial, have been compelled to admit the truth of deniers' claims: "We are told that it is 'anti-Jewish' to question orthodox assertions about German criminality. Yet we find that it is Jews themselves like Mayer, Bauer, Hier, Hilberg, Lipstadt and others who beginning [*sic*] to challenge the establishment Holocaust story." This notion—that deniers have exposed the truth and mainline historians are scrambling to admit it—remains a linchpin of the deniers' strategy. It has two objectives: to make it appear that Jewish scholars are responding to the pressure of the deniers' findings and to create the impression that Holocaust deniers' "questions" are themselves part of a continuum of respectable scholarship. If establishment scholars, particularly those who are Jews, can question previously accepted truths, why is it wrong when Bradley Smith does the same?

Alan Dershowitz, a Harvard law professor and one of the country's most prominent constitutional scholars, argues that the decision to run or not run the advertisement [denying the facts of the Holocaust] is not a First Amendment issue. Rather it is solely a policy or standard issue that is strictly an internal matter of the paper. In his opinion, consistency is the key issue here. If one runs an ad on Holocaust revisionism, then one should be willing to run an ad presenting the position that Afro-Americans are racially inferior or that women deserve to be raped.

Carlos C. Huerta, in his "Revisionism, Free Speech, and the Campus," in Midstream, *April 1992.*

Though much of the ad consisted of familiar rhetoric, Smith added a new twist that had a particular resonance on American college campuses. Since the 1980s the concept of "political correctness" has been a source of academic conflict. Conservative political groups have accused the "liberal establishment" of labeling certain topics politically incorrect and therefore ineligible for inclusion in the curriculum. Smith framed his well-worn denial arguments within this rhetoric, arguing that Holocaust revisionism could not be addressed on campus because "America's thought police" had declared it out of bounds. "The politically correct line on the Holocaust story is, simply, it happened. You don't debate 'it.' " Unlike all other topics students were free to explore, the Holocaust story was off limits. The consequences, he charged, were antithetical to everything for which the university stood. "Ideology replaces free inquiry, intimidation represses open debate, and . . . the ideals of the university itself are exchanged for intellectual taboos." While most students who had to decide whether the ad should be published did not overtly succumb to CODOH's use of the political correctness argument, many prove prone to it, sometimes less than consciously—a susceptibility evident in their justifications for running the ad. Among the first universities to accept the ad were Northwestern, the University of Michigan, Duke, Cornell, Ohio State, and Washington University.

At the University of Michigan the saga of the ad had a strange twist. Smith mailed camera-ready copy directly to the *Michigan Daily.* According to the paper's business manager, the ad "slipped through without being read." When it appeared the business staff was appalled to learn what they had allowed to happen. On the following day they placed a six-column ad in the paper apologizing for running Smith's ad and acknowledging that its publication had been a mistake. They declared it a "sorrowful learning experience for the staff." The manager told the *Detroit Free Press,* "We make mistakes like any organization."

The story might well have ended here—an example of faulty monitoring by a segment of the staff of the *Michigan Daily*—but the issue became more complicated when, despite the fact that those responsible for running the ad acknowledged doing so as a mistake, the editorial board attempted to transform a blunder into a matter of principle. They recast a snafu as an expression of freedom of speech. On the same day that the advertising staff published its apology, the front page carried an editorial explaining that, though the editors found the ad "offensive and inaccurate," they could not condone the censorship of "unpopular views from our pages merely because they are offensive or because we disagree with them." Editor in chief Andrew Gottesman acknowledged that had the decision been in his hands, he would have printed the ad. He argued that rejecting it constituted censorship, which the editorial board found unacceptable.

The following day a campus rally attacked both Holocaust denial and the paper's editorial policies. Stung by student and faculty condemnations and afraid that its editorial was being interpreted as an endorsement of CODOH, the editorial board devoted the next issue's lead editorial to the topic. Condemning Holocaust denial as "absurd" and "founded on historical fiction and anti-Jewish bigotry," they dismissed it as irrational, illogical, and ahistorical propaganda. The editors accurately assessed the ad as lacking intellectual merit. Nonetheless, they continued to

support its publication. Their powerful condemnation of Holocaust denial in general and Smith's ad in particular appeared under a banner quoting Supreme Court Justice Hugo Black's opinion on free speech: "My view is, without deviation, without exception, without any ifs, buts, or whereases, that freedom of speech means that you shall not do something to people either for the views they have or the views they express or the words they speak or write."

The strange set of circumstances at Michigan—snatching a constitutional principle from the jaws of a mistake—was further complicated by the entry of the university's president, James Duderstadt, into the debate. In a letter to the *Daily* he declared the ad the work of "a warped crank" and proclaimed that denying the Holocaust was to "deny our human potential for evil and to invite its resurgence." But he, too, defended the paper's decision, which was more of a nondecision, to run the ad. The president asserted that the *Daily* had a long history of editorial freedom that had to be protected even when "we disagree either with particular opinions, decisions, or actions." Most disturbing was Duderstadt's elevation of Smith's prejudices to the level of opinions.

There was no doubt about the message the editors and the president were trying to convey: As absurd, illogical, and bigoted as the ad may be, First Amendment guarantees were paramount. The dictates of the American constitution compelled the *Daily* to publish. None of those involved seemed to have considered precisely what the First Amendment said: "Congress shall make no law . . . abridging the freedom of speech or of the press." Those who argued that free speech guarantees acceptance of the ad ignored the fact that the First Amendment prevents *government* from interfering in any fashion with an individual's or group's right to publish the most outlandish argument. The *New York Times* made this point in an editorial when it adamantly repudiated the notion that this was a First Amendment question: "Government may not censor Mr. Smith and his fellow 'Holocaust revisionists,' no matter how intellectually barren their claims."

To call rejection of the ad censorship was to ignore the fact that, unlike the government, whose actions are limited by the First Amendment, these papers do not have a monopoly of force. If the government denies someone the right to publish, they have no other option to publish in this country. But if a paper rejects someone's column, ad, or letter, there are always other publications. The First Amendment does not guarantee access to a private publication. It is designed to serve as a shield to protect individuals and institutions from government interference in their affairs. It is not a sword by which every person who makes an outlandish statement or notorious claim can invoke a Constitutional right to be published. Nor did the *Michigan Daily* seem to notice how Justice Black, whom they quoted, framed it: "you shall not do something to people. . . . " No one was advocating "doing" anything to Smith.

One of the most ardent advocates of the free-speech argument was the *Duke Chronicle.* In an editorial column the editor in chief, Ann Heimberger, justified the paper's decision by acknowledging that while the paper knew it could reject the ad, it "chose" to accept it as an expression of the paper's desire to "support the advertiser's rights." The editorial board believed that it was not the paper's responsibility to protect "readers from disturbing ideas," but to "disseminate them."

Echoing his Michigan colleague, Duke University president Keith Brodie repeated the free-speech defense in a statement that, though it contained a strong refutation of the ad, was more vigorous in its support of the *Chronicle*'s publication of the ad. To have "suppressed" the ad, he argued, would have violated the university's commitment to free speech and contradicted its "long tradition of supporting First Amendment rights."

When the *Cornell Daily Sun* ran the ad, the editors justified the decision in an editorial statement warning that "page twenty will shock most readers" but proclaimed that it was not the paper's role to "unjustly censor advertisers' viewpoints." Echoing their colleagues on many of the other campuses that printed the ad, the editors declared that they decided to print it because the "First Amendment right to free expression must be extended to those with unpopular or offensive ideas." Neeraj Khemlani, the editor in chief of the *Daily Sun,* said his role was not to "protect" readers. Cornell president Frank H. T. Rhodes joined his colleagues at Duke and Michigan in defending the paper's decision.

The University of Montana's paper, the *Montana Kaimin,* also used the First Amendment to defend its publication of the ad. The editor contended that it was not the paper's place to "decide for the campus community what they should see." The University of Georgia's paper, the *Red and Black,* expressed the hope that publishing the ad would affirm America's unique commitment to "allowing every opinion to be heard, no matter how objectionable, how outright offensive, how clearly wrong that opinion may be." After the ad appeared the paper's editor defended the decision by describing it as "a business decision," arguing that "if the business department is set up to take ads, they darn well better take ads." Given the juxtaposition of these two explanations, there was, as Mark Silk, an editorial writer for the *Atlanta Constitution,* pointed out, something dubious about "this high-minded claim."

After an extensive debate Washington University's *Student Life* decided to run the ad. When the ad appeared in the paper, Sam Moyn, the opinion editor, was responsible for conveying to the university community the reasoning behind the staff's "controversial action." The editors, he wrote, conceived of this as a free-speech issue: "The abridgement of Mr. Smith's rights endangers our own." The *St. Louis Post Dispatch* defended the students' actions. Declaring the ad "offensive, provocative and wrong," it praised the student newspaper's courage to print it and stated that its actions strengthened the cause of freedom of speech. The University of Arizona also depicted its actions as protecting the First Amendment. The editor in chief, Beth Silver, proclaimed that the mission of student newspapers is "to uphold the First Amendment and run things that are obviously going to be controversial and take the heat for it." This attitude—we have to do what

is right irrespective of the costs—was voiced by a number of papers. Ironically, it echoed a theme frequently voiced by the deniers themselves: We will tell the truth, the consequences notwithstanding.

At Ohio State University the decision-making process was complex. The *Lantern*'s advertising policy is in the hands of a publications committee comprising faculty, students, editorial board members, and the paper's business manager. University policy requires committee approval before acceptance of an ad designating a religious group. The committee voiced five to four to reject CODOH's submission. But the story did not end there. Enjoined by the committee's decision from running the ad, the *Lantern*'s editor, Samantha G. Haney, used her editorial powers to run it as an op-ed piece, explaining that the paper had an "obligation" to do so. This decision gave Smith added legitimacy and saved him the $1,134 it would have cost to place a full-page ad in the paper.

A lengthy editorial explaining the *Lantern*'s decision condemned Bradley Smith and his cohorts as "racists, pure and simple" and the ad as "little more than a commercial for hatred." Nonetheless the newspaper had to publish it because it could not only "run things that were harmless to everyone." Haney and her staff rejected the suggestion that they turn to the Ohio State History Department to "pick apart" the ad fact by fact. That, they explained, might suggest that the ad had some "relevancy" and some "substance," which they were convinced it did not. Given that one of the rationales the *Lantern* offered for publishing the article was that "truth will always outshine any lie," its refusal to ask professional historians to elucidate how the ad convoluted historical fact seemed self-defeating. It seemed to reflect an understandable reluctance to accord denial legitimacy. There is no better example of the fragility of reason than the conclusion by these editorial boards that it was their obligation to run an ad or an op-ed column that, according to their *own* evaluation, was totally lacking in relevance or substance.

In contrast to the position adopted by James Duderstadt at the University of Michigan, Ohio State's president, Gordon Gee, attacked the decision to give Smith space in the newspaper, declaring the deniers' arguments "pernicious" and "cleverly disguised" propaganda that enhanced prejudice and distorted history.

When this issue was being debated at Ohio State, a CBS reporter came to that campus to film a segment on Holocaust denial for a network show on hatred and extremism in the United States. Alerted in advance to the pending controversy, the cameras were conveniently present when the editor received a call from Smith congratulating her for running the ad and standing up for the principles of free speech and free press. When Haney hung up, the television reporter, who was standing nearby, asked how she felt. She turned and somewhat plaintively observed that she thought she had been had.

Not all the papers subscribed to the First Amendment argument; indeed, some explicitly rejected it. The University of Tennessee's *Daily Beacon* dismissed the idea that not running the ad harmed the deniers' interests: It was not "censorship or even damaging." Pennsylvania State University's *Daily Collegian,* which had been one of the first to receive an ad from Smith, denied that the issue was one of free speech. After seeing student leaders and numerous individuals on campus inundated with material by deniers, the paper reasoned that those behind the ad had sufficient funds to propagate their conspiracy theory of Jewish control without being granted space in the paper.

In an eloquent editorial the *Harvard Crimson* repudiated Smith's claim to a free-speech right to publish his ad. To give CODOH a forum so that it could "promulgate malicious falsehoods" under the guise of open debate constituted an "abdication" of the paper's editorial responsibility. The University of Chicago *Maroon* agreed that while the deniers "may express their views," it had "no obligation at anytime to print their offensive hatred."

The argument that not publishing the ad constituted censorship was not only a misinterpretation of the First Amendment but disingenuous. The editorial boards that reached this decision ignored the fact that they all had policies that prevented them from running racist, sexist, prejudicial, or religiously offensive ads. (Some of the papers in question even refuse cigarette ads.) How could they square their "principled" stand for absolute freedom of speech with policies that prevented them from publishing a range of ads and articles? Why was Bradley Smith entitled to constitutional protection while an ad for an X-rated movie, *Playboy,* the KKK, or Marlboros was not? Recognizing this inconsistency, some of the boards tried to reconcile these two seemingly contradictory positions by adopting a stance that drew them even further into the deniers' trap. They argued that Holocaust denial was not antisemitic and therefore not offensive. The *Cornell Daily Sun* editorial board determined that the "ad does not directly contain racist statements about Jewish people." Valerie Nicolette, the *Sun*'s managing editor, told the *Chronicle of Higher Education* that the editors had evaluated the ad based on their standards of "obscenity and racism" and decided that it passed. When a group of Jewish students at Duke met with the editorial board of the *Duke Chronicle* to protest the running of the ad, they were told that the paper's policy was not to run any ad that was "racist or contained ethnic slurs" but that this ad did not fall into that category.

Andrew Gottesman, who vigorously argued that he could not condone "censorship" of Smith's advertisement and whose *Michigan Daily* published its ringing denunciation of Holocaust denial under Justice Hugo Black's interpretation of the First Amendment, admitted that there were ads he would not run in the paper. This ad, however, did not deserve to be "banned from the marketplace of ideas, like others might be." Among those he would ban were a Ku Klux Klan announcement of lynching or a beer ad with a woman holding a beer bottle between her breasts. For Gottesman keeping such sexist and racist ads out of the paper would not constitute censorship; keeping Smith's out would. When Washington University's *Student Life* published the ad, an editorial explained that it did so in the interest of preventing "freedom of ideas from disappearing from its newspapers." Yet the same paper in-

cludes the following policy statement on its advertising rate card: "*Student Life* reserves the right to edit or reject any advertisement which does not comply with the policies or judgment of the newspaper."

The claim that the rejection of the ad constituted censorship also revealed the failure of editorial staffs and, in certain cases, university presidents to think carefully about what their papers did regularly: pick and choose between subjects they covered and those they did not, columns they ran and those they rejected, and ads that met their standards and those that did not. The *Daily Tar Heel,* the paper of the University of North Carolina, proclaimed that as soon as an editor "takes the first dangerous step and decides that an ad should not run because of its content, that editor begins the plunge down a slippery slope toward the abolition of free speech." What the *Tar Heel* failed to note was that newspapers continuously make such choices. As Tom Teepen, the editor of the *Atlanta Constitution*'s editorial page, observed, "Running a newspaper is mainly about making decisions, not about ducking them." In fact the *Duke Chronicle,* whose editor had wondered how newspapers founded on the principles of free speech and free press could "deny those rights to anyone," had earlier rejected an insert for *Playboy* and an ad attacking a fraternity.

While some papers justified their decision by arguing that the ad was not antisemitic and others leaned on the censorship argument, an even more disconcerting rationale was offered by many papers. They argued that however ugly or repellent Smith's "ideas," they had a certain intellectual legitimacy. Consequently it was the papers' responsibility to present these views to readers for their consideration. Those editors who made this argument fell prey to denial's attempt to present itself as part of the normal range of historical interpretation. That they had been deceived was evident in the way they described the contents of the ad. The editor in chief of the *Cornell Daily Sun* described the ad as containing "offensive *ideas.*" The *Sun* argued that it was not the paper's role to "unjustly censor advertisers' *viewpoints*" however "unpopular or offensive." In a similar vein the *University of Washington Daily* defended giving Smith op-ed space because the paper must constitute a "forum for diverse *opinions* and *ideas.*" Ironically, six weeks earlier, when it rejected the ad, it had described Smith's assertions as "so obviously false as to be unworthy of serious debate." The paper insisted that the op-ed column it eventually published was different because it was Smith's "opinion" and did not contain the "blatant falsehoods" of the ad. In the column Smith asserted that for more than twelve years he has been unable to find "one bit of hard evidence" to prove that there was a plan to "exterminate" the Jews, and that the gas-chamber "stories" were "allegations" unsupported by "documentation or physical evidence."

The *Michigan Daily* engaged in the same reasoning. It would not censor "unpopular *views*" simply because readers might disagree with them. In a show of consistency, two weeks after Smith's ad appeared, the *Daily* supported the decision by Prodigy, the computer bulletin board, to allow subscribers to post Holocaust denial material. Prodigy, they contended, was similar to a newspaper, and like a newspaper it must be a *"forum for ideas."* In another suggestion that Smith's views were worthy of debate, the editor in chief of the *Montana Kaimin* argued that "this man's *opinions,* no matter how ridiculous they may be, need to be heard out there." According to the editor in chief of Washington University's *Student Life,* the board voted to run the ad because "we didn't feel comfortable censoring offensive *ideas.*"

The *Ohio State Lantern*'s explanation of why it let Smith have his "public say" despite the fact that it condemned Smith and CODOH as "racist, pure and simple," was more disturbing than the decision itself. The *Lantern* argued that it was "repulsive to think that the quality, or total lack thereof, of any idea or opinion has any bearing on whether it should be heard." It is breathtaking that students at a major university could declare repulsive the making of a decision based on the "quality" of ideas. One assumes that their entire education is geared toward the exploration of ideas with a certain lasting quality. This kind of reasoning essentially contravenes all that an institution of higher learning is supposed to profess.

The editors of Washington University's *Student Life* demonstrated a similar disturbing inconsistency. They dismissed Smith's claim to be engaged in a quest for the truth, describing him as someone who "cloaks hate in the garb of intellectual detachment." They believed that Smith was posing as a "truth seeker crushed by a conspiratorial society." Given their evaluation of Smith, his tactics, and the way conspiracy theorists have captured the imagination of much of American society, what followed was particularly disconcerting. Notwithstanding all their misgivings, the editors decided that they must give "Mr. Smith the benefit of the doubt if we mean to preserve our own rights." In an assertion typical of the confused reasoning that student papers nationwide displayed on this issue, the *Student Life* editors acknowledged that they could have suppressed Smith's views "if we attributed motives to him that contradict his statements. But we cannot in good conscience tell Mr. Smith that we 'know' him and his true intentions." Was not the fact that he was denying a historical fact about whose existence there is no debate among any reputable scholars indicative of something significant? The editorial board had concluded that "if we refused Mr. Smith's advertisement, we could censor anyone based on ulterior motives that we perceive them to harbor." At what point would the board feel it was appropriate to make a decision based on the objective merits of the information contained in the ad?

In this instance what the paper considered to be ulterior motives is what scholars call coming to a conclusion based on a wide variety of facts, including historical data. In giving Smith the "benefit of the doubt," the editors fell prey to the notion that this was a rational debate. They ignored the fact that the ad contained claims that completely contravened a massive body of fact. They transformed what the *Harvard Crimson* described as "vicious propaganda" into iconoclasm.

The most controversial interpretation about precisely what this ad represented was expressed by the *Duke Chronicle*. In a column justifying the paper's decision to run the ad, Ann Heimberger contended that "Revisionists are . . . reinterpreting history, a practice that occurs constantly, especially on a college campus." In a private meeting with Jewish student leaders on the Duke campus, the editors reiterated this argument. The students were told that the ad was neither racist nor antisemitic but was part of an ongoing "scholarly debate." The Duke editorial board viewed the advertisement more as "a political argument than as an ethnic attack." In editorials, articles, and interviews, those at the helm of the *Duke Chronicle* repeatedly referred to Holocaust denial as "radical, unpopular *views,*" and "disturbing *ideas*" and argued that the ad was not a "slur" but an "*opinion.*" By doing so they not only clung to their First Amendment defense, they gave the ad historical and intellectual legitimacy.

The *Chronicle*'s acceptance of the ad and the editor's defense of having done so elicited two reactions. Bradley Smith, quite predictably, praised Heimberger's column as "fantastic" and an example of sound reasoning. A less laudatory response came from the Duke History Department, which, in a unanimously adopted statement, asserted that the ad aimed to "hurt Jews and to demean and demonize them." It was particularly vehement about Heimberger's contention that the ad was nothing more than a reinterpretation of history. The department observed that the "scholarly pretensions" of the ad were effective enough to deceive Heimberger so that she believed the ad's claims were part of the "range of normal historical inquiry." The statement continued:

> That historians are constantly engaged in historical revision is certainly correct; however, what historians do is very different from this advertisement. Historical revision of major events is not concerned with the actuality of these events; rather it concerns their historical *interpretation*—their causes and consequences generally.

If the ad convinced Heimberger, one can only imagine its impact on individuals who have had less exposure to history and critical thinking.

There were, of course, those college newspapers that had no problem evaluating the ad's intellectual value. The *Harvard Crimson* repudiated the idea that the ad was a "controversial argument based on questionable facts." In one of the most unequivocal evaluations of the ad, the *Crimson* declared it "vicious propaganda based on utter bullshit that has been discredited time and time again." More than "moronic and false," it was an attempt to "propagate hatred against Jews." The editorial board of the University of Pennsylvania's *Daily Pennsylvanian* argued that "running an ad with factual errors that fostered hate" was not in the best interests of the paper.

The *MIT Tech* simply decided that it would not accept an ad that it knew "did not tell the truth." For the *Brown Daily Herald* the ad was "a pack of vicious, antisemitic lies" parading as "history and scholarship." The *Daily Nexus,* the publication of the University of California at Santa Barbara, refused the ad because of its "blatant distortions of truth and its offensive nature." The paper described receiving the ad itself and the more than one thousand dollars to print it as "chilling." The *Dartmouth Review,* no stranger to controversy, also rejected the ad. It acknowledged that by so doing it was denying "someone a forum through which to speak to the paper's readership" but explained that it had a "bond of trust" with the public, which expected it to abide by "standards of accuracy and decency." Accepting an ad "motivated by hatred and informed by total disregard to the truth" would be to violate that trust. The *Chicago Maroon* saw no reason why it should run an ad whose "only objective is to offend and incite hatred." The *Yale Daily News* "simply" let Smith know that it found the ad "offensive."

Some of the papers that ran the ad did so on the basis of what may be called the light-of-day defense, a corollary of the free-speech argument: In the light of day, truth always prevails over lies. Neeraj Khemlani of the *Cornell Sun* believed that by running the ad he had done the Jewish people a favor—reminding them that there were a "lot of people out to get [them]," which was something they needed to know. This attitude is reminiscent of the concept of "saving the Jews (or women, African Americans, or any other potentially vulnerable group) despite themselves." Michael Gaviser, business manager of the *Daily Pennsylvanian,* decided to run the ad because of his belief that Smith was a "dangerous neo-Nazi" of whom the public had to be aware. (His decision was reversed by the editorial board.)

A number of the nation's most prominent national papers echoed the light-of-day position. A *Washington Post* editorial rejected the freedom-of-the-press argument but accepted the light-of-day rationale. Acknowledging that college newspapers had no obligation to accept the ads, it argued that it was "bad strategy" automatically to "suppress" them. What the ad needed was the "bracing blast of refutation." The *Post* did not seem to consider the possibility that an article fully analyzing the ad would have served the same purpose. In an archetypal deniers' move Smith cited the *Post*'s editorial as proof that the paper believed it both "ethical and permissible" to debate the "Holocaust story." He made the same claim about a *New York Times* editorial that left it up to each newspaper to decide whether to publish Smith's "pseudo-scholarly" and "intellectually barren" tract.

The Rutgers *Daily Targum* contended that publication of the ad constituted a means of defeating Smith. The editors argued that "you cannot fight the devil you cannot see." Exposing Smith's views through publication of his ad could thwart his objectives. The *Targum* correctly understood that the First Amendment did not apply— ("CODOH was wrapped itself so tightly in the First Amendment it borders on suffocation.")—and the claim to be engaged in historical investigation was dismissed as "a sham." Nonetheless it chose to reprint Smith's ad in full on the editorial page, surrounding it with three op-ed pieces and an editorial, all of which attacked the ad's contents. In addition, an editors' note introducing the column noted that the ad had originally been rejected by the paper's business section because of "its false content and antisemitic nature." The editorial board argued that despite all this it was necessary to print the advertisement

in full because, "more than anything else, [it] makes it painfully obviously that a clear and present danger exists." Reiterating this point in a letter to the *New York Times,* *Targum* editor Joshua Rolnick argued that publishing the ad in its entirety was the best way of "mobilizing the community in opposition to its hateful ideas."

The *Targum*'s decision to print the ad as a column and surround it with dissenting opinion won it the editorial praise of the *New York Times*: "The editors thus transformed revulsion into education." Nevertheless there is reason to question that decision. First of all it saved Smith the approximately five hundred dollars it would have cost to purvey his extremist arguments. The paper proudly proclaimed that it had "not accepted any payment" from him, as if the acceptance of money made them accomplices. In fact it was Smith, Rolnick acknowledged, who had "encouraged" him to run it as an op-ed piece. Smith may well have recognized that, the dissenting articles notwithstanding, the full text of his ad was likely to win converts to his cause even as it mobilized some people against him. Given the space the *Daily Targum* devoted to the topic, a lengthy analytical piece quoting heavily from the ad and demolishing it point by point would have served the same purpose and given Smith less of a chance to lay out his "argument." Some wonder what was the danger of allowing Smith his say, particularly when surrounded by articles that firmly and swiftly refuted him. But the *Daily Targum* had given Smith just what he wanted: They made him the other side of a debate. Although it may not have been evenly balanced, although more room may have been given to the articles that surrounded his, and although editorials may have condemned him, he had nonetheless been rendered a point of view. Smith seems to be acutely cognizant of the efficacy of even bad publicity. That may well be why, when a rally at Rutgers denounced Holocaust revisionism and his ad, he declared himself "grateful and delighted" that the rally was held.

In the spring of 1992 Smith began to circulate a second ad that was essentially a reprint of an article from the *Journal of Historical Review* by Mark Weber. The article, entitled "Jewish Soap," blamed the postwar spread of the rumor that the Nazis made Jews into soap on Simon Wisenthal and Stephen Wise—a claim that has no relationship to reality. Echoing the first ad, it charged that historians of the Holocaust have "officially abandon[ed] the soap story" in order to "save what's left of the sinking Holocaust ship by throwing overboard the most obvious falsehoods." The point of this second effort, Smith acknowledged, was to submit a piece that was thoroughly "referenced." The ad was submitted with a cover letter that claimed that the original ad had been rejected by a number of papers because it was not "sourced." In contrast, every "significant claim" in the second ad was backed up by sources. Entitled "Falsus in Uno, Falsus in Omnibus [False in one thing, false in all] . . . The 'Human Soap' Holocaust Myth," the essay on soap was preceded by a statement citing Roman law: If a witness could not be "believed in one thing, he should not be believed in anything."

Most universities that received the second ad, including

those who had accepted the first, rejected it out of hand. When it was submitted to the *Ohio State Lantern,* the editor immediately refused it, observing that "the only news value in this is that Bradley Smith is approaching schools again." Having been burned once, the editor seemed far more cognizant of Smith's motives. "The fact that it is Holocaust Remembrance Week indicates that he's in to ruffle some feathers and stir up trouble again." The arguments about the First Amendment and censorship no longer seemed to apply.

At the University of Texas the deliberations about the second ad were directly linked to what had occurred with the first ad. The editor of the *Daily Texan,* Matthew Connally, had wanted to run the first. However, after familiarizing himself with the "group behind the ad," he reversed his decision. "They were not only showing a disregard for the truth but they were doing it with malicious intent." The Texas Student Publication Board (TSPB), which has ultimate authority over the paper's advertising and financial affairs, supported Connally and voted to reject the ad. After hearing Connally's arguments, TSPB member Professor John Murphy, who initially voted in favor of running the ad, decided to oppose it.

But that was not the end of the story at Texas. In April the paper received Smith's second ad. Though the *Daily Texan*'s editorial board was firmly against running it, they quickly discovered that the decision was not in their hands: They were told by the TSPB that they must run it. "We do not want to do this. But we're being told we must follow orders," a member of the editorial board told me sadly. This time Professor Murphy emerged as the ad's most vociferous supporter. According to the *Houston Chronicle,* Murphy, joined by other faculty members on the TSPB, argued that the paper needed to publish "divergent and unpopular opinion." Facing a situation in which it would be forced to publish something it "detested," the editorial board considered leaving all the pages blank except for the ad. (They were told that since this would affect advertising revenues, they did not have the authority to do so.)

The ad was scheduled to run on Holocaust Memorial Day, Yom HaShoah, 1992. Students opposed to the ad discovered that the internal regulations of the TSPB prohibited the newspaper from printing opinion ads unless all persons cited in those ads had granted permission to be quoted. I was among the scholars quoted in the ad. Fortuitously, I was scheduled to visit the campus to deliver a lecture on Holocaust denial the day before the ad's scheduled publication. When I indicated my opposition to being cited in the ad, an emergency meeting of the TSPB board was called to discuss the matter. I informed the board that I had not given my permission to be quoted in the ad and was opposed to being associated with it. I pointed out that the ad specifically violated their own regulations. Despite my objections and my announcement that I would explore the possibility of legal remedies should the ad be published, the TSPB voted to run it, postponing publication for a few days so that my name could be dropped and a rebuttal prepared. Two days later the university's legal counsel suggested that because individuals quoted in the

ad had protested—by this time other professors mentioned in the ad had joined the protest—the ad should be dropped. The TSPB then voted to reject the ad. But the story did not end here. In February 1993 the TSPB compelled the paper to accept an ad promoting a video exposé of the gas chambers by a CODOH member claiming to be a Jew. Based on advertisements and articles by this young man, the video apparently contains the same recycled arguments deniers have been making for years. Though the editorial board and the university president opposed the ad because it was "deceptively rigged," the TSPB ran the ad. The TSPB's three faculty members, two working professionals, and five of its six students voted for the ad.

During this period students were not the deniers' only campus targets. For more than two years—not for the first time—deniers had tried to insinuate themselves into the scholarly arena by finding ways to place Holocaust denial on the agenda of organizations of professional historians. They sought to force these groups to treat denial as a legitimate enterprise. In the spring of 1980 all members of the Organization of American Historians (OAH) received a complimentary copy of the first issue of the *Journal of Historical Review.* It was quickly revealed that the IHR had purchased the OAH's twelve thousand member mailing list. Some OAH members protested the sale of the list to this neo-Nazi group. Others argued that to deny anyone the right to purchase the list would be to abridge intellectual freedom. The executive secretary of the OAH proposed to resolve the issue by inviting a panel of "well-qualified historians" to analyze the *Journal* and evaluate it based on the "credentials of the contributors and the use of evidence." He would then transmit this evaluation to the OAH executive board so it could decide how to treat the matter.

Lucy Dawidowicz, a fierce critic of the OAH response, wondered what those historians would evaluate: "Perhaps that the neo-Nazis did not have proper academic credentials or that they failed to use primary sources?" Carl Degler, a past president of the OAH, defended the suggestion that the OAH should sponsor an analysis of the *Journal.* He argued that once historians begin to consider the "motives" behind historical research and writing, "we endanger the whole enterprise in which the historians are engaged." Following the same pattern as the student editors who described the contents of the denial ad as opinions, views, and ideas, he described the articles contained in the *Journal* as "bad historical writing." Given the *Journal*'s contents and its publisher's identity, Degler's categorization of it as bad history was described by Dawidowicz as a "travesty."

A far-less-ambiguous position was adopted by the editors of the *Journal of Modern History,* when the Liberty Lobby bought its subscription list and sent out antisemitic material. The journal's editors sent a letter of apology to its subscribers acknowledging that an "antisemitic hate organization" had obtained its mailing list. It "repudiate[d] and condemn[ed] the propaganda" that readers had received and apologized that both the readers and the academic discipline had been "abused in this thoroughly scurrilous manner."

Another attempt to force professional historians to treat Holocaust denial as a legitimate enterprise began in 1990, when members of various university history departments began to receive letters soliciting support for "Holocaust revisionism." That same year the American Historical Association's (AHA) annual meeting was disrupted by pickets calling for recognition of a book charging Gen. Dwight Eisenhower with consciously causing the death of a million German POWs at the end of the war. The AHA issued a statement noting that 1995 marked the fiftieth anniversary of the defeat of Nazism and calling on scholars to "initiate plans now to encourage study of the significance of the Holocaust."

The AHA statement referred to the Holocaust but did not explicitly say that the Holocaust was a fact of history. According to the then-president of the AHA, William Leuchtenburg, it did not want to "get into the business of certifying what is and is not history." Moreover, he believed that for a group of historians to say there had been a Holocaust was tantamount to "an organization of astronomers saying there is a moon." The press, he believed, would simply ignore such a statement. In December 1991 the AHA unanimously adopted a statement deploring the "attempts to deny the fact of the Holocaust" and noting that "no serious historian questions that the Holocaust took place." Leuchtenburg opposed allowing deniers a table at the convention because the AHA was a professional organization and they were not professionals. It would be the equivalent of the AMA allowing quacks to hawk miracle cures at its meetings.

The OAH was also a target of the deniers. In November 1991 the OAH's executive committee agreed to allow its newsletter to publish a call by the IHR's *Journal of Historical Review* for "revisionist" papers. This action was taken after David Thelen, the editor of the OAH's scholarly journal, the *Journal of American History,* refused to list articles by deniers because it was the responsibility of an academic publication to "make judgments on the quality of scholarship." He felt it was harder to refuse them space in the association's newsletter because it contained both scholarly and nonscholarly information. Joyce Appleby, OAH president, protested the executive committee's decision to accept the announcement in the *OAH Newsletter.* "This is not a question of respecting different points of view but rather of recognizing a group which repudiates the very values which bring us together," Appleby wrote. It was the responsibility of a professional organization to make "professional judgments" and, Appleby asserted, "these people are not professionals and to allow them to advertise is to legitimate them."

Mary Frances Berry, a former president of the OAH and a history professor at the University of Pennsylvania, disagreed with Appleby. She compared the debate within the OAH to campus codes against "hate speech," to which she objected. Her primary concern was "guaranteeing civil liberties for everyone." She argued that since the OAH did not have a general policy regarding advertisements it would accept or reject, it was obligated to accept everything it received. The next issue of the *OAH Newsletter* contained a series of letters regarding the decision to

include the ad and Appleby's dissent. A group of prominent historians, including Thelen and Berry, wrote in support of the inclusion of denial announcements. They argued that however "abhorrent" the goals of the *Journal of Historical Review,* the constitutional principle of free speech as well as the OAH's commitments to freedom of expression and the search for historical truth demanded that the ad be printed. In an apparent attempt to "balance" their support of the ad, they suggested a variety of strategies for dealing with the future efforts by the *Journal of Historical Review* and other deniers to place ads in OAH publications. One idea was that the OAH "pressure" the deniers' journal to abide by international standards of scholarship, including that experts in appropriate fields evaluate articles submitted to the journal. Given the way they handle documents and data, it is clear that deniers have no interest in scholarship or reason. Most are antisemites and bigots. Engaging them in reasoned discussion would be the same as engaging a wizard of the Ku Klux Klan in a balanced and reasoned discussion of African Americans' place in society. But on some level Carl Degler was right: Their motives are irrelevant. Some may truly believe the Holocaust a hoax—just as hundreds of antisemites believed the *Protocols* genuine. This does not give the contents of their pronouncements any more validity or intellectual standing. No matter how sincerely one believes it, two plus two will never equal five. Among the historians' other suggestions was that a "truth-in-advertising" group be created to unmask the misleading claims in denial notices and announcements and that this group insist that their exposure be published along with the deniers' claims. But such a suggestion would imply that a debate was being conducted by mainline historians and "revisionists." The historians' ideas, offered in the name of an attempt to resolve a situation that confounds many academics, played directly into the deniers' hands. Given the response of such eminent teachers of history, it is not surprising that the *Daily Northwestern,* Northwestern University's student newspaper, writing in support of inviting Arthur Butz to debate his "unorthodox view" of the Holocaust, declared that "even outrageous and repugnant theories sometimes deserve a forum." Students emulated exactly what these professors had done. They had elevated what the *Harvard Crimson* had properly characterized as "utter bullshit" to the level of a theory deserving of a forum. After the IHR's announcement appeared, the executive board voted to establish a policy henceforth to exclude such advertisements and announcements from the newsletter. There was significant debate within the OAH's leadership on this matter, and the decision to exclude denial ads in the future passed by one vote.

Writing in support of Appleby, the *Los Angeles Times* provided an interesting slant to the argument. It pointed out that the First Amendment guaranteed freedom of association as well as freedom of speech. As a result the OAH had the right to "exclude fake historians from its ranks." It was probably the most appropriate and possibly the most creative citation of the First Amendment during this entire debate. The responses to Holocaust denial by both students and faculty graphically demonstrate the susceptibility of an educated and privileged segment of the American population to the kind of reasoning that creates a hospitable climate for the rewriting of history. There were a variety of failures here. All of them are sobering indicators of the ability of Holocaust denial to gain legitimacy. There was a failure to understand the true implications of the First Amendment. There was also a failure by student editors to recognize that their high-minded claims about censorship were duplicitous, given their papers' policies of rejecting a broad range of ads and articles. In fact, campus policies are often more restrictive than those of the commercial press.

There was a failure to look at the deniers' own history and to understand what they represented. The observation of the *Ohio State Lantern* rings hauntingly in my ears: "It is repulsive to think that the quality, or total lack thereof, of any idea or opinion has any bearing on whether it should be heard." It is a response likely to make professors nationwide cringe. But, as we have seen, professors also showed their confusion on this matter.

Most disturbing was the contention voiced by students, faculty members, and university presidents that however ugly, the ad constituted an idea, opinion, or viewpoint—part of the broad range of scholarly ideas. However much they disassociated themselves from the content of the ad, the minute they categorized it as a "view," they advanced the cause of Holocaust denial. That students failed to grasp that the ad contravened all canons of evidence and scholarship was distressing. But those at the helm sometimes also failed to grasp that the ad was not advocating a radical moral position but a patent untruth. Writing in the *Cornell Daily Sun,* President Frank Rhodes couched the discussion in terms of freedom of the press, arguing, "Free and open debate on a wide range of ideas, however outrageous or offensive some of them may be, lies at the heart of a university community." Rhodes was positing that Holocaust denial should be considered an idea worthy of inclusion in the arena of open debate.

This assault on the ivory tower of academe illustrated how Holocaust denial can permeate that segment of the population that should be most immune to it. It was naive to believe that the "light of day" can dispel lies, especially when they play on familiar stereotypes. Victims of racism, sexism, antisemitism, and a host of other prejudices know of light's limited ability to discredit falsehood. Light is barely an antidote when people are unable, as was often the case in this investigation, to differentiate between reasoned arguments and blatant falsehoods. Most sobering was the failure of many of these student leaders and opinion makers to recognize Holocaust denial for what it was. This was particularly evident among those who argued that the ad contained ideas, however odious, worthy of discussion. This failure suggests that correctly cast and properly camouflaged, Holocaust denial has a good chance of finding a foothold among coming generations.

This [essay] ends where it began. Given the fact that even the papers that printed the ad dismissed Smith's claims in the most derogatory of terms—absurd, irrational, racist, and a commercial for hatred—one might argue that the entire affair had a positive outcome. Rarely did the ad appear without an editorial or article castigating Holocaust denial. Students were alerted to a clear and present danger that can easily take root in their midst. Courses on the Holocaust increased in number. One could argue that all this is proof that CODOH's attempt to make Holocaust denial credible backfired.

My assessment is far more pessimistic. It is probably the one issue about which I find myself in agreement with Bradley Smith. Many students read both the ad and the editorials condemning it. Some, including those who read neither but knew of the issue, may have walked away from the controversy convinced that there are two sides to this debate: the "revisionists" and the "establishment historians." They may know that there is tremendous controversy about the former. They may not be convinced that the two sides have of equal validity. They may even know that the deniers keep questionable company. But nonetheless they assume there *is* an "other side." That is the most frightening aspect of this entire matter.

On Holocaust denial literature in library collections:

There is little doubt that the established view of Nazism is universally available; nevertheless the relative prominence given to extreme interpretations when they appear in small library collections bears contemplation, particularly where the total collection may be insufficient in size to allow ready evaluation of all relevant statements cited in the debate.

David Irving's *Hitler's War* is a case in point. Nearly nine hundred OCLC locations report holding the work, which was a book club selection. Irving's thesis, that Hitler was too weak a leader to be held responsible for the acts of his lieutenants, has been criticized strongly both in reviews and in subsequent books in the field of modern German history. To take up one specific instance, Irving advances a short memorandum by Himmler as evidence that Hitler ordered "no liquidation" of Jews in December 1941. Sebastian Haffner carefully rebuts this argument in *The Meaning of Hitler* by setting the evidence in a wider context, one that makes clear its misleading and exceptional nature. Almost as many libraries report copies of Haffner on their shelves as do those with Irving, but they are not necessarily the same libraries. In fact, 341 OCLC sites own Irving's book but not Haffner's rebuttal. In fairness, it must be noted that other basic texts on the Holocaust, such as Raul Hilberg's *Destruction of the European Jews* or Lucy S. Dawidowicz's *The War Against the Jews* are widely owned; yet it is troubling that portions of the debate are unavailable to many patrons.

Steven W. Sowards, in his "Historical Fabrications in Library Collections," Collection Management, *1988.*

LIBRARY ACCESS TO HOLOCAUST DENIAL LITERATURE

Jeffrey Katz

SOURCE: "Revisionist History in the Library: To Facilitate Access or Not to Facilitate Access?" in *Canadian Library Journal,* Vol. 48, No. 4, October, 1991, pp. 319-24.

[In the following essay, Katz addresses the major questions that have been raised over the acquisition and dissemination of Holocaust denial literature in Canadian libraries.]

In her very provocative article, "Lies about the Holocaust," (1980) Lucy Dawidowicz describes the concept of "historical revision" (the practice of "reinterpreting the past") as a necessary part of the historian's job. Herself an eminent historian of the Jewish Holocaust, Dawidowicz makes the observation that "every historical subject has undergone revision as each new generation rewrites the history of the past in the light of its own perspectives and values."

New information and the discovery of hitherto unknown documents or artifacts can change entirely the generally accepted picture of a particular event, era, person, or civilization—even if that picture has lasted for centuries. Consider the Trojan War, dinosaurs, the Etruscans and William Shakespeare. Public officials, national leaders, and celebrities are notorious for witholding information about their personal and professional lives which is eventually "unearthed" by historians when the luminaries in question have departed this life.

In short, the stuff of history is *evidence,* and when a new bit of evidence seems to outweigh an older bit of evidence in terms of authenticity, the historian must acknowledge this fact and proceed to *revise.*

However, once we move away from the rather loose, non-threatening concept of "historical revision" and towards the more precise term "revisionism," we experience (as Dawidowicz also makes clear) an extremely radical shift in meaning. For, unlike "historical revision," which refers to the practice of *updating* history on the basis of accurate, well-researched facts, "revisionism" concerns the *distortion* of history by individuals whose primary motivation is the advancement of a personal (often bizarre) ideological position.

Although the term has been used by conscientious historians to describe cases of historical fabrication and tampering (Steven W. Sowards, for example, makes use of the term in his discussion of Samuel Eliot Morison's *John Paul Jones*), the most common usage of the term "revisionism" has been in relation to the Jewish Holocaust (1933–1945).

Those individuals referred to as "Revisionist Historians" deny flatly that a Nazi plan to exterminate the Jews of Europe ever existed and attempt to "prove" that concentration camps, gas chambers, and the entire concept of genocide was just one huge "hoax" concocted by "Zionists" and their cohorts, in order to discredit Germany and advance their own (naturally greedy) causes.

As one might expect, such "Revisionist Historians" (who refer to their opposition as "traditionalists" or, less politely, as "exterminationists") have produced a small but not insubstantial body of literature, which they work fervently to distribute far and wide. One target of this literature, of course, is the library. As a result, the entire "Revisionist" Holocaust history issue is also a *library* issue.

This article attempts to identify the major questions that have been (and continue to be) raised over the acquisition and dissemination of such "Holocaust-denial" literature in the library, and to discuss whether or not there is any hope that these volatile questions can ever be answered conclusively.

Over the past ten years, Holocaust-denial literature has become one of the most controversial issues in librarianship. Indeed, as a result of the existence of such literature (and the many subsequent decisions that librarians must make regarding its acquisition and public accessibility), the entire library profession has been forced once again to examine its basic philosophy and its fundamental role in society.

At the core of the controversy is the issue of free speech. Purists, like John C. Swan, have maintained that libraries have an obligation to make such material, however distasteful, available and easily accessible to the general public. The concept of intellectual freedom, according to Swan, requires that we place no ideological limits on our collections but, instead, make every effort to provide our library patrons with as wide a body of literature as possible, in order that these patrons might have the opportunity to make their own decisions and choose their own intellectual paths. For support, he cites the intellectual freedom statements that exist in both the United States and Canada.

On the other hand, a large number of librarians have argued against the presence of "Revisionist" Holocaust works in the library because of the essentially *racist* and *hateful* nature of this literature. According to librarians of this opinion, who are represented here by Steven Sowards, Noel Peattie, and Grant Burns, librarians in general are under no obligation whatsoever to purchase or acquire Holocaust-denial literature, since such books may be looked upon not only as untrue, but also as designed specifically to promote bigotry and to incite violence against a particular religious or ethnic group.

Also claiming the right of free speech, librarians such as Peattie and Burns maintain that while the publishers of Holocaust-denial literature are at liberty to print whatever they wish (provided it does not violate federal law), they too—as librarians—are at liberty to keep such material out of the library. Holocaust "Revisionists," to quote Burns, "have as much right to propagate their views as any of us," but this "does not mean the rest of us have to go out and facilitate their efforts."

Of course, there are still others, such as Morton Weinfeld and Mark Pendergrast, who recognize the potential research value a "Revisionist" Holocaust text might have for a serious student of, say, anti-Semitism. But they insist that great care be taken within the library insofar as the handling and access of such a text is concerned. Harm could be done, it is felt by Weinfeld and Pendergrast, if no attempt is made by the library to distinguish clearly between a "Revisionist" approach to the Holocaust and a so-called "standard" one.

Accordingly, both Weinfeld and Pendergrast call on reference and technical services librarians to give serious thought to special classifications, shelf locations, catalogue notes, and even labeling, for Holocaust-denial literature. In this way the patron will be alerted to the fact that books such as *The Hoax of the Twentieth Century,* and periodicals such as the *Journal of Historical Review,* are not works of history, but rather of hate. Such practices in a library, of course, are themselves potentially dangerous and we shall address this problem later.

In a sense, once we acknowledge the fact that "Revisionist" Holocaust history is considered by so many people to be nothing more than thinly disguised hate literature, we deepen the entire controversy in terms of the library. For, although the library strives (or at least should strive) to present a balanced collection of material representing "all points of view on current and historical issues," there are some very real problems created for the librarian when a book's particular "point of view" is at once distorted, constructed upon a foundation of lies, and intentionally harmful to others.

At this point, the librarian might begin to question the accepted ethical policies and the official standards of the profession (as they relate to collection management) and choose, instead, to place greater emphasis on the "good of the community" whose "best interests" would not be served by housing such material.

Once again, of course, we tread upon fairly dangerous ground when we start talking about librarians deciding what is or is not "beneficial" to any particular community. Nevertheless, it does seem rather clear that there is a need for librarians to consider very carefully the actual purpose that is meant to be served by Holocaust-denial literature.

Librarians, as Swan points out, may be dependent more upon freedom than truth as a fundamental professional *cause.* However, it can be said that librarians have an obligation to be wary of those individuals who would take advantage of the library's great respect for the concept of intellectual freedom in order to give greater voice to their own less-than-respectful ideologies.

That the Holocaust—the wilful destruction of millions of Jews from 1933 to 1945—is a fact, is indisputable. Innumerable documents, eyewitness accounts of both survivors and perpetrators, and well-researched, widely respected historical texts exist which provide proof of its tragic, utterly horrific existence. What then is the motivation of the "Revisionists"?

Dawidowicz, Seidel, and countless others have demonstrated quite clearly that the essence of the Holocaust-denial movement is anti-Semitism and a fanatical devotion to the doctrines of Nazism, and that the publishers and writers of Holocaust-denial literature can be traced to

some neo-Nazi or white supremacist group whose primary goal is the achievement of power.

As librarians, of course, it is not our business to "investigate" every item on our shelves in order to determine whether or not its author or publisher is a rabid fascist. However, when we are confronted by a certain group of books, which we can identify as having been created and generated by racists, for the purpose of promoting racism, we are forced to ask some very serious questions about the acquisition and handling of Holocaust-denial literature and its place inside the library.

Should we or should we not, as librarians, acquire material that seeks quite plainly to deny an indisputable historical fact? This question is extremely difficult to answer and has been the subject of much scholarly debate. On opposite sides of the fence sit John C. Swan and Noel Peattie.

Swan, a great champion of free speech and intellectual freedom, insists (as we have seen) that libraries have an obligation, as upholders of the Right to Read, to get the material and put it into circulation. Citing the *ALA Intellectual Freedom Manual,* Swan declares that "freedom is indivisible" and contends that the librarian must be "committed both to the search for truth and the freedom of expression of untruth." Holocaust-denial literature, therefore, has a right to sit on the shelves of a library just as much as those works which prove that "Revisionism" is a pack of lies. As Swan makes very clear, he himself is fully aware of the "untruth" of the Holocaust-denial literature, but does not deny its right to be accessed in a library:

> [Revisionist] arguments will never turn out to be true, and "Creation Science" will always be apologetics masquerading as empiricism, but both have a place in our libraries.

Noel Peattie, on the other hand, argues against the granting of a forum to "racist" literature, since such literature is characterized by "deliberate" falsehoods, "uttered to deceive and hurt people." So-called "Revisionist" history, according to Peattie, is *dangerous* and must be thought of as being a *conscious effort* to distort the truth. Peattie, in this sense, would find an ally in Dawidowicz, who likens Holocaust-denial literature to a possible series of books seeking to "prove" that slavery of Africans had never existed in the United States but, instead, was a huge hoax created by blacks in order to gain money and power.

The issue of collection "balance" in this instance becomes quite meaningless since, as Peattie points out, we do not collect books that contain proven falsehoods in order to balance our collection of books that are true. Peattie uses the example of the Flat Earth Society, stating that librarians do not attempt to balance their collection of "round earth books" by stockpiling ones which promote the "flat earth" theory. In short, Peattie finds Swan's devotion to the tenets espoused in the *Intellectual Freedom Manual* to be admirable but unacceptably restrictive:

> We need to understand what intellectual freedom is, what relation it bears to reality, how much of it is unconscious or concealed abuse of privilege, and how we justify using it. We need to understand that if freedom is indivisible, so is

human dignity. This would result in a complete rewriting of the Library Bill of Rights which . . . isn't doing us much good anyway.

Additionally, of course, there is a need to decide which libraries—which *kinds* of libraries—should be dealing with Holocaust-denial literature in the first place. Most critics agree that academic and research libraries are perfectly justified in acquiring such materials. As S. D. Neill observes: "An academic library could develop a collection of racist materials for research purposes." Indeed, some of the most extensive collections of Holocaust-denial materials in North America may be found in the major Jewish libraries (e.g. the Jewish Public Library in Montreal and the Jewish Theological Seminary of America in New York City).

However, the big problem—the most serious point of contention—seems to involve the position of the *public* library in the acquisition of such literature. Some public libraries choose to collect whatever they feel the public will demand. Operating on the same philosophy as that of Swan, the attitude of some public libraries is that the *patron* has the right to decide what he or she will not read, not the library. Edmonton Public Library is one such example and will be discussed later in greater detail.

Other public libraries, however, do *not* collect Holocaust-denial titles because they are viewed as examples of hate literature and are considered either "inappropriate" for the community, or completely unjustifiable in a time of tight budgets. Vancouver Public Library, for example, carries none of the most notorious "Revisionist" histories. Such institutions, of course, will generally be quite willing to order Holocaust-denial titles upon request, through the interlibrary loan system. However, in such cases patrons must *know* what they are looking for, since the books in question would be impossible to find in the library by simple browsing.

In many instances, the entire problem of acquiring "Revisionist" histories is solved by federal law; after all, once a book is banned by the government, there is no longer any issue (unless your library wishes to defy the law for some particular reason). Material that is *questionable* but not yet banned, though, can be a *very* tricky issue. Because of the uncertain status of all "Revisionist" histories, some libraries might be ambivalent about making an effort to acquire such materials. As Leonidas Hill states: "Laws are vague," and any title could be suppressed at any time as "hate propaganda."

This is especially true here in Canada, where the trials of Jim Keegstra and Ernst Zundel have prompted both the courts and common citizens to be much more careful about books and materials that present an "unconventional" (to put it mildly) approach to the Holocaust. Of course, while certain "Revisionist" works, such as Arthur Butz's *The Hoax of the Twentieth Century,* have been banned (UBC's copy is now in Special Collections), other titles, such as Walter N. Sanning's *The Dissolution of Eastern European Jewry* remain unsuppressed.

More problems await the library or librarian once a "Revisionist" Holocaust history text has been ordered and re-

ceived. At this stage, it becomes necessary to decide precisely *how* the controversial item should be classified and entered into the catalogue. Additionally, it must be decided precisely where in the library the item should be located. Predictably, the critics are quite varied in their suggestions and, equally without surprise, the Library of Congress makes life no easier for the librarian in need of assistance in this matter.

Some of the fundamental questions facing the librarian in this situation include: a) should the item be classified as history or anti-Semitism (or something in between) b) should the item be given a special subject heading, (such as "Holocaust-denial Literature" or the lone LC contribution, "Holocaust, Jewish [1939-1945]—Errors, inventions, etc."), or should it be provided with a more "standard" history heading? c) should the item be labeled—either in the catalogue and/or directly on the cover of the book—as a book of "Historical fabrication?" and d) should the item be placed on a special "Revisionist History" shelf; on a shelf with standard historical texts; on a shelf containing anti-Semitic materials; or in a restricted access area, where it could not be retrieved without the assistance of a librarian?

Such questions, of course, require serious consideration by the librarian and do not lend themselves to answers which are particularly clear-cut. The belief held by many librarians is that *some* effort must be made to separate or distinguish such potentially volatile material. Indeed, the placement of a Holocaust-denial text on the same shelf as that of a "valid" history of the Holocaust is looked upon by many as both insulting and misleading.

As Peattie points out, we would not expect to find the aforementioned "flat earth" and "round earth" books sitting together comfortably in the geology section of the library. Why then should we as librarians choose to shelve a "Revisionist" work, such as Richard Harwood's *Did the Six Million Really Die?* in the very same area that contains such "authentic" histories of the Holocaust as Raul Hilberg's *The Destruction of European Jews,* and Gerald Reitlinger's *The Final Solution.*

Perhaps, as Swan observes, the "sorting out" should be left to the patron. This would not only follow official association guidelines, but would also be a recognition of the patron's ability to make the "best" choices. However, certain scholars argue that such a "transfer of responsibility" might turn out to be more damaging than fruitful.

For example, if a student doing a report comes into the library in search of books on the Nazi persecution of Jews during the Second World War, it is very possible that he or she will be misled if Holocaust-denial works are mixed in with the "standard" works in the field. Moreover, if a "Revisionist" history of the Holocaust is provided in the catalogue with a "standard" subject heading (e.g. "Jews-Europe, Eastern-History" for Sanning's *The Dissolution of Eastern European Jewry*), could it not also be said that the patron, in a sense, is being misled?

Works such as *The Protocols of the Elders of Zion,* or Henry Ford's sponsored writings from his newspaper, *The Dearborn Independent-The Internationalist Jews,* are classified in the McGill University Library at DS 145, which comprises examples and studies of anti-Semitism. Their classification here—and not in social thought or general history—provides a useful signal to the reader.

Morton Weinfeld, in his "The Classification of Holocaust Denial Literature by the Library of Congress," in* Judaica Librarianship, *1986-87.

It is clear that a very definite impression may be created in the user's mind by a book's simple location on the shelf or by the access points with which it is furnished in the library catalogue. When a single "Revisionist" Holocaust history is found on the same shelf as fifteen "standard" works, that single text is afforded a certain "dignity" or, as Sowards says, a certain "implied stature." While certainly not *endorsing* the position taken by the book, the library may confer on a Holocaust-denial text a certain respectability by the seemingly simple act of classifying or shelving.

In order to illustrate the problems we have discussed in this article, it might be worthwhile to describe very briefly the recent case involving the Edmonton Public Library (EPL) and its collection of Holocaust-denial literature.

In 1984, a $2,300 federal grant was received by EPL in order to "strengthen [its] collection of Holocaust-related materials." The grant was obtained largely through the efforts of the Jewish Federation of Edmonton, and the titles chosen, subsequent to receipt of the grant, were selected by a team consisting of librarians and representatives of the Holocaust Resource Committee. The idea of "balancing" the collection with "Revisionist" material was neither considered nor discussed at the outset.

In about a year, though, a decision was made to "balance" the Holocaust history collection by adding a group of "Revisionist" histories. The decision, according to EPL Director, Vincent Richards, was based upon the demand created by the Keegstra and Zundel trials, as well as the desire to present an opposing "viewpoint." To quote Richards:

> It is the duty of a public library to provide a cross-section of the available literature, both good and bad. . . . Presumably people who come to our library are literate and trained to engage in some level of actual thinking. We have to give them access to both the revisionist books and the more conventional sources and let them decide for themselves which is valid.

The reaction to the discovery of such Holocaust-denial literature in the EPL was very strong. Led by Wojiciech Buczynski, secretary of the Polish Culture Society of Edmonton, many groups and individuals protested the existence of such material in the library. Buczynski, who came across the questionable titles while browsing the recently-expanded Holocaust section, called for the removal of every Holocaust-denial text: "(Public) libraries should not be depositories of rubbish."

On the other hand, the response of the equally-astonished Jewish Federation was that the books should remain in the library ("the library is free to buy whatever it likes") but there was a need for reclassification and restricted access. The point was made that, in spite of Richards' contention that all "Revisionist" items were "appropriately designated in the catalogue," much of the material boasted subject headings that were misleading: *Is the Diary of Anne Frank Genuine?* was catalogued by EPL under "Frank, Anne; Jews; Netherlands, Biography."

Throughout the ordeal, EPL kept the books on the shelves and defended its right to continue to keep them there, but promised to discuss the entire matter at length. While Richards expressed sympathy for those who were offended by the material and continued to deny that the mere existence of the material in the library was any indication of EPL's own philosophy, he never swayed from his opinion that such "Revisionist" literature presented an opposing viewpoint to the generally-accepted account of the Jewish experience in World War II. The debate, as of this date, goes on.

The existence of Holocaust-denial literature in the library and, in particular, the public library, has created (and will continue to create) a tremendous amount of anxiety and debate throughout the world. Such anxiety and debate, indeed, is unavoidable. There are no easy answers when it comes to deliberating between free speech and the literary propagation of hatred and lies.

What is especially intriguing about the entire issue is how supportive of the right to speak freely are those who espouse the Holocaust-denial. Doug Christie, lawyer for both Keegstra and Zundel, and founder of the ultra-rightwing Western Canada Concept, cries out: "Let freedom solve the problem of any hatred and intolerance," while Vancouver journalist Doug Collins bemoans the treatment handed out to Zundel and to the works of the "Revisionists" by declaring boldly that "witch-hunts and book burnings are as bad now as ever they were . . . the Ministry of Truth is here."

It cannot be denied that Holocaust-denial literature is designed to distort the truth, promote hatred, and advance a racist ideology. It also cannot be denied that free speech is, indeed, a right, and that the most fundamental ethic of the library profession is intellectual freedom. The problem for the librarian, therefore, is to find a way to reconcile both truths.

THE AUTHENTICITY OF ANNE FRANK'S DIARY

David Barnouw

SOURCE: "Attacks on the Authenticity of the Diary," in *The Diary of Anne Frank: The Critical Edition,* edited by David Barnouw and Gerrold van der Stroom, translated by Arnold J. Pomerans and B. M. Mooyaart-Doubleday, Viking, 1989, pp. 84-101.

[*In the following essay, Barnouw answers Holocaust revisionists who deny the authenticity of Anne Frank's diary.*]

The earliest attacks on the authenticity of Anne Frank's diary we could discover in print come in two articles published in November 1957 in the Swedish paper *Fria Ord* under the heading of "Judisk Psyke—En studie kring Anne Frank och Meyer Levin [Jewish Psyche—A Study Around Anne Frank and Meyer Levin]." Their author was Harald Nielsen, a Danish literary critic. Basing himself on a brief factual report in *De Telegraaf* of April 11, 1957, Nielsen alleged that the diary owed its final form to Meyer Levin. In support of this opinion, he produced such spurious arguments as the claim that Anne and Peter were not Jewish names. He went on to delve into the Jewish background of Meyer Levin's writing. He concluded his articles with the comment that Levin's reminiscences, published in 1951 in a book entitled *In Search,* had the advantage of undisputed authenticity.

In March 1958 the Norwegian paper *Folg og Land,* the organ of the former SS Viking Division, referred to Meyer Levin's lawsuit and went on to allege that Anne Frank's diary was very probably a forgery. One month later, part of this article was published in translation in the *Europa Korrespondenz* in Vienna, and another month later it appeared in *Reichsruf, Wochenzeitung für das nationale Deutschland,* the weekly journal of the extreme right-wing *Deutsche Reichspartei,* founded in 1950.

It is not clear whether Otto Frank himself or any of his publishers ever saw these or other attacks on the diary; in any case no legal action was taken by any of them.

This was not the case with Lothar Stielau, a high school teacher of English at the Lübeck *Oberschule zum Dom.* Stielau, who was born in 1908, had joined the NSDAP (Nazi Party) and the SA (storm troopers) in 1932 and had been a Hitler Youth leader. Ten years after the war he joined the *Deutsche Reichspartei* and in 1957 he became district chairman of the party in Lübeck. On October 10, 1958, he wrote a review of the play *Tom Sawyers grosses Abenteuer (The Adventures of Tom Sawyer)* for the *Zeitschrift der Vereinigung ehemaliger Schüler und der Freunde der Oberschule zum Dom e. V. Lübeck* (Journal of the Association of Former Students and Friends of the Lübeck *Oberschule zum Dom*), which contained the following passage:

> The forged diaries of Eva Braun, of the Queen of England and the hardly more authentic one of Anne Frank may have earned several millions for the profiteers from Germany's defeat, but they have also raised our own hackles quite a bit.

One month later Fischer Verlag had its attention drawn to Stielau's article by the *Zentralrat der Juden in Deutschland* (Central Council of German Jews) and a week later Otto Frank, who had come to the publishing house for a meeting, heard about it as well.

The Ministry of Culture in the federal state of Schleswig-Holstein then decided to determine whether Stielau, who had clearly "caused offense," had also breached his professional obligation of political neutrality. On December 5, Stielau was given the opportunity to explain the passage objected to in front of a senior official. At this interview he conceded that there was no doubt that Anne Frank had kept a diary, but went on to allege that none of the published versions of any of the diaries was anything like the original. He referred to the earlier article in the *Reichsruf* and said that he should have used the word *verfälscht* instead of *fälschen* (while *fälschen* signifies that something is entirely fake, *verfälschen* refers to an original to which greater or smaller alterations have been made). For the rest he insisted that he had been punctilious in the performance of his pedagogic duties.

That was also the view of Heinrich Buddeberg, chairman of the *Deutsche Reichspartei* in Schleswig-Holstein, who wrote a letter to the *Lübecker Nachrichten,* published on January 6, 1959, in which he described Stielau as a political victim of the Social Democrats who, with others, had been pressing for Stielau's suspension. And he, too, came up with the distorted account of the Meyer Levin story, quoting this time from the *Deutsch-Amerikanische Bürger-Zeitung* of October 2, 1958.

Buddeberg, born in 1893, was a farmer at Woltersdorf über Büchen in Schleswig-Holstein. Unlike Stielau, he refused during the preliminary examination to say anything about his political past other than that from 1933 to 1945 he had been *Kreisbauernführer* (District Farmers' Leader), which had earned him two years' internment.

On the day Buddeberg's letter was published, the first official steps were taken to have Stielau disciplined. He was alleged to have neglected his duties and to be unworthy of the respect and confidence to which the teaching profession is entitled. As a teacher, he had propagated political attitudes in conflict with his educational duties. The Ministry of Culture ordered his temporary suspension.

In January 1959, Dr. A. Flesch, a Frankfurt advocate acting for Otto Frank, and a few days later for the two publishing houses as well, laid criminal charges against Stielau and Buddeberg before the public prosecutor of the Lübeck *Landgericht*. The charges included libel, slander, insult, defamation of the memory of a dead person and anti-Semitic utterances. Dr. Flesch stated in his indictment that the manuscripts written by Anne Frank were in Amsterdam and that their authenticity could be checked. He next explained the difference between the actual diary and the Hacketts' dramatization, and emphasized that what Stielau had done was to impugn the authenticity of the diary itself and not that of the play.

The public prosecutor's office reacted very quickly: within two days of the complaint being lodged it confirmed receipt and inquired when Otto Frank had first become aware of Stielau's article.

That same month, too, the Federal Minister of Justice in Bonn asked the Schleswig-Holstein Minister of Justice to keep him informed because of the special interest of the case. The preliminary examination could begin.

In April the public prosecutor set out at the end of a long preamble the reason why it was necessary to determine the authenticity of the diary by court action, namely:

> Given the delicate nature of the attitude of foreign countries towards Germany and her people due to their National Socialist past, a judicial inquiry is the only way of arriving at a satisfactory conclusion.

If there were a conviction the court would have to take into account the accused's inner attitude (*"innere Einstellung"*) toward Jews, toward the persecution of the Jews and toward Anne Frank. Moreover, Stielau's attitude as a teacher would also be a factor.

The public prosecutor further noted that an inquiry into the authenticity of the diary would prove extraordinarily difficult, and referred to a recent article in *Der Spiegel*. The magazine, which had focused attention on Cauvern, quoted the latter as saying: "At the beginning I made a good many changes." It also claimed that the well-known clergyman J. J. Buskes had served as a spiritual guide to Otto Frank, who had granted him "censorship rights." The impression that the translation was inadequate was confirmed by a number of obvious inconsistencies in it. The article ended with the following statement by Baschwitz: "I believe that the solution of this case lies in the speedy publication of a word-for-word edition of the diary."

Stielau's first appearance before the examining magistrate, on June 18, was entirely devoted to establishing his background, past and political views. He declared that, because he had considered communism a grave threat, he had joined the NSDAP before the war, but "I was never particularly interested in questions of race, the Jewish question included." After the war he had looked for a party that suited him, one that was "unreservedly pro-German," and had ended up in the *Deutsche Reichspartei*.

Seven days later, when the examination was resumed, Stielau made the astonishing allegation that in his article he had not been referring to the published version of the diary, *Das Tagebuch der Anne Frank,* but to the play. The examining magistrate pointed out that this was something he had failed to mention to the Ministry of Culture.

Stielau wisely refused to be drawn, although he had to admit that at the time he himself had neither read the play nor seen a performance of it. He referred, however, to a number of articles in the press that had given him cause to doubt the authenticity of the diary.

It was not until April 25 of the next year that Stielau was examined again. He now refused to discuss the statements of other witnesses or the expert opinion that had meanwhile been prepared, and stuck by his earlier declaration that in 1958 he had been referring to the play. Otto Frank had been interviewed two weeks after the examination, on

July 2, 1959, of one of Stielau's colleagues about the *Journal of the Association of Former Students*. Frank stated on what date he had first been told about Stielau's article and then explained what his daughter had written originally, that those writings had been handed to him by Miep after the war, and what he had done with them after that. According to him, Cauvern had merely corrected Germanisms and grammatical errors, and that was all there was to the claim by *Der Spiegel* that Cauvern had "made a good many changes." Otto Frank had himself given information to *Der Spiegel* but was not very happy with the way his words had been reported.

The next day, during his continued examination, Otto Frank denied that any pressure had been put on him "by the clergy." He did not know the Reverend J. J. Buskes personally. He was in favor of an official investigation into the authenticity of Anne's writings; an expert was free to study all the relevant documents in Basle. The dispute with Meyer Levin was also brought up. Finally, Otto Frank agreed to appear as a witness in Lübeck if that proved necessary; all he wanted was to help remove any doubts about the authenticity of his daughter's diary.

On September 29, Bep Voskuijl and Miep and Jan Gies were heard. Each of them gave a separate account of events in the Annexe at 263, Prinsengracht, declared they had known about Anne keeping a diary, and mentioned the discovery of the diaries and the loose sheets and their return to Otto Frank.

For an expert opinion on the authenticity of the diary, the examining magistrate turned to the *Institut für Zeitgeschichte* in Munich. The Institute, however, advised that the case called for philological and graphological rather than historical expertise. Moreover, since no member of the Institute was proficient in the Dutch language they could do no more than recommend two professors of Dutch studies, one in Münster and the other in Berlin.

It was decided to look closer to home, and at the end of September 1959, Dr. Annemarie Hübner of Hamburg University declared herself willing to prepare an expert assessment of *Das Tagebuch der Anne Frank*. She would investigate whether there had been crucial changes between the so-called Typescript II and the German edition, and what the omissions and additions amounted to. In addition she would try to determine whether the German could be considered a "true" and "faithful" translation of the original.

The Hamburg handwriting expert Minna Becker, for her part, was asked to determine whether the diaries in the possession of Otto Frank and the loose sheets had been written by the same person who had written a letter on December 13, 1940, and two postcards on July 25, 1941, and July 5, 1942, all of which had been signed "Anne."

After formal instruction on October 13, 1959, Dr. Hübner, Mrs. Becker and Dorothea Ockelmann—who had been added by the examining magistrate to the panel of experts at a later stage—traveled to Basle to make their investigations on the spot. Mrs. Becker and Mrs. Ockelmann concluded in their report, dated March 7, 1960, and running to 131 pages, that all the written entries in Diaries

1, 2 and 3, including the pages that had been pasted in, the loose sheets and all improvements and additions were "identical" with the specimen handwriting of Anne Frank. They did not mention that a pasted-in letter from Otto Frank, a card from "Jacque" and a birthday card from Ruth Cauvern had been included in Diary I.

The examining magistrate also asked them to determine which had been written first—Diaries 1, 2 and 3 or the loose sheets? Mrs. Becker and Mrs. Ockelmann both concluded that the loose sheets had not been written before Diaries 1, 2 and 3.

A month later Dr. Hübner handed in her report to the examining magistrate. Although it had not been part of her brief, she had perforce looked first of all into the relationship between the manuscripts and Typescript II. Her conclusion:

> The text of the printed manuscript [= Typescript II] must be considered authentic by virtue of its substance, the ideas expressed in it and its form.

> The translation must be considered to correspond [to the original] and on the whole to be factually correct. There are mistakes in translation and these are to be deprecated, but most of them can be considered minor faults which are immaterial to an understanding of the total context.

Dr. Hübner concluded that "the text published in German translation as *Das Tagebuch der Anne Frank* may be considered true to its sources in substance and ideas."

Stielau was defended by Professor Dr. Noack and by Dr. Noack, both from Kiel. In May 1960, they submitted their objections to Dr. Hübner's opinion to the examining magistrate in writing. They questioned Dr. Hübner's qualifications, arguing that her academic status (*"Dozent ohne Lehrauftrag,"* literally "lecturer without a teaching assignment") was not such as to entitle her to give an expert opinion in the field of "comparative philology." Her opinion was therefore dismissed by them as "worthless." This argument appeared to impress the public prosecutor, who communicated it to the Schleswig-Holstein Minister of Justice and added that it seemed advisable, even during the preliminary investigation, to appoint an *Obergutachter* ("senior assessor").

One month later the public prosecutor commented on Dr. Hübner's actual findings. There were two central questions, namely, whether *Das Tagebuch der Anne Frank* was authentic in "documentary" respects (which seemed unlikely in view of the changes) and whether it was authentic in literary respects. The second question could not be answered by Dr. Hübner because she lacked the qualifications to do so.

In July 1960, Professor Dr. Friedrich Sieburg, a well-known publicist and a contributor to the *Frankfurter Allgemeine Zeitung,* was formally asked to be the senior assessor and to prepare an expert opinion, though the precise terms of his brief were not made clear.

Stielau's lawyers had other strings to their bow. In a letter to the examining magistrate they complained that the preliminary investigation had started from the wrong premise, since the article to which the plaintiff objected had referred to the play, not to the book. Moreover, Stielau had been shocked by the fact that adaptations not faithful to the text had been used to make money, and also by the fact that the U.S. edition had contained a photograph, not of Anne, but of one of the actresses who had played her. Further, Noack and Noack submitted that Albert Hackett, and to a lesser extent his wife, had been Communist fellow travelers since 1937; their source for this information was a series of reports by the California Un-American Activities Committee. In the circumstances, it was not at all surprising that Stielau had not wanted to see the play.

Although Noack and Noack had argued earlier that Dr. Hübner's opinion was "worthless" they felt free to make use of it. After all, she had discovered differences between the original "document" and the translation, and Noack and Noack concluded that the translation was no longer "a document": "A document must be authentic word for word, or else it is not a document."

On October 30, 1960, Sieburg concluded his expert opinion, and Noack and Noack turned their attention to it in December that year. They argued, with justification, that it was difficult to come to grips with the expert opinion since it had not been addressed to any specific question: "It is impossible to tell from the opinion which question the expert is actually trying to answer, nor is it known which question he should have answered."

Sieburg had confined himself in his report to the content and the importance of *Das Tagebuch der Anne Frank*; he did not consider it his task to review the manuscripts or the quality of the translation, not least because he had no Dutch. He did nevertheless refer to Diaries 1, 2 and 3, the loose sheets and the "Tales," though his comments were clearly based on Dr. Hübner's opinion, a fact he failed to mention. Sieburg seemed to think that, in view of the large number of loose sheets (which he had never seen), it must have been necessary to make a selection from them. However this selection in no way affected the picture that Anne Frank had drawn of her life.

An important part of Sieburg's evidence concerned the absurdity of forging the diary of a completely unknown person. Moreover the diary contains references to events, for instance the persecution of the Jewish people, which had been confirmed from thousands of historical sources.

Noack and Noack dismissed this expert opinion, too, as completely "worthless," and returned to the changes discovered by Dr. Hübner, the better to prove that the diary "lacked youthfulness and had been schematized and systematized."

In fact, Mrs. Becker's and Mrs. Ockelmann's conclusion that everything in the diary was by Anne's hand was not correct, in view of the pasted-in letter, the postcard and the birthday card, none of which had been written by her. . . .

There are also several objections to Dr. Hübner's conclusion that the German translation must be judged by its substance and the ideas expressed. There is no doubt that the translator made Anne "more adult" than she was and omitted items from the translation that the German public might have found "embarrassing."

The purpose of Sieburg's expert opinion remains unclear. His contribution is no more than an essay on the importance of *Das Tagebuch der Anne Frank.*

A few weeks after Noack and Noack's last letter, the public prosecutor was ready to present his case against Stielau and Buddeberg. The indictment was characterized by its thoroughness. It contained a summary of what the accused had done, what the witnesses had stated, and of the evidence three of the expert witnesses had submitted. Next it went into why Stielau's belated assertion that he had been referring to the play and not to the diary was unacceptable. Stielau's wording, the comparison with the two other diaries, the framework within which the remark had been made, Stielau's statement to the official in the Ministry of Culture, the newspaper articles he had quoted, none of which dealt with the play, together with the fact that Stielau was not even familiar with the dramatization of the diary—all served to rebut the submissions of the defense.

Stielau and Buddeberg had furthermore been guilty of *"üble Nachrede"* (libel: Article 186 of the German Penal Code) by denying the authenticity of the diary, and of *"Beleidigung"* (defamation: Article 185) by using the term "profiteers from Germany's defeat." These offenses were punishable with a fine or a maximum prison sentence of two years. The public prosecutor asked for the case to be heard before the *Landgericht* (regional court) in Lübeck.

In their objection Stielau's lawyers repeated that their client had been referring to the play and not to the book. For an opinion of the play they asked the court to call Hans Gomperts, drama critic of *Het Parool,* who, according to *Der Spiegel* of October 10, 1956, had described the dramatic adaptation as "Kitsch sailing under false colors." Now, Gomperts had admittedly used these words in his review of the U.S. premiere of the play, but he reversed that opinion in his review of the Dutch premiere.

In June the Third Criminal Division of the Lübeck *Landgericht* concluded that Stielau and Buddeberg had a case to answer.

In the end, on October 17, 1961, three years after Stielau had published his article, the whole case simply petered out. Before it had a chance to come to court, Stielau's and Buddeberg's lawyers on the one hand, and Otto Frank's and the publishers' lawyers on the other, had arrived at a settlement. All that the court had left to do was to assess costs. The settlement was put in writing.

Stielau and Buddeberg declared that the preliminary investigation had convinced them that Stielau had had no grounds for claiming that the diary was a forgery—the expert opinions and the evidence of witnesses had persuaded them of the contrary. They expressed regret for their statements, which they had made with no attempt at verification. Stielau also withdrew the phrase "profiteers from Germany's defeat" with expressions of regret.

Stielau and Buddeberg declared further that they had

meant no offense to either Otto Frank or the publishers, or to sully the memory of Anne Frank. Otto Frank and the publishers, for their part, acknowledged that preliminary examination had revealed no anti-Semitic tendencies on the part of the defendants.

The defendants agreed to the publication of the terms of this settlement, and Otto Frank and the publishers declared that they would drop criminal proceedings. Stielau agreed to contribute DM 1,000 to the legal costs.

From newspaper reports about the case and statements made later by Otto Frank it appeared that the presiding judge had pressed them to reach a settlement. He had argued that if the injured party declared itself satisfied with a public apology by the offender this was to be preferred to a judicial sentence. Moreover, according to the judge, the continuation of the case would have raised domestic and foreign issues which, although not directly, or at most marginally, connected with it, could have invited unwelcome repercussions.

This was a nebulous argument but one that was given more concrete form perhaps by a letter from Otto Frank to Heinz Roth in which we read that his lawyer had told Otto Frank on October 17 that, had the case been continued, the defendant would have received a very light sentence. The judge was afraid that he would then have been accused by a large section of the press of being too lenient in his treatment of Nazis. Because he, Otto Frank, was not concerned with revenge but only with the authenticity of the diary, he had agreed to the settlement.

The question of the high costs of the preliminary examination was also settled in a somewhat unsatisfactory manner. Stielau offered to contribute DM 1,000, but Buddeberg refused to pay anything, and the bench agreed that he need not. The remaining sum, DM 10,000, would be paid by the state.

On the day after the hearing, *Vrij Nederland* quoted approvingly a headline from the West German *Bildzeitung*: "High school teacher libels Anne Frank [. . .] but judge lets him off."

Otto Frank may have been satisfied at the time, but later he regretted the settlement. "Had I but known that there would be people who would consider a settlement in this case as insufficient proof [of the authenticity of the diary], I should certainly not have dropped the case."

The fact that the bench had established the authenticity of Anne Frank's diary did not put an end to the allegations.

In January 1959, even before the Stielau case, the Vienna *Europa Korrespondenz* had published an article with the title "Der Anne Frank-Skandal. Ein Beitrag zur Wahrheit [The Anne Frank Scandal. A Contribution to the Truth]," in which Dr. Louis de Jong, until 1979 director of the Netherlands State Institute for War Documentation, was alleged to have been the real author of the diary.

> The father came back to Amsterdam after the war, learned about the alleged diary, did not want to publish it, but was practically forced to do so by his friends. The Dutch journalist Louis

de Jong, now director of the Netherlands State Institute for War Documentation, was crucially involved in the diary, and from the publications it is clear that De Jong is the author of the book.

In October 1957, De Jong had admittedly written an article on Anne Frank which had appeared in the *Reader's Digest,* and later in foreign editions of that magazine, but there is nothing to indicate that De Jong ever had anything to do with the publication of *Het Achterhuis.*

In the course of the next few decades the authenticity of the diary was to be challenged in various journals and writings.

Thus, in the summer of 1967, Teressa Hendry took aim at the diary's authenticity in the *American Mercury.* She claimed that its real author had been Meyer Levin and went on to quote in English what was allegedly a summary of the *Fria Ord* articles published in the *Economic Council Letter* on April 15, 1959:

> History has many examples of myths that live a longer and richer life than the truth, and may become more effective than truth.

> The Western World has for some years been aware of a Jewish girl through the medium of what purports to be her personally written story, "Anne Frank's Diary." Any informed literary inspection of this book would have shown it to have been impossible as the work of a teenager.

> A noteworthy decision of the New York Supreme Court confirms this point of view, in that the well known American Jewish writer, Meyer Levin, has been awarded $50,000 to be paid him by the father of Anne Frank as an honorarium for Levin's work on the "Anne Frank Diary."

> Mr. Frank, in Switzerland, has promised to pay to his race-kin, Meyer Levin, not less than $50,000 because he had used the dialogue of Author Levin just as it was and "implanted" it in the diary as being his daughter's intellectual work.

However, neither the judgment of the court nor the sum mentioned appeared in the two *Fria Ord* articles.

The *American Mercury* article is typical of the way in which right-wing extremists have challenged and continue to challenge the authenticity of the diary: they like to refer to earlier publications and to quote from them in such a way as to suggest that what has merely been alleged is "really true." Several years later the article in the *Economic Council Letter* was used again, in a pamphlet called *Did Six Million Really Die? The Truth at Last.* Its author was Richard Harwood, a pseudonym of Richard Verrall of the extreme-right-wing British National Front. German and Dutch translations of the pamphlet were published in 1975 and 1976 respectively.

Teressa Hendry had used a question mark at the end of the title of her article: "Was Anne Frank's Diary a Hoax?"; Harwood, however, wrote unequivocally: "Bestseller a hoax." His article ended with: "Here, then, is just one more fraud in a whole series of frauds in support of the 'Holocaust' legend and the saga of the Six Million."

In 1975, David Irving, the extreme-right-wing British historian, had this to say in the Introduction to his book *Hitler und seine Feldherren* (Hitler and His Generals):

> Many forgeries are on record, as for instance that of the "Diary of Anne Frank" (in this case a civil lawsuit brought by a New York scriptwriter has proved that he wrote it in collaboration with the girl's father).

Otto Frank protested successfully to the publishers, and the passage was omitted when the book was reprinted. However, because a large number of copies of the first impression had been sold, Otto Frank also asked for damages to be paid to the Anne Frank Foundation in Amsterdam; this too was done.

That same year Richard Harwood's publishers brought out a book by an American, A. R. Butz, called *The Hoax of the Twentieth Century,* a mainly demographic study in which the author denied the "Final Solution." He went at length into the existing literature, the better to suggest that he was a serious scholar. Here again Anne Frank's diary played a part, albeit a subsidiary one:

> The question of the authenticity of the diary is not considered important enough to examine here; I will only remark that I have looked it over and don't believe it. For example, already on page 2 one is reading an essay on why a 13 year old girl would start a diary, and then page 3 gives a short history of the Frank family and then quickly reviews the specific anti-Jewish measures that followed the German occupation in 1940. The rest of the book is in the same historical spirit.

The first book of any size to be devoted exclusively to the so-called unmasking of the diary appeared in 1978. *Anne Frank Diary—A Hoax?* was written by Ditlieb Felderer from Sweden, whose own publishing house, Bible Researcher, had also published such books as *Zionism: The Hidden Tyranny.*

Felderer conceded that there was no truth in the story that Meyer Levin had written the diary but used a different line of attack, as witness some of his chapter headings: "Drug Addict at Tender Age" ("proven" by the fact that Anne wrote on September 16, 1943, that she swallowed valerian pills every day); "Anne's Character—Not Even a Nice Girl"; "Teenage Sex"; "Sexual Extravaganza" (Anne's entries about her growing love for Peter are styled by Felderer "the first child porno"). Felderer went on to "unmask" the diary as "a forgery, a monstrous travesty."

In the United States people were not yet ready to drop the Meyer Levin myth; on May 1, 1978, Teressa Hendry's article was reprinted in the Washington weekly *The Spotlight.*

That year also saw the foundation of the Institute for Historical Review in Torrance, California, by Willis Carto, director of the Noontide Press, a man closely involved in the *American Mercury* and the Liberty Lobby, publishers of *The Spotlight.* The Institute championed the so-called revisionist approach to history, and to the history of the Second World War in particular. Now, there had been a trend among a small group of American historians ever since the First World War to take a special interest both in the question of war guilt and in why the United States had become involved. This trend resurfaced after the Second World War. It included serious historians, who, for example, reexamined the causes of, and responsibility for, the outbreak of the war, as well as a number of persons who wrote of Nazi Germany in nothing but positive terms, minimizing Nazi war crimes. This second group took on itself the title of "revisionists." The group's "revisions" were so many denials of the persecution of the Jews and the existence of the gas chambers.

The Institute for Historical Review tried to act as an umbrella organization for all these separately operating "revisionists" by distributing "revisionist" and blatantly Nazi literature and, from 1979 onward, by organizing an annual Revisionist Conference at which European "revisionists" were also welcome. The first issue of the quarterly *Journal of Historical Review,* devoted in the main to the lectures delivered at the annual conferences, appeared in 1980.

The obvious purpose of all these activities was to provide anti-Semitism and neo-Nazism with an ostensibly scientific foundation.

In Germany, too, there were fresh stirrings. In 1976, Anne Frank's diary was again the subject of a court case, heard this time by the *Landgericht* in Frankfurt following the activities of Heinz Roth, an architect from Odenhausen, north of the city.

In 1975, Roth, whose own publishing house issued neo-Nazi brochures, began to distribute pamphlets with such titles as '*Anne Franks Tagebuch—eine Fälschung (Anne Frank's Diary—A Forgery)* and *Anne Franks Tagebuch—der grosse Schwindel (Anne Frank's Diary—The Big Fraud)*. Quoting Irving and Harwood, he referred again to the old story that Otto Frank had written the diary with the help of a New York playwright. In December 1975 a quotation from one of his pamphlets appeared in the *"Leserbriefe"* (readers' letters column) of the Austrian periodical *Neue Ordnung*. When Otto Frank heard about this, he made a request to the editor of *Neue Ordnung* that a letter by himself be published in the same column setting out the successful outcome of his protests against David Irving's Introduction, and stating that the Lübeck *Landgericht* had established the authenticity of the diary. We do not know whether or not this letter was in fact published.

Otto Frank sent a copy of his letter to Heinz Roth, who continued to maintain in the ensuing correspondence that he was concerned with the *"reine historische Wahrheit* [pure historical truth]," and continued to refuse to enter into Otto Frank's detailed arguments.

Roth's activities had not escaped the notice of the German Department of Justice, and after a preliminary legal investigation had been ordered against a distributor of one of Roth's pamphlets, the Bochum public prosecutor inquired of Otto Frank in February 1976 if he had already laid criminal charges. The public prosecutor wanted to know when Frank had first heard about the pamphlet in ques-

tion; this because of the statute of limitations. Otto Frank replied a few weeks later; he had first heard about the pamphlet in September 1975 and although he had been indignant he had taken no steps because of his age and his health. He enclosed photocopies of his correspondence with Wappen Verlag, the publishers of *Neue Ordnung* (who had not replied), and with Roth, and added that the latter was "stubborn and intractable." This was written by Otto Frank following a performance of the Anne Frank play on February 3, 1976, in Hamburg at which Roth's pamphlet had been distributed, and he asked if it would be possible to proceed not only against the distributor of Roth's pamphlet but also against Roth himself. On July 16, 1976, following the publication of one of Roth's later pamphlets, *Das Tagebuch der Anne Frank—Wahrheit oder Fälschung? (The Diary of Anne Frank—Truth or Forgery?)*, Otto Frank applied for an injunction to restrain Roth from using certain expressions in the future.

From the information available, we gather that the Frankfurt *Landgericht* decided on July 22, 1978, that Heinz Roth would incur a maximum fine of DM 500,000 or a maximum prison sentence of six months if he repeated any of the following statements in public:

> a) "Anne Frank's diary—a forgery."

> b) "This world-famous best-seller is a forgery."

> c) "Millions of schoolchildren have been forced and are still being forced to read this fake . . . —and now it turns out that it is the product of a New York scriptwriter in collaboration with the girl's father!"

> d) "This fraud was exposed for the first time not just recently but over a decade ago!"

From its deliberations it appears that the bench considered the expert opinions given at the preliminary examination in Lübeck and the statements of the various witnesses carried sufficient weight to refute Roth's allegations. Roth's lawyers had also submitted an expert opinion, which was to play an important part over the years in attacks on the authenticity of the diary. It took the form of a study by Robert Faurisson, to which we shall now turn our attention.

Faurisson, of the Department of Literature at the University of Lyons, produced his expert opinion, written in German, in 1978. It was published two years later in France under the title of *Le Journal d'Anne Frank est-il authentique? (The Diary of Anne Frank—Is It Authentic?)*. In 1985 a Dutch translation was published in Belgium under the title of *Het Dagboek van Anne Frank—een vervalsing (The Diary of Anne Frank—a Forgery)*, this time without the question mark. For the purposes of his investigation, Faurisson had examined the published diary in the French translation, compared the Dutch edition with the German, spoken to Otto Frank in Basle and gone into the circumstances of those who had been in hiding and of their arrest in August 1944.

It goes without saying that a life in hiding carried countless risks; the possibility of discovery was ever present, and many thousands of those who hid from the Germans did indeed fall into enemy hands as a result of betrayal, accident or their own carelessness.

From the diary it appears that the inhabitants of the Annexe, too, had to brave many dangers, not least the chance that they might make too much noise and be overheard. Faurisson, however, did not examine the overall picture of life in hiding in any depth, or concern himself greatly in this context with the fact that the Frank family and their fellow fugitives were in the end arrested. On the contrary, he used his findings only in order to demonstrate that it must have been impossible to hide in the Annexe and that therefore the diary could not have been written by Anne Frank.

A typical example of his approach is the way in which he examined the problem of noise as presented in *Het Achterhuis:*

> Let us take the case of noise. The people in hiding, we are told, are not allowed to make the slightest noise, to the extent that if they cough they are made quickly to take some codeine. The "enemies" might hear them. The walls are so "thin" (March 25, 1943). The "enemies" are very numerous: Lewin, who "knows the whole building well" (October 1, 1942), the men in the warehouse, the clients, the tradesmen, the postman, the *charwoman,* Slagter the *nightwatchman,* the sanitary department, the bookkeeper, the police flushing people out of their homes, neighbors near and far, the owner of the building, etc. It is therefore improbable, even inconceivable, that Mrs. van Daan should have been in the habit of using *the vacuum cleaner* daily at 12:30 (August 5, 1943). Vacuum cleaners at that time were exceptionally noisy. I must ask: "Is this credible?" My question is not just a formality. It is not rhetorical. Its purpose is not to astonish. My question is simply a question. An answer will have to be found. That question could be followed by forty others concerning noise. The use of an *alarm clock,* for instance, needs explanation (August 4, 1943). The noisy *carpentry* must be explained: dismantling wooden stairs, turning a door into a movable cupboard (August 21, 1942), making a wooden candlestick (December 7, 1942). Peter chops wood in the loft in front of the open window (February 23, 1944). There is mention of making "a few little cupboards for the walls and other odds and ends" with wood from the attic (July 11, 1942). There is even talk of building a little compartment in the attic as a place to work in (July 13, 1943). There is the almost constant noise of the *radio,* the *slamming of doors,* the *incessant shouting* (December 6, 1943), the *rows,* the *crying,* the *clamor,* the *"noise . . . enough to waken the dead"* (November 9, 1942), "a *great din and disturbance* followed [. . .] I was doubled up with *laughter"* (May 10, 1944). The episode described on September 2, 1942, cannot be reconciled with the need for keeping quiet and for discretion. We see the people in hiding sitting at table. They *chatter gaily.* Suddenly there is *a piercing whistle* and they hear Peter's voice *calling* down the chimney saying that he isn't coming down anyway. Mr. van Daan springs to his feet, his napkin

falls to the floor and scarlet in the face he *shouts*: "I've had enough of this." He goes up to the attic and then we hear *a good deal of resistance and stamping.* The episode recorded on December 10, 1942, was of the same type. We see Mrs. van Daan being attended to by the dentist, Dussel. With his scraper he touches a bad tooth. Mrs. van Daan utters "incoherent cries." She tries to pull the thing out of her mouth. The dentist stands with hands against his sides calmly watching the little comedy. The rest of the audience *"roared with laughter."* Anne is not in the least anxious about the screams and the roars of laughter. Instead she says: "It was rotten of us, because I for one am quite sure that I should have screamed even louder."

Given the above extract, we have no need to subject all the examples mentioned by Faurisson to review. We shall make use of just three examples in order to highlight Faurisson's method.

A comparison with the diary will show that to prove his point Faurisson relates his chosen examples in part only. Thus the fact that Mrs. van Daan should have used the vacuum cleaner daily at twelve-thirty (August 5, 1943) is indeed mentioned by Anne on that date, but the sentence before reveals: "The warehousemen have gone home now."

On December 6, 1943, Anne refers to "resounding . . . laughter" (the "incessant shouting" is our translation of Faurisson's *"cris interminables"* whereas the French translation of *Het Achterhuis* has *"éclats de rire interminables").* Again Faurisson fails to mention that Anne sets this scene on a Sunday evening (December 5).

On November 9, 1942, Anne recorded that a sack of brown beans had burst open and that "the noise was enough to wake the dead." Faurisson omits to quote the next sentence: "(Thank God there were no strangers in the house.)"

In the spring of 1977, Faurisson called on Otto Frank, and in the presence of Frank's wife asked a number of questions concerning his time in hiding and the way *Het Achterhuis* had come to be written. Faurisson's account of this conversation gives the impression that Otto Frank was entangled in all sorts of contradictions: "The interview turned out to be grueling for Anne Frank's father." Eighteen months later Otto Frank, in a written commentary on Faurisson's study and in particular on Faurisson's report of their conversation, challenged most of what Faurisson had put into his mouth.

A few items examined by Faurisson have already been discussed. They concern the background of *Het Achterhuis,* the disparities between *Het Achterhuis* and the translations, particularly the German, and the course of events surrounding the arrest of the Frank family.

One point will suffice to clarify Faurisson's work method. In his story of the arrest he mentions a witness "who, I believe, is well informed and of good faith and at the same time has a good memory. [. . .] I have promised to keep his name secret. [. . .] The name and address of this witness [. . .] have been noted in a sealed envelope." A photograph of this sealed envelope is printed as an appendix to Faurisson's "investigation," albeit only in the French version of 1980; the publisher of the Dutch version had the sense to leave out this piece of evidence.

In the same year that the French edition of Faurisson's study appeared, his new book, *Mémoire en défense,* was published in Paris. In it he denied, not for the first time, the existence of the gas chambers and defended himself against those who accused him of falsifying history. The introduction by Noam Chomsky, the distinguished U.S. linguistic philosopher and well-known opponent of United States policy in Vietnam, caused a sensation. Chomsky declared that he would defend freedom of speech everywhere and at all times, even if Faurisson were an anti-Semite or a fanatical Nazi apologist.

In 1981, Faurisson was called before a French judge in order to substantiate his statement on the radio and in various publications that the gas chambers had never existed. He received a three-month suspended prison sentence and was ordered to pay fines and damages for defamation, incitement to discrimination, race hatred and racial violence. The sentence was confirmed on appeal.

And it was Faurisson's study that was presented as expert evidence during Roth's appeal to the Frankfurt *Oberlandesgericht* (Higher Regional Court) against his sentence. Roth continued to insist that his doubts concerning the authenticity of the diary were justified. He based that claim on the *Der Spiegel* article of April 1959 and also on statements by Harwood, Butz and Faurisson. The court, however, did not seem very impressed and found that Roth had been unable to substantiate his allegations. His appeal was rejected on July 5, 1979; after having taken all the submissions into consideration, the court concluded:

> From the foregoing we must concur with the *Landgericht* that the accused has not succeeded in establishing the truth of his allegations, and that he has failed to submit any evidence that would result in a different conclusion. As a consequence the plaintiff is entitled to demand that he cease from making these claims and from propagating them in future.

Although Roth had died in November 1978, the *Bundesgerichtshof* (the Federal High Court) referred the case back to the Frankfurt *Oberlandesgericht* on December 6, 1980. In the view of the *Bundesgerichtshof* the case concerned not only the good name of Otto Frank but also the not unimportant role of "proprietary interests," by which the court was probably referring to royalties, although no specific mention of them was made. Otto Frank died on August 19, 1980, so that the question now involved his heirs. The *Bundesgerichtshof* took the view that the court had confined itself to the question of whether Meyer Levin and Otto Frank had jointly written the diary, a claim that had proved to be false. Roth had not, however, been given enough opportunity to prove his allegations that the diary was a *"Fälschung* [forgery]"; he was to be given that opportunity during the review of the case. The fact that the accused had been dead for two years was plainly irrelevant.

While the case against Roth came to a rather unsatisfacto-

ry conclusion, two other cases actually ended in aquittals. In July 1978, E. Schönborn, chairman of the extreme-right-wing *Kampfbund Deutscher Soldaten* (Combat League of German Soldiers), distributed pamphlets outside the Anne Frank Schools in Frankfurt and Nuremberg claiming, *inter alia,* that the diary of Anne Frank was "a forgery and the product of a Jewish anti-German atrocity propaganda campaign intended to support the lie about the six million gassed Jews and to finance the state of Israel." So read the report in *De Volkskrant.*

According to the same daily newspaper, the prosecution asked for a ten-month suspended sentence, but the judge held that Schönborn, too, had the right of free speech. Schönborn, the judge went on to say, had acted within the law inasmuch as he had not denied human rights to any Jews. He was therefore acquitted. The judge, according to *De Volkskrant,* did not exonerate Schönborn, he had simply held that a sentence for defamation must be consequent upon charges being laid by those personally affected.

The second case was heard in Stuttgart. Here a former Hitler Youth leader called Werner Kuhnt, who after the war became editor-in-chief of the extreme-right-wing monthly *Deutsche Stimme,* was charged with *Volksverhetzung* (incitement of the people) and defaming the memory of a dead person. Kuhnt had stated in the issue of October 1979 that Anne Frank's diary was "a forgery" and "a fraud," that it had not been written by Anne and that it was the result of "collaboration between a New York scriptwriter and the girl's father." In June 1980, Kuhnt was acquitted by the Stuttgart *Amtsgericht* (district court). The public prosecutor entered an appeal.

On October 27, 1980, the appeal was heard before the Stuttgart *Landgericht* (regional court), which found that the charge of inciting the people could not be substantiated, that there had been no evidence of anti-Semitism and that Kuhnt had in no way insulted human dignity. As far as the misleading statement in Kuhnt's article was concerned, the bench found that Otto Frank should have lodged a complaint, which he had failed to do. The appeal was therefore dismissed and Kuhnt acquitted.

At the end of February and the beginning of March 1976 it came to the notice of the police in Hamburg that pamphlets had been handed out after performances of the play there. The pamphlets were headed "Best-Seller—a Fraud" and repeated the old Meyer Levin allegation. The pamphlet was, in fact, a reprint of two pages from the German translation of Harwood's *Did Six Million Really Die? The Truth at Last,* and had been distributed, it appeared, by Ernst Römer, born in 1904. On January 13, 1977, almost a year later, Römer was fined DM 1,500 for defamation by the Hamburg *Amtsgericht.* He appealed, and his case was heard on August 21, 1978, before the Hamburg *Landgericht.* During the hearing the journalist Edgar Geiss, born in 1929, distributed pamphlets in the courtroom alleging in effect that the diary was "a fraud."

Geiss was also taken to court, and in April of the following year the *Amtsgericht* sentenced him to one year in prison for defamation. His sentence was more severe than Römer's because he had several previous convictions.

Geiss, too, appealed, and three months later the *Landgericht* decided to hear the cases of Römer and Geiss jointly.

The *Bundeskriminalamt* (the BKA, or Federal Criminal Investigation Bureau) in Wiesbaden was charged with preparing an expert opinion on whether it was possible "by an examination of paper and writing material to establish that the writings attributed to Anne Frank were produced during the years 1941 to 1944."

The investigation—in the spring of 1980—was therefore restricted by this limited brief. The BKA came to the conclusion that the types of paper used, including the covers of Diaries 1, 2 and 3, as well as the types of ink found in the three diaries and on the loose sheets, were all manufactured before 1950-51 (and could thus have been used during the stated period). On the other hand:

> Some of the corrections made subsequently on the loose pages were [. . .] written in black, green and blue ballpen ink. Ballpen ink of this type has only been on the market since 1951.

The BKA report ran to a mere four pages. The precise location of the corrections on the loose sheets and their nature and extent are not mentioned, nor is the number of such corrections.

In itself this was a less than sensational report and did not touch upon the authenticity of the diary as such. That was not, however, the view of *Der Spiegel,* which on October 6, 1980, published a long article with the following introductory paragraph printed in bold type:

> Proved by a *Bundeskriminalamt* report: "The Diary of Anne Frank" was edited at a later date. Further doubt is therefore cast on the authenticity of that document.

It was a suggestive article in other respects too. Without asking when the writing in ballpoint had been made on the loose sheets, what the nature of these corrections was or whether they had been incorporated in the published texts, the author of the article, instead of referring to *Korrecturen* (corrections) as the BKA had done, wrote of "additions to the original that up till now had always been considered to be in the same hand as the rest of the text."

In support of the phrase "up till now had always been considered," the reader was referred to Minna Becker's mistaken 1960 opinion. *Der Spiegel* added: "Now if the handwriting of the original entries matched that of the additions, then there must have been an impostor at work," which, the magazine generously conceded, "cannot be seriously maintained even now in view of the controversial nature of graphological evidence."

It is only towards the end of the article that *Der Spiegel* quotes briefly from the BKA report and uses the term "*Korrekturen*"; before that, however, the reader had been told that the published diary had been subjected to countless "*Manipulationen* [manipulations]."

True, *Der Spiegel* also pointed out that those who had cast doubt on the authenticity of the diary had done so for the purpose of establishing "the truth about the persecution of the Jews," in manner, as the magazine remarked critically, of "one of the pamphlet distributors at the Römer trial who wanted to put a stop to the 'gas chamber fraud.' "

David Irving, too, was portrayed critically, as was the "oft-repeated legend" that Otto Frank had incorporated quotations from a film script (what was meant, of course, was from the text of a play) into the diary.

The article aroused great interest both in Germany and abroad. *Der Spiegel*'s message seemed clear: there was something wrong. Members of the Anne Frank Foundation let it be known in the Dutch press that, at the request of Otto Frank, Kleiman had made minor corrections to the manuscript after the war but that these had simply been clarifications.

We have just called the *Spiegel* article suggestive. The magazine had, however, been indirectly encouraged to take this line by the failure of the *Bundeskriminalamt* to publish the concrete data on which it had based its findings, thus rendering any kind of verification impossible.

We asked the *Bundeskriminalamt* to put these data at our disposal. The reply was that no such data were in their possession.

On December 20, 1985, at our request, the BKA then used the State Forensic Science Laboratory of the Netherlands Ministry of Justice in Rijswijk in an attempt to give concrete expression to the findings of their report.

They were in part successful. The reader is referred to Chapter VI of the State Forensic Science Laboratory's report [in *The Diary of Anne Frank. The Critical Edition*], which also discusses the relevance of the ballpoint writing to the authenticity of the diary.

The BKA was unable to indicate where just one alleged correction in green ballpoint ink was to be found.

Ian R. Barnes and Vivienne R. P. Barnes

SOURCE: "A 'Revisionist Historian' Manipulates Anne Frank's Diary," in *Patterns of Prejudice*, Vol. 15, No. 1, January, 1981, pp. 27-32.

[*In the following essay, the critics address the contention of Swedish revisionist Ditlieb Felderer that Anne Frank's diary is a falsified document.*]

To assert that Anne Frank constitutes the 'pinnacle of the Holocaust theory' is a gross distortion of history. The claim is made by the Swedish 'revisionist historian' Ditlieb Felderer who strives his utmost to expose Anne's diary as a fraud. The allegations and accusations levelled in his book continue the type of 'yellow press' writing found in his *Bible Researcher,* run from the Stockholm suburb of Täby. This 'broadsheet' indulges in revisionist 'history', attacks upon the Anne Frank diary, and spiteful vituperation towards the recently deceased Otto Frank. Anne's father is accused of participating in a form of racist activity by spreading hate towards and denigrating Arabs. He is seen as part of a 'fascist gang of dictatorial hoodlums', who purvey an 'Anne Frank concoction to be a fake used in foisting support for Zionist gangsterism and to peddle the now so odious Zion-Racism.' Felderer writes:

> All the way back in antiquity the Zionists have peddled their ware, a disease far worse than the leprous plague. In this way they have brought havoc, confusion, butcheries, cruelties and death to millions of innocent people. Wherever they have tread—crime, corruption, perversion and pornography has come. Whoever has aligned himself with them has finally become victim of their crime and succumbed to their satanism. The Zion-racists continue on to our present day to whore their race merchandise, often under the guise of equality, brotherhood and democracy. In truth, their form of 'democracy' is no other thing but a chronic state of demonocracy—a rule by incarnated demons.

Felderer apparently subscribes to the old conspiracy theory. His attacks upon the Diary continue his basic theme of a plot by people with unmentionable habits. A complete section of his book is concerned with proving that Jews have a preoccupation with the anus. This is used to explain why the Diary indulges in 'lavatorial' descriptions, ignoring the fact that the Diary is a faithful reflection of a distinctly cramped environment providing very little privacy.

Prior to examining Felderer's work, an investigation into his wider environment and activities will clarify his political position, and the basis of his intellectual pornography. In Sweden, Felderer has distributed leaflets at schools urging pupils to question orthodox accounts of Nazi crimes. So far his impact does not seem to have been significant: Ulf Lindström at the Department of Political Science, University of Umeå in Sweden, who researches into Swedish rightwing radicalism, has heard of neither the *Bible Researcher* nor Felderer. This might explain Felderer's move to the international arena where he can receive more attention, especially in the USA.

His book has been published by the California-based Institute for Historical Review which has a United Kingdom distributor in the Historical Review Press, Chapel Ascote, Ladbroke, Southam, Warwickshire. The Institute has held two conventions: the first in 1979 at Northrop University, Los Angeles, and the second, dedicated to the memory of the French 'revisionist historian', Paul Rassinier, in August 1980 at Pomona College, Ontario, California. The first convention resulted in the publication of the *Journal of Historical Review* containing contributions to the convention. Felderer contributed an article in company with several notorious 'revisionists', Arthur R. Butz, Robert Faurisson, Austin J. App, and Udo Walendy. Others present included John Bennett and Jim Martin. The Pomona convention had similar participants. Felderer provided a slide show on Auschwitz, according to the Institute's advertisement.

Felderer's cognitive environment is rooted in an expanding organization of the extreme right which pursues neo-Nazism, denies the Holocaust, repudiates Hitler's guilt, resurrects the world conspiracy theory, and claims that an exterminationist 'myth' has been invented to extort money

from Germany in order to win material and political aid for the Israeli state at the eventual expense of the Palestinians. Most 'revisionist historians' tend to concentrate upon vindicating some of Hitler's policies while refurbishing his image as a conservative anti-Communist hero; they cast doubt on documented evidence of the extermination of European Jewry as a whole, or claim deaths were much fewer than six million; and they claim the Allies were guilty of crimes equal to those 'allegedly' perpetrated by Nazi Germany. Thus, Felderer's fixation upon the Anne Frank diary is a departure from the mainstream of 'revisionist' writing, even though Butz and Harwood have made a few brief comments on its authenticity.

Felderer questions the veracity of the Diary, by focussing on historical aspects which he attempts to analyse. He argues that it was nonsensical or strange for Anne and Margot Frank to be shipped to Bergen-Belsen via Auschwitz-Birkenau and Westerbork. 'How anyone in a time of full-scale war, where transportation and food supplies are severely hampered, can proceed in this manner to "exterminate" people is beyond our comprehension.' However, much is beyond his comprehension. Dutch men and women destined for concentration camps were sent to Westerbork for sorting into categories prior to onward shipment. Why Nazi Germany should move people around from camp to camp during the final stages of the Second World War has frequently appeared nonsensical to historians. The explanation is simple. Nazism was and is a totally irrational ideology maintaining that a worldwide Jewish conspiracy exists behind 'Jewish Communism' and 'Jewish capitalism'. Based upon this was a Nazi messianism whose 'holy' task consisted of requiring an elite (SS) to sacrifice its conscience when eliminating Jews in order to bring about a better German future. This 'higher necessity' demanded genocide as an end in itself, a task with absolute priority. This explains why significant proportions of German army vehicles and transport were used to convey Jews to gas chambers, rather than utilizing them against the advancing armies of the Soviet Union.

Felderer's limited perception is clearly demonstrated when he provides two photographs of Anne's writing which appear to be totally different. One shows a fine, mature, and regular script while the other portrays an obviously irregular and clumsy, childish style. Felderer automatically assumes that the Diary is a literary joint-effort, or certainly suspect in some way. But such an assumption is entirely superficial. First, one piece of writing is 'joined-up', the other is printed: therefore, they are bound to look dissimilar. Secondly, the original piece of printing had Anne's genuine signature appended as if added at a later date. This can be easily checked against the same photograph in Serge Thion's book, *Verité historique ou verité politique?* which tries to evaluate Robert Faurisson's attack on the Diary. An obvious possibility, if one refuses to accept that the two styles emanate from the same time period, is that Anne eventually signed an earlier piece of printing which she wrote prior to hiding. Also, the printing is attached to a photograph of a young Anne imagining it is for Hollywood, a fantasy she enjoyed while collecting photographs of film stars, her hobby. This would again strengthen the view that Anne added her signature to an early picture/piece of printing at a later date.

In his attempts to undermine the authenticity of the diary, Felderer indulges in a series of twisted assumptions, peculiar arguments and inexact translations. The front cover of *A Hoax* shows a photograph of Otto Frank holding part of the Diary. Felderer makes much of this: it is neither 'small' nor 'little' when according to Anne's own description of it, it should be. Furthermore, Felderer states that the diary was found inside exercise books, therefore assuming it must be 'not only small in width and length but also rather thin.' He wonders how such a diary can be published in its well-known Cardinal edition of 230 pages. This view, typical of Felderer's simplistic approach, ignores the lexical differences in meaning.

A careful, critical reading of both the Diary and Felderer's book reveals the bankruptcy of Felderer's methodology. Three further illustrations can be cited. First, Felderer accuses those in hiding of living luxuriously, possessing much tobacco and assorted quantities of canned vegetables, dried pulses, and potatoes. This is to 'destroy' the 'myth' of a group living under starvation conditions, while Germans suffered worse hardships. Felderer ignores the friends who smuggled provisions to the Frank family and their fellow-fugitives. Furthermore, he omits statements about periods when they lived on a daily diet of two spoonfuls of porridge plus rotten potatoes, spinach and lettuce—the very opposite of a well-balanced nutritional diet. Secondly, in trying to prove the presence or otherwise of sundry stoves in the hiding place, Felderer states: 'Likely it was their own stove which she tells about when she wrote of "Daddy's bedroom slippers warming in front of the fire" as "in bygone days" '. This is an out of context quotation designed to mislead. Compare it with the original Diary entry: 'We are quite used to the idea of going into hiding, or "underground", as in bygone days one was used to Daddy's bedroom slippers warming in front of the fire.' One need say no more.

Thirdly, Felderer attempts to deny the veracity of the Diary by accusing Anne Frank of sexual perversion. This form of intellectual pornography shows a lack of education about child development and psychology. Felderer asserts that the Diary is not written by a healthy child. He believes it was the work of someone attempting to fabricate a child's mind, and sexy parts have been inserted to render the Diary more saleable.

Felderer contends that 'in some respects the diary can be claimed to be the first paedophile pornographic work to come out after World War II and sold on the open market. In fact, the descriptions by a teenage girl over her sex affairs may likely be the first child porno ever to come out.' Completely and deliberately misunderstanding a sensitive Diary entry in which Anne shows the natural developing awareness an adolescent girl has of her body, Felderer accuses her of incipient lesbianism. He then proceeds to attack her for her friendship with Peter van Daan, carefully selecting Diary extracts in such a way as to give them high sexual overtones.

To put Felderer's distortions into perspective one can quote from a paediatrician's manual for teachers by Professor Illingworth of the University of Sheffield:

> By about nine children enter the homosexual phase, wanting friends of the same sex, and teasing children of the opposite sex. At the age of puberty they commonly develop intense friendship with someone of the same sex—so intense, sometimes, that it may guide a child in the choice of career; he wants to take up the same work as his hero so that he can be with him. . . . There is then a gradual change to heterosexuality so that in early adolescence a crush for someone in the opposite sex may develop. . . .

Felderer's book is an exceptionally poor example of recent 'revisionist' writing. This genre has recently avoided the pitfalls of bad printing, poor writing and simplistic argument. Felderer tries to emulate such writers as the academic 'revisionists' Butz and Faurisson, but fails. His tract utilizes all the most unsophisticated pseudo-academic and pseudo-scientific jargon. Furthermore, the obsessive malice displayed towards the Anne Frank Diary is self-defeating.

Reasons why credence is sometimes given to the claims of Holocaust denial literature:

Holocaust deniers play upon contemporary society's tendency toward historical amnesia, and its fuzzy notion of "tolerance" that cannot distinguish between an open mind and an empty mind. Thus a young reporter for a respected magazine interviewing [Deborah E.] Lipstadt (without having read her book) asked this question: "What proof do you include in your book that the Holocaust happened?" That reporter passed through college unmarked by information about even the largest events of the century, but acquired the conventional skepticism of the emptyheaded: When in doubt, doubt.

People as ignorant as that reporter know nothing, so they doubt everything except how sophisticated they are when they assume that nothing is certain. This assumption is irrigated in the badly educated by fashionable academic theories of epistemological indeterminacy. The vocabulary and mentality of literary "deconstruction" seeps everywhere, relativizing everything, teaching that history, like all of life, is a mere "narrative," a "text" with no meaning beyond what any individual reads into it. No event, no book, nothing has a fixed content; the individual's "perception" or "reaction" to it is everything.

George Will, in his "Trying to Deconstruct the Holocaust," in New York Newsday, *August 29, 1993.*

Jon Connell and Antony Terry

SOURCE: "Anne Frank's Diary Goes on Trial," in *The Sunday Times,* London, November 30, 1980, p. 15.

[*Connell is an English journalist. In the following essay,*

Connell and Terry report on a trial that took place in Hamburg, Germany, to determine the validity of allegations that Anne Frank's diary is not authentic.]

The Diary of Anne Frank is one of the Second World War's most poignant testimonies to Jewish endurance. But is it genuine?

Over the years, right-wing propagandists have made determined efforts to suggest that it is not really the work of Anne Frank—the young girl who spent two years hiding in Amsterdam with her family before being betrayed to the Nazis in 1944.

But the latest assault on its authenticity is the most serious yet: this suggests that certain words in the diary were written with a ball-point pen which was invented in 1951 and so could not have been available to Anne Frank; and that these words are in handwriting identical to that of the main text. The inference is clear—the diary was compiled *after* the war, by which time Anne had died in a German concentration camp.

These claims will be tested early next year in a court case in Hamburg, but already our inquiries suggest that the case against the diary is deeply flawed:

Ernst Roemer, the man behind that latest allegations, is a former Nazi who served with the notorious Geheime Feldpolizei, the secret field police responsible for rounding up Jews in occupied Europe.

The initial impetus for the attack came from a mysterious group of apologists for Adolf Hitler in England.

The words in ballpoint are in fact corrections made long after the diary was first written, almost certainly by a family friend who wanted to clarify the text.

The campaign to prove that the diary was a fake goes back to February, 1976, when Ernst Roemer, a 76-year-old Hamburg pensioner, began distributing an emotive pamphlet to theatre-goers attending a dramatised version of the Diary of Anne Frank.

The pamphlet, entitled *Did Six Million Really Die?*, claimed that the holocaust was a myth, and that Anne's diary was a forgery. It purported to be the work of an Englishman called Richard Harwood—described in the blurb as "with the University of London"—and published by the Historical Review Press in Richmond. Although London University has never heard of Harwood, and the Historical Review Press is no more than a forwarding address, Roemer began using the pamphlet as part of a protracted campaign "to establish the truth."

Roemer continued distributing the pamphlet, until finally the play's director called police to the theatre. Roemer was eventually fined 1,500 Deutschmarks for defaming the diary, and therefore the play. He appealed, and when the hearing opened in March, 1978, his lawyers won an adjournment so that the diary could be subjected to a rigorous analysis to establish, once and for all, whether or not it was genuine.

In April this year forensic scientists from West Germany's Federal Crime Bureau in Wiesbaden flew to Basle in Swit-

zerland, the home of Otto Frank, Anne's father and the only member of the family to survive the war. Here, armed with stereo-microscopes and ultraviolet lamps, the scientists pored over random pages of the diary, subjecting paper and ink to a wide range of chemical tests. By early summer their work was complete.

They discovered that certain words in the manuscript had been written with three separate ballpoints—black, green and blue. Although ballpoints were available during the war, the report is quite specific in its conclusion that the type used was not invented until 1951. This in itself was not necessarily damming evidence—after all, the corrections could have been added by one or more of the many family friends who handled the manuscript.

But what *was* devastating was the earlier testimony of a graphologist, attached to the report, which stated that "the penmanship . . . in the three bound books, including all notes and additions . . . is identical with the handwriting of Anne Frank."

If this was true, and the forensic report accurate, then the diary stood condemned. Last month *Der Spiegel,* the German news magazine, leaked details of the report, saying that it "provided new fuel for the slanderers."

The man who could have shed light on the matter—Otto Frank, who for 30 years had made the diary his life's work, was no longer on hand to offer an explanation. In August, before *Der Spiegel*'s report appeared, he died.

His widow, an Austrian Jew who had met Otto at the end of the war and become his second wife, took up the case. She pointed out that the handwriting report had simply presented an overall assessment of the text and did not refer to specific words. So she commissioned Erhard Friess, a Swiss graphologist, to carry out a new test.

Friess quickly identified the words in green ballpoint—nine in all—and his report, which we have seen, is adamant that they are in a different hand. Moreover it stresses that most of the "offending" words were inserted where ink blots had obscured the original text, and were therefore straight-forward clarifications.

The words in black and blue, however, presented a problem: Friess could not identify these because he lacked the necessary equipment. To the naked eye they are indistinguishable from the fountain pen ink used in the bulk of the narrative.

However, Dr Alois Werner who compiled the forensic report, told us that the words in black and blue ballpoint were similar to those in green, adding that all were "individual word corrections and never whole passages or pages or sections."

And, in support of the diary, his report is positive that the fountain pen, the ink and the paper used can be firmly dated to wartime manufacture.

The evidence is, therefore, overwhelming that Anne herself wrote the diary during her years in hiding. She used pen and ink (and some pencil); then, several years after she died, a family friend went through the diary, making corrections and using three different ball-point pens. One possible candidate for this role is Johannes Kleiman who features in the diary as Mr Koophuis, and who risked his life to bring food to the Frank's hideout.

Inevitably, the campaign to undermine the diary will go on. The English historian, David Irving, who argues that Hitler was unaware of the holocaust, says he cannot accept that the diary was the work of a 13-year-old girl. "I think it's sad that people have accepted it as genuine," he said last week. "I compare it to *Oliver Twist,* which doesn't lose anything because it's a novel."

Deborah E. Lipstadt

SOURCE: "The Diary of Anne Frank," in *Denying the Holocaust: The Growing Assault on Truth and Memory,* The Free Press, 1993, pp. 229-35.

[*In the following essay, Lipstadt reviews the controversy concerning the authenticity of Anne Frank's diary.*]

Anne Frank's diary has become one of the deniers' most popular targets. For more than thirty years they have tried to prove that it was written after the war. It would seem to be a dubious allocation of the deniers' energies that they try to prove that a small book by a young girl full of musings about her life, relationship with her parents, emerging sexuality, and movie stars was not really written by her. But they have chosen their target purposefully.

Since its publication shortly after the war, the diary has sold more than twenty million copies in more than forty countries. For many readers it is their introduction to the Holocaust. Countless grade school and high school classes use it as a required text. The diary's popularity and impact, particularly on the young, make discrediting it as important a goal for the deniers as their attack on the gas chambers. By instilling doubts in the minds of young people about this powerful book, they hope also to instill doubts about the Holocaust itself.

On what do these deniers and neo-Nazis build their case? A brief history of the publication of the diary, and of some of the subsequent events surrounding its production as a play and film, demonstrates how the deniers twist the truth to fit their ideological agenda.

Anne Frank began her diary on June 12, 1942. In the subsequent twenty-six months she filled a series of albums, loose sheets of paper, and exercise and account books. In addition she wrote a set of stories called *Tales From the Secret Annex.* Anne, who frequently referred to her desire to be a writer, took her diary very seriously. Approximately five months before the family's arrest, listening to a clandestine radio she heard the Dutch minister of education request in a broadcast from London that people save "ordinary documents—a diary, letters from a Dutch forced laborer in Germany, a collection of sermons given by a parson or a priest." This would help future generations understand what the nation had endured during those terrible years. The next day Anne noted, "Of course they all made a rush at my diary immediately." Anxious to publish her recollections in book form after the war, she rewrote the first volumes of the diary on loose copy paper. In it she changed some of the names of the principal char-

acters, including her own (Anne Frank became Anne Robin.)

When Otto Frank was liberated from Auschwitz and returned from the war, he learned that his daughters were dead. He prepared a typed edition of the diary for relatives and friends, making certain grammatical corrections, incorporating items from the different versions, and omitting details that might offend living people or that concerned private family matters, such as Anne's stormy relationship with her mother. He gave his typed manuscript to a friend and asked him to edit it. (Other people apparently also made editorial alterations to it.) The friend's wife prepared a typed version of the edited manuscript. Frank approached a number of publishers with this version, which was repeatedly rejected. When it was accepted the publishers suggested that references to sex, menstruation, and two girls touching each other's breasts be deleted because they lacked the proper degree of "propriety" for a Dutch audience. When the diary was published in England, Germany, France, and the United States, additional changes were made. The deniers cite these different versions and different copies of the typescript to buttress their claim that it is all a fabrication and that there was no original diary. They also point to the fact that two different types of handwriting—printing and cursive writing—were used in the diary. They claim that the paper and the ink used were not produced until the 1950s and would have been unavailable to a girl hiding in an attic in Amsterdam in 1942.

But it is the Meyer Levin affair on which the deniers have most often relied to make their spurious charges. Levin, who had first read the diary while he was living in France, wrote a laudatory review of it when Doubleday published it. Levin's review, which appeared in the *New York Times Book Review,* was followed by other articles by him on the diary in which he urged that it be made into a play and film. In 1952 Otto Frank appointed Levin his literary agent in the United States to explore the possibility of producing a play. Levin wrote a script that was turned down by a series of producers. Frustrated by Levin's failures and convinced that this script would not be accepted, Frank awarded the production rights to Kermit Bloomgarden, who turned, at the suggestion of American author Lillian Hellman, to two accomplished MGM screenwriters. Their version of the play was a success and won the 1955 Pulitzer Prize.

Levin, deeply embittered, sued, charging that the playwrights had plagiarized his material and ideas. In January 1958 a jury ruled that Levin should be awarded fifty thousand dollars in damages. However, the New York State Supreme Court set aside the jury's verdict, explaining that since Levin and the MGM playwrights had both relied on the same original source—Anne's diary—there were bound to be similarities between the two.

Since it appeared that another lawsuit would be filed, the court refused to lift the freeze that Levin had placed on the royalties. After two years of an impasse, Frank and Levin reached an out-of-court settlement. Frank agreed to pay fifteen thousand dollars to Levin, who dropped all his claims to royalties and rights to the dramatization of the play. Levin remained obsessed by his desire to dramatize the diary. In 1966 he attempted to stage a production in Israel, though he did not have the right to do so, and Frank's lawyers insisted that it be terminated.

It is against this background that the deniers built their assault on the diary. The first documented attack appeared in Sweden in 1957. A Danish literary critic claimed that the diary had actually been produced by Levin, citing as one of his "proofs" that names such as Peter and Anne were not Jewish names. His charges were repeated in Norway, Austria, and West Germany. In 1958 a German high school teacher who had been a member of the SA and a Hitler Youth leader charged that Anne Frank's diary was a forgery that had earned "millions for the profiteers from Germany's defeat." His allegations were reiterated by the chairman of a right-wing German political party. Otto Frank and the diary's publishers sued them for libel, slander, defamation of the memory of a dead person, and antisemitic utterances. The case was settled out of court when the defendants declared that they were convinced the diary was not a forgery and apologized for unverified statements they had made.

In 1967 *American Mercury* published an article by Teressa Hendry, entitled "Was Anne Frank's Diary a Hoax?" in which she suggested that the diary might be the work of Meyer Levin and that if it was, a massive fraud had been perpetrated. . . . Hendry's allegations were repeated by other deniers as established fact. This is their typical pattern of cross-fertilization as they create a merry-go-round of allegations. In *Did Six Million Really Die? The Truth at Last,* Harwood repeated these charges, unequivocally declaring the diary to be a hoax. In one short paragraph in his book, Arthur Butz likewise stated that he had "looked it over" and determined that the diary was a hoax.

In his 1975 attack on the diary, David Irving relied on the familiar charge that an American court had "proved" that a New York scriptwriter had written it "in collaboration with the girl's father." In 1978 Ditlieb Felderer, publisher of the sexually explicit cartoons of Holocaust survivors, produced a book devoted to certifying the diary as a hoax. He repeated the Levin charge but then went on to label Anne a sex fiend and the book "the first child porno." (Some of his chapter titles are indicative of his approach: "Sexual Extravaganza" and "Anne's Character—Not Even a Nice Girl." Felderer's charges are designed to build on what is often part of the inventory of antisemitic stereotypes: Jews, unnaturally concerned about sex, are also producers of pornography designed to corrupt young children.)

In 1975 Heinz Roth, a West German publisher of neo-Nazi brochures, began to circulate pamphlets calling the diary a forgery actually written by a New York playwright. He cited Irving's and Harwood's findings as "proof" of his charges. When asked to desist by Otto Frank, he refused, claiming, in the familiar defense used by deniers, that he was only interested in "pure historical truth." At this point Frank took him to court in West Germany. Roth defended himself by citing statements by Harwood and Butz declaring the diary to be fraudulent. In ad-

dition, Roth's lawyers produced an "expert opinion" by Robert Faurisson, among whose charges to prove the diary fictitious was that the annex's inhabitants had made too much noise. Anne wrote of vacuum cleaners being used, "resounding" laughter, and noise that was "enough to wake the dead." How, Faurisson asked, could people in hiding, knowing that the slightest noise would be their undoing, have behaved in this fashion and not been discovered? But Faurisson quoted the diary selectively, distorting its contents to build his case. When Anne wrote of the use of the vacuum cleaner, she preceded it by noting that the "warehouse men have gone home now." The scene in which she described resounding laughter among the inhabitants of the annex took place the preceding evening—a Sunday night—when the warehouse would have been empty. When she wrote that a sack of beans broke open and the noise was enough to "wake the dead," Faurisson neglected to quote the next sentence in the diary: "Thank God there were no strangers in the house."

In his description of his visit to Otto Frank, Faurisson engaged in the same tactics he used in relation to his encounter with the official from the Auschwitz museum. He tried to make it appear as if he had caught Frank in a monstrous lie: "The interview turned out to be grueling for Anne Frank's father." Not surprisingly Frank's description of the interchange differs markedly, and he challenged the veracity of much of what Faurisson claimed he said. Faurisson also claimed to have found a witness who was "well informed and of good faith" but who refused to allow his name to be made public. Faurisson assured readers that the name and address of this secret witness had been placed in a "sealed envelope." As proof of this evidence he included a photograph of the sealed envelope as an appendix to his "investigation." In 1980 the court, unconvinced by Faurisson's claims, found that Roth had not proved the diary false.

In 1977 charges were again brought against two men in the West German courts for distributing pamphlets charging that the diary was a hoax. The Bundeskriminalamt (The BKA, or Federal Criminal Investigation Bureau) was asked to prepare a report as to whether the paper and writing material used in the diary were available between 1941 and 1944. The BKA report, which ran just four pages in length, did not deal with the authenticity of the diary itself. It found that the materials had all been manufactured prior to 1950-51 and consequently could have been used by Anne. It also observed, almost parenthetically, that *emendations* had been made in ballpoint pen on loose pages found with the diary. The ink used to make them had only been on the market since 1951. (The BKA did not address itself to the substance of the emendations, nor did it publish any data explaining how it had reached this conclusion. When the editors of the critical edition of the diary asked for the data they were told by the BKA that they had none.)

Given the history of the editing of the diary it is not surprising that these kinds of corrections were made. This did not prevent *Der Spiegel* from publishing a sensationalist article on the diary which began with the following bold-face paragraph: " 'The Diary of Anne Frank' was edited at a later date. Further doubt is therefore cast on the authenticity of that document." The author of the article did not question whether these corrections had been substantive or grammatical, whether they had been incorporated into the printed text, or when they had been made. Nor did he refer to them as corrections as the BKA had. He referred to the possibility of an imposter at work and charged that the diary had been subjected to countless "manipulations."

These sensationalist observations notwithstanding, *Der Spiegel* dismissed the charge made by David Irving and other deniers that Levin wrote the diary as an "oft-repeated legend." It also stressed that those who wished to shed doubt on the diary were the same types who wished to end "gas chamber fraud."

On Otto Frank's death in 1980, the diary was given to the Netherlands State Institute for War Documentation. By that time the attacks on it had become so frequent and vehement—though the charges that were made were all essentially the same—that the institute felt obliged to subject the diary, as well as the paper on which it was written, glue that bound it together, and ink to a myriad of scientific tests in order to determine whether they were authentic. They also tested postage stamps, postmarks, and censorship stamps on postcards, letters, and greeting cards sent by Anne and her family during this period (in addition to the diary the institute examined twenty-two different documents containing writings by Anne and her family). Forensic science experts analyzed Anne's handwriting, paying particular attention to the two different scripts, and produced a 250-page highly technical report of their findings.

The reports found that the paper, glue, fibers in the binding, and ink were all in use in the 1940s. The ink contained iron, which was standard for inks used prior to 1950. (After that date ink with no, or a much lower, iron content was used.) The conclusions of the forensic experts were unequivocal: The diaries were written by one person during the period in question. The emendations were of a limited nature and varied from a single letter to three words. They did not in any way alter the meaning of the text when compared to the earlier version. The institute determined that the different handwriting styles were indicative of normal development in a child and left no doubt that it was convinced that it had all been written in the same hand that wrote the letters and cards Anne had sent to classmates in previous years.

The final result of the institute's investigation was a 712 page critical edition of the diary containing the original version, Anne's edited copy, and the published version as well as the experts' findings. While some may argue that the Netherlands State Institute for War Documentation used an elephant to swat a fly, once again it becomes clear that the deniers' claims have no relationship to the most basic rules of truth and evidence.

DAVID IRVING AND THE "NORMALIZATION" OF HITLER

Martin Broszat

SOURCE: "Hitler and the Genesis of the 'Final Solution': An Assessment of David Irving's Theses," in *Yad Vashem Studies,* Vol. XIII, 1979, pp. 73-125.

[Broszat was a German historian and a respected authority on the Holocaust. Director of the Munich-based Institute for Contemporary History for seventeen years, he argued that the Nazi plan to exterminate the Jews was not fully formed before World War II. Rather, he believed the strategy of extermination evolved during the war years in response to the pressures of the conflict. In the following essay, Broszat offers an assessment of David Irving's book Hitler's War.*]*

The English Edition of David Irving's Hitler book [*Hitler's War*], published in the spring of 1977, two years after the expurgated German edition, has created a furore both in England and elsewhere. The British author, who gained a reputation as an *enfant terrible* with earlier publications on contemporary history, has propounded a thesis which is embarrassing even to some of his friends and admirers.

Hitler, according to Irving, had pursued the aim of making Germany and Europe *judenfrei,* that is, clear of Jews; he had not, however, desired the mass murder of the Jews and had not ordered it; this had been instigated by Himmler, Heydrich and individual chiefs of the civilian and security police in the East.

This essay endeavours to re-examine the subject beyond shedding light on David Irving's contentious arguments, an issue already treated unequivocally by internationally recognized historians and Hitler researchers. In view of the confusion which may be sensed by those readers of this well-written book, particularly teachers of history who are insufficiently versed in the details, it seems pertinent to combine a critical analysis of Irving's arguments and text with a documentation of the significant sources which, although known to the author and copiously cited in his work, are nonetheless frequently obscured by him.

Despite their faulty reasoning Irving's theses do however afford the challenge of tracing the arguments relating to the origins of the Nazi extermination of the Jews, which remain controversial until this day; these arguments also touch on an explicit annihilation order issued by Hitler, if such ever existed.

What is important, after all, is the context. The author of this treatise is not concerned solely or directly with a review of the history of the National Socialist Jewish policy; Irving is primarily engaged in a re-evaluation of Hitler himself, claiming a solid foundation on known and hitherto unknown sources.

Perhaps one day after he was dead and buried, an Englishman would come and write about him in an objective manner. Hitler is said to have made this remark some time in 1944. Irving grasps at it eagerly in his Hitler book. He seems determined in his own way to make this apocryphal remark come true. His book would finally bring about a de-demonization of Hitler, so he asserts in his introduction with a sideswipe at Joachim Fest who anticipated him, without—according to Irving—finding it necessary to comb the archives for new sources. Irving claims, on the basis of newly discovered documents, to draw Hitler as he really was, the real human being: "An ordinary, walking, talking human, weighing some 155 pounds, with graying hair, largely false teeth and chronic digestive ailments."

He emphatically promises the reader to purge Hitler's image of the accumulated contamination of the legends of allied war propaganda and post-war accusations. The tone is set by compensatory overpressure on the part of the author who makes it his business to point out their omissions to his colleagues, and to overturn current concepts about Hitler. For years, according to Irving, historians had only copied from one another: "For thirty years, our knowledge of Hitler's part in the atrocities has been based on interhistorian incest."

The author's mastery of his sources, at least regarding the limited scope of his presentation, is incontrovertible; he has also managed to produce a number of remarkable and hitherto unknown contemporary notebooks, diaries and letters of the National Socialist period. These stem mainly from Hitler's inner circle at the Führer's headquarters, and from liaison officers of the Wehrmacht as well as from individual Reich ministers, adjutants, secretaries, valets and stenographers. These documents are not of equal significance; although they contribute to a clearer understanding of the events at the Führer's headquarters (primarily the "Wolf's Lair" at Rastenburg in East Prussia) and illustrate the atmosphere in Hitler's immediate vicinity, they add hardly anything at all to our understanding of major military or political decisions and actions on Hitler's part, and hardly justify the author's exaggerated claims of innovation. The discovery and utilization of contemporary primary sources has long been a sort of adventuresome passion of Irving the historian. However, the unprejudiced historian and researcher is obstructed by the passionately partisan author whose insistence on primary sources lacks the control and discipline essential in the selective interpretation and evaluation of material.

He is too eager to accept authenticity for objectivity, is overly hasty in interpreting superficial diagnoses and often seems insufficiently interested in complex historical interconnections and in structural problems that transcend the mere recording of historical facts but are essential for their evaluation. Spurred by the ambition of matching himself against professional historians in his precise knowledge of documents, he adopts the role of the *terrible simplificateur* as he intends to wrest fresh interpretations from historical facts and events and spring these on the public in sensational new books.

Earlier theses of Irving's revealed the obstinacy of which he is so proud; his Hitler book proves it anew. The perspective of the presentation, however effective it may be from a publicity point of view, shows *a priori* a narrowing of scope in favour of Hitler. In an attempt to illustrate as far as possible the flux of political and military events from Hitler's point of view, from "behind his desk," Irving attaches exaggerated importance to the antechamber aspect of the Führer's headquarters and to testimonies of employees, in many cases subordinate officials, his new sources there. This "intimacy with Hitler" and his claims to objectivity are proved mutually contradictory from the beginning.

The manner of their presentation lends them a particular character. Irving positions and hides himself behind Hitler; he conveys a military and political evaluation of the situation as well as the cynical utterances of the Führer concerning his opponents (Churchill and Roosevelt) and the alleged failure of his own generals and allies, mostly with no comment. Beside Hitler all other characters remain merely pale shadows. This subjective likeness of Hitler (as documented by the author) forms the skeleton of a biography and war account.

A great part of the apologetic tendencies of the work stems from this conceptual arrangement, in spite of its reliance on documentation. The terse chronological description of the ever-shifting military and political problems which were brought before Hitler (others are not noted) causes the spotlight to fall mainly on Hitler. As a result, military and political developments appear incomplete since they are not presented in their true perspective.

This lack of critical comment on the part of the author who pretends merely to describe events in chronological order, reveals his bias. Quite two-thirds of the book, which numbers over 800 pages, deals with Hitler's conduct of the war, with military events and problems. This is not the author's first description of World War II from the German point of view, others are yet to come. The struggle of the German Wehrmacht under the command of Adolf Hitler holds a spell for the author. What emerges "between the lines" of this detailed and well-documented chronicle is the fascinating story of the superior leader and general and the superior army, who could but yield, after an heroic struggle, to the overwhelming masses of men and *matériel* of an inferior enemy. This is a later version of Ernst Jünger's interpretation of World War I. David Irving, according to an English critic's pointed remark, has remained the schoolboy who during the war stared fascinated at the wreckage of a Heinkel bomber. As an historian he turns his "childhood war" upside down and fixes his attention on the techniques of armament and strategy and the great and heroic battles of destiny. Above all, his talents as a writer are engaged; on occasion he totally disregards reliable documents. The author is writing a war novel. He describes the Polish campaign as follows:

> Hitler's positive enjoyment of the battle scenes was undeniable. He visited the front whenever he could, heedless of the risk to himself and his escort . . . At a divisional HQ set up in a school within range of the Polish artillery he made the acquaintance of General von Briesen, who towered head and shoulders above him. Briesen had just lost an arm leading his division in an action which warded off a desperate Polish counterattack of four divisions and cavalry on the flank of Blaskovitz's eighth army; he had lost eighty officers and 1,500 men in the fight, and now he was reporting to his Führer not far from the spot

where his father, a Prussian infantry general, had been killed in the Great War . . .

Bravery in mastering a crisis—this is the endlessly varied theme on which the author places his greatest semantic emphasis. He introduces his description of the lurking disaster in Russia in the winter of 1941/42 with these words:

> In the dark months of that winter Hitler showed his iron determination and hypnotic powers of leadership. We shall see how these qualities and the German soldier's legendary capacity for enduring hardship spared the eastern army from cruel defeat that winter.

Such inserts set the tone for the evaluation of Hitler even when Irving refers back to facts and documents which also include material damaging to Hitler. The author's opinion of the Officers' Plot of July 20, 1944 is revealed solely by the chapter heading: "The Worms Turn."

The "strategy" of de-demonization is based simply on the attempt to shunt ideological and political considerations onto the broad periphery of purely military events. For instance, actions like Hitler's secret euthanasia order just after the outbreak of the war are frequently (and wrongly) connected with, or justified by military exigencies. In some cases Irving dispenses entirely with reference to documentary evidence.

To this class belongs the newly revived theory (against all well-founded judgements) that Hitler's campaign in Russia forestalled a Soviet attack. Mysterious versions of aggressive speeches secretly made by Stalin to officers of the Red Army at the Kremlin on May 5, 1941, extensively quoted without any proof by Irving are mustered in support of Irving's thesis of a preventive war. It is on such pseudo-documentation that he bases his rationale for Hitler's orders concerning the liquidation of Soviet commissars: "Now the Soviet Union began to reap the harvest she had sown." The shooting of the commissars, according to Irving, was Hitler's answer to the projected "eradication of the ruling classes" in the western countries which the communists intended to attack—an interpretation which would have been truly congenial to Hitler.

Irving does not conceal isolated acts of killing or annihilation which can be traced to Hitler, but he describes them apologetically and sometimes distortedly and obscures their basic differences. The fanatical, destructive will to annihilate, he defines as mere brutality and he encompasses Hitler in the common brutality of warfare in which the total partisan warfare in the East and the bombing raids of the Allies in the West played equal parts. War itself, the main character in this book, becomes the great equalizer of violence. In this respect Hitler is no longer an exceptional phenomenon.

The predominance of war in Irving's presentation also furnishes him with an explanation concerning the structure and the distribution of power within the National Socialist regime during the war: the "powerful military Führer" played but a small part in the country's domestic policy during the war. While Hitler was conducting his war, it was Bormann, Himmler, Goebbels and others who ruled the Reich: "Hitler was a less than omnipotent leader, and

his grip on his immediate subordinates weakened as the war progressed." Irving himself designates this as his central theme. However, while it might not be entirely mistaken in this generalized form, it is completely erroneous when one applies it, as does the author, to Hitler's part in the annihilation of the Jews during the war. It becomes evident that the policy of the mass murder of the Jews does not fit into the picture of generalized brutality of war as drawn by Irving. Without the unreserved acquittal of Hitler on this, the greatest crime in German history, no "normalization" of Hitler could be possible.

Somewhat more is involved than just Hitler and his responsibility, for otherwise we could disregard Irving's thesis or even welcome it as a necessary contribution to the controversial interpretations of German contemporary history, where Hitler's sole responsibility, if not explicitly assumed, is at least occasionally implied. Irving's thesis touches the nerve of the credibility of the recorded history of the National Socialist period. It was not with Himmler, Bormann and Heydrich, not even with the Nazi party, that the majority of the German people so wholeheartedly identified themselves, but rather with Hitler. This poses a particular problem for German historians in their review of the National Socialist period. To bear the burden of such a disastrous mistake and to explore the meanings without minimizing them will remain a difficult task for German historical scholarship, but without doing so, the inherent truth would be lost. The distorted picture of Hitler as a mere madman, which Irving pretends to destroy, has long ceased to exist for serious contemporary historical research, if indeed it ever existed. Hitler's place in history does not admit of any such caricature. But the catastrophic influences which he set in motion and which he bequeathed to posterity also preclude any "normalization" towards which there seem to be some tendencies, mainly in the Federal Republic, using Irving as a reference. Hitler's power, based above all on his capacity to personify and mobilize the fears, aggressions and utopias of his time and society as no other could—and to make this faculty appear as solid statesmanship—cannot be separated from the mediocre falsehoods, the disgusting monstrosity of the mental and spiritual makeup of this "nonperson," his totally irresponsible, self-deceiving, destructive and evilly misanthropic egocentricity and his lunatic fanaticism which confront the unbiased historian on all sides. All of this cannot be made to disappear through an appreciation of the "greatness" of his historical influence or through later "over-Machiavellization" or rationalization of Hitler and even less through "antechamber" humanization of the subject.

Irving himself, near the end of his book cites an utterance that testifies significantly against his Hitler image. In his last address before *Gauleiters* of the NSDAP, on February 24, 1945, in the face of the ruins of his policy and conduct of the war, this Führer who had so long been worshipped by such a great part of his people and who was no longer prepared to make a public speech to them, declared that if the German people now defected to the enemy, they deserved to be annihilated. The monstrosity (not the monster of the caricature) revealed by such utterances can in no way be transformed into the image of a normal war leader.

Comprehensive descriptions of the "final solution of the Jewish problem" which have existed for years, may mask the fact that many aspects of the genesis of this programme are still obscure. Careful examination has been checked to a degree by the tendency to regard the extermination of the Jews as a sort of metahistoric event which could have been "logically" predicted long before 1933 on the basis of Hitler's radically dogmatic anti-Semitism and from his preformed psychological motive of destruction. As crucial as this point—Hitler's pathological philosophy—may be for the explanation of the whole, this does not release us from the responsibility of clarifying the historical question of how this ideology came into being and under what conditions, and by what institutional and personal levers it was "transmitted" and possibly "distorted."

Definite as our knowledge seems to be of the various phases, arenas and modes of the execution and of the act of annihilation, based on contemporary documents and later statements of the perpetrators and victims, we know but little of the murderous final step towards the radicalization of Nazi policy *vis-à-vis* the Jews, of those who had shared in the decision-making and of the precise content of these decisions; we know equally little of the form and the manner of their transmission to the special commandos and official agencies who were charged with their execution. In spite of the destruction of the pertinent files, mainly those of the *Sicherheitspolizei* (Security Police) who were primarily responsible, and the methodical removal of all traces after the actions, as well as the misleading phrasing of the documents themselves, the acts as such could not be hidden. Given the centralization of all decision-making, however, the attempts to obscure evidence were to a large extent successful.

It is doubtful whether the files of the SD chief, who on July 31, 1941 was charged with the organization of the "final solution," the files of the Führer's Chancellery, which supplied the gassing specialists (formally employed in the euthanasia programme), or Bormann's personal files at the Führer's headquarters could have provided unequivocal answers to these questions even if this material had not been largely destroyed before the end of the war. It is remarkable that prominent Nazi figures who had had frequent dealings with Hitler during the war and who were connected at least partially with the Jewish question and who after the war were still available as witnesses (for instance Göring, Ribbentrop, Hans Frank) or who left extensive notes (like the diaries of Goebbels), while obviously informed about the annihilation of the Jews, could make no statement about a specific secret order on the part of Hitler. This not only indicates that all agreements about the ultimate aim of the "final solution" were adopted and transmitted verbally but also shows that the physical liquidation of the Jews was set in motion not through a one-time decision but rather bit by bit.

The first extensive liquidation act, the mass execution in the summer and fall of 1941, of hundreds of thousands of Jews in the occupied Soviet territories by the *Einsatzkommandos* of the security police and the SD was no doubt carried out on the personal directive of Hitler. This, like the order to shoot all Soviet commissars, was obviously based on the fanatical determination of the National Socialist leadership to eradicate "Jewish Bolshevism" root and stem. This does not yet necessarily signify that physical liquidation, including the Jews of Germany, was the overall aim of Nazi Jewish policy, and had already been adopted at that time, nor that Göring's order to Heydrich for the preparation of a comprehensive programme for the deportation of Jews dated July 31, 1941, should be interpreted in this sense. Uwe Dietrich Adam in his study of the National Socialist Jewish policy had rejected this theory some years before, and with good cause.

While the mass murder of Jews (including women and children) as first perpetrated in the occupied Soviet territories necessarily contributed to the adopting of this means of liquidation as the "simplest" form of the final solution, plans then being formulated for the deportation of the German Jews remained to a great extent undetermined, as was the question of their destination and treatment. All emphasis and decisions were aimed at one target: to get rid of the Jews, and above all to make the territory of the Reich *judenfrei*, i.e. clear of Jews, since earlier plans to deport the Jews from Germany in the winter of 1939/40 had to be postponed.

When in the summer and fall of 1941 in their discussions and written communications the participants spoke only in vague terms of deportation "to the East," this was not merely semantic obfuscation—it was typical of the manner in which Hitler, Himmler and Heydrich approached the problem of a "radical solution" to major racial, social and folkish-political questions. Extensive actions for the transport of masses of people were begun without any clear conception of the consequences. Regarding the deportation of Jews to the East, conceived and planned ever since the summer of 1941 and begun, in fact, in the middle of October 1941, in all probability there existed only a vague idea: to employ the Jews in the East, in ghettos and in camps, at forced hard labour. Many of them would perish; as for those incapable of work, one could always "help along" their demise, as had been done in German concentration camps and in the labour camps of Poland. They were governed by the concept that the enormous spaces to be occupied in the Soviet Union would in any case offer a possibility for getting rid of the Jews of Germany and of the allied and occupied countries, and above all, of the multitudes of Jews in the ghettos of the General Government, which since 1940 was visualized as a settlement area for the Germanization of the East.

In the summer and autumn of 1941, it was clearly Hitler himself who voiced the imminent possibility of deporting Jews to the East to some of the Reich *Gauleiters,* to the Reich Protector of Bohemia and Moravia and to the Governor General of the occupied Polish territories, as well as to the Axis satellite governments; he himself urged its realisation and thereby in a way set off a lively competition to make their respective territories *judenfrei* as quickly as possible.

Some relevant testimonies of this phase show that in spite of the determination of the National Socialist leadership to handle the Jewish question radically, no clear aims existed with respect to the subsequent fate of the deportees. Alongside the Russian East, the old Madagascar plan still figured with Hitler and the competent officials of the SD as an alternative scheme.

The diary of the Governor General (Hans Frank) notes on July 17, 1941:

> The Governor General wishes to stop the creation of further ghettos, since according to an express declaration of the Führer of June 19, the Jews will be removed in due course from the General Government, and the General Government is to be, so to speak, only a transit area.

In conference with the Croatian Marshal Kvaternik on July 17, 1941 Hitler remarked, according to the minutes:

> The Jews were the scourge of humanity, the Lithuanians as well as the Estonians are now taking bloody revenge on them . . . When even one state, for any reason whatsoever, tolerated one single Jewish family in its midst, this would constitute a source of bacilli touching off new infection. Once there were no more Jews in Europe there would be nothing to interfere with the unification of the European nations. It makes no difference whether Jews are sent to Siberia or to Madagascar. He would approach every state with this demand . . .

A certain light is also shed on the planning and thinking of this phase by some parts of Goebbels' diaries which surfaced a few years ago and which have not yet been published; they contain the following remarks under the date August 8, 1941, concerning the spread of spotted typhus in the Warsaw ghetto:

> The Jews have always been the carriers of infectious diseases. They should either be concentrated in a ghetto and left to themselves or be liquidated, for otherwise they will infect the populations of the civilized nations.

On August 19, 1941, after a visit to the Führer's headquarters, Goebbels notes:

> The Führer is convinced his prophecy in the *Reichstag* is becoming a fact: that should Jewry succeed in again provoking a new war, this would end with their annihilation. It is coming true in these weeks and months with a certainty that appears almost sinister. In the East the Jews are paying the price, in Germany they have already paid in part and they will have to pay more in the future. Their last refuge is North America but even there they will have to pay sooner or later . . .

The next day, August 20, 1941, Goebbels supplements the impressions he brought back with him from the Führer's headquarters:

> . . . even if it is not yet possible to make Berlin a city entirely free of Jews, the Jews should no longer be seen in public; the Führer has promised me, moreover, that immediately after the conclusion of the campaign in the East, I can deport the Jews of Berlin to the East. Berlin must

be cleared of Jews. It is revolting and scandalous to think that seventy thousand Jews, most of them parasites, can still loiter in the capital of the German Reich. They not only spoil the general appearance of the streets, but also the atmosphere. This is going to change once they carry a badge but it can only be stopped once they are removed. We must approach this problem without any sentimentality.

Other testimonies of this time also confirm that Hitler set the targets of this, by now accelerated, activity. On September 18, 1941 Himmler wrote to the *Gauleiter* and Reich Governor of the Warthegau, SS-*Obergruppenführer* Greiser:

> The Führer wishes that the Old Reich and the Protectorate should be emptied and freed of Jews from the West to the East as soon as possible. I shall therefore endeavour to transport the Jews of the Old Reich and the Protectorate as far as possible this year; as a first step, into the newly acquired eastern regions that were annexed by the Reich two years ago, in order to deport them further to the East in the spring. Over the winter I intend to send about sixty thousand Jews of the Old Reich and the Protectorate into the ghetto of Litzmannstadt, which, as I hear, is barely able to accommodate them. I ask you not to misunderstand this measure which will no doubt entail difficulties and troubles for your district, but to support it wholeheartedly in the interests of the whole Reich.

It is possible that Himmler's communication, according to which the placing of the Jews in Litzmannstadt was intended as a temporary solution until they could be transported further to the East the following spring, was a feint while their murder in the occupied Polish areas was already planned at this point.

At the beginning of October of 1941, serious controversies broke out over the possible absorption of 20,000 Jews from the territory of the Reich between the governor of Litzmannstadt, SS-*Brigadeführer* Übelhör, and Himmler, and, after deportation had started (in the middle of October), between Übelhör and the security police, because the governor categorically refused to concede any absorptive capacity for the ghettos. This would be hard to explain if the plan for the extermination of the Jews had already been decided upon. Goebbels, too, was informed by Heydrich at the Führer's headquarters on September 23, 1941 that (possibly because the transport trains were required by the army and because of the limited capacity of the available camps and ghettos in the East) there were still temporary difficulties in the smooth deportation of the Jews of Berlin. In his notes of a discussion with Heydrich on September 23, 1941 (entry in diary 24.9.1941—partly or totally indecipherable), Goebbels states:

> This could occur as soon as we arrive at a clarification of the military situation in the East. They [the Jews] shall finally be transported into the camps which have been erected by the Bolsheviks . . . these [were erected by the Jews themselves] . . . [what could be more fitting

than] . . . that they should now also be populated by Jews . . .

Elsewhere (September 24, 1941) in the diary, concerning
his visit at the Führer's headquarters, Goebbels writes:

> The Führer is of the opinion that the Jews are
> to be removed from Germany step by step. The
> first cities that have to be cleared of Jews are
> Berlin, Vienna and Prague. Berlin will be the
> first of these and I hope that we shall manage to
> deport a considerable portion of the Jews of Ber-
> lin in the course of the current year.

A month later Goebbels was to learn that a rapid and
wholesale deportation of the Jews of Berlin into occupied
Soviet territory was not feasible. He notes in his diary on
October 24, 1941:

> Gradually we are also beginning with the depor-
> tation of the Jews to the East. Some thousands
> have already been sent on their way. They will
> first be brought to Litzmannstadt.

On October 28, 1941, Goebbels again complained in his
diary about the opposition that prevented the evacuation
of Jews from Berlin in the "shortest possible time." Steps
such as the evacuation had a more negative propaganda
influence in the capital than in other cities since "we have
here all the diplomats and the foreign press." He noted on
November 18, 1941:

> Heydrich advised me of his plans concerning de-
> portations from the area of the Reich. The prob-
> lem is more difficult than we had originally en-
> visaged: 15,000 Jews must remain in Berlin as
> they are employed in the war effort and in dan-
> gerous jobs. Also a number of elderly Jews can
> no longer be deported to the East. A Jewish
> ghetto could be set up for them in a small town
> in the Protectorate . . .

On November 21, 1941, Hitler, who had also come to Berlin, obviously had to damp the hopes of the Minister of
Propaganda and *Gauleiter* of Berlin regarding the pace of
the deportations. Goebbels noted the following day:

> He [the Führer] desires an aggressive policy to-
> wards the Jews which, however, should not
> create unnecessary difficulties for us.

Considerable difficulties indeed arose, mainly through the
unexpectedly arduous progress and, finally, the standstill
of military operations in the East and the extra burdening
of the already overloaded transportation system.

The situation into which the National Socialist leadership
had manoeuvered itself in the planning of large-scale deportations of Jews becomes sufficiently clear through the
documents already cited. As is clear from Hitler's declarations, Hitler, Himmler and Heydrich launched preparations for the wholesale deportation of Jews as a matter of
ideology to be pursued with fanatical eagerness. They
made this principle clear in their contacts with the *Gauleiters* of the cities with overwhelmingly large Jewish populations (Goebbels in Berlin, Schirach in Vienna) or the Governor General of Poland. The Chief of the Security Police
(Heydrich) and his expert on Jews (Eichmann) had prepared plans for the deportation and had sent their "advis-

ers" on Jewish questions to the southeastern satellite governments with large Jewish communities. These "experts"
had been sent to Bratislava, Bucharest and Agram (Za-
greb) with the objective of including Jews of these areas
in the deportations to the East. Hitler obviously had no
intention of halting the plan for the massive evacuation of
the Jews even when the military situation in the East
proved more difficult than had been assumed in the summer of 1941. It was for this reason that the original plans
for deportation were curtailed on the one hand, while on
the other decisions were made aimed at eventually remov-
ing at least part of the evacuated Jews "by other means,"
i.e. planned killing operations.

It thus seems that the liquidation of the Jews began not
solely as the result of an ostensible will for extermination
but also as a "way out" of a blind alley into which the
Nazis had manoeuvered themselves. The practice of liquidation, once initiated and established, gained predominance and evolved in the end into a comprehensive "programme."

This interpretation cannot be verified with absolute certainty but in the light of circumstances, which cannot be
discussed here in detail, it seems more plausible than the
assumption that there was a general secret order for the
extermination of the Jews in the summer of 1941.

The first massacre of Jews deported from the Reich took
place in November of 1941. The Jews of some transports
that had been diverted to the *Reichskommissariat* Ostland,
mainly to Riga, Minsk and Kovno, were not assigned to
the local ghettos or camps, as were the majority of the
later transports; these Jews were shot upon arrival together with the local Jews in the executions already started by
the *Einsatzkommandos* of the Security Police and the SD,
as for instance in Riga on the so-called Bloody Sunday of
November 30, 1941. At about the same time (November
1941), in the *Reichsgau* of Wartheland the "Lange Special
Commando" arrived in Chelmno (Kulmhof) and pro-
ceeded to construct temporary extermination facilities,
such as the gas vans of the type used by this commando
during the euthanasia killings in the transit camp of Sol-
dau, and as of December 1941 for the killing of Jews,
mostly from the ghetto of Litzmannstadt. The action in
Chelmno was obviously closely connected with the disputes that had arisen concerning the transport of German
Jews to Litzmannstadt. The idea that was initiated the
previous summer in Posen, according to which the situation in the ghetto could be relieved through the killing of
Jews unable to work "by means of a quick-acting medium," had apparently fallen on fertile ground. The erection
of Chelmno was intended mainly for this limited purpose—to create room for the second and third waves of
Jewish transports from the Reich which would be "temporarily" lodged in Litzmannstadt during the winter of
1941/42. The ghetto should be cleared of those unable to
work (above all women and children), who would be
brought to Chelmno for gassing. This action was mainly
completed by the summer of 1942 (with the annihilation
of about 100,000 Jews). Its *ad hoc* character becomes clear
from a letter by *Reichstatthalter* Greiser addressed to

Himmler and dated May 1, 1942. With a frankness unusual in a written communication, he reports:

> The action for the special treatment of about 100,000 Jews in my province that has been approved by you in agreement with the chief of the RSHA, SS-*Obergruppenführer* Heydrich, will be concluded in the next two or three months.

Only relatively few transports reached Chelmno after the summer of 1942: the installations were dismantled in March 1943 and all traces of the killings were removed. (Only in the spring of 1944 were the buildings again required for further killings). This process illustrates that the initiative for this partial action originated from the local Security Police staff and the office of the *Reichsstatthalter*. It was however in all probability initiated within the general context of decisions on the increased use of liquidation measures adopted after October-November 1941. An additional document shows that at that time there existed no general order for the annihilation of Jews but rather sporadic liquidation measures prompted by an inability to carry out the programme of deportations as planned. This is the draft of a letter by the expert on Jewish questions of the Reich Minister for the Occupied Eastern Territories to the *Reichskommissar* for Ostland, dated October 25, 1941, concerning the use of a gassing van for the killing of Jews; the chief of the Führer's Chancellery Viktor Brack (who was responsible for gassing methods after the euthanasia action), had promised to manufacture and deliver it. He writes among other things:

> May I point out that *Sturmbannführer* Eichmann, the expert on Jewish questions at the RSHA, agrees to this process. According to reports by *Stumbannführer* Eichmann, camps will be erected for the Jews at Riga and Minsk which may also be used for the accommodation of Jews from the Old Reich. Jews evacuated from the area of the Old Reich will be brought to Litzmannstadt and also to other camps to be later assigned to forced labour in the East (to the extent that they are able to work). With the present state of affairs, there should be no hesitation about doing away with those Jews who are unable to work, with the aid of Brack's expedient. In this manner occurrences like those at the time of the execution of Jews at W[ilna], as described in a report I have before me, prompted by the fact that the executions were carried out in public in a way that can hardly be tolerated, will no longer be possible . . .

The practice of annihilation became even more widespread and at this stage was discussed with cynical frankness at the German agencies of administration in the East. Hans Frank declared on December 16, 1941 at a government session in the office of the Governor of Cracow in connection with the imminent Wannsee Conference:

> Regarding the Jews, to start with, principally, there is one concern—that they disappear. They have to go. I have started negotiations with the aim of deporting them [the Polish Jews in the General Government] to the East. A major conference on this question will convene in Berlin in January to which I shall appoint Assistant Secretary Dr. Bühler as a delegate. The meeting will take place at the RSHA office of SS-*Obergruppenführer* Heydrich. This will mark the beginning of a great Jewish migration. What however shall happen to the Jews? Do you believe that they will be accommodated in settlement villages in the East? In Berlin they say, why all this bother. We have no use for them either in Ostland or in the *Reichskommissariat,* liquidate them yourselves . . . In the General Government we have an estimated two and a half and, with half-Jews and their families, three and a half million Jews. These three and a half million Jews we cannot shoot, we cannot poison, yet we must take measures that will somehow result in extermination so that this will be in concert with the major campaign launched by the Reich. The General Government must be as *judenfrei* as the Reich . . .

This additional evidence confirms the impression gained from other documents of this period: the various authorities of the National Socialist regime were ready in late autumn of 1941 for the extermination process aimed at reducing the number of Jews; there existed no real capacity to absorb the mass deportations which everybody urged and, further, the campaign in the East, which had reached a stalemate in the winter, offered no prospect for sending the Jews "behind the Urals." There were other reasons as well: the ghettos which had been created in order to isolate and select the Jews for deportation (in occupied Poland as early as 1939-1940) spread destitution and disease, which were now regarded by those responsible as typically Jewish "sources of pestilence" that were to be wiped out. Epidemics and a high mortality rate suggested the possibility of "helping nature along" in a systematic fashion.

The Jews had to be "exterminated somehow." This fatal expression recurs again and again in documents of various origins at this stage (autumn 1941), revealing evidence of the "improvisation" of extermination as the "simplest" solution—one that would, with additional extermination camps in occupied Poland, finally generate the accumulated experience and the institutional potential for the mass murders. It could also be exploited in the course of later deportations from Germany and from occupied or allied countries in Europe.

If we base our interpretation on the concept that the annihilation of the Jews was thus "improvised" rather than set off by a one-time secret order, it follows that the responsibility and the initiative for the killing were not Hitler's, Himmler's or Heydrich's alone. This does not however free Hitler of responsibility.

We know almost nothing about the way in which Hitler spoke about these matters with Himmler and Heydrich, who bore institutional responsibility for the acts of liquidation performed by the SD- and SS-Commandos, and who at this time frequently visited the Führer's headquarters. We shall discuss the reasons that prompted him to hide the full truth even from high-ranking associates; we shall also examine the fact that these strictly unlawful measures could be ordered only by verbal instructions on the part of Hitler and not by way of legally binding formal directives (written communications). Hitler's responsibility for the murder of the Jews can in any case be established only indirectly: the idea that it would be possible to "prove" this by means of some document signed by Hitler as yet undiscovered or destroyed before 1945 is derived from false suppositions: Hitler, as is well known, rarely processed files himself, and his signature or handwriting on documents of the Third Reich, except in the case of laws and ordinances, is hardly ever found.

Indications pointing at his responsibility are nevertheless overwhelming. A great number of documents concerning anti-Jewish legislation during the National Socialist period, as for instance the official definition of the concept "Jew" (in this case Hitler had no need to hide his participation), prove that Hitler concerned himself with numerous details of the planned anti-Jewish measures and that these were contingent on his decisions. It could not be hidden from any prominent functionary of the National Socialist regime that Hitler had the greatest interest possible in the solution of the Jewish question. To assume that such important decisions as the measures for the destruction of Jewry could be usurped by any individual in 1941-1942 without Hitler's approval is tantamount to ignoring the power-structure and hierarchic framework of the *Führerstaat*. It is especially baseless with respect to Himmler, whose loyalty to the Führer, especially in questions of basic ideology, was at this stage absolute. Such a concept is also untenable as the preparations for the extermination of the Jews (e.g. the question of transportation and the release of Jews from work essential to the war effort) interfered directly with the interests of the Wehrmacht (and frequently collided with it) and could not at any rate be implemented by Himmler or Heydrich, in view of their limited competence, without the backing Hitler alone could impose. Goebbels reveals in his diaries that every important stage of the deportation of the Jews from the capital of the Reich required the approval of Hitler: at the Wannsee Conference (January 20, 1942), which convened to discuss the "final solution of the Jewish question," Heydrich makes pointed reference to the necessary "previous authorization by the Führer." All this leads of necessity to the conclusion that the Führer specifically vested authority in the *Reichsführer*-SS and the Chief of the Security Police with regard to the massive actions of liquidation, regardless of who might have proposed these measures. (It is indeed possible that it was only with Himmler and Heydrich that the matter was discussed openly). That Hitler knew of this already in 1941-1942—even while trying to hide it from any wider circle of listeners—becomes clear from the notes of participants in confidential conversations with him at this time (winter 1941/42).

At a "table talk" at the Führer's headquarters on October 25, 1941, in the presence of Himmler and Heydrich, Hitler remarked:

> From the rostrum of the *Reichstag* I prophesied to Jewry that, in the event of war's proving inevitable, the Jew would disappear from Europe. That race of criminals has on its conscience the two million dead of the First World War, and now already hundreds of thousands more. Let nobody tell me that all the same we can't park them in the marshy parts of Russia! Who's wor-

rying about our troops? It's not a bad idea, by the way, that public rumour attributes to us a plan to exterminate the Jews. Terror is a salutary thing. . . .

On January 23, 1942, three days after the Wannsee Conference, during a "table talk" at the Führer's headquarters in the presence of Himmler and Lammers, Hitler again referred to the Jewish question:

> One must act radically. When one pulls out a tooth, one does it with a single tug, and the pain quickly goes away. The Jew must clear out of Europe. Otherwise no understanding will be possible between Europeans.

Further on in the same "table talk," after Hitler had cited the discrimination that the Roman Church State had levelled in former centuries against the Jews, he referred with a mixture of obvious cynicism and hypocritical obscurity to the current deportations and occasional acts of annihilation:

> For my part, I restrict myself to telling them they must go away. If they break their pipes on the journey, I can't do anything about it. But if they refuse to go voluntarily, I see no other solution but extermination. Why should I look at a Jew through other eyes than if he were a Russian prisoner-of-war?

> In the p.o.w. camps, many are dying. It's not my fault. I didn't want either the war or the p.o.w. camps. Why did the Jew provoke this war?

Four days later (January 27, 1942) Hitler again said on the occasion of a "table talk" at the Führer's headquarters:

> The Jews must pack up, disappear from Europe. Let them go to Russia. Where the Jews are concerned, I'm devoid of all sense of pity. They'll always be the ferment that moves peoples one against the other. They sow discord everywhere, as much between individuals as between peoples.

> It's entirely natural that we should concern ourselves with the question on the European level. It's clearly not enough to expel them from Germany. We cannot allow them to retain bases of withdrawal at our doors. . . .

On February 24, 1942 Goebbels notes in his diary after a visit of Hitler's to Berlin:

> The Führer again voices his determination to remorselessly cleanse Europe of its Jews. There can be no sentimental feelings here. The Jews have deserved the catastrophe that they are now experiencing. They shall experience their own annihilation together with the destruction of our enemies. We must accelerate this process with cold brutality; by doing so we are doing an inestimable service to humanity that has been tormented for thousands of years . . .

The accumulation of Hitler's aggressive statements and destructive will regarding the Jewish question, at this stage, as well as the allusions inherent therein to concrete measures for the Jews' expulsion and decimation, are sufficiently conclusive when interpreted within their historical context. They clearly reveal Hitler's fixation concerning the Jewish question and show his passionate interest in it. These facts preclude any possibility of his indifference to the continuing progress of the solution of the Jewish question.

At a much later period, in a secret speech of Hitler's to generals and officers of the Wehrmacht on May 26, 1944, in which he expounded on the liquidation of the Jews which had meanwhile been largely completed, he let drop a remark which seems to confirm that the annihilation of the Jews, as it "developed" in the winter of 1941/42, was a radical "expedient" adopted as an escape from the difficulties into which the Nazis had led themselves. "If I remove the Jews," according to Hitler's justification at a later stage of the war, "I have removed any possibility of the development of revolutionary cells or sources of infection. Someone might ask me: could this not have been achieved in a simpler manner—or, rather, not simpler, *because anything else would have been more complicated*—but solved more humanely . . . ?"

David Irving has correctly deduced that the annihilation of the Jews was partly a solution of expedience, "the way out of an awkward dilemma." However, he finds himself on an apologetic sidepath if he concludes, contrary to all evidence, that some of the subordinate SS and party leaders had instituted the murders in cynical extrapolation of Hitler's remarks and against his will.

In his book about Hitler, David Irving has not presented in any systematic way either the factual events of the "final solution" or Hitler's manifold utterances about the treatment of the Jews during the war. His revisionist theory is not derived from any incontrovertible historical conclusion; rather the arguments mustered in its support to which he constantly refers, often arbitrarily scattered in the text and footnotes, are in the main controversial, drawn from a dozen different sources, citing only specific aspects and documents relating to "Hitler and the extermination of the Jews." He marshals inconclusive arguments to which he authoritatively appends irrelevant and erroneous inferences, presenting them as foregone conclusions or to be assumed as such. Once the author had committed himself to this theory, no shred of seeming evidence was too shabby to support it.

The other Irving appears again and again behind the laboriously spliced argument of his revisionist theory, with ambition and great acrimony vaguely citing all pertinent documents even when these barely relate to the main argument. And within the categorical vindication of Hitler one suddenly encounters thoughtful and cautious reflections and formulations: Hitler's role in the context of the "final solution" was a "controversial issue" and "the negative is always difficult to prove." In another place:

> Hitler's was unquestionably the authority behind the *expulsion* operations; on whose initiative the grim procedures at the terminal stations of this miserable exodus were adopted, is arguable.

Irving poses the justified question: what exactly did Hitler mean when he promised the Governor General (of Po-

land) in June 1941 to expel the Jews "further to the East": " . . . did Hitler now use 'East' just as a generic term, whose precise definition would be perdition, oblivion, extermination? The documents at our disposal do not help us."

Unfortunately the author did not confine himself to such cautious questions. He blocked the path for new insights for himself and others by presenting false stereotypes and artificial argumentation clearing Hitler.

In his introduction the author already reveals what he regards as his principal discovery: Hitler ordered on November 30, 1941, that there was to be "no liquidation of the Jews." In a facsimile of the original documents which Irving appends to his book, the reader can see for himself: a page from Himmler's hand-written telephone notes dating from the years 1941 to 1943. Although nothing is found there concerning Hitler or any general prohibition of the liquidations, Irving, in his senseless yet literal interpretation of this note, would like to make us believe so in various parts of his book. This document reveals one fact only: Himmler held a telephone conversation from the Führer's bunker at the Wolf's Lair with Heydrich in Prague at 13:30 hours on November 30, 1941, and as one of the subjects of the conversation he noted: "Jew transport from Berlin, no liquidation." Whether Himmler had spoken to Hitler before this conversation and if its contents derived from Hitler is questionable. In any case, this contention cannot be substantiated, nor can it be conclusively stated that Himmler relayed an order of Hitler's to Heydrich. The contents of the note prove one thing: the words "no liquidation" are connected with "Jew transport from Berlin." This was a directive or an agreement concerning a *particular* situation, and not a *general* order. It is not possible to determine precisely the occasion and the subject of the conversation from these few words; however, what can be determined with certainty, is that they were connected with the execution of Jews from the Reich that had taken place some days before in Kovno (Kaunas). The purpose of the telephone conversation between Himmler and Heydrich was evidently to forestall the liquidation of another Jewish transport from Berlin that had left for Riga on November 27, 1941, which obviously could not have been prevented. On precisely that day (November 30, 1941) an extensive mass execution took place near Riga and this was the reason that Himmler telephoned Heydrich once again on December 12, 1941. These semi-public executions as well as the treatment of the German Jews who had been deported to the East, had been attracting considerable attention among the German military authorities, as well as among some members of the civil administration in the Ostland. *Gauleiter* Kube, the *Kommissar* General of White Ruthenia who the day before had visited the German Jews who had newly arrived in Minsk, to the surprise of the local SS and Security Police, had remarked angrily that in his view a number of persons whose close relatives served at the front had been unjustly deported. Heydrich was forced to contend with these reproaches for months to come.

It might have been this intervention or the particularly sensitive situation in Berlin, where American journalists had begun to evince interest in the fate of the deported Jews—until the entry of the USA into the war even Hitler had to take this mood into consideration—that made the liquidation in Kovno or Riga of the Jews of Berlin which could not be kept secret, seem undesirable either to Hitler or to Himmler. This and no more can be inferred from the telephone note. This is additional evidence pointing to the improvisatory character of the annihilation, still typical for this phase, with all its contradictions and occasional misunderstandings between those who had been charged with the execution of the "final solution" and those who issued the orders. Even assuming that the telephone conversation between Himmler and Heydrich was based on Hitler's directive (with the aim of preventing the transport of Berlin Jews on their way to Riga from being executed upon arrival, as had been done once before in Kovno), one cannot conclude, as Irving does, that Hitler was not aware of the murder of the Jews. On the contrary: the exceptional directive (in *this* case) would indicate that Hitler knew in principle about the practice of annihilation.

Irving's interpretation, that Hitler had on November 30, 1941 issued a general prohibition against the liquidation of the Jews which would also be binding for the years to come is, however, totally mistaken. In fact it was at this point that the more institutionalized and better "regulated" way of carrying out the "final solution" began. On January 20, 1942 the Wannsee Conference in Berlin took place, which made it clear, even in vaguely worded minutes, that those in charge intended to make sure that a great part of the deported Jews would not long survive deportation.

The first extensive mass execution of Polish, German and Slovak Jews began in the spring of 1942 at Auschwitz and in the newly erected extermination camp of Belźec in the Eastern part of the General Government (the first of four extermination camps under the supervision of SS and Police Führer Globocnik at Lublin). Goebbels notes this in his diary on March 27, 1942:

> Beginning with Lublin, the Jews under the General Government are now being evacuated eastward. The procedure is pretty barbaric and is not to be described here more definitely. Not much will remain of the Jews. About 60 per cent of them will have to be liquidated; only about 40 per cent can be used for forced labour.

> The former *Gauleiter* of Vienna, who is to carry out this measure, is doing it with considerable circumspection and in a way that does not attract too much attention. Though the judgment now being visited upon the Jews is barbaric, they fully deserve it. The prophecy which the Führer made about them for having brought on a new world war is beginning to come true in a most terrible manner. One must not be sentimental in these matters. If we did not fight the Jews, they would destroy us. It's a life-death struggle between the Aryan race and the Jewish bacillus. No other government and no other regime would have the strength for such a global solution as this. Here, once again, the Führer is the undismayed champion of a radical solution, which is made necessary by existing conditions

and is therefore inexorable. Fortunately a whole series of possibilities presents itself to us in wartime which would be denied us in peace. We shall have to profit by this. The ghettos that will be emptied in the cities of the General Government will now be refilled with Jews thrown out of the Reich. This process is to be repeated from time to time. Jewry has nothing to laugh at.

One feels, on reading this document, that Goebbels, who apparently had just heard of the new practice of murder through gassing, was talking himself out of his feeling of horror and clinging desperately to the bacillus theory of his Führer whom he calls "the spokesman of a radical solution."

Irving's interpretation of this well-known diary entry is revealing. He mentions it without citing it in detail and above all, conceals the explicit reference to "the Führer." He even manages to indicate the reverse by his accompanying remark. Basing himself on his theory of Hitler's prohibition of the liquidation, he submits that the Minister of Propaganda as well as Himmler and Heydrich were one with the plotters whose purpose was to hide from Hitler the fact that new acts of murder had begun on the largest possible scale. Goebbels, so he writes, entrusted his diary with a frank description of the horrible events in the death camps "but he obviously kept silent when he met Hitler two days later." Further, so the author doggedly insists when writing about this conference, Goebbels had noted in his diary only the following expressions of Hitler concerning the Jewish question: "The Jews must pack up, disappear from Europe; if necessary we have to apply the most brutal means." Since there is no record of Hitler using the word gassing, he knew nothing about it; this is the manner in which Irving arrives at his "faithfully documented" deductions to prove his point, here as well as in other parts of his book. When examining Irving's thesis the historian, who is obliged to be sceptical as well as critical, might wonder why Hitler's statements concerning the Jewish problem during the war contain—contrary to Irving's statement—words like extermination and annihilation which are by no means scarce, and generally reveal Hitler's murderous intentions but make hardly any direct references to various phases or specific aspects of the extermination of the Jews.

The fact that no written order signed by Hitler concerning the exterminations has come down to us, cannot be recognized as a decisive factor. We have already indicated that it is quite possible that such a one-time general order to wipe out the Jews never existed. It might be added that the act of mass execution according to legislation still in force at that time made *a priori* a written confirmation of the order by the head of the German Reich quite unthinkable, unless Hitler was prepared to risk causing extreme embarrassment to the orderly administration and the judicial authorities of the Reich which were still fundamentally based on law and justice. This was the advantage of strict adherence to rules of semantics: the various branches of the civil administration, without whose organizational cooperation it would not have been possible to carry out the mass actions of the "final solution," were informed "officially" only about those aspects or portions of the general action which were still just permissible from a legal point of view: about "evacuations," "Jew transports," etc. Those parts of the action which were totally criminal and unlawful—the liquidations—occurred under the formal responsibility of special bodies in the Security Police and the SD who were above the law. More or less open mention of these matters was therefore acceptable on occasion, as can be seen on inspecting written communications between the SS and police authorities or between them and the heads of civil administration in the occupied areas of the East, who were outside the scope of the ordinary administration of the Reich.

Hitler as Head of State had to be far more formal and punctilious than, for instance, Himmler, about the process of law and order in the regular administration of the country. He had ample reason to refrain from any explicit verbal or written reference that a third party could have interpreted as an official directive on the unlawful annihilation of the Jews. It is also known that at the time of the euthanasia programme Hitler was patently unwilling to furnish even a minimum of formal confirmation in the form of an obscure handwritten "authorization" (by no means "order"). However, confirmation was unavoidable in 1939, for with the killing of the mentally deficient being carried out within the boundaries of the German Reich, i.e. within the sphere of competence of regular civil administration and judicial authority, the euthanasia doctors and specialists had to be in a position, if necessary, to cite a formal authorization on the part of Hitler. But as far as the killing operations in the occupied territories were concerned, within the framework of the prevailing emergency situation, the manifold restrictions within the jurisdiction of the civil administration obviated this necessity. Here Hitler could content himself with verbal authorizations that were kept strictly secret.

Thus, when Himmler, at a later date, for instance in his secret speeches at Posen before SS commanders and district governors on October 4, and 6, 1943, spoke openly about the annihilation of the Jews, he called this "the heaviest task" of his life; the reason probably was not that "faithful Heinrich" had acted behind the Führer's back in the extermination of the Jews, or had voluntarily "relieved" him of this burden—as Irving claims contrary to all evidence—but obviously that Himmler could not cite any official mandate because Hitler entrusted him not only with the massacre of the Jews but, in addition, expected him to keep the order strictly secret. The extent to which Hitler took pains to keep that "last" truth about the fate of the Jews from the German public, is also revealed in Bormann's confidential circular addressed to Reich and district governors of the NSDAP, dated July 11, 1943. He prohibits "by order of the Führer" any mention of a "future overall solution" in public dealings on the Jewish question and advises only mentioning "that the Jews are being employed in gangs as a labour force."

It was very likely that not only formal considerations led Hitler to refrain from referring explicitly to the extermination of the Jews. With the sure instinct of the demagogue, and such he remained at his table conversations, he knew just what demands he could make on his listeners. In his official speeches during the war any declaration of his virulent anti-Semitism—his desperate determination to take "revenge" on the Jews—was received with applause (as for instance in his speech of January 30, 1942); any description of an actual massacre of the Jews however would have (as in the case of Goebbels) aroused quite different emotions. Since our knowledge of Hitler's attitude towards the Jewish question during the war is based almost exclusively on records of his conversations and speeches, our interpretation is confined by the limits of his demagogic point of view.

There is, however, some indirect evidence about Hitler's intervention in measures connected with the annihilation of the Jews. We may take as an indication the stepping-up of the killings that became operative in the summer of 1942 with the "running in" of Sobibor and Treblinka in the General Government. Himmler as well as SS and Police Commander Globocnik were, for reasons of secrecy, anxious to carry out the action "as quickly as possible." There was some resistance on the part of the Wehrmacht, because of the need for Jewish labour (for instance regarding the c. 400,000 Warsaw Ghetto Jews) and further, due to the still chronic shortage of transport trains, for which the Wehrmacht had other priorities. For that reason Himmler required Hitler's full support. It was obviously on this subject that he conferred with Hitler at the Führer's headquarters on July 16, 1942 and it was from there, on the same day, that his liaison officer to Hitler, SS-*Obergruppenführer* Wolff, made an urgent telephone call to the Assistant Secretary in the Ministry of Transport, concerning the availability of additional transport trains. It was three days later, only after these conditions had been met, that Himmler could, on July 19, 1942, issue the directive to the senior SS and Police Commanders that the accelerated resettlement of the entire Jewish population of the General Government was to be carried out and terminated by December 31, 1942. Exempted should be solely the Jews in some of the labour camps. On July 28, 1942, Assistant Secretary Ganzenmüller issued Wolff this comforting communication:

> Since July 22, one train per day with five thousand Jews was leaving Warsaw for Treblinka, and that twice a week a train was leaving Przemysl with five thousand Jews for Belzek [!] . . .

Wolff expressed his gratitude on August 13, 1942 for the efforts in this matter and declared that it gave him "special pleasure" to learn that "daily trainloads of five thousand members of the Chosen People are going to Treblinka and that we are thus being enabled to accelerate this migration." Wolff's intervention on the day of Himmler's conference with Hitler is only one of the indications that deportation and extermination activities were repeatedly granted special priority by the Führer's headquarters.

It is all the more fantastic when Irving claims that not only Hitler's secretaries and stenographers, but Wolff who accompanied Himmler while inspecting Auschwitz, as well as Globocnik at Lublin, in the summer of 1942 still knew nothing about the killings. It was in this vein that Wolff pleaded against charges of complicity in the killings at his trial in the Munich District Court in 1964. The court could not, as recorded in its judgement "accept the claim of the defendant since it is not in accordance with the truth." Nevertheless, Irving treats Wolff's version as if it were a proven fact and makes no mention of the dissenting opinion of the court although he was aware of this.

On the whole it seems that the author owes a great debt to Wolff. It was the latter who in the early 50's was the first to propound the theory that Himmler, in his bizarre zeal for the Führer and the Führer's ideology, saw it as his task to personally relieve the Commander-in-Chief, engaged in an external war with the world, and to take upon himself the anti-Semitic objectives without burdening Hitler himself. This theory of Irving's was obviously supported by the evidence of the author's witnesses of preference, Hitler's junior staff, who knew Hitler from a servant's perspective only as a more or less charming "boss." They could well imagine that "A.H." (as they were still calling him) was once again kept in the dark, as Hitler had claimed often enough, and deceived on account of his good nature and naivete. Even Hitler's valet, Krause, whose memoirs lend wholehearted support to the popular refrain "if only the Führer knew about this," has not been shunned by David Irving as a source of information. On the other hand Irving often failed to take into consideration, or treated with impatience, the post-war statements of witnesses who were personally involved in the killings or who had had access to secret information. He refers to the statements by Walter Blume and Otto Ohlendorf, the former commander of the *Einsatzgruppen,* confirming the 1941 verbal instructions to commanders about the killings, expressly issued under Hitler's instructions; although these are cited by the author they are distorted in the reproduction. He completely ignores the remarkable statement of the former SD officer Wilhelm Höttl [The critic adds in a footnote: "Höttl stated during the Eichmann Trial in Jerusalem in June 1961: The leader of *Einsatzgruppe* A, Dr. Stahlecker, had explained to him during the war that the orders to the *Einsatzgruppen* concerning the annihilation of the Jews 'came from Hitler personally and were communicated to the *Einsatzgruppen* by Heydrich.' Höttl further stated that as witness in Nuremberg in the years 1945-1947 he spoke with former leading functionaries: 'the unanimous understanding of these people' had been 'that the physical annihilation of the Jewish people should definitely be traced back to Hitler personally.' "] and those of the commander of Auschwitz, Rudolf Höss. The testimony of Adolf Eichmann, too, is passed over and declared misleading.

Irving claims that the only evidence of the fact that Hitler had ordered the annihilation of the Jews came from the former SD officer and expert on Jewish questions in Bratislava, Dieter Wisliceny, but is of no value. Irving attempts to refute this testimony by citing a particularly weak parallel—"Given the powerful written evidence that Hitler again and again ordered the 'Jewish problem' set aside until the war was won." He refers to the conversations with Bormann, Goebbels and others in the summer of 1941 concerning oppositional stirrings within the Catholic Church (Count Galen), in which Hitler opposes the tendency to apply radical measures against the opposition spokesmen of the Catholic clergy suggested by the

NSDAP and particularly by Bormann in order to forestall opposition of the Church-going public. Just as in the case of the Church, Irving claims that Hitler sought to postpone the Jewish problem until after the war. That Irving does not hesitate to manipulate his documentary evidence in order to add conviction to a thesis that is misleading *ab initio,* reveals the obstinacy of his reasoning.

This argument is obviously intended to support Irving's main thesis that Hitler was too busy with the conduct of the war to attend to the Jewish question himself and left Heydrich and others to deal with it. Irving's want of historical understanding and his lack of textual cohesion become especially obvious in this thesis. Even a cursory inspection of Hitler's wartime declarations concerning the Jews makes it clear that there was a widely motivated and powerful link in Hitler's thinking and will between military operations, particularly the war against the Soviet Union, and his ideological war against the Jews. It is precisely this very obvious connection that robs Irving's revisionist theses of all conviction, especially since without this ideological-pathological linkage between the war and the annihilation of the Jews (in Hitler's world-view) the latter could hardly be explained.

If one seeks to grasp the full significance of this philosophy as a motivating force, it does not suffice to trace it back to a paradigm of rational ideological interactions. Hitler's philosophy, and especially the anti-Jewish components, had always been a non-wavering dogma, combined with sudden outbursts of paranoic aggressiveness. Anyone considering only the first portions necessarily concludes that there had been neither evolution nor radicalization. The final solution of the Jewish problem appears as a realization of a long-established programme methodically and "logically" carried out step by step. Closer inspection of the National Socialist Jewish policy shows that such a hypothesis is incorrect and does not adequately explain some important facts. The violent *Reichskristallnacht* which opened the door for the lawless persecution of the Jews, is a particularly telling example. Ever since, Hitler's fixation and impatience for a solution of the Jewish question were reinforced—evident from the frequency and intensity of his official utterances and the diplomatic activities with which he approached the Jewish question at the beginning of 1939—and cannot be explained on the basis of Hitler's ideology alone. Whichever explanation—with its inevitable concomitant psychological undertones—one prefers, be it the overwhelming euphoria of success to which Hitler was then subject and which drove him to exceed his still rational, political aims, means and calculations; or the later (post-winter 1941) and by no means insignificant motive of revenge and retribution for the unsuccessful conduct of the war, it is certain that Hitler's dogmatic ideological anti-Semitism was not independent of factors of time and events. Its development was not merely programmatic but rather pathological and was weakened or intensified by current events; these fluctuations were at least as important a motive for decision and action as was a fixation on a specific dogma. This is mirrored in the alternately spontaneous or constrained nature of actions relating to the Jewish policy and the killings, which did not proceed smoothly and according to plan but rather in an improvised and jerky fashion.

From this angle the interdependence between the war and the Jewish question gains even greater importance. The war did not only offer—as noted cynically by Goebbels in his diary on March 27, 1942—opportunities for violent procedures that did not exist in peacetime, but was *welcomed* (and not only *risked* for political imperialist reasons). Hitler's prophesied destruction of Jewry, made on January 30, 1939, in the event of a new world war which has subsequently been cited so frequently, was from a psychological point of view not only a "warning" but in itself part of the motivation.

The war, however, in its further course, offered ideal fuel for the constant "recharging" of a manic-aggressive anti-Semitism, and not to Hitler alone. The confrontation with the masses of *Ostjuden* in occupied Poland, in the Baltic states and in Russia, provided emotional nourishment and confirmation for an imperialist racial ideology that had until then been propagated only in the abstract; there now existed a concrete picture of an inferior race which had to be eradicated. The psychologically cheapest and most primitive form of self-confirmation and self-fulfilling prophecy could now be set in motion: the discriminated against, crowded, tormented and frightened Jews in the East finally looked the way they were caricatured in the anti-Semitic periodicals. Epidemics in the ghettos made them a threat to the health of the general population; their terrified flight into the forest created the danger of "Jewish gangs" that one pretended to remove prophylactically just as one had to eradicate their expected propagation of defeatist ideas and plots in the occupied or allied neighbouring countries. All this and other motives were exploited not only by Hitler and Himmler but also by Goebbels and Ribbentrop and by the district military and civil administration chiefs. They were also employed by diplomats charged with the pressuring of the Allies into further intensification of the final solution in Europe, and were used and produced especially in the last stages of the deportations and exterminations in 1943-1944. These motives can be understood not only as semantic rules for the accomplishment of real ideological objectives, but rather as a conglomeration of various factors stemming from ideology, propaganda and, first and foremost, unexpected reactions of the individual which exceeded objectives set forth by racist ideology and brought into play so many "accomplices" and "assistants."

With Hitler, too, the assessment of the motives mirrored in his remarks on the Jewish question during the second half of the war is of major significance. As the military struggle appeared to become hopeless, the "war of fate" against Jewry was promoted as the real war (which would be won). The death of hundreds of thousands of German soldiers had to be expiated and biologically revenged through the liquidation of an even greater number of Jews. Also with Hitler the "security" problem came to the fore; Jews had to be eliminated, otherwise he feared that there could be internal unrest due to increased partisan warfare in the rear, defeatism and defection of Axis countries. It was for that reason the final intensification of radicalism

took place in Hitler after Stalingrad, and seems to be one of the motives for the intensified measures that aimed to encompass, if possible, all the Jews within the German sphere of influence into the extermination programme.

Hitler's numerous references to the interrelation of the war and the Jewish question show with sufficient clarity how untenable Irving's argument is. One example of Hitler's increased intervention in the final solution after Stalingrad is his discussions with the Rumanian head of state, Marshal Antonescu, and with the Hungarian Regent Admiral Horthy in April 1943. We shall examine these records in more detail at the close of this discussion, since not only do they once more document Hitler's intransigence and his way of thinking, but also give us an opportunity to demonstrate how the author of the Hitler book manipulates such documents. By describing the anti-Jewish measures in Germany (in the area of the Reich there remained only a few thousand Jews), Hitler attempted to persuade both heads of state to adopt a similar radical line towards the Jews of their respective countries. He bluntly expressed himself to Horthy on April 16-17, 1943. It had aroused his particular dissatisfaction that Hungary's 800,000 Jews could, in spite of some anti-Jewish laws that were promulgated in 1938, still move about with relative freedom. On April 16, 1943 Horthy answered the reproaches levelled against him on this matter by enumerating the manifold measures that had been taken by his government to restrict the Jewish influence; he closed his remarks with a clear allusion to the reports known to him about the German measures for the liquidation of the Jews: "He had done everything that could decently be done against the Jews, but it was after all impossible to murder them or otherwise eliminate them." Hitler, who was obviously embarrassed by this hint, declared, according to the records: ". . . there is no need for that; Hungary could put the Jews into concentration camps just as had been done in Slovakia . . . " He continued by counter-attacking while twisting the argument in his typical manner: "When there was talk of murdering the Jews, he [the Führer] had to state that there was only *one* murderer, namely the Jew who had provoked this war . . . " Hitler and Ribbentrop did not give up and on the next day (April 17) brought up the subject again. The most important parts of the record read:

> In reply to Horthy's question, what should be done with the Jews after he had deprived them of almost any means of existence—to murder them is not possible—the Foreign Minister answered that the Jews must either be destroyed or put in concentration camps—there is no other way.

Hitler complemented the straightforward speech of his Foreign Minister first by a long-winded dissertation on the decay that the Jews caused wherever they were found and, with a typical mixture of openness and obscurity, arrived at the heart of the matter: the massacre of the Jews in the concentration camps, as Horthy had alluded.

> They [the Jews] are just parasites. This state of affairs had not been tolerated in Poland; if the Jews there refused to work, they were shot. Those who could not work just wasted away.

They had to be treated as tuberculosis bacilli which could infect a healthy organism. This was by no means cruel when one considered that even innocent creatures like hares and deer had to be put down to prevent damage. Why should the beasts that had brought Bolshevism down on us, command more pity.

These documented statements on the part of Hitler could not be ignored even by Irving. He reproduces some passages but attempts to modify their significance methodically by a number of manoeuvers: Ribbentrop's declaration in the presence of Hitler (that the Jews must either be destroyed or put in concentration camps) is concealed in a footnote to the appendix of the book. Hitler's own remark (in Poland the Jews who refused to work were shot and those who could not work perished) Irving introduces with the reference to the Warsaw Ghetto Revolt which had been suppressed shortly before (and that had not even been mentioned in the conference with Horthy); he thus makes it falsely appear as only referring to an action that was limited in scope and carried out for a specific reason. In order to completely obscure the impression that the Führer's utterances, which could hardly be misunderstood, were indeed a confirmation of this policy of annihilation, Irving allows the discussion with Horthy to terminate, contrary to the documented facts, with Hitler's evasive remark of the previous day (April 16, 1943) in reply to Horthy's direct question if he should murder the Jews ("there is no need for that"). Irving cites these words at the end of his quotation and they are the only ones he cites *verbatim* and stresses with quotation marks. Irving finally ends the thoroughly manipulated course and content of the conference with some further remarks that are intended to relieve Hitler of responsibility and are typical for Irving's apologetic interpretation. As an illustration we shall quote them *verbatim*:

> What had prompted the earthier [!] language now employed? It is possible to recognize the association in his mind of certain illogical ideas; half were unconscious or the result of his own muddled beliefs, but half had deliberately been implanted by trusted advisers like Himmler and Goebbels: the Jews had started the war; the enemy was the international Jew; the most deadly of the Bolsheviks, like Stalin's propagandist Ilya Ehrenburg, were Jews: Ehrenburg and the Jews behind Roosevelt were preaching the total extermination of the German race. The saturation bombing of German cities, their blasting and burning, were just the beginning. In his warning to Horthy that the "Jewish Bolsheviks" would liquidate all Europe's intelligentsia, we can identify the influence of the Katyn episode . . . But the most poisonous and persuasive argument used to reconcile (!) Hitler to a harsher treatment of the Jews was the bombing war. From documents and target maps recently found in crashed bombers he knew that the British aircrews were instructed to aim only at the residential areas now and to disregard the industrial targets proper. Only one race murdered, he told the quailing Horthy, and that was the Jews, who had provoked this war and given it its present character against civilians, women and chil-

dren. He returned repeatedly to this theme as 1943 progressed; in 1944 it became more insistent; and in 1945 he embodied it in his Political Testament, as though to appease his own conscience and justify his country's actions.

With these "explanations" our author has done it again: without the British bombing war that had been initiated by Churchill, Hitler would not have been such a hater of the Jews. The prejudice of the author, transforming his hatred of Churchill into an apology for Hitler, is apparent in this passage, and indeed, characterizes the whole book.

It is not possible, and indeed it is quite unnecessary to delve into Irving's distorting interpretation. Over and above our criticism, it is a point in the author's favour that we are provided an opportunity to re-examine the subject. In spite of his mistaken conclusions Irving has drawn our attention to some of the hitherto inadequate information and existing interpretations.

Bradley F. Smith

SOURCE: "Two Alibis for the Inhumanities: A. R. Butz, *The Hoax of the Twentieth Century* and David Irving, *Hitler's War*," in *German Studies Review,* Vol. I, No. 3, October, 1978, pp. 327-35.

[*Smith is an American historian and author of numerous studies of the Nazis. In the following essay, he reviews* The Hoax of the Twentieth Century *by A. R. Butz and* Hitler's War *by David Irving.*]

In his closing statement to the Nürnberg Tribunal, the American Chief Prosecutor, Justice Robert Jackson, predicted that the war crimes trial's "mad and melancholy record" would "live as the historical text of the twentieth century's shame and depravity." Yet here we are 30 years later not only facing a bewildering range of scholarly interpretive and factual assertions about Nazism, but also a book by an American university professor (Butz) which contends that no Nazi exterminations of the Jews ever took place, and a volume by an English specialist on the Second World War (Irving) which concedes that Jews were exterminated, but claims that Hitler did not order the killings.

So much for those who hoped to produce a permanent historical record about Nazism which would bind and control the future! Times change, and the emotional experience of one generation cannot be completely transferred to the next, no matter how strong the emotion or deep the pain. This is the main reason why the purists are wrong when they advise that scholars should not give attention to "mad" or "crazy" works such as those by Butz or Irving. The very existence of these two books indicates that the feelings of the present, no matter how base or petty they may appear on occasion, can be more intense than the loftiest sentiments carried over from an earlier time. In 1978 a reader who is under the age of 35 can no more have had direct experience of the Nazi era than he, or she, can have participated in the Boer War or the burning of witches. The post-1945 generation may only develop a personal feeling for the Nazi period through study and by trying to share the emotional experience of others. But to expect that this feeling or attitude will, in every case, run in the same channels and with the same intensity as that of the war's chief victims is totally unrealistic. The events of the Third Reich and World War II are now being made to serve the whole range of emotional, ideological and political demands of the present. Obviously these can take forms which, as in these two volumes, are difficult for many of us to emotionally accept, but such is the ultimate law of history. Even in the case of historical atrocities, time does not stand still, and we either face things as they are now, or leave the historical opinion formation of the present generation to the whims of public fancy and the works of [A. R.] Butz or [David] Irving.

Of the two volumes before us, that by Butz should have the least claim to our attention if we judge impact solely on the basis of whether a book might produce large over-the-counter sales. *The Hoax of the Twentieth Century* is a dull, badly printed volume of 200 pages, produced by an obscure English provencial press. Its general tone and the quality of the writing are not significantly higher than that in the anti-Semitic, anti-Communist, and pro-Nazi tracts which lie around bus stations and skid row bookstores. But Butz is a professor of electrical engineering and computer sciences at Northwestern, and his assertions are bound to be quoted by his ideological (rather than his academic) colleagues as the height of scientific erudition. Furthermore, when the book appeared in the summer of 1977, it immediately produced a long wire service story which, in turn, caused articles about the volume to appear in many American newspapers. On the heels of this first burst of publicity came a second, occasioned by controversy at Northwestern, and by denunciations of Butz and the University's handling of the affair, from the Anti-Defamation League.

So Butz is with us, and on the bar and parkbench circuit his views will probably enjoy a wide circulation. Butz's main contention is one common to elements of the radical right that the historical fact of a Nazi murder of 6 million Jews is nothing but a myth concocted by communists and Zionists for their own devilish political purposes. According to Butz and his friends, the Nazis were rather decent fellows who only wanted to put Jews to work in order better to defend Germany against the Reds and misguided, Jewish dominated fools in the Western democracies. After the war, in Butz's view, Bolsheviks and Zionists gathered up the Jews who had been contentedly laboring in camps in the East, and either absorbed them into the Soviet Union or smuggled them into the United States and Israel. So to believe Butz is to deny that mass killings occurred and to hold that the historical reality of extermination is only a plot, a "hoax" to create sympathy for Israel and "Jewish" Communism.

Even after taking a deep breath it is difficult to take in all this, especially as Butz tries to produce a scholarly gloss for his assertions by the use of some 450 footnotes. Therefore one must begin by stressing that Butz's "conclusions," which are also his premises, are totally false. We are fortunate to have a recently published scholarly German study by Ino Arndt and Wolfgang Scheffler ["Or-

ganisierter Massenmord an Juden in Nationalsozialistischen Vernichtungslagern," *Vierteljahrshefte für Zeitgeschichte*] which systematically refutes all the assertions and alleged statements of fact made by current German right-wing publications of what may come to be called the "Butz school." This splendid survey is as applicable to Butz as it is to his German comrades, and should be studied by everyone able to read German.

But even for those able to read Arndt and Scheffler, it is important to understand the particular methods Butz uses to support his "conclusions," for it is from a superficial appearance of scholarly inquiry that *The Hoax* may gain some credence. Butz uses a whole series of methodological tricks and gimmicks in addition to misleading or erroneous footnotes and the confusing half-truths which are the stock and trade of polemical writing. Butz is a master of deceptive selection. His favorite device is to reject broad categories of evidence on the ground that the sources are tainted. Thus any document or testimony which originated in the Soviet Union or Israel is dismissed out of hand, as are most statements by individual Jews or Russians. Butz also easily convinces himself that the Nürnberg trials were a Communist-Zionist plot, so all of this material is cast away. There is virtually no end to his categorical rejections. In a typical Butz explanation, he dismisses all evidence from the American Office of Strategic Services (OSS), Office of War Information (OWI), and War Refugee Board (WRB) on the ground "that two 'internationals,' the Communist and the Zionist, played important roles" in these agencies. By the time one has subtracted all the material that Butz wants rejected, little remains of World War II documentation except a few Nazi records and the apologia of SS men.

Yet even when dealing with the records of the Third Reich, Butz has a special gift for selecting and arranging in a way that produces the maximum confusion and uncertainty. One may ask, for example, how he could hope to explain away the numerous references to the "Endlösung" and "Sonderbehandlung" in SS documents? He does it simply by denying that these words actually mean extermination and killing. He asserts that *Endlösung* merely indicated that Jews were being transferred to the east, while *Sonderbehandlung* referred to anything from special correspondence privileges for prisoners to specialized procedures for handling abortions. Butz scampers through published document collections—including ones he elsewhere rejects as "Zionist"—until he finds a document in which a specific word like *Sonderbehandlung* is not used in a perfectly clear way. In most such cases he misreads or misinterprets the document until he can claim a harmless meaning, and then crows to his readers that *Sonderbehandlung* did not necessarily mean killing. The important consideration here is not that he twists a particular document to come up with this conclusion, but that he passes over scores of documents in the same collections which show beyond any sane margin of doubt that *Sonderbehandlung* was the cover word used by the SS to mean execution or killing. Obviously we are faced with a conscious effort to misrepresent the evidence.

In a related piece of slight-of-hand, Butz loves to jump on

a weak source while ignoring any formidable account with which he does not want to cope. For example, in discussing the operation of concentration camps, he waxes eloquent on the weak points of an obscure book of memoirs published by Christopher Burney in 1946, but is careful not to take on any piece of significant concentration camp literature such as Kogan's *Der SS Staat,* or the recent detailed studies of the camp system which have been published in Germany. Regarding documentary sources too, he can speculate endlessly on such inane questions as the authenticity of the published version of Himmler's speech to the SS leaders in Posen on October 4, 1943. The reason Butz needs to discredit such items is obvious because in this speech, and many others, Himmler frankly discussed the extermination of Jews. So Butz floats up every imaginary reason why the printed text might contain errors, but he pays no attention either to published commentaries on the speeches, or the original texts and recordings of them which are in the National Archives. Butz claims that he visited the Archives, but if so he did not check the original Himmler speech materials or the thousands of other primary source documents in the collection which would have quickly demolished his wild speculations about the validity of the crucial published materials.

One could go on and on, citing instances of Butz's mania for distortion and misleading selection, but the pattern should by now be clear. Butz's book is a contrived sham, dangerous only because of its possible impact on naive and confused general readers. For the specialist, or those with a general grasp of World War II conditions however, *The Hoax of the Twentieth Century* is a sitting duck.

After struggling through this polemic by Butz, it is easy to see that the second work under consideration, *Hitler's War* by David Irving, is a different, and historically more serious animal. Irving is a technically competent student of the Second World War, and he is, after a fashion, trying to understand what happened. *Hitler's War* simply suffers very seriously from a basic flaw that has marked a number of the author's previous works. Irving cannot rise above his own intense emotional response to Britain, Germany, and the events of World War II. Perhaps already alienated from his own country at the time the war ended, Irving made the rather unusual decision to leave Britain and, while still a young man, went to Germany—the land of the defeated enemy in the late 1940s—where he toiled for a year as a factory worker. Although he then returned to Britain, this period seems to have left a strong mark upon him. In those years he developed a passionate interest in the history of the Second World War, a sure grasp of the German language, a great love for Germany, and a sharp hostility, if not contempt, for wartime Britain and its leaders, especially Winston Churchill.

One suspects that only such a peculiar personal history could lead a professional writer to produce a volume for the Anglo-American public that approaches the Second World War uncritically, even enthusiastically, from Hitler's point of view. The title is no misnomer. Irving assumes Hitler's vantage point so totally that it is often difficult to tell where the views of the Führer end and those of the author begin. Irving only puts before us the facts

and issues which surviving records and interviews indicate that Hitler saw. He then argues and badgers us in an effort to make his readers believe that Hitler's judgment and his orders were usually reasonable and justified. It is as if Irving had walked into Hitler's headquarters, sat down at his desk, donned the same blinders that Hitler wore, and then presented the Führer's memoirs as if they were history.

As a tour de force it is intriguing at first, especially because Irving's narrative makes use of some unknown and genuinely significant new documentary sources. It is also satisfying to see him demolish the post-war excuses and self-justifications of the many Hitler servants who have long tried to heap all responsibility for Nazi errors and atrocities on the head of the dead Führer. But since the text is 823 pages long, the myopia becomes ever more depressing, especially when it emerges that Irving is not just playing at being Hitler for illustrative purposes. To him this is not a tour de force but a realistic point of view, and the reader gradually finds himself gripped by disgust and the same kind of otherworldly panic which occasionally took possession of those wretched souls who actually lived through the madness that was Hitler's wartime headquarters.

Volumes could, and probably will, be written on the ways Irving's vision distorts every conceivable aspect of the history of World War II, but here we are only concerned with his claim that although Adolf Hitler did order the deportation of the Jews, he did not command that they be exterminated. Building his case on the lack of any direct written order by Hitler to exterminate, Irving gathers together a series of garbled documentary scraps and concludes that Hitler's aides carried out the killings behind his back, and without his knowledge. These assertions are so singular that they have brought forth a number of harsh popular reviews as well as extended negative critiques by four of the world's leading specialists on Nazi Germany: Alan Bullock, Hugh Trevor-Roper, Eberhard Jäckel and Martin Broszat. All four authorities agree that Irving's conclusions are wrong and that he misinterprets or distorts the evidence. Martin Broszat also convincingly demonstrates that the absence of a written killing order by Hitler is neither surprising nor interpretively very significant. The command system in the occupied Eastern territories, and the complex evolution of Nazi anti-Semitic measures combined so that an oral order from Hitler to Himmler and Heydrich was a more "natural" development than a written authorization moving through bureaucratic channels.

In his extended analysis, Broszat shows that the core of the trouble with Irving's book is the author's decision to try to stand in Hitler's shoes and allow the whole range of World War II events to swirl around him. By so doing he and the reader lose sight of the way the *Endlösung* killing system developed; each murderous event simply floats by in the narrative as if it was an isolated incident having no connection with what came before. Irving examines each phase, such as the *Einsatzgruppen* murders in Russia in the summer of 1941, or the beginning of gas chamber execution of Jews at the end of that year, but concludes there is no overwhelming evidence extant to trace responsibility for any particular case directly to Hitler. As

Broszat stresses, Irving has to give more ground on some incidents than others, but he is careful never to draw attention to the cumulative case that points toward Hitler.

Broszat's 35 page critique is too long and too detailed to permit even a cursory summary in these pages, but the validity of his major point, that Irving's explanation fails as soon as the *Endlösung* is examined systematically, can be demonstrated if we apply it to one simple question—who does Irving indicate was responsible for the killings if it wasn't Hitler? To my knowledge none of Irving's critics have posed this question, but it is obviously critical to the *Endlösung* thesis in *Hitler's War*. Immediately beneath Hitler in the chain of command stood Himmler, then Heydrich, and finally the SS and Party leaders in the Eastern territories. For Irving's argument to be taken seriously it is crucial to establish whether he is saying that Himmler duped Hitler, or whether the Reichsführer-SS is also supposed to have been duped. We know that Himmler had an incredible *Paladinkomplex* which makes the first alternative implausible. The simple law of probability would suggest that one can't extend the "duped chain" indefinitely, so even if we ignore the numerous documentary references showing that Himmler issued killing orders, the second choice also seems doubtful. Irving is in a tight corner, which way does he go?

As one might expect, he goes every way. When speaking of the killing of Polish Jews in 1939, Irving says that "Himmler and Heydrich provided the initiative and drive themselves." He also makes use of a modified form of this assertion when first discussing the killings in Russia in late 1941. "Responsibility for what happened to Russian Jews and (sic) to European Jews after their arrival in 'the east,'" Irving writes, "rested with Himmler, Heydrich, and the local authorities there." But six pages later, while still discussing the extermination of Jews in Russia he asserts that "It was Heydrich and the fanatical Gauleiters in the east who were interpreting with brutal thoroughness Hitler's decree that Jews must 'finally disappear' from Europe; *Himmler's personal role is ambivalent.*" Finally near the end of the book, when describing the frank speeches on the exterminations which Himmler made in October 1943, the author remarks that Himmler must have felt impregnable because his speeches amounted—in Irving's twisted view—to an open admission "that he had disregarded Hitler's veto on liquidating the Jews all along."

Without resorting to caricature one might capsulize Irving's statements as follows: The responsibility for the extermination of the Jews was not Hitler's; it was Heydrich's, but sometimes it was also the Eastern Gauleiters, and Himmler's too, but the latter point is not certain even though the Reichsführer-SS was the one who did it behind Hitler's back. This is not an explanation of the murder of Jews, or of anything else. It is merely an accumulation of vignettes which Irving has used to drape the reality that he cannot present any plausible alternative to a Hitler order for the *Endlösung*. Irving has thereby failed to produce a viable revisionist interpretation of the exterminations.

In conclusion, it is important to stress that while Butz is vicious, Irving is merely frivolous, if irresponsibly so. Yet because he is so technically skilled, Irving through his impact on historians could have a more pernicious influence than Butz. With public interest in the mass murders heightened by the recent television series, "The Holocaust," both the general reader and the historian need a new, corrective English language handbook on the exterminations. Until it appears, the works by Arndt, Scheffler and Broszat cited above, are still the best buttresses we have for the cause of historical sanity.

The response of the Canadian press to Holocaust denial:

In May 1983, the *Calgary Sun,* a sensationalist tabloid, ran the headline " 'Holocaust a lie,' " in inch-high letters, across a full-page article on Jim Keegstra. A large photo showed the Eckville teacher smiling in an easy chair, reading an issue of *Holocaust News* with the headline " 'Holocaust' Story an Evil Hoax." In a Sunday edition, the *Edmonton Sun* published one article in which a professor of history at the University of Alberta stated that "the basic facts of the Holocaust are beyond doubt," and another article in which Keegstra claimed that six million Jews could not possibly have been murdered during the war. In yet a third instance, this time in the *Lethbridge Herald,* an anonymous letter writer was allotted thirty-four column inches to detail the "Holocaust as hoax" and Jewish world-conspiracy myths. Sometimes even a serious paper lost its perspective, as occurred when a *Calgary Herald* story was headlined: "City Jews insist Holocaust real," as though this were not a documented fact.

To an extent, the treatment was predictable: the serious journalistic publications approached a sensitive issue in a professional manner; the others gave it the same sensational treatment which some of their material receives. More often than not, the press coverage of the Keegstra affair was thorough and objective, while editorial and feature comment reflected disapproval and rejection of the Eckville mayor and his teachings. In this way, the press added to its traditional role of disseminator of information an additional one of moral guide and persuader.

David Bercuson and Douglas Wertheimer, in their A Trust Betrayed: The Keegstra Affair, *Doubleday Canada Limited, 1985.*

Alan Bullock

SOURCE: "The Schicklgruber Story," in *The New York Review of Books,* Vol. XXIV, No. 9, May 26, 1977, pp. 10-15.

[*Bullock is an English historian whose book* Hitler: A Study in Tyranny *(1952) is considered one of the most important books on the Nazi dictator. In the following excerpt, he considers arguments advanced in David Irving's* Hitler's War.]

"It seems likely," Robert Waite begins his book [*The Psychopathic God, Adolf Hitler*], "that more will be written about Adolf Hitler than about anyone else in history with the exception of Jesus Christ." This is a depressing prospect indeed. Why Hitler should continue to arouse such interest is a subject worthy of a major essay, for which *The New York Review* might well offer a prize. At the bottom of his first page Professor Waite prints this quotation:

> The more I learn about Adolf Hitler, the harder I find it to explain and accept what followed. Somehow the causes are inadequate to account for the size of the effects. It is offensive to our reason and to our experience to be asked to believe that the [youthful Hitler] was the stuff of which the Caesars and Bonapartes were made. Yet the record is there to prove us wrong. It is here, in the gap between the explanation and the event, that the fascination of Hitler's career remains.

Although this comes from an introduction I wrote twenty years ago, I should not want to alter it today; but the passage of thirty years since Hitler's death has naturally extended the spectrum of comment in a way which is well illustrated by three of the four books I have been reading.

At one end of the spectrum is David Irving, an Englishman, whose book [*Hitler's War*] was first published in Germany in 1975 (*Hitler und seine Feldherren*). Further printing, however, was stopped after two days as a result of a dispute between author and publishers, apparently over his view of Hitler's responsibility for the "Final Solution." The book begins rather abruptly at the outbreak of war in 1939, with no discussion of the events leading up to this, and then takes 800 pages to cover in detail the five and a half years separating this from Hitler's defeat and suicide.

Mr. Irving's strength is in the persistence with which he pursues new evidence. This is a virtue recognizable by any historian and since I am critical of the use Mr. Irving makes of the evidence I want to be fair and acknowledge the energy and resource he has shown as a researcher.

There is no danger that anyone will overlook these. Mr. Irving rarely misses an opportunity to reiterate his claim that this is "not another biography of Hitler drawing on the same tired, mutually-supporting material" that other historians have used, but one entirely based on firsthand research "eschewing published sources."

It is a pity, in view of this claim, that he has not devoted more space to discussing the material he has used. At first sight the eighty pages of notes would appear to offer everything one wants, but it is often difficult without considerable research to distinguish between the claim to have unearthed new material which has never been seen before and the claim to have gone back to original sources already known and not relied on copying out quotations from other people's books. It is no less important to distinguish new material which adds something important to what is already known from that which, while not used before, adds only a few unimportant details or merely provides confirmation, perhaps with minor variations, of

something known before. This is another distinction which Mr. Irving frequently fails to make.

From a number of cases where I have made checks in following up the notes, my own conclusion is that the basis of Mr. Irving's account remains evidence known to and used by other historians before him. He has certainly worked over this evidence again for himself and in doing so thrown up a number of omissions and suppressions; he has also, without doubt, added to it, but not all his geese have proved to be swans, and I suspect that quite a lot of the additional material which he has gathered does not add substantially to what was known before.

It would not be worth spending so much time on this question of sources if it were not for Mr. Irving's further claim that his researches have "disclosed a picture of the man that nobody until now had suspected." I do not believe, as I shall go on to argue, that this claim is justified. But in so far as he does strike out an original line of argument, it is important that the reader should not allow himself to be stunned by the barrage of references to hitherto unpublished or unexploited material and be led to conclude that Mr. Irving's view follows necessarily, or even plausibly, from new evidence which he has brought to light.

The scope of Mr. Irving's book is unusual. It is not a biography of Hitler, since it deals only with the last five and a half years of his life when he was already over fifty years old. On the other hand, it is not a history of the war, even seen from the German point of view. It deals in great detail with the war but "in each case," Mr. Irving says, "this book views the situation as far as possible through Hitler's eyes, from behind his desk." Mr. Irving's method is to scour every source in order to establish what was said by Hitler and others in his wartime conferences and conversations. This is the substance of the book and the scene throughout is the Führer's headquarters. It is not easy reading, partly because the author introduces so little variation in the chronicle form as one conference follows another in the Führer's headquarters. No attempt is made to analyze the content or function of these meetings or, except in a perfunctory way, to look at the organization of the German war economy and the production of armaments.

But there is a more serious criticism to be made of Mr. Irving's method. He lays great stress on providing an accurate record of what was said on these occasions but inevitably the reader asks how far this can be accepted as reliable evidence of what actually happened even on the German side of the war. Thus, for example, a good deal of space is devoted to the argument between Hitler and his generals about who was to blame for the disastrous outcome of the Russian war. One can accept Mr. Irving's argument that the generals are biased witnesses and have had it too much their own way; but is Hitler, whom he quotes at length to the effect that it was the generals' fault and not his, any less biased or more reliable a witness? Is Mr. Irving still "viewing the situation through Hitler's eyes" or is he playing the role of a historian offering his own independent valuation of what was said? I am not sure that Mr. Irving has ever faced this question of his own position; if he has his answer seems to me ambiguous.

His answer is not even ambiguous when he discusses Hitler's opponents. Churchill and Roosevelt were warmongers in Hitler's eyes and it would be hard to find a sentence in these 800 pages which suggested that Mr. Irving took a different view. In the case of Britain he quotes with approval the Duke of Windsor's suspicion in July 1940 that the war was continued "purely so that certain British statesmen could save face," and argues that it was the British refusal to make peace with Hitler then that condemned the Western world to so much unnecessary suffering and destruction, including the death of six million Jews. The premise for this is Mr. Irving's "discovery"—which has been known for many years—that Hitler admired rather than hated the British and would have preferred to have them as allies rather than enemies.

Of course he would, since this would have given him a free hand in Europe. But why, Mr. Irving asks, were such "momentous alternatives" not considered by the British? To which the answer is that they were. The whole object of the policy of appeasement (to which Mr. Irving never once refers) was precisely to find such an alternative, and it broke down, not because the British thought Hitler hated or threatened them directly, but because they reluctantly concluded in the light of his record in the Thirties that it was impossible to make terms with him that he would keep, and that if he was allowed to go on and conquer the whole of Europe, Britain would lose its independence.

If the British *had* made a compromise peace after the fall of France, there is no reason at all to suppose that Europe would have been spared a continuation of the war—since Hitler would have gone on to attack Russia all the more readily—or that once he had come to rule all Europe Hitler would have left the Jews their lives or the British their independence. If Mr. Irving is going to discuss British policy he ought surely to take some account of what the British themselves thought and not simply see them through Hitler's eyes.

One quotation in Mr. Irving's book seems to me revealing. In talking with Hitler one day, a doctor asked him if he had ever read the life of the Kaiser by the Englishman J. D. Chamier. Hitler had and admitted that, though the author was English, the Kaiser had emerged well—perhaps better than he deserved. The doctor's note of the conversation continues:

> Hitler then said that a foreigner probably finds it easier to pass judgment on a statesman, provided that he is familiar with the country, its people, language and archives. . . . Hitler said that for some time now he has gone over to having all important discussions and military conferences recorded for posterity by shorthand writers. And perhaps one day after he's dead and buried an objective Englishman will come and give him the same kind of objective treatment.

Was Mr. Irving thinking of himself when he copied down this quotation? At the very least, it points up the question which I believe he fails to answer, perhaps even to himself, whether he regards "viewing the situation through Hitler's eyes" as the same thing as "objectivity."

Mr. Irving claims that his researches have not only enabled him to place Hitler's foreign policy in a different light but have disclosed "a picture of the man that nobody until now had suspected." "My central conclusion," he writes, "is that Hitler was a less than omnipotent Führer and that his grip on his immediate subordinates weakened as the war progressed." If Mr. Irving means that Hitler was never interested in administration and after the outbreak of war left such matters to be fought over by Bormann, Himmler, and the other satraps, this has been one of the commonplaces of the history of the Third Reich for twenty-five years. If, however, Mr. Irving is talking about *power* rather than administration—and he goes on to say that "Hitler was probably the weakest *leader* Germany has known in this century"—then there is so great a volume of evidence against such a view that it is astonishing anyone can seriously suggest it.

I was so surprised by Mr. Irving's conclusion, which seems to me to do less than justice to his own book, that I cast around for an explanation. In part, it seems to me to reflect his concentration on the war years and his omission of the 1930s, which must surely be counted as brilliant a decade of success as any political leader has ever enjoyed. But I believe the real explanation is to be found in Mr. Irving's desire, as he puts it, to "de-demonize" Hitler, leading up to his *coup de théâtre,* Hitler and the "Final Solution."

The connection between the two is obvious. The revisionist version of Hitler has hitherto stopped short at his foreign policy, which is represented as no different from anyone else's, and the responsibility for the war, from which he is absolved. For what happened inside Germany, however, Hitler has hitherto remained responsible. But if he was ignorant of and did not approve the greatest of all crimes, the extermination of five to six million Jews, then a very different picture emerges; then Hitler can be seen and understood as a normal person in domestic as well as foreign affairs or, as Mr. Irving describes him, "an ordinary, walking, talking human being weighing some 155 pounds, with graying hair, largely false teeth, and chronic digestive ailments." It is this final step in the normalization of Hitler which Mr. Irving now proposes.

He starts from the fact, long familiar to historians, that no order signed by Hitler for the extermination of the Jews has ever been found, and (a fact which always impresses Mr. Irving more) that what other researchers have failed to find he has not found either. He does not question the fact that the massacres took place and he admits that

> if this book were simply a history of the rise and fall of Hitler's Reich, it would be legitimate to conclude: "Hitler killed the Jews." He after all created the atmosphere of hatred with his anti-Semitic speeches in the 1930s; he and Himmler created the S.S.; he built the concentration camps; his speeches, though never explicit, left the clear impression that "liquidate" was what he meant.

Nonetheless, Mr. Irving goes on to maintain that historians have refused to face up to the difference made by the absence of a written order—or of documentary evidence of what Hitler and Himmler may have said *"unter vier Augen"*—and have simply gone on repeating that he was personally responsible without taking the trouble to look at the evidence.

No one denies that the evidence is incomplete and equivocal. This is hardly surprising considering the monstrosity of the crimes being committed, the massacre of several million people. Elaborate precautions were taken to confine knowledge of the facts to as small a circle as possible, denials were issued which Mr. Irving himself characterizes as "the purest humbug," and the ghastly reality was camouflaged by a series of euphemisms (such as the "Final Solution") which were employed even between those who knew what was taking place. Thus as late as July 1944—and even Mr. Irving admits that by October 1943 Hitler knew what had taken place—he notes that Himmler still continued to speak to Hitler only of the "expulsion" (*Aussiedlung*) of the Jews.

The process was spread over two years or more and was halted from time to time for reasons of expediency. (This could very well be the explanation of Himmler's telephone message of November 30, 1941 that Jews were not to be liquidated, of which Mr. Irving makes so much.) Mr. Irving agrees that Hitler was "unquestionably" the authority behind the "expulsion" of the Jews, their uprooting and "re-settlement" in the occupied areas of the East. But he asks us to believe that the man who claimed as his greatest discovery the identification of the Jew as the bacillus causing all decay in society, the man who from beginning to end of his career made the cleansing of Germany of its Jewish population a main plank of his program and spoke openly of his intentions, had no knowledge of or interest in what happened to the Jews when they got to the East. There are many people in Germany and Austria, Mr. Irving says, who have an interest in putting the blame on Hitler. He evidently believes that they knew what was happening, as did Goebbels and Hans Frank—to mention only two of the Nazi leaders about whose knowledge there is no doubt—but not Hitler. This is a lot to ask us to believe on the strength of not finding evidence which, given the nature of what was being done, it would be far more surprising to learn ever existed.

After getting Hitler to agree on August 18, 1941 to the requirement that Jews wear the Star of David and to the deportation of the 70,000 Berlin Jews to the East, Goebbels noted that Hitler had reminded him of his January 1939 Reichstag speech. He had said he was convinced that the prophecy he uttered then—that if the Jews provoked another world war it would end with their destruction (*Vernichtung*)—was "coming true these weeks and months with a dread certainty that is almost uncanny. In the east the Jews will have to square accounts." This was a few weeks before the first massacres took place. In a speech of February 24, 1943 Hitler referred to the extermination (*Ausrottung*) of European Jewry and on June 19 insisted to Himmler on pushing through radically (*radikal*) the "evacuation" of the Jews.

In October of that year, Himmler told conferences of the S.S. Gruppenführers and the Gauleiters that by the end of the year the last Jews in occupied Europe would have been physically exterminated, and he accepted responsibility for what had been done. But Himmler was not the man to have acted without Hitler's authority. In May 1944 he told an audience of generals that he had "uncompromisingly" solved "the Jewish problem." "You can imagine how I felt *executing this soldierly order issued to me, but I obediently complied* and carried it out to the best of my convictions" (my italics).

Mr. Irving does his best to explain away evidence like this and such is the immediate attraction of any revisionist thesis, especially if it offers to cut the portent of Hitler down to size, that his book will attract attention for this attempt alone. But I am convinced that, once the fuss has died down, Mr. Irving's thesis will not be accepted by the majority of historians who have worked on the period, and that the answer to the problems posed by Hitler will not prove to be that his power and his responsibility for what happened between 1933 and 1945 have been exaggerated. . . .

FURTHER READING

Bercuson, David, and Wertheimer, Douglas. *A Trust Betrayed: The Keegstra Affair.* Toronto: Doubleday Canada Limited, 1985, 241 p.

> Focuses on the trial of Jim Keegstra, a Canadian teacher accused of using anti-Semitic and revisionist books and tracts in his classroom.

Bolton, Judith. "Holocaust Revisionism: Editing the Past." *Congress Monthly* 59, No. 5 (July-August 1992): 9-12.

> Briefly discusses the impact of Holocaust denial on historical study, and concludes: "Rather than resist it by reinventing, rearranging, or downgrading it, the Holocaust must be acknowledged as well as anchored with ethical and moral imperatives."

Braham, Randolph L. "Historical Revisionism and the New Right." In *Remembering for the Future, Working Papers and Addenda, Vol. II: The Impact of the Holocaust on the Contemporary World*, pp. 2093-2103. Oxford: Pergamon Press, 1989.

> Examines the preponderance of Holocaust deniers in ultra-rightist political groups.

Butovsky, Avriel. "Radical Round Up: The Holocaust on Trial in Canada." *Patterns of Prejudice* 19, No. 3 (July 1985): 34-6.

> Briefly discusses the trial of Ernst Zundel, a German immigrant in Canada who was convicted under Canada's anti-hate-mongering laws for his Holocaust denial writings.

Davies, Alan. "A Tale of Two Trials: Antisemitism in Canada 1985." *Holocaust and Genocide Studies* 4, No. 1 (1989): 77-88.

> Summarizes the trials of Jim Keegstra and Ernst Zundel and addresses the more general issue of anti-Semitism in Canada.

Drobnicki, John A., Goldman, Carol R., Knight, Trina R.,

and Thomas, Johanna V. "Holocaust-Denial Literature: A Bibliography." *Bulletin of Bibliography* 51, No. 1: 17-24.

Comprehensive bibliography of Holocaust denial primary and secondary sources.

Gutman, Yisreal. *Denying the Holocaust.* Jerusalem: The Hebrew University of Jerusalem, 1985, 46 p.

Transcription in English of a lecture and discussion held on 13 May 1984 at the Study Circle on Diaspora Jewry.

Hill, Leonidas E. "The Trial of Ernst Zundel: Revisionism and the Law in Canada." *Simon Wiesenthal Center Annual* 6 (1989): 165-219.

Detailed examination of Ernst Zundel's trial, as well as an analysis of the Canadian laws under which Zundel was prosecuted.

Huerta, Carlos C. "Revisionism, Free Speech, and the Campus." *Midstream* XXXVIII, No. 3 (April 1992): 10-11.

Focuses on Bradley Smith and the controversial decision of university student newspapers to run his Holocaust denial ad.

King, Dennis. "The Jewish Question." In his *Lyndon LaRouche and the New American Fascism*, pp. 38-46. New York: Doubleday, 1989.

Examines the ties of Libertarian leader Lyndon LaRouche and his followers to anti-Semitism and Holocaust denial.

Lipstadt, Deborah E. *Denying the Holocaust: The Growing Assault on Truth and Memory.* New York: The Free Press, 1993, 278 p.

Book-length study of the Holocaust denial phenomenon, including discussion of its initial stirrings immediately after World War II, major figures in the Holocaust denial movement, and the contemporary controversy over Holocaust denial and First Amendment rights.

May, Michael. "Denying the Holocaust: The Background,

Methods and Motives of the 'Revisionists'." *Index on Censorship* 14, No. 6 (December 1985): 29-33.

Offers a concise discussion of the main issues, publications, and individuals involved in the Holocaust denial movement.

Mintz, Frank P. "Anti-Zionism and Holocaust Revisionism." In his *The Liberty Lobby and the American Right: Race, Conspiracy, and Culture*, pp. 107-26. Westport, Conn.: Greenwood Press, 1985.

Analyzes the anti-Semitic and revisionist strains within the American right-wing organization known as the Liberty Lobby.

Shapiro, Shelly, ed. *Truth Prevails. Demolishing Holocaust Denial: The End of "The Leuchter Report."* New York: The Beate Klarsfeld Foundation and Holocaust Survivors & Friends in Pursuit of Justice, 1990, 135 p.

Collection of responses to The Leuchter Report—a "forensic" study of the Auschwitz concentration camp in Poland financed by Ernst Zundel to be used in his defense at his trial—discrediting both the findings of the report and its author's credentials.

Vidal-Naquet, Pierre. *Assassins of Memory: Essays on the Denial of the Holocaust.* Translated by Jeffrey Mehlman. New York: Columbia University Press, 1992, 205 p.

Collection of essays on Holocaust denial.

Weinfeld, Morton. "The Classification of Holocaust Denial Literature by the Library of Congress." *Judaica Librarianship* 3, Nos. 1-2 (1986-87): 50-5.

Weinfeld's response to an article by Vincent Richards in which Richards defends unlimited access to revisionist literature in Canadian libraries. The article also reprints Richards's article, as well as an earlier article on the subject by Weinfeld.

Latin American Literature

INTRODUCTION

Latin American literature encompasses the national literatures of South and Central America, Mexico, Cuba, Puerto Rico, and parts of the West Indies. Its roots lie in European language and literary traditions, combined with themes and images drawn from the physical landscape and indigenous cultures of the South American continent. As early as the 1600s European colonists documented their experiences in the New World. When Latin American colonies began to declare independence from Europe in the early part of the nineteenth century, the climate of rebellion fostered a desire among many writers to create a literature that accurately reflected the lives and concerns of Latin Americans. While the tradition of Romanticism that developed in Europe during the nineteenth century had been favored by early Latin American novelists and poets, this style gradually gave way to greater realism, increased focus on the lives of ordinary people, and, with few exceptions, an intense concern with social and political reform. Magical realism, or the introduction of supernatural or uncanny elements into otherwise realistic narrative, also became a common feature in the works of many Latin American writers during the second half of the twentieth century. Since the 1940s and the "Boom" period of the 1960s, Latin American literature has become increasingly available to a worldwide audience. Writers such as Jorge Luis Borges, Juan Carlos Onetti, Juan José Arreola, Julio Cortázar, Carlos Fuentes, Gabriel García Marquez, and Miguel Angel Asturias have been internationally recognized for their contributions to world literature. The often chaotic political atmosphere of contemporary Latin America continues to generate writing that is both artistic and activist in nature. Recent decades have seen an increase in works devoted to the specific struggles of blacks, indigenous peoples, and other minorities. With the exception of Brazilian literature, which is written primarily in Portuguese, nearly all Latin American literature is in Spanish, and is often designated by critics as "Spanish-American" or "Hispanic-American" literature.

REPRESENTATIVE WORKS

Alegría, Ciro
  La serpiente de oro (novel) 1935
  [*The Golden Serpent,* 1943]
  El mundo es ancho y ajeno (novel) 1941
  [*Broad and Alien Is the World,* 1941]
Arguedas, Alcides
  Raza de bronce (novel) 1919
Arreola, Juan José
  Confabulario (short stories and essays) 1952
  [*Confabulario and Other Inventions,* 1964]
Asturias, Miguel Angel
  El señor Presidente (novel) 1946
  [*The President,* 1963]
  Hombres de maíz (novel) 1949
  [*Men of Maize,* 1975]
Azuela, Mariano
  Los de abajo: Novela de la revolución mexicana (novel) 1916
  [*The Underdogs,* 1929]
Bioy Casares, Adolpho
  La invención de Morel (novel) 1940
  [*The Invention of Morel, and Other Stories,* 1964]
Borges, Jorge Luis
  Ficciones (short stories) 1944
  [*Fictions,* 1965]
  El Aleph (short stories) 1949
  [*The Aleph, and Other Stories,* 1971]
Cabrera Infante, Guillermo
  Tres tristes tigres (novel) 1967
  [*Three Trapped Tigers,* 1980]
Carpentier, Alejo
  El reino de est mundo (novel) 1949
  [*The Kingdom of This World,* 1957]
  El acoso (novel) 1956
  [*Manhunt,* 1959]
Carrasquilla, Tomás
  Frutos de mi tierra (novel) 1896
  Grandeza (novel) 1910
  La marquesa de Yolombó (novel) 1929
Cortázar, Julio
  Rayuela (novel) 1963
  [*Hopscotch,* 1966]
  La vuelta al dia en ochenta mundos (novel) 1967
  [*Around the Day in Eighty Worlds,* 1986]
Dario, Rubén
  Azul (poetry and short stories) 1888
  Los raros (poetry) 1893
  Prosas profanas (short stories) 1896
  Cantos de vida y esperanza, Los cisnes, y otros poemas (poetry) 1905
de Castro, Eugenio
  Horas (poetry) 1891
del Campo, Estanislao
  Fausto (poetry) 1866
di Benedetto, Antonio
  Zama (novel) 1956
Fuentes, Carlos
  La región más transparente (novel) 1958
  [*Where the Air Is Clear,* 1960]
  Las buenas conciencias (novel) 1960
  [*The Good Conscience,* 1961]
  Aura (novel) 1962
  La muerte de Artemio Cruz (novel) 1962
  [*The Death of Artemio Cruz,* 1964]

Gringo viejo (novel) 1985
[*The Old Gringo,* 1985]
Gallegos, Rómulo
Doña Bárbara (novel) 1929
García Marquez, Gabriel
Cien años de soledad (novel) 1967
[*One Hundred Years of Solitude,* 1970]
El amor en los tiempos del cólera (novel) 1985
[*Love in the Time of Cholera,* 1988]
Gorostiza, José
Muerte sin fin (poetry) 1939
[*Death without End,* 1969]
Güiraldes, Ricardo
Don Segundo Sombra (novel) 1926
[*Don Segundo Sombra: Shadows on the Pampas,*
1935]
Guzman, Martín Luis
*El águila y la serpiente: Memorias de la revolución mex-
icana* (novel) 1928
[*The Eagle and the Serpent,* 1930]
La sombra del caudillo (novel) 1929
Henríquez Ureña, Pedro
Seis ensayos en busca de nuestra expresión (essays)
1928
Hernández, José
El gaucho Martín Fierro (poetry) 1872
La vuelta Martín Fierro (poetry) 1879
Icaza, Jorge
Huasipungo (novel) 1934
[*The Villagers,* 1973]
Lezama Lima, José
Paradiso (novel) 1966
[*Paradise,* 1974]
Lynch, Benito
Los caranchos de la Florida (novel) 1916
El inglés de los güesos (novel) 1924
El romance de un gaucho (novel) 1933
Machado de Assis, Joaquim María
Memórias pósthumas de Braz Cubas (novel) 1881
[*Epitaph of a Small Winner,* 1952]
Quincas Borba (novel) 1891
[*Philosopher or Dog?,* 1954]
Dom Casmurro (novel) 1899
[*Dom Casmurro,* 1953]
Marechal, Leopoldo
Adán Buenosayres (novel) 1948
La batalla de José Luna (drama) 1970
Martinez Moreno, Carlos
El paredón (novel) 1963
Neruda, Pablo
Residencia en la tierra (poetry and prose) 1935
Canto general (poetry) 1950
Onetti, Juan Carlos
La vida breve (novel) 1950
[*A Brief Life,* 1976]
El astillero (novel) 1961
[*The Shipyard,* 1968]
Juntacadaveres (novel) 1964
Paz, Octavio
Aquila o sol? (poetry) 1951
[*Aquila o sol? Eagle or Sun?,* 1970]
Blanco (poetry) 1967

Vuelta (poetry) 1975
Quiroga, Horacio
Cuentos de amor, de locura y de muerte (short stories)
1917
La gallina degollada, y otros cuentos (short stories)
1925
[*The Decapitated Chicken, and Other Stories,* 1976]
Rivera, José Eustacio
La vorágine (novel) 1924
[*The Vortex,* 1935]
Roa Bastos, Augusto
Hijo de hombre (novel) 1960
[*Son of Man,* 1965]
Rojas, Manuel
Hijo de ladrón (novel) 1951
[*Born Guilty,* 1955]
Rosa, João Guimarães
Grande Sertão: Veredas (novel) 1956
[*The Devil to Pay in the Backlands,* 1963]
Rulfo, Juan
El llano llamas (short stories) 1953
[*The Burning Plain, and Other Stories,* 1967]
Pedro Páramo (novel) 1955
Sabato, Ernesto
Sobre héroes y tumbas (novel) 1961
[*On Heroes and Tombs,* 1981]
Uslar Pietri, Arturo
Las lanzas coloradas (novel) 1930
[*The Red Lances,* 1963]
Vargas Llosa, Mario
La ciudad y los perros (novel) 1963
[*Time of the Hero,* 1966]
La casa verde (novel) 1966
[*The Green House,* 1968]
Elogio de la madrastra (novel) 1988
[*In Praise of the Stepmother,* 1990]
Yañez, Agustín
Al filo del agua (novel) 1947
[*The Edge of the Storm,* 1963]

HISTORICAL AND CRITICAL
PERSPECTIVES

Alan Cheuse

SOURCE: "Books in Flames: A View of Latin American
Literature," in *The Antioch Review,* Vol. 36, No. 2, Spring,
1978, pp. 141-53.

[*Cheuse is an American novelist and critic. In the following
essay, he traces the influences and evolution of Latin American literature.*]

The flat, swampy, low jungle of the Yucatan peninsula is
hot enough even in winter for its inhabitants to live without using fires at night for heating purposes. But in the
Mayan city of Mani, eighteen kilometers south of Merida,
the state's present capital, in the year 1562, a great fire
roared for days outside the walls of a convent newly con-

structed from the stones of a Mayan temple. Tens of thousands of religious articles and every extant Mayan holy manuscript that the priests, led by Bishop Diego de Landa, could find in the territory fed the flames in a book-burning that was much more devastating than those we have seen in films of the Nazi period in Europe. In the age of mechanical reproduction, book burning is a symbolic act. In sixteenth-century Mexico, the priests attempted to destroy an entire culture, the mind of a people, their past, their present, and their future. Nothing was more dangerous to the conquering theologians than the beautiful designs and colors of the Mayan hieroglyphic narratives. For several times a year, as Diego de Landa himself writes in his account of the Mayan culture he worked for decades to destroy,

> The priests would take out the books and extend them on cool foliage they had for this purpose . . . while they diluted a bit of verdigris in a glass with virgin water that they asserted was brought from the mountain where no woman treads, and they would anoint the wooden covers of the books with it . . . and the most learned of the priests would open a book and look at the omens for that year and make them known to those present.

These holy books, with their stately processions and knotted groups of kings and warriors, books of virgin water and succoring foliage, were painted in profound blues, rich golds, deep greens, and earthy reds, on both sides of thin sheets of pounded bark of the indigenous fig tree, and finished with a layer of calcium carbonate obtained from local rocks. Of their actual content, we still know quite little. "Of five apparent distinct varieties of pictowriting, the first treated years and times, the second days and festivals, the third dreams, delusions, vanities, and omens, the fourth baptism and the naming of children, and the fifth rites and ceremonies related to marriage." As the Mexican art historian Maria Sten describes it, the content of the manuscripts gave the Mayas an entire world.

It was not merely the content of the books which the priests destroyed. To the Mayans, the act of painting the narratives was holy in itself. As the legend has it, Quetzalcoatl, the plumed serpent of the Mexican pantheon, came to the Yucatan, in the form of the deity Kukulkan, and before anything else taught the Mayan people how to create the painted books. In this tropical territory, fire remained secondary in importance to the act of creating narratives. The coolness of an orderly universe stood first in importance. To combat the serpent god's invention, the priests plunged the books into the flames.

The discovery of America was thus not an act of uncovering a continent unknown to cultured human beings. As the Colombian historian Germán Arciéniegas has written, it was not so much an act of *descubriemiento* as of *cubriemiento,* not a discovery but a covering over, the burial of a great culture by the agents of another. For more than two centuries, the Spanish *criollo* ruling class bricked over indigenous Indian folkways, supplying the American continent with an imported theology in exchange for a stage where Spain, undergoing tumultuous social change from within and military and political defeat without, might

continue to reenact the tattered glories of its pre-Armada past.

However, colonial rule across oceans can only work well for the mother country if the imagination of the colony remains in its thrall. Ironically, the very allegiance to the traditions and mores of Spain which kept Spanish America in harness for several centuries produced the conditions which led to the burgeoning New World movements. In the eighteenth century, the Latin American ruling class, true to its sense of itself as a European-oriented group, opened wide its arms to the methods of European science, technology, and educational methods. Rationalism and liberalism took hold among an increasingly enlightened young generation and congress with Spain led to congress with Europe as well, a Rousseau-ist Europe in which man was everywhere throwing off his unnatural bondage to monarchy. In the wake of Bolivar's revolutions there emerged a group of independent Latin nations no longer enslaved by European imperialism. Now, however, they freely chose a way of life that was essentially European in nature. While the Indians toiled on, Madrid and Paris became centers of liberalism and bastions of middle-class hegemony, and served as the intellectual capitals of the newly independent American countries ruled by the *criollo* landowners and professionals.

In his seminal study of Argentine society, *Facundo, or Life in the Days of the Argentinian Tyrants,* author and statesman Dominigo Sarmiento describes the events of his nation's history as a struggle between the forces of civilization and barbarism. This analysis grew out of his understanding of the early period of Argentine post-Independence politics and the battles that raged between the educated creoles of Buenos Aires and the ragged, rugged uneducated cowboy armies of the countryside which from time to time threw up a leader to take over the urban seat of national power. Sarmiento boldly shows his sympathy for the European-oriented ruling group of the city. He never doubts the necessity for struggling against the rise of dictators from the pampas such as Facundo Quiroga, the figure who stands in his essay for the forces of misrule, anti-democracy, and the destruction of culture. Barbarism represents for him a return to the murder, rampages, and brutal tyranny that obtained during the short period of Facundo's rule.

Yet it also exerts a powerful attraction for the citified, Europeanized Sarmiento. He reserves his finest prose for the description of life among the barbaric gauchos of the pampas. His passages devoted to the skills and talents of the rough-riding gauchos, such as his abilities as a hunter and tracker, horseman, and singer of ballads, present us with a type reminiscent in its mythic stature of our own nineteenth century's Natty Bumpo, the Deerslayer of James Fenimore Cooper. The sections dedicated to the evocation of the landscape, the stage upon which these heroic gauchos ride, strut, sing, and shoot, rival in power and visionary force those of Sarmiento's model, the eighteenth-century French aristocrat Chateaubriand. The vast romantic vista of the pampas becomes a sight worthy of ranking alongside the North American landscapes in *Atala* and Cooper's "Leatherstocking Tales." The line between earth and sky becomes sublimely blurred as indigenous Homers of the plains wander past, singing of victories over the Indians while herding their great droves of cattle from one hazy horizon to the next. Like the first generation of conquerors, Sarmiento seems to admire what he considers most dangerous in indigenous American culture.

The paradox inherent in Sarmiento's work characterizes the next hundred years and more of Latin American literary production. For while it was not true, as he suggested, that all culture in the New World grew from the struggle between the forces of civilization and barbarism, it was evident that those who held the power in the Latin American nations behaved as though it were true. Thus brutal dictatorships arose from time to time throughout the continent, more often again than not in the name of civilization and the European way of life, and creole writers produced slavish imitations of European romantic fiction. As Alejo Carpentier has put it, there was an abundance in this period of novels with the names of women, the foremost example being *Maria* by the Colombian Jorge Isaacs. Poetry turned stale, the fragile tranquillity broken now and then by outcries that at last Venezuela had her Virgil or Brazil her Homer (noises akin to our own nineteenth-century proclamations, such as those made by William Cullen Bryant that the U.S. at last had matured to the point where it might make a poetry of its own, with a diction and stress pattern distinct from that of England's). Independence, which came early in the nineteenth century for nations such as Argentina, Venezuela, and Chile, and as late as 1902 for Cuba, did not necessarily mean economic freedom. Certainly it did not mean cultural independence.

For more than a century thereafter, most Latin American novelists applied the techniques of European artists to the materials of their own culture in unashamed imitation. To the ruling practitioners of the time, such models, whether romantic or naturalistic, did not seem "foreign" at all. Since they felt themselves bound to the progress of European culture, these nineteenth-century artists worked as willing slaves to a foreign tradition. The rise of the European regional folkloric novel produced a slight but important turn. Although today most of their works are best left to the specialists, the European writers—Jean Giono, Liam O'Flaherty, Ladislao Raimond—who practiced this sub-genre had a great effect on the first generation of twentieth-century Latin American intellectuals. As Alejo Carpentier, born in 1904, has written of his own encounter with these novels,

> In the face of an incredible boredom produced by a day of reading a novel about the customs of Alsatians, I asked myself "Why not do the same to them in Europe with novels about the customs of Cuban peasants or Gauchos or Yucatecans?"

That day, the Cuban novelist asserts, he became the author of *Ecue-Yamba-O!,* his first novel. Written when the author was twenty-five, it grew out of his research into the customs of black Cuban cane-cutters whose lives had been largely ignored by the educated, European-oriented creoles of the cities and large farms.

In similar fashion across Latin America, the Sarmientos of the present day looked beyond the romantic imagery of their predecessors to search out in serious, scientific fashion the facts of the daily life of the large masses of the Indian population of the continent, lives which up until then had been "discovered" only to be covered over by the dominant creoles. The Indians possessed no literature which the curious ethnologists, novelists, poets, and nascent anthropologists might immediately consult. Bishop Diego de Landa had seen to that. But their music, tribal language, work habits, tools, and designs on ceramics or cloth were readily available to the visitors from the urban centers, though most of their ancient cities still lay in vine-covered ruin. This marked the first phase of the true discovery of America by her own inhabitants. Paradoxically, the role of Europe in this major renovation of the Latin American imagination cannot be ignored. To Carpentier, and his Guatemalan contemporary Miguel Angel Asturias, sojourns to the Continent were instrumental in their own personal discoveries of America. What few manuscripts survived the holocaust at Mani in 1562, and the earlier destruction of Montezuma's library in Tenochtitlan when Cortez brought down the pillars of the Aztec empire, could only be found in Paris and Germany. To study the roots of their own culture, these young artists had to study in Europe.

It was in Paris in the 1920s that Carpentier first encountered the manuscripts that would inspire him to return to Cuba and study first-hand the history of his native island. It was in Paris in the 1920s that Asturias first read the *Popol-Vuh,* the sacred book of the Quiché-Maya whose language and imagery would affect his own fiction for nearly fifty years afterward. But while Europe in the 1920s was a place to study in, Europe in the 1930s became a place to flee. As Alfonso Reyes, the Mexican essayist put it, the continent began to disintegrate before the eyes of the world. The clouds gathering over the concentration camps gave notice that the culture of the Conquerors had fallen into a decadence no Aztec priest, hair smeared with blood of sacrificial victims, could ever have imagined. Europe offered no more idols to worship.

Latin American intellectuals, writers, artists, painters, poets, musicians, suddenly found themselves "exiled" in their own countries. Those who had not already turned their eyes toward the arts and traditions of their own population had no other place to turn. In 1945, Carpentier began the composition of his short novel based on the Haitian Revolution led by Toussaint L'Ouverture, *El Reino de este Mundo* [*The Kingdom of this World*] which would dramatize the break between Latin American "magical realist" writers and the European surrealist tradition which had nurtured them. In this same period, parallel with the rise of the continent's first indigenous socialist parties, Asturias published *El Señor Presidente,* a ferocious indictment of a Central American dictator in which he employed linguistic and narrative techniques indigenous to Guatemalan Indian narratives. His *Hombres de Maiz* [*Men of Maize*] followed shortly thereafter, signalling a break with the naturalist tradition in Latin America. Even the anomalous genius Borges, the eternal cosmopolitan, wrote in his unique "universal" style of city dwellers who dreamed of hand-to-hand combat with murderous gauchos. More than just the rejection of the hegemony of European culture united these men. Like the painters of the Mexican Revolution, Rivera, Siqueiros, and Orozco, they had finally uncovered their personal connection to the period of the Conquest and found themselves on the other side of the Sarmiento paradigm from civilization in a new world rich with aesthetic possibility and political adventure.

Four hundred years after the burning of the Mayan scriptures, Latin America could once again boast of a literature. Before the end of World War II, the best fiction writers of the continent's first modern generation of intellectuals (specifically, Borges, Carpentier, Asturias, the Brazilian Joao Guimaraes Rosa, and the Uruguayan Juan Carlos Onetti) had not yet published any of their major work in book form. But between 1944 and 1952, each of them produced at least one novel or collection of short stories which brought his name to the attention of a small but intensely interested national reading public. By the end of the fifties, a second younger group of writers had made its debut, including Julio Cortázar (born in 1914 and thus really a figure who links the two generations) from Argentina, Juan Rulfo in Mexico, Gabriel García Márquez in Colombia, Carlos Fuentes, another Mexican, and the Peruvian Mario Vargas Llosa.

Taken together, this group forms what critic Luis Harss has definitively proclaimed as the "mainstream" of modern Latin American prose narrative. Although aficionados might wish to add the names of Peruvian novelist Jose Maria Arguedas, or the Puerto Rican novelist Pedro Juan Soto, these nine can be viewed as major artists who leaped the boundaries of their individual countries and won international reputation. Asturias, for example, won the Nobel Prize for Literature in 1967. Carpentier has won several major literary prizes in France and Spain, been applauded both in Moscow and Peking, and had the honor of having his novel *Los Pasos perdidos* [*The Lost Steps*] reissued five years after its initial appearance in New York by the same major American publishing house. *Pedro Paramo,* Juan Rulfo's only novel, a mysterious narrative about life among the dead in a small Mexican village, is currently in print in the same North American edition after twenty years. For a long time, the novels of Carlos Fuentes have rivalled those of Gide and Camus among American college students, but now that the paperback edition of García Márquez' *Cien Años de Soledad* [*A Hundred Years of Solitude*] has gone into its eleventh printing, it seems that the Colombian writer has no rival on U.S. campuses, not even among the Yankees Vonnegut and Pynchon. Julio Cortázar's novel *Rayuela* [*Hopscotch*] wins new converts each day. Less well known are Onetti and Vargas Llosa, but the former's best novel, *La Vida Breve* [*A Brief Life*], has just been published in translation here after nearly thirty years of life in Spanish. Front-page reviews of Vargas Llosa's *Conversación en la Catedral* [*Conversation in the Cathedral*] and the growing popularity of the paperback edition of his *La Casa Verde* [*The Green House*] suggest that these writers may become as widely known as Fuentes and García Márquez. Borges, of course, remains as famous as Kafka.

Every generation has its fads, fiction writers both native and foreign, who mean much more at a special moment in the life of a student than they ever will again, and the "marvelous realities" of García Márquez and Carpentier serve that function, I'm sure, in the imagination of some younger readers. But for others, the current bloom in Latin American writing is no mere fad. It is as much a "discovery" for them as it was a "discovery" for those of us who taught some of the books to them, those of us for whom Spanish was once only one language among many foreign tongues, and for that matter a lesser one than any one of a number of European languages. We welcomed the tyranny of European culture and called our education complete. We never burned any books—but we left some important volumes unopened.

Modern Latin American fiction has helped us all to become a bit more civilized and a bit more barbarian.

—Alan Cheuse

Modern Latin American fiction has helped us all to become a bit more civilized and a bit more barbarian. The fruits of an economic system we call "under-developed," it instructs us, paradoxically, in the most sophisticated fashion on the root questions of life. Consider, for example, the Guatemalan masterpiece *Hombres de Maiz*. The story of the war between the small cultivators of native corn in the Guatemalan countryside and the military forces who work on behalf of economic centralization, the narrative employs local dialects and local mythologies in tandem with Spanish prose and Christian imagery. The strife between the old Indian corn farmers and the new technocrats who manipulate the army becomes a battle for reality itself. Pre-Conquest myth challenges Christian ideology for possession of the reader's imagination, and the seemingly loose development of the plot, with its shifts from one time period to another and from one seemingly unrelated group of characters to the next, becomes emblematic of the practice of *nagualismo* or the benevolent lycanthropy indigenous to the beliefs of the region (which allows a postman to turn into a coyote and back into a postman again in order to speed along the mails). In this fiction, the leader of the peasant revolt rises again and again in the collective imagination of his followers like the shaman, called the "deer of the seventh fire," whom he has supposedly killed. Each time a cornfield goes up in flames, the Indian guerrilla chief rises in rebellion. Though the North American reader of this difficult but rewarding novel may sometimes feel as he makes his way through the alien territory of Asturias' story as though he were trying to track the evanescent coyote-postman himself, he recognizes that he remains in the hands of a narrative master quite unlike any other he has encountered before. The power and the force of the *Popol-Vuh,* the sacred book of the Quiché-Maya, hovers constantly on the horizon of Asturias' modern-day Guatemalan countryside. The ancient and the modern stamp its pages with a character similar to other recent works of Latin American literature but quite unlike any outside of the region.

The fusion of ancient mysteries and contemporary political struggle, the yoking of the disparate polarities of Latin American culture since the Conquest into a single, unified action, occurs within Alejo Carpentier's *El Reino de este Mundo,* published in the same decade as *Hombres de Maiz.* In this short novel, what Carpentier calls "the marvelously real" of the constituents of the Haitian Revolution becomes a metaphor for radical political and social change. The action is presented from the point of view of Ti-Noel, a Haitian of African descent who is first a slave under French rule and then a *houngan* or master of voodoo who struggles against the reactionary mulatto successors in the regime of Toussaint L'Ouverture. Ti-Noel, like Asturias' coyote-postman, possesses metamorphic powers. Like Mackandal, the leader of the initial rebellion against French rule, he can change back and forth from human to animal form in order to further the cause of Haitian independence. The mode of *El Reino* is itself metamorphic, weaving back and forth between, on the one hand, creole rationalism and, on the other, indigenous belief in magical transformation as though there were no actual distinctions between the two modes of thought. Here, Carpentier's enlistment of surrealist narrative technique in the service of the revolutionary ideal strikes a fresh and pleasing new style quite unlike the social fantasies of European writers from Gogol to Hoffman. Reality in this novel is a marvelous realm in which one sees no distinction between what the Haitian revolutionaries believe to be true and what appears to be true. At the novel's conclusion, we learn that Mackandal and other revolutionaries had disguised themselves as animals,

> to serve man, not to abjure the world of men. It was then that the old man (Ti-Noel), resuming his human form, had a supremely lucid moment. He lived, for the space of a heart beat, the finest moment of his life; he glimpsed once more the heroes who had revealed to him the power and the fullness of his remote African forebears, making him believe in the possible germinations the future held. He felt countless centuries old. A cosmic weariness, as of a planet weighted with stones, fell about his shoulders shrunk by so many blows, sweats, revolts. . . . Now he understood that a man never knows for whom he suffers and hopes. He suffers and hopes and toils for people he will never know, and who, in turn, will suffer and hope and toil for others who will not be happy either, for man always seeks a happiness far beyond that which is meted out to him . . . man finds his greatness, his fullest measure, only in the Kingdom of This World.

Then, as if to suggest the ephemeral nature of such rhetoric, Ti-Noel challenges the new mulatto tyrants to battle and fades away into a great green wind that blows in from the Caribbean, a Dionysian figure who came into the world to set things right and then disappears into the sea, leaving nothing but "trails of salt on the flanks of the mountains."

Other more recent works by members of this group of writers further the convention of the "marvelously real" narrative complete and self-contained within the covers of a book which nevertheless demands an active and immediate response from its readers. The person who holds Julio Cortázar's *Rayuela* in his hands is literally instructed how to play hopscotch back and forth between the scores of short narrative sequences between its covers, and thus dramatize the passage, willy-nilly, between European and American culture, the I and the Other, This Side and The Other Side, inner and outer consciousness, past and present, life and death, passages which the main character, an Argentinian expatriate named Horacio, attempts to enact within the formal narrative itself. Because of Cortázar's radical impressment of the reader in the unfolding of his novel, some critics have called the work the *Ulysses* of Latin American literature. But it is a *Ulysses* on the side of change rather than stasis, a novel which, rather than celebrating the repetition, in ever apparent Viconian spirals, of the old, calls out to its readers to give themselves over to the invention of new modes of consciousness.

The novels of the Peruvian writer Mario Vargas Llosa are long, difficult, but fascinating works in which the rot and sterility of his nation's psychic and spiritual life are exposed with Balzacian exactitude. Because of their ties to the European naturalist tradition, they point up with striking clarity the important transformation of Continental traditions modern Latin American writers have wrought. In his first novel, *La Ciudad y los Perros* [*The*

Alejo Carpentier.

Time of the Hero], Vargas Llosa employed Joycean interior monologues in a ferocious exposé of social conditions at a Lima military academy. The success of his experiment—the yoking of high-culture, Mandarin literary technique and naturalist social imperative—may be measured by the fact that the administrators of the academy he had attended in Lima bought up every available copy of the novel and burned them, some six hundred in number, in the main courtyard of the school. Shades of Bishop Diego de Landa! In subsequent novels, Vargas Llosa further refined his use of interior monologue, breaking down the components of the Spanish-American sentence itself in order to convey new states of feeling, and employing Flaubertian finesse in the dramatization of the lives of the near-primitive inhabitants of the Peruvian jungle as well as the cafés and mansions of the Lima middle-class. In *La Casa Verde,* published in 1965, he portrayed the schism between city life and jungle life which comprises one of the major paradoxes of Peruvian society in such a way as to turn Sarmiento on his head. Further, and perhaps more importantly, he took apart tense and time itself, completely reorienting the reader's sense of past and present and thus demonstrating that the rift between regions and subcultures may be seen as a struggle between distinctive conceptions of time itself.

Time, as Georg Lukács wrote, is the single major constitutive element of the novel. Poised between the end of the period of European Conquest and the beginning of a new epoch of individual and political independence, Latin American writers have recognized themselves, in the words of the epigram from Lope de Vega which Carpentier employs at the head of his story collection called *Guerra de Tiempo,* as soldiers in the war of time. A number of interesting and innovative younger writers have added their names to this cadre, among them the Chilean Jose Donoso, the Argentinian Manuel Puig, and the Cuban exile Guillermo Cabrera Infante. But for many North American readers of Latin American literature, the most effective depiction of how this struggle for the invention of a new mode of being in the world may be waged, if not won, can be found in the pages of Gabriel García Márquez' *Cien Años de Soledad.* One hundred years, a century, of solitude. The title itself orders time in the same moment that it presents the problem of being in time. This narrative history of the Buendía clan enhances our understanding of this basic contradiction of Latin American society, the opposition of intellect and feeling, rationalism and intuition, the Apollonian and the Dionysian modes of being, and exposes such paradigms as Sarmiento's as mere rhetorical presentations of situations which can only be understood as living problems, the dialectic made flesh within a clearly defined period of temporal passage. In other words, it is the first major Latin American novel to embrace all of the self-conscious paradoxes of modern Latin American thought in a wholly credible, every-day situation whose nature is entirely unlike any of the major works of Continental fiction.

> Many years later, as he faced the firing squad, Colonel Aureliano Buendía was to remember that distant afternoon when his father took him to discover ice. At that time, Macondo was a vil-
> lage of twenty adobe homes, built on the bank of a river of clear water that ran along a bed of polished stones, which were white and enormous, like prehistoric eggs. The world was so recent that many things lacked names, and in order to indicate them it was necessary to point.

The opening lines of the novel mark a good place to conclude this hurried survey of much more than a hundred years of strife, solitude, false sentiment, and new solidarity. In the face of impending death, Aureliano Buendía, the eponymous protagonist, casts his mind back to a time of origins, childhood, and the early days of the Colombian village of Macondo, but also, given the resemblance of the polished stones along the stream bed, to a prehistorical moment, to an age of ice, a time before language, before fire. His mental gesture seems highly appropriate to recall the task of the Latin American writer, which as Carpentier has written, is the task of Adam: he must give names to the component parts of the magical region that he calls home. García Márquez does precisely that, teaching us how to match language and reality in such a way as to invent a new world with a fresh history. In the face of the fact that most of the indigenous New World texts had been burned by the conquerors in the sixteenth century, no labor less than the creation of living narratives from their ashes will do. The result, as Vargas Llosa has suggested, is a "literature of fire" that illuminates the contradictions of contemporary Latin America but serves at the same time as its greatest creation. In the ice-age of contemporary North American culture, it serves us well to huddle close to this life-giving flame.

José Luis Martínez

SOURCE: "Unity and Diversity," in *Latin America in Its Literature,* edited by César Fernández Moreno, Julio Ortega, and Ivan A. Schulman, translated by Mary G. Berg, Holmes and Meier Publishers, Inc., 1980, pp. 63-83.

[In the following essay, Martínez provides a historical overview of movements and major figures in Latin American literature.]

> We are a small human species; we possess a world apart, surrounded by vast seas, new in nearly all the arts and sciences although, in a certain sense, old in the experience of civil society.
>
> Simón Bolívar

The most unique aspect of Latin America is that it exists as such, that is, as a group of twenty-one countries, with such profound historical, social, and cultural ties that they constitute a single unit in many senses. Other groups of countries may be related by their history and by their race, by their language, and by their religion, or by political or economic pacts. But it is not often that all these connections are found simultaneously, and it is even less frequent that, as in the case of Latin America, the common traits are stronger than the will to individualize and stronger than any dissidence.

Occupying more than half of the American hemisphere,

these nations were conquered and colonized in the beginning of the sixteenth century by the Spanish and Portuguese. Since then nineteen of them have retained the Spanish language, and only one, as large as a continent, has retained the Portuguese. They have all experienced parallel histories, cultural formations, and literary developments. But, on the other hand, autochthonous populations and cultures and particular geographical conditions have existed in each zone of America. Common Iberian patterns were imposed upon men, cultures, and nature that encouraged a blending or unifying process, that is, the creation of the community of nations we call *Latin America,* which are very similar in language, cultural formation, religion, ethnic composition, and economic and social structure.

This complex of particular circumstances—that is, recognition of itself as an American extension of European cultures, the acknowledgment of Indian roots of different thicknesses and depths, and the self-awareness of itself as part of a community made up of countries which are identical in many aspects—can explain the insistent questions which Latin American intellectuals tend to ask themselves about their own identity, their originality, and the nature of their culture. Throughout the nineteenth century, American thinkers reflected constantly about the existence, the condition, and the destiny of America; and in our century, a new cycle of more systematic self-questioning began with Pedro Henríquez Ureña's *Seis ensayos en busca de nuestra expresión* [*Six Essays in Search of Our Expression*] (1928). This mood soon moved on to inquiries into the essential nature of each of the cultural nationalities. The collapse of Europe at the end of the Second World War and the existentialist philosophy which was then in fashion encouraged these inquiries into the existence and the destiny of American and the autonomous qualities of national cultures. Since the vogue has passed, now Latin Americans, instead of theorizing, extend their literature in the world and speak and write about the excellence of their poets and novelists, no longer concerned about whether or not they express America or their respective countries.

Nineteenth-century Latin American literature pertains to an era of apprenticeship and formation. The first apprenticeship had to be that of liberty and identity. The new countries were formally independent by then and thus felt obliged to extend that independence to matters of spirit, to achieve that which was then called *mental emancipation,* and, consequently, to create an original culture. During the first third of the nineteenth century, literature acquired an intense ideological change which caused it to participate strongly in the complex process of cultural elaboration. No later enterprise in Latin America will possess the force of that initial thrust which proposed to secure our literary emancipation because its struggle was to establish the very existence of America's own literary expression.

In effect, the Latin American generations which appeared during the 1830s, when the new republics began to resolve their internal conflicts—except for Brazil, which was an independent kingdom until 1899 when it changed over to the republican system—undertook the creation of a litera-

ture which would express our nature and our customs. In all the countries of the region, poets, novelists, dramatists, and essayists dedicated themselves eagerly to the task of singing the splendors of American nature and of describing and exploring the particular qualities of our character and customs, above all the popular ones which had the greatest flavor and picturesqueness.

From the complex literary panorama of nineteenth-century Latin America, from its ranks of thousands of writers and from the multiplicity of trends and literary currents, three outstanding and representative aspects may be singled out: *costumbrista* narrative, poetry about gauchos and common people, and the prose of thinkers.

The *cuadro de costumbres,* or "descriptive sketch," was easily adapted to the literary description of the most evolved Latin American societies in the mid-nineteenth century, in which everyday customs and popular types could be clearly defined. The *costumbristas* described a society in transition: colonial models and customs continued to survive in the upper classes, but the still recent independence had caused many problems to arise and had increased the conspicuousness of the conflicts and social inequalities which the sketches or descriptive articles so humorously satirized.

The extent to which *costumbrismo* became fashionable, especially in Peru, Mexico, Cuba, Colombia, Chile, and Venezuela, was not exclusively due to the desire to imitate Spanish models, such as Mesonero Romanos, Larra, and Estébanez Calderón, but it was also a response to the urgent need for identity which our writers felt and to a search for national and original expression.

The strongest branch of Latin American *costumbrismo* is the novel. However, the simple accumulation of descriptive sketches did not suffice to create a novel of quality, and perhaps because they understood this, only the most highly endowed intellects of the era accepted the challenge and undertook more profound and ample descriptions of the new societies. When they took up the challenge, some of the best novelists, who were stimulated by the weight of the *costumbrista* characters and scenes, shifted, sometimes consciously, from romanticism to realism, thus announcing the maturity of the novel in Latin America.

The relative peace which Brazil enjoyed during the nineteenth century—in contrast with the chronic agitation of Hispanic-America—contributed to the flourishing of the novel in this country during the second half of the century, a novel which in its totality constituted the most important body of fiction in Latin America during this period.

Joaquim María Machado de Assis (1839-1908) is the most eminent figure in Brazilian letters. His life was a pathetic and silent struggle. Born a mulatto, poor, a stutterer, and an epileptic, he defeated his adversities so radically that his works are untouched by any of those shadows of his infancy and are centered only upon man, that is, ordinary men and women of the Brazilian middle class, with the vulgar passions and problems of body and soul. He also turned his back on the jungle, on telluric man, who was anguished by febrile passions, and on stylistic exuberance, in order to present another picture of his country, one of repose and sobriety, of delicate humor which enchants his readers with its acute perceptiveness and sensitivity. As he wrote of Alencar, Machado de Assis's words really explain his own style: "There is a way of seeing and of feeling," he said, "which strikes the intimate note of nationality, independent of the external face of things." In his great novels, *Epitaph of a Small Winner* (1880), *Philosopher or Dog* [*Quincas Borba*] (1891), *Dom Casmurro* (1900), and in his splendid stories, Machado de Assis, intimately Brazilian, is one of the finest universal storytellers.

Colombia also had good novelists of manners and customs during the second half of the nineteenth century, among whom Tomás Carrasquilla (1858-1940) represents one of the peaks of Latin American *costumbrismo*. The case of this nearly forgotten Colombian writer is unique. If one considers the dates of publication of his works (1896-1935), he coincides with the height of Modernism and even with the beginnings of the modern novel. And although he was well acquainted with the writers of his time, he closed himself within his Antioquean region in order to find himself and to try to understand the men of his time. He achieved thus a body of work which formally must be considered within *costumbrista* realism, already out of fashion by then, but which reveals a rare aesthetic quality, a penetrating human vision and a re-creation of the popular language which he found in himself and made part of his literary style. He wrote many stories and four extensive novels. *Frutos de mi tierra* [*Fruits of My Land*] (1896), about the people of his region; *Grandeza* [*Greatness*] (1910), about Medellín society; *La marquesa de Yolombó* [*The Marchioness of Yolombó*] (1926), about an Antioquean city during the eighteenth century; and *Hace tiempos* [*In Times Past*] (1935-1936), a vast evocation of his own experiences and of places he knew. Carrasquilla is a great extemporaneous novelist whose fame has perhaps begun to be celebrated in the narrative magic of some of his countrymen.

The Mexican *costumbrista* novel has two outstanding narrators, Payno and Inclán. Manuel Payno's (1810-1894) most important novel, *Los bandidos de Río Frío* [*The Bandits of Rio Frio*], is a charming human comedy about Mexican life during the first half of the nineteenth century. Written as a serialized romance, it is not lacking in gory detail. In addition to these qualities, however, it includes *costumbrista* details of nearly all the social classes of the epoch, portrayed with great sympathy and narrative efficacy. A unique personality is encountered in Luis G. Inclán (1816-1875), merely a "rancher" whose perceptive words leave us his testimony of love for the land and for the "charrerías" [the doings of the cowboys]. His principal work, *Astucia* [*Cunning*] (1865-1866), a vast account of the adventures of a band of *charros* [cowboys] who are tobacco smugglers, is a highly colored and cordial panorama of rural Mexican life during the middle of the nineteenth century.

The variety and the contrasts among the classes of Cuban colonial society may be found in realistic descriptions in *Cecilia Valdés* (1839-1879), by Cirilo Villaverde (1812-1894), the first Cuban novelist. The narrator of Chilean life during the second half of the nineteenth century was Alberto Blest Gana (1830-1920). Influenced by Balzac, he described Chilean situations and the lack of communication between the social classes.

In the mid-nineteenth century, the expanse of Argentinian territory was very thinly populated. "The problem which afflicts the Argentine Republic," wrote Sarmiento in *Facundo* (1845), "is that of extension; the desert surrounds it on every side." On those enormous prairies, on the pampas, while the Indians were being persecuted and annihilated, and the nineteenth century had just begun, there developed a type of nomadic cowboy, Creole or mestizo, who would come to be called a *gaucho*. Those unique inhabitants of the pampas survived, thanks to the abundance of wild horses and cows. Dressed in characteristically distinctive clothing, they wandered ceaselessly from place to place. A picturesque legend was built up around them and their way of life, around the *rastreador* ("tracker"), the *baquiano* ("pathfinder"), the bad gaucho, and the *cantor* or *payador* ("wandering minstrel"), described by Sarmiento in masterful pages.

The wandering life of the gauchos, the distinctive dialect in which they expressed themselves, their adventures, their wisdom, and their decadence were taken up by a series of poets in Argentina and in Uruguay who transformed that mythology into a unique literary creation, gaucho poetry. Like the Mexican *corridos,* these poems are yet another resurgence of the old Spanish ballads, and they are both written, with few exceptions, in octosyllables. The gaucho poems were exceptionally popular, were printed in hundreds of editions, were read around campfires while *mate* was being passed, and many people memorized long sections of them. In 1894 Unamuno celebrated the Hispanic roots of *Martín Fierro,* and a year later, Menéndez y Pelayo affirmed that the gaucho poems were "the most original works of South American literature" and that *Martín Fierro* was "the masterpiece of the genre."

The first poet to write in the gaucho dialect, the Uruguayan Bartolomé Hidalgo (1788-1822) wrote *cielitos* and patriotic dialogues from 1811 on. He anticipated the tone of the great gaucho poems as well as their motifs and characteristic scenes. Like his contemporary, the Mexican Fernández de Lizardi, Hidalgo peddled the *cielitos* he wrote in the streets of Buenos Aires. Hilario Ascasubi (1807-1875), an Argentine Creole, lived multiple experiences. He was a sailor and soldier in the civil wars, traveled through Europe and America, and held various jobs. He played cards with the caudillo Facundo Quiroga and heard him recite entire chapters of the Bible. Among his many gaucho writings, *Santos Vega* (1850-1872) stands out, an enormous poem made up of brief tales and descriptions of pampa customs.

The second generation of gaucho poets is made up of the Argentinians Estanislao del Campo (1834-1880) and José Hernández (1834-1886). Like his friend Ascasubi, whom he admired, del Campo also participated in his country's civil wars. He wrote poems in a conventional language, but he owes his fame to *Fausto* [*Faust*] (1866), a poem which narrates the conversation of two gauchos, one of whom has attended a performance of Gounod's opera *Faust* and, with wit and humor, tells about it, comments upon it, and analyzes it as though the opera were a series of real events. José Hernández knew and learned about gaucho life thanks to his father's business dealings in the country. He was a public functionary, legislator, and combative journalist. *El gaucho Martín Fierro* [*The Gaucho Martín Fierro*] (1872), his masterpiece, is the culmination and summary of the genre. This first poem is the story of the rebellion of Martín Fierro, a *payador,* against civilization, which for him is injustice and oppression. Torn away from his happy life, the primitiveness and miseries of military service on the frontiers have been imposed upon him until he deserts and becomes a *gaucho malo,* quarrelsome, drunk, and a killer. The second part, *La vuelta de Martín Fierro* [*The Return of Martín Fierro*] (1879), recounts the life of the hero with the Indians, among whom he has taken refuge, and his return to the white world. Here Martín Fierro is an old man who remembers and reflects.

One of the merits of *Martín Fierro* is the human truth of its hero. Misfortunes have involved him in evil, but he retains a core of incorruptible honesty, a profound respect for an unwritten code of valor and decency. There is also a very fortunate contrast between the youthful action of the first part and the evocative and sententious tone which dominates the second. Throughout the poem, a superior command of language and its resources is maintained. As employed by José Hernández, gaucho dialect achieves the height of its power.

A unique phenomenon may be found in nineteenth-century Latin America. The best prose is not to be found in pure literature but rather in sociological meditations about the ills of our societies, in allegations in favor of civic causes, in historical reflections, in polemical and combative writings and, sometimes, in literary criticism. Perhaps this profound urgency, this burning passion or this anger which give rise to the writings of the Latin American thinkers are what give them their affecting truth and their validity as literary creations.

During the course of the century, nearly all of the countries had men who, beyond ambitions and contingencies, fought generously for liberty and culture. Some of these men were also very fine writers, like the Venezuelan Andrés Bello (1781-1865), the Argentinian Domingo Faustino Sarmiento (1811-1888), the Ecuadorian Juan Montalvo (1833-1889), the Puerto Rican Eugenio María de Hostos (1839-1903), the Peruvian Manuel González Prada (1848-1918), the Mexican Justo Sierra (1848-1912), the Brazilian Ruy Barbosa (1849-1923), and the Cubans Enrique José Varona (1849-1933) and José Martí (1853-1895). And even among the great soldiers, an occasional excellent writer could be found. The Venezuelan Simón Bolívar (1783-1830), author of more than three thousand letters and two hundred speeches and proclamations, wrote with distinctive liveliness and elegance, and was as revolutionary in his style as with arms.

In the case of Bolívar, the pen was only a complement of the sword. In contrast, the Latin American thinkers depended principally upon words. The majority were great polemicists or sustained long ideological campaigns, like Montalvo's against the theocratic dictatorship of García Moreno, and González Prada's against the social injustice

and obscurantism of Peruvian society. Nevertheless, side by side with his combative works, the liberalism of which seems naïve to us today, Montalvo wrote the *Capítulos que se le olvidaron a Cervantes* [*Chapters That Cervantes Forgot*] (1898) and *Geometría moral* [*Moral Geometry*] (1917), both published posthumously, and remarkable for the elegance and the purity of their prose. And González Prada, in addition to having stimulated the awakening of the social conscience of his country, was a poet who, while he occasionally continued the satiric violence or the political caricatures of his combative prose, did not disdain to re-create ancient forms or to evoke the Indian past of Peru.

In 1842, when they both met in Chile, Bello and Sarmiento carried on a magnificent polemic about the purity of the language or the romantic liberty of expression. Despite all this, Bello's temperament was more suited to the tasks of the scholar and the teacher, although certainly with an eye to reform. He was one of the forerunners of literary emancipation in the two splendid poems called *Silvas americanas* which sing to the landscape and the past of America. Toward the middle of the century, when the Latin American community seemed to have greater coherence, Bello, from Caracas, was invited to Santiago de Chile where he would be the reorganizer of education and of the university, as well as one of the authors of the civil code (1853-1856). His *Filosofía del entendimiento* [*Philosophy of Understanding*] (1843) was written during those years, as well as his scholarly studies and his treatises on grammar which, together with those of the Colombian Rufino José Cuervo, constitute the most important American contribution in this field.

Sarmiento, on the other hand, was a torrential spirit who possessed equal quantities of combative passion and desire to civilize. His was one of the most intense and productive lives. He fought against tyrannies both with arms and with the pen; he left a masterful treatise, *Facundo* (1845), a lucid diagnosis of Argentine reality and the dilemma of civilization versus barbarism; as president of his country (1868-1874), his accomplishments were substantial. His best works, in addition to *Facundo, Viajes* [*Journeys*] (1849), *Recuerdos de provincia* [*Recollections of Provincial Life*] (1850), and so many speeches and journalistic pages, are certainly written hurriedly and tumultuously, as by someone who has a great deal to say and many tasks to tend to, but which, at the same time, expressed his ideas in organic concepts and with perceptiveness. Like Martí, Sarmiento was a natural-born writer and one of the most authentic teachers America has had.

Other American thinkers were also decisive in the moral and cultural formation of their countries. Ruy Barbosa, renowned Brazilian jurist, was the organizer of the republic proclaimed in 1889, an impassioned fighter for the abolition of slavery and a writer of multiple curiosities in his *Cartas de Inglaterra* [*Letters from England*] (1896). Eugenio María de Hostos, although he was above all an excellent literary critic (*Juicio crítico de Hamlet* [*Critical Judgment of Hamlet*], 1872), a moralist (*Moral social* [*Social Morality*], 1888), and a promoter of education in Santo Domingo, had the supreme ambition that his country, Puerto Rico, should achieve independence and form part of a West Indian confederation. Justo Sierra, who was the organizer of Mexican education, founder of the National University—at the inauguration of which (1910) he gave a speech in which he pointed out the necessity of a philosophy and a science "which will defend our country"—and generous guide of national culture, was also a poet, literary critic, and historian in the great *Evolución política del pueblo mexicano* [*Political Evolution of the Mexican People*] (1900-1901). Although Enrique José Varona, intellectual and skeptic, did not always succeed in his political ambitions, he served Cuban education and was an intellectual stimulus and a writer of polished style in his brief essays and literary criticism (*Desde mi Belvedere* [*From My Belvedere*], 1907, and *Violetas y ortigas* [*Violets and Nettles*], 1917).

José Martí was one of those exceptional personalities in whom the passion for a political cause was transformed into a written expression of high literary quality. While still an adolescent, he began to fight with his pen for the independence of Cuba, was condemned to forced labor, and left in exile for Spain (1871). He spent the better part of his life in exile, with the exception of a short stay in Cuba between 1878 and 1879. Nevertheless, he dedicated much of his writing to Cuba and its political problems, although he also wrote a great deal about art, letters, politics, personalities, and events in the Latin American and European countries he visited. He also wrote a long series of chronicles about the United States, where he spent his last fourteen years. When he finally managed to unify his desires and organize the war for independence, he returned to Cuba to die. And although he felt that his hour had come, the patriot and the writer continued to be fused; during his last days he made notes in his diary (*De Cabo Haitiano a Dos Ríos* [*From the Haitian Cape to Dos Ríos*]), which are full of poetic intent and of observations about nature, side by side with accounts of guerrilla incidents, right up until the night before his death.

Perhaps with the exception of his dramatic and novelistic attempts, in which he let himself be defeated by the rhetoric of the epoch, the rest of Martí's written work, poetry and essays, is of a quality and an authenticity which are very moving. "What will I have written without bleeding?" he asked. And on his pages his spirit bleeds, both in truth and in literary mastery, with a sense for verbal precision as well as an instinct for the felicitous and expressive turn of phrase. Both in his poetry and in his prose, Martí avoids clichés and abstract images or feelings in order to depict concrete entities, familiar, sometimes picturesque and full of personal emotion, and he knows how to transmit them so well that, in the torrent of his prose, they crystallize into palpitating and perfect expressions. This hurried writer, who only wrote to serve his country or to earn his living; this man who gave himself entirely to the cause of liberty for his people and to the cause of America was at the same time a literary innovator and one of the best writers of Latin America.

No other literary movement in the cultural history of Latin America, either colonial or independent, provides such evidence of the unity and originality of literature in this part of the world as does Modernism. Over a period of forty years, all the countries of the region participated in Modernism; half of them produced twenty or more important writers—among whom would be found the major poet of Hispanic America—who wrote at least thirty significant books, superior to those which had heretofore been written in their line, and which imposed their influence upon their entire area and, for the first time, upon Spain.

With Modernism, Hispanic America exists as a unit, the internal circulation of which has suddenly become fluid. The first manifestations of the movement appear in Mexico, around 1875, with the simultaneous appearance of twenty-two-year-old José Martí and sixteen-year-old Manuel Gutiérrez Nájera, who begin to manifest new stylistic devices and, above all, a new sensibility. Modernism is already substantially outlined. The clarion call which will give it vitality everywhere and will extend it throughout the continent is heard next in Valparaiso, the opposite geographic corner, where a young Nicaraguan, Rubén Darío (1867-1916), publishes in 1888 a collection of poems and stories with a suggestive title: *Azul. . . ,* which, especially in its prose, introduces an exceptional lyric and an innovative voice. During these years, in Havana and Bogotá, people are reading the poems of Julián del Casal

Dust jacket for Julio Cortázar's 1963 novel, Rayuela.

(1863-1893) and José Asunción Silva (1865-1896), sensitive, refined, and tragic.

But the creators of Modernism are still ruled by romantic fate and they die young. By 1896 only Darío remains, if not as the chief, at least the major poet of a constellation which is multiplying itself: in Mexico, with Salvador Díaz Mirón (1853-1928), Luis G. Urbina (1868-1934), Amado Nervo (1870-1919), José Juan Tablada (1871-1945), and Enrique González Martínez (1871-1952); in Colombia, with Guillermo Valencia (1873-1943); in Venezuela, with Manuel Díaz Rodríguez (1868-1927) and Rufino Blanco Fombona (1874-1944); in Peru, with José Santos Chocano (1875-1934); in Bolivia, with Ricardo Jaimes Freyre (1868-1933); in Argentina, with Leopoldo Lugones (1874-1938) and Enrique Larreta (1875-1961); in Uruguay, with José Enrique Rodó (1872-1917) and Horacio Quiroga (1878-1937); and in Chile, with Carlos Pezoa Véliz (1879-1908). After 1896, which represents the peak of Modernism with Darío's *Prosas profanas* [*Profane Prose*] and *Los raros* [*The Strange Ones*], the culminating books of the movement are published one after another, until approximately 1915, in Mexico and Buenos Aires, Bogotá and Lima, Caracas and Montevideo.

The collection of studies which Darío called *Los raros* was important because it discussed the principal literary figures of the moment, the French symbolists and Parnassians, in addition to writers of other nationalities like Poe and Ibsen. Such an observant and opportune guide concludes with homage to the Cuban José Martí and a lecture about the Portuguese poet Eugenio de Castro, who introduced free verse poetry in *Horas* [*Hours*] (1891), which had great influence during those years.

The intense literary activity is manifest also in the magazines which publish, together with local writing, that of the Modernists of other countries as well as French, Italian, and English translations. The most representative of these publications, the *Revista Azul* [*Blue Journal*] (Mexico, 1894-1896), presided over by Gutiérrez Nájera until his death, is both American and universal to an exceptional extent. During its three years of publication, it includes contributions by ninety-six Latin American authors from sixteen countries, who are followers of Modernism, without counting the Mexicans. Darío heads the list with fifty-four contributions and is followed by del Casal and Chocano, with nineteen each, and Martí with thirteen. Sixty-nine French writers appeared in translation, among them Baudelaire, Barbey d'Aurevilly, Coppée, Gautier, Heredia, Hugo, Leconte de Lisle, Richepin, Sully Prudhomme, and Verlaine. They appropriately outnumber the Spaniards, who are represented by only thirty-two contributions. And from other nationalities, there are translations of Heine, Wilde, Ibsen, D'Annunzio, of the great Russian novelists, and of Poe, who had already been translated in Mexico in 1869. During years of precarious communications, the extent to which the Modernists managed to become acquainted with each other's work, and to expose their own writings in literary magazines, seems truly remarkable.

Thus for Latin American writers at the turn of the century, Modernism was a taking possession of the world, but it was also a becoming aware of their own time. Seeking beyond the exhausted Spanish romanticism, the creators of the movement perceive, however vaguely, that a vast revolutionary movement of formal renovation and of sensibility has begun in the world, and they decide to form part of it with their own expression. Refusing to accept the vulgarity of the language, they find a first approach in the rigor of French Parnassianism, and new possibilities of refinement, musicality, and imagination in symbolism. Poe, Heine, Whitman, and D'Annunzio will also contribute, but the final result of this synthesis will be entirely original: it will deal with predominantly lyric voices which participate through affinity in a common movement of renovation.

During the initial period and that of the movement's peak, which may be designated as 1905 with the appearance of Darío's *Cantos de vida y esperanza* [*Songs of Life and Hope*], Modernism creates a distinctive thematic mythology of exotic escapism. A Parnassian and Renanesque Greece is turned to by Gutiérrez Nájera in his *Odas breves* [*Brief Odes*], del Casal in *Las oceánidas* [*The Ocean-Nymphs*], and in *Mi museo ideal* [*My Ideal Museum*], Darío in *Coloquio de los centauros* [*Colloquium of the Centaurs*] and in the "Responso a Verlaine" ["Prayer for Verlaine"], and Rodó when he sketches a synthesis of Hellenic civilization in *Ariel* (1900). An Orient more imagined than actually known, and limited to China and Japan, appears in some of Darío's stories, in poems by del Casal, and will serve not only as a thematic but also as a formal inspiration in various books by Tablada which introduce the Japanese haiku into Spanish. On the other hand, Valhalla and the Grail, elves and fairies, Loke and Odín, Wagnerian and Nordic appear in Jaimes Freyre's *Castalia bárbara* [*Savage Castilian*] (1897). The traditions and personalities of the Old Testament and of the Middle Ages are recreated in stories and poems by Darío ("El arbol del rey David," "Las tres reinas magas," "Los motivos del lobo") and in poems by Valencia ("Palemón el estilista"). An eighteenth-century France, of elegant parties in the manner of Verlaine and of Watteau, appears in poems by Darío, Chocano, and Tablada; and in the general tone of Gutiérrez Nájera and Darío breathes that Francophilia that Juan Valera called "Gallicism of the mind."

Modernism seems to forget American and Hispanic themes. However, Martí and Gutiérrez Nájera used them often, and Darío's stay in Chile moved him to evoke the Herculean strength of Caupolicán in a sonorous sonnet in *Azul*. . . . After a few years in which autochthonous motifs almost disappear, they reappear in the last phase of Modernism in poets like Valencia, Chocano, and Lugones, together with praise of the Hispanic world and with popular themes. Darío knew Spain and its history very well and also wanted to be the "poet of America." He would succeed in this both through the splendor of his lyricism and because he made himself the spokesman of the Hispanic world ("Salutación del optimista," "A Roosevelt"), of the great Spanish heroes like the Cid and Don Quijote, and because he wrote so many poems ("Triptico de Nicaragua," "Intermezzo tropical," "Oda a la Argentina") in which the presence or the nostalgic memory of his own land and of the American landscape gleam.

Two recurrent symbols also form part of the Modernist mythology, the *azul* or "blue" of Darío's first important book and of Gutiérrez Nájera's *Revista Azul,* perhaps because, as Hugo had said, "l'art c'est l'azur," and the swan, symbol of gratuitous beauty, much employed by Parnassians and symbolists, which will appear in the first Modernists and, in an obsessive manner, in Darío, who, associating it with the myth of Leda, converts it into an emblem of the new poetry. When González Martínez, in 1910, writes the sonnet which begins "Tuércele el cuello al cisne de engañoso plumaje" ["Wring the neck of the swan of deceptive plumage"], and proposes the "wise owl" as a new reflexive symbol, the hour of the swan and of Modernism has reached its end.

These new and old themes and symbols of Modernism, nevertheless, only serve to characterize it. The more profound renovation or revolution of the movement takes place in language and in sensibility; it begins by reacting against careless expression and makes an effort to renovate images and simplify syntax. A distinctive Modernist vocabulary comes into being which seems to limit itself to luxury and to beauty. Poetic language should be a unique and surprising creation, and a continual series of discoveries, such as Darío and Lugones achieved, the former in his maturity in the "Epístola a la señora de Lugones" (1907)—a poem which magnificently introduces colloquial language into Spanish-language poetry—and the latter in his *Lunario sentimental* [*Sentimental Lunarian*] (1909).

The Modernist poets also accomplished a more complex renovation, that of versification. This renovation took place in three ways: first, they sought in the past old forms that were in disuse, like the classic hexameter or ancient meters and forgotten Spanish combinations, like the monorhyme or the hendeca-syllable with various accentuation patterns. Second, they gave greater agility and harmony to verse in general and put all the known meters into active use. When Latin American readers shuddered as they read José Asunción Silva's "Nocturno" which begins "Una noche, una noche toda llena de murmullos . . . " ["A night, a night all filled with whispers . . . "], some supposed that a new metric form was being employed; but the poet explained once that the morbid beauty originated formally in a very ordinary fable by Iriarte which says:

> A una mona
> muy taimada
> dijo un día
> cierta urraca
>
> [To a very sly monkey a certain magpie said one day]

However, Silva had put the feet or tetrasyllabic verses together in irregular groups. And third, the Modernists created new meters; they attempted; as did Darío ("Heraldos" in *Prosas profanas,* 1896) and Jaimes Freyre (*Castalia bárbara,* 1897), metric liberty, free verse, and they even theorized about the topic just as Jaimes Freyre did in his *Leyes de versificación castellana* [*Rules of Spanish Versification*] (1912).

The Modernists frequently sought impressionistic effects based on sensations, like groupings of synesthesias, the visual transpositions of the colors or exercises of monochromatic variations. Vocabulary, themes, symbols, versification, and special effects, all these formal renovations were intended to find adequate expression for a new sensibility. In the moment of Modernism's triumph, Rubén Darío, who said everything and divined everything, thus summarizes the new sensibility in the opening poem of *Cantos de vida y esperanza* (1905):

> Y muy siglo dieciocho y muy antiguo
> y muy moderno; audaz, cosmopolita,
> con Hugo fuerte y con Verlaine ambiguo,
> y una sed de ilusiones infinita.
>
> [And every eighteenth century and very ancient / and very modern; bold, cosmopolitan / strong with Hugo and ambiguous with Verlaine, / and an infinite thirst for illusions.]

But this thirst for illusions and this desire to embrace simultaneously the ancient and the modern will flow easily into doubt, uneasiness, and disenchantment; that is, into a desire to escape and, finally, into a collision against "the black infinite where our voice does not reach." The great poets of the Modernist apogee—Darío, Lugones, Herrera y Reissig, Urbina, and Nervo—show both the triumphal, sensual, and plastic face of life as well as the other, nocturnal and perturbed, which, after the festivities are over, must confront reality and death.

In its totality, Modernism was a unanimous movement in Latin America which fundamentally signified a formal renovation and the full conquest of original expression and modernity. It was a powerful attempt to form part of the world and of the time, to cause all the important voices of the hour to resound in this America and to be heard right along with them. As has been said so many times, with Modernism Latin America takes the initiative and moves ahead of Spain. Now it will be the Spanish writers of the Generation of '98 who will follow the lead of America and recognize the authority of the movement and, above all, of Rubén Darío.

Brazil also experienced a movement of renovation parallel to that of Spanish America, although it was related to it only through coincidences of epoch and of influences. Nor did the Brazilian movement have that unanimous and fervent spirit; it consisted exclusively of the appearance of new trends, among which the Parnassian at first dominated, with Alberto de Oliveira Correa (1857-1937) and Olavo Bilac (1865-1918), excellent poet in *O caçador de esmeraldas* [*Hunter of Emeralds*] (1904). Later the symbolist group appeared, about 1899, the outstanding poet of which is João de Cruz e Sousa (1863-1898), follower of Verlaine and of Mallarmé in *Broqueis* and *Missais* (1893). Another distinction is that in Brazil the term *Modernism* is not applied to the work of early twentieth-century writers, but rather to those of the vanguard movement, which was begun in 1922 by Mario de Andrade and Manuel Bandeira.

> In Latin America, poetry flows along naturally, and from time to time great poets emerge: Darío, Vallejo, Neruda, Paz. By contrast, the creation of a vigorous and original novel has been one of the greatest literary ambitions of various generations, but judgment has always been withheld as to whether the battle has finally been won.
>
> — *José Luis Martínez*

Considered in its totality, Latin American literature after 1920 reveals two conspicuous trends, vanguardism and social concern, which at certain times have been considered to be antagonistic to each other. The desire to participate in the revolution of artistic expression and meaning, which began at the end of the nineteenth century and was fulfilled during the 1920s, was seen as an exercise in pure literature for those who preferred that literature not serve the cause of its own revolution but rather that of the social and political one which stirs up the world. Although the names of the trends have changed, the two fundamental and still dominant attitudes have remained the same. In more recent years, a new trend has begun to appear, still imprecisely defined, which seems to unite innovation and experimentation with social concern, and which intends to accomplish a more radical revolution of social structures, of sensibility and of conduct, as well as of language and literary forms.

Following the traditional genre categories, that of drama has been the artistic activity which, in this region, has still not fully reached that transcendence which would provide testimony of its literary importance. During the first decade of the twentieth century, there emerged in Argentina and Uruguay an interesting movement of *costumbrista* theater. It was centered around a family of theatrical impresarios, the Podestás, who were of Italian origin, and their most famous author, the Uruguayan Florencio Sánchez (1875-1910), who did his writing in Buenos Aires. Both Sánchez and his followers wrote social criticism about conflicts between the city and the country, the assimilation of the immigrants, and the moral problems of a still provincial society which was serving its apprenticeship in cosmopolitanism. In Buenos Aires, Montevideo, and Santiago, this theatrical movement acquired authentic vitality. The spectators could recognize their own faces and problems and even their own language in those fictional presentations.

The first steps toward the modernization of the Latin American theater were taken by the following dramatic authors of this period: the Argentinians Conrado Nalé Roxlo (1898) and Samuel Eichelbaum (1894); the Uruguayan Vicente Martínez Cuitiño (1887); the Chilean Armando Moock (1894-1942); and the Mexicans Xavier Villaurrutia (1903-1950), Celestino Gorostiza (1904-1967), and Salvador Novo (1904-). They organized the groups and the theatrical seasons called *Teatro Ulises* [Ulysses Theater] (1928) and *Orientación* [Orientation] (1932).

These eager interests in renovation and in the vanguard were followed by other important movements, like that of the theater of criticism and interpretation of national problems. Contributors included authors like the Brazilian Claudio de Souza (1876-1954), the Mexican Rodolfo Usigli (1905), the Peruvian Bernardo Roca Rey (1918), the Cuban José Antonio Ramos (1885-1946), the Nicaraguan Pablo Antonio Cuadra (1912), and those of the Areyto group, founded in 1935 in Puerto Rico by Emilio Belaval. Theater after 1940 deals with the problematical existence of contemporary man, his solitude, his insecurity, and his confusion, and the conflicts which his sense of responsibility sets for him as he is confronted by violence and injustice.

The exhaustion of Modernism during the second decade of the twentieth century does not in the least imply the debilitation of poetry in Latin America. From 1920 until the present day, generations of new poets have appeared who form a great current which is designated initially as vanguard poetry and later, as contemporary poetry. Since the twenties there have been two major trends: one made up of the poets who reacted against certain aspects of Modernism in order to emend excesses or defects in what was called *postmodernism;* and the other composed of more audacious poets who wished to explore the most radical consequences of the tendency of Modernism toward individual creation and the liberty of the artist, denying and destroying the past in a movement which was called *ultramodernism*. The first group's forms of reaction—a search for simplicity and lyric intimacy, reactions against the classic tradition, against romanticism, or against Modernist sensibility and forms by means of irony—in themselves inform us that this group included those who preferred moderate variations on conventional tastes and themes, although that did not preclude the inclusion of such original and interesting poets as the Colombians Porfirio Barba Jacob (1883-1942) and Luis Carlos López (1883-1950); the Argentinians Baldomero Fernández Moreno (1885-1950), Enrique Banchs (1888-1968), and Carlos Mastronardi (1900); the Peruvian José María Eguren (1882-1942); and the Puerto Rican Luis Lloréns Torres (1878-1944).

The *"ultras,"* on the other hand, were the nonconformists and the revolutionaries, the advocates of the "tradition of rupture." Coinciding with the European vanguard movements which appear after the First World War, Latin American poets like the Chilean Vicente Huidobro (1893-1948), the Peruvian César Vallejo (1892-1938), and the Argentinian Jorge Luis Borges (1899) participated actively around 1920, in association with the Spaniards who shared their worries and concerns—Gerardo Diego, Federico García Lorca, Juan Chabás, and Antonio Espina—in movements like that of creationism and other less important ones, which grouped together were called *ultraism*. It was the youthful and iconoclastic era of the isms, of the free imagination, which manifested itself above all in such magazines as the Argentinian *Prisma* [*Prism*] (1921-1922), *Proa* [*Prow*] (1922-1923), and *Martín*

Fierro (1924-1927); the Mexican *Horizonte* [*Horizon*] (1926-1927), *Ulises* [*Ulysses*] (1927-1928), and *Contemporáneos* [*Contemporaries*] (1928-1931); the Cuban *Revista de Avance* [*Vanguard Review*] (1927-1930); the Peruvian *Amauta* [*Inca Sage*] (1926-1932); and the Uruguayan *Los Nuevos* [*The New Ones*] (1920) and *Alfar* [*Clay*] (1921-1955).

A parallel movement of renovation was taking place in Brazil. It was begun by the poets Mario de Andrade (1893-1945) and Manuel Bandeira (1885-1968) with the celebration of the Week of Modern Art in São Paulo in 1922. The celebration included expositions of paintings and sculpture, concerts and conferences, a clamorous launching of the vanguardism which the Brazilians would call *Modernism*. That same year saw the publication of a book of poems by de Andrade, *Paulicéia desvairada* [*Demented Paulicéia*], which proposed all of the liberties of a new era for Brazilian poetry: free verse, prosaic and colloquial language, personal and ironic expression, and the search for Indian and popular themes. The writer who was then at the height of his powers, Graça Aranha (1868-1931), would speak out clearly in favor of Brazilian Modernism with his speech-manifesto at the Academy (1924), and he would be joined or followed right to our day by poets such as Jorge de Lima (1893-1953), Rui Ribeiro Couto (1898-1963), Cecilia Meireles (1901-1964), Carlos Drummond de Andrade (1902), Murilo Mendes (1902), and Augusto Federico Schmidt (1906-1965), who as a group constitute one of the most brilliant periods of Brazilian poetry.

Soon the most aggressive and boisterous aspect of those *isms* would subside, but permanent conquests of that vast poetic current would remain: free verse, the elimination of rhyme, the use of typographic compositions, liberty in metamorphic invention, colloquial language, and the enrichment of poetic experience proposed by surrealism. Along beside these characteristics were certain periods of insistent themes like *nativism,* which would involve such poets as the Mexican Ramón López Velarde (1888-1921); the Brazilian Jorge de Lima; the Puerto Rican Luis Palés Matos (1898-1959); the Cuban Nicolás Guillén (1902), and, during certain periods of their work, César Vallejo, Jorge Luis Borges, the Ecuadorian Jorge Carrera Andrade (1902), and the Chilean Pablo Neruda (1904-1973). They gave poetic value to Negro rhythms, to provincial turns of phrase, to the neighborhood epic, and to the secret of the Indian worlds.

These allusions led almost necessarily to the social themes which concerned almost all the nativists and particularly Neruda, perhaps the major poet of Latin America during this period because of his two great poetic corpora, *Residence on Earth* (1931, 1935), and *General Song* (1950).

In addition to these themes and general characteristics of contemporary Latin American poetry, there are many others which only pertain to each of the great poets who have appeared between 1920 and 1940. Thus, the verbal inventiveness and the uneasy spirit of Ramón López Velarde; the acid and original voice, full of human pain and pity, of the Chilean Gabriela Mistral (1889-1957); the classic and popular accents in the vast poetic world of the

Mexican Alfonso Reyes (1889-1959), who is also the master of prose and of intellectual curiosity during this period; the lyric refinement of the Cuban Mariano Brull (1891) and of the Argentinian Ricardo E. Molinari (1898). Note also the descriptive sensuality and the verbal imagination of the Argentinian Oliverio Girondo (1891-1967) and of the Mexican Carlos Pellicer (1899); the mixture of vanguardism and classicism in the Nicaraguan Salomón de la Selva (1893-1959); the complex sensibility and the lyric fantasy of the Colombian León de Greiff (1895); the radical and tragic humanity which affects us so in the poetry of César Vallejo; the creation of a universe of intellectual fictions and the rigorous poetic sensibility of Jorge Luis Borges, one of the most influential and original writers; the perceptive poetry of the Mexican José Gorostiza (1901), whose *Muerte sin fin* [*Death Without End*] (1939) is the most important poem in Latin America during this period. Note also the theological lyricism of the Argentinian Leopoldo Marechal (1900-1970); the formal purity, lyric contention, and humanism of the Mexican Jaime Torres Bodet (1902); the metaphysics of the senses and of the experiences in the Mexican Xavier Villaurrutia (1903-1950) and the Chilean Rosamel del Valle (1900-1963); the tenderness, irony, and colloquial poetry in the Mexican Salvador Novo (1904); and the trace of surrealism in the Guatemalan Luis Cardoza y Aragón (1904).

Since 1940 a new Latin American poetic generation has revealed itself vigorously, with very few traits in common among its members except for their position as witnesses of an unjust and torn-up world. Before such confusion, the following diverse voices are raised: the Argentinians Enrique Molina (1910) and César Fernández Moreno (1919); the Brazilians Vinicius de Moraes (1913) and João Cabral de Melo Neto (1920); the Mexican Octavio Paz (1914); the Chilean Nicanor Parra (1914); the Colombian Alvaro Mutis (1923); the Peruvian Sebastián Salazar Bondy (1924-1965); and the Nicaraguan Ernesto Cardenal (1925). The most outstanding among them is the intense, profound lyric voice of Paz, an extraordinarily lucid spirit in whom the conflicts and cultural experiences of history and of our time intercross.

While modern poetry in Latin America presents an organic development, without solutions of continuity, the novel has had a troubled, if not dramatic, development. In Latin America, poetry flows along naturally, and from time to time great poets emerge: Darío, Vallejo, Neruda, Paz. By contrast, the creation of a vigorous and original novel has been one of the greatest literary ambitions of various generations, but judgment has always been withheld as to whether the battle has finally been won. However, there have been two significant peaks: the first occurred between 1924 and 1930, and is somewhat diminished by now; the second, the boom of the Latin American novel, began in the sixties and we still live in its blaze.

Barely past the time of Modernism, the novel attracted extraordinary attention with its great narratives about the Mexican Revolution. The following novels may be of interest to the reader: *The Underdogs* by Mariano Azuela (1873-1952)—which, although it was originally published in 1915, would only be discovered literarily after its sixth edition in 1925; *The Eagle and the Serpent* (1928) and *La sombra del caudillo* [*The Leader's Shadow*] (1929), by Martín Luis Guzmán (1887); a bitter novel of social denunciation, *Raza de bronce* (1919), by the Bolivian Alcides Arguedas; two excellent novels, the dominant theme of which is the struggle of man with nature: *The Vortex* (1924) by the Colombian José Eustacio Rivera (1889-1928), and *Doña Barbara* (1929), by the Venezuelan Rómulo Gallegos (1884-1968). A delicate counterpoint to this tense dramatism will be provided by two Argentinian narrators: Benito Lynch (1885-1951), who would concentrate on the conflicts of the people of the pampas in a series of novels which begins with *Los caranchos de la Florida* [*The Carancho Birds of Florida*] (1916) and includes *El inglés de los güesos* [*The Englishman of the Bones*] (1924) and *El romance de un gaucho* [*The Ballad of a Cowboy*] (1930); and Ricardo Güiraldes (1886-1927), who would convert man's encounter with nature into poetic imagery in *Don Segundo Sombra* (1926).

However, the works of this generation of founders of the modern novel are regarded with less enthusiasm today than when they first appeared. In effect the vision that those novelists had of the peasant who fights for his land, of the revolutionary who struggles for justice, and of the conflict of man with nature and with barbarism was still a Romantic vision, sometimes Indianist, and the stylistic devices and methods of composition they had at their disposal were elementary and continued to be linked to realism and naturalism. They were still living in the natural and legendary era, with the historic era only dimly in the future. Nevertheless, those novelists captivated various generations of readers and offered the world a first image of America, thanks to an uncommon quality: authenticity and the vigor of their narrative talent. A page, apparently free of rhetorical artifice, by Azuela, Guzmán, Gallegos, or Lynch is still a masterpiece.

The years which followed this flowering were not very fertile, even when the first important novels appeared during the thirties: *Las lanzas coloradas* [*The Red Lances*] (1930) by the Venezuelan Arturo Uslar Pietri (1905); *The Villagers (Huasipungo)* (1934), by the Ecuadorean Jorge Icaza (1906); *The Golden Serpent* (1935), by the Peruvian Ciro Alegría (1909-1967); and *Angustia* [*Anguish*] (1936), by the Brazilian Graciliano Ramos (1892-1953). In general, it is a lackluster decade, characterized by the social novel, which is important in Brazil for the group of novelists headed by Jorge Amado (1903). The germane analysis by the Peruvian critic Luis Alberto Sánchez, *América: novela sin novelistas* [*America: Novel Without Novelists*] (1933), speaks for this period.

As often happens, facts would soon contradict this pessimistic view, for the decade of the forties saw the appearance of two of the most original narrators of Latin America, the Argentinian Jorge Luis Borges and the Cuban Alejo Carpentier (1904), and of novels and stories which are remarkable for their formal rigor and their novelistic density. Naturalism has been left behind, and a critical attitude in the observation of reality prevails, as in *Yawar fiesta* [*Yawar Holiday*] (1943), by the Mexican José Revueltas (1914), *The President* (1946), by the Guatemalan

Miguel Angel Asturias (1899), *The Edge of the Storm* (1947), by the Mexican Augustín Yáñez (1904), and *Adán Buenosayres* (1948), by Leopoldo Marechal. An imagination ruled by intelligence may also prevail, as in *The Invention of Morel* (1944), by the Argentinian Adolfo Bioy Casares (1914), in *Ficciones* [*Fictions*] (1944), by Borges, or *The Kingdom of This World* (1949), by Carpentier. For the novelists of this period—as Emir Rodríguez Monegal has observed—their relationship with the vanguard movements is important: "They are, above all, renovators of a vision and of a concept of the language."

During the fifties, writers like Borges and Carpentier reached their moment of greatest productivity, and novelists just beginning to publish important fiction included Juan Carlos Onetti (1909)—*La vida breve* [*A Brief Life*], 1950—the Chilean Manuel Rojas (1896)—*Hijo de ladrón* [*Born Guilty*], 1951—and the Venezuelan Miguel Otero Silva (1908)—*Casas muertas* [*Dead Homes*], 1955. Three Mexican narrators were introduced: Juan Rulfo (1918), with the stories of *The Burning Plain* (1953) and the novel *Pedro Páramo* (1955); Juan José Arreola (1918), with the extraordinary prose pieces of *Confabulario* [*Collection of Schemes*] (1952) in which fiction and essay blend; and Carlos Fuentes (1929), who, with *Where the Air is Clear* (1958), opens a new period of the Latin American novel, together with an exceptional Argentinian narrator, Julio Cortázar (1914), who in 1959 published his first memorable book, the stories of *Las armas secretas* [*The Secret Weapons*].

Thus, through this accumulation of experiences, through this slow conquest of liberty and imagination, through this gradual apprenticeship of techniques and styles, through this struggle with language in which the major expressive concern becomes central, and coinciding with the development of a larger phenomenon of demythification and rejection of social and cultural structures, of sexual revolution, of new norms and life-styles, of dissolving demarcations between the genres and the artistic forms, which together characterize the creation of a sensibility and a style which belong to the present years, the recent apogee of the Latin American novel is produced.

The first period of excellent novels, between 1924 and 1930, was based upon the work of only six major novelists, scattered across Latin America. Now there are almost twice that many, and, whether they write in their own countries, or in other Latin American or European ones, they have established very active communications and alliances among themselves. Their success, the ample and opportune exegesis which their works have received, and the fact that they have achieved an exceptionally widespread readership in their own language and in numerous translations are not unrelated to the parallel appearance of a remarkable generation of critics: the Uruguayans Mario Benedetti (1920), Emir Rodríguez Monegal (1921), and Angel Rama (1926); the Mexicans Emmanuel Carballo (1929) and Carlos Monsiváis (1938); the Chileans Fernando Alegría (1918) and Luis Harss (1936); the Cuban Severo Sarduy (1937); and the Peruvian Julio Ortega (1942).

Here are the names of the novelists who form part of this

generation and the titles of their most celebrated works: the Paraguayan Augusto Roa Bastos (1917), with *Son of Man* (1960); Carlos Fuentes, with *The Death of Artemio Cruz* (1962) and *A Change of Skin* (1967); the Brazilian João Guimarães Rosa (1908-1967), with *The Devil to Pay in the Backlands* (1963); the Argentinians Julio Cortázar, with *Hopscotch* (1963) and *La vuelta al día en ochenta mundos* [*Around the Day in Eighty Worlds*] (1967) and Ernesto Sábato (1912), with *Sobre héroes y tumbas* [*On Heroes and Graves*] (1962); the Uruguayans Carlos Martínez Moreno (1917), with *El paredón* [*The Execution Wall*] (1963), and Juan Carlos Onetti, with *The Shipyard* (1961), *Juntacadáveres* [*Corpse-gatherer*] (1965), and his *Cuentos completos* [*Complete Stories*] (1967); the Peruvian Mario Vargas Llosa (1936), with *Time of the Hero* (1963) and *The Green House* (1966); the Cubans José Lezama Lima (1912), with *Paradiso* (1966) and Guillermo Cabrera Infante (1929), with *Three Trapped Tigers* (1967); and the Colombian Gabriel García Márquez (1928) with *One Hundred Years of Solitude* (1967).

This list is neither closed nor definitively established. With the exception of the deceased Guimarães Rosa, they are all at the height of their creativity, and alongside them are novelists of previous generations who continue to write, as well as new writers who are just starting out. Nor can the list of memorable works be considered as comprehensive of all those which form part of this Latin American battering ram which attracts the attention of the world. Some of them will only retain a certain critical esteem and will be forgotten by posterity. All of them reveal a liberty of language and of invention, an undisguised combativeness and a definite participation in the conflicts and currents of contemporary thought which make them significant and alive for the modern reader of our language or any other. Provincialism has been left behind. Of all these novels, one has already achieved, in various languages, a fame which is not only literary but popular, perhaps because it is the masterpiece of this period, García Márquez's *One Hundred Years of Solitude*. It is a book of love and of imagination. It includes everything: history and myth, protest and confession, allegory and reality. Everything is recounted with an ancient art which, when it really appears, defeats all literary formulae. This is a gift as well as a product of the mind and of the spirit, the old secret of storytelling which captivates us once again.

John S. Brushwood

SOURCE: "From *Pedro Páramo* to *Rayuela* (1956-1962)," in *The Spanish American Novel: A Twentieth-Century Survey,* University of Texas Press, 1975, pp. 211-48.

[*Brushwood is an American writer and educator, and the author of several book-length studies and articles on Latin American literature. In the following excerpt, he discusses some major Latin American novels published between 1956 and 1962.*]

Although the terms "new Latin American novel" and "the boom" sometimes appear synonymous, they really indicate two different aspects of a single phenomenon—

Julio Cortázar.

the maturity of fiction in Latin America. Specifically with reference to the Spanish-speaking countries, it is convenient to think of the new novel as dating from the late 1940s, the years of the reaffirmation of fiction. The boom, on the other hand, best describes the unprecedented international interest enjoyed by Spanish American novelists in the 1960s, and the spectacular increase in the number of high-quality novels they produced. Although nobody thought of it as a boom until several years later, the change is readily apparent in the years following *Pedro Páramo*. The foundations had been laid: Spanish American novelists were technically sophisticated and sure that the novel was a valid artistic expression. The overwhelming number of good novels published in the period 1956-1962 could easily justify division into several chapters. Nevertheless, they belong in a single showcase of a remarkable period—one in which two generations are notably productive, in which there is wide variation in techniques and themes, and a period when Spanish American authors write with more confidence in their art than at any earlier time.

In order to provide an organization for the panorama, the present study will deal first with some of the younger novelists most closely associated with the boom. Then a review of the works published in 1956-1962 by established writers will show the relationship of the boom to the new novel. After that, some general thematic classifications of novels by other young writers will illustrate the diversity of fiction during these years. Some novels deal with specific, national scenes; within this classification are some works based on current politics while others are more concerned with the cultural heritage of the nation or region. Another large classification is a far more intimate kind of novel, more overtly concerned for people than for places or politics; within this group are some that are anguished to the point of nihilism while others are more objective studies of human relationships. Such classifications, of course, are oversimplifications of what the novels are. All classifications of this kind should be taken as organizational devices, never as critical opinions.

If someone were to make a survey, asking which Spanish American novelists are the best representatives of the boom, the chances are that the most frequently mentioned names would be Julio Cortázar, Carlos Fuentes, Gabriel García Márquez, and Mario Vargas Llosa (mentioned here in alphabetical order). In addition to their obvious excellence as writers, they share several other characteristics associated with the boom. They belong to an international literary set, travel extensively, spend much time in residence abroad (in some cases even most of the time), but find inspiration in their cultural heritage. To some extent they consider themselves handicapped by the unsympathetic cultural milieu of their native countries. There are practical reasons for this attitude; however, the reaction is occasionally similar to the *poète maudit* syndrome. Awareness of the creative act of making fiction causes the boom novelists to comment willingly (and sometimes eagerly) on the nature of fiction. Together they make an impressive declaration, in the forum of world literature, of the excellence of Spanish American letters; and it may be even more important that they have stimulated communication among writers of the Spanish American countries—a condition that has never been as productive as during the 1960s. One undesirable effect of the boom is that a few writers in the spotlight tend to be lionized while many good writers are ignored. Such an effect is by no means the intention of the best-known writers, and, although their fame may shine brighter than the reputations of many worthy colleagues, it is equally true that they have attracted attention to a body of literature that badly needed publicity. The boom is not four novelists, or even six or seven. A large number of writers participate in the activities, attitudes, and rewards of the boom. Indeed, the rewards have benefited many novelists who probably would not even consider themselves part of the boom.

Three of the four big names appear as novelists during the 1956-1962 period. The fourth, Vargas Llosa, published an important volume of short stories, *Los jefes,* during this period, but his first novel, *La ciudad y los perros,* did not appear until 1963, the year of Cortázar's *Rayuela.* Cortázar himself published *Los premios* in 1960, a good novel that has been eclipsed by the fame of *Rayuela,* García Márquez published two works, *El coronel no tiene quien le escriba* (1961) and *La mala hora* (1962), that resemble his *La hojarasca* in two ways: they are generically somewhere between a short story and a novel, and are creations preliminary to the main event that turned into *Cien años de soledad* in 1967. The most active of the four was Carlos

Fuentes, who established himself as a major writer through the excellence and variety of four works in a time span of five years: *La región más transparente* (1958), *Las buenas conciencias* (1960), *La muerte de Artemio Cruz* (1962), and *Aura* (1962).

Fuentes's first novel is complicated in structure, long, often discursive, but also highly entertaining. It is a panorama of life in modern Mexico City and, at the same time, an analysis of what it means to be Mexican, including what the Revolution has to do with that condition. There is hardly a reader who does not find the book exciting, yet almost everyone feels compelled to point out some imperfection. The objection may be to the author's unabashed and freely confessed adaptation of the styles of other novelists, most notably of John Dos Passos. Or some may object to the definition of Mexicanism, on the grounds that national cultural identity is out of style. Someone else may object to the melodramatic prose poems that open and close the novel. More than a few have felt the novel attempts too many things. All these objections, and more, have some degree of validity. What it amounts to is that we may call Carlos Fuentes a pretentious novelist, without really speaking ill of his work. He is pretentious in the sense that he does not hesitate to undertake whatever strikes his creative fancy. It might be more accurate to say he is a flamboyant novelist. Whatever the word, in many respects his fiction comes close to being excessive, and it spills over at different places depending on where an individual reader's tolerance level is lowest.

In *La región más transparente,* Fuentes segments the narrative to achieve simultaneity in place-time relationships. By means of references that relate one segment to another, we know that two events separated in space are happening at the same time. The focal point at the beginning of the novel is a party attended by Mexico City's cocktail crowd. The basic scene is more than a view of life in a particular city; it is a revelation of some of the most superficial aspects of western culture. The overall picture, however, includes all social classes in the city, with economic and moral corollaries.

The central character in the novel's basic structure is an old revolutionary named Federico Robles. He is a financial tycoon, a self-made man whose power grew from the Revolution. As we know him in the novel, however, his position among the power elite has no real meaning since it serves only to feed itself. Robles has to find special relationships to maintain his hold on reality. His story is one of financial ruin and possible self-discovery. If this story were the central incident of the novel, it would be a far more compact work than it is in fact. The importance of Robles—and of the Robles story—is to provide a unifying factor that relates many lives and problems so that they form a mosaic of life in Mexico City; it is in this sense that Robles is the central character. Not through him, but in relation to him, we appreciate the reality of post-Revolutionary Mexico—a society changed in many ways from the years preceding, but one that is certainly not revolutionary in any common understanding of the term.

In spite of the very careful characterization of Federico Robles and the use of helpful narrative devices in the manner of Dos Passos, the basic narrative structure of *La región más transparente* apparently does not serve to create the complex of feelings and ideas desired by the author. Therefore, he adds two important characters, Manuel Zamacona and Ixca Cienfuegos, who are laced into the narrative structure without being essential factors. They are interesting and important to what Fuentes apparently wishes to say, but the Robles story could stand without them. Zamacona is an intellectual poet who thrives on discussions of the meaning of being Mexican. His discourses—and the dialogues in which he participates—are more like essays than fiction. Cienfuegos is harder to define. He is a representation of the Indian influence in Mexican life. Part man and part myth, he suffers some human limitations, but goes beyond these limitations in his ability to be everywhere, inexplicably yet undeniably. We can never know exactly who he is, and this quality is an important element in his symbolic value; that is, the indigenous factor in Mexican culture is generally recognized but not well defined. Cienfuegos, even more than Zamacona, seems to exist in order to make a statement the author considered essential but could not express in any other way.

Fuentes pursues many of the same ideas and attitudes in *La muerte de Artemio Cruz,* his best novel. His technical virtuosity is as apparent as in *La región más transparente,* but is more controlled in a novel whose structure is essential to its meaning. The protagonist, Artemio Cruz, is similar in many ways to Federico Robles. The novel opens at a time shortly before his death and creates a multi-faceted biography of the man, using narrative voices in first, second, and third persons. The first-person narrative is absolute present—Artemio Cruz taking account of his actual situation. The second-person voice (the familiar "you" in Spanish) moves back into the past and, from that point, looks toward the future. This future is, of course, already past in terms of the novel's basic present time. The use of a second-person narrative voice, though fairly common in very recent fiction, still tends to be a distracting technique that requires an act of generous acceptance by the reader. The effect it creates seems to depend not only on the author's intent, but also on the individual reader's reaction to the surprise. Some are put off, for example, by the imperative tone of the "you" sections of *La muerte de Artemio Cruz.* The fact is that several readings are possible. One reasonable and satisfying understanding of this narrative perspective is that Artemio Cruz is beside himself, observing his actions as a normally integrated personality. In addition to this placement of the narrator, the "you" passages exploit the time factor as a means of characterizing the protagonist. This narrative voice does not look back; the view is toward the future. This impulse is one of the major factors in the character of Artemio Cruz. It explains some of his actions, illuminates the tragedy of the moment of his death, and amounts to a moral commentary.

The third-person voice belongs to an omniscient narrator who recounts past incidents in the life of Cruz. Each episode is specifically placed in time. They are important moments rather than a full narration, and their placement is not in chronological order, but in a sequence that produces meaningful associations. Fuentes alternates the

three narrative voices to create a fascinating character whose life represents modern Mexico—not as a symbol, but as a real person. The connotations of the characterization of Artemio Cruz are practically limitless. In very general terms, it is probably accurate to say that power is the protagonist's goal, the only thing he really values. He has very little sense of belonging—to another person, to a place, or to a culture. What little inclination he has in this direction falls victim to his will to be powerful. This attitude—still speaking in very general terms—is one way of describing Fuentes's sensitivity to the failure of the Revolution. These novels were published during a period that saw a strike of railroad workers summarily broken by the army in 1959 and the imprisonment of David Alfaro Siqueiros, the leftist painter, for "social dissolution," in 1960. It is not necessary to take sides on these specific issues to understand how they might symbolize the exercise of power at the expense of social justice that is part of the revolutionary ideal.

Fuentes is so skillful a technician that we can easily identify certain narrative procedures as the dynamic factors of his novels—the source of the change that takes place within the work, or the agent that transforms anecdote into art. These observations, however, can still leave much unsaid, because they do not necessarily indicate how interesting his novels are. It is a sad fact that, in recent fiction, some of the most spectacular narrative techniques grace some painfully dull novels. Not so in the works of Fuentes—at least not in those of the years 1956-1962. What analysis of technique cannot possibly communicate is the sheer joy of a mother-daughter dialogue on the correct pronunciation of Joan Crawford's last name, the insidious presence of old age in an episode about sugar-daddy Artemio in Acapulco with his luscious young dolly, or the combination of fun and cruelty among some lower-class fans at a bullfight. The author's sensitivity to reader interest makes him as competent a novelist on the small canvas as he is in the panoramic, murallike works.

A fine example of this small-canvas writing is Fuentes's second novel, *Las buenas conciencias* (1960). Rather than Mexico City, the scene is Guanajuato, a provincial town. Jaime Ceballos, a minor character in *La región más transparente,* is the protagonist. The book deals with well-meaning people who are inhibited by custom and tradition to the point of being unwittingly frustrated. *Las buenas conciencias* is in many ways the opposite of *La región más transparente,* almost as if Fuentes intended to show his critics how he could organize a novel economically and use traditional techniques effectively. *Las buenas conciencias* was originally intended to be the first of a series, later abandoned and, unfortunately, almost forgotten. It is an interesting link between the heroically proportioned novels and the more intimate works of writers like Sergio Galindo, Pedro Orgambide, and Haroldo Conti.

Aura (1962) is a novella that reveals another important aspect of Fuentes as a novelist—his love for the mysterious. In this respect, *Aura* recalls a number of his short stories and also the elusive Ixca Cienfuegos in *La región más transparente.* In the novella, a young scholar-narrator is employed by an elderly woman whose life reaches incredibly far back into history. However, she is also a young woman—the product of her own will. It is not likely to surprise many readers that the narrator falls in love with Aura (the young version) and finally discovers he has been duped. Here indeed is the novel's great fault: not many readers will be surprised by any of it. As a mystery story, it fails because the author gives away his secret. Attempts to find other meanings in the story include a social-protest reading which sees the old woman as a representation of the superannuated impediments to social progress in Mexico, the ash that covers the fire and refuses to move. A more interesting aspect of the double personality is the question it raises concerning identity, and the second-person narrative tends to incorporate the reader into the identity problem, unless he rejects this narrative technique and removes himself from participation. Fuentes loves the identity game and plays it well, albeit too frequently, in his later work. This particular interest, however, shows Fuentes's relationship to still another group of recent novelists: those who play tricks with reality, almost always producing a problem of identity.

The two short novels of García Márquez continue the story of Macondo that begins in *La hojarasca* and culminates in *Cien años de soledad*. The epic quality of this body of fiction derives from a profound sense of history that mythologizes a culture, rather than from a panoramic vision like that of Fuentes. The retired colonel of *El coronel no tiene quien le escriba* is a combination of pathos and dignity. The story concentrates on him, but it suggests much more than it actually says. The man is a victim of dehumanized bureaucracy, for example; yet he continues to hope while trying to hide from others the fact that he is hopeful. This set of circumstances suggests—but only suggests—a detailed biography of the protagonist. *La mala hora* is a distillation of the fear and distrust that are essential parts of *la violencia* in Colombia. Someone puts up placards around the town undermining the security of the people who live there. What the placards actually say is not in itself of such devastating import. Much of it is equivalent to common gossip. However, two factors give them a special importance: the message is written, and no one knows who is posting them. The possibility of civil war turns to probability.

Except for a few devices like the multiple narrative voice in *La hojarasca,* García Márquez's narrative techniques tend to be rather conservative. His storyteller's imagination is the major creative tool. He has not the slightest doubt about his right to invent. Much of the unreality of his work, most of the feeling of myth, and a large portion of the humor come from this uninhibited invention. Often he deals with the extraordinary as if it were entirely commonplace. The colonel keeps his gamecock tied to the foot of his bed, and he does it as matter-of-factly as he pours a cup of coffee. Some of the inventions are preposterous. The newly arrived doctor in *La hojarasca* asks for grass for dinner, and we never find any explanation or exploitation of this unusual appetite. Wherever the inventions are used (and even where withheld information is itself a form of exaggeration), they create a special atmosphere—a new reality that springs from one that is more familiar.

Los premios (1960) is Julio Cortázar's major step toward *Rayuela* (1963), though he had written many short stories. This first novel is a playful yet serious consideration of a set of human destinies. The basic situation of the story is highly artificial—a diverse collection of *porteños* (people from Buenos Aires) are on a sea voyage because each has won the trip in a lottery. They are interesting as types recognizable in *porteño* society. Luis Harss points out that this fact is of secondary interest to the author. Nevertheless, it would be foolish to overlook this factor of identity in a novel that deals with the problem of identity. In any work of this kind, there is a counter-pointing of two qualities: one that emanates from the author's experience of belonging and another that comes from his experience of creating. They are not categorically separated, of course, but they certainly are recognizable as they function side by side. Carlos Fuentes, for example, might say he is only secondarily interested in the definition of the Mexican character, that he is really seeking the human reality beyond that definition. On the other hand, he might say exactly the opposite, and neither statement would change what he has written. So also with Cortázar. *Los premios* can be enjoyed as a gallery of types. Moving to an entirely different level, we experience the inconclusive self-identification of people who do not understand their destinies. As the novel develops, a sense of impenetrable mystery grows. The stern of the ship is forbidden to the passengers. Something strange—probably malevolent—is going on. We never find out what it is.

This withheld information is a major use of a technique that García Márquez uses in a minor way. In *Los premios,* it creates an atmosphere that should be enough of a message in itself. Cortázar, however, like Fuentes in *La región más transparente,* apparently thinks the basic structure of his novel does not say enough, so he inserts a character, Persio, who functions as an invented narrator. In expository passages that bear a limited resemblance to interior monologue (and printed in italics), Persio sees the group as a whole. The unifying effect is aesthetically desirable; but Persio is a presumptuous intruder, a nonentity who does not correspond to author, character, or reader, and his metaphysical wanderings are a bore. The diversity of the passengers is the interesting factor, whatever the level of appreciation. Among the several possibilities, one rather far-fetched one has a certain insistent appeal: that these *porteño* types, taken collectively, may represent the world view of a particular culture in their restricted understanding of their own reality, with a consequent accumulation of doubts and forebodings.

Whatever the shortcomings of particular works by these three writers who became big names in the boom, there is no doubt they are excellent novelists. It is important to notice, however (and it may be surprising to casual readers of Spanish American fiction), that they are not very notable for their technical innovation. In all fairness, the novelists themselves have never made that claim; critics and scholars have tended to emphasize their technical adventures because of a universal tendency to ignore their direct predecessors in Spanish America while eulogizing some of the least imaginative novels the region has produced. Carlos Fuentes freely admits his indebtedness to non-Hispanic novelists, and particularly to some in the United States. What he does not point out is that practically all the narrative techniques he learned reading North American novels had been used also in Spanish American fiction, by authors frequently not well known and, in many cases, not as gifted as Fuentes or the major writers who influenced him.

A number of the established writers who were productive during the period 1956-1962 belong to that delayed generation that tried its wings in the vanguardism of the late 1920s and early 1930s, and then went through a quiet period before participating in the reaffirmation of fiction in the late 1940s. Some established writers show little or no change from their earlier works; others are clearly different. Some participate in the boom, though not as intensely as the newer writers.

The works of Miguel Angel Asturias during this period belong to the negative side of his ledger. Protest dominates them—perfectly justifiable protest against the United States' imperialism, economic and political. Justifiable protest, however, does not necessarily make art; in some instances, Asturias's anxiety makes his work ridiculous. Agustín Yáñez continues to produce the portrait of Mexico begun in *Al filo del agua*. He never again achieves that excellence, but he comes very close in *Las tierras flacas* (1962). This is a novel of the high country—the land is poor and the people are persistently enduring. One of the major techniques used to portray these people is the proverb, the folk saying, not simply placed in dialogue, but used as the basis of stream-of-consciousness narration or as interior monologue. These sayings create a feeling of the sparseness of the land. The most basic representative of a technological age, a sewing machine, serves to illuminate the frustrations and faith of the people.

In a very carefully balanced narrative structure, the author sets this primitive technology against a more complicated one, and also the general concept of technological progress against the primitive endurance of the people.

Both Yáñez and Eduardo Mallea wrote novels on the creative act: Yáñez in *La creación* (1949) and Mallea in *Simbad* (1957). *La creación* is about a musician—a very difficult way to deal with creativity when the author is confined to words. The novel contains interesting suggestions about the process of making an artistic work, but there is no satisfactory communication of the feeling of the process itself. The novel is more interesting for its picture of the artistic world in post-Revolutionary Mexico. Mallea wisely creates a protagonist who is a writer. *Simbad* is an enormous book, a kind of stocktaking of the writer's relationship to the world. In this respect, it is reminiscent of *La bahía del silencio*—in principle, not in detail. Mallea's protagonist, Fernando Fe, imagines a work in which Simbad will end his quest, discovering his dream world. Fernando's imagined world overlaps with his real world, and this circumstance is the means of highlighting the nature of creativity. The author uses one of his favorite narrative devices: the double plot line. In this case the two are clearly related to each other, but create entirely different impressions of the duration of time. The five sections of the novel tell the life story of Fernando Fe; however, each of the sections has a prelude that deals with the protagonist's action during a short but crucial period of his life. Here, as in earlier novels, Mallea narrates defining. It is possible that the habits and customs of the characters (mostly intellectual bourgeoisie) may have some intrinsic interest, but the principal communication of the book is the never-ending quest of man as artist and as ordinary human.

Both Alejo Carpentier and Juan Carlos Onetti produced their best novels between 1956 and 1962. Carpentier's *El acoso* (1957) is a short novel generally recognized as a technical tour de force. The plot, basically a manhunt, develops in time and tension that accord with a performance of Beethoven's Third Symphony. The tension created by this structural requirement harmonizes with the emotional tension of the plot. The characters are recognizable Havana types, but that fact, as in Cortázar's *Los premios,* is secondary unless the reader is looking specifically for that characteristic.

El acoso is a virtuoso performance, but *El siglo de las luces* (1962) is the best of Carpentier's major works. He finds the basis of his magic in history, as in *El reino de este mundo*. The time is the French Revolution and the Napoleonic era. The protagonist is an obscure figure in French history, Victor Hugues. His exploits bring him into contact with an aristocratic family in colonial Havana. The story deals with the family and also with the partially separate line of Hugues's adventures. Cuba, the whole Caribbean area, France, and Spain are brought together in the story, so the concept of cultural heritage develops jointly with the idea of revolution. All this is another part of the New World experience. Carpentier's way of dealing with history, here as elsewhere, gives it a magical quality. Hugues is the man of action, ideas put in motion. The principle of revolution, along with its relationship to ambition and success, appears in a historical frame, but the transfer to contemporary implications is easy enough. Undoubtedly, Carpentier thinks of the Cuban Revolution as a restatement of a historical constant.

The lack of meaning that bedevils the characters of Juan Carlos Onetti becomes a kind of gamesmanship in *El astillero* (1961), one of the best novels—possibly the best—written by the dour Uruguayan. The title of the novel is the Spanish word for shipyard. This enterprise is located in Onetti's mythical town of Santa María. The protagonist, Larsen, returns to the town determined to make a name for himself. A position as general manager of the shipyard seems to be the perfect opportunity. Its owner, Petrus, is an aging businessman who pretends that the shipyard's affairs are about to take a turn for the better. The fact is that it is a collection of rusty machinery, a skeleton of what once existed. There is no business except the illicit activity of selling what remains of the machinery, without the owner's permission. General manager Larsen has two employees: a technical administrator and a business manager who pore over disintegrating blueprints and keep imaginary accounts of transactions that never happen. Everybody knows perfectly well that they're just playing a game, going through a set of motions. Larsen even courts the boss's daughter, a mentally retarded girl who lives in a musty old house about as lively as the shipyard.

The narrator tells the story of *El astillero* as if he himself witnessed part of it and learned the rest from other people. This point of view keeps the reader aware that the novel's characters do not see some facts that ought to be apparent to them. Therefore, we react to Larsen and the others not as we might toward people who are being deceived, but as we might toward those who deceive themselves. One reaction is to feel that they must hold on to this pretense because it is all they have. Another is that life amounts to playing a game that has no meaning beyond the game itself. It is impossible to dismiss *El astillero* without thinking about Uruguayan politics, which allow government by committee to promote civic inertia and the consequent corrosion, material and spiritual, of the nation. The exposé of life as a game demands more than a political answer, but the answer is not found in Onetti's novel.

Ernesto Sábato's *Sobre héroes y tumbas* (1962) tends to overwhelm readers. An initial experience with it creates an impression of a great mural depicting the present (last years of the Perón regime) and past of Argentina, with an extra dimension provided by the third of the novel's four parts, a penetrating interiorization of Fernando Vidal, possibly the novelist's protagonist. Even after several readings, many questions remain unanswered, and two readers can easily become completely absorbed in asking each other what Sábato means by this or that character or act. Angela Dellepiane does the best job of relating his essays to his novels and it is through her analysis that we begin to see *Sobre héroes y tumbas* as an examination of values, an attempt to reindividualize human beings in the context of contemporary society.

Sábato contrasts two characters, Alejandra and Martín, particularly in the first two parts of the novel. She is impure and belongs to a family that includes an unusually high percentage of the famous names of Argentine history. Martín, on the other hand, is innocent and is virtually without family ties and tradition. These two antithetical people seem irresistibly attracted to each other. Indeed, one of the less attractive features of the novel is the author's insistence on this deterministic relationship. It is a love affair more for a novel of the early nineteenth century than for one of the late twentieth. However, the telescoping of the emotion-time effect is one of the novel's narrative techniques. An account of the retreat of General Lavalle, a historical event of more than a century ago, functions as one element in the mural of contemporary Argentina and is particularly significant in its communication of a sense of honor and loyalty. There is a suggestion of the decadence of tradition, set forth in the character of Alejandra and the relationship within her family; but the Lavalle account is strongly affirmative. Martín, on the other hand, is devoid of tradition even to the point of being denied by his own mother; yet he is the character who carries the novel's spark of optimism. It is possible to suppose that Sábato wishes to set forth human values in such a way that they cannot possibly be confused with the process of passing time. Such an understanding would be far removed from an initial reading, because the story of the fatally attracted lovers plus a melodramatic development worthy of *King's Row* (incest, murder, suicide) overwhelm more subtle appreciations.

One critic provides a unified understanding of the novel through the archetypal explanation of Fernando as a hero. He sees a pairing of General Lavalle and Fernando, the latter's interior descent into hell working as a contemporary parallel to Lavalle's heroic act. The nucleus of this reading is the third part of the novel, "Informe sobre ciegos," which may be taken as the journey through the underworld—an interior experience that recalls the journey of *Adán Buenosayres*. It is possible to find, in Fernando's experience, the seeds of Martín's salvation. This analysis, however, is a lot neater than the novel; it can illuminate the book, but should not be taken as an equivalent to the experience of the novel itself.

Manuel Mujica Lainez, already known for his aesthetic interests and his nostalgic novels based on the changing social structure of Buenos Aires, published *Bomarzo* in 1962. This book provided the story for Alberto Ginastera's opera. It is a historical novel that creates the flavor of the Renaissance. The author has been the art critic for the newspaper *La Nación* and for several years was con-

Dust jacket for the English translation of Gabriel García Márquez's 1985 novel, Love in the Time of Cholera.

nected with a museum. His sensitivity is not simply the enjoyment of artistic creations, but includes also a reaction of delight in the very act of evoking a past era. This evocation is one of the two important factors that make *Bomarzo* interesting. The other is the incorporation into the story of many well-known historical personages: Cervantes, Michelangelo, Lotto, Cellini, Charles V, and others. Mujica Lainez's work reveals his aristocratic attitude, and it is also a representative of the Argentine literary world's sophistication. The author is a latter day member of the Florida fellowship; his works contain many of the qualities that provoked the rebellion of the parricides, the revisionist writers of the Viñas group.

Another important writer, Ezequiel Martínez Estrada, may seem a strange addition to a group of established novelists, since he is more often thought of as an essayist. Actually he has made distinguished contributions to literature also as a poet and as a writer of fiction. While none of his works in the latter category have ever been considered major, they might well have enjoyed more attention if his essays had been less remarkable. The excellence of his stories and short novels is the result of several factors of great importance in the development of the genre: transformation of philosophical attitudes into fiction, association of narrative invention with the creative impulse, and use of stylistic variation to communicate the experience of the story.

His "Viudez" (1956) is the portrayal of a widow's confusion, indecisiveness, and eventual recognition of her state of being alone. The dynamic factor in the novel is the progressively nightmarish quality of its three episodes. The scene is rural—the home and family of a small farmer. The first episode contains a labyrinth experience when the woman gets lost among the cattle (it is night) while going to seek aid from a neighbor. The second episode turns Carnival into a dead clown. The third tells of relatives who come and, instead of being helpful, make a fiesta that gets in the way of work the woman has to do. The reader identifies easily with the protagonist because the narrative, although in the third person, sees the situation as she would see it. It is also interesting that from this position the narrator is able to ask questions and answer them. They do not appear obtrusive because they seem to be the woman's natural questions. This advantage is a large contributing factor in the transformation of philosophical attitude into fictional experience.

Marta Riquelme is a Borgesian piece that cloaks subjectivity with a presumed objectivity. The story pretends to be a prologue written by Martínez Estrada for Marta Riquelme's memoirs. The book itself is presumed lost. It was supposedly given to Martínez Estrada for editing, by Arnaldo Orfila Reynal, who actually was director of Mexico's Fondo de Cultura Económica at one time. This setup gives the piece a desirable ring of authenticity. Beyond that, *Marta Riquelme* is a multiple satire: on the family-history type of novel, on literary scholarship of the "detective" kind, and on interpretive literary criticism. It is a stylistic tour de force because Martínez Estrada says most of what he wishes to say simply by changing from one style to another. He uses at least four major style tones: scholar-

ly exposition, the style used by the editor whose personal interest makes the prologue more intimate, Marta Riquelme's own style, and a style that may possibly not be Marta's.

The established novelists writing in the period 1956-1962 reveal few important changes in narrative technique. They did not need innovation. Their works of ten to fifteen years earlier established them as modern novelists. Even the best known of the younger writers used the same techniques. If it is possible—admittedly it is risky—to establish a difference between a large-screen, muralistic novel and a small-screen, salon-type book, it is correct to say that the large-screen type is more common among the established novelists. It is doubtful, however, that this preference indicates a generational choice. Among the younger novelists, the muralistic concept is very common. In any case, the established novelists of this period make up an unusual generation, because the fruition of their productive period was delayed so they often appear younger than they really are.

Separation of the new novelists of this period from the big names of the boom does not in any way mean that they are inferior writers. The well-known figures of the boom serve to define the phenomenon; they do not dominate it artistically. Another pitfall in discussing the boom is the temptation to separate writers who belong to it from those who do not; or, even worse, to make a complicated scale of relative "in-ness." If we allow consideration of the boom to go deeper than reaction to personalities, all the current novelists in Spanish America participate in the phenomenon in some way and to some extent.

Among the newer novelists of the period 1956-1962, a substantial number wrote novels that fall into our general classification of large screen or muralistic. Almost always these works are concerned with some understanding or explanation of a national (or regional or cultural) situation, developing it in terms and by means of techniques that make it a vital experience rather than a set of statistics or an objective account of an event already terminated. Making a subordinate classification within this large one, it appears that some novels are primarily political, while others are more concerned with the heritage, history, or tradition of the place. The political concern seems to emphasize three countries: Colombia, Argentina, and Cuba.

One of the most vital political novels is *La calle 10* (1960) by Manuel Zapata Olivella. Its factual basis is the assassination of Jorge Eliécer Gaitán and the subsequent rioting in 1948. The novel was probably written at a time closer to the event than to the date of publication. It has a sense of immediacy; however, this particular vitality persists through repeated readings, probably because a compelling impression of mass insurrection operates in balance with portraits of individuals who are genuinely appealing. This way we feel the excitement of the mass movement while, at the same time, the attractive individuals create a natural sense of brotherliness. The association makes exhortations to brotherhood unnecessary, and the result is much more convincing.

The narrator opens with a morning scene: a cadaver, a

family waking up, a man with a cart, a mule, and a dog. The prose is clear, direct, sparse. Yet it creates a feeling of great tenderness when the narrator speaks of emotions, always with simplicity that is convincing because it is unadorned. He brings the crowd to life by using unidentified dialogue. The narrative darts from one street scene to another. There is enough relationship between scenes to provide a sense of group unity, but the narrator does not develop a conventional plot line. That is, there are always people or situations that connect one scene with another, but these relationships may be of little importance in the total action that takes place in a given scene. There are moments that recall *Los de abajo*. The momentum of the novel develops in three stages: the circumstance seen in terms of an individual, then in the movement of mass insurrection, and finally back to an individual. Zapata Olivella portrays abject poverty without dramatic protest, but with tenderness. Class differences become apparent, but the novel's emphasis is on contrast rather than on indignation. The tone becomes disgust when politicians destroy the momentum of the rebellion by declaring, via radio, that they are the voice of the people and the people are triumphant. Finally, back once more to communication through an individual, one disillusioned rebel starts to break his rifle, but another stops him saying he will soon have use for it. This prediction—somewhat dramatic in the cold atmosphere of today's news report—is an entirely credible promise, even a consolation, in the context of the novel.

The feeling of frustration produced in *La calle 10* has a counterpart in another Colombian novel of the same period, Fernando Soto Aparicio's *La rebelión de las ratas*. It is a social protest novel, and, although it is not based on a specific political incident or problem, it deals with the dehumanizing effect of power. The circumstance is exploitation of the worker by a mining company. Soto Aparicio sets the tone, with no great subtlety, at the beginning of the novel: the advent of the mining company interrupts the bucolic quiet of the locale. Soto Aparicio moves from the general scene to the family of Rudecindo Cristancho and then shifts to the ideas of Rudecindo, his protagonist.

If someone were to make a survey, asking which Spanish American novelists are the best representatives of the boom, the chances are that the most frequently mentioned names would be Julio Cortázar, Carlos Fuentes, Gabriel García Márquez, and Mario Vargas Llosa.

— *John S. Brushwood*

The time span of the novel is very specific, with narrative divisions indicated by days from February 10 to February 19. During this time, Cristancho's family suffers all the trials of poverty and exploitation by the company. Rudecindo is reduced to a number, sees his domestic happiness de-

stroyed, and loses his life in a revolt against his exploiters. The narration is consistently third person, but from the standpoint of several different people. This procedure relates the social protest to the question of individual dignity. Therefore *La rebelión de las ratas* does not suffer from the doctrinaire effect that clutters the fictional experience of many proletarian novels.

The Argentine crisis of awareness is still acute during the years 1956-1962. David Viñas produced three novels that show he is as adept at the intimate study as he is in the muralistic books. *Los años despiadados* (1956) is the story, possibly autobiographical, of a schoolboy who feels imprisoned by the traditions of his family. It is important to note that they are not aristocratic but middle class. Even so, he feels restricted by a way of life that seems to him to belong to another age. Viñas states the message in one of his favorite ways—the development of an opposite. The protagonist's friend and opposite is the son of immigrants, and, so far as the protagonist can see, is not inhibited by any traditions. He has no apparent need to create any particular image or earn the approval of anyone. He is proletarian, *peronista,* even somewhat cruel; and his need for the protagonist's friendship is primitive. Although the novel deals only with this personal situation, we can hardly avoid the reference to change in Argentine society.

The narrative techniques Viñas uses are intended to emphasize a certain point he wishes to make. Sometimes the point is preconceived and the technique designed to bring it out. The author risks becoming didactic when he does so, but usually he is clever enough to make his characters so vital they mask his planning. That is the case in the development of the opposite. For the same reason, Viñas uses typographical effects, especially italics. The first three parts (there are six in all) of *Los dueños de la tierra* (1959) are in italics, which properly set them apart because they are historical background. The novel, whose title means "the owners of the land," deals with the expansion into Patagonia, a frontier movement something like the United States' conquest of the West. In the three introductory parts of the novel, Viñas chooses three important moments in the history of the southward expansion: the Indian wars, development of the wool industry during World War I, and labor troubles between ranchers and peons in 1920.

The novel's present time—that is, the action that takes place in the last three parts—coincides with the third historical moment. President Irigoyen sends Vicente Vera to Patagonia as a conciliator. The change from italics signals the narrator's change from background to novel proper, and Vera becomes a symbol of what Viñas finds wrong with the official regime. The mood created by the story of Vera is surprisingly like the reaction to the protagonist of Los *años despiadados*. Vera, like the boy protagonist of the other novel, is so controlled by formulas there is little or no hope of his accomplishing anything. His approach is platitudinous. The difference between him and the boy is that Vera does not even know he is caught. In the next-to-last section Viñas sets up an opposite in the person of Yuda, a schoolteacher with progressive ideas. The love affair between Vera and Yuda softens the contrast, just as friendship shades the difference between the two boys in *Los años despiadados*. It is unproductive so far as Vera's mission is concerned. His government is too far removed from the nation's reality for him to be able to accomplish anything.

Beatriz Guido's *Fin de fiesta* (1958) is a successful though discouraging picture of the persistence of *caudillismo*. Guido, who likes to use young people as her protagonists, tells the story primarily through four cousins who grow up in the household of their *caudillo* grandfather. Multiple point of view contributes substantially to the effect of the novel, which alternates passages of first-person and third-person-omniscient narration. The presentation of the four cousins develops from their relationships during their early teens and continues into their political awareness. The death of the old *caudillo* fades into the rise of a new one (Perón, though he is not identified in the novel). The story suggests possible change in the quality of *caudillismo,* but it also suggests its indestructibility as an institution.

Concentration of power in one individual is the theme of *La alfombra roja* (1962), by Marta Lynch. It is a psychological study of what happens to several people during an election campaign which the protagonist, Doctor Aníbal Rey, wins. The focus is on his use of people and their reaction to him. The narrative point of view is the most important technical factor. It is consistently first person, but the identity of the first-person narrator varies from chapter to chapter. The chapter titles indicate who the narrator is in each case. The time perspective is also important—the narration is retrospective, but refers to the immediate past. The tone usually has an effect similar to a diary. The narration produces a more logical sequence of events than is characteristic of interior monologue, but the revelations made by the narrators are more intimate than we normally expect from a first-person narrator who functions in the novel on equal terms with the other characters.

Each chapter places emphasis on the person speaking, but we always learn something about the others. The candidate himself narrates chapter one (he also narrates several others) and reveals his growing taste for manipulating the crowd. In the same chapter, this euphoric demagogue introduces some of his supporters, so it is quite natural for one of them to act as the narrator of the second chapter. The technique of changing from one narrator to another produces a certain amount of simultaneity in the time covered by the various chapters. As the presidential campaign comes to a close, Lynch brings the novel to a climax. In one chapter (Beder), Rey's publicity man views the change that has taken place in the candidate. This episode is one of several where the first-person narration actually produces the effect of third-person omniscient. It is a description of the transformation of an intellectual into a power-myth: " . . . although the image of Rey that is current among the people has connection with reality, his myth is already in the making, created partly by himself, partly by history."

The remaining chapters of *La alfombra roja* really constitute an epilogue. They all occur on election day; and the last, in which Rey is again the narrator, is called "El Señor Presidente," rather than "El Doctor." The basic facts of the campaign and election are commonplace, so the psychological insight into several characters is more interesting than the event itself. This fact, however, makes the mechanics of the campaign seem so cold and impersonal that its significance in the lives of human beings takes on a terrifying quality. Rey uses people more and more to gain his own ends, as he thinks of himself increasingly as a man of destiny. When Beder describes the transformation of the candidate, he describes him as unreal. By the end of the novel, the circumstance and the man are dehumanized—that is, they are not what we hope humanity is. The concluding chapters reveal the sacrifice of individuals to destiny, and at the end of the novel Aníbal Rey stands quite alone in his new residence.

The experience of political concern in these novels is preeminently one of objection to the concentration of power. There is also a strong revolutionary feeling—not in the specific threat or prediction of an uprising, but in the feeling that established political patterns must change. Nevertheless, hovering over the scene is the presence of the *caudillo,* the leader who will run the country. Marta Lynch's contribution to the literary life of this myth is portrayal of the change that takes place in the man as a corollary to the concentration of power. *La alfombra roja* deserves a place with *El Señor Presidente* and *La sombra del caudillo* in the literary picture of the phenomenon. . . .

Speaking in broad, general terms, the novels of 1956-1962 are a somber lot, although many of them are excellent. They initiate an intense bourgeois self-flagellation that still goes on in 1970. However, the years following 1962 saw several innovations or intensifications of tendencies already begun and related to the century's anguish. The most widely cultivated is the segmented narrative. This technique is valuable for creating new appreciations of reality. It also reflects the fragmented nature of contemporary society, and segmented narration turns out to be alternately centrifugal and centripetal.

No doubt in some instances readers may ask what became of the story. With this reaction in mind, it is important to point out that the raconteur's art has not disappeared. One important witness to this fact is Fernando Alegría's *Caballo de copas* (1957), a Damon Runyon-type story about a race horse imported into the United States from Chile. It is what Graham Greene calls an "entertainment"— smooth, professional writing, fun to read, no profound implications but quite a few matter-of-fact revelations of what life is like. Many novelists, particularly the innovative ones, would do well to learn from *Caballo de copas* or similar novels, and then innovate. The results could be rewarding, as in the case of *La muerte de Artemio Cruz.* Actually, the departure from an expected order of narration varies in nature. Many contemporary novelists tell the story fairly straight, but without explanations. Others do the unexpected, but take care that we follow them. Still others leave their readers to struggle.

The story is there; or, if it is not, there is a substitute. What has happened is that ways of presenting the story have changed, and, in addition, a circumstance may have taken the story's place. By 1962, the novelist is extremely aware of his creative function, though he talks about it more later on. Since he is so aware of creating, experience becomes more important than denouement. Of course, the experience of any novel is always the most important consideration, but it can become confused with or even hidden by the traditional plot-development sequence. The novelists after 1962 depend to a very great extent on the importance of experience.

THE NOVEL

Helen E. Haines

SOURCE: "Fiction from Latin America," in *What's in a Novel,* Columbia University Press, 1942, pp. 169-96.

[*In the following essay, Haines provides an overview of several Latin American novels published during the early 1940s.*]

> There must come a conception of life which, without denying the fundamental union between man and the earth would lift him past the barriers that had held him back until then to lead him to the more complete forms of existence.

> —Ciro Alegría: *Broad and Alien Is the World*

To the vast majority of readers in the United States, Latin American fiction is more remote, more exotic, than any of the fiction of Europe. The two Americas share a hemisphere; they have never shared a common understanding. Underlying their deep separation are fundamental differences in folk roots, in historical development, in religion, in social and cultural conditions that set up barriers to mutual sympathetic response and that are not resolved by friendly trade relations or political agreements. With the rise of world conflict "hemispheric solidarity" has become not simply a pious phrase of political aspiration but a profound and urgent necessity. There is deepening realization in both continents of the need of closer social and cultural ties—of reciprocal relations in education, and of a much more extensive exchange of literature between the Latin American countries and the United States—if any real bond of understanding is to be established between them.

Many cultured Latin Americans read English and are familiar with the work of North American writers, many of whose books also have been translated into Spanish; English is required in the schools of ten of the Latin American countries, and its study is steadily increasing in all. But Latin American literature is virtually unknown to the general reading public of the United States. That the most widely known novel (*The Thatched Hut*) of the Ecuadorian novelist José Icaza should have been translated into six languages, one of them Chinese, but not into English, shows this limitation of our literary horizon. Yet the mind of a people reveals itself in that people's literature, and through the books of Latin American writers it is possible to gain a knowledge and understanding that otherwise can come only from personal experience.

Since the early 1920's there has been a sporadic endeavor to acquaint cultivated readers in the United States with the variety and vitality of contemporary Latin American fiction. Isaac Goldberg, Waldo Frank, Anita Brenner, Carleton Beals have been among the leaders in this endeavor; and about thirty novels by Mexican and South American writers were published in English translation in this country during this period. They reached only a limited audience; commercially, they must have registered loss rather than profit. But their publication marked a step toward fuller representation in our current book production of this young American literature, that, like our own, is an expression of American culture, and that, also like our own, holds portent of American development and American destiny. A further step was taken in 1940, when a prize contest for the best book, preferably a novel, by a Latin American author was initiated by the New York publishing firm of Farrar & Rinehart, with the aid of the Division of Intellectual Coöperation of the Pan-American Union and of literary groups in the different Latin American countries. Ciro Alegría, exiled Peruvian novelist, was awarded the prize in March, 1941, for his novel *Broad and Alien Is the World;* and three other novelists received honorable mention: Enrique Gil Gilbert, of Ecuador, for *Our Daily Bread;* Cecilio J. Carneiro, of Brazil, for *The Bonfire;* Miguel Angel Menéndez, of Mexico, for *Nayar.* Other similar contests are to follow, to include fiction, nonfiction (biographic, sociological, or philosophic), and a book for children. To make this fresh-flowing stream of Latin American fiction—so varied, so significant—more available in English translation, to strengthen and stimulate appreciation of its interest and potential values should be a more effective means of realizing aims and ideals of intracontinental relationship than chamber of commerce excursions, scholastic dissertations, or political oratory.

Much Latin American fiction undoubtedly carries an impact of shock to many North American readers. The shock is less than it would have been a few years ago, before so many of our own novelists had turned to harsh transcription of brutal experience in their recording of social and economic evils; but its immediate effect may be painful or benumbing. The exotic pictorial vividness of these novels seems crude or garish; their violence of action, their mingling of primitive barbarism with sophisticated European culture, gives a sense of unreality; in structure and development they may lack coherence and climax; often they reek of human suffering and are veined with cruelty, as they picture oppression and exploitation, political corruption, and revolutionary conflict. All this, however, represents the creation of a self-sufficient, individual literary culture. Latin American novelists have broken the traditional bond with nineteenth-century Spanish letters. They have drawn their substance from their native soil, and their qualities of expression, in exuberance, in abruptness, in disorder and intensity, are the manifestations of the life they delineate. Their preoccupation with social problems, their dominant tendency to the tragic, their absorption in natural settings of savage beauty, impart an inner unity to what is essentially a literature of national and social transmutation. Russian fiction nearly a century ago extended the boundaries and enlarged the horizons of the novel in its exploration of the human spirit; today Latin American fiction opens for exploration the processes of social evolution in the New World that is part of, but completely different from, our own.

Mexican fiction has had very little representation in the influx of books about Mexico that came into being about 1928, under the influence of D. H. Lawrence, Anita Brenner, Stuart Chase, Carleton Beals, and Waldo Frank, and that still continues, though in lessened volume. But the few Mexican novels that are available in English translation illuminate significant backgrounds of the contemporary scene and give color and reality to the folk life of the people.

The Under Dogs, Mariano Azuela's novel of the revolution of 1911-17, is the most famous modern Mexican novel. First published when its author was in exile in El Paso, it went unheeded for ten years; but by 1927 its fame had spread throughout the Spanish-speaking literary world, and it will long remain a vital evocation of the break-up of a country under the sudden flare of civil war, assassination, hate, the uprising of the "under dogs" from centuries of servitude into a savage freedom of fighting, comradeship, and brutal pillage. Azuela, by profession a physician, went himself as military doctor with the guerrilla band that was transformed into a Villa army which swarmed like locusts, burning, killing, looting, and carousing through the states of Zacatecas and Jalisco. From this experience he drew the material for his novel; its last scene, we are told, was written in a cave overlooking the annihilation of the band, and the rest was composed later, in exile. The book is short: direct, dramatic, vivid. Its central figure is the guerrilla leader, driven from his patch of land, his hut and cows and wife and child, drawing about him followers like himself; half-naked *pelados,* swept into the whirlpool of revolution, hardly knowing how or why; victims and perpetrators alike of ruthless violence and brutal crime. One savage, picturesque scene follows another in extraordinary flesh-and-blood reality; and through all the tragedy, futility, coarseness, high exploits, and abysmal cruelties there is conveyed a sense of pity for the poor and ignorant, to whom Villa was the reincarnation of the old legend: "Villa as Providence, the bandit, that passes through the world with the blazing torch of an ideal: to rob the rich and give to the poor."

Beside Azuela's novel must stand the narrative of Martín Luis Guzmán, *The Eagle and the Serpent,* often regarded as fiction, though it is in fact personal reminiscence in dramatic dialogue form, which gives a first-hand record of the revolution during the years of Villa's power. Personal experience, adventure, vigorous character etching, quickly moving drama, mingle in this absorbing, authentic narrative. It is detailed, following no single plot-thread, with the flavor of mixed good humor, sardonic indifference and devil-may-care casualness which is characteristic of the Mexican temperament, even in grim danger or tragic circumstance. There is no artificiality, no writing for effect; even the most monstrous scenes of ruthless cruelty are invested with a direct simplicity. Guzmán, like Azuela,

wrote from his own experience. He was a follower and champion of Villa, never deserted him, and sees him always with admiring eyes—even his cruelty, ruthlessness, irresponsibility, infantile pomposity, crass sentimentalities. Both books have continuing value as historical material.

Azuela has written many other novels; his work as a whole forms a broad fictional canvas of the social-revolutionary struggle, from the last days of the Diaz regime, with the dominance of the rich landowners, through the rise and fall of Madero, the devastating conflicts of rival parties, and the disillusion, corruption, and persecutions of later years. Always he deals with the exploited classes: the Indian peon, the tenant farmer, the middle class, helpless under political rascality; all under dogs in a complex social struggle. Of these novels only one has appeared in English translation: *Marcela*—a passionate love story of Indian peons on a feudal estate ruled by a cruel and dissolute owner, its folk life curiously mingling subtlety and fierceness, its pervading superstition blending ancient Indian lore and Catholic ritual; its feuds and lusts and cruelties pervaded by the exotic beauty of its natural setting.

More limited but of deep significance is the aspect of Mexican life portrayed in *El Indio,* the novel by Gregorio López y Fuentes, that won Mexico's first National Prize of Literature, in 1935. This is a study of the Mexican Indian in his own tribal life and in his traditional fear and distrust of white or mestizo civilization. It deals with a remote Indian village, high in the Mexican mountains; its people, proud, quiet, wary of strangers, speak Aztec, not Spanish. None of them are named, for they are not only individuals but also, as López y Fuentes sees them, symbols of a conquest that has continued for more than four hundred years; yet they have individuality, and their everyday living takes on a warm and moving reality. Their story runs through a period of years. It opens with the arrival of white prospectors, greedy and treacherous, bringing terror and violence and leaving suffering in their wake; it closes with requisitions of food and conscription of labor imposed by officials of the towns in the valley below—the exactions of a government that regards these people only as materials for exploitation. Dramatic and moving episodes are woven into the texture of this primitive living. There is dignity, integrity, courage and devotion in individual experiences; and the communal folkways, with their witch-doctor miracles, their council meetings that give judgment in controversies, their fiesta that opens with solemn ritual and closes with machetes flashing in drunken fight, their ancient sports that have come unchanged from the Aztec past, all compose a fascinating and impressive pattern. There is a quality of classic beauty in the calm simplicity, the stoic dignity, with which the tale is told.

Although they are very different, a certain similarity exists between *El Indio* and *Nayar,* the novel by Miguel Angel Menéndez that received honorable mention in the Latin American prize novel contest. Both books are a manifestation of the deepening Indian—as opposed to Spanish—influence in contemporary Latin American literature, which accepts the elemental pattern of tribal Indian life and the qualities and powers of the race as potential

Dust jacket for Juan Carlos Onetti's 1950 novel, La Vida breve.

sources of a rich indigenous national culture, and seeks to expose exploitation and oppression exercised under the civil, military, and religious domination rooted in Spanish conquest. The scene is a remote province (Nayarit) on the west coast of Mexico, a region of mountains, forest jungles, salt marshes, and obscure villages, where the remnants of two primitive Indian tribes lead a harassed existence, victimized by both whites and mestizos, held in bonds of poverty, ignorance, superstition, and magic, and in a sudden flaring of civil and religious conflict ultimately crushed between opposed forces of government and revolutionaries. *Nayar,* however, has an emotional exuberance, an intensity of color and action, far removed from the restraint of *El Indio;* the work of a poet (later, Mexican minister to China), it weaves a complex social problem into a vivid, uneven web of tragedy.

Even a partial gleaning from the South American fiction that is available in English translation will reveal its rich variety of content and its historical and social significance. For such a gleaning we have books by representative novelists from seven of the South American countries. These, following a rough topographical order from north to south, are: Venezuela, Colombia, Peru, Brazil, Chile, Argentina, and Uruguay. Countries from which no fiction is represented are Ecuador, Bolivia, and Paraguay. Of course, in these a native literature exists; in Ecuador, espe-

cially, novelists of talent are exploring their country's composite human elements; but it must be remembered that very little of the whole body of South American fiction has been translated into English; and in the translations that have been made, the work of Argentinian, Brazilian, Colombian, and Venezuelan writers predominates.

Perhaps a word should be said first concerning the whole field of South American fiction. The Latin Americans have always been a literary people; they have as heritage the traditions and the culture of the Roman Catholic Church, and that heritage found expression through the four centuries of their history in a continuous, changing flow of literary productions. Prose narratives and heroic poems of conquest and discovery mirror the early colonial period. Dramas, poems, and devotional writings were strongest in the static years of undisturbed Spanish rule. The opening of the nineteenth century and the rise of the Napoleonic era saw the advent of the revolutionary years and the birth of an entirely different literature of national aspiration and passionate purpose, as the struggle for independence from the mother country plunged the Spanish colonies into ruthless war. Yet throughout most of the nineteenth century the colonial spirit and manner of life persisted. Not until the last quarter of that century did the rising wave of reform and innovation wash away traditional literary conventions and disclose a new creative spirit. No general literacy yet exists in South America; until the turn of the century public education bore the stamp of medieval Europe rather than that of the modern world. Literature has been the field of an intellectual élite, which cultivated it as the means and the sign of culture. Authorship in the past did not mean earning a living; even today few of the leading South American authors depend on their books for their full income—they are usually also journalists, teachers, lawyers, doctors; most of the older men can look back on a common life experience of revolution, prison, political vicissitudes; nearly all were pamphleteers, poets, and dramatists before they became novelists. This has meant that the literature they produce is generally of high literary quality: their books are written, not for commercial reasons, but to express convictions, ideals, or the inner urge of the spirit.

Within the twentieth century the audience for South American writers has greatly increased, and since 1930 a native book production has come into existence that has broken down former literary border lines between the different countries and virtually eliminated the "literary colonialism" that depended on Spain for its book supply. The publishing house of Ercilla, established in Santiago de Chile in 1932, has become a center for publication and distribution throughout South America. Whereas formerly Argentine books were little known in Ecuador, and Venezuelan writers found fewer readers in Chile, the Ercilla firm now handles books by all Latin American authors and makes them available to all Latin American readers. During the first five years of its existence (to January, 1937) it published 1,120 books by many hundreds of authors, including not only the work of writers from every Latin American country but also books of leading French, Italian, German, Russian, English, and North American authors, issued in Spanish translation. Influences for growth and strength have flowed into Latin American literature from Spain's tragedy. The extinction of the Spanish Republic under fascist victory and the resulting extirpation of Spain's modern thought and culture by destruction and interdiction of books, restriction of education, and exile of writers and scientists, have brought deepening and widening intellectual life to Spanish America. In Mexico publishing, printing, educational, scientific, and literary activities have been centered, under sponsorship of the Spanish Government in Exile, in Mexico City. Exiled Spanish writers, scholars, and artists in many fields are also at work in other Latin American countries; and the dissemination of modern continental and English literature in Spanish translation steadily increases.

This expanding audience, this birth of a continental spirit, finds its manifestation in the rise of fiction. Poetry has always been the leading form in Latin American literature, the mark of culture and idealism. But within a generation, while poetry holds its place, there has been widespread development of novels and short stories, by writers who have disregarded the older aristocratic limitations, who are going for their material to life itself, reflecting and interpreting the common experience of the world and the people amid which they live. Of this contemporary fiction Waldo Frank says:

> There are novelists like the Mexican, Mariano Azuela, who are depicting the life of the Mexican Indian, soldier, mestizo, in the passionate years of revolution. There are novelists like the Colombian, José Eustacio Rivera, who bring the cruel and deep suffering of mankind in the jungles into their pages. Argentinians, like Ricardo Güiraldes, Leopold Lugones, Horacio Quiroga, tell the tales of the gaucho, of the small country village lost on the pampa, of the northern forests where gigantic snakes still dispute the land with the pioneers. Venezuelan novelists, like Rufino Blanco-Fombona, reveal the political and social fabric of their complex world; and like Teresa de la Parra the struggle of women to be free of the medieval trammels of the church. In Chile, there is a whole school of admirable novelists devoted to the pastoral life of the villages beneath the Andes.

In summarizing the books of the novelists chosen, the most effective course seems to be to follow the map, opening with the most northern country, moving southward, then westward, then south again; and attempting to trace in these novels the backgrounds, historical and social, of the countries whose life they reflect.

For Venezuela we have Rufino Blanco-Fombona, one of the older leading figures in contemporary Latin American literature, whose life is part of his country's annals of revolution; and the younger novelist, Rómulo Gallegos, most widely popular of present-day Venezuelan writers.

Blanco-Fombona, born in Caracas, in 1874, of old Spanish aristocratic stock, represents the mingling of the aristocratic and insurrecto strain as it was exemplified in Simón Bolívar, "The Liberator,"—also born in Caracas nearly a century earlier—and in the young creole aristocrats who died by thousands for the cause of independence. In a volume of critical and biographical essays (*La Lámpara de Aladino,* 1915) he has written his own epitaph:

> This man, like one beloved of the gods, died young. He knew how to love and to hate with all his heart. He loved fields, rivers, fountains; he loved good wine, he loved marble, steel, gold; he loved nubile women and beautiful verses. He despised the timorous, the presumptuous, and the mediocre. He hated traitors, hypocrites, calumniators, venal spirits. . . . In the midst of his injustice he was just. . . . He attacked only the strong. He had ideals and struggled and made sacrifices for them. . . . Only one thing did he ever refrain from giving: advice. . . . It is not known whether he was moral or immoral or amoral; but he placed beauty and truth—his truth—above all. He enjoyed and suffered much, spiritually and physically. . . . His life was illogical. His thought was contradictory. His one unchanging attribute was his sincerity, both in feeling and thought. . . . He preached liberty by example; he was free. He was a soul of the sixteenth century and a man of the twentieth. He rests in peace for the first time. May the earth, which he loved, be propitious to him.

Very evident here is the quality of oratory, the flow of rhythmic eloquence, that is so strong an element in Latin American politics and literature and that finds intensified emotional expression in fiction.

His stormy political and public career, his varied literary work, in poetry, criticism, sociology, politics, and fiction, make Blanco-Fombona an important contemporary figure. From the age of eighteen, when he was a volunteer in the revolution against President Andueza, he participated in his country's many political struggles, held consular and governmental positions, twice visited the United States (where he contracted a violent dislike for the country and its people), suffered imprisonment, fought duels, escaped assassination; traveled widely in South America as well as in Europe; and lived in Paris and Madrid.

As a novelist, his reputation has long been established. *The Man of Gold,* translated into English by Isaac Goldberg in 1929, is a companion novel to his previous book, *The Man of Iron,* considered his most important work, which was written when he was in prison in 1907 and has not, so far as I know, appeared in English translation. These two novels, as Goldberg points out, form an ideological unity—the second the natural outgrowth from the first. Both titles are ironic: *The Man of Iron* is an honest, simple, creature of passive nature, easily molded, the victim of his virtues; *The Man of Gold* is a creature of alloy, a repulsive miser and usurer, whose single passion is gain and whose story is an ironic composition on the theme of the triumph of evil over good. Both novels are placed in the romantic, languorous setting of Caracas, and both apply stinging satire and bitter irony to social and political conditions in Venezuela under the Castro regime. *The Man of Gold* strikes most vigorously at the machinations and greed of politicians, undoubtedly veiling in caricature some recognizable figures in the political annals of Caracas. Its central figure is the miser and moneylender, withered and hideous, who lives in filthy penury with his crippled, miserable old housekeeper and who is brought into business relationship with three well-born spinsters and their beautiful young niece, Olga, the single object of their devotion. Olga, selfish and ruthless, conceives the idea that the youngest of her aunts should marry the miser: she will undoubtedly outlive him and inherit his wealth, and Olga will be her heiress. On this purpose the plot is woven, carrying the miser to growing political importance as his wealth brings about him sycophants and corrupt officials. There is a play of satirical humor throughout; cruel, sometimes vulgar, realism and harsh physical details are curiously combined with limpid charm; and the vivid portrayal of many different types conveys a sense of varied, distinctive life.

Very different is *Doña Barbara,* the slight but vivid and fascinating novel by Rómulo Gallegos which mirrors ranch life on the Venezuelan plains. It mingles realism and romanticism, and it unrolls a memorable panorama of magnificent natural backgrounds, of wild and vigorous life amid wide streams and vast savannahs, with the far-ranging herds, the lighthearted swaggering plainsmen, and the primitive isolated ranches set down in illimitable expanses. Especially interesting are the contrasts and similarities of this exotic frontier with our own early western cattle country, and the differences of temperament and tradition between the Latin American plainsman and his Nordic counterpart. The story centers on the fortunes of an old Venezuelan family, decimated by an ancient feud, still keeping its great homestead on the plains, though it has fallen into ruin and is being gradually absorbed through the chicaneries of the nearest ranch owner, the powerful, notorious Doña Barbara, a woman of half-Indian blood and lawless background who has made herself despot of the region. The only son and survivor of the ancient family has been educated in Caracas and admitted to the law, but the heritage of his plains ancestry still lives in him. He returns to the half-abandoned ranch to consider selling the property; and then his childhood memories, his inborn nature of the plainsman, reassert themselves. He remains, to regain and restore the family domain and to inaugurate, so far as possible, an era of justice and fair dealing. But he is confronted by the power, greed, and passions of Doña Barbara and by the rascalities of the North American hunter and trader ("the foreigner"), who has established himself in squatter sovereignty on Doña Barbara's land. The courts are corrupt, and the very law that young Santos-Luzardo seeks to invoke has been enacted through the influence of his enemies. His anger is roused, and he determines to fight them in their own fashion; but his natural high principles hold him to honest dealing, and in the end he wins victory through finer means. A love story that is both dramatic and appealing is woven into the plot. The charm and dramatic interest of the novel lie in the portrayal of the plainsman's life: the herding and branding of the cattle, the breaking of the horses, the details of ranch management, the personalities of the plainsmen themselves, their superstitions and customs; and the impressive, beautiful panoramic background of the plains under all the changes of the seasons.

Gallegos is regarded as the most important present-day literary figure in Venezuela. He displays high dramatic ability and a romantic spirit, yet he writes objectively, without expressing personal intensities of feeling, as does Blanco-Fombona. He understands the psychology, landscape, and language of his country, and in some half-dozen novels he has given brilliant portrayal of different turbulent or formative periods in Venezuelan history.

We pass now to Colombia—that country of which most North Americans know very little, set in the northwest corner of South America, adjoining the isthmus of Panama. Bogotá, the capital, center of the country's literature as of its social and political life, is one of the most remote and inaccessible of cities, far in the interior, behind great mountain ranges and mighty rivers, raised up on its high tableland to an elevation of 8,500 feet. To reach Bogotá required in the old days a journey of at least three weeks; today there is a modern air service, but those who do not fly must give nearly a week to the transit. On account of this isolation the people have kept many of the ancient native and Spanish characteristics, and life has changed comparatively little from its earlier pattern. The intellectual class has held to aristocratic traditions; in literature, poetry has been predominant, and it is only within recent years that liberal forces have begun to find expression among the younger writers. Fiction of the older type is represented in Colombia by the most widely read novel written by any South American: the famous romance *María,* by Jorge Isaacs, published in 1867, still one of the standard school "classics," familiar in Europe and the United States. This is an idyl of young love cut short by death, picturing benign and patriarchal home life on a great estate in the valley of the Cauca; traditional in its lachrymal sensibility, it is simple and charming in its details of family relationship, picturesque in its vivid incidents of hunting and its depiction of native customs.

More representative of modern literary art is *Pax,* by Lorenzo Marroquín, who died in 1918: a novel that deserves to rank with the serious and powerful anti-war fiction of the present day. *Pax* is a long novel, elaborate, somewhat overweighted with detail, but colorful and moving in its presentation of love, intrigue, religion, politics, and revolution. It is infused with a passionate sincerity of desire to portray evils that consume a beloved country. Lorenzo Marroquín knew his people and their customs, the landscape, the social and historical backgrounds, the vanishing nobility and its ideals, the rising lower classes and their purpose. His sympathies were with aristocratic ideals, with religious faith, and with patriotic self-sacrifice for both; but his deepest feeling was of the waste and horror and futility of war. It is the same feeling that underlies *The Four Horsemen of the Apocalypse* and the later war novels, from Remarque to Hemingway; and it is expressed in his title, which symbolizes "a war-sick world crying 'Peace! Peace!' through the silenced voice of sacrificed youth." The tale opens in peace time and shows a cross-section of Colombian life—in the city and in the country, at home, at the opera, at the race track, in business offices, in political departments at banquets, weddings, and funerals, in church, and in literary assemblies. Then comes outbreak of civil war, bursting forth from political strife over a national industrial project (what we should probably call a battle of rival interests over public utilities), and destruction and death are let loose over the country. Youth is drawn into the vortex, revolutionary forces meet in conflict, there are burning cities, ravaged fields, fleeing refugees, congested hospitals, and battlefields strewn with dead and dying. The novel moves to a somber tragic climax in its vision of war, its passionate appeal for peace; but it holds sustained human interest in the fortunes of the many characters, the lights and shadows of experience, the romance and caricature and satire that are part of its fabric. It is a book that will repay careful reading; for it imparts social, historical, and human understanding of a country and a people.

The Vortex, the single novel of José Eustacio Rivera, is probably the most remarkable production of Latin American fiction. It was born of personal experience in the rubber forests of the Rio Negro, where the author, distinguished poet and diplomat, served on the commission that traced the definite boundary between Colombia and Venezuela. His book was conceived in the heart of the jungle, where, like the hero of his novel, he trudged "through leech-infested swamps, bare-footed, half-starved, crazed by mosquitos and fevers," writing, not on paper, but in his mind, and reciting in the evening what he had "written" during the day; his death, in 1928, was caused by a mysterious malady contracted at that time. This is the fevered, brilliant narrative of a youthful poet and lover, who has fled with his sweetheart from Bogotá to escape pursuit of the law, invoked by the girl's parents. The two find haven first in the grasslands, on a great cattle ranch, in a wild, primitive existence of feuds, round-ups, drinking, cockfights, gambling, and promiscuous lovemaking. Then violence and betrayal separate them; the youth, again a fugitive, plunges deeper into the wilderness and is caught, with other miserable human beings, in the vortex of the rubber jungles, to be held in a slavery of hopeless labor, starved, tortured by ants, leeches, and poisonous insects, cheated by sadistic traders, surrounded by appalling cruelties, experiencing love, lust, exaltation, horror, and despair. The monstrous conditions of the rubber traffic, as exposed in the famous Casement report on the Putomayo jungles in Brazil, live again in this extraordinary narrative, which combines introspection and objectivity, romantic lyric emotionalism and starkly brutal realism.

Peru has a long tradition of literary art, flowering in poetry and in essays, fruitful in serious works of research, but with little representation of fiction, except in the form of the *cuento,* or short story. The only contemporary Peruvian novel that has been brought in translation to American readers is *Broad and Alien Is the World,* by Ciro de Alegría, prize winner in the Latin American novel competition of 1940. Alegría, as a member of the Apra revolutionary political party, which was defeated in 1932 and later outlawed, went into exile after a term of imprisonment and makes his home in Chile. His novel may be considered an expression of the "Aprismo movement" in Peruvian literature, dedicated to the social-political struggle and the championship of the native Indian race against oppression and exploitation. There is a close relationship between this novel and *El Indio,* although the Mexican Indian folk life depicted by López y Fuentes is less civilized and more isolated than is that of the Peruvian Indian community,

which, unchanging through centuries, still carries traces of the communal socialist pattern that shaped the ancient Inca civilization of Peru. Here in colorful panoramic narrative, with intricate variation of scene and incident yet with complete unity of the whole, unfolds the tragedy of the small Indian village of Rumi, high up in the Peruvian Andes. For generations it has maintained a happy and industrious communal agrarian existence, primitive and toilsome, but giving independence and livelihood to its people. There is poverty, ignorance, and superstition, but there is also tolerance, communal loyalty, sturdy self-respect, and dimly sensed abilities for self-development. Government is in the hands of a mayor and four councillors, elected to their office; and the mayor, Rosendo Maqui, whose life is followed from youth to death, is the central figure: rugged, wise, shrewd, the father of his people, their fellow worker and leader, dying in prison, still their defender. The fate of Rumi is portended when Don Alvaro Amenabar, rich and predatory landowner of the town in the valley, institutes suit against the community, charging that the land it had occupied for generations rightfully belonged to him. The land itself has no value; but he owns silver mines in the region beyond, and cheap labor for them may be gained by dispossession of the Indians. Upon Rosendo Maqui falls the responsibility to fight Don Alvaro in the courts and try to save his people, panic-stricken and helpless.

This life-and-death struggle against hopeless odds is the substance of the novel. We see the Indian community cheated by tricky lawyers and corrupt officials, uprooted and bewildered, moving silently up the mountainside to more barren lands to begin again to establish their community, to meet privation, difficulties, despair; again to be attacked by military force as a center of revolt, machine guns sweeping the cliffs where only the sick, women, and children remain, in a final triumph of tragic repression. We follow individual victims into strange servitudes in a broad and alien world: to the long-drawn-out miseries of the malarial coca plantations; to the terrible purgatory of the rubber swamps and jungles; to the hopeless lot of the Indian soldier, herded to fight in strange causes of which he knows nothing. Some, the bolder and stronger, become bandits; the countryside, once peaceful, is torn by violence, menaced by danger. Powerful, deeply moving, picturesque and vital in characterization, there is a strong poetic quality in Alegría's novel; tragic and compassionate, it is also challenging in its portrayal of Indian dignity and integrity and of native abilities that need only education and opportunity to fulfill themselves. The leader who in the second community succeeds Rosendo Maqui strives for such fulfillment. He carries out draining of the land by dynamiting a channel from an "enchanted lake," haunt of a Chaco, or evil spirit. That would bring more crops, the village would thrive, a school would be established: "once they had a school, then in ten or twenty years nobody would believe in enchanted lakes or Chacos." He, too, perishes under machine guns and Mauser bullets. The pitiful, unequal conflict, in its essence and its implications is the conflict that grips the world today—freedom against despotism.

Brazil, bordering Venezuela, Colombia, and Peru, stretch-

Juan Rulfo.

ing far southward beside Bolivia and Argentina, is a world in itself: a mighty empire—Portuguese, not Spanish, in its European origin and language—a union of states greater in area than our own, underpopulated, undeveloped in relation to its size and resources, but holding unpredictable power in the future of the Americas. To the literature of Brazil, Isaac Goldberg devoted a substantial close-packed volume; but very little has appeared in translation for English readers. Four Brazilian novels, however, that have been made available in English represent a varied literary art and illuminate Brazilian life in past and present aspects. Oldest and most famous of these is *Canaan,* by the scholar and diplomat Graça Aranha, among whose numerous works this is considered by many the masterpiece of Brazilian literature. It is, indeed, a philosophic-realistic-symbolic epic of human brotherhood rather than a novel; its theme, the quest in the New World of a simpler, more humane, more moral, freer and happier society than European civilization can ever attain to. The quest is futile: the German immigrant who seeks in Brazil this promised land, finds there only a continuing re-enactment of the eternal tragedy of man's hatreds, selfishness, brutalities, hypocrisies, egotism, and injustice. Long, elaborate, ranging from abstract philosophical disquisition to ruth-

less scenes of horror, with backgrounds that shift from city to wilderness, the book has remarkable qualities: rich and powerful imagery, vivid descriptive rendering of tropical beauty, distinctive characterizations, and an ingrained spiritual fervor.

Irony and realism dominate Aluizio Azevedo's tale of the making of a Brazilian millionaire, *A Brazilian Tenement.* Set in the late nineteenth century, it is a picturesque, episodic chronicle of ruthless greed and of mounting power over the lives of others: the building of a fortune by way of petty, obscure rascalities, exploitation of workers, ownership of a teeming tenement, speculation in real estate, to the emergence of a great capitalist with far-reaching "interests."

Brazilian history is reflected in *Domitila,* by Paulo Setúbal, one of the writers most loved in his native country. Setubal had originally intended to be a lawyer, but he began writing poetry and gave up a legal career to devote himself to historical romances that should make the history of Brazil their theme. *Domitila* is a rapid, dynamic novel, rendering one of the dramatic incidents of the region of Dom Pedro I, first emperor of Brazil, it must be remembered, discovered by the Portuguese in 1500, became a Portuguese colony and is today the only country in the western world that speaks the Portuguese language. It was ruled by an imperial governor until 1808, when the King of Portugal fled before Napoleon's invasion, and taking his court of 1,200 persons transferred his seat of government to Brazil. This changed Brazil from a colony to the governing capital of the Portuguese world. For twelve years this continued; then, in 1820, after Napoleon's downfall, the king returned to Portugal, leaving his son, Dom Pedro, to govern Brazil. In 1822 the young prince yielded to the growing Brazilian movement for independence, proclaimed Brazil independent of Portugal, and became Dom Pedro I, founder of a new empire in a new world. He ruled until 1831, when he abdicated and returned to Portugal and was succeeded by his son, the famous emperor Dom Pedro II, who ruled for the next half century and abdicated in 1889, when the Brazilian revolution was accomplished and Brazil became the present republic of federated states, the United States of Brazil. Setúbal's novel deals with the reign of Dom Pedro I, from the proclamation of Brazilian independence, in 1822, until 1829. It centers in the rise to power, the triumph, and the downfall of the beautiful Domitila, mistress of the emperor, who for ten years held the strings of political power and who came within a hair's breadth of achieving her passionate ambition of being crowned as empress after the death of Dom Pedro's wife. Historical fact is closely followed; most of the characters are actual persons, politicians, courtiers, officials of the days of the first empire. Costumes and customs, letters and documents quoted and referred to, dramatic incidents, and the whole sequence of events are part of historic record. It is a brilliant, picturesque evocation: a mingling of Old World magnificence and the tropical luxuriance of the semi-barbaric New World. Character portrayal, psychological values, and realistic detail are negligible; the tale is essentially a vivid, pictorial unfolding of passion and intrigue, of a woman's consuming ambition, and of the absolutism and selfish pleasure-seeking of a young ruler, swayed only by his emotions. While the novel has romantic and dramatic interest, its significance is as a reflection of the brilliance, luxury, and tense political conflict of this chapter of Brazil's history.

On the novel by Ferreira de Castro rests the enormous shadow of the jungle. Here the high-keyed intensity of Rivera's phantasmagoria of the Colombian rubber forests is transposed and stabilized into a tempered, thorough, sympathetic, and deeply interesting presentation of life on a rubber plantation in the Rio Madeira jungle of southwestern Brazil. *Jungle: a Tale of the Amazon Rubber-Tappers* has continuing values of firsthand knowledge and of bringing to simple, clear reality the remote, savage little colonies whose existence centered in the struggle to obtain rubber. Undercurrents of exploitation, of suffering and cruelty, are here; there is psychological insight and distinctive character portrayal; and the mysterious, terrifying atmosphere of the jungle is infused into this story of a young university student, a political exile from his native Portugal, who is suddenly thrust into the barbarous, almost hopeless life of a rubber tapper, but who rises from the slavery of "the avenues" and at last returns to freedom.

Chile's most famous novelist is Alberto Blest Gana, whose ambition was to be the American Balzac. His life spanned nearly a century (he was born in 1830 and died in 1922), and in its two periods of literary activity, separated by thirty years of diplomatic service in Europe, he produced more than a dozen novels concerned with Chilean history and with critical, penetrating study of contemporary society. *Martin Rivas,* published in 1862, is his masterpiece. It is a long, elaborate novel, old-fashioned in manner, but a mirror of the life and character of its day and place. It is set in Santiago, about 1850. Martin Rivas (truly a hero of the Victorian stamp of nobility and rectitude!) is a young man from the country who makes his home with the family of a wealthy financier, who had built up his riches by fraudulently gaining from Martin's father the silver mine that was the source of his fortune. In this household Martin becomes indispensable; while carrying on his own studies at the law, he is also secretary and adviser to the father, friend and helper to the silly, foppish son, and cherishes a deep, hidden devotion for the beautiful and willful daughter, Leonor. The mother is lazy and luxury loving, devoted to her lapdog; and there is an attractive young cousin, whose unfortunate love affair educes the dramatic and tragic elements of the plot. This family of wealth and pretensions, ambitious for social advancement, is set in contrast with a lower-class family (mother, two daughters, and worthless, scheming son) in a very interesting portrayal of caste lines and differences in customs and manners of living. There are intricate love involvements, resulting feud and complexities, and Martin's participation in the revolutionary uprising of 1851. He is arrested and condemned to death; his danger brings Leonor to realization of her love, and she manages to enlist influences that enable him to escape, so that a "happy ending" is successfully accomplished. In spite of its length and its Victorian qualities, the variety of scenes and the complex interest of events make the story move rapidly and hold its interest to the end. Reality and vitality are established: the

reader steps into a living world, into social and home life, into politics, into the festivities and cross currents that made the everyday existence of Chileans of that particular period, all conveying the historic and human reality which is the achievement of fine fiction.

Argentine fiction is more generously represented in English translation than is that of any other Latin American country. In these novels we may find the historical aspect, reflecting the fierce civil wars of the second quarter of the nineteenth century; the aspect of modern social problems and changing economic conditions; the romantic and dramatic rendering of regional and local backgrounds. Argentina made its first definite impact upon English readers early in the present century, when belated recognition came to W. H. Hudson's novel, *The Purple Land,* with its exotic, pictorial backgrounds, its powerful portrayal of the violent years of struggle against the tyrant-dictator Rosas. Those years, in fact, brought an uprush of passionate expression from Argentine writers, for the whole country was torn and convulsed under the conflict. To understand this, it should be said that after the separation from Spain, Argentina was organized as a centralized or "unitarian" republic, with the capital in Buenos Aires. The provinces, however—the vast plains, with their great ranchos and the half-Spanish, half-Indian gauchos who made up most of the population—refused to accept the rule of the city, rose in rebellion, and demanded a federal republic with a large measure of local autonomy. There were years of civil war; the unitarian party was beaten by the federalists under the leadership of Juan Manuel Rosas, who for twenty-three years, until his downfall in 1852, exerted absolute power and carried on merciless extermination of his enemies. Not until nearly fifty years later was the political conflict finally resolved, when Buenos Aires was made a federal district and capital of the republic. Rosas represented the gauchos of the interior, what would probably today be called the proletariat; his policy of extermination was directed against the intellectual and aristocratic elements, so that the struggle against him was inspired and maintained by the educated classes, the journalists, poets and writers. Many fled to Chile, where they brought a freshening vigor to Chilean literature and infused in it their own vehement protest against despotism.

Foremost among the Argentine writers of this period is José Mármol (1817-71), whose novel *Amalia* lives as a passionate exposition of the tyranny and degradation of the Rosas dictatorship. Mármol at the age of twenty was imprisoned as a conspirator, scribbling on the walls of his cell a quatrain denouncing the tyrant. This denunciation he continued through years of danger and of exile, in long poems, in quatrains, and in his memorable novel. *Amalia* conveys the incandescent intensity of his hatred and gives also a remarkable social study of this period in Argentine history, by one who was himself an actor in the events he portrays and who experienced the feelings he describes. It is a long, elaborate historical novel, patterned on Sir Walter Scott, which centers on the tyranny and ferocity of Rosas and the social degradation existing in Buenos Aires under his rule. Its chief actor is a young man, Daniel Bello, enlisted in the struggle against the dictator, but protected in his operations because he is the son of one of

Rosas's supporters, and so working skillfully and subterraneously with those who are plotting Rosas's overthrow. The love story, which is a central thread, is woven about Amalia, Daniel's cousin, and a young rebel who is wounded and left for dead in an attack by police and hidden in her house, where she nurses him back to health. The youth is tracked down by Rosas's agents; danger and intrigue menace the lovers and bring the tale to a tragic climax. The novel has unity, power, and sustained interest; a depth of personal feeling and a vividness of description and characterization that give it value as an evocation of time and place and personal experience.

Manuel Gálvez, in *Nacha Regules,* represents the Argentine novelist of modern development, studying the problems and mores of the life he knows. This was the first important postwar novel of Argentina, and for it the city of Buenos Aires awarded Gálvez the prize for letters for the year 1920. One of the leading authors of his own country, his work has been widely translated into other languages, and his name has been put forward for the Nobel prize for literature. Nacha Regules is a girl of the streets, who by chance wakens the pity and interest of a Buenos Aires lawyer, a thinker and an idealist. The story tells of his efforts to save her from degradation and suffering and to bring home to society a realization of evils for which it is ultimately responsible. A Tolstoyan touch of idealistic and humanitarian philosophy is evident throughout, but there is Latin emotionalism in the contest of mutual self-sacrifice that is carried on between Nacha and Dr. Monsalvat. The conclusion is one of defeat and disillusion on the surface; but with love and idealism unextinguished and spiritually triumphant. *Holy Wednesday,* Gálvez's second novel to be translated into English, is slighter, simpler, and has a similar undercurrent of idealism. In it we hear the sins of a great city through the grating of a confessional box as we follow one day in the life of Father Solanas, the most popular confessor in Buenos Aires.

The romantic, the dramatic, and the pictorial prevail in the work of Gustavo Martínez Zuviría ("Hugo Wast"), most popular and prolific Argentine novelist, several of whose books have been translated into English. Of these, *The Stone Desert* should have interest and fascination for any reader; it is the author's own favorite—the novel, he says, which he "most desired to write." Its title comes from the name of a tract of land at the upper end of a great ranch near the top of a remote mountain zone of central Argentina. The old and childless owner of the ranch has received in his home a nephew, whose daughter of twenty is left to maintain and carry on the management. Her struggle and the dangers she encounters are woven into a dramatic, exciting plot, accompanied by strange, impressive natural backgrounds, glimpses of primitive, picturesque ways of life, and arresting characterizations. *Black Valley* is the Zuviría novel that received a prize from the Royal Spanish Academy. It, too, has strong romantic and dramatic, often melodramatic, flavor, and it strikes a deeper note of tragedy than *The Stone Desert.* It is set in the same remote, mountainous locale—which is the author's native region—a lonely, haunting valley, a place of storms and silence; it weaves a complex plot of inherited feuds, family enmities, and deep-channeled passions, and it

closes on a note, not of romantic fulfillment, but of renunciation. *The Strength of Lovers* is a re-telling of one of the famous tragedies of the Discovery era: the story of Captain Sebastian Hurtado and his beautiful, valiant wife, Lucia Miranda, who were members of the Sebastian Cabot expedition that sailed from Spain for the new world in 1526 and who met death together at the hands of the Indians of the Paraná River region. English readers may remember that in Charles Kingsley's *Westward Ho!* this story is related by Don Guzman, the Spaniard captured by Amyas Leigh and held for ransom in Devon, as an example of the devotion and courage of his countrymen.

For the traditional life of the Argentine pampas, Ricardo Güiraldes's novel *Don Segundo Sombra* will long remain a modern classic. It has been called the South American *Huckleberry Finn*; and in its portrayal of boyhood and youth in the cattle country it has, for all its exotic background and Latin spirit, qualities that justify the comparison. Don Segundo is the philosophical old gaucho under whom the boy who has fled from his home to escape restrictions and monotony serves his apprenticeship as herdsman and for whom he has unwavering reverence and affection. A story thread is entwined in the vivid, roughcast chronicle of the hard work on the pampas, the casual loves, the friends and associates and adventures of the wandering young herdsman, who comes at last to his own family rights and assured well-being. Unusual in warmth and rich human vitality, charm and delicacy are here, in spite of brutality and harshness and rough realism of speech. This is one of the South American novels that linger in memory as do the books of W. H. Hudson.

Don Segundo Sombra is linked in such illuminating relationship with *Martin Fierro,* the famous folk ballad of the gaucho, by José Hernández, that a word should be said of that national epic of the Argentine. Hernández's poem, of which the first part was published in 1872 and the second part seven years later, both immortalizes and symbolizes the gaucho, in the figure of Martin Fierro, who, as Walter Owen says, stepped out of its pages "to become the embodiment of his hardships and rugged virtues, the champion of his wrongs, the spokesman of his class for social justice." It is a verse narrative of gaucho life, mingling the epic and the lyric, redolent of the pampas, of the rank, pristine living of plain and outpost, of round-up, and cattle brand, and Indian raid. A series of vivid, authentic pictures of a life and a time now past, it challenges the government practice of forced recruiting, the official corruption and injustice of which the plainsmen were victims. Translated by Walter Owen into English verse that is designed to keep the chanting, ballad form of the original, it was published in a limited English edition in 1935 and in facsimile American issue a year later, and it should be known and enjoyed by many English readers.

Varied aspects of Argentina's literary art, as of its life and backgrounds, are revealed in Waldo Frank's volume *Tales from the Argentine.* Here are gathered seven stories by writers who were masters in their fields, reflecting conditions and scenes that are now part of the country's past. These tales open vistas of the tangled jungles, of the primitive villages of the pampas, of the secret wild creatures of the great rivers and the forest wilderness; they depict different human types, the gaucho, the vagabond, the dwellers in country towns; and they convey the color and fever of life in Buenos Aires during the stormy days of the past. Most original and fascinating is the story that closes the volume: "The Return of Anaconda," by Horacio Quiroga, native Uruguayan, who is the leading Argentine short story writer of today. This is a little masterpiece of fantastic, imaginative conception: the tale of the strong and beautiful young serpent, Anaconda, who leads a rebellion of the jungle against man, the intruder, sweeping down through her vast hunting grounds on the turbulent flood waters of the mighty river, swollen and irresistible after the deluge of rain; only to meet disaster through the overpowering force on which she had planned her triumph.

Last in this gleaning is Uruguay, represented by a selection of Quiroga's remarkable short stories and by one novel in English translation. This, *Castanets,* is the work of Carlos Reyles, leading novelist of the Rio de La Plata region; but it is Spanish, not South American, in theme and setting: a swift, passionate tale of prewar Seville, exhaling the traditional atmosphere of bullfight and dance.

THE SHORT STORY

Kenneth Fleak

SOURCE: "Latin American Short Fiction," in *Studies in Short Fiction,* Vol. 20, No. 4, Fall, 1983, pp. 297-306.

[*In the following essay, Fleak provides an overview of the Latin American short story and its relationship to the novel.*]

The critical history of the short story is both brief and incomplete. In an article entitled "The Modern Short Story: Retrospect," H. E. Bates refers to different studies on the recent development of short fiction: "The paradoxical answer is that the history of the short story, as we know it, is not vast but brief. 'The short story proper,' says Mr. A. J. J. Ratcliff, 'that is, a deliberately fashioned work of art, and not just a straightforward tale of one or more events, belongs to modern times'; 'the short story is a young art,' says Elizabeth Bowen, 'as we know it, it is a child of this century'." [H. E. Bates, "The Modern Short Story: Retrospect," in *Short Story Theories,* ed. Charles E. May, 1976]. William Peden states that "as a conscious literary form, the short story is a comparatively recent addition to the family of literary types" [*Short Fiction: Shape and Substance,* 1971].

In Latin America, the time that bridges the period between the genre's beginnings and the modern age is indeed short. But in spite of this brevity, in contemporary literature the popularity of the Latin American short story is unquestionable. As a relatively young art form, the genre has experienced a growth that is especially notable since the mid-twentieth century. In large measure, this is a direct result of its development through the three prevailing literary trends during the first half of the century: natural-

ism, modernism, and *criollismo.* Short story writers from this time who quickly come to mind include Rubén Darío, Manuel Gutiérrez Nájera, Manuel Díaz Rodríguez, Amado Nervo, Leopoldo Lugones, Baldomero Lillo, Horacio Quiroga, Javier de Viana, and Mariano Latorre.

Interestingly enough, however, the short story has not experienced the same popularity in other parts of the world. Enrique Pupo-Walker sees the situation in Latin America as "lo contrario de lo que ocurre hoy en países como Inglaterra y Estados Unidos, donde es cada vez más difícil publicar un cuento" ["Prólogo: Notas sobre la trayectoria y significación del cuento hispanoamericano," in *El cuento hispanoamericano ante la crítica,* ed. Enrique Pupo-Walker, 1973]. Julio Cortázar states that the short story "tiene un especial interés para nosotros, puesto que casi todos los países americanos de lengua española le están dando al cuento una importancia excepcional que jamás había tenido en otros países latinos como Francia o España." ["Algunos aspectos del cuento," *Cuadernos hispanoamericanos,* 253 (marzo 1971).] In his study of contemporary Spanish American literature, Jefferson Rea Spell also indicates this extensive development in the short story: "Among the forms of fiction for which writers of Spanish America have shown a decided preference, particularly during the present century, is the brief prose narrative, or *cuento*" [*Contemporary Spanish-American Fiction,* 1968]. Although the short story is one of the most difficult genres in which to succeed and simultaneously receive a universal recognition, it has experienced a steady cultivation since its beginning, and especially in recent decades.

In Latin America two factors have aided the short story writer: the increase in the number of national anthologies devoted to the genre and the extensive availability of the small literary magazine. Enrique Pupo-Walker asserts that "the number of collections of stories already published and being published in Spanish America is simply staggering" ["The Contemporary Short Fiction of Spanish America: An Introductory Note," *Studies in Short Fiction,* 8 (Winter 1971)]. Such collections occur either as those of individual writers or as anthologies which are unified by a certain theme or generation. Enrique Lafourcade's three anthologies of the short story from the Chilean Generation of 1950 represent but one example. Like Lafourcade, most major novelists share a parallel interest in the short story. We should note, however, that the short story appears mainly in national journals; this explains in part why, as a form, it does not receive the same attention as the novel. Unless the short story writer first succeeds in the novel, his short fiction normally does not achieve universal acclaim. José Donoso, a contemporary Chilean novelist, is but one example. It is only after the publication of his novels that his short stories begin to receive some universal critical consideration.

In spite of the vitality of the Latin American short story in recent literary history, in most Latin American countries it is second only to the novel in popularity with readers, the genre is yet to receive the critical appreciation that it merits. In Chile, for example, Ricardo Latcham has explained the importance of the Generation of 1950 in relationship to these two genres: "La generación existe porque sus hechos lo confirman. La generación de 1950 ha dado un impulso desconocido a la novela y el cuento" [Enrique Lafourcade, "La nueva literatura chilena," *Cuadernos americanos,* 128, No. 4 (1962)]. However, critical studies of the Generation focus almost entirely on the novel, and such is the case in country after country in Latin America. In critical studies of the short story, few names come to mind: Luis Leal, Enrique Pupo-Walker, Seymour Menton. Unfortunately, the critical history by Luis Leal is the only one that offers a continental view of the development in the short story. Although Enrique Pupo-Walker's book contains a variety of important critical essays, it by no means gives us a source for the whole of the genre. As for Seymour Menton's study, it can more accurately be classified as an anthology whose primary aim is to present a broad range of styles of short stories; the critical commentaries are extremely brief and superficial.

The case is quite different with the novel; a quick glance at critical works includes names such as Fernando Alegría, Ángel Flores, Raúl Silva Castro, John Brushwood, Zunilda Gertel, Jorge Lafforgue, Luis Harss, José Donoso, Carlos Fuentes, Gabriel García Márquez, Mario Vargas Llosa, Emir Rodríguez Monegal, Donald Bleznick, Juan Loveluck, Julio Ortega, Walter Langford, Alfred MacAdam, Joseph Sommers, and many others.

In Latin America, few writers have attempted to define the short story. Horacio Quiroga (Uruguay, 1878-1937), writing in the early part of the twentieth century, represents the earliest real success in defining and promoting the short story. Few would dispute the premise that Quiroga is the unquestionable father of the genre in Latin America. Quiroga's best known comment on the short story is the "Decálogo del perfecto cuento," in which he emphasized the debt owned to universally recognized authors of the short story: Poe, Maupassant, Kipling, and Chekhov.

Perhaps because of the paradoxical combination of brevity and complexity inherent in the form, the short story almost defies definition. In modern Latin American literature, Juan Bosch (Dominican Republic, 1909) and Julio Cortázar (Argentina, 1918) are among the few authors who have written any noteworthy studies on short fiction. Many of the writers considered to be members of the Chilean Generation of 1950 recognize the difficulty in defining what the genre involves. Pablo García is but one writer among several who refers to the writer's need to discover his own individual definition.

Nevertheless, as readers and critics, we are able to perceive certain factors that point to the general characteristics of the short story. It is indeed a paradox that the short story and the novel are in so many ways related but at the same time so different. Perhaps it is more a hindrance than an aid to compare the short story too closely to the novel. Many critics and writers see the short story as a writer's apprenticeship for the more expansive form of the novel. Jaime Laso, a Chilean writer, asserts that the short story is a "verdadera *maquette* de la novela." We find it necessary, however, to reject totally these ideas. Indeed, for many writers a vast gulf separates the two genres. Two

twentieth-century novelists in particular, Carlos Fuentes and William Faulkner, have pointed out the complex and separate form of the short story. William Faulkner explained the immense demands imposed by certain genres: " 'I'm a failed poet,' he said. 'Maybe every novelist wants to write poetry first, finds he can't, and then tries the short story, which is the most demanding form after poetry. And failing at that, only then does he take up novel writing' " [Thomas A. Gullason, "The Short Story: An Underrated Art," in *Short Story Theories,* ed. Charles E. May, 1976]. Carlos Fuentes sees the same complexity: "Es más difícil la estructura del cuento que la de la novela" [Emmanuel Carballo, *Diecinueve protagonistas de la literatura mexicana,* 1965].

The difference between the novel and the short story is so distinct that many authors find it impossible to cross that line successfully. Poe, Maupassant, Chekhov, and Quiroga stand out as masters in the field of the short story. We can note the significance of the fact that each excels in short fiction, but finds it impossible to move successfully to the parallel but vastly different genre of the novel. Jorge Luis Borges, Juan José Arreola, and Baldomero Lillo are also writers who rarely experiment with the novelistic form, if at all. The inverse may also be true. Writers such as Zola, Dos Passos, Pérez Galdós, and Balzac all apparently felt that only the more expansive form of the novel was capable of containing their conception of literature. Carlos Fuentes explains his preference for the novel in this vein: "Es el único género en que se puede decir todo." ["La novela es el único género en que puede decirse todo: Carlos Fuentes," *El día,* 14 marzo 1967.] Still, certain writers are able to excel in both the short story and the novel, for example, Carlos Fuentes, Gabriel García Márquez, José Donoso, and Julio Cortázar. As we will see in this study, however, the difference in style and conception between genres is totally distinct. Parallel success in both art forms indicates a creative talent that few writers possess.

The view that holds the short story as a product of the youthful writer, and the novel of the experienced author, is only partially acceptable. As a more structured and limited art form, writers may find it much easier to begin with the short story. However, it is impossible to accept the restricted view that short fiction is the special province of the young writer. The Latin American new novelists have not abandoned the form; instead they periodically return to it. Carlos Fuentes' first publication was a collection of short fiction, *Los días enmascarados* (1954). But after the experimental techniques that he employs in the novels entitled *La región más transparente* (1958) and *La muerte de Artemio Cruz* (1962), he once again returned to the short story with *Cantar de ciegos* (1965). Fuentes has recently published a collection of four novellas entitled *La ciudad perdida.* In 1962 Gabriel García Márquez, best known for his novels, published *Los funerales de mamá grande.* In an article which appeared in *El Espectador* in 1980, he stated his preference for the more difficult form of the short story. García Márquez also revealed that he was working on sixty new stories, and the number would have been even greater if he had not lost a notebook that contained forty short stories. The alternate appearance of short stories and novels is also evident in José Donoso's fiction. He begins with the short story, *Veraneo y otros cuentos* (1955), turns to the novel, *Coronación* (1957), only to return to the short story, *El charlestón* (1960). Then, after three successive novels, he publishes three novellas in *Tres novelitas burguesas* (1973). Finally, of the major contemporary Latin American authors, Julio Cortázar is perhaps the most productive in the short story: *Bestiario* (1951), *Final de juego* (1956), *Las armas secretas* (1959), *Todos los fuegos el fuego* (1967), and *Octaedro* (1974).

Conceivably, the best definitions of the short story derive their significance through a comparison with other genres. It is our opinion that the short story resembles the intensity required by both poetry and drama more than it does the novel. V. S. Pritchett characterizes short fiction as a "hybrid" form of art. Because the short story captures moments of existence, he finds it is more closely related to poetry, drama, and the cinema than to the totality of the novel ["Short Stories," in *What is the Short Story,* ed. Eugene Current-García & Walton R. Patrick, 1961]. Frank O'Connor and Elizabeth Bowen are additional critics who support this theory.

Claudio Giaconi, a twentieth century Chilean writer and critic, relates short fiction more closely to poetry through his description of the genre as "un género de sonoridades puras." María Elena Gertner, also Chilean, sees the short story as "una línea melódica expresada con palabras." We may relate a concentration on a definitive technical awareness to the requirements of both drama and poetry. As

João Guimarães Rosa.

with poetry and the cinema, the short story captures the impact of a given situation. Because of the emphasis on technical perfection, it is common to place the genre on the outer boundaries of prose.

As the most prolific writer of short stories from the group of contemporary Latin American novelists, Julio Cortázar's views are especially pertinent to this study. He gives us several points of comparison that allow us to see how the short story is essentially different from the novel. Cortázar states that if both were compared to a boxing match, the novel would win by points and the short story by a knockout. In this obvious reference to the essential element of intense impact, we also see the relationship to poetry that we have just noted. Cortázar also conceives of the short story form as a sphere. For Cortázar short fiction is a type of catharsis which engulfs and controls the writer: "El sentimiento de la esfera debe preexistir de alguna manera al acto de escribir el cuento, como si el narrador, sometido por la forma que asume, se moviera implícitamente en ella y la llevara a su extrema tensión" [Flora H. Schiminovich, "Cortázar y el cuento en uno de sus cuentos," in *Homenaje a Julio Cortázar*, ed. Helmy F. Giacoman, 1972]. Inherent with Cortázar's idea of the sphere are three important revelations. The precision and limited range the form requires tie in closely with Quiroga's precept of the genre's boundaries: "Toma a tus personajes de la mano y llévalos firmemente hasta el final, sin ver otra cosa que el camino que les trazaste" [Horacio Quiroga, "Decálogo del perfecto cuento," in *Sobre literatura* (Montevideo: ARCA, 1970)]. Wholeness of shape demands perfection. Finally, because the writer must constantly consider the sphere as a basic element of the genre, the idea of form must precede the act of writing.

Cortázar's most perceptive insight is his analogy between the novel as movie and the short story as photograph, which contrasts in some degree to the comparison by such critics as Elizabeth Bowen who relates short fiction to both drama and the cinema. While the movie normally consists of multiple segments and an unlimited chronology, the photograph is in itself a precise limitation on both time and space. This contrast establishes a basic reversal in concept between the two genres. Cortázar's points of comparison and contrast all relate the short story to an art form that is consistently concerned with conciseness and perfection.

Two elements, then, that we may consider basic to the short story are perfection, and the necessary degree of tension. To be successful, the writer of short fiction must achieve both within certain spatial limitations. The two characteristics that we have cited reveal abstract considerations that are consistently pertinent to the history of the short story writer. Edgar Allan Poe, the recognized "father" of short fiction as a universal form of literature, conceived the genre's success in such terms. At a much later date in Latin America, Horacio Quiroga characterized the short story in similar terms: "No empieces a escribir sin saber desde la primera palabra adónde vas. En un cuento bien logrado, las tres primeras líneas tienen casi la importancia de las tres últimas." In the contemporary Latin American short story, these same concerns continue to dominate. Juan Bosch speaks of the constant fluency [*Teoría del cuento,* 1967]. Julio Cortázar emphasizes considerations that are parallel to both Poe's and Quiroga's. To a large extent we may compare his interest in the theory of the genre to that of Poe and Quiroga, and this is manifest in Cortázar's two lengthy studies on the short story: "Algunos aspectos del cuento" and "Del cuento breve y sus alrededores." It is difficult to believe it mere coincidence that Cortázar translated the complete prose works of Poe. Poe's concept of the unity of effect is evident in Cortázar's statement on the inner rhythm of the short story: "Cada vez que me ha tocado revisar la traducción de uno de mis relatos (o intentar la de otros autores, como alguna vez con Poe) he sentido hasta que punto la eficacia y el sentido del cuento dependían de esos valores que dan su carácter especial al poema y también al jazz: la tensión, el ritmo, la pulsación interna, lo imprevisto dentro de parámetros pre-vistos, esa libertad fatal que no admite alteración sin una pérdida irrestañable" [Julio Cortázar, "Del cuento breve y sus alrededores," in *Último round,* 1969]. The external limitations in the form of this genre make it necessary for the writer of short fiction to reflect constantly on every device he employs according to its unifying effect.

Although form must be uppermost in the mind of the author of short fiction, neither can the genre be considered to possess a rigid and mathematical construction. At best, the qualities we have cited as being consistent from Edgar Allan Poe to our own time are abstract and elusive. This inconsistency becomes even more obvious when we speak of the modern short story. Ian Reid states that "the history of the modern short story embraces diverse tendencies, some of which have stretched, shrunk or otherwise altered previous conceptions of the nature of the genre" [*The Short Story,* 1977]. Length, perfection, and the impact of tension form the general boundaries of the genre. Other than these general characteristics, each individual author must decide for himself where a true definition for short fiction lies. Therefore, the short story is an intensely personal art form.

The development of the contemporary Latin American short story, in comparison to the novel, is an interesting point of consideration. Since the nineteenth century the novel has held the indisputable position as the preferred literary genre in the Western world. In contemporary literature we only need to think of the direction that Robbe-Grillet gives to the "nouveau roman" or of the experimental techniques of Cortázar and Fuentes in Spanish America and Saul Bellow, Donald Barthelme, Kurt Vonnegut, and Ken Kesey in North America. Emir Rodríguez Monegal sees the beginning of the development of the new Latin American novel as a "boom pequeño" that starts shortly after World War II. During the period between 1940 and the late 1950's important works are published that represent an introductory state for the beginning of the new novel that may be said to begin in 1963 with Julio Cortázar's *Rayuela.* The following novels are the most influential along the path leading to *Rayuela: Invención de Morel* (1940), Adolfo Bioy-Casares; *El señor presidente* (1946), Miguel Asturias; *Al filo del agua* (1947), Agustín Yáñez; *El túnel* (1948), Ernesto Sábato; *Adán Buenosayres*

(1948), Leopoldo Marechal; *El reino de este mundo* (1949), and *Los pasos perdidos* (1953), Alejo Carpentier; and *Pedro Páramo* (1955), Juan Rulfo. Although novels were published simultaneously throughout the large cultural centers of Latin America, there was, at the time, no coherent sense of the impact that was to be felt on the international scene in the years following the publication of *Rayuela.* At this early stage, we can speak of national movements that were creating the necessary conditions for the novel that would be influential within a universal context. In the 1960's, with writers such as Julio Cortázar, Carlos Fuentes, Gabriel García, Márquez, José Lezama Lima, Mario Vargas Llosa, Severo Sarduy, and José Donoso, the so-called "boom" of the Latin American novel reached an international recognition. Although Jorge Luis Borges is an obvious exception, the short story remains more a matter of national interest. The novel's movement from national to universal attention may be explained in part by the expansion of literary journals: *Siempre, El Nacional, Amaru, Review, Books Abroad, La nueva narrativa,* and especially *Mundo nuevo.* The stimulus that such journals offer through their sponsorship of literary awards in the field of the novel have also been important to the genre's development. Institutions and publishing companies like Casa de las Américas and Seix-Barral have also been significant factors in the promotion of the novel. And translation into major European languages, and into English, is a factor that cannot be overlooked.

Because of the greater prominence of the novel, the recognition due the modern short story has been considerably obscured. Nevertheless, it is possible to trace a parallel movement leading to the modern short story. In Latin America we may appropriately speak of four periods in the development of the genre.

The introductory epoch may be found in the nineteenth century, in the beginnings of Romanticism. Esteban Echeverría's story entitled "El matadero" (1837) is generally considered to be the first written in Latin America. Ricardo Palma's *Tradiciones peruanas* represent another influential work in short fiction from this same literary period.

The second movement in the short story history begins around 1880 and continues through 1940, during which time the genre is truly developed as a popular and important literary form. We have already referred to Horacio Quiroga as the "father" of the Latin American short story. His "Decálogo del perfecto cuento" becomes a significant factor in the recognition of this new art form. In general the authors of this period follow a traditional story line according to three different literary styles: modernism, naturalism, and *criollismo.*

Another age in the history of short fiction is defined by the years between 1940 and 1960. Writers continue with *criollista* themes, and within a traditional orientation. Nevertheless, important works appear in the short story, as in the novel, which represent the initial stages of the modern short story. The following collections are the most influential: *El jardín de senderos que se bifurcan* (1941), *Ficciones* (1944), and *El aleph* (1949), Jorge Luis Borges; *Varia invención* (1949) and *Confabulario* (1952), Juan José Arreola; *Bestiario* (1951) and *Final de juego* (1956), Julio Cortázar; *Un sueño realizado y otros relatos* (1951), Juan Carlos Onetti; *El llano en llamas* (1953), Juan Rulfo; and *Veraneo y otros cuentos* (1955), José Donoso.

What we can designate as the new Latin American short story definitely reaches its strongest and most noticeable manifestation around 1960. This is precisely at the time that Jorge Luis Borges, the most influential writer in Latin American short fiction, began to receive universal acclaim. The importance of Jorge Luis Borges as the leader in the contemporary short story is undeniable. Carlos Fuentes goes so far as to state that without Borges, there would simply not be the modern novel in Latin America.

As we have already stated, the majority of the contemporary Latin American novelists have also contributed significantly to the new short story. Many of these novelists recognize the debt that they owe to short fiction, a genre that they often view to be superior. The interrelationship between the two genres is evident. Yet in this correlation, the short story can never be seen as an inferior art form.

The modern Latin American short story is obviously less uniform than that of preceding generations. Even so, certain basic concepts of the short story genre that we have already cited remain intact. Peter G. Earle states that short fiction is produced more in the sense of a tradition because "the writer as story-teller is more conscious of his role as a craftsman" ["Dreams of Creation: Short Fiction in Spanish America," *University of Denver Quarterly,* 12 (Fall 1977)].

Because of the limitation imposed by length, short fiction is obviously not free to pursue the complex and intricate digressions of the novel. Nevertheless, many changes have occurred in the last thirty years through the incorporation of experimentation in structure, unresolved or open endings, metaphysical, intellectual, and individualized themes, and urban settings. Recent writers in this genre have demonstrated a definite ability to vary considerably in modes: psychological, social, fantastic, satirical, humorous, and detective. At times even *criollista* elements tend to be part of the overall concept present in modern short fiction.

It is evident then that the Latin American countries have witnessed a steady growth in short fiction. Since 1960, this development represents the birth of the modern short story, in which the new writers pursue diverse levels of experimentation in both theme and structure. While this movement cannot be considered as a "boom" in the same sense as the novel, the genre definitely experiences changes that are notable and important. Especially in the modern age, the short story is what each individual author chooses it to be. Short fiction is a genre that demands both preciseness and perfection. Perhaps the only true criterion that the writer of short fiction must fulfill is to achieve totality of effect. A complete definition for the genre is difficult, if not impossible. It is our opinion that both poetry and drama allow us a more basic and realistic insight into what constitutes the short story than does the novel. In Latin America, the last thirty years represent a period rich in short fiction and worthy of study as a unique literary genre

because of its pursuit of multiple avenues of change and experimentation.

DRAMA

Diana Taylor

SOURCE: "Theatre and Crisis: The Making of Latin American Drama," in *Theatre of Crisis: Drama and Politics in Latin America,* University Press of Kentucky, 1991, pp. 22-63.

[*In the following excerpt, Taylor examines the connection between politics and contemporary Latin American drama.*]

While commentators studying Latin American theatre generally recognize the dramatic transformation that has taken place in the quantity and quality of the plays produced from the 1960s onward, we still do not have a good name to describe the process (or perhaps multiple processes), or a very clear understanding of its (their) complexity or periodization. Various terms have been proposed. Beatriz Risk enumerates them in her work *El nuevo teatro latinoamericano: Una lectura histórica:* "theatre of identity, revolutionary theatre, committed theatre, historical theatre, theatre of violence, theatre of social criticism, documentary theatre, avant-garde, popular theatre"; she herself opts for "new theatre." Several studies have traced the history of that term and its practical applications, notably Rosa Eliana Boudet's *Teatro nuevo* and Marina Pianca's *Diógenes.* The term has gradually gained a degree of currency in Latin American studies, although it is doubtful whether everyone using it refers to the same phenomenon. While my use of "theatre of crisis" only partially overlaps with what is generally understood as "new theatre," the latter deserves a brief analysis both because of its widespread use and because it has a certain limited applicability. My comments on the several features characterizing the term will, I hope, clarify my use of it throughout this work and the differences I perceive between new theatre and theatre of crisis.

For Risk and Pianca, new theatre seemingly applies to the entire theatrical movement that developed toward the end of the 1950s (coinciding with the Cuban revolution of 1959), which broke with inherited, especially bourgeois, models and became revolutionary and "dialectical," following Brecht's theatre. The movement spread gradually throughout the Latin American continent and finally reached Hispanic American communities in the United States. The "new" theatre addresses a "new" proletariat and peasant audience, forming part of a wider socioeconomic and political confrontation in which the underclasses struggle for decolonization and for the appropriation of methods of production, including theatrical production. Risk, Pianca, and Boudet all equate new theatre with popular theatre, which does not clarify it significantly because the term "popular theatre" is also open to interpretation.

The definition proposed by Risk, Pianca, and Boudet is, paradoxically, both too general and too specific to prove helpful or meaningful in understanding the profusion of plays produced since the late 1950s and early 1960s. On the one hand, the concept of new theatre signals a widespread commitment to social inquiry and change on the part of the playwrights. In the most global sense, all the serious drama written after the late 1950s which tried to change the situation of the dispossessed is a form of new theatre, characterized by what Leon Lyday and George Woodyard describe as "a spirit of revolution, both in terms of aesthetics and often of sociopolitical values." On the other hand, however, the term also refers to a particular methodological approach (a dialectical or Brechtian model), a clearly defined ideological position (Marxist-Leninist for Boudet), and a specific proletarian audience. So while the dramatists presented in my study unanimously endeavor to demystify sociopolitical obfuscation and alter social attitudes, none of their work—not even that of Enrique Buenaventura, whom Risk uses as her model— falls into the category of new theatre. The use of the term to refer both to a demythifying theatre that profoundly and critically examines society and its own role within it and to a propagandistic theatre that imposes a "correct" political attitude and world view raises a host of contradictions. How can one kind of theatre simultaneously expose and impose an ideology?

The equation of "new theatre" with "popular theatre" further complicates the issue. Questions about what popular theatre is and whose interests it serves are by no means resolved. Discussion about the term's meaning continues in Latin America as well as other parts of the world: for example, in Nigeria and South Africa. Without exhausting all the possible issues the term "popular theatre" raises, two major positions on the subject clarify its use in the context of this study. Many theatre practitioners and scholars accept a "by the people, for the people" definition of popular theatre. Karin Barber's study of the Yoruba traveling companies in Nigeria typifies this stance. Their plays, staged by Yoruba practitioners, reflect the rural audience's values and tastes without attempting to analyze or alter them. From Barber's examples, however, it seems clear that even though these plays are written in Yoruba and performed for audiences unaccustomed to drama, they can in fact reaffirm negative stereotypes and divert the audience's attention from the widespread sociopolitical corruption in Nigeria resulting from the recent flow of *petro-naira* (oil-generated dollars). Though not intentionally "antipopular," such plays can undermine the position of their audience by, for example, idealizing wealth or feminine submission without providing a context for analysis or question. Throughout this study I refer to this "by the people, for the people" theatre as "people's theatre."

The conscious political use and abuse of people's theatre has been noted by such activists as Frantz Fanon and Augusto Boal, who argue that such traditional popular events as carnival and vodun (or voodoo) rites, placed within the framework of colonization, can prove to be antipopular: thus, "the native's relaxation takes precisely the form of a muscular orgy in which the most acute aggressivity and the most impelling violence are canalized, trans-

formed, and conjured away." Those in power not only allow but often promote "native," "folkloric," or "traditional" cultural products and events, thereby controlling, co-opting, and often reifying them. Sometimes the ministries of culture promote this art, claiming to bring it international recognition and thus to secure personal fame for the artist and good press and tourism for the nation. Sometimes the promotion of "native" art takes a more sinister turn. South Africa provides an example of people's culture used against the people: the Nationalist Party claims that apartheid and "separate development" helps protect "Bantu" culture.

The other definition of popular theatre, the one I use throughout this work, takes into account that theatre plays an instrumental part in shaping ideology, whether it is an agitational, integrative, or demystifying kind of theatre. Therefore, it defines a theatre as "popular" if it advances and supports the interests of the oppressed and marginalized groups within a society. Popular theatre, as Boal and other practitioners recognize, need not necessarily be written by members of the oppressed classes or even address a popular audience as long as it furthers the position of the disadvantaged within the system. Many dramatists want to reach as wide an audience as possible, hoping to transform the social structure both from without and from within. Theatre can undermine the assumptions and expectations of the audience and in this sense, perhaps, can prove most effective where its efficacy is least anticipated. Popular theatre, then, refers less to specific spectacles, audiences, and methods of production than to the *aims* this theatre serves. By means of intense examination and self-examination, popular theatre attempts to liberate both its audience and itself from the constraints and blinders imposed (however imperceptibly) by the hegemonic cultural discourse.

Yet like people's theatre, this popular theatre also manifests its own ideological blind spots, thereby possibly perpetuating oppressive relationships. The black consciousness movement promotes a male ideology ("Black man, you are on your own"), as does its theatre. Male Latin American political revolutionaries, as Buenaventura points out in *La requisa*, also tend to infantilize or marginalize women. Sometimes, as Wolff's *Paper Flowers* or Eldridge Cleaver's *Soul on Ice* illustrate, the "revolutionary" discourse can exclude and even actively attack other oppressed groups—in this case, women. For Cleaver, "rape was an insurrectionary act" attacking "the white man's law" through his object, woman. This theatre, too, is a product of society and reflects its prejudices. In fact, it is naive to suppose that "new theatre" can escape the cultural limitations inherent in any and all art forms.

Again, one cannot overlook the potential political manipulation of popular theatre. Like people's theatre, it can impose, rather than propose or expose, a vision. Do the university students and radical intellectuals have a moral right to instruct the underprivileged on a "better" life? How does doing so differ from religious proselytizing? Is it merely a coincidence that a similar conflation of educational and religious zeal occurred after the Mexican Revolution with the initiation, by José Vasconcelos (Mexico's minister of education) of a program of traveling educators known as "missionaries?" Can the literate, usually from the bourgeois class, even presume to understand or voice the concerns of the illiterate and semiliterate underclass? How does this presumption differ from the official claims that government works in the best interests of the populace? What happens when popular theatre becomes institutionalized? When "popular theatre" groups such as Cuba's Grupo Teatro Escambray and the Conjunto Dramático de Oriente (which Boudet uses as the prototypes for her analysis of new theatre) formally adopt rules that "the actor must possess and practice marxist-leninist principles . . . in a constant and systematic manner." one can again question whose interests are being served.

One of the problems I perceive in the term "new theatre" is the implicit and, in the case of Boudet, Risk, and Pianca, explicit automatic legitimation of theatrical activity perceived as "popular." The terms "new" and "popular," posited in such a way as to reflect and authorize each other, tend to place the subject above discussion and criticism, rather than—as their claims insist—open the field to inquiry. Theatre, precisely because it is process rather than object, always lends itself to multiple uses and abuses, onstage and off. Popular theatre and people's theatre are no exceptions. Without entirely discrediting or discarding the concepts of new and popular theatre, it is important to recognize that they cannot in themselves legitimate or endorse theatrical activity as politically "correct" or socially liberating. Again, as with all theatrical activity, the context defines theatre's ultimate role and character. Popular theatre, then, as I understand and use the term, incessantly questions and rigorously analyzes its own position and ideology.

Another of the major drawbacks in the term "new theatre" is the facile but erroneous assumption made by commentators that if the goals of these plays are similar (social equality, personal and political freedom), their methodology is too. Somehow the diversity and originality with which the plays themselves propose critical revisions of reality has not been duplicated in the criticism. "New theatre" criticism, rather than exploring alternative modes of theatrical discourse, usually legitimates *one,* the Brechtian, claiming that new theatre is epic theatre, collective theatre, and so forth. The repeated critical appeal to specific models or methodologies proves limiting. It fails to account for the multiple anti-Aristotelian, antihierarchical forms that sprang up after the 1960s: *loas* (a form that had almost disappeared after the nineteenth century), farces (by definition an anarchic genre), *el grotesco* (an Argentine genre developed by playwright Armando Discepolo [1887-1971] which advances its own alienation techniques), the *sainete,* short skits or gags dating back to Spain's Golden Age. Conversely, some playwrights (Egon Wolff, for one), take the "well-made play" and demolish it before our eyes. But surely these too are profoundly popular forms and aspirations that continue the earliest attempts made by Latin Americans to express their own local realities in their own voices.

Another disadvantage in the term "new theatre" has to do with periodization: after thirty years, one may justifiably

question the validity of the adjective. In a sense, we can say that "new" serves a symbolic rather than practical function. Risk, Boudet and Pianca, as I noted, relate new theatre to the Cuban revolution, and in a sense the word supports the revolutionary aspirations for a new beginning, new dating systems and calendars, new men and women.

Pianca tries to reconcile the symbolic with the practical by dividing the development of new theatre into three consecutive stages: during 1959-68 it developed on a national level; from 1968 to 1974 it became international through Latin American theatre festivals; and from 1974 to the present, it began "under the sign of exile, atomization and repression" but experienced a "restructuring and a new hope." In raising the fundamental issue of periods, Pianca's 1-2-3 approach seems to set up an untenable dichotomy between national and international theatrical development within Latin America. It also introduces a final note of optimism which, given the current reality of sociopolitical acts of repression and continuing genocide carried out in some Latin American countries today (particularly in Central America), seems unsustainable. While she correctly notes that individual theatre groups started working on a national level in universities and cultural centers during the 1960s, the impetus and the energy stemmed from a revolutionary consciousness that was affecting all of Latin America and a large portion of the rest of the world as well. Pianca, like most scholars, recognizes the connection between the emergence of the new theatre and the Cuban revolution in 1959, but she downplays the relationship between the individual national "drama" and what I perceive, in consciously theatrical terms, as Latin America's "major drama of liberation," corresponding to the first stages of the Cuban revolution. The revolution was of course in the most literal sense a national phenomenon—it did not in fact extend beyond the island—but in another sense it was clearly an international phenomenon . . . . [The] revolution proved a suspenseful drama. For Latin Americans who aspired to self-government and self-definition, it was a heroic epic: the oppressed conquered their oppressors; David slew Goliath. For the antirevolutionaries in the United States and elsewhere, the revolution signaled the danger of a "Communist takeover" and led to the disastrous Bay of Pigs attempt. On the basis of the relationship I see between the new theatre and two stages in the revolutionary impetus of the 1960s (the initial revolution and the subsequent institutionalization or, as some argue, *failure* of the revolution), I would expand Pianca's first stage to the end of the 1960s and divide it into two parallel movements. Even though labeling does tend to be self-legitimating and to promote its own fiction of validity, the need to distinguish between concepts and categories makes it impossible to dispense with the practice altogether. Therefore, I propose the following terms: the theatre of revolution and the theatre of crisis, to signal two general, often overlapping kinds of theatrical activity.

As we have noted thus far, most of the serious, noncommercial theatre of the late 1950s and throughout the 1960s was a revolutionary theatre in spirit and form. This is not to suggest that revolution "sparked" this new theatre; several of the plays within the category were actually written before the Cuban revolution. Rather, the conflicts and changing perspectives that led to revolution also shaped this new theatrical perspective. The very constant threat posed by the United States to Latin America throughout this century became increasingly obvious and alarming. I am not referring simply to overt invasions and political meddling—the overthrow of the government of President Jacobo Arbenz Guzmán in Guatemala in 1954, or the thwarted invasion of Cuba in 1963; perhaps of greater long-term consequence was the subsequent CIA counterinsurgency campaign, which initiated the use of terrorist tactics and the now infamous practice of "disappearances" throughout Central and South America. (The term *desaparecido* was used in the Latin American press for the first time in conjunction with U.S. counterinsurgency in Guatemala). The increasingly hostile relationship between the United States and Latin America provoked a revision of the colonial self/other tension: the imperialist, now *other*, was to be rejected in favor of the redefined heroic self.

The Latin American revolutionary movement was linked to a larger, polyphonic revolutionary discourse worldwide. According to Fidel Castro and Ché Guevara, political power could be achieved only by means of armed struggle. Régis Debray, the French philosopher and student of Louis Althusser, announced through his *Revolution in the Revolution?* that the 1960s marked the end of an epoch, the "death of a certain ideology" and "the beginning of another, that of total class warfare, excluding compromise solutions and shared power." Previously pacifist approaches such as Martin Luther King's nonviolent civil rights movement became increasingly militant. At this point, there was a romanticization not only of revolution but also of the violence deemed necessary to bring the revolution about. While the escalating confrontations did not meet with the ultimate success that Castro, Ché, or Debray might have desired, in many ways Debray's title itself sums up the proliferating and conflicting left-wing philosophies that sprang up around the world during the 1960s. In the United States, two main lines of revolutionary thinking—best represented iconographically by means of the clenched fist and the peace symbol—typified the discourse. On one hand were the then militant civil rights movement, student rioting on college campuses, the growing feminist movement, and anti-Vietnam protests—only a few examples of political agitation in the United States. On the other was the so-called "sexual" revolution, which many political revolutionaries must have deemed, at best, antirevolutionary and decadent.

Both forms of revolutionary discourse manifested themselves in other countries, sometimes in combination with other kinds of attacks on political and institutional authority. The civil rights movement, influenced by the Cuban revolution, in turn influenced the formation of the black consciousness movement in South Africa in 1968. Armed struggle against Portuguese domination during the late 1950s and early 1960s, directly linked Angola's Popular Movement for the Liberation of Angola (MPLA) and Mozambique's Front for the Liberation of Mozambique (Frelimo) to Castro's Marxism, both financially and ideologically. These struggles eventually led to national independence and Marxist governments for those two African countries in the 1970s. The Prague Spring (1968) signaled an internal rupture within Communism itself; it raised hopes of a nonauthoritarian, liberating Communism in eastern Europe, which was then crushed by Soviet Stalinism. The 1968 Cultural Revolution in China also tightened its definition of "revolution" and proposed to "purify" or purge it of stagnating elements. In Paris, during the revolt of May 1968, the student left not only questioned the "the truth of knowledges" and rejected the university (in the words of Althusser) as "the dominant ideological State apparatus in capitalist social formations"; they also contested different varieties of Communism, from Stalinism and Maoism to the cult of anarchism, situationist "created chaos," and Trotskyism. In Mexico in October 1968 the raised fist emblematized one trend in the revolutionary thinking: left-wing students challenged the Institutionalized Revolutionary Party (PRI), which has dominated Mexico since the 1910-20 revolution. They were massacred in Tlatelolco, a working-class housing compound in the middle of Mexico City, two weeks before the Olympics. Throughout the 1960s, however, the "sex, drugs, and rock-and-roll" trend also affected Mexican youth in what was known as the *onda,* the wave.

The revolutionary movement promised to cast Latin America in a leading role on the world's political and cultural stages. The 1960s provided a new theatrical infrastructure for the marginalized, the oppressed, and the repressed. Radical theatre companies such as Bread and Puppet and the San Franscisco Mime Troupe were on the move; there were national festivals and international festivals. There was renewed hope that Latin America, theatrically as well as politically, would find acceptance not as an inferior other but as a revitalizing, revolutionizing self. Yet, Latin American theatre, with the exception of Triana's *Night of the Assassins* (staged by the Royal Shakespeare Company as *The Criminals* in 1968), was not taken up by the European and U.S. practitioners. And at home, the new feeling of liberation eventually collided with the reality of oppressive power.

The Cuban revolution, aside from providing the hope of viable political alternatives for Latin America, also produced a riveting theatrical image. In other words, though the revolution worked primarily on the real order (a political event, which I leave to political theorists), it had a significant symbolic component. Without reducing the revolution to a spectacle, it is important to notice that its spectacular components served a vital, *real* function. They captured worldwide attention; they rallied followers and admirers by ennobling the revolutionaries while delegitimizing their opposition. The compelling figure of Ché and to a lesser degree the figure of Castro dominated the imagination of a huge portion of the population of Latin America. The revolution generated images of epic proportions, which coincided with Brechtian terminology; Ché's heroic quest embodied the continent's hopes for liberation. The entire sequence was highly spectacular: a new world was being created out of conflict, a new beginning, a new hero or "revolutionary man." The self-representation of the revolution was also powerfully theatrical: the frozen frame of Ché in his beret; the green fatigue uniforms of the *Castristas;* the Brechtian *gestus* as the revolutionary attitude of "men" in action; the episodic plot described by Ché in his diary, his continuing struggle to move the revolution to Bolivia and then to other oppressed regions of Latin America; the enthralled popular audience. Events reactivated the "revolutionary myth" envisioned by José Carlos Mariategui. And just as scholars argue that theatre provides one means of forging a collective identity, the revolution too created a sense of national and international identity mediated through an image. Instead of twenty-five politically marginal, economically and culturally dependent countries, Latin America could envision itself as a united, coherent entity, a producer (rather than importer) of cultural images.

Notwithstanding its epic proportions, the "drama of liberation," even when applied to the revolution, cannot be "read" according to strictly Brechtian terminology. Although it was a politically liberating event (to a degree), sided with the oppressed against an oppressive and corrupt government, and tried to expose a bourgeois, capitalist, imperialist ideology, it also imposed its own reality. The contradictions underlying many discussions of "new" or "popular" or "revolutionary" Latin American theatre reflect the paradox that lies at the heart of this and perhaps every revolution. If we continue to examine it according to theatrical terminology (discussions of "revolutionary" theatre tend to conflate the two), we detect a significant overlap with Artaud's dramatic theory as expressed in his collection of essays *The Theater and Its Double.* Unlike the Brechtian dialectical theatre, which insists on space for critical distancing—"Spectator and actor ought not to approach one another but to move apart"—the theatricality of the Revolution encouraged an Artaudian identification, even a merging, with those heroic figures "capable of imposing this supreme notion of the theater, men who [would] restore to all of us the natural and magic equivalent of the dogmas in which we no longer believe." Artaud's theory calls for collective fusion in the name of metaphysical transcendence; the individual assumes the image and takes on the "exterior attitudes of the desired condition." Likewise, the revolution encouraged subsuming the personal to the collective ideal. The individual surrender to the ideal creates a new real in both theatrical and revolutionary discourse. The actor, committed to the process of creating a new real, "makes a total gift of himself," as Jerzy Grotowski advocated, following Artaud's lead, and "sacrifices the innermost part of himself." But not only in theatre do people give themselves up like Artaud's "victims burnt at the stake, signaling through the flames." The mythification of violence as a source of liberation, whether self-directed or other-directed, in Artaudian theories of a total, essential, and heroic theatre—the "theatre of cruelty"—also forms part of revolutionary thinking, a factor as much in its discourse as in its military strategy. Images of self-sacrifice and surrender characterize works on revolution. Fernando Alegría, in *Literatura y revolución* describes "the bloody operation" of self-examination and recrimination through revolutionary literature, in which authors and their public undergo a painful and glorious striptease: they unmask, "wash, scrub, fumigate themselves, burn their clothing and expose their flesh to merciless scrutiny." Moreover, revolutions themselves are

almost synonomous with violence; though people do speak of "nonviolent revolutions," the term seems contradictory. Hannah Arendt argues in *On Revolution* that revolutions "are not even conceivable outside the domains of violence." This is a position the Cuban revolutionaries themselves, maintaining that the struggle for political power was inseparable from armed warfare, would have accepted.

This giving oneself up to the revolution, however, is not a Brechtian critical or dialectical position. A sudden linguistic shift occurs at the point where one would follow the Brechtian terminology to its logical conclusion, to critical awareness and emotional distancing. Here, the surrender to the revolution is described in natural rather than theatrical terminology: one *becomes* a revolutionary and creates a new real by giving oneself up to the seemingly irresistible force or process. In this sense, the meaning of "revolution" as the steady motion of heavenly bodies in orbit, which follow laws of physics beyond human control, carries over into the modern usage of the term. For one commentator on Latin American popular theatre, "the new socialist hero" will be neither a pessimist nor a conflicted, tortured individual but "a man caught up in the revolutionary whirl-wind."

Just as the Cuban revolution was theatrical, much of the so-called "revolutionary" theatre of this period incorporated and furthered revolutionary ideology, identity, and

Juan Carlos Onetti.

images. The theatre of revolution, while functioning primarily on the symbolic order, also aimed at real, political consequences and saw itself as an important instrument in the social struggle. During the 1960s, collective theatres began to reinforce the grassroots movements with their emphasis on leadership, unity, mass mobilization, and combined force. This theatre manifested the widespread preoccupation with war, either reaffirming or decoding military terminology. Augusto Boal, for example, speaks of theatre as a "weapon" in overthrowing systems of oppression and describes theatrical "raids" staged in 1963 during the Cuban crisis: "A group of actors meet on a corner and begin arguing about politics to the point of threatening physical violence; people gather around them and the group suddenly begins an improvised performance that deals with the most urgent political issues. Only midway through the performance does the crowd realize that it is attending a play." In Cuba, theatrical groups such as the Conjunto Dramático de Oriente (started in 1961) and the Grupo Teatro Escambray (1968) gradually moved away from scripted theatre and staged collective acts of group definition and affirmation. Revolutionary theatre is a pragmatic, educational, *useful* theatre, conceived as a practical exercise in learning about the revolutionary process and encouraging "public participation in [revolutionary] solutions. Theatre is an excellent vehicle to detect and combat problems." Theatrical performances also became acts of collective affirmation and group definition.

It is easy to see the considerable overlap and the blurring of boundaries between the theatricality of revolution and the revolutionary theatre. For one thing, both function concurrently on the real and the symbolic level. Both work as double images, W. J. T. Mitchell's "hypericons." They are simultaneously images and generators of images. They provide not only spectacles but scenarios in which one can envision oneself otherwise, take an image and embody it, become it. The theatricality of the roles and parts does not suggest that these are not socially real or efficacious. By assuming the images of power, one can obtain power—therein lies the real power of images: "the robe makes the man" and "a dog's obeyed in office."

The drama of revolution, both onstage and off, orchestrated images to support the revolutionary drive to overthrow both those in power and the ideology associated with that power structure. As the examples noted above suggest, for images to be politically powerful they must be selected carefully; they must signal one unequivocal message. The *theatricality* of revolution, like theatre's *revolutionary* potential, lies in one basic strategy: the elimination (rather than the accumulation) of signs. This theatre, not surprisingly, is often univocal in its attempt to further its ideology. This is its strength as an instrument of change, and its weakness as theatre.

Not all the plays of the 1960s, however, even the socially committed ones, looked to the Revolution for their goals and identity or unquestioningly accepted the revolutionary myth of liberation. Contradictory images, formulated in some of the major plays of 1965-70, reflect the beginning of an ideological crisis. As the revolution within the revolution split factions on the left, the Cuban revolution underwent crisis from within. Opposition also increased from the outside as right-wing governments steadily gained power. The Brazilian military dictatorship of 1964 was the first of a wave of repressive governments that began to take over in Latin America. The triumphalist drama of liberation gave rise to another, far more complex, and problematic depiction of reality. The word "revolution" itself meant no one thing, appropriated as it had been by parties old and new, as varied and unrevolutionary as Mexico's Institutionalized Revolutionary Party, Juan Carlos Onganía's authoritarian Revolución Argentina of 1966, and Guatemala's "third revolutionary party" (1966) headed by Julio César Méndez Montenegro and characterized by death squads. The word "revolution," clearly, had a potent symbolic function that justified its indiscriminate application. As early as 1965 Triana's *Assassins* was already suggesting a disenchantment with revolution in general and with the Cuban revolution in particular, insinuating that "revolution" did not necessarily mean "liberation." The revolutionary process in Cuba was undergoing critical systemic change as it compromised its principles in order to adhere to the Soviet program. Basing its original liberating ideals on José Martí's visions of a revolution grounded in love and self-determination, the Cuban revolution initially considered itself strong enough to tolerate many kinds of ideas. In 1965 with the uneasy reception of Triana's *Assassins* and in 1968 with the famous Padilla affair, it became evident that the *fidelistas,* like Latin American parties before and after them, also felt the need to restrict, censor, and condemn ideas. As Triana's play makes clear, the concepts of revolution and repression, which had in the romanticization of revolution been conceived as antithetical binaries, now seemed indistinguishable. The conflict between the old order and the new had ultimately failed to generate a new language, a new order, new images, new paradigms for historical process.

Dreams of liberation and self-determination gradually gave way to a new authoritarian order, but one which (like the Mexican Revolution) integrated the revolutionary vocabulary and images—new images that also proved recreations of the old. Ché's heroic though almost predictable downfall replayed yet again the extinction of a heroic race, another Cuauhtemoc. Like Demetrio, the hero of *Los de abajo,* Mariano Azuela's novel about the Mexican Revolution of 1910-20, Ché and his followers were ambushed in a ravine and fought to the last man. Real events, echoing fiction, acquired a *déjà vu* quality. So too the new image of a Latin American "self" stemming more from a rejection of the other than from any real sense of affinity or identity, proved fictitious and unsustainable. The characters, like the societies they represent, continued to be marginal and economically dependent. One of the hopes for the revolution, as expressed by H. A. Murena in 1960, was that it would "free man from the myths that oppress him," so that he "could become once again his own master." Yet, the revolution seemed to recreate, rather than dispel, the old myths.

For many writers who believed that revolution could free the oppressed, the Cuban revolution became another repressive institution. For those who believed that Latin

America had reached a new level of democratization and liberty, the 1968 massacre of the students in Tlatelolco proved that neither the powerful elites at home nor the U.S. government supporting them were about to relinquish their grip without open warfare. For those who believed in progress, the new wave of authoritarian governments recalled Bolivar's Sisyphean view of Latin American history, his disillusioned, "I've ploughed the sea." Revolution/repression, self-determination/colonization, progress/repetition, triumph/extinction—the dream of differentiation collapsed into a nightmare of monstrous sameness. The theatre of crisis stems from this collapse.

After the brief historical overview of theatre and theatricality as instruments of oppression in Latin America, it may seem arbitrary to designate a body of theatre produced between 1965 and 1970 as a theatre of crisis. And, of course, in a way it is. There have been many periods of crisis, not only in Latin America but the world over, and hence, one might argue, many theatres of crises. Though in the broadest sense this is true, we can still perceive differences between various manifestations of crisis theatre. What do the theatre of the Holocaust, protest theatre in black townships in South Africa, theatre of the absurd, and commercial "hits" have in common? While we may note that the differences between them are more interesting than the similarities, we cannot overlook that all have been analyzed in terms of crisis, whether political, ideological, or economic. The issues these theatrical activities raise range from ethical ones (Adorno's contention that art after the Holocaust is barbaric) to purely financial ones (how will theatre in Buenos Aires or on Broadway survive as a viable industry if it prices itself out of the consumer market?).

The theatre of crisis that I propose to study builds upon two crisis theories, the social and the scientific. A combined social-scientific theory brings together two determining factors: the *subjective* experience of crisis and personal decomposition with *objective* systemic shifts, ruptures, or delegitimation. In other words, the individual or group's response to crisis is inseparable from the concrete, usually violent or spasmodic, rifts within social systems and institutions. Individuals and groups have boundaries, identities, goals. As Jürgen Habermas points out in *Legitimation Crisis,* the same is true of systems. When those boundaries, identities, and goals are significantly undermined, or when the maintenance of boundaries alters the identity of the system, either ossifying or subverting its structures, we can say that the system is in crisis. However, as Habermas notes, systems can tolerate varying degrees of disturbance without entering into crisis: "Only when members of a society experience structural alterations as critical for continued existence and feel their social identity threatened can we speak of crises. . . . Crisis states assume the form of a disintegration of social institutions."

This objective/subjective definition of crisis excludes from discussion several other kinds of theatre; theatre of protest and theatre of the absurd, for example, express only one of the two facets of crisis, the objective and subjective respectively. Theatre of protest often signals objective systemic strife, as in the case of black theatre in South African townships, yet one of its notable features is its affirmation of personal and group cohesion and identity. The filmed version of Percy Mtwa's play *Bopha!* exemplifies my point. While fighting and explosions turn the streets into a stage for what Wole Soyinka calls "the deadly drama enacted daily in the streets and suburbs of South Africa," and while apartheid is recognized as posing a potent and invidious threat to black integrity, the political crisis only accentuates the urgency of reaffirming the blacks' solidarity and sense of identity.

The theatre of the absurd, on the other hand, represents a crisis ideology, the subjective rather than objective experience of crisis. The theatre of the absurd, both as Martin Esslin defines it and as we note in the plays generally associated with it, uproots the disintegrating characters and refuses to recognize the sociohistoric context that gave rise to their rootlessness and existential anguish in the first place. Esslin develops his idea of the theatre of the absurd from Camus's definition of absurdity in *The Myth of Sisyphus:* "In a universe that is suddenly deprived of illusions and of light, man feels a stranger. His is an irremediable exile as much because he is deprived of memories of a lost homeland as because he lacks the hope of a promised land to come. This divorce between man and his life, the actor and his setting, truly constitutes the feeling of Absurdity." This theatre's separation of the subjective and objective factors of crisis, combined with the loss of memory, makes the objective sociopolitical specificity of the catastrophe inaccessible to the characters. Moreover, while the theatre of the absurd reflects the consciousness of a moral and philosophical collapse following World War II, this theatre was produced in a period of social, political, and economic consolidation in Europe and the United States.

The theatre of Holocaust stems from the same sociopolitical crisis that generated the theatre of crisis, World War II, but unlike the theatre of the absurd, it vows never to forget the historic events that gave it rise. In the same "universe" deprived of illusions and light, such writers as Elie Wiesel make a new start: "In the beginning there was the Holocaust, we must therefore start all over again." The theatre of the Holocaust shares many of the characteristics with the theatre of crisis and, one could argue, is another manifestation of a theatre of crisis as I use the term. Griselda Gambaro's *The Camp* (1967), for example, exposes the concentration camp universe in a way that resembles what Lawrence Langer later called the "literature of atrocity" in his 1975 study, *The Holocaust and the Literary Imagination.* While Langer mainly (though not exclusively) equates the literature of atrocity with the literature of the Holocaust, Gambaro continues the tradition, finding that the *univers concentrationnaire* aptly conveys the horror also of Argentine fascism with its exterminators and death camps. The main difference between the theatre of crisis and theatre of the Holocaust, then, is that the entire focus of the latter is fixed on one historic event, and it is therefore necessarily more limited in application. Another important difference is that while the theatre of atrocity is a theatre of crisis, the opposite does not hold—the theatre of crisis is not always atrocious. The theatre of crisis invariably deals with violence but with many different kinds of violence, from the subtle, deforming pressures exerted on individuals by oppressive forces or authority figures (Carballido, Triana), to racial and sexual violence (Buenaventura, Wolff), to the spectacular cruelty of torture and terrorism (Gambaro, Wolff, Buenaventura). Not all forms of violence express the hideous, irrational, unmitigated horror that Langer associates with the "aesthetics of atrocity."

Nevertheless, like the theatre of crisis, the theatre of the Holocaust signals both the objective and subjective reality of crisis. Both (and one could include most protest theatre as well) emphasize collective suffering, point to an "official" enemy responsible for the systematic annihilation of people(s), refer to concrete sociohistoric reality, and combine "historical fact and imaginative truth." Like the theatre of crisis, the theatre of the Holocaust subverts the lines of demarcation traditionally used to distance the spectators; on the contrary, it implicates them as accomplices in the onstage violence. However, one could also argue that the theatre of the Holocaust takes a step—temporally and ideologically—*beyond* crisis in that it isolates the problem and assumes a position in the face of it. And whereas the theatre of the Holocaust fixes its attention on a historically limited and unique past, and protest theatre generally looks forward to a happier future, the theatre of crisis is grounded in contradiction; it shapes undifferentiation. We can call it a theatre of crisis precisely because the historic point of reference, like all else, blurs into decomposition.

The theatre of crisis by definition, then, involves objective systemic change: that is, the dissolution or the transformed identity of social institutions and structures attempting to cope with or stave off systemic rupture or collapse. Crisis is not linked to the collapse of any specific political ideology, however, of either the left or the right. It can, for example, result from other, nonpolitical factors. Sophocles' *Oedipus Rex* (430 B.C.), perhaps the prototypical model of the theatre of crisis, a play *of* and *about* crisis, was written during an outbreak of the plague and against the background of the Peleponnesian wars (431 B.C.). It manifests the characteristics associated with crisis thus far—the loss of identity and the collapse of boundaries leading to "contagious" crimes such as parricide and incest. The subjective and objective factors of crisis are inseparable and mutually fueling. Oedipus's crimes ostensibly "cause" or provoke the Theban crisis, and his own crisis (his own awareness of his unhappy situation) directly stems from his attempts to resolve the social catastrophe. Not only is the play overtly violent—Oedipus stabs out his eyes, and Jocasta hangs herself—but Thebes as a city is drowning in a sea of violence and disease. Or, crisis can result from the fracture between competing, irreconcilable ideologies or "isms." The abyss into which the *indiano* Don Alvaro hurls himself, in Duque de Rivas's *Don Alvaro o la fuerza del sino* (1835), represents the no-man's-land, the ruptured ideological, political and cultural frames of the early nineteenth century. Chekov's plays also belong, in a general sense, to a theatre of crisis. They focus on the moment of transition between two economic and cultural systems, a moment that provokes feelings of decomposition and despair in those caught in the middle

of the social transformation. However, the violence in Chekov's plays, the murders and suicides, can hardly be called atrocious; nor does the chopping down of the cherry trees, though violent within the context of the play and world-shaking in its sociopolitical implications, constitute what we normally think of as a hideous act of violence. Chekov's disintegrating characters and waning worlds quietly fade away.

During the period under examination in Latin America, the *causes* of system transformations and disintegrations vary from country to country—from the crisis within the revolution on the left to the rise of quasi-fascist totalitarianism on the right. In Cuba the entire social apparatus taken over from Batista was dismantled and restructured to serve the sociopolitical and economic ends of the new revolutionary government. Early in its history, however, the Cuban revolution underwent major internal, structural changes as it increasingly compromised its original agenda and became incorporated into Soviet Communism. In Argentina, Onganía's government (which came to power with the repressive *coup d'état* of 1966) called itself "the Argentine revolution" and intended not only to eliminate and reconstruct existing institutions but to override constitutional limits and remain in power indefinitely. Colombia, in the 1960s, saw the end of a decade of widespread civil strife known simply as *La Violencia,* which had left 300,000 people dead. It also experienced the intensification of other kinds of violence associated with the growing drug trade, which escalated to such a degree that

Carlos Fuentes.

at present murder is the leading cause of death in males between the ages of eighteen and forty. Mexico, by comparison, seemed relatively stable, yet the PRI government (an undemocratic oligarchy) came under extreme fire during the late 1960s. Civil confrontation became critical in 1968: government tanks patrolled Mexico City's main streets; hundreds (some estimates say thousands) of students were massacred in Tlatelolco, and their bodies were burned or dumped into the ocean. The crisis in Chile did not occur until slightly later, but ideological confrontations had gradually intensified through the late 1960s. The heated competition between the PDC (the Christian Democratic Party, heavily backed by the U.S. CIA) and the FRAP (the anticapitalist, antiimperialist socialist-communist alliance) led to the victory of the PDC in the 1965 elections and then, because of increased dissatisfaction among major elements of the population, to the election of the FRAP and Salvador Allende in 1970. Before Allende's presidency could be ratified by the Chilean Congress, however, the Chilean military with United States backing initiated the series of assaults that led to Allende's death in 1973 and the imposition of Augusto Pinochet's military regime. For all their differences, then, many Latin American countries in the 1960s underwent profound crisis; their societies were either threatened with civil war or became embroiled in revolution culminating in military dictatorships. What we are dealing with here is full-fledged sociopolitical and economic crisis, rather than a subjective crisis of consciousness or ideology.

Notwithstanding the different *causes* of crisis in these various contexts, the *effects,* as manifested through the theatre of crisis, remain surprisingly constant in both content and representation. The similarities, quite obviously, were not intended. Nor do they reflect a school of thought, a dramatic tradition, or even a coherent, shared ideology—except perhaps the shared rejection of Western hegemony evident in these Latin American plays—but rather a crumbling set of beliefs and structures: myths of democracy and personal freedom, progress and utopia, Marxism, liberal humanism, and revolution. The inability to subscribe to them as possible solutions leaves a void, attesting to the difficulty of finding another sustaining ideology. The concept of liberal nationalism failed early in the century, creating its own disillusionment. Democratic socialism had no roots in Latin America. Therefore intellectuals found themselves floundering, seeking a nonmythifying ideological basis in which to ground beliefs. The common denominator of these plays, then, is not intertextual but extratextual.

Still, common denominators do exist, and the analysis of the similarities in conjunction with the differences allows us to map out the parameters of a Latin American theatre of crisis between 1965 and 1970. Produced in the moment of suspension provoked by a systemic schism, this theatre shows society balanced between destruction and renovation, subject to change and open to question. The moment of crisis is one of rupture, of critical irresolution, the "in between" of life and death, order and chaos. And because these plays combine feelings of decomposition with the threat of imminent extinction, they often reflect the moment of annihilation and/or terror. The characters, locked

in a dreadful present, perceive time as a contradiction. The historical moment is lived as ahistorical. As Anthony Kubiak notes, the "moment of terror, like the instant of pain, is a moment of zero time and infinite duration. Although terror can only exist in history, it is felt as naked singularity, existing outside all possible representation." The temporal displacement implicit in crisis is accompanied by spatial dislocation as well; the characters in the plays presented in this study have no safe home of their own—they live in houses either owned or taken over by someone else. Nor do the houses shelter or protect; often they are prisons, with barred windows and locked doors. Sometimes, the house itself becomes a weapon, an instrument of oppression or torture. Often, too, the structures collapse: walls fall in or break down, either crushing the inhabitants or exposing them to the violence from outside. The inner spaces merge with the outer; the sociopolitical conflicts are fought out on city streets, in homes, on human bodies. Crisis, as rupture, suspends boundaries, denying the characters the possibility of temporal and spatial shelter; there is no place to hide, no future to look forward to. "To think disaster," as Maurice Blanchot observes in *The Writing of Disaster,* "is to have no longer any future in which to think it." The theatre of crisis is fragmented, inconclusive. It offers no resolution, no restorative harmony, no cathartic relief.

René Girard, in *The Scapegoat,* notes the uniformity in various and culturally divergent depictions of crisis, suggesting that the similarities in the social and personal experience of crisis lead to similarities in its representation. What, then, are the effects of crisis? What happens to individuals in a society whose boundaries, goals, and identity are being attacked? Societies that are not in crisis respect authority and maintain hierarchies, resort to a judicial system in times of conflict, tolerate diversity, "name" and differentiate between members; societies confronting crisis initially—for that second of suspension—do none of the above. When systems are attacked, the effectiveness and legitimacy of authority become suspect and, as frequently happens in Latin America, vulnerable to violent contention. The notion of legitimate government, of due process and judicial integrity, of moral and ethical safeguards all interconnect to such a degree that the challenges posed to one threaten the others.

When all basis for positive (noncrisis) differentiation has been undermined, these societies respond in two sequential ways. First, they experience the "monotonous and monstrous" sameness of crisis that negates difference; they fail to name, differentiate, valorize, or make distinctions. Michel Foucault's description of the plague in seventeenth-century France reveals all the stereotypes of crisis: the "suspended laws, lifted prohibitions, the frenzy of passing time, bodies mingled together without respect, individuals unmasked, abandoning their statutory identity." Artaud also describes the plague as a crisis in which "social forms disintegrate. Order collapses"; crisis is accompanied by "every infringement of morality, every psychological disaster."

Second, because this sameness is threatening and intolerable, those who exert some power combat disorder with a vigilant, oppressive order. This is the deadly "society shrouded in an order so orderly that its chaos was far more intense than anything that had preceded it" described by Michael Taussig in his *Shamanism, Colonialism, and the Wild Man*. If crisis provokes disorder, then, the "solution" to crisis would seemingly entail the imposition of strictest order, states of emergency, law, and penalties, and the application of what Foucault calls the "disciplinary mechanism" that monitors individuals precisely by naming them, locating and compartmentalizing them, and controlling their movements by means of either visual surveillance (the Panopticon) or computers (the threat to black liberation posed by computers in South Africa). People are compartmentalized, subjugated: "All events are recorded . . . [the] uninterrupted work of writing links the centre and the periphery . . . power is exercised without division, according to a continuous hierarchical figure." Crisis, experienced as a profound disorder that threatens power, hierarchy, social systems, and individual identity, sets in motion an "ordering" mechanism of surveillance, of social and individual control.

Aside from the imposition of centralized, vigilant order, which epitomizes crisis governments from South Africa's Afrikaner Nationalist party to Pinochet's military regime, societies in crisis also set in motion a mechanism of exclusion; they invent false differences and convert members of society into grotesque and apparently threatening others. Initially, this attack on the other also passes as a solution to crisis—if crisis is equated with undifferentiation, surely the politics of differentiation provides the way out of crisis. Systemic crisis often results in persecution and scapegoatism because selective violence, as Girard argues in *Violence and the Sacred*, is conceived as channeling the community's aggression. Instead of destroying each other, members of the community agree to focus their aggression on a "safe," expendable victim. Moreover, as these plays demonstrate, violence is perceived as a *defense* against crisis, rather than as an *effect* of it. By participating in the creation of difference and in the politics of segregation and exclusion, people can comfort themselves that they are doing something to solve the problem; they not only differentiate but rigorously maintain boundaries. Yet because the "difference" is generally a false one, a created one, the hatred, exclusion, and persecution of the other often masks a deeper hatred and self-hatred. The violence associated with sociopolitical crisis, then, is self-perpetuating, coming back to destroy the individuals who initiated the violence as a form of self-defense.

The similar depictions or descriptions of crisis evident in this theatre reflect the uniformity of the experience of social, systemic crisis. In the theatre of crisis analyzed in this study, the sets concretely depict the struggle for spatial control in the face of structural collapse. When walls cave in, crumble, or disappear, inner is inseparable from outer and private from public. The blurred and obliterated boundaries reveal worlds in ruin, both onstage and off. The physical destruction reflects disintegrating judicial, moral, and physical frameworks, distinctions that will not hold, partitions that fail to separate or protect.

The same annihilating undifferentiation is evident in the depiction of the characters. The overwhelming majority of characters in these works have no distinguishable identity; few even have names. They are socially marginal, physically infirm, or malformed to the point of monstrosity. Waves of violence wash over previous distinctions and hierarchies: children kill their parents; the police violate the innocent; personal violence and state violence mingle and feed on each other.

One of the significant features of crisis, as attested both by this theatre and by theorists as divergent as Girard and Habermas, is that it incapacitates the subject to deal effectively with the situation. The theatre of crisis abounds in examples of passive characters unable to react constructively to the situation at hand. The characters' ineffectuality may stem, in part, from powerlessness. Habermas, who introduces the concept of crisis in medical terms, compares the subject of crisis to a patient in critical condition: "Crisis cannot be separated from the viewpoint of the one who is undergoing it—the patient experiences his powerlessness *vis-à-vis* the objectivity of the illness only because he is a subject condemned to passivity and temporarily deprived of the possibility of being a subject in full possession of his powers." It is only later, when the characters are in a sense beyond crisis, that they can gain the lucidity to assess what occurred. However, we should resist interpreting this powerlessness and passivity as either historically or biologically determined. It is not a personality defect on the part of the victims, as critics of the indigenous victims of the Conquest or of the Jews in the concentration camps (to signal out only two groups), seem to suggest. Rather, it is situational, positional; the victims are caught in a deadly and complex web of circumstances and cannot effectively judge, from their position *within* it, how to best

Gabriel García Márquez.

extricate themselves. Usually, they need outside help from those who are not themselves trapped in the critical situation.

The characters' sense of being trapped, of being unable to deal with crisis, results in the creation of both victims and victimizers. Several of the most vicious characters in these plays see themselves as victims of crisis and claim to be coping with their predicament when they attack others who, they feel, are responsible for provoking it. As Girard notes, "Rather than blame themselves, people inevitably blame either society as a whole, which costs them nothing, or other people who seem harmful for easily identifiable reasons." Hitler, in *Mein Kampf*, exemplifies perhaps the most extreme position of crisis culminating in mass victimization, blaming what he saw as the humiliation of the German nation after World War I not on military defeat (the "outward symptom of decay") but on "toxins," "harmful poisons," and an "alien virus" undermining the national "body." Only the extermination of the Jews, according to his thinking, could restore "health." Unable to identify the true causes of crisis, the "victims" can become the victimizers, willing to kill for a "cure." Within the context of the plays, the protagonists who experience crisis—Lalo, the Torturer, the Hake, Lorenzo, and even SS Officer Franco—consider themselves its victims. In order to "defend" themselves, they rationalize exterminating others on the grounds that they are "Communist" (Buenaventura and Gambaro), or "bourgeois" (Wolff), or hurtful and harmful in some way (Carballido and Triana). Therefore, it is deemed necessary to marginalize the "dangerous" individuals or kill them. While the individuals thus singled out as victims may in fact be guilty of some crime, it is not the catastrophic, earthshaking crime for which they are being persecuted and punished. The victims of the kind of violence associated with persecution, as opposed to judicial law, are usually members of marginalized social groups: poor, black, female, and so on.

It is interesting to note throughout these plays that the objects of attack in times of crisis are precisely the boundaries—physical, moral, legal, or discursive—that previously maintained social hierarchies, family and personal integrity, law and order. All the crimes associated with crisis, such as parricide, infanticide, and incest, "seem to be fundamental," Girard notes. "They attack the very foundation of the cultural order, the family and the hierarchical differences without which there would be no social order." Buenaventura's cycle of plays depicts violence as both the result of the imposition of social and class boundaries and an attack on those hierarchies regarded by the outcasts as exclusionary and oppressive. In *The Menu,* the boundaries are literally painted on the stage in the shape of various colored circles; the Beggars are fumigated before they are permitted to cross from one ring to another to pick up the leftovers that the charitable ladies graciously throw their way. Notwithstanding the insistence on maintaining difference, however, the enforced distinctions only underline the fact that all these characters are very much the same. While the poor are unwashed, infirm, greedy, deformed by poverty and degradation, the wealthy ladies themselves are freaks and hybrids: the Wo/Man, the Fatso, the Dwarf. The colonized, having internalized the colonizer, incarnate contradiction; they are simultaneously victim and victimizer, the embodiment of the two-in-one, grotesque self/other. The monstrosity and violence in the privileged circle is no different from the monstrosity and violence of the beggars. The painted lines maintain power rather than difference—or, more precisely, they maintain power by insisting on false difference. In Triana's *Assassins,* Lalo's "crime" reeks of incest; he pretends to penetrate his parents with his knife and roll in their blood. His world becomes a nightmare of undifferentiation in which life is indistinguishable from death and refuse. The bedroom, as site of reproduction and incorporation, "becomes" the bathroom, the site of excretion and expulsion. In Gambaro's *Siamese Twins,* Lorenzo's personal need to annihilate his twin is physically carried out by the police who, though theoretically upholders of law and justice, torture and kill Ignacio and dump his body in an unmarked grave. The play opens up spiraling worlds of violence in which the violence *inside* the home and the individual and the violence of the systems and structures *outside* augment each other. Ultimately, the violence ends in a whirlwind of terrorism, which, by invading the streets, homes, and private lives of individuals, "gets us where we live" and deterritorializes us. In Wolff's *Paper Flowers,* the Hake's destruction of Eva attacks both class and gender, for he substitutes the real, tangible woman's body for an incorporeal, "effeminate," middle-class body politic. Wolff has so effectively—that is, so *invisibly*—transposed one site of aggression (the middle class) onto another (the woman) that almost without exception commentators read the The Hake's violence as a political act, the more-or-less justifiable attack by a social underdog on an exclusive system of power. The fact that it is also a misogynist act (in which a physically powerful man destroys a powerless woman), and an example of scapegoating, has passed without comment.

The plays examined in this study, while not all violent, are about violence, a term that is hard to define in the best of times and almost impossible to pin down in a discussion of oppression and crisis. I discuss the various kinds in individual chapters and in the concluding remarks, but it is worth noting here that the plays as a whole emphasize two major, interrelated spheres of violence: crisis and oppression. The paradigm of crisis, as I have noted, includes the initial subjective-objective collapse that provokes disorder and undifferentiation, followed by the implementation of the strictest order, the differentiation and exclusion of a group into a grotesque other, and the persecution and scapegoating of the marginalized group or individual. The paradigm of oppression includes the deforming, though often less overt, violence that casts the victim as grotesque other in the repressive self/other binary—the distanced, underdeveloped, childlike, ignorant, inferior, helpless, passive, feminized, persecuted other whose "permanent dream," according to Frantz Fanon, is to become the self, the defining power, "the persecutor." In connection with these two major paradigms, we see numerous secondary manifestations: revolutionary violence (response to oppression), institutionalized or professionalized violence (criminal governments, torture and terrorism associated with both oppression and crisis), behavioral disorders and seemingly gratuitous acts of cruelty (again, related to both crisis and oppression).

While there is significant overlapping between the two paradigms of violence, crisis and oppression, they are not inherently connected. Crisis, as I noted, can stem from factors such as plague or war that are not directly or even indirectly related to oppression. Moreover, even when crisis derives from clear sociopolitical clashes resulting from oppression, crisis threatens the legitimacy of the ruling power (insofar as it threatens all objective and subjective frameworks), while oppression need not. This is not to say that oppressive societies are morally or ethically "legitimate" but merely that their existence is not questioned or contested in any manner that will seriously jeopardize their continuity. Oppressive systems are usually so consolidated, so deeply cemented in institutions, laws, and ideology, that their legitimacy is taken for granted not only by the oppressors but often by the oppressed themselves. These systems can last decades without experiencing or provoking crisis, in part because their violence has been rendered natural, almost invisible. It was long considered "natural" for women to serve men, for blacks to serve whites, and so forth. Studies in law, history, human nature, and biology among others—by means of which "man" came to represent "mankind," proved how natural a state it was. Some scholars go so far as to deny that we can use the word "violence" to describe institutionalized oppression. Even Hannah Arendt states that a "legally unrestricted majority rule, that is, a democracy without a constitution, can be very formidable in the suppression of the rights of minorities and very effective in the suffocation of dissent without any use of violence." Here I disagree with Arendt; rather than thinking in terms of violence and nonviolence (power) in regard to oppression, we might more accurately think in terms of explicit and implicit violence. Explicit, or overtly physical, violence is easy enough to recognize. No less real, though perhaps just as damaging in the long run, is the implicit violence of naming and directing the other, of *naturalizing* distinctions based on gender, race, and class, of limiting the others' options and casting them in symbolic if not literal servitude. My broader definition of violence includes the violence Emmanuel Levinas refers to in *Totality and Infinity:* "Violence does not consist so much in injuring and annihilating persons as in interrupting their continuity, making them play roles in which they no longer recognize themselves, making them betray not only commitments but their own substance, making them carry out actions that will destroy every possibility for action." While I oppose Levinas's downplaying of explicit violence, I believe that no one has better delineated the corrosive effects of what I call implicit violence.

Even though oppression and crisis are not necessarily related, this study illustrates the process by which implicit violence becomes explicit, by which the age-old violence associated with oppression bursts into the reactive violence of the oppressed. The process of decolonization is violent and perhaps, as Fanon suggests, *"always* violent" (my emphasis). What interests me here, however, is that the violence of decolonization precipitates crisis. Fanon describes the objective systemic shifts and the subjective transformations I have associated with crisis as inherent in decolonization: "A whole social structure [is] being changed from the bottom up," and "there is a total, complete, and absolute substitution" by means of which "a certain 'species' of men" is replaced by another. That crisis, then, marks both the culmination of distress and the uncertainty for the future—the question of "whether or not the organism's self-healing powers are sufficient for recovery." Recovery here should not signal a return to an earlier noncrisis state in what would constitute the politically conservative or reactionary move toward reestablishing the status quo. Rather, "recovery" and "self-healing" suggest that the state and individual strive for self-definition, autonomy, nonviolence. The problem, of course, is that the process threatens to be circular and self-perpetuating. If decolonization precipitates crisis, and if crisis (as the paradigm indicates) throws systems and individuals into abeyance and undermines structures of definition (which is not necessarily bad, as Fanon points out, but always critical), resulting in a situation that then triggers strict repressive measures, where will it end? That is what these plays ask us to consider.

POETRY

Jorge Carrera Andrade

SOURCE: "Poetry and Society in Spanish America," in *Reflections on Spanish American Poetry*, State University of New York Press, 1973, pp. 21-38.

[*Carrera Andrade was an Ecuadoran poet, essayist, and diplomat. In the following essay, he discusses the relationship between poetry and society in Latin America.*]

"We are passing through calamitous times, during which it is not possible to speak or to keep silent without danger": these words which seem to allude to our epoch were written by the great Valencian thinker Juan Luis Vives in the sixteenth century. From then on, the two tendencies, toward acquiescence or toward dissent, were already emerging in the terrain of ideas, which means in today's vocabulary that men of letters took positions either in the ranks of *conformity* or of *nonconformity*. The most debated questions were the Counter Reformation, the right of Spain to conquer the New World, the crusade to redeem the Indians, known as infidels. While it is very true that the literature of protest and revolutionary literature are contemporary phenomena which are responsive to the present stage of sociological progress, it is an equally indisputable fact that Spanish-American literature from its beginnings was the fruit of social conditions in the colonies. In the colonial period there was none of what is properly called escape literature. The writer found himself *committed* from the first days of the Discovery, as can be seen in the attitude of the poets who felt themselves responsible before society and the "Christian conscience."

It must not be forgotten that writers had to submit to ecclesiastical censorship, to the Council of the Indies, and to the censors of the Holy Tribunal of the Inquisition. This obliged authors to express themselves cautiously, to resort to skillful expedients and to veil their intentions by artistic distortions of form. In his *Elegías de Varones Ilustres de Indias,* Juan de Castellanos put acerbic criticism of the Spanish conquest in the mouth of Drake. This did not escape the keen eyes of the censor for the Council of the Indies, who ordered 650 lines of the *Discurso* of the English corsair destroyed; actually this did not involve a significant cut in the length of the poem, which comprises 150,000 verses and constitutes the longest rhymed chronicle about the Discovery and Conquest of the New World. The rector of Tunja, an old fisher of pearls, possessed enough mental vigor to write throughout his long life, but he was not endowed with the chromatic vision of the world which characterizes Alonso de Ercilla. He was only a modest amanuensis of poetry who noted events in his book in hendecasyllabic verses "in the Italian style." Ercilla had a Renaissance background and knew how to appreciate and interpret the American scene; he constructed most vivid metaphors with his original perception. In the last years of the sixteenth century and the first of the seventeenth, new cultivators of poetry followed these models and published *El Peregrino Indiano,* "rhymed diary of the military operations of Hernán Cortés," by Saavedra Guzmán, *Arauco Domado* by Pedro de Oña, *Grandeza Mexicana* by Bernardo de Balbuena, *Armas Antárticas* by Juan de Miramontes. Poetry was the mirror which reflected all ideas and events of the epoch as well as the experiences of the new society.

The voyages, the reconnoiterings of unknown coasts, the landings and expeditions to the interior of virgin lands, the combats with Indians, and the hostilities between Spaniards constituted a thematic out-pouring into the narrow molds of *octavas reales*. The epic poem became a historic document which helps us to understand the nascent social organization of the colonies. *Armas Antárticas* tells, among other episodes, about the battle of Iñaquito, which was fought by Gonzalo Pizarro, chief of the encomenderos opposed to Viceroy Blasco Núñez de Vela, who was in turn upholder of the royal ordinances for the protection of the Indians against the misbehavior of the conquistadors. The poem denounces the fact that the Spaniards brought to America the seed of civil war. The poets did not hide their sympathy for one or another of the opposing factions, though in general they took a conformist position in favor of the royal power and the church.

The colonial society was not simply Spanish society transported to the New World, rather it was also enriched by the manners and customs of the conquered peoples. The city, the street, the square, the dwelling, were not wholly Spanish: the city had more space available and was laid out on a geometric plan of parallel streets; the street was a stage on which the comedy of good manners was presented daily, the characters of which were the encomendero, the ecclesiastic, the pettifogging lawyer, and the soldier. The principal square constituted the appropriate place for popular diversions, bullfights, the market, and civic displays. It was the heart of the city and for this rea-

son all the symbols of pontifical and royal power and of popular representation were concentrated there; these included the episcopal palace, government house, the municipal palace or guildhall, and finally the prisons and the gallows. The civil architecture copied the religious in such a way that a house was a convent in miniature, with its square interior patio and its paunchy columns supporting lofty galleries. In America the Spaniard found ease and time in which to practice religion as well as to enjoy a gathering of friends and a game of cards. At times the evening gatherings were stirred by criticism of the colonial institutions, the taxes, and the bad public administration. In the epic poem *Arauco Domado,* Pedro de Oña resorted to the well-known device of having a character's dream draw his reader's attention to another extreme of America and tell how the people of Quito rebelled against the sales taxes and the consequent punishment of their leaders. The poet had been not only an eyewitness but an actor in that drama of a people. When the general of archers, Pedro de Arana, raised a mercenary army to march against the rebels, Pedro de Oña offered his services, and he was rewarded with the office of corregidor of Jaén de Bracamoros. In the midst of the exuberant vegetation of that equatorial land, de Oña found the peace and leisure propitious for writing his strophes in praise of the captains who smothered the first authentic popular movement in America, the sales-tax revolution, at the end of the sixteenth century. But the court poet, flatterer of the viceroy of Lima, neglected to burn incense at the feet of some authorities of the Royal Audience of Quito, who then obtained the suppression of the first edition of *Arauco Domado* even though the poem praised the methods used by colonial policy to keep the people in subjection. Nevertheless the poem incorporated many facts about daily life in that period and there are allusions to Spanish-American flora and fauna, as well as some well-chosen metaphors for water: the river is a "transparent pane of crystal," the stream is "made of pure glass," the "liquid and serene material" in which the trees are reproduced makes it impossible to guess "which is the real bough—the one above or the one below." In another poet of the same period poetry assumes a civil character. Bernardo de Balbuena, highly esteemed by colonial society, wore the mitre as bishop of Puerto Rico, but he had a nostalgic love for the city of Mexico, in praise of which he composed the poem *Grandeza Mexicana,* which is a manual of lyric eulogy and a compendium of that town's social activity, "flower of cities, glory of the west." It has been said that the poet wished to praise the powerful in Mexico, and there can be no doubt of this, but it is necessary to point out that in Chapter IV of the poem, its author does not exalt wealth or position but rather learning, creative ability, and wisdom. He places the lecture halls of Mexico on the level of those of Salamanca, Alcalá, Louvain, and Athens in letters and sciences. And with great eloquence he affirms in his musical tercets that in Mexico there are more eminent men "in all the arts and sciences / in human and divine letters / eternal seekers of verities."

Spanish America is a land of paradoxes. In a society where education was exclusively in the hands of the church and where the people had no access to the university but only to primary schools, writers enjoyed general appreciation.

Miguel Angel Asturias.

Spanish-American poetry of the twentieth century—particularly from 1930—is not only the fruit of the diffusion of ideas; even more it tends to transform the society from which it proceeds.

— *Jorge Carrera Andrade*

The case of sor Juana Inés de la Cruz is illustrative of how much social consideration poetry attained in those days. It would seem that Juana's illegitimacy did not prevent the viceregal court from opening its doors to her and lavishing attentions upon her. But her disillusionment with the world soon led her to the convent and this attitude corresponded with the period, which was a Spanish one of human and metaphysical disillusionment. Sor Juana expressed this idea lucidly in a sonnet about her portrait, which she called a "colored imposture." In truth she could have applied this expression to the world as a whole, because in poetic language it means a mirage, an illusion, the evanescence of life, disguised by attractive but ephemeral colors. Sor Juana suffered from an inner conflict between science and faith, or more clearly between her rationalist thinking, which sought the truth, and her intimate feelings, which inclined toward religious dogma. It was a dramatic battle between the mind and the heart, between scientific restlessness and duty. Sor Juana Inés de la Cruz reflected in her poetic creation the state of the society in which her life was spent.

Juan Bautista Aguirre, Pablo de Olavide, and Juan de Velasco are already poets of the Enlightenment. Their works are linked with the social vicissitudes of their times, which witnessed the expulsion of the Jesuits from America, confidence in the Enlightenment, or rather in public and lay education, and the appearance of a new political and social philosophy incarnate in the French Revolution. Aguirre and Velasco were exiled to Italy because they were members of the Ignatian order, but they found appreciation in the land which offered them hospitality. Velasco, poet and historian, wrote an anthology, *El Ocioso en Faenza,* in which he brought together the best works of his Jesuit comrades and his own poems—among them an elegy to Mirabeau—to show Europe the great culture achieved by America; with this he anticipated the type of literary Americanism that was to flourish in the nineteenth century.

Juan Bautista Aguirre, thanks to his learning, came to hold very important positions in the Royal Audience of Quito, his native city. Anticipating Pasteur he maintained the theory, revolutionary in those days, that illness was not produced by supernatural causes but by "corpuscles," as he called microbes. During the exile of the Jesuit order, he was theological consultant to Bishop Chiaramonti of Tívoli, who later was to receive the pontifical tiara under the name of Pius VII. The personality of Father Aguirre stands out in the eighteenth century because, like that of Clavijero in Mexico, it represents Jesuit humanism, which

Francisco de Terrazas, Jacinto de Evia—called "master" by his contemporaries—and Hernando Domínquez Camargo lived surrounded by an aura of public admiration in their respective countries. The dominant traits of these poets were religiosity, a feeling for nature, a resigned acceptance of the colonial organization, the search for metaphysical truths. But a new subterranean current of ideas was opening up which expressed its nonconformity with the society of the times through satire. Mateo Rosas de Oquendo and Juan del Valle Caviedes are figures representative of this tendency. Their mocking darts were not aimed at the political power, however, but only against certain practices vulnerable to criticism: the ignorance of physicians and healers, feminine intrigues, the servility of courtiers. Toward customs the satire had a moralizing purpose. This current was joined by the appearance of the scientific spirit in the colonies. The Mexicans Carlos de Sigüenza y Góngora and sor Juana Inés de la Cruz showed in their lives and their works the conflict between the baroque and scholastic century in which they lived and the ideas of the Enlightenment which reached full maturity in the following century. Sigüenza y Góngora received the highest honors in recognition of his intellectual worth.

prepared the way for the independence of the Spanish-American people. Among the poems of Aguirre, one of the most famous is the *Carta a Lizardo,* in which the concept that "everything born dies twice" is repeated at the end of each strophe, creating an atmosphere of mystery. The poet philosophically defines nothingness as death. Every being comes from nothing and returns to nothing—a concept with little religion in it, which incorporates a materialistic, Encyclopedist idea. Father Aguirre on occasion elaborated a hermetic poetry which needs an intellectual key to be deciphered. The poet had no hope for a future life for man; he believed in liberty and intervened to promote the rights of the people. In the Mutiny of the Monopolies which took place in Quito in 1763, Aguirre showed himself to be an eloquent and persuasive orator, who led the multitude to a temporary triumph.

It is not easy to understand Spanish-American evolution without examining the lives and works of men like Pablo de Olavide in the frame of the eighteenth century, when the Enlightenment began to reform society in order to obtain greater justice and to try out more rational economic measures. Olavide, born in Lima, reached the greatest heights of social and political influence, not only in America but also in Spain and France. In Spanish territories he put through his original project of agrarian colonization in the Sierra Morena, cultivated the friendship of Jovellanos, Aranda, Floridablanca, and other ministers of Carlos III, and maintained a "philosophical salon," from which the ideals of the Encyclopedists were disseminated. Olavide was a man completely committed to the philosophy of the French Revolution and to the independence of the Spanish-American colonies. Persecuted by the Inquisition, which made an auto-da-fé of his works and condemned him to imprisonment in a monastery, the thinker took refuge in France, where the Convention decreed high honors for him and a civic crown for the services he had rendered society. His friends included Diderot, Voltaire, and Grimm. When he lost his fortune in the bankruptcy of the House of Gueméenée, Catherine of Russia sent him money so that he could live decently. He never abandoned his stand in support of Spanish-American independence. The representatives of the peoples of America, gathered in Paris, entrusted Olavide and Miranda with the mission of negotiating with England for material aid for the campaign of emancipation. Miranda was able to see his aspirations partly realized, but the octogenarian Olavide could not harvest the fruits of his labors. The personal drama in the last days of his life was the scientific-religious conflict. Olavide exercised a great influence on the society of his time. He announced the change in orientation of American consciousness toward the guiding light of France and the new political doctrine of the rights of man and the sovereignty of the people.

In the nineteenth century poetry thrust its roots into the social condition, fruit of the evolution or advance of the colonial society toward a republican society. The poets were singers of democratic equality under the aegis of liberty. Nations were born in America. Patriotism inspired the poems of José Joaquín de Olmedo, who sang of Bolívar, the liberator of five nations. The poet participated in the insurrection of the Creoles against Spanish domina-

tion. He was a member of the first government junta established in Guayaquil and later deputy to the Cortes of Cádiz, where he was distinguished by his position in support of abolishing the institution of *mitas* which required unpaid work from the Indians. Such an injustice, as well as the Inquisition and other anachronistic institutions, were suppressed by the Cortes, thanks to the efforts of the deputies from the New World. The Cortes announced a political constitution according to which the Spanish nation would not recognize King Ferdinand VII as sovereign as long as he would not swear obedience to the said supreme law. The document was signed by the majority of the Spanish-American deputies, Olmedo among them. But a little later an absolutist reaction was imposed. Ferdinand VII returned to the throne and persecuted the men who had signed the famous constitutional document. Olmedo escaped to France, together with other liberal deputies, and returned to his native land when the campaign of Bolívar and San Martín to consolidate the American independence movement was beginning. The poet wrote *La Victoria de Junín* in praise of the decisive battle of that war. With this poem the epic style appears again in Spanish America, but as a song to the liberty of peoples, as a Pindaric poem in which new myths arise. Olmedo was named minister plenipotentiary in London and Paris. In his time he enjoyed not only international celebrity but also the appreciation of his people, which made possible his candidacy for the presidency of the republic, although he was defeated in the voting of the Constituent Assembly.

The predominantly mestizo republican society which had succeeded the colonial society gave primary importance to teaching trades and exalted work on the land. The republican government decreed the emancipation of negro slaves and laid down special arrangements for the protection of the Indians. The feudal estate was converted into the plantation, tilled in the same way as in the past. Royal benefices were wiped out and covenants between the Vatican and the nascent states were signed. The new social structure is reflected in the poetry of Andrés Bello, in the fables of García Goyena, and in the satires of Irisarri. The first of these authors celebrated agricultural labor in the tropics and exalted the dignity of the countryman. He made his poem into a proclamation against the civil war and a call for civilized and fruitful peace. At the beginning Bello held the office of secretary of the Society of Friends of the Country, an institution which was a nursery for patriots and literary talents. He was the teacher of Bolívar and later minister plenipotentiary to the English court. He lived for twenty years in London, where he maintained friendly relations with banished Spanish and American poets. A typical poem of Andrés Bello was in *Carta de Londres a París, por un americano a otro,* in which he points out some truths regarding the Spanish-American situation and shows that the work of emancipation had not yet brought happiness to the people. The letter is addressed to Olmedo, his close friend, who held a high diplomatic position in Paris. The characteristic note of Bello's poetry is his optimism regarding the destiny of America, for this he has been called "the Virgil of the New Age." Like the Latin poet who, on the threshold of the Christian Era, sang the coming "golden age," the great Venezuelan announced the Golden Age of independence, democracy, and progress.

But the predictions were not fulfilled. After emancipation, the New World found itself in a state of economic ruin and chaos, because it was unable to solve the principal political and social problems such as oligarchic domination, the feudal structure of landholding, and above all the fragmentation of the "American homeland" into states. It was the epoch of military chiefs and the economic penetration into America of the European powers, principally England, which gained control of commerce through its investments and credits. The church intervened in politics in order to maintain its old colonial privileges: the direction of teaching; the administration of hospitals and cemeteries; the registration of births, marriages, and deaths; the exclusion of other forms of worship. Romanticism was to be confronted with new realities.

During this period the poets became involved in the political struggle for the rights of the people against the dictatorships and for affirmation of the national physiognomy. The Cuban Heredia, the Argentine Echeverría, Mármol, Hernández, the Peruvian González Prada and others suffered persecutions and deportations for their attitudes of opposition to tyranny and ignorance. Their dissatisfaction with the material world was a part of their romantic anguish. José María Heredia lived in exile in Mexico, José Mármol fought against the tyrant Rosas, for which he was imprisoned. Esteban Echeverría founded the first socialist group with the character of a secret society. José Hernández, creator of *Martín Fierro,* knew the harshness of exile but also the jubilation of triumph when, the tyranny having been routed, he was elected a delegate to the National Congress. All gaucho poetry can be catalogued within the literature devoted to supporting the rights of the pampa mestizo. Effective in vindicating this social class, gaucho poetry expresses itself through the simple form of the ballad in the vernacular. The circumstances created by government action hastened the decline of gaucho life, but *Martín Fierro* endures because it is a song of friendship, it exalts local color, it represents nationalism at its best in those days, and it condemns social injustices.

Gonzáles Prada and José Martí were social reformers. Both possessed a great capacity for rebellion and inexhaustible generosity. The first was a defender of the Indian and the worker, that is to say, of the underprivileged social classes. Martí dedicated all his energy to the independence of Cuba, to which he made the supreme gift of his life. He was the purest voice of the Cuban conscience. Simplicity and liberty constituted the two great themes of his poetry, in which he expresses the most complex feelings with great verbal richness and facility, in a condensed and detailed style impressive for its captivating sincerity.

We have run through more than three centuries of Spanish-American poetry in long strides, until we arrive at the last five years of the nineteenth century, on the threshold of modernism, where the tormented figures of Gutiérrez Nájera, Julián del Casal, and José Asunción Silva are situated. The three poets, modernists in their musical form but basically romantics, disdained modern life and bourgeois society. Nevertheless their nonconformist attitude was not combative but rather resigned. They cultivated the secret desire to abandon life in the fullness of youth. Silva did so through the false door of suicide. The trademark of this generation of late-blooming romantics was lack of restraint and love of death in contrast to the group headed by Darío, who proclaimed moderation and love of life. But there was a common denominator to both groups: artistic refining.

In his book *The Modern Culture of Latin America (Society and the Artist),* Jean Franco states that the poet is an "outsider" in Spanish-American society. To reenforce this concept, she evokes among others the names of Lugones, Silva, Darío, and adds: "Long before writing, several of the modernists had already verified in the harsh terrain of experience the cruelties and dangers of a world governed by money and force." This declaration does not correspond wholly to reality, because Darío and Silva were precocious poets who began to write before reaching the age of experience. Besides, the fact that power or money predominates does not imply that the poet is an intruder, a stranger, alien to the society to which he belongs. In no period of Spanish-American cultural evolution has the poet been an "outsider." Quite the contrary: we have seen that from the first days of the formation of Spanish-American society the poet has participated in its vicissitudes or has taken a position against it in defense of justice. There have been various degrees of commitment to this position, from the inflamed satires of the colonial poets,

Ciro Alegría.

the devastating criticisms of Gonzáles Prada and the holocaust of Martí, to the nihilism of Casal and Silva. The modernist poets understood that poetry should fulfill a social function of esthetic education for the people. They did not withdraw from the world as claimed by the myth of the "ivory tower" spread by those who did not penetrate the meaning of modernism and thought it was only an innovation in form and a decadent art for initiates. Modernism was somewhat more complex: it was a search for American originality, a rhythmic revolution, a thematic renewal and its amplification on a universal scale, as well as the acceptance of modernity and an understanding of the future. Before his revelation of a new art, Darío at the age of sixteen was already the first civic poet of his country and had dedicated a thousand verses to exalting the book as one of the great human creations. Admired by several presidents of the republic, the poet was able to leave the land of his birth and discover new horizons. He did not suffer from loneliness, which sets him apart from Spanish poetry, nor did he intend to create a work of social content, although on several occasions he was the spokesman of the Spanish-American conscience in support of peace, hope, and progress. In Ruben's work, there are isolated examples of the four modes of social poetry—the historical, the national, the political, and the humanitarian—a classification made by Pedro Salinas. In the historical mode, the luminous poem *Tutecotzimí* stands out; in the national mode, the greater part of the work prior to *Azul, Tríptico de Nicaragua,* and other poems. The political and humanitarian modes were fused in various songs where Darío cried out for the elimination of violence. A year before his death, while passing through New York, he read at Columbia University his poem *Pax,* in which he presented a picture of Europe at war, and counselled: "Take honey and roses to the altar of peace. Peace to immense America. Peace in the name of God."

During the first decade of our century Spanish-American society underwent various changes due to penetration by opposed ideological trends: socialism, positivism, anticlerical liberalism, the new idealism. The socialist doctrine, utopian in its beginnings and later romantic, was transformed into scientific socialism and began to get organized with the assistance of the working class. In Paris the French Socialist party movement started with Jaurés in 1904; these were the days when Darío and other modernist poets were travelling through Europe. The Mexican Revolution, initiated by Madero in 1908, triumphed two years later and opened the era of socioeconomic transformation in which the rural class performed its sacrificial role in the civil conflict. The currents of ruralism and exaltation of the simple life appear in poetry with Lugones, Ramón López Velarde, Luis C. López, and Enrique González Martínez, who in a sonnet evocative of Verlaine's advice to "wring the neck of eloquence," asks that the same be done to the swan of "lying plumage," symbol of sumptuous exoticism and an aristocracy devoid of sensibility.

Rooted deeply in the social subsoil is the poetic production of Leopoldo Lugones, who declared himself a socialist from the very early period of *Las Montañas de Oro,* but in the last years of his life he abandoned that doctrine and proclaimed his sympathy for a diametrically opposite philosophical policy based on force. Nevertheless many of his poems constitute a song to the collective Argentine spirit, to the laborious life of the countryside. The teachings of Andrés Bello seem to have germinated in the work of Lugones, who offers us in great murals a picture of the pastures where the herds are fattened and of the wheat, "golden tribes" whose riches overflow in the "immensity of the pampa." New bucolic poems, georgics of the New World, the *Odas Seculares,* the *Estampas Rurales,* and the *Poemas Solariegos* represent a deliberate attempt to create an authentic poetry of the customs, the people, and the works of a free and active society. The immigrants, the farmers, millers, spinners, peasants, water-carriers, harp players, and other simple people march in review through the descriptive poems of Lugones, whose esthetic realisations qualify him as the greatest modernist poet after Darío and as the greatest poet of Spanish-American rural life.

In the field of social faith, Guillermo Valencia had a reversal of attitude similar to that of Lugones. In his youth Valencia wrote the poem *Anarkos*—in which he evokes the feats of the French anarchists—but in his maturity he paradoxically defended the most extreme conservative doctrines. The plastic quality and Parnassian coloring of his verses won him great popularity which brought him to occupy a seat in the Senate of Colombia.

Within much more limited horizons Luis Carlos López, a man from Cartagena de Indias, presented in the humorous gallery of his poetry the portraits of the principal personages of village society: the mayor, the unmarried girls, the priest, the talkative barber "who follows the Mass on his knees and speaks well of Voltaire." The work of the Cartagenian poet is an animated and burlesque little world, a "tropical comedy," as it has aptly been called.

In his poetry César Vallejo took a stand against official shibboleths. He interpreted the anguish of contemporary man threatened by all the perils of a society based on the usurpation of political and economic power. Vallejo's trajectory began with *Los Heraldos Negros,* a book of direct, bitter poetry, full of allusions to the daily life and habits of the Indians and mestizos in his native land. In his evocation of local people and things, the poet hits the mark with a typical mixture of colors: the "gay procession of lights," the muleteer "fabulously glazed with sweat," the "rural Romeo," the long narrow cart that "conveys a feeling of fasting," the vendor of lottery tickets who "comprises no one knows what aspect of God." Some time later, in the cell where he was imprisoned for his political activity, Vallejo wrote in a visceral, enigmatic idiom the poems of his second book, *Trilce;* with this step he initiated his ascent to the sphere of transcendental poetry. Notwithstanding his attitude of permanent rebellion against social injustices and solidarity with the oppressed classes, the poet did not condescend to introduce the facile elements of political proselytism into his poetry. In an article which he published in 1928—later included in his book *Literatura y Arte*—he said: "When Haya de la Torre underlined for me the need for artists to help revolutionary propaganda in America with their works I told him again that as a man I find his demand politically very significant and sincerely sympathize with it, but as an artist I do not accept any label or objective, my own or from outside, which even if backed by the best of intentions would subject my esthetic freedom to the service of this or that political propaganda."

This was the period when the doctrine of incorporating the Indians into the national life was diffused through the South American countries and the teachings of the Russian Revolution were flourishing. In the regions where there was a large Indian population, indigenous poets made their appearance. In Peru and Bolivia they went so far as to incorporate Quechua words into their poems, which limited the poetry to circulation within the very social class that it claimed to be rescuing. Furthermore, much of this class was made up of illiterates, which explains the slight response to the poetry of Alejandro Peralta, José Varallanos, or Gamaliel Churata, who were genuine advocates of the rise of the native class. Many other poets, readers of Tolstoy and Gorky, wrote poems to the oppressed and the revolution, in Chile, Argentina, and particularly in Mexico, where the atmosphere was stirred up by the "Strident" movement, which was represented by figures with a broad literary background such as Maples Arce. Mixed in with Stridency were some echoes of more advanced schools such as Creationism and Vanguardism. The truth was that the poets referred to were not Stridents but rather coiners of new metaphors whose essential element of surprise was oriented toward political reality. This was demonstrated by Maples Arce, who was able to catch in his poems some of the characteristic images of the social struggle. An example is the very well-known poem in which he compares the resplendence of the afternoon with a "bloody riot in the suburbs."

The Spanish Civil War broke out, arousing the conscience of the world and naturally that of the Spanish-American man. Poets like Vallejo, Neruda, Nicolás Guillén, and Octavio Paz wrote books in praise of the people and of the Republic. Others kept silent but maintained an attitude of sympathy for democratic principles. In this group were included the Mexicans Jaime Torres Bodet and José Corostiza, the Venezuelan Andrés Eloy Blanco, the Guatemalans Miguel Angel Asturias and Luis Cardoza Aragón. Their position has not prevented society in their respective countries from recognizing their high intellectual value as was proved by the fact that almost all of them have received the investiture of ambassador extraordinary. Torres Bodet, Blanco, and Corostiza have also held the high post of minister of foreign affairs.

Spanish-American poetry of the twentieth century—particularly from 1930—is not only the fruit of the diffusion of ideas; even more it tends to transform the society from which it proceeds. The poet is a social man who aspires to be a guide for his people and who helps the collective effort by publishing his works, despite certain adverse conditions that include book publishing, which is an underdeveloped industry in Spanish America. Its anachronistic efforts are not on a par with the high level of its literature nor with the growth of the modern city. The backwardness of the publishing business has been overcome in only one case, that of Neruda, who has found a large audi-

Jorge Luis Borges.

ence among the masses. Thirty years ago the poet confessed his proselytizing work in a hymn to his native country:

> I went forth throughout the earth to find you
>   sons,
> I went forth to tend the fallen with your name
>   of snow,
> I went forth to build a house with your pure
>   wood,
> I went forth to bring your star to the wounded
>   heroes.

Time would take care of turning these aspirations into reality. In every corner of Spanish America, "social poetry" found an echo which has not yet been extinguished and which seems consubstantial with the expression of the man of our time; but this poetry must not be confused with propagandistic poetry, which was fashionable around the middle of the century but has now disappeared definitely from the literary horizon. Today's social poetry is nourished by biological and ontological elements and represents a form of human experience.

In his book about culture and society which has been referred to before, Jean Franco comes to categorical conclusions, among them a very significant one which reinforces our thesis: "The greatest difference (between Latin American culture and that of the rest of the world) is not the obvious one of a diversity of race and landscape, but it is rather related to the fundamental ideas about the ultimate aims of art. While a considerable part of occidental art is principally interested in individual experience and in relations between the sexes, the best Latin-American literary works, and even its paintings, are preoccupied with greatest intensity with social ideals and phenomena." Later Jean Franco names a love for humanity as the most notable characteristic of Spanish-American poetry. These affirmations rest upon solid foundations. Our epoch is characterized by the awakening of the collective conscience and by the realization of a great adventure: the advance of humanity toward new horizons. This fact has been very clearly expressed by Torres Bodet, one Spanish-American poet shaken by a new humanism:

> We will not see the promised land
> nor will we taste its golden honey
> nor will its lamps of perfumed oil
> light our dreams in the night.

> . . . . .

> We will not see the promised land.
> We are born and die in the times of the Exodus.

The present era is one of transition. Man lives harried by all sorts of tensions, physical, spiritual, collective, and international. We traverse our period of time as if it were a vast inhospitable expanse, like the "sterile earth" of Eliot, at the end of which will be found the springs we have sighed for which will slake our thirst. At this crossroads of the most recent years, human society has begun to disdain poetry, considering it a useless exercise. The French critic Roger Caillois has pointed out with reason two contemporary phenomena: first, the ever more restricted role played by poetry, and second, the diminution of its importance relative to the culture as a whole. In reality these are two facets of the same problem of dehumanization, already more than half a century old, which finds its culmination in the new mechanical and economic myths. Society is experiencing the progressive decline of spiritual life, as some prophetic voices had announced in the nineteenth century. But this decline fortunately shows signs of being transitory. Man will reach the frontiers of the void and will turn in his tracks, using poetry as an instrument of salvation. It will be the end of the Exodus and the beginning of an era of universal understanding.

THE WRITER AND SOCIETY

Doris Meyer

SOURCE: An introduction to *Lives on the Line: The Testimony of Contemporary Latin American Authors,* edited by Doris Meyer, University of California Press, 1988, pp. 1-11.

[*Meyer is an American writer and educator, and the author of several books on Latin American literature. In the fol-* *lowing excerpt, she provides an overview of the role of the Latin American writer throughout history.*]

> We can say without irony or lack of respect that in order to speak solely of Latin American literature today one has to create an environment similar to that of an operating room with specialists who only look at the patient lying on the stretcher and the patient can be called novel or short story or poem. In all honesty I can say that the few times I have been in those operating theaters of literary criticism I have gone out into the street with a burning desire to drink wine in a bar and to look at girls in the buses. And each day that passes it seems more logical and necessary to approach literature—whether we are writers or readers—as one approaches the most basic encounters of one's existence, such as love or death, knowing that they form an inseparable part of the whole, and that a book begins and ends much before and much after its first and last word.

> —Julio Cortázar

The integral relationship between life and literature in Latin America would seem to be an obvious fact. Yet, all too often, the well-intentioned reader—especially the non-Latin American reader—lacks the information to make this relationship meaningful. To read Latin American literature today without a sense of the reality lived by its writers is to miss what makes it most vibrant and stimulating. And also to miss what Carlos Fuentes has called "an urgent literature" [in *Latin American Fiction Today: A Symposium,* Rose S. Minc, ed., 1980].

Before the first word and after the last comes the writer's experience as a self in a vivid, personal circumstance. This is the informing substance of literature, the subjective drama of human life. It is made up of incidents large and small, which are transposed by the imagination into creative texts. What differentiates contemporary Latin American literature from other world literatures is the nature of the relationship between the writer and the environment: the context in which he or she prepares for a literary calling, the milieu (cultural, political, socioeconomic) in which that vocation is exercised, and the awareness of self-as-writer in a given place and time. . . .

By their own testimony, Latin American writers, with few exceptions, confess to an engagement with reality that is *entrañable* or visceral, and it would seem that the vitality of their writing is connected to the urgency with which they perceive and experience that reality. According to Carlos Fuentes, the act of writing in Latin America is an act of faith:

> The paradox of writing on a continent where the majority is illiterate isn't so great; perhaps the writer knows he's writing to keep alive the connection with that prodigious cultural past that only rarely found correspondence in politics. Not to do it would be a way of admitting defeat, and one need only walk along the streets of Bogotá, Mexico City, or Lima to know that the quota of Latin American defeats is already filled.

More than anywhere else in the so-called Third World,

writers from Latin America have proven their willingness to put their lives on the line, both in the literary and the physical sense of the expression.

Today more than ever, the writer in Mexico, Central America, the Caribbean, and South America feels the critical nature of his role in society both as witness and social conscience—his "double responsibility," in the words of Uruguayan author Mario Benedetti, "to his art and to his surroundings" [in "Situación del escritor en América Latina," *Casa de las Américas* 45]. This attitude is not new, as excellent studies of Latin American intellectual history by Martin Stabb and Jean Franco, among others, have shown: since the nineteenth century, the writer in Latin America has not only addressed the most vital concerns of his society but has also traditionally wielded enormous influence as a man of letters in a society where men of politics were mistrusted. (My emphasis on the masculine gender is intentional here; with rare exception, women were excluded from positions of intellectual or political authority in a male-dominated Latin American culture until very recently.)

Deeply embedded in this sense of responsibility, since the last century as well, has been a desire to define a Latin American identity, both on a universal and a regional (national) level. Roberto González Echevarría has called it "the main theme of Latin American thought" [in *The Voice of the Masters: Writing and Authority in Modern Latin American Literature,* 1985], with its own "mythology of writing" in the essay as well as in the novel and poetry, that has yielded ambiguous results. What is not ambiguous is the intensity with which writers from Sarmiento and da Cunha to Paz and Cabrera Infante have expressed their fascination with Latin American identity. Indeed it has been an obsession born of unique historical, geographical, and cultural circumstances.

Briefly summarized, from the sixteenth to the nineteenth century, Latin America's history was that of a colonized continent ruled by a highly institutionalized and oppressive foreign empire—more so in the case of Spain than of Portugal, and thus the difference in Brazil's path to independence. Three hundred years of such occupation led to a "colonized mentality" much harder to overcome than that of the English colonies in North America. Geographical remoteness—between Latin American cities and between the continent and Europe or North America—and the hostility of the terrain produced a feeling of solitude and isolation. In addition the *mestizaje,* or mixture of Indian, European, and African races, has enriched the culture of Latin America but has made it much harder to define its values. Many essayists have pondered the sociological and psychological complexities related to these factors, particularly after the Spanish-American War of 1898, the Mexican Revolution of 1910, and the First World War served to heighten disillusionment with Eurocentric positivism, a popular philosophy at the turn of the century in Latin America.

The influence of the North American writer, Waldo Frank, and the Spanish philosopher, José Ortega y Gasset, cannot be underestimated in the increase in Latin American essays, from the 1930s on, relating to the quest for identity. In different ways, both men were persuasive in their call for self-knowledge and authenticity as a means to achieving a true Latin American destiny. Ortega, in particular, focused on the importance of individual experience in a given historical context—the interaction between self and circumstance as a basis for action. His example, interpreted on a nationally introspective level, spawned such works as Ezequiel Martínez Estrada's *X-ray of the Pampa* (1933), Gilberto Freyre's *Roots of Brazil* (1936), Octavio Paz' *The Labyrinth of Solitude* (1950), and Luis Cardozo y Aragón's *Guatemala, The Lines of Your Hand* (1955). Some of the most fertile mythology of Latin American culture was the legacy of these writers and their contemporaries to the younger generation of writers today. The problem of self and circumstance continues to feed the Latin American imagination with more urgency than ever before.

The period of the early 1960s to early 1970s (especially in reference to the novel) has come to be known as "the Boom in Latin American literature"—a popular expression that continues to resonate despite the efforts of some critics to silence it. . . . It was, without doubt, an explosive period in the history of literature in Latin America.

When the term was first used in 1966 in a Buenos Aires magazine, it was meant to highlight the success of the "new novel" in Latin America. The most remarkable aspect of this success was the international profile that certain authors and works had begun to achieve. In 1961, for example, Jorge Luis Borges (who had been publishing in

Lezama Lima.

Latin America for forty years prior to that) was awarded along with Samuel Beckett the prestigious Formentor Prize in Paris. The following year, Spain's Seix Barral Prize for the best novel written in Spanish went to Mario Vargas Llosa, the first Latin American recipient; thereafter, the prize was won by Latin Americans in all but two of the next seven years, making the names of Carlos Fuentes, Julio Cortázar, Gabriel García Márquez, and others, instant literary celebrities at home and abroad. In 1967, Guatemalan author Miguel Angel Asturias became the second Latin American (after Gabriela Mistral in 1945) to win the Nobel Prize for Literature, followed in 1971 by the Chilean poet Pablo Neruda. At the same time, García Márquez' *One Hundred Years of Solitude* (1967) was breaking international sales records for a Latin American work in translation.

Unquestionably, the quality of their writing justified the attention these authors received, but it is not the whole story. For the first time, a handful of Latin American writers were seen as commercially valuable and were treated as marketable commodities, with their own literary agents and publishing houses. Their works were publicized and reviewed on a scale never before accorded to Latin Americans, thus stimulating further book sales. True, this applied to less than a dozen authors—notably all male and all acquainted with one another, to the point that envious colleagues called them "the Mafia." Nonetheless, recognition from the literary elite in countries like Spain, France, and the United States—where Latin American literature had the reputation of being exotic and (since it was unknown) inferior—was a symbolic triumph for a continent of writers.

But the Boom was not just a literary phenomenon; political and economic developments gave it cohesion, and primary among them was the Cuban Revolution of 1959. More than the War of 1898 or even the Mexican Revolution, Fidel Castro's overthrow of the Batista dictatorship focused world attention on problems in Latin America and the forces in conflict there. It also raised the self-consciousness of Latin American intellectuals. Although divided in their reaction to a Marxist government in their midst, they were united in their awareness that Latin America was replacing Europe as a battleground for opposing political ideologies. In the early 1960s, many leftist writers supported the Castro regime, praising the Cuban ideal of social justice and condemning the autocratic heritage that had exploited Latin America since the Colonial period. A climate of free expression—despite known cases of government censorship—prevailed in Cuba in those years, following decades of repression. With the founding of the Casa de las Américas to promote Cuba's cultural relations with other countries in Latin America, Havana became a major center of intellectual exchange. The revolution seemed to engender a spirit of unity and optimism among many writers of the Boom generation who visited Cuba and took part in literary activities there.

After the invasion of Czechoslovakia in 1968, Castro aligned himself more closely with the Soviet Union. Communist ideology was more strictly enforced in Cuba, and the government increased its censorship of dissenting intellectuals, unequivocally reaffirming the orthodox view that art should serve the cause of the people's revolution. One incident, particularly explosive in its effect upon the Latin American intellectual community, involved the poet and journalist Heberto Padilla. Padilla had been a Castro supporter and foreign correspondent for the government newspaper, but he fell into disfavor for criticizing the regime. He was arrested, imprisoned, interrogated, and eventually forced to publicly retract his views and denounce his fellow writers (including his wife, Belkis Cuza Malé) in order to regain his freedom. This took place in 1971. That same year the Cuban Congress of Education and Culture officially defined the limits of tolerance of artistic freedom and excluded "pseudo-leftist bourgeois intellectuals" from taking part in the culture of the revolution.

The "Padilla affair" produced widespread disillusionment among Latin American writers who had openly or tacitly backed Castro. Jose Donoso, in *The Boom in Spanish American Literature: A Personal History* (1972), suggests that the discord it engendered tolled the death knell of the Boom. Controversy about the role of literature in a revolution and the nature and extent of a writer's involvement had been brewing for years; between 1969 and 1971 the pages of the Uruguayan journal *Marcha* recorded an ideological debate between several prominent authors. Another blow to the Boom was dealt by the economic recession of the 1970s, which forced many publishing houses to close. Even more disruptive was the return of right-wing political regimes to intellectually active countries like Argentina, Brazil, Uruguay, and Chile. (The CIA's role in toppling Chilean president Salvador Allende confirmed the worst fears of many leftist writers who were also dismayed by Castro's persecution of Padilla.) The diaspora of artists and intellectuals began in earnest. As early as 1968, political intrusion put an end to the effective influence of *Mundo Nuevo,* a literary journal edited in Paris by the influential critic Emir Rodríguez Monegal. *Mundo Nuevo* had published Boom writers and brought their works to international attention. Its demise, and the general deterioration of the cultural atmosphere in Latin America in the early 1970s, signaled the advent of a new era of urgency in Latin American letters.

In 1972, Carlos Fuentes wrote the following in the journal *Triquarterly:*

> To write on Latin America, from Latin America, for Latin America, to be a witness of Latin America in action or in language is now, will be more and more, a revolutionary fact. Our societies don't want witnesses. They don't want critics. And each writer, like each revolutionary, is in some way that: a man [*sic*] who sees, hears, imagines and says; a man who denies we live in the best of worlds.

Male or female, the Latin American writer of the 1970s or 1980s knows both the history and reality of his society's institutional penchant for discouraging free speech or critical thinking of any kind. The Catholic Church, responsible for the spread of culture during the Colonial period, also cast a long Inquisitorial shadow across the Atlantic: it regulated the importation of books and set the tone for all future intellectual endeavors. Colonial censorship took many forms: from the burning of Mayan bark-paper "books," effectively silencing an entire indigenous culture, to the cloistering of women's minds, virtually denying female participation in the power structure. Overall, its effect was to limit the reading public to an educated few, whose literary taste was urbane and elitist; writers who weren't also statesmen or churchmen were suspect, or worse, ignored.

Over the centuries, the writer's situation has changed for the better. Yet it still remains a risky venture on many fronts. Less than twenty years ago, Mario Vargas Llosa of Peru—who, like many others, began his writing career as a journalist—observed that "a few have managed to conquer the hostility, the indifference, the scorn that exists in our countries toward literature, and they wrote, published and were even read. It is true that not all could be killed off by starvation, oblivion or ridicule. But these fortunates constituted the exception" [in "Fate and the Mission of the Writer in Latin America," *Haravec* 4]. In Brazil, the situation was equally dismal, according to literary historian Afrânio Countinho: "Brazilian literary people are scattered among heterogeneous activities or are prisoners of public administration, where everything conspires against the spirit" [*An Introduction to Literature in Brazil*, 1969]. In the face of chronic illiteracy, cultural isolation, and economic hardship so severe that even the populace who reads can rarely afford to buy books, Latin American writers have been quick to acknowledge the Quixotesque quality of trying to succeed in their profession—despite the success of the Boom. In the 1970s, in authoritarian countries, their very lives were in danger: many writers were imprisoned, tortured, and "disappeared" under regimes more brutal than the Catholic Inquisition. Violence from both the right and the left essentially foreclosed any possibility of a normal intellectual existence, and emigration to neighboring countries—to Europe or the United States—increased. For those remaining, internal exile and self-censorship could be even more damaging than voluntary or involuntary exodus.

And yet this very inhospitable climate has bred a contemporary writer—male and female—who is extraordinarily attached to his homeland, and far more inclined than his European or United States counterpart to discuss the writer's role in society. Whether living at home or in exile, he or she is more likely to acknowledge a basic expectation among the Latin American public: that the writer's vocation entails a moral imperative to speak out on issues of national concern—or when this is not feasible, to encode political dissent into the pages of "creative" literature. At times, the pressure to voice a commitment on the sociopolitical level is strongest from a writer's peers—generally those of Marxist persuasion. Authors who have chosen to avoid politics (rarely possible in the course of a Latin American life) have often been disparaged for their "aloofness" or "elitism." Jorge Luis Borges, whose life was completely absorbed by the company of books, was one of those repeatedly criticized by leftists, some of whom suggested that by virtue of his preference for European literature, he wasn't even Latin American. Nowadays, such manifest xenophobia is the exception rather than the rule

among Latin American intellectuals, who freely acknowledge their indebtedness to American films and rock music as much as to Sartre or Kafka. But the xenophobic does represent a current of thought in Latin America, going back as far as the turn of the century when nationalists and universalists took sides against each other.

It is interesting to note that women authors have remained outside many of these literary-political debates until recent years, due in part to their marginalized status in both arenas. A woman's personal struggle to become a writer was often lonelier and fraught with more obstacles than a man's; her chances of being taken seriously as a professional, much smaller. Because of her gender experiences, she tended either to immerse herself in a private world of literature (Clarice Lispector and Victoria Ocampo, for example) with primarily male mentors (for lack of a female network of support), or she identified strongly with the oppressed (Rosario Castellanos and Elena Poniatowska) and devoted her works to their cause. Today, women authors are becoming more politically active and their works reflect a wider range of personal involvement.

Beyond the political sphere, the larger profile accorded women's writing in Latin America has focused attention on another side of human experience and has thereby called into question certain assumptions about societal values in a historical context. Because women's voices were not heard publicly for several centuries, their role in private and public life remained obscured by patriarchal dominance, but today this is no longer the case. Women are writing about the problems of being female in Latin America, and their words have a healthy, subversive resonance. Old mythologies regarding male and female relationships are undergoing reevaluation, and many male authors have responded with new awareness on their part. As forgotten works by women authors are brought to light, the true picture of life in Latin America—both past and present—will emerge and force a revision (in both senses of the word) of Latin American social and cultural history.

The integral relationship between life and literature in Latin America would seem to be an obvious fact. To read Latin American literature today without a sense of the reality lived by its writers is to miss what makes it most vibrant and stimulating.

— Doris Meyer

In the 1980s the Central American crisis has captured world attention in the way Cuba did twenty years earlier, stimulating a renewed cohesiveness among Latin American intellectuals. Most decry the Reagan administration's intervention in the regional affairs of Nicaragua, El Salvador, and Honduras. Even writers who have been skeptical or critical of Sandinista policies are calling for a Latin American solution to the conflict. At the same time, the reestablishment of elected democracies in southern-cone countries such as Argentina and Uruguay has brought a new and potentially disruptive intellectual crisis. Many expatriate writers are returning, or contemplating a return, to their homelands after years in exile. They are finding, however, that the process of *desexilio* (or "disexile"), as Mario Benedetti has named it, can be as traumatic as the original decision to flee repression; the temptation toward reproach—on the part of those who left and those who stayed—must be tempered, says Benedetti, by an effort toward understanding.

Less apt to grasp at quick solutions, today's Latin American writers concentrate instead on asking questions fundamental to their continent's future. They are probing the implications of dependency and underdevelopment, and questioning the viability of inherited myths and cultural assumptions, including the notions of "modernity" and "progress." The very sense of "otherness" that brought despair to an earlier generation of Latin American writers is, in the words of Carlos Fuentes, what makes for "an eccentric culture"—indebted to the Mayan *Popul Vuh* as well as to the Judeo-Christian Bible—and thus potentially richer for its cultural *mestizaje*. . . .

Latin American writers are affirming a plurality of cultures within a larger sense of being "Latin American": Pablo Neruda's love affair with Spanish ("It's a fine language we inherited from the fierce conquistadors"); Augusto Roa Bastos's effort to ransom the Paraguayan-Guaraní "ancestral voice" ("A language without writing that in another time contained within itself the very essence of the soul-word"); and Nélida Piñon's travels through "the archipelagos of language"—before she could arrive at the conviction that "[g]uided by language and its historical process, the Brazilian writer must learn that mythologies and intrigues were created in such abundance in this country that they can never be exhausted or diminished." For despite similarities in historical background, what defines the Latin American identity is not one but many ways of being rooted in Latin American reality. And each writer, with each book, has the possibility of writing that identity based on his or her own experience or "reading" of it, through the medium of language.

Fred P. Ellison

SOURCE: "The Writer," in *Continuity and Change in Latin America,* edited by John J. Johnson, Stanford University Press, 1964, pp. 79-100.

[*Ellison is an American educator and the author of several books on Latin American literature. In the following essay, he evaluates the role and status of the writer in Latin American society and politics.*]

The writers of Latin America are, like their counterparts everywhere, intellectuals, who, in Edward A. Shils' definition, are particularly "enquiring, and desirous of being in frequent communion with symbols which are more general than the immediate concrete situations of everyday life, and remote in their reference in both time and place"

["The Intellectuals and the Powers," *Comparative Studies in Society and History,* I (Oct. 1958)]. Such men have social influence out of proportion to their relatively small number. They may be members of the liberal professions, educators, priests, administrators, lawmakers, historians, writers, artists, or musicians. Here, attention will be directed to the writer as creator of *belles lettres,* be he poet, novelist, dramatist, or essayist.

The last category may include philosophers, educators, historians, political writers, journalists, and others not ordinarily associated with *belles lettres,* provided they have literary style—that is, a way of writing that pretends to beauty. Stylistic distinction is highly valued in Latin America. The pervasive influence of literature and related stylistic preoccupations on Brazilian education has been noted by the sociologist Fernando de Azevedo: "Literature is but one of the elements of general culture; but, because of the specific conditions of our formation, which was almost exclusively literary, it was the first, the strongest, the most persistent, the most expressive element of our culture" [*A Cultura brasileira,* 1944]. K. H. Silvert has emphasized style in speaking of the entire Latin American intellectual community: "To be counted in this prestigious company the individual must manipulate ideas of a philosophical nature and communicate them in an artistic fashion" [*The Conflict Society: Reaction and Revolution in Latin America,* 1961].

Here, however, the emphasis will be not on evaluation of individual works or the creative process, but on the sociology of the writers: their social provenance, their economic situation, and their status and role in society, particularly in politics. Literature, after all, is a social institution, and its creators are members of society. Admittedly there are inherent limitations in such a generalized approach, especially in a field so vast and relatively unexplored.

The existence of a national group consciousness among writers is attested not only by the statements of literary historians and sociologists, but also by the existence of numerous nationwide professional organizations, such as the Sociedad Argentina de Escritores, the Asociación Venezolana de Escritores, and the União Brasileira de Escritores. It is not uncommon for the writers to compare their own national standing with that of their opposite numbers in the United States. From such comparisons emerges a generic profile: the Latin American man of letters has high social prestige as an artist, but is ill rewarded for his creativity; he may, as a writer, hold the highest positions of public trust, usually as a result of a well-developed political aptitude, but in most cases does not enjoy independent professional status as a writer; he is frequently entrusted with the loftiest educational, political, and cultural responsibilities, and even more frequently must live in exile, see his books burned, or face arrest or economic reprisals for his views.

Continental group consciousness is more tenuous. Latin American writers know each other's work less well than one might think, and there is truth in the quip that the concept of Latin America exists only in the United States, where "Latin American studies" are pursued. The Argen-

Juan Jose Arreola.

tine novelist Jorge Luis Borges offers this explanation: "We feel that we are very much alike in the various regions of Latin America, and for that reason, the work of a writer from a given region does not arouse much curiosity among the writers of another region. . . . On the other hand, if we read European writers we think we're going to find something different" [quoted by Rodolfo Vinacua in "Borges on Literature," *Américas*, XIII (Dec. 1961)].

Improved transportation and communication are changing the situation, but even now it is possible to speak of a continental spirit, to refer, as Alberto Zum Felde has done, to the "continental literary unity upon which Spanish American criticism is based." He sees this as a consequence of the countries' common language, common cultural and historical origins, and common concern with what he calls "telluric" problems [*Indice crítico de la literatura hispanoamerica: los eusayistas,* 1954]. The Mexican critic José Luis Martínez has justly observed that "the poetry, drama, and novel of the countries of America have crossed their own borders to make us conscious of the peculiar meaning of their ways of life, their ideas, and even their dark infamies; and because of these worthy efforts at friendly interchange, it may be possible to speak of the existence of an American consciousness" [*Problemas literarios,* 1955]. Literary historians have begun to include Brazilian literature in their panoramas, and since the last presidential term of Getulio Vargas, Spanish American writers are being studied in Brazilian universities.

The radical left, especially the Communists, seek to encourage this latent continental consciousness among the writers of Latin America through writers' congresses, publications, and so forth. A significant gathering of Cuban and Latin American writers was the First Congress of Cuban Writers and Artists, held in Havana on August 17-22, 1961. On its agenda were: "The creative responsibility of the writers and artists vis-à-vis the Revolution and the Cuban people"; "Exchanges, contacts, and cooperation of Cuban artists and intellectuals with those of Latin America and all other countries, in defense of the people's culture, national sovereignty, and universal peace"; and "Organization problems of Cuban writers and artists." Among the principal speakers were the poet Nicolás Guillén, the novelist Alejo Carpentier, and the critics José A. Portuondo and Roberto Fernández Retamar. In his speech, Carpentier commented on the sense of community that existed among many of the Latin American writer-politicians in the nineteenth century, their intercommunication and shared values, especially their hatred for Spain. He chided present-day writers for their failure to take political action in concert. "We Cubans are more like the nineteenth-century intellectuals," he said, proclaiming a national and hemispheric group spirit he hopes to see increase throughout Latin America.

Changes in educational practice inevitably have been reflected in literature. Certain literary concerns identifiable with nationaiism in nineteenth-century Brazil can be attributed directly to the growing prestige of Brazilian educational institutions. Because of its Jesuit heritage the Brazilian educational system long maintained an aura of humanism and aristocratic values, which was reflected in Brazilian literature until quite recently. Since the 1920's and early 1930's intellectual activity has taken on a distinctly anti-traditional and anti-academic tone, in response to major social and economic changes. Speaking of Brazil, Fernando de Azevedo said that new social forces "contribute to breaking the hold of the traditional school, inaugurating . . . an era of restlessness, and the tapping of sources of the most modern and singularly fecund inspiration to the literary milieu. Now, it is not through its direct influence, but outside the school, and in opposition to it, that criticism, fiction, poetry, and the theater revive and develop" [*A Literatura no Brasil,* 1956]. And elsewhere in Latin America, as a consequence of the University Reform movement, members of the working classes and lower-middle sectors receive higher education and join the literary force.

Speaking at the Congress of Cuban Writers and Artists, [in 1961] Nicolás Guillén berated the colonial system of education in Cuba for what he called its stifling effects on literature and general culture and its alienation of the writers. He promised that the new Marxist-Leninist system would be "of positive value for the intellectual worker. Ahead of him looms a reality different from the one in which he lived until now—a reality not only different, but superior, because his work will stop being profitable principally for the capitalist, who under other regimes, in diverse and subtle ways, lives off the intellectual production of others."

In his speech Guillén reflected the Marxist thesis that intellectuals cannot be identified with a single social class. Similarly, the sociologist Karl Mannheim holds that intellectual activity is now the domain of "a social stratum which is to a large degree unattached to any social class, and which is recruited from an increasingly inclusive area of social life." While this may be true in Europe, Silvert has accurately observed that, socially, the Latin American intellectuals "are invariably rooted in middle or upper classes." In literature, the distinction between middle and upper classes was not important, for many aristocrats of Spanish America who made important contributions to letters in the nineteenth century defended the liberalism of the middle groups.

During the nineteenth and early twentieth centuries in Brazil, literature was primarily the province of the aristocracy; but especially during the reign of Dom Pedro II, himself an amateur writer and generous patron, writers from the middle sectors profited from literature's great prestige. Until the end of World War I, the rising group of writers from the middle sectors tended to emulate the literary values of the elite that were perpetuated by the Brazilian Academy of Letters. Many Brazilian writers still represent traditional ruling families who, if no longer affluent, own distinguished names. The situation in Chile, however, is more typical of Latin America; there "literature is no longer the province of the ruling class; . . . it no longer has anything to do with military and political power; and . . . there is now a lively sensitivity, an alert literary consciousness that contemplates its own universe, whether to express disapproval or delight" ["The Writers of Chile," *Américas,* XIV (Oct. 1962)]. Though literature itself may have little direct connection with political power, literary men may have a great deal, as will be shown later. Suffice it to say here that we can expect fresh and often strong points of view from the writers of the lower-middle strata.

The current trend toward professionalism among writers reflects new economic circumstances. Literary men in the nineteenth century undoubtedly had little professional status *qua* writers; literary activity was a sideline of politicians, journalists, members of the liberal professions, and so forth. There was prestige, glory, and power to be had through writing, but little pecuniary reward and hence no professional status. Men of letters belonged to the aristocracy and upper middle classes, which monopolized positions of affluence. Many writers treated creative writing as an incidental activity to be pursued until they became established as lawyers, politicians, or bureaucrats. In the view of Brazilian critic Nelson Werneck Sodré, only with the rise of the middle class in Brazil at the close of the nineteenth century did it become "possible to distinguish literary activity from some of its earlier nonspecific manifestations, in which it appeared as an ornamental or auxiliary element. Among the lists of authors, it is possible henceforward to separate those who utilized the spoken or written word merely as a vehicle, within specialized and even professional activities, from those who used it for artistic creation" [*Historia da literatura brasileira: seus fundamentos económicos,* 1960]. There were similar developments in the Spanish-speaking nations, led by the Nicara-

guan poet Rubén Darío. Literature now ranked with diplomacy and politics as a career, though there were still few literary men who could support themselves by their writing.

This remains true even today, despite the demand of a wider literate public and technological advances. Contemporary writers are perhaps more sensitive to their economic plight than ever, since a good many come from the lower classes and lack the support available to their more well-to-do predecessors. The following is typical of complaints heard throughout Latin America:

> Writing is not remunerative work. It becomes impossible for intellectuals to concentrate the best of their energies on such work, since they must cling to bureaucratic and other jobs for the sake of their own livelihood. As a rule Brazilian writers are dilettantes—that is, they compose their novels and poems in moments stolen from their normal rest, often by dint of anti-sleep stimulants and gallons of bitter black coffee. [Consuelo dos Reis e Mello, "Resposta sôbre literatura," *Leitura,* XIX, No. 57 (March 1962); and her "Remuneração de escritor," *Leitura* XIX, No. 50 (Aug. 1961)]

The high illiteracy rate, prohibitive costs of paper and equipment, ineffective distribution of books (especially to the interior), the low purchasing power of the populace, and inflation all contribute to the financial insecurity of the writer. Recent studies of the book trade in Argentina, Chile, Peru, Colombia, and Brazil confirm the jeopardy of writing as a career. And fragmentary research on the reading public in Rio de Janeiro, where the rate of illiteracy is less than 10 per cent, established that books are "strange and unknown objects to the vast majority of *cariocas* [residents of Rio]" ["Por que lemos tão pouco?" *Para todos,* Ano I, No. 7 (Aug. 1956)].

Propaganda of the extreme left has been aimed at the writers' dissatisfaction with their economic situation, and it has stressed defense of professional requirements. The Communists have been alert in subsidizing writers whose works have propaganda value, with translation royalties and expense-paid trips to Russia, China, and other Iron Curtain countries. The United States, too, would like to play host to Latin American writers, but, to our embarrassment, immigration regulations have barred many highly respected writers suspected of Communist sympathies. The exclusion of novelist José Lins do Rego, who wanted to visit his daughter in Washington, D.C., caused a furor in Brazil, where critics have always considered him politically moderate.

As one might expect, there are signs of an eventual improvement in the writers' financial situation—expanding mass media, government subsidies, and professional movements in Brazil, Argentina, Venezuela, and Cuba. The União Brasileira de Escritores, for example, is working toward the adoption by the publishing industry of advanced methods of marketing and distribution, and toward legislation protecting writers' contract and copyright interests. The federal government supports the writers' organization and a similar association of Brazilian playwrights.

The French tradition of state patronage has undoubtedly served as a model in many Latin American countries. The governments of Venezuela, Colombia, Ecuador, Mexico, and Brazil have sponsored publications, the building and maintenance of theaters, libraries, archives, and academies, as well as cultural campaigns designed to enhance the professional status of the writer. But most intellectuals find the government's support insufficient, particularly those who favor state intervention in many areas of national life. The writers' economic well-being has not been substantially improved by these state-supported measures, though their indirect influence on culture should not be underestimated.

Considerable expansion in education and mass communications characterizes almost all Latin America. One might expect the writers to have benefited from the expansion of the reading public and from the financial rewards of radio, television, and mass-circulation newspapers and magazines. This is not necessarily the case, however, to judge from the apprehension of, and outright hostility to, the newer media on the part of many noted writers. Despite the possibilities of increased earnings, such writing lacks the value and prestige associated with more traditional forms.

Journalism deserves special mention, for now, as in the past, it is closely tied to literature. The distinguished critic Baldomero Sanín Cano proudly called himself a "journalist." Rubén Darío and many of his followers, though poets of the most refined taste, were also newspaper correspondents, columnists, and editorial writers. This is partly because, as one critic notes, "The newspaper continues to be the ordinary citizen's library as well as news headquarters. Almost invariably literary works have appeared in newspapers long before their advent in book form" [Martin E. Erickson, "Trends in Central American Literature," in *Intellectual Trends in Latin America,* 1945]. Brazilian critics have debated the question and are apparently agreed that journalism is in many respects a literary activity.

> In Brazil, beyond a doubt, those who have created the most legitimate and authentic literature were, are, and will always be journalists. In a land without cultural periodicals, the literary supplements of the great Rio newspapers are true literary journals. They have, for example, an extraordinary importance and usefulness, and, with contributors of the highest category, are truly precise and faithful mirrors of Brazil's cultural panorama. [Peregrino Junior, "Alocução," *Curso de jornalismo,* 1958]

While writers have yet to make a satisfactory adjustment to their changing social and economic circumstances, they continue in their traditional role as the creative and critical conscience of society. Success in serving the nation as intellectuals and artists compensates for shabby treatment in the market place. John Gillin observes that it is their quest for ultimate values and ideals "that in large measure makes life worth living for many Latin Americans of middle status" ["Some Signposts for Policy," in *Social Change in Latin America Today*]. The *pensadores* carry on the tradition of nineteenth-century political theorists and social

philosophers (Simón Bolívar, José Bonifácio, Esteban Echeverría, Domingo Faustino Sarmiento, Joaquín Montalvo, José Martí) in their concern for national and continental problems. The Mexican government has recently summoned the philosopher and writer Leopoldo Zea to formulate the goals of the Partido Revolucionario Institucional, and the poet (and industrialist) Augusto Frederico Schmidt received a similar commission from President Juscelino Kubitschek. In government positions of great responsibility and trust, one finds distinguished poets, novelists, and essayists. As Gillin notes, "They receive such posts not only because of their prestige, but also because of a genuine belief that their success in aesthetic pursuits fits them for posts of national responsibility and leadership."

Writers have served not only democratically constituted governments, but also totalitarian ones. As Zum Felde pointed out, "The difference between the 'enlightened' dictatorships and the simply 'barbarous' ones is defined by the attitude of the intellectual minorities with respect to them." In these terms, Porfirio Díaz and Guzmán Blanco would qualify as enlightened and Anastacio Somoza and Rafael Trujillo as barbarous. Clearly, the majority of intellectuals have stood against the most benighted dictatorships. They may have relaxed their usual scruples in the case of Getulio Vargas, himself a literary man of sorts. In his dictatorial phase, Vargas and his infamous DIP (Departamento de Imprensa e Propaganda) burned books and jailed writers of the extreme left; but at the same time he did much to support the writing profession, founding, for example, the Instituto Nacional do Livro (National Book Institute). The dictator Juan Perón "felt the immediate necessity of having his own ideology, with a respectable philosophical basis, and he surrounded himself with a team of university men under the leadership of Father Benítez in order to create a new political doctrine, which they called *justicialismo,* derived from 'social justice' " [Francisco Miró Quesada, "The University and Society," *Americás,* XII (Dec. 1960)].

But most dictators, including Perón, have regarded writers as enemies, and have sought to destroy or restrict their time-honored role as social critics with a heightened sense of responsibility. Censorship, the closing of universities, book burning, arrest, imprisonment, and exile are familiar hazards in mid-twentieth-century Latin America. For Arturo Torres-Rioseco, "the greatest obstacle to the development of art and literature in Spanish America is the lack of freedom" [*Ensayos sobre literatura latinoamericana,* 1958]. As long as they are not denied freedom of expression, the writers of Latin America may be expected to contribute to national development in its broadest sense.

Naturally, writers have been active agents of intellectual progress, and have shown a remarkable spirit of innovation. The Spanish critic Ricardo Gullón has related Hispanic letters (we can include Portuguese) to the whole complex of new forms and attitudes in western art that arose between 1890 and the beginning of World War II, to which he applies the term *modernismo,* giving it broader significance (somewhat like Renaissance or Enlightenment) than it had in the earlier—and still-current notion limiting it to the Parnassian-symbolist school. *Modernismo* reflects a widespread quickening of creative vitality, and of receptivity to cultural currents flowing between Europe and America. This concept embraces many disparate and often conflicting artistic movements that have arisen in the last half century, and reconciles such disparate works as the subjective symbolist novel and the naturalist novel of social protest, the escapist poems of a Leopoldo Lugones and the social poetry of a Drummond de Andrade. The fundamental attitudes in modernist literature derive from the unstable, revolutionary ferment of romanticism, and the humanitarian and more tolerant reformist ideals of liberalism. These ideals are expressed in the modernists' "opposition to all forms of exploitation of man by man, and to all political repression"—opposition exemplified by Martí, Unamuno, Díaz Mirón, Valle Inclán, and Antonio Machado.

Because of the preciosity and taste for the ornate of some early modernists, literary historians and critics (as well as many "vanguardist" writers of the 1920's) overlooked their relation to more conventional revolutionary currents. Exoticism and *indigenismo* are, as Gullón observes, forms of escapism that reveal deep dissatisfaction with the late-nineteenth-century world. These escapist tendencies, like the anti-bourgeois sentiments that accompanied them, were assimilated by avant-garde movements in Europe and America during and immediately following the First World War. In the present context, the writers wish to transform society and popularize the best new cultural forms among their compatriots through the education art provides.

The writers' leadership and prestige stem from their traditional role as men of uncommon vision placed at the service of important national and hemispheric causes. Their special status is due to the rich cultural life of the middle sectors, which, as Gillin notes, "has an aesthetic tone which middle-class North Americans of today do not often permit themselves." Outstanding characteristics of Latin American culture are the persistent esteem for humanistic education, the high regard for poetry and poets, and the comparatively widespread interest in reading literary criticism in newspapers. The public deference shown writers is well illustrated by the success of two Bahian writers, Jorge Amado and Luis Viana Filho, in having writers exempted from the income tax on royalties. In short, as Frank Tannenbaum puts it, the writer in Latin America has "a basis for leadership in the nation which is both admirable and unique. It is admirable because he is independent, and unique because he cannot be deprived of the following that he has, or lose it except by ceasing to write and publish" ["Toward an Appreciation of Latin America," in *The United States and Latin America,* 1959].

This sort of leadership has been exercised by a few Latin American writers who, according to Tannenbaum, "are almost household words among the literate people in the entire area, particularly in the eighteen Spanish-speaking countries." His list comprises names from both the humanities and social sciences: Alfonso Reyes, Germán Arciniegas, Mariano Picón Salas, Rómulo Gallegos, Luis Alberto Sánchez, Gilberto Freyre, José Luis Romero, and Fernando Ortiz. To these should be added the late Nobel Prize winner Gabriela Mistral, Jorge Luis Borges, Pablo Neruda, and Jorge Amado. With few exceptions, all these writers have achieved both artistic excellence and consequent European recognition.

This high estimate of the writer's social prestige is not quite unanimous. The most vigorous dissenter is Francisco Ayala, a Spanish writer who has lived in many Latin American countries and in the United States. He laments the disappearance of a "qualified" elite of intellectuals and authors, which in the nineteenth century helped shape the values of the ruling classes, and blames "mass society" for the absence of any group that exercises authority by virtue of its particular qualifications. He concludes that "the proportions and relations within the social framework have been altered to such an extent that [the writer's] figure, once obvious in the foreground, has become insignificant and marginal" [*El Escritor en la sociedad de masas,* 1956]. Latin America is not the only place, of course, where writers, as bearers of a humanistic tradition, find themselves opposed to many values of mass society and are afraid of losing identity, prestige, and influence.

Writers continue to wield actual political power through public office and party activity, and exert considerable political pressure through their writings. The majority of literary men in Brazil now belong to left-of-center parties. The same is true of most other Latin American countries. However, since there are writers of almost every political persuasion, and precise information is wanting, generalizations on this subject are necessarily impressionistic and tentative.

In nineteenth-century Latin America, writers by and large supported progressive constitutional regimes, opposed the usurpation of power by force, and advocated the extension of social and political liberties. A few rightists—Andrés Bello, Gabriel Moreno, Rafael Núçez, and Carlos Reyes—justified conservative or authoritarian governments. The political role of writers was a great one. In the apt words of Peruvian Luis Benjamín Cisneros, "In Spanish America, where the republican form of government gives each individual a direct role in political life, where truly imperishable literature is still in the process of gestation and therefore subject to the most heightened passions, names abound to confirm this observation. In the entire chain of republics that extend along the Pacific, there is hardly a literary name that is not at the same time a political name" [Cited by Emilio Carilla, *El Romanticismo en Hispanoamérica,* 1958]. Throughout Latin America there were writer-politicians or politician-writers in positions of power and leadership. The literary historian Pedro Henríquez Ureña gives an incomplete list of some thirty writers who were presidents of their respective countries in the nineteenth and early twentieth centuries.

He laments that the Cuban writer and political idealist José Martí was "the last of the great Spanish American men of letters who were at the same time political leaders" [*Las Corrientes literarias en la América Hispánica,* 1954]. In his view the so-called modernists—e.g., Darío, Ricardo Jaimes Freyre, Amado Nervo—accepted a "division of labor" and by choice abandoned politics, at least during the first twenty years of this century.

Though perhaps attenuated, the tradition of writers' intervention in political affairs clearly was not broken even among the followers of Darío. Indeed, some of his contemporaries were deeply involved in social movements. For example, the literary successors of Justo Sierra and Antonio Caso in Mexico were challenging positivism, and the little band led by José Ingenieros in Argentina represented an awakening interest in dialectical materialism. Gonzales Prada, as both man of letters and political leader, contributed to the rise of the indigenous Marxist movement of the Peruvian José Mariátegui and his Amauta group.

Later developments that involved writers in politics were the Mexican Revolution, the beginnings of the APRA movement in Peru, the rise of the Socialist party in Ecuador, the pre-revolutionary ferment of the 1920's in Brazil—to which the "Semana de Arte Moderna" group in São Paulo and the Regionalist movement of Gilberto Freyre in the Northeast are both related—and the demand for social reform from every corner of the continent during the economic crisis of 1929-30.

Pedro Henríquez Ureña insists that though the writers since 1920 "have begun to return little by little to their traditional course of participation in public affairs," they have had only limited success in achieving political office, mainly because as revolutionists they challenge the established order. "Men of letters who take part in our public life rarely manage to get into government: they belong to the opposition, and customarily spend much more time in prison than in office, not to mention life in exile, whether forced or voluntary." Even when their parties achieve power, the writers may hold points of view more advanced than those of their own party. The election in 1963 of the novelist Juan Bosch as president of a free Dominican Republic, as well as the presidencies held in recent years by the novelist Rómulo Gallegos (Venezuela), the poet and essayist Natalicio González (Paraguay), and the political essayist Juan José Arévalo (Guatemala), indicates the continuing role of literary men in high office—and the difficulties they face once they achieve it.

It is difficult to measure the extent of political influence exerted by poets, novelists, playwrights, and essayists in their nonpolitical writings. Certainly most of them joined, if they did not anticipate, the demand for social reform that has been constantly heard since the Mexican Revolution. Though there are many writers whose work has no connection with politics, political import, reforming zeal, and the pursuit of social objectives are fundamental characteristics of Latin American literature.

The high point in combative writing, especially propaganda novels, seems to have been reached in the 1930's, when "socialist realism" in the novel and proletarian literature of all sorts flourished. The battle between literary right and left was perhaps fiercest among the novelists of Ecuador, with the left virtually eliminating the opposition before the war. Literature was closely identified with political participation, as the names Enrique Gil Gilbert, Joaquín Gallegos Lara, Alfredo Pareja Díez-Canseco, Jorge

Icaza, and Humberto Salvador testify. An extensive literature in Mexico dealt with the problems of the Revolution, after Mariano Azuela and Martín Luis Guzmán had shown the way. Every Latin American country could offer similar lists, particularly Brazil, where in the 1930's a vital literary movement was headed by the Northeastern novelists José Lins do Rego, Graciliano Ramos, Jorge Amado, Rachel de Queiroz, and José Américo de Almeida. All these writers represented left-of-center political philosophies, and wrote works full of implied or explicit social protest. They wrote in behalf of the Negro, the rural and urban workers, the drought-stricken *sertanejos* (backlands people). They surveyed the social and economic consequences of the latifundia system, which came under attack from a number of directions. And elsewhere in Brazil other voices echoed their protests.

In Brazil as elsewhere in Latin America, proletarian literature continues to be produced, but writers and critics have generally forsaken it for less explicitly propagandistic forms. This generation has been just as relentless in attacking the established order, but the visions of poets, novelists, and playwrights have taken an intensely poetic form that reflects new aesthetic preoccupations. One thinks of parts of Pablo Neruda's *Canto general,* of Graciliano Ramos' *Memórias do cárcere,* Miguel Angel Asturias' *El Señor Presidente,* Carlos Fuentes' *La Región más transparente,* Jorge Amado's *Gabriela, cravo e canela.*

Though the aesthetic value of this literature may have increased, its usefulness as propaganda has doubtless declined. The political and social influence of twentieth-century writing is also limited by the vast gap between the men of letters and the general reading public, not to mention the illiterate masses. Brazilian critics trace the phenomenon to the rise of the Parnassian and symbolist movements at the end of the nineteenth century. Even authors of proletarian novels have lamented that they would never be read by those they were intended to serve. The Peruvian critic Augusto Salazar Bondy has recently observed that in his country there is no "social support" for the arts, and that such pursuits are "a task of minorities for minorities, carried out against the background of a vast illiterate community" ["Imagen del Perú de hoy," *Cuadernos americanos,* CXX, No. 1 (Jan.-Feb. 1962)].

The writers' left-of-center allegiance seems to have become particularly marked after World War II. The rise of *fidelismo,* to be discussed below, is perhaps the most dramatic example. The concept of "littérature engagée," that is, of social and political participation through writing, is still important, though it has been rejected by many.

Robert G. Mead, Jr., found in 1956 that Mexican writers were divided into two opposing factions: a Marxist-nationalist group that proclaimed "Mexico for the Mexicans" in a literary debate, and a more cosmopolitan group he described as "universalists":

> Indeed, if we discount certain inevitable differences, this controversy between the two groups can be interpreted as the form that is assumed today by the age-old conflict in Mexican literature, that is, the struggle between the defenders of a narrow chauvinistic nationalism against the

universalists, who have defended the prerogative of Mexican authors to enjoy complete freedom in shaping their artistic creations and to undergo the influence of writers and literatures from other countries. [*Temas hispanoamericanos,* 1959]

Professor Mead's distinction may well be applied to all Latin America, though subject to the usual limitations of any taxonomic device. In general, the Marxist-nationalists expect the writers to take up social themes and to express, at least by implication, a political point of view. While the Marxist-nationalists can easily be identified with the left, the cosmopolitan-universalists may represent the right, center, or left, without ideological conformity being demanded of them. Perhaps more than the Marxist-nationalists, they seek to harmonize the autochthonous with the universal. The poet and social philosopher Octavio Paz, the critics Enrique Anderson-Imbert, José Luis Martínez, and Arturo Torres-Rioseco prolong the quest for spiritual renovation and beauty undertaken by the followers of Rubén Darío. This group's outstanding representative was Alfonso Reyes, until his recent death Latin America's most distinguished man of letters. Undoubtedly these men have fulfilled their civic and political obligations, but their work has never had to hew to an ideological line.

Since World War II, the chief organization of Brazilian writers has wavered between a strong position on political issues and complete withdrawal from politics. An ABDE (Associação Brasileira de Escritores) congress in 1945 voted a series of strong statements supporting middle-sector reformist principles and opposing the dictator Vargas. Three years later the ABDE split over outlawing the Communist party. A number of anti-Communists withdrew, and for several years thereafter the Association supported radical politics. A reconciliation was reached in 1957 when the two factions were reunited in the purely professional UBE (União Brasileira de Escritores), whose statutes expressly forbid members and officers to take political positions in its name.

There is strong sentiment in Brazil today for a professionalism that will free literature from involvement with politics. This is particularly the position of the so-called New Critics—who have their analogues in other Latin American countries. The leader of the Brazilian group, Afrânio Coutinho, has bemoaned the fact that men of letters must, because of the shortage of intellectuals, fulfill a multiplicity of social functions, especially political ones, with the result that writers become amateur politicians and, as he notes, politicians dabble in letters. In recent years, Coutinho has headed a rather successful movement to liberate critics from all activity that is not essentially literary. A fruit of his campaign was the First Brazilian Congress of Literary History and Criticism at Recife, August 7-14, 1960. In describing the meeting, Coutinho recently wrote:

> Another matter made clear at the Congress was the independence of critical activity, that is, the notion that literary criticism must be, above all, literary—an autonomous activity, with its own individuality, not subsidiary to other intellectual pursuits. Such a distinction will become more

and more precise among us: the literary critic can be only that, and his function possesses a high dignity without its being necessary for him to be also a sociologist, a historian, a politician, a journalist, a poet or a novelist, in order to take his place in the intellectual community. ["1960, Ano crucial," in *Anuário da literatura brasileira, 1961*]

Greater professionalism, however, does not imply a loss of interest in politics. The consensus of center-left and leftist sentiment (leaving aside the question of Communism, which splits the left in many countries) has apparently convinced many writers that they can gain their political objectives in Brazil without concerted campaigns. Since the death of Stalin, militant leftists have soft-pedaled or abandoned the Communist theme. An indication of a developing tolerance of leftist ideas, even in so traditionally conservative a body as the Academia Brasileira de Letras, is the award of the Sylvio Romero Prize of 1959 to Luiz Pinto Ferreira for his *Interpretação da literatura brasileira,* a Marxist history of Brazilian literature.

The rise of *fidelismo* pinpoints the tendency of writers to coalesce at the left of the political spectrum. Since 1959, the Castro government has boasted of widespread support by writers throughout the continent. Manifestos of adherence to Castro and his movement were given by hundreds of writers, including some of the most noted. A guarded statement by the Mexican Alfonso Reyes shortly before his death was accorded much prominence. Of course, the Cuban government's lists of supporters, published in 1960, do not necessarily include only Marxist-Leninists or even radical leftists. It is too early to estimate what effect Castro's public avowal of Marxism-Leninism late in 1961 and Khrushchev's intervention in Cuba in 1962 may have had on the writers' enthusiasm for the Cuban revolution. Nearly all the leading Cuban writers continue to back Castro—the defection of the novelist Lino Novás Calvo was a resounding exception. Another was the denunciation of Castro by the Argentine Jorge Luis Borges, who was in turn immediately attacked by writers of the left.

John J. Johnson has argued that "the original middle-sector leaders and their successors have tended to assume a centrist position and now face the prospect of being overwhelmed by the forces they fathered in the not-too-distant past" ["Whither the Middle Sectors?" *The Virginia Quarterly Review,* XXXVII (Autumn 1960)]. The writers' idealism, civic responsibility, and concern for humane values make it unlikely that they will defend a centrist emphasis on a rather narrow, economically oriented program that, as Johnson notes, tends to exclude "moral values and the dignity of the individual."

Since the 1930's, a small but prestigious company of Latin American writers has placed its talent and influence at the service of international Communism. A list of these should include Aníbal Ponce, José, Carlos Mariátegui, César Vallejo, Joaquín Gallegos, Enrique Gil Gilbert, Graciliano Ramos, Astrojildo Pereira, Aimé Césaire, Pablo Neruda, and Jorge Amado. In addition, an impressive array of Cubans actively supports Castro. The best known are Juan Marinello, Alejo Carpentier, Nicolás Guillén, José Antonio Portuondo, and Fernández Retamar. Such respected figures are used by the Communists to foster a sense of Latin American cultural superiority vis-á-vis the United States. They are perhaps more effective in bringing intellectuals into front groups than in getting them into the Party. They also head "cultural" congresses and petition campaigns, and are generally "useful to the Party in establishing Communist influence in professional and other organizations which have great prestige in the national life of the various countries" [Robert J. Alexander, *Communism in Latin America,* 1957]. The Communist writers' role is thus an important one, especially given the Latin American tendency to ignore the international implications of supporting Communist causes and paying respect to distinguished Party members.

The idealistic writers are particularly sensitive to the appeal of Communism and especially *fidelismo* for social justice. Communism invokes seductive visions of a better and happier society. George Steiner observes that "Communism . . . has been a central force in much of the finest of modern literature; and personal encounter with Communism has marked the sensibility and career of many of the major writers of the age." After all, the creed of Marx, Engels, Lenin, and Trotsky "is a creed penetrated from the very moment of its historical origin by a sense of the values of intellect and art" [George Steiner, "The Writer and Communism," *Problems of Communism,* X, No. 3 (May-June 1961)].

Though ideological positions vary, they have many common features. The ten-point plan for the "Second Independence Movement" of the Ecuadorian critic Benjamín Carrión summarizes goals common to many writers of the center-left and left: (1) agrarian reform, "to abolish the feudal system," (2) assimilation of indigenous elements and the rural workers in an improved socioeconomic system, (3) social security, (4) civil liberties, (5) equal rights for women, (6) international equality, (7) revision of political structures, (8) a campaign against underdevelopment, (9) greater inter-American cooperation, and (10) peace ["Teoría y plan de la Segunda Independencia," *Cuadernos americanos,* CXIV, No. 1 (Jan.-Feb. 1961)].

There has always been agreement on the urgency of improving public education, but in Brazil, for instance, a strong attack has recently been made by the leftist UNE (União Nacional de Estudantes) on the Diretrizes e Bases (Norms and Bases of Education) law of December 20, 1961. And the same organization has recently struck the national universities in an attempt to gain greater student influence in university administration. In addition to attacking "curricular unilateralism," "political-ideological discrimination," corruption, and other alleged evils, the students cite "imperialist infiltration in our educational system, through Point IV and the Ford and Rockefeller Foundations, and even through the Alliance for Progress. These sabotage university instruction through a useless kind of technology [*tecnicismo*]. They do not afford learning that might be useful to students and permit our economic development, because that would merely mean the economic independence of our country from the imperialist yoke" ["Universidade do ponto de vista político-social," *O Metropolitano* (official weekly newspaper of the

UNE, circulated with the *Diário de Notícias* of Rio de Janeiro on Saturdays), April 7, 1962]. Marxist-nationalist writers have generally supported the students.

Many Latin American writers deplore the masses' non-participation in politics and rejoice in the formation of new political parties to replace the old "liberals" and "conservatives." Until recently, on behalf of the Brazilian Communist Party, Jorge Amado worked to instill political awareness in the apathetic masses. There are also left-wing writers like Octavio Paz and Alfredo Pareja Díez-Canseco who unhesitatingly attack "totalitarian socialism" and the police-state morality of Communist Russia.

Paz voices the now frequently heard suggestion that the so-called underdeveloped countries of Latin America join forces with the beleaguered countries of Asia and Africa to promote mutual economic growth. In Brazil, the new Afro-Asian Institute, under government sponsorship, fosters "an effective cultural policy" toward the African and Asian countries. The Brazilian literary critic Adonias Filho mentions important new books by Eduardo Portella, José Honório Rodrigues, and Adolfo Justo Bezerra de Menezes that were stimulated by the Institute. According to many writers, the nations of Latin America must also renew their efforts for hemispheric cooperation, independent, of course, of what is widely considered the economic imperialism of the United States.

The theme of *antiyanquismo* is sounded constantly in Latin American writing today, and no topic could be of greater importance to this country. After enjoying great prestige in Latin America during the early years of the nineteenth century, the United States saw its moral leadership and influence seriously questioned at the end of the century by a number of writers. They admired some aspects of North American civilization, but feared its technological encroachment and scorned its pragmatism, materialism, and apparent disregard for humane values. The Uruguayan modernist José Enrique Rodó gave literary form to this resentment in his artistically written *Ariel* (1900), which Zum Felde has called "the most widely read essay in Spanish America." The influence of this book is still felt, and from it has arisen the name *arielismo,* which has come to mean a refined but critical approach to the United States and suspicion of its role in Latin America. The viability of the image of the United States as the corrupting imperialist exploiter is confirmed by the frequency with which it is still evoked. The writer who attempts to alter its outlines is rare indeed, no doubt because so many are convinced of its essential truth. In 1962 the prestigious *Cuadernos americanos* of Mexico published an anthology, *Hispanoamérica en lucha por su independencia,* a collection of selections from Latin American leaders, beginning with Bolívar and Miguel Hidalgo and ending with Castro and Lázaro Cárdenas, that reinforces this image.

Nationalism may take countless forms, from narrow xenophobia and programmatic *antiyanquismo* to the widest range of concerns considered peculiarly Latin American, especially vis-á-vis Europe and the United States. Literary nationalism dates from the *americanismo* and romanticism of the writers of the Independence movement. They considered writing of the people, the customs, the history, the flora and the fauna of their native land a patriotic service. Since Domingo Sarmiento's day, the men of letters have given increasing thought to the problems of their nation and continent. In his extensive study of the Spanish American essay, Zum Felde has found a preponderant interest in American topics, and the same may be said for the novel. The regionalist concerns of Gilberto Freyre and his group are but a modern variant. Every Latin American literature has its interpreters of the national "reality," and critics who examine accepted values in an unremitting search for the national identity. The search for *argentinidad* by such writers as Eduardo Mallea, Jorge Luis Borges, and Ezequiel Martínez Estrada is applicable to all America, "because the 'profound' or essential man, whether Argentinian or American, is universal man himself, and universally valid." It should be stressed that this broad kind of nationalism (which does not exclude universal implications, as Freyre is always quick to point out) is the most characteristic theme of Latin American writing, embracing not only the humanities but the social sciences as well.

At least passing mention must be made of the related theme of the writer's alienation, much discussed in the United States as well as Latin America. Marxist and nationalist writers hold that the intellectual is cut off from reality by a "colonial" mentality that keeps him from seeing himself and his nation as they actually are, and that similar impediments have hindered Brazil's national development. The opposing argument has been stated thus: "The thinker who hurls the charge of *alienation* against our Nation's entire past, who refuses to take into account the goodly number of national values modeled by time in a long process of sedimentation, actually represents an ideological current that can very justly be situated at the antipodes of nationalism. For he rejects out of hand the Brazilian nation and its culture, the only Brazilian nation and culture that really exist" [José Carlos Barbosa Moreira, "O Problema da cultura nacional," *Jornal do Brasil* (Rio de Janeiro), May 18, 1962].

Since the era of Darío and Rodó, the value of technology and industrialization has been generally accepted, but few well-known writers would endorse them enthusiastically. A modern writer, Benjamín Carrión, is stung by the disparity between technology and ethics. This is because technology, which a Latin American has called the "mystique of today," conflicts with many humanistic values, a conflict well expressed by the critic Enrique Anderson-Imbert:

> Our countries of Hispanic tradition have not had an Industrial Revolution nor have we had technical progress or scientific preparation. We are behind the times in comparison with the countries of Western civilization who are leading the world through a tremendous mechanization, one of whose resources is the atomic bomb. On the other hand, we maintain the basic ideas of the older humanism. The individual and his own efforts to express himself still constitute our measure of value. Of course we are becoming modernized. We accept the results of industrial transformation. We indeed slip into the social and political process of our time. But, for having

> arrived late, we feel keenly the cultural impulses of the past. Our intellectuals have not suffered the devastations of industrial civilization and are in a position to affirm their own individuality against totalitarian cruelty and capitalistic mediocrity. [*La Crítica literaria contemporánea*, 1957]

An extensive study of attitudes of Latin American writers toward technology concludes that hardly any writers treat technology as a legitimate or valuable contribution to Hispanic culture, though it has won a grudging acceptance, particularly by historians and essayists. The high value on leisure and a centuries-old hostility to practical, as opposed to theoretical, pursuits strengthen the resistance. Indicative of a fresh approach to the problems of modern Brazil, with its basic conflict between a static rural order and "a dynamic urban structure impelled and transformed by the process of industrialization," is the young critic Eduardo Portella's appeal to the writers to accept the challenge and creative stimulus provided by "the complexity and dynamism of our contextual reality" ["A Literatura do desenvolvimento," *Anuário da literatura brasileira, 1960*]. His article is significantly titled "The Literature of Development."

By now it should be apparent that the men of letters are powerful agents of political change. One recalls Edward A. Shils' observation that "modern liberal and constitutional politics have largely been the creation of intellectuals with bourgeois affinities and sympathies, in societies dominated by land-owning and military aristocracies." The statement is applicable to most of the writer-politicians and politician-writers of nineteenth-century Latin America. Shils has further noted that there is a close connection between "ideological politics" and the intellectuals. Indeed, "the function of modern intellectuals in furnishing the doctrine of revolutionary movements is to be considered as one of their most important accomplishments." As we have seen, the writers have exercised intellectual leadership not only in the cultural but also in the political sphere, and in the twentieth century their voices most often have been raised to advocate change. They have increasingly aligned with leftist ideologies advanced by the middle sectors. A few of the most outstanding writers in recent years have been Communists, and large numbers have been associated with Communist front activities. Their influence has been the greater because of the widespread respect they command as men of letters.

Creators of change, the writers are also subject to it. Changing patterns of education in the twentieth century, for example, tend to lessen the influence of the traditional school on literary creativity. Educational reform has enlarged the sector from which writers may emerge, and they no longer represent the elite so preponderantly. The rise of the middle sectors has contributed to the professionalization of literary pursuits, although journalism, diplomacy, and the bureaucracy remain essential to the writers' livelihood. Less closely identified with the elite, writers are more sensitive to financial pressures; the majority of writers, despite professional intentions, are still unable to live by writing alone. Governments have lent some material assistance, and the Communists have on occasion ministered to the writers' sense of economic insecurity. The mass media and the expanded general reading public have not been the answer to their quest for professional independence. Paradoxically, the gap between writers and their public has widened since the end of the nineteenth century, when literature became more esoteric. The monolithic works of socialist realism and outright propaganda notable in the 1930's have given way to a more poetic expression of the aspirations of man and society.

The writers insist on performing their time-honored tasks as political and social thinkers, and society, as always, accords them high prestige and great responsibility. In ideological terms, many Latin American men of letters are obviously out of sympathy with some attitudes and values basic to the civilization and culture of the United States. If this country has not been entirely successful in the communication of ideas, it may be because it has not learned to engage in mutually advantageous dialogue with Latin American intellectuals, especially the writers.

David William Foster

SOURCE: "The Sociopolitical Matrix," in *Gay and Lesbian Themes in Latin American Writing,* University of Texas Press, 1991, pp. 62-93.

[*Foster is an American writer and educator, and the author of numerous books on Latin American literature. In the following excerpt, he examines the manner is which recent Latin American novels have portrayed social and political issues associated with homosexuality.*]

From the concept of the noble savage in the writings of Jean-Jacques Rousseau and in Claude Lévi-Strauss's lamentation, *Tristes tropiques,* drawn from his experience as an anthropologist in Brazil, on the destruction of the observed by the observer (H. V. White), it has been widely held that the founding of Latin American culture meant a tragic conflict between *natura* and *cultura.* Although the *indianista/indigenista* component of Latin American thought maintains the more strictly anthropological view that pre-Columbian nature has been suffocated by the imposition of European culture, other translations of the conflict concern popular versus elite ways of viewing and experiencing the world and the disjunction between the New World as a new beginning for humanity and the New World as the rearticulation of the dominant ideologies of the colonizing powers.

Aguinaldo Silva's *No país das sombras* (*In the Land of Shadows,* 1979) is one of the author's several attempts to understand the conditions of the homosexual experience within the larger context of Brazilian social reality, in consonance with the prevailing Latin American view that issues like feminism and countercultural identities are essentially questions concerning a sociopolitical reality that affects everyone, not just feminists or gays and lesbians. . . . For this reason, Silva frames his novel in terms of two basic narrative axes: a homosexual "crime" as metonymic of a founding act of social repression and the typological echoes that exist between contemporary political experience and successive historical events. The narrator, as a journalist and historical researcher who stumbles upon an obscure event in early Brazilian colonial history that comes to assume for him the proportions of a master schema, ultimately reaches the unequivocal conclusion that "a única função do passado era explicar o presente e ajudar a modificá-lo." Written against the backdrop of violent acts of social repression, the narrator's text, unfortunately, is unable to do much to modify the present and, at the end of the novel, the narrator becomes also a victim of police brutality.

Paralleling Carlos Fuentes's *Terra nostra* (1975), or, earlier, *Cambio de piel* (1967; *Change of Skin*), the novels of the Argentines Ricardo Piglia, *Respiración artificial* (*Artificial Respiration,* 1980), and Martha Mercader, *Juanamanuela mucha mujer* (*Juanamanuela, Quite a Woman,* 1980), or the Brazilian Haroldo Maranhão, *O tetraneto del-rei* (*The Great-Great-Grandson of the King,* 1982), Silva frames his novel as an exercise in historical research that will reveal the expanding synecdochic relationship between founding acts of violence and an abiding social code based on the hypocritical justification of repression and the cynical justification of social and political dissidence.

Specifically, *No país das sombras* deals with two young soldiers who, during the first decades of the Portuguese occupation of the New World, enter into a homosexual relationship. One of them, however, is the object of desire of the chief of the military garrison, who apparently harbors behind the façade of his proper marriage and social rectitude a sexual preference for young men. Determined to separate the young man he desires from his lover, the *general-provedor* informs them that they will be posted to separate stations. Rather than accept this separation, the two men lure the *general-provedor* to a secluded spot and murder him. Seen leaving the jungle area where the body is later discovered, the two men are arrested, accused of murdering their officer as part of a plot to revolt against Portuguese rule, tortured to extract a confession to this effect, and hanged. Although the majority of the scarce remaining documents echo the allegations of sedition, Silva's narrator is able to ferret out an alternate reading of history whereby the official explanation is a smoke screen for a tawdry episode involving sexual jealousy and revenge.

One of the narrator's documentary sources is a diary, in bad Latin, by Tália, a Venetian courtesan who provides colonial Olinda with her versions of the glittering debaucheries of the European courts. Befriending the two lovers, Tália, who understands very well how her profession, working in tandem with the cynical Jesuit religious leader, fulfills an important function in the establishment of an extended Portuguese culture in the New World, and she recognizes how the two lovers represent a version of "natural" human destiny that is excluded from the cultural sign system of which she is part. She recalls witnessing their execution:

> Os dois tremiam e—como desejei que o fizessem—em nenhum momento se olharam. Para meu consolo, pensei que talvez já estivessem muito longe dali, tão adiante de tudo, e sempre juntos. Foi isso o que me fez suportar a

Guillermo Cabrera Infante.

execução (ah, a dança lenta do carrasco, seu capuz negro como a cara da própria morte), a certeza de que, ainda ali—e apesar de tudo o que lhes ocorrera—eles ainda se amavam. Foi nisso que pensei quando o alçapão se abriu repentinamente e os dois, durante breves segundos, se sacudiram no ar. E depois, quando todos já tinham ido embora e eu ainda estava lá, sozinha, diante dos seus cadáveres pendurados, era ainda sobre isso que eu meditava—eles, afinal, não haviam feito outra coisa senão obedecer ao que lhes ditara essa boa e poderosa natureza.

The "good and powerful nature" to which Tália refers includes, of course, the exuberance of the New World, the sights, sounds, and smells of which the European authorities distrust—along with the "uncivilizable" natives—as contributing to the corruption of soldiers and settlers. Control, by whatever means, becomes necessary in order to staunch the seemingly nature-inspired rebellion of the New World citizenry. Establishing a model that will, it is implied, become the official ideology of Brazilian society, first the *general-provedor* and then, after his murder, the Capitão-General inaugurate a text of lies that legitimates a multiplicity of persecutions in the name of Social Order.

The primary locus of Silva's narration thus becomes the discontinuities between historical and social reality and the disingenuous rewritings (or partial and ambiguous

representations) of events in favor of a more compelling authoritarian imperative. Confronting successive layers of historical truth, the narrator works his way through evermore revealing documents, watched over by the blind librarian of the Biblioteca Nacional, Luís Borges, who is a sly reincarnation of the celebrated Argentine writer and librarian, Jorge Luis Borges, who held an equally salutary view regarding the oppressive qualities of cultural constructs.

As an interpretation of the social role of homosexual love, Silva's novel offers the image of a profoundly natural and emotionally satisfying human experience that is both the object of a destructive jealousy hidden behind the cynical mask of public morals and a gesture of authentic social rebellion. In the first guise, the love affair between the two soldiers is the pretext for a spectacle of execution as an example to anyone who would subscribe to principles of social dissolution in defiance of the supremacy of the Portuguese king's authorities. From this point of view, the two men, falsely accused of the sedition that they acknowledge under torture, are sacrifices in an attempt to ward off any sort of challenge to the prevailing order. Silva thus presents two soldiers as inaugurating a gallery in Brazilian history of tortured and unjustly executed political prisoners as part of the authoritarian repression of "natural" forms of human dissent from a monolithic official culture that has its roots in the first vestiges of colonial control. . . .

However, Silva's narrator discovers, almost by accident, that in reality the two men may not have been innocent of the charges against them. The narrator comes into possession of the memoirs of the Jesuit who was present at the proceedings against them (a document that the narrator has to "steal" back from an American historian who, in the continued tradition of the plundering of Latin America by self-serving imperial authorities, is about to spirit it out of the country). Thus, he is able to read the priest's revelation of the confession of one of the soldiers (this quote follows the priest's transcription of the Capitão-General's charge that the Church is under the obligation to cooperate in making the facts of the alleged crime fit the political exigencies of the moment):

> E na conclusão dos documentos ele reproduzia "para uma comparação também futura," a confissão do mesmo prisioneiro, que ajudara a forjar, e que foi a única citada no processo—aquela pela qual os dois soldados foram condenados:

> " . . . Após nossos encontros e as muitas vezes em que nossos corpos se enlaçaram passamos a ver que a vida fora feita para muito mais: cabe ao homem gritar suas razões e defendê-las. Pensando assim, partimos para observar o que nos cercava, e nos deparamos então com a mais cruel das injustiças. A colônia sofria os resultados da ganância desenfreada da Coroa. Aqui todos morriam, apenas este direito lhes cabia, enquanto lá vivia o Rei e tudo era faustoso. E ainda aqui, em meio aos infelizes, havia os que, cruelmente, contra eles trabalhavam. Daí partimos para conclusões sempre mais exatas e um dia, quando afinal nos demos conta, tinhamos feito um círculo em torno dos nossos pensamentos e

concluído que era preciso lutar contra as forças que nos consumiam. Antônio Bentes me dizia que os soldados nossos irmãos tinham sido transformados em máquinas de conduzir a injustiça—e quem eram os culpados? Já éramos, então, dois místicos. Nossos encontros passaram do amor febril à condução febril das nossas idéias. Nem nos amávamos mais, porque éramos um só, havíamos formado uma maldita aliança. E nos lançamos então à conspiração final. Retomo a pergunta—quais os culpados? Foi a partir daí que nós e nossos amigos planejamos matar uma a uma as autoridades da Coroa . . . "

In this version of events, which must assumedly be taken at face value because they are the revealed sacred confessions of one of the accused, the outlawed sexual relations between the two soldiers evolve into a generalized revolutionary repudiation of Eurocentered military authority. Thus, the execution of the *general-provedor* is *both and together* the first step in the elimination of the agents of Portuguese domination and the elimination of a threat to the homosexual union between lovers. Love defined as immoral by the conventions of a dominant culture is transformed into a revolutionary solidarity against the exploitations of the riches of nature in the New World.

Silva's novel enjoys an inverted intertextuality with the utopian feelings of colonial chronicles of the Conquest that saw the New World as the opportunity to fulfill the Renaissance ideals of European culture. The executed lovers are the victims of a dystopian repression that judges them both for their outlawed sexual behavior and for the stimulus to social revolt it engenders in them. One conclusion of Silva's juxtaposition of sexuality and political history is that participation in outlawed sexual activity gives one a glimpse of what it could be like to engage in other forms of rebellion. As a founding act of Brazilian social history, the homophobic persecution of the soldiers the narrator recovers in his research (which he at first hopes will win him the support of the Instituto Nacional do Livro, only to realize that the story he has to tell cannot hope for official endorsement) installs a dynamic of social repression. The narrator himself, more than three hundred years later, inevitably falls victim as well to its projections into the modern day.

. . . . .

Arturo, la estrella más brillante (1984; *The Brightest Star*), by the Cuban Reinaldo Arenas, is a novel of radical separation, of schizophrenic dissociation in the face of a social dynamic whose compact structures of exclusion for Arturo are so unchallengeable in their inability to accommodate his personal identity that the only options available to him are forms of madness and, eventually, suicide as a way of challenging the authorities of the prison where he is incarcerated for antisocial behavior to kill him for refusing to obey an order. The option of suicide as a desperate flight from an uncomprehending world or as a calculated determination to close a personal life cycle is not uncommon in writing about homosexuality—or, for that matter, in any cultural text about the radical disjunction between the higher moral nature of the individual and an inhumanly oppressive society.

Arenas's novel is of speical interest within the spectrum of contemporary Latin American literature in that it locates this general question, manifested in terms of the specific issue of homosexuality, within the context of the Castro revolution and the social programs it created. The most controversial aspect of those social programs, because it has become widely viewed as an infamous transgression of human rights and because, as the direct consequence of this embarrassment, it is a taboo subject for leftists (who, at least, seem to eschew public discussion of antigay policies in Cuba out of a sense of loyalty to the revolution), is the treatment of alleged homosexuals after the revolution. . . . It should be noted that the subject is also distinctly taboo among the anti-Castro right: the identification with an established Catholic morality makes it difficult to generate much sympathy for the concentration of homosexuals in work camps by the Castro government. The subject is a complex one, because it is fair to assume that the early Castro government was not particularly interested in repressing the personal dignity that the socialist revolution was interested in affirming, and that it did in fact enhance personal and social life in the case, say, of blacks, women, the rural disenfranchised, and the urban dispossessed. Yet Castro's government subscribed to the legendary (nineteenth-century social engineering) antipathy of Marxism-socialism-communism (and parallel revolutionary movements like anarchism) toward homosexuality as socially nonproductive behavior and toward homosexuals as paradigms of upper- and middle-class decadence that exploited poor youths as part of the overall disease of prostitution. Moreover, Havana was notorious for its public display of homosexuality, and homosexuality was an integral part of the extensive commercialization of sex in the Cuban capital, which mostly served the needs of local and foreign (i.e., American) exploiters and the raunchy tourism they serviced (at a time, to be sure, when a city like Havana was an easily accessible escape valve for Ozzie and Harriet America). Guillermo Cabrera Infante's novels recall, with a considerable degree of nostalgia, this Havana of a bygone era.

But whereas female prostitutes were "redeemed" by medical treatment and incorporation into a productive society as defined by the new social programs, male prostitutes and anyone suspected of being homosexual (one need not rehearse all of the tiresome classificational problems of distinguishing between forms of homosexual identity and their lack of comforting alignment with male hustling as a form of survival) were rounded up and sent to forced labor camps. It is questionable whether any attempt was made to "redeem" these men and to offer them the opportunity for social integration. Arenas's novel is grim in its depiction of the contrary: the *locas* are not only left to recreate, mostly undisturbed by the authorities, their former microsociety in the camps—to dress and make themselves up as they please, to have the social interaction they please—but they are also allowed to be readily available objects of exploitation for the camp guards. This exploitation takes two forms: the guards may use the prisoners as handy objects of verbal and physical abuse, and the guards may use them for sex as they wish, as long as they are not public about it.

Arenas's novel is noteworthy because it casts the well-established pattern of scapegoating and the rape of the publicly vilified queer within the context of a revolution that proclaims the establishment of a political and economic order that will respect the rights of individuals and accord them dignity and worth by incorporating them into a just social dynamic. Just as Edmund White said that one's attitude toward outrageous fairies is an index of the ability to take sexual freedom and its display seriously for oneself and others, the treatment of alleged homosexuals, whether fairies or simply nonconformists vis-à-vis the code of machismo, can be taken as an index of a socialist society's willingness to take seriously the question of human dignity. For this reason, Julio Cortázar, one of the most loyal of Castro's supporters among Latin American intellectuals and artists, in his essays on the Nicaraguan revolution, made an eloquent plea for the Sandinista government not to repeat the Cuban folly of the persecution of alleged homosexuals (*Nicaragua tan violentamente dulce* [*Nicaragua So Violently Sweet*]). To the best of one's knowledge, no attempt was ever made to identify and deal specifically with lesbians, and the safe assumption is that they were probably grouped together for a number of reasons with female prostitutes (Cuban lesbians are included in the study by Lourdes Argüelles and B. Ruby Rich).

What makes Arturo of special interest is that he is represented as something other than the stereotypical example of the screaming queen, the most overt manifestation of a putative gay identity, at least from the perspective of a straight world. Rounded up with others after a concert by a Soviet pianist whom the gay community turns out to hear in its best finery, Arturo is incarcerated with a group of men with whom he feels no personal affinity. Eschewing their pack mentality and their acquiescence to stereotypic behavior (which the guards seem to demand, reinforce, and reward, in order to engage in scapegoating and exploitation), Arturo is doubly an outcast within the concentration camp, a transparent synecdoche (like Solzhenitsyn's cancer ward for Stalinized Russia) for the new Cuban society. Automatically an object of degradation at the hands of the guards because he has been identified as a *maricón* (queer, fag) by being rounded up and incarcerated (i.e., social treatment has assigned him an identity, rather than merely acting in accord with a previously established identity), Arturo is subject to the same mistreatment at the hands of the guards that the other prisoners receive, including being required to sexually service one of them at least once a week. But because he prefers to withdraw within himself and to refuse the role of preening fairy, he is scorned and roughly abused by his fellow prisoners. Thus, "la eterna tragedia del sometimiento" comes from all directions, and Arturo becomes the scapegoat of scapegoats, as the prisoners accept and elaborate on the system of oppression of their oppressors, thus, in the time-honored logic of prison society (whether literal or metaphoric) reinforcing the efficiency of that system.

Arturo, la estrella más brillante is a novel of the forging of a self-identity within the circumstances described above. If Arturo is out of place in general society because of his sexual needs, the triumph of a social revolution, rather than affording him a new dignity, formalizes his degradation by making him even more of an outcast (homosexuality, while ridiculed, was widely tolerated in pre-Castro Cuba, as it tends to be in Latin American society in general, with the possible exception of Argentina [Whitam and Mathy]). The outcast victim of society's outcasts, Arturo engages in mutiple strategies to protect himself, and he becomes "la estrella más brillante" of the queens, beating them at their own game by performing as a witty cabaret star. Only when newer prisoners upstage him after he has been incorporated into the prison society of the *locas* is Arturo able to withdraw into himself.

This withdrawal impels him to literature. The most interesting aspect of Arenas's novel is that, in the pop-Freudian framework of literature as a form of psychoanalytical therapy, Arturo is finally able to establish some dignity for himself by the creation of an *él* (it is italicized in the text), an alter ego transcending the *él* of his daily persona that is an integral part of the system of humiliation and degradation. This *él* is also in opposition to the *ellos* of the other prisoners, who, as has been said, are part of the routine of submission. What is particularly ironic about all of this is that the need for escape into a fantasy, the need for a literature of evasion, comes within the context of a social revolution promising the full integration of the individual with dignity into society. Only by a strategy of opting out of the social dynamic as represented by the subworld of the synecdochal prison, can Arturo finally achieve any sense of personal worth: "esa misma noche decidió que para salvarse tenía que comenzar a escribir inmediatamente." Of course, writing in prison is a risky business. Aside from the possibility of being discovered and punished for transgressive conduct, the prisoner has the perennial problem of obtaining writing materials. Fortunately, because of the array of personal effects permitted the imprisoned *locas,* personal effects that encourage them to retain the antisocial identity for which they were imprisoned in the first place, justify their continued incarceration, and sustain them as functional elements in the prison economy (forced labor, scapegoating, and exploitation), Arturo has no problem hiding his writing. He solves the acute problem of paper, however, by stealing prison documents and posted announcements. These examples of writing transcribe the official versions of the new socialist society; Arturo literally covers that writing over with his own countercultural writing:

> las libretas traídas por Rosa [su hermana] se fueron saturando de una letra mínima, veloz, casi ilegible, ilegible para él mismo, había que darse prisa, había que darse prisa, había que seguir, rápido, y, tomando precauciones—se hacían registros, se prohibía llevar diarios, cosas de maricones, decían los tenientes como justificación oficial, irrebatible y reglamentariamente se violaba toda la correspondencia—, las libretas, las contratapas, los respaldos, los márgenes y forros de los manuales de marxismo leninismo y de economía robados de la Sección Política fueron garrapateados furtivamente, rápidamente, cuando nadie vigilaba, bajo la sábana, de pie en el excusado, en la misma cola para el desayuno, hasta los márgenes de los grotescos carteles políticos instalados en las paredes y murales para uso interno del campamento sufrieron

la invasión de aquella letra microscópica y casi indescifrable en tarea interrumpida incesantemente y a la vez constante [. . .] había que seguir, había que seguir y Arturo continuó garabateando las cartas de sus compañeros robadas a medianoche, las consignas ofensivas y airadas del momento [. . . y] una noche descubrió en el Departamento de Fiscalía un baúl repleto de actas sobre consejos de guerra, sin titubear se apoderó de ellas y tuvo material para trabajar por varias semanas [. . .]

However, rather than affording him a private world that would allow him to continue functioning without setbacks in the public realm, Arturo's writing becomes more and more lost in the realm of his other *él,* and he begins to have visions and waking fantasies. He escapes twice from the camp, and the second time he is shot for, it is alleged, resisting the order to give himself up; at the moment of his death, really a form of suicide, Arturo is able to feel that he is moving definitively into the realm of the complex fantasy he has created for himself. When the guards go through his effects, they find his reams of writing, the illegible counter-text that he has created at the expense of the materials of both his fellow inmates and the prison officials—and, hence, the destructive reality of both their languages and their social codes:

el primer teniente ordena un registro en los trastos de Arturo, y todo ávidos, pensando encontrar cigarros, dinero, alguna lata de leche, quien sabe si hasta joyas ("de un maricón todo se puede esperar"), registran, revuelven; cartas y fotos de maricones, dice uno, y las tira; potes de crema, dice otro y los lanza contra el suelo, y papeles, papeles, cartones, pancartas, afiches, actas de consejos de guerra, y todo escrito hasta los mismos bordes; las actas que se habían perdido, dice el teniente, qué haría ese verraco con ellas, y toma una y, con trabajo, lee, al instante, asqueado, mira al cabo y le entrega uno de los documentos garabateados, qué te dije, dice, con esta gente hay que tener mucho cuidado, éste no sólo no se conforma con desmoralizarse a sí mismo, sino que también nos desmoraliza a nosotros, al país, a la patria, mira lo que escribe, contrarrevolución, contrarrevolución descarada; y el cabo lee, trabajosamente, algunas palabras que no entiende [. . .]

As a consequence, writing, the creation of a radically private text, becomes Arturo's only form of salvation and, yet, paradoxically, also the confirmation of his need to escape through an induced suicide from the prisonhouse of his oppression as a human being. Writing is a form of definitive, if pathetic liberation for Arturo. In his colophon to the novel, Arenas explains that it is based on the story of his friend Nelson Rodríguez Leyva, who was shot in 1971 while attempting to hijack a Cuban plane. Rodríguez Leyva's own writings during his stay in a *campo de concentración* like the one described in the novel were apparently destroyed by the authorities.

. . . . .

La otra mejilla (The Other Cheek, 1986) by Oscar Hermes Villordo concerns the intersection of a love story and the account of a political murder. Like other Latin American works that deal with renovation based on the restructuring of official societal values, Villordo's novel has an explicitly Biblical title and overt religious references (one of the most famous examples is the Paraguayan Augusto Roa Bastos's *Hijo de hombre* [*Son of Man,* 1960]). In this fashion, the murder victim, Víctor, assumes Christological dimensions that must surely be the source of discomfiture and bemusement for readers uneasy about the conjunction of the cause of sexual liberation and the repression often associated with Christianity, at least through its institutional hierarchies and conventionalized moralities. However, the sense of Villordo's novel is clear: as one of the major spokespersons for the gay experience in a recently redemocratized, post-military-dictatorship Argentina, Villordo has in this, as well as in his 1984 novel *Con la brasa en la mano* (*With the Burning Coal in His Hand*), a message of a social regeneration that accords the same dignity to the homosexual quest for identity and recognition as it must strive to do for an entire range of formerly proscribed and repressed political convictions and individual forms of behavior (D. W. Foster, "Narrativa testimonial").

The love story told within the three-day frame of reference of the narrative is the conquest by the narrator of a young man, Lucio, who seeks his assistance in finding work. Almost ridiculously successful in his conquest (which, in its outlines is reminiscent of magazine romances; cf. Villordo's 1985 novel, *Consultorio sentimental* [*Miss Lonely-Hearts*]), the narrator describes the perfect meeting of mind and body between himself and Lucio, in what surely ought to be a figure for the sort of star-blessed union possible in a society that has transcended mindless prejudices against homoerotic love.

Unfortunately, the Argentina of the narrative hasn't achieved this degree of transcendence, and the narrator's liaison with Lucio is intersected strategically by a series of persecutions of increasing seriousness that culminate in the assassination of Víctor, the narrator's friend, the prototype of the perennially abused Romeo. First in the form of a generalized queer-baiting in the context of workplace jealousies, these persecutions grow in intensity to include harassment and exploitation by the police (who may require prisoners to have sex with them, as in Arenas's novel), the intimidating violence of anonymous hit squads, to culminate in the murder of Víctor by unknown agents who will, of course, never be identified and never brought to justice.

There is little question that the essential social backdrop for *La otra mejilla* is the Argentina of the military dictatorships of the mid-1970s and early 1980s that made police persecution of homosexuals by gangs of thugs condoned by authorities an integral part of a policy of social control that sought to extirpate all vestiges of countercultural defiance. By the same token, for the middle-aged characters in the novel, such violence is an encoded sign of a collective experience of anonymous but systematic violence. Ernesto, whose birthday celebration is the point of reference for the second half of the novel, recalls a traumatic childhood act of witness:

Pero para entender el porqué de esta manera de ser—de los estallidos que no podía contener en momentos como éstos—tal vez haya que recordar el episodio de su infancia, lejano y perdido en su memoria, pero claro y preciso cada vez que lo evocaba, de los muertos en la plaza de pueblo, contemplados, por dos niños inocentes, uno de los cuales (él [Ernesto]) develaba al mirar la escena el misterio del amor acabado violentamente. "Yo era muy chico cuando vi por casualidad el primer crimen contra homosexuales—me contó—. Vestidos con nuestros guardapolvos blancos y con nuestras carteras de escolares golpeándonos las espaldas, mi amiguito y yo corrimos hasta el lugar donde se amontonaba la gente. El quedó atrás y yo me adelanté. Vi, mudo de asombro, que el muerto tendido boca arriba en el cantero, bajo los naranjos agrios [. . .], era Fernando, el muchacho del aserradero que yo conocía y que, según los mayores, tenía 'malas costumbres.' "

The death of Víctor, just like the death of Fernando that Ernesto relives in his memory, is an act of political assassination. Paralleling the violent arrests, often in public during the height of the military's so-called dirty war in the late 1970s and the subsequent permanent disappearance of the many thousands detained both by the regular police and by unidentified agents, the victims of antihomosexual persecution in *La otra mejilla* are designed to be read as synecdoches of an issue of sociopolitical intolerance of far larger proportions than the right to a personal life style of a specific sexual minority.

In this way, Villordo inscribes his novel within a specific Latin American tradition that sees that the quest for gay liberation not only as the generalized struggle against a variety of self-serving intolerances, but also as an effort to counter forms of political repression that define deviance in many but ultimately confluent ways. This explains why the enormous success of the 1981 Argentine production of Martin Sherman's *Bent,* which deals with the persecution of homosexuals in Hitler's Germany, was due in great measure to its perception as an allegory of Nazi-like campaigns of extermination under the Christian moral order touted by the military tyranny.

But *La otra mejilla* is more than a sensational account of Víctor's murder and the romance magazine detailing of an exemplary falling in love. Both of these narrative nuclei are essentially stereotypes, despite the legitimate—and antithetical—poles of experience, success versus defeat, love versus death, fulfillment versus destruction, that they represent. These nuclei are foregrounded as specific references to homosexual identity. But they also form part of a process of storytelling that refracts them into a multiplicity of individual experiences.

Villordo's novel, like *A Thousand and One Nights,* is a narrative about narratives, and in some instances it is a narrative about narratives about narratives, as a mosaic of personal stories crisscross in a complex network of intersecting identities. While the narrator is engaged in telling his own story of falling in love with Lucio, he is also occupied in repeating the stories of others, as well as their stories of others. These stories, particularly as regards the street-

wise Ernesto and the repeatedly abused Víctor, constitute a selective typology of gay experiences in the context of an Argentine society seen as repressive and hypocritical in its public morality. Significantly, key acquaintances reappear in these personal histories, providing a panorama of the countercultural world that exists on the fringes of Argentine social life.

Through the telling of these interwoven stories, the narrator seeks to complete for himself a sense of the proscribed underworld of which he is a part. As a consequence, he is preoccupied with the difficulties of grasping the elusive meaning of what he is being told and of specifying the nature of the individuals whose stories he repeats. Tags referring to understanding, to the discovery of meaning, and to the postponement of comprehension abound in the narrator's discourse, as do references to events as a theatrical *escena* that requires an act of interpretation:

> Detuve la mano que iba a golpear con los nudillos sobre el vidrio porque, aunque estaba acostumbrado a las sorpresas de Víctor, la escena no podía dejar de llamarme la atención. Como Ernesto sus encuentros, yo solía contar las andanzas de Víctor. Lo hacía de modo que los hechos resultaran graciosos en la sucesión disparatada, a falta de explicación, como él narraba sus aventuras exagerando el cuento para que causaran risa. Pero mi manera de contar era sólo la forma de decir la extrañeza ante lo inexplicable. Podía entender, sí, las razones—ya me las contaría—por las cuales ahora estaba hablando con la guardia en pleno hospital, pero que eso sucediera con tanta naturalidad y después de escenas como las que acabábamos de vivir hacía unas horas, no. Porque me preguntaba: ¿Cuál es Víctor? ¿El de la comisaría que siembra billetes en el piso para que los recoja un preso que los necesita? ¿El del departamento del portero que cae de rodillas y transforma con su rezo a quienes lo rodean? ¿El robado? ¿El engañado que se deja engañar? ¿Ese que pide que venga—porque sabe que iré—y está riéndose y haciendo reír a los médicos mientras habla? Golpeé.

In the search for a language capable of characterizing crucial human experiences that are aggressively persecuted by the police and the public that supports it, *La otra mejilla* opts for an assertively colloquial register. This register derives from the fact that its readers will know that organized police oppression of homosexuals has been suspended in redemocratized Argentina, along with the official censorship of culture, while at the same time these readers are to understand that homophobic attitudes continue to prevail among the majority. Thus, as a novel that conjugates texts that read like personal diaries, romance-magazine fictions, crime news, and a Spanish translation of *The Joys of Gay Sex, La otra mejilla* is written with a nonchalant colloquial register that runs counter to the highly metaphorized language of sexuality to be found in novels published during periods of military repression and in conformance with cultural taboos circumscribing the transcription of frank discussions on the subject. Eschewing both the "poetic" encodings of writers like Manuel Mujica Láinez and the sort of inverted modernism of a William Burroughs (a form of sexual writing brilliantly developed in Spanish by the Cuban Severo Sarduy), Villordo turns to a documentary literalness in the style of Edmund White. The result is a narrative texture that is, in comparison with previous narrative treatments of the subject, strikingly unmediated by any form of euphemism, and it is accompanied by a commitment to the narrator's recording of his stories with admirable explicitness.

NATIVE AMERICANS IN LATIN AMERICAN LITERATURE

Carmelo Virgillo

SOURCE: "Primitivism in Latin American Fiction," in *The Ibero-American Enlightenment,* edited by A. Owen Aldridge, University of Illinois Press, 1971, pp. 243-55.

[*In the following essay, Virgillo examines the distorted image of the Native American in romantic Latin American literature of the nineteenth century.*]

> L'enfant de la nature abhorre l'esclavage;
> Implacable ennemi de toute authorité,
> Il s'indigne du joug; la contrainte l'outrage;
> Liberté c'est son voeu; son cri c'est liberté.
> Au mépris des liens de la société,
> Il réclame en secret son antique apanage.
>
> *Les Éleuthéromanes*—1772

These lines, written over two centuries ago, on the eve of the French Revolution, upheld the Indian as the product of a happy primeval society—a tangible dream for the freedom-starved European who longed to cut the bonds of social injustice. Today it is difficult to think of anybody who has been more abused and enjoys less autonomy than the American Indian, who, far from having impressed anything on the white man, remains, no doubt, the least recognized and understood inhabitant of the New World. This tragic fact is particularly true of most of Latin America, where the primitive who once was absolute master of his surroundings is today either extinct or excluded, a stranger in his own country. Ironically, his survival depends largely, if not exclusively, on his giving up the little land still in his possession and on his merging into the mainstream of modern, urban-minded civilization which refuses to understand the primitive's plight for his freedom and independence.

In spite of the efforts of today's writers to present a realistic picture of the Indian, most of us still rely on the stereotyped version fashioned by nineteenth-century romantic literature, and this, in general, has been the downfall of the oldest native American.

After briefly outlining the earliest misconceptions surrounding the primitive, and discussing the role France played in creating the myth of the Noble Savage, we shall examine four representative romantic Latin American novels in an effort to show this distorted image and the consequences of such a distortion. The novels are José de Alencar's *O Guarani* (1857) and *Iracema* (1865, Brazil),

Juan León Mera's *Cumandá* (1879, Ecuador), and Zorrilla de San Martín's *Tabaré* (1886, Uruguay).

As far as we know, the misconceptions about the Indian date back to 1492, when Columbus returned to Spain with six tribal dignitaries dressed in full regalia and presented this stereotyped group as the definitive image of the native inhabitant of the New World. In the ensuing years, the primitive was paraded through Europe, where he came to be regarded as a real curiosity, while reports from the New World were so subjective and far-fetched as to create more confusion than anything else about the Indian. France, from the start, took a special interest in the primitive, and soon the poets of the Pleïade were singing the praises of the "enfant de la Nature," idealizing him but not really shedding any light on him or his society. Montaigne, however, was to take a more realistic look at the primitive, and, after meeting some Tupinambá Indians from Brazil at the court of Charles IX in Rouen, was so impressed with their wisdom and simplicity that he came to regard the American aborigine as the epitome of instinctive goodness, which he claimed resulted from an ideal free society close to God because it was close to Nature. Thus began the myth of the Noble Savage, and there are those who report that Montaigne, inspired by his encounter with the savages and by their account of society in the wilderness, was to trace a clear outline of what was later defined as "class struggle" and "social revolution."

It wasn't, however, until the Enlightenment that the primitive and his society became the center of much interest, particularly in France, where, by the middle of the eighteenth century, the original sketch of Montaigne had become the blueprint of a real social revolution in the works of the enlightened *philosophes*. In Rousseau's *Discours* (1750) and three years later in his *Discours sur l'inégalité parmi les hommes* the primitive appears definitely established as the embodiment of natural goodness and representative of an ideal equalitarian society from which the white civilized man had much to learn. Obviously, what Rousseau really advocated was not that civilized man adopt the savage and his society but that the distorted product of an unjust, unnatural society become undistorted, keeping all the virtues of civilization but at the same time returning to the simplicity of the primitive. Unfortunately, Rousseau was taken literally, and a generation of *éleuthéromanes,* or nature maniacs, came into being. As we all know, many of these fled the shores of Europe to seek shelter in the world of the savage, only to return to their native countries shocked and disillusioned by cold reality. As I see it, the situation did not become critical for the primitive until this disillusionment affected the arts, particularly literature. We see this in Chateaubriand, who, upon his return from North America, disenchanted with the natives and with the perils of his journey to the wilderness, refashioned in his works both the primitive and his environment to fit his neurotic self in search of an imaginary world. Thus begins the systematic destruction of the oldest native American. For, too intent on recreating the beauty of the exotic settings in which he had wished to become lost but had failed, and set on forgetting the primitive he had actually met, Chateaubriand turned the native into a prop whose main purpose was to highlight the scenery and give vent to the writer's "mal du siècle." In short, Rousseau's happy Indian had been replaced by a sad would-be Indian whose only real identity lay in his feathers and moccasins.

In American primitivist fiction this image is paramount in the works of James Fenimore Cooper and other Indianist writers inspired by him in whose hands the Noble Savage becomes the tool of sentimentalism. Conforming to romantic tradition, the primitive is cast as a rebel fighting the oppressing forces of civilization, namely the white man, who wants to enslave him and deprive him of his natural freedom. As one might have expected, the Indian hero is fashioned after his white European counterpart, thus conforming to the white man's standards of valor, intelligence, and physical prowess. However, alongside this "noble" savage there appears a "savage" savage who couples the worst elements of the white villain of romantic European tradition with the least desirable traits of his own race. He is deceitful, animalistic, ignorant of the white man's ways, and unwilling to bow to the *conquistador*. He is labeled as a bad Indian, therefore a nonentity.

In the same tradition of his North American brother, the Latin American primitive appears in nineteenth-century fiction as possessing the instinctive natural goodness attributed to him by Rousseau and the fatalistic, hypersensitive, and quasi-pathological personality created for him by Chateaubriand. Unreal as this fictional primitive might sound, he fulfilled an urgent need for the Latin American countries, which had just achieved independence from Spain and Portugal. A national literature had to be created to unite the indigenous elements in each country. In view of the fact that no one had been subjected more to the treachery of the European colonists than the Indian, he was the logical choice for a symbol of national identity in the struggle against the foreign invader. What better opportunity to clear the conscience of the wealthy oligarchy and forge a national tradition at the same time than to turn the clock on the mistreatment of the primitive and place the blame for this on the founding fathers—the European *conquistadores* who had started abusing the primitive centuries before! Ironically, it was the powerful land-owning intellectuals of Latin America, converted for the occasion into romantic writers, who brought the Indian skeleton out of the closet hoping to redeem him artistically. The result was the creation of an unbelievable Indian who might be called a combination Tonto and René.

Thus a literature was born filled with disconsolate, frustrated primitives whose main problem seemed to stem from their inability to mix with the white race. This sentimentalism appealed, no doubt, to the sensitive feelings of the lady of the mansion who would while away her time enthralled by heart-warming tales of ill-fated friendships between Indians and whites. She had plenty of time to do this, for in her household and out in the fields numerous Indians slaved away to provide her with wealth and leisure. In Brazil many hearts among the land-grabbing upper classes must have been stirred by José de Alencar's sentimental novels filled with touching scenes of brotherly love between white Portuguese noblemen and their Indian companions. Taking a closer look at this relationship one notices, however, that the Noble Savage as portrayed in these works, though physically compatible with his natural environment, is otherwise fashioned after the white man's conception of the romantic hero. In short, on the outside he may be a primitive, but inwardly he is a European with all the attributes of white nobility. In *O Guarani,* Indian Peri, a handsome son of the wilderness, saves the life of Cecília, daughter of the Portuguese *fidalgo* Dom Antônio de Mariz, who therefore befriends the Indian because down deep Peri is a nobleman in the body of a savage. On another occasion the Indian's intelligence is praised: vigorous as the vegetation of his native soil, says Alencar, Peri is guided by common sense and prudence worthy of civilized man. After another act of supreme altruism, Dom Antônio is carried away by his enthusiasm and tells Peri that his deeds would classify him as a veritable *fidalgo,* then throws his arms around the Indian and assures him that his savage heart should not feel ashamed to beat over the heart of a Portuguese nobleman. As can be seen here, contrary to the enlightened man's concept that true nobility, symbolizing virtue, comes naturally to the unspoiled savage, it would appear that it is instead an attribute associated with civilized man in general and white European aristocracy in particular. At best all the primitive can expect is to equal it.

> In spite of the efforts of today's writers to present a realistic picture of the Indian, most of us still rely on the stereotyped version fashioned by nineteenth-century romantic literature, and this, in general, has been the downfall of the oldest native American.
>
> —*Carmelo Virgillo*

If in the romantic Indianist novel, supposedly fostering national unity, the author's intention was to advocate a harmonious coexistence of all the inhabitants of his country, no trace of this can be seen in the four works representing the very best in their genre. Definitely not in *O Guarani,* where Indian Peri is portrayed as a misanthrope who prefers to live a sad and lonely existence in a cabin near the white settlement of Dom Antônio. Peri saves Cecília from the hostile Indians at whose hands her family perishes but declines her invitation to go live with her in Rio, certain that he could not survive in the world of civilized man. In *Iracema* Martim marries an Indian maiden and settles in her world. He soon discovers, however, that the wilderness and the accompanying bucolic life are not meant for a civilized Portuguese. He returns to civilization with his child and his Indian companion, proving that if the Indian cannot get along in the white man's world, the same is true of civilized man, who has no alternative but to put up with the ills of his complex white world.

In Harriet Beecher Stowe's *Uncle Tom's Cabin,* happiness for the American Negro is defined as being sheltered by a devout white patriarch who teaches him how to sing religious hymns, behave like a child, and learn what is good for him. Thus Thomas Paine's *The Rights of Man* is reinterpreted to mean the rights of the nonwhite to imitate the white. What started as a sentimental novel has come to mold the Negro's image in the eyes of the majority of white Americans. May we suggest that the Latin American counterpart, the romantic Indianist novel, did just as great an injustice to the primitive south of the border.

In Juan León Mera's *Cumandá,* one is shown what happiness means to the Záparo tribesmen inhabiting the *reducción* of Fray Orozco. The once-proud Indian warriors appear as a community of zombies who have switched from an Indian *cacique* to blind obedience to a white Dominican friar of whom they must ask permission before they can take one step. As we recall, attending pagan tribal festivities for the Záparos becomes a major issue until Orozco's son Carlos decides to attend and the Indians are allowed to go. Let us remember that such Dominican *reducciones* were a very poor substitute for the Jesuit Latin American utopias which Spain and Portugal had seen fit to eliminate for a number of reasons. Foremost, it would seem, was the threat which the enlightened Christianity of the Society of Jesus posed to those two powers who, far from wishing to educate the savage and bring about his self-sufficiency, preferred instead to make him dependent on them to better exploit him.

According to the pattern of the primitivist novel in Latin America, the difference between a human being and an Indian is almost always determined by the savage's acceptance of the orthodox Christian faith, which will raise him from the rank of *tigre* to that of *hermano.* This is not really saying that he is elevated to the status of the white man. In military terms one might call an Indian convert a noncommissioned officer. Spain's destiny, claims Zorrilla de San Martín in *Tabaré,* was to fight the savage monster that lurked in the New World and bring Christianity into the wilderness. Tabaré is outstanding among his tribesmen, not because he is a blue-eyed mestizo, but more because deep inside his savage body there beats a Christian heart, for his white mother was a Christian. Likewise, Cumandá's Christian faith sets her apart from the Indians who raised her, and she remains unbelievably pure and angelical in the midst of the wildest savages a writer's mind could possibly conceive.

Christian salvation invariably serves as the *deus ex machina* of the sentimentalist novel, providing the author with the opportunity of gathering the loose ends of his plot while carrying the melodrama to its inevitable climax. In *Iracema* Martim, realizing that becoming an Indian warrior has brought down a divine curse upon him and his Indian bride, who eventually dies, rejoins Christianity more fervently than ever, and for good measure converts even his good Indian friend Poti. In *O Guarani* Peri accepts conversion to Christianity on the spot in order to escape from his master's burning home and be allowed to carry Cecília with him to safety. Christianity plays an important role also in the dénouement of *Cumandá.* The heroine, really Fray Orozco's daughter Julia, loses her life in a horrible sacrifice while Orozco, whose timely arrival could

save her, gives top priority to converting Indian Tongana, spending precious hours to save his soul.

As one can see, the Enlightenment's Noble Savage—instinctively good, naturally free, and socially independent—is reshaped in Latin American fiction to fit the image of an animal on trial whose redemption depends on serving God in Heaven and white man on earth, being protected and guided by both. Having come to this conclusion, one naturally assumes that under such tutelage the Indian lived happily ever after.

In much the same fashion as television and movie writers nowadays create productions filled with Negro neurosurgeons and Oxford-educated Indians, Latin American landowner-writers filled their books with noble, disproportionate Indian chiefs suffering from *mal du siècle* and not necessarily social injustice. This expedient is an easy way out because it allows the sentimentalist writer to blame everything on fate without having to suggest any solution to the racial conflicts that were the core of his plots. Moreover, the writer points to the revolt of the oppressed—the primitive—as a source of divine as well as human punishment, thus advocating the status quo in a genre that should suggest revolutionary measures. This is evidenced in *Cumandá,* in which the 1790 Indian uprising in Ecuador is seen by Mera as having brought down the wrath of God upon thousands of innocent people, among whom are some of his characters. From this it would appear evident that the Latin American Indian is doomed and his fate considered inevitable and quietly accepted as such.

If one examines closely the ill-fated, marked-for-death protagonists of a romantic primitivist novel one cannot help but notice the following cliché: to be an Indian, to have any Indian blood, or to become involved with an Indian engenders cataclysmic results, as it brings down divine wrath. In reality, this can only be interpreted as the social stigma placed upon the primitive by the writer. It is quite interesting to note how consistent this cliché is in Latin American primitivist fiction. Indian Peri's love for Cecília causes her death as God suddenly sends down a horrible deluge that drowns the ill-fated lovers just as they are about to fulfill their dream. In *Iracema* Martim's love for the Indian vestal is the cause of the near extermination of her family as well as the cause of her own death.

If love between the members of two cultures—the Indian and the white—leads to disaster, no better fated is the fruit of that love: the mestizo. While in romantic European literature the hero is ordinarily forced by fate to pay for an unintentional yet unpardonable sin, in Latin American romanticism this victim of fate is the mestizo, and his unforgivable sin is his mistake of racial integration. As we see, the primitivist who claims to be writing a national epic based on the union of the two cultures, the European and Indian, is actually doing no more nor less than painting a bleak picture of such a union. It would appear from this genre that the Latin American hybrid race has resulted from an unfortunate set of circumstances which could not be avoided or helped since they were predetermined by destiny. While on the one hand the North American James Fenimore Cooper does not try to conceal his disapproval of racial integration, the Latin American primitivist shows greater subtlety in dealing with this issue. According to Leslie A. Fiedler, Cooper rejects the idea of marriage even in Heaven between white Cora and Indian Uncas in *The Last of the Mohicans,* thus making his position quite clear. Hypocritically, Cooper's Latin American counterpart will strongly endorse the union of his racially incompatible lovers after death, although seldom if ever allowing them to marry on earth. This is evidenced in *O Guarani* where Isabel, the sensual, illegitimate mestizo daughter of Dom Antônio, shows the indelible traits of her race: she is madly in love with a white nobleman, Dom Álvaro. When he reciprocates this feeling, he is immediately punished by José de Alencar, who sends him off to die at the hands of non-Christian Indians. Isabel then chooses to poison herself and lies down next to Álvaro to achieve in death what was impossible in life. Dom Antônio also pays with his life for having loved the Indian maiden who was Isabel's mother. Similarly, Tabaré's blond, blue-eyed mother dies as the result of her abduction and physical union with the mighty Indian chief Caracé. Taberé makes the mistake of falling in love with a white girl, and this is enough to bring upon him the usual curse that marks him for inevitable death. In *Cumandá* the heroine dies as a result of her marriage to Indian warrior Yahuarmaqui.

The fear of miscegenation seems to haunt the Latin American primitivist writer. Poorly concealed behind unfulfilled love, this fear is evident in almost every plot and could not fool even the least-aware reader. Death, however, is the writer's check valve, and he uses it generously to prevent physical union from occurring while he appropriately remains within the boundaries of romantic tradition. When Christianized Peri is finally alone in the jungle with his beloved Cecília, death surprises them in the form of a deluge which, with biblical implications, cleanses the evil which is about to be committed on earth. The pair die unfulfilled but pure. Julia Orozco also dies by water before her marriage to Yahuarmaqui is consummated. Mestizo Tabaré and Blanca will never be joined in marriage because a sword puts an end to Tabaré's life at the very moment when Blanca might have been able to make a plea for her noble savior. However, Tabaré is allowed to die in Blanca's arms in the presence of a sympathetic monk, which should be of some consolation to him. An unusual circumstance is employed in Alencar's *Iracema* to justify physical union between two races. Martim first implores Christ to save him from succumbing to the Indian maiden Iracema's passionate advances. When this fails to work Martim then begs the maiden herself to put him to sleep with her magic potion that can induce wishful dreams. This precursor of LSD eventually accomplishes what Martim's conscious mind would never have allowed.

Undoubtedly the Latin American primitivists all agree on the strong attraction between the Indian and the white man, and this is made obvious by the contrast between the physical characteristics of the lovers. To be sure, the white maidens are depicted more along the lines of Sir Walter Scott's fair lasses than the rugged, southern, dark-skinned Spanish and Portuguese belles. Peri is spellbound by the divine features of Cecília, the stereotyped white *conquistadora*—very blond, blue-eyed, and ethereal. For her he re-

jects his most beautiful Indian maidens and even leaves his mother. Isabel, half-Indian and quite dark, confesses that she envies Cecília's fair features and deep inside hates the Indian in herself, a hatred which she turns against Indian Peri. Peri, recognizing why he is hated, cannot help but hate her. By the same token, chief Yahuarmaqui chooses white Cumandá over hundreds of maidens to be his favorite wife. Writer Mera states openly that Cumandá's superior beauty sets her apart from her fellow tribesmen. Zorrilla de San Martín would have one believe that Tabaré feels attracted to Blanca because he sees in her the Virgin Mary-like image of his own mother. Actually, what the writer has in mind and is afraid to express is the plight of the unfortunate mestizo who would like to forget the Indian half of him and is desperately attracted to the fair race.

Reinforcing our proposition that the Noble Savage in romantic Latin American literature is but a mere artistic creation of little human consequence, Emilio Carilla states: "El indio aparece—literariamente—defendido, idealizado, pero no exactamente como ideal de vida o cultura."

In short, the Indian is seen as a tool of the sentimentalist writer who uses the primitive as a bad copy of the white man. The Noble Savage's salvation, as nineteenth-century romantic Indianist fiction suggests, is seen as his adaptation to the world of his white master, whose characteris-

Dust jacket for Juan Jose Arreola's Confabulario.

tics he must inherit if he is to survive. For it is the Noble Savage who must conform to the distorted society of the European and not the other way around, as Montaigne and later the French encyclopedists advocated. To be sure, the corrupt and class-conscious society which the eighteenth-century *philosophes* condemned so vehemently appears to have been transplanted to the once-peaceful wilderness of the New World. The native American described by Diderot and his fellow encyclopedists as the "implacable ennemi de toute authorité" would appear in the works discussed in this paper as a subculture resigned by fate to play second fiddle to blond, blue-eyed *consquistadores,* envious of the master's white skin and desperate to lose its native traits. These traits, sentimentalist novelists would have one believe, the Noble Savage would gladly relinquish for the chance to be a little less dark, less pagan, less instinctive, less free, less natural, less Indian. The Noble Savage, as portrayed in Latin American primitivist fiction, is an allegory rather than a human being of flesh and blood. He is an abstraction symbolizing both evil and virtue, as some fictional Indians are made out to be more savage than others, but always stereotyped and unreal. In the melée it is difficult to imagine what the Noble Savage is really like, and, since most of us have still to understand him as an individual with his own particular needs and desires, it is easier for us to keep on destroying him physically just as he has been destroyed artistically.

Braulio Muñoz

SOURCE: "The Indian and the Literary Tradition" in *Sons of the Wind: The Search for Identity in Spanish American Indian Literature,* Rutgers University Press, 1982, pp. 33-74.

[*Muñoz is a Peruvian-born American writer and educator who wrote his book,* Sons of the Wind, *as a response to "the almost total neglect of the Indians' point of view in the understanding of Latin American culture." In the following excerpt from that work, Muñoz discusses the pre-Columbian origins of the* indigenista *novel.*]

The treatment of the Indian in indigenista novels is the culmination of a long literary tradition developed by Indian, Spanish, and Spanish American writers. Over the centuries, this tradition has shown important continuities as well as ruptures caused by different views of the Indian and his world. The main continuities and ruptures in the literary tradition up to the end of the nineteenth century are discussed in this chapter with reference to the underlying social factors that affected them. Before proceeding, however, it is important to state as clearly as possible who is considered Indian in this work in order to avoid a possible misunderstanding of the discussion that follows.

Figures concerning the actual size of the Indian population before the Spanish conquest vary, and no definitive one has been reached; estimates range from about 13 million to about 150 million. What is certain is that a large number of Indians died during the first decades of colonial rule due to massacres, plagues, and forced labor. Calculations prepared by the Berkeley school of historians and demographers show that in Central Mexico alone there were an estimated 25,200,000 Indians in 1519, the year Cortés landed in Veracruz; 13 years later, there were 16,800,000 Indians left. By 1580, 60 years after the conquest, the Indian population had been reduced to only 1,900,000! These figures give an idea of the genocide that accompanied the conquest of Spanish America.

Despite the tremendous demographic collapse, Indians were able to endure. This was particularly the case where they had developed large and integrated societies; that is to say, in the regions generally referred to as nuclear America: the Andes zone in South America, Central America, and central and southern Mexico. After the first centuries of colonial rule, the bulk of the Indian population was circumscribed in these areas, where their demographic density made possible the retention of their culture as they retreated from the coastal regions to the less accessible highlands. Where their numbers were small, as in large portions of present-day Argentina, for example, the Indians dissolved both culturally and biologically into the mestizo within the first centuries of colonial domination.

Population estimates of present-day Indians also vary. Some argue that there are only about 10 million Indians left in Spanish America compared with about 160 million or so whites and mestizos. But these estimates should be viewed with caution, for there is no general agreement as to who is Indian in Spanish America. Are, for example, those who walk barefoot Indians? Those who do not speak Spanish? Those who are dark? Those who dress like Indians? Indeed, as it has been pointed out by several writers, figures concerning existing Indian populations vary according to the criteria each investigator uses in calculations.

There are three basic criteria for classifying a person as an Indian: biological, cultural, and social. Biologically speaking, there are few pure Indians in Spanish America; yet, phenotypically speaking, no one can deny their great number in the area. In fact, were Spanish Americans to classify Indians phenotypically, as blacks are classified in the United States, for example, the majority of Spanish Americans could be classified as Indian; Haya de la Torre and his followers based their claim for an Indo-America on these grounds. The biologic basis for classification does not, however, do justice to the complexity of the Indian problem in Spanish America. Phenotypic characteristics are crucial classification factors only when used in conjunction with other cultural and social criteria.

The interpretation of the Indian problem as a cultural one has been widespread in Spanish America since the first years of indigenismo, the movement whose goal was to redeem the Indian. Racial prejudice, it has been argued, is really cultural prejudice. If Indians were to learn Spanish, dress in western fashion, and so forth, they would cease to be Indian and become mestizo; their Indianness would fall off like a change of skin. No doubt, this view of the Indian problem has some basis in reality, but it ignores too much. Deculturation is not sufficient for a change of skin. As a mestizo, the deculturated Indian will still be discriminated against by the whiter population and remain at the bottom of his nation's economic ladder.

The noble battle waged by indigenistas against those who argued for a biological interpretation of the Indian problem soon became spurious. For sociologically speaking, one of the things to remember when dealing with discrimination in Spanish America is that there are people who look, think, feel, and live differently from Westerners and who are considered Indians by these Westerners. While it may be true that pure Indians are slowly facing biological extinction, be it through intermarriage or rape, it is also true that less pure Indians encounter discrimination in Spanish America because of their phenotypic appearance. Sociologists would do well to remember W. I. Thomas's insight: If the situation is defined as real, it is real in its consequences. In Spanish America, if a person is defined as Indian, he is treated as one and discriminated against whether or not he is biologically pure. Biology does play a part in discrimination in Spanish America, however mistaken its basis may be. In attempting to disprove racist arguments, adherents of the cultural conception of the Indian problem downplay its biological aspects.

Ever since the famous essays by Mariátegui, there have been social scientists who argued that racial prejudice hides unequal and unjust economic relations between two groups of unequal power. This thesis, too, has basis in reality, and the most cursory view of Spanish American history bears it out. Today, for example, the majority of the poor are darker skinned than the privileged few. The Indian problem was clearly used to mask economic interests in the case of the *científicos* in Mexico who, following positivist and evolutionist philosophies, argued that by natural laws the white (fittest) rose to the top of the economic ladder and the Indian (unfit) remained at the bottom. Exploiting Indians and dark mestizos for the benefit of the small oligarchic group was thus justified. But to argue from there to a purely economic interpretation of the Indian problem in Spanish America is to be guilty of bad faith, and the staunchest proponents of the thesis know this and acknowledge the limitations of their analysis. Even if racial discrimination is often fostered and sustained by the class system in Spanish America, the fact that there is discrimination based on phenotypic characteristics can not be ignored.

What seems clear is that neither of these factors alone sufficiently explains the Indian problem in Spanish America. Phenotypic characteristics and cultural prejudices make it possible to justify an unjust economic order where the Indian is usually at the bottom. Alternatively, the low economic position of the Indian supports the ruling class's negative attitude toward the Indian's culture and the phenotypic characteristics that single him out.

With these issues in mind and for the purpose of this study, I shall adopt the following criteria when referring to Indians: Indians are those so defined by the rest of the Spanish American population and who evidence phenotypic characteristics and cultural traits associated with the definition. This concept of Indianness follows from that of race as a social rather than a genetic category while at the same time allowing for the impact of phenotypic characteristics on classifying people into distinct races.

A brief excursus on pre-Columbian history is necessary for two reasons: First, the role of the writer and literature in Spanish America can be understood only when seen in its sociocultural context of which the ancient world and its demise are a part; second, many Indian novels in the nineteenth century and particularly the twentieth century cannot be understood without reference to Indian life before Columbus. The major problems of much of the research on Spanish American society and culture steam from the basically ahistoric approach of the research. What everyone knows must be rescued from what is taken for granted: The fact that the Indian's life has involved endless suffering with little or no change for the better over the centuries must not prevent historians from recounting it. We cannot close our eyes to what has been and expect to grasp what is. . . .

[Pre-Columbian] nuclear America was governed by a succession of small groups of people who cemented their power through force. The majority of the Indians did not enjoy the full benefit of their labor, and many suffered the consequences of being a conquered people. Even in the Andes, if the Indians were not slaves, they also were not free. It is important to keep in mind that tribute, repression, and even slavery were not brought by the Spaniards to the New World; there never was a utopia in nuclear America. The twentieth-century novelist's exaltation of pre-Columbian America hides the truth about the past in order to criticize the present more. But for all this, it must not be forgotten that the Spanish conquest cut short the development of a remarkable people and condemned them to perpetual suffering. The coming of the Europeans did not bring respite to the Indian; rather, it augmented oppression to unheard-of proportions.

The literature of nuclear America, marking the onset of Indian culture, shows a remarkable development. To be sure, as in most societies of that time (ca. 1000 B.C.-A.D. 1500), literary production and enjoyment among the Indians reflected the social stratification of the society between the aristocratic few and the rest of the population. The most accomplished pre-Columbian literature was basically a literature of theopolitical ruling classes.

From the remnants of this literary tradition, it can be deduced that pre-Columbian literature lacked what might be called a critical tendency. Tragedies, for example, which involve a close analysis of the sociocultural complexities of society are conspicuously absent. Even the fable, perhaps one of the most indirect ways of criticizing ruling powers, did not develop here in that direction. Moreover, due to its theopolitical character, thematic changes in literature within regions (for example, Aztec and Incan societies) seem to have developed as different cultures competed with one another. This is one of the factors supporting the view that cultural unity of what is now Spanish America was not even remotely considered in pre-Columbian times. Finally, it should also be noted here that pre-Columbian literature did not develop as literary genres, such as poetry, drama, epic, and so on; the Indians combined theology, medicine, history, myth, and literature in a single work.

Pre-Columbian literature is an important aspect of the literature of today's Spanish America; it records the Indian's glory, hopes, fears, and fate. Surely, pre-Columbian literature translates the vision of a world that neither a white nor a mestizo can totally penetrate, but it constitutes a voice from the past that present-day Spanish Americans can hardly ignore.

— Braulio Muñoz

Written pre-Columbian literature was developed to the highest degree by the Mayas. In addition to inscriptions on stone, the Mayas had a large number of sacred books or codices. Evidence so far indicates that they did not develop an alphabet; the characters of the codices represent ideas or objects rather than sounds. But like Aztec writing, Mayan writing was moving toward syllabic phonetics through the use of rebus writing, where sounds of a word are represented by combining pictures or signs of things whose spoken names resemble sounds in the words to be formed. Unfortunately, most of these codices were burned by the conquering Spanish priests; only three are extant today.

Besides written texts, the Mayas, Aztecs, Incas, and other pre-Columbian people had a large body of myths, legends, poetry, and traditional history that was transmitted orally from generation to generation. The excerpts on philosophy and art that follow are examples of the few remnants of ancient nuclear America's cultural developments. They are part of an oral tradition that was finally written down during the early days of conquest. The first text relates Quetzalcoatl's vision of Ometeotl, the dual god and fundamental being in Nahuatl cosmology. He is depicted as having a masculine countenance and features that are at the same time feminine. Ometeotl is master of what is near and far, master of everything that is. He is the origin; he dresses in stars like a maiden and vests himself in black and red, colors symbolizing wisdom.

> And it is stated and said that
> Quetzalcoatl called upon, as his
> proper god, one who dwells in the
> interior of the heaven.

> He invoked her, surrounded by a skirt of
> stars,
> him who gives light to all things;
> Mistress of our flesh, lord of our flesh,
> She who clothes herself in black,
> He who clothes himself in red,
> She who established the earth firmly,
> He who gives activity to the earth.

> Thither did he direct his words,
> thus did he know himself,
> toward the place of the duality
> and of the nine crossbeams

in which the heaven consists.
And as he knew,
He called on him who dwelled there,
directed supplications to him,
living in meditation and in retirement.

The second text concerns the Aztecs' conception of knowledge, tradition, and of those who develop and transmit it. The figure of the tlamatini, he who knows something, pre-figures the more modern Spanish American writer-critic. Master of black and red, the symbols of wisdom, the tlamatini illuminates the world and man as "a full torch that does not smoke." He thinks and writes down his thoughts in the sacred books of paintings. He is a teacher who attempts to give humans a proper face, a proper personality and character so that they "become prudent and careful." He desires to know and guide his pupils on the path to the mysteries of the Upper World (*Topan*) and Under World (*Mitlan*); he shows forth his light over the world and knows what is above us and the region of the dead. It is thanks to him that men humanize their desires, fortify their hearts, and receive a strict instruction.

> The tlamatini: a light, a torch,
> an ample torch that does not smoke.
> A mirror pierced through,
> A mirror full of holes on both sides.
> His is the ink black and red,
> his are the codices,
> he is the master of the books of paintings.
> He is himself the scripture and the wisdom.
> He is the way, the true guide for others.
> He leads persons and things,
> he is the guide in human affairs.

> The good tlamatini is careful (like a doctor)
> and guards the tradition.
> His is the wisdom handed down,
> he is the one who teaches it,
> he follows the truth
> and he does not desist from counseling.
> he makes strange faces wise,
> he makes them develop it.
> He opens their ears, he illuminates them.
> He is the master of guides,
> he gives them their path,
> and one depends on him.

> He puts a mirror before the others,
> he makes them prudent, and careful;
> he makes them acquire a face.
> He establishes things,
> regulates their path,
> disposes and orders.
> He turns his light upon the world.
> He knows that which is above us (Topan)
> and the region of the dead (Mitlan).

> He is a thoughtful man;
> everyone is comforted by him,
> is corrected, is taught.
> Thanks to him, the people humanizes its
> desire
> and received a strict instruction.

> Comforter of the heart,
> comforter of the people,
> help and remedy,

he brings healing to all.

Among the many tlamatinimi who enlightened pre-Columbian America, the best known was Nezahualcoyotl. Born in 1402, the son of a king, he became one of the most influential men of his time. He opposed the Aztecan practice of human sacrifice and the wars of flowers, while seeking the possibility of overcoming death. He searched for a root that would allow man to escape time and change. The third text shows Nezahualcoyotl's awareness of the effects of time on man and world.

> Perhaps one with root truly lives upon the
>   earth?
> Not forever on the earth;
> Only for a short time here.
> Even if it be of jade it will be broken,
> even if it be of gold it will be shattered,
> even if it be the plumage of a bird that rends
>   itself.
> Not forever on the earth;
> only for a short time here.
>
> Only for an instant does the meeting endure,
> for a brief time there is glory. . . .
> None of your friends has root,
> only for a short time are we given here as
>   loans,
> your lovely flowers. . . .
> Everything that flourishes in your mat or in
>   your chair,
> nobility on the field of battle,
> on which depends lordship and command,
> your flowers of war . . .
> are only dried flowers.
>
> I am inebriated, I weep, I am afflicted,
> I think, I say,
> within myself I find it;
> if I would never die,
> if I would never disappear.
> There where there is no death,
> there where death is conquered,
> there will I go.
> If I would never die,
> if I would never disappear.

Nezahualcoyotl's fears and anxiety foreshadow the fate of his people a few years after his death: With the arrival of the Spaniards, Indian cultures disappeared. In their haste to dominate, the Spaniards were swift to destroy, not only native political and economic structures, but the Indian's cultural world as well.

Fortunately, not all Spaniards came to destroy; some came to salvage what was being destroyed. Among the latter were priests and other humanists, who guided the efforts of young Indians writing down some of their fading literature. To be sure, precisely because of this guiding effort, the literature written down by the Indians for the most part treated their destroyed culture nostalgically and made excuses for that destruction. (In these works one finds the earliest manifestations of the Dream of a mestizo Spanish America.) Even recording pre-Columbian history was aimed at preserving and incorporating it into the new ideology supporting the new order. Nonetheless, among the bulk of recorded history and lore, there are crucial remnants that are an awesome testimony of the conquest.

This testimony remains in the Spanish American memory, bearing witness to the fact that the mestizo culture was born of rape. To forget this past would entail the mestizo's self-denial; a self-denial that has never been possible, despite many attempts.

In their testimony, the Aztecan cultural elite, for example, tell how the Spanish conqueror treated the treasures of their civilization. In a naïve attempt to save his empire, Moctezuma took the Spaniards to his treasure house in Teucalco; there, the Spaniards carried out all the cultural treasures. "Immediately, the gold was taken from war shields and from other emblems. They made a huge mound of gold and set everything else afire. They burned, burned everything that was not gold, no matter how valuable: Thus everything went to ashes" [Miguel León-Portilla, *Visión de los vencidos: Relaciones indígenas de la conquista,* 1958]. Unable to stop the ransacking of their cultural world, the tlamatinime contemplated the destruction of their ancient knowledge of the world, the vision of the heavens. The books of Chilam Balam preserve the lament of the ancient teachers over the destruction of their lessons by a horde of "damned bearded foreigners: Lost will be science, lost will be wisdom" [*El libro de los libros de Chilam Balam,* trans. Alfredo Barrera Vásquez and Silvia Rendón, 1969] and they describe the violence and destruction of the gods:

> You tell us
> that our gods are untrue.
> This is a new thing
> that you tell us,
> it disturbs us,
> it fills us with grief.
> For our ancestors,
> those who were before us,
> those who lived on the earth,
> were not accustomed to tell us so.
> And now should we destroy
> the ancient rule of life? . . .
> Truly we cannot believe it,
> we do not accept it as the truth
> even though it offends you.

In the end, however, an end that came centuries later, the Indians had to admit the death of their gods; the destruction all around them demanded it. Their fears were to become prophecies:

> Let us die then,
> Let us perish then,
> For our gods are already dead!

True, beneath their vision of doom, the Indians kindled a hope of enduring, of returning—a forever truncated hope. "This is our genealogy," says the testimony of the Cakchiqueles, "which will never be lost because we know our origin and shall never forget our forefathers [*Anales de los cakchiqueles,* trans. Adrian Recinos, 1950]. But remembrance is a double-edged sword; when the past becomes a refuge, the future turns opaque. Memory can be a catapult to action, but it is also the pastime of a people without a vision of the future. In the long travail that constitutes the Indian's history since the conquest, the effects of memory of the past have alternated like Ometeotl. For long periods, it has been a sedative: The Indian and his descendant, the mestizo, have retreated to the memory of better times and failed to act in the present. At other times, memory has spurred the same Indian and mestizo to rebellion. (By prohibiting Indian plays where the Incan past was recalled, as in Peru in 1782, the Spaniards showed awareness of the revolutionary potential of collective memory.) Over the years, however, the Indians have lost even the memory of their past. In the twentieth century, the Indians are a people with almost no conscious history; whites and mestizos have become the keepers of the memory. Consequently, the potential for liberation stored therein has left their hands. Here lies one of the reasons why Indian rebellions in the twentieth century have increasingly been directed by mestizos and not by Indians themselves.

Pre-Columbian literature is an important aspect of the literature of today's Spanish America; it records the Indian's glory, hopes, fears, and fate. Surely, pre-Columbian literature translates the vision of a world that neither a white nor a mestizo can totally penetrate, but it constitutes a voice from the past that present-day Spanish Americans can hardly ignore. As such, this literature has become a source of pride as well as shame, guilt, and hatred for modern Spanish Americans. In these testimonies, Spanish America relives the conquest and colonization. As things stand, it is highly unlikely that today's Indians will ever produce a literature that presents a vision of the world in terms other than Western. Indian literature production ceased in the early days of the conquest and, from then on, the literature of Spanish America was to be written in Spanish or by individuals with basically a Western world view.

Two important aspects of the Indian's literary legacy should be stressed. First, much of this literature already points to the coming of a mestizo culture, which was permeated by an apologetic tendency from the very beginning. This effort to forgive and forget the violence of origins began with Spanish American history, since the audience intended for these works was not the Indians themselves but their white masters. Secondly, it must also be stressed that the literature of protest in Spanish America and the role of the writer as social critic began with using literature as a testimony of the genocide days of conquest. The tradition began, therefore, with the protest, however veiled, of a disintegrating civilization aware of its tragedy. And the dual tendency to apologize while protesting that is present in the first Spanish American literature has permeated all subsequent literary production by or about Indians in the region.

A detailed account of the Indian's social conditions during the 300 years of colonial domination is not possible here; suffice it to note the following: The Indian's welfare deteriorated drastically as colonial rule became more secure. As a subject to the Spanish crown, the Indian was required to pay tribute either in gold or work or both, a situation from which Spaniards living in America profited by making the Indian work without wages. Millions of Indians died because of disease, wars, and physical exhaustion resulting from extreme forms of forced labor under the *mita, repartimiento,* and *encomienda* systems. Moreover, the Spanish conquerors saw themselves as racially superior,

and, therefore, they exploited the Indian not only physically by securing his labor without payment but psychologically as well by demanding the obedience and submission of a slave. In other words, the genocide days of the conquest were extended to the colonial period. For centuries the social, economic, and political privileges of colonial society rested on the servitude of the Indian people.

In the literature of conquest, the Indian was depicted as a mixture of warrior and savage. Through this literary image, the Spanish chroniclers sang of Spanish courage and the triumph of civilization. In their literary vision, the writers of this period transformed the Indian's culture and psychology to fit preconceived models. Alfonso de Ercilla y Zúñiga (1533-1594), the most gifted writer of this period, for example, presented the Indian in his long poetic work *La araucana* (1569-1589) as an unhappy cross between a European classical mythopoetical being and a savage. In this work, it is not uncommon for savages to deliver their thoughts in the most classical Spanish, and less gifted writers were equally inaccurate in their portrayal of the Indian. This image of the Indian remained in Spanish American literature for centuries to come.

This view of the Indian was a matter of course, given the literary tradition and the audience of the time. As were most writers of the period, Ercilla was a Spaniard who wrote for a Spanish audience for whom the classical form was required for writing good poetry. As Concha Meléndes has noted in her well-known analysis of literature about Indians written during this period, the authors carried with them their classical culture "intercepted between the physical object and their vision" [Concha Meléndes, *La novela indianista en Hispanoamérica: 1832-1889,* 1939].

During the ensuing years of colonial domination, the Indian's image did not change substantially; however, elements introduced in the literature of Spanish America by Indians who survived the demise of their society were further accentuated. As noted, the work of Indian chroniclers was tinged with nostalgia and apology for the violence committed by the Spaniards. One hundred years into the colonial period, Inca Garcilaso de la Vega, the illegitimate son of an Incan princess and a Spanish captain, fully developed this dual tendency in his famous *Comentarios reales,* published in 1609.

Garcilaso's work is one of the most knowledgeable accounts of Incan culture, but, like the work of all Indian chroniclers, the *Comentarios reales* tends to apologize for the conquest. In fact, Garcilaso viewed the conquest of the Incas by the Spaniards as the end of a long process of preparing the Andean Indians for salvation—a preparation that had begun with founding and expanding the Incan empire itself. Some of the passages most critical of the Spanish conquest deal with the lack of missionary zeal on the part of Spanish conquerors. Conquest and colony were thus justified by an appeal to the sublime Christian God and superior Western culture. It is no accident that Garcilaso presented his case to whites and no longer to Indians; that he did so in a highly stylized and erudite Spanish (he identified Cuzco with Rome in the preface and in several places within the text, and biblical and Greek references abound) shows to what extent he had internalized his father's culture as his own.

As did other chroniclers, Garcilaso emphasized the past, not the present or future of the Indians: The beautiful narrative of the *Comentarios reales* is nostalgic. But in a masterful dialectic move, Garcilaso transformed this nostalgia into a vision of utopia; in this work, Incan leaders appear godlike, and their society approaches perfection—except for a few drawbacks such as their pagan religion. In transforming the past into a utopia, Garcilaso made one of his most important contributions to Spanish American culture. For by positing an Incan utopian past, Garcilaso subtly but forcefully protested against the injustice of the Indian's conditions in his time. True, Garcilaso's protest was devoid of militancy and did not seek to marshal soldiers for a cause; it only attempted to enjoin the sympathies of the conquerors. Nonetheless, showing the Spaniards that the Incas had had a complex culture and a high sense of justice, honor, and pride constituted a tacit act of protest against the Indian's present state and the Spaniards' arrogance.

This view of a utopian Indian past has been used again and again as an ideological weapon; it was used by Bolívar and his generation in the nineteenth century and by the indigenista movement and various political parties in the twentieth century. In this sense, Garcilaso's work must be seen as one of the foundations of the indigenista novel. Also, by maintaining the dual tendency noted, Garcilaso contributed to developing the Spanish American tradition of the writer as critic (witness to injustice) and literature as a means to socioethical ends, while maintaining ambivalence toward the benefactors of this protest.

If Garcilaso wrote with nostalgia, Fray Bartolomé de Las Casas, a Spanish Dominican priest, did so with compassion. Of all those who defended the Indian throughout Spanish American history, none surpasses Bartolomé de Las Casas in kindness, perseverance, and courage. His denunciation of the violence that accompanied the Spanish conquest of America has always inspired intellectuals, men of science, and social revolutionaries and influenced their attitude toward the Indian problem in Spanish America.

Bartolomé de Las Casas's work, however, situated as it was in the period of conquest, could not free itself from some idealization of the Indian and his world. In his passionate defense, the Dominican priest presented the Indian as virtuous, innocent, and submissive. He set Indian life before conquest in a quasi-utopian world, in a state of social tranquility reminiscent of the childhood of the human race. With the pangs of civilization not having reached such a world, the Indian was thought to live in a most harmonious relationship with nature in a self-contained paradise.

No two other men were to influence ideas about the Indian of the Americas held by the nineteenth-century European romantic writers as did the Dominican Bartolomé de Las Casas and the mestizo Garcilaso de la Vega. They gave European writers the image of the noble savage, the uncorrupted, happy, natural man. This image of the Indian before his encounter with the civilization that put him in chains helped European romantic writers to rise above history to the realm of abstract human nature.

When nineteenth-century Spanish American writers rediscovered the Indian, such a rediscovery did not involve the Indians around them, that is, the poor and exploited Indian. Rather, it involved the Indians of the French intellectuals; in other words, the virtuous, noble, savage Indian whom their European mentors first knew through the work of Bartolomé de Las Casas and Garcilaso de la Vega. As a consequence of this importation, the Indian of literary creation in nineteenth-century Spanish America was the transformed, rarefied, ahistorical Indian presented in the works of Voltaire, Rousseau, Saint-Pierre, Chateaubriand, Marmontel, and others. Thus, the real Indian was overlooked by the Spanish American literary imagination and was largely supplanted by an imagined Indian—a poetic Indian extracted from the works of conscientious and pious men. In this importation of the Indian character, the profound cultural dependency of the Spanish American cultural elite during the nineteenth century is most clearly seen.

This romantic rediscovery of the Indian by Spanish American writers coincided with movements for independence from Spain; in fact, both political ideology and literary romanticism were mutually reinforcing. The leaders of the revolutionary movement were romantic visionaries who made the Indian a symbol of their cause. In their manifestos, programs, and personal correspondence, these caudillos evoked a romantic Indian past; a poem by the Venezuelan patriot Andrés Bello (1781-1865) is significant:

> Not for long would the Spanish foreigners
> usurp the Kingdom of the Sun,
> nor, in seeing his throne in such disgrace,
> the ghosts of Manco Capac moan.

To reiterate, the wars for independence in Spanish America were led by members of the creole and mestizo elite who claimed the political and economic power that had always been in the hands of the Spanish king and his representatives. Ideologically, the wars for independence were fought with vague notions of liberty, equality, and fraternity that Spanish American elites had learned from the French Revolution. These revolutionaries advanced the interests of creole and mestizo elites who were guided by tenets of economic liberalism because they found colonial rule fettered their economic development.

The changes in political and economic power that took place during the wars for independence did not, however, substantially change the lot of the majority of the Spanish American people. The Nation became fragmented, largely due to the lack of radical social transformations. Indians, blacks, and the majority of poor mestizos, who had fought the war, gained little or nothing either as a class or an ethnic group. When, in February 1825, Bolívar claimed in Lima that the revolution had broken the Indian's chains, he was carried away by his own rhetoric. In fact, in the transfer of power from the Spanish kings to the local oligarchies, the Indian lost both economically and politically. For, if in the past, the Indian had been exploited, he at least had had the protection of colonial laws that gave him some security for his lands. With the abolition of the legal colonial structure, the Indian was more thoroughly exploited by his new masters who introduced laws aimed at dispossessing him of more of his lands. In the ensuing years, through deception and outright violence, the Indian lost much of his land to creole and upper-class mestizo landlords.

It is important to emphasize that during the period of activity to found a united Spanish America, the Indian was used not only physically as a soldier but symbolically as well. In both cases, he was used to advance the interests of his eventual exploiters. Of course, since real Indians were an indispensable support for the revolutionary armies, the leaders of these revolutions did not ignore the Indian's situation while the fighting was going on. Some steps were taken to better his lot although, more often than not, these steps were ineffective and even counterproductive. After the revolution, when the transfer of power permitted old aristocrats to become presidents of new republics, the Indian was no longer a viable political or military force. And once his symbolic and military role had been exhausted, the interest granted his condition by the elites also began to fade. Thus, the Indian reverted to his position of beast of burden in the eyes of the new Spanish American society.

As political activity to found a united Spanish America gave way to the Dream, so, too, the combination of symbolism and reality, literature and politics, which the Indian represented, gave way to a purely literary romanticism. Significantly, the Argentine Esteban Echeverría (1805-1851) laid the foundation for the romantic literary movement in 1834. That is, the romantic movement achieved a comfortable separation from politics and a degree of cohesiveness as a literary school only when the local oligarchies were secure in their positions of power. The Indian, whose image during the wars of independence supported a call to combat, throughout the rest of the nineteenth century became a purely nostalgic and exotic element in Spanish American letters.

Due to its abstractness and generalities, when the romantic notion of human nature that fostered the brotherhood of mankind was transported from Europe to Spanish America, it enabled the Spanish American writer to disregard the Indian's real situation. As a literary movement, romanticism in Spanish America failed to deal with the Indian's psychology, culture, or objective social position. Bent on proving their national pride, many of the post-independence romantic writers took flight into the Indian's golden past. And by doing so, they idealized the Indian until he was little more than a product of their imagination. In this context, the Ecuadorian writer Juan León Mera (1832-1894) was able to write that "everything indigenous exists as a historic remembrance, and I do not see any inconvenience in its being useful in a poetic work, be it as a principal or secondary theme [in Cometta Manzoni's *El indio en la poesía de América española,* 1939]. There can be little doubt that for the romantic writers the Indian was long since dead. One of the last writers in this tradition, the Uruguayan Juan Zorrilla de San Martín (1855-1931), presents the romantic writers' view of the Indian [in Augusto Tamayo Vargas, *Literatura en Hispano América,* vol. 1]:

> He is silent
> Silent forever, like time
> Like his race,
> Like the desert
> Like a grave that the dead has abandoned.

The Indian seemed to be no more than a memory. But if this view could be held with some justification by Argentine or Cuban writers in whose countries the Indian population during the nineteenth century was small and rapidly disappearing, the fact that Juan León Mera was able to share such a view is indicative of the romantic period as a whole—his Andean country Ecuador was one where the majority of the population was Indian. . . .

A final point should be made before discussing the social factors that made indigenista novels possible. While Indian novels in the nineteenth century were basically romantic, indigenista novels in the twentieth century were basically realist. This literary rupture, as might be expected, followed in the footsteps of a similar rupture in the European tradition, namely, the broad transformation from romanticism to realism in literature.

European realism arrived in Spanish America in the 1860s. By the time it developed into a significant school there at the turn of the century, its influence in Europe, especially in France, where it had been the strongest, had diminished; nonetheless, the strong influence that French writers had on Spanish American letters during the wars for independence continued under realism. Like Chateaubriand and Marmontel in the romantic period, Balzac and especially Zola became the mentors of Spanish American writers of Indian novels during the realist period.

To be sure, transplanting European realism in Spanish America did not take place without fundamental changes. In Europe, for example, such French writers as Balzac and later Zola shared their eminence with the great realists of Russia, Tolstoy and Dostoyevsky. In Spanish America, the Spanish cultural elite, always fond of French letters, was not decisively influenced by Russian writers. Tolstoy's work, with its heavy dose of mysticism, did not constitute one of the pillars of realism in Spanish America, nor did Dostoyevsky's insights into, and fascination with, psychology gain many followers.

In addition to the Spanish American elite's predilection for French letters, there were other reasons for the lack of influence by Russian writers. For one thing, at the time realism arrived in Spanish America, the cultural elite was going through a period of optimistic faith in science. And scientific positivism as a philosophy of art or politics was too strong to allow mysticism in Tolstoy's tradition. Influenced by Mexico's positivist thinkers (the científicos) and Peru's Gonzáles Prada, a wave of anticlericalism swept across Spanish America, announcing the age of enlightenment. Instead of mysticism, therefore, it was anticlericalism that later became one of the principal characteristics of the indigenista movement in Spanish America.

The near absence of Tolstoy's influence did not mean, however, that nonscientific concerns were unimportant to the indigenistas; even at the height of the movement, Spanish America's indigenista writers never ceased to preach morality. What happened was that the old individual morality, basically Catholic and mainly concerned with salvation and the soul, gave way to a kind of *social morality* concerned with the Indian's salvation. From the 1860s until at least the 1950s, realists, indigenistas prominent among them, were perhaps the most moral of all writers in Spanish America. In this sense, Zola, and not Balzac, became the true master of indigenismo. From its very inception, indigenismo was engaged in a moral crusade to stamp out the evils of society; literature was a tool for regeneration. This original moral stance of indigenismo survived the demise of its initial ally, scientific positivism, and continued invigorated under Marxist socialism. It is true that socialist writers did not openly call for moral regeneration, nor did they draw their inspiration primarily from a religious conception of the world; nonetheless, a deep moral stance is evident throughout their work. Marxism in the hands of these writers, particularly in the Andes, became the light that showed how to destroy the evils of society. These writers endeavored to liberate man from social sins.

European realism underwent other changes with its introduction in Spanish America; two of these changes were the near absence of pessimism before the evils of society and the negligible treatment of sexual behavior. Spanish American indigenismo, for example, inspired as it was first by scientific positivism and its faith in science and progress and later by socialism based on Marxist thinking, could not have easily become pessimistic. In fact, as Marxism displaced positivism in the 1930s, indigenista literature became even more optimistic, so that the denunciation of social evils was paired, if not with a program, then with a hope for their solution and abolition.

As to the shady side of sexuality, Spanish American elites had not yet thrown away their long cherished *pudor,* their sense of shame. Naturalistic writing on sex was not in good taste; besides, to the indigenista writers, worse than sexual perversion was the corruption of social, political, and economic institutions, the exploitation by the rich of the workers in general, and the Indians in particular. The crudest scenes ever depicted in Spanish American literature up to the middle of the twentieth century were those in Jorge Icaza's *Huasipungo* (1934), a novel about the social, economic, political, and spiritual exploitation of Indians by the ruling classes in Ecuador. The Indians in this novel appear almost subhuman, with the result that such a presentation is an indictment against the ruling classes, which are portrayed as greedy and morally corrupt.

Perhaps the best way to characterize the changes in perspective that accompanied the shift from romanticism to realism in Indian novels is to view them as obeying different gestalts. On the one hand, the romantics view Spanish America as a country composed of beautiful and unexplored landscapes, noble and savage Indians, and heroes who die romantic deaths; in short, according to this view, Spanish America is suspended in an ideal world. The realist school, on the other hand, depicts a society led by a morally bankrupt elite supported by a corrupt military

machine and clergy, all of whom live off the Indian's labor. According to this view, Spanish America is divided into a wealthy and corrupt minority and a sick, exploited, hungry, and dehumanized majority. To the indigenista writer, especially under the influence of Marxism, Spanish America had a long history of corruption and oppression; however, deliverance is foreshadowed, that is, the solution and transcendence of evil in the future.

FURTHER READING

Anthologies

Cohen, J. M., ed. *Latin American Writing Today.* Harmondsworth, England: Penguin, 1967, 267 p.
>   Contains poetry and short fiction by authors such as Jorge Luis Borges, César Vallejo, Pablo Neruda, Octavio Paz, Carlos Fuentes, and Gabriel García Marquez.

Secondary Sources

Anderson Imbert, Enrique. *Spanish-American Literature: A History,* translated by John V. Falconieri. Detroit: Wayne State University Press, 1963, 616 p.
>   Provides an inclusive chronology of authors and literary movements from the Spanish conquest through 1963.

Brotherston, Gordon. *Latin American Poetry: Origins and Presence.* London: Cambridge University Press, 1975, 228 p.
>   Analyzes Latin American poetry in its historical context, and discusses the work of poets such as Rubén Dario, Octavio Paz, Pablo Neruda, and César Vallejo.

——. *The Emergence of the Latin American Novel.* London: Cambridge University Press, 1977, 164 p.
>   Analyzes the novels of authors such as Alejo Carpentier, Juan Carlos Onetti, Julio Cortázar, and Gabriel García Marquez.

Brushwood, John S. *Genteel Barbarism.* Lincoln: University of Nebraska Press, 1981, 233 p.
>   Discussion of eight Spanish-American novels of the nineteenth century, with a bibliography of history, criticism, and theory.

Crow, John A. "Some Aspects of Spanish American Fiction." In *South Atlantic Studies for Sturgis E. Leavitt,* edited by Thomas B. Stroup and Sterling A. Stoudemire, pp. 109-25. Washington, D.C.: Scarecrow Press, 1953.
>   Analyzes several contemporary Latin American novels.

DeCosta, Miriam, ed. *Blacks in Hispanic Literature: Critical Essays.* Port Washington, N.Y.: Kennikat Press, 1977, 157 p.
>   Discusses Caribbean fiction and poetry, and explores such topics as the image of blacks and the portrayal of slavery in Latin American literature.

Esquenazi-Mayo, Roberto. "Social Aspects of the Contemporary Spanish American Novel." In *Artists and Writers in the Evolution of Latin America*, edited by Edward Davis Terry, pp. 73-83. University, Ala.: University of Alabama Press, 1971.
>   Explores the Latin American novel, with emphasis on the works of Colombian writer Caballero Calderon.

Forster, Merlin H. "Latin American *Vanguardismo:* Chronology and Terminology." In *Tradition and Renewal,* edited by Merlin H. Forster, pp. 12-50. Urbana: University of Illinois Press, 1975.

Examines the influence of several modern literary movements, such as Futurism, Surrealism, and Ultrism, on Latin American literature.

Foster, David William. "Latin American Documentary Narrative," *Publications of the Modern Language Association of America* 99, No. 1 (January 1984): 41-55.

Includes a bibliography of literature and criticism in Spanish and English.

————, ed. *Handbook of Latin American Literature,* 2nd ed. New York: Garland Publishing, 1992, 799 p.

Provides overviews of fiction, drama, and poetry in twenty-one Latin American countries, as well as sections on Latino writing in the United States, paraliterature, and film.

Franco, Jean. *An Introduction to Spanish-American Literature.* Cambridge: Cambridge University Press, 1969, 390 p.

Includes essays on topics such as literature and nationalism, the avant-garde in poetry, and regionalism in the novel and short story.

Henriquez-Urena, Pedro. *Literary Currents in Hispanic America.* Cambridge, Mass.: Harvard University Press, 1949, 345 p.

Charts the development of Latin American literature from the Spanish conquest through 1940.

McMurray, George R. *Spanish-American Writing since 1941: A Critical Survey.* New York: Ungar, 1987, 340 p.

Discusses major figures and movements in modern Latin American fiction, poetry and drama.

Ortega, Julio. "The New Spanish-American Narrative." In his *Poetics of Change,* translated by Galen D. Greaser, pp. 3-10. Austin: University of Texas Press, 1984.

Examines stories and novels by five authors as part of a discussion of the changing nature of Latin American narrative.

Pring-Mill, Robert. "The Poetry of Protest." *Times Literary Supplement,* No. 3882 (6 August 1976): 994.

Reviews Robert Marquez's *Latin American Revolutionary Poetry,* and collections by five Latin American poets.

Sosnowski, Saul. "Spanish-American Literary Criticism: The State of the Art." In *Changing Perspectives in Latin American Studies,* edited by Christopher Mitchell, pp. 163-82. Stanford: Stanford University Press, 1988.

Focuses on "the content and praxis" of contemporary academic criticism of Latin American literature.

Spell, Jefferson Rea. *Contemporary Spanish-American Fiction.* Chapel Hill, N.C.: University of North Carolina Press, 1944, 323 p.

Examines early modern Latin American fiction, including the work of Eduardo Barrios, Horacio Quiroga, José Eustacio Rivera, and Jorge Icaza.

Virgillo, Carmelo, and Lindstrom, Naomi, eds. *Woman as Myth and Metaphor in Latin American Literature.* Columbia, Mo.: University of Missouri Press, 1985, 199 p.

Anthology of essays on the role of women in Latin American literature. The collection also includes discussion of myth and folk-culture.

Zubatsky, David. *Latin American Authors: An Annotated Guide to Bibliographies.* Metuchen: Scarecrow Press, 1986, 332 p.

Alphabetical listing of authors with bibliographical sources.

The Modern Essay

INTRODUCTION

Michel de Montaigne is considered by most commentators to be the first essayist, introducing the form in 1580 when he published *Essais*, a collection of brief, informal prose pieces. Montaigne's title, which means "attempts," suggested the searching, sometimes rambling nature of his prose, which, although stylistically polished, was intended to present the author's discursive thought process as he investigated a variety of topics. Most of the characteristics that remain intrinsic to the modern essay derive from Montaigne's example: subjective point of view, informal tone, unstructured form, brevity, and an accomplished prose style. The essay has traditionally been a forum for writers to investigate and present their opinions, concerns, and interests from a personal point of view using a variety of forms, including letters, reviews, criticism, memoirs, nature and travel writing, philosophical and ethical meditations, and newspaper and magazine columns. The modern essay had its early exemplars in writers such as Virginia Woolf, J. B. Priestley, and A. C. Benson who, in 1932, asserted that "the point of the essay is not the subject, for any subject will suffice, but the charm of personality." The varied and informal nature of the essay has led to much debate during the last century as to whether the form can justifiably stand as a distinct literary genre. In 1910, Georg Lukács vigorously defended the essay as a unique and creative form of literature in the introduction to his *Soul and Form*. The last half of the twentieth century has seen a return of the personal element in the modern essay, with the emergence of New Journalists such as Joan Didion, Norman Mailer, and Tom Wolfe, authors whose writing moves beyond reportage to provide personal perspectives and interpretations of issues and events.

REPRESENTATIVE WORKS

Baldwin, James
   Notes of a Native Son 1955
   The Fire Next Time 1963
Beerbohm, Max
   And Even Now 1920
   A Peep into the Past, and Other Prose Pieces 1972
Belloc, Hilaire
   On Nothing and Kindred Subjects 1908
   On Everything 1910
   One Thing and Another: A Miscellany from His Uncollected Essays 1955
Benchley, Robert
   Of All Things 1921
   No Poems, or, Around the World Backwards and Sideways 1932

Benson, A. C.
   The Upton Letters, by T. B. 1905
   From a College Window 1906
   Beside Still Waters 1907
Berry, Wendell
   The Long-Legged House 1969
   The Hidden Wound 1970
Chesterton, G. K.
   Twelve Types 1902
   Come to Think of It . . . 1930
   The Common Man 1950
Didion, Joan
   Slouching towards Bethlehem 1968
   The White Album 1979
Dillard, Annie
   Pilgrim at Tinker Creek 1974
   Teaching a Stone to Talk 1982
   The Annie Dillard Reader 1994
Eliot, T. S.
   The Sacred Wood: Essays on Poetry and Criticism 1920
   The Use of Poetry and The Use of Criticism: Studies in the Relation of Criticism to Poetry in England 1933
Lawrence, D. H.
   Phoenix 1936
   Phoenix II 1968
Liebling, A. J.
   The Road Back to Paris 1944
   The Most of A. J. Liebling 1963
   Liebling at the New Yorker: Uncollected Essays 1994
Lopate, Phillip
   Bachelorhood: Tales of the Metropolis 1981
Mailer, Norman
   Existential Errands 1972
   Pieces and Pontifications 1982
McPhee, John
   The John McPhee Reader 1976
   Coming into the Country 1977
Mencken, H. L.
   Prejudices. 6 vols. 1921-1928
   A Vintage Mencken 1955
Morley, Christopher
   Off the Deep End 1928
   Streamlines 1936
Orwell, George
   Such, Such Were the Joys 1952
Ozick, Cynthia
   Art and Ardor 1983
   Metaphor and Memory 1989
Pickering, Jr., Samuel
   A Continuing Education 1985
   The Right Distance 1987
   Trespassing 1994
Priestly, J. B.
   Papers from Lilliput 1922

OVERVIEW

Mary E. Rucker

SOURCE: "The Literary Essay and the Modern Temper," in *Papers on Language & Literature,* Vol. 11, No. 3, Summer, 1975, pp. 317-35.

[*In the following essay, Rucker outlines the evolution of the modern essay.*]

Although a generic definition is conspicuously absent in the large body of periodical literature devoted to the essay between 1880 and 1950, many American and British journalists and essayists debated its viability and its capacity to express the modern sensibility. The issue underlying the debate was, ultimately, the function of art in an era of dramatic social change. The seemingly blithe humanism that allowed the essay to reach its apogee in the early nineteenth century was rapidly undermined by the deterministic sciences and by the colossal growth of technology and industry. Each of these developments tended either to deny or to undercut the validity of spiritual realities and the imaginative constructs predicated upon them. Not idealism but rather pragmatism and empiricism, systems of thought that focus upon the immediate, progressive, and existentially vital, became the focal point of politics, education, philosophy, and eventually the fine arts.

Granted that the bulk of the criticism of the essay was written by non-academicians whose concepts of the subject matter and style of the form were varied, this criticism nevertheless reveals popular opinion, which may or may not be sanctioned by literary historians. It was of crucial importance in that it reflected the taste of that audience to which the weeklies and monthlies were addressed. Because of its brevity, the essay has relied upon the periodical press, which, in meeting the demands of its readers, finally imposed upon the genre a content and method appropriate to the social order. Traditionally, the familiar essayist presented his reflections upon commonplace incidents and objects and appealed to the emotions of his readers, who sought not intellectual food but rather lyricism. If he assumed the role of the philosopher, he pretended to be no more than the arm-chair philosopher whose loose cogitations upon human destiny were primarily to entertain. The essay has been a form for a consideration of non-momentous matters, and its existence presupposed in society a well-being that allowed for the detached observer and for the appreciation of often eccentric individuality. With the emergence of the deterministic sciences and the industrial and technological developments of the past century, however, the aloof yet familiar stance of the essayist began to smack of gentility; his art was judged neither organically related to nor pragmatically functional in that society of which it was a part. Consequently, during the last decades of the preceding century, the traditional essay began either to evolve into or to be replaced by the article, which emphasizes the polemic. By the 1930s, both editors and a majority of readers won their demand for a periodical literature addressed to the biological and existential needs of man. This development did not, of course, result in the immediate extinction of the essay, which has had its defenders and practitioners even during the most hectic decades of this century. And the new journalism of, for example, Norman Mailer and Tom Wolfe is to a degree a resurgence of the personalism that characterizes the essay. In general, however, the cultural context of the last hundred years or so has been such that the delicate art of the familiar essay has been judged mere escapism.

> With the emergence of the deterministic sciences and the industrial and technological developments of the past century, the aloof yet familiar stance of the essayist began to smack of gentility; his art was judged neither organically related to nor pragmatically functional in that society of which it was a part.
>
> —*Mary E. Rucker*

The desired relation between art and the social order resulting from an emphasis upon the empirical and the pragmatic was formulated by José Ortega y Gasset and George Santayana, both of whom criticized what they perceived to be a split between the intellectual and the existential life of American and European cultures. In *The Modern Theme* Ortega argued that the values set up by culture are never fulfilled under existential conditions because they bear no relation to the biological and historical needs of man. As Ortega saw it, "The 'Good, the Beautiful and the True' only achieve estimable importance in the service of culture. The doctrine of culture is a kind of Christianity without God. The attributes of the latter sovereign reality—Goodness, Truth and Beauty—have been amputated or dismantled from the divine person, and once they were separated became deified. Science, Law, Morality, Art, etc., are activities . . . which the culturist only appreciates in so far as they have been antecedently disintegrated from the integral process of vitality which creates and sustains them." Ortega opted for the vital and the existential, and this preference accounts for his essentially positive attitude toward the younger generation of the 1920s who rejected not only culturalism but also the two inherited methods of dealing with the antinomy between life and culture: relativism and rationalism. Not willing to sacrifice either truth or life, one of which is demanded by either system, the younger generation chose perspectivity, which finds truth from the point of view of the observer and thus makes truth and culture depend from life. Hence the new artists debunked art, declaring it to be a thing of no transcendent value. Whereas the culturist deemed art of value because it is a copy either of lived realities or of realities humanized by the artist's temperament and because it deals with human destinies, the new artist believed that art is a mere image, a transparency devoid of human or real substance and hence is not a vehicle for the redemption and salvation of man. Art is art only insofar as it dehumanizes, derealizes reality; and to the extent that the dehumanization of art served spontaneous man, it was made subservient to the existential.

Very similar to Ortega's vitalism is Santayana's naturalism. Certainly Santayana's belief in the dependence of essence and spirit on matter underlies his charge against American culture: that its intellectual life has no direct relation to its practical life. In his famous "The Genteel Tradition in American Philosophy," Santayana asserted that

> America is . . . a country with two mentalities, one a survival of the beliefs and standards of the fathers, the other an expression of the instincts, practice and discoveries of the younger generations. In all the higher things of the mind—in religion, in literature, in the moral emotions—it is the hereditary spirit that still prevails. . . . The truth is that onehalf of the American mind, that not occupied intensely in practical affairs, has remained . . . slightly becalmed; it has floated gently in the back-water, while, alongside, in invention and industry and social organisation the other half of the mind was leaping down a sort of Niagara Rapids.

This split is symbolized by the colonial mansion and the sky-scraper. "The American Will," Santayana wrote, "inhabits the sky-scraper; the American Intellect inhabits the colonial mansion. The one is the sphere of the American man; the other, at least predominantly, of the American woman. The one is all aggressive enterprise; the other is all genteel tradition."

Both Ortega and Santayana argued for an organic relation between imaginative constructs and social existence. So did those critics who contended that the familiar essay was warped by gentility. They held that neither its conventional subject matter nor its technique was organically related to society and that, given the crucial issues that readers confronted in their practical lives, the form was trivial. The opponents agreed that the modern sensibility made inevitable the rejection of a genre incompatible with its existential needs. Significantly, other critics defended the genre because it was not geared to the immediate and practical. Believing in an essentially humanistic function of literature, they maintained that because the essay could nourish the soul, which they saw threatened by many aspects of modern history, it should be fostered even though its vitality did not come from the social order.

Perhaps the most important characteristic of a society in which the essay flourishes is a relatively homogenous system of values providing a sense of community to which the essayist may appeal whether he is castigating the town or reflecting upon old china. Although commentators on American society both deny and affirm its having fostered a community such as that of England in the early nineteenth century, it is generally agreed that the culture of both countries was fragmented by industrial and technological developments. Among the earliest commentators on the implications of this fragmentation for the essay was an anonymous writer in the *Cornhill Magazine* for September 1881. He noted that the England of Addison, Steele, and Lamb offered both a homogenous culture upon which their art was predicated and a specific means of experiencing community: the club. In the 1880s, however, the club had deteriorated to a mere crowd of strangers, and the larger social order was no more than "a shifting caravanserai, a vague aggregate of human beings, from which all traces of organic unity [had] disappeared." The closest approximation to the club was the clique, but its emphasis on the cosmopolitan and on uniformity proved to be destructive of the individuality necessary to the essay. American critics too complained of the absence of community. Fragmentation, they suggested, was an inevitable consequence of the acquisitiveness and aggressiveness demanded by the frontier. Although America necessarily promoted the individualism upon which the essayist's art was built, it also fostered action at the expense of reflection and independence at the expense of community. The factors that destroyed community in England thus further prohibited in America not only the emergence of community but also, as a critic noted in the *Saturday Review of Literature* for 23 August 1930, the development of the contemplative mind and the meditative temperament necessary to an appreciation of the familiar essay.

The no-nonsense pragmatism of American culture did not, however, preclude the emergence of an essay believed to be organic to that culture. There were, of course, writers such as C. S. Brooks and Richard Le Galliene who sought to perpetuate the Lambian essay. But the form that critics such as Henry S. Canby judged indigenous was the humorous essay of the 1920s. The Lambian essay, Canby argued, was antithetical to the frankness and pragmatism which define the American, and writers who consciously strived to be "literary" by engaging in "pretty writing about trivial things—neighbors' back yards, books I have read, the idiosyncrasies of cats, humors of the streets—the sort of dilettantish comment that nations writing of a more settled, richer civilization can do well" were out of the mainstream of their society. Americans, Canby contended, are temperamentally prone to exaggerated humor and are inspired by the follies of the crowd rather than by the whimsical aspects of cultured leisure. While many other critics have protested this levelling tendency of democracy, Canby seemed to accept it and used the literature that it had produced as a measure of the essay. The dominant characteristics of this literature are first "a hard-hitting statement, straight out of intense feeling or labored thought," as one finds in Emerson, and second, the "easy-going comment on life, often slangy and colloquial and frequently so undignified as not to seem literature," as one finds in humorists such as Twain and Billings. Exaggerated humor and directness in dealing with the follies of the crowd were, for Canby, the foundations of the essay that emerged in the 1920s, when humorists were deepening their casual perceptions, expanding the pithy sentence into developed thought, and expressing their perceptions more artistically.

Insofar as Canby and others conceived of the essay in terms of the social order, they avoided the antinomy between life and art of which Ortega and Santayana spoke and could declare the form viable despite the forces that threatened its existence. If the absence of community and the pace of life in an industrial society caused some critics to lament the desuetude of the essay while others woefully noted the ways in which it had been transformed, those who accepted literary evolution defended both the viability of the genre and its capacity to express the modern sensibility. In their defense, however, critics such as Florence Finch Kelley too often abandoned all standards to praise any essay that smacked of democracy or Americanism. In the *Bookman* of February 1916 she welcomed the democratization of the Lambian essay and offered Frank Crane's *Just Human,* the individual pieces of which are characterized by the brevity, pith and plainness consonant with democracy, as the apogee of the American essay. She bestowed upon the author questionable praise for skirting literary graces and for platitudinously discussing the obvious. Kelly's values are implicit in her assertion that although Crane "is prone to skip rapidly along the surface of his subject and [although] his observation is often inaccurate and his reasoning faulty," his essays are praiseworthy in that they reveal his fundamental and comprehensive democratic feeling. In the August 1920 issue of the same journal Berton Braley proffered a less irresponsible comment on the changes in the essay which, in his opinion, had ceased to be a "precious, precious thing," a "delicately exclusive snob which can endure association only with a strictly selected number of other snobs. . . . " In addressing the masses, he contended, the American essayist is closer to Dugan in his back lot than to Fauntleroy.

The question which these critics indirectly raise is crucial but not readily answered: to what extent may a particular genre evolve before it becomes another genre? Or, to put it another way, just how far may the traditional essay as it was shaped by Montaigne adapt to a dynamic social order without becoming the polemic article? The earlier mentioned writer in the *Cornhill* at one point declared the essay a lost art and at another stated that it had undergone radical changes toward the article. In a 1902 *Harper's* "Editor's Study" William Dean Howells noted the changes in the genre effected by the modern temper and denied an evolutionary relationship between the essay and the article:

> . . . the moment came when the essay began to confuse itself with the article, and to assume an obligation of constancy to premises and conclusions, with the effect of so depraving the general taste that the article is now desired more and more, and the essay less and less. It is doubtful, the corruption has gone so far, whether there is enough of the lyrical sense left in the reader to appreciate the right essay; whether the right essay would now be suffered; whether if any writer indulged its wilding nature, he would not be suspected of an inability to cultivate the growths that perceptibly nourish, not to say fatten, the intellect.

But whether the article is a distinct genre or merely a development of the essay, the fact is that the traditional essay failed to express the modern sensibility and to meet the needs of its would-be readers. An unsigned article in the issue of *Saturday Review* for 23 July 1932 presents the case succinctly: twentieth-century man not only moves too fast but also thinks too little; he is "too impatient of the speculative, and too avid of accomplishment to tolerate the ruminative discursiveness of the easy chair philosopher." If this critic and Howells suggested that the failure of the form was due to a corruption of society, others believed that it was due to an inherent weakness in the form. G. K. Chesterton, for instance, compared the essay to the thesis and warned that despite the tendency of the modern mind to think in terms of the essay, that is, to make no attempt to come to conclusions, the essay had strayed too far from the structured thesis. Its lack of direction and its impressionism that often conceal sophistry and illogicality were perilous because of the essayist's relation to the masses: "the wandering thinkers have become our substitute for preaching friars. And whether our system is to be materialist or moralist, or sceptical or transcendental, we need more of a system than that [of the wandering essayist]. After a certain amount of wandering the mind wants either to get there or to go home."

The modern temper was such that the well-ordered polemical article willy-nilly displaced the essay as a form of expression. Critical reaction to this change that was noticeable as early as the 1880s was varied. Most essayists, of course, defended the traditional form by indicating its humanitarian and aesthetically utilitarian values, while those journalists who tended to embrace the immediate and the pragmatically utilitarian welcomed the factual, realistic article and denounced the essay because of its gentility. The journalists won the day in part because of the clamor of the 1930s and 1940s and the very real need of their readers for direction in a topsy-turvy world. The conventional subject matter and method of the essay may have been able to nourish one's soul, yet there was the more pressing problem of nourishment for the body, and journals were expected to offer their audience direction in meeting their biological and other existential needs.

Agnes Repplier was among the traditional essayists who defended their art against the changes imposed by the social order. In the 1890s she naively attacked the factualism of the current journals with the bland assertion that the public craved not facts but rather "the maddest and wildest impossibilities" of romance. And, as if morally to justify this craving for romance which the essay could satisfy and to prevent charges of escapism, she asserted that the traditional subject matter of the form effectively strengthened man's faculties and broadened his "sympathies for all that is finest and best." The reader whose sensibility is refined by the essay is more serviceable than the proselytizing activist to his downtrodden neighbors. Repplier's argument is obviously a conventional defense of the fine arts, but it ceased to carry weight for her when World War I magnified the antinomy between the social order and the familiar essay. The Lambian essay, Repplier was compelled to admit, had been blasted by the War, and any writer who continued to practice the art did so at great cost: "the price he pays for his steadfastness is that his words, whether grave or gay, seem to his readers to have been written in some unstirred prehistoric days with which we have lost connection" (*Yale Review,* January 1918). The gentility hinted at here is the crux of John P. Waters's "A Little Old Lady Passes Away" (*The Forum,* July 1933) in which the author comments on the deterioration of the quality of the essay and on the complexities of the 1930s. The era was such that readers once content to indulge in reverie "now groped bewilderingly for *facts,* explanations, anything to help them realign their lives before new discoveries, new techniques, drove out all meaning from life itself." This same note dominates Nathaniel Peffer's rejection of the too genteel essay and his defense of the article that reflects the milieu. Whereas the pre-War world was a world of fixed values and such relatively minor social issues that it could easily accommodate the placid comments of the familiar essay, Peffer wrote, the world of 1935 was chaotic: "nothing can be certain for more than the day thereof, and if there are verities at all, no two men agree on what they are. The social order is being unmade and re-made under our eyes amid fierce but confused contention over what form it shall take and who shall have the right to determine its form." In an unstable world threatened by war, widespread poverty, a precarious economy and the loss of individual rights and authority, editors were obligated to deal realistically with social issues (*Harper's,* December 1935). The demand was for articles on, for example, economic determinism, collectivism, social trends, Hitler, the gold standard, Manchukuan tariffs, and even the state of hogs in Kansas.

The popularity of the article reveals the extent to which periodical literature, at least, is shaped by audience. Even the old-line magazines were affected by the vast changes in society; by the 1920s there had occurred, as Leon Whipple noted in *The Survey* (1 November 1926, 1 January 1927), a "revolution on quality street." In their initial stages, the *Century,* the *Atlantic, Scribner's* and *Harper's* had perpetuated the Brahmin tradition of the Atlantic sea-board. Although they condescendingly recognized local colorists as "native" writers, their editorial policies were determined by the belief that only polite literature, philosophy, and the fine arts were sure indications of a civilized culture. Editors, then, addressed themselves to the elite, for whom the quality magazines were an assurance that life was utopian. The magazines were, in short, essentially an escape from the world of affairs. Whipple quotes Robert Underwood Johnson on the *Century*: its contents revealed "no straining after effect, no simulated robustness, no cocksureness, no 'punch and pep,' no revolutionary madness. In keeping with our tradition it had grace and serenity, and honest sentiment and natural gaiety. . . ." Such a magazine could well house the familiar essay.

However, after the establishment of muck-raking magazines that dealt with vital sociological issues, and after the flood of cheap magazines that reached a large audience and thus obtained more advertising to allow higher payments to contributors, the quality magazines were in financial difficulty. F. L. Allen, an editor of several old-line magazines, noted in the *Atlantic* for November 1947: "what had caused the procession to the graveyard was not a vulgarizing of American taste or even the rise of the mass-production principle in journalism, so much as the editorial—and business—complacency of the onetime leaders of the American magazine world. Unable to find their way out of the ivory tower of learned gentility into the flesh-and-blood world of affairs, they gradually lost touch with American leadership. Only those among them who were able to rediscover the stuff of life were able to carry on." To succeed, therefore, the quality magazines began to recognize the world of affairs and their readers' need for explanations and guidance.

The changes in editorial policy and several essayists' objection to them reflect the tension in America between cultural democracy and cultural elitism. If editors of magazines such as *transition* or the *New Yorker* could at one point say "the plain reader be damned," they were eventually forced to realize that "the consumer is king" and to accept what Theodore Peterson has called the social responsibility theory of the press growing out of urbanization and the industrial and technological revolution. The commercial basis of the press, the redistribution of income resulting from urbanization, and the collectivist theory of society disallowed the elitism which characterized the quality magazines of the early nineteenth century, and as the mass media were institutionalized, many magazines ceased to be primarily literary. They were not only democratized but also standardized in content and technique, tending to perpetuate the status quo as they assumed their responsibility to readers in a world that has often been too complex to experience at first hand. In an important way, then, the minority magazines assumed an organic relation to society. Yet insofar as they merely reflected the social order, it was impossible for essayists at least to shape that order by reaffirming values that appeared outmoded or by perceiving it from that perspective which has traditionally been granted the artist and is too readily labelled "elitist."

If the belief that old-line magazines should shape society, not by escaping the world of affairs, but rather by placing those affairs in a larger perspective is in fact a pejoratively elitist belief, it was, nevertheless, the point of view from which Katherine F. Gerould attacked the periodical press of the 1930s (*Saturday Review of Literature,* 29 December 1934; *North American Review,* December 1935). Equating polemicism, propaganda and journalism, she maintained that even though the War had created a demand for information, editors of old-line magazines were derelict in their publishing merely factual, propagandistic articles that tended to dehumanize man in that they prohibited the meditative process by which he determines the meaning of the world in which he lives. To counteract this negative effect Gerould pleaded for the recognition of the essay; significantly, her conception of the genre was a happy compromise between democracy and elitism or organicism and gentility. Although the form is always based upon a proposition, she wrote, it is neither polemical nor propagandistic because the proposition represents a personal point of view only and because the essayist persuades through the meditative process in which the reader participates. Through meditation, essayist and reader place facts in perspective (the essayist either explicitly or implicitly treats information from the perspective of "his whole knowledge of life") and discover their meaning. Insofar as the essay is a vehicle which allows reader and writer to reason together and attain truth, it both provides information and promotes humanism and civility. It is organic to society in that it takes cognizance of the workday world, yet it is also "aloof" in the positive sense: it allows for reflection upon the social order to determine essences. Certainly such a conception of the genre avoids the dichotomy between art and life.

Many commentators on the essay during the period under study made no distinction between the formal and the informal or familiar essay: any relatively short prose composition that revealed a "voice" reflecting upon issues as disparate as sunsets and Greek genius was considered to belong to the genre. This same blurring of lines occurred in comments on the essay and the article. For instance, in defending editors of old-line magazines against the charges of Gerould, Peffer, although he did not insist on a label for their productions, argued that the monthlies did, in fact, offer more than reportage: "when you have the purveying of fact as fact you have journalism. When facts are selected with reference to broader ideas and ordered in relation to those ideas, you have not journalism but serious writing, whether the subject be Nazi Germany, crop control, communism in China, modern painting, or the decaying art of conversation, and whether the product be called an essay, a treatise, or an article." The term *essay* has, of course, been appropriated for treatises, for example Locke's *Essay on Human Understanding.* Nevertheless, there is a generally recognized distinction between the strictly utilitarian short prose composition and that composition which, although it may be formally structured and deal with "non-literary" issues, is primarily belletristic. Such is the distinction between the essay and the article that Peffer seemingly ignored.

Other journalists of the 1930s, however, insisted upon the difference. Aware of the chaos of the era and the concomitant desire for facts and explanations, they instructed would-be journalists in the art of the article which, they agreed, must be factual, direct, and concise—or, in other words, pragmatically utilitarian rather than belletristic. Edward Weeks, an editor of the *Atlantic,* noted that neither the literary quality of the formal essay nor the familiarity of the informal essay met the needs of a non-thinking, no-nonsense democratic society. He indicated that because readers want raw facts rather than the shared thought of the essay, experienced journalists "switch on the glare of electricity, they gather up an index, a mass of figures, charts, and typewritten reports, and with this information they prepare a magazine article which will correct any grievances or tip over any monument that an editor may suggest." In presenting his facts, the journalist also realizes that Americans are apt to be annoyed by sarcasm and perplexed by irony; his approach, therefore, is always positive and forthright.

If Weeks instructed journalists in the propaganda that Gerould believed dehumanizing, the instruction of other journalists was in the essay as she conceived of it although they called the form an article. Both Gerould and Alan Devoe, realizing that the Zeitgeist made the conventional subject matter of the familiar essay unacceptable, sought to adjust the form to the social order rather than abandon it completely, as Weeks did in condoning thorough democratization. Although Devoe at one point stated that the article is "primarily a recitation or a chronicle" designed to convey facts, he also saw the form as an amalgamation of the familiar essay and the newspaper feature. Focusing on place of publication, he wrote that the rambling essay once housed by the monthlies had been "routed by the brisk and analytical temper of the times" and that the often slap-dash feature lacked sufficient depth and literary merit to warrant publication in either weeklies or monthlies. Hence the magazine article that, like the feature, reports facts but goes beyond the merely reportorial to offer interpretation. And like the essay, the article has depth of thought and literary meticulousness yet shuns its randomness. Thus unlike the familiar essay, the article proved suitable to the social order because of its concise treatment of the factual and of the conclusions that it offered.

The dominance of the article and the virtual displacement of the familiar essay attest to that strain in American culture that has allowed it always to meet the challenge of the pragmatic and the democratic. Yet there is another strain in our culture that balances its pragmatism: the social idealism manifest in its emphasis upon realization of self, freedom, and equality, and the yearning for spiritual idealism typified by Emerson and Hawthorne. It is this latter strain that has protested the acquiescence to the pragmatic. Very few Americans have been able to unite both strains and achieve a monism similar to that of Benjamin Franklin or of the Thoreau who lived at Walden Pond. Consequently, when several critics protested the capitulation to the pragmatic and sought to recall the genteel tradition amidst the clamor of the 1930s and 1940s, they unavoidably perpetuated the antinomy between the cultural and the existential that Santayana believed characteristically American. But whether these critics who called for the recrudescence of the familiar essay be called elitist or genteel, they indicate the failure of the pragmatic and the existentially vital to satisfy all of man's needs. An organic literature may have its value, they seemed to suggest, but if it fails to transcend the material, there is a validity also in that literature which inhibits "the ivory tower of learned gentility."

For this reason, an anonymous writer in the *Saturday Review* for 23 July 1932 held that the essayist's larger and detached perspective and his ability to see above the instant to a realm of infinite possibilities could serve as a cure for the great ill of the decade, the tendency to live "so fiercely in the instant." His mildness of mood and his agility of fancy could provide adventure of the spirit and thus at least a temporary escape from the harshness of reality. In the same periodical for 16 February 1935 another critic used the familiar essay as a barometer by which to gauge the decade and asserted that if readers could not respond to the essay "without a nervous feeling that the writer is taking his time when there is no time to take from a hurrying year in which war or revolution or a dictatorship may be declared in the next headline," the fault lay not with the essay but rather with the times. Those who insisted that the leisurely and reflective approach of the genre was inappropriate to the era were, "by the necessity of the moment, untrue to one of the permanent needs of a culture worthy the name—untrue to second thought, to meditation, to the inner life." In the issue of *Scholastic* for 27 February 1937 Calvin T. Ryan insisted that even during an era "when people are hungry, when floods overwhelm cities, when pastures dry up and cattle have to be killed, when crops die and wither . . . and the whole family needs shoes," the familiar essay has its value. For Americans have an indomitable cheerfulness which responds to the essayist's sense of play. But the essay offers more than entertainment. Ryan, as Repplier did, noted that it could purify the emotions and make the reader "susceptible to greater sympathy for his fellow man" in a way that articles exposing fallacies and advocating causes could not.

Even after the eruption of World War II there were sporadic pleas for the revival of the essay as a means of effecting the salvation of man in a nearly dehumanized world. For instance, James Norman Hall offered "A Word for the Essayist" (*Yale Review,* 1942) and echoed Gerould's belief that the essay keeps man civil. He contended that essayists were essential to any body politic that considered itself civilized in that they "somehow hold fast to urbanity" despite wars and other social conflicts. As Hall saw it, a state that lacks urbanity is only a conglomeration of men who "find themselves eating, without relish, while glaring and snarling at one another, the stale bread of mere economic existence" offered in the journalism that focused too intently upon the present. To the extent that the essayist shunned the polemic and placed the present in perspective, his "exhilarating give-and-take discussion over the hills and dales of common experience, common humanity" offers salvation from boredom and from the depressions caused by the complexities of the social order.

Walter Prichard Eaton's defense of the genre (*Virginia Quarterly Review,* 1948) put to rout the happy compromise offered by Gerould and Devoe, who suggested that sociological facts could, if treated properly, be converted into the stuff of art. Without denying the possibility, Eaton asserted that sociology, politics, and international affairs could seldom be converted into literature, the material of which must issue from the writer's individuality. As other critics who defended the genre had done, Eaton too assured his readers that in dealing with his personal vision the artist affects society insofar as he makes manifest in a forceful way the value of sympathy, tolerance, and respect for human rights. Thus, Eaton concluded, the familiar essays of writers such as Lamb, Thoreau, and E. B. White are, despite their impressionism, valid and penetrating statements that foster humanism much more effectively than polemics do. "I could feel more cheerful about the future of the human race," he declared, after becoming " 'the contemporary and familiar friend' of a modern Montaigne or Lamb or Hazlitt than after struggling through a mass of predictions by 'experts' on everything from the devaluation of the franc to the establishment of a full-fledged law school in Oklahoma over the weekend."

Joseph Wood Krutch's recognition of the dehumanizing tendencies of the deterministic sciences and of technology and his recognition of the value of art as a means of humanizing both nature and man are the bases of his plea for the familiar essay ("No Essays, Please!," *Saturday Review of Literature,* 10 March 1951). Just as Gerould and Eaton did, Krutch protested the eschewal of the personal in favor of the "machine-made article." Admitting, as Waters and Peffer did, that the essay died of anaemia in that it came to represent the genteel tradition at its feeblest, Krutch still maintained that its disappearance had deprived man of an effective means of dealing with that area of human experience that is neither startlingly momentous nor absurdly trivial. As he conceived of it, the form is a device for treating human problems in a personal rather than an objective, pseudo-scientific manner which fragments man into, for example, the physical man, the I.Q. man, the economic man. "Literature is the only thing which deals with the whole complex phenomenon at once," Krutch dramatically asserted, "and if all literature were to cease to exist the result would probably be that in the end whatever is not considered by one or another of the sciences would no longer be taken into account at all and would perhaps almost cease to exist." Hence the desuetude of the familiar essay led him to "wonder whether or not we have now entered upon a stage during which man's lingering but still complex individuality finds itself more and more completely deprived of the opportunity not only to express itself in living but even to discover corresponding individualities revealing themselves in the spoken or written word." The desperation of Krutch's comment stemmed from his belief, developed in *The Modern Temper* and *The Measure of Man,* that man can save himself from spiritual suicide only if he asserts the reality and validity of consciousness and the moral and aesthetic values that pertain to it.

Since the late 1950s the periodical press has undergone further change. Mid-century writers protested the factual article, even though it had been personalized by journalists such as Joseph Mitchell and A. J. Liebling, because of its formulaic quality. But the most revolutionizing force was the socio-cultural changes that reached a peak during the 1960s. The old journalism was not judged an adequate means for handling the events that mined the foundations of American society: the free speech movement of Berkeley; the protests against the Viet Nam war; the black power movement; the Jesus movement; the hippie and yippie movements; the assertion of women's rights; the sexual revolution; the flaunting use of drugs, etc. The truth of these facets of the counter-culture and of other events such as the interest in ecology was not captured by the conventional article that tended to deal with the surface of events in a relatively standardized manner (who, what, when, why, where) and to perpetuate the status quo. The old journalism, precision journalism, alternative journalism, and the new journalism (or new nonfiction). Only the new journalism, which attempts to capture the meaning beneath the surface of events, is relevant to this study in that it treats the social scene in terms of the journalist's personal vision and strives to raise reportage to the status of art.

Norman Podhoretz noted the artistic potential of the article in the July 1957 issue of *Harper's*. As Tom Wolfe and Dan Wakefield would do later, Podhoretz debunked the novel because it shuns reality, and he maintained that the reportage of accomplished journalists offered "a more exhaustive and more accomplished investigation of our morals and manners than the bulk of contemporary fiction." Judging the nonfiction of James Baldwin and Isaac Rosenfeld to be more imaginative and more truthfully complex than their fiction, he accounted for the artistic value and the appeal of that nonfiction in terms of its functionalism. By no means did Podhoretz condone the demand for the topical, the occasional, the newsworthy, the utilitarian; the imaginative or the creative, he noted, should not be considered useless. Yet, given the reality of readers' demand for the utilitarian, the article-writer is able to succeed in a way that neither the essayist nor the writer of fiction can—first because the article deals with the socially or politically relevant (hence it is functional) and second, because this given relevance frees the writer to create. As Podhoretz put it, "we have all, writers and readers alike, come to feel temporarily uncomfortable with the traditional literary forms because they don't *seem* practical, designed for 'use,' whereas a magazine article by its nature satisfies that initial conditional and so is free to assimilate as many 'useless,' 'non-functional' elements as it pleases. It is free, in other words, to become a work of art." Podhoretz made the best of a situation that is admittedly bad.

Truman Capote, Tom Wolfe, Jimmy Breslin, Gay Talese, and Joan Didion are among the writers who seek to make journalism as artistic as fiction. Although the so-called nonfiction novel which Capote claims to have established with *In Cold Blood* was for him an alleged escape from his personal vision into complete objectivity, other new journalists are as subjective as the traditional essayist in their effort to re-create the sights, sounds, and nuances that surround the facts reported. In the final analysis, their perceptions and responses are at least as important as the events. As Dan Wakefield notes, in becoming an "I" rather than an impersonal "eye," the new journalist invades the territory of emotion and feeling to achieve the end that James Agee did in *Let Us Now Praise Famous Men*. If Ca-

pote's attempt to be objective resulted in the failure to make art out of the Kansas murder by allowing his consciousness or moral imagination to transform without distorting the facts of the case, Agee, according to one new journalist, succeeded in making facts yield art. In the opinion of Wakefield, Agee "recognized and made art and illumination of the presence and personality of the reporter as he entered and inevitably affected the scene and events he was watching . . ." (*Atlantic,* June 1966). Similarly, Norman Mailer becomes his own hero in *The Armies of the Night* and dares to illuminate the march on Washington as the events impinge upon his vision. The rationale behind the new journalism is that the truth of an event is ascertained only insofar as the journalist fully absorbs that which he reports, immerses himself in the event in order to re-create its setting and emotional dimensions, and personalizes his account by focusing not so much on what happened but rather on how it affected him and the other people involved. In his writing he dares to create a sense of immediacy through the use of dialogue, drama, scene, point-of-view and other devices usually associated with fiction.

The new journalism is, it seems to me, an amalgamation of the conventional article and the familiar essay. For although it relies on the techniques of fiction, it is grounded in facts as the article is, and it allows for the expression of individuality as the essay has done. It is this often overwhelming subjectivity to which many critics have legitimately objected on the basis that the primary aim of journalism is to inform readers of facts in a manner that is as objective as possible. From the perspective of conventional journalism Dwight Macdonald dismissed the writings of the new journalists as para-journalism: it resembles journalism (" 'the collection and dissemination of current news' ") but aims to entertain rather than inform. And the chief crime of the parajournalists is their intimacy not only with the reader but also with their subject: "the parajournalist cozies up, merges into the subject so completely that the viewpoint is wholly from inside. . . . There is no space between writer and topic, no 'distancing' to allow the most rudimentary objective judgment, such as for factual accuracy. Inside and outside are one" (*The New York Review of Books,* 26 August 1965). Herbert Gold complained in the August 1971 issue of the *Atlantic* that the use of the first person had reached epidemic proportions, and he accused Mailer and Wolfe of decadence: the parading of their personalities caused them to lose sight of their object in writing—to tell and share their experiences. Gold recognized the value of personalism: "at its best, the first person singular can reflect the context of events, give a passionate depth sounding, resonate with social need, answer for a moment the avidity for touch and intimacy which is one of the diseases of mass society, and thus truly justify what *this writer* says, feels, suffers." A degree of personality, he admitted, is necessary to persuasion. Nevertheless, the rampant self-display of contemporary journalism is, in Gold's opinion, a mere game that denies importance to anything beyond self and fails to give magazine readers that knowledge of the world, rather than of the writer, that they desire. Michael J. Arlen levelled a similar charge: the new journalist disdains facts. Insofar as he offers a merely personal account of events, he is "less a journalist than an impresario" who insists that reality be viewed from his perspective alone (*Atlantic,* May 1972). Both Gold and Arlen called for more objectivity.

There is no gainsaying the need for facts and for a validating principle in journalism. Nor is it possible to deny that these negative reactions to the new journalism are symptomatic of "the pursuit of loneliness" and the concomitant disengagement that Philip Slater analyzes in his study of the breaking point of American culture. The individualism theoretically so dear to America and the lack of permanence resulting from its super-industrial society have led to a distrust of *engagement.* Worse still for a revival of the personal element in popular literature is the notion that man is helpless before the external world—note the new novel that offers the self as a mere observing consciousness incapable of acting or of effecting events. Only a society that frustrates interpersonal communion could lead to phenomena such as the flower children and the elaborately planned assertions of self and the confrontation of others associated with Esalen. These protests against the isolating and dehumanizing forces of society, however, have failed to affect in any significant manner the status quo with its preference for the safely objective, the safely impersonal. Yet if it is true that the virtue of being human is man's capacity to express his uniqueness and that psychological and spiritual growth is predicated upon dialogue, the new journalism is valuable in that it attests to the validity of the private and the subjective. Despite the inevitable failures resulting from an attempt to perceive life as art, and despite the impermanence of an art based squarely upon the topical and the occasional, the new journalism represents an effort to free the self from mere facts and from things that annihilate individuality and deny community. It bridges the gap between life and culture and in its own way offers dialogue as an antidote to what any humanist worth his salt must believe to be an unwilled pursuit of aloneness.

THE ESSAY IN THE EARLY TWENTIETH CENTURY

Arthur Christopher Benson

SOURCE: "The Art of the Essayist," in *Types and Times in the Essay,* edited by Warner Taylor, Harper & Brothers Publishers, 1932, pp. 3-12.

[*Benson was an English educator and author. Although he was a prolific poet, novelist, and biographer, he is best known for such volumes of essays as* The Upton Letters *(1905),* From a College Window *(1906), and* Beside Still Waters *(1907). In the following essay, Benson offers an overview of the characteristics of the essay form.*]

There is a pleasant story of an itinerant sign-painter who in going his rounds came to a village inn upon whose signboard he had had his eye for some months and had watched with increasing hope and delight its rapid progress to blurred and faded dimness. To his horror he found

a brand-new varnished sign. He surveyed it with disgust, and said to the inn-keeper, who stood nervously by hoping for a professional compliment, "This looks as if someone had been doing it himself."

That sentence holds within it the key to the whole mystery of essay-writing. An essay is a thing which someone does himself; and the point of the essay is not the subject, for any subject will suffice, but the charm of personality. It must concern itself with something "jolly," as the schoolboy says, something smelt, heard, seen, perceived, invented, thought; but the essential thing is that the writer shall have formed his own impression, and that it shall have taken shape in his own mind; and the charm of the essay depends upon the charm of the mind that has conceived and recorded the impression. It will be seen, then, that the essay need not concern itself with anything definite; it need not have an intellectual or a philosophical or a religious or a humorous motif; but equally none of these subjects are ruled out. The only thing necessary is that the thing or the thought should be vividly apprehended, enjoyed, felt to be beautiful, and expressed with a certain gusto. It need conform to no particular rules. All literature answers to something in life, some habitual form of human expression. The stage imitates life, calling in the services of the eye and the ear; there is a narrative of the teller of tales or the minstrel; the song, the letter, the talk—all forms of human expression and communication have their anti-types in literature. The essay is the reverie, the frame of mind in which a man says, in the words of the old song, "Says I to myself, says I."

It is generally supposed that Montaigne is the first writer who wrote what may technically be called essays. His pieces are partly autobiographical, partly speculative, and to a great extent ethical. But the roots of his writing lie far back in literary history. He owed a great part of his inspiration to Cicero, who treated of abstract topics in a conversational way with a romantic background; and this he owed to Plato, whose dialogues undoubtedly contain the germ of both the novel and the essay. Plato is in truth far more the forerunner of the novelist than of the philosopher. He made a background of life, he peopled his scenes with bright boys and amiable elders—oh that all scenes were so peopled!—and he discussed ethical and speculative problems of life and character with vital rather than with a philosophical interest. Plato's dialogues would be essays but for the fact that they have a dramatic colouring, while the essence of the essay is soliloquy. But in the writings of Cicero, such as the *De Senectute,* the dramatic interest is but slight, and the whole thing approaches far more nearly to the essay than to the novel. Probably Cicero supplied to his readers the function both of the essayist and the preacher, and fed the needs of so-called thoughtful readers by dallying, in a fashion which it is hardly unjust to call twaddling, with familiar ethical problems of conduct and character. The charm of Montaigne is the charm of personality—frankness, gusto, acute observation, lively acquaintance with men and manners. He is ashamed of recording nothing that interested him; and a certain discreet shamelessness must always be the characteristic of the essayist, for the essence of his art is to say what has pleased him without too prudently considering whether it is worthy of the attention of the well-informed mind.

The essay is the reverie, the frame of mind in which a man says, in the words of the old song, "Says I to myself, says I."

— *Arthur Christopher Benson*

I doubt if the English temperament is wholly favourable to the development of the essayist. In the first place, an Anglo-Saxon likes doing things better than thinking about them; and in his memories, he is apt to recall how a thing was done rather than why it was done. In the next place, we are naturally rather prudent and secretive; we say that a man must not wear his heart upon his sleeve, and that is just what the essayist must do. We have a horror of giving ourselves away, and we like to keep ourselves to ourselves. "The Englishman's home is his castle," says another proverb. But the essayist must not have a castle, or if he does, both the grounds and the living-rooms must be open to the inspection of the public.

Lord Brougham, who revelled in advertisement, used to allow his house to be seen by visitors, and the butler had orders that if a party of people came to see the house, Lord Brougham was to be informed of the fact. He used to hurry to the library and take up a book, in order that the tourists might nudge each other and say in whispers, "There is the Lord Chancellor." That is the right frame of mind for the essayist. He may enjoy privacy, but he is no less delighted that people should see him enjoying it.

The essay has taken very various forms in England. Sir Thomas Browne, in such books as *Religio Medici* and *Urn-Burial,* wrote essays of an elaborate rhetorical style, the long fine sentences winding themselves out in delicate weft-like trails of smoke on a still air, hanging in translucent veils. Addison, in the *Spectator,* treated with delicate humour of life and its problems, and created what was practically a new form in the essay of emotional sentiment evoked by solemn scenes and fine associations. Charles Lamb treated romantically the homeliest stuff of life, and showed how the simplest and commonest experiences were rich in emotion and humour. The beauty and dignity of common life were his theme. De Quincey wrote what may be called impassioned autobiography, and brought to his task a magical control of long-drawn and musical cadences. And then we come to such a writer as Pater, who used the essay for the expression of exquisite artistic sensation. These are only a few instances of the way in which the essay has been used in English literature. But the essence is throughout the same; it is personal sensation, personal impression, evoked by something strange or beautiful or curious or interesting or amusing. It has thus a good deal in common with the art of the lyrical poet and the writer of sonnets, but it has all the freedom of prose, its more extended range, its use of less strictly poetical effects,

such as humour in particular. Humour is alien to poetical effect, because poetry demands a certain sacredness and solemnity of mood. The poet is emotional in a reverential way; he is thrilled, he loves, he worships, he sorrows; but it is all essentially grave, because he wishes to recognise the sublime and uplifted elements of life; he wishes to free himself from all discordant, absurd, fantastic, undignified contrasts, as he would extrude laughter and chatter and comfortable ease from some stately act of ceremonial worship. It is quite true that the essayist has a full right to such a mood if he chooses; and such essays as Pater's are all conceived in a sort of rapture of holiness, in a region from which all that is common and homely is carefully fenced out. But the essayist may have a larger range, and the strength of a writer like Charles Lamb is that he condescends to use the very commonest materials, and transfigures the simplest experiences with a fairy-like delicacy and a romantic glow. A poet who has far more in common with the range of the essayist is Robert Browning, and there are many of his poems, though perhaps not his best, where his frank amassing of grotesque detail, his desire to include rather than exclude the homelier sorts of emotion, his robust and not very humorous humour, make him an impressionist rather than a lyrist. As literature develops, the distinction between poetry and prose will no doubt become harder to maintain. Coleridge said in a very fruitful maxim: "The opposite of poetry is not prose but science; the opposite of prose is not poetry but verse." That is to say, poetry has as its object the kindling of emotion, and science is its opposite, because science is the dispassionate statement of fact; but prose can equally be used as a vehicle for the kindling of emotion, and therefore may be in its essence poetical: but when it is a technical description of a certain kind of structure its opposite is verse—that is to say, language arranged in metrical and rhythmical form. We shall probably come to think that the essayist is more of a poet than the writer of epics, and that the divisions of literature will tend to be on the one hand the art of clear and logical statement, and on the other the art of emotional and imaginative expression.

We must remember in all this that the nomenclature of literature, the attempt to classify the forms of literary expression, is a confusing and a bewildering thing unless it is used merely for convenience. It is the merest pedantry to say that literature must conform to established usages and types. The essence of it is that it is a large force flowing in any channel that it can, and the classification of art is a mere classification of channels. What lies behind all art is the principle of wonder and of arrested attention. It need not be only the sense of beauty; it may be the sense of fitness, of strangeness, of completeness, of effective effort. The amazement of the savage at the sight of a civilised town is not the sense of beauty, it is the sense of force, of mysterious resources; of incredible products, of things unintelligibly and even magically made; and then too there is the instinct for perceiving all that is grotesque, absurd, amusing, and jocose, which one sees exhibited in children at the sight of the parrot's crafty and solemn eye and his exaggerated imitation of human speech, at the unusual dress and demeanour of the clown, at the grotesque simulation by the gnarled and contorted tree of something human or reptile. And then, too, there is the strange property in human beings which makes disaster amusing, if its effects are not prejudicial to oneself; that sense which makes the waiter on the pantomime stage, who falls headlong with a tray of crockery, an object to provoke the loudest and most spontaneous mirth of which the ordinary human being is capable. The moralist who would be sympathetically shocked at the rueful abrasions of the waiter, or mournful over the waste of human skill and endeavour involved in the breakage, would be felt by all human beings to have something priggish in his composition and to be too good, as they say, to live.

It is with these rudimentary and inexplicable emotions that the essayist may concern himself, even though the poet may be forbidden to do so; and the appeal of the essayist to the world at large will depend upon the extent to which he experiences some common emotion, sees it in all its bearings, catches the salient features of the scene, and records it in vivid and impressive speech.

The essayist is therefore to a certain extent bound to be a spectator of life; he must be like the man in Browning's fine poem "How it strikes a Contemporary," who walked about, took note of everything, looked at the new house building, poked his stick into the mortar.

> He stood and watched the cobbler at his trade,
> The man who slices lemons into drink,
> The coffee-roaster's brazier, and the boys
> That volunteer to help him turn its winch;
> He glanced o'er books on stalls with half an eye,
> And fly-leaf ballads on the vendor's string,
> And broad-edge bold-print posters by the wall;
> He took such cognizance of men and things!
> If any beat a horse, you felt he saw—
> If any cursed a woman, he took note,
> Yet stared at nobody—they stared at him,
> And found less to their pleasure than surprise,
> He seemed to know them, and expect as much.

That is the essayist's material; he may choose the scene, he may select the sort of life he is interested in, whether it is the street or the countryside or the sea-beach or the picture-gallery; but once there, wherever he may be, he must devote himself to seeing and realizing and getting it all by heart. The writer must not be too much interested in the action and conduct of life. If he is a politician, or a soldier, or an emperor, or a plough-boy, or a thief, and is absorbed in what he is doing, with a vital anxiety to make profit or position or influence out of it; if he hates his opponents and rewards his friends; if he condemns, despises, disapproves, he at once forfeits sympathy and largeness of view. He must believe with all his might in the interest of what he enjoys, to the extent at all events of believing it worth recording and representing, but he must not believe too solemnly or urgently in the importance and necessity of any one sort of business or occupation. The eminent banker, the social reformer, the forensic pleader, the fanatic, the crank, the puritan—these are not the stuff out of which the essayist is made; he may have ethical preferences, but he must not indulge in moral indignation; he must be essentially tolerant, and he must discern quality rather than solidity. He must be concerned with the pageant of life, as it weaves itself with a moving tapestry of scenes and figures rather than with the aims and purposes of life. He must, in fact, be preoccupied with things as they appear, rather than with their significance or their ethical example.

I have little doubt in my own mind that the charm of the familiar essayist depends upon his power of giving the sense of a good-humoured, gracious and reasonable personality and establishing a sort of pleasant friendship with his reader. One does not go to an essayist with a desire for information, or with an expectation of finding a clear statement of a complicated subject; that is not the mood in which one takes up a volume of essays. What one rather expects to find is a companionable treatment of that vast mass of little problems and floating ideas which are aroused and evoked by our passage through the world, our daily employment, our leisure hours, our amusements and diversions, and above all by our relations with other people—all the unexpected, inconsistent, various, simple stuff of life; the essayist ought to be able to import a certain beauty and order into it, to delineate, let us say, the vague emotions aroused in solitude or in company by the sight of scenery, the aspect of towns, the impressions of art and books, the interplay of human qualities and characteristics, the half-formed hopes and desires and fears and joys that form so large a part of our daily thoughts. The essayist ought to be able to indicate a case or a problem that is apt to occur in ordinary life and suggest the theory of it, to guess what it is that makes our moods resolute or fitful, why we act consistently or inconsistently, what it is that repels or attracts us in our dealings with other people, what our private fancies are. The good essayist is the man who makes a reader say: "Well, I have often thought all those things, but I never discerned before any connection between them, nor got so far as to put them into words." And thus the essayist must have a great and far-reaching curiosity; he must be interested rather than displeased by the differences of human beings and by their varied theories. He must recognise the fact that most people's convictions are not the result of reason, but a mass of associations, traditions, things half-understood, phrases, examples, loyalties, whims. He must care more about the inconsistency of humanity than about its dignity; and he must study more what people actually do think about than what they ought to think about. He must not be ashamed of human weaknesses or shocked by them, and still less disgusted by them; but at the same time he must keep in mind the flashes of fine idealism, the passionate visions, the irresponsible humours, the salient peculiarities, that shoot like sunrays through the dull cloudiness of so many human minds, and make one realize that humanity is at once above itself and in itself, and that we are greater than we know; for the interest of the world to the ardent student of it is that we most of us seem to have got hold of something that is bigger than we quite know how to deal with; something remote and far off, which we have seen in a distant vision, which we cannot always remember or keep clear in our minds. The supreme fact of human nature is its duality, its tendency to pull different ways, the tug-of-war between Devil and Baker which lies inside our restless brains. And the confessed aim of the essayist is to make people interested in life and in themselves and in the part they can take in life; and he does that best if he convinces men and women that life is a fine sort of game, in which they can take a hand; and that every existence, however confined or restricted, is full of outlets and pulsing channels, and that the interest and joy of it is not confined to the politician or the millionaire, but is pretty fairly distributed, so long as one has time to attend to it, and is not preoccupied in some concrete aim or vulgar ambition.

Because the great secret which the true essayist whispers in our ears is that the worth of experience is not measured by what is called success, but rather resides in a fulness of life: that success tends rather to obscure and to diminish experience, and that we may miss the point of life by being too important, and that the end of it all is the degree in which we give rather than receive.

The poet perhaps is the man who sees the greatness of life best, because he lives most in its beauty and fineness. But my point is that the essayist is really a lesser kind of poet, working in simpler and humbler materials, more in the glow of life perhaps than in the glory of it, and not finding anything common or unclean.

The essayist is the opposite of the romancer, because his one and continuous aim is to keep the homely materials in view; to face actual conditions, not to fly from them. We think meanly of life if we believe that it has no sublime moments; but we think sentimentally of it if we believe that it has nothing but sublime moments. The essayist wants to hold the balance; and if he is apt to neglect the sublimities of life, it is because he is apt to think that they can take care of themselves; and that if there is the joy of adventure, the thrill of the start in the fresh air of the morning, the rapture of ardent companionship, the gladness of the arrival, yet there must be long spaces in between, when the pilgrim jogs steadily along, and seems to come no nearer to the spire on the horizon or to the shining embanked cloudland of the West. He has nothing then but his own thoughts to help him, unless he is alert to see what is happening in hedgerow and copse, and the work of the essayist is to make something rich and strange of those seemingly monotonous spaces, those lengths of level road.

Is, then, the Essay in literature a thing which simply stands outside classification, like Argon among the elements, of which the only thing which can be predicated is that it is there? Or like Justice in Plato's Republic, a thing which the talkers set out to define, and which ends by being the one thing left in a state when the definable qualities are taken away? No, it is not that. It is rather like what is called an organ prelude, a little piece with a theme, not very strict perhaps in form, but which can be fancifully treated, modulated from, and coloured at will. It is a little criticism of life at some one point clearly enough defined.

We may follow any mood, we may look at life in fifty different ways—the only thing we must not do is to despise or deride, out of ignorance or prejudice, the influences which affect others; because the essence of all experience is that we should perceive something which we do not begin by knowing, and learn that life has a fulness and a richness in all sorts of diverse ways which we do not at first even dream of suspecting.

The essayist, then, is in his particular fashion an interpreter of life, a critic of life. He does not see life as the historian, or as the philosopher, or as the poet, or as the novelist, and yet he has a touch of all these. He is not concerned with discovering a theory of it all, or fitting the various parts of it into each other. He works rather on what is called the analytic method, observing, recording, interpreting, just as things strike him, and letting his fancy play over their beauty and significance; the end of it all being this: that he is deeply concerned with the charm and quality of things, and desires to put it all in the clearest and gentlest light, so that at least he may make others love life a little better, and prepare them for its infinite variety and alike for its joyful and mournful surprises.

J. B. Priestley

SOURCE: "In Defence," in *The Saturday Review,* London, Vol. 148, No. 3853, August 31, 1929, pp. 235-37.

[*Priestley was the author of numerous popular novels that depict the world of everyday, middle-class England. His most notable critical work is* Literature and Western Man *(1960), a survey of Western literature from the invention of movable type through the mid-twentieth century. In the following essay, Priestley makes a plea for the essay as a serious literary genre.*]

It is not often that we essayists are attacked. This does not mean that our portion is praise. It is the custom to ignore us, and it is a mystery to me why we go on or why editors and publishers trouble to throw a few guineas our way. The large public demands that an essayist shall have been dead a long time or, alternatively, be an American journalist writing easy slop about the Open Road, before it condescends to buy and read him. The smaller and more intelligent public calls us charming fellows and then promptly thinks about something or somebody else. "Ah, yes," they say, "I saw a nice little thing of yours in the *Saturday* the other week. It was—er—about what-the-calling-it, you know, that thing." And when the volume arrives they bring out the small type and yawn through the same old tepid praise—"Variety of subjects—sense of humour—pleasant fancy—readable." For two weeks, sometimes three in a stirring season, the publisher puts your book in his advertisements—"Another charming volume," he says, wistfully. A schoolmaster in Newcastle and a retired civil servant in Dorset write to point out one or two mistakes in grammar. Six months later, an assistant professor in Saskatoon writes to ask if he may include the worst essay in the book in an anthology he is preparing. The rest is silence.

Being a vain man, I would rather be attacked than ignored, rather be thrown out than left unnoticed. Therefore I was glad to discover Mr. Stonier, who apparently contributes a literary causerie to the *Clarion,* the last number of which was sent to me the other day. This is not the *Clarion* I remember—it seems centuries ago—the penny weekly that was written by innumerable Blatchfords and had a passion for cycling clubs. (Many a time have I seen the *Clarion* enthusiasts streaming out, on fine Sunday mornings, in the West Riding of my childhood.) It is now a sixpenny monthly, quite handsome, and more dignified, though still rather dashing in the old cycling-club style. I read it all through and enjoyed it. But we must return to Mr. Stonier, who, in the course of a review of an "omnibus" book of essays, made the following observations:

> The conventional idea of an essay is this whimsical, childish-charming play with fancies. Almost all living essayists adopt this pose (sometimes successfully); with slight variations they present the same picture of an absent-minded, untidy, rambling, talkative but lovable amateur rather resembling Mr. Horace Skimpole. They write on the same topics without apparent effort every week in the literary reviews and book columns of newspapers. If only they had one word which they really felt bound to say, if only they did not spend all their time in practising a way of saying it! Mr. Belloc once wrote a book of essays which he called *On Nothing,* and though I have not read it, I am prepared to believe that the title described the book. There has been too much table-talk in recent essays, not enough of the pulpit or the soap-box. In short, what these writers lack is sincerity . . .

Well, there is one essayist who has at last one word he feels bound to say, and that is "Boo!" And if this only calls up yet another "childish-charming fancy," namely, that Mr. Stonier is perhaps a goose, I cannot help it.

Let us first examine this pose that our critic says nearly all living essayists adopt. With one or two of the adjectives we cannot quarrel. It is true that we all pretend to be talkative. There may be essayists who pretend to be very taciturn, but of course we do not know anything about them, because their pose forbids them to write at all. As for being "lovable," the pretence, such as it is, is all the other way. Thus, Messrs. Belloc, Chesterton, Beerbohm, Lynd seem to me lovable men who are all pretending in their essays to be less lovable than they actually are. For the rest, I have not noticed Mr. Belloc's attempt to persuade us he is absent-minded, or Mr. Beerbohm's that he is untidy. But that, of course, is only the beginning. We must now face the charge expressed in the third sentence, in which, by the way, Mr. Stonier makes the mistake of assuming that essays appear in the book columns of newspapers. The charge is that we write on the same topics every week. Now that, it seems to me, is precisely what essayists do not do. Indeed, they are the only contributors to the Press or contemporary literature who do not write for ever on the same topics. Members of Parliament, leader-writers, women novelists, foreign correspondents, dramatic critics, stern young Socialists, retired Indian Army officers, clergymen, publicists, general busybodies, all these people can be discovered every day writing on the same old topics. But not the essayists. Heaven only knows what Mr. Chesterton or Mr. Lynd will be writing on next. The editor of this paper does not know what will be my next subject. I do not know myself. If Mr. Stonier knows, I wish he would drop me a line before next Tuesday.

He is prepared to believe that Mr. Belloc's title, *On Nothing,* describes the book. If so, he is prepared to believe anything. He tells us, with a frankness that does him credit (he must be new to the game), that he has not read this particular volume of essays. I find it difficult to believe that he has read any volume of essays by Mr. Belloc. If you

wanted to suggest that men who write essays are vague-minded triflers, with no opinions, no beliefs, of their own, mere butterflies, could you find, in all the assembled literatures of Europe, a worse example, a more damning instance, than Mr. Belloc? Here is an essayist whose dense mass of opinion, whose arrogant conviction, almost crush the reader, and who affects at all times to be severely objective and concrete, and he of all men is singled out as an example of having nothing to say. I should have thought it obvious that a writer of some experience who dared to call a book *On Nothing* knew very well—and assumed his readers knew very well—that he had something quite definite to say on nearly every subject under the sun. I have read books that really were on nothing, but they always bore such titles as 'The Decentralization of the Unconscious' or 'The Awareness of Graduality.' And no essayist ever wrote one.

To say there is too much table-talk in recent essays is to complain that there is too much meat in recent sausages. The essay, as we understand the essay nowadays, is table-talk in print. If Mr. Stonier does not like table-talk, then he does not like essays; and there is an end of it. Apparently, he favours the introduction of the pulpit and the soap-box. Here, he may congratulate himself, for he is with the majority. Most people prefer the pulpit and the soap-box in print to the dinner-table, and that is why essays are so comparatively unpopular and why some other kinds of writing pay so well. The popular Press has now said good-bye to the essay and the essayists, but it welcomes the preacher and the tub-thumper every morning. If an editor wants to have more than a million readers, he takes care to set up a pulpit and a soap-box on his leader-page. He also takes care to keep the table-talker out of the office. Is this because the table-talker, the essayist, is so insincere? Is the essayist insincere?

It is Mr. Stonier's word, this sincerity, and not mine. Perhaps because I have so little of the quality myself, perhaps for other and sounder reasons, I mistrust this word. It should be handled as carefully as dynamite. If the essayists, talking freely about themselves, their habits, their tastes, their hopes and fears, their weaknesses and little vanities, lack sincerity, what writers have it? Is it the possession of the philosophers, the critics, the historians, the biographers, the romancers? Why, they are even beginning to suspect the very prophets. Who has it, this sincerity? He that died o' Wednesday.

It is true that we essayists, even on Mr. Stonier's showing, have achieved something, for though, as he complains, we spend all our time practising a way of saying our nothings (sedulous apes to a man), yet, as he says, we write every week "without apparent effort." This means that we are very clever fellows, unless there happens to be a flaw in Mr. Stonier's logic, and it is not the business of one of your whimsical, fanciful, childish-charming laddies to suggest such a thing. But Mr. Stonier, I take it, is a man who likes philosophy, opinions, beliefs, a point of view, in a writer, and he misses these things in the essayists. But because he misses them he must not jump to the conclusion that they are not there. He has been in too much of a hurry, perhaps; a trifle deafened, it may be, by those pulpit and soap-box orations that he prefers. Table-talk has its own manner, and sometimes its nonsense is the sanest sense, just as the gravest or most passionate sense of the pulpit and the soap-box sometimes contrives, after being carried home to the table, to turn into the silliest nonsense.

H. Belloc

SOURCE: "An Essay upon Essays upon Essays," in *New Statesman,* Vol. XXXIV, No. 862, November 2, 1929, p. 123.

[*At the turn of the century Belloc was one of England's premier literary figures. His characteristically truculent stance as a proponent of Roman Catholicism and economic reform—and his equally characteristic clever humor—drew either strong support or harsh attacks from his audience, but critics have found common ground for admiration in his poetry. W. H. Auden called Belloc and his longtime collaborator G. K. Chesterton the best light-verse writers of their era, with Belloc's* Cautionary Tales *(1907) considered by some his most successful work in the genre. In the following essay, Belloc defends the proliferation of modern essays.*]

There has been a pretty little quarrel lately—it will probably be forgotten by the time this appears, but no matter—a quarrel between those who write essays and those who have written an essay or two to show that the writing of essays is futile. These last seem to be particularly annoyed by the foison of essays in the present generation. They say it has burst all restraint, and is choking us under a flood.

Of old the essay appeared here and there in some stately weekly paper. Then it dignified once a week some of the more solemn of the daily papers. Then it appeared in another, and another more vulgar. Then, not once a week, but twice a week, in these last: at last, every day. And now (say they) it is everywhere. And the enemies of the essay—or at least of this excess of essays, this spate of essays, this monstrous regiment of essays—are particularly annoyed by the gathering of the same into little books, which they think a further shocking sin against taste. It is bad enough (they say) to drivel away week by week, or even day after day, for your living, but you may be excused (poor devil!), for a living you must get. What is quite unpardonable is to give this drivel the dignity of covers, and to place it upon shelves.

The enemies of the modern essay go on to say that it cannot possibly find sufficient subject-matter for so excessive an output. And so on.

Now here let me break modern convention at once and say that I am a good witness and in a good position also to plead in the matter. I have written this sort of essay for many weary years. I know the motive, I know the method, I know the weakness, but also all that is to be said for it. And I think that, upon the whole, the modern practice is to be supported.

I certainly do not say that with enthusiasm. It would be better for literature, no doubt, and for the casual reader (who reads a great deal too much) if the output were less. It would certainly be better for the writer if he could afford

to restrict that output. But I know that, in the first place, the level remains remarkably high in this country (where there are a dozen such things turned out to one in any other), and that it does so remain high is an argument in favour of the medium. For a sufficient standard maintained in any form of writing should be proof that there is material and effort sufficient to that form: that there is a need for that form to supply, and that it is supplied.

These modern essays of ours may be compared to conversation, without which mankind has never been satisfied, which is ever diverse (though continually moving through the same themes), and which finds in the unending multiplicity of the world unending matter for discussion and contemplation. It lacks the chief value of conversation, which is the alternative outlook: the reply. That cannot be helped. But I fancy the reader supplies this somewhat in his own mind, by the movements of appreciation or indignation with which he receives what is put before him. Indeed, sometimes his indignation moves him to provide free copy in protest; though I am afraid that the corresponding pleasure does not get the same chance of expression. I do indeed note, especially in the daily papers nowadays, continual letters from correspondents approving (usually) the more horribly commonplace pronouncements, or those which have been put in to order, as part of some propaganda or other undertaken by the owner of the sheet. These letters I suspect. I believe they are arranged for. But the letters of indignation are certainly genuine, and editors get a good many more than they print. When such letters are written in disapproval of what I myself have written, I nearly always agree with them.

I can also claim to give evidence as a reader of other people's essays. For I can read this kind of matter with less disgust than any other in the modern press. Yes, I prefer it even to murders. And I cannot tell you how much I prefer it to ignorant comment upon the affairs of Europe, or conventional rubbish upon affairs domestic: the presentation of little men as great, of falsehood as truth, of imaginaries as realities.

As for a dearth of subject, I see no sign of it at all. If I consider any one man of that half-dozen or so whom I read regularly, my colleagues in this same trade, I can name no one except myself who tends to repetition. And there is no reason why a fairly well-read man, still active and enjoying occasional travel, let alone the infinite experience of daily life, should lack a subject. Stuff is infinite. The danger lies not in the drying up of matter, but in the fossilisation of manner. Nor do I find much trace of *that* in my contemporaries.

I have, indeed, the contrary fault to find with the English essay to-day, and that is the restriction of matter. There are whole departments of the highest interest to man which are, by convention, avoided. For instance, until quite lately (when the ice was courageously broken by one group of newspapers) a discussion of the ultimate truths and of whether those truths could be discovered or stated—in other words, a discussion of what is generically called "Religion"—was forbidden. Now that the ice *has* been broken, editors have discovered—a little to their astonishment, I think—that the pioneer was right: that there is nothing for which the public has a stronger appetite than theology.

Another form of restriction is the absence of a devil's advocate; and that absence is more clearly marked and of worse effect here than abroad. The *really* unpopular, or the *really* unusual, point of view cannot get stated in pages of general circulation. And that means the absence of creative friction; for conflict is the mother of all things.

The opposition is, indeed, allowed to appear in small, obscure sheets which are devoted to nothing else. But that is of no great public service. What would be of public service would be eager and general discussion, and the perpetual presentation of argument and fact which the public are not allowed to have.

Take such a simple point as that of Communism. It is a very living issue in our time. It is an active threat in the French commonwealth, a triumphant one in the Russian; it is a subject of immediate anxiety to every Government in Europe, and though it has less place here than in any other industrial country, it does indirectly leaven a wide area of thought even here.

But to get it stated—to have said in its favour all that can be said in its favour—one must turn to small publications which are ignored by the principal newspapers and reviews. In these last you never get the Communist position fully and strongly put. You get it vaguely if violently abused—but without definitions and without concrete details; you feel that it is always there in the background, and yet you are never allowed to see it.

Let no one flatter himself that opposition can be heard because certain points of view supposedly unpopular are sometimes put in what are called "daring" or "paradoxical" essays. These are *never* true opposition. They are always either a jest or that worst form of demagogic flattery which consists in telling people what they really think but what they have not hitherto dared to say. Of true opposition in English letters we have to-day none. And English letters are badly the worse for the lack of it.

Simeon Strunsky

SOURCE: "The Essay of Today," in *English Journal,* Vol. XVII, No. 1, January, 1928, pp. 8-16.

[*In the following review of* Essays of 1925, *edited by Odell Shepard, Strunsky delineates the defining characteristics of the modern essay.*]

Confronted with the task of defining the novel, you might do much worse than say that a novel, as a rule, is something that is written by a novelist. The generality of mankind is not very well informed on the laws of plot, character, situation, and the inner life; but we know Dickens, Tolstoy, and William Dean Howells when we see them. Similarly, it is possible, in the absence of a thorough acquaintance with the textbooks from Aristotle down, to define drama as something written by a dramatist, and poetry as something offered for sale by a poet, and a picture as something committed by a painter. People will understand, and nine times out of ten will not go astray.

But now look at the essay. Among a dozen writers brought together by Odell Shepard in *Essays of 1925,* I find one United States senator, three journalists, two or three journalists who have attained the dignity of publicists, one poet and novelist, one literary critic. In the dozen names I find just two which at first sight connote the essay; they are E. S. Martin and Zephine Humphrey. This is not intended to suggest that there is anything in the Constitution of the United States or in the jurisdictional rules of the essayists' labor union to prevent anybody from trying his hand at Montaigne's trade. That there is no such labor organization in this particular field is precisely the point with which I have set out. Freedom from every sort of restriction on immigration from other domains of literature has characterized the essay almost from the beginning. It is particularly true of the contemporary essay.

Nevertheless, Mr. Shepard foresees an air of bewilderment on his reader's face, and he hastens to explain. It appears that he really holds much more rigorous views on the essay than the present writer does:

> Really excellent humorous writing is hard to find in the magazines of the year. What is more important, there is little play of mind for its own sake, little amiable and graceful trifling of the kind inherited by English writers from Charles Lamb. . . . I may as well record that one man at least, while reading his way through the nonfictional prose of recent magazines, has often sighed for more frequent oases of urbane and civilized laughter, little zones of leisure remote from the drum-fire of argument.

Plainly, Mr. Shepard feels that topics like government regulation of business, or prohibition and the Ku Klux, or international peace, or the career of William J. Bryan are not essay topics. It simply happened that 1925 was a poor year. If better essays had been made in 1925 he would have collected them.

What is this ideal essay form which Mr. Shepard has only approximated in the absence of the real thing? It is the thing which Addison and Charles Lamb wrote. It is the thing which Christopher Morley has in mind when he says, in his introduction to the first series of *Modern Essays,* that "the essay is a mood rather than a form." It is the thing which others have in mind when they speak of the essay as "meditation." It is the aggregation of qualities of which most of us think when we think of the essay, though we would turn pale at any peremptory request to define the word. It is the short expository prose that is informal, urbane, tolerant, pedestrain, reverent, quietistic, tentative, concerned with spiritual or emotional values or translating physical circumstance into personal values— Mr. Morley's "mood." It is intuition, speculation, reverie, whimsy, and in every instance easy going. What the essay, as we usually conceive it, must never do is kill its subject. The essayist is a man who does not know where he is going, but is happy to be on his way. Or if he does have some dim sense of the compass directions, he is never in any haste to get there. The essay suggests; but if you don't quite see the point it does not make much difference, and if you disagree there are no bones broken. After all, "What know I?" said the Frenchman who first essayed the essay.

So, in true essay fashion, we come back right to where we started from, after a pleasant little promenade. The essay, as we think of it without attempting to define it, is the sort of thing Addison and Elia were so good at turning out.

What this popular impression does is to beg the question—which, in the true essay spirit, we are of course at liberty to do. But if you say only Addison and Lamb, you will have to dismiss perhaps the greater part of your modern essays and a very important number of the Pioneers and the Founding Fathers of the essay. What is the first example of the essay with which the high-school student is confronted? If the fashions in secondary school English have not greatly changed since the war it would still be the Essay on Milton. Perhaps the student has had a touch of Elia; but he has met him as an isolated tidbit in the *Dissertation on Roast-Pig,* as a reading "selection," and not as an example of the essay. Perhaps the student has met Addison, but by way of the *Roger de Coverley Papers*; and unless secondary-school psychology has changed greatly, a paper is not often identified as an essay. The boy and the girl are first directly aware that they are traveling in essay land when they meet Mr. Macaulay on Milton.

Take, then, Thomas Babington Macaulay and test him by the popular specifications laid down previously, specifications drawn from our vague but clinging belief of what an essay should be. It will emerge that Macaulay, one of our super-essayists, is pretty nearly everything that an essayist should not be. He is not exactly urbane. He is not—to put it mildly—tolerant. He has no "mood," unless by mood you mean iron convictions. And on the formal side Macaulay of the swelling organ tones and of the magnificently wrought sequences is not what you would call the ambling wayfarer or the felt-slippered dreamer in the easy chair. Macaulay knows where he is going before he starts out, and he knows every minute of the day that he is on the right road. If Montaigne was an essayist, then Macaulay ought not to be one; yet, unfortunately for our peace of mind at the present moment, he is. That is why we cannot say that something is an essay because it is written by an essayist. Macaulay was not an essayist. Emerson is reputed to have written essays; but how many of us think of Emerson as an essayist?

But if a definition, or a stab at a definition, is unavoidable, then one might reverse Christopher Morley, and say, certainly on the basis of the modern essay and with fair reason on the basis of the entire history of the essay, that the essay is a form rather than a mood. The essay is a short piece of expository prose, and that is as far as we can go. Mood is often present, though, far less frequently in the modern essay than in the earlier record. But mood is not an essential part, if definition is suited to data instead of data to definition. And even if you insist on mood you cannot insist on the mood of Addison, of Elia, of Max Beerbohm, or Hilaire Belloc in his gentler phases, of the late Samuel McChord Crothers—in whom we have just lost the Addison of our own day—of Mr. Morley himself when he is alone at home in Paumanok with old Thomas Burton. You must allow for, and give entry to, other moods: to Chesterton when he is writing about capitalists and vegetarians; to Belloc when he is writing about modernists;

and to H. L. Mencken. Why is not the editor of the *American Mercury* represented in the anthologies? Because he calls his essays *Prejudices*? Allowing for historical changes in vocabulary and reticence, Mr. Mencken is not much more prejudiced against Methodists than Macaulay was against Tories, than Ruskin was against the industrial system, or than Chesterton is against this same system. Mr. Mencken, I cannot help feeling, is the victim of established notions among the anthologists. His urbanity, tolerance, quietism, lack of self-confidence, and gift for understatement do not exactly leap to the eye. But by the definition of the essay as a short prose piece he belongs. He has written some very noticeable short pieces. And incidentally, there is a prudential reason. If you refuse Mr. Mencken admission to the anthologies for the use of high-school and college youth, he will bust right in, despite the *Polizei,* and carry your student youth off with him.

It is, then, with the contemporary essay as it has been with the essay at all times, only much more so. The essay can be, and is, anything and everything. You cannot define the essayist as someone who doesn't know too much about anything but is willing to try. In that case you would have to deport W. C. Brownell, who can be easily convicted of knowing a great deal about literature, and Frenchmen, and the American scene in general. You would have to deport William Beebe because he knows altogether too much about the jungle and the sea and the people who go down to both. You would have to deport Santayana. From nearly every collection of American essays you would have to exclude the late Stuart P. Sherman, because in respect to American literature and American tradition Stuart Sherman knew. And on the other hand you would have to expel an entire host of younger and very young writers whom as a matter of fact you often include in your anthologies. As against Brownell, Beebe, Sherman, who would be disfranchised from the essay on the ground of knowing too much, some of the young men might well qualify. But the difficulty is that although they sometimes do not know very much, and are thus entitled to write essays, they are not willing to wait and try. Because of their irritating refusal to say "What know I?" or "Perhaps," or "Does it not then seem?"—because of their insistence that they do know and are going to tell you whether you like it or not—they would, by the mood and meditation test, be excluded. And yet there they are. They have written fine short pieces and must be reckoned with.

The essay, then, as we find it today in America—which includes, of course, the British Isles and the Dominions—is in theme and spirit everything. If Mr. Shepard had looked hard enough for the year 1925 he would have found a few essays in the Montaigne-Addison-Lamb tradition to make a juster balance against the articles on government regulation and Ku Klux, without excluding the latter. Other editors have been more successful. Mr. Morley, of course, was never in such danger. Starting out with a strong emotion for Addison and Lamb, his problem was the opposite one: to give adequate recognition to the younger writers of essays who will not be put off with urbanity or abstract speculation or a timid questioning of life. They want to speak about the visible, social, political, financial, sexual world about them. Mr. Morley went some distance in admitting a piece on Mussolini in his second series of *Modern Essays,* published after three years. By 1924 the world had made such progress away from the inner life to the hard external facts that even the essay had to take note and come out now and then from the ivory tower.

In going part of the way to meet the modern world the essay of Addison and Lamb has not made a surrender of itself. It has only consented to take up residence by the side of essay which is not Addison or Lamb, but a speech by President Coolidge, a study of the international temper by Alfred E. Zimmern, a study of the frontier influence in American life by Professor Turner. These three articles I find in McCullough and Burgum's excellent collection, *A Book of Modern Essays,* by the side of such "truer" essays as Stuart P. Sherman's "What Is a Puritan?" and the "ideal" essay: Galsworthy on "Castles in Spain," Kenneth Grahame on "Day-dreams," A. Clutton-Brock on "Friendship," and Meredith Nicholson on "The Cheerful Breakfast Table." So in the University of Michigan's compilation, *Adventures in Essay Reading,* you will find among the modern representatives Le Baron Briggs, President Meiklejohn and Wu Ting Fang busying themselves with concrete problems in the company of Samuel McChord Crothers and Agnes Repplier and G. K. Chesterton embodying the more traditional type.

The perfect state would be, of course, where the traditional type of essay did more than live in neighborhood with the modern, concrete, militant article or chapter; where the old urbanity and reverie borrowed something of the new iron and "punch," and lent something of its own easy grace to the two-fisted newcomers. And that frequently happens. There is charm as well as edge in Charles Merz's study of our new filling-station civilization in his piece on "The Once Open Road" in the McCullough and Burgum collection. There is charm as well as bite in Robert Littell's "Let There Be Ivy" and "Pigskin Preferred" in Warner Taylor's *Essays of the Past and Present.* On the other side of the line, Samuel McChord Crothers has shown that a training in the earlier spirit of the essay does not immunize one against the gift for satire. His last essay on "The Literary Slums," in the *Atlantic Monthly,* will testify to his ability to rub in the salt where it will do most good. Agnes Repplier knows how to bring the older method to the exploitation of modern instances.

And thus you will find the modern essay, in the sense of time, representative of the history of the essay of all time, either in a blend of qualities or in the pure example. We have young essayists, in this country and England, who can write essays of first-class criticism and write other essays of pure whimsy. I have in mind in this country the aforesaid Robert Littell, and on the other side of the ocean, J. B. Priestley, in the latter of whom there is obviously an exceptional talent at play. John Burroughs and William Beebe are in the tradition of Walden. On his own level I find Walter Pritchard Eaton's nature essay maintaining the amateur tradition in which the English-speaking world has been so rich. In the essays of the late Frank Moore Colby, the spirit of Montaigne has come to life again, though expressing itself at times in the staccato of modern times. For a striking combination of the old hu-

mane background with the modern energy and vocabulary, for a combination of urbanity and acid, it will more than repay the student to consult the essays of Elmer Davis. For the essay of pure whimsy reinforced by extraordinary observation and colored with tenderness there are the several volumes of Robert Cortes Holliday, in whom, at every reading, I catch the ring of genius; he certainly has earned his place in the *entourage* of Charles Lamb. The essay, which very soon after its beginning grew to be anything and everything, from sermon to dream, from epigram to pamphlet, has its examples among our writers today, in the pure type of every *genre,* and in almost every blend.

And as all the forms of the essay have survived, there has survived also—and to my mind that is of far greater importance—the spirit of the essay, asserting itself in every form though in varying degree, and with but few exceptions. To say that there is a single thing which may be called the spirit of the essay would seem at first to contradict the thesis I have been stressing, namely, that the essay may be anything and everything; may be Montaigne or Macaulay. What I mean is that, taking this literature of short or comparatively short prose, we do find that for the *corpus* as a whole there is a single spiritual trait; and that trait is moderation, restraint, the sense of proportion. Montaigne's skepticism has been a little more than enough to outweigh Macaulay's dogmatism. The amateur talents of a Lamb mix with the wisdom of an Emerson or the specialized knowledge of a Brownell to make the essay, in the total, more or less incurably and beautifully amateur, tentative, wandering, wondering. Almost it seems inevitable that when a man sits down to write an essay he finds it impossible always to say "I know it all." The hereditary virtue of "What know I?" persists; the sense of modesty; the sense of proportion.

Now a sense of proportion is something to be thankful for today. Mr. Shepard has grasped this outstanding virtue of the essay when he remarks of the pieces in his collection that, hard-hitting though most of them are, they cannot be said to belong to "the Literature of Despair." You will find plenty of despair lying around today in the novels and in the biographies and the Outlines. But in the contemporary essay you will find the corrective and sometimes the antidote to that despair. Take as an example Aldous Huxley. In his novels life is disillusion and disenchantment. In his essays life manages to keep a good many of its old truths and its old values. To put it quite roughly, Aldous Huxley in his essays is much more sane, much more faithful to the truth of things, much more guarded in his affirmations and denials, than the people in his novels are. Is it the spirit of Montaigne looking over his shoulder and whispering, "What, after all, know you?" Is it the spirit of Addison politely suggesting that this is a world full of many kinds of people and a life full of all sorts of values, and one should not be too rough? Is it the spirit of Lamb lisping, "Well, now, really?" This much is certain: that in an age of disenchantment and revolt and "debunkage" it is in the essays that you must chiefly look for the sense of humor and the sense of proportion. Always excepting Mr. Mencken, a modern essay setting forth the full thesis expounded by Sinclair Lewis in *Elmer Gantry* is inconceivable. The ancestral spirits of the essay simply will not allow it. When you sit down to the composition of an essay, of a most modern, contemporaneous essay, something within you urges you to stop and look and listen—and think twice.

Virginia Woolf

SOURCE: "The Modern Essay," in *Collected Essays, Vol. II,* Harcourt Brace Jovanovich, 1925, pp. 41-50.

[*One of the most prominent figures in twentieth-century literature, Woolf rebelled as a novelist against traditional narrative techniques, developing a highly individualized style that employed the stream-of-consciousness mode. She was also esteemed for her critical essays, which cover a broad range of topics and contain some of her finest prose. In the following review of the five-volume collection* Modern English Essays, *edited by Ernest Rhys, Woolf considers the essential qualities of the modern essay.*]

As Mr. Rhys truly says, it is unnecessary to go profoundly into the history and origin of the essay—whether it derives from Socrates or Siranney the Persian—since, like all living things, its present is more important than its past. Moreover, the family is widely spread; and while some of its representatives have risen in the world and wear their coronets with the best, others pick up a precarious living in the gutter near Fleet Street. The form, too, admits variety. The essay can be short or long, serious or trifling, about God and Spinoza, or about turtles and Cheapside. But as we turn over the pages of [*Modern English Essays,*] containing essays written between 1870 and 1920, certain principles appear to control the chaos, and we detect in the short period under review something like the progress of history.

Of all forms of literature, however, the essay is the one which least calls for the use of long words. The principle which controls it is simply that it should give pleasure; the desire which impels us when we take it from the shelf is simply to receive pleasure. Everything in an essay must be subdued to that end. It should lay us under a spell with its first word, and we should only wake, refreshed, with its last. In the interval we may pass through the most various experiences of amusement, surprise, interest, indignation; we may soar to the heights of fantasy with Lamb or plunge to the depths of wisdom with Bacon, but we must never be roused. The essay must lap us about and draw its curtain across the world.

So great a feat is seldom accomplished, though the fault may well be as much on the reader's side as on the writer's. Habit and lethargy have dulled his palate. A novel has a story, a poem rhyme; but what art can the essayist use in these short lengths of prose to sting us wide awake and fix us in a trance which is not sleep but rather an intensification of life—a basking, with every faculty alert, in the sun of pleasure? He must know—that is the first essential—how to write. His learning may be as profound as Mark Pattison's, but in an essay it must be so fused by the magic of writing that not a fact juts out, not a dogma tears the surface of the texture. Macaulay in one way, Froude in another, did this superbly over and over again. They have

blown more knowledge into us in the course of one essay than the innumerable chapters of a hundred text-books. But when Mark Pattison has to tell us, in the space of thirty-five little pages, about Montaigne, we feel that he had not previously assimilated M. Grün. M. Grün was a gentleman who once wrote a bad book. M. Grün and his book should have been embalmed for our perpetual delight in amber. But the process is fatiguing; it requires more time and perhaps more temper than Pattison had at his command. He served M. Grün up raw, and he remains a crude berry among the cooked meats, upon which our teeth must grate for ever. Something of the sort applies to Matthew Arnold and a certain translator of Spinoza. Literal truth-telling and finding fault with a culprit for his good are out of place in an essay, where everything should be for our good and rather for eternity than for the March number of the *Fortnightly Review.* But if the voice of the scold should never be heard in this narrow plot, there is another voice which is as a plague of locusts—the voice of a man stumbling drowsily among loose words, clutching aimlessly at vague ideas, the voice, for example, of Mr. Hutton in the following passage:

> Add to this that his married life was very brief, only seven years and a half, being unexpectedly cut short, and that his passionate reverence for his wife's memory and genius—in his own words, 'a religion'—was one which, as he must have been perfectly sensible, he could not make to appear otherwise than extravagant, not to say an hallucination, in the eyes of the rest of mankind, and yet that he was possessed by an irresistible yearning to attempt to embody it in all the tender and enthusiastic hyperbole of which it is so pathetic to find a man who gained his fame by his 'dry-light' a master, and it is impossible not to feel that the human incidents in Mr. Mill's career are very sad.

A book could take that blow, but it sinks an essay. A biography in two volumes is indeed the proper depository; for there, where the license is so much wider, and hints and glimpses of outside things make part of the feast (we refer to the old type of Victorian volume), these yawns and stretches hardly matter, and have indeed some positive value of their own. But that value, which is contributed by the reader, perhaps illicitly, in his desire to get as much into the book from all possible sources as he can, must be ruled out here.

There is no room for the impurities of literature in an essay. Somehow or other, by dint of labour or bounty of nature, or both combined, the essay must be pure—pure like water or pure like wine, but pure from dullness, deadness, and deposits of extraneous matter. Of all writers in the first volume, Walter Pater best achieves this arduous task, because before setting out to write his essay ('Notes on Leonardo da Vinci') he has somehow contrived to get his material fused. He is a learned man, but it is not knowledge of Leonardo that remains with us, but a vision, such as we get in a good novel where everything contributes to bring the writer's conception as a whole before us. Only here, in the essay, where the bounds are so strict and facts have to be used in their nakedness, the true writer like Walter Pater makes these limitations yield their own quality. Truth will give it authority; from its narrow limits he will get shape and intensity; and then there is no more fitting place for some of those ornaments which the old writers loved and we, by calling them ornaments, presumably despise. Nowadays nobody would have the courage to embark on the once-famous description of Leonardo's lady who has

> learned the secrets of the grave; and has been a diver in deep seas and keeps their fallen day about her; and trafficked for strange webs with Eastern merchants; and, as Leda, was the mother of Helen of Troy, and, as Saint Anne, the mother of Mary . . .

The passage is too thumb-marked to slip naturally into the context. But when we come unexpectedly upon 'the smiling of women and the motion of great waters', or upon 'full of the refinement of the dead, in sad, earth-coloured raiment, set with pale stones', we suddenly remember that we have ears and we have eyes, and that the English language fills a long array of stout volumes with innumerable words, many of which are of more than one syllable. The only living Englishman who ever looks into these volumes is, of course, a gentleman of Polish extraction. But doubtless our abstention saves us much gush, much rhetoric, much high-stepping and cloud-prancing, and for the sake of the prevailing sobriety and hard-headedness we should be willing to barter the splendour of Sir Thomas Browne and the vigour of Swift.

Yet, if the essay admits more properly than biography or fiction of sudden boldness and metaphor, and can be polished till every atom of its surface shines, there are dangers in that too. We are soon in sight of ornament. Soon the current, which is the life-blood of literature, runs slow; and instead of sparkling and flashing or moving with a quieter impulse which has a deeper excitement, words coagulate together in frozen sprays which, like the grapes on a Christmas tree, glitter for a single night, but are dusty and garish the day after. The temptation to decorate is great where the theme may be of the slightest. What is there to interest another in the fact that one has enjoyed a walking tour, or has amused oneself by rambling down Cheapside and looking at the turtles in Mr. Sweeting's shop window? Stevenson and Samuel Butler chose very different methods of exciting our interest in these domestic themes. Stevenson, of course, trimmed and polished and set out his matter in a traditional eighteenth-century form. It is admirably done, but we cannot help feeling anxious, as the essay proceeds, lest the material may give out under the craftsman's fingers. The ingot is so small, the manipulation so incessant. And perhaps that is why the peroration—

> To sit still and contemplate—to remember the faces of women without desire, to be pleased by the great deeds of men without envy, to be everything and everywhere in sympathy and yet content to remain where and what you are—

has the sort of insubstantiality which suggests that by the time he got to the end he had left himself nothing solid to work with. Butler adopted the very opposite method. Think your own thoughts, he seems to say, and speak them as plainly as you can. These turtles in the shop window which appear to leak out of their shells through heads and feet suggest a fatal faithfulness to a fixed idea. And so, striding unconcernedly from one idea to the next, we traverse a large stretch of ground; observe that a wound in the solicitor is a very serious thing; that Mary Queen of Scots wears surgical boots and is subject to fits near the Horse Shoe in Tottenham Court Road; take it for granted that no one really cares about Æschylus; and so, with many amusing anecdotes and some profound reflections, reach the peroration, which is that, as he had been told not to see more in Cheapside than he could get into twelve pages of the *Universal Review,* he had better stop. And yet obviously Butler is at least as careful of our pleasure as Stevenson; and to write like oneself and call it not writing is a much harder exercise in style than to write like Addison and call it writing well.

But, however much they differ individually, the Victorian essayists yet had something in common. They wrote at greater length than is now usual, and they wrote for a public which had not only time to sit down to its magazine seriously, but a high, if peculiarly Victorian, standard of culture by which to judge it. It was worth while to speak out upon serious matters in an essay; and there was nothing absurd in writing as well as one possibly could when, in a month or two, the same public which had welcomed the essay in a magazine would carefully read it once more in a book. But a change came from a small audience of cultivated people to a larger audience of people who were not quite so cultivated. The change was not altogether for the worse. In volume iii. we find Mr. Birrell and Mr. Beerbohm. It might even be said that there was a reversion to the classic type, and that the essay by losing its size and something of its sonority was approaching more nearly the essay of Addison and Lamb. At any rate, there is a great gulf between Mr. Birrell on Carlyle and the essay which one may suppose that Carlyle would have written upon Mr. Birrell. There is little similarity between *A Cloud of Pinafores,* by Max Beerbohm, and *A Cynic's Apology,* by Leslie Stephen. But the essay is alive; there is no reason to despair. As the conditions change so the essayist, most sensitive of all plants to public opinion, adapts himself, and if he is good makes the best of the change, and if he is bad the worst. Mr. Birrell is certainly good; and so we find that, though he has dropped a considerable amount of weight, his attack is much more direct and his movement more supple. But what did Mr. Beerbohm give to the essay and what did he take from it? That is a much more complicated question, for here we have an essayist who has concentrated on the work and is without doubt the prince of his profession.

What Mr. Beerbohm gave was, of course, himself. This presence, which has haunted the essay fitfully from the time of Montaigne, had been in exile since the death of Charles Lamb. Matthew Arnold was never to his readers Matt, nor Walter Pater affectionately abbreviated in a thousand homes to Wat. They gave us much, but that they did not give. Thus, some time in the nineties, it must have surprised readers accustomed to exhortation, information, and denunciation to find themselves familiarly addressed by a voice which seemed to belong to a man no larger than themselves. He was affected by private joys and sorrows, and had no gospel to preach and no learning to impart. He was himself, simply and directly, and himself he has remained. Once again we have an essayist capable of using the essayist's most proper but most dangerous and delicate tool. He has brought personality into literature, not unconsciously and impurely, but so consciously and purely that we do not know whether there is any relation between Max the essayist and Mr. Beerbohm the man. We only know that the spirit of personality permeates every word that he writes. The triumph is the triumph of style. For it is only by knowing how to write that you can make use in literature of your self; that self which, while it is essential to literature, is also its most dangerous antagonist. Never to be yourself and yet always—that is the problem. Some of the essayists in Mr. Rhys' collection, to be frank, have not altogether succeeded in solving it. We are nauseated by the sight of trivial personalities decomposing in the eternity of print. As talk, no doubt, it was charming, and certainly the writer is a good fellow to meet over a bottle of beer. But literature is stern; it is no use being charming, virtuous, or even learned and brilliant into the bargain, unless, she seems to reiterate, you fulfil her first condition—to know how to write.

This art is possessed to perfection by Mr. Beerbohm. But he has not searched the dictionary for polysyllables. He has not moulded firm periods or seduced our ears with intricate cadences and strange melodies. Some of his companions—Henley and Stevenson, for example—are momentarily more impressive. But *A Cloud of Pinafores* has in it that indescribable inequality, stir, and final expressiveness which belong to life and to life alone. You have not finished with it because you have read it, any more than friendship is ended because it is time to part. Life wells up and alters and adds. Even things in a bookcase change if they are alive; we find ourselves wanting to meet them again; we find them altered. So we look back upon essay after essay by Mr. Beerbohm, knowing that, come September or May, we shall sit down with them and talk. Yet it is true that the essayist is the most sensitive of all writers to public opinion. The drawing-room is the place where a great deal of reading is done nowadays, and the essays of Mr. Beerbohm lie, with an exquisite appreciation of all that the position exacts, upon the drawing-room table. There is no gin about; no strong tobacco; no puns, drunkenness, or insanity. Ladies and gentlemen talk together, and some things, of course, are not said.

But if it would be foolish to attempt to confine Mr. Beerbohm to one room, it would be still more foolish, unhappily, to make him, the artist, the man who gives us only his best, the representative of our age. There are no essays by Mr. Beerbohm in the fourth or fifth volumes of the present collection. His age seems already a little distant, and the drawing-room table, as it recedes, begins to look rather like an altar where, once upon a time, people deposited offerings—fruit from their own orchards, gifts carved with their own hands. Now once more the conditions have changed. The public needs essays as much as ever, and perhaps even more. The demand for the light middle not exceeding fifteen hundred words, or in special cases seventeen hundred and fifty, much exceeds the supply. Where

Lamb wrote one essay and Max perhaps writes two, Mr. Belloc at a rough computation produces three hundred and sixty-five. They are very short, it is true. Yet with what dexterity the practised essayist will utilize his space—beginning as close to the top of the sheet as possible, judging precisely how far to go, when to turn, and how, without sacrificing a hair's-breadth of paper, to wheel about and alight accurately upon the last word his editor allows! As a feat of skill it is well worth watching. But the personality upon which Mr. Belloc, like Mr. Beerbohm, depends suffers in the process. It comes to us not with the natural richness of the speaking voice, but strained and thin and full of mannerisms and affectations, like the voice of a man shouting through a megaphone to a crowd on a windy day. 'Little friends, my readers', he says in the essay called 'An Unknown Country', and he goes on to tell us how—

> There was a shepherd the other day at Findon Fair who had come from the east by Lewes with sheep, and who had in his eyes that reminiscence of horizons which makes the eyes of shepherds and of mountaineers different from the eyes of other men. . . . I went with him to hear what he had to say, for shepherds talk quite differently from other men.

Happily this shepherd had little to say, even under the stimulus of the inevitable mug of beer, about the Unknown Country, for the only remark that he did make proves him either a minor poet, unfit for the care of sheep, or Mr. Belloc himself masquerading with a fountain-pen. That is the penalty which the habitual essayist must now be prepared to face. He must masquerade. He cannot afford the time either to be himself or to be other people. He must skim the surface of thought and dilute the strength of personality. He must give us a worn weekly halfpenny instead of a solid sovereign once a year.

But it is not Mr. Belloc only who has suffered from the prevailing conditions. The essays which bring the collection to the year 1920 may not be the best of their authors' work, but, if we except writers like Mr. Conrad and Mr. Hudson, who have strayed into essay writing accidentally, and concentrate upon those who write essays habitually, we shall find them a good deal affected by the change in their circumstances. To write weekly, to write daily, to write shortly, to write for busy people catching trains in the morning or for tired people coming home in the evening, is a heart-breaking task for men who know good writing from bad. They do it, but instinctively draw out of harm's way anything precious that might be damaged by contact with the public, or anything sharp that might irritate its skin. And so, if one reads Mr. Lucas, Mr. Lynd, or Mr. Squire in the bulk, one feels that a common greyness silvers everything. They are as far removed from the extravagant beauty of Walter Pater as they are from the intemperate candour of Leslie Stephen. Beauty and courage are dangerous spirits to bottle in a column and a half; and thought, like a brown-paper parcel in a waistcoat pocket, has a way of spoiling the symmetry of an article. It is a kind, tired, apathetic world for which they write, and the marvel is that they never cease to attempt, at least, to write well.

But there is no need to pity Mr. Clutton Brock for this change in the essayist's conditions. He has clearly made the best of his circumstances and not the worst. One hesitates even to say that he has had to make any conscious effort in the matter, so naturally has he effected the transition from the private essayist to the public, from the drawing-room to the Albert Hall. Paradoxically enough, the shrinkage in size has brought about a corresponding expansion of individuality. We have no longer the 'I' of Max and of Lamb, but the 'we' of public bodies and other sublime personages. It is 'we' who go to hear the *Magic Flute*; 'we' who ought to profit by it; 'we', in some mysterious way, who, in our corporate capacity, once upon a time actually wrote it. For music and literature and art must submit to the same generalization or they will not carry to the farthest recesses of the Albert Hall. That the voice of Mr. Clutton Brock, so sincere and so disinterested, carries such a distance and reaches so many without pandering to the weakness of the mass or its passions must be a matter of legitimate satisfaction to us all. But while 'we' are gratified, 'I', that unruly partner in the human fellowship, is reduced to despair. 'I' must always think things for himself, and feel things for himself. To share them in a diluted form with the majority of well-educated and well-intentioned men and women is for him sheer agony; and while the rest of us listen intently and profit profoundly, 'I' slips off to the woods and the fields and rejoices in a single blade of grass or a solitary potato.

In the fifth volume of modern essays, it seems, we have got some way from pleasure and the art of writing. But in justice to the essayists of 1920 we must be sure that we are not praising the famous because they have been praised already and the dead because we shall never meet them wearing spats in Piccadilly. We must know what we mean when we say that they can write and give us pleasure. We must compare them; we must bring out the quality. We must point to this and say it is good because it is exact, truthful, and imaginative:

> Nay, retire men cannot when they would; neither will they, when it were Reason; but are impatient of Privateness, even in age and sickness, which require the shadow: like old Townsmen: that will still be sitting at their street door, though thereby they offer Age to Scorn . . .

and to this, and say it is bad because it is loose, plausible, and commonplace:

> With courteous and precise cynicism on his lips, he thought of quiet virginal chambers, of waters singing under the moon, of terraces where taintless music sobbed into the open night, of pure maternal mistresses with protecting arms and vigilant eyes, of fields slumbering in the sunlight, of leagues of ocean heaving under warm tremulous heavens, of hot ports, gorgeous and perfumed. . . .

It goes on, but already we are bemused with sound and neither feel nor hear. The comparison makes us suspect that the art of writing has for backbone some fierce attachment to an idea. It is on the back of an idea, something believed in with conviction or seen with precision and thus compelling words to its shape, that the diverse company which includes Lamb and Bacon, and Mr. Beerbohm and Hudson, and Vernon Lee and Mr. Conrad, and Leslie Stephen and Butler and Walter Pater reaches the farther shore. Very various talents have helped or hindered the passage of the idea into words. Some scrape through painfully; others fly with every wind favouring. But Mr. Belloc and Mr. Lucas and Mr. Squire are not fiercely attached to anything in itself. They share the contemporary dilemma—the lack of an obstinate conviction which lifts ephemeral sounds through the misty sphere of anybody's language to the land where there is a perpetual marriage, a perpetual union. Vague as all definitions are, a good essay must have this permanent quality about it; it must draw its curtain round us, but it must be a curtain that shuts us in, not out.

CHARACTERISTICS OF THE MODERN ESSAY

Scott Russell Sanders

SOURCE: "The Singular First Person," in *Essays on the Essay: Redefining the Genre,* edited by Alexander J. Butrym, The University of Georgia Press, 1989, pp. 31-42.

[*Sanders is an American educator, fiction writer, and essayist. In the following essay, he discusses the personal nature of the essay form.*]

The first soapbox orator I ever saw was haranguing a crowd beside the Greyhound station in Providence about the evils of fluoridated water. What the man stood on was actually an upturned milk crate, all the genuine soapboxes presumably having been snapped up by antique dealers. He wore an orange plaid sports coat and a matching bow tie and held aloft a bottle filled with mossy green liquid. I have forgotten the details of his spiel except his warning that fluoride was an invention of the Communists designed to weaken our bones and thereby make us pushovers for a Red invasion. What amazed me, as a tongue-tied kid of seventeen newly arrived in the city from the boondocks, was not his message but his courage in delivering it to a mob of strangers. It would have been easier for me to jump straight over the Greyhound station than to stand there on that milk crate and utter my thoughts.

To this day, when I read or when I compose one of those curious monologues we call the personal essay, I often recall that soapbox orator. Nobody had asked him for his two cents' worth, but there he was, declaring it with all the eloquence he could muster. The essay, although enacted in private, is no less arrogant a performance. Unlike novelists and play-wrights, who lurk behind the scenes while distracting our attention with the puppet show of imaginary characters—and unlike scholars and journalists, who quote the opinions of others and take cover behind the hedges of neutrality—the essayist has nowhere to hide. While the poet can lean back on a several-thousand-year-old legacy of ecstatic speech, the essayist inherits a much briefer and skimpier tradition. The poet is allowed to quit in less than a page, but the essayist must generally hold forth over several thousand words. It is an arrogant and foolhardy form, this one-man or one-woman circus, which relies on the tricks of anecdote, memory, conjecture, and wit to hold our attention.

It seems all the more brazen or preposterous to address a monologue to the world when you consider what a tiny fraction of the human chorus any single voice is. At the Boston Museum of Science an electronic meter records with flashing lights the population of the United States. Figuring in the rate of births, deaths, emigrants leaving the country, and immigrants arriving, the meter calculates that we add one fellow citizen every twenty-one seconds. When I looked at it recently, the count stood at 242,958,483. As I wrote the figure in my notebook, the final number jumped from 3 to 4. Another mouth, another set of ears and eyes, another brain. A counter for the earth's population would stand somewhere past 5 billion at the moment and would be rising in a blur of digits. Amid this avalanche of selves, it is a wonder that anyone finds the gumption to sit down and write one of those naked, lonely, quixotic letters to the world.

A surprising number do find the gumption. In fact, I have the impression that there are more essayists at work in America today, and more gifted ones, than at any other time in recent decades. Whom do I have in mind? Here is a sampler: Edward Abbey, James Baldwin, Wendell Berry, Carol Bly, Joan Didion, Annie Dillard, Stephen Jay Gould, Elizabeth Hardwick, Edward Hoagland, Barry Lopez, Peter Matthiessen, John McPhee, Cynthia Ozick, Paul Theroux, Lewis Thomas, and Tom Wolfe. No doubt you could make up a list of your own—with a greater ethnic range, say, or fewer nature enthusiasts—and one that would provide even more convincing support for my view that we are blessed right now with an abundance of essayists. We have no one to rival Emerson or Thoreau, but in sheer quantity of first-rate work our time stands comparison with any period since the heyday of the form in the mid-nineteenth century.

In the manner of a soapbox orator, I now turn my hunch into a fact and state boldly that in America these days the personal essay is flourishing. Why are so many writers taking up this risky form, and why are so many readers—to judge by the statistic of book and magazine publication—seeking it out?

In this era of prepackaged thought, the essay is the closest thing we have, on paper, to a record of the individual mind at work and at play. It is an amateur's raid in a world of specialists. Feeling overwhelmed by data, random information, and the flotsam and jetsam of mass culture, we relish the spectacle of a single consciousness making sense of a portion of the chaos. We are grateful to Lewis Thomas for shining his light into the dark corners of biology, to John McPhee for laying bare the geology beneath our landscape, to Annie Dillard for showing us the universal fire blazing in the branches of a cedar, to Peter Matthiessen for chasing after snow leopards and mystical insights in the Himalayas. No matter if they are sketchy, these maps of meaning are still welcome. As Joan Didion observes in her own collection of essays, *The White*

Album, "We live entirely, especially if we are writers, by the imposition of a narrative line upon disparate images, by the 'ideas' with which we have learned to freeze the shifting phantasmagoria which is our actual experience." Dizzy from a dance that seems to accelerate hour by hour, we cling to the narrative line, even though it may be as pure an invention as the shapes drawn by Greeks to identify the constellations.

The essay is a haven for the private, idiosyncratic voice in an era of anonymous babble. Like the blandburgers served in their millions along our highways, most language served up in public these days is textureless, tasteless mush. On television, over the phone, in the newspaper, wherever humans bandy words about, we encounter more and more abstractions, more empty formulas. Think of the pablum ladled out by politicians. Think of the fluffy white bread of advertising. Think, Lord help us, of committee reports. In contrast, the essay remains stubbornly concrete and particular: it confronts you with an oil-smeared toilet at the Sunoco station, a red vinyl purse shaped like a valentine heart, a bow-legged dentist hunting deer with an elephant gun. As Orwell forcefully argued, and as dictators seem to agree, such a bypassing of abstractions, such an insistence on the concrete, is a politically subversive act. Clinging to this door, that child, this grief, following the zigzag motions of an inquisitive mind, the essay renews language and clears trash from the springs of thought. A century and a half ago, Emerson called on a new generation of writers to cast off the hand-me-down rhetoric of the day, to "pierce this rotten diction and fasten words again to visible things." The essayist aspires to do just that.

As if all these virtues were not enough to account for a renaissance of this protean genre, the essay has also taken over some of the territory abdicated by contemporary fiction. Pared down to the brittle bones of plot, camouflaged with irony, muttering in brief sentences and grade-school vocabulary, today's fashionable fiction avoids disclosing where the author stands on anything. Most of the trends in the novel and short story over the past twenty years have led away from candor—toward satire, artsy jokes, close-lipped coyness, metafictional hocus-pocus, anything but a direct statement of what the author thinks and feels. If you hide behind enough screens, no one will ever hold you to an opinion or demand from you a coherent vision or take you for a charlatan.

The essay is not fenced round by these literary inhibitions. You may speak without disguise of what moves and worries and excites you. In fact, you had better speak from a region pretty close to the heart, or the reader will detect the wind of phoniness whistling through your hollow phrases. In the essay you may be caught with your pants down, your ignorance and sentimentality showing, while you trot recklessly about on one of your hobbyhorses. You cannot stand back from the action, as Joyce instructed us to do, and pare your fingernails. You cannot palm off your cockamamie notions on some hapless character. If the words you put down are foolish, everyone knows precisely who the fool is.

To our list of the essay's contemporary attractions we

should add the perennial ones of verbal play, mental adventure, and sheer anarchic high spirits. The writing of an essay is like finding one's way through a forest without being quite sure what game you are chasing, what landmark you are seeking. You sniff down one path until some heady smell tugs you in a new direction, and then off you go, dodging and circling, lured on by the songs of unfamiliar birds, puzzled by the tracks of strange beasts, leaping from stone to stone across rivers, barking up one tree after another. Much of the pleasure in writing an essay—and, when the writing is any good, the pleasure in reading it— comes from this dodging and leaping, this movement of the mind. It must not be idle movement, however, if the essay is to hold up; it must be driven by deep concerns. The surface of a river is alive with lights and reflections, the breaking of foam over rocks, but beneath that dazzle it is going somewhere. We should expect as much from an essay: the shimmer and play of mind on the surface and in the depths a strong current.

To see how the capricious mind can be led astray, consider the foregoing paragraph, in which the making of essays is likened first to the romping of a dog and then to the surge of a river. That is bad enough, but it could have been worse. For example, I began to draft a sentence in that paragraph with the following words: "More than once, in sitting down to beaver away at a narrative, felling trees of memory and dragging brush to build a dam that might slow down the waters of time . . . " I had set out to make some innocent remark, and here I was gnawing down trees and building dams, all because I had let that "beaver" slip in. On this occasion I had the good sense to throw out the unruly word.

I might as well drag in another metaphor—and another unoffending animal—by saying that each doggy sentence, as it noses forward into the underbrush of thought, scatters a bunch of rabbits that rush off in all directions. The essayist can afford to chase more of those rabbits than the fiction writer can but fewer than the poet. If you refuse to chase any of them, and keep plodding along in a straight line, you and your reader will have a dull outing. If you chase too many, you will soon wind up lost in a thicket of confusion with your tongue hanging out.

The pursuit of mental rabbits was strictly forbidden by the teachers who instructed me in English composition. For that matter, nearly all the qualities of the personal essay, as I have been sketching them, violate the rules that many of us were taught in school. You recall that we were supposed to begin with an outline and stick by it faithfully, like a train riding its rails, avoiding sidetracks. Each paragraph was to have a topic sentence pasted near the front, and these orderly paragraphs were to be coupled end to end like so many boxcars. Every item in those boxcars was to bear the stamp of some external authority, preferably a footnote referring to a thick book, although appeals to magazines and newspapers would do in a pinch. Our diction was to be formal and dignified, shunning the vernacular. Polysyllabic words derived from Latin were preferable to the blunt lingo of the streets. Metaphors were to be used only in emergencies, and no two of them were to be mixed.

And even in emergencies we could not speak in the first person singular.

Already as a schoolboy, I chafed against those rules. Now I break them shamelessly, in particular the taboo against using the lonely capital *I*. My speculations about the state of the essay arise from my own practice as reader and writer, and they reflect my own tastes, no matter how I may pretend to gaze dispassionately down on the question from a hot-air balloon. As Thoreau declares in his brash manner on the opening page of *Walden*: "In most books the *I*, or first person, is omitted; in this it will be retained; that, in respect to egotism, is the main difference. We commonly do not remember that it is, after all, always the first person that is speaking. I should not talk so much about myself if there were anybody else whom I knew as well." True for the personal essay, it is doubly true for an essay about the essay: one speaks always and inescapably in the first person singular.

We could sort out essays along a spectrum, according to the degree to which the writer's ego is on display—with John McPhee, perhaps, at the extreme of self-effacement and Norman Mailer at the opposite extreme of self-dramatization. Brassy or shy, stage center or hanging back in the wings, the author's persona commands our attention. For the length of an essay, or a book of essays, we respond to that persona as we would to a friend caught up in a rapturous monologue. When the monologue is finished, we may not be able to say precisely what it was about, any more than we can draw conclusions from a piece of music. "Essays don't usually boil down to a summary, as articles do," notes Edward Hoagland, one of the least summarizable of companions, "and the style of the writer has a 'nap' to it, a combination of personality and originality and energetic loose ends that stand up like the nap of a piece of wool and can't be brushed flat." We make assumptions about that speaking voice, assumptions that we cannot validly make about the narrators in fiction. Only a sophomore is permitted to ask how many children had Huckleberry Finn. But even literary sophisticates wonder in print about Thoreau's love life, Montaigne's domestic arrangements, De Quincey's opium habit, Virginia Woolf's depression.

Montaigne, who not only invented the form but perfected it as well, announced from the start that his true subject was himself. In his note "To the Reader," he slyly proclaimed: "I want to be seen here in my simple, natural, ordinary fashion, without straining or artifice; for it is myself that I portray. My defects will here be read to the life, and also my natural form, as far as respect for the public has allowed. Had I been placed among those nations which are said to live still in the sweet freedom of nature's first laws, I assure you I should very gladly have portrayed myself here entire and wholly naked." A few pages after this disarming introduction, we are told of the Emperor Maximilien, who was so prudish about displaying his private parts that he would not let a servant dress him or see him in the bath. The emperor went so far as to give orders that he be buried in his underdrawers. Having let us in on this intimacy about Maximilien, Montaigne then confessed that he himself, although "bold-mouthed," was equally prudish, and that "except under great stress of necessity or voluptuousness," he never allowed anyone to see him naked. Such modesty, he feared, was unbecoming in a soldier. But such honesty is quite becoming in an essayist. The very confession of his prudery is a far more revealing gesture than any doffing of clothes.

Every English major knows that the word "essay," as adapted by Montaigne, means a trial or attempt. The Latin root carries the more vivid sense of a weighing out. In the days when that root was alive and green, merchants discovered the value of goods and alchemists discovered the composition of unknown metals by the use of scales. Just so the essay, as Montaigne was the first to show, is a weighing out, an inquiry into the value, meaning, and true nature of experience; it is a private experiment carried out in public. In each of three successive editions, Montaigne inserted new material into his essays without revising the old material. Often the new statements contradicted the original ones, but Montaigne let them stand, since he believed that the only consistent fact about human beings is their inconsistency. Lewis Thomas has remarked of him that "he [was] fond of his mind, and affectionately entertained by everything in his head." Whatever Montaigne wrote about, and he wrote about everything under the sun—fears, smells, growing old, the pleasures of scratching—he weighed on the scales of his own character.

It is the *singularity* of the first person—its warts and crotchets and turn of voice—that lures many of us into reading essays and that lingers with us after we finish. Consider the lonely, melancholy persona of Loren Eiseley, forever wandering, forever brooding on our dim and bestial past, his lips frosty with the chill of the Ice Age. Consider the volatile, Dionysian persona of D. H. Lawrence, with his incandescent gaze, his habit of turning peasants into gods and trees into flames, his quick hatred and quicker love. Consider that philosophical farmer, Wendell Berry, who speaks with a countryman's knowledge and a deacon's severity. Consider E. B. White, with his cheery affection for brown eggs and dachshunds and his unflappable way of herding geese while the radio warns of an approaching hurricane.

E. B. White, that engaging master of the genre, a champion of idiosyncrasy, introduced one of his own collections by admitting the danger of narcissism:

> I think some people find the essay the last resort of the egoist, a much too self-conscious and self-serving form for their taste; they feel that it is presumptuous of a writer to assume that his little excursions or his small observations will interest the reader. There is some justice in their complaint. I have always been aware that I am by nature self-absorbed and egoistical; to write of myself to the extent I have done indicates a too great attention to my own life, not enough to the lives of others.

Yet the self-absorbed Mr. White was in fact a delighted observer of the world and shared his delight with us. Thus, after describing memorably how a circus girl practiced her bareback riding in the leisure moments between shows

("The Ring of Time"), he confessed: "As a writing man, or secretary, I have always felt charged with the safekeeping of all unexpected items of worldly or unworldly enchantment, as though I might be held personally responsible if even a small one were to be lost." That statement may still be presumptuous, but the presumption is turned outward on the world.

Such looking outward on the world helps distinguish the essay from pure autobiography, which dwells more complacently on the self. Mass murderers, movie stars, sports heroes, Wall Street crooks, and defrocked politicians may blather on about whatever high jinks or low jinks made them temporarily famous and may chronicle their exploits, their diets, and their hobbies in perfect confidence that the public is eager to gobble up every least gossipy scrap. And the public, according to sales figures, generally is. On the other hand, I assume that the public does not give a hoot about my private life (an assumption also borne out by sales figures). If I write of hiking up a mountain, with my one-year-old boy riding like a papoose on my back, and of what he babbled to me while we gazed down from the summit onto the scudding clouds, I do so not because I am deluded into believing that my baby, like the offspring of Prince Charles, matters to the great world. I do so because I know that the great world produces babies of its own and watches them change cloud-fast before its doting eyes. To make that climb up the mountain vividly present for readers is harder work than the climb itself. I choose to write about my experience not because it is mine but because it seems to me a door through which others might pass.

On that cocky first page of *Walden,* Thoreau justified his own seeming self-absorption by saying that he wrote the book for the sake of his fellow citizens, who kept asking him to account for his peculiar experiment by the pond. There is at least a sliver of truth to this, since Thoreau, a town character, had been invited more than once to speak his mind at the public lectern. Most of us, however, cannot honestly say that the townspeople have been clamoring for our words. I suspect that all writers of the essay, even Norman Mailer and Gore Vidal, must occasionally wonder whether they are egomaniacs. For the essayist, in other words, the problem of authority is inescapable. By what right does one speak? Why should anyone listen? The traditional sources of authority no longer serve. You cannot justify your words by appealing to the Bible or some other holy text; you cannot merely stitch together a patchwork of quotations from classical authors; you cannot lean on a podium at the Atheneum and deliver your wisdom to a rapt audience.

In searching for your own soapbox, a sturdy platform from which to deliver your opinionated monologues, it helps if you have already distinguished yourself at some other, less fishy form. When Yeats describes his longing for Maud Gonne or muses on Ireland's misty lore, his words are charged with the prior strength of his poetry. When Virginia Woolf, in *A Room of One's Own,* reflects on the status of women and the conditions necessary for making art, she speaks as the author of *Mrs. Dalloway* and *To the Lighthouse.* The essayist may also lay claim to our attention by having lived through events or traveled through terrains that already bear a richness of meaning. When James Baldwin writes his *Notes of a Native Son,* he does not have to convince us that racism is a troubling reality. When Barry Lopez takes us on a meditative tour of the far north in *Arctic Dreams,* he can rely on our curiosity about that fabled and forbidding place. When Paul Theroux climbs aboard a train and invites us on a journey to some exotic destination, he can count on the romance of railroads and the allure of remote cities to bear us along.

Most essayists, however, cannot draw on any source of authority from beyond the page to lend force to the page itself. They can only use language to put themselves on display and to gesture at the world. When Annie Dillard tells us in the opening lines of *Pilgrim at Tinker Creek* about the tomcat with bloody paws who jumps through the window onto her chest, why should we listen? Well, because of the voice that goes on to say: "And some mornings I'd wake in daylight to find my body covered with paw prints in blood; I looked as though I'd been painted with roses." Listen to her explaining a few pages later what she is about in this book, this broody, zestful record of her stay in the Roanoke Valley: "I propose to keep here what Thoreau called 'a meteorological journal of the mind,' telling some tales and describing some of the sights of this rather tamed valley, and exploring, in fear and trembling, some of the unmapped dim reaches and unholy fastnesses to which those tales and sights so dizzyingly lead." The sentence not only describes the method of her literary search but also displays the breathless, often giddy, always eloquent and spiritually hungry soul who will do the searching. If you enjoy her company, you will relish Annie Dillard's essays; otherwise you will not.

Listen to another voice which readers tend to find either captivating or insufferable:

> That summer I began to see, however dimly, that one of my ambitions, perhaps my governing ambition, was to belong fully to this place, to belong as the thrushes and the herons and the muskrats belonged, to be altogether at home here. That is still my ambition. But now I have come to see that it proposes an enormous labor. It is a spiritual ambition, like goodness. The wild creatures belong to the place by nature, but as a man I can belong to it only by understanding and by virtue. It is an ambition I cannot hope to succeed in wholly, but I have come to believe that it is the most worthy of all.

The speaker is Wendell Berry writing about his patch of Kentucky. Once you have heard that stately, moralizing, cherishing voice, laced with references to the land, you will not mistake it for anyone else's. Berry's themes are profound and arresting ones. But it is his voice, more than anything he speaks about, that either seizes us or drives us away.

Even so distinct a persona as Wendell Berry's or Annie Dillard's is still only a literary fabrication, of course. The first person singular is too narrow a gate for the whole writer to pass through. What we meet on the page is not the flesh-and-blood author but a simulacrum, a character who wears the label *I*. Introducing the lectures that be-came *A Room of One's Own,* Virginia Woolf reminded her listeners that " 'I' is only a convenient term for somebody who has no real being. Lies will flow from my lips, but there may perhaps be some truth mixed up with them; it is for you to seek out this truth and to decide whether any part of it is worth keeping." Here is a part I consider worth keeping: "Women have served all these centuries as looking-glasses possessing the magic and delicious power of reflecting the figure of man at twice its natural size." It is from such elegant, revelatory sentences that we build up our notion of the "I" who speaks to us under the name of Virginia Woolf.

What the essay tells us may not be true in any sense that would satisfy a court of law. As an example, think of Orwell's brief narrative, "A Hanging," which describes an execution in Burma. Anyone who has read it remembers how the condemned man as he walked to the gallows stepped aside to avoid a puddle. Only an eyewitness should be able to report such a haunting detail. Alas, biographers, those zealous debunkers, have recently claimed that Orwell never saw such a hanging; that he reconstructed it from hearsay. What then do we make of his essay? Or has it become the sort of barefaced lie that we prefer to call a story?

Frankly, I do not much care what label we put on "A Hanging"—fiction or nonfiction, it is a powerful statement either way—but Orwell might have cared a great deal. I say so because not long ago I found one of my own essays treated in a scholarly article as a work of fiction. When I recovered from the shock of finding any reference to my work at all, I was outraged. Here was my earnest report about growing up on a military base, my heartfelt rendering of indelible memories, being confused with the airy figments of novelists! To be sure, in writing the piece I had used dialogue, scenes, settings, character descriptions, the whole fictional bag of tricks; I had picked and chosen among a thousand beckoning details; and I had downplayed some facts and highlighted others. But I was writing about the actual, not the invented. I shaped the matter, but I did not make it up.

To explain my outrage, I must break another taboo, which is to speak of the author's intention. My teachers warned me strenuously to avoid the intentional fallacy. They told me to regard poems and plays and stories as objects washed up on the page from some unknown and unknowable shores. Now that I am on the other side of the page, so to speak, I think quite recklessly of intention all the time. I believe that, if we allow the question of intent in the case of murder, we should allow it in literature. The essay is distinguished from the short story, not by the presence or absence of literary devices, not by tone or theme or subject, but by the writer's stance toward the material. In composing an essay about what it was like to grow up on that military base, I *meant* something quite different from what I mean when I concoct a story. I meant to preserve and record and help give voice to a reality that existed independently of me. I meant to pay my respects to a minor passage of history in an out-of-the-way place. I felt responsible to the truth as known by other people. I wanted to speak directly out of my own life into the lives of others.

You can see I am teetering on the brink of metaphysics. One step farther and I will plunge into the void, wondering as I fall how to prove there is any external truth for the essayist to pay homage to. I draw back from the brink and simply declare that I believe one writes, in essays, with a regard for the actual world, with a respect for the shared substance of history, the autonomy of other lives, the being of nature, and the mystery and majesty of a creation we have not made.

When it comes to speculating about the creation, I feel more at ease with physics than with metaphysics. According to certain bold and lyrical cosmologists, there is at the center of black holes a geometrical point, the tiniest conceivable speck, where all the matter of a collapsed star has been concentrated and where everyday notions of time, space, and force break down. That point is called a singularity. The boldest and most poetic theories suggest that anything sucked into a singularity might be flung back out again, utterly changed, somewhere else in the universe. The lonely first person, the essayist's microcosmic "I," may be thought of as a verbal singularity at the center of the mind's black hole. The raw matter of experience, torn away from the axes of time and space, falls in constantly from all sides, undergoes the mind's inscrutable alchemy, and reemerges in the quirky, unprecedented shape of an essay.

Now it is time for me to step down, before another metaphor seizes hold of me, before you notice that I am standing, not on a soapbox, but on the purest air.

Samuel Pickering, Jr.

SOURCE: "Man of Letters," in *The Virginia Quarterly Review,* Vol. 61, No. 1, Winter, 1985, pp. 130-45.

[*Pickering is an American critic and educator. In the following essay, he describes the pleasures of writing the familiar essay.*]

Occasionally I write familiar essays. When I send them to editors, I usually explain that I am trying to write my way to a new car, adding that I have done well recently and have earned the front half of a station wagon, the automatic transmission, power brakes, and a luggage rack. Of course, that's not true. My essays will never earn me a new car. Besides I am happy with my 1973 Pontiac. Although it is rusting around the edges and the sun has so bleached it that it looks like a tired, old dachshund, it is comfortable and suits me. Other people, though, want to see me in "better circumstances," as a friend put it. After I was towed for the second time last year, he advised me to look at Toyotas, saying they were "splendidly efficient."

Efficiency, however, is not something I think much about. If anything, I am afraid of it. The second time my car broke down was on the Interstate at 7:30 Labor Day morning. I was headed for a road race in New Haven and wore blue sneakers without socks, jeans that should have been in the ragbag months before, and an orange T-shirt. On the front in brown was a picture of four runners and

the inscription "Woodstock 10 K"; on the back "Linemaster America's Foot Switch Leader" stood out in bold letters three inches high. Some years ago when I broke down on the road with my wife, I had to wait two hours before someone stopped. Although I looked like an escapee from Danbury prison, things were different this time. I got out of the car and, climbing onto the roof, held up my running shoes. The first car along pulled over, and a girl rolled down the window and said, "Going to the race?" "Yes," I answered, "my car stopped." "Nothing to that," she said. "Hop in, John, here," she continued, gesturing to the driver, "is an engineer at Pratt and Whitney; he can fix anything, and after the race will get you going again." In I hopped, and after the race and lunch and some lies about running, John repaired my car, and I drove home feeling good about life and the people who live it.

No, efficiency is not for me. If it were, I would not write personal essays. Certainly they will never bring me acclaim or money. Years ago when I started, I was naïve and, hoping to make a "big hit," sent *The New Yorker* a familiar essay on my athletic doings. "A bit too familiar" the rejection said. The flip tone hurt, and for a while I gave up personal essays and concentrated on scholarly writing. Since I teach at the University of Connecticut, I feel obligated to research subjects and write a fair amount about them. Actually research and academic writing are enjoyable. In fact, they are so seductive that months frequently pass without my writing a personal essay. Becoming an expert in a narrow area is not difficult. I know a lot, for example, about early children's books, and when scholars have questions about Giles Gingerbread or Goody Two-Shoes, they write me. These inquiries appeal to my vanity and make me want to write more. I dream of my little reputation growing so large that graduate students at the best universities will know my name and the Modern Language Association will solicit my opinions on things academic. Because it tempts me to become efficient and concentrate my energy and life, the dream bothers me and I struggle against it. Sometimes the struggle is difficult.

This past winter I went to New York to be interviewed for a post at a big state university. The interview was held in the New York Hilton, one of the hotels hosting the Modern Language Association Convention. Academics bustled about in the hotel lobby, and after the interview as I made my way to the street, a young woman pushed through the crowd and throwing her arms over my shoulders said, "You are the most wonderful scholar; keep up your good work." Before I could think of a witty answer, she kissed me on the cheek and melted back into the crowd. "You bet your sweet article in *PMLA* I'll keep it up," I mumbled while I stood on the curb looking for a taxi. New York makes me nervous, though, and I am not very efficient at catching taxis. By the time one stopped for me, I concluded the woman had made a mistake. Since I had not come to New York to attend the convention, I was not wearing a name tag, and although my last book had received some good reviews, my picture did not appear on the jacket. "A case of mistaken identity," I muttered, and beating down the temptation to covet and pursue reputation as a scholar, I decided that the kiss foreshadowed the familiarity into which academic writing would thrust me. How much better to write personal essays and remain unknown, I thought, as I rode the bus back to Connecticut and planned an essay on picking up sticks.

I write about the little things of life like starlings or dandelions or picking up sticks. I do so because the little things are about all most people have. None of my friends live romantic lives vibrant with excitement; instead they jog through the quiet byways of ordinary existence, with its leaves and laundry, unread newspapers, diapers and matchbox cars, and Masterpiece Theater on Sunday night. I also write about small things because they bring me letters. I live in a rambling, old-fashioned house; since I will never earn enough from my essays to redecorate it, I have let it decorate me. Big bundles of faded pink roses cover the wallpaper in my study, and on my desk is an old chamber pot, covered like the walls with roses. In it I keep my correspondence, and whenever one of my essays appears in print it overflows with wondrous mail. These letters are not part of the academic world and its momentary intellectual conflicts; they never bring those feelings of cagey rivalry that come over me when I learn that a younger, and perhaps better, critic has published a study of children's books. The letters come from a cleaner place. The wallpaper suits them, and they are redolent of simpler lives in a simpler time.

My wife's family owns a farm in Nova Scotia. The farm is in Beaver River, a little town north of Yarmouth on the Bay of Fundy. Vicki and I spend summers there and almost every day take walks with our children through fields or along the shore. The letters come from that world, and as I read them, I drift from words to goldenrod and Queen Anne's lace, salt marshes and peatbogs and patches of blue and green and white as the coast juts out around Black Point before sweeping into Cape St. Mary's. At night Vicki and I sleep upstairs in a dark Victorian bed with a headboard that towers solidly above us. Through the window blows the sea and the wash of stones down the beach. Sleep comes simply and naturally; I don't dream, and early in the morning I wake fresh and thankful for life. Like those nights, the letters I receive renew me; and although they do not offer hope for the world in which I work my way for most of the year, they bring happiness and moments in which I forget self and want to give more to life than I receive.

Last spring *Yankee* magazine printed an essay I wrote on the box turtle. In the essay I appeared as a slow-moving, gentle bachelor, a turtle of a man, alone and out of step with the age. The first hint that the essay was a success occurred when an elder neighbor who had taken little notice of my wife and me when we moved into our house and who I thought resented our children's breaking the morning's quiet, brought us a caramel cake. We invited her in for tea and cookies, and conversation meandered pleasantly along until she said, "I read your article in *Yankee* and I have a question." "What's that," I answered. "Well, I really liked the article," she said, "but I want to know if it has any deeper meaning." "No," I replied. "Oh," she said smiling, "I am so glad"; and with that she turned to Vicki who sat beside her on the couch and taking her hands into hers said, "I must get to know you and those adorable little boys of yours better." That day letters began to trickle in about the essay. In September, *Reader's Digest* reprinted it, and the trickle became a flood.

Many of my correspondents described their love for, as one called them, "my slow moving hinged friends." Most of the writers were old, and turtles often reminded them of the past. The owner of Timmy, a woman with grandchildren aged 21 and 23, wrote that her husband had "been a turtle lover since early childhood when he roamed the mountains near his home at Delaware Water Gap." Exercising in a "private plastic bathtub" and dining on lean hamburger, bananas, and strawberries, Timmy led an idyllic life. From October to the first of April, he stayed close to a warm radiator and slept in a tunnel made from pillows. His favorite occupations were basking in the sun and listening to relaxing music.

In my essay I said that on the road outside my house I had put up signs reading "Box Turtle Crossing. Slow Down." And actually, whenever I see a turtle on or near a highway, I stop, jump out of my car, pick up the turtle, and after guessing which way he or she is going, I carry it across the highway and turn it loose as far from the road as I can. I have done this ever since I was a child. Perched high on my knees in the front seat of our Ford, I would scan the roadside while my parents drove. Sometimes eight turtle stops would break the six mile drive from my grandfather's farm in Hanover, Virginia, to the grocery store in Ashland. Last year, I showed up with stickers on my socks and trousers and slightly late for a talk in Farmington because I had rescued a turtle. I felt guilty, but after I explained what delayed me, the audience clapped and the talk was a success. Still, I sometimes feel foolish when I stop for turtles, or at least I did until my article appeared. Now I know that hundreds of people behave like me.

"I was traveling down a rural highway," Peggy wrote, "when Golda came into my life. She was sitting on the middle line with a paw over her head. She'd been clipped by cars and had several small holes in her shell." Fortunately Golda's shell rejuvenated, and she now lives safely with Cynthia and Helmet, both of whom Peggy saved from callous owners. Peggy discovered Helmet in a pet store. When she asked why there was no food or water in Helmet's aquarium, the owner answered that box turtles only needed water and food "a couple of times during their lives." Infuriated by the man's ignorance, Peggy bought Helmet. Cynthia led a better if more sheltered existence than Helmet. For five years she had been a child's pet, so much so, Peggy explained, "she has no idea about turtle life. On seeing an earthworm, she dived into her shell and wouldn't come out until she smelled hamburger." Such a creature was not fit for the wild, and when Cynthia's owner became more interested in petting boys than turtles, the girl's parents decided to abandon Cynthia in the park. Peggy did not think Cynthia could survive and took her home as a companion for Golda and Helmet. Cynthia was so pleased by the change that this past year she laid an egg. Peggy promised to write me if it hatched.

Like Peggy, people that save turtles usually have more

than one, and I received many letters describing "turtlariums." "Since about 1978," Jane wrote from Alabama, "I have been picking up Box Turtles from roads and placing them in my fenced back yard." Although her backyard was only half an acre, Jane said, it contained 35 to 40 pine trees and supported "a substantial turtle population." During winter the turtles hibernated under the trees and on hot summer days they "spend a good bit of time burrowed down in pine needles." Although turtles themselves are sluggish particularly in the heat, "turtle owners" are lively. "My normal day," Jane recounted, "begins around 6:30 at which time I make Turtle Rounds. I usually see three or four at this time. Some are in concrete blocks (the foundation of one end of the fence). Others are munching away at tomato peels or cantaloupes rotting on the compost heap." Compared to some owners' yards, Jane's was large. In Virginia, George's yard was only 20 by 30 feet and included a four-by-eight foot fishpond. Happily for the turtles, though, pines and shrubs filled the yard, and worms, snails, and crickets abounded. Around the yard ran a board fence under which George had sunk concrete blocks to prevent the turtles from digging their way out. At one time George owned four adults, but one drowned in the pond and another came out of hibernation too early and died. Now he reckoned he had the two remaining adults and two to four babies born in September 1981.

People who have, as George put it, "a love affair with Box Turtles" are slow and patient, like the turtle itself, and generally seem apart from the bustle of modern living. I imagine the women sitting in rocking chairs on small screened-in porches drinking iced tea and talking about things past, "memories of Pensacola" or "barefoot days on Missouri country roads where I would paddle along in the dust." The men I see coming around to the front porch after digging in their gardens. Wiping their hands on their trousers, they sit down, and like George, they laugh and delight in breaking the slow rocking and nostalgia. "Have you ever witnessed their mating," George asked me. "I can tell you," he continued, warming to the subject, "that the act is not exactly earthshaking—nor does it call for athletics, but for endurance it must be tops. I have seen one pair mate for over two hours. And later that same day they were at it again! The female was one of those that died. Did not bother the male at all."

Universities are rarely communities. Both students and faculty are migrants. Even if faculty members spend their entire careers at one school, they, if they resemble me at least, spend much time thinking about going elsewhere. Such thoughts inhibit the growth of those rich sentimental ties that bind a person like ivy to people and place. Research and academic writings undermine the community and contribute to an individual's isolation. Because the very nature of a specialty is particularity, the expert usually can share little of his research with others. Moreover, publication and reputation make thinking about taking a "better" post at another institution not merely a dream but a possibility to be considered and forever reconsidered. In contrast, writing familiar essays enlarges the sense of community as the writer is touched by the hopes and fears of all kinds and ages of people. Not long ago, a member of my department died unexpectedly. At the funeral we

sang "Abide with Me," and as I walked out of the church, I felt loss and was convinced that I was a part of something. The next week a search began for a replacement, and as I thought about the kind of person we could hire, I became upset—not at the department for looking for "new blood" but at myself for being so alone that death would diminish me so little and that I could forget the dead so quickly. In another job, I wondered, would things, even heartache, last longer? Wouldn't other people, then, I almost pleaded with myself, be a greater part of my life?

I could not answer my questions. I did know, though, that many of the letters written in response to my article on the box turtle stirred feelings which lasted comparatively long. For months I carried around tears evoked by a letter from Boston, written by "a country girl lost in the city." "I can really understand how you feel about turtles," she began, "as I had a baby turtle left with me while a friend of my son's went into the army but he didn't want him back and after 5 years Squeaky has grown to be 12 1/2 pounds and has gone from a deep ashtray to a punch bowl then to a ten gallon tank to a 50-gallon tank and now has taken over my tub." The country girl had long since become old, and being feeble and living in a bad neighborhood, rarely left her house. Squeaky was one of the last pleasures of her life. "He is very smart," she wrote, "and lets the water out by flipping over the plug and then stands up and really is fun to watch. He has thrived on cat food and gets a spoon each morning and again at night. He and Princess the cat, the only cat I know that has a pet, she sits on the toilet and watches him and gets very excited if he starts climbing. But he has to go," she continued; "he needs his own kind of life but I've been wondering if he could hibernate and live in water. Please tell me and I'm curious about what you call a box turtle."

A picture accompanied the letter and showed Squeaky pushing a brick about in the tub. Clearly, Squeaky was not a box turtle. He was a snapping turtle, the kind my grandfather said would bite and not let go until there was a thunderstorm. Unfortunately, although the country girl had tamed an aggressive turtle, she could not tame time or circumstance. "Being handicapped," she told me, "I've got to find a home for Squeaky. My son can't help me as he passed away last New Year's eve. I'd like to find a place where I wouldn't have to worry about sick-minded teenagers catching him and being cruel as they were near here." The teenagers, she said, had caught a turtle and tying a shoelace around its neck hanged it from a fence and used it for target practice, throwing rocks and bottles at it. A policeman discovered the boys and made them cut the turtle down, bury it, and even say a prayer. After describing the incident, the old woman said, "I couldn't take it, knowing Squeaky went through this," and she asked me to "find a turtle farm for Squeaky." A farm in the country, she suggested, would be better than one near Boston because fish and ducks were dying in nearby rivers, and she wanted "Squeaky kept healthful."

She gave me her address and telephone number, and although I wrote her I did not do as I should have done: gone to Boston and brought Squeaky back to Storrs and turned him loose in a horse pond. I told myself that I did not go because her letter arrived in the middle of the semester when I was busy grading mounds of undergraduate papers. Of course, my car was also old and liable, I thought, to break down on a long trip. Furthermore, cities made me nervous, and I wondered what would happen if I broke down in Boston. My journey to New York in December was out of character. Until then I had not been to New York during the six years I lived in eastern Connecticut. For that matter I have never been to Boston or Providence and only been in Hartford twice. Like the country girl, I decided, I would be lost in Boston and so I stayed home. Now I feel guilty and suspect that I am lost in a way the country girl is not.

I received many letters from people who were more at home in the past and the country than they were in the city and the present. "I envy anyone the ability to write," a woman wrote from Chicago; "I am just a music teacher and that's all I can do. But I had the most wonderful, talented mother I'd love to tell everyone about. She played piano, was the best cook in seven counties, made hats, ran a switch-board, could mend fences like a trooper. People came from miles around to see her beautiful flowers. Once she walked back in the woods, found a rocky hillside where she planted flowers and small evergreens among the trees, looking down on a big sycamore and a babbling brook. Every time she had the weight of the world on her shoulders, she'd walk back and sit on a rock. Soon her problems disappeared. She could shoot—oh how she could shoot a gun. She'd have me walk up the road behind the fence row hedge, beating the bushes as I went. She walked down the road slightly to my rear—the gun pointed. Any rabbit I scared out of the hedge—ping—she got him on the run. Well, you can see, I could go on and on."

In writing me the woman had herself walked back into a woods, and when she felt better, had come out hesitatingly and sheepishly, wanting to write more yet aware that she had revealed her heart. I was sorry when she stopped describing her mother, and when the letter ended I thought about my own mother who had also been a good shot. When I was growing up in Nashville, Nelson Leasor worked in our yard occasionally. Mr. Leasor was from east Tennessee and was as angular as the Clinch Mountains. He worked only when he felt like it, and my father wanted to get rid of him, telling mother he would never be reliable. Mother disagreed and said, "Just you wait." And wait we did until one day when Mr. Leasor knocked on the door and said, "Mrs. Pickering, I'm going home. There is no sense in raking these leaves. The squirrels chew up so many hickory nuts that every load I carry out back is mostly nuts." "That bothers you does it, Mr. Leasor," mother said. "Yes, ma'am," he answered in as contrary a tone as he could. "Well, I'll take care of that," mother said and went to the bedroom and got her shotgun out of that closet. "Mrs. Pickering, what are you going to do," Mr. Leasor asked when he saw the gun. "I am going to get you a little meat for Brunswick stew," mother replied. "You can't shoot that gun in the city," he said. "And who is going to stop me," mother said going out the door, "not you—come along." Mr. Leasor followed quietly and that evening after he finished raking the yard, he carried home 14 squirrels. He was not late for work again,

and whenever I saw him in later years, even on his deathbed, he would say, "Sammy, I have never seen a woman shoot like Mrs. Pickering. Right in the city—14 shots and 14 squirrels and some of them in Mr. Knox's yard."

Maybe in writing about turtles I was unconsciously escaping from my sandy present and searching for solid rock on which I could sit and renew myself. Turtles had once been very important to me. Every summer in Virginia, the children who lived on grandfather's farm and I spent our days catching things in order to win four contests: the lizard, the frog, the locust (cicada), and the turtle. I didn't have fast hands, and I never won the frog or locust contests, but I was observant and always found the most turtles. After grandfather died, grandmother sold the farm and moved to a smaller house near the post office and the train station. Although the contests ended, I still searched for turtles. Almost every day I walked north along the tracks toward Fredericksburg. About a mile and a half up the tracks at the edge of a pine woods near a swamp was a real turtle crossing. Attempting to go from one side of the track to the other, turtles would scrape gravel from under the rails and burrow through. Long, slow freights did not bother them, but fast passenger trains often flipped them onto their backs, and before they could right themselves, many were killed by the sun. The sight of dead turtles upset me, and so I saved as many as I could, righting those on their backs and carrying others across the roadbed and into the swamp. Those that were dead I took home and let rot. Then I cleaned and shellacked them and put them on a bookcase in my room. I still have one shell. Since 1958, I have kept it in the glove compartment of every car I have owned. Occasionally Vicki suggests taking it out, saying we need more room for maps. I usually answer that since we don't travel anywhere we don't need to carry maps in the glove compartment. In any case I don't want to remove the shell. It is itself, I suppose, a kind of map, a map of my past reminding me where I came from.

Academic readers learn not to take any writing, even the personal essay, as completely autobiographical. In contrast, many of the people that wrote me about turtles accepted my essay as entirely true. In the essay I reflected on the turtle's courtship ritual and depicting myself as an aging bachelor, lamented that I had never met an old-fashioned girl like Miss Box Turtle, who responded shyly to her suitor's ardor by retreating into her shell and peeking out "the front door" demurely. Several people took my lovelorn state to heart and tried to cheer me up. "Samuel," one person wrote, "you just keep studying the box shell and learn from his widsom, and one day the Lord will send you an old-fashioned girl and you will live happily every after." The study of "God's creatures," a man wrote from Iowa, could make up for not having a wife. "I spend happy hours," he said, "watching the birds come to the feeders and in summer love to watch the antics of the many raccoons that pay nightly visits to the patio to get corn, stale bread, and sometimes marshmellows." "Hope your life will be filled with peace and love," another man concluded; "stay in good spirits. I am sure that someday soon you will meet an old-fashioned girl like Miss Box Turtle. God bless you."

I answered every letter I received and tried to write something which would appeal to the reader. I began by describing catching turtles when I was young. Then I became philosophical. The person who moves slow enough to see beauty in the ordinary, who was "a lover of life in all its endless variety," I wrote, would be happier than one who rushed quickly through days in pursuit of wealth or position. Usually I ended by talking about my plans for future essays and said I wanted to write next about the daddy-longlegs. "Where," I wrote, "were Mommy and Baby and grandma and grandpa longlegs?" It was time, I said, that somebody wrote about the whole family. Not all the letters I received, though, were easy to answer. Unlike scholarly writing, which is often abstract and which entails little responsibility because it appeals primarily to readers' minds and moves them only to intellectual play, the familiar essay is particular. Because it frequently appeals to and so moves emotions that people act, it forces responsibility upon the writer. In contrast to the footnotes generated by my academic writings, the essay on the box turtle brought me notes from the heart. "Sometimes it takes me a long time to get around to things," a woman wrote, "and sometimes I am shy about approaching people I do not know. However, I firmly believe that it's never too late to express appreciation, and I wanted you to know how very much I enjoyed your ruminations about the box turtle." "I have never known any," she went on, "but I am sure that is my loss. I think of myself as a quiet woman; I don't go along with rushing around or being assertive. In those respects, I suppose I am like a box turtle too." "I'm frequently late to work in the spring and early summer," a woman wrote from Georgia, "because I'm helping turtles across the road. Leaving earlier doesn't work because then I see more turtles and my boss doesn't understand. My dream is to have a box turtle sanctuary and to have turtle crossings under every U.S. highway. People think I'm weird, but I figure you'll understand." " 'The Very Thought of Turtles,' " she concluded, "was delightful and next spring I plan to put up some turtle crossing signs. The only problem with your not marrying is that you need to produce offspring that will be turtle lovers too."

As letters like this and that from the "quiet woman" began to stream in, I thought I understood, but initially I was not sure how to respond. It "sounds like you are in my fantasy island," a woman from Minnesota wrote; "you kind of reveal yourself as being old-fashioned and shy. I personally don't think that being an old-fashioned person is a bit dull at all. Maybe it is true to the outgoing persons, but I simply believe that old-fashioned people are the most reliable persons that one can trust. They also are the types of persons who can be very interesting, affectate, romatic and the best companion one can find—after you get to truly know them. I myself is very old-fashioned person too. I did overcome my shyness in last couple of years, but I always prefer my old ways. I treasure every thing I own such as my thoughts, my old friends."

In writing familiar essays I suppose I have built a personal fantasy island, far from the main currents of life, a place where everyday, as one man put it, seems "one of those wonderfully lazy Sunday afternoons." In answering the letters of those people whose loneliness led them to respond warmly and nakedly to my narrator's isolation, I tried not to break the gentle peace of a Sunday afternoon. The lies which lead to disappointment with our world are everywhere, and if the life described in my essay had not actually been led, I now wanted my correspondents to believe that the emotions behind the essay were true. Initially, I told curious friends in the university that I wrote the essay as an exercise in gilding the mundane. Now I hoped my motivation ran deeper and richer. Whatever the case, though, I knew the feelings revealed in the letters were good, and if I could not prolong my correspondents' fantasy of a bittersweet bachelor dreaming of the right wife, I thought that I might be able to substitute another but still decent picture for it. And so in responding to letters like that written by the very old-fashioned person, I talked about the pleasures writing brough me and then described the real loves of my life, my family, Vicki and my two little boys, Francis and Edward.

Writing about my family made me happy, but I worried about the effect the transformation of a turtle-loving bachelor into a husband and father would have on my correspondents. I underestimated the letter-writers, and I soon learned there was no reason for anxiety. "Hello Samuel Pickering," one wrote back, "how are you today. I enjoyed your letter and am so glad you have your Miss Box Turtle and the two little boys. I am making items at present for a craft bazaar. I have never made any box turtles, but thought you might like a Teddy bear decoration to hang in your little boys' bedroom. If they are in separate rooms, let me know and I'll send you another one. Take good care of Miss Box Turtle and the precious little ones. Please write more articles. God Bless."

This letter invigorated me. And in truth almost all the people who answered my letters said they were eager to read more of my essays. "Where may I find additional pearls of Pickering ponderings," a woman asked lightly, while a man urged me, "don't ever stop writing. I hope your daddy longlegs article will be in *Reader's Digest*." So did I, and off I rushed to the library and checked out a dozen books. At first all went well, and I was sure I had found the subject for a pearl of an essay. Some 3,200 species of daddy longlegs lived in the world, I learned; and they were known by a wealth of names: haymakers, harvestmen, and grandfather greybears. Three and a half centuries ago in England they were called shepherd spiders. In his *Theater of Insects* (1634) Thomas Muffett explained the name, writing "the English call it Shepherd either because it is pleased with the Company of Sheep or because Shepherds think those fields that are full of them to be good wholesome Sheep-pasture." When I realized that this Muffett was the famous entomologist and the father of Patience, most certainly the heroine of the nursery rhyme "Little Miss Muffet," I thought my essay was as good as sold. I even told Vicki that we could afford a radio in our new car and suggested that we visit a few junk shops to see if we could find a second chamber pot to accommodate all the letters that would arrive after the essay appeared. "One with daffodils or violets on it would be nice," I said. Alas, I spoke without knowing enough about the daddy longlegs. I soon learned, though. The spider, I reluctantly concluded, that disrupted Miss Muffet's snack of curds and whey must have been a shepherd spider. The legs are not the only long thing on the daddy longlegs. If a person gently squeezes the sides of the male harvestman, down from an internal sack will drop its penis, an organ, I read, "remarkable for its great size, often exceeding the creature's body in length." Although I had not read Freud for 20 years, he came suddenly to mind, and eager to be accused of "daddy longlegs envy," I closed the book I was reading. Then I got up from the desk and, taking the notecards for the essay into the kitchen, dropped them into the trash can. That night I began an "academic article" on "Liars and Tattle-Tales in 18th-Century Children's Books."

William Howarth

SOURCE: "Itinerant Passages: Recent American Essays," in *The Sewanee Review,* Vol. XCVI, No. 4, Fall, 1988, pp. 633- 43.

[*An American educator and critic, Howarth has written and edited several books on the life and writings of Henry David Thoreau. In the following essay, Howarth discusses American essays written after 1965.*]

How to begin? A screen door opens, light and air spread into the room, a voice calls out. A man crossing a snowfield suddenly halts in mid-stride, having glimpsed a fox. A lone car sweeps north, only its driver awake to see the dawn. These are opening moments from some of my own essays, and I am struck by how often they begin with motion, the setting forth on a journey.

Since the days of Herodotus writers have sent readers traveling, but essays seem to have their own brand of itinerancy. As texts they open doors, take to the road, launch a stream of discourse. Their authors begin and move out, heading for uncertain destinations, carrying readers through a succession of events that pass like the flow of experience. Essays provide us with safe passage to ideas, arguments, stories with characters and dialogue—always unfolded as an ongoing process.

Process is a word now much in fashion, used by everyone from writing teachers to the makers of synthetic cheese. In its narrowest meaning a process is motion between two points, from here to there. The motion may be unique or recurring, and therein lies an important difference. A recurring process invokes order and certainty, the successions that establish traditional patterns—a line of monarchs, a rally in tennis. A unique process is eccentric and finite, coming to a definite end.

In American essays written after 1965, these two forms of motion often coexist in jostling opposition. During the tumultuous sixties many writers turned instinctively to orthodox prose forms. Such counterculture classics as *Armies of the Night, Zen and the Art of Motorcycle Maintenance, Fear and Loathing in Las Vegas,* and *The Electric Kool-Aid Acid Test* all share the pattern of a cross-country journey, an epic quest that searches for personal and national identity. These songs of the open road reflect an old American faith in westering, the hope that traversing the continent will bind us to its immense sprawl and expand our moral capacity.

Vietnam may have stirred this desire, for that land persistently eluded American possession. The war in southeast Asia had no clear battlefront or enemy; its daily events presented no itinerary to Americans—only appalling chaos and stasis. Michael Herr best captures those qualities in *Dispatches,* six essays that vigorously resist causal integration and deny the usual mapping structures that link space or time. Reading a map of Vietnam, he writes, "was like trying to read the wind." The same anomie affected civilian life, Michael Arlen observes in *Living-Room War,* a collection of essays on television, because that medium fractures continuity into a channel-flipping maze of unexplained events. For both writers Vietnam was a harrowing journey, but definitely not America's traditional saga of exploration and settlement.

Something of that pioneer story reappeared after 1975, in such works as *Pilgrim at Tinker Creek* and *Coming into the Country,* which celebrate back-to-the-soil lives and rugged American spaces. Yet neither Annie Dillard nor John McPhee follows a single itinerary: their books unfold as a series of essays, loosely related by different locales and seasons in Virginia and Alaska. This meditative structure enhances the authors' cool unsentimental observations, as they observe the food chain impose its cheerless economy on all creatures, great and small. A far more strategic vision of competitive strife dominates *Of a Fire on the Moon* and *The Right Stuff,* two accounts of journeys by astronauts that are built with strong novelistic designs.

The decade that began in 1985 will surely bring us new varieties of essay, but among them the itinerant motif will endure. McPhee is now composing a multivolume series, *Annals of the Former World,* which describes his journeys across America with professional geologists. Spanning all the books is Interstate 80, a national corridor that crosses the continent but also cuts deep into its surface. Pausing at frequent road cuts, McPhee reveals how geologists can imagine the history of continental evolution—events that vastly predate human imagination. Such journeying in time has grown increasingly complex in McPhee's writing, including briefer works. Here is a suggestive passage from "Atchafalaya" (1987).

> If you travel by canoe through the river-swamps of Louisiana, you may very well grow uneasy as the sun is going down. You look around for a site, a place to sleep, a place to cook. There is no terra firma. Nothing is solider than duckweed resting on the water like green burlap. Quietly you slide through the forest, breaking out now and again into acreage of open lake. You study the dusk for some dark cap of uncovered ground. Seeing one at last, you occupy it, limited though it may be. Your tent site may be smaller than your tent. But in this amphibious new world, you have found yourself terrain. You have established yourself in much the same manner that the French established New Orleans. So what does it matter if your leg spends the night in the water?

This passage is about passage, the moving planes of space,

time and thought. In a few hundred words the journey of a lone canoeist evolves into a broad survey of regional history. By casting his lot with a tentative second-person voice, "If you travel by canoe," McPhee aligns himself with readers, leading us toward a shared hypothesis: "So what does it matter if your leg spends the night in the water?" The journey ends as it began, in speculation, remaining an exploratory foray into an "amphibious new world." Amphibious means double-lived, in this case both fluid and solid, familiar and strange. Through these dualities McPhee effectively enacts the experience of discovery, the human "establishment" in unknown realms.

That theme takes its shape from an itinerary. As the canoe glides through forest and water, their passing images propel a smooth flow of motion toward "a dark cap of ground," a point of pause and rest. Once reached, this island becomes a ground for larger inquiry, the vision of founding New Orleans. The camp site provides a stable, central locus—positioned at the center of this passage, which itself stands near the essay's midpoint. That formal congruency presents an imaginative process, while the intimacy of "you" helps us to enact its procedures. In a conditional amphibious world McPhee has located terrain—and established us upon it.

Recognizing the itinerancy of a text also means accepting its serial conventions. Texts are progressive, moving within and along a linear matrix. The glyphs become words, phrases and sentences follow, and soon great volumes of prose are sliding along. Text is a chain, a road, a voyage. We scan the lines from side to side and top to bottom, turning pages as we go; and these sequences immerse us in the stream of language. Texts *are* journeys; as Aristotle noted, their language represents a series of related actions that form a plot, a continuous line of events from beginning to end.

Since Montaigne introduced the principle of casual rumpled discourse, essays do not march smartly forward. To the linear models we could add that text is also a web, a maze, a dark and tangled forest. In that essay on Louisiana McPhee often breaks apart his line of narration, jumping away from the abecedarian chain of history, ignoring an obvious beginning to settle in a later, more original point of insertion. His early piece on Atlantic City, "The Search for Marvin Gardens," presents a scatter-shot narrative, as mixed and kaleidoscopic in temporal sequence as Faulkner's deconstructions of story-telling.

For many recent essayists, chaos and turbulence have become staple themes, reflecting anxieties about the breakdown of orderly culture structures. This apocalyptic urgency ironically has arrived on the wings of high technology. Satellite transmission now links the global village, but cannot deliver it from greed, suspicion, and ignorance. We recall Thoreau's response to the magnetic telegraph: "But Maine and Texas, it may be, have nothing important to communicate." Or remember Henry Adams's warning that velocity destroys a culture's unity. In this age of Artificial Intelligence, the current joke runs, nothing is more powerful than Real Stupidity. Amid pervasive fears of collapse the contemporary essay would not seem to offer much security.

For essays are not usually broad comprehensive projects but "pieces" wrought on assignment and published diversely—in magazines, newspapers, even literary quarterlies. Much later, after the original occasions have faded, writers may gather these scatterlings into collections—never a best-selling genre with the public. The etymology of "essay" suggests *trial* or *experiment,* work not fully or finally formed. Collecting such material naturally arouses their author's expectations: how did these pieces emerge? do they form a body of work? The process of review often yields a metaphor that arranges and defines part of a career. Often as not, the metaphor describes a journey.

In her thirty-ninth year Alice Walker sifted through nearly two decades of lectures, reviews, and articles for a collection, *In Search of Our Mothers' Gardens.* The book's structure is not chronological but thematic, arranged in four parts under a title Walker first used in 1974, for an essay in *Ms.* about southern black women. Her phrase *our mothers' gardens* descends from Virginia Woolf's "a room of one's own," but Walker has taken it outdoors, transforming a solitary closed image of femininity into expansive fertile spaces.

Walker's book unfolds as a searching journey for those imagined gardens, many Edens to reclaim. Her title phrase is deliberately inclusive, she explains, since the search for mothers is "a personal account that is yet shared, in its theme and its meaning, by all of us." That pluralism also invokes her subtitle, "Womanist Prose," meaning feminist writing that is strong and inclusive, "Committed to the survival and wholeness of entire people, male *and* female." As her search reveals, one life has many mothers, in all guises and colors.

One of Walker's maternal figures is the novelist and folklorist Zora Neale Hurston (1901-1960), who was largely forgotten until Walker edited *The Zora Neale Hurston Reader.* In "Looking for Zora" Walker dramatizes this history of neglect by retelling her journey to Fort Pierce, Florida, to find Hurston's grave. After much searching she finally located the unmarked site in an abandoned cemetery, full of weeds and imagined snakes. Walker buys a tombstone, inscribes it with Jean Toomer's phrase *A Genius of the South,* and then gathers stories about Zora from townspeople. To gain their confidence, she pretends to be Zora's niece: "Besides, as far as I'm concerned, she *is* my aunt—and that of all black people as well."

Walker's searching invariably leads back to the sources of her life as a writer. In "Beyond the Peacock: The Reconstruction of Flannery O'Connor," she goes with her mother to Milledgeville, Georgia, to visit two homes, her own and Flannery O'Connor's. The essay begins in a mood of resentment, posing herself and O'Connor as racial and cultural opposites, but eventually she comes to acknowledge their shared values. This turning begins with a conversation between the mother and daughter, held over lunch in a once-segregated restaurant. In that setting the "reconstruction" of a famous white artist unfolds.

Both women ask why O'Connor kept peacocks in her garden. As the mother observes, "Those things will sure eat up your flowers." Walker raises the ante slightly, saying

"They're a lot prettier than they'd be if somebody human had made them." Although she is a religious skeptic, this response casts a metaphysical light upon the peacock's owner. Says the mother: "She must have been a Christian person, then," to which Walker assents: "She believed in everything, including things she couldn't see." Coming to this accord completes the reconstruction of O'Connor. Her mother asks, "Is that why you like her?" And, with a trace of surprise, Walker realizes: "I like her because she could *write*."

This passage has the force of revelation, like "the shock of recognition" Melville felt on first reading Hawthorne. Walker's epiphany arises from a generational dialogue, the searching reexamination of old prejudices. To understand the peacocks, she learns to see "beyond" them to the transcendent values they incarnate. That act of imagination grasps what all three women share, a will to believe in the unseen. Both mother and daughter, Christian and writer, can thus accept O'Connor as a figure who shares and reconciles their attributes. And by including this essay in her collection, Walker continues to journey beyond the peacocks, asking her original ideas to open and expand.

Collections induce recollection, seeing how works have shaped a career. This principle shapes McPhee's "Pieces of the Frame" (1972), in which stories about the Loch Ness monster assemble within an enclosing frame, the image of human cruelty and monstrosity. A similar progression arranges Oliver Sacks's *Awakenings,* a series of case histories about patients emerging from long Parkinsonian comas. Dr. Sacks wrote half of his stories for medical or literary journals, the rest for publication as a book. In creating a single volume he discovered entirely new ways of seeing the patients' response to therapy by drugs. The book thus recounts his own awakening, as he comes to see his role in the healing process: "Diseases have a character of their own, but they also partake of our own character."

In most volumes of essays the title metaphor yields entitlement, an author's self-definition. By gathering a series of essays under the title *Teaching a Stone to Talk,* Annie Dillard declares her pervasive interest in language: "We are here to witness. There is nothing else to do with those mute materials we do not need." The world's mystifying silence raises a necessary question for her—why bother with words? Teaching stones to talk is a Zen-like riddle, she finds; one must shed language and accept silence, learn to hear what a wordless, stony existence has to say. Of course, she must use words to convey this very thought; but in her essays the itinerant mood is always contradictory and intuitive.

Frequently essays are presented to novice writers as models of the logical process. Mainly they chart the mind's motion, slipping from principle to example, and through a series of examples to another principle. In teaching writing today we stress sequence and coherence, but too often the students remain mute as Dillard's stones, unable to speak. In the present clamor for cultural literacy we may not be properly hearing this silence. Core curricula and rote learning will achieve results, but they are not conclusively the best modes of instruction for developing minds.

Joan Didion often voices her despair about the survival of thought in a brutal irrational world. Yet paradoxically her essays portray nervous breakdown and self-annihilation in a cool, elegantly sculptured prose. The title of her first essay collection, *Slouching Towards Bethlehem,* alludes to Yeats's "The Second Coming," a poem that for her predicted "the evidence of atomization, the proof that things fall apart" that characterized the 1960s. In that decade the world she knew collapsed into shards, robbing her of both voice and audience. As a writer she came to suspect the worst, "that nobody out there is listening."

Didion's second collection of essays, *The White Album,* appropriates '60s pop culture less despairingly, by replacing Yeats with the icons of rock musicians. Her title alludes to the Beatles' last album, actually called *The Beatles* but universally identified by its blank white cover. A largely non-collaborative set of songs, this album forecast the coming end of both the group and their era. While Didion's voice fears such closures, her essays cathartically purge that dread. In one cinematic "flash cut" she enters a clinical report on her neurological condition: depression and catatonia, exacerbated by chronic episodes of migraine. Writing about this collapse becomes reconstructive, the act of self-healing.

By naming her disorders she subordinates and arranges them into text, where she maintains an authority. Narration is the traditional basis of healing, as patients describe symptoms and doctors interpret their stories. Hence Didion no longer fears that no one is listening: *she* hears these tales and they justify her purpose. Writing becomes not futile but heroic, shaping significance out of life's inchoate experiences. Thus she begins *The White Album*: "We tell ourselves stories in order to live. . . . We live entirely, especially if we are writers, by the imposition of a narrative line upon disparate images. . . . Or at least we do for a while."

To write such a beginning anticipates the end of *The White Album*—that Didion survived her fears by writing them down. This victory is not merely personal, but an offer of reassurance to the culture at large. Her tales of survival recall *The Crack-Up,* a book Edmund Wilson assembled from Scott Fitzgerald's uncollected essays of the 1930s. That, too, was a shattered decade—the national economic crisis mirrored in Fitzgerald's own spiritual collapse. In the pages of *Esquire* he cast aside his celebrated Jazz Age image and confessed to breakdown—yet the essays describing this process were taut polished pieces of writing that renewed his confidence. After them he went on to finish *Tender Is the Night* and begin *The Last Tycoon,* flawed novels but distinguished by their considerable ambition.

Coming through her own soul's dark night, Didion closes *The White Album* with a section entitled "On the Morning After the Sixties." There she writes of lifeguards and orchidists, pastoral figures who protect and nurture life, surviving even in the face of California's high seas and brush fires. She recounts their stories of disaster and survival, moving beyond apocalypse to a morning dawn. At the end, she reports: "The fire had come to within 125 feet of the property, then stopped or turned or been beaten back, it was hard to tell. In any case it was no longer our house."

Her first line, about telling stories to live, still echoes, for here "it was hard to tell" is both a composing of experience—and an admission that it ultimately resists composition.

Didion's work reminds us that essays fulfill but also surprise our expectations, because they are both designed and improvised. After all the preliminary study and thought, the writing process still takes unexpected turns, reveals unforeseen connections. Asked if he planned his writing, E. M. Forster replied: "How do I know what I think until I see what I have said?" The itinerancy of writing, its own being in motion, generates and arranges thoughts, and they take form from their movement, not their mass. Writers think less *about* writing than *through* it: they watch it unfold and grasp its meaning as it emerges. "If I know what I'm doing," Didion once wrote, "then I can't do it."

The "process-writing" movement that now dominates college composition courses recognizes that writing is motion, a journey through constantly recurring cycles. The circuit spins repeatedly, through steps of gathering material, compiling and arranging it, then synthesizing a draft. Successive revisions follow, a learning process that reveals what to say and how to find a form—often a form that rehearses the writing journey. This faith in continuity values loose and imprecise forms, devoted to an ecological web of relationships rather than strict hierarchies. Whitman envisioned such a cosmology in his poetic catalogs, linking the soprano in the loft with the carpenter cutting his beam. In contemporary American essays high and low cultures often fuse; Yeats and the Beatles bear witness to the same general truths.

Process writing recognizes the itinerancy of text; its makers see composition as ongoing, constantly in motion. Robert Frost's definition of poetry held that texts can make "a momentary stay against confusion." That balanced phrase suggests that art is a refuge, but only for a moment. Joan Didion assembles such moments into a collage that she calls an album. Albums gather scraps of experience along a line of narration, offering a momentarily coherent account of fragmented times.

Writers like Didion have also journeyed through the world of publishing, learning the procedures that put texts before a public. At magazines such as *Vogue* and *Life* she saw that editors have strong notions about "the book" and had to find her own way, following but also subverting the house standards to maintain her own. The personal essays she writes, with their curious divisions of anxiety and confidence, measure the ambiguity of this training.

In years to come we may see how other external factors—such as writing on computers—affect essayists. That machine renders text as a rolling scroll, in motion on a seamless journey. Concerns about this new medium have mounted with its popularity. Writing in the *New Republic,* Edward Mendelson warns: "The computer eases the mechanical task of composition while quietly undermining coherence and truth." What no medium can alter is the fundamental linearity of text—and its attendant qualities of motion. Through their itinerancy, essays will continue to take us on passages—to bits of land where we may pass a night, sleeping with one leg in the water.

MODERN ESSAYISTS

Spencer Brown

SOURCE: "The Odor of Durability," in *The Sewanee Review,* Vol. LXXXVI, No. 1, Winter, 1978, pp. 146-52.

[*Brown is an American poet and critic. In the following review, he commends the essays of E. B. White and John McPhee.*]

Two of our foremost essayists have appeared almost simultaneously in retrospective volumes. E. B. White's selection from his own essays [*Essays of E. B. White,* 1977], is a companion to his collected letters published in 1976, and an anthology from John McPhee's dozen books [*The John McPhee Reader,* 1977], has been edited with great understanding and taste by William L. Howarth.

White describes himself alternately as essayist and as journalist. McPhee clearly considers himself a journalist. White being intensely personal and McPhee apparently impersonal, they have little in common but excellence and the same employer—the *New Yorker,* whose pages they have enriched and influenced. White's influence and enrichment, of course, are the greater; he is older by a generation.

White's position in the essay, indeed, is that of the schooner *America* off the Isle of Wight. "Who is second?" asks Queen Victoria. "Madam, there is no second." White has been our preeminent essayist so long that many would say there is no other. If you want to know what the modern informal essay is, you must read *One Man's Meat* or *The Second Tree from the Corner* or *The Points of My Compass.* Here you find both the best and the only true exemplar—a precise definition of a classic, as, for example, Milton *is* the English epic. When White tells us that he has chosen a few of his pieces that seem "to have the odor of durability clinging to them," we feel confident that here, as always, his nose knows. Yet I am a bit disappointed that he didn't wish to be remembered also by "The Door"—if it is an essay—surely one of his most remarkable achievements. Perhaps he considers it already anthologized enough, or bravura and therefore too easy.

Elsewhere I have tried to make a case for White as poet. He is so in part but not altogether. The poet writes with his ear cocked for sounds: for him, in the beginning was the Word. White writes more with his eye on the object. He seeks and often attains a precision so deft that it does soar off the ground into poetry. He is also so enchanted by the very words that he often adopts the other, the poet's, direct way—especially in his reminiscence "Years of Wonder," which recounts his journey to Alaska in 1923, drawing heavily and amusedly from his journal kept on the voyage. "Alaskan towns," wrote White of 1923, "are just murmurings at the foot of mountains." White of

1961 writes: "Sandburg had me by the throat in those days." Later: "A lookout had been posted on the forecastlehead and Tony, the giant Negro watchman, was heaving the lead. Although I was busy getting squared away in my new job, my journal for that date contains a long, fancy description of the heaving of the lead. I was tired, but not too tired for a burst of showy prose." Self-mockery, the lightest fluff of romantic irony, makes the best of both past and present.

Like White's letters this essay suggests the extraordinary unity of his career. He portrays himself as socially gawky, financially feckless, vocationally indecisive; also singleminded in his ambition for literary success, into which, over the years, he continually sidles, each time as astonished as Dumbo to find himself up so high and yet gratified that dedicated skill has won superiority over a slovenly and illiterate world.

"The essayist," says White in his foreword, "is a self-liberated man, sustained by the childish belief that everything he thinks about, everything that happens to him, is of general interest." It is, if you can write like White. One such thing, for him, is birds, from city pigeons to the Harris's sparrow he saw in Maine, "at least a thousand miles from where he belonged"; and one of the pleasantest of the essays is "Mr. Forbush's Friends," concerning a three-volume work on the birds of Massachusetts. White's professional conscience only moderates his admiration: "If Edward Howe Forbush's prose is occasionally overblown, this results from a genuine ecstasy in the man, rather than from a lack of discipline. Reading the essays, one shares his ecstasy." So too is White's ecstasy genuine, though the prose is scarcely overblown.

Even casual readers of the *New Yorker* have long been aware of White's style and observing eye. The author has generously included in his selection a number of such long-esteemed or even famous pieces as "Coon Tree," "Death of a Pig," "Bedfellows," and "Once More to the Lake." These and others like them, about his farm and life in Maine, give the characteristic flavor to the book—a flavor compounded of shrewd insight, hindsight, and artfully rambling structure. "Bedfellows," ostensibly a memorial for White's disreputable and mendacious dog Fred, actually ruminates on politics, democracy, the nurture of heterodoxy, and the shadow of death—not Fred's death, but, one might say,

> It is the blight man was born for,
> It is E. B. White you mourn for.

The structure of a White essay resembles the configurations of a *corps de ballet,* in its confusing and harmonious and interlacing whirls of snowy tutus, gliding long-legged on point (in what Noel Coward once called a *pas de tout*) into the predestined arrangement. White's genius is in expatiation, in byways. He is not a thinker; he is a wry observer; but he achieves peripheral vision.

Yet his elegantly controlled digressions are less remarkable than the sentences they ride on. And since we are more familiar with his notes on Maine than with his Florida pieces, it is in the latter that we can best admire his quality. In "The Ring of Time," after a tenderly ironic picture of a girl training as a rider in the circus winter quarters, he writes:

> It has been ambitious and plucky of me to attempt to describe what is indescribable, and I have failed, as I knew I would. But I have discharged my duty to society; and besides, a writer, like an acrobat, must occasionally try a stunt that is too much for him. At any rate, it is worth reporting that long before the circus comes to town, its most notable performances have already been given. Under the bright lights of the finished show, a performer need only reflect the candle power that is directed upon him; but in the dark and dirty old training rings and in the makeshift cages, whatever light is generated, whatever excitement, whatever beauty, must come from original sources—from internal fires of professional hunger and delight, from the exuberance and gravity of youth. It is the difference between planetary light and the combustion of stars.

Like the two greatest American poets, Dickinson and Frost, White can become exasperatingly cute; but normally he is saved from cuteness by humor that they achieve only irregularly. Though he may pose as much as they, his poses are more natural and less noticeable. Wilbur, the hero of *Charlotte's Weh,* is SOME PIG, but at the last triumphs by being HUMBLE.

White's sentences can be sharp and memorable. His first view of Siberia: "On shore we could see dogs curled up asleep among patches of tired snow." On the USSR: "The West has a real genius for doing approximately what the East wants it to do." "The side that enjoys numerical superiority stands to gain by disarmament, the side that does not have any intention of remaining unarmed for more than a few minutes stands to gain, and the side that uses the lie as an instrument of national policy stands to gain. If disarmament carried no chance of advantage, Mr. Khrushchev would not be wasting his breath on it." On Thoreau: "It is probably no harder to eat a woodchuck than to construct a sentence that lasts a hundred years."

The essay on Thoreau, "A Slight Sound at Evening," deliberately points up the differences between White and Thoreau. Thoreau's humor—what there is of it—is savage. White's is tolerant—with teeth. Thoreau's finest sentences are those of an angry man. Says White: "Henry went forth to battle when he took to the woods, and *Walden* is the report of a man torn by two powerful and opposing drives—the desire to enjoy the world (and not be derailed by a mosquito wing) and the urge to set the world straight. One cannot join these two successfully, but sometimes, in rare cases, something good or even great results from the attempt of the tormented spirit to reconcile them."

White loves the past. His is true nostalgia, full of detailed knowledge, avoiding stock responses. He is too humorous to be overtly sentimental, and usually too accurate. The Model-T Ford, which he eulogizes as mechanically uncanny in "Farewell, My Lovely!", was really not better than its successor. "Here Is New York" shows the city in 1948 as safer and kinder than it is now. White considers this essay a period piece, written about New York emerging from the depression. He loved it, though its face even then was pockmarked.

He is at his best when nostalgia merges with current observation and when the drift toward sentimentality turns to genuine emotion:

> Here in New England, each season carries a hundred foreshadowings of the season that is to follow—which is one of the things I love about it. Winter is rough and long, but spring lies all round about. Yesterday, a small white keel feather escaped from my goose and lodged in the bank boughs near the kitchen porch, where I spied it as I came home in the cold twilight. The minute I saw the feather, I was projected into May, knowing that a barn swallow would be along to claim the prize and use it to decorate the front edge of its nest. Immediately, the December air seemed full of wings of swallows and the warmth of barns. Swallows, I have noticed, never use any feather but a white one in their nestbuilding, and they always leave a lot of it showing, which makes me believe that they are interested not in the feather's insulating power but in its reflecting power, so that when they skim into the dark barn from the bright outdoors they will have a beacon to steer by.

In contrast to all this, John McPhee is journalist rather than essayist, not the only journalist though one of the best. McPhee rejoiceth not in uniquity but rejoiceth in the truth. Perhaps his vision of truth is what makes him appear unique.

William L. Howarth's brilliant introduction focuses on McPhee's awesomely organized methods of work: weeks, months of interviews, neutral listening (utterly unlike the television interviewer's pushiness: "And how did you *feel* when you saw your baby burned to death?"), acres of notes, shuffling and reshuffling of index cards, decisions on structure; the writing comes last of all.

McPhee's range is so extensive that it is astonishing how one man can encompass it. Surely no one could be an expert in tennis and basketball, nuclear physics, irrigation and river control, urban blight, the wilderness, and artistic treasures and forgeries—a partial summary of *The McPhee Reader*. Presumably his interest in each field is what originally dictates his choice of subject. Once made, the choice demands total research and total recall, since so much material comes from conversations and scenes that could not be fully noted on the spot. (He does not use a tape-recorder, for fear of inhibiting his speakers.) Like a top-flight novelist McPhee has the knack of creating at least the illusion of mastery, through his skill in setting down characteristic speech and his excellence in narrative.

Ernest Hemingway says that the extent and accuracy of a writer's knowledge of some activity will altogether determine the quality of his writing about it. The slightest ignorance will betray itself or will make the reader uneasy. (Hemingway implies, of course, that his own profound competence in all human arts, from sex to war to hunting and bullfighting, produces the splendor of his style.) McPhee writes as if he subscribes to this principle. He seems to sound the depths of whatever he studies, yet his approach is almost always through a person rather than directly toward a subject. His exposition depends on the methods of fiction, and his best pages remind us forcibly of the best stories of Kipling, or the marvelous technical descriptions in Richard Hughes's *In Hazard*—the same clarity and offhand savoir faire. McPhee makes every reader wish to be an expert in each field of discourse. He is both a stimulator of intellectual curiosity and a showman who plays on the gee-whiz emotion.

McPhee likes to work on a frame. Sometimes it is a little gimmicky, as in "The Search for Marvin Gardens," where he laminates bits of description of the decay of Atlantic City with bits of the game *Monopoly*, which happens to use the street-names and geography of that city. Sometimes it is a structure that he himself arranged: the furious dialogue between conservationist David Brower and dam-builder Floyd Dominy grew out of a trip down the Colorado that McPhee maneuvered them into; or the tennis match between Arthur Ashe and Clark Graebner, a videotape of which McPhee used to draw from each player just how he had felt and thought at each point. In "The Pine Barrens" and "A Roomful of Hovings" he is more direct, though he plunges in medias res and flashes back and forward freely in time and place. (In *Coming into the Country*, a study of Alaska not included in *The McPhee Reader*, he uses the proposed relocation of the state capital as the thread to string exploration and interviews on.)

"The Curve of Binding Energy" and "The Deltoid Pumpkin Seed" are more ambitious, studying respectively: effects of atomic bombs and the chances of their extracurricular manufacture, and an extraordinary series of experiments with the idea of an airship (not an airplane—an airship). Both demonstrate McPhee's peculiar strength and also a weakness in the *Reader*. Wishing to show as many sides of McPhee as possible in a compendious book, Howarth has necessarily limited the length of each selection. Consequently a reader unfamiliar with the whole work thus abridged may easily be confused. The fault is partly McPhee's: it is nearly impossible to figure out (even in the original length) what happened and what would happen to the Deltoid Pumpkin Seed—though I doubt if many readers stop reading, so compelling is the narrative drive. But this book does have the inevitable defect of an anthology of fragments: it cannot but distort.

Many of McPhee's pieces resemble the biographical sketches in Dos Passos's *U.S.A.*—in overwhelming richness of detail, in speed, in absorption with the person. But Dos Passos is more outside his character, usually satirical, always detached. And though McPhee is well aware of his characters' flaws, he so sinks himself into another man that his own vigorous personality vanishes; it comes as a shock when *I* appears *in propria persona*, complete with glinting wit.

His ability to merge with a character can lead him astray. In his study of Frank Boyden, "Headmaster," McPhee's admiration climbs through the words, and a kind of preachiness takes over; he forgets to *show* us and *tells* us instead. We are less than convinced. Somewhat similar is "A Roomful of Hovings." Hoving is no doubt a genius;

but some of his mental feats here recorded stretch credulity; and not everything he and his family have done is admirable. The elder Hoving, enormously wealthy, refused to pay his son's graduate-school tuition; so Hoving won a scholarship—which someone else would have really needed.

McPhee's "nature is subdued to what it works in, like the dyer's hand." If this is sometimes a defect, it can also account for the superb coloring of everything he does. The material is the style—seemingly only functional yet possessed of sharp individuality. If you chance to open the *New Yorker* in the midst of a McPhee profile, you spot it at once: the direct, subject-verb, connectiveless sentences; the infallible vocabulary; the richness and speed. Like the Colorado River through the canyon in his unsurpassed description, he sweeps you along.

McPhee and White are not really alike except in one way: in the preface to *Lyrical Ballads* Wordsworth said he sought "a certain colouring of imagination, whereby ordinary things should be presented to the mind in an unusual aspect"; and he wished "to make these incidents and situations interesting by tracing in them, truly though not ostentatiously, the primary laws of our nature." The poet's prosy formulation states what these two distinguished prose writers have consistently achieved.

J. P. Riquelme

SOURCE: "The Modernist Essay: The Case of T. S. Eliot—Poet as Critic," in *The Southern Review,* Louisiana State University, Vol. 21, No. 4, Autumn, 1985, pp. 1024-32.

[*An American educator and critic, Riquelme is the author of book-length studies of James Joyce and T. S. Eliot. In the following essay, Riquelme analyzes Eliot's "Tradition and the Individual Talent" as an "exemplary Modernist essay."*]

> The triumph is the triumph of style. . . . Vague as all definitions are, a good essay must have this permanent quality about it; it must draw its curtain round us, but it must be a curtain that shuts us in, not out.
>
> —Virginia Woolf, "The Modern Essay"
>
> Criticism is no more to be judged by any low standard of imitation or resemblance than is the work of poet or sculptor.
>
> —Oscar Wilde, "The Critic as Artist"

The modernist essay emerges as part of the reaction against Matthew Arnold that is characteristic of Modernism. Arnold expresses his sense of the secondary function of criticism in his famous 1864 lecture at Oxford on "The Function of Criticism at the Present Time." There he asserts that the "aim of criticism" is not the passing of judgment, though it is judgment's precursor, but the achieving of accurate perception through procedures exercised by a "disinterested curiosity." The critic strives "to see the object as in itself it really is." The most forceful early counter to Arnold's attitude toward criticism as less independent

and less worthy than creation comes from Oscar Wilde in his volume *Intentions* (1891), especially in the essay in dialogue form, "The Critic as Artist," originally published as "The True Function and Value of Criticism: with Some Remarks on the Importance of Doing Nothing." For Wilde, criticism's aim is to see the object as it is not, and this aim is never disinterested and never just a procedure. And it need not be pursued through the style of high seriousness that Arnold adopted. By both assertion and example, Wilde makes claims for criticism that are at least as wide-ranging and, in the results, at least as successful as any we encounter nowadays. With the combined force of Ruskin and Pater as precursors to aid him, Wilde is able to create a crucial, liberating turning point in late nineteenth-century English letters. Wilde heralds the essay's importance as a literary form that would become the sibling of Modernist poetry and fiction in the first half of the twentieth century, but one that academic literary criticism continues largely to neglect. Despite this relative neglect, a surprising number of essays written by Wilde's Modernist descendants—Yeats, D. H. Lawrence, Eliot, Pound, Virginia Woolf, Jorge Luis Borges and Samuel Beckett, among others—have achieved the status so many contemporary critics desire for their works in prose: the status of being recognized as literature.

The Modernist essay is not easy of definition, and that is one of its characteristics, for it is not produced by an academic writer interested in adhering to the conventions of argumentation and decorum practiced by a community of established literary critics. The refusal of adherence takes on a variety of stylistic manifestations, markedly different from those of conventionally expository and interpretative literary critical essays. Because of its multiplicity and difference, the Modernist essay cannot be conveniently fitted either into the category of literary criticism or into literary criticism's categories. In part out of lack of another term, we call it an *essay* because it is a relatively short work in prose, but neither a short story nor a scientific or quasi-scientific report. Generally, it is a commentary dealing with art or literature whose function is not primarily expository and whose mode of procedure is not necessarily strictly logical. Its function is to help make possible the creation of a new kind of artwork, of which it may itself be an example and not just a precursor. Our response upon encountering an example of the form may resemble Samuel Beckett's in "Three Dialogues," where he says, "I don't know what it is, having never seen anything like it before." On this unashamedly flexible and general account, even a portion of another text, such as the "Scylla and Charybdis" episode of *Ulysses,* if taken in isolation from its fictional context, could be considered a Modernist essay. In this case, the episode is, in fact, one of the precursors of Beckett's "Three Dialogues," which is both essay and literary text masquerading as an interview. The clear distinctions between genres have largely disappeared.

I take as an exemplary Modernist essay, but by no means as a paradigm—this particular literary form always refusing to conform to any prescriptive pattern—, T. S. Eliot's "Tradition and the Individual Talent." Several reasons stand behind the choice. Eliot has consistently been the most badly treated of the major Modernist writers by the contemporary neo-Romantic reaction against Modernism that, in one of its forms, wishes to see the emergence of a creative criticism. Such a creative criticism has already been achieved in this and other Modernist essays. In addition, this specific essay is quite possibly the most widely anthologized literary essay of the twentieth century. It was so widely anthologized by 1964 that Eliot complained of its omnipresence in the preface to the reissuing of *The Use of Poetry and The Use of Criticism,* a volume that he hoped might provide anthologists with other material. The essay has now become so familiar to us that we take it largely for granted. It has been put to rest—buried as a dead part of the tradition—by our excessive contact with it. To read the essay as if it were readily intelligible, that is, under our control, is a serious failure of literary understanding, for such a reading is unable to recognize the continuing and permanent nature of the essay's radical qualities. It is not merely revolutionary in a specific historical situation that has now passed; it is perpetually revolutionary because of certain curious and compelling features of style.

Eliot's achievement as an essayist has been considerably misunderstood by those who claim that his reformulations of the English poetic tradition failed to turn back through logical argument the assertion that the poems of Dryden and Pope were, in Arnold's catchy phrase, "classics of our prose." Eliot was, in fact, not involved in redefining the canon only by means of conventional literary critical argumentation. In addition, through his *writing practice,* he changed our understanding of the possibilities for expression in prose. He answered Arnold in effect by taking the writing of prose seriously. For Eliot, who sees the real possibility of something new coming into being, something that transforms the way we think in the present, thereby transforming the past, the *critical* project is indistinguishable from the *poetic* one. That something new need not be limited to poetry; it may well occur through and as prose.

In his writing practice Eliot implicitly rejects the simplistic association of literary forms with separable functions of mind. Prose need not be seen as a mimetic manifestation of critical, rational thinking, for it can involve a mixture in which creative and critical have indissolubly merged. Such prose may at times be both necessary to the creating of poetry and in many ways identical to it as to function and certain aspects of style. One function of prose so conceived is to act as both evidence and occasion for the bringing of new work into existence, perhaps quite different work implicated in the writing of the prose, but even the prose work itself as that something new. The style of such new work, whether in verse or in prose or possibly in both, strives to reach a maximal intensity, expressing and evoking a meaning and experience that could not be otherwise expressed and evoked. Section two of part five of *A Portrait of the Artist as a Young Man,* in which Stephen Dedalus writes his villanelle, would be an example of a work that uses both verse and prose in order to represent the verse's creation. That representation embedded in prose is itself an example of the truly new text, though in this case it is a work of fiction. If the prose is really new, then the technical means employed to reach the necessary intensity will vary from other works. "Tradition and the Individual Talent" involves the creating of something new

in both ways: as one of the precursors of *The Waste Land* and simultaneously as that poem's prose counterpart, going beyond the conventional literary essay to reach the status of literature. The essay reaches that status because, despite its ostensible familiarity, the more closely we look at its argument, organization, and even sentence structure, the stranger it becomes.

We can see this strangeness especially clearly at the end of the essay, in the oft-quoted concluding sentence of part III:

> And he [the poet] is not likely to know what is to be done unless he lives in what is not merely the present, but the present moment of the past, unless he is conscious, not of what is dead, but of what is already living.

At the beginning of this final section, only a single paragraph in length, Eliot claims that the essay "proposes to halt at the frontier of metaphysics or mysticism, and confine itself to . . . practical conclusions." But it does not halt at the frontier of what might be expected in the style and structure of a literary essay in the Arnoldean tradition. It crosses that frontier most prominently in the final sentence. We might recall at this point the distinction Eliot makes briefly in the concluding pages of *The Use of Poetry and the Use of Criticism* (1933) between poems that have " 'meaning' " in order "to satisfy one habit of the reader, to keep his mind diverted and quiet, while the poem does its work upon him" and those other poems, presumably Modernist ones, that pursue different possibilities entirely through the attenuating of meaning in the ordinary sense. The conclusion of "Tradition" also pursues those different possibilities. This is not to say that the sentence is nonsense, but it goes beyond the making of ordinary sense because of its resonance and complexity, generated by repetition and contrast within the sentence and within the essay at large. The repetition and contrast within the sentence are clear enough. They are part of the reason we do not grasp any simple, determinate significance when we read or hear the whole sentence and attempt a semantic interpretation: it is too complicated to be taken in all at once. But the sentence also does not yield an easily restatable meaning when we break it into parts for analysis, for it is organized antithetically, by contrasts that work through both multiple repetition and multiple antitheses. If we follow the to-and-fro, fro-and-to shifting, our engagement is decidedly temporal, in a way that does not result in a meaning that can be grasped instantaneously in overview.

Both grammatically and logically, the sentence is a multiple antithetical construction. The basic construction clearly announces an apparently controlling contrast through the use of "not" in counterpoint to "unless" and "but." Eliot uses constructions involving such contrasts regularly in the other essays collected in *The Sacred Wood,* for example, in the short pieces grouped under the rubric "Imperfect Critics." None of these other sentences, however, achieves a comparable complexity of structure and implication, for in "Tradition," the negation by contrast is repeated and then repeated again. Each repetition, which is also a contrast, modifies our sense of all the others. The contrast between "not likely to know" and the first dependent clause beginning with "unless" seems clear enough and easily graspable, until we reach the relative clause, "what is not," used as a substantive within the dependent clause, for the second "not" repeats the first one literally at the same time as it stands in contrast to it in context. The complications increase when we discover that the second "not" is linked to the "but" that follows shortly. Now, not just "not," but "not . . . but" repeats the whole "not . . . unless" construction while it also forms a part of it. And the antithesis with reversal is repeated again in the second, parallel subordinate clause, with its "unless . . . not . . . , but." When we compare the parallel dependent clauses, the contrasts that are also virtually repetitions proliferate. "What is not . . . but" is matched, but not repeated in form or meaning by "not of what is . . . , but of what is. . . ." "Merely the present" and "the past" occupy the same respective positions in the first as "what is dead" and "living" do in the second. The repetitions create alignments of meaning where semantically a contrast would otherwise stand. The connotations and the repetitions in structure, together with variations and reversals, combine to make each contrast and each repetition modify the possible meanings of their counterparts and antitheses in other parts of the sentence. In the other essays of *The Sacred Wood,* the constructions employing "not" and "but" generally function as part of Eliot's effort to achieve the sort of balanced judgments through point-counterpoint that he praises in his commendation of Samuel Johnson as a model for critics in the "Introduction." The wildly complicated construction at the end of "Tradition" has little to do with balance, unless we understand that concept anew, dynamically, as an uneasy equilibrium produced by antitheses in interaction.

Such an analysis can help clarify the sentence's potentially dizzying effect on the reader, but it does not provide a clue to its meaning that can be applied semantically to produce a convincing, explanatory translation. The analysis suggests instead that the sentence's meanings are in flux, though not necessarily haphazardly so. It complicates rather than simplifies our sense of the reading process, which we now realize involves an encounter with multiple antitheses in a series of repetitions. Tropologically, we can describe the construction as a rhetorical process of transformation structured as a chiasmus within a chiasmus. We have a repetition and reversal, as in chiasmus, with the complication that the repetition and reversal have also been repeated in such a way as to include reversals. To use a German word, which Eliot himself employs in his essay on Massinger to describe some lines by Tourneur and Middleton, we find "meanings perpetually *eingeschachtelt* into meanings." The word evokes something like the fitting of Chinese boxes inside one another. Or we might think of anastomoses, the way veins in plants and animals merge with other veins through a system of tiny, articulating connections. This is a special kind of sentence in Eliot's prose, though by no means unique, whose resonance and appeal arise in part from syntactical and semantic complexities crafted into a rhythmic sequence of contrasts within contrasts. Such complexities can set us into a kind of mental activity in response that is not often engendered by a literary essay. But the sentence from "Tradition" exerts a special *concluding* force, because it has the rest of the essay as prelude and context. The essay has already given us, through the two analogies of parts I and II, a double antithetical structure, like the structure of meaning we are able to realize through our enactment and enact through our realization of the ending's syntactical and rhetorical play. In addition, through the shifts in style and focus from part to part, a stylistic pressure and thematic dissonance have built up that are brought to fulfillment by the reversals within reversals of the final sentence.

The large structure of the entire essay is reflected in the ending. The congruence amidst and by means of heterogeneous complications between whole and part gives the essay a great deal of its special force. It does so because the whole-to-part relationship of synecdoche is combined inextricably with the disjunctive, dialectical interplay of irony. Part reflects whole but only by reflecting the whole as an uneasy interaction of parts. This conjoining of synecdoche with irony amounts to a Modernist critique and revision of Organicist attitudes. As in the sentence, the parts of the essay may be said to overlap, that is, to interact, and to be in parallel at the same time as they differ significantly. The overlap is indicated in a straightforward way at the end of the first two parts, when the focus is shifted toward what will be developed in the part to come. The essay is structured like a complex sentence in which two segments, parts I and II, are set in parallel at the same time as they stand in antithetical relationship to one another. This structure of simultaneous contrast and parallelism is most obvious in Eliot's use of analogies in place of more conventional argumentation to make his case, which, bluntly stated, is a case against Romanticism as a tradition that had become a moribund cliché still refusing to die. Eliot carefully chooses his analogies to propose antithetical alternatives to conventional Romantic ones; that is, the alternatives are at once antithetical to the conventions and to one another. How fair Eliot is to Romanticism is not at issue here, for the essay is not working in service to balanced judgment but in service to an impulse to write that must express itself in new ways.

Eliot's strategy is to attack Organicist visions of both literary history and literary creation, which he sees as the debased, unusable tradition of Romantic thinking. In part I, he rejects the notion that literary history, and by implication history in any form, is teleologically oriented, developing with a clear direction like an organism either growing or evolving toward a higher state that carries with it in some direct way the stages that have preceded. In place of growth and evolution, he describes a model that also has an organic aspect but not the same one. This aspect is something like homeostasis. Literary history is not to be thought of as growing and improving gradually in a foreseeable direction but as simply changing in response to new stimuli on the way to achieving again temporary homeostasis. This conception of history as involving mutation, or disruption, and eventual homeostasis rather than continuous growth stands in contrast to both the ideology of Imperialism—that is, of Social-Darwinism—and the tenets of Marxism, with their common heritage of teleological views of history. The other aspect of Organicism that Eliot rejects is the notion of the poet's mind as sensitive plant. Here his choice of analogy from *inorganic* chemistry, the catalyst that remains unchanged in the chemical reaction though it enables it, is antithetical to the conventional Romantic conception of the poet's role.

With the introduction of the second analogy, the complications, like those of the sentence's construction, arise, for this analogy is built around an inorganic process, while the first one is still basically organic, though not teleologically so. Both analogies challenge by implication the debased Romantic conventions, but they also reflect through the antithesis of organic with inorganic a sensitivity to an abiding dissonance. As Eliot understood, such dissonance accompanies any serious attempt to conceptualize about history and mind together rather than about one or the other separately. The recognition that this and related dissonances are incapable of being assimilated smoothly into any conceptual system relying primarily on one kind of rhetorical figure, as Organicism relies on synecdoche, forms another, perhaps the boldest, aspect of the position Eliot takes against Romanticism and its heritage. The essential role of contradiction in the critique of Romanticism, understood as aligned with Organicist attitudes toward history and mind, helps explain and justify the complexity of the essay's final sentence.

The intensity that the style of "Tradition" reaches in its ending belies the clear distinction many critics have tried to make between Eliot's work as poet and his work as critic. In his well-known essay, "Poetry and Drama" (1951), Eliot formulates in one way the stylistic ideal he strives for, here with specific reference to his attempt to write verse drama:

> . . . if our verse is to have so wide a range that it can say anything that has to be said, it follows that it will not be "poetry" all the time. It will only be "poetry" when the dramatic situation has reached such a point of intensity that poetry becomes the natural utterance, because then it is the only language in which the emotions can be expressed at all.

Achieving this ideal of a flexible style is also one goal of Eliot's work three decades earlier in both verse and prose. We can reformulate Eliot's statement for this earlier, and in certain regards more general, context pertaining to the relationship of prose to verse: If our prose is to have so wide a range that it can say anything that has to be said, it follows that it will at times come close to being "poetry." It will only do so when the critical situation has become critical in another sense; when the issues and the argument reach a point of such intensity that prose of the usual sort is left behind, because then the new style is the only one in which the necessary complexity can be expressed at all. The fact that Eliot continued working in both poetry and prose throughout his career points to his abiding interest in developing a range of styles. Within that range, the wide latitude in style and the resulting possibility of new juxtapositions and combinations of styles make possible the simultaneous representation and evocation of aporia. This evocation is one of the goals of the flexible style. As in the ending of "Tradition," the style communicates the grounds for its own intensity by reflecting in its movement the contradictory structure of the dissonance as source.

Because of that movement, the essay remains permanently outside what we can call, following Beckett, "the domain of the feasible."

The Modernist essay, for which I have taken "Tradition and the Individual Talent" as primary example, is a literary form that cannot justifiably be evaluated by a mimetic standard. This is true in at least two senses. It is not merely a reflection of either some ostensible object of study or of a faculty of mind that we might just as well call reason rather than the critical faculty. It moves beyond the function of critical exposition and outside the control of the conventionally assumed Arnoldean constraints of both the object and reason. Its power inheres largely in its style, which it draws round us, shutting us in, not out, by giving us an experience of meaning that goes beyond semantics. We can say of Eliot, as of other writers of Modernist essays, what Eliot said of F. H. Bradley: "Certainly one of the reasons for the power he still exerts, as well as an indubitable claim to permanence, is his great gift of style." Eliot's most original contribution as a critic is his prose style, through which he responds effectively to the Arnoldean distinction in value between poetry and prose. In reading "Tradition and the Individual Talent," we can experience the aporia of the title when the essay's structure and style evoke in us the interplay of reciprocal relations in a continuous process of exchange. This process in itself is not wholly describable by means of the formulations of reason yoked to the thematic semantics of critical exposition. We can come close to an adequate description in one way by comparing its images and structure to those of some Modernist poems. We encounter, to our surprise and against our expectation, because the form is prose but not fictional, a phenomenon closer to Yeats's "Byzantium" and "Those images that yet / Fresh images beget" than to anything Matthew Arnold was able to write in either prose or verse. The triumph is the triumph of style.

Charles O'Neill

SOURCE: "The Essay as Aesthetic Ritual: W. B. Yeats and *Ideas of Good and Evil*," in *Essays on the Essay: Redefining the Genre,* edited by Alexander J. Butrym, The University of Georgia Press, 1989, pp. 126-36.

[*O'Neill is an American-born educator and critic. In the following essay, he discusses William Butler Yeats's essays collected in* Ideas of Good and Evil *as reflective of aesthetic and philosophical principles that were current in the late nineteenth and early twentieth centuries.*]

Virginia Woolf claims that the essay "should lay us under a spell with its first word, and we should only wake, refreshed, with its last." These words apply literally to the essays of William Butler Yeats. Most often consulted as explanatory material for the poetry and plays, Yeats's many essays exist in their own right as unique examples of the modern essayist's art. I will consider Yeats's early essays with a view to accounting for the "spell" they cast no matter how often they are read.

At the end of his career, Yeats wrote, "As I altered my syntax I altered my intellect." This statement applies as much to his prose as to his poetry. Yeats wrote essays throughout his life for many purposes: to create audiences for his diverse interests, to explain his esoteric beliefs, and to reflect on his art and on his life. The *Autobiographies* volume is actually a series of more or less self-contained essays composed over many years and in differing styles. From the luxuriant rhythms of his earliest prose to the astringency of his last, Yeats's essays reflect not only the evolution of a commanding literary sensibility but also the evolution of the modern essay itself.

Ideas of Good and Evil collects the best and most suggestive of the essays Yeats wrote between 1895 and 1903, from his thirtieth to his thirty-seventh year. In this period the poet was committed both to creating an audience for Irish literature and to the symbolist aesthetic in art and thought. These early essays differ from other modern essays and from Yeats's own later work. Whether appraisals of other writers, reflections on the nature of art, or investigations into occult ideas, the essays in *Ideas of Good and Evil* employ symbolist thought and technique to suggest a version of "reality" in which the imagination—and not science—is the central good.

In his essay "Magic," Yeats asks rhetorically, "Have not poetry and music arisen, as it seems, out of the sounds the enchanters made to help their imagination to enchant, to charm, to bind with a spell themselves and the passersby?" For Yeats, the purpose of this spell or enchantment was nothing less than the transformation of the modern world. In the new age that symbolist art is heralding, the imagination will reassert its ancient authority over empirical reality. "I cannot get it out of my head," Yeats writes in 1895, "that this age of criticism is about to pass, and an age of imagination, of emotion, of moods, of revelation, about to come in its place." Symbolist in manner and matter, the essays collected in *Ideas of Good and Evil* attempt to indicate, as much as Yeats's poems of the 1890s, the art of that "new age."

Kenneth Burke, in *Counter-Statement*, writes that "if the artist's 'revelations' are of tremendous importance to him, he will necessarily seek to ritualize them, to find a correspondingly important setting for them." In the nineteen essays of *Ideas of Good and Evil*, Yeats attempts to "ritualize," through complex patterns of syntax and symbol, the "revelation" of the new age he anticipated. According to Burke, "Revelation is 'belief,' or 'fact.' Art enters when this revelation is ritualized, when it is converted into a symbolic process." The early essays of Yeats are works of art: while announcing the "revelation" of a new age, they also, by means of evocative symbol and complexly cadenced prose, deliver that "revelation" in "ritual." The best of these essays go beyond the traditional rhetorical ends of the form to enter the nonparaphrasable realm of poetry. From the great mass of his early essays, book reviews, and journalism, Yeats selected only those works which, in manner as well as matter, announce a new age.

Yeats, with his avowed hostility to objective truth, logic, "the restraints of reason," and a corresponding faith in subjectivity, intuition, and revelation, works without many of the traditional tools of the essayist in designing his "aesthetic rituals." In an essay entitled "The Moods," Yeats explains: "Literature differs from explanatory and scientific writing in being wrought about a mood, or a community of moods, as the body is wrought about an invisible soul; and if it uses argument, theory, erudition, observation, and seems to grow hot in assertion or denial, it does so merely to make us partakers at the banquet of the moods." This brief essay, only a paragraph in length, replaces argument by a patterned repetition of words and phrases in the manner of a poem. It is, in effect, a "spell" that Yeats seeks to cast over his readers. The nineteen essays together constitute "a community of moods" that persuade by suggestion and evocation. Yeats writes, "Everything that can be seen, touched, measured, explained, understood, argued over, is to the imaginative artist nothing more than a means, for he belongs to the invisible life, and delivers its ever new and ever ancient revelations." Thus as an imaginative artist Yeats comes to the essay, employing symbolist thought and technique to deliver this "revelation."

The beliefs that organize and motivate *Ideas of Good and Evil* are presented most succinctly in the essay "Magic." Yeats declares, "I believe in the practice and philosophy of what we have agreed to call magic," and he then lists three articles of faith or "doctrines": "(1) That the borders of our mind are ever shifting, and that many minds can flow into one another, as it were, and create or reveal a single mind, a single energy. (2) That the borders of our memories are as shifting, and that our memories are a part of one great memory, the memory of Nature itself. (3) That this great mind and great memory can be evoked by symbols." The essay "Magic" treats, in detail, the poet's own efforts to evoke "spirits" by means of magical symbols. "I cannot now think symbols less than the greatest of all powers," Yeats writes, "whether they are used consciously by the masters of magic, or half consciously by their successors, the poet, the musician and the artist." All artists, in other words, work in the same essential manner and to the same end: casting spells to evoke the "great memory," they thereby enchant their audiences. Yeats claims, "If I can unintentionally cast a glamour, an enchantment, over persons of our own time who have lived for years in great cities, there is no reason to doubt that men could cast intentionally a far stronger enchantment, a far stronger glamour, over the more sensitive people of ancient times, or that men can still do so where the old order of life remains unbroken." With *Ideas of Good and Evil*, Yeats will announce the imminent return of the "old order of life."

Yeats took the book's title from William Blake. According to Yeats, Blake "announced the religion of art," the one "true" religion of the modern world. "In our time," Yeats writes, "we are agreed that we 'make our souls' out of some one of the great poets of ancient times" or out of such modern poets as Blake, Shelley, or Wordsworth. The role of the artist in this "soul-making" is that of a priest: "We who care deeply about the arts find ourselves the priesthood of an almost forgotten faith, and we must, I think, if we would win the people again, take upon ourselves the method and the fervour of a priesthood."

In such a religion of art, the "ideas of evil" would include rhetoric, allegory, the will, reason, Nature, and time; those of "good" would include revelation, symbol, imagination, art, and Eternity. The central "good" is, of course, the imagination. The goal of such a faith would be "to come at least to forget good and evil" in what Yeats calls "an absorbing vision of the happy and unhappy." The imagination, in these terms, is beyond good and evil.

If William Blake is behind much of the matter of this volume, Walter Pater inspired its manner. In his 1918 poem "The Phases of the Moon," Yeats recalls "that extravagant style / He had learned from Pater." He employed that style in his fiction and essays of the 1890s. In *The Renaissance,* Pater, following Buffon, noted that " 'the style is the man'—and it is his plenary sense of what he really has to say, his sense of the world." Hating what he called "that straight-forward logic, as of newspaper articles," Yeats, when he deployed his own prose style most deliberately, dispensed with argumentation, "manifest logic," and "clear rhetoric" in favor of evocation, poetic citation, and suggestive rhythm. Yeats can be seen as having turned his back on the three most popular modes of the nineteenth-century essay: the familiar essay (Hazlitt), the critical essay (Arnold), and the scientific essay (Huxley). In this, he followed Pater, who, in his essay on "Style," insisted that a writer is "vindicating his liberty in the making of a vocabulary, an entire system of composition, for himself, his own true manner."

Pater's sinuous, allusive prose style was perfectly suited to Yeats's symbolist aesthetic. Late in his career, Yeats printed a passage from Pater's description of the Mona Lisa as free verse, contending that it was a poem, one which had arisen "out of its own rhythm." For Yeats, poems often did arise, not from ideas, but from rhythms, and the acoustic singularity of a cadence or phrase frequently led him to an insight not consciously intended. In like manner, Yeats felt that Pater's subtly cadenced prose rhythms were able to transform a rhetorical description into a poetic incantation. It was the "extravagant style" he needed for his own early prose.

Yeats's debt to Pater goes well beyond the influence of the latter's prose rhythm. In essays written throughout his long career, Yeats practices what Pater, in the preface to *The Renaissance,* calls "aesthetic criticism." Pater required the "aesthetic critic" to ask: "What is this song or picture, this engaging personality presented in life or in a book, to me? What effect does it really produce on me?" The essays on art and artists collected in *Ideas of Good and Evil* examine their subjects for the sake of what they mean to Yeats and, specifically, to his sense of an imminent "revelation." Yeats's essays are examples of what Pater calls "the literature of the imaginative sense of fact." The artist, for Pater, transcribes "not . . . mere fact, but his . . . sense of it" and concludes, "All beauty is in the long run only *fineness* of truth, or what we call expression, the finer accommodation to that vision within." Yeats's "vision" in his early poems, stories, and essays was of a world about to undergo a complete change of mind, or "mood," and he accommodated his "speech" on the art and ideas of others to that personal "vision within." Throughout *Ideas of Good and Evil,* literary criticism, historical speculation, poetry, philosophy, the occult, and

personal experience are woven together to illustrate what Yeats calls "the continuous indefinable symbolism which is the substance of all style."

In an essay entitled "The Symbolism of Poetry," Yeats describes the change of style the "new age" will bring:

> With this change of substance, this return to imagination, this understanding that the laws of art, which are the hidden laws of the world, can alone bind the imagination, would come a change of style, and we would cast out of serious poetry those energetic rhythms, as of a man running, which are the invention of the will with its eyes always on something to be done or undone; and we would seek out those wavering, meditative, organic rhythms, which are the embodiment of the imagination, that neither desires nor hates, because it has done with time, and only wishes to gaze upon some reality, some beauty; nor would it be any longer possible for anybody to deny the importance of form, in all its kinds, for although you can expound an opinion, or describe a thing, when your words are not quite well chosen, you cannot give a body to something that moves beyond the sense, unless your words are as subtle, as complex, as full of mysterious life, as the body of a flower or of a woman.

This singular sentence makes up what I would call an "aesthetic ritual"; the "revelation" of a "change of style" is delivered in the "ritual" of the sentence's incantatory cadences. Instead of argument or description, Yeats, following symbolist procedure, suggests this coming "change" with the "wavering, meditative, organic rhythms" of the sentence itself. From individual sentence to entire volume, *Ideas of Good and Evil* is as deliberately composed as the "sacred books of the arts" it anticipates: form and content are inextricably fused.

In an essay entitled "Symbolism in Painting," Yeats declares, "All art that is not mere story-telling, or mere portraiture, is symbolic, and has the purpose of those symbolic talismans which medieval magicians made with complex colours and forms, and bade their patients ponder over daily, and guard with holy secrecy; for it entangles, in complex colours and forms, a part of the Divine Essence." As much as any symbolist poem, the essays in *Ideas of Good and Evil* are designed to "entangle," on the formal levels of sentence, essay, and collection, the "patient" reader as well as whatever "part of the Divine Essence" the poet can capture. For Yeats constructs both sentence and essay as "symbolic talismans" that require pondering before they yield a meaning.

Yeats's famous essay "On the Philosophy of Shelley's Poetry" can bring his essayistic strategies into focus. Written in a style of Paterian extravagance, it is a striking example of symbolist procedure applied to the essay form. Dispensing with logic, reason, and argumentation, and relying on evocation, suggestion, and incantation, the essay is a symbolic talisman that proposes the image of Shelley as a symbolist poet. All of the volume's themes are woven into this prose reverie: symbolism, magic, Irish folklore, and the "revelation" that Yeats hoped for. Yeats's "Shelley" is as much a creation of a Paterian "vision within" as Pater's own "Mona Lisa."

Like a familiar essay, it opens with a personal reminiscence: "When I was a boy in Dublin," Yeats writes, "I was one of a group who rented a room in a mean street to discuss philosophy." Yeats then announces his "one unshakable belief": "I thought that whatever of philosophy has been made poetry is alone permanent." After years of observing "dreams and visions," he is now "certain" that "the imagination has some way of lighting on the truth that the reason has not, and that its commandments, delivered when the body is still and the reason silent, are the most binding we can ever know." This sequence of beliefs, which we recognize from other essays in the volume, serves as a prelude to the discussion of Shelley. Yeats's "imagination," then, sets the conditions in which Shelley will be seen. We can expect that when *Prometheus Unbound* is introduced, it will be seen as a Yeatsian "sacred Book." He writes of it: "I remember going to a learned scholar to ask about its deep meanings, which I felt more than understood, and his telling me that it was Godwin's *Political Justice* put into rhyme, and that Shelley was a crude revolutionist, and believed that the overturning of kings and priests would regenerate mankind." Yeats, who felt that a new "revelation" would soon regenerate mankind and that Shelley was one of its prophets, uses these lines to dismiss academic criticism: it is the "scholar," and not Shelley, who is revealed to be crude; Yeats's "feeling" for the book is the "standard" of judgment.

Yeats then assimilates Shelley to his symbolist pantheon. By a careful selection of quotations from *A Defense of Poetry,* Yeats insists that Shelley exalts the imaginative faculty and denigrates reason, "the calculating faculty." "The speaker of these things," Yeats writes, "might almost be Blake, who held that the Reason not only created Ugliness, but all other evils." Yeats is, clearly, creating in Shelley a precursor in order to provide further proof that "all art that is not mere story-telling . . . is symbolic."

After "proving" that Shelley was an early symbolist, Yeats concludes the first section of the essay by assimilating Shelley's work to his own world of Irish folk belief:

> I have re-read his *Prometheus Unbound* for the first time for many years, in the woods of Drimna-Rod, among the Echtage hills, and sometimes I have looked towards Slieve ná nOg where the country people say the last battle of the world shall be fought till the third day, when a priest shall lift a chalice, and the thousand years of peace begin. And I think this mysterious song utters a faith as simple and as ancient as the faith of those country people, in a form suited to a new age, that will understand with Blake that the Holy Spirit is 'an intellectual fountain,' and that the kinds and degrees of beauty are the images of its authority.

Shelley, Blake, Yeats himself, and the unlettered Irish "country people" are all united in receiving influences from what he calls here, with a nod to orthodoxy, "the Holy Spirit" but in the next paragraph the "great Memory."

The longest sentence of the entire volume begins, "Alastor passed in his boat along a river in a cave." It continues, paratactically, for thirty-four lines and draws on at least seven separate poems by Shelley in order to exhibit his recurring symbols. In the essay "Some Post-Symbolist Structures," Hugh Kenner notes that Yeats adopted Mallarmé's "syntactic legerdemain" in some poems of the 1890s. Kenner proves that Yeats's poem "He Remembers Forgotten Beauty" "proceeds by systematic digression from its formal structure." And Kenner claims, "The effect is to move our attention as far as may be from the thrust of subject-verb-object. The structure is formal, elaborate, symmetrical, and syntactically faultless; and yet only by a very great effort of attention is the reader like to discover it is." Yeats's prose, likewise, "proceeds by systematic digression"; in doing so, it creates true talismanic labyrinths, sentences to wander lost in, hypnotized by rhythm and word choice. We are finally convinced of the "truth" of the sentence, not by its logic or cogency, but by the elaborate formal "ritual" we have undergone to reach its end.

The conclusion of "On the Philosophy of Shelley's Poetry" reveals the true import of the essay. Here Yeats is imagining a Shelley born into a culture in which the older imaginative traditions are still in force:

> I think too that as he knelt before an altar where a thin flame burnt in a lamp made of green agate, a single vision would have come to him again and again, a vision of a boat drifting down a broad river between high hills where there were caves and towers, and following the light of one Star; and that voices would have told him how there is for every man some one scene, some one adventure, some one picture that is the image of his secret life, for wisdom speaks first in images, and that this one image, if he would but brood over it his life long, would lead his soul, disentangled from unmeaning circumstance and the ebb and flow of the world, into that far household where the undying gods await all whose souls have become as quiet as an agate lamp.

In this "talismanic sentence," Shelley's own images—the "caves and towers," "Star," and drifting boat—are the pretext for Yeats's own "critical creation." It is, in fact, a belief of Yeats's—that for every man there is "one image" which will redeem his soul from the entanglements of reality—that is being "revealed" in the "aesthetic ritual" of the sentence. Yeats's own beliefs, finally, and not "The Philosophy of Shelley's Poetry," are the real subject of this essay. Shelley's own work is judged inadequate throughout and nowhere more than in the concluding sentence. There Yeats writes: "But [Shelley] was born in a day when the old wisdom had vanished and was content merely to write verses, and often with little thought of more than verses." With these abrupt words, the "spell" that the essay cast is broken, and we are left impatiently waiting for the day when the "old wisdom" will return.

The question that "The Philosophy of Shelley's Poetry" asks—and it is the question posed by *Ideas of Good and Evil* as a whole—might be "How does the Great Memory work in the modern world?" Yeats's answer is that it works through symbols. But as an "answer" impossible of "proof," it is given through suggestion and repetition. Yeats's "dialogue" with Shelley, with his symbols considered as "philosophy," can extend only so far; Shelley is not Yeats, and the "dialogue" is finally internal.

If, as I have claimed, each essay in *Ideas of Good and Evil* is a "mood," the entire volume makes up what Yeats calls "a community of moods." Whatever the ostensible subject of each essay, they have a common style, content, and purpose. All, in some degree, seek to announce a "revelation"; each does so by "ritualizing," with rhythm and symbol, its contents. On receiving the volume, Yeats's oldest friend A. E. (George Russell) wrote to the poet: "I did not think I would like the book so well as I do for I had only read one or two of the essays before, but read together they throw a reflected light on each other and the book has a perfect unity." In a reverie on the future of the arts entitled "The Autumn of the Body," Yeats concludes with the prophecy:

> I think that we will learn again how to describe at great length an old man wandering among enchanted islands, his return home at last, his slow gathering vengeance, a flitting shape of a goddess, and a flight of arrows, and yet to make all these so different things "take light from mutual reflection, like an actual trail of fire over precious stone," and become "an entire world," the signature or symbol of a mood of the divine imagination as imponderable as "the horror of the forest or the silent thunder in the leaves."

In this passage, the images are from Homer, the quoted phrases from Mallarmé: the oldest Western poetry and, as of 1903, the newest, are drawn together by Yeats as embodiments of that "invisible life" which, he believes, perpetually "delivers its ever new and ever ancient revelations."

The essays in *Ideas of Good and Evil,* like poems, finally resist paraphrase. Their intricate thematic, syntactical, and sonic patterns, sometimes descending into obscurity, often rising into poetic lucidity, make them works of art. Their contribution to the later poetry of Yeats has been, I believe, overlooked. In managing the syntactical complexities of his talismanic sentences and in the sudden "leaps" of poetic and intuitive "logic" the essays make, Yeats went a long way toward the intricate stanzas and sharp contrasts of his finest poetry.

Essays are written for many reasons: to describe, to persuade, to inform, to record personal impressions. Yeats himself had these as goals but felt compelled to work toward them in his own way. He declared: "The scientific movement brought with it a literature which was always tending to lose itself in externalities of all kinds, in opinion, in declamation, in picturesque writing, in word-painting . . . , and now writers have begun to dwell upon the element of evocation, of suggestion, upon what we call the symbolism in great writers." The symbolist essay, as Yeats developed it in this volume, seeks to persuade and inform by "suggestion" and "evocation," to make his readers susceptible to an imminent "revelation" by involving them in the "aesthetic rituals" of sentence and essay. It is not a direction that most other essayists of the twentieth century have followed.

Yeats himself changed the direction of his prose. When reading the proofs of *Ideas of Good and Evil,* he had a meeting with the young James Joyce, who made him self-conscious and doubtful about the "generalizations" the books contained. Yeats then wrote, but did not publish, an "introduction" containing these criticisms. He did, however, write a letter to A. E. which casts light on his formal and thematic intentions:

> I am no longer in much sympathy with an essay like "The Autumn of the Body," not that I think that essay untrue. But I think that I mistook for a permanent phase of the world what was only a preparation. The close of the last century was full of a strange desire to get out of form, to get to some kind of disembodied beauty, and now it seems to me the contrary impulse has come. I feel about me and in me an impulse to create form, to carry the realization of beauty as far as possible.

Yeats's "strange desire to get out of form" helped create the incantatory rhythms and the subjective development of these early essays.

If Yeats himself became disenchanted with the millenarian aspirations of *Ideas of Good and Evil,* the essays in which he elaborated them still possess the power that Virginia Woolf sought in the modern essay: "It must draw its curtain around us, but it must be a curtain that shuts us in, not out." These symbolist essays of Yeats enable us, reading them, to participate in an "aesthetic ritual" while we ponder, in the prose itself, a poetic "revelation."

Carl H. Klaus

SOURCE: "On Virginia Woolf on the Essay," in *The Iowa Review,* Vol. 20, No. 2, Spring-Summer 1990, pp. 28-34.

[*In the following essay, Klaus analyzes Virginia Woolf's "The Modern Essay."*]

> Even things in a book-case change if they are alive; we find ourselves wanting to meet them again; we find them altered. So we look back upon essay after essay by Mr. Beerbohm, knowing that, come September or May, we shall sit down with them and talk.

When I first encountered this haunting passage from Virginia Woolf's "The Modern Essay," some thirty-seven years ago, I took no more note of it than I did of any other passage in the essay. To tell the truth, I didn't pay much attention to anything in that piece, compared to the time I spent on her other essays in *The Common Reader.* They were assigned reading for an undergraduate survey of modern British literature, and I made my way through them, as I did through the essays of T. S. Eliot, E. M. Forster, and George Bernard Shaw—to discover Woolf's ideas about literature, especially about great authors, great books, and the great literary forms. Essays, of course, didn't belong anywhere in that pantheon. They were *about* literature and therefore couldn't *be* literature too. So, it didn't seem especially important to hear what she had to say about the modern essay. Never mind that three out of twenty essays in *The Common Reader* were about essayists and the essay. Never mind that she, the doyenne of the Bloomsbury Group, had achieved her reputation as much for her essays as for her novels. Never mind that her reflections on the modern essay resonated with so vivid a play of personality that I might well have taken the piece for a dramatic monologue. I was one and twenty, no use to talk to me:

> Even things in a book-case change if they are alive; we find ourselves wanting to meet them again; we find them altered.

Twenty-five years later, I did find myself wanting to sit down again with Woolf's essay. No longer the cocksure honors student, his sights trained on the big time and the big forms, I was instead revising a little textbook piece on the essay as a form of literature, and I hoped her essay might provide me with a few suggestive ideas or passages. Having cut through it so quickly during my salad days, I had no idea of what I would find, so imagine my surprise when I heard her refer to the essay right off as one of the "forms of literature," whose controlling "principle . . . is simply that it should give pleasure." Heady stuff that, even for someone already predisposed to look upon the essay as literature. Pleasure, after all, is hardly what I'd thought of as the purpose of essays, nor what I'd led my writing students to think about them, though upon reflection then I couldn't help admitting that the essays I'd been reading at the time—pieces by the likes of Arlen, Baldwin, Didion, Dillard, Eiseley, Ephron, Hoagland, and Mailer—had been giving me a good deal of pleasure. And the pleasure, as I thought more about it, seemed to emanate, just as Woolf claimed, from my passing "through the most various experiences of amusement, surprise, interest, indignation. . . ."

What I couldn't accept so readily—or perhaps more accurately what I couldn't understand—was her equally bold assertion that the essay "should lay us under a spell with its first words, and we should only wake, refreshed, with its last," that it "must lap us about and draw its curtain across the world." How, I wondered, could such a trance-like, other-worldly state of mind be induced by essays, given their so frequent immersion in the world of human experience, in the press of human affairs? But I didn't puzzle over this troubling question very long, for Woolf's conception of the essay as a virtually magical or hypnotic kind of writing seemed to endow it with the imaginative power ordinarily attributed to literature, which was all I really wanted to avow at that point in my little textbook piece on the essay. So, as it happens, I didn't on that occasion bother to read any further than the first few paragraphs of Woolf's essay—and thus didn't notice how she returns to the theme of hypnosis in her concluding declaration that the essay "must draw its curtain round us, but it must be a curtain that shuts us in, not out." Having shut myself out of Woolf's essay once again, I also didn't notice that within the hypnotic circle of her essay Woolf herself seems to be more vividly and variously present than the host of essayists who figure in her observations.

> Even things in a book-case change if they are alive; we find ourselves wanting to meet them again; we find them altered.

Five years later, I once again found myself wanting to revisit Woolf's essay, and this time I stayed long enough to read it all the way through, two or three times in fact. I could hardly do otherwise, for I had assigned it as required reading in a graduate essay course I was then teaching—a speculative course in which a handful of students and I were trying to generate ideas about the most distinctive aspects and elements of the essay. Lacking a body of theory and criticism, I had suggested that we look at what the essayists themselves had to say, and Woolf, as it happened, had more to offer than most of her colleagues, for her essay was devoted to reviewing Ernest Rhys' *Modern English Essays,* a five-volume collection, published in 1920, of representative essays and essayists from each of the preceding five decades. But, as it turned out, her general reflections on the essay were so closely interwoven with her critical comments on the essayists in Rhys' collection that I initially found it quite difficult to disentangle the one from the other. Worse still, I was familiar with the writing of only a handful of the modern essayists she referred to—Pater, Beerbohm, Conrad, Belloc, and Leslie Stephen. The rest were unknown to me even by name—Mark Pattison, Mr. Hutton, Mr. Birrell, Henley, Mr. Lucas, Mr. Lynd, Vernon Lee, Mr. Squire, Mr. Clutton-Brock. No wonder I didn't pay any attention to this piece during my undergraduate days! No wonder the graduate students were having trouble with it! No sooner did those thoughts come to mind than I began to wonder how many of our own modern essayists would be known some sixty or eighty years from now. And what would people think of them then? For that matter, what would Woolf think of them, I wondered, if she were reviewing a five-volume collection of representative pieces from the last five decades? Would she find them beset by the same problems she had perceived in her own time—some "stumbling drowsily among loose words, clutching aimlessly at vague ideas," others "strained and thin and full of mannerisms and affectations, like the voice of a man shouting through a megaphone to a crowd on a windy day"?

Idle speculations, of course, especially compared to what I should have been most curious about, namely the essays in Rhys' collection. Had I tracked down his collection and worked my way through it, I might not have been so puzzled as I then was by Woolf's heavy emphasis on style as "the first essential" art of the essayist, on the necessity that the essayist "know . . . how to write." Had I read through Rhys' collection then, as I did a few years later, I'd have seen enough stylistic clumsiness, and self-consciousness, and affectation to convince me too that "it is no use being charming, virtuous, or even learned and brilliant, unless . . . you . . . know how to write." Lacking sufficient grounds for that intense conviction, I considered her view of the essay to be so aesthetically self-conscious as to be art-for-art sakeish, especially because her preoccupation with style seemed to be occasioned primarily, if not exclusively, by its power to induce a hypnotic state—"to sting us wide awake and fix us in a trance which is not sleep but rather an intensification of life—a basking with every faculty alert in the sun of pleasure." More than that, she seemed to be so carried away by the supremacy of style as to denigrate the importance of content. How else to construe her assertion that "learning. . .in an essay must be so fused by the magic of writing that not a fact juts out, not a dogma tears the texture of the surface"? How else to account for her painstaking attempts to identify the point at which stylistic polish gives way to stylistic decoration? Such questions, I later discovered, would not have been troubling me then had I also paid more attention to the range of Woolf's voice, to the play of her personality, and to her intense concern with the personality of the essayist:

> Even things in a book-case change if they are alive; we find ourselves wanting to meet them again; we find them altered.

Five years later, I did find myself wanting to sit down again with Woolf's essay, for I was writing a piece about essayists on the essay, and I planned to discuss her as the exponent of a highly aesthetical approach to its form. But in the process of making my way through her essay again, I found numerous points at which the piece didn't really match my prior impressions and recollections of it. Oh yes, I did hear her once again insisting upon the hypnotic power of the essay, especially in her first few paragraphs, and growing out of that discussion I did again find her worrying at length about matters of style. At the same time, however, I noticed that she gradually seemed to be working up to a more substantial and complex view of the essay—a paradoxical view that she announces most clearly midway through her piece when she celebrates Beerbohm as "an essayist capable of using the essayist's most proper but most dangerous and delicate tool. He has brought personality into literature, not unconsciously and impurely, but so consciously and purely that we do not know whether there is any relation between Max the essayist and Mr. Beerbohm the man. We only know that the spirit of personality permeates every word that he writes. The triumph is the triumph of style. For it is only by knowing how to write that you can make use in literature of your self; that self which, while it is essential to literature, is also its most dangerous antagonist. Never to be yourself and yet always—that is the problem."

Given so heavy an emphasis on the essayist's persona, and given such a paradoxical conception of it as both an authentic reflection and a fictionalized construction of personality, I could see more clearly why Woolf had been so preoccupied with style, for an essayist's persona is, after all, inseparable from the style in which and through which it is voiced. Remembering that truth, I could then also see why she might think that "to write like oneself and call it not writing is a much harder exercise in style than to write like Addison and call it writing well." So, it seemed, she was invoking an elaborate form of artful artlessness, a thought that put me in mind of Montaigne's reflections on his own essay writing, which he frequently referred to as an equally elaborate form of self-portraiture. Recognizing the kinship between Woolf and Montaigne made me feel much better about her essay—and about my self. And in the days and weeks to come I was to continue feeling better on both counts, as I recognized the kinship between

her thoughts on the essayist's personality and the thoughts of other essayists, such as Hazlitt, Lamb, Hoagland, White, and perhaps most interestingly her father, Leslie Stephen, who also had written an essay on the essay. Published in 1880, it offered a synoptic view of the essay from Montaigne through the mid-nineteenth century, so I could not help wondering if Woolf's reflections on the modern essay had been engendered by the knowledge of her father's piece, as if she were picking up where he had left off, especially because she seemed to be worrying about some of the very same issues—about a shrillness of voice in her own time akin to what he had been hearing in his. Exploring such connections distracted me temporarily from a renewed sense of puzzlement about her belief in the hypnotic power of the essay, so I didn't return to that problem until a year later when I was rereading the essay again in preparation for a class discussion of it, and I finally happened to notice that haunting passage I had inadvertently been ignoring for so long:

> Even things in a book-case change if they are alive; we find ourselves wanting to meet them again; we find them altered. So we look back upon essay after essay by Mr. Beerbohm, knowing that, come September or May, we shall sit down with them and talk.

My first reaction to the passage was, of course, an extraordinary sense of surprise at not having noted it before, especially because of its pertinence to Woolf's essay, to my own continuing desire to meet it again and again, to my sense of finding it altered upon each visit, and by extension to finding myself altered each time as well. But my surprise on those counts was followed quickly by surprise about another oversight—namely, my failure to notice that arresting metaphor in which she conceives of reading a good essay as comparable to carrying on a highly civilized acquaintance or friendship with someone:

> So we look back upon essay after essay by Mr. Beerbohm, knowing that, come September or May, we shall sit down with them and talk.

Looking back over the paragraph in which that passage occurs, I then noticed that she invokes the metaphor several sentences earlier in talking of Beerbohm's essay, "A Cloud of Pinafores," which she refers to as having "that indescribable inequality, stir and final expressiveness which belong to life and to life alone. You have not finished with it because you have read it, any more than friendship is ended because it is time to part. Life wells up and alters and adds." How, I wondered, could she possibly conceive of an essay—and of reading an essay—in such intensely familiar terms, unless she found it to be suffused with the sense of a human presence? Not just with a voice to be heard, nor with a personality to be observed, but with a virtually living presence to be encountered and engaged in talk, as if one were in the presence of it! And how could that be possible, I suddenly realized, unless one were stung wide awake and fixed in a trance "which," as Woolf says in the beginning of her piece, "is not sleep but an intensification of life"? And as if to confirm this supposition, I suddenly felt in that passage I had never noticed before the overwhelming sense of a human presence, engaging me directly in thought and feeling, evoking for me in word and phrase and image the drawing-room ambiance of Beerbohm's essays, where "there is no gin about; no strong tobacco; no puns, drunkenness, or insanity," where "ladies and gentlemen talk together, and some things, of course, are not said."

Feeling as I did at that moment, I could not imagine what more Woolf's essay might hold in store for me, so my sense of elation with it was tinged with the melancholy feeling that we might have nothing more to talk about. But I had not yet reckoned with the conclusion of her piece, as I realized a year later when I was reading it yet again to prepare for another offering of that graduate course on the essay. Then I heard her saying things that I had noticed but had not taken sufficient account of before—in particular, "that the art of writing has for backbone some fierce attachment to an idea." Having always believed that to be a fundamental premise of essay-writing, I suppose I must have thought it needed no saying. So I had more or less ignored it during prior readings of the piece as simply a gesture on Woolf's part toward an axiomatic truth about the essay that she had previously not bothered to acknowledge in her discussion. But here she was, I realized, saying it not just once but at length in the peroration of her essay: "It is on the back of an idea, something believed in with conviction or seen with precision and thus compelling words to a shape, that the diverse company which included Lamb and Bacon, and Mr. Beerbohm and Hudson, and Vernon Lee and Mr. Conrad, and Leslie Stephen and Butler and Walter Pater reaches the farther shore." And as if to challenge all that she had previously said about the essay, or to throw it into a new and more complicating framework, here she was crediting "an obstinate conviction" with the power to lift "ephemeral sounds through the misty sphere of anybody's language to the land where there is a perpetual marriage, a perpetual union." So it suddenly appeared as if neither style nor personality alone were sufficient to produce the hypnotic state that Woolf attributed to the essay—"some fierce attachment to an idea" was also needed. That seemed to me to be Woolf's final and definitive word on the matter, until I thought again of her remarks about the experience of reading a good essay:

> You have not finished with it because you have read it, any more than friendship is ended because it is time to part. Life wells up and alters and adds. Even things in a book-case change if they are alive; we find ourselves wanting to meet them again; we find them altered.

THE ESSAY AS A LITERARY GENRE

Georg Lukács

SOURCE: "On the Nature and Form of the Essay: A Letter to Leo Popper," in *Soul and Form*, translated by Anna Bostock, Merlin Press, 1974, pp. 1-18.

[A Hungarian literary critic and philosopher, Lukács is acknowledged as one of the leading proponents of Marxist

> **Of all forms of literature, however, the essay is the one which least calls for the use of long words. The principle which controls it is simply that it should give pleasure; the desire which impels us when we take it from the shelf is simply to receive pleasure.**
>
> **—*Virginia Woolf***

---

theory. His development of Marxist ideology was part of a broader system of thought which sought to further the values of rationalism (peace and progress), humanism (Socialist politics), and traditionalism (Realist literature) over the counter-values of irrationalism (war), totalitarianism (reactionary politics), and modernism (post-Realist literature). In major works such as Studies in European Realism *(1950) and* The Historical Novel *(1955), Lukács explicated his belief that art is wasteful and harmful if not made consonant with history and human needs. The following letter, originally published in Hungarian in 1910, appeared as the introduction to a collection of Lukács' essays titled* Soul and Form.]

My friend,

The essays intended for inclusion in this book lie before me and I ask myself whether one is entitled to publish such works—whether such works can give rise to a new unity, a book. For the point at issue for us now is not what these essays can offer as "studies in literary history", but whether there is something in them that makes them a new literary form of its own, and whether the principle that makes them such is the same in each one. What is this unity—if unity there is? I make no attempt to formulate it because it is not I nor my book that should be the subject under discussion here. The question before us is a more important, more general one. It is the question whether such a unity is possible. To what extent have the really great writings which belong to this category been given literary form, and to what extent is this form of theirs an independent one? To what extent do the standpoint of such a work and the form given to this standpoint lift it out of the sphere of science and place it at the side of the arts, yet without blurring the frontiers of either? To what extent do they endow the work with the force necessary for a conceptual re-ordering of life, and yet distinguish it from the icy, final perfection of philosophy? That is the only profound apology to be made for such writings, as well as the only profound criticism to be addressed to them; for they are measured first and foremost by the yardstick of these questions, and the determining of such an objective will be the first step towards showing how far they fall short of attaining it.

The critique, the essay—call it provisionally what you will—as a work of art, a genre? I know you think the question tedious; you feel that all the arguments for and against have been exhausted long ago. Wilde and Kerr merely made familiar to everyone a truth that was already known to the German Romantics, a truth whose ultimate meaning the Greeks and Romans felt, quite unconsciously, to be self-evident: that criticism is an art and not a science. Yet I believe—and it is for this reason alone that I venture to importune you with these observations—that all the discussions have barely touched upon the essence of the real question: what *is* an essay? What is its intended form of expression, and what are the ways and means whereby this expression is accomplished? I believe that the aspect of "being well written" has been too one-sidedly emphasized in this context. It has been argued that the essay can be stylistically of equal value to a work of the imagination, and that, for this reason, it is unjust to speak of value differences at all. Yet what does that mean? Even if we consider criticism to be a work of art in this sense, we have not yet said anything at all about its essential nature. "Whatever is well written is a work of art." Is a well-written advertisement or news item a work of art? Here I can see what so disturbs you about such a view of criticism: it is anarchy, the denial of form in order that an intellect which believes itself to be sovereign may have free play with possibilities of every kind. But if I speak here of criticism as a form of art, I do so in the name of order (i.e. almost purely symbolically and non-essentially), and solely on the strength of my feeling that the essay has a form which separates it, with the rigour of a law, from all other art forms. I want to try and define the essay as strictly as is possible, precisely by describing it as an art form.

Let us not, therefore, speak of the essay's similarities with works of literary imagination, but of what divides it from them. Let any resemblance serve here merely as a background against which the differences stand out all the more sharply; the purpose of mentioning these resemblances at all will be to limit our attention to genuine essays, leaving aside those writings which, useful though they are, do not deserve to be described as essays because they can never give us anything more than information, facts and "relationships". Why, after all, do we read essays? Many are read as a source of instruction, but there are others whose attraction is to be found in something quite different. It is not difficult to identify these. Our view, our appreciation of classical tragedy is quite different today, is it not, from Lessing's in the *Dramaturgy*; Winckelmann's Greeks seem strange, almost incomprehensible to us, and soon we may feel the same about Burckhardt's Renaissance. And yet we read them: why? On the other hand there are critical writings which, like a hypothesis in natural science, like a design for a machine part, lose all their value at the precise moment when a new and better one becomes available. But if—as I hope and expect—someone were to write a new *Dramaturgy*, a *Dramaturgy* in favour of Corneille and against Shakespeare—how could it damage Lessing's? And what did Burckhardt and Pater, Rhode and Nietzsche do to change the effect upon us of Winckelmann's dreams of Greece?

"Of course, if criticism were a science . . ." writes Kerr. "But the imponderables are too strong. Criticism is, at the very best, an art." And if it were a science—it is not so impossible that it will become one—how would that change our problem? We are not concerned here with replacing something by something else, but with something essentially new, something that remains untouched by the complete or approximate attainment of scientific goals. Science affects us by its contents, art by its forms; science offers us facts and the relationships between facts, but art offers us souls and destinies. Here the ways part; here there is no replacement and no transition. In primitive, as yet undifferentiated epochs, science and art (and religion and ethics and politics) are integrated, they form a single whole; but as soon as science has become separate and independent, everything that has led up to it loses its value. Only when something has dissolved all its content in form, and thus becomes pure art, can it no longer become superfluous; but then its previous scientific nature altogether forgotten and emptied of meaning.

There is, then, a science of the arts; but there is also an entirely different kind of expression of the human temperament, which usually takes the form of writing about the arts. Usually, I say, for there are many writings which are engendered by such feelings without ever touching upon literature or art—writings in which the same life-problems are raised as in the writings which call themselves criticism, but with the difference that here the questions are addressed directly to life itself: they do not need the mediation of literature or art. And it is precisely the writings of the greatest essayists which belong to this category: Plato's *Dialogues,* the texts of the mystics, Montaigne's *Essays,* Kierkegaard's imaginary diaries and short stories.

An endless series of almost imperceptible, subtle transitions leads from here to imaginative writing. Think of the last scene in the *Heracles* of Euripides: the tragedy is already over when Theseus appears and discovers everything that has happened—Hera's terrible vengeance of Heracles. Then begins the dialogue about life between the mourning Heracles and his friend; questions akin to those of the Socratic dialogues are asked, but the questioners are stiffer and less human, and their questions more conceptual, less related to direct experience than in Plato. Think of the last act of *Michael Kramer,* of the *Confessions of a Beautiful Soul,* of Dante, of *Everyman,* of Bunyan—must I quote further examples?

Doubtless you will say that the end of *Heracles* is undramatic and Bunyan is. . . . Certainly, certainly, but why? The *Heracles* is undramatic because every dramatic style has this natural corollary, that whatever happens within human souls is projected into human actions, movements and gestures and is thus made visible and palpable to the senses. Here you see Hera's vengeance overtaking Heracles, you see Heracles in the blissful enjoyment of victory before vengeance is upon him, you see his frenzied gestures in the madness which Hera has dealt to him and his wild despair after the storm, when he sees what has happened to him. But of what comes after you see nothing at all. Theseus comes—and you try in vain to determine by other than conceptual means what happens next: what you see and hear is no longer a true means of expression of the real event, and that the event occurs at all is deep down a matter of indifference to you. You see no more than that Theseus and Heracles leave the stage together. Prior to that some questions are asked: what is the true nature of the gods? Which gods may we believe in, and which not? What is life and what is the best way of bearing one's sufferings manfully? The concrete experience which has led up to these questions is lost in an infinite distance. And when the answers return once more into the world of facts, they are no longer answers to questions posed by real life—questions of what these men must do or refrain from doing in this particular situation. These answers cast a stranger's eye upon all facts, for they have come from life and from the gods and know scarcely anything of Heracles' pain or of its cause in Hera's vengeance. Drama, I know, also addresses questions to life, and in drama, too, the answer comes from destiny—and in the last analysis the questions and answers, even in drama, are tied to certain definite facts. But the true dramatist (so long as he is a true poet, a genuine representative of the poetic principle) will see *a life* as being so rich and so intense that almost imperceptibly it becomes *life*. Here, however, everything becomes undramatic because here the other principle comes into effect: for the life that here poses the question loses all its corporeality at the moment when the first word of the question is uttered.

There are, then, two types of reality of the soul: one is *life* and the other *living*; both are equally effective, but they can never be effective at the same time. Elements of both are contained in the lived experience of every human being, even if in always varying degrees of intensity and depth; in memory too, there is now one, now the other, but at any one moment we can only feel one of these two forms. Ever since there has been life and men have sought to understand and order life, there has been this duality in their lived experience. But the struggle for priority and pre-eminence between the two has mostly been fought out in philosophy, so that the battlecries have always had a different sound, and for this reason have gone unrecognized by most men and have been unrecognizable to them. It would seem that the question was posed most clearly in the Middle Ages, when thinkers divided into two camps, the ones maintaining that the *universalia*—concepts, or Plato's Ideas if you will—were the sole true realities, while the others acknowledged them only as words, as names summarizing the sole true and distinct *things*.

The same duality also separates means of expression: the opposition here is between image and "significance". One principle is an image-creating one, the other a significance-supposing one. For one there exist only things, for the other only the relationships between them, only concepts and values. Poetry in itself knows of nothing beyond things; for it, every thing is serious and unique and incomparable. That is also why poetry knows no questions: you do not address questions to pure *things,* only to their relationships, for—as in fairy-tales—every question here turns again into a thing resembling the one that called it into being. The hero stands at the crossroads or in the midst of the struggle, but the crossroads and the struggle are not destinies about which questions may be asked and answers given; they are simply and literally struggles and crossroads. And the hero blows his miraculous horn and the expected miracle occurs: a thing which once more orders life. But in really profound criticism there is no life of things, no image, only transparency, only something that

no image would be capable of expressing completely. An "imagelessness of all images" is the aim of all mystics, and Socrates speaks mockingly and contemptuously to Phaedrus of poets, who never have nor ever could worthily celebrate the true life of the soul. "For the great existence which the immortal part of the soul once lived is colourless and without form and impalpable, and only the soul's guide, the mind, can behold it."

You may perhaps reply that my poet is an empty abstraction and so, too, is my critic. You are right—both are abstractions, but not, perhaps, quite empty ones. They are abstractions because even Socrates must speak in images of his "world without form", his world on the far side of form, and even the German mystic's "imagelessness" is a metaphor. Nor is there any poetry without some ordering of things. Matthew Arnold once called it *criticism of life*. It represents the ultimate relationships between man and destiny and world, and without doubt it has its origin in those profound regions, even if, often, it is unaware of it. If poetry often refuses all questioning, all taking up of positions, is not the denial of all questions in itself an asking of questions, and is not the conscious rejection of any position in itself a position? I shall go further: the separation of image and significance is itself an abstraction, for the significance is always wrapped in images and the reflection of a glow from beyond the image shines through every image. Every image belongs to our world and the joy of being in the world shines in its countenance; yet it also reminds us of something that was once there, at some time or another, a somewhere, its home, the only thing that, in the last analysis, has meaning and significance for the soul. Yes, in their naked purity they are merely abstractions, those two limits of human feeling, but only with the help of such abstractions can I define the two poles of possible literary expression. And the writings which most resolutely reject the image, which reach out most passionately for what lies behind the image, are the writings of the critics, the Platonists and the mystics.

But in saying this I have already explained why this kind of feeling calls for an art form of its own—why every expression of this kind of feeling must always disturb us when we find it in other forms, in poetry. It was you who once formulated the great demand which everything that has been given form must satisfy, the only absolutely universal demand, perhaps, but one that is inexorable and allows of no exception: the demand that everything in a work must be fashioned from the same material, that each of its parts must be visibly ordered from one single point. And because all writing aspires to both unity and multiplicity, this is the universal problem of style: to achieve equilibrium in a welter of disparate things, richness and articulation in a mass of uniform matter. Something that is viable in one art form is dead in another: here is practical, palpable proof of the inner divorce of forms. Do you remember how you explained to me the living quality of human figures in certain heavily stylized mural paintings? You said: these frescoes are painted between pillars, and even if the gestures of the men depicted in them are stiff like those of puppets and every facial expression is only a mask, still all this is more alive than the columns which frame the pictures and form a decorative unity with them.

Only a little more alive, for the unity must be preserved; but more alive all the same, so that there may be an illusion of life. Here, however, the problem of equilibrium is posed in this way: the world and the beyond, image and transparency, idea and emanation lie in the two cups of a scale which is to remain balanced. The deeper down the question reaches—you need only compare the tragedy with the fairy-tale—the more linear the images become, the smaller the number of planes into which everything is compressed, the paler and more matt the radiance of the colours, the simpler the richness and multiplicity of the world, the more mask-like the expressions of the characters. But there are other experiences, for the expression of which even the simplest and most measured gesture would be too much—and too little; there are questions which are asked so softly that beside them the sound of the most toneless of events would be crude noise, not musical accompaniment; there are destiny-relationships which are so exclusively relationships between destinies as such that anything human would merely disturb their abstract purity and grandeur. I am not speaking here of subtlety or depth: those are value categories and are therefore valid only within a particular form. We are speaking of the fundamental principles which separate forms from one another—of the material from which the whole is constructed, of the standpoint, the world-view which gives unity to the entire work. Let me put it briefly: were one to compare the forms of literature with sunlight refracted in a prism, the writings of the essayists would be the ultra-violet rays.

There are experiences, then, which cannot be expressed by any gesture and which yet long for expression. From all that has been said you will know what experiences I mean and of what kind they are. I mean intellectuality, conceptuality as sensed experience, as immediate reality, as spontaneous principle of existence; the worldview in its undisguised purity as an event of the soul, as the motive force of life. The question is posed immediately: what is life, what is man, what is destiny? But posed as a question only: for the answer, here, does not supply a "solution" like one of the answers of science or, at purer heights, those of philosophy. Rather, as in poetry of every kind, it is symbol, destiny and tragedy. When a man experiences such things, then everything that is outward about him awaits in rigid immobility the outcome of the struggle between invisible forces to which the senses have no access. Any gesture with which such a man might wish to express something of his experience would falsify that experience, unless it ironically emphasized its own inadequacy and thus cancelled itself out. A man who experiences such things cannot be characterized by any outward feature—how then can he be given form in a work of literature? All writings represent the world in the symbolic terms of a destiny-relationship; everywhere, the problem of destiny determines the problem of form. This unity, this coexistence is so strong that neither element ever occurs without the other; here again a separation is possible only by way of abstraction. Therefore the separation which I am trying to accomplish here appears, in practice, merely as a shift of emphasis: poetry receives its profile and its form from destiny, and form in poetry appears always only as destiny; but in the works of the essayists form *becomes* destiny, it is the destiny-creating principle. This difference means

the following: destiny lifts things up outside the world of things, accentuating the essential ones and eliminating the inessential; but form sets limits round a substance which otherwise would dissolve like air in the All. In other words, destiny comes from the same source as everything else, it is a thing among things, whereas form—seen as something finished, i.e. seen from outside—defines the limits of the immaterial. Because the destiny which orders things is flesh of their flesh and blood of their blood, destiny is not to be found in the writings of the essayists. For destiny, once stripped of its uniqueness and accidentality, is just as airy and immaterial as all the rest of the incorporeal matter of these writings, and is no more capable of giving them form than they themselves possess any natural inclination or possibility of condensing themselves into form.

That is why such writings speak of forms. The critic is one who glimpses destiny in forms: whose most profound experience is the soul-content which forms indirectly and unconsciously conceal within themselves. Form is his great experience, form—as immediate reality—is the image-element, the really living content of his writings. This form, which springs from a symbolic contemplation of life-symbols, acquires a life of its own through the power of that experience. It becomes a world-view, a standpoint, an attitude vis-à-vis the life from which it sprang: a possibility of reshaping it, of creating it anew. The critic's moment of destiny, therefore, is that moment at which things become forms—the moment when all feelings and experiences on the near or the far side of form receive form, are melted down and condensed into form. It is the mystical moment of union between the outer and the inner, between soul and form. It is as mystical as the moment of destiny in tragedy when the hero meets his destiny, in the short story when accident and cosmic necessity converge, in poetry when the soul and its world meet and coalesce into a new unity that can no more be divided, either in the past or in the future. Form *is* reality in the writings of critics; it is the voice with which they address their questions to life. That is the true and most profound reason why literature and art are the typical, natural subject-matter of criticism. For here the end-point of poetry can become a starting-point and a beginning; here form appears, even in its abstract conceptuality, as something surely and concretely real. But this is only the typical subject-matter of the essay, not the sole one. For the essayist needs form only as lived experience and he needs only its life, only the living soul-reality it contains. But this reality is to be found in every immediate sensual expression of life, it can be read out of and read into every such experience; life itself can be lived and given form through such a scheme of lived experience. Because literature, art and philosophy pursue forms openly and directly, whereas in life they are no more than the ideal demand of a certain kind of men and experiences, a lesser intensity of critical capacity is needed to experience something formed than to experience something lived; and that is why the reality of form-vision appears, at the first and most superficial glance, less problematic in the sphere of art than in life. But this only seems to be so at the first and most superficial glance, for the form of life is no more abstract than the form of a poem. Here as there, form becomes perceptible only through abstraction, and there as here the reality of form is no stronger than the force with which it is experienced. It would be superficial to distinguish between poems according to whether they take their subject-matter from life or elsewhere; for in any case the form-creating power of poetry breaks and scatters whatever is old, whatever has already been formed, and everything becomes unformed raw material in its hands. To draw such a distinction here seems to me just as superficial, for both ways of contemplating the world are merely standpoints taken up in relation to things, and each is applicable everywhere, although it is true that for both there exist certain things which, with a naturalness decreed by nature, submit themselves to one particular standpoint and others which can only be forced to do so by violent struggles and profound experiences.

As in every really essential relationship, natural effect and immediate usefulness coincide here: the experiences which the writings of the essayists were written to express become conscious in the minds of most people only when they look at the pictures or read the poem discussed and even then they rarely have a force that could move life itself. That is why most people have to believe that the writings of the essayists are produced only in order to explain books and pictures, to facilitate their understanding. Yet this relationship is profound and necessary, and it is precisely the indivisible and organic quality of this mixture of being-accidental and being-necessary which is at the root of that humour and that irony which we find in the writings of every truly great essayist—that peculiar humour which is so strong that to speak of it is almost indecent, for there is no use in pointing it out to someone who does not spontaneously feel it. And the irony I mean consists in the critic always speaking about the ultimate problems of life, but in a tone which implies that he is only discussing pictures and books, only the inessential and pretty ornaments of real life—and even then not their innermost substance but only their beautiful and useless surface. Thus each essay appears to be removed as far as possible from life, and the distance between them seems the greater, the more burningly and painfully we sense the actual closeness of the true essence of both. Perhaps the great Sieur de Montaigne felt something like this when he gave his writings the wonderfully elegant and apt title of "Essays". The simple modesty of this word is an arrogant courtesy. The essayist dismisses his own proud hopes which sometimes lead him to believe that he has come close to the ultimate: he has, after all, no more to offer than explanations of the poems of others, or at best of his own ideas. But he ironically adapts himself to this smallness—the eternal smallness of the most profound work of the intellect in face of life—and even emphasizes it with ironic modesty. In Plato, conceptuality is underlined by the irony of the small realities of life. Eryximachos cures Aristophanes of hiccups by making him sneeze before he can begin his deeply meaningful hymn to Eros. And Hippothales watches with anxious attention while Socrates questions his beloved Lysis—and little Lysis, with childish malice, asks Socrates to torment his friend Menexenos with questions just as he has tormented him. Rough guardians come and break up the gently scintillating dialogue, and drag the boys off home. Socrates, however, is more amused than anything else: "Socrates and the two boys wanted to be friends, yet were not even able to say what a friend really is." I see a similar irony in the vast scientific apparatus of certain modern essayists (think only of Weininger), and only a different expression of it in the discreetly reserved manner of a Dilthey. We can always find the same irony in every text by every great essayist, though admittedly always in a different form. The mystics of the Middle Ages are the only ones without inner irony—I surely need not tell you why.

We see, then, that criticism and the essay generally speak of pictures, books and ideas. What is their attitude towards the matter which is represented? People say that the critic must always speak the truth, whereas the poet is not obliged to tell the truth about his subject-matter. It is not our intention here to ask Pilate's question nor to enquire whether the poet, too, is not impelled towards an inner truthfulness and whether the truth of any criticism can be stronger or greater than this. I do not propose to ask these questions because I really do see a difference here, but once again a difference which is altogether pure, sharp and without transitions only at its abstract poles. When I wrote about Kassner I pointed out that the essay always speaks of something that has already been given form, or at least something that has already been there at some time in the past; hence it is part of the nature of the essay that it does not create new things from an empty nothingness but only orders those which were once alive. And because it orders them anew and does not form something new out of formlessness, it is bound to them and must always speak "the truth" about them, must find expression for their essential nature. Perhaps the difference can be most briefly formulated thus: poetry takes its motifs from life (and art); the essay has its models in art (and life). Perhaps this is enough to define the difference: the paradox of the essay is almost the same as that of the portrait. You see why, do you not? In front of a landscape we never ask ourselves whether this mountain or that river really is as it is painted there; but in front of every portrait the question of likeness always forces itself willy-nilly upon us. Give a little more thought, therefore, to this problem of likeness—this problem which, foolish and superficial as it is, drives true artists to despair. You stand in front of a Velasquez portrait and you say: "What a marvellous likeness," and you feel that you have really said something about the painting. Likeness? Of whom? Of no one, of course. You have no idea whom it represents, perhaps you can never find out; and if you could, you would care very little. Yet you feel that it is a likeness. Other portraits produce their effect only by colour and line, and so you do not have this feeling. In other words, the really significant portraits give us, besides all other artistic sensations, also this: the life of a human being who once was really alive, forcing us to feel that his life was exactly as shown by the lines and colours of the painting. Only because we see painters in front of their models fight such a hard battle for this ideal expression—because the look and the battle-cry of this battle are such that it cannot be anything else than a battle for likeness—only for this reason do we give this name to the portrait's suggestion of real life, even though there is no one in the world whom the portrait could be like. For even if we know the person represented, whose portrait we may call "like" or "unlike"—is it not an abstraction to say of an arbitrarily chosen moment or expression that *this* is that person's likeness? And even if we know thousands of such moments or expressions, what do we know of the immeasurably large part of his life when we do not see him, what do we know of the inner light which burns within this "known" person, what of the way this inner light is reflected in others? And that, you see, is more or less how I imagine the truth of the essay to be. Here too there is a struggle for truth, for the incarnation of a life which someone has seen in a man, an epoch or a form; but it depends only on the intensity of the work and its vision whether the written text conveys to us this suggestion of that particular life.

The great difference, then, is this: poetry gives us the illusion of life of the person it represents; nowhere is there a conceivable someone or something against which the created work can be measured. The hero of the essay was once alive, and so his life must be given form; but this life, too, is as much inside the work as everything is in poetry. The essay has to create from within itself all the preconditions for the effectiveness and validity of its vision. Therefore two essays can never contradict one another: each creates a different world, and even when, in order to achieve a higher universality, it goes beyond that created world, it still remains inside it by its tone, colour and accent; that is to say, it leaves that world only in the inessential sense. It is simply not true that there exists an objective, external criterion of life and truth, e.g. that the truth of Grimm's, Dilthey's or Schlegel's Goethe can be tested against the "real" Goethe. It is not true because many Goethes, different from one another and each profoundly different from *our* Goethe, may convince us of their life: and, conversely, we are disappointed if our own visions are presented by others, yet without that vital breath which would give them autonomous life. It is true that the essay strives for truth: but just as Saul went out to look for his father's she-asses and found a kingdom, so the essayist who is really capable of looking for the truth will find at the end of his road the goal he was looking for: life.

The illusion of truth! Do not forget how slowly and with how much difficulty poetry abandoned that ideal. It happened not so very long ago, and it is highly questionable whether the disappearance of the illusion was entirely advantageous. It is highly questionable whether man should want the precise thing he sets out to attain, whether he has the right to walk towards his goal along straight and simple paths. Think of the chivalresque epics of the Middle Ages, think of the Greek tragedies, think of Giotto and you will see what I am trying to say. We are not speaking here of ordinary truth, the truth of naturalism which it would be more accurate to call the triviality of everyday life, but of the truth of the myth by whose power ancient tales and legends are kept alive for thousands of years. The true poets of myths looked only for the true meaning of their themes; they neither could nor wished to check their pragmatic reality. They saw these myths as sacred, mysterious hieroglyphics which it was their mission to read. But do you not see that both worlds can have a mythology of their own? It was Friedrich Schlegel who said long ago that the national gods of the Germans were not Hermann

or Wotan but science and the arts. Admittedly, that is not true of the *whole* life of Germany, but it is all the more apt as a description of *part* of the life of every nation in every epoch—that part, precisely, of which we are speaking. That life, too, has its golden ages and its lost paradises; we find in it rich lives full of strange adventures and enigmatic punishments of dark sins; heroes of the sun appear and fight out their harsh feuds with the forces of darkness; here, too, the magic words of wise magicians and the tempting songs of beautiful sirens lead weaklings into perdition; here too there is original sin and redemption. All the struggles of life are present here, but the stuff of which everything is made is different from the stuff of the "other" life.

We want poets and critics to give us life-symbols and to mould the still-living myths and legends in the form of our questions. It is a subtle and poignant irony, is it not, when a great critic dreams our longing into early Florentine paintings or Greek torsos and, in that way, gets something out of them for us that we would have sought in vain everywhere else—and then speaks of the latest achievements of scientific research, of new methods and new facts? Facts are always there and everything is always contained in facts, but every epoch needs its own Greece, its own Middle Ages and its own Renaissance. Every age creates the age it needs, and only the next generation believes that its fathers' dreams were lies which must be fought with its own new "truths". The history of the effect of poetry follows the same course, and in criticism, too, the continuing life of the grandfather's dreams—not to mention those of earlier generations—is barely touched by the dreams of men alive today. Consequently the most varied "conceptions" of the Renaissance can live peacefully side by side with one another, just as a new poet's new Phèdre, Siegfried or Tristan must always leave intact the Phèdre, Siegfried or Tristan of his predecessors.

Of course there is a science of the arts; there has to be one. The greatest essayists are precisely those who can least well do without it: what they create must be science, even when their vision of life has transcended the sphere of science. Sometimes its free flight is constrained by the unassailable facts of dry matter; sometimes it loses all scientific value because it is, after all, a vision, because it precedes facts and therefore handles them freely and arbitrarily. The essay form has not yet, today, travelled the road to independence which its sister, poetry, covered long ago— the road of development from a primitive, undifferentiated unity with science, ethics and art. Yet the beginning of that road was so tremendous that subsequent developments have rarely equalled it. I speak, of course, of Plato, the greatest essayist who ever lived or wrote, the one who wrested everything from life as it unfolded before his eyes and who therefore needed no mediating medium; the one who was able to connect his questions, the most profound questions ever asked, with life as lived. This greatest master of the form was also the happiest of all creators: man lived in his immediate proximity, man whose essence and destiny constituted the paradigmatic essence and destiny of his form. Perhaps they would have become paradigmatic in this way even if Plato's writing had consisted of the driest notations—not just because of his glorious form-giving—so strong was the concordance of life and form in this particular case. But Plato met Socrates and was able to give form to the myth of Socrates, to use Socrates' destiny as the vehicle for the questions he, Plato, wanted to address to life about destiny. The life of Socrates is the typical life for the essay form, as typical as hardly any other life is for any literary form—with the sole exception of Oedipus' life for tragedy. Socrates always lived in the ultimate questions; every other living reality was as little alive for him as his questions are alive for ordinary people. The concepts into which he poured the whole of his life were lived by him with the most direct and immediate life-energy; everything else was but a parable of that sole true reality, useful only as a means of expressing those experiences. His life rings with the sound of the deepest, the most hidden longing and is full of the most violent struggles; but that longing is—simply—longing, and the form in which it appears is the attempt to comprehend the nature of longing and to capture it in concepts, while the struggles are simply verbal battles fought solely in order to give more definite limits to a few concepts. Yet the longing fills that life completely and the struggles are always, quite literally, a matter of life and death. But despite everything the longing which seems to fill that life is not the essential thing about life, and neither Socrates' life nor his death was able to express those life-and-death struggles. If this had been possible, the death of Socrates would have been a martyrdom or a tragedy—which means that it could be represented in epic or dramatic form. But Plato knew exactly why he burned the tragedy he wrote in his youth. For a tragic life is crowned only by its end, only the end gives meaning, sense and form to the whole, and it is precisely the end which is always arbitrary and ironic here, in every dialogue and in Socrates' whole life. A question is thrown up and extended so far in depth that it becomes the question of all questions, but after that everything remains open; something comes from outside—from a reality which has no connection with the question nor with that which, as the possibility of an answer, brings forth a new question to meet it—and interrupts everything. This interruption is not an end, because it does not come from within, and yet it is the most profound ending because a conclusion from within would have been impossible. For Socrates every event was only an occasion for seeing concepts more clearly, his defence in front of the judges only a way of leading weak logicians *ad absurdum*—and his death? Death does not count here, it cannot be grasped by concepts, it interrupts the great dialogue—the only true reality—just as brutally, and merely from the outside, as those rough tutors who interrupted the conversation with Lysis. Such an interruption, however, can only be viewed humoristically, it has so little connection with that which it interrupts. But it is also a profound life-symbol—and, for that reason, still more profoundly humorous—that the essential is always interrupted by such things in such a way.

The Greeks felt each of the forms available to them as a reality, as a living thing and not as an abstraction. Alcibiades already saw clearly what Nietzsche was to emphasize centuries later—that Socrates was a new kind of man, profoundly different in his elusive essence from all other Greeks who lived before him. But Socrates, in the same

dialogue, expressed the eternal ideal of men of his kind, an ideal which neither those whose way of feeling remains tied to the purely human nor those who are poets in their innermost being will ever understand: that tragedies and comedies should be written by the same man; that "tragic" and "comic" is entirely a matter of the chosen standpoint. In saying this, the critic expressed his deepest life-sense: the primacy of the standpoint, the concept, over feeling; and in saying it he formulated the profoundest anti-Greek thought.

Plato himself, as you see, was a "critic", although criticism, like everything else, was for him only an occasion, an ironic means of expressing himself. Later on, criticism became its own content; critics spoke only of poetry and art, and they never had the fortune to meet a Socrates whose life might have served them as a springboard to the ultimate. But Socrates was the first to condemn such critics. "It seems to me," he said to Protagoras, "that to make a poem the subject of a conversation is too reminiscent of those banquets which uneducated and vulgar people give in their houses. . . . Conversations like the one we are now enjoying—conversations among men such as most of us would claim to be—do not need outside voices or the presence of a poet. . . ."

Fortunately for us, the modern essay does not always have to speak of books or poets; but this freedom makes the essay even more problematic. It stands too high, it sees and connects too many things to be the simple exposition or explanation of a work; the title of every essay is preceded in invisible letters, by the words "Thoughts occasioned by. . . ." The essay has become too rich and independent for dedicated service, yet it is too intellectual and too multiform to acquire form out of its own self. Has it perhaps become even more problematic, even further removed from life-values than if it had continued to report faithfully on books?

When something has once become problematic—and the way of thinking that we speak of, and its way of expression, have not become problematic but have always been so—then salvation can only come from accentuating the problems to the maximum degree, from going radically to its root. The modern essay has lost that backdrop of life which gave Plato and the mystics their strength; nor does it any longer possess a naïve faith in the value of books and what can be said about them. The problematic of the situation has become accentuated almost to the point of demanding a certain frivolity of thought and expression, and this, for most critics, has become their life-mood. This has shown, however, that salvation is necessary and is therefore becoming possible and real. The essayist must now become conscious of his own self, must find himself and build something of his own out of himself. The essayist speaks of a picture or a book, but leaves it again at once—why? Because, I think, the idea of the picture or book has become predominant in his mind, because he has forgotten all that is concretely incidental about it, because he has used it only as a starting-point, a springboard. Poetry is older and greater—a larger, more important thing—than all the works of poetry: that was once the mood with which critics approached literature, but in our time it has had to become a conscious attitude. The critic has been sent into the world in order to bring to light this *a priori* primacy over great and small, to proclaim it, to judge every phenomenon by the scale of values glimpsed and grasped through this recognition. The idea is there before any of its expressions, it is a soul-value, a world-moving and life-forming force in itself: and that is why such criticism will always speak of life where it is most alive. The idea is the measure of everything that exists, and that is why the critic whose thinking is "occasioned by" something already created, and who reveals its idea, is the one who will write the truest and most profound criticism. Only something that is great and true can live in the proximity of the idea. When this magic word has been spoken, then everything that is brittle, small and unfinished falls apart, loses its usurped wisdom, its badly fitting essence. It does not have to be "criticism": the atmosphere of the idea is enough to judge and condemn it.

Yet it is now that the essayist's possibility of existence becomes profoundly problematic. He is delivered from the relative, the inessential, by the force of judgement of the idea he has glimpsed; but who gives him the right to judge? It would be almost true to say that he seizes that right, that he creates his judgement-values from within himself. But nothing is separated from true judgement by a deeper abyss than its approximation, the squint-eyed category of complacent and self-satisfied knowledge. The criteria of the essayist's judgement are indeed created within him, but it is not he who awakens them to life and action: the one who whispers them into his ear is the great value-definer of aesthetics, the one who is always about to arrive, the one who is never quite yet there, the only one who has been called to judge. The essayist is a Schopenhauer who writes his *Parerga* while waiting for the arrival of his own (or another's) *The World as Will and Idea,* he is a John the Baptist who goes out to preach in the wilderness about another who is still to come, whose shoelace he is not worthy to untie. And if that other does not come—is not the essayist then without justification? And if the other does come, is he not made superfluous thereby? Has he not become entirely problematic by thus trying to justify himself ? He is the pure type of the precursor, and it seems highly questionable whether, left entirely to himself—i.e., independent from the fate of that other of whom he is the herald—he could lay claim to any value or validity. To stand fast against those who deny his fulfilment within the great, redeeming system is easy enough: a true longing always triumphs over those who lack the energy to rise above the vulgar level of given facts and experiences; the existence of the longing is enough to decide the outcome. For it tears the mask off everything that is only apparently positive and immediate, reveals it as petty longing and cheap fulfilment, points to the measure and order to which even they who vainly and contemptibly deny its existence—because measure and order seem inaccessible to them—unconsciously aspire. The essay can calmly and proudly set its fragmentariness against the petty completeness of scientific exactitude or impressionistic freshness; but its purest fulfilment, its most vigorous accomplishment becomes powerless once the great aesthetic comes. Then all its creations are only an application of the measure which at last has become undeniable, it is then some-

thing merely provisional and occasional, its results can no longer be justified purely from within themselves. Here the essay seems truly and completely a mere precursor, and no independent value can be attached to it. But this longing for value and form, for measure and order and purpose, does not simply lead to an end that must be reached so that it may be cancelled out and become a presumptuous tautology. Every true end is a real end, the end of a road, and although road and end do not make a unity and do not stand side by side as equals, they nevertheless coexist: the end is unthinkable and unrealizable without the road being travelled again and again; the end is not standing still but arriving there, not resting but conquering a summit. Thus the essay seems justified as a necessary means to the ultimate end, the penultimate step in this hierarchy. This, however, is only the value of what it *does*: the fact of what it *is* has yet another, more independent value. For in the system of values yet to be found, the longing we spoke of would be satisfied and therefore abolished; but this longing is more than just something waiting for fulfilment, it is a fact of the soul with a value and existence of its own: an original and deeprooted attitude towards the whole of life, a final, irreducible category of possibilities of experience. Therefore it needs not only to be satisfied (and thus abolished) but also to be given form which will redeem and release its most essential and now indivisible substance into eternal value. That is what the essay does. Think again of the example of the *Parerga*: whether they occurred before or after the system is not a matter simply of a time-sequence; the time-historical difference is only a symbol of the difference between their two natures. The *Parerga* written before the system create their preconditions from within themselves, create the whole world out of their longing for the system, so that—it seems—they can give an example, a hint; immanently and inexpressibly, they contain the system and its connection with lived life. Therefore they must always occur before the system; even if the system had already been created, they would not be a mere application but always a new creation, a coming-alive in real experience. This "application" creates both that which judges and that which is judged, it encompasses a whole world in order to raise to eternity, in all its uniqueness, something that was once there. The essay is a judgement, but the essential, the value-determining thing about it is not the verdict (as is the case with the system) but the process of judging.

Only now may we write down the opening words: the essay is an art form, an autonomous and integral giving-of-form to an autonomous and complete life. Only now would it not be contradictory, ambiguous and false to call it a work of art and yet insist on emphasizing the thing that differentiates it from art: if faces life with the same gesture as the work of art, but only the gesture, the sovereignty of its attitude is the same; otherwise there is no correspondence between them.

It was of this possibility of the essay that I wanted to speak to you here, of the nature and form of these "intellectual poems", as the older Schlegel called those of Hemsterhuys. This is not the place to discuss or decide whether the essayists' becoming conscious of their own nature, as they have been doing for some time past, has brought perfection or can bring it. The point at issue was only the possibility, only the question of whether the road upon which this book attempts to travel is really a road; it was not a question of who has already travelled it or how—nor, least of all, the distance this particular book has travelled along it. The critique of this book is contained, in all possible sharpness and entirety, in the very approach from which it sprang.

T. W. Adorno

SOURCE: "The Essay as Form," translated by Bob Hullot-Kentor and Frederic Will in *New German Critique*, Vol. 11, No. 2, Spring-Summer, 1984, pp. 151-71.

[*A German-born philosopher, literary and cultural critic, musicologist, and sociologist, Adorno greatly influenced the intellectual foundations of revolutionary thought in postwar Europe. He is closely associated with the Frankfurt Institute for Social Research, a center for Marxist studies, and aided development of the Institute's "Critical Theory." Critical Theory is an approach to the analysis and criticism of philosophies and ideologies intended to allow movement toward an objective and creative view of society untainted by false theories and inherited assumptions. In* Minima Moralia *(1951) and* Dialektik der Aufklarung *(1947; Dialectic of Enlightenment, 1972), Adorno stated that the arrogant denial of our oneness with nature is the original sin of our society. In the following essay, he discusses the essay as a unique literary form.*]

That in Germany the essay is decried as a hybrid; that it is lacking a convincing tradition; that its strenuous requirements have only rarely been met: all this has been often remarked upon and censured. "The essay form has not yet, today, travelled the road to independence which its sister, poetry, covered long ago; the road of development from a primitive, undifferentiated unity with science, ethics, and art" [George Lukács, *Soul and Form*]. But neither discontent with this situation, nor discontent with the mentality that reacts to the situation by fencing up art as a preserve for the irrational, identifying knowledge with organized science and excluding as impure anything that does not fit this antithesis: neither discontent has changed anything in the customary national prejudice. The bestowal of the garland "writer" still suffices to exclude from academia the person one is praising. Despite the weighty perspicacity that Simmel and the young Lukács, Kassner and Benjamin entrusted to the essay, to the speculative investigation of specific, culturally predetermined objects, the academic guild only has patience for philosophy that dresses itself up with the nobility of the universal, the everlasting, and today—when possible—with the primal; the cultural artifact is of interest only to the degree that it serves to exemplify universal categories, or at the very least allows them to shine through—however little the particular is thereby illuminated. The stubbornness with which this stereotypical thought survives would be as puzzling as its emotional rootedness if it were not fed by motives that are stronger than the painful recollection of how much cultivation is missing from a culture that historically scarcely recognizes the *homme de lettres*. In Germany the essay provokes resistance because it is reminiscent of

the intellectual freedom that, from the time of an unsuccessful and lukewarm Enlightenment, since Leibniz's day, all the way to the present has never really emerged, not even under the conditions of formal freedom; the German Enlightenment was always ready to proclaim, as its essential concern, subordination under whatever higher courts. The essay, however, does not permit its domain to be prescribed. Instead of achieving something scientifically, or creating something artistically, the effort of the essay reflects a childlike freedom that catches fire, without scruple, on what others have already done. The essay mirrors what is loved and hated instead of presenting the intellect, on the model of a boundless work ethic, as *creatio ex nihilo*. Luck and play are essential to the essay. It does not begin with Adam and Eve but with what it wants to discuss; it says what is at issue and stops where it feels itself complete—not where nothing is left to say. Therefore it is classed among the oddities. Its concepts are neither deduced from any first principle nor do they come full circle and arrive at a final principle. Its interpretations are not philologically hardened and sober, rather—according to the predictable verdict of that vigilant calculating reason that hires itself out to stupidity as a guard against intelligence—it overinterprets. Due to a fear of negativity *per se,* the subject's effort to break through what masks itself as objectivity is branded as idleness. Everything is supposedly much simpler. The person who interprets instead of unquestioningly accepting and categorizing is slapped with the charge of intellectualizing as if with a yellow star; his misled and decadent intelligence is said to subtilize and project meaning where there is nothing to interpret. Technician or dreamer, those are the alternatives. Once one lets oneself be terrorized by the prohibition of going beyond the intended meaning of a certain text, one becomes the dupe of the false intentionality that men and things harbor of themselves. Understanding then amounts to nothing more than unwrapping what the author wanted to say, or, if need be, tracking down the individual psychological reactions that the phenomenon indicates. But just as it is scarcely possible to figure out what someone at a certain time and place felt and thought, such insights could not hope to gain anything essential. The author's impulses are extinguished in the objective substance they grasp. The objective abundance of significations encapsulated within each spiritual phenomenon, if it is to reveal itself, requires from the person receiving them precisely that spontaneity of subjective fantasy that is chastised in the name of objective discipline. Nothing can be interpreted out of a work without at the same time being interpreted into it. The criteria of this process are the compatibility of the interpretation with the text and with itself and its power to release the object's expression in the unity of its elements. The essay thereby acquires an aesthetic autonomy that is easily criticized as simply borrowed from art, though it distinguishes itself from art through its conceptual character and its claim to truth free from aesthetic semblance. Lukács failed to recognize this when he called the essay an art form in a letter to Leo Popper that serves as the introduction to *Soul and Form*. Neither is the positivist maxim superior to Lukács' thesis, namely the maxim which maintains that what is written about art may claim nothing of art's mode of presentation, nothing, that is, of its autonomy of form. The positivist tendency to set up every possible examinable object in rigid opposition to the knowing subject remains—in this as in every other instance—caught up with the rigid separation of form and content: for it is scarcely possible to speak of the aesthetic unaesthetically, stripped of any similarity with its object, without becoming narrow-minded and *a priori* losing touch with the aesthetic object. According to a positivist procedure the content, once rigidly modelled on the protocol sentence, should be indifferent to its presentation. Presentation should be conventional, not demanded by the matter itself. Every impulse of expression—as far as the instinct of scientific purism is concerned—endangers an objectivity that is said to spring forth after the subtraction of the subject; such expression would thus endanger the authenticity of the material, which is said to prove itself all the better the less it relies on form, even though the measure of form is precisely its ability to render content purely and without addition. In its allergy to forms, as pure accidents, the scientific mind approaches the stupidly dogmatic mind. Positivism's irresponsibly bungled language fancies itself to be responsibly objective and adaquate to the matter at hand; the reflection on the spiritual becomes the privilege of the spiritless.

None of these offspring of resentment are simply untruth. If the essay disdains to begin by deriving cultural products from something underlying them, it embroils itself only more intently in the culture industry and it falls for the conspicuousness, success and prestige of products designed for the market place. Fictional biographies and all the related commercial writing are no mere degeneration but the permanent temptation of a form whose suspicion toward false profundity is no defense against its own turning into skillful superficiality. The essay's capitulation is already evident in Sainte-Beuve, from whom the genre of the modern essay really stems. Such works—along with products like the biographical sketches of Herbert Eulenberg, the German model for a flood of cultural trash-literature, all the way to the films about Rembrandt, Toulouse-Lautrec, and the Holy Bible—have promoted the neutralizing transformation of cultural artifacts into commodities, a transformation which, in recent cultural history, has irresistably seized up all that which in the eastern bloc is shamelessly called "the cultural heritage." This process is perhaps most striking in the instance of Stefan Zweig, who in his youth wrote several discerning essays, and who finally, in his book on Balzac, stooped so low as to describe the psychology of the creative artist. Such writing does not criticize basic abstract concepts, mindless dates, worn-out clichés, but implicitly and thereby with the greater complicity, it presupposes them. The detritus of an hermeneutic psychology is fused with common categories drawn from the *Weltanschauung* of the cultural philistines, categories like those of personality and the irrational. Such essays mistake themselves for that kind of feuilleton journalism with which mistake themselves for that kind of feuilleton journalism with which the enemies of form confuse the form of the essay. Torn itself becomes unfree and sets itself to work in the service of the socially performed needs of its customers. The moment of irresponsibility, in itself an aspect of every truth that does not exhaust itself in responsibility toward the status quo, will account for itself when faced with the needs of the established consciousness; bad essays are no less conformist than bad dissertations. Responsibility, however, respects not only authorities and committees but the object itself.

The bad essay chats about people instead of opening up the matter at hand; in this the essay form is somewhat complicitous. The separation of knowledge from art is irreversible. Only the naiveté of the literary entrepreneur takes no notice of this separation; he thinks of himself as at least an organizational genius, and simply chews up good art-works into bad ones. With the objectification of the world in the course of progressing demythologization, science and art have separated from each other. A consciousness in which perception and concept, image and sign would be one is not, if it ever existed, to be recreated with a wave of the wand; its restitution would be a return to chaos. Only as the completion of the mediating process would such a consciousness be thinkable, as a utopia just as that on which idealist philosophers since Kant had bestowed the name of creative intuition, and which failed them whenever actual knowledge appealed to it. When philosophy supposes that by borrowing from art it can do away with objectifying thought and its history—with what is usually termed the antithesis of subject and object—and indeed expects that being itself would speak out of a poetic montage of Parmenides and Jungnickel, it only approximates a washed-out pseudo-culture. With peasant cunning legitimated as primordiality, it refuses to honor the obligation of conceptual thought to which it has subscribed as soon as it has employed concepts in statements and judgments. At the same time its aesthetic element remains a second-hand thinned-out cultural reminiscence of Hölderlin or Expressionism, or possibly of *art nouveau,* simply because no thought can entrust itself to language as boundlessly and blindly as the idea of a primal utterance deceptively suggests. Out of the violence that image and concept do to one another in such writings springs the jargon of authenticity in which words tremble as though possessed, while remaining secretive about that which possesses them. The ambitious transcendence of language beyond its meaning results in a meaninglessness that can easily be seized upon by a positivism to which one thinks oneself superior; and yet, one falls victim to positivism precisely through that meaninglessness that positivism criticizes and which one shares with it. The playing chips of both are the same. Under the spell of such developments, language, where in the sciences it still dares to stir, approximates pseudo-art; and only that scientist proves, negatively, his fidelity to the aesthetic who in general resists language and instead of degrading the word to a mere paraphrase of his calculations prefers the charts that uninhibitedly admit the reification of consciousness and so produces a sort of form for reification without resorting to any apologetic borrowing from art. Of course art was always so interwoven with the dominant tendency of the Enlightenment that it has, since antiquity, incorporated scientific discoveries in its technique. Yet quantity becomes quality. When technique is made absolute in the art-work; when construction becomes total, eliminating what motivates it and what resists it, expression; when art claims to be science and makes scientific criteria its standard, it sanctions a crude preartistic manipulation of raw material as devoid of meaning as all the talk about "Being" (*Seyn*) in philosophical seminars. It allies itself with that reification against which it is the function of functionless art, even today, to raise its own however mute and objectified protest.

But although art and science have separated from each other in history, their opposition is not to be hypostatized. The disgust for anachronistic eclecticism does not sanctify a culture organized according to departmental specialization. In all of their necessity these divisions simply attest institutionally to the renunciation of the whole truth. The ideals of purity and cleanliness bear the marks of a repressive order; these ideals are shared by the bustle of authentic philosophy aiming at eternal values, a sealed and flawlessly organized science, and by a conceptless, intuitive art. Spirit must pass a competency test to assure that it will not overstep the offical culture or cross its officially sanctioned borders. The presupposition is that all knowledge can potentially be converted into science. Theories of knowledge that distinguish prescientific from scientific consciousness have therefore grasped this distinction as one of degree only. The fact that this convertibility has remained a mere assertion and that living consciousness has never really been transformed into scientific consciousness, points to the precariousness of the transition itself, to a qualitative difference. The simplest reflection on the life of consciousness would reveal just how little acts of knowledge, which are not just arbitrary premonitions, can be completely caught by the net of science. The work of Marcel Proust, no more lacking than Bergson's in scientific-positivistic elements, is a single effort to express necessary and compelling perceptions about men and their social relations which science can simply not match, while at the same time the claim of these perceptions to objectivity would be neither lessened nor left up to vague plausibility. The measure of such objectivity is not the verification of asserted theses through repeated testing, but individual experience, unified in hope and disillusion. Experience, reminiscing, gives depth to its observations by confirming or refuting them. But their individually grasped unity, in which the whole surely appears, could not be divided up and reorganized under the separated *personae* and apparatuses of psychology and sociology. Under the pressure of the scientific spirit and of an everpresent desire latent in every artist, Proust attempted, by means of a scientifically modelled technique, a sort of experimentation, to save or reproduce a form of knowledge that was still considered valid in the days of bourgeois individualism when the individual consciousness still trusted itself and was not yet worried about organizational censure: the knowledge of an experienced man, that extinct *homme de lettres,* whom Proust once again conjures up as the highest form of the dilettante. No one would have thought to dismiss as unimportant, accidental or irrational the observations of an experienced man because they are only his own and as such do not lend themselves readily to scientific generalization. Those of his discoveries which slip through the meshes of science certainly elude science itself. Science, as cultural science (*Geisteswissenschaft*), negates what it promises to culture: to open up its artifacts from within. The young writer who wants to learn at college what an art-work is, what linguistic form, aesthetic quality, even aesthetic technique are, will only haphazardly learn anything at all about the matter; at best he will pick up information ready culled from whatever modish philosophy and more or less arbitrarily slapped on to the content of works currently under discussion. If he turns, however, to philosophical aesthetics he is beleagured with highly abstract propositions that have neither a connection with the works he wants to understand, nor with the content after which he is groping. The division of labor within the *kosmos noetikos* (intelligible world) into art and science is not, however, altogether responsible for this situation; the internal boundaries between art and science will not be obviated by good will or over-arching planning. Rather, the spirit irretrievably modeled on the pattern of the control of nature and material production forgoes both recollection of any surpassed phase that would promise any other future and any transcendence vis-à-vis the frozen relations of production; this cripples the technical intelligence's own specialized procedure precisely with regard to its specific objects.

With regard to scientific procedure and its philosophic grounding as method, the essay, in accordance with its idea, draws the fullest consequences from the critique of the system. Even the empiricist doctrines that grant priority to open, unanticipated experience over firm, conceptual ordering remain systematic to the extent that they investigate what they hold to be the more or less constant preconditions of knowledge and develop them in as continuous a context as possible. Since the time of Bacon, who was himself an essayist, empiricism—no less than rationalism—has been "method." Doubt about the unconditional priority of method was raised, in the actual process of thought, almost exclusively by the essay. It does justice to the consciousness of non-identity, without needing to say so, radically un-radical in refraining from any reduction to a principle, in accentuating the fragmentary, the partial rather then the total. "Perhaps the great Sieur de Montaigne felt something like this when he gave his writings the wonderfully elegant and apt title of *Essays.* The simple modesty of this word is an arrogant courtesy. The essayist dismisses his own proud hopes which sometimes lead him to believe that he has come close to the ultimate: he has, after all, no more to offer than explanations of the poems of others, or at best of his own ideas. But he ironically adapts himself to this smallness—the eternal smallness of the most profound work of the intellect in face of life—and even emphasizes it with ironic modesty" [Lukacs, "On the Nature and Form of the Essay," in *Soul and Form,* 1974]. The essay does not obey the rules of the game of organized science and theory that, following Spinoza's principle, the order of things is identical with that of ideas. Since the airtight order of concepts is not identical with existence, the essay does not strive for closed, deductive or inductive, construction. It revolts above all against the doctrine—deeply rooted since Plato—that the changing and ephemeral is unworthy of philosophy; against that ancient injustice toward the transitory, by which it is once more anathematized, conceptually. The essay shys away from the violence of dogma, from the notion that the result of abstraction, the temporally invariable concept indifferent to the individual phenomenon grasped by it, deserves ontological dignity. The delusion that the *ordo idearum* (order of ideas) should be the *ordo rerum* (order of things) is based on the insinuation that the mediated is unmediated. Just as little as a simple fact can be thought without a concept, because to think it always already means to conceptualize it, it is equally impossible to think the purest concept without reference to the factual. Even the creations of phantasy that are supposedly independent of space and time, point toward individual existence—however far they may be removed from it. Therefore the essay is not intimidated by the depraved profundity which claims that truth and history are incompatible. If truth has in fact a temporal core, then the full historical content becomes an integral moment in truth; the *a posteriori* becomes concretely the *a priori,* as only generally stipulated by Fichte and his followers. The relation to experience—and from it the essay takes as much substance as does traditional theory from its categories—is a relation to all of history; merely individual experience, in which consciousness begins with what is nearest to it, is itself mediated by the all-encompassing experience of historical humanity; the claim that social-historical contents are nevertheless supposed to be only indirectly important compared with the immediate life of the individual is a simple self-delusion of an individualistic society and ideology. The depreciation of the historically produced, as an object of theory, is therefore corrected by the essay. There is no salvaging the distinction of a first philosophy from a mere philosophy of culture that assumes the former and builds on it, a distinction with which the taboo on the essay is rationalized theoretically. The intellectual process which canonizes a distinction between the temporal and the timeless is losing its authority. Higher levels of abstraction invest thought neither with a greater sanctity nor with metaphysical content; rather, the metaphysical content evaporates with the progress of abstraction, for which the essay attempts to make reparation. The usual reproach against the essay, that it is fragmentary and random, itself assumes the giveness of totality and thereby the identity of subject and object, and it suggests that man is in control of totality. But the desire of the essay is not to seek and filter the eternal out of the transitory; it wants, rather, to make the transitory eternal. Its weakness testifies to the non-identity that it has to express, as well as to that excess of intention over its object, and thereby it points to that utopia which is blocked out by the classification of the world into the eternal and the transitory. In the emphatic essay, thought gets rid of the traditional idea of truth.

The essay simultaneously suspends the traditional concept of method. Thought acquires its depth from penetrating deeply into a matter, not from referring it back to something else. In this the essay becomes polemical by treating what is normally held to be derived, without however pursuing its ultimate derivation. The essay freely associates what can be found associated in the freely chosen object. It does not insist stubbornly on a realm transcending all mediations—and they are the historical ones in which the whole of society is sedimented—rather the essay seeks truth contents as being historical in themselves. It does not concern itself with any supposed primeval condition in order to contravene society's false sociality, which, just because it tolerates nothing not stamped by it, ultimately tolerates nothing indicative of its own omnipresence and nec-

essarily cites, as its ideological complement, that nature which its own praxis eliminates. The essay silently abandons the illusion that thought can break out of *thesis* into *physis,* out of culture into nature. Spellbound by what is fixed and admittedly deduced, by artifacts, the essay honors nature by confirming that it no longer exists for human beings. The essay's Alexandrianism replies to the fact that by their very existence the lilac and the nightingale, wherever the universal net allows them to survive, only want to delude us that life still lives. The essay abandons the main road to the origins, the road leading to the most derivative, to being, the ideology that simply doubles that which already exists; at the same time the essay does not allow the idea of immediacy, postulated by the very concept of mediation, to disappear entirely. All levels of the mediated are immediate to the essay, before its reflection begins.

As the essay denies any primeval givens, so it refuses any definition of its concepts. Philosophy has completed the fullest critique of definition from the most diverse perspectives, including those of Kant, Hegel and Nietzsche. But science has never adopted this critique. While the movement beginning with Kant, a movement against the scholastic residues in modern thought, replaces verbal definition with an understanding of concepts as part of the process in which they are temporally embodied, the individual sciences insist stubbornly on the pre-critical job of definition—and do so for the sake of the undisturbed security of their operation. In this regard the neopositivists, who identify philosophy with scientific method, agree with Scholasticism. The essay, in contrast, takes the antisystematic impulse into its own procedure, and introduces concepts directly, "immediately," as it receives them. They gain their precision only through their relation to one another. In this, however, the essay gets some support from the concepts themselves. For it is a mere superstition of a science exclusively concerned with the appropriation of raw materials to believe that concepts are in themselves undetermined, that they are first determined by their definition. Science requires the image of the concept as a *tabula rasa,* in order to secure its claim to domination; the claim to be the sole power at the head of the table. Actually, all concepts are already implicitly concretized through the language in which they stand. The essay begins with such meanings and, itself being essentially language, it forces these meanings on farther; it wants to help language, in its relation to concepts, to grasp these concepts reflectively in the way that they are already unconsciously named in language. That effort is already envisaged by the procedure of meaning-analysis in phenomenology; only there the relation of concepts to language is fetishized. The essay remains as skeptical of this as it is of definition. Without apology the essay draws on itself the reproach that it does not know beyond a doubt just what is to be understood as the real content of concepts. For the essay perceives that the longing for strict definitions has long offered, through fixating manipulations of the meanings of concepts, to eliminate the irritating and dangerous elements of things that live within concepts. Yet the essay can neither do without general concepts—even language that does not fetishize the concept cannot do without concepts—nor does it treat them arbitrarily. It therefore takes the matter of presentation more seriously than do those procedures that separate out method from material and are indifferent to the way they represent their objectified contents. The *how* of expression should rescue, in precision, what the refusal to outline sacrifices, without, however, betraying the intended matter to the arbitrariness of previously decreed significations. In this Benjamin was an unequaled master. Such precision, however, cannot remain atomistic. Not less, but more than the process of defining, the essay urges the reciprocal interaction of its concepts in the process of intellectual experience. In the essay, concepts do not build a continuum of operations, thought does not advance in a single direction, rather the aspects of the argument interweave as in a carpet. The fruitfulness of the thoughts depends on the density of this texture. Actually, the thinker does not think, but rather transforms himself into an arena of intellectual experience, without simplifying it. While even traditional thought draws its impulses from such experience, such thought by its form eliminates the remembrance of these impulses. The essay, on the other hand, takes them as its model, without simply imitating them as reflected form; it mediates them through its own conceptual organization; it proceeds, so to speak, methodically unmethodically.

The way in which the essay appropriates concepts is most easily comparable to the behavior of a man who is obliged, in a foreign country, to speak that country's language instead of patching it together from its elements, as he did in school. He will read without a dictionary. If he has looked at the same word thirty times, in constantly changing contexts, he has a clearer grasp of it than he would if he looked up all the word's meanings; meanings that are generally too narrow, considering they change depending on the context, and too vague in view of the nuances that the context establishes in every individual case. Just as such learning remains exposed to error, so does the essay as form; it must pay for its affinity with open intellectual experience by the lack of security, a lack which the norm of established thought fears like death. It is not so much that the essay ignores indisputable certainty, as that it abrogates the ideal. The essay becomes true in its progress, which drives it beyond itself, and not in a hoarding obsession with fundamentals. Its concepts receive their light from a *terminus ad quem* hidden to the essay itself, and not from an obvious *terminus a quo*. In this the very method of the essay expresses the utopian intention. All of its concepts are presentable in such a way that they support one another, that each one articulates itself according to the configuration that it forms with the others. In the essay discreetly separated elements enter into a readable context; it erects no scaffolding, no edifice. Through their own movement the elements crystallize into a configuration. It is a force field, just as under the essay's glance every intellectual artifact must transform itself into a force field.

The essay gently defies the ideals of *clara et distincta perceptio* and of absolute certainty. On the whole it could be interpreted as a protest against the four rules that Descartes' *Discourse on Method* sets up at the beginning of modern Western science and its theory. The second of these rules, the decomposition of the object into "as many parts as possible and as might be necessary for its adequate

solution," formulates that analysis of elements under whose sign traditional theory equates a conceptual order with the structure of being. But the object of the essay, the artifact, refuses any analysis of its elements and can only be constructed from its specific idea; it is not accidental that Kant treated art-works and organisms analogously, although at the same time he insisted, against all romantic obscurantism, on distinguishing them. The whole is to be hypostatized into a first principle just as little as is the product of analysis, the elements. In opposition to both, the essay is informed by the idea of that interaction which in fact tolerates the question of elements as little as that of the elementary. Neither are the specific elements to be developed purely out of the whole, nor vice versa. The artifact is a monad, yet it is not; its elements, as such of a conceptual kind, point beyond the specific object in which they gather themselves. But the essay does not follow these elements to that point where they legitimize themselves, on the far side of the specific object; otherwise it would turn into a bad kind of infinity. Rather, the essay comes so close to the here and now of the object, up to the point where that object, instead of being simply an object, dissociates itself into those elements in which it has its life.

The third Cartesian rule, "to conduct my thoughts in such an order that, by commencing with the simplest and easiest to know, I might ascend by little and little, step by step, to the knowledge of the more complex," is sharply contravened by the form of the essay in that it begins with the most complex, not the most simple, which is in every instance the habitual. The essay as form will be a good guide for the person who is beginning to study philosophy, and before whose eyes the idea of philosophy somehow stands. He will hardly begin by reading the easiest writers, whose common sense will skim the surface where depth is called for; he will rather go for the allegedly difficult writers, who shed light on what is simple and illuminate it as a "stance of the mind toward objectivity." The naiveté of the student, to whom the difficult and formidable seems good enough, is wiser than the adult pedantry that admonishes thought with a threatening finger to understand the simple before risking that complexity which alone entices it. Such a postponement of knowledge only prevents knowledge. In opposition to the cliché of the "understandable," the notion of truth as a network of causes and effects, the essay insists that a matter be considered, from the very first, in its whole complexity; it counteracts that hardened primitiveness that always allies itself with reason's current form. Whereas science treats the difficulties and complexities of an antagonistic and monadologically split reality according to the expectation of this society by reducing them to simplifying models and then belatedly differentiates them with fabricated material, the essay shakes off the illusion of a simple, basically logical world that so perfectly suits the defense of the status quo. Its differentiation is no supplement, but its medium. Established thought readily ascribes that differentiation to the mere psychology of the author and then thinks that it has adequately dealt with it. The pompous scientific objections to oversophistication actually do not aim at the impertinently unreliable method but at the irritating aspects of the object which the essay reveals.

The fourth Cartesian rule that one "should in every case institute such exhaustive enumerations and such general surveys" that one "is sure of leaving nothing out"—this ultimate principle of systematic thought—reappears unchanged in Kant's polemic against Aristotle's "rhapsodic" thought. This rule corresponds to the particular objection to the essay that, in the words of the schoolmaster, it is not exhaustive, while it is clear that every object, and above all a cultural object, encloses endlessly many aspects, the choice among which can only be determined by the intention of the knower. The "general survey" would only be possible if it were determined in advance that the object in question can be fully grasped by the concepts which treat it; that nothing is left over that could not be anticipated by these concepts. Following that assumption, the rule requiring the exhaustive enumeration of the individual elements claims that the object can be presented in an airtight deductive system: a supposition of a philosophy of identity. As a practical technique of thought, as for example in its insistence on definition, the Cartesian rule has outlived the rationalistic theorem on which it was founded: a comprehensive general view and a continuity of presentation is urged even upon empirically open scientific procedure. In this fashion the intellectual conscience that should, in Descartes' philosophy, keep watch over the necessity of knowledge is transformed into the arbitrariness of a "frame of reference." In order to satisfy a methodological need and to support the plausibility of the whole, it becomes an axiomatic doctrine that is being set up as the gateway to thought while no longer being able to demonstrate its own validity or proof. Or, in the German version, it becomes a "project" (*Entwurf*) that, with the pathos-laden claim of reaching into being, simply suppresses its subjective conditions. The insistence on the continuity of thought's process tends to prejudice the inner coherence of the object, its own harmony. A continuous presentation would contradict material that is full of antogonisms as long as it did not simultaneously define continuity as discontinuity. Unconsciously and far from theory, the need arises in the essay as form to annul the theoretically outmoded claims of totality and continuity, and to do so in the concrete procedure of the intellect. If the essay struggles aesthetically against that narrow-minded method that will leave nothing out, it is obeying an epistemological motive. The romantic conception of the fragment as an artifact that is not complete in itself but openly striding into infinity by way of self-reflection, advocates this anti-idealist motive even in the midst of idealism. Even in its manner of delivery the essay refuses to behave as though it had deduced its object and had exhausted the topic. Self-relativization is immanent in its form; it must be constructed in such a way that it could always, and at any point, break off. It thinks in fragments just as reality is fragmented and gains its unity only by moving through the fissures, rather than by smoothing them over. The unanimity of the logical order deceives us about the antagonistic nature of that on which it was jauntily imposed. Discontinuity is essential to the essay; its concern is always a conflict brought to a standstill. While the essay adjusts concepts to one another by virtue of their function in the parallelogram of the forces of the materials, it shrinks back from the over-arching concept under which particular concepts should be subordinated; what the over-arching concept merely pretends to accomplish, the essay's method recognizes as insoluble while nevertheless attempting to accomplish it. The word "essay"—in which thought's utopia of hitting the bull's eye unites with the consciousness of its own fallibility and provisional nature—indicates something, like most historically surviving terminologies, about the form, the importance of which is magnified by the fact that it results not programmatically but as a characteristic of the form's groping intention. The essay must let the totality light up one of its chosen or haphazard features but without asserting that the whole is present. It corrects the isolated and accidental aspects of its insights by allowing them to multiply, confirm, and restrict themselves—whether in the essay's proper progress or in its mosaic-like relation to other essays; and it does so not by abstracting characteristic features from its insights. "Thus the essay distinguishes itself from a scientific treatise. He writes essayistically who writes while experimenting, who turns his object this way and that, who questions it, feels it, tests it, thoroughly reflects on it, attacks it from different angles, and in his mind's eye collects what he sees, and puts into words what the object allows to be seen under the conditions established in the course of writing" [Max Bense, "Über den Essay und seine Prosa," *Merkur* (1947)]. The discontent with this procedure, the feeling that it could all go on indefinitely, has its truth and untruth. Its truth, because in fact the essay comes to no final conclusions and makes explicit its inability to do so by parodying its own *a priori*; it is then saddled with the guilt that is actually incurred by those forms that erase every trace of arbitrariness. Yet that discontent with the essay is at the same time untrue because, as a constellation, the essay is not arbitrary in the way that it seems to a philosophical subjectivism which translates the exigencies of the object into those of its conceptual organization. The essay is determined by the unity of its object, together with that of theory and experience which have migrated into the object. The essay's openness is not vaguely one of feeling and mood, but obtains its contour from its content. It resists the idea of the master-work that reflects the idea of creation and totality. Its form follows the critical thought that man is no creator, that nothing human is creation. The essay, always directed towards artifacts, does not present itself as a creation; nor does it long for something all-embracing, the totality of which would resemble creation. Its totality, the unity of a form thoroughly constructed in itself, is that of non-totality; one that even as form does not assert the thesis of the identity of thought and thing, the thesis which in its own content the essay rejects. Freedom from the pressure of identity occasionally provides the essay (and this is lacking in official thought) with an aspect of ineffaceability, of inextinguishable color. In Simmel certain foreign words—*cachet, attitude*—betray this intention, without it being treated theoretically as such.

The essay is both more open and more closed than traditional thought would like. It is more open in so far as, through its inner nature, it negates anything systematic and satisfies itself all the better the more strictly it excludes the systematic; residues of the systematic in the essay such as the infiltration of literary studies with ready-made, wide-spread philosophical commonplaces, by which these studies try to make themselves respectable, are of no more value than psychological banalities. On the other hand, the essay is more closed in that it labors emphatically on the form of its presentation. The consciousness of the non-identity between presentation and presented material forces the form to make unlimited efforts. In that respect alone the essay resembles art; otherwise, on account of the concepts which appear in it and which import not only their meaning but also their theoretical aspects, the essay is necessarily related to theory. To be sure, the essay relates itself to theory as cautiously as to the concept. It neither deduces itself rigidly from theory—the cardinal fault of all Lukács' later essayistic work—nor is it a down-payment on future syntheses. Disaster threatens intellectual experience the more strenuously it ossifies into theory and acts as if it held the philosopher's stone in hand. And yet, intellectual experience itself strives by its own nature toward such objectification. This antinomy is mirrored by the essay. Just as it absorbs concepts and experiences, so it absorbs theories. However, its relation to them is not that of a standpoint. If this lack of a standpoint is no longer naive and dependent on the prominence of its objects; if the essay rather uses the relationship to its objects as a weapon against the spell of beginnings, it parodically practices the otherwise only feeble polemic of thought against mere standpoint philosophy. The essay swallows up the theories that are close by; its tendency is always toward the liquidation of opinion, even that from which it takes its own impulse. The essay remains what it always was, the critical form *par excellence*; specifically, it constructs the immanent criticism of cultural artifacts, and it confronts that which such artifacts are with their concept; it is the critique of ideology. "The essay is the form of the critical category of our mind. For whoever criticizes must necessarily experiment; he must create conditions under which an object is newly seen, and he must do so in a fashion different from that of a creative author. Above all the fragility of the object must be probed, tested; this is precisely the meaning of the small variation that an object undergoes in the hands of its critic" [Bense]. If the essay is accused of lacking a standpoint and of tending toward relativism because it recognizes no standpoint lying outside of itself, then the accusation implicitly contains the conception of truth as something "ready-made," a hierarchy of concepts, an image of truth that Hegel destroyed in his dislike of standpoints: in this the essay touches its polar opposite, the philosophy of absolute knowledge. The essay would like to cure thought of its arbitrariness by taking arbitrariness reflectively into its own procedure instead of masking it as spontaneity.

Hegelian philosophy, to be sure, remained trapped in the inconsistency that it criticized the abstract, over-arching concept, the mere "result," in the name of an internally discontinuous process, while at the same time, in the idealist tradition, speaking about dialectical method. Therefore the essay is more dialectical than the dialectic as it articulates itself. The essay takes Hegelian logic at its word: neither may the truth of the totality be played off immediately against individual judgments, nor may truth be reduced to individual judgments; rather, the claim of the particular to truth is taken literally to the point where there is evidence of its untruth. The risked, anticipatory, and incompletely redeemed aspect of every essayistic detail draws in other details as negation; the untruth in which the essay knowingly entangles itself is the element of its truth. Untruth certainly also resides in the essay's basic form, in its relation to what is culturally preformed and derived as though it were something in-itself. But the more energetically the essay suspends the concept of some first principle, the more it refuses to spin culture out of nature, the more fundamentally it recognizes the unremittingly natural essence of culture itself. Up to the present day, a blind natural interconnectedness, myth, perpetuates itself in culture. It is precisely this upon which the essay reflects: its proper theme is the interrelation of nature and culture. It is not by coincidence that, rather than "reducing" the artifact, the essay immerses itself in cultural phenomena as in a second nature, a second immediacy, in order through persistence to remove the illusion of immediacy. The essay deceives itself as little as the philosophy of origins about the difference between culture and that which underlies it. Yet for the essay, culture is not some epiphenomenon superimposed on being that must be eliminated, but rather what lies underneath is itself artificial (*thesei*), false society. Thus, for the essay, origins have no priority over the superstructure. The essay owes its freedom in its choice of objects, its sovereignty vis-á-vis all priorities of fact or theory to the circumstance that for it all objects are equally near the center, to the principle that casts a spell over everything. The essay refuses to glorify concern for the primal as something more primal than concern for the mediated, because to the essay primacy itself is an object of reflection, something negative. It corresponds to a situation in which the primal, as a standpoint of the mind within the falsely socialized world, becomes a lie. It covers a wide territory from the enshrinement as primal words of historical concepts extracted from historical languages, to academic instruction in "creative writing"; from craft-shop primitiveness to recorders and finger-painting: in every instance the pedagogical necessity sets itself up as a metaphysical virtue. Thought is not exempt from Baudelaire's rebellion of poetry against nature as a social reservation. Even the paradises of thought are only artificial, and in them the essay indulges. Since, according to Hegel's dictum, there is nothing between heaven and earth that is not mediated, thought may only hold true to the idea of immediacy by way of the mediated, but it becomes the prey of the mediated the instant it grasps directly for the unmediated. Cunningly, the essay settles itself into texts, as though they were simply there and had authority; without the illusion of the primal, it gets under its feet a ground, however dubious, comparable to earlier theological exegesis of holy writings. The essay's impulse, however, is the exact opposite of the theological; it is critical: through confrontation of texts with their own emphatic concept, with the truth that each text intends even in spite of itself, to shatter the claim of culture and move it to remember its untruth—the untruth of that ideological façade which reveals culture's bondage to nature. Under the glance of the essay second nature becomes conscious of itself as first nature.

If the truth of the essay gains its momentum by way of its untruth, its truth is not to be sought in mere opposition to what is ignoble and proscribed in it, but in these very things: in its mobility, its lack of that solidity which science demands, transferring it, as it were, from property-relationships to the intellect. Those who believe they must defend the intellect against the charge of a lack of solidity are the enemies of intellect: intellect itself, once emancipated, is mobile. As soon as it wants more than simply the administrative repetition and manipulated presentation of what already exists, it is somehow exposed; truth abandoned by play would be nothing more than tautology. Thus historically the essay is related to rhetoric, which the scientific mentality, since Descartes and Bacon, has always wanted to do away with; that is, until, appropriately in the age of science, rhetoric decayed and became a science *sui generis,* the science of communication. Of course rhetoric has always been a form of thought which accommodated itself to communicative language. It directed itself to the unmediated: the substitute-satisfaction of its audience. Yet the essay preserves in the very autonomy of its presentation, through which it distinguishes itself from the scientific mode of communication, traces of the communicative with which science dispenses. The pleasures which rhetoric wants to provide to its audience are sublimated in the essay into the idea of the pleasure of freedom vis-à-vis the object, freedom that gives the object more of itself than if it were mercilessly incorporated into the order of ideas. The scientific consciousness, which is directed against any anthropomorphic idea whatsoever, was always closely bound up with the reality principle and similarly hostile to happiness. While happiness is supposedly the goal of all domination over nature, it always appears to the reality principle as regression to mere nature. This can be seen even in the highest philosophies, including Kant's and Hegel's. Reason, in whose absolute idea these philosophies have their pathos, is denounced by them as something both pert and disrespectful as soon as it challenges the established system of values. Against this inclination the essay rescues a sophistic element. The hostility to happiness of official critical thought can be felt particularly in Kant's transcendental dialectic: it wants to eternalize the boundary between understanding and speculation, and, according to its characteristic metaphor, to prevent any "roaming around in intelligible worlds." While self-critical reason should, according to Kant, keep both feet planted on the ground, indeed should ground itself, it follows its innermost principle and seals itself off against anything new as well as against curiosity, the pleasure principle of thought, that is also upbraided by existential ontology. What in the content of his thought Kant projects as the goal of reason, utopia, the production of humanity, is disbarred by the form of his thought, the theory of knowledge; it forbids reason to go beyond the realm of experience, which, caught in the machinery of mere material and unchangeable categories, is reduced to that which always was. But the object of the essay is the new as something genuinely new, as something not translatable back into the staleness of already existing forms. By reflecting the object without doing violence to it, the essay silently laments the fact that truth has betrayed happiness and thus itself; this lament incites the rage against the essay. In the essay the persuasive aspect of communication, analogously to the functional transformation of

many traits in autonomous music, is alienated from its original goal and converted into the pure articulation of presentation in itself; it becomes a compelling construction that does not want to copy the object, but to reconstruct it out of its conceptual *membra disjecta*. But the objectionable transitions in rhetoric, in which association, ambiguity of words, neglect of logical synthesis all make it easy for the auditor, yoking him to the speaker's will: all these are fused in the essay with its truth-content. Its transitions disavow rigid deduction in the interest of establishing internal cross- connections, something for which discursive logic has no use. It uses equivocation neither out of slovenliness nor in ignorance of their proscription by science, but to clarify what usually remains obscure to the critique of equivocation and its mere discrimination of meanings: whenever a word means a variety of things, the differences are not entirely distinct, for the unity of the word points to some unity, no matter how hidden, in the thing itself; however, it is obviously not the case that this unity, as claimed by contemporary restorative philosophies, can itself be taken simply as a unity of linguistic affinities. Here as well the essay verges on the logic of music, the stringent and yet aconceptual art of transition; it aims at appropriating for expressive language something that it forfeited under the domination of a discursive logic which cannot be circumvented, but may be outwitted in its own form by the force of an intruding subjective expression. For the essay is not situated in simple opposition to discursive procedure. It is not unlogical; rather it obeys logical criteria in so far as the totality of its sentences must fit together coherently. Mere contradictions may not remain, unless they are grounded in the object itself. It is just that the essay develops thoughts differently from discursive logic. The essay neither makes deductions from a principle nor does it draw conclusions from coherent individual observations. It co-ordinates elements, rather than subordinating them; and only the essence of its content, not the manner of its presentation, is commensurable with logical criteria. If, thanks to the tension between presentation and what is presented, the essay—compared with forms which indifferently convey a ready-made content—is more dynamic than traditional thought, it is at the same time, as a constructed juxtaposition of elements, more static than traditional thought. In that alone rests the essay's affinity to the visual image; except that the essay's static quality is itself composed of tensions which, as it were, have been brought to a standstill. The slightly yielding quality of the essayist's thought forces him to greater intensity than discursive thought can offer; for the essay, unlike discursive thought, does not proceed blindly, automatically, but at every moment it must reflect on itself. This reflexion, however, does not only extend to the essay's relation to established thought, but also to its relation to rhetoric and communication. Otherwise the essay, while fancying itself meta-scientific, would become vainly pre-scientific.

The relevance of the essay is that of anachronism. The hour is more unfavorable to it than ever. It is being crushed between an organized science, on one side, in which everyone presumes to control everyone and everything else, and which excludes, with the sanctimonious praise of "intuitive" or "stimulating," anything that does not conform to the status quo; and, on the other side, by a philosophy that makes do with the empty and abstract residues left aside by the scientific apparatus, residues which then become, for philosophy, the objects of second-degree operations. The essay, however, has to do with that which is blind in its objects. Conceptually it wants to blow open what cannot be absorbed by concepts, or what, through contradictions in which concepts entangle themselves, betrays the fact that the network of their objectivity is a purely subjective rigging. It wants to polarize the opaque, to unbind the powers latent in it. It strives to concretize content as determined by space and time; it constructs the interwovenness of concepts in such a way that they can be imagined as themselves interwoven in the object. It frees itself from the stipulation of those attributes which since the definition in the *Symposium* have been ascribed to ideas; the notion that ideas "exist eternally and neither come into being nor pass away, neither change nor wane"; "A being eternally created in itself and for itself "; and yet the essay remains idea, in that it does not capitulate under the burden of mere being, does not bow down before what merely is. It does not measure what is by some eternal standard, rather by an enthusiastic fragment from Nietzsche's later life: "If we affirm one single moment, we thus affirm not only ourselves but all existence. For nothing is self-sufficient, neither in ourselves nor in things: and if our soul has trembled with happiness and sounded like a harpstring just once, all eternity was needed to produce this one event—and in this single moment of affirmation all eternity was called good, redeemed, justified, and affirmed" [Friedrich Nietzsche, *The Will To Power*]. This with the exception that the essay mistrusts such justification and affirmation. For the happiness that Nietzsche found holy, the essay has no other name than the negative. Even the highest manifestations of the intellect that express happiness are always at the same time caught in the guilt of thwarting happiness as long as they remain mere intellect. Therefore the law of the innermost form of the essay is heresy. By transgressing the orthodoxy of thought, something becomes visible in the object which it is orthodoxy's secret purpose to keep invisible.

Richard Kostelanetz

SOURCE: "Innovations in Essaying," in *Essaying Essays: Alternative Forms of Exposition,* edited by Richard Kostelanetz, Out of London Press, 1975, pp. 1-9.

[*An American author who is prolific in many genres, Kostelanetz is one of the major supporters of later twentieth-century avant-garde literature. He has edited several anthologies, including* The Young American Writers: Fiction, Poetry, Drama, and Criticism *(1967) and* Breakthrough Fictioneers *(1973), devoted to the work of young experimental artists. In* The End of Intelligent Writing: Literary Politics in America *Kostelanetz discusses what he perceives as a conspiracy against experimental artists by established literary groups. In the following essay, he explores alternative forms of the modern essay.*]

> It's odd that while the essay as a distinctive form in modern literature is so well cherished and enjoyed, it has received so little expert attention. Books upon the drama, upon poetry in its many

phases, upon the novel even, a thing comparatively of yesterday, are as leaves in Vallembrosa for number, but books on the essay—where are they?
> —Richard Burton, "The Essay as Mood and Form" (1901).

Essays differ from fiction in that they are about something particular, which remains outside the work itself. Stories and novels, by contrast, tend to fabricate an artificial universe of related activity that, though it reflects outside reality, defines itself as fictional through internal coherence and consistency. Compared with poets and novelists, essayists deal more directly with what is perceived to be "the real world"—the domains of personal experience and extrinsic circumstance. In practice, essays are used for exposition and description, as well as argument and narration, each purpose reflecting a different perspective upon both the materials of life, on one hand, and the processes of communication, on the other. The essay is literature's most common genre, as nearly all of us read more essays than poetry or fiction.

However, most writings in this genre are not called "essays" at all but something else, such as "history", "criticism", "articles", "reviews", "reports", "letters" or any of a score of other comparably less august terms. The epithet "essay" is commonly used as an honorific term to identify expositions that, for reasons of style, do more than merely expose (and thus can, for one measure, be reprinted in permanent books).

Since essays tend to document what the author knows before he begins to write, rather than what he discovers in the course of creation, they proceed not from interior understanding but from exterior knowledge. Whereas poetry or fiction represents an author's imagination and feeling, essays represent his thought (informed, no doubt, by imagination and feeling). Whereas poetry and fiction can be "unreal", essays must relate to verifiable experience; their frame of reference is exterior rather than interior. Essays are generally more premeditated than other literary genres; if stories and poems sometimes "write themselves", essays are customarily *written*, out of consciousness, in order to distill their authors' prior perceptions. It is true that essays resemble certain kinds of poetry, especially lyric expressions, in their creative orientation and manner of communication, as both are what Northrop Frye calls *thematic genres*: "Works of literature in which no characters are involved except the author and his audience".

However, essayists differ from lyric poets in favoring prose over verse, denotative language over connotative, declaration over suggestion, explicitness over mystery. Because an essay endeavors to communicate something definite about a particular subject, it honors the ideals of clarity, accuracy, and force; the kinds of obscurity and ambiguous interpretations that are tolerable in poetry or even in fiction are typically unacceptable in essays. Poems are usually shorter than essays, though size alone is not a crucial criterion, as essays vary in length from a single page to a whole book.

Essays are so common that literary scholars and critics

have scarcely examined the genre; that is one reason why formal differences in "essays" are so rarely perceived. Most people learned in their childhoods to write the classical form, historically epitomized by Montaigne (1533-92), in which a subject or thesis is announced in an opening paragraph (that echoes the essay's title), while the ensuing text of paragraphs, composed of sentences that are usually written in a direct and graceful style, provides a series of illustrations, anecdotes, digressions, possible objections and then refutations, customarily running from the least important to the most consequential. All of these parts ideally reenforce, with roughly syllogistic reasoning, the opening points, which are usually reiterated in the essay's final sentences. (Indicatively, each Montaigne essay was originally set as a single paragraph). Most of the essays written today, from newspaper editorials to academic monographs, approximately observe this traditional form.

Essays are so common that literary scholars and critics have scarcely examined the genre; that is one reason why formal differences in "essays" are so rarely perceived.

— *Richard Kostelanetz*

Those of us who have reported for newspapers had to master a different structure, customarily called "the pyramid style", which requires that all of the essential information be crammed into the opening paragraph, called "the lead", while the remaining paragraphs provide progressively less essential elaborations of the original data. As there is no definite conclusion in this kind of essay, one advantage of this form is that an individual report can be easily clipped, from the bottom up, to a length appropriate to its place and space in the newspaper. An older, more solemn variation of this inverted-funnel structure is the Ramean essay, favored by Puritan divines, who open with a theological proposition, parts of which are explained and elaborated in all subsequent statements, the essay as a whole proceeding from a universal assertion to numerous particulars. In other words, the subsequent axioms are derived from the initial proposition, for all of the lower bricks support, so to speak, the top of the pyramid. As a didactic form that structurally forbids caveats and counter-arguments, this is, of course, especially appropriate to an ideology that permits no doubts. The intellectual historian Perry Miller observed that this essayistic structure, like the Ramean logic informing it, was designed to represent "a formal description of the image of God", and this peculiar form influenced subsequent New England essayists.

Many of us have also written numerical essays, in which a succession of statements, customarily of equal import, are numbered, usually to emphasize the autonomy of (or distances between) the particular propositions. Legislative documents are usually expressed in this form, later parts often citing earlier ones (by number, rather than by subject). The philosopher Ludwig Wittgenstein used a more complex enumeration, adapted from scientific writing, to plot the differing relationships between his various assertions, the assumption being that a proposition preceded by the number "4.1", say, has a different relationship to "4.0" than the one prefaced "5.0". As Wittgenstein himself noted in his *Tractatus Logico-Philosophicus* (1921), "The propositions *n*. 1, *n*. 2, *n*. 3 are comments on the proposition no. *n*; the propositions *n.m.* 1, *n.m.* 2, etc. are comments on the proposition no. *n.m.*; and so on". This formally resembles the popular contemporary structure of separate vignettes—a narratively discontinuous form used in both reportage and fiction—which reflects, in turn, the impact of cinematic montage.

In a conventional non-tabloid newspaper, the multi-headlined front page can be regarded as a multi-part essay about the previous day's major events, but it would be more correct to say that this "essay on yesterday" ushers the page-turning reader into several different essays about particular occurrences—the discontinuous whole introducing the continuous parts. One reason why the daily newspaper is customarily read in random, undirected ways is that it lacks both a focused "beginning" and a definite "end". A newspaper is designed for "browsing" and "scanning", rather than for systematic scrutiny, like a book. Questionnaires with blank spaces require us to write comparably fragmented essays, our itemized responses ideally telling our examiner what he wants to know (usually about ourselves); and our everyday lives are filled with expository surrogates, such as resumés, chronologies, or tables of contents, in which a list, based upon a familiar convention, assumes the essayistic function of outlining an experience and/or defining a reality.

Among the other established essay forms are aphorisms, in which thoughts are not argued but asserted, ideally condensed into pithy, quotable sentences, which tend to be severe in tone, general in outlook, abstract in perspective, and disconnected in overall structure. The classic exemplars are Francis Bacon (1561-1626) in England, La Rochefoucauld (1613-80) in France, and Georg Christoph Lichtenberg (1742-99) and then Friedrich Nietzsche (1844-1900) in Germany, all of whom were attempting to transcend the leisurely paced prose of their predecessors. Contemporary aphorists of note include Norman O. Brown, especially in his most recent writings, Eric Hoffer (at his best), and the Frenchman Malcolm de Chazel. As the American poet and critic Richard Burton noted of Francis Bacon, "He clarified and simplified the prevailing diction, using shorter words and crisper sentences, with the result of a closer-knit, more sententious effect".

One popular contemporary essayistic form is the published interview, which customarily consists of a series of short, spatially separated, informally phrased remarks; but in spite of such virtues as spontaneity and accessibility, interviews nearly always suffer from expository simplicity and intellectual imprecision. Most of the letters we write have a similarly disconnected structure, as we tend, after an opening sentence of introduction or acknowledgment, to comment separately on points raised before and then to divulge new information or ask new questions, before concluding with a summary or a request for a reply. (The post-script, if any, is invariably articulated in a different tone, further separating it from "the body" of the letter).

Another increasingly familiar form reflects the influence of Charles Olson, an American poet who followed the examples of both Ezra Pound and William Carlos Williams in developing a stylistically impulsive, almost notational, tonally conversational, formally open-ended essay that, like comparable poetry, scrupulously eschewed facile formulations. In this kind of essaying, the author's confusions remain as evident as his conclusions, while the reader must "work" harder than usual in drawing the necessary linkages and definitions. Indeed, such a diffusion of energy and perception tends, especially in Olson's own prose, to make individual sentences (and the authorial personality) more prominent than any overarching theme.

Certain essayistic forms are not as new as they might initially seem. For instance, expository pastiche, which weaves quotations (and commentary) from disparate sources (and perspectives) rather closely resembles the traditional "commonplace books", in which a discriminating, wisdom-loving author collected all the choice aphorisms and personal observations that he thought worth preserving. (As this medium historically preceded the impact of the Montaigne essay, pre-Renaissance exposition echoed the digressive disconnectedness, along with the penchant for allusions, of the commonplace books). What is commonly called "the new journalism" represents an innovation not in essayistic form but in reportorial perspective, for its practitioners eschew pure objectivity to let their intelligences and emotional responses function actively in their reportage. While such "subjective realism", to use Richard Goldstein's term, may be innovative in strictly journalistic contexts, it is scarcely new in the tradition of essay-writing; even Montaigne, after all, was a rather active presence in his prose.

Indeed, nearly all of the great contemporary essayists, partially in rejection of the nineteenth-century (and academic) value of objectivity, emphasize authorial voice and informal tone, for it is the ideal, as Leslie A. Fiedler notes, "to achieve on the page the lucid, direct, orderly and vivid flow of conversation, which conversation, itself interrupted and half-hearted, seldom attains". What distinguishes the true essayist from the academic scholar is that the latter is enslaved to his circumscribed subject, while the essayist is inclined to let his mind roam free, his remarks typically tending to be more suggestive than exhaustive. As the essayist writes for a general public, rather than for an audience of fellow scholars, he talks about fairly familiar experience in the common tongue.

Although the word "essay" implies not only a liberal outlook but a willingness to experiment, most essays are written without consciousness of form (or formal possibility); for remarkably few practitioners have essayed how different forms might follow from traditional functions—or how a form might be invented to suit a particular function.

> With a new form comes a new content. Form thus determines content.

—Alexei Kruchenykh (c. 1916), as quoted in Vladimir Markov, *Russian Futurism* (1968).

Genuinely innovative essays are those that move decidedly beyond earlier kinds of essays—beyond not only the classical traditions of linear and/or aphoristic exposition but also beyond modernist essays with their emphasis upon personality and disjunctive structure. Innovative essays are those that confront not just dimensions of extrinsic reality but also the intrinsic, literary problem of how else essays might be written. Since they tend to be based upon radically different structural and stylistic assumptions, they expose twice over not only their particular subjects but also the reader's possible perception of printed communication. As essays depend upon organization, rather than fabrication, formal changes instill a re-essaying of a chosen subject; precisely because a different form reveals connections and perspectives that were not previously available, structural invention can change the essayist's thoughtful perception. (In the writing of fiction, by analogy, the shift from first-person narrator to third, or vice versa, performs a similar function of generating a new perspective upon fictional material.)

One kind of innovation is the conceptually resonant chart, which ideally realizes the essayistic function of compressing a large body of perceptions and/or contentions into remarkably little space. Though necessarily simplifying, a chart offers the compensating advantage of vividly documenting the entire picture—a concise image of the whole that reveals contrasts and connections that would not be so apparent if spread over many pages of prose. A chart is particularly useful in documenting multiple relations among several discontinuous elements. Since charts tend to lack explicit beginnings or definite ends, they cannot be read in the conventional way—steadily in one predetermined direction, at an even speed. Instead, charts must be read around and about, indeterminately, much like geography maps which are, after all, visual essays of a different sort; for a rich chart offers many levels of meaning, generalization and relatedness. (One reason why charts can pack so much perception into so little space is their avoidance of superfluous language; another is their allowance for sequential discontinuity.) Both maps and charts oblige the reader to draw his own lines between fixed points (e.g., to write his own connecting sentences, usually in his head), and both pack signposts that tell the reader when he has "finished" receiving the available message. Indeed, charts resemble the front pages of newspapers in that the whole is usually perceived before the parts are selectively examined. Evidence suggests that some charts are already too familiar for artistic use (e.g., box scores, financial statements) and that some kinds of perceptions and information are more conducive to charting than others. Nonetheless, there is no doubt that an effective chart is worth more than a thousand words. . . . Precisely in their emancipation from oral speech, essays in this graphic form realize a mediumistic integrity indigenous to printed communication.

Other experimental essays endeavor to excise those connectives that move the traditional essay along—conjunctions, adjectives, and comparably secondary linguistic baggage; and this syntactical diminution produces a skeletal essay, which likewise compresses large amounts of understanding into comparatively little space. One prominent practitioner in this vein is the literary critic Ihab Hassan, who speaks of his latest work, which he calls "paracriticism", as "experiments with a discontinuous medium, mixing literary and non-literary materials, mixing expository and other modes of discourse"; and he uses visual techniques, such as unusual typography and design, to represent emphases and relationships that would, in conventional essaying, generally be articulated in words. Especially in contrast to Hassan's more standard criticism, this new way of writing essays seems to "free" his critical mind to generate more perceptions and insights in far fewer pages. To discern how formal inventions can enhance critical intelligence, one need only compare Hassan's seminal essay on "POSTmodernISM" (1971) . . . with his stolid, book-length survey of *Contemporary American Literature* (1973), in which the conventions of academic style seem to confine, if not suppress, his knowledge and consciousness. In my judgment, the latter *says less* about its subject in 216 pages than the former does in 26. Given the prestige of "criticism" as a higher form of essaying, it is not surprising that some of the more substantial experimental essays should deal with the realities of contemporary culture. ("The best criticism will be", in John Cage's suggestion, "the doing of your own work [of art].") At the extreme of elliptical writing is, of course, essayistic minimalism, in which thoughts are compressed into isolated sentences that, like Ad Reinhardt's brilliant polemics, echo the traditions of aphorism and yet realize something decidedly different. One-page visual essays such as Kenneth Burke's "Cycle of Terms" or Robert Rauschenberg's "Autobiography" (1966) also suggest that aphorism is *not* the only form of essayistic minimalism.

Some innovative essays are entirely visual, consisting only of pictures (either drawn or photographed) that define a certain reality or document an event (rather than telling a story). And just as words can be visually enhanced to make a point that would not be possible in conventional language and or typography, so can the essayist employ an ideographic logic to add clarity, accuracy and force to an initially verbal statement. For instance, the circular, hand-drawn, intrinsically endless theses of my own "Manifestoes" (1970), make polemical points that would be less effective if printed in conventional horizontal lines (e.g., "The truth of fiction is the power of artifice is the truth . . ."). Not only do the structure and the content of this one-page essay complement each other, but the visual dimension also serves to introduce the reader to the modes of articulation characteristic of my own visual poetry. Visual essays in this form also move beyond post-Bauhaus exposition, epitomized by Moholy-Nagy's book on *Vision in Motion* (1947) and echoed by Marshall McLuhan and Quentin Fiore in *The Medium Is the Massage* (1967), in which rectangular blocks of type ("captions") accompany rectangular pictures, each "illustrating" the other.

Since this essay seems on the verge of suggesting that crystalline prose might be the least interesting virtue in contemporary essaying, I should add that one sure index of innovation in prose literature is a radically remarkable style. The distinguishing marks of Marvin Cohen's essays, for instance, stem from imposing a hyperbolic, idiosyncratic, essentially fictive style upon initially expository purposes. In truth, had not Sir Thomas Browne's "Urn Burial" (1658) been published so long ago, it would probably seem "new" today.

The American poet and critic J. V. Cunningham remarked, in *The Journal of John Cardan* (1960), "It is apparent that in our society we have too many choices", but that is untrue, particularly in the writing of essays. Expository writers trying to cope with the unprecedented forms of modern life presently have scarcely enough formal choices available to them. That also explains why discriminating readers rarely come across essays that "seem true" to the texture of contemporary experience of essays that resemble innovative art in challenging their capacities for perception and organization (simply because they must be "read" in unusual ways). It appears that the formal revolutions of artistic modernism have hardly affected the writing of essays, as remarkably few expository writers have considered how else "essays" might be written—or what might be the *most appropriate* form for confronting a particular experience. Especially in comparison to other literary genres, the art of the essay seems untouched by the great modern theme of increasing the pool of possibilities.

Phillip Lopate

SOURCE: "The Essay Lives—in Disguise," in *The New York Times Book Review,* November 18, 1984, pp. 1, 47-9.

[*Lopate is an American author who has published in a variety of genres. His collection of personal essays,* Bachelorhood: Tales of the Metropolis *(1981), derives its title from Lopate's feeling that his perceptions are shaped to a great degree by his marital status. In the following essay, Lopate discusses current popular forms of the essay and how they differ from the traditional essay form.*]

The informal or familiar essay is a wonderfully tolerant form, able to accommodate rumination, memoir, anecdote, diatribe, scholarship, fantasy and moral philosophy. It might have an elegant form or an amoebic shapelessness, held together by little more than the author's voice. Working in it liberates you from the structure of the "well-made" short story and allows you to ramble in a way that reflects the mind at work. You have an added freedom at this historical moment, because no one is looking over your shoulder. Nobody much cares. Commercially, essay volumes rank even lower than poetry.

I know, because my last book, a personal essay collection called *Bachelorhood*, received lovely critical notices but was less welcomed by booksellers, who had trouble figuring what niche or category to put it in. Autobiography? Short fiction? Self-help? I felt like telling them, "Hey, this category has been around for a long time—Montaigne, Addison and Steele, Hazlitt, remember? I didn't invent it." Yet, realistically, they were right: what had once been a thriving popular tradition had ceased being so. Readers who enjoyed the book often told me so with some surprise, because they didn't think they would like "essays." For them, the word conjured up those dread weekly compositions they were forced to write on the gasoline tax or the draft.

Essays are usually taught all wrong: instead of being celebrated for their delights as literature, they are harnessed to rhetoric and composition, in a two-birds-with-one-stone approach designed to sharpen the students' skills at argumentative persuasion. Equally questionable is the anthology approach, which assigns an essay apiece by a dozen writers along our latest notion of a representative spectrum. It would be much better to read six apiece by two writers, since the essay (particularly the familiar essay) is so rich a vehicle for displaying personality in all its willfully changing facets.

> **Essays are usually taught all wrong: instead of being celebrated for their delights as literature, they are harnessed to rhetoric and composition, in a two-birds-with-one-stone approach designed to sharpen the students' skills at argumentative persuasion.**
>
> — *Phillip Lopate*

Essays go back at least to classical Greece and Rome, but it was Michel de Montaigne, generally considered the "father of the essay," who first matched the word to the form around 1580. Reading this contemporary of Shakespeare (whom the Bard himself is rumored to have read), we are reminded of the original, pristine meaning and intention of the word, from the French verb *essayer*: to attempt, to try, to make an experimental leap into the unknown. Montaigne understood that, in an essay, the track of a person's thoughts struggling to achieve some understanding of a problem *is* the plot, is the adventure. The essayist must be willing to contradict himself (for which reason an essay is not a legal brief), to digress, and even to end up in an opposite place from where he started. Particularly in Montaigne's magnificent late essays, freefalls that go on for a hundred pages or more, it is possible for the reader to lose all contact with the shore, ostensible subject, top, bottom, until there is nothing to do but follow the companionable voice of Montaigne, thinking alone in the dark. Eventually, one begins to share his confidence that "all subjects are linked with one another," which makes "any topic equally fertile."

It was Montaigne's peculiar project, which he claimed rightly or wrongly was original, to write about the one subject he knew best: himself. As with all succeeding literary self-portraits—or stream-of-consciousness, for that matter—success depended on having an interesting consciousness, and Montaigne was blessed with an undulatingly supple, learned, skeptical, sane and self-attentive one. In point of fact, he frequently strayed onto other subjects, giving his opinion on everything from cannibals to coaches, but we do learn a lot of odd things about the man,

down to his bowels and kidney stones. "Sometimes there comes to me a feeling that I should not betray the story of my life," he writes. On the other hand: "No pleasure has any meaning for me without communication."

A modern reader may come away thinking that the old fox still kept a good deal of himself to himself. This is partly because we have upped the ante on autobiographical revelation, but also partly because Montaigne was writing essays, not confessional memoirs; and in an essay it is as permissible, as candid, to chase down a reflection to its source as to confess some past misdeed. In any case, having decided that "the most barbarous of our maladies is to despise our being," he did succeed via the *Essays* in learning to accept himself, by making friends with his mind.

Montaigne's generous development of the essay form, taking it to its outer limits right away, was also daunting. Afterward came an inevitable specialization, which included the very un-Montaignean split between formal and informal essays. It is difficult even now to draw a firm distinction between the two, because elements of one often turn up in the other, and because most of the great essayists were adept at both modes. However, the official version states that the formal essay derived from Francis Bacon and is (to quote the New Columbia Encyclopedia) "dogmatic, impersonal, systematic and expository" and written in a "stately" language, while the informal essay is "personal, intimate, relaxed, conversational, and frequently humorous."

Informal, familiar essays tended to seize on the parade of everyday life: odd characters, small public rituals, vanities, fashions, love and disappointment, the pleasures of solitude, reading, going to plays, walking the streets. It is a very urban form, and it enjoyed a terrific vogue in the coffeehouse London society of the 18th and early 19th centuries, when it enlisted the talents of such stylists as Jonathan Swift, Dr. Johnson (in his "Rambler" series), Addison and Steele, Charles Lamb, William Hazlitt, and the visiting American, Washington Irving. This golden age of the familiar essay was given a boost by the phenomenal growth of newspapers and magazines, all of which needed "smart" copy (of the kind inaugurated by the *Spectator* papers) that functioned as instructions on manners for their largely middle-class readership.

Much of the casual, *feuilleton* journalism of this period was not as memorable as Addison and Steele—it was, in fact, cynical hackwork. However, the journalistic situation was still fluid enough to afford original thinkers a platform within the public press. The British tolerance for eccentricity seemed especially to encourage their commentators to develop idiosyncratic, independent voices. No one was as cantankerously marginal, in his way, or as willing to write against the grain, as Hazlitt. His energetic prose registered a temperament that passionately, moodily swung between sympathy and scorn. Anyone capable of writing such a bracingly candid essay on "The Pleasures of Hating" could not—as W. C. Fields would say—be all bad. At the same time, Hazlitt's enthusiasms could transform the humblest topic, such as going on a country walk or seeing a prizefight, into descriptions of visionary wholeness.

What many of the best essayists have had—what Hazlitt had in abundance—was quick access to their own blood reactions, so that the merest flash of a prejudice or taste-discrimination might be dragged into the open and defended. Hazlitt's readiness to pass judgment, combined with his receptivity to new impressions, made him a fine critic of painting and the theater; but he ended by antagonizing all of his friends, even the benign, forgiving Charles Lamb. Not that Lamb did not have his contrary side. He too was singled out for "his perverse habit of contradiction," which helped give his prose its peculiar bite. Lamb's "Elia" essays are among the most pungent and funny in the English language.

How I envy readers of the *London Magazine*, who could pick up a copy in 1820 and encounter a new essay by Hazlitt, Lamb, or both. After their deaths, the familiar essay continued to attract gifted practitioners, like Robert Louis Stevenson, Thomas DeQuincey and Mark Twain, but somehow a little of the vitality seeped out of it, and by the turn of the century it seemed rather toothless and played out. As Stevenson confessed, "Though we are mighty fine fellows nowadays, we cannot write like Hazlitt." Perhaps the very triumph of the early essayists in exploiting the familiar essay form so variously contributed to its temporary decline.

The modernist esthetic was also not particularly kind to this sort of writing, relegating it to some genteel, antiquated nook, "belles lettres"—a phrase increasingly spoken with a sneer, as though implying a sauce without the meat. If "meat" is taken to mean the atrocities of life, it is true that the familiar essay has something obstinately nonapocalyptic about it; the very act of composing such an essay seems to implicate the writer in rationalist-humanist assumptions, which have come to appear suspect under the modernist critique.

Still, it would be unfair to pin the rap on modernism, which Lord knows gets blamed for everything else. One might as well "blame" the decline on what happened to the conversational style of writing. Familiar essays were fundamentally, even self-consciously, conversational: it is no surprise that Swift wrote one of his best short pieces on "Hints Toward an Essay on Conversation"; that Addison and Steele were always analyzing true and false wit; that Hazlitt titled his books *Table Talk, The Plain Speaker* and *The Round Table,* that Montaigne wrote his own "Of the Art of Discussion" or that Oliver Wendell Holmes actually cast his familiar essays in the form of breakfast table dialogues. Why would a book like Holmes's *The Autocrat of the Breakfast Table,* a celebration of good talk that was so popular in its time, be so unlikely today?

I cannot go along with those who say, "The art of conversation has died," because I have no idea what such a statement means. If it did pass on, it happened long before I came on the scene; and I hope I may be forgiven by those with longer memories for not knowing the difference between the real article and those pleasurable verbal exchanges in my life. No, conversation grows and changes as does language; it does not "die." What has departed is conversationally-flavored writing, which implies a speaking relationship between writer and reader. How many

readers today would sit still for a direct address by the author? To be called "Gentle Reader" or *"Hypocrite lecteur,"* to have one's arm pinched while dozing off, to be called to attention, flattered, kidded like a real person instead of a privileged fly on the wall—wouldn't most current readers find such devices archaic, intrusive, even impudent? Oh, you wouldn't? Good, we can go back to the old style, which I much prefer.

Maybe what has collapsed is the very fiction of "the educated reader," whom the old essayists seemed to be addressing in their conversational remarks. From Montaigne onward, essayists until this century have invoked a shared literary culture: the Greek and Latin authors and the best of their national poetry. The whole modern essay tradition sprang from quotation. Montaigne's *Essays* and Robert Burton's *The Anatomy Of Melancholy* were essentially outgrowths of the "commonplace book," a personal journal in which quotable passages, literary excerpts and comments were written. Though the early essayists' habit of quotation may seem excessive to a modern taste, it was this display of learning that linked them to their educated reading public and ultimately gave them the authority to speak so personally about themselves.

Such a universal literary culture no longer exists; we have only popular culture to fall back on. While it is true that the old high culture was never really "universal," excluding as it did a great deal of humanity, it is also true that, without it, personal discourse has become more barren. Not only is popular culture not strong enough to cleanse the air of narcissism, but the writer's invocation of its latest bandwagon successes, be it "Indiana Jones" or cabbage patch dolls, comes off as a pandering to the audience.

The average reader of periodicals becomes conditioned to digest pure information, up-to-date, with maybe a smattering of viewpoint disguised as objectivity, and is ill equipped to follow the rambling, cat-and-mouse game of contrariety played by the great essayists of the past. Very few American periodicals today (shall we say none?) support house-essayists to the tune of letting them write regularly and at comfortable length on whatever topics they may choose, however non-topical. The nearest thing we have to that are columnists. The best of these, like Russell Baker, Ellen Goodman and Leon Hale, are in a sense carrying on the Addison and Steele tradition; they are so good at their professional task of hit-and-run wisdom that I only wish they had the space sometimes to try their essayistic wings for real. The problem with the column format is that it becomes too tight and pat: One idea per piece.

Fran Lebowitz, for instance, is a very clever writer and one not afraid of presenting a cranky persona; but her one-liners have a cumulative sameness of effect that inhibits a true essayistic movement. In the future, I hope, her structures may become more receptive to self-surprise, so that she might say, with Lamb, "I do not know how, upon a subject which I began treating half seriously, I should have fallen upon a recital so eminently painful."

From time to time, I see hopeful panel discussions offered on "The Resurgence of the Essay." Yes, it would be very nice, and it may come about yet. The fact is, however, that very few American writers today are essayists primarily. A good number of the essay books issued each year are essentially random collections of book reviews, speeches, articles and prefaces by authors who have made a name for themselves in other genres. The existence of these collections owes more to the celebrated authors' desire to see all their words between hard covers than it does to any real devotion to the essay form. A tired air of grudgingly graceful civic duty hovers over many of these performances. Still, there are exceptions, like Cynthia Ozick, who seems to have brought her freshest energies to the essays in *Art and Ardor.*

I do not want to overstate the case for decline. While any boom in the essay will be held back by its commercial sluggishness, at the same time the form seems to have powerful attractions, esthetically at least, for many good writers working today. The essay offers the chance to wrestle with one's own intellectual confusion and to set down one's ideas in a manner both more straightforward and more exposed than in fiction (where it is always possible to attribute opinions to the characters or narrator instead of the author).

As for the familiar essay, it is very much alive today, if you choose to track it down under its various disguises. Shards of the form, more or less complete, appear in the work of newspaper columnists, as mentioned; under the protective umbrella of New Journalism (Joan Didion being the most substantial personal essayist to emerge from that training ground); in autobiographical-political meditations (Richard Rodriguez, Adrienne Rich, Ntozake Shange, Norman Mailer); naturalistic and regional essay-writing (John Graves, Wendell Berry, Lewis Thomas, Edward Abbey, Annie Dillard); humorous pieces (Max Apple, Roy Blount Jr., Calvin Trillin); literary criticism (Susan Sontag, Cynthia Ozick, Vivian Gornick, Seymour Krim); and travel writing (Mary McCarthy, Eleanor Clark and Paul Theroux). E. B. White is in a class of his own, as was the late William Saroyan. I am sure I have left out some other first-rate essayists and regret not having the space here to analyze the individual contributions of those listed; the point is, however, to indicate the range of activity and continuing viability of the form, especially when linked to a compelling subject that makes the reader temporarily overlook his or her hostility to essays.

In Europe, the essay stayed alive by taking a turn toward the speculative or philosophical, as seen in writers like Walter Benjamin, Theodor Adorno, Simone Weil, E. M. Cioran, Albert Camus, Roland Barthes, Czeslaw Milosz and Nicola Chiaramonte. All are offspring of the epigrammatic, belletristic side of Nietzsche, in a sense. This fragmented, aphoristic, critical tradition of essay writing is only now beginning to have an influence on American writing. One sees it, curiously, in much of the experimental new fiction—in Renata Adler, William Gass, Donald Barthelme, Elizabeth Hardwick, John Barth. Their novelistic discourse often reads like a broken essay, personal and philosophical, intermixed with narrative elements. The tendency of many post-modernist storytellers to parody the pedantry of the essay voice speaks both to their in-

tellectual reliance on that tradition and their unsureness about adapting the patriarchal stance of the Knower. This is why the essay must remain "broken" for the time being.

In one of the most penetrating discussions of the essay form, Georg Lukacs put it this way: "The essay is a judgment, but the essential, the value-determining thing about it is not the verdict (as is the case with the system) but the process of judging." Uncomfortable words for a non-judgmental age. The familiar essayists of the past may have been non-specialists—indeed, it was part of their attraction—but they knew how to speak with a generalist's easy authority.

That is precisely what we contemporary essayists have a hard time doing; we are too well aware of the superiority experts have over us in technical information. The last generalist-essayist who seemed able to write comfortably, knowledgeably, opinionatedly on everything under the sun was Paul Goodman; we may not see his like again soon.

Still, the willingness of contemporary writers to try the form, if not necessarily commit themselves to it, speaks well of its chances for survival. If we do offend, we can always fall back on Papa Montaigne's "Que scayje?": What do I know?

George Core

SOURCE: "Stretching the Limits of the Essay," in *Essays on the Essay: Redefining the Genre,* edited by Alexander J. Butrym, The University of Georgia Press, 1989, pp. 207-20.

[*In the following essay, Core discusses the development of fictional qualities in the modern essay.*]

The rise of the familiar essay in this country can be charted largely in the pages of a single magazine, and it will surprise no one when I say that the magazine is the *New Yorker.* In the fall of 1985 I published an issue of the *Sewanee Review* largely devoted to the *New Yorker* and to some of the major figures of its early history. One of the essays involved was "Modernism and Three Magazines: An Editorial Revolution" by Earl Rovit. In it Mr. Rovit argues that the *New Yorker, Time,* and the *Reader's Digest* all contributed significantly to modernism as we now know and understand it, particularly the transmission of information in the new world that emerged after World War I. And all developed distinctive formats and tones for conveying information. None of these magazines was engaged in strict reportage, as Rovit makes plain.

The distinctive contribution of the *New Yorker*—cartoons, news-breaks, casual pieces, and even poetry and fiction aside, not to mention the magazine's distinctive format, with neat columns of print swimming strongly through high seas of advertising—lies in the realm of the essay. This is worth reconsidering, even though in recent times the magazine's venerable and recently retired editor, William Shawn, allowed many of his staff writers—especially the writers of profiles and book-length serials involving public issues—to become wordy and otherwise self-indulgent.

In the *New Yorker's* salad days there were at least four great essayists working on the staff—E. B. White, who did more than any other person to establish the stylish tone of the magazine; James Thurber, who was probably the magazine's most famous and popular writer for most of his professional life; A. J. Liebling, who had the greatest range of the essayists involved and was the most learned and wily while superficially appearing to be the least sophisticated; and Joseph Mitchell, who is still connected with the *New Yorker,* but who has written little or nothing that has been published—at least under his own name— since his book on Joe Gould in 1965. I am deliberately neglecting other essayists whose stars are now blear—for instance, Frank Sullivan, S. J. Perelman, Robert Benchley, Wolcott Gibbs, and John Lardner. It would be stretching things to include such writers as Edmund Wilson, who were not primarily devoted to writing familiar essays.

Each of the writers in question wrote in many forms aside from the essay: you think immediately of Thurber's short stories and fables, of White's parodies and poems, of Liebling's critical articles on the press, of Mitchell's sketches in *My Ears Are Bent.* But each of these writers is essentially—quintessentially—an essayist; and in each case the writer's best essays often partake of the qualities of fiction.

I will not beat around the bush—or engage into providing a subtle inductive argument. My fundamental point is simple but worth restating: each of these essayists, in distinctive ways, moved the familiar essay toward fiction. Joseph Mitchell, who I sometimes think is the best of them as an essayist—even in some respects as a stylist—has in fact always called his essays *stories,* not reports or essays or memoirs or something else—*stories.* If you look in the author's note to *McSorley's Wonderful Saloon,* you will find that word; it reappears in the author's notes for *Old Mr. Flood* and *The Bottom of the Harbor.*

In the note to *Old Mr. Flood,* Mitchell, a taciturn man when it comes to his methods as a writer, becomes almost garrulous. He explains that "Mr. Flood is not one man; combined in him are aspects of several old men who work or hang out in Fulton Fish Market, or who did in the past." The author continues, making a sharp distinction: "I wanted these stories," he says, "to be truthful rather than factual, but they are solidly based on facts." (Had Alistair Reid's essays been presented in an equally honest light, his revelations about them a few years ago would not have been so controversial.)

In any case, as far as Mitchell is concerned, the bedrock providing the foundation for his essays is factual—a combination of scholarship and reportage, both of which are all but concealed, especially the scholarship. If you are interested in this aspect of the man whom Malcolm Cowley has called the paragon of reporters, read his "Joseph Mitchell: The Grammar of Facts" (1943) or Noel Perrin's "The Paragon of Reporters" (1983). Both Cowley and Perrin stress the factual side of Mitchell, a side that we see in all essayists worth their salt. Both also stress Mitchell's genius at depicting character, what Henry James would call "character expressed and exposed" (*The Future of the Novel*); indeed Mitchell's skill at depicting reality springs from his inveterate interest in character, especially the

characters of eccentric folk who often remind you of Dickens. Cowley clinches his clinically exact description of Mitchell's methods as a writer by observing: "You might say that he tries—often successfully—to achieve the same effects with the grammar of hard facts that Dickens achieved with the rhetoric of imagination." The *grammar of hard facts*—that is a phrase for us to conjure with. Perrin shrewdly amplifies Cowley's statement in saying, quite properly: "Part of Joe Mitchell's secret" is "that whatever he writes about he tends to know better than anybody else in the world."

For some years it has been rumored that Joseph Mitchell has another book in the making—probably a Mitchell Reader. I hope this rumor is true because such a book would naturally and inevitably bring him back into the eye of the reading public and make it plain that he is one of the great essayists of our time. Were I editing such a reader, I would probably make it a book of his essays in character, showing how he—to quote James again—has "the trick of investing some conceived or encountered individual . . . with the germinal property and authority" (*The Art of the Novel*). For Mitchell, of course, those people are usually connected with what A. J. Liebling would unabashedly call low life or what some of us might be inclined to call little people, but in the author's note to *McSorley's* Mitchell calls this latter phrase "patronizing and repulsive" and says that there are no "little people" in his work. "They are as big as you, whoever they are," he adds. Some of these people—and the stories about them—appear in "Professor Sea Gull," his first account of Joe Gould; "Mazie," which Brooks and Warren thought plenty good enough to anthologize; in "King of the Gypsies"; and in "A Sporting Man," all from *McSorley's*; they also appear in the whole of *Mr. Flood* and in most of *The Bottom of the Harbor.* These and other pieces by Mitchell on New York City add up to an informal history of that great city, especially the waterfront, the Bowery, and other places outside the borough of Manhattan. The key to this history lies in the accumulated experience of the people about whom Mitchell has chosen to write. And, as James tells us, "a character is interesting as it comes out, and by the process and duration of that emergence; just as a procession is effective by the way it unrolls, turning to a mere mob if all of it passes at once." A character like Mazie, whom Perrin has deliciously characterized as the toughtalking Mother Teresa of the Bowery, is emphatically one such germinal figure. Mazie is revealed largely through her conversation, and few authors deriving from any time or place and working in any literary mode can rival Mitchell for the exactness of his dialogue. Consider her closing speech. Mazie is speaking of the bums who occupy her days and nights and whom she mothers in a spirit of exasperation and affection: "To hear them tell it," she says, "all the bums on the Bowery were knocking off millions down in Wall Street when they were young, else they were senators, else they were the general manager of something real big, but, poor fellers, the most of them they wasn't ever nothing but drunks" (*McSorley's*), says the Lady from Boston. One of her "clients," whom she calls Pop, says of himself: "I come from a devout family of teetotallers. . . . They was thirteen in the family, and they called me the weakling because I got drunk on Saturday nights. Well, they're all under the sod. Woodrow Wilson was President when the last one died, and I'm still here drinking good liquor and winking at the pretty girls." In that brief monologue we get the sad history of a protracted and largely wasted life.

A. J. Liebling's world has much in common with Mitchell's, but it is far broader, encompassing France, North Africa, Louisiana, the West, and still other places in addition to New York City. His range of subjects is also broader than Mitchell's. The most obvious difference between Joe Liebling and Joe Mitchell is that Liebling is often the protagonist of his essays, while Mitchell is never more than a bystander and is often invisible. In this sense John McPhee, the greatest of the present generation of *New Yorker* essayists, learned more from Mitchell's retiring ways than from Liebling's cheerful and unabashed egotism. McPhee, as I think his skillful editor William Howarth would agree, has also learned a vast amount about the use of fact from Mitchell.

Liebling's earmarks are the most distinctive of the writers we are considering with the possible exception of White. And let us not forget that each of these men has a strong and distinct signature. What are the elements of Liebling's signature? As I have already suggested, he has the same gusto for life, especially low life, that marks Mitchell's; and Liebling's collection of human instances is at least as broad as Mitchell's, but Liebling does not sink himself so deeply into the character of others as Mitchell regularly and naturally does. Fact is an important element in Liebling—but, again, it is not as extensive or essential as in Mitchell. Liebling regarded himself as a reporter, "a chronic, incurable, recidivist reporter," and he once said, "a good reporter, if he chooses the right approach, can understand a cat or an Arab." We may ask ourselves what approaches Liebling chose.

In certain ways Liebling pushes us still closer to fiction than Mitchell, in part because his facts are a good deal harder for the famous Checking Department of the *New Yorker* to verify.

In writing of himself and the press Liebling said: "Sinbad, clinging to a spar, had no time to think of systematic geography. To understand perfectly a new country, new situation, the new characters you confront on an assignment, is impossible. To understand more than half, so that your report will have significant correlation with what is happening, is hard. To transmit more than half of what you understand is a hard trick, too, far beyond the task of the so-called creative artist, who if he finds a character in his story awkward can simply change its characteristics." Liebling then adds: "Even to sex, *vide* Proust and Albertine. Let him try it with General DeGaulle." Liebling continues: "It is possible, occasionally, to get something completely right—a scene, or a pattern of larceny, or a man's mind. These are the reporter's victories, as rare as a pitcher's home runs" (*The Most of A. J. Liebling*).

If we look for a moment at a characteristic piece by Liebling, we can see what engages this writer's attention and affection. "Tummler," one of the best pieces that he ever published, deals with a con man named Hymie Katz, who,

as one of his admirers says, "is a man what knows to get a dollar." Hymie's specialty is opening nightclubs; in between the flush times when one of his clubs is open and making money he plays the horses and runs various hustles of dubious legality; he is at his most imaginative and enterprising with the nightclub. Liebling quickly and surely gives us the facts involving such a business—especially how Hymie uses his money, which is all borrowed, to get the enterprise going. After explaining the various details Liebling says: "Despite all Hymie's forethought, exigencies sometimes arise which demand fresh capital." So the promoter then takes in partners. Liebling now writes of his hero: "He usually bilks his partners for the principle of the thing. He is not avaricious. Dollars, Hymie thinks, are markers in a game of wits as well as a medium of exchange. He refuses to let his partners keep any markers." Business goes nicely for a while, but as Liebling explains, "finally the creditors close in, or the entertainer either loses his brief vogue or goes on to a large club. Hymie returns to the horse-tipping business. He has written one more chapter in his saga." That saga, as Liebling deftly reveals it, includes Hymie's early life and an unforgettable vignette with his aged father (who when he comes out to meet his son locks the door of his jewelry shop from the outside so as to converse with his son safely on the sidewalk). What Liebling has presented in a 5,000-word essay might well be a picaresque novel.

Liebling's war reportage, with himself as a humorous observer of action that is often distinctly unhumorous, has novelistic qualities as well. Again the emphasis is on character, and like a fiction writer Liebling often concentrates on what James calls the "great central region of passion and motive, of the usual, the inevitable, the intimate." You find these qualities in "Quest for Mollie," "Madam Hamel's Cows," "My Little Louise," and many other pieces that he wrote about World War II. He told us much more about that war than any other reporter and probably any other writer, including various novelists, Hemingway among them. An essay such as "That Will Stay with You," published in 1949, could well be presented now as fiction. In it Liebling comes to an earned conclusion better than what you can find in most short stories as his protagonist, Marvin Bloom, a survivor of the carnage at Omaha Beach, asks a bartender: "Mac, did you ever see a deck covered with blood and condensed milk, all mixed together?" "No," replies the bartender, who adds: "Well, that'll stay with you." This image—of blood and condensed milk mixed together—is one of this reporter's victories. This piece, unlike the other war pieces that I have mentioned, does not appear in *The Road Back to Paris* or his other collections about World War II and returning to France. Instead it is derived from a long report, "Cross-Channel Trip," in which Liebling plays a considerable part; it is one of the best essays in *Mollie & Other War Pieces*. But Liebling the reporter does not appear as a character in "That Will Stay With You": he has disappeared.

All of this is to say that with Liebling we not only find the exact ear for dialogue and the profound interest in character, especially low-life characters, that characterize Mitchell's essays, but we also encounter other fictive qualities such as the controlling image. On occasion we even get the rudiments of plot.

With E. B. White we are confronted by still another breed of cat. In some ways White is the slyest and subtlest of the *New Yorker*'s writers. He offhandedly tells us more about the familiar essay than nearly anybody, including those who make heavy weather of the subject. "Only a person who is congenitally self-centered has the effrontery and the stamina to write essays," he writes in prefacing his selected essays. "Some people," he goes on to observe, "find the essay the last resort of the egoist, a much too self-conscious and self-serving form for their taste; they feel it is presumptuous of a writer to assume that his little excursions or his small observations will interest the reader" [*Essays of E.B. White,* 1977]. With such an author we may wonder how his essays may partake of fiction. Nevertheless they often do enter into the realm of fiction—and not merely when he is unwinding a grown-up children's story such as *Charlotte's Web.* "Death of a Pig," one of White's best and most characteristic essays, is in some respects a short story, an account of a comical and pathetic reversal in the usual pattern of buying a pig in the spring to fatten through the summer and butcher in the fall. White, by identifying himself with the pig, is able to present an unconventional parable, a melodrama, punctuated by moments of hilarity and pathos, about life and death. "The Death of a Pig" complements not only *Charlotte's Web* but what is White's most famous essay, "Once More to the Lake," which among other things is devoted to generational likenesses and indifferences as seen through the lens of memory. At the end of "Once More to the Lake," as you will remember, we are given an image of death and of life as White's ten-year-old son, Joel, buckles the cold soggy swimming trunks about his vital parts and his father, watching, feels a chill in the groin. It is a perfect image that compares with Liebling's image of blood and milk.

My own favorite of White's essays is the first part of "The Ring of Time," a superficially transparent allegory about the circus as a microcosm of life; the ring of time as presented here is a beautifully sustained image and symbol. White gives us at the same time a running commentary about his efforts as "recording secretary" or "writing man . . . charged with the safekeeping of all unexpected items of worldly or unworldly enchantment." The success of the moment—and of White's account of it—depends largely on the unrehearsed nature of the girl's ride as she stands easily on the back of a horse and turns around the ring. At this moment in her life, White tells us, "She believes she can go once around the ring . . . and at the end be exactly the same age as at the start."

Again the image has fictive precision and rightness, and with a change here and there we might well have a short story—say, a tale turning on a conflict between the girl and her mother or the mother and the circus's manager.

The poetry of White's essays is obvious here, as it is in "Once More to the Lake," "The World of Tomorrow," "The Years of Wonder," most of the pieces in *One Man's Meat,* and many another essay. White is a poet of the city—of Manhattan—just as much as he is a poet of the country, particularly the salt water country in his part of Maine. White, following in the line of Thoreau, has done much to celebrate nature and in so doing to sound the alarm about what we are doing to the environment, a theme sounded in the work of many of the great American essayists of our century from John Muir to Loren Eiseley to Edward Hoagland and John McPhee. But White is a subtler reformer than most of these writers, especially Thoreau, as you will see in even an antiutopian essay such as "The Morning of the Day They Did It."

The element that you regularly encounter in White's essays, as in Mitchell's and Liebling's, one that strikes you as quintessentially fictive is scene. Scene is the sine qua non of fiction, as nearly anyone—perhaps even the most "advanced" theoretical critics of the present time—will readily admit who is not daft. Scene separates the true fiction-writer from the popular novelist, whether the latter writes thrillers or detective fiction or drugstore romance. The popular or pulp writer cannot write a scene if his or her life depends upon it: on that you may bet this month's mortgage payment and have a sure thing. Mitchell, Liebling, and White can; and that is especially true of Mitchell and Liebling. What this all boils down to is explained by James in the preface to *The Ambassadors*: "To report at all closely and completely of what 'passes' on a given occasion is inevitably to become more or less scenic."

James, in praising Turgenev, approaches scene from an entirely different perspective. Of course, as James, Percy Lubbock, and other critics have stressed, what is of first importance in fiction is "the dramatic incident or scene," and "to the scene . . . all other effect" should be "subordinated." (I quote Lubbock's *The Craft of Fiction.*) Yet James sees Turgenev's brilliance—what he calls the constant "element of poetry"—as depending upon "the mere particularized report" (*The Future of the Novel*). It is that cumulative effect gotten through the closely observed and carefully chosen detail that characterizes the best essays of Mitchell, Liebling, and White.

What, then, you may ask, separates the best essays of these writers—say Mitchell's "Mazie," "King of the Gypsies," and *Old Mr. Flood*; Liebling's "Tummler," "Quest for Mollie," and "That Will Stay with You"; and White's "The Ring of Time," "Death of a Pig," "Once More to the Lake," "The Years of Wonder," and "The World of Tomorrow"—from fiction? The short answer is that often there is no definite line, as in Liebling's "That Will Stay with You," which you will recall my saying was dramatized from an earlier and more straightforward journalistic account of the same essential incident. Part of the answer is that your ordinary essay, no matter how good, doesn't have a plot in the usual sense that we apply that term to fiction. (Indeed, as White says in his foreword, "Most of my essays have no plot structure.") It may very well have all the constituents that I have mentioned—character presented in the round, cumulative use of related representative detail, the scenic element (including exactly rendered dialogue), a controlling image or extended metaphor—without being fiction in the traditional or classic sense; but it will probably lack the pattern of conflict, crisis, and resolution that is imbedded in the best fiction;

and of course the author will usually be standing four-square in the middle of the essay or off to the side of the action (but still unmistakably there)—and, of greater importance, the essay will be in large part about him or her and about the author's reaction to the action as it is told and interpreted.

All of this is to say that the familiar essay, as I have been measuring it, is finally closer to reportage on the one hand and to autobiography on the other than it is to fiction, even if, on occasion, the essayist strays from fact into making up details and into taking fictive license with his or her material.

To some of you—perhaps to all of you—I have mounted my hobbyhorse and ridden simultaneously and furiously off in all directions. What have you been driving at, you may quite properly ask? Or where does this leave us?

You will remember that I promised a little history of the rise of the familiar essay as seen through the *New Yorker*'s best essayists. I deliberately did not consider James Thurber, whose work is now fading badly; to some extent I scanted E. B. White, now the most famous of the four; I stressed two—Joseph Mitchell and A. J. Liebling who have been neglected, especially Mitchell.

What these writers and others nearly as good accomplished was to make the essay into an art form. They did this, on the whole, with no illusions. As late as 1977 White could say, with some asperity: "I am not fooled about the place of the essay in twentieth-century American letters—it stands a short distance down the line. The essayist, unlike the novelist, the poet, and the playwright, must be content in his self-imposed role of second-class citizen. A writer who has his sights trained on the Nobel Prize or other earthly triumphs had best write a novel, a poem, or a play, and leave the essayist to ramble about, content with living a free life and enjoying the satisfactions of a somewhat undisciplined existence." When White wrote those lines, he must have remembered his old friend Thurber's pretensions about winning the Nobel Prize for literature. Toward the end of his life Thurber thought of himself as the Henry James or Mark Twain of the *New Yorker* and whined about being neglected when in fact he had been lionized by T. S. Eliot and others. Then Thurber began believing his press notices.

Liebling, like White, never expected to be lionized. He enjoyed his position as a "mere" reporter and essayist, often poking fun at literary critics and other academic types, saying for instance, "I feel as naked as a critic without a fellowship, or a professor of communications without a grant" (*The Most*), or using locutions like "as the boys on the literary quarterlies would say" often indulging himself in self-deflating jokes. One of the best of these jokes appears in a boxing sketch in which Liebling says: "I have been to the country myself. I went to a college in New Hampshire [Dartmouth]. But I seldom mention this, because I would like to be considered quaint and regional, like William Faulkner." In some respects Liebling was the Faulkner of American essayists, but in other ways Mitchell is even closer to that honor than Liebling.

In any event—to remount my hobbyhorse—these writers gave the informed general reader the familiar essay in all the forms that White mentions when he says: "There are as many kinds of essays as there are human attitudes or poses, as many essay flavors as there are Howard Johnson ice creams." "The essayist," White continues, "can pull on any sort of shirt, be any sort of person, according to his mood or his subject matter—philosopher, scold, jester, raconteur, confidant, pundit, devil's advocate, enthusiast." We see most of these poses in these writers—particularly Liebling, who fulfills them all.

All of this is well and good for the reader such as myself who repairs to the essay in the long innings of sleepless nights, but it is far better for the essayists who have inherited the mantels of White, Mitchell, Liebling, and Company—and who are trying to become worthy of their fathers and are too intelligent to think that parricide is the appropriate answer to what is now grandly called the Anxiety of Influence.

The leading essayists among us now, whether they be chiefly essayists or writers of another ilk, have profited immensely from the example of their immediate predecessors—note that I refuse to use Harold Bloom's term precursor—and can draw on that accumulated capital. One reason that ours is the Age of the Essay, as I have said in print once or twice and will now say again, is that such writers as Joan Didion, M. F. K. Fisher, John McPhee, Larry L. King, Edward Hoagland, Noel Perrin, Richard Selzer, Jane Kramer, Joseph Epstein, Roy Reed, Lewis Thomas, Carol Bly, and many another good essayist has profited by the examples of the writers we have been considering thus far. I do not mean to suggest that any of these writers is slavishly following in the paths of White, Mitchell, Liebling, and the rest; and I think it good that one can find first-rate familiar essays in a wide range of periodicals now—not merely in, say, the *New Yorker* or the *Atlantic* but also in the *Virginia Quarterly Review*, the *Yale Review*, the *American Scholar*, and other quarterlies. There are more good essayists now than fifty or even ten or twenty years ago, and their work is appearing in a greater variety of magazines. That development is all to the good. For some time the *New Yorker* came close to dominating the field so far as the familiar essay is concerned.

For anyone who is still with me and who wants to know my answer to the question Are any of our current essayists as good as Mitchell, Liebling, and White? I would say no; but some of them at their best—especially McPhee, King, and Epstein—come very close—and reasonably often—to rivalling these classic essayists. And why shouldn't they? For, as I have said, they have the example of this earlier generation. The same thing is beginning to look true for some of the best younger essayists in this country—and my list is by no means exhaustive. Indeed it is short largely owing to my own spotty reading. Robert Atwan could easily expand my list. I would call the names of Sam Pickering, Rob Schultheis, Alec Wilkinson, Mark Singer, and Bill Barich in this connection, knowing all too well that there are at least as many other good younger essayists.

These essayists have learned the essential secret that any good writer must always discover in order to be good and to find his or her own niche. This matter applies equally well to any other writer—but especially to the fictionist. The writer of fiction, long or short, must post himself or herself precisely in order to examine and dramatize the fictive country that is the individual writer's bailiwick. The same applies to the familiar essayist: once that writer finds the right post of observation or the right place on the stage, he or she can see the world in a fresh and distinctive way and can find the right tone in which to write about that world. If you look at some of the early work of the younger writers whom I have just mentioned—say Pickering's essays predating those in his first collection, *A Continuing Education,* or Wilkinson's *Midnights,* or Barich's *Laughing in the Hills,* you can see the author groping hesitantly toward finding his voice by searching for the precise place to pose himself. (Pickering has found the right distance, the title of his new collection.) With Liebling or White that place, you will remember, is center stage; but with Mitchell it is just barely on the stage—or perhaps in the wings or even outside the theater. The familiar essayist today is often in the middle of things, and in this sense the familiar essay is often deeply autobiographical, as you would expect. But the world of the essayist is often simply a small part of the world outside that is being encountered, and the familiar essay of late has involved everything from the environment, as I have said, to matters seldom discussed in this way or from this vantage until recently—moonshiners, science and medicine, betting, life in England, cowboying, oranges, Monopoly, small hydroelectric dams, houses of prostitution, popular entertainers (including politicians), police work, and countless other subjects.

In general it is abundantly clear that the essay's limits have been extended and amplified in technical and substantive senses. All of this is obvious if you read but a few of the best essays published in the last five or ten years. You can read the *New Yorker* or other magazines or Robert Atwan's *Best American Essays* or the work as it has appeared in collections by the writers that I have mentioned.

In other words the familiar essay is alive and well. To my mind it is not merely alive and well but is flourishing. It is battening because this form of the essay is so constituted that it can bear additional bulk and weight without strain, provided that writers like McPhee and Selzer and Didion and Epstein continue to carry out their business as they already have done brilliantly. That business depends not only upon their having marshalled the various techniques that I have discussed but upon their marshalling the facts that will always provide the bedrock that must underlie any familiar essay. The best essays in this vein have always been bound to what E. B. White called the eloquence of fact; McPhee and the others have not forgotten that.

Throughout this essay I have quoted James, and I cannot resist using his language to point out a difficulty in my own presentation—what he would have called a misplaced middle, which is to say that my scrutinies of Mitchell, Liebling, and White—of the classic essay as it appeared in the salad days of the *New Yorker* magazine—have been too detailed in comparison to what has followed. You must therefore take the subsequent generalizations largely on faith.

What I have attempted to show—and I believe that I have shown—is that the best writers working regularly in the broad and deep vein that we are calling the familiar essay use the techniques of fiction as well as the techniques that we associate with the essay and upon which the essay always to some extent must depend, especially exposition and description.

Oddly enough, in recent fiction—especially the short story in its most popular forms today—the fiction writer often mechanically is using the techniques of the essay—particularly exposition—for his or her stories. Minimalism—the congeries of devices popularized—at first almost by accident—in the work of Raymond Carver, Ann Beattie, and other writers over the past decade depends largely on description and exposition. The result is a fiction that is founded on relentless exposition and that bulges with detail, often excessive detail devoted to arcane processes and to the superficial appearance of people and places. In the latter sense much contemporary fiction is old-fashioned, recalling Scott and Dickens and Hardy. The psychology tends to be primitive because the characters are often flat—shallow and uncomplicated. The action of the typical minimalist fiction entails a chronicle of everyday middle-class life and so in this sense it is often more nearly a report of mundane life than what appears in the best of our familiar essays.

That this situation is replete with irony I would be among the first to say. I am not announcing the end of the novel or the short story; I am talking about a particular form of fiction now in vogue that few critics have taken to task because they have failed to see beyond its apparent virtues—the dazzling surface of its maker's prose.

To see my point you need only read the annual anthologies of prizewinning fiction, especially *The Best American* series of the past few years.

In his famous dictionary Samuel Johnson defined the essay as "a loose sally of the mind"; he also deemed it "an irregular, indigested piece, not a regular and orderly composition." White reminds us of the latter definition in the foreward to his selected essays. In any case we would be bound to consider it, for Johnson himself was no mean essayist. And, no matter how many definitions we consider, we will have to determine that the essay is impossible to define. For White it is a ramble through the basement or the attic of the essayist's mind. As Sam Pickering says, "the essay saunters, letting the writer follow the vagaries of his own willful curiousity. . . . The essay ruminates and wonders" [*The Right Distance,* 1987].

In this essay I have sauntered and meandered through the work of a few writers, examining aspects of their work that make it enduring—which is to say rereadable. We cannot legitimately ask more of literature than it stand the acid test of rereading.

As I have written elsewhere, the literature of fact—not the new journalism—has secured its place as a distinctive form of literature and mode of discourse in our time. The House of Literature has many mansions. The personal essay may not be the grandest of these, but it is solid and tight and respectable while providing a splendid view of human circumstance. In some respects the familiar essay is the most elastic, succinct, and engaging of all literary forms; and it is the linchpin that draws the grander forms of letters into a closer and more familial connection.

One of the most salutary aspects of the present-day literary scene is that the canon of literature has been opened up to include modes that have previously been neglected, and I think that the personal report is the most significant of these forms. If you ask me What about the nonfiction novel and how does it differ with what you have said about Mitchell and Liebling or you say How can you fail to give minimalist fiction its due, I can only helplessly reply, ladies and gentlemen, those are other stories—subjects for other essays, other rambles. This particular ramble is over. So much then for this particular instance of what White has called a mask and an unveiling.

FURTHER READING

Anthologies

Johnson, Burges. *Essaying the Essay*. Boston: Little, Brown, and Company, 1927, 317 p.
> Collection intended to assist in teaching essay writing through a selection of exemplary essays. Samples of such early modern essayists as G. K. Chesterton, Max Beerbohm, and Christopher Morley are included.

Kazin, Alfred. *The Open Form: Essays for Our Time*, 2nd ed. New York: Harcourt, Brace & World, Inc., 1961.
> Collection of modern essays that demonstrates the variety of forms that the modern essay takes and the types of sources in which it can be found, such as biographies, collections of personal writing, popular magazines, and scholarly journals.

Lopate, Phillip, ed. *The Art of the Personal Essay: An Anthology from the Classical Era to the Present*. New York: Anchor Books, 1994, 777 p.
> Collection covering the tradition of the personal essay including a wide selection of unabridged essays.

Secondary Sources

Boetcher Joeres, Ruth-Ellen, and Mittman, Elizabeth, eds. *The Politics of the Essay*. Bloomington: Indiana University Press, 1993, 230 p.
> Collection of essays by radical feminist writers, activists, and political progressives, covering such topics as form, tone, and purpose in women's essays.

Butrym, Alexander J., ed. *Essays on the Essay: Redefining the Genre*. Athens: The University of Georgia Press, 1989, 309 p.
> Collection of critical essays providing several perspectives on the modern essay, including studies of form, pedagogy, the essay's place in literature, and its history.

Earle, Peter G. "On the Contemporary Displacement of the Hispanic American Essay." *Hispanic Review* 46, No. 3 (Summer 1978): 329-41.
> Compares the fate of the modern essay in Hispanic-American and English literature, contending that the essay, which has suffered a demise in popularity in English literature, losing its distinction from other forms such as the novel and literary criticism, is still a fairly independent, well-recognized aspect of Hispanic-American literature.

Fernald, Anne. "*A Room of One's Own,* Personal Criticism, and the Essay." *Twentieth Century Literature: A Scholarly and Critical Journal* 40, No. 2 (Summer 1994): 165-89.
> Argues that personal criticism is more than just autobiographical revelation; it is "a passionate and candid critique written from a self-consciously individual perspective."

Hartman, Geoffrey. "Crossing Over: Literary Commentary as Literature." *Comparative Literature* XXVIII, No. 3 (Summer 1976): 257-76.
> Asserts that the critical essay is a creative form of literature that should not be considered subordinate to the subject it covers.

Mailhot, Laurent. "The Writing of the Essay." *Yale French Studies,* No. 65, (1983): 74-89.
> Provides a historical overview of the Quebecois essay and analyzes its form and function.

Stabb, Martin S. "Not Text but Texture: Cortázar and the New Essay." *Hispanic Review* 52, No. 1 (Winter 1984): 19-40.
> Studies Julio Cortázar as an example of a "genuine essayist" amidst the decline of the essay form in Spanish American literature. Stabb examines whether the traditional essay form can express the concerns of modern society.

The New Yorker

INTRODUCTION

Founded in 1925 by Harold W. Ross as a humorous weekly concerned with people and events in New York City, the *New Yorker* achieved renown as a forum for stylish, high-quality fiction, poetry, essays, and cartoons. From its inception Ross's magazine and its illustrious contributors exerted a strong influence on American writing and culture. Many eminent figures in American literature and illustration launched their careers in the pages of the *New Yorker,* including authors E. B. White, James Thurber, and John Updike and artists Peter Arno, Helen Hokinson, and Charles Addams. As the focus of the magazine's content broadened, the *New Yorker* became known for its highly polished journalistic essays, which ranged from "profiles" that examined the lives and careers of notable figures to such painstakingly reported accounts of current events as Truman Capote's study of homocide which was subsequently published as the nonfiction novel *In Cold Blood.* Having undergone a variety of editorial changes, particularly during the 1980s and 1990s, the *New Yorker* continues to be an important showcase for American literature, journalism, and art.

OVERVIEWS

Philip Hamburger

SOURCE: "Thoughts about the 'New Yorker'," in *The New Leader,* Vol. LXXV, No. 9, July 13-27, 1992, pp. 10-12.

[*An American author, Hamburger worked as a staff writer for the* New Yorker *beginning in 1939. In the following essay, he reminisces about various figures and editorial characteristics associated with the magazine.*]

Writers have memories, not crystal balls. Moreover, it is extremely dangerous to speculate about the future; matters rarely turn out the way one expects. So when I heard (an overwhelming din) and read (much of it misleading and superficial) that a new editor was to replace the gifted Robert Gottlieb at the *New Yorker,* the best I could do was sit down, keep calm and think about the past. And the past, in my case, goes back a long way.

I went to work at the magazine in 1939, the 15th year of its existence. I was 25. Like so many other would-be writers, I was drawn by its magical mix of fact, fiction, wit, art and comment, but mostly by its intellectual honesty, civilized skepticism and gentle irreverence. I started out as a reporter for the "Talk of the Town" section. This brought me face to face with the volcanic founding editor, Harold

W. Ross, since he had a habit of sitting down with a young reporter and going over his piece line by line. Ross cast a spell, a compound of fierce candor, bubbling humor and an almost messianic quest for clear, truthful writing. Above all, truthful.

One of the many clichés that make up the so-called "mystique of the *New Yorker*" is the old saw that Ross was not putting out a magazine for the old lady from Dubuque. Ross, in his wisdom, would have been delighted to have the Iowa lady subscribe, and today there are 127 *New Yorker* subscribers in that lovely Mississippi River town. (I'm a sucker for river towns, having been born on the Ohio.) Ross was quixotic, but he knew what he wanted. The magazine, he said, should "be good, be funny and be fair," a healthy prescription for a general state of well-being.

Another hapless notion has it that there is "a *New Yorker* style"—everybody writing in the same predictable tone. Just try to find the common denominator in the work of, say, E. B. White, Roger Angell, Rachel Carson, Edmund Wilson, James Baldwin, Janet Flanner, Andy Logan, William Maxwell, A. J. Liebling, Adam Gopnik, and Joseph Mitchell. Or similarity in the art of Peter Arno, Helen Hokinson, Charles Addams, Roz Chast, George Price, Gretchen Dow Simpson, and George Booth.

A few years ago, in the Introduction to *Curious World,* a collection of some of my *New Yorker* pieces, I put down a few recollections of sessions with Ross in his office, and I think they are relevant here: "His questions were deeply penetrating. 'Facts,' he would say, 'give me the facts.' Detail fascinated him. The human comedy fascinated him. From time to time, looking up from the copy on his desk, he would say, 'Never go cosmic on me, Hamburger,' or 'Circulation is rising too fast—a very dangerous business,' or 'Don't expect literary fame—it's like lightning, either it'll strike or it won't.' . . . 'I saw your wife on the street today . . . For Christ sake, she's pregnant. You have one child already, where in hell you going to put the next one? *Writers!* I called your landlord, and I think he'll give you a larger apartment.' " The next day my landlord, Vincent Astor, did call, offering larger space.

There was a familial sense to the place. During World War II, the "Letter from London" was written by Mollie Panter-Downes, who became in the minds of many of the staff a sort of Mrs. Miniver, a symbol of indomitable Great Britain. Neither Ross nor William Shawn, his de facto managing editor (titles were frowned upon), had ever met her, but a number of us, traveling either during or just after the War, had the pleasure of knowing her in London or Haslemere, Surrey, where she lives. Soon after the War she announced that she would visit New York. Ross felt this called for high ceremony. He stationed Clifford Orr, a brilliant, waspish writer (now, like so many others, lost to the past) on the roof of the office at 25 West 43rd Street to keep a lookout down the Hudson for the first glimpse of her steamer, heading upriver. "She's coming! She's coming!" Orr shouted down to those who knew her, and off went the group, pell-mell, to greet the incoming heroine at the pier.

The word "profile" as a form of biography seems to have gone into the language. Even if the sketch of a personality consists of one paragraph, practically every publication calls it a profile. The *New Yorker* spells it with a capital P. Profiles are a special form, initiated under Ross, and many a current biographer addicted to thousand-page, hernia-inducing tomes, could do worse than examine the succinctness, cutting edge and character-revealing aspects of most of them. Ross paid special attention, not meeting these writers face to face but flooding them with myriad queries. One night in 1949, as a Profile by me of Dean Acheson, then Secretary of State, was about to go to press there was a sudden knock on the door of my office, followed by a blast of air as a disturbed Ross burst in. "I'm told you haven't showed proofs to Acheson," he said. "Good God! There's a Cold War! Suppose we're saying something. . . ." I interrupted to say that I never showed proofs, didn't think we needed to, but if it would put his mind at rest I would call Acheson at home and put the question to him. I did, and the Secretary said, "Certainly not. I'll read it when it comes out. I trust the *New Yorker*."

Ross had a naïve, almost child-like quality. I recall that when I visited the rubble of the Third Reich, at Berchtesgaden (having been sent overseas by Ross and Shawn), I spied on the floor of Hitler's massive, picture-windowed meeting room a heavily engraved calling card, just lying there in the midst of the debris. I scooped it up. It was the calling card of Herr Hermann Wolfgang Goering. I brought it back to Ross. His delight in this gift was touching; you might have thought I had given him a complete set of Lionel trains. He promptly framed the card and hung it on the wall in his office.

Ross and Shawn worked closely together for many years. The contrast in personalities was dramatic: Ross always audible, direct to the point of bluntness, Shawn shy, soft spoken, exceedingly polite. But when it came to editorial integrity and vision and a passion to honestly reflect the world in which they lived, these men were spiritual twins. And by no means incidentally, they worked harder than any two I have ever known. The *New Yorker* became their lives.

After Shawn took over, in 1952, he broadened and deepened the magazine. He reached out to writers everywhere. No idea seemed alien to this man, and a writer presenting one for a possible piece would find that Shawn not only grasped it with the speed of light, he had already formed in his mind the editorial shape it would take. His magazine powerfully defended the environment, eloquently condemned bias and hatred, and made clear to readers that the proliferation of atomic weapons was suicidal.

I find it hard to write about Shawn, for in addition to being my editor for many years, he has been a close friend. These days, the press continually refers to him as "legendary."

That is true enough, yet sad, since it implies an artifact in a glass case. Shawn was an inspiring editor. He gave me a free hand to travel the United States, and I turned out some 58 pieces for him under the rubric "Notes for a Gazetteer," visits to middle-sized American cities, picked at random. He never suggested a city, and never turned one down. I received only one editorial directive: All the pieces were to be written in the third person. No "I" was to appear anywhere in the text. I was to be an objective, outside visitor. "You'll find the form yourself," he said quietly.

Gazetteers bring me to Raoul Fleischmann, the publisher of the magazine at the time, and a man who passionately believed in the separation of church and state: i.e. editorial and business. One of my chance travels took me to Wilmington, Delaware (Alt. 255 ft., Pop. 110,356), and in the course of the piece I dreamed up an imaginary gathering of high-powered Du Pont executives, whooping it up at the Du Pont Country Club, which flies a nylon flag. I invented some characters who might pose there for a group photograph, mixing real people like Henry Francis du Pont with Orlon M.B. du Pont, and Lammot du Pont Copeland with Teflon du Pont. Shortly after the piece appeared Fleischmann asked me to stop by his office, one floor above and several hundred miles from Editorial.

When I walked in, he handed me a letter, and with his usual Old World courtesy said, "*Mon Vieux,* read this." It was a communication from a mighty vice president of Du Pont, that began, "Dear Raoul, You will recall, old chap, the days we played golf together on the Island," and called for the summary dismissal of the rude correspondent who had so defiled the Du Pont name. "What are you going to do about it?" I asked Fleischmann. "F—it!" he said, tossing it in his waste basket.

And then came Gottlieb. He arrived under dauntingly difficult conditions: There were protests, petitions, much hubbub. He handled himself with awesome grace. Although he, too, reached out to new writers, no cataclysmic changes occurred. He had respect for the traditions of the magazine. He kept "Notes and Comment" on a high plane, paying close note to human rights and the rule of law, and commenting forcefully on political sleaze and hypocrisy in high places. He didn't shrink from the dreaded L word.

Gottlieb was a completely hands-on editor who bustled about from office to office at all hours. He always kept his door open, and the sight of him banging away at his Olympia upright typewriter was comforting to staff members passing by. He made the wise decision to transfer many of the *New Yorker* archives to the New York Public Library, and supervised the move. The collection will be available in perpetuity to scholars and others studying the literature of the 20th century.

I liked Gottlieb's easy, informal, accessible way, his humor, and the swiftness with which he would read a piece and get back to the writer. I also appreciated his response when presented with an editorial idea that pleased him. "Go for it!" he would say.

Not a bad idea.

Scott Donaldson

SOURCE: "The *New Yorker,* Old and New," in *The Sewanee Review,* Vol. LXXXIII, No. 4, Fall, 1975, pp. 676-85.

[*Donaldson is an American critic and educator who has written several studies of twentieth-century American literary figures, including Ernest Hemingway and John Cheever. In the following excerpt from a review of several books about the* New Yorker, *Donaldson examines changes in the magazine's content and editorial policies over the years.*]

The dust jacket of *Here at The New Yorker,* with its cartoon gallery of thirty-six of the magazine's present and past luminaries, promises much the sort of anecdotal reminiscence that Brendan Gill delivers within. But there is only one cartoon of Gill himself, which hardly suggests how ponderously he bulks in his own version of the *New Yorker's* history. To some extent this is inevitable, for Gill is after all a survivor, having labored among the cubicles on West 43rd Street since 1936, and over that space of time having, as he disingenuously confesses, written more words published in the magazine than anyone else alive or dead. For all that, readers may learn more about Gill and his bitchiness than they care to know, for his strategy in the book is to ingratiate himself, establish his qualifications, and then lay about him with a blunt axe.

From behind a veneer of modesty Gill reveals that he emerged from a prosperous and literate family, that he triumphed as a prep-school poet, that at college he was tapped for Skull and Bones (a name "held in awe, and not at Yale alone"), that he wrote a damnably good if widely unread novel, that writing is not work but play to him, that he loves parties and enjoys his life, and that he considers Wallace Stevens a greater poet than Robert Frost (apparently because Stevens did not resort to "an unseemly scrambling to attain a place at the top of the steeple" and was altogether nicer and more respectable).

A similar bias against the unseemly seems to lie at the root of the malice with which Gill attacks Harold Ross. Ross, who founded the magazine and edited it from its inception in 1925 until his death in 1951, has since been the subject of three books, including James Thurber's bittersweet and moving *The Years with Ross.* The most striking thing about the editor, all critics agree, was the contrast between his rough-hewn appearance and gutter language and the sophistication and polish of the magazine that he built to such indisputable eminence. For that accomplishment, however, Gill allows him very little credit indeed. Ross was more lucky than good. As a young reporter he had been "conspicuously raffish and incompetent." As an editor his aggressive ignorance led him to pose such classic queries as "Is Moby Dick the whale or the man?" (Jane Grant, who was married to Ross, maintains that he affected such ignorance as a way of intensifying the paradox between the elegant magazine and his own background as a Colorado boy who never went to college.) What's more, according to Gill, Ross's editing consistently disimproved his copy. The editor's sole virtues, in Gill's view, were that he insisted on absolute fidelity to the facts and that the endless stream of queries issuing from his office forced the *New Yorker's* contributors, through some alchemy, to write better than they knew how.

Gill reserves his most withering comments for his former editor's personal, not professional, failings. Ross, one is told, gambled foolishly, clung to unlovely bigotries, blasphemed continually, and "was a notorious coward." Worst of all, with his gap-toothed "monkey face agape," sloping shoulders, and arms hanging almost to his knees, he offended Gill by looking more like an ape than a man and by behaving accordingly on social occasions. Even in his Fabian Bachrach portrait, according to Gill, Ross stared "into the camera with the air of a small-town crook arrested for having tried to hold up a bank with a water pistol." Unlike Gill he did not love parties, and at weddings or nightclubs he "radiated a continuous intensity of unease." The poor chap simply had no manners at all. Once, in the Oak Room of the Plaza Hotel, Ross pelted the Gills' table with spitballs; belatedly, and with heavier firepower, Gill has returned the barrage.

Here at The New Yorker, it should be admitted, has at least one hero besides its author, and that is William Shawn, the shadowy figure who took over as editor of the magazine in 1951 and still holds the reins. Gill also includes graceful good-natured sketches of several of the *New Yorker's* artists, including Saul Steinberg, William Steig, and Peter Arno. But those who are his manifest superiors as writers do not fare so well. Toward Edmund Wilson Gill is uneasily respectful; toward Stanley Edgar Hyman, gently condescending; toward John O'Hara and Thurber, openly nasty. These two are pilloried through apostrophe ("Oh, but John O'Hara was a difficult man!") and apposition ("Thurber, that malicious man" and "Thurber, that incomparable mischief-maker"). Gill fell out with both of them after Thurber, practicing one of his frequent—and frequently cruel—practical jokes, persuaded O'Hara that Gill's unfavorable review of *A Rage to Live* (for most of his career on the *New Yorker,* Gill has been a reviewer of books, films, or plays) had really been written by Wolcott Gibbs. It is not entirely clear why Thurber should have insisted on this falsehood, except that, as Gill puts it, it was in his nature "to wish to inflict pain," or why O'Hara should have swallowed the misinformation whole, except that he was forever suffering, in Gill's phrase, from "fancied slights." In any event the incident had the effect of cooling whatever potential friendships may have developed between Gill and either of those two masters of short fiction, though once Gill relented long enough to take his son Michael, a Thurber devotee, around to the Algonquin where they both listened as the "old, blind, witty, dying cockatoo" talked a blue streak at them.

There is another explanation for Gill's antipathy toward such illustrious figures as Ross, Thurber, and O'Hara: for all his longevity on the *New Yorker,* Gill has not until recently ranked as one of the magazine's insiders. Dale Kramer in *Ross and The New Yorker* (1951) mentions Gill but once. Jane Grant's *Ross, The New Yorker, and Me* (1968) contains no reference to him at all, and neither does Burton Bernstein's detailed and thorough *Thurber,* published in 1975. Only half a dozen times in fifteen years, Gill admits, did he and Ross lunch together; "given the difference in our temperaments," he explains, "there was no likelihood that I would be one of Ross's buddies." No, nor one of O'Hara's or Thurber's or even E. B. White's, who shared an office with Thurber and, Gill thinks, taught him practically everything about writing. . . .

Though the *New Yorker* is far from dead—indeed, it may be a more important national periodical now than ever before—it too has become decidedly less humorous in its advancing age. Brendan Gill returns time and again to invidious comparisons between the shaggy Ross and the elegant Shawn, contrasting the former's nicotine-stained fingers, for example, with their nails "grossly rimmed with dirt," to the latter's large, well-kept pianist's hands. But he takes no account of a more important distinction suggested by Shawn's own assessment of his predecessor. Ross, his successor wrote, served as the magazine's "final authority on humor. His element was humor. He generated it, he sought it out, he needed it, and he lived by it. If he thought something was funny, it was funny." When Ross died, almost exactly at the midpoint of the *New Yorker*'s fifty years, it began to miss that sure sense of the comic which, up to 1951, had been the magazine's trademark and its glory.

In the beginning Ross had modelled his fledgling magazine after *Punch*. Like its model it ran cartoons and illustrations but placed primary emphasis on text. The format of the text betrayed further influences: the *New Yorker*'s typographical restraint, its front-running "Talk of the Town" (a straight steal from *Punch*'s "Charivari" of London gossip), its short-fiction pieces (still called "casuals" after the British style), and its character sketches or "profiles" are all directly traceable to its famous and long-lived English progenitor. Ross mixed into the pot his own obsessions with accuracy and readability. A perfectionist, he established a checking department and sought each week to produce a technically flawless issue. He insisted, too, on excision of all highfalutin language and elimination of all possible confusions in the copy which crossed his desk— and everything crossed his desk then just as everything crosses Shawn's now. Moreover he had the gift of attracting brilliant talents to work at his side, most notably White and Thurber; and with their aid he began to reshape the *New Yorker*'s humor into something quite different from that published across the Atlantic.

Punch's forte has always been wit of a satiric bent. But the developing *New Yorker,* especially the sketches of White and Thurber, fashioned a gentler, tenderer humor. One of White's earliest contributions . . . illustrates the distinction. A waitress at a Child's restaurant clumsily spilled a full glass of buttermilk over his new suit, and in her distress uttered an abject "In the name of God," began to sob, and fled to the kitchen. "The waitress came trotting back," to let White tell his own story, "full of cool soft tears and hot rough towels. She was a nice little girl, so I let her blot me. In my ear she whispered a million apologies, hopelessly garbled, infinitely forlorn. And I whispered back that the suit was four years old, and that I hated dark clothes anyway. One has, in life, so few chances to lie heroically." In this short piece White laughs at no one's expense, and he even enlists our sympathy on behalf of the hapless wait-

ress. Thurber accomplished much the same effect in depicting the funny but touching misadventures of his bumbling Little Man. Though the *New Yorker* has never entirely abandoned satire, it achieved its finest moments in pieces like these, where wit gave way to humor, the barb to the benediction.

In 1965 the irreverent Tom Wolfe published an acid dissection of the *New Yorker* in the rival *New York,* then the Sunday *Herald Tribune* magazine. Wolfe excoriated Shawn for his aversion to personal publicity and subjected him and his publication to a vicious ad hominem attack. Though the *New Yorker*'s reputation had prospered until, according to Wolfe, it had "become—new honors!—the most successful suburban woman's magazine in the country," it had actually deteriorated and "mummified" because of Shawn's insistence, as "the smiling embalmer," on changing nothing about Harold Ross's creation. Wolfe's attack was not only cruel but quite wrong, for the *New Yorker* in 1965 resembled the one of 1950 more in appearance than in reality, and the changes are still more pronounced ten years later. The *New Yorker* has become more serious and much wordier. Where Ross generated humor and attracted its practitioners, Shawn's gift is for locating talented "fact" writers and giving them their head. As his latest book demonstrates, Sid Perelman is still occasionally doing his business at the old stand, making his marvelous lists (his impressions of India encompass "the quaint customs, the colorful temples, the succulent food buzzing with flies, and the deep wisdom that we in the West could learn from their philosophy"), inventing his wonderful names ("Mr. Fleischkopf, who had wisely refrained from Anglicizing his name to Meathead," the yummy Chinese Candide Yam, the stockbroker Worthington Toushay), striking mock-heroic poses as lover and fighter ("the rogue's impertinence tempted me to box his ears, but since they were obscured by a luxuriant growth of hair, I had no time to hunt for them"), and poking extravagant fun at the booboisie (a Yahoo asks him as a writer to discuss the relative merits of Jacqueline Susann and Harold Robbins, provoking the answer: "Gosh, who can say? It's like trying to compare Balzac with Tolstoy. I mean, they're two colossi"). But Perelman's comedy is basically logomachic, and no true humorists have come along (not even the clever Donald Barthelme nor the super-hip Woody Allen) to replace the long-dead Thurber and the semiretired White.

Instead the *New Yorker* under Shawn has vastly intensified its capacity for indignation and its eagerness to express itself on national and international issues. Shawn not only published all of Rachel Carson's *Silent Spring,* for example, but found in John McPhee an amazingly readable interpreter of the natural environment. Similarly the *New Yorker* not only printed all of John Hersey's *Hiroshima* and inveighed early and often in Notes and Comments against the war in Vietnam; but in Jonathan Schell, whose long series on the Nixon administration ran this past summer, and in Richard Harris, author of the terrifying *If You Love Your Guns,* the magazine has added to its staff two of the nation's most incisive reporters of the political scene. *New Yorker* fiction does not seem quite so good now as twenty years ago, but both Calvin Trilin and Michael

J. Arlen have recently published affecting literary portraits from the twenties, Trillin's on Gerald and Sara Murphy, Arlen on his father.

On the basis of *Levels of the Game,* the best book about tennis since William T. Tilden's *Match Play and the Spin of the Ball* forty years ago, and the brilliant articles in his new *Pieces of the Frame* (there's a fine one on Wimbledon, and a stunner on an animal lover and her travels in Georgia) the prolific McPhee qualifies as the best of the impressive stable that Shawn has recruited, nearly all of whom have been carefully ignored by Gill. Still the *New Yorker* is not nearly so much fun to read as it used to be, and nostalgia for those good old days probably has a lot to do with the commercial success of Gill's book. In 1960 the *New York Times* described the *New Yorker* as "the best literary magazine in the English-speaking world, big or little." If that's true, and many readers would agree that it still is, it says a good deal about the present perilous state, in that world, of both fiction and, especially, humor.

Peter Salmon

SOURCE: "*The New Yorker*'s Golden Age," in *The New Republic,* Vol. 140, No. 26, June 29, 1959, pp. 19-20.

[*In the following review of James Thurber's* The Years with Ross, *Salmon reflects on what he considers the "golden age" of the* New Yorker.]

An over-zealous younger editor of *The New Yorker* could, if he tried, find material for at least half a dozen of that magazine's "Newsbreaks" in James Thurber's *The Years With Ross.* There are obvious candidates for the "Forgetful Authors" Department and others that could be twisted into one of the "Infatuation With the Sound of " Series. And one shudders to think what the current crop of the magazine's book reviewers could say about Thurber's organization, which has all of the faults that are frequently to be found in a book that derives from a series of articles originating in a magazine—in this case in *The Atlantic.* Such a reviewer, moreover, could legitimately argue that the book never really explains what it was that made Ross a great editor.

In any event, I am confident that not even the most self-righteous purist could take serious notice of any of the faults. For the faults are those of genius and *The Years With Ross* is quite simply, if may use an over-worked phrase, a great book. It should win the Pulitzer Prize for biography; a National Book Award (in fiction, nonfiction or poetry: it qualities in all three categories), and anyone with contacts in Stockholm should notify the Swedish Academicians that now is the time for all of Thurber's work to be accorded the Nobel Prize it deserves.

The Years With Ross is an illuminating portrait of its subject, its author, and that American institution, the magazine they both served. One of the most interesting things about the book is that, directly or indirectly, it asks more questions than it answers; and one of these questions is: Now that we have read about *The New Yorker* in the days of its greatness, what about the magazine today?; while we still take it, we have come to take it for granted.

As one reads *The Years With Ross,* the conclusion cannot be escaped that Thurber has his own worries about this problem. Speaking of John Mosher, who once rejected a story because it was "a tedious bit about an adolescent female," Thurber remarks: "I sometimes wonder what Mosher would say, if he were alive now, about *The New Yorker*'s flux of stories by women writers dealing with the infancy, childhood, and young womanhood of females. 'We are in a velvet rut,' Ross once said many years ago." More and more of today's stories fit this pattern, a pattern which comes out of the old *Delineator* rather than the old *New Yorker.*

Reading later in the book how Ross "gave up slowly and reluctantly his old original belief that the weekly ought to be confined to the scenes and peoples and goings on" in New York City, one wonders what he would think of the endless stream of stories set in South Africa, India, England and even (*pace* Frank O'Connor) Ireland. *The New Yorker*'s fiction department remains the last stronghold of the British Empire. You may or may not agree that there are no new good fiction writers in this country but the fact remains that the significant younger American writers seldom appear in *The New Yorker* today. John Updike, of course, is an exception to this generalization, and maybe he is enough for the magazine to keep its franchise, but I doubt if Ross would have agreed. And before somebody brings up Salinger, let me hasten to point out that he got his start in the days of Ross.

It is true that the level of the magazine's nonfiction has remained fairly high. In addition to the consistently good foreign reporting, there are the regular contributions of such stalwarts as John Brooks and Berton Roueché. But we read much of their smooth work out of habit and a nagging sense of duty, before turning elsewhere for more real provocation to thought. As for the "Profiles" (a word invented by Ross), there has been a definite deterioration, best exemplified by Geoffrey Hellman's recent job on Bennett Cerf as compared to Wolcott Gibbs' earlier, annihilating profile of Henry Luce.

In the departments of criticism the magazine's record is more uneven. John Lardner's Television reviews are probably among the best available in a field that offers little competition. With the arrival of Kenneth Tynan and Donald Malcolm as drama critics, the pages of that department are the most stimulating to be found in the magazine. On the other hand, the regular book reviewers do not sustain the former critical standards, grace of writing and authority.

A friend of mine recently commented that twenty years ago he would have had called to his attention, either angrily or enthusiastically, two or three things in every issue; ten years later the average had dropped to one a week; currently, months can go by without anyone's mentioning *The New Yorker* to him. Years ago, he said, he had given up the old weekly ritual of reading the magazine from cover to cover. On the other hand, I know from firsthand experience that today's undergraduates, in the Eastern colleges, at least, are regular and devoted readers. It may be that there is a limit to the number of years during which one may remain faithful to a magazine as stylized as this one. To those whose ardor for *The New Yorker* has dimmed with the passage of time, I recommend a reading of *The Years With Ross.* In its pages are to be found anew all of the old excitement and glory.

Russell Maloney

SOURCE: "Tilley the Toiler: A Profile of the *New Yorker* Magazine," in *The Saturday Review of Literature,* Vol. XXX, No. 34, August 30, 1947, pp. 7-10, 29-32.

[*In the following excerpt, Maloney discusses "legends" concerning various personalities and practices associated with the* New Yorker.]

This article is the work of a man who spent just under eleven years on the staff of *The New Yorker* magazine, wrote two million words for it, more or less, went through five hundred and seventy-odd weekly deadlines, and resigned at last because he felt rather middle-aged and pooped.

Once a year, on the anniversary of the first issue of *The New Yorker,* there appears on its cover a portrait by Rea Irvin, the magazine's first art editor, of the mythical character known around the office as Eustace Tilley. Tilley, who is represented as scrutinizing a butterfly through a single eyeglass, is a supercilious fellow dressed in the height of Regency foppishness, complete with beaver hat and high stock. He is the embodiment of *The New Yorker* legend, which is surely the most voluminous body of fact, fiction, and conjecture ever attached to any enterprise, let

Harold Ross.

alone the relatively simple one of publishing a twenty-cent weekly magazine.

Next February Tilley will make his twenty-third appearance on *The New Yorker*'s cover. His survival is symbolic of the fact that the editorial staff has always worked as hard at being legendary as at the routine chores of writing and editing. The faithful subscriber, who follows the gossip columns and reads the pieces about *The New Yorker* that have appeared occasionally in other periodicals, can recite all the classic *New Yorker* stories in detail: for instance, Thurber tipping over the telephone booth in the reception room, powdering his face, lying down in the booth, and pretending to be a corpse; or the card-index system, keyed to a series of colored tabs, which was prepared for the benefit of a new managing editor who turned out to be color-blind.

Aside from the legend, the actual accomplishments of the actual *New Yorker* magazine are impressive. The current idiom of American humor derives directly from *The New Yorker.* The illustrated he-and-she joke, which was once sold in quantities to the readers of *Judge* and the old pre-Luce *Life,* has been replaced by the one-line cartoon gag, in which picture and text are equally important. Further, these pictures are based on real current events or observation of human character, and not on the hack humorist's dreary world, in which Dusty Rhodes, the tramp, knocks on the door and asks for a piece of pie, in which Little Willie tearfully rebels against his Saturday night bath, or plays hookey from the little red schoolhouse to go fishin' with a bent pin.

To the generally barren field of day-to-day journalism, *The New Yorker* brought a fresh style and enthusiasm. The mannered but severely accurate Talk of the Town reported little happenings unnoticed by the newspapers. Prominent or notorious citizens were the subjects of Profiles—a word that has become part of the language, despite occasional screams from *The New Yorker*'s lawyers about copyright. The Reporter at Large series gave scope to writers with a story too big to be handled in Talk. Talk very soon in *The New Yorker*'s career was taken over by James Thurber and E. B. White. By ordinary city-editor standards, both were very bad reporters, and they had actually proved this by working on newspapers—White in Seattle and Thurber in New York. Their contribution to Talk, however, did much to revive the moribund art form known in city rooms as the feature story. Before long examples of their work were being reprinted in textbooks and were solemnly analyzed by professors of journalism. Reporters on other publications were stirred to emulation. Journalism began to look up.

Meanwhile, E. B. White, in the Notes and Comments department, was setting *The New Yorker*'s editorial style—editorial policy would be too strong a term. Comment, through an inspired piece of bad make-up, has always appeared under the Talk of the Town heading, although it is a separate enterprise. Comment occupies the first page, Talk the second, third, fourth, and fifth pages. Except for a five-year hegira, from 1938 to 1942, when he lived on a farm on the Maine coast and contributed a monthly department to *Harper's Magazine,* White has always been the leading Comment writer, accepting odd thoughts or bits of information from staff men or readers, combining them with his own observations, and blending the whole into a mellow and stylistically impeccable page. Before Hitler became an active menace, *The New Yorker*'s editorial stand, as defined by White, was simple and, theoretically, not impossible to put into action. *The New Yorker* was on record as being against the use of poisonous spray on fruit, and against the trend in automobile design which narrows the driver's field of vision by lowering the front seat.

Wartime Comment, which was not entirely by White, was not much above the level of other wartime prose; but he has since become a fervent internationalist and has written lyrically and persuasively of his convictions. The tone of the magazine, taking pictures, reporting, criticism, and fiction into account, has been increasingly liberal, pro-New Deal, and internationalist. At any rate, *The New Yorker* has grown beyond the stature of a funny magazine; there was nothing incongruous in the August 31 issue of this year, which was devoted completely to John Hersey's thirty-thousand word dispatch about the destruction of Hiroshima, later issued in book form.

Inextricably mingled with the story of *The New Yorker* is the story of Harold Ross, founder and editor. Unfortunately it is a story which nobody is able to tell. No man—no man, that is, if we make an exception of the entire field of theology—has been the subject of so much analysis, interpretation, and explanation, with so little concrete result. For more than twenty-one years he has belched and wrangled and improvised and compromised and given his subscribers a magazine every seven days. He still works hard; except for a few sports columns and foreign newsletters which come in over the week end, he works on every bit of copy that goes into the magazine. He stalks through the dirty corridors of his editorial domain, gaunt, gap-toothed, his black hair tousled and his mouth agape like that of a man who has just established contact with a bad oyster, watching the next issue grow and arguing minute points of fact, taste, punctuation, or policy. He is, arbitrarily and inexplicably, an authority on the migratory habits of eels and the customs of the harem, subjects on which he likes to expatiate for hours, usually to some anxious minion who is trying desperately to make a press deadline. It is not unusual for a writer to work in *The New Yorker* office for several years without once meeting his editor. The elevator men have strict instructions not to greet him by name, lest he be accosted by some tactless writer or artist in the same car. He is a man of no perceptible learning, and he does not seem to be inordinately impressed by experience. He has relatively few friends and a number of enemies of whom he is, on the whole, rather proud. "A journalist can't afford to have friends," he is fond of saying. In a time when people are vociferous about politics, it is difficult to decide just where he stands; probably he is a lukewarm rightist despite the underlying liberal tone of the magazine itself.

A whole generation of journalists has got into the habit of thinking of Ross as a mystery man, and it suits Ross well enough to have it that way. Actually, there is no more up

his sleeve today than there was thirty-odd years ago, when he left Aspen, Colorado, to seek his fortune. It is not a pose when the editor of *The New Yorker* refers to the local smart set as "dudes." They *are* dudes, as far as he's concerned; always will be. Ross's editing might be described as the apotheosis of honest ignorance. All he asks is that a piece of writing be completely comprehensible to him. (He now asks this even of poets. "God damn it!" he suddenly yelled, one day back in 1938, "after this I'm not going to buy any verse I don't *understand!*") Ross will not pretend he understands something he doesn't understand, nor will he hope that others may be quicker than he. He has no intellectual arrogance, and will happily turn over his valuable magazine to the mismanagement of somebody he has brought in off the street to be managing editor. As soon as the incumbent's incompetence becomes clear, Ross fires him—a process that takes anywhere between one and two years, the editor meanwhile continuing at full salary while his responsibilities are gradually whittled down. Ross would rather hire than fire, with the result that his editorial roster today is near a hundred, or twice what it was ten years ago. His effect on *The New Yorker,* so far as taste, policy, and other intangibles are concerned, is mainly negative. He has harnessed some of the nation's most fractious wits. *The New Yorker*'s quarrel with Woollcott, for instance, resulted simply from Ross's refusal to let Woollcott devote his polished style to the narration of smoking-car stories, and old ones at that.

Next to Ross, Thurber and White have most deeply impressed their personalities on the magazine. Thurber, because of increasingly severe eye trouble, has not been very active at *The New Yorker* for the past six or seven years, but he has left a permanent impression—a little private Thurber legend, you might say, preserved within *The New Yorker* legend. Before he appeared on the literary scene, magazine writers were not regarded as terribly glamorous figures. They were the sort of men who took pepsin tablets after lunch and wore rubbers on cloudy days. Thurber brought the neuroses to English prose. A tall, thin, spectacled man with the face of a harassed rat, Thurber managed to convey to his office associates something of his own sense of impending doom.

In E. B. White's phrase, Thurber in those days trailed a thin melancholy after him. It was catching, too. Any humorist—for that matter, any subjective writer—is a potential neurotic. In the Gothic atmosphere which Thurber established at *The New Yorker,* the potential was actualized. One after the other, a string of slapdash newspaper writers hired by Ross in the hope that they could dash off a few profiles or Reporter at Large pieces were turned, before his very eyes, into Byronic figures who could barely summon the energy once a week to grope their way down the block to the Guaranty Trust Company and cash their drawing-account checks. It even became the thing, for a time, to be voluntarily institutionalized, and new managing editors would solemnize their promotion with a nervous breakdown.

One of E. B. White's great contributions to *The New Yorker* was his insistence, against almost overwhelming opposition, that Thurber was a funny artist whose pictures should appear in the magazine. Not even Thurber thought this; but White collected his random doodlings from his waste-basket, inked over the penciled lines, submitted the pictures to the art editor, and finally had his way. Probably more people think of Thurber as an artist than as a writer, though Thurber himself has always said he puts writing first. White, in the same defiant way, is inclined to pooh-pooh his taut and wonderful prose; he likes to think he's a poet, a title for which he is disqualified by his inordinate fondness for the word "doth."

White's Comment paragraphs can hardly be called inimitable, since they have been successfully forged by lesser staff members. Nevertheless he was the inventor, and is still the surest practitioner of this style, which is modest, sly, elliptical, allusive, prim, slightly countrified, wistful, and (God help us) whimsical. And if White's style can be forged, the New York of which he writes remains his own property. It is a microcosm with fewer orange peels and bloodstains than its original; White regards it fondly, like a spinster looking at her tank of guppies. Slight and nervous, modestly dressed and undistinguished in feature, White is a triumph of big-city protective coloration. He is never seen at cocktail parties, though he goes to one now and then.

There is an editor in the White household, too. She was Katherine Angell when, in the Twenties, she went to work editing fiction and poetry. When she and White were married, they established the first *New Yorker* dynasty: young Roger Angell, Mrs. White's son by an earlier marriage, has already sold his first piece to the magazine. Though the week-to-week drudgery of buying and printing poetry and short stories has been delegated to others, Mrs. White descends on the office every now and then for a brisk bout of editorial housecleaning.

Wolcott Gibbs, who will thank you to pronounce his first name "Woollcott," must be mentioned among the founders of *The New Yorker* legend. Alice Duer Miller, his aunt, was a close friend of Ross, and her efforts on his behalf landed Gibbs at *The New Yorker*. His first printed contribution was a sparkling verse parody titled "I Have A Rendezvous with Debt" and, in the fine old phrase, he has never looked back. He soon proved that any ambitious young man could become an acceptable amalgam of Thurber and White. In fact, during White's unadvertised absences from the Comment job, the principal contributor has been Gibbs; and most of his essays—*The New Yorker* staff calls them "casuals"—have been in the Thurber vein of the superior and highstrung man frightened by a piece of machinery or a woman. Under the tutelage of Mrs. White he became an excellent editor, his talent for parody enabling him to handle copy without violating the author's style. Gibbs gave up editing when he became the play reviewer.

Ross seldom talks about the early days of *The New Yorker,* and positively refuses to look at the early issues, the ones that came out in 1925-6. None of his present staff was with him then. Contributors were recruited from the Algonquin "round table" set, the lunchtime wits—Marc Connelly, Dorothy Parker, Robert Benchley, George Kaufman, and their lesser friends. They worked for all but

nothing, presumably spurred on by the new magazine's slogan. "Not for the old lady from Dubuque." This touch of Greenwich Village defiance was quietly buried after a few years, and Ross would undoubtedly be happy to have it forgotten. It was this period that saw the birth of *The New Yorker* legend; the organized effort that was to produce the present-day *New Yorker* began later.

A fact about *The New Yorker* which is not part of *The New Yorker* legend is that the job of editor or staff writer is physically debilitating, mentally exhausting, and a form of social suicide.

There are not titles at *The New Yorker* except in the business department. The most definite statement possible about the staff is that the excellence of most *New Yorker* prose is due partly to the fact that it passes through the hands of men named Shawn, Vanderbilt, Maxwell, Lobrano, Whitaker, Packard, and Weekes, none of whom have any definite titles and few of whom are known to the public.

There are several factors that make an editorial job at *The New Yorker* a more desperate affair than another editorial job. The worst, of course, is the glum fact of *The New Yorker's* perfection; because perfection, in the mind of Harold Ross, is not a goal or an ideal, but something that belongs to him, like his watch or his hat.

Another factor that makes editing *The New Yorker* something of a nightmare is the number and variety of items in each issue. There are Comment and Talk paragraphs, pictures, poems, short stories, essays, a Profile or Reporter at Large, half a dozen critical departments, a dozen or so newsbreaks, and the Goings-On Department, which covers movies, plays, restaurants, and night clubs. Talk is made up according to a loose but inevitable formula requiring four short anecdotes at least, and a selection of four long stories including one "dope" story, one personality story, and if possible a "visit" or personally reported story by a Talk rewrite man. Talk must be made up so that there are no conflicts with other items in the issue: that is, no mentions of subjects mentioned elsewhere in the magazine. Thus, if one of the Talk personality stories is about a dog-breeder who took a prize at the Westminster Kennel Club show, there must be no dogs in other Talk stories, nor in any of the drawings, short stories, or essays as well. Newsbreaks, poems, and other fillers—even the tiny spot drawings used as type ornaments—are scrutinized until the last press deadline, for fear of possible conflicts.

The third factor which produces a good magazine once a week and keeps editorial nerves on the stretch is an insane complexity of action. The trend is always away from simplicity. Twenty years ago a man-about-town named Fillmore Hyde used to come in and write three thousand words of Talk on Thursday afternoon. Lately, Talk has been taking up the entire working week of four reporters. The breezy titles of the various factual departments—Profiles and A Reporter at Large, as well as Talk of the Town, are merely memories of days when *The New Yorker* took life and journalism much less seriously than at present. A Profile, for instance, could be reported and written in a couple of days, once upon a time; the intention then was merely to present an offhand impression of the subject, literally a profile. Nowadays it is not unusual for a writer to spend three months gathering his material, a month writing the Profile, and another month answering queries and preparing the piece for the press. Ross is no longer content with a profile; he requests also a family history, bank reference, social security number, urinalysis, catalogue of household possessions, names of all living relatives, business connections, political affiliations, as well as a profile. The pieces have expanded enormously; there are numerous two-part profiles, some three-part ones, and now and then a five-part one, such as McKelway's painstaking dissection of Walter Winchell and John Bainbridge's study of *The Reader's Digest*. Back in 1926 *The New Yorker* would probably have had some pretty caustic things to say about a publication which printed a twenty-five-thousand word biographical study and called it a profile.

Some amateur statistician at the magazine recently estimated that if every staff writer contributed only one piece every six months, there would be a sufficient supply of Talk, Profiles, Reporters, and other fact pieces. *The New Yorker* is prodigal with drawing accounts. The indebtedness of departing writers is usually carried in the books, the fiction being that he will return some day, write seven or eight Profiles, and clear his account. Nobody, staff writer or free lance, is ever commissioned to do a piece—that is, given an assignment with a guarantee of payment.

Fiction and poetry being almost but impossible to regiment, *The New Yorker* handles such contributions pretty normally. By and large, it is no harder to write a *New Yorker* short story now than it was fifteen or twenty years ago. Sally Benson once sent in a story about some adventure or other that happened to a man who lived in a cabin on a mountainside. Her author's proof included a fretful Ross query: "How he come to be living on mountainside? Better explain." Miss Benson penciled an answer: "I don't know how he came to be living on a mountainside. This is just a story I made up, and I didn't make up that part."

"Art meeting" is one of the great *New Yorker* institutions: the process, hardly changed by the passage of the years, by which the drawings are bought. It has always been attended by Ross and Rea Irvin, the first art editor. The current art editor attends; so does one of the fiction editors; Mrs. White does if she is in town. These people sit four abreast at a conference table, while the pictures, one after another, are laid on an easel in front of them. At each place is a pad, pencil, ashtray, and knitting needle. The knitting needle is for pointing at faulty details in pictures. Ross rejects pictures firmly and rapidly, perhaps one every ten seconds. "Nah . . . nah . . . nah." A really bad picture wrings from him the exclamation "Buckwheat!"—a practical compromise between the violence of his feelings and the restraint he feels in the presence of Mrs. White or a lady secretary. "Who's talking?" he will ask occasionally; this means that the drawing will get sent back to the artist, to have the speaker's mouth opened wider. Now and then Ross gets lost in the intricacies of perspective. "Where am *I* supposed to be?" he will unhappily inquire,

gazing into the picture. If nobody can say exactly where Ross is supposed to be, out the picture goes.

It might be noted that the business department of *The New Yorker* is just like the business department of any successful enterprise. There is an unwritten and inviolable non-fraternization rule, encouraged by Ross and meekly accepted by Raoul Fleischmann, the owner: no business-office men in the editorial room unless by strict invitation. The advertising salesmen are happy fellows, hampered only by Ross's objection to such advertisements as those mentioning deodorants, contraceptives, or even kiss-proof lipstick. The circulation is pushing three hundred thousand, and could probably go much higher if it were not for the standard *New Yorker* advertising contract, which guarantees the advertiser that half the circulation is within metropolitan New York. Fleischmann, who put up the bulk of the original investment, has been out of the red for eighteen years. There are reports that Henry Luce with whose magazine *The New Yorker* had been feuding for more than twenty years, is now a fairly large stockholder in the New Yorker Magazine, Inc. The why, when, and how-much of the transaction have not been disclosed; but blocks of *New Yorker* stock have been available from time to time at something over fifty, there being several dozen stockholders in all. In any event, accidentally, or otherwise, there have been few recent evidences of editorial swiping—at least in print—between *The New Yorker* and *Time,* Inc.

A guided tour of *The New Yorker* offices would reveal little of the spiritual turmoil that goes on there. It is an unusually dirty and inconvenient office, to be sure; but impersonal. There are no rugs at the *New Yorker,* no curtains, no decorations, and little feeling for order or cleanliness. Carrying on the Thurber tradition of drawing on the walls, the office boys have left quite a few dirty and meaningless hen-tracks. The water-coolers are filled at the mop-closet sink, though the containers bear the name of a famous bottled water. Hidden in a corner is a photostat machine; once, long ago, Ross thought that a multiplicity of photostat copies would expedite the handling of last-minute copy, forgetting that it took time for the prints to dry. The automatic pencil-sharpener is gathering dust in a corner, too. The very soft pencils demanded by Ross tended to break in the user's hand after being put through the automatic sharpener. An edict went out that all Ross pencils had to be hand-sharpened and personally tested by his personal secretary. While Ross was basking in this luxury, the secretary fleeced him of thousands of dollars by presenting him with blank checks to sign and making them out to himself, lost the money on the horses, and evaded justice by way of the gas-oven.

The New Yorker is, in the end, merely a state of mind, a relationship between Ross and his minions, between staff and readers. The readers are important; they contribute all the Talk anecdotes and all the newsbreaks, suggest Talk stories, profiles, and other factual pieces, and (in Ross's guilty imagination) have miscarriages at the sight of saucy pictures or stories. Ross is a puritan, and he flew into a rage, back in 1927, when *The New Yorker*'s one suggestive drawing was explained to him. It was the one showing a man and a girl, carrying between them the back seat of an automobile, saying to a rural policeman, "We want to report a stolen car." It was this picture, or something equally uninhibited in the text, that caused a lady reader to have a miscarriage; or so she wrote to Ross. He has never forgotten it.

The most significant single fact about *The New Yorker* is not the financial statement, impressive as this frequently has been; it is the fact that, at present, none of *The New Yorker* people except Ross has an ulcer. It's when the boss begins delegating his ulcers to somebody else that a magazine begins to slip.

Stanley Edgar Hyman

SOURCE: "The Urban New Yorker," in *The New Republic*, Vol. 107, No. 3, July 20, 1942, pp. 90-2.

[*As a longtime literary critic for the* New Yorker, *Hyman rose to a prominent position in American literature during the middle decades of the twentieth century. He is noted for his belief that much of modern literary criticism should depend on knowledge received from disciplines outside the field of literature, and many of his critical essays rely on theories gleaned from such disciplines as cultural anthropology, psychology, and comparative religion. In the following excerpt, he provides an overview of the writers and editorial features that characterized the* New Yorker *in 1942.*]

There is no other magazine quite like *The New Yorker,* which is perhaps just as well. There is a *Rural New Yorker,* but it is an unabashed farm paper, and will not be mentioned in this review again. Its urban cousin, *The New Yorker,* is unique of its kind, and it is this rather terrifying uniqueness that regularly fascinates critics and reviewers, so that no critical season is complete without at least one learned article attempting to define what makes *The New Yorker* tick. The most recent of these critical efforts was Lionel Trilling's in *The Nation* of a few months ago. Beginning with the "polite" relation that existed between reader and writer in Fielding and Dickens, Mr. Trilling worked inexplicably into a dismissal of the body of *New Yorker* fiction as both "cruel" and "dead," and ended on a note of rapturous tribute to the "bright humanism" of Ludwig Bemelmans, who is surely one of the smaller, if one of the more amiable, of the *New Yorker* talents. His central point was the contradiction between the magazine's "grimly moral" short stories and its "more genial contents"; the stories consistently denying the polite tradition that the rest of the magazine affirms.

It is here, I am afraid, that Mr. Trilling fumbles the ball just before starting on his pretty touchdown run, tripping over the same obstacle that defeated most of the earlier analysts, the assumption that *The New Yorker* has any fixed and consistent tone or attitude against which a given feature may be judged. Here, the fact that his review confined itself wholly to fiction probably misled him, for even the most cursory analysis of the magazine's "more genial contents," if it did nothing else, would at least have tossed that "genial" right in his eye.

The heart of *The New Yorker* is the section called "The

Talk of the Town," and *its* heart is the editorial first page entitled "Notes and Comment," which is what editors of English textbooks for college freshmen reprint to show the influence of the magazine's "scintillating" prose on contemporary writing. The chief author of this page for many years, and the man who seems to have established its highly stylized form as an extension of his own rare personality, was E. B. White, who has just published a book of what Lionel Trilling would probably call "genial" personal essays. Although all but three of these pieces appeared, not in *The New Yorker,* but in White's monthly column in *Harper's,* and although the three from *The New Yorker* are among the slightest in the book, it would be hard to find a better exhibit of the magazine's editorial characteristics than these essays. Like the *New Yorker* paragraphs, White's pieces take anything of interest for their subject matter, from the brooder stove on his saltwater farm in Maine to a personal plan for world peace, and distill it down to a moral conclusion. The touch is always light, but the punch can be heavy and full of conviction, and it is surprising to see how frequently something gently tapped (like the Townsend Plan) goes right down for the count.

White's style is the essence of what gets called "*New Yorker* style." Its ingredients are a meticulous ear for sound (his chapter on Maine Speech is something to make a phoneticist's recording blush for shame) and a fresh use of words that always looks effortless and almost never is. An example is the much-discussed phrase, "the unspeakably bright imploring look of the frustrated," in his great short story, "The Door." Change the "unspeakably" to its uncle "terribly" and you have reduced a perfect and momentous expression to a merely good one. White is currently on a Thoreau jag, and some of the lines in his book could have been cribbed directly from the Old Hermit himself: ("From such adaptable natures [those who can adjust to fascism] a smell rises. I hold my nose." ". . . for if freedom were denied me by force of earthly circumstance, I am the same as dead and would infinitely prefer to go into fascism without my head than with it, having no use for it any more and not wishing to be saddled with so heavy an encumbrance.") But ignoring the Gems from Thoreau, *One Man's Meat* is *New Yorker* editorial writing at its best, and its best is plenty good.

In sharp contrast to the magazine's editorial section, *New Yorker* reporting is markedly amoral, as two recent books of collected reportage, mostly from *The New Yorker,* by Meyer Berger and A. J. Liebling, make clear. The interest is in people, and whether they are Roy Howard or Frankie (the Dasher) Abbandando is almost irrelevant. This stimulates a curious sense of acceptance in the reader, and things like Berger's scientific report on the slow trial-and-error evolution of the technique of ice-pick murdering in his amazing piece on Murder, Inc., seem quite reasonable and not at all shocking. What raises *New Yorker* reporting above the level of comparable newspaper stuff, and puts some of it among the best reportage of our time, is elaborate and careful fact-gathering for interest and accuracy, plus the inevitable lightness of touch, rather than any specific "*New Yorker*" angle. The editorial slant, of course, comes in with the selection of material, but the writing is rarely satirical or critical and never opinionated. *The New*

Yorker, particularly in its "Profiles" section, has run some scathing pieces (some of the memorable ones that come to mind are the gleeful dissection of Walter Winchell; Wolcott Gibbs's beautiful job, written in a parody of Time-style, on Henry Luce; and the complete demolition of Dewey the magazine performed when he was a candidate for the Republican nomination in 1940), but they get their effects wholly from factual documentation, never from moral slant. Sometimes this method backfires, and a piece that could have been incisive ends up tediously noncommittal, like the Profile on Willkie and Matthew Josephson's recent whitewash-by-omission of Knudsen. The technique is literally that of the anthropologist, and Liebling's exhaustive study of the Telephone Booth Indian in "The Jollity Building" is a fine example. In all seriousness, he has studied the telephone-booth chiseler as though he *were* an Indian, and has carefully surveyed his behavior, explored his habitat and catalogued his speech in the best anthropological manner. But funny, which is perhaps the difference as well as the secret of *New Yorker* reporting.

Probably the most reprinted items in the magazine, to which it owes its unfortunate popular reputation as a "comic" paper, are the strictly funny pieces, the things *The New Yorker* calls "casuals," that is, amorphous pieces neither fiction nor fact. Robert Benchley, one of the Old Guard of professional humorists, has been writing these at a furious clip for twenty years, and he (or someone) has recently selected what are supposed to be the best pieces from his ten books. Some unforgettable pieces have been inexplicably left out ("Another Uncle Edith Christmas Story," "Happy Childhood Tales," some of the fine and bitter book reviews from "Love Conquers All," etc.), but enough good things have been included (The Opera Synopses, the Fascinating Crimes, "Romance in Encyclopedia Land," "Paul Revere's Ride" and others) to make the book at least as good as the average Selected Works. Selections from Benchley are a fairly accurate cross-section of all *New Yorker* funny pieces, and include most of the forms: dilemma, parody, *reductio ad absurdum,* riding a book or clipping, sheer nonsense; and even most of the stock pieces: A Visit to the Dentist, The Jukes Family on the Radio, Vacation Days, etc. Other humorists have written some of the stock pieces funnier, and a number of them have developed specialties further (Perelman's nonsense, for example, is better, as are the parodies of Wolcott Gibbs and Corey Ford and the games that Frank Sullivan plays with names) but a collection of Benchley's work is about as consistently good as *New Yorker* funny pieces come, and where the hell do the movies get off, etc.?

The greatest concession (aside from Howard Brukaber) that *The New Yorker* makes to the idiot third of its readers is the serial stories. Some of these are good, and when they are they are magnificent (like Thurber's series published in book form as *My Life and Hard Times*), but generally they are not, and when they are not they stink, as has been said about the little girl with the curl. The principal occupational hazard of this stuff is *lapsosis,* or the falling off from week to week, nothing being harder to sustain than a series of weekly funny pieces about the same people. Most of the serials are fictionalized reminiscence, like Clarence Day's series on his father, Ruth McKenney's on

early days in the Village, or Mencken's on his newspaper days, but many of them are simply light serial fiction, such as Arthur Kober's series on the Bronx (and his strained pieces, now running, on a Hollywood agent) or John O'Hara's on Pal Joey. Two books of serial pieces have just been published; one by Emily Hahn on an incredible Chinese of her acquaintance or imagination, and one tedious reminiscence of childhood in St. Louis by Sally Benson, which is only stopping off in *The New Yorker* long enough to catch its breath before heading for the stage, Hollywood and a radio program with Shirley Temple.

The two outstanding characteristics of *The New Yorker*'s serious stories are their strong social edge and their surprisingly high quality. (It is worth noting that *The New Yorker,* allegedly a "humor" magazine, prints a higher percentage of good serious stories than any of the heavy literature magazines like *Story,* and prints very little real tripe.) True, the *New Yorker* story is almost as rigid a form as the *New Yorker* editorial paragraph, and there is little or no place for experimental or "different" writing, but within these limitations the stories are excellent. Most of the regular authors—Kay Boyle, Irwin Shaw, Edward Newhouse, John O'Hara, Jerome Weidman, John Cheever and half a dozen others—write roughly the same sort of thing (a few, like John Collier and Sylvia Townsend Warner, manage to avoid the pattern): tight, objective sketches with a strong undercurrent of emotion, aimed at capturing a mood, a feeling or a situation. Many of these have a strong social emphasis, and there are always a bewildering few by genuinely left-wing authors on unmincing left-wing themes (Albert Maltz is perhaps the best example). One of the punchiest and most horrible stories about chauvinism against the Negro ever written appeared in *The New Yorker* of September 27, 1941. It was called "An Action Photo Has Been Taken . . . ", by an unknown (at least to me) named Alex Gaby, and it is one of the unforgettable stories of recent times. A rare and really fine form *The New Yorker* occasionally runs is the quiet, impressionistic piece of the type of White's "The Door," Thurber's "One Is a Wanderer" and the Robert M. Coates sketches from his novel *Yesterday's Burdens.* Deeply moving, generally complex and (literally) parenthetical in thought, highly stylized, this sort of thing is perhaps the best expression today for certain aspects of frustration, bewilderment and loneliness in our civilization.

New Yorker light verse tends to be even more formalized than *New Yorker* fiction, as recent collections of light verse by Morris Bishop and Richard Armour make clear. The subjects are all the stock light-verse subjects: the discomforts of the country, the incredible behavior of women, the loathing for children, the tedium of week-end visits, etc., all adding up to what might be called the Light Verse Attitude, a combination of the ostentatiously blasé, the scornfully urban, the proudly incompetent and the generally wicked in a mild 1920 pattern. The total effect of both volumes, and in fact much of *The New Yorker*'s light verse, is an impression of flawless technical competence combined with a fine dose of boredom after reading more than a few poems at a sitting. From this sweeping judgment are exempt: most of Ogden Nash, which is always fresh and individual, if not always successful, and the light verse of such people as Phyllis McGinley and E. B. White, which is light in form but rarely in content. (White's "I Paint What I See" and Miss McGinley's verse-criticism of Auden and his merry men, "Public Journal," are outstanding examples.)

The New Yorker's serious verse, like the serious fiction, is surprising for both its quality and its degree of social content. Some of the principal modern poets, William Carlos Williams, Conrad Aiken, Kenneth Fearing, W. H. Auden, Rolfe Humphries and others are regularly printed in the magazine, as are many of the liveliest of the newer poets, people like Harry Brown, George Allen and a very promising young man named Judd Polk.

With our entry into the war, *The New Yorker* suddenly went all-out. For the first few weeks, "The Talk of the Town" was given over entirely to tributes to Colin Kelly and comparable subjects, most of the cartoons were devoted to bespectacled Japanese, and the magazine even dug up a bad story by Edward Newhouse (who has written some pretty good ones) that managed to mention Pearl Harbor before the smoke had cleared away. This hysteria gradually abated, "The Talk of the Town" returned to a relative if somewhat more serious normal, the cartoonists recalled that other things besides the Japanese might be funny, and no stories quite so frantically topical turned up. The magazine's reportage section, which had been running impressive material on the war for months before Pearl Harbor (much of it sent from England by A. J. Liebling), has stayed in its groove, and continues to print sharp articles on the shipping situation, the housing shortage and similar subject matter that Lionel Trilling would surely assume to be the prerogative of weightier periodicals. It is unlikely that *The New Yorker* will be markedly affected by the war (although its luxury advertising will certainly suffer), since it now has about the ultimate in both-ends-against-the-middle coverage; enough straight stuff on the war to satisfy the most demanding war-bulletin fiend and enough escape material to please his ostrich cousin.

The final clue to *The New Yorker* is probably that paradox of inclusiveness. If you think of it as a funny paper or a snob paper, what are you going to do with its strong weekly dose of social criticism; if you think of it as a slick-paper *New Masses,* Sally Benson comes up behind and trips you. Its outstanding feature is a catholicity wide enough to include prim moral judgments and wholly amoral reporting; sharp social satire and columns telling what it assumes to be its readers where they can get thousand-dollar hairbrushes with each bristle torn from a different Siberian boar; some of the best and toughest contemporary writing and incredible silliness; maniac humor and bitter attacks on injustice. The word "urban" first turned up in this review in a gag about another periodical aimed at the farm trade, but "urban" (not, for God's sake, "urbane") might well be the key. *The New Yorker* was founded to reflect the life and times of New York, and in a city of seven or eight million people, it seems you can find just about every damn thing to reflect.

Theodore Peterson

SOURCE: "New Leaders: The Missionaries," in *Magazines in the Twentieth Century,* second edition, University of Illinois Press, 1964, pp. 223-61.

[*Peterson is an American educator and critic who has written numerous works on magazines and journalism. In the following excerpt, he traces the growth of the* New Yorker *from its origin through 1964.*]

As Time Inc. expanded into a global operation and took the world for its beat, another missionary was deliberately cultivating a relatively small following and was focusing his editorial attention on a single city. Harold Ross and his *New Yorker* kept their eyes on New York; and although they regularly peered across the ocean at Europe and occasionally looked across the United States at Hollywood, they largely ignored the America west of the Hudson. Yet Ross's *New Yorker* was an influential magazine. It changed the character of American humor, introduced a new approach to magazine biography, set high standards of reporting, and thereby influenced the course of American journalism in general.

In 1952 when Dale Kramer published a book about Harold Ross and his *New Yorker,* some of the persons most closely associated with the magazine disavowed the book on principle. No outsider, they insisted, could possibly handle the subject adequately. A number of writers before Kramer, some of them staff members of the *New Yorker,* had tried to tell what Ross was like. "Unfortunately, it is a story which nobody is able to tell," Russell Maloney, who had worked with Ross for eleven years, admitted in his own attempt in 1947. "No man . . . has been the subject of so much analysis, interpretation, and explanation, with so little concrete result."

For twenty-six years, from the first issue in February, 1925, until his death in December, 1951, the *New Yorker* was unmistakably the product of Harold Ross. He worked on every piece of copy which went into the magazine, apart from a few sports columns and foreign newsletters which came in over the weekend, Maloney recalled; and he stalked "through the dirty corridors of his editorial domain, gaunt, gap-toothed, his black hair tousled and his mouth agape like that of a man who has just established contact with a bad oyster, watching the next issue grow and arguing minute points of fact, taste, punctuation, or policy."

By all accounts, Ross was aloof, tactless, rude, given to outbursts of temper and profanity, a man with relatively few friends. Yet the friends he had were remarkably loyal; and he was indisputably a demanding editor, a meticulous one, a great one. The *New Yorker* reflected Ross's personality; but, curiously, his personality and that of the urbane, witty, sometimes acid *New Yorker* were totally unalike.

Harold Ross was not a native *New Yorker,* not even an Easterner. He was born in Aspen, Colorado, in November, 1892, and moved to Salt Lake City with his family when he was seven. He never completed high school. At the end of his sophomore year, he quit to take a job with the Salt Lake City *Tribune*; and as a young man of college age, he was a tramp newspaperman whose driftings took him to Sacramento, Atlanta, Panama City, New Orleans, and San Francisco. His biographer has described him as a "happy-go-lucky, poker-playing, hard-swearing" reporter, competent but not outstanding. His newspaper associates in San Francisco nicknamed him "Rough House."

In 1917 Ross enlisted in the railway engineers' corps, was among the first American troops to arrive in France, and went to an officers' training camp there. But when he learned that a newspaper for enlisted men was to be published in Paris, he went absent without leave to get a job on it. He became editor of that newspaper, *Stars and Stripes,* after leading a revolt which deposed the officer in charge of publication. The journalists with whom he worked on the paper and spent his off-duty hours at a restaurant in Montmartre included Alexander Woollcott, Franklin P. Adams, John Winterich, and Grantland Rice.

After the war, Ross edited *Home Sector,* a short-lived veterans' magazine staffed by former *Stars and Stripes* men, which tried unsuccessfully to capitalize on the wartime popularity of *Stars and Stripes* among the troops. From *Home Sector* he went to the editorship of the official publication of the *American Legion,* which he left for a brief term as editor of *Judge.* Meanwhile he was planning a magazine of his own. Meanwhile, too, he was admitted into the select circle of wits who lunched at the famous Round Table in the Algonquin Hotel—Dorothy Parker, Robert Benchley, Marc Connelly, Franklin P. Adams, Edna Ferber, and a few others—and played poker with some of them on Saturday nights.

At one of the poker games Ross met Raoul Fleischmann, whose family had made a fortune from a bakery and yeast business. Fleischmann agreed to help finance Ross's projected magazine, a weekly of high quality humor and satire. The idea for the magazine seems to have grown out of Ross's experiences on *Stars and Stripes* and *Judge,* tempered by his association with the Round Table sophisticates. Just as *Stars and Stripes* had been written by enlisted men for enlisted men and had shown no respect for officialdom, so the new magazine would be written by the urbane for the urbane and would make no concessions to a mass audience. The humor in *Judge* was broad and obvious because the magazine was addressed to a large audience, and it was often stale because of the big spread between deadline and publication date. By seeking a New York audience, the new magazine could be produced fast enough to preserve the freshness of its humor and commentary; more than that, it could publish what Ross thought was the most successful type of humor, humor with a local flavor like that in Franklin P. Adams' newspaper column.

Ross put his ideas for his magazine into a prospectus which, as it turned out, was a good description of the *New Yorker* during the twenty-six years of his editorship:

> The *New Yorker* will be a reflection in word and picture of metropolitan life. It will be human. Its general tenor will be one of gaiety, wit and satire, but it will be more than a jester. It will not be what is commonly called radical or highbrow. It will be what is commonly called sophisticated, and will be fur-

in that it will assume a reasonable degree of enlightenment on the part of its readers. It will hate bunk.

> As compared to the newspaper, the *New Yorker* will be interpretive rather than stenographic. It will print facts that it will have to go behind the scenes to get, but it will not deal in scandal for the sake of scandal nor sensation for the sake of sensation. Its integrity will be above suspicion. It hopes to be so entertaining and informative as to be a necessity for the person who knows his way about or wants to.

> . . . . .

> The *New Yorker* will be the magazine which is not edited for the old lady in Dubuque. It will not be concerned in what she is thinking about. This is not meant in disrespect, but the *New Yorker* is a magazine avowedly published for a metropolitan audience and thereby will escape an influence which hampers most national publications. It expects a considerable national circulation, but this will come from persons who have a metropolitan interest.

Since Ross's interests were primarily editorial, his biographers have disagreed over whether or not he foresaw the commercial possibilities of his metropolitan magazine. There was no good reason that he should have overlooked them. In retrospect, the idea was simple enough: through a local magazine, an advertiser could reach a sizable number of well-to-do consumers in the New York area with far less expense and waste circulation than he could through metropolitan newspapers or through national magazines. After readers outside of the city came to far outnumber those in New York, the magazine offered advertisers a screened circulation; and even then, advertisers could still buy space in only a special New York edition until 1960, when it was discontinued as anachronistic. Simple as the idea seemed, it failed when publishers tried it in other large cities in imitation of the *New Yorker.* . . .

The idea almost failed for Ross at first. He set to work translating his prospectus into the words and drawings of a first issue, and to help him he had a staff consisting only of Philip Wylie, Tyler Bliss, an advertising salesman, two secretaries, and a telephone switchboard operator. The first issue appeared on February 19, 1925. By general agreement, it was terrible. Ross knew little about New York, lacked the sort of material he wanted to publish, and did not have the ability to write it himself. He hoped for an eventual circulation of 50,000 to 70,000. His first issue sold 15,000 copies, his third 12,000, his fourth 10,500. Circulation had dropped to 8,000 by April, and the magazine was losing $8,000 a week. In May, Fleischmann, who was covering the losses, held a conference on the fate of the magazine. He decided to kill it. But as he walked away from the meeting, he overheard an associate remark that "it is like killing a living thing." He was so bothered by the idea that he told Ross he would keep the magazine going a little longer while he sought new capital.

Ross had originally estimated that the *New Yorker* could be started on $50,000. He had contributed $20,000 and had drawn only a third of his salary; Fleischmann had furnished $25,000. Their first issues, scanty of advertising as well as of circulation, rapidly depleted their initial capital. Its backers invested $225,000 in the *New Yorker* during its first year of publication, and Fleischmann provided all but $35,000 of it. A total of $710,000—$550,000 from Fleischmann alone—went into the *New Yorker* before it began paying its own way in 1928. Thereafter it made a profit every year.

When Fleischmann gave the *New Yorker* its reprieve, Ross, aware that his Round Table friends could not fill the magazine in their leisure time, began building up a staff which, as it enlarged, included Ralph Ingersoll, who later went to Time Inc. and then on to the newspaper *PM;* Morris Markey, whom Ross lured away from *Collier's;* Joseph Moncure March; Lois Long; and Corey Ford, a frequent contributor to *Vanity Fair.* Getting the sort of staff he wanted was a frantic business; Ross is said to have fired about a hundred staff members in the first year and a half of the magazine's existence. The week after the first issue appeared, Fleischmann had sought assistance from John Hanrahan, a publishers' consultant and "magazine doctor," who offered to help manage the *New Yorker* in exchange for stock in the company. Hanrahan has been credited with recruiting personnel for all departments other than editorial and with having a strong hand in a series of advertisements which promoted the *New Yorker* among advertising men in the fall of 1925.

At that time there were signs that the *New Yorker* would survive. Legend credits a series of articles by Ellin Mackay, a young society woman, with establishing the success of the magazine. Miss Mackay was the rebellious daughter of Clarence H. Mackay, president of Postal Telegraph, and she had decided to become a writer. She sent the *New Yorker* a manuscript written in longhand and impressively bound in leather. Ross had staff members rewrite the article, then ran it under the title "Why We Go to Cabarets," with the subtitle "A Post-Debutante Explains." Miss Mackay's explanation was that society girls frequented cabarets to escape the stag lines of society affairs. Newspapers reprinted parts of the article because it was somewhat iconoclastic and because its author was a member of high society, and the result was a good deal of publicity for the *New Yorker.* Miss Mackay wrote additional articles for the magazine before she caused another stir by marrying Irving Berlin, the song writer, against her father's wishes. Her articles supposedly brought the *New Yorker* to the attention of the Park Avenue set. Whether they did or not, the *New Yorker* ended 1925 with a rising circulation and a growing number of advertising contracts.

In its early years the *New Yorker* acquired some of the staff members whose names were associated with it at mid-century. E. B. White, a graduate of Cornell who had served unhappily in an advertising agency, joined the staff in 1926. James Thurber, a native of Columbus, Ohio, was hired away from a newspaper in 1927 and thereafter brightened the pages of the *New Yorker* with prose and sketches. By ruthless hiring and firing, Ross found the other editors, writers, and artists he wanted: Katherine Angell, who married E. B. White in 1929, Alva Johnston,

Wolcott Gibbs, John O'Hara, S. J. Perelman, Ogden Nash, Helen Hokinson, O. Soglow, Peter Arno.

It was a staff whose escapades provided an unending succession of anecdotes about the *New Yorker.* Ross, intrigued by the weekly editorial teas of *Punch,* established a private speakeasy to create a bond between the *New Yorker* and its contributors. One morning the employee who opened it discovered two contributors of opposite sexes stretched out in a stupor, and Ross permanently closed down the establishment. Another day Ross was acquainting a new managing editor with office routine. "I am surrounded by idiots and children!" he complained. Just then a copy boy rushed in shouting, "Mr. Thurber is standing on a ledge outside the window threatening to commit suicide." Ross turned to the new editor. "See?" A man in the financial district once submitted an essay by Stephen Leacock as his own contribution. The *New Yorker* published it without recognizing it as Leacock's. Ross and Wolcott Gibbs soon learned of the plagiarism, but they took no legal action against the offender. Instead they requested that he write a financial letter each week. They returned each contribution with a note saying that the article was not quite what they wanted but that he was getting close.

Working for the *New Yorker* as editor or staff writer, Russell Maloney concluded after eleven years of it, was "physically debilitating, mentally exhausting, and a form of social suicide." It was not just the escapades which made it so; it was Ross's insistence upon perfection. For Ross, perfection was "not a goal or an ideal, but something that belongs to him, like his watch or his hat."

Ross's mania for perfection was exemplified in the Profile, a term registered by the *New Yorker* to designate its probing biographical studies. The Profiles developed from casual sketches of Manhattan personalities into detailed dissections of character and motives. Their development, Wolcott Gibbs once observed, was "the story of Ross' ferocious curiosity about people—struggling against the mechanical limitations of a fifteen-cent magazine and the lethargy of authors generally. . . . " The Profile became a distinctive form of biography. Clifton Fadiman suggested that the Profile was perhaps no less specific a form of composition than the familiar essay, the sonnet, or the one-act play.

Profiles in the early years were, as the term literally suggests, offhand impressions of the subject which an author could report and write in a few days. As Ross sought perfection, the Profile became increasingly long and complex. By the end of World War II, a reporter sometimes devoted five months to preparing one—three months to collecting his facts, a month to writing his article, and another month to revising it for publication. Ross was no longer content with mere outlines of character; he demanded "a family history, bank references, urinalysis, catalogue of household possessions, names of all living relatives, business connections, political affiliations."

The Profiles, without doubt, helped to improve the quality of magazine biography generally and demonstrated that a person need be neither successful nor significant to be worthy of treatment. Before the *New Yorker,* magazines had run biographies of successful businessmen, the lives of historical figures, sentimental sketches of lovable characters; but the *New Yorker* gave attention to persons who, in Clifton Fadiman's words, had "made a success, not of their bank-balances, but of their personalities." Subjects of the Profiles were sometimes eminent citizens, sometimes raffish characters from New York's byways, sometimes persons of accomplishment, sometimes persons of doubtful integrity; but all of them, as Fadiman noted, had one common quality: their personalities were literally outstanding. Reporters conveyed not just a surface impression but explored deep into their characters in a manner of which Plutarch would have approved.

Because of Ross's obsession for completeness, accuracy, and lucidity, the *New Yorker* established a checking system comparable perhaps only to the research department of Time Inc. Checkers examined and re-examined every fact that went into the magazine. Writing that satisfied Ross could not be done hastily. In the midtwenties, Fillmore Hyde could write the entire 3,000 words of the "Talk of the Town" department in a single afternoon; in 1947 four reporters devoted their entire working week to it.

To what seemed the perpetual astonishment of its executives, the *New Yorker* prospered handsomely. A share of its stock valued at about $30 in 1925 was worth $1,440 in 1960. The magazine had to ration advertising because it attracted so much. Its profit record was one of the best in the industry. Its income of $2,028,186 on gross revenues of $19,843,337 in 1962 came to 10.2 per cent as compared with an average of less than 2 per cent for many other major publishers. With virtually no bargain offers, it kept its circulation growing at a faster rate than the population after 1950.

Inevitably perhaps, the *New Yorker* became a regular target for critics as it grew old and wealthy. On the ninth anniversary of Ross's death, *Time* took a page to complain that the magazine was not what it once had been. No brilliant writers had replaced its original crew, who had died, retired, or become infrequent contributors, *Time* said, and its editorial formula of the twenties and thirties sat ill with the sixties. Its shapeless, plotless fiction was pedestrian, its cartoons trite. A reviewer noted that the significant young writers, almost without exception, rarely appeared in it. Its Profiles had deteriorated, and although the other nonfiction was of high quality, one read it out of a nagging sense of duty instead out of any provocation to thought. When James Baldwin contributed an angry essay on the degradation of the Negro, another reviewer remarked on the irony of its appearing amidst advertisements for $1,300 chinchilla furs and $18,500 diamond clips and bracelets. Even James Thurber had his say. He worried, he said, about the increase in size, wealth, and "matronly girth": "We have got into a thing that Ross dreaded all his life—the magazine is turning grim and long."

Such complaints had some validity, but it was easy to exaggerate their basis. Executives of the *New Yorker,* wearing their success with an air of pleasant disbelief mingled with constant apprehension, did seem uneasy about changing an extremely profitable pattern. Indeed, after

World War II, the magazine was probably more notable for innovations in advertising than in editorial matter. Editorial copy did trickle in slender streams between mountains of advertising, as critics charged, and flowed on at sometimes inordinate length. The magazine did show signs of greater preoccupation with remote regions of Asia and obscure English villages than with the New York scene.

On the other hand, William Shawn followed an editor who had become almost an institution, and any comparison of his magazine with Ross's was bound to be tinged with nostalgia. Some of the developments that critics complained of, in fact, had begun while Ross was still editor. By any standard, the *New Yorker* was still an excellent, provocative magazine in the fifties and sixties. It first carried Rachel Carson's warning about the dangers of pesticides, which in 1962 touched off a national debate and a governmental investigation, for instance, and Hannah Arendt's significant series on the Eichmann trial, which engaged intellectuals in controversy in 1963.

Certainly over the years the *New Yorker* influenced American journalism all out of proportion to its relatively small circulation, about 468,000 in 1963. Perhaps no other magazine in a similar period published as many articles, stories, cartoons, and verses that later appeared in book form. Any listing of such books—and each year brought a fresh dozen or so—would be purely arbitrary; but among them were Clarence Day's *Life with Father,* James Thurber's *My Life and Hard Times,* Sally Benson's *Junior Miss,* Ruth McKenney's *My Sister Eileen,* John O'Hara's *Pal Joey,* John Hersey's *Hiroshima,* to which the magazine unprecedentedly devoted an entire issue in 1946, John Updike's *Pigeon Feathers,* Rachel Carson's *Silent Spring,* and Alan Moorehead's *The Blue Nile.* At one time in 1941 four comedies based on *New Yorker* pieces were simultaneously hits on Broadway: *Mr. and Mrs. North, Pal Joey, Life with Father,* and *My Sister Eileen.*

Although the *New Yorker* was not a "funny" magazine, it raised the level of American humor. It showed that humor could take other forms than the traditional "he-she" jokes. Ross's prejudice against that sort of humor was so strong that he published one joke, its lines transposed, in each anniversary issue:

POP: A man who thinks he can make it in par.

JOHNNY: What is an optimist, pop?

The *New Yorker* helped to popularize the cartoon with caption intimately related to picture. Cartoons in *Judge* and the old *Life* were merely appendages to two-line jokes which could have stood without illustration. Ross developed the one-line caption, made pointed by rewriting, and he insisted that readers know at a glance which character in the picture was speaking.

In less apparent fashion, the conscientious reporting by Rebecca West, Alva Johnston, Joseph Mitchell, Richard Rovere, St. Clair McKelway, Lillian Ross, A. J. Liebling, Daniel Lang, E. J. Kahn, Jr., and others surely affected the standards of American journalism. Richard Watts, Jr.,

The *New Yorker*'s Prospectus:

The New Yorker will be a reflection in word and picture of metropolitan life. It will be human. Its general tenor will be one of gaiety, wit and satire, but it will be more than a jester. It will not be what is commonly called radical or highbrow. It will be what is commonly called sophisticated, in that it will assume a reasonable degree of enlightenment on the part of its readers. It will hate bunk.

As compared to the newspaper, *The New Yorker* will be interpretative rather than stenographic. It will print facts that it will have to go behind the scenes to get, but it will not deal in scandal for the sake of scandal nor sensation for the sake of sensation. Its integrity will be above suspicion. It hopes to be so entertaining and informative as to be a necessity for the person who knows his way about or wants to.

The New Yorker will devote several pages a week to the covering of contemporary events and people of interest. This will be done by writers capable of appreciating the elements of a situation and, in setting them down, of indicating their importance and significance. *The New Yorker* will present the truth and the whole truth without fear and without favor, but will not be iconoclastic.

Amusements and the arts will be thoroughly covered by departments which will present, in addition to criticism, the personality, the anecdote, the color and chat of the various subdivisions of this sphere. *The New Yorker*'s conscientious guide will list each week all current amusement offerings worth-while—theatres, motion pictures, musical events, art exhibitions, sport and miscellaneous entertainment—providing an ever-ready answer to the prevalent query, "What shall we do with this evening?" Through *The New Yorker*'s Mr. Van Bibber III, readers will be kept apprised of what is going on in the public and semi-public smart gathering places—the clubs, hotels, cafés, supper clubs, cabarets and other resorts.

Judgment will be passed upon new books of consequence, and *The New Yorker* will carry a list of the season's books which it considers worth reading.

There will be a page of editorial paragraphs, commenting on the week's events in a manner not too serious.

There will be a personal mention column—a jotting down in the small-town newspaper style of the comings, goings, and doings in the village of New York. This will contain some josh and some news value.

The New Yorker will carry each week several pages of prose and verse, short and long, humorous, satirical and miscellaneous.

The New Yorker expects to be distinguished for its illustrations, which will include caricatures, sketches, cartoons and humorous and satirical drawings in keeping with its purpose.

The New Yorker will be the magazine which is not edited for the old lady in Dubuque. It will not be concerned with what she is thinking about. This is not meant in disrespect, but *The New Yorker* is a magazine avowedly published for a metropolitan audience and thereby will escape an influence which hampers most national publications. It expects a considerable national circulation, but this will come from persons who have a metropolitan interest.

Quoted by Margaret Case Harriman, in her The Vicious Circle: The Story of the Algonquin Round Table, *Rinehart, 1951.*

succinctly expressed the essence of the *New Yorker*'s reportage:

> It doesn't encourage the stuffed shirts and it has a warm place in its heart for the more amiable misfits; it certainly isn't radical, but it can give the reactionaries an expert dressing down; it is often annoyingly supercilious, but it likewise can be perceptive and understanding. Best of all, it not only has a frequent kind of frank honesty which the newspapers too often lack, but it is so professionally skillful that it impresses the journalistic journeymen it tends to despise and serves as a good example for them. I suspect it of being the most forceful influence in American newspaper writing today.

Newsweek

SOURCE: "Alarms and Issues," in *Newsweek*, Vol. LXXVI, No. 15, October 12, 1970, pp. 129-30.

[*In the following excerpt, the critic notes changes in the editorial stance and subject matter of the* New Yorker *as a possible reaction to the social and political upheavals of the late 1960s.*]

"We had been hoping to hear from our old friend Ernest M. Frimbo," began the lead article in the only magazine that could begin like that. Some pages on, however, a reader of the Sept. 26 *New Yorker* came across what seemed to be a radical departure from the sort of urbane, good-humored, politically unprovocative fare that once made the magazine as predictable in its way as a Sears, Roebuck catalogue.

The article in point is "The Greening of America," a 39,000-word essay by Yale University law professor Charles A. Reich. No popular magazine has ever published a more comprehensive and unforgiving indictment of America's consumer culture—or at least no magazine that has traditionally taken so much of its tone from that culture. In the presence of gilt-edged ads for Caribbean cruises and exotic furs, Reich charges that Americans have created "a society that is unjust to its poor and minorities, is run for the benefit of a privileged few, lacks its proclaimed democracy and liberty, is ugly and artificial, destroys the environment and the self, and is, like the war it spawns, 'unhealthy for children and other living things'."

Obviously, that sort of thing strikes a new note for a publication that, for decades after its birth in 1925, seemed dedicated to the proposition that outrage was unpardonable and that politics, like a rainy summer at the shore, was a distasteful reality to be borne with good grace and composure. But the Reich article was no isolated phenomenon. Last week's *New Yorker* featured a wry but alarming report on the National Guard by Renata Adler. Paired with Richard Harris's 1968 indictment of the National Rifle Association, the Adler article may well convince the extreme right that *The New Yorker* is out to disarm the nation. A year ago, before the public furor over the Song My affair, the magazine printed "Casualties of War," Daniel Lang's powerful account of the rape and murder of a Vietnamese girl by four GI's. And following the Cambodian invasion this spring, *The New Yorker* devoted its Notes and Comment section to an impassioned protest against President Nixon's "act of usurpation." Casual readers remark that even the matchless cartoons seem to be growing more topical and militant.

If *The New Yorker* is on its way to becoming the *Ramparts* of the carriage trade, only one man has to answer for it. The magazine's shabby editorial offices on 43rd Street are the personal kingdom of William Shawn, 63, a kindly and courtly man who inherited the editorship from Harold Ross, *The New Yorker*'s perfectionist founder, in 1952. Granting a rare interview last week—but retaining at least a semblance of his cherished privacy by typing out the answers to some of the questions—Shawn pointed out that there was nothing droll or cozy about such *New Yorker* offerings as John Hersey's "Hiroshima" (1946), James Baldwin's "The Fire Next Time" (1962), Rachel Carson's "Silent Spring" (1962) and Hannah Arendt's "Eichmann in Jerusalem" (1963).

"It's been my theory that the notion of 'frothiness' goes back to the 1920s, and is a rumor of a rumor." Shawn told *Newsweek*'s Judith Gingold. "As I see it, people are always discovering that *The New Yorker* is more serious, less frothy than they thought it was. Every few years, the same discovery is made again." Shawn does allow, however, that the magazine's "seriousness" has at least been accelerated by the seething '60s. "This is a time of crises, emergencies, alarms and issues," he explained, "and since *The New Yorker* is, as it's always been, a journalistic magazine, it inevitably deals with all of these one way or another. I wish the world were otherwise, and if it ever becomes otherwise, I imagine *The New Yorker* will become otherwise, too."

Shawn may be selling his own role a bit short, for if *The New Yorker* reflects the tone of its times it also reflects the singular mind of William Shawn. The 1930s, after all, were also a time of "crises, emergencies, alarms and issues," but one would have hardly deduced any of that from perusing Harold Ross's magazine. Several years ago, New Journalist Tom Wolfe dismantled *The New Yorker* in a pair of articles that characterized Shawn as "the museum curator, the mummifier, the preserver-in-amber, the smiling embalmer . . . for Harold Ross's *New Yorker*." On that occasion, a number of Wolfe's facts didn't check, and five years later his unflattering portrait of Shawn doesn't check well either. If *The New Yorker* has moved with relative ease from social banter to reform and dissent,

much of the credit goes to the editor and his ready acceptance of young writers and young ideas.

One of these young writers, 27-year-old Rick Hertzberg, finds his boss "receptive, incredibly respectful of writers, and extremely generous." "Shawn and the magazine are so confident, so unaffected, that nothing threatens them," says the shaggy-maned Hertzberg. "I've never noticed the slightest reaction to long hair at *The New Yorker,* or any relation between long hair and the kind of stories I cover." Notes and Comment, once the special province of E.B. White, is now frequently given over to Vietnam comment by Jonathan Schell, who is 27. And when students took to the streets last spring to protest the Cambodian invasion, it was with *The New Yorker*'s editorial blessing.

Although none of his staffers even hint that Shawn might change his editorial policies to reap an extra dollar, the magazine's new tone seems at least partly attributable to some unpleasant economic realities. The entire magazine business is in a general slump this year, but *The New Yorker* has been witnessing a slow, steady drop in its advertising revenue since 1967, and its circulation—which now stands at 456,000—has fallen 4 per cent during the same period. And although *New Yorker* men steadfastly refuse to recognize the existence of any real competition, Manhattan's breezy, fast-growing *New York* magazine has been making steady gains in the ad race.

All this long ago suggested that it was time for *The New Yorker* to jettison the quaint, somewhat arrogant assumption that the people who deserved the magazine would somehow discover it. And recently *The New Yorker* has begun to act on that realization. In April the magazine named a new ad agency, Lord, Geller, Federico and Partners, which promptly launched an intensive attempt to increase *The New Yorker*'s circulation. As part of its pitch to the young, Harold Ross's haughty old slick has at last offered itself on the electronic media and even gone one step beyond—to an advertisement in the *Village Voice,* the hip, Greenwich Village weekly. Not that *The New Yorker* is about to compete with the underground press on its home turf. In matters sexual, for example, the magazine has chosen to ignore the vanguard and remain as verbally squeamish as that little old lady in Dubuque.

William Shawn admits that his embargo on cursing and copulation has cost him some good writing through the years, but he plans no changes. And certainly few top writers mind dropping a few expletives for a place in Mr. Shawn's showcase. Happy writers, in fact, are the magazine's best advertisements. Charles Reich, the painstaking polemicist of "The Greening of America," admits he had second thoughts about publishing a revolutionary manifesto in such a stronghold of conspicuous consumption. After working with *The New Yorker* editors for five months, however, Reich sounded eminently enthusiastic. "I've had twenty years of this sort of work and I've never had a better experience," he said, "Those people are consummate professional craftsmen. It's the last vestige of something different—an example of what an institution would look like after the world changes the way I want it to."

Time, **New York**

SOURCE: "New Politics, New *New Yorker,*" in *Time,* New York, Vol. 99, No. 18, May 1, 1972, pp. 34, 39.

[In the following excerpt, the critic offers observations on the more liberal social and political attitudes reflected by the New Yorker *during the volatile era of the late 1960s and early 1970s.]*

In more ways than the obvious visual ones, *The New Yorker* since its founding in 1925 has seemed almost immune to dramatic change. It has had only two editors in those 47 years, Harold Ross and the man who took over after Ross's death in 1951, William Shawn. The devotion to low-key fiction and gentlemanly criticism has persisted, as have the horse-racing column and such self-mocking images as Eustace Tilly and an imaginary correspondent called "The Long-Winded Lady."

So would you believe that *The New Yorker* is today one of the most socially activist and politically polemical among major magazines? That it vibrates in tones of tough liberalism and occasionally radical outrage?

"The President," said a recent editorial about busing, "seems determined to keep the people's fear and hatred at the peak until election time, whatever the cost to the nation's children and to its laws." An editorial on the expanded bombing of Viet Nam: "The war that this country's government is waging now is war trivialized . . . and involves us all in the dishonor of killing in a cause we are no longer willing to die for." An article about the Nixon Administration's record on civil liberties, by Richard Harris: "No one can say that the President has willfully set out to undermine the Constitution that he swore to uphold. But how would the results be different if he had?"

"*The New Yorker* has always run articles about public issues," Editor Shawn says; the magazine can cite such warnings as Rachel Carson's *Silent Spring* and James Baldwin's *The Fire Next Time* ten years ago. But Shawn agrees that both the urgency and frequency of political pieces have increased sharply. In his view, the turning point was the 1970 Cambodian invasion. Richard Goodwin, once a Kennedy speechwriter, wrote a denunciation of Nixon's "usurpation" of power; Shawn used it as an editorial. After that "Notes and Comment," once the fluffy lead-in to each issue, frequently became the magazine's most somber instrument.

The change coincided with some of the roughest weather *The New Yorker* had ever encountered in the narrow, sometimes viciously choppy New York publishing pond. Back in 1965, *New York* had run Tom Wolfe's satiric attack on Shawn and his magazine. Though shallow and unfair, Wolfe's article generated talk and crystallized the notion that *The New Yorker* had become musty and irrelevant. Then, in the late '60s, like other magazines, it began experiencing a money crunch. It continued to be profitable, but income shrank dramatically.

Outsiders naturally assumed that Shawn's response to adversity was new politics for *The New Yorker*—an impression strengthened by an advertising campaign that emphasized the stinging prose. But Shawn and his staff insist that

there was no connection. "Even when things were at their worst," Shawn told *Time*'s Horace Judson recently, "I have never felt any pressure. I can't imagine what the pressure could have been. I did hear murmurings in the background, people in the advertising community who thought we were too sedate in our appearance. But we liked the way we looked. We always felt that we were in advance in what we said."

As Shawn and his writers agree, the real reason for *The New Yorker*'s political preoccupation lies in the subtle relation between them. *The New Yorker,* with hardly any hierarchical structure, could be described as a participatory dictatorship. Though Shawn shapes the magazine each week ("I approve everything we publish"), only very rarely does he initiate a direct assignment or even set a deadline. Instead, he chooses from what the writers suggest and submit.

The altered tone and emphasis have come "not because of a deliberate or calculated change in policy, but simply because certain authors—responding to the heightened sense of trouble at the end of the '60s and since—have become interested in saying certain things, and we, the editors, are sympathetic."

Shawn deals with his writers the way he approaches the outside world—combining intellectual interest and personal detachment. In a city where editors think of themselves as public figures, Shawn, 64, is so retiring as to be invisible, a trait to which he adds a genuine but rigidly old-fashioned courtesy. "I've known him 20 years," says Rich-

Katherine Angell White.

ard Harris, a staff writer, "and we are still Mr. Shawn, Mr. Harris." "Behind Shawn's manner," adds Richard Goodwin, "is a fantastically acute steel mind. I've never had editing like it. He went over my Cambodian piece word by word, with me sitting by his desk. He has a great instinct for bringing out what you are trying to do."

Shawn's own profound disquiet about the dangers to mankind evidently has early roots. Born in Chicago, he dropped out of the University of Michigan, worked as a newspaper reporter in New Mexico, then in 1933 joined *The New Yorker* as a "Talk of the Town" reporter. He was an editor by 1935. The only piece he ever signed in the magazine was a brief and melancholy fantasy in 1936 titled *The Catastrophe,* which tells how a meteorite neatly obliterated "all five boroughs of Greater New York," and how the entire notion of New York eventually was forgotten. Ten years later, as managing editor, he persuaded Ross that John Hersey's account of the obliteration of Hiroshima was so important that it should take up the entire editorial space of one issue.

The recent changes seem to be grounded, paradoxically, in a kind of classical conservatism: "We have defended certain things that we do believe in and cherish," Shawn says. "We have written whenever we thought the democracy as we saw it or the constitutional processes were threatened." He thinks back: "I remember Rachel Carson, when she was working on *Silent Spring,* just hated having to do it. With her kind of love of nature, the sea and birds, she felt she was using up the last years of her life on something repugnant. It is often that way now. You do these things out of a feeling of duty."

J. H. Rutledge and P. B. Bart

SOURCE: "Urbanity, Inc.: How *The New Yorker* Wins Business Success Despite Air of Disdain," in *The Wall Street Journal,* June 30, 1958, pp. 1, 6.

[*In the following excerpt, Rutledge and Bart examine reasons for the financial success of the* New Yorker.]

A. J. Russell, *The New Yorker* Magazine's urbane, well-tailored advertising director, still looks sheepish when he recalls it. "It was awfully corny," he mumbles, shifting his position uneasily.

Until recently, it seems, it was the custom at *The New Yorker* for the advertising staff to toll a ship's bell whenever an important new account was landed. Upon hearing the signal, all hands would adjourn to the nearby Harvard Club to clink glasses and enjoy good fellowship.

But now the high-spirited ad men, aware that their frivolity is inimical to *The New Yorker*'s urbane atmosphere, have retreated to their desks in quiet embarrassment. "At *The New Yorker*," as one staff member explains firmly, "being corny is more than a minor indiscretion."

And no wonder. *The New Yorker*'s carefully cultivated air of sophistication has helped transform this once lean magazine into a remarkably prosperous business enterprise—one which even now is piling up some notable, if rather corny, records in the magazine industry.

To wit: While the recession has drained much of the advertising linage from the big national weeklies (*Life*'s linage is down 23%, *Saturday Evening Post*'s down 14% in the first five months of 1958 from the like period last year), *The New Yorker* has been bounding merrily along, even showing a slight (3%) improvement over 1957 levels. Among general circulation consumer magazines no other publication carries so many pages of advertising as *The New Yorker,* according to figures of the Publishers Information Bureau, although it is topped by *Business Week,* a specialized business magazine.

These gains look even better when it's considered that *The New Yorker*'s ad rate per thousand of circulation is perhaps the highest of any national consumer magazine—nearly twice *Life*'s rate. Moreover, *The New Yorker*'s fastidious editors annually reject as much as $250,000 of advertising which they deem to be beneath the magazine's dignity, such as ads which take a particularly blatant approach to the problem of body odor. "You might say we are anti-armpit," quips suave Stephen B. Botsford, the magazine's president.

The New Yorker's top officials are as reticent in circulation promotion as they are about armpits. President Botsford says he spent a scant $9,323 to lure more readers in 1956 "while the *Reader's Digest* spent $2.4 million on postage costs alone for subscription offers." Even this expenditure Mr. Botsford deemed excessive: In 1957 he cut it to $645.07.

Despite these unorthodox economies, the magazine's circulation has climbed to 420,000—modest in these days of multi-million circulations, but reassuring to the magazine's editors who cringe at the image of *The New Yorker* as a "mass magazine." In their very first announcement, they emphasized that *"The New Yorker* will be the magazine which is not edited for the old lady in Dubuque." Yet today even Dubuque has its 76 subscribers. Overall, 80% of the readers are outside of New York City, with 21,600 in Los Angeles alone.

"The most remarkable thing about *The New Yorker*'s circulation is that it's genuine," notes Bernard P. Gallagher, a leading magazine broker and operator of two magazine subscription agencies. "When you subscribe you pay the price on the masthead; other magazines roll up a lot of phony circulation by flooding the mails with cut-rate subscription offers."

Most publishers, of course, insist there is nothing "phony" about circulation gained by cut-price offers; a subscriber is a subscriber no matter what price he is charged. But some do concede that special-discount subscribers may not be deeply interested and often fail to renew, *The New Yorker,* which sells 71% of its copies by subscription and the rest on the newsstands, claims a renewal rate of about 76%, regarded as exceedingly high in this industry.

The upshot of all this is profits—handsome profits. The magazine earned a net of $1.6 million in 1957, nearly three times its net five years ago. And industry insiders note that *The New Yorker*'s fat 10% profit margin (profit after taxes as a percentage of sales) is probably the highest in the field.

Big Time, Inc., pulls in far higher revenues—$254 million last year to *The New Yorker*'s $15.5 million. But its net profit margin was less than 5%, or half *The New Yorker*'s. For the magazine industry as a whole—which is a notably poor profit performer—the margin was a mere 2.7% in 1956, the last figure available.

No publisher, too, sticks more resolutely to its knitting than does *The New Yorker*. Time, Inc., gathers its dollars from such diverse fields as radio and TV stations and paper manufacturing as well as from its magazines, which include *Time* and *Life*. Other magazine firms operate subscription agencies, book departments and the like.

"Our only business is putting out our magazine," says Vice President Eugene R. Spaulding. While a number of collections of *New Yorker* stories and cartoons have appeared in book form, all profits have been turned over to the contributors.

The prospect of sizable profits seemed remote indeed 33 years ago when wealthy Raoul H. Fleischmann first supplied most of the funds to launch the venture. Mr. Fleischmann, still an active board-chairman at 72, recalls he had to pour in "over $700,000" before lifting his frail magazine out of the red.

Mr. Fleischmann's secret weapon, however, was not money but manpower—specifically a cantankerous free-wheeler from Colorado named Harold Ross. Although he never finished high school and looked, according to Alexander Woollcott,; "like a dishonest Abe Lincoln," the gaunt shaggy Ross commanded a remarkable circle of literary friends. Among them: Woollcott himself, Mark Connelly, Robert Benchley, George S. Kaufman and Dorothy Parker. Before long Ross' contributors included such as Ernest Hemingway, F. Scott Fitzgerald, E. B. White and James Thurber along with famed cartoonists Charles Addams, Peter Arno and Rea Irvin.

Despite or maybe because of this abundance of talent, *The New Yorker*'s early years were anything but tranquil. For one thing, Editor Ross engaged in perpetual guerrilla warfare with his benefactor. Reminisces Mr. Fleischmann: "Ross and I never got along. He was sore because I put in the dough, or maybe because I had the dough to put in."

"Ross always was threatening to quit and take his stable of writers to another magazine," recalls one former *New Yorker* staff member who was around in the old days. "At one point Ross even sold his stock to Henry R. Luce out of spite." Mr. Luce, editor-in-chief of all Time, Inc., publications, and a target of one of *The New Yorker*'s more acid profiles, later sold out.

The combative brand of individualism which Ross exuded still prevails throughout *The New Yorker*'s cramped, bustling offices. As one business staff member relates: "Ross' legacy was that of a balance of terror between the editorial and business departments—with the editors creating most of the terror."

Although considerably less terrifying than his predecessor, William Shawn, current *New Yorker* editor, nonetheless wields great personal influence. Significantly, while most veterans refer to septuagenarian Fleischmann as

"Raoul," the 50-year-old editor is usually called "Mr. Shawn."

Another yardstick of the editor's power: Any inquiry or other message which the business department wishes to convey to the editorial department must be channeled through Fred Norman, the official "liaison man." Yet Editor Shawn himself, if so inclined, may step right in and veto an advertisement set to run in an issue—even though the ad already has received the sanction of the advertising manager and the president. This is an extraordinary setup, of course, in the ad-oriented magazine world.

Nonetheless, Editor Shawn is not at all hesitant in using his prerogatives. He'll often veto an ad on the grounds that it is in "poor taste" or that it claims to offer "proof" as to the quality of a product.

Advertising officials themselves also are on the lookout for material which fails to fit into the magazine's "style," of course. President Botsford keeps a fat "Rejection Book" in his office containing ads turned down by editorial or business department heads. The loose-limbed Mr. Botsford, stepson of Chairman Fleischmann, points to one rejected ad portraying an inexpensive clothing product and shrugs:

"We can't serve these people and Brooks Brothers at the same time. We want to give the magazine a Brooks Brothers and Tiffany sort of flavor."

The New Yorker also turns down thousands of dollars in liquor advertising in keeping with its formula which limits liquor to 16% of total annual advertising. Ad men also reject material heralding the virtues of vitamins, hangover cures, yogurt, feminine hygiene products and other items.

These restrictive policies, coupled with *The New Yorker*'s frequent demands for revisions of advertising copy, cause more than a little brow-furrowing along Madison Avenue. As Promotion Manager Philip Ewald concedes with characteristic understatement: "We sometimes place an agency in a difficult position with its client by seeming to cast doubt upon the agency's judgment. It's awkward when agencies say to us, 'Aren't our accounts good enough for you?'"

While editors often encroach upon the ad men's realm in vetoing advertising, there'd be scant chance of survival for an advertising man who trespassed on the editorial floor. Editor Ross himself made sure of that over 20 years ago when he personally cast out a hapless night club space salesman who had come in search of some editorial favors.

Mr. Shawn and his subordinates obviously take pride in this tradition. "If it's possible to single out a single reason for the magazine's success, you can say it's due to the writers' freedom from the whims of the business department," remarks one veteran writer. "There's never any pressure to add or delete an item because of an advertising tie-in."

In April, 1955, when the *Reader's Digest* decided to accept ads *The New Yorker* ran a facetious story which offered a "welcome to the wicked fold." The piece went on to advise *Reader's Digest* editors: "When the advertising manager makes the mistake of showing up in the editor's office, however, he should be rubbed out."

At *The New Yorker,* even President Botsford carefully avoids invading the editorial domain. On those infrequent occasions when he conducts a visitor around the magazine's quarters, he walks briskly up and down the editorial halls, opening no doors, greeting no one. Smiling nervously, he will say: "We have to make it a quick tour today—the editors are very busy."

Though strangers in their own house, *New Yorker* business executives nonetheless strive mightily to emulate their magazine's "style" in their own frequent public utterances before publishing and advertising groups. They lean on the low-key quip, the urbane understatement.

Tall, natty Philip Ewald, the promotion director, will lace a talk at the Harvard Club by tossing off a "story Picasso tells about the two cannibals." President Botsford will drop a quote like, "My idea of heaven is eating pate de fois gras to the sound of trumpets," and add characteristically: "Then hell must be eating Harvard Club chicken to the sound of Stephen Botsford."

All this, it is hoped, somehow conveys *The New Yorker* atmosphere—but it's all very painful for the orators themselves. As Mr. Botsford told an audience recently: "This is my farewell as a public speaker because they can't make Miltown fast enough to keep me in oratory."

The writers, too, find *The New Yorker* mood a hard one to sustain. As one former editor states: "The magazine plainly has fallen into the formula approach—there are too many interminable stories about sensitive adolescents, too many cartoons about desert islands and talking animals."

Editor Shawn, however, disputes this charge. "*The New Yorker* follows no formulas," he asserts in one of his highly infrequent conversations with reporters. "People used to call our stories 'slice of life' fiction because of their plotless style, but that's just not correct. We run all types of stories."

Humor poses the most serious problem. "Perhaps we're just not as funny as we used to be—there aren't so many funny writers around any more," reflects Mr. Fleischmann.

The editors, though highly secretive about their policies, have tried to meet these problems in various ways. They pay more for the first 1,500 words of a piece than for the remainder to encourage brevity. And they often pay more for a humorous work than for a sullen one. Some prolific writers are said to earn over $30,000 annually.

Many leading contributors, of course, bolster their pay with outside literary efforts. Among these writers: Ogden Nash, S. J. Perelman, Peter De Vries, John Hersey, John Cheever and James Thurber.

In format, *The New Yorker* has not undergone much change in recent years. It still opens with Talk of the Town, with its casually written items ("Our interest in nimble oldsters led us to an uncommonly energetic one the other day . . ."). Its stories and articles still hide their by-lines at the bottom of the final paragraph. And its one-paragraph items (Department of Understatement, Department of Utter Confusion, Social Notes From All Over) still derive humor from the typographical faux pas of other magazines and newspapers.

Perhaps *The New Yorker*'s most famous trademarks are its covers which, as President Botsford proudly asserts, boast "no bands, no strips, no stickers, no other gimmicks telling of the goodies inside." Once each year, in fact, Eustace Tilley himself reappears on the cover—Tilley being the name given to the caricature of a Victorian dandy peering through his monocle which appeared on the first cover.

To assemble its weekly issues, *The New Yorker* employs an editorial staff of nearly 100. Each week about 2,000 unsolicited editorial contributions and 2,000 cartoon ideas are processed in the small cubicles lining the editorial halls. In addition, the editors meticulously scrutinize, rewrite, check and counter-check material sent in by regular contributors. The extent to which they call for revised proofs, on glossy paper, is a constant irritant to the business department.

New Yorker writers enjoy a high degree of freedom. They come and go as they please; some arrive at their offices at noon, some later. Instead of drawing paychecks on an article-by-article basis, some 30 writers operate on "cash drawing accounts." Money is advanced from the account and, at year's end, article payments are balanced against the amount drawn. Recalls one veteran writer: "At one point I got several thousands of dollars behind, and no one ever said a word to me." Most writers, however, come out well ahead.

"We're a relatively quiet, simple band of people," says one writer. "Very few characters among us." There's no back-slapping or frivolity in the corridors, he notes.

Still, many writers vehemently protest such words as "urbane" or "sophisticated" when used to describe *The New Yorker* or its staff. Both words, in fact, usually are crossed out when they turn up in copy.

"What puts the magazine over is its integrity, not its urbanity," asserts one writer with vigor. "We try to tell the truth, to say simple things simply. We're often sentimental—we use words like 'love.' Why, I think the old lady from Dubuque enjoys our magazine much more than the jaded sophisticate from the big city," he adds.

Editorial staff members generally feel strongly that their magazine's success stems from this "integrity" rather than from any "Brooks Brothers" air of sophistication. Their belief: That the writers' freedom from the pressures of the business department forms the basis of the magazine's strength. Says one writer: "No space salesman has ever told me what I could or couldn't write, and if one ever did, I'd pack up and go home."

Still, the advertising and circulation departments have their own explanations as to the reasons for their magazine's success—and they also have done very well on the pay side. Ad salesmen draw salaries of from $6,500 to $19,000 a year, not counting 25% bonuses. In addition, many advertising hands partake of a stock plan effective after three years of employment which earns them 60 salable shares of stock a year for five years. In some cases, the five-year period is extended.

The leading stockholders, of course, remain the Fleischmann family which now includes the chairman, Raoul Fleischmann, President Botsford and Peter Fleischmann, treasurer, who is Mr. Fleischmann's son. Mr. Fleischmann says he retains 25% of the stock of his company, which now has total assets of $8.2 million (including *The New Yorker* trade name valued at $1).

MAJOR FIGURES

William Shawn

SOURCE: An excerpt from *Here at the "New Yorker,"* by Brendan Gill, Random House, 1975, pp. 388-95.

[*Shawn joined the staff of the* New Yorker *in 1933 as a reporter for the magazine's "Talk of the Town" section and succeeded Harold Ross as editor of the magazine in 1952. In the following excerpt, he discusses Ross's editorship of the magazine.*]

Harold Ross presented himself to the world as a raucous, clumsy, primitive, somewhat comic figure. He said extremely funny things spontaneously and intentionally, and in his conversation and in his physical bearing he was funny unintentionally, or almost unintentionally, as well. He lent himself to anecdote. Because of this, and because his personal qualities were large in scale and included a formidable charm and magnetism, the serious and inspired work that he did as an editor tended at times to be lost sight of. Occasionally, when contemporaries of Ross talked about the old days on *The New Yorker,* one got the impression that he did very little to create it or run it—that in spite of his inadequacies, and somehow over his protest, a number of other people did what was necessary to put out the magazine each week. The implication was that Ross spent much of his time getting in the way of the talented people who worked for him. None of this, of course, is true. Ross founded *The New Yorker,* but he did far more. He gave it its character, he shaped it, he guided it through its formative period, he determined its basic policies and principles, and he edited it in its every detail for twenty-seven years. Some of the magazine's innovations—the characteristic literate, observant, very particularized, light-handed, timely writing that was to revolutionize the American magazine article; the Profile, the 'Talk of the Town' story, the 'letter' from abroad, all three in form and intention unlike anything that had gone before; the cartoon with the one-line caption—were there from the beginning. So was the then novel orientation toward New York City.

Of all the people Ross might have gathered around him, he selected those who had the talent, the temperament, and the outlook that were right for *The New Yorker.* They gravitated to *The New Yorker* for a reason, and they re-

mained for a reason. Whatever gaps there were in Ross's own taste and understanding and appreciation he tried to compensate for through other editors. Once he had found his way, by trial and error, to a number of editors who supplied him with what he knew was missing in him, he came to trust them utterly. He would sometimes say of a piece of writing, 'This is over my head,' by which he meant that it was slightly beyond the normal boundaries of his taste; but he trusted the judgment of the other editors, and, besides, it wasn't over his head. With a few exceptions, Ross was not adept at working directly with writers and artists. From a distance, he greatly admired them, and he was sympathetic to their professional and personal problems; in their presence, he was ill-at-ease, and could be awkward, tactless, or confusing. But he swiftly discovered, or developed, a remarkable group of editors which included Katharine White, Wolcott Gibbs, William Maxwell, Gus Lobrano, and James Geraghty. By nature strikingly unsystematic, Ross dreamed of systems that would take care of virtually everything: a system that would serve as the magazine's memory; a system that would anticipate as many 'operational contingencies' as possible; a system that would keep track of the flow of proofs and memoranda; a system that would coordinate what the various members of the staff were doing; a system that could jump into the breach and turn out an issue by itself if necessary. He found an editor to design systems and watch over them. Ross wanted the magazine to be accurate. What he had in mind, however, was not approximate, or human, accuracy; it was absolute accuracy. Therefore, he established the first magazine checking department, the purpose of which was to back up the writers by checking every checkable fact that went into print, and he placed at its head an erudite editor equipped to take accuracy as far as it could go. Ross knew, roughly, what he wanted the magazine to look like, but he had no idea of how to go about making it look that way. His knowledge of typography and layout was sketchy. Nevertheless, within months he found the one make-up editor in the world, the legendary Carmine Peppe, who could provide him with the chaste and lovely pages that would properly set off whatever we published—and to this day the pages are Peppe's pages. Ross had no aptitude for keeping an organization running smoothly and in a relatively happy state, but he found people who could help him do that, too. He presided over it all—justly, nervously, and, for the most part, benevolently.

Every issue of *The New Yorker* represented hundreds of editorial choices, hundreds of decisions; Ross chose, and Ross decided. Somebody had to say what went into the magazine and what stayed out; Ross was the one who said it. He read proofs of everything that went into the magazine, and respectfully 'queried' anything he thought was questionable; his queries, in the course of time, influenced writers and other editors, set technical and literary standards, established a canon of taste, and laid the basis for a tradition of good writing which still flourishes. It was not someone else who led the magazine to avoid whatever was shoddy, shabby, cynical, petty, sensational, gossipy, exploitative, opportunistic, coarse, pedestrian, or banal; it was Ross.

Ross was an enormously intelligent man who worked almost entirely by instinct and intuition. He was not naturally analytical in his approach to a piece of writing or to a drawing. If he had a favorable response to something, or an unfavorable one, he felt no need to know why. If he laughed at a cartoon, that was enough for him; that meant it was funny, and he didn't think that his reaction or the humor itself should be, or could be, analyzed. He was unintellectual, at times even anti-intellectual. He once told me, half seriously, that he didn't want to know what any writer thought. And in a way he didn't. He was not at home with ideas, theory, speculation—abstract thought of any kind. He liked what he regarded as pure information. His working assumption, at least, was that there was such a thing as objective reporting. He wanted to know about events; he did not want to know what a writer's subjective response to the events was. It was hard for him to face the rumored possibility that a writer could approach a journalistic story with preconceptions, with a bias, with a point of view; and he appeared to hope that if these impurities were present, the writer would transcend them. At a minimum, he expected that the writer's point of view would not be expressed explicitly but would be implicit in the facts. Because Ross was suspicious of 'thinking,' the magazine that he founded and edited did not publish either essays or what are called articles of opinion. It was, fundamentally, a magazine of reporting, humor, fiction, and criticism. His feeling for reporting, humor, and criticism was sure and confident; his feeling for fiction was less so, and his feeling for poetry still less, and in these spheres he therefore relied rather more on the judgment of others. He shied away from the words 'art' and 'literature.' For many years, the word 'literary,' applied to some piece of writing—including fiction—was a house pejorative. But Ross enjoyed and was stirred by, valued and encouraged much that was in fact literary.

Ross was an editor who doted on immaculate writing and on stylish writing, which is to say writing that had style. He had a natural taste for simple, direct, colloquial writing, but he never failed to take delight in good writing of any sort, even writing that was elaborate or exquisite. He was equally open-minded in the field of comic art. He may have had his preferences in styles, but he was receptive to as many styles as there were talented and original comic artists. He never talked aesthetics—again, he would have shunned the word—but he was highly sensitive to graphic art. And, though he would have been embarrassed to admit it, he recognized beauty when it appeared. It was certainly not the least of Ross's talents that he was able to see talent in writers and artists before it was plainly visible to everyone. Also, he understood that talent developed more slowly in some than in others, and he was willing to wait. He gradually learned that the primary function of the magazine's editors, including him, was to create a structure and an atmosphere—a little world apart from the world—within which the writers and artists could fulfill themselves. The entire editorial staff was there, Ross realized, to serve the writers and artists, and then to bring their work to the reader in an appropriate setting.

Every publication must consider itself to be interested in the high quality of the work it publishes, but in Ross, I think, this interest ran especially deep. Not only was he determined to publish the best writers and artists he could find; once he had found them, he did everything possible to stimulate and encourage them to do the best work they were capable of. By being hospitable to the best, and expecting the best, he often received the best. Something else contributed to the high quality of the work published in *The New Yorker.* Unlike some editors, Ross was not diverted by external considerations. He did not care about 'names' or reputations; he published material he thought had merit, no matter who had done it. If a writer had a name, or acquired one, that did not rule him out, but it did not rule him in, either; he was treated like anyone else. If his work was seen to have merit and to be right for *The New Yorker,* it was accepted; if not, it was rejected. Unknown writers and artists were as welcome as known writers and artists; it was the quality of the work that mattered. Also, Ross did not have commercial considerations on his mind. He did not worry about whether what we published attracted advertisers or drove them off. Nor did he concern himself with building a large circulation. He concentrated on the quality of the magazine, and let the circulation find its own level. He did not think of how many people might like what we published. And he was indifferent to fashion. We published what pleased us, and we ignored the question of whether or not it was fashionable.

I have never been sure just what Ross really thought about facts. All I know is that he loved them. They were an end in themselves; they were self-justifying. I doubt whether he gave any thought to why it was good to gather facts and present them in journalistic form; he simply took it for granted that that was worth doing. As a young editor working for Ross, I never questioned the usefulness of facts. It was only in later years that I realized that facts in themselves might be meaningless or worthless, or might need defending. Ross was not tormented by questions of this kind. Scores of articles were written for *The New Yorker* because he himself was curious about something; he wanted to find out about a particular situation or person or event. He wanted the magazine to report on something not because he thought the public—or some hypothetical reader—wanted to know about it, or ought to know about it, but because he wanted to know. The impulse was not professional, it was personal. He used to say, 'We don't cover the news; we parallel the news.' But he had marvellous news judgment, and he knew what news to parallel. He had a vast, though not indiscriminate, curiosity, and it was that curiosity which set the magazine on the course it is still following. His appetite for facts was not unlimited, but it was large, and perhaps this explains why the magazine's reporting became as thorough as it did—for among the new standards he set were standards of thoroughness. Facts steadied him and comforted him. Facts also amused him. They didn't need to be funny facts—just facts. A series of factual statements set down with complete gravity could make him laugh because they took him by surprise or amazed him in some inconsequential way. Above all, facts—or some facts—were interesting to him. What was interesting to Ross, I always thought, really was interesting. What was dull to Ross really was dull. As far as I was concerned, Ross was the final authority on facts. Ross was also the final authority on humor.

His element was humor. He generated it, he sought it out, he elicited it, he needed it, and he lived by it. If he thought something was funny, it was funny.

Ross was devoted to clarity and stood in awe of grammar. Poets, he recognized—with some displeasure—had to be ambiguous and obscure at times, but he saw no excuse for ambiguity or obscurity in prose. He wanted every sentence of prose in the magazine to be intelligible, and he struggled hard to achieve that aim. The words 'fuzzy,' 'cloudy,' and simply 'unclear' turned up often in his queries. He also wanted impeccable grammar. This seeming fanaticism about clarity and grammar, I think, was a form of courtesy to the reader. He didn't want the reader to be stumbling around in the murk, or to have to take time to decipher what someone was trying to say, or to be distracted from what was being said by the faulty mechanics of how it was said. 'We don't print riddles,' he often remarked. And we don't. (Being a non-formulator, he would not have thought of it this way, but his high standards of accuracy were a token of his more important high standards of truthfulness. In the same way, his high standards of grammar were a token of his more important high standards of journalistic and literary content, and of style.) In a refinement of his effort to attain total clarity, Ross tried to do away with indirection in writing—particularly in factual writing. He did not want facts to come in one moment later than they should. He wanted the reader to know everything he should know at each step of the way, and not be taken unawares by information he should have had at an earlier point. He did not want a writer to say that a character took off his hat unless it had been established that the character was wearing a hat. I interpret this avoidance of indirection, too, as a form of courtesy. Moreover, he did not want a writer to raise questions of any sort in the reader's mind (synonymous with his own mind) without answering them—if possible, immediately: he did not want the reader to be, as he said, 'tantalized.' (He said, 'A writer should never arouse curiosity without satisfying it'—and he was a man whose curiosity was easily aroused.) Finally, Ross asked for sense. He wanted everything in the magazine to make sense, to be rigorously logical. To assist him in his pursuit of clarity, grammar, and sense, he assembled a group of gifted editors who specialized in those matters.

Ross's ability to detect falseness of any sort and in any form was one of his important attributes as an editor. He was naturally drawn to what was genuine, authentic, real, true. His eye and his ear—and another sense or two that he peculiarly possessed—were affronted by a word, a phrase, a sentence, a thought, a bit of information, a line of dialogue, a short story, a piece of reporting, that was not the real thing, that was in one way or another specious, spurious, meretricious, dishonest. Although the branch of writing he knew best was journalism, his senses worked just as reliably with fiction. Even when a piece of writing was too rarefied for his taste, or outside the normal range of his interests or knowledge, or—in extreme cases—basically incomprehensible to him, he could tell whether it was the real thing or counterfeit. He could spot any kind of pretension or affectation instantly. Conversely, he looked for truth in a piece of fiction, a reporting piece, a cartoon, and he knew just what it was when he saw it. Without, I'm sure, realizing it, he was a connoisseur of authenticity.

Of Ross's own qualities, perhaps the most important was his honesty. The idea of distorting information, of tampering with facts, of saying something that you knew was incorrect or that you didn't mean, repelled him. From time to time, he referred to 'journalistic integrity,' by which he meant many things, some of which he could identify and some of which he could not. In any event, journalistic integrity was a religious matter for him. When, once, he said that *The New Yorker* was not a magazine but a cause—and Ross was a man who fled from 'causes'—he was speaking, in a sense, of integrity. Ross was no moral philosopher, and his social conscience was shaky, and he knew nothing whatever about politics, but he had a profound ethical sense when it came to journalism. The truthfulness and accuracy were part of it. The aversion to falseness was part. But there was something more. He held to some resolve—scarcely ever hinted at in words—never to publish anything, never to have something written, for a hidden reason: to promote somebody or something, to pander to somebody, to build somebody up or tear somebody down, to indulge a personal friendship or animosity, or to propagandize. There were no ulterior motives, no hidden purposes, however worthy; no concealed explanations. Everything that was published in *The New Yorker* was precisely what it purported to be, was published for its own sake. In addition, Ross was fair-minded, and he saw to it that the magazine was fair-minded. That meant being fair to every person we wrote about, and also being fair to the facts, whatever they were. These aims were seldom articulated. Ross was a secret idealist. He would have been unable to formulate his journalistic principles, but the principles were there, in his bones.

As a managing editor working for Ross, I always felt that he had some vision—never defined, never described, never mentioned—of what he thought a magazine should be, what he wanted *The New Yorker* to be, and I was trying to give it to him. I imagine that it was much the same for several other editors. If those of us now who are loosely bound together in this common enterprise manage every once in a long while to bring out an entire issue that might be called a work of art, it is because Ross, who thought he scorned works of art, prepared the way. In the early days, a small company of writers, artists, and editors—E. B. White, James Thurber, Peter Arno, and Katharine White among them—did more to make the magazine what it is than can be measured. Over the years, many other people contributed heroically to the mixture. But at the source, abounding in promise, was Ross.

Charles S. Holmes

SOURCE: "*The New Yorker*: Early Days," in *The Clocks of Columbus: The Literary Career of James Thurber*, Atheneum, 1972, pp. 90-112.

[*Holmes was an American critic and educator. In the following excerpt, he discusses James Thurber's early years at the* New Yorker.]

Joining *The New Yorker* in March of 1927 was the turning point in [James] Thurber's career, and perhaps in that of the magazine as well. He was thirty-two years old (older than most of the *New Yorker* staffers), a frustrated writer and wandering journalist who had not yet found himself or a place where he could do what he wanted to do. The magazine was in the process of developing from a doubtful experiment into an established reality, and Thurber brought to it the versatility and the kind of comic talent it was looking for. *The New Yorker* gave him the chance he needed to practice his craft as a humorist, and more important, it brought him into close association with two men who had a considerable influence on the shaping of his style at this critical moment in his development—Harold Ross and E. B. White.

In 1927 the magazine was moving into the black financially, and its special formula of original cartoons, superior reporting, and a miscellany of light essays and stories was beginning to take shape. E. B. White's "Notes and Comment" led off the magazine, and set the tone of intelligent observation and civilized prose which has been its hallmark ever since. "The Talk of the Town" (at that time done by Russel Crouse) followed, with its verbal snapshots of the New York scene; such soon-to-be-famous features as "A Reporter at Large" (chiefly the work of Morris Markey, who was to become one of Thurber's close friends), "The Wayward Press" (in those days done by Robert Benchley), and the profiles of interesting contemporary people were beginning to establish themselves; and, perhaps the most original feature of all, the remarkable cartoons by such artists as Helen Hokinson, Peter Arno, Otto Soglow, and Garrett Price were giving the struggling new magazine a special luster.

The first two years of *The New Yorker* had been shaky, and few of Harold Ross's friends had given it much chance to survive. It first appeared on February 22, 1925, an unimpressive little magazine of thirty-six pages and very little advertising. The best thing about it was Rea Irvin's cover, showing the top-hatted nineteenth-century dandy inspecting a butterfly through a monocle. The public response was apathetic. Circulation dropped from an opening issue of 15,000 copies to a low of 2700 in August, and the magazine was losing $5000 a week. As Thurber put it in *The Years with Ross, "The New Yorker* was the outstanding flop of 1925, a year of notable successes in literature, music, and entertainment." Ross was driven to extraordinary measures to keep the magazine afloat. On one occasion, he tried to get new money by entering a poker game with some of the high rollers of the Thanatopsis Literary and Inside Straight Club, a little circle within the Algonquin circle, and managed to lose $29,000. He was saved at the last moment when Raoul Fleischmann, the original angel of *The New Yorker,* and Hawley Truax, who managed its business affairs for many years, went out and raised enough money to give the magazine a fresh start. Ross's rates were very low at first, and he sometimes had to pay his writers in stock rather than cash. The slenderness of the magazine's resources in the early days is neatly summed up in the anecdote in which Ross, meeting Dorothy Parker somewhere, asked her why she hadn't been in the office the day before to do a piece she had promised

him, and she is reported to have replied, "Because someone was using the pencil."

Harold Ross himself seemed to have few of the qualifications for launching a magazine designed to appeal to a well-to-do New York audience. He had grown up in Colorado and Washington and had quit school early to follow the life of an itinerant newspaperman. He got his first newspaper job (on the Salt Lake City *Tribune*) when he was fourteen. In the early years of World War I he knocked around from city to city and from paper to paper, developing the fierce independence and the hardboiled pragmatism of the old-time reporter. During the war, he was on the editorial staff of the *Stars and Stripes* in Paris, where two of his colleagues were Captain Franklin P. Adams and Corporal Alexander Woollcott. After the war, he held a variety of editorial jobs, one on the *American Legion Magazine* and another (his last before starting *The New Yorker*) on *Judge,* the old family humor magazine.

Ross was self-educated, and his intellectual and aesthetic tastes were simple. Herbert Spencer was his philosopher, and the only writers he really liked were the manly ones, like Conrad, Twain, and O. Henry. He knew nothing of modern fiction and never did get anything out of music, painting, or poetry. (He once instructed an assistant, "Never leave me alone with poets.") In experience, character, and manner he was the Western type: physically he was rawboned, his face was craggy, his hair stiff and unruly; his manner was casual and informal (meeting Sherwood Anderson for the first time, he said, "Hi, Anderson," and launched into a lecture on English usage, one of his favorite subjects).

Yet for some obscure reason, this ex-newspaperman from Salt Lake City was determined to put out a magazine which would appeal to a wealthy and sophisticated New York audience. His experience with *Judge* had convinced him that the old two-line He-She joke had had its day, and that no humor magazine could survive the attempt to reach a national middle-class family audience. His new magazine would be aggressively parochial. In the "Prospectus" which he drew up to attract backers, he announced that it would be "a reflection of metropolitan life." It would not be "edited for the old lady in Dubuque," he added, somewhat gratuitously. Its tone would be marked by "gaiety, wit and satire," and it expected to be "distinguished for its illustrations." This last turned out to be Ross's most accurate prediction, since he was lucky enough to get Rea Irvin to act as art director from the very beginning.

In spite of its low rates and uncertain future, *The New Yorker* attracted outstanding contributors from the beginning, precisely because it was new, open to experiment, not yet committed to a formula, and because Ross made it clear that he was looking for excellence. Early issues of the magazine carried pieces by Ernest Hemingway (a parody of Frank Harris's *My Life and Loves*), John O'Hara (a satiric look at the world of Ivy League alumni), and Elmer Rice (a series of reminiscent essays on his New York childhood), and its cartoons were making it the center of American comic art. By 1929 there was a solid ballast of expensive advertisements, and there was little doubt that *The New Yorker* stood alone as the magazine for the upper-middle-brow, upper-middle-income audience.

Ross had his limitations and eccentricities, but he was a great editor. He was a perfectionist with a special passion for clarity and accuracy. He had "an almost intuitive perception of what was wrong with something," Thurber recalled, and his marginal comments and opinion sheets were classics of meticulous editing—badgering, questioning, prodding, suggesting, until, as Thurber put it, you knew your story and yourself better than you had before. His famous questions, "Who he?," "What mean?," and such notations as "unclear" and "cliché" show his dedication to the ideals of precision and accuracy in style. He surrounded himself with dictionaries, especially Fowler's *Modern English Usage* and the *Oxford English Dictionary,* which he read, says Thurber, "the way other men read fiction." Sometimes his obsession with detail led him into ludicrous blind alleys. Coming across an allusion in a piece by S. J. Perelman to "the woman taken in adultery," he queried, " 'What woman? Hasn't been previously mentioned.' "

In the weekly art conferences where the cartoons and covers were discussed and selected, he showed the same concern for clarity and accuracy. One story has it that when a cartoon was submitted showing two elephants looking at their baby, with the caption, "It's about time to tell Junior the facts of life," Ross asked, " 'Which elephant is talking?' " On another occasion, when a drawing of a Model T delivery truck driving along a dusty country road was up for discussion, Ross turned to his assistant and said, " 'Take this down, Miss Terry. . . . Better dust.' " The famous checking department of *The New Yorker* was simply an extension of Ross's passion for accuracy. His great dream was to get out a magazine free from all taint of error, and he used to say that despite the telephone company's careful checking, it had never yet got out a directory with fewer than three mistakes.

The ordeal of submitting copy to Ross's demanding examination was a valuable experience for Thurber, and he acknowledged the debt time and again. Looking back at the nature of Ross's influence from the vantage point of 1955, he told George Plimpton and Max Steele that while Ross was not the man to develop a writer, his passion for clarity was a healthy influence on all those who wrote for the magazine. "He was a purist and a perfectionist and it had a tremendous effect on all of us: it kept us from getting sloppy," he said. His admiration was not uncritical, however, and in later years he became increasingly uneasy about Ross's fussy precisionism, worrying in particular about its possibly damaging effects on writers with highly original styles like John McNulty. Ross's addiction to the comma as the key to clarity was always a source of contention, and he was capable of insisting that the phrase "the red, white, and blue" be punctuated in this way, while Thurber countered that it was better without any commas at all. Once, when he had had all he could take, Thurber sent Ross a stanza from Wordsworth's "She Dwelt Among the Untrodden Ways" punctuated according to Ross:

She lived, alone, and few could know

When Lucy ceased to be,
But, she is in her grave, and, oh,
The difference, to me.

Ross never set down his ideals of style in any systematic fashion, but implicit in all his editing was a demand for accurate reporting, stylistic clarity, and a casual, offhand manner. He set great store by the casual style as the proper trademark of the magazine as a whole. Hence the title of his departments—"Notes and Comment," "Profile," "A Reporter at Large," and so on. He liked to refer to the short pieces of fiction and humor featured by the magazine as "casuals." He wanted to avoid anything labored, studied, or arty, and much of his admiration for White and Thurber was based on the easy informality of their prose.

One of the chief reasons for Ross's astonishing success as an editor was his ability to surround himself with talent. Among those on the *New Yorker* staff in the late Twenties and early Thirties were Dorothy Parker, Robert Benchley, Russel Crouse, Alexander Woollcott, Frank Sullivan, St. Clair McKelway, Ogden Nash, Clifton Fadiman, Clarence Day, and Robert M. Coates; and the list of those who were frequent contributors would include S. J. Perelman, Marc Connelly, Ring Lardner, Sally Benson, John O'Hara, Kay Boyle, John Collier, and Morris Bishop.

Certain people were particularly important in the shaping of the magazine in the early days. In addition to White and Thurber, there were Katharine Angell, Ralph Ingersoll, and Wolcott Gibbs. Katharine Angell (later Mrs. E. B. White) was the literary editor. She joined the magazine six months after it started, and Ross depended on her in all matters involving taste and culture. A staffer of those days said, "She had a sure, cold sense of what was good, what was bad, what was in poor taste. She balanced Ross." Ingersoll was with the magazine from 1925 until 1930, when he quit to become an editor of *Fortune*. Thurber recalls that it was he who created the formula for "The Talk of the Town" and who took care of the hundreds of managerial details necessary to keep the department going. "Without his help and direction . . . I could never have got "Talk of the Town' off the ground," he said.

Wolcott Gibbs was one of the three men Ross considered indispensable—the other two were, of course, White and Thurber. "If you and White and Gibbs ever left this magazine, I would leave too," Ross once told Thurber. Gibbs joined the magazine in 1927, just a few months after Thurber did, and like White and Thurber, he brought to it a remarkably versatile talent. He substituted for White on "Notes and Comment," he did some of *The New Yorker*'s most famous profiles (those on Henry Luce and Alexander Woollcott are masterpieces of witty malice), he wrote short stories and superb parodies ("Death in the Rumble Seat" is surely one of the best of Hemingway parodies), and he conducted the theater and occasionally the movie reviews, where his wittily expressed disapproval of practically everything made him the delight and despair of readers across the land. " 'Maybe he doesn't like anything,' " Ross once said to Thurber when they were discussing an article in *Harper's* complaining about Gibbs's crotchets as a reviewer, " 'but he can do everything.' "

In addition to his other talents, he was, in Thurber's

words, "the best copy editor *The New Yorker* ever had."
In 1935 or 1936 he sent Ross a memo entitled "Theory
and Practice of Editing New Yorker Articles," a distillation of the ideals of style which guided the magazine for
many years. Thurber reprinted it in *The Years with Ross*.
The emphasis in the memo is on a clean, functional, informal style, and it was just these standards which Thurber
encountered when he first joined the magazine, at a time
in his career when he was ready to give up journalese and
find a voice of his own. Association with Ross and the
early *New Yorker* writers was undoubtedly important in
shaping Thurber's style, but with one notable exception,
the influence was one of generally shared assumptions
about writing rather than of the clearly demonstrable effect of one man on another. The exception was E. B.
White, whose influence on his artistic development Thurber often and generously acknowledged.

White had been on the magazine less than a year when
Thurber joined the staff. He was a graduate of Cornell,
where he had edited the university paper, and he had tried
his hand at newspapering in Seattle, where he found that
feature-writing suited him better than conventional reporting. He came to New York in 1923, hoping to make
his way as a writer, and went to work for an advertising
agency. His literary models were the great columnists of
the day—Don Marquis, F. P. A., and Heywood Broun—
and he spent his spare time writing verse and short prose
sketches. He began to sell to *The New Yorker* in 1925, and
late in 1926 Katharine Angell hired him at a salary of $30
a week.

He was a sharp observer of the human and natural scene,
and he liked to wander the streets of New York or to sit
in Grand Central Station, watching the people. He was
shy and reflective by nature, and he had always wanted to
be a poet. The world he liked best was the rural village
world of barns and horses and fields and trees. He carried
a copy of *Walden* with him wherever he went. He had a
natural easy prose style which could report the surface as
well as suggest expansions of meaning, and this is probably what Marc Connelly meant when he said appreciative-
ly of White that he "brought the steel and music to the
magazine." His versatility was exactly what Ross needed
in the early days, and he made *The New Yorker* famous
for two of its departments—the "newsbreaks," those typographical garbles which unintentionally enliven the columns of many a newspaper, and the "Notes and Comment" page which opened the magazine.

The newsbreaks show White's talent as a professional humorist. They are, in general, unexpected explosions of the
absurd in the midst of the commonplace, and his sure taste
in selecting the best of these, and his comic inventiveness
in creating the categories under which they were to appear—"Raised Eyebrows Department," "Neatest Trick of
the Week," and "How's That Again?"—raised a standard
feature of the humor magazine (both *Punch* and *Judge*
collected newsbreaks) to the level of comic art.

Thurber's favorite among the thousands selected by White
was this:

The Departure of Clara Adams

[From the Burbank (Cal.) Post]

Among the first to enter was Mrs. Clara Adams
of Tannersville, Pa., lone woman passenger.
Slowly her nose was turned around to face in a
southwesterly direction, and away from the han-
gar doors. Then, like some strange beast, she
crawled along the grass.

But it was the White of "Notes and Comment" that Thurber had in mind when he said that he "learned about writing from Andy White." In this weekly page of deceptively
simple paragraphs and essays, White exercised his remarkable talent as observer and critic of the contemporary
scene as well as poet and amateur philosopher. His manner was casual, offhand, and lightly ironic. His effects were
always underplayed. What he did best was to take one of
the small facts of everyday life and give it a sudden surprising extension of meaning. A good example of his material and method is the little essay "Accomplishment,"
which appeared in "Notes and Comment" April 20, 1929.
It is a defense of jaywalking as one of the last possible expressions of individualism in an over-organized society.
White develops the theme in a series of mock-heroic comparisons which invest the unthinking behavior of twentieth-century pedestrians with surprising significance.

We are a people of dangerous intent, and courage. The superannuated messenger, bundle
under arm, faces death with a balance, a rhythm,
a sense of time and motion that would make an
American Indian walking the forests seem clumsy. Every citizen is capable of making crossings
where the slightest error of judgment or faulty
timing would crush him out. And for all his artistry, there is a fine simplicity in his performance, a lack of ostentation. He survives because he is fit. This is our security, our protection against invasion by the Visigoths. Strong
men may come down, but they will never be able
to cross our vehicular boundaries; hiding behind
a phalanx of Checker cabs we will meet the
enemy and they will be ours.

Thurber and White shared a closet-sized office for several
years and found themselves in sympathy from the beginning. White was shy at first, and when Thurber suggested
that they go out to lunch together one day, White de-
murred, saying, "I always eat alone." Soon, however, they
were lunching together, drinking together, going to the
fights at Madison Square Garden and to ball games together, and establishing a personal and creative rapport
which was to last until the end of Thurber's life. After
1937, when White moved to Maine, where he stayed until
1943, they saw less of each other, but they sustained their
friendship in a warm and lively correspondence which
continued until the late 1950's. Their letters are full of domestic anecdotes, private jokes, and news of friends, as
well as exchanges of opinion on public affairs, discussions
of current literary projects, and mutual encouragement
and appreciation. In their relationship, White was the
older brother. Thurber always felt that it was White who
had really discovered his talent; his first book was done in
collaboration with White, it was White who insisted that
The New Yorker use his drawings, and it was White's introduction to *The Owl in the Attic* which launched Thur-

ber as a literary personality. When Thurber needed literary advice or help, it was White he turned to, as he did in 1943 with *Many Moons* and in 1950 with *The Thirteen Clocks*. Writing for the *Saturday Review of Literature* in 1938, Thurber called White "the most valuable person on the magazine," and spoke of his "silver and crystal sentences which had a ring like the ring of no one else's sentences in the world."

Thurber acknowledged few influences on his work. Among living authors he usually named only two—Robert O. Ryder and White. Ross and Gibbs were influences, to be sure, but in their editorial capacities rather than as creative examples. The influence of White was direct and personal. In a 1956 letter he pays tribute to White and gives a curious account of the state of his own writing at the time he joined *The New Yorker:*

> I can see by "Credos and Curios" that I matured slowly. Until I learned discipline in writing from studying Andy White's stuff, I was a careless, nervous, headlong writer, trailing the phrases and rhythms of Henry James, Hergesheimer, Henley, and my favorite English literature teacher at Ohio State, Joe Taylor.
>
> I would use "in fine," "as who should say," and the like. . . . The precision and clarity of White's writing helped me a lot, slowed me down from the dog-trot of newspaper tempo and made me realize a writer turns on his mind, not a faucet. I rewrite most things five to ten or more times.

Thurber's debt to White was very real, but nowhere in his early *New Yorker* pieces is there badness of the kind he accuses himself of here. The charge applies to the self-indulgence of the Chicago *Tribune* Riviera edition feature story of the Wills-Lenglen tennis match, written early in 1926, but he had purged himself of this sort of thing before he began to write for *The New Yorker* in 1927. His generous statements of indebtedness (made many years after the fact) should not be taken too literally, but as affectionate hyperboles, speaking the truth, but overstating it for dramatic effect. What they really mean is that Thurber felt himself to be at a turning point when he joined *The New Yorker,* and that White stood out as a model of the kind of style he was developing on his own. White gave Thurber confidence in what he was already trying to do, and confirmed him in the direction he wanted to go. Specifically, he demonstrated to Thurber the artistic values of simplicity and understatement. . . .

During Thurber's first two years on the magazine, Ross refused to pay him extra for his contributions to the literary department, on the grounds that not getting paid for writing would make him concentrate better on his editorial duties. But Thurber turned out a steady stream of short pieces notwithstanding, and finally Ross relented and began to pay him the regular rates. Most of this work between 1927 and 1929 is best described by that over-used term, "transitional." He stayed within the established patterns of American literary humor with which he had been experimenting since college days—the paragraph, the anecdote of personal experience (usually dealing with the trivial misadventures of everyday life), the comic essay (a flexible form adaptable to a great range of subjects and modes), the parody, and light verse. Looming up behind most of these forms was the inescapable figure of Robert Benchley.

In a review of a posthumous collection of Benchley's work, Thurber called him "the humorists' humorist." This was not mere conventional praise of a departed colleague, for it was Benchley, more than anyone else, who gave definitive shape to the forms and subject matter of American literary humor in the 1920's and early '30's. Like Stephen Leacock, to whom he always acknowledged his debt, he saw the great comic subject of modern life as the predicament of the ordinary man confronted by a complex technological-business society which he neither understands nor approves, and by a host of minor domestic problems which he can never quite handle. Benchley's protagonist is usually the well-meaning bumbler, either as harassed father and husband or as slightly stuffy businessman, politician, or scientist. Thurber took over this figure and reshaped it to express his own temperament and personality, making it into a darker, more neurotic and complex character than Benchley's.

Benchley's art is essentially the art of parody, whether his subject is the style and form of a novelist or the language and values of popular culture. His literary parodies are humor and criticism of a high order. Who can ever feel quite the same about Dreiser after reading "Compiling an American Tragedy"? Thurber's own favorite was the parody of Galsworthy called "The Blue Sleeve Garter," and he once said in a letter, "I would rather have Benchley's 'The Blue Sleeve Garter' and Cyril Connolly's parody of Huxley than all the junk written between Washington Irving and the end of the Civil War." More than once he said that he would rather have Benchley's praise than anyone else's, and he summed up his view of Benchley as a force felt by a whole generation of writers of humor in his review of *Chips Off the Old Benchley,* in 1949:

> Benchley got off to a fast start ahead of all of us on the *New Yorker,* and our problem was the avoidance of imitation. He had written about practically everything, and his comic devices were easy to fall into. White once showed me something he'd written and asked anxiously, "Did Benchley say that?" In a 1933 preface I said that we were all afraid that whatever we had engaged on had probably been done better by Robert Benchley in 1924.

Thurber's talent took its own shape, and his mature work is very different from Benchley's, but the lines it followed during its early development were the lines laid down by Benchley.

One of the first pieces Thurber sold to the magazine, an ironic fable entitled "News of the Day" (April 2, 1927), recalls Benchley's satiric treatment of popular sentimental attitudes. It is more flippant and superficial than Thurber's later fables, but one can see in this early piece the preparations for such classic reversals of popular folklore as "The Little Girl and the Wolf," with its moral, "It is not so easy to fool little girls nowadays as it used to be." The brief anecdote tells the sad tale of little Marjorie Morrison, aged eleven, whose father has gone to Canada with a stenographer who subsequently murdered him, and whose mother has just killed her lover by choking him with an oil mop. A kindly adult world shields her from the ugly facts, but one day little Marjorie disappears and everyone is sure that she has learned the truth and killed herself.

> And then along about five P.M. the next day little Marjorie came back to her aunt's house in the Bronx.
>
> "My precious!" cried her happy aunt, "where has Aunty's precious been?"
>
> "I'm booked solid for twenty-six weeks in vaudeville at five grand a month," said little Marjorie.

He followed the Benchley model in several anecdotes of personal misadventure, like "Camera vs St. Bernard" (June 7, 1928), dealing with the tribulations of the American tourist trying to get a camera repaired in Paris, and he did a number of parodies as well. Most of them are best forgotten, but one, a parody of Hemingway entitled "A Visit from Saint Nicholas" (December 24, 1927), gives promise of better things to come. It is a re-telling of "'Twas the Night Before Christmas" in the Hemingway manner, and the comic incongruity between subject and style is effectively developed.

> I went to the chimney and looked up. I saw him get into his sleigh. He whistled at his team and the team flew away. The team flew as lightly as thistledown. The driver called out, "Merry Christmas and good night." I went back to bed.
>
> "What was it?" asked Mamma. "Saint Nicholas?" She smiled.
>
> "Yeah," I said.
>
> She sighed and turned in the bed.
>
> "I saw him," I said.
>
> "Sure."
>
> "I did see him."
>
> "Sure you saw him." She turned farther toward the wall.

In addition to the Benchley-style anecdotes and parodies, Thurber did a number of short stories and a rather unsuccessful profile of Myron T. Herrick in his first two years on the magazine. The profile was a new form, original with *The New Yorker,* and it was just in the process of development when Thurber tried his first one. The traditional journalistic biographical piece was almost always a success story with strong moralistic and inspirational overtones, but the *New Yorker* writers, after some early backing and filling, worked out the detached, ironic, somewhat skeptical view of the subject which has since become a trademark of the magazine.

He had already written a feature story on Herrick for the Kansas City *Star* Magazine in 1925, and the difference between the two pieces suggests the kind of influence *The New Yorker* had on Thurber as a writer. "The Evolution of an Ambassador" is a conventional journalistic feature article, praising the good work, personal charm and democratic instincts of an admirable American abroad. To the French, he will always be a hero for his famous response to those who urged him to leave Paris for a safer place in 1914: "There are times when a dead ambassador is of greater service than a live one." "Master of Ceremonies," Thurber's profile of Herrick in *The New Yorker* (July 21, 1928), takes a rather ironic view of Herrick's success story, balancing the record of his achievements against the implication that his position owed more to his nice smile and his cultivation of the right people than to his intellectual or political talents. The profile emphasizes Herrick's magnetism and his talent for the theatrical, citing as an example the famous quotation about the dead ambassador. This time, Thurber wickedly adds a detail absent from his earlier account: "Embassy men smile when you ask them if Herrick really said that. But the French will doubtless carve it some day on a monument to him."

Many of these early *New Yorker* pieces show Thurber staking out his own territory, assimilating the examples of Benchley and White, but shaping them to his own artistic purposes. "The Thin Red Leash" (August 13, 1927) is his version of the anecdote of humiliating experience, and he handles it in the way of White rather than in the way of Benchley. Benchley almost always employed the persona of the bumbler or the victim, and his anecdotes were usually heightened and stylized for strong comic effect. Thurber did many pieces in the Benchley manner throughout his career, but his own way was to draw more directly on autobiographical experience, to appear as himself, more or less, rather than to use a persona, to manipulate the material as little as possible, letting it assume a natural form, following White here, but unlike White, to treat it more fictionally than essayistically; that is to say, to treat it as a specific dramatic occasion rather than to generalize upon it. . . .

Thurber worked hard to develop his skills in the humorous essay and the fictional sketch, but between 1927 and 1935, when Russell Maloney took over, he did most of his writing for "The Talk of the Town." They were eight years of wandering the city and writing about its places and people. "I wrote about a million words for Talk in my time," he once recalled. Ross attached particular importance to this department and to White's "Notes and Comment" page which preceded it, because it was here that the tone of informal conversation which was his ideal for the magazine as a whole was to be established. In the early days there were weekly "Talk" conferences, attended by Katharine Angell, White, Ingersoll, and Thurber, during which Ross worried over the style and content of the department with the full force of his neurotic perfectionism. "Talk" was a group enterprise, depending on the reportorial energies and imaginations of a number of different people. Ralph Ingersoll and Bernard A. Bergman were the chief idea men for the department in Thurber's day, and Charles H. Cooke (the original "our Mr. Stanley") was the best reporter. Thurber was the rewrite man. He did his own legwork on a few items each week, but his chief job was reworking facts and anecdotes submitted by others.

Ross was always hard to please, and at first he was convinced that Thurber had worked too long on newspapers to do "Talk" properly. " 'He can't write Talk the way I want it. He'll always write journalese,' " he said, and for three months he rewrote nearly every one of Thurber's contributions, filling them up with favorite expressions of his own like "and such," which he thought would give them a casual, offhand air. Thurber's "The studio walls are hung with oils and water colors, with here and there a gouache and silverpoint" became "The studio walls are hung with oils and watercolors, and such." It was not until the issue of December 2, 1927, after what Thurber called "three months of slavery" that Ross accepted and praised a piece by Thurber, and this only after forcing him to rewrite it six times. " 'Now you got it,' he said. 'Write it the way you would talk to a dinner companion.' " The piece in question, "A Friend of Jimmy's," was a brief character sketch of a man named William Seeman, a friend of Mayor Walker's and president of the White Rose salmon cannery. It is an undistinguished sketch, but Thurber remembered it as a second turning point in his relationship with Ross.

Even so, the early days were full of conflict between editor and rewrite man. Ross's revisions were sometimes heavy-handed or finicky, and more than once he spoiled a good anecdote. On occasion, when things were at an impasse, Thurber would rewrite Ross's revisions and fake his "R" of approval on the sheet. Gradually the tension relaxed, as Ross came to realize that Thurber was exactly what the department needed. "Talk" was to be an entertaining miscellany of anecdotes about interesting people and events on the New York scene. It needed an easy informal style, blending the reportorial and the essayistic, and a strict economy of means. This is exactly what Thurber had to offer. His mastery of the art of paragraphing, which he had learned from the peerless Robert O. Ryder of the *Ohio State Journal,* was the ideal apprenticeship for "The Talk of the Town." As Robert M. Coates, his old friend and colleague on the magazine, once observed, " 'Talk' was just made for him, as he was made for it, and it is no more than simple fact to say he 'made' the department . . . into its present image." . . .

"The Talk of the Town" was Thurber's first unqualified success. It was in doing this weekly stint of informal reporting and commentary that he found the style he had been looking for—casual, economical, flexible. Looking back on Thurber's many accomplishments, Robert M. Coates said, "I think . . . that in some ways he was proudest of all his exploits in the old 'Talk' days, when after briefly studying some anecdote or other small item that had been sent in to us he would put it down beside his typewriter in the jammed-up little office we happily shared and proceed to rewrite it equally swiftly, giving it just the right turn of phrasing that added point and pungence—or when, seizing on a 'visit' suggestion, he would put on his hat and, demon reporter-like, go out to get the material for a piece on some landmark or other in our ever-beguiling city and come back and write it in time for our Thursday deadline."

The late Twenties and early Thirties were the high-water mark of "Talk." After a while, the weekly conferences were abandoned, and Ross's interest shifted to other departments. Thurber himself wearied of the routine after eight years, and quit in 1935. Thereafter it was handled by a succession of able writers, but in Ross's view, it was never the same after Thurber dropped out. Writing to Thurber in 1946, Ross lamented the decline of his favorite department: "Give me you, Shawn, and Cooke and I'll get out a Talk department," he said. "It's up to God to send some young talent around this place, and He's been neglecting the job. That's the trouble."

Looking back on his experience, Thurber described the "Talk" formula and the *New Yorker* form and style generally in a long letter to John McNulty written in the late Thirties. McNulty had joined the magazine in 1937, and during his first year or two he despaired of ever getting the hang of doing pieces for "The Talk of the Town" and "Notes and Comment." Thurber was by this time an acknowledged master of the *New Yorker* forms, and he could look at the magazine with some objectivity. His letter is primarily an effort to help and encourage his friend, but it is also a remarkable piece of informal literary criticism. He is sympathetic with McNulty's frustration, because he went through the same ordeal himself: "Ross ran my stuff through his typewriter for months, threw it away by carloads, often rewrote the things so I didn't find a phrase of mine left. I would try to imitate his rewrites of my rewrites, keeping in mind what he always said 'limber it up, make it easy and off-hand, like table-talk.' What came out often sounded like the table talk of bindle stiffs." Listening to Ross's advice will probably be more confusing than helpful, he says. "He's likely to fill you up with too many ideas and maxims and instructions!"

> He could rattle off "Don't build it up, make it limber, we don't have to know too much, we want goddam it like table talk, interesting stuff, full of facts, to hell with the facts, we don't have to be experts, let yourself go, thousand interesting things in the city, for Christ's sake, etc. etc." I got bewildered. I finally figured what he wanted, in a way: "A man we know was telling us the other day about gaskets. Seems they are little funny kind of what's-its-names. Fellow named Pritch or Feep invents them, or imports them, or something of the sort. Otto H. Kahn has ninety-two and a Mrs. Bert Geefle of the Savoy Plaza seven. Nobody else has any, except Madame Curie who was presented with four thousand by the city of Nantes for telling the city what time it was one night when it called Meridian 1212 and got her by mistake."

Writing for "Talk" is chiefly a matter of learning the formula, and the formula is one of style. White "was the first guy to write perfect Talk pieces," and "everybody has in a sense imitated him." "It is a formula, all right," Thurber concedes, although it is not as tight as the sonnet. Everyone writing for "Talk" or "Comment" has to follow it— "John Steinbeck, Walt Whitman, Evelyn Waugh, and Shakespeare would all have to get the knack of it, if they got any stories printed."

Thurber then points out, reassuringly, that "Talk" and "Comment" are not typical of the magazine as a whole;

in the other departments, the writer can write as he pleases. "People sometimes speak of a *New Yorker* style," he says, "but they are either thinking of Talk or of the form and shape of the casuals; what makes them look alike is their length and form. Where nothing runs much over 2 or 3 thousand words—as in casuals—there is bound to be a similarity of form." There is a subtle danger in this sameness of form, he confesses. Years of writing casuals have probably shaped his imagination for life, he says. "I find most of my stories, after I have typed them, run to 6 and a half or seven pages. I haven't tried for that. My brain has unconsciously formed that kind of mould for them. In a way this is bad, because everything I start—play, two-volume novel, or what-not, finally rounds itself out into 6 or 7 pages—seems complete, too." He goes on to define the casual. It is a form of its own, "neither essay nor short story, but a little of each. . . . Slighter than the short story, stronger than the essay." Ross always said that he would never use a short story, says Thurber. "I think he vaguely means by a short story something with more than four characters and at least three changes of scene." Sally Benson writes the purest casuals, in Thurber's opinion. "You never confuse her stuff with a real short story." Robert M. Coates, on the other hand, "has ingeniously managed to get short stories into the casual form."

The trademark of the *New Yorker* casual is the inconclusive ending. "We have invested, or perfected, something that is neither a happy ending nor an unhappy ending. It might be called the trailing off." Thurber is obviously a bit puzzled by this phenomenon, and he reaches out to baseball and ballet for analogies. "We seem to find a high merit in leaving men on bases," he says. "It's the ballet finish; rather than the third act tag or the black out. More people are left standing and looking in ballets and *New Yorker* casuals than in any other known art forms."

After having described the *New Yorker* form, Thurber warns McNulty not to try too hard to imitate it. "I don't care what the fashion in casuals is, nor should you," he says. "I read very few of them. It is easy to get *New Yorker* glut, casual fag. Don't read the magazine too consistently. If you read it from cover to cover it's like eating a two pound box of candy." It is bad to read it so much that "its little tricks of form and style keep running through your head." Finishing the letter the next morning, he adds a few maxims ("Don't let the magazine new-yorker you, mcnulty the magazine") and words of encouragement ("There's nothing more you have to learn from the *New Yorker*—the rest is what it's got to learn from you").

NEW YORKER STYLE

Don Hausdorff

SOURCE: "Politics and Economics: The Emergence of a *The New Yorker* Tone," in *Studies in American Humor*, n.s., Vol. 3, No. 1, Spring, 1984, pp. 74-82.

[*Hausdorff is an American critic and educator. In the fol-*

lowing excerpt, he analyzes the editorial tone of the New Yorker *as revealed by its contributors' treatment of political and economic subjects during the 1920s and 1930s.*]

In 1925, when *The New Yorker* made its first appearance, the Jazz Age was at its peak. John Held, Jr.'s flappers were dancing and smoking through the pages of *College Humor;* Gloria Swanson and Babe Ruth were being ballyhooed in the tabloids; and the cocktail party crowd, between snorts from their hip flasks, were chattering about Freud and Picasso. High Culture was big business, as *Vanity Fair* was demonstrating, and so too was the iconoclasm of H. L. Mencken in the pages of the *American Mercury*. The consumerist society, replete with cars, appliances, fads and fashions, and easy credit, was in full swing.

True, Scott Fitzgerald's *Great Gatsby* and Theodore Dreiser's *An American Tragedy* were both published in 1925, similar in their insistence that America was a land of false illusions and broken promises. But after all, the Great War had faded into history, Europe's problems were far away, and Calvin Coolidge ("the business of America is business") had just polled almost 72% of the electoral votes. For America's reading public, it was party time and, wow, look at those stock prices soar!

At its inception, accurately reflecting its era, *The New Yorker* was a melange of sophistication and crude effects. Founder Harold Ross had worked on the venerable humor magazine *Judge* and other publications, and had also come to know and admire many of the writers and illustrators associated with the cosmopolitan "new humor": Alexander Woollcott, Franklin P. Adams, Robert Benchley, Gluyas Williams and George S. Kaufman, among others. Early issues of the magazine unevenly blended the talents of these artists with the more raucous laugh-that-off! gag styles of *Judge* and *Life* (both of which dated back to the 1880s); the suave manner of *Vanity Fair;* and the sharp satire of the old British humor magazine *Punch*. Constant infusions of capital and continual replacements of editors and contributors marked the magazine's first few years.

In the late 1920s a group of young writers and cartoonists joined that staff: Ogden Nash, James Thurber, Wolcott Gibbs, E. B. White, Peter Arno and Helen Hokinson—all of whom remained solidly identified with the magazine for the next several decades. They gradually created for *The New Yorker* a distinctive stamp, one marked by an articulate and sharp humorous perspective. Where *Vanity Fair* often seemed like a buffet table of cultural curiosities, *The New Yorker* began to acquire a uniform tone. It minimized the helter-skelter effects borrowed from the humor magazines. And it slid away from the iconoclastic manner of the *American Mercury*.

To some extent, Mencken's justified irritation at the complacencies of Coolidge-Hoover prosperity was also present in *The New Yorker,* but Ross and his staff were less interested in a fervent assault on what Mencken called the "booboisie" than in a skeptical, quietly amused scrutiny of day-to-day events.

The magazine did not completely eschew consideration of political and economic matters. After all, it was directed at a reasonably educated urban readership. Rather, it channeled these two topics in two unique ways. For one thing, it inserted political and economic comments right into the mainstream of all the other exciting events of the time, suggesting an equivalence of significance. Additionally, it consistently converted large issues into small-scale, even miniature perceptions. Capitalistic excess would not be excoriated loudly or at length; instead it might be compressed into a Peter Arno cartoon parody of a fat and foolish capitalist.

Almost from the beginning, two ambivalences were present. *The New Yorker* poked fun at conspicuous consumption, even while it paraded numerous examples of it, in columns and advertisements, in every issue. And while the magazine's humorists bemoaned the demise of "enlightened individualism" in the city and nation, its own efforts often were largely the product of group process and editorial conference. A caption worked over by two writers might be attached to sample illustrations drawn by two or three cartoonists. In short, *The New Yorker* was hostage to the consumer society and the group ethic right from the outset.

A simple contrast might demonstrate *The New Yorker*'s usual perspective. When Tudor City, an expensive residential complex, was erected on New York's east side in 1929, a *New Masses* writer pointed to the irony of sumptuous dwellings rising within whispering distance of dreadful slums. But a *New Yorker* cartoonist drew hundreds of faces peering, astonished, from Tudor City windows at the one resident who had the effrontery to *ride* to work. The issue was not economic discrepancy, but the impact of a single deviant on an otherwise uniform mentality. No polemic, just poking fun.

Political humor in the late 1920s in *The New Yorker* often was confined to cynical flippancies in such columns as Howard Brubaker's "Of All Things." "After painstaking research," Brubaker once wrote blithely, "we have at last discovered what the Mexican revolution is about. It is about over." Another columnist wrote, ". . . our sympathy goes out to Mussolini. It must be pretty discouraging to find that he has not scared anybody after all." Of course, this was better than *College Humor,* in which Ezra Pound could be found extolling the virtues of Fascist Italy. And *The New Yorker* was also warning, if rather gently, against Father Coughlin in 1931, three years before the formation of the Fascist-minded Christian Front. Periodically too, Adolf Dehn's sinister little cartoons on German decadence appeared in its pages.

But in most important matters in politics and economics, *The New Yorker*'s tone reduced them to frivolity. Small farmers had been in crisis for several years, but they made their only appearance in the magazine as bumpkins in cartoons. Even during such a violent and prolonged labor struggle as the Gastonia, N.C. textile strike, *The New Yorker*'s focus on idiosyncratic elements in the news led to its treatment of widespread symptoms of labor unrest in much the same way that it summarized April Fool's Day pranks.

So problems of magnitude could be neatly reduced to

whimsy. Peter Arno's absurdly pompous walrus-moustached roués were properly punctured, but they remained charming—and the corporate practices that they embodied were simply ignored. Ignored, too, were the business manipulations that helped to create the dramatic imbalances in the economy.

Late in October 1929 the stock market suffered two successive disasters. On Oct. 24, "Black Thursday," almost 13,000,000 shares of stock changed hands, in what the New York *Times* called "the most disastrous decline in the biggest and broadest stock market of history." On Oct. 29, "Tragic Tuesday," an estimated eight to nine billion dollars were lost, as over 16,000,000 shares were traded. The next day, *Variety* magazine set the tone for the initial response of American humor. What was to emerge as the worst peacetime economic collapse in modern history was shrunken to a Show Biz cliché: WALL STREET LAYS AN EGG.

The New Yorker added its voice to the wisecrack mood. "The collapse of the market . . . couldn't help but be amusing," remarked a columnist. "It is amusing to see a fat land quivering in paunchy fright." The metaphor suggested that only Peter Arno's fat capitalists were in danger.

The following week, the same blasé, cocktail-party chit-chat tone was extended, to suggest that at least this fresh topic offered a welcome change from the Same Old Thing: "There was one feature of the stock market unpleasantness of last week which was not entirely without charm. It gave the newspapers something to print besides what the political candidates were saying."

Surely, the "Great Flurry," as *The New Yorker* liked to refer to the incipient Depression, was a temporary phenomenon. Just a few days after the crash and a few days before the song "Happy Days Are Here Again" was published, the magazine noted: "What finally stemmed the tide and averted an actual panic in Wall Street was not the intervention of the bankers but the arrival in town of the Rodeo."

Another early reaction was to needle political leaders. *The New Yorker,* always keeping one eye cocked for the marginalia on the inside pages, noted that ex-President Calvin Coolidge had just purchased a large estate in Northampton. This prompted an ironic jab demonstrating that "business has turned the corner and is definitely on the upgrade":

> Probably few people realize how bad for a nation's morale it was to have an ex-president . . . living in half of a two-family house and paying thirty-two dollars a month rent. It hardly spoke well for the condition of business, and it tended to make everybody hold back. . . . Now, with the Coolidges in a sixteen-room house, everything will open up. Mills and factories will soon be running again at full blast, oil wells will be drilled, stocks will show a decided strong tendency, and grain elevators of the West will be full to the brim, and the Sun will shine on a happy and prosperous people. . . .

It didn't happen of course, and soon the irony began to

harden. "Depression has a strange effect on America," a late 1930 column began:

> We observed . . . the changed look on the faces of the dummies in the department-store windows. These silent ladies, fashionably poised, used to exemplify—in prosperous times—beauty, sophistication, worldly wisdom, the charm of decadence. The ones you see now are quite the opposite type. . . . Seemingly America has developed a new feminine ideal, in keeping with the slump. No longer can the Ultimate Consumer afford a worldly-wise woman who requires a sable collar to hide her lifted chin in; what he wants is a helpmeet with a schoolgirl complexion, who wants to make ends meet, and who has only a rather sketchy idea of how complicated life can really get.

A brief flurry of guarded optimism developed after the turn of the year. *The New Yorker* found new "symptoms of recovery" where it could, although it could hardly keep pace with the fountain of good cheer emanating from politicians and economists. By 1931, there had been such a plethora of optimistic, usually platitudinous, predictions, that an entire book of them was published, with the appropriate cynical title, *Oh Yeah? The New Yorker,* for its part, devoted two full pages in one issue to "An Anthology of Hope, Compiled by Those Incorrigible Optimists, the Editors of the New Yorker, Who for Two Years Have Felt the Almost Daily Inspiration of the Country's Leaders of Thought." Centered in the spread was a cartoon by Otto Soglow, featuring his well-known man-in-a-manhole. From the depths of the sewer, he could be heard proclaiming, "I am convinced, Joe, that the country is fundamentally sound." Veteran satirists Reginald Marsh and Al Frueh, who had been drawing theatrical scenes for the magazine, now turned up with satires on industrialists. On at least one occasion, *The New Yorker*'s cover, which usually was filled with romping roués, giddy clubladies or colorful yachting pageants, came close to being a paean to the proletariat; it depicted, non-humorously, a group of industrial workers. *New Masses* could have used it.

Even the farmer, usually an object of rustic stereotypes in *The New Yorker,* came in for sympathy. On the occasion of the Administration's crop-destruction proposal, the editors turned bitter:

> We have read, every month or so for years, an article predicting that man would eventually be destroyed by insects. . . . Now it appears that the bugs will be too late: long before they overrun the earth, we will have been destroyed by simple economic disintegration, leaving, for the insects, the vast hoppers full of wheat that we were unable to distribute equitably among ourselves.

Such dry irony was becoming commonplace in *The New Yorker.* By the end of 1931, the tendency in the magazine was to categorize almost every event or official pronouncement as a symptom—of official avarice, indifference, or simply bunk. And yet the magazine was usually incapable of dealing directly with explosive issues: old habits die hard. When, in the spring of 1932, the bonus army, consisting largely of unemployed veterans, descended on Washington, and some thousands of them encamped after the Senate voted down the bonus bill, *The New Yorker* commented: "If Henry Ford wants to do his government a good turn, he will go to Washington and get the bonus expeditionary force out of the trenches."

And when General MacArthur, on orders from President Hoover, brutally dispersed the bonus army, declaring that it was "a mob. . . animated by the essence of revolution," *The New Yorker* cavalierly commented:

> [The bonus army] attracted largely an assemblage of economists, men who turned to the study of economics, because it supplies a substitute for job-hunting and loafing. Ostensibly they made a demonstration to compel Congress to give them a hand-out, but unquestionably they liked the life or they wouldn't have gone to Washington—that is, they preferred it to any other life they could have worked out for themselves at the moment. The Bonus-Army veterans are students of a sort; and we will wager that most of them could talk your ear off on almost any subject you might bring up, and would rather talk than eat.

The next item was on society notes.

With no lightening of the economic situation, the magazine staff seemed to become bored with the topic. Sometimes they viewed the Depression philosophically, as just one in a group of continually recurring events in the topsy-turvy, but withal charming history of mankind—along with saloons, traffic laws, the five-day week, shorthand, pyorrhea, short skirts and bobbed hair. By late 1932, a *New Yorker* writer was asking: "What Depression?" Staff regulars Thurber, Benchley and Adams offered humorous tidbits about the depression, but they seemed to be mining, almost mechanically, the old humorous veins: Business was flat on its back, Over-Confidence was a Bad Thing, and the Horatio Alger myth was not true.

In the Presidential campaign of 1932, which the *New Republic* called an "obscene spectacle" because major-party candidates seemed to equivocate on every issue, the *New Yorker* confined itself to sniping. The magazine had been sarcastic about Hoover's round-the-corner prosperity for some time; it was not equally unenthusiastic about FDR, who "could even straddle the bundling issue." In October, a columnist wrote, "It is hard for us to make up our mind whom to vote for, darn it."

Toward third parties, the *New Yorker* was contemptuous: "The Communists have been at us," wrote an editor, "to join up with them, flattering us with sly references to our 'intellectual' side and classifying us a 'professional worker.'" (Such intellectuals as Clifton Fadiman, Edmund Wilson, Upton Sinclair and Sherwood Anderson had made positive comments on various Communist positions.) But for the *New Yorker* the Communists, like all radicals, were immature in their boisterous enthusiasms and denunciations, and in their idealism. In a typical cartoon, "Evolution of a Socialist," militant, revolutionary youth "progressed" to cynical, reactionary, chauffeur-driven capitalists. "A successful revolution," a Communist wrote, "will require the finest sort of organization, whereas the typical Red cannot make his right foot cooperate with his left." Alexander Woollcott wrote from Moscow that everything connected with the Five Year Plan was far less significant industrially than the production of photographs of Stalin.

After the election, the *New Yorker* remarked that it preferred the election of the Lord Mayor of London, because at least that had "style." But the excitement engendered by the flurry of early New Deal legislation, which gradually lifted the spirit of Depression America, was not lost on the *New Yorker*'s acute observers. It had consistently parodied collectivism and bureaucracy, but by the end of 1933, a columnist could write ". . . the long, long dreams of a planned society are coming true, the way things look now. . . . Industry is learning its lesson."

When the NRA made its appearance, the *New Yorker* sported its own little NRA eagle, and when it reported "symptoms of recovery," it now did so without sarcasm. Its tendency, still, was to convert issues—in this case, the complex new program—into recognizable, humanized dimensions. In one cartoon, a man relaxes with his feet up on a table, while his wife complains to a friend: "It's Johnson this an' Johnson that ever since he won his blue iggle." And a new awareness of the significance of economic security was sometimes being manifested, as in one cartoon where a rich roué is shown propositioning a young lady: ". . . and when you're 63 you'll have a hundred a month the rest of your life."

A basically positive attitude about the nation's health began to be built into the magazine now, despite the vicissitudes of the long Depression years that still lay ahead. "The figures on reemployment look hopeful," wrote Howard Brubaker. "In a couple of years there will be useful work for everybody—except John Garner"

The rise in national optimism was accompanied by an upturn in advertising volume, and the *New Yorker* was an obvious beneficiary. As the 1930s moved along, the magazine grew fatter and more confident, even as the magazines which anachronistically embodied the Jazz Age spirit declined and died.

The *New Yorker*'s success in wooing advertisers was achieved despite its steady sniping at hucksterism, a pattern inherited from the joke-a-second flamboyance of the 1920s, and intensified after the stock market crash. *The New Yorker* gently satirized the irresistible onrush of advertising—in public conveyances, over the airwaves, in the streets. In 1932, poet Ogden Nash offered a definitive statement on the trend: "I think that I shall never see / A billboard lovely as a tree. / Perhaps, unless the billboards fall, / I'll never see a tree at all."

The *New Yorker* continued to run its "There'll Always Be an Adman" department, mocking fatuous or snobbish ads (as it has to this day), despite the presence of similarly absurd marketing appeals that filled its own advertising columns. Editor and author Alexander King noted that the *New Yorker* always knew precisely what it was doing: "It deals with personalities irreverently yet preserves enough tact to maintain the good will of its advertisers." King, who had edited the bitterly satirical *Americana* magazine

early in the Depression, found out where his own bread was buttered. When *Americana* folded, he moved to an editorial desk at *Time* magazine.

Although Harold Ross, according to biographer Dale Kramer, was the first editor of a major modern magazine to achieve complete independence from the business side of the publication, it is obvious that Ross's editorial "formula" included shrewd techniques for attracting "class" advertising. The magazine's earliest and heaviest backer was Raoul Fleischmann, a yeast manufacturer.

Coolidge and Hoover were gone and business leaders had taken their lumps, but to read through the *New Yorker* in the 1930s was to feel that day-to-day life was mostly a matter of buying and selling. As usual, the *New Yorker* cartoons took an intimate perspective: generally, a one-on-one relationship between an aggressive, sometimes charmingly silly, salesman and his victim. To a slightly suspicious customer, a friendly neighborhood store-keeper says in one cartoon: "Fish is an old story with us, Mrs. Burbank, but when this cod was unpacked we all pricked up our ears."

Occasionally, *New Yorker* writers manifested exasperation, especially when the English language was abused. Alexander Woollcott once railed: "I find my own mind giving way under this persistent spectacle of the American business man sitting with his finger in his mouth and lapsing into a vintage coquetry that was already losing its charm when David Copperfield's child-wife practiced it a hundred years ago." As for what one critic of advertising called its worst sin, the "systematic manipulation of anxieties," the *New Yorker* managed to hit at such trauma even while cushioning its barb with cuteness: one cartoon presented a grinning door-to-door salesman saying, "Good morning, sir. Have you given thought to the possibility of complete paralysis?"

The New Yorker's middle-of-the-road adaptability in this area, as in so many others, proved successful. Step by step it had shed most of the superficial resemblances to the older humor magazines on the one hand, and to the chic-Culture publications on the other. Quietly but effectively, the *New Yorker* had been pioneering a different manner, one emphasizing moderation, in an almost eighteenth-century spirit, in all things. It stressed nuances rather than sharp contrasts, turning its well-tailored back on sweeping indictments. Satirical magazines that arose during the early Depression, such as *Ballyhoo* and *Americana* were either too rambunctious or too vitriolic to outlive the decade. Unlike both of them the *New Yorker* never quite confronted the worst implications of the Depression at all.

The *New Yorker*'s moderation and detachment also led to a disappearance of overt "villains" in its humor. Such traditional enemies in magazine humor as the brutal police officer and the corrupt clergyman made fitful appearances in cartoons in the late 1920's; by the 1930's they underwent a humanizing process, even as the capitalist had become a comic, rather than a vicious, figure. All of these figures were portrayed as rather ordinary folks, foibles and all, caught up in a genial society that defied ready-made distinctions between good and evil.

An important result of this rounding-out of character and the resultant softening of moral overtones, was that distinctions of a moral sort became increasingly difficult to recognize, not unlike the marginal differences between competing name brands on virtually identical products. Infinite nuances of judgment created a blurring effect: if there was less of the old-fashioned good-vs.-evil tension, there was also a less clear value structure. What was important and what wasn't?

"Notes and Comment" moved freely, abruptly, from short

The *New Yorker*'s imitators:

In imitation of the successful *New Yorker,* local magazines addressed to the sophisticates of both sexes sprang up in major cities across the United States.

The local magazine of gossip and chitchat for socialites was nothing new. Colonel William Mann founded *Town Topics* for New York society before the turn of the century, for instance, and it lasted until 1932, when it collapsed after the attorney general of New York accused its publishers of forcing wealthy persons to buy stock in the company to keep out unsavory items about themselves and the court enjoined it from selling any more stock. The new local magazines that appeared in the twenties and thirties, while they owed something to such society organs as *American Sketch* and *Tatler,* were nevertheless of a different stamp. They much more obviously emulated the *New Yorker,* and even the names of some showed their debt: *Bostonian, Chicagoan, New Orleanian, Philadelphian, San Franciscan,* and *Washingtonian.* Cleveland had *Parade,* a "social, semi-humorous, and pictorial weekly," and Minneapolis and St. Paul had *Golfer and Sportsman.* Washington in 1939 got the *Senator,* a weekly published by Harry Newman of *Judge,* which sought a national readership but which concentrated on affairs within 150 miles of the capital in much the way that the *New Yorker* did for New York City.

The success of those imitators of the *New Yorker* was slight at best, and their mortality rate was high. Even granting that their goal was an upper-class audience, their circulations were low; the *Chicagoan* was selling only about 23,000 copies when it was enlarged and redesigned in the summer of 1931. Perhaps the magazines failed to hold readers because they tried too hard to transplant the *New Yorker* to their own localities instead of developing as indigenous products. The audiences they did attract were not large enough to be worth the attention of the big national advertisers whose accounts were essential if a publication were to become financially successful. The *New Yorker,* as its national circulation grew, may well have eliminated any economic justification for its local imitators, for through the *New Yorker,* a national advertiser could perhaps reach as large a discriminating audience in, say, Chicago as he could through a local Chicago magazine.

Theodore Peterson, in his Magazines in the Twentieth Century, *University of Illinois Press, 1964.*

---

jottings about international crises to Lily Daché hat designs. As the choice between different styles of lapels received equal attention with the choice between conflicting armies, there often was, in philosopher Suzanne Langer's phrase, "a general trivialization of the human battle." It might be said that the *New Yorker* built on the tabloids' crazyquilt approach to the human panorama, and it also anticipated the "mosaic" miscellany that Marshall McLuhan later found intrinsic to television presentations.

The genuine achievement of the *New Yorker*'s humor, perceptive and civilized, need not be detailed here. But it is also true that in some ways this same humor represented a narrowed purview. "Hamlet lost a kingdom," someone said, and "Benchley lost a tooth." What often was lost in this new individualized humor was a sense of scale and the possibility of really trenchant satire. Radical views of individuals and events, like radical solutions to social problems were not, in general, subjects for serious consideration.

And always, of course, the advertiser and the world of goods supplied a special context, providing motive and means for the full efflorescence of the consumerist, self-oriented society. A triumphant new magazine founded in 1934 was *Esquire.* It incorporated many of the features that had made the *New Yorker* successful: articulate contributors, cartoons scattered throughout its pages, strong appeals to fashion and luxury consumption, and even a cute little capitalist, "Esky," walrus-moustache and all.

Gerald Weales

SOURCE: "Not for the Old Lady in Dubuque," in *The University of Denver Quarterly,* Vol. 8, No. 2, Summer, 1973, pp. 65-83.

[*Weales is an American novelist, critic, and educator. In the following excerpt, he provides an overview of the humorous writings that appeared during the early years of the* New Yorker.]

When the *New Yorker* was young, it could still laugh at itself. During its first year, Corey Ford contributed a series, "The Making of a Magazine," which presumably took the reader behind the scenes and showed him how Eustace Tilley managed to get the whole thing together. The joke, which was more characteristic than it was funny, was that the tone of the pieces was primly professional while the events described ranged from the purely amateur to the serenely absurd. In the early days, each anniversary number led off with an item in "The Talk of the Town" congratulating the magazine on still being alive; in 1927 (February 19), the note said, somewhat wryly, "We may even, in the next twelve months, develop a Righteous Cause or two and become Important." Not that an occasion was needed for a self-deprecating plug. In "A Reader's Tribute" in the issue of September 11, 1926, Elmer Davis compared the *New Yorker* favorably with "Uncle Cyrus Curtis's weekly." "What with the editorial page and Hergesheimer's stories," Davis explained, the *Saturday Evening Post* had become so heavy that it was not as useful as the *New Yorker* for killing mosquitoes: "the loathsome insects can always hear it coming in time to get out of the way." In one case—a Ralph Barton cartoon—an inside joke had serious implications about what the magazine wanted to be, what it was and what it would become. The cartoon appeared in the issue for December 12, 1925, when the magazine was less than a year old. It shows an attractive matron, wearing a typical short dress of the period; she appears to be dancing and, in the process, kicking over a cocktail shaker and toppling the cigarette out of her elegantly long holder. The caption: "Disturbing Effect of the Spirit of Christmas on the Old Lady in Dubuque, As Revealed in a Christmas Card Received by The New Yorker from That Worthy Dame." The reference, of course, is to the prospectus that Harold Ross wrote when the *New Yorker* was still in the making. Its most famous proclamation was that "The New Yorker will be the magazine which is not edited for the old lady in Dubuque." Ross wanted "a magazine avowedly published for a metropolitan audience," and, particularly in the early days, it was as relentlessly provincial as it had promised to be, mainly concerning itself with the minutiae of New York City life. Yet, as the Barton cartoon suggested, there was not that great a distance between the old lady in Dubuque and the boys and girls from Salt Lake City, Columbus, Ohio, and Mount Vernon, New York, who put out their insular journal. Within a few years, the best of the *New Yorker* contributors—first the humorists, then the short-story writers—found a following far beyond the Hudson River.

"I reflect that not everyone has little pieces published in magazines," wrote E. B. White in a "little piece" about the dangers of not wearing a hat. "*Almost* everyone does, but not everyone" ("No Hat," November 27, 1926). The first few years of the *New Yorker* show how right E. B. White was. Not only do those writers who became identified with the *New Yorker* appear—White, James Thurber, Robert Benchley, Dorothy Parker, John O'Hara, Frank Sullivan—but there are frequent contributions from men like Elmer Davis and Gilbert Seldes, who went on to do other kinds of writing in other places. Actors as different as Leslie Howard and Groucho Marx turn up, being funny, or trying to be, and there are comic pieces from Ernest Hemingway, Upton Sinclair, F. Scott Fitzgerald. What's more, Hemingway's is genuinely amusing ("My Own Life," February 12, 1927). The "little piece," the "casual," to borrow one of Ross's words, was not exactly a *New Yorker* invention. *Judge,* which Harold Ross edited for a while, and the old *Life,* and even *College Humor* and *Vanity Fair,* in their very different ways, had their versions of the "little piece." The minuscule piece, one might say, for some of the contributions in *Life* and *Judge* ran for no more than a paragraph or two, but then neither did some of the early offerings in the *New Yorker*. Ross's magazine finally turned its back on its nearest relatives, but not until it had borrowed the best of their writers and cartoonists, and an occasional idea as well.

As these other magazines faded away and the *New Yorker* solidified its position, the brief, humorous essay began to be identified as "*New Yorker* humor." The label is misleading if it is supposed to define with any exactitude a particular kind of prose work, for the range within the "little pieces" is great—from verbal slapstick to philosophic ruefulness. Still, there is a generic sameness within the variations. The types were established very early. The most common device was for the writer to take a recognizable current event as a place to begin and to build on it an intricate framework of fantasy or simple comment. In "The Seed of Revolt" (May 29, 1926), Robert Benchley contemplates the pedestrians' problem in a city beset by new construction, using as his starting point an actual fire on the wooden staging around a construction site; in "How I Became a Subway Excavator" (January 23, 1926), the building of a new subway becomes the excuse for one of Frank Sullivan's characteristic descents—or ascents—into autobiographical lunacy. When the events were of more than local interest—national and international news stories, real or manufactured—the *New Yorker* writers returned to them again and again; thus, in the early years of the magazine there were a great many pieces that grew out of the Lindbergh flight, expeditions to the North Pole, the Hall-Mills case. Calvin Coolidge was the butt of a great many jokes in both the cartoons and the essays. In "Kamp Koolidge Nights" (June 5, 1926), Robert Benchley imagines the President putting on "that property pair of overalls that was used for photographic publicity purposes during the campaign" and telling stories around the campfire: "A reggeler ghost story about th' time up Bostin way when I run inter a hull tribe er strikin' policemen and held 'em at bay, singlehanded." The piece, however, is the usual one based on a newspeg, in this case the announcement that the Summer White House would be in the Adirondacks. Unless some such news story triggered the essay, Coolidge's name was likely to appear simply as one of a number of familiar names of the period—Herbert Bayard Swope, William Lyon Phelps, Grover Whalen—which for some reason the writers found funny the way radio comedians used to depend on a mention of Brooklyn or Sheboygan to get a laugh. There was obviously a deal of political acumen in the mock election analyses that Frank Sullivan wrote during the Hoover-Smith campaign, and his response to that election was the most partisan essay I can remember seeing in the early *New Yorker*. For the most part, *New Yorker* humor was not political.

Among *New Yorker* writers in search of a subject, the private incident was almost as popular as the public event. E. B. White got an amiable short piece ("Petit Dejeuner," September 18, 1926) out of trying and failing to explain to an uncomprehending French waiter how to serve the shredded wheat he was so delighted at having discovered in a grocery in Paris. James Thurber, working somewhat more broadly, edged into farce in his account of the aftermath of a pre-sailing party ("My Trip Abroad," August 6, 1927). This kind of piece, in the hands of White and Thurber, became a cross between personal anecdote and social comment. On the one hand, then, it shared the characteristics of those perennial pieces which catalogued the difficulties and the indignities which one faced when one went shopping, went abroad, tried to mail a letter, entered a bank, went to or gave a party, rented a summer cottage—the list is endless. Sometimes, in the hands of Robert Benchley or Donald Ogden Stewart, such material was newly funny; more often, even the masters nodded, and anyone leafing through the pages of the old *New Yorker* is likely to shudder and say, oh, no, here comes another embarkation party. On the other hand, the personal incident began to move toward the character sketch, the short story. Although E. B. White can make me believe he observed a real drunk when he went to see the Lunts in *Caprice* ("Interpretation," April 13, 1929), there is no real reason why the incidents that the humorists used could not be fictional. Certainly, very early in the *New Yorker*'s history writers like Dorothy Parker, Arthur Kober and Marc Connelly began to invent not only the incidents but the voices that described them. A typical example is Arthur Kober's "Just a Pal" (March 31, 1928). A girl whom the *New Yorker* readers had met in an earlier Kober piece complains about her friend Florrie for whom she will never again do a favor. When Florrie was delayed in the subway on the way home from work, the narrator kindly agreed to go out with Florrie's boyfriend, just to save the waste of a ticket, but when she discovered that the show was at Carnegie Hall ("and, believe me, I saw a lotta foreign element"), she walked out at intermission and came home to tell Florrie how lucky she was to have missed it. She cannot understand either Florrie's tears or her ingratitude. Such sketches were a first step toward what came to be known as the *New Yorker* story.

Either the personal incident or the public event—more often the second—could be approached through parody, and that form became one of the *New Yorker* standards. It has always been an attractive genre to comic writers whether they really tried to imitate the original they were kidding or whether they went for burlesque and buried a recognizable source under a load of grotesque overstatement. The form was particularly popular in the 1920s, both in book-length works and in the comic magazines that preceded the *New Yorker*. Many of the writers who came over to Harold Ross's new magazine brought a reputation for parody with them. Donald Ogden Stewart is a prime example. His first book was *A Parody Outline of History* (1921), in which he recounts events in American history in a variety of styles, ranging from that of James Branch Cabell to that of Thornton W. Burgess; his second book, *Perfect Behavior* (1922), was a burlesque etiquette manual. There are parody elements in many of his *New Yorker* contributions—the practical advice article peeks through "How I Got My Rabbits to Lay" (April 7, 1928) and "How We Made Both Ends Meet in the Middle" (April 28, 1928)—but there were so many parodists in the *New Yorker* pages that Stewart was barely noticeable in the crowd. Parke Cummings turned up with a description of a bridge contest in a competent sports page style ("Clubs Is Trumps," March 13, 1926), and Nunnally Johnson described a bathroom whistler as though he were writing a music review ("Good Clean Fun," May 15, 1926). Most forms of popular journalism and literature were cycled through the parody mill, and, of course, the more serious writers were fair game. One of James Thurber's early contributions to the magazine was "A Visit from Saint Nicholas" (December 24, 1927), a version of Clement Moore's Christmas poem retold "In the Ernest Hemingway Manner." Hemingway's own *New Yorker* piece was ostensibly a parody of Frank Harris's *My Life and Loves*. As a critic, I admit a certain difficulty with the parodists. I admire individual pieces that range from E. B. White's "Worm Turning" (October 1, 1927), a take-off

on Alexander Woollcott at his worst—which could be most anytime—to Peter De Vries's parody of Elizabeth Bowen ("Touch and Go," January 26, 1952). Yet, it is not a genre I warm to. Corey Ford's "New Light on the Rothstein Theory" (March 2, 1929), which discusses the traffic problem in scientific terminology, is an efficient, restrained piece that sticks to its initial conception, but, for me, it is dead after one paragraph. On the other hand, Ring Lardner's "Miss Sawyer, Champion" (September 10, 1927), which begins as a parody of tennis reporting and ends somewhere near surrealism, is the kind of comic writing that remains alive although it kills its first parodic impulse as it grows. *New Yorker* writers, depending on whether they wanted to demonstrate their ear or their imagination, vacillated between restraint and exuberance in their use of parody; particularly in the early days, they tended to walk on the wild side.

Although the best of the *New Yorker* humorists developed unmistakable literary personalities and the styles to express them, there is a storehouse of comic devices and verbal tricks which most of them used on occasion. The non sequitur, for instance, and its cousin, the irrelevant aside. Listen to the parenthetic remark in this sentence from Robert Benchley's "Sex is Out" (December 19, 1925): "According to Dr. Max Hartmann (I used to have a dentist named Dr. Hartmann, but he was a dentist) there is no such thing as absolute sex." Or take this sentence from Ring Lardner's "Miss Sawyer, Champion": "Yesterday's event was attended by the largest crowd of the season, attracted not only because it was the championship final, but also by the fact that the former Miss Stevens's birthplace in Portugal gave the match an international odor." The line almost makes sense, and then one realizes that its spurious plausibility is completely undone by the fact that there is no Miss Stevens anywhere else in the article. There is something so gentle about E. B. White and something so logical about his writing that it takes a second or two to recognize his personal variation on the standard non sequitur in a line like, "Let a man's leg be never so shapely, sooner or later his garters wear out" ("Garter Motif," June 5, 1926).

Repetition is another of the comic devices. The narrator in Dorothy Parker's "Dialogue at Three in the Morning" (February 13, 1926) is a little bit drunk which might explain her saying, "Trouble with me is, I'm too kind-hearted. That's what everybody always told me. 'Trouble with you is, you're too kind-hearted,' they said." But almost exactly the same line can be found in Frank Sullivan's "How I Became a Subway Excavator," published a month earlier: "The folks, I guess, think I'm more interested in digging that subway than I am in my job. 'You're more interested in that subway than you are in your job,' they tell me." The joke, I assume, lies in the almost confessional tone of the lines, the suggestion that the alteration of a word or two or the movement from indirect to direct address brings with it a new revelation. Another favorite repetition joke can also be found in the work of Frank Sullivan. He has always been obsessive about fashionable names, as his annual holiday poem for the *New Yorker* indicates, but in an early piece, a mock society column ("The Costume Balls," March 13, 1926), his list of celebrities is designed so that certain names keep appearing. The device is not simply comic, as the repetition of any sounds might be, but satiric as well. The implication is that certain figures manage to elbow their way to a real lion's share of public attention. Elmer Davis makes this specific in his use of the joke. In "Now It Can Be Told" (October 16, 1926), an eye witness gives a list of the famous people on hand the night of the Hall-Mills murders. After mentioning Herbert Bayard Swope six times, she says, "Oh, dear, I've gone and mentioned Mr. Swope twice; but really that is precisely the impression which he makes upon me." Still another variation in the repetition technique is the line that keeps returning like a refrain. In a parody of syndicated columns that peddle exotic New York to local papers ("Metropolitan Nature Fakers," July 23, 1927), Nunnally Johnson describes each of his exciting New Yorkers as "a collector of rare first editions and an admirer of Nietzsche." He caps the gag by changing the wording the last time the line appears; his chorus girl "has an excellent collection of rare first editions including one of 'Thus Spake Zarathustra.'" The switcheroo—as they say in show business—may not be all that funny, but Johnson's comic instincts are sound; the correct finish to that kind of refrain is to deny and fulfill the audience expectations at the same time.

Another popular comic device and one that may have had a deleterious effort on the *New Yorker* at its most serious is the use of excessive incidental detail. Originally, of course, the detail itself was supposed to be funny. Thus Frank Sullivan introduced a "Mrs. Maud Fetterdetsch, tester of police whistles" into "How I Became a Subway Excavator," and Corey Ford, writing a fictional history of the magazine ("The Anniversary of a Great Magazine"), turned out this sentence: "In those halcyon days, for example, a stage-line started at the Public Library (destroyed by fire in 1889, owing to a carelessly-tossed cigarette), circled Bryant Park to avoid the construction which had just started, crossed over to Broadway and ran down James G. Blaine, after which it was discontinued." The honorable ancestry of that kind of comic line can be seen in Crabtree's description of a pistol shot in *The School for Scandal*: "the ball struck against a little bronze Shakespeare that stood over the fireplace, grazed out of the window at a right angle, and wounded the postman, who was just coming to the door with a double letter from Northamptonshire." That kind of extended line was not the only, not even the most conventional way of playing with detail; as often as not, a single phrase, a specific name or location would be imbedded in an ordinary sentence. When Corey Ford mentioned "a prominent manufacturer named Meebles" in one of his essays on traffic problems ("How D'You Get What Way?" January 9, 1926), he probably thought the name Meebles funny—which it may be to some people—but the important part of the phrase is the man's occupation which gives a bogus authority to the whole invention. Perhaps a better example can be found in E. B. White's "Interview with a Sparrow" (April 9, 1927): "I stopped a sparrow recently at the Seventy-second Street entrance to the Park and put the question bluntly." In this case, the exact location plays against the unspecific "recently" and the whole air of accident—as though he had just happened to meet the sparrow—and

gives the fantasy an almost repertorial substance. The *New Yorker*'s preoccupation with detail turned finally to the kind of cataloguing which now makes the magazine almost unreadable. I picked up a recent issue (February 12, 1972) and found an item in "The Talk of the Town" which began, "Having been invited by the Brody Corporation, a hydra-headed association of restaurant operators, whose responsibilities include L'Étoile, Gallagher's Steak House, and the Rainbow Room, to drop in at the last of these during . . ." The sentence went on for another half column. And it was not even meant to be funny. If Frank Sullivan had written it thirty years ago, it would have been funny and a great deal easier to read aloud.

I might have used Corey Ford's description of the stage-line that ran down James G. Blaine as an example of something other than the *New Yorker* absorption in detail. It also represents a kind of conscious overwriting used for comic effect. Sometimes the elaboration comes from the misuse of metaphor, as in this line, also from Corey Ford: "All too late the lily of truth, crushed to earth beneath the heel of Industry, tears the bandage from its eyes to behold the handwriting on the wall" ("The Bleakest Job," May 29, 1926). In time, such lines almost disappeared from the casuals, but they turned up as filler at the bottom of the page in the series of accidentally funny newsbreaks labeled "Block That Metaphor." Oddly enough, the pun, one of the standard forms of comic ornamentation, appeared infrequently in the early days of the *New Yorker*. One of Wolcott Gibb's first pieces was built around the phrase "neither beer nor there," ("On Working That Line Into the Conversation," February 25, 1928), but it did not really try to inflict the pun on the reader; instead, it was a first-person account of a man's attempt to work the phrase into a conversation and his failure when the occasion arose. It was not until a master punner arrived that the form came into its own in the *New Yorker*. Of all the outrages committed by Peter De Vries, I prefer the response he swears he never made to the woman who said she saw the geese fly south: "Migratious!" ("Compulsion," January 17, 1953). The master of ornamentation at the *New Yorker*, at least since the 1930s, has been S. J. Perelman. His rich and scarcely appropriate vocabulary is one reason why his prose is so lush, but a look at a reasonably commonplace sentence of his will show that his effects are also syntactical. He can take the simplest sentence and convert it into a grandiosity by stuffing it with clause upon clause, phrase upon phrase. "Every woman cherishes a dream" is the kind of direct declarative sentence that might be an appropriate opening for a casual, but look what happens to it in S. J. Perelman's hands: "Every woman worth her salt, and even the few unsalted ones I have known, cherishes somewhere in her heart midway between the auricle and the ventricle a lovely, pastel-tinted dream." There is no more compelling indication of the variety in the *New Yorker* "little piece" than to consider this kind of prose alongside that of E. B. White and James Thurber, who, as the years passed, became increasingly spare in their effects.

Most of the familiar *New Yorker* names have appeared in the examples I have cited, but my attempt to define the genre and the shared literary devices necessarily buries the individual in the group. There is hardly time in a short lecture to discuss each of the writers, but let me take a few minutes to comment on some of those who seem to me most characteristic of the magazine and its humor. Since most of them wrote for other publications as well, a few of my examples come from non-*New Yorker* pages, but so mild an impurity should not obscure the general picture. When Donald Ogden Stewart and Nunnally Johnson went off to Hollywood in the early 1930s, they practically ceased to write except for the films. Their identification with the *New Yorker* was necessarily brief, and I doubt that either man's name would occur to anyone who grew up with the magazine in the 1930s and 1940s. Yet, Johnson's workmanlike pieces represent the kind of occasional essay that was the magazine's stock-in-trade in the 1920s, and he left behind him at least one magic line. I have still not mastered the implications of a sentence of his that begins, "This fact was brought home, or even worse, early last Thursday morning . . ." ("Good Clean Fun"). Stewart was at his best in the strange historical essays in which he leavened a demented family chronicle with a touch of social comment. In "The President's Son" (December 10, 1927), an illogical extension of Nan Britton's revelations about President Harding, Stewart tells an idyllic tale of the meetings between his mother and an unidentified president—first, at a White Elephant sale in New Britain, Connecticut; then, at Grant's Tomb; finally, in a tree during the Johnstown Flood. This kind of invention has its verbal equivalent in lines like, "But daisies, like the cat who bit John D. Rockefeller, Jr., are often 'all too human,' and this year I'm going to tell" ("After Christmas—What?" December 31, 1927). Frank Sullivan worked a similar vein when he first began to write for the *New Yorker*. For instance, in "Three Methods of Acquiring Loam" (May 26, 1928), he converts the sidetrack into the main road. He explains, almost parenthetically, that the British stripped Manhattan of its loam when they evacuated it during the Revolutionary War, which leads him to Luther Burbank and his separation of "hoats" into "two distinct varieties . . . hay and oats." At another point in the same essay, illustrating the way to show your friends that you would like loam as a gift, he writes a conversation which somehow turns into an attempt to pick up a girl on Fifth Avenue and, then, into a musical comedy with a love song which ends incredibly with "They needed a tenor in Heaven so they took Caruso away." One of Sullivan's later inventions is Mr. Arbuthnot, the cliché expert, who appears in a great many dialogue pieces. The character is a treasurehouse of bromidic answers—a testimony to Sullivan's good ear—but the Arbuthnot exchanges are too restrained to show Sullivan at his best. He is most himself at his most irrelevant—for instance, when, apropos of nothing at all, he suddenly says, "Succotash had not yet, however, come into its own" ("Down the Ages with the Social Center," March 6, 1926).

Presumably most of the *New Yorker* humorists began writing in college, but Corey Ford and S. J. Perelman somehow stayed closer to their campus origins. Ford, who had edited the *Jester* at Columbia, went downtown and began to contribute to *Judge, Life, Vanity Fair* and, as soon as it was founded, the *New Yorker*. Perelman came down from Brown, where he had edited the *Brown Jug,*

to work for *Judge* and to contribute to *Life* among others. It was not until the 1930s that he began to write for the *New Yorker*. The two humorists differ in that Ford worked in a variety of styles, adapting himself to the immediate needs of the situation and the subject; Perelman early adopted a personal style that has hardly changed between the 1920s and the 1970s. What the two men have in common is that the work of both of them seems very strained; it gives off an air of conscious cleverness that harks back to the editorial rooms of the college humor magazines from which they came. It is this quality in Ford's work, I assume, that kept him from building a large following as so many of the *New Yorker* writers did—this quality, plus an almost complete absence of literary personality. S. J. Perelman, on the other hand, has—or once had—legions of admirers. If I may wax autobiographical, for a moment, I was once among them. In my college days in the late 1940s, when humor magazines were just beginning to die, I was a Perelman enthusiast at a time when I was no more than an admirer of Thurber and White. I now find it very difficult to read period Perelman. When he calls himself "the present troubadour" ("*Whose* Lady Nicotine?") or says that "Mr. Farber recently sat himself down" ("Hell in the Gabardines"), I squirm a little and try to catch a glimpse of the old imagination behind the fancy wordwork. Perelman is probably in better control in most of his pieces than are Donald Ogden Stewart and Frank Sullivan in the essays I applauded earlier, but a controlled outrageousness has its limits. What he lacks, I think, is a genuine wildness.

It is not particularly evident in his first contributions to the *New Yorker,* but Robert Benchley is the comic in this group who developed the firmest personality. That may be because the character he created—the voice in most of his pieces—had a life both on and off the page. He was a busy and successful journalist in 1923 when he went on stage, in the third *Music Box Revue,* and first performed his famous monologue, "The Treasurer's Report." In 1928, the "Report" was filmed and Benchley went on to make more than forty film shorts in which he tried, with a kind of placid desperation, to make something simple seem complicated; during the 1940s, he played variations on his likable bumbler in feature films. The Benchley character was also clearly delineated in the caricature that Gluyas Williams created to illustrate the many Benchley books. More important, of course, is that the character emerges in the short pieces that Benchley continued to write even after he became a movie star. The character is a little vain, always willing to strut a few steps before he falls into a real or imaginary manhole. He is a touch ponderous as he tries to explain things, and he is constantly viewing with mild alarm. Embarrassment is almost a disease with him. He is sometimes fictional—working in the planetarium with Mr. MacGregor, the old Navy man—but more often simply an after-image of the author himself. As I have described him, he is not unlike a great many other comic characters, the little man beset by the intricacies of life, catching whatever transient pleasures he can. There is, however, a dark side to this man. He would never say so directly, but mortality and an unfriendly universe are also after him. This is clear in "My Trouble," in which he wonders "Do all boys of 46 stop breathing when they go to bed?" and in "Duck, Brothers!" in which he is quite certain that "a full-fledged rain of ten-ton flame-balls" is heading directly for him: "I know where I'm not wanted." These pieces are as funny as the lighter ones, but they do have a disquieting undertone, which may indicate that Benchley was a more serious comic writer than he was ever willing to admit.

James Thurber and E. B. White are the two humorists most closely associated with the *New Yorker*. One could almost say that they were created by the magazine, but they in turn helped create it. It was their work that separated the "little piece" from the slapstick of the early days, that let it turn gentle, ruminative, even somber on occasion. E. B. White came to the *New Yorker* first, when it was only a few months old, and, as Marc Connelly once said, "brought the steel and the music to the magazine." In the early days, White did almost everything, from theater reviews to cartoon captions, but it was in the casuals that he established his authority. There is a sentimental side to the man which expresses itself in spongy lyricism and the kind of rue that grows in Dorothy Parker's garden. Most of that sentimentality was happily milked off in the verse that White wrote in the 1920s. In his prose, that quality was contained, became genuine sentiment, expressed an affection for places and people and the time of day that few other writers have been able to equal. White was quite capable of fooling around in the Frank Sullivan manner. In the collection of society notes that he calls "Fin de Saison—Palm Beach" (April 7, 1934), he uses all the familiar devices—funny names, ludicrous juxtaposition, abrupt irrelevancy—and the result is one of the funniest burlesques to come out of the *New Yorker*. Yet, that is not the kind of piece which one identifies with E. B. White. The best of his work is in one of two forms, both allied to the short story—the personal anecdote and the parable. He came to the first quite early. In 1925, he made a characteristic piece ("Child's Play," December 19) out of having buttermilk spilled on him in a restaurant. He manipulated the material more obviously than he probably would have in later years, but he clearly established both a sense of the situation and the character of the narrator—qualities which would continue to mark his anecdotal pieces. In the parables, he displays greater range. It is wry intelligence that shows through "The Wings of Orville" (August 8, 1931), in which the sparrow's wife comes to share her husband's crackpot dream; in "The Door" (March 25, 1939), the irony turns frightening as his narrator's world becomes the rat's cage of the behavioral scientist.

It was 1927 when James Thurber first turned up in the pages of the *New Yorker*—with two poems that are of historical interest only. With his next appearance, "An American Romance" (March 5, 1927), the Thurber tone—or one of them—was already established. "Romance" tells the story of a "little man in an overcoat that fitted him badly at the shoulders" who took refuge in a revolving door and would not come out until he had become a public hero. " 'I did it for the wife and children,' he said." That piece and another early one about a man who tries to take a straw hat to the cleaners ("The Psyching of Mr. Rogers," April 27, 1929) have an undertone of pain

and panic that weaves all through Thurber's work. It surfaces lightly in "A Note at the End" of *My Life and Hard Times* (1933), and it grows pervasive in Thurber's last years, as *Further Fables for Our Time* (1956) indicates. There are other Thurbers who have to live with the dark humorist of the *Fables*. There is the word crank who can be traced from the early series on "Our Own Modern English Usage" through the dialect games of "What Do You Mean It *Was* Brillig?" (January 7, 1939) to the children's author of *The Wonderful O* (1957). There is the writer who, beginning with "The Thin Red Leash" in 1927 (August 13), has described the most unlikely company of dogs in modern letters. There is the autobiographer of *My Life and Hard Times,* who went again to his past in *The Thurber Album* (1952) and built solid memoirs on ground that had already supported some of the best and funniest comic writing in America. It seems to me that what all these Thurbers have in common is the writer who insisted on being rational in the cause of irrationality—at least, insofar as that word can stand for fantasy, variety, openness, surprise and a healthy distrust of all rules. That Thurber is implicit in the cartoonist whose characters hear seals bark, crouch on bookcases, "come from haunts of coot and hern." He is explicit in *Let Your Mind Alone* (1937), the mock-serious discussion of popular psychology in which he says, "The undisciplined mind . . . is far better adapted to the confused world in which we live. . . . This is, I am afraid, no place for the streamlined mind."

The world is more confused in the 1970s than it was in the 1930s, but today there is apparently not even room for the undisciplined mind. At least, there is no room for the kind of comic writing that these humorists represent. S. J. Perelman still turns up in the pages of the *New Yorker,* but he is like a literary Rip Van Winkle come home to a village that does not recognize him. The magazine prints occasional casuals by Woody Allen, who out-Perelmans Perelman, and by Roger Angell, among others, but it has grown turgid and heavy, it has—as that 1927 note suggested—developed "a Righteous Cause or two and become Important." Hardly the home for the "little piece" that E. B. White had in mind when he contemplated the dangers of going hatless. Nor is there any other home. In a world in which there are fewer magazines and in which the remaining ones tend to be very serious or fakily flashy or aimed at a non-general audience, no magazine editor wants the kind of comic writing that made the *New Yorker* famous. No newspaper editor, either. Except for a few regional columnists, the remaining newspaper humorists are almost completely political. Times change, tastes change. The *New Yorker* humorists have gone the way of Mark Twain and Mr. Dooley and Artemus Ward, into the libraries or into oblivion. It is my job as scholar and critic to record the fact, coldly, and pass on. But somehow this sounds like a lament. That may not be inappropriate. Not only has a kind of comic writing disappeared, but an attitude as well. "Quo Vadimus?" (May 24, 1930) is a case in point. In that piece, E. B. White stops a man in East Thirty-fourth Street and asks "Quo vadis?" He chides the man for giving his time and energy to pointless activities that obscure his simple wants, but before the piece ends it turns back on the author, sees him as one with the harried man and justifies the plural of the title. What all these writers share is a sense of complicity. Even when they are not their own subjects, there is an implicit recognition that only a fine line separates the satirist from his target, the humorist from his subject, the teller from the told. They know that all of us are clumsy, confused, vain and mortal, and that we build the wrong monuments to the wrong gods on the wrong quicksand. Perhaps one can no longer know that and still retain a deep affection for imperfect man and his unlikely works.

For all I know, there may no longer be an old lady in Dubuque.

Edward A. Martin

SOURCE: *"The New Yorker,"* in *H. L. Mencken and the Debunkers,* The University of Georgia Press, 1984, pp. 177-91.

[*Martin is an American critic and educator. In the following excerpt, he examines the development of a distinctive brand of humor and satire in the* New Yorker.]

Developing the energy of American English into a distinctive American style became an implicit mission for the *New Yorker* as it grew in the 1930s into a magazine of unusual cultural significance and achievement. The *New Yorker* began as a magazine of debunking satire and wit, but prior to 1930 its satirical tone was uneven and its facetiousness unsure. During the years between 1925 and 1930 there were some exceptions, some prefigurings of the comic spirit it was to display in the 1930s, but its initial success came primarily during the years of the Depression, and grew out of the comic way in which it treated Depression-related subjects.

In the late 1920s and the early 1930s the *New Yorker* was publishing debunking commentary by some of America's best satirists. These few years were also the years of the *New Yorker*'s greatest success as a magazine of humor. This humor was not of the sort that celebrated the smiling aspects of American life. It was debunking humor: urbane, witty, satiric. Its subjects were those identified and worked by the debunkers: provincialism, Puritanism, Americanism, Philistinism, and the defective language that was the common vehicle of such subjects.

Other ingredients contributing to the success of the magazine's humor were brevity, simplicity of format, and topicality. The principle that humorous articles and facetious commentary must be brief had been learned from the venerable comic weeklies, *Puck, Judge,* and *Life. Time* magazine, three years older than the *New Yorker,* had also demonstrated that capsule treatment of contemporary events was effective. The relationship among humor, satire, and contemporary events was one that was understood by the editors of the older comic weeklies; it was a relationship exploited by journalists throughout the nineteenth century, and it had been proved, in the 1910s and 1920s, by the popularity of the feature pages of newspapers such as *New York World,* the *New York Evening Sun,* and the *New York Tribune.* The *New York World* had featured Adams's "The Conning Tower," Broun's "It Seems to Me," Sullivan's "Out of a Clear Sky" and the writings of

Benchley. Marquis had written "The Sun Dial" column for the *Evening Sun* and "The Lantern" for the *Tribune.* For most newspaper humorists the shift from the feature page of the newspaper to the pages of comic weeklies was easy and natural. The *New Yorker* preserved the brevity and topicality necessary to the writing of the journalist. It used the narrow newspaper column as an aid to rapid reading, and in so doing imitated *Puck, Judge,* and *Life,* all of which had begun to imitate newspaper layout around 1916.

More indirect influences on the *New Yorker* were some of the "little" magazines that had preceded it. Like them, the *New Yorker* was able with assurance, almost from the very beginning, to represent and project an attitude and point of view. Its attitude flattered the urbane reader; its point of view was satiric. Such a combination of characteristics had not figured prominently in American humor before the advent of debunkers such as Mencken and Marquis. Satire, with a few exceptions (Bierce is one), had been possible in the nineteenth century only for those American humorists who assumed an unsophisticated comic mask. Usually the satire was delivered in a rustic dialect by a wise fool from the provinces. The twentieth-century shift of comic posture, to which the *New Yorker* responded, was from the provincial to the urbane. Two late nineteenth-century journalistic prefigurations of the shift were magazines briefly published in metropolises on opposite sides of the country: *M'lle New York* and, in San Francisco, the *Lark.* With them the *New Yorker* shared simplicity of format, the effective use of drawings and cartoons, and the planned appeal to a limited readership. The *Lark* and *M'lle New York* did not survive into the new century. Obviously, the *New Yorker* conceived of a different audience. Nevertheless, it accepted from the beginning the principle that the satiric attitude could be at once entertaining and effective.

Puck magazine, begun in 1877, was the immediate progenitor in the field monopolized by the *New Yorker* after the early 1930s. *Puck* had conceived of itself as a comic and satiric magazine; it was also an instrument of partisan political commentary, leaning heavily toward the Democratic Party. A survey of issues in the late 1870s and the early 1880s shows satiric treatment of some of the subjects which the debunkers of the twentieth century handled in similar fashion. There was the "Puck's Sensational Novels" series, which parodied tales of adventure and sentimental fiction. The "Puck's Essential Oil of Congress" series spoofed activities and inactivities in Washington. Mock histories of the United States prefigured Stewart's historical parodies in the 1920s. There was also a series called "Fitznoodle in America," in which the impressions of a traveling Englishman were recorded in comic fashion. The affected, snobbish, and effeminate Fitznoodle was depicted as ridiculous and pathetic as he confronted the masculine crudities of American life. The twentieth-century debunkers' hostility was an inversion of this, for theirs was directed not at the Englishman or European but at the provincial American. *Puck* in the depression of 1893 expressed antipopulist attitudes which also pointed toward the comic antiprovincial hostility that was a persistent attitude and an important ingredient of the *New Yorker*'s early success. British mannerisms and traditions continued to be a source of *Puck*'s material in the 1890s. H. C. Bunner wrote a series called "The People in the Fog—Being Desultory Dips into the Gray Matter of the British Brain." The debunkers, especially writers for the *New Yorker,* borrowed this satiric tone to ridicule Americans who lived in what they took to be the provincial fog of the Midwest.

There was a good deal of antipapist sentiment in *Puck,* satire of papal politics and of the doctrine of papal infallibility. *Puck* insisted that it was ridiculing the way the church was administered, not Catholicism itself, but genteel Protestant readers must have assumed otherwise. The tendency of the debunkers was to ridicule organized religion in general, with the emphasis on the Puritan roots of American culture, since the middle class in America was primarily Protestant. In 1893 and 1894 *Puck* initiated an antipuritanism campaign, aimed at those who wanted to force blue laws on the Chicago World's Fair—such restraints as Sunday closing and art censorship. The debunkers, many of them in the pages of the *New Yorker,* continued to deride the Puritan minority which tried with frequent success to impose its morality on everyone else.

In the twentieth century *Puck* continued very much as it had in the 1890s. There was little change in format unitl 1916, when the neater, easier-to-read, three-column page was introduced. With the change in format, the magazine promised that it would develop a "new school of satire." To that end it called for contributions from newspapermen; perhaps it hoped for debunking material from journalists such as Marquis and Mencken. During the prewar years the tenor of its humor was much the same as it had always been. Women's rights movements were ridiculed (as they had been in the 1870s). Special targets for comic treatment were the tycoons J. P. Morgan, Andrew Carnegie, John D. Rockefeller, and Theodore Roosevelt, with his quadrennial presidential aspirations. The Armory Show of 1913 provoked satiric commentary about modern art. Most of the debunkers, the *New Yorker* writers among them, continued to be offended by the avant-garde in art; here was an easy way to elicit the hostile laughter of middle-class citizens whose tight moral attitudes the debunkers, paradoxically and inconsistently, attacked in so many other areas. *Puck,* always Democratic, gave its vehement allegiance to Woodrow Wilson, and its comic tone was lost in pro-American, antialien, prowar polemics. After 1916 it did try to bring itself up to date by publishing some of the younger satirists. There were cartoons by John Held, Jr., and Ralph Barton, both *New Yorker* contributors. Among the writers appearing in issues during its last two years of publication were Samuel Hoffenstein and George S. Chappell, parodists who wrote frequently for *Vanity Fair.* But *Puck* was hopelessly outdated, in spite of the addition of numerous photographs of enticingly draped female models. After being sold to Hearst's International Magazine Company in 1917 it reverted to the kind of gentility it had once debunked, and the last issue appeared in September 1918. The comic weekly field was left to two very similar *Puck* imitators, *Judge* and *Life.*

Like *Puck, Judge* and *Life* had for years been the reposito-

ries for homespun humor which relished the cheerful character of American life. Thomas L. Masson was a typical early twentieth-century contributor to both magazines. There were many he-she jokes: early issues of the *New Yorker* did not disdain this venerable comic affliction either. There were pictures of handsome, healthy young women, suitable for admiration in the parlors of the American home. That the *New Yorker* scorned such pictures was a sure sign of sophistication and of an attempt to appeal to emancipated feminine readers, who saw themselves as something other than attractive parlor centerpieces. There was some political commentary in *Judge* and *Life,* frequently on presidential candidates. In 1912 *Judge* ran a cartoon which showed "Wouldgrow Wilson" trying to get into Bryan's oversize presidential suit. *Judge* also in each 1912 issue devoted a page to "The Modern Woman," spoofing the energetic enthusiasms of the militant female suffragists. The *New Yorker* discovered that women, who paid their advertisers, were no longer suitable comic material; like it or not, a magazine that aspired to a general readership in America had to take women seriously.

By 1925 *Judge* and *Life* had adjusted somewhat to the times. Keeping their national circulations in mind, they made fun of the frantic lives of hard-drinking urbanites, but tried to maintain their urban appeal at the same time by printing jokes and cartoons about quaint life in the provinces. The *Judge* cover girls wore less clothing and thus revealed more of their wholesomeness, but their pulchritude was never especially suggestive. Nevertheless, that they were present at all was evidence of *Judge*'s bias toward the masculine reader. The magazine displayed a fatal disregard for the tastes and interests of a female America that had just been given the right to vote. The advertisements, which were national in scope, contrasted sharply with what was to appear in the *New Yorker;* the somewhat unsophisticated emphasis was on trusses, health cures, and how-to-be-a-success-in-love-and-business books. *Judge* did see the humorous possibilities of all this nonsense when, on 11 April 1925, it published a burlesque advertising issue, which debunked the elaborate claims of manufacturers. Norman Anthony, the editor responsible for the issue, left *Judge* to become editor of *Life* in 1929.

Anthony had tried as editor of both *Judge* and *Life* to find a formula that would maintain the reputations and circulations of these magazines. Both of them foundered in the 1930s. The title *Life* was sold to Time, Incorporated, in 1936, while *Judge* lingered on uncertainly and unsuccessfully. Anthony himself, upon leaving *Life* after a year, produced a new humorous magazine that had brief but spectacular fame. The magazine, *Ballyhoo,* first appeared in 1931. *Ballyhoo* used the burlesque technique which Anthony had developed in 1925 as editor of *Judge.* Advertisements were flamboyantly parodied. Sex was used freely both as a weapon for parody and as a circulation booster in itself. The appeal of the magazine was primarily to New Yorkers; one printing in 1931 exceeded two million copies. It seemed at first that Anthony had found a formula which could rival the *New Yorker*'s. Advertisers, discovering that derogatory burlesques of their products led to increased sales, frequently paid for *Ballyhoo* advertisements which satirized their products. Such a peculiar inversion of standards led to the further deterioration of *Ballyhoo*'s original debunking intentions. The novelty soon wore off; burlesque advertisements were not enough to sustain a general-circulation magazine. The fad died quickly, although *Ballyhoo* did not expire completely until 1939. The *New Yorker* in the 1930s had little left in the way of competition.

Some competition at the start came from Mencken's and Nathan's *American Mercury.* While the early *New Yorker* was much more flippant in appearance and style, it borrowed Mencken's antiprovincialism so thoroughly that at first there seemed to be little else. It looked and sounded much like the *Smart Set* because its initial appeal was to "cleverness" and to "minds that are not primitive."

While the *Smart Set* continued as a Hearst publication, it was radically changed from a magazine of cleverness and satirical wit. Probably the *New Yorker* acquired some of the *Smart Set*'s subscribers, although many must have followed Mencken and Nathan to the *Mercury,* which appealed to much the same audience. After 1927 the circulation of the *Mercury* decreased while the *New Yorker* enlarged and consolidated its readership. Initially its subjects for satire were the same as the *Mercury*'s: provincialism, puritanism, Americanism, and the pretensions of aesthetes. It imitated the *Mercury*'s "Americana" section by using as column fillers self-parodying excerpts from the American press. Its "Profiles" were shortened forms of the *Mercury*'s biographical essays. Like the *Mercury,* the *New Yorker* was able to demonstrate successfully that Americans had come of age, that there were in America enough aspirers to a native urbanity and wit to support a magazine which both flattered and directed their sense of superiority.

Another magazine that was aimed at some of the same circulation the *New Yorker* hoped to attract was *Vanity Fair.* Begun in 1914 with Frank Crowninshield as editor, *Vanity Fair* made its suave and glossy appeal to those elements of society who were flattered by the reassurance that their artistic tastes were at once catholic, avant-garde, and European in flavor. *Vanity Fair* provided vignettes of, and writings by, the people who mattered in society, sports, drama, and the visual arts. It also sought out for ridicule the unknowing Philistines and those newly arrived in the outer parlors of high culture. Its most effective weapons in these campaigns were parody and the two departments of the magazine that with equal assurance made nominations for the "Hall of Fame" or for "Oblivion."

Humorists who appeared regularly in *Vanity Fair* during the 1920s were Benchley, Ford, Stewart, George S. Chappell, Nancy Boyd (Edna St. Vincent Millay), Samual Hoffenstein, and Edgar Dalrymple Perkins. Stewart wrote often from the point of view of the Ivy League socialite giving facetious hints to young ladies from the Midwest who were about to attend Eastern schools. Chappell was perhaps best remembered for his "Rollo" series: Rollo was the young son of a family, recently come from the provinces to live in New York, whose efforts to become cultured urbanites were hampered by the hayseed which

clung to them. Millay, under the pseudonym "Nancy Boyd," wrote many "he-she" dialogues, which chronicled the manners and problems of young, urban married couples. Ford was the most persistent contributor, frequently appearing under his own name and a pseudonym in the same issue. *Vanity Fair,* like the *New Yorker,* depended primarily on satire for its success during the 1920s. There were, of course, other departments, but satire made up the bulk of each issue.

Vanity Fair's decline began around 1930. Cleveland Amory and Frederic Bradlee blame this decline on the Depression. It is true that *Vanity Fair* changed very little during the Depression years. There was the same flamboyance, the same features, and with Prohibition dying a natural death the magazine nevertheless campaigned vigorously for its repeal, as if the issue were still fresh. The satiric tone of the magazine in the 1930s was upheld almost entirely by the glib ironies of Clare Boothe Brokaw (whose addition to the staff as a satiric writer had been hailed in 1930), and by Ford's astonishing productivity. But the main reason for the decline and fall of *Vanity Fair* was that the *New Yorker* was a far better magazine, both in its humor—which remained predominantly debunking humor in the 1930s—and in its other offerings. *Vanity Fair* tried to change the trend by becoming a picture magazine (color photography and reproduction became commercially feasible in the early 1930s) and by frankly imitating the *New Yorker* in some respects. There were many short biographies of prominent people, in imitation of the *New Yorker*'s series of "Profiles." Perhaps both magazines were responding to *Time* magazine's capsule technique in the news field. In December 1932 and thereafter, *Vanity Fair* acknowledged the *New Yorker*'s potency by imitating its format: the narrow column, three to a page, was used. Even the covers began to look like the *New Yorker*'s. But these cosmetic alterations were to no avail, since the *New Yorker* had the advantage over *Vanity Fair* in the quality of its satire. Often *Vanity Fair*'s satiric commentary rambled and became tedious, but the *New Yorker* insisted on brevity, whether in humor or features. *Vanity Fair,* more expansive and flamboyant, was less carefully edited. And the *New Yorker* provided an American, New York-centered sense of sophistication, whereas *Vanity Fair*'s orientation was more European.

The *New Yorker* had, however, begun by trying to imitate some of the mannered superiority of *Vanity Fair.* It was trying to be a reliable, worldly, amusing guide for the social, cultural, and material needs of well-to-do New Yorkers. Bringing these elements into harmony was not easy. For the first few years the magazine was an uneven comic hodge-podge. The format of the pages was cluttered. The effect was a little like that of the feature pages of the *New York World* and *New York Evening Sun.* But gradually the *New Yorker* cleaned up its pages, simplified its format, established its weekly departments, and drastically reduced the number of drawings and cartoons, as well as the many inane and gossipy jokes about its friends and enemies. In 1935 and 1936 the old *Life,* just before it was taken over by Time, Inc., acknowledged the *New Yorker*'s success, as had *Vanity Fair,* by imitating its format, layout, covers, and typeface.

The *New Yorker* began in 1925 as a magazine of debunking humor; there were other departments and kinds of writing in the first years, but it was primarily through satiric writing that Ross hoped to reflect the urbanity and vitality of New York. Jokes, short anecdotes, and humorous "casuals" were the meat of the early issues. It was not until the 1930s that short, nonhumorous stories began to appear with regularity. Gradually longer and longer contributions were printed; the climax of this tendency was the one-issue Hiroshima article by John Hersey in 1946. The tendency toward length has also led away from humor; the essence of the humorous piece is brevity. Thus (disregarding weekly features, which have remained nearly unchanged) the *New Yorker* has changed over the years from a humor magazine with occasional articles and stories to a magazine of articles, stories, and poetry which occasionally prints humor. But in the early 1930s it was not unusual to find satiric writing in each issue. These pieces almost invariably were produced by several of the same group of writers: Ford, Stewart, Davis, Parker, Benchley, Lardner, White, Thurber, Gibbs, Sullivan, and Perelman. Other writers appearing less frequently as humorists were Fillmore Hyde, Thomas Beer, Stephen Leacock, Nunally Johnson, and Heywood Broun. The *New Yorker* conceived of urbanity in terms of humor and wit; there were other ingredients, but humor came first. The success and tone of the magazine depended upon a combination of editorial policy and the kind of contributions available.

Ross had no talent as a writer, but as editor of the *New Yorker* his first and lifelong interest was in comic writing. Satire and burlesque were the modes of expression that appealed to him, and in these preferences he was like the writers he most appreciated, one of them being Mencken. He was like Mencken in his professed rejection of the genteel, and in his need for the recognition and applause of sophisticated people. Both were outspoken in their prejudices. Ross's ignorance of culture and literature appalled those who thought that the editor of the *New Yorker* should have been more obviously cultured, like *Vanity Fair*'s Frank Crowninshield. Ross said loudly and in public that he distrusted the female and femininity in general, but his own mother and later his daughter were important exceptions (he was married three times). In a book which admiringly perpetuated Ross's carefully contrived aura of the enigmatic, Thurber wrote that he was plagued by a "truly severe Momism." Ross said, "Men don't mature in this country, Thurber, They're children. . . . I think it's the goddam system of women school teachers." Ross insisted that he was surrounded and oppressed by women and children: he claimed that he looked constantly and unsuccessfully for a superman who could run his magazine smoothly. In his vague, comic, and half-nostalgic public statements about an ideal masculinity he was very like Mencken. In fact, the writers who surrounded him were men—Dorothy Parker was one of the exceptions—but Ross must have realized that many, perhaps most of the readers of his magazine were women. Like Mencken, he must have sensed that relationships between male and female in America were changing gradually but irrevocably.

Part of Ross's nature was captured in a parody *New York-*

er cover; it was drawn for a burlesque issue which was privately printed on the magazine's first anniversary in 1926. The figure of Eustace Tilley, the dapper dandy who adorns all the anniversary issues of the *New Yorker,* was given the scowling features of Ross. In the perennial cover by Rea Irwin, Eustace strikes the pose of Walt Whitman in the famous photograph, but the butterfly he is examining has the head of Alexander Woollcott. Woollcott and Ross were both friends and enemies all their lives. Woollcott typified the kind of cultured superiority that Ross both longed to emulate and hated for its snobbishness.

The magazine that Ross created in 1925 conformed to his rather limited concept of urbanity. His concern for precision of language echoed the sensibilities of all the debunkers who ridiculed inflated, abusive rhetoric everywhere around them. Ross has been frequently pictured as a perfectionist, and it is true that he developed a mania for fact-checking, clarity of expression, and conformity to Fowler's *English Usage.* Perfectionism may have been a belligerent defense that he developed after his magazine had been laughed at by some of the urbane readers he wanted most to impress. It was also a sign of his anxiety for his magazine's success and a compensation for his general cultural naiveté. He responded as an editor especially to parody and to writing that ridiculed excessive pompousness both in language and in attitude.

Ross had been a wandering reporter before the war, and during the war was editor of *Stars and Stripes* in Paris. Just before beginning the *New Yorker* he worked briefly for *Judge* magazine. *Judge,* and to a lesser extent, *Life,* were previews of what he hoped to do with the *New Yorker.* Ross thought he could publish a successful magazine by aiming directly at middle-class New York readers; to this end he sought advertising material which would have local appeal. *Life* and *Judge* differed: both were magazines that tried to be national in scope.

From its superior vantage point in the citadel of New York, the *New Yorker* persistently in its early years deprovincialized the rest of America through ridicule and satire. In the first issue (21 February 1925), the magazine announced "that it is not for the old lady in Dubuque. By this it means that it is not of that group of publications engaged in tapping the Great Buying Power of the North America Steppe region by trading mirrors and colored beads in the form of our best brands of hokum." Some of the other voices in the early issues, however, were not as sure of their sophistication. Certain anecdotes and gossip items had a hometown flavor which was not quite appropriate to the big city, and which betrayed a naiveté more often found in college humor magazines. For example: "Don Marquis sort of satisfied a boyhood dream when he playacted as a bartender at a 'pope night' down at the Players. Don's just been seriously noticed by 'Doc' S. P. Sherman, but it don't seem to have gone to his head much yet." In the "Washington Notes" of the same issue there was a comment on Henry Cabot Lodge which began: "He wasn't so darned high-hatty." Even at its most facetious the mature voice of the *New Yorker* was never guilty of such lapses in its assured tone and meticulous English usage. Nevertheless, the rest of the "Washington Notes" in which the comment on Lodge appeared was a devastating, deadpan indictment of Coolidge's provincialism—a clear imitation of subject and attitude found in issue after issue of the *American Mercury.*

During 1925 many other subjects which became perennial *New Yorker* topics were fondly introduced: taxis and their drivers, smog, flamboyant building projects that changed the face of the old town, Prohibition, suburban life, commuter life, Hollywood, the problems encountered while weekending in the country. Also making their debut in 1925 were some writers and artists of note, or who would shortly become noteworthy: there were, for example, sketches by Reginald Marsh, and writings by Sullivan, White, Stewart, Benchley, Maxwell Bodenheim, and Elmer Davis.

The most persistent debunking campaign of the early years involved ridicule of those regions of the country so unfortunate as to lie outside of New York. The urban sophisticate seemed never to get enough reassurance of his superiority. Davis, who came from Indiana, was a contributor in this vein: in "On the Banks of the Wabash," he borrowed both Menckenian hyperbole and Menckenian scorn. The piece was

> the first installment of the report of *The New Yorker*'s expedition to explore the Unexplored Area lying southeast of Chicago and northwest of Cincinnati, known to the ancient cartographers as Indiana. . . . The principal hazard encountered by the inexperienced traveller is the streams of tobacco juice which spurt geyserlike in all directions on the streets of Indianapolis. . . . Threading my way through a crowded corridor, I found myself about to step on a citizen who looked pretty much like a cockroach. "Don't do that!" cried my companion in horror. "It may be a Grand Dragon."

Provincialism as a subject was practically inexhaustible. In 1932 there was this in the "Notes and Comments" department: "A lot of people in Darke County, Ohio, and in Kansas, Louisiana, Oregon, etc., think that one of the candidates for President this fall is the late Theodore Roosevelt, a man who, they feel, is greatly needed at the helm of State in these times."

Other familiar debunking subjects appeared frequently. Morris Markey, who wrote the weekly feature variously titled "In the News," "The Current Press," and finally "A Reporter at Large," borrowed the burlesque tone of Mencken's polemic and at least one of Mencken's favorite subjects. He wrote on the origin of Prohibition that "a group of tightwad puritans: hard-fisted, greedy—more deeply concerned in the end with their wads than their morals—that vast body of the vulgate lying to the South and West of us, precipitated the calamity." The first sustained issue against which the *New Yorker* measured its superiority was fundamentalism. Throughout 1925 there were jokes, anecdotes, and "casuals" about William Jennings Bryan, and also a profile of him. The Scopes trial took place that year in Dayton, Tennessee.

Many pretensions to culture and urbanity were debunked. In "Up the Dark Stairs—" Benchley wrote that the trouble with journalism "began about ten years ago when the Columbia School of Journalism began unloading its graduates on what was then the *New York Tribune.* . . . Every one of the boys had the O. Henry light in his eyes, and before long the market report was the only thing in the paper that didn't lead off with 'up the dark stairs at———.' "

Corey Ford provided many burlesques in the early years; one series in 1925 was on creative art in New York. Some of the sources of "the native art that springs untrammeled from the heart of a free people" were billboards ("every subway station shows this craving for expression"), blotters, laundry bills, sand, and shattered glass ("observe what a devastating effect the unknown artist has achieved by the simple process of pasting a horsehide baseball against the pane of glass"). Published frequently in *Life, Judge,* and *Vanity Fair* (under the pseudonym "John Riddell"), Ford did not appear very often in the *New Yorker* after 1930. His humor eventually (in the 1950s) was found suitable by the *Saturday Evening Post* and by *Reader's Digest.* His most notable writings were parodies and burlesques of heroic tales of adventure and exploration; his spoofs of the adventurer June Triplett had a wild ebullience borrowed from the burlesque theatre, and in them one finds both the monotony and hilarity of burlesque. When the *New Yorker* around 1930 ceased to print Ford's writings, it seemed to be rejecting the kind of humor that had sustained *Life* and *Judge* for years. Yet it had been Ford to whom Ross had turned in 1925 when he was looking for a writer who could give substance to the *New Yorker*'s sense of cosmopolitanism. Ford, using Rea Irwin's first-issue cover picture for his inspiration, had created Eustace Tilley in a series called "The Making of a Magazine," which was begun on 3 August 1925 and was printed on the insides of the covers of the magazine.

Davis was another frequent early contributor whose offerings dwindled as the *New Yorker* became surer about its attitudes and style. Davis had learned a great deal from Mencken, especially from the bathtub hoax. One of his pieces was a burlesque profile of the typical, successful American novelist. This attack on aestheticism presented a composite portrait: "He began his literary career, in the approved manner, with a spiritual Autobiography. . . . It was casual; and the critics called it the authentic voice of tortured and groping youth." Then the novelist went to war and wrote a novel "spelling out for the benefit of etymologists certain Anglo-Saxon terms often heard but rarely written, except with chalk." Picture rights were sold; when Hollywood drastically altered the plot of the novel (which was pro-Communist), the novelist "called in the reporters and denounced the smug vulgarians of Hollywood who had Falsified His Artistic Concept, and a thousand editorials praised him." Next he "discovered that the curse of America was the conspiracy of silence about Sex. Fearlessly he broke the taboo in a novel which the critics called searching and masterly." He began to have trouble with his wife, "so his next book dealt with the hopeless situation of the artist with a Rotarian wife, in a Rotarian civilization. . . . He went abroad, and from his villa in Capri wrote an article for *Vanity Fair* explaining that life in America is impossible for the artist."

By 1928, the *New Yorker* had developed enough of a manner and style to be ridiculed by one of its ablest contributors. Lardner wrote and published in the *New Yorker* a parody of one of its favorite departments—a bit of frivolity probably only possible in the more carefree days of the *New Yorker's* youth. He wrote a mock profile entitled "Profiles: Dante and ————." The thin thread of logic in the piece had to do with Beatrice Kaufman's pursuit of and marriage to George S. Kaufman. Beatrice was also referred to as Lotta Fairfax, who had in turn assumed the name of Beatrice Lillie. As in the typical *New Yorker* profile, there was deliberate violation of logic and of normal biographical sequence: Beatrice-Lotta-Beatrice is described as having "written many plays under the sobriquet of Owen Davis, and in 1926 she won the women's national tennis championship as Mrs. Bjurstedt." She had arrived in the United States as a stowaway on a Gaelic ship and her first glimpse of New York was from the steeple of a church in South Orange, New Jersey. On seeing New York she says: "Oh, mumsey, (mother) . . . please take me to New York so I can marry a Kaufman."

Also ridiculed here was the *New Yorker's* method of reporting, a method which even in 1928 had become characteristic. The method, a modification of the satiric catalog, hinges on the facetious effect produced when unrelated facts, names, or ideas are telescoped and presented to the reader in juxtaposition. Mencken was a master of such catalogs. The style, actually highly contrived, gives the impression of casual yet articulate sophistication; there is usually a hint of irony suggested by the carefully balanced incongruity in the sequence. There was a close parallel to, and perhaps source of, this development in the concurrent growth of *Time* magazine's condensed style, particularly in its creation of portmanteau words. Both magazines thought they had similar journalistic problems: *Time* strained mightily to hold the interest of the tired executive, who did not have the time or ability to read more eloquent English; the *New Yorker* struggled to flatter its readers with the illusion that they were bored literati who had read too much. *Time* had set an iconoclastic pattern for journalistic English and the *New Yorker* in its probably unconscious way followed where Henry Luce had led, although at some unlocatable point imitation may have become parody. It is a striking testimony to the sharpness of Lardner's ear and eye for language and to his sensibilities as a humorist that he, as early as 1928, recognized that the *New Yorker* was developing a style which could be parodied. And it is to the credit of the editors that they were willing to print this spoof of what became a central affectation. However, one *New Yorker* contributor did not completely concur; in 1929 Woollcott wrote his own mannered profile of Kaufman. He commented on Lardner's effort: "In it, for the first time in this series of Profiles, the spirit of whimsy reared its ugly head." Woollcott's own spirit and temperament were usually better suited to the pages of *Vanity Fair*.

Insofar as the *New Yorker* has had an editorial voice, the "Notes and Comments" section has been that voice, and White was the most consistent writer of the section. He came to the *New Yorker* in 1926; even in the early issues the "Notes and Comments" showed the style of writing and imagination that he was to bring to them for years. The comments covered a wide range of attitudes and subjects. They could be serious, facetious, whimsical, satiric, indignant, nostalgic. Frequently White's commentary was on subjects which had been given wide and overly serious treatment in the week's news. During the early 1930s there was a great deal of subject matter exactly suited to the *New Yorker's* pointed commentary. These were the years when the *New Yorker* solidified its success, because it recognized in the Depression and in the administrations in Washington rich sources of comic material. Certainly, too, it was not above catering to the gentility of its middle-class readers, many of whom were Republicans. Yet at the same time it avoided any overt political commitment. Thus it was able to appeal to both liberal and conservative elements in its middle-class audience. It chose not to be solemn about America's embarrassment as the home of free enterprise, and this attitude was exactly right for the intelligent readers in whose existence Ross had always believed.

In the late 1930s the *New Yorker* began to take on what Thurber has described as "matronly girth." The quality and tenor of its humorous writing changed. Lardner, a frequent contributor in the early 1930s, had died in 1933. Sullivan turned more and more to reminiscences for his comic effects. Thurber wrote about life in the provincial city of Columbus, Ohio, with nostalgic affection. Toward the end of the war White took up the United Nations as a cause and used the *New Yorker* as an editorial rostrum. The days for relentlessly debunking life and manners in the provinces were over; too many *New Yorker* readers lived in them (by 1958, 80 percent of the *New Yorker's* circulation was outside of New York.) Parody continued as the main form of satiric writing; but there was less and less comic hyperbole of the sort leveled at the provinces, or like that shaped as a weapon in Lardner's short crusade against radio. Gradually during these years the *New Yorker* attracted and published America's best writers of fiction, a function which in the *Mercury* had deteriorated in the early 1930s under the dictatorial editorship of Mencken. For example, it published Thurber and Kay Boyle after they were rejected by the *Mercury*. Initially the *New Yorker* had fallen heir to the prestige of the *Mercury* in the 1920s by reflecting more successfully a spectrum of interests in satire, literature, politics, manners. Later, its humorists not only entertained but provided an accurate expression of the anxiety of sensitive Americans about the serious economic, political, and social problems of the 1930s. Finally, the *New Yorker's* initial success depended on a combination of editorial direction and the quality of the satiric writing that was available to it.

The *New Yorker* conveyed the most central concern of all the debunkers; again and again, the feelings of the mimics, parodists, and satirists about the abuse of language ranged from amusement to outrage. The *New Yorker* accepted this concern for the purity of language as its own. In the nonsatiric writing, in the expository prose, fiction, and poetry that it published more and more after the early 1930s, the *New Yorker* developed rigorous standards of usage and style. Its enhancement of the art of writing in America has been of far-reaching effect. One aspect of that enhancement has been its emergence as one of the most significant journals for the publication of contemporary poetry and fiction. In retrospect we can look back on the satire it published in its formative years as a kind of crusade for the preservation of the medium sacred to all writers. The *New Yorker* writers and editors of these years were not purists or traditionalists, but they were responsive to the vitality and potential of American English. Perhaps more consistently than any other twentieth-century journal, the *New Yorker* has preserved and promoted that vitality and potential. The active, participatory concern of its writers had an aloof scholarly counterpart in Mencken's *American Language* and its supplements; several articles by Mencken on the American language were first published in the *New Yorker*.

William H. Whyte, Jr.

SOURCE: "You, Too, Can Write the Casual Style," in *Harper's Magazine,* Vol. 207, No. 1241, October, 1953, pp. 87-9.

[*Whyte is an American author who wrote several studies of American business, including* The Organization Man *(1956). In the following excerpt, he provides a satirical study of the prose style employed by various* New Yorker *writers.*]

A revolution has taken place in American prose. No longer the short huffs and puffs, the unqualified word, the crude gusto of the declarative sentence. Today the fashion is to write casually.

The Casual Style is not exactly new. Originated in the early Twenties, it has been refined and improved and refined again by a relatively small band of writers, principally for the *New Yorker,* until now their mannerisms have become standards of sophistication. Everybody is trying to join the club. Newspaper columnists have forsaken the beloved metaphors of the sports page for the Casual Style, and one of the quickest ways for an ad man to snag an award from other ad men is to give his copy the low-key, casual pitch; the copy shouldn't sing these days—it should whisper. Even Dr. Rudolf Flesch, who has been doing so much to teach people how to write like other people, is counseling his followers to use the Casual Style. Everywhere the ideal seems the same: be casual.

But how? There is very little down-to-earth advice. We hear about the rapier-like handling of the bromide, the keen eye for sham and pretension, the exquisite sense of nuance, the unerring ear for the vulgate. But not much about actual technique. The layman, as a consequence, is apt to look on the Casual Style as a mandarin dialect which he fears he could never master.

Nonsense. The Casual Style is within everyone's grasp. It has now become so perfected by constant polishing that its devices may readily identified, and they change so little that their use need be no more difficult for the novice than for the expert. (That's not quite all there is to it, of course. Some apparently casual writers, Thurber and E. B. White, among others, rarely use the devices.)

The subject matter, in the first place, is not to be ignored.

Generally speaking, the more uneventful it is, or the more pallid the writer's reaction to it, the better do form and content marry. Take, for example, the cocktail party at which the writer can show how bored everyone is with everyone else, and how utterly fatuous they all are anyhow. Since a non-casual statement—*e.g.,* "The party was a bore"—would destroy the reason for writing about it at all, the Casual Style here is not only desirable but mandatory.

Whatever the subject, however, twelve devices are the rock on which all else is built. I will present them one by one, illustrating them with examples from such leading casual stylists as Wolcott Gibbs, John Crosby, John McCarten, and (on occasion) this magazine's "Mr. Harper." If the reader will digest what follows, he should be able to dash off a paragraph indistinguishable from the best casual writing being done today.

(1) *Heightened Understatement.* Where the old-style writer would say, "I don't like it," "It is not good," or something equally banal, the casual writer says it is *"something less than* good." He avoids direct statement and strong words—except, as we will note, where he is setting them up to have something to knock down. In any event, he qualifies. "Somewhat" and "rather," the bread-and-butter words of the casual writer, should become habitual with you; similarly with such phrases as "I suppose," "it seems to me," "I guess," or "I'm afraid." "Elusive" or "elude" are good, too, and if you see the word "charm" in a casual sentence you can be pretty sure that "eludes me," or "I find elusive," will not be far behind.

(2) *The Multiple Hedge.* Set up an ostensibly strong statement, and then, with your qualifiers, shoot a series of alter-

James Thurber

nately negative and positive charges into the sentence until finally you neutralize the whole thing. Let's take, for example, the clause, "certain names have a guaranteed nostalgic magic." Challenge enough here; the names not only have magic, they have guaranteed magic. A double hedge reverses the charge. "Names which have, *I suppose* [hedge 1], a guaranteed nostalgic magic, *though there are times that I doubt it* [hedge 2]. . . ."

We didn't have to say they were guaranteed in the first place, of course, but without such straw phrases we wouldn't have anything to construct a hedge on and, frequently, nothing to write at all. The virtue of the hedge is that by its very negating effect it makes any sentence infinitely expansible. Even if you have so torn down your original statement with one or two hedges that you seem to have come to the end of the line, you have only to slip in an anti-hedge, a strengthening word (*e.g.,* "definitely," "unqualified," etc.), and begin the process all over again. Witness the following quadruple hedge: "I found Mr. Home entertaining *from time to time* [hedge 1] on the ground, *I guess* [hedge 2], that the singular idiom and unearthly detachment of the British upper classes have *always* [anti-hedge] seemed *reasonably* [hedge 3] droll to me, *at least in moderation* [hedge 4]." The art of plain talk, as has been pointed out, does not entail undue brevity.

If you've pulled hedge on hedge and the effect still remains too vigorous, simply wipe the slate clean with a cancellation clause at the end. "It was all exactly as foolish as it sounds," says Wolcott Gibbs, winding up some 570 casual words on a subject, "and I wouldn't give it another thought."

(3) *Narcissizing Your Prose.* The casual style is nothing if not personal; indeed, you will usually find in it as many references to the writer as to what he's supposed to be talking about. For you do not talk about the subject; you talk about its impact on you. With the reader peering over your shoulder, you look into the mirror and observe your own responses as you run the entire range of the casual writer's emotions. You may reveal yourself as, in turn, listless ("the audience seemed not to share my boredom"); insouciant ("I was really quite happy with it"); irritated ("The whole thing left me tired and cross"); comparatively gracious ("Being in a comparatively gracious mood, I won't go into the details I didn't like"); or hesitant ("I wish I could say that I could accept his hypothesis").

(4) *Preparation for the Witticism.* When the casual writer hits upon a clever turn of phrase or a nice conceit, he uses this device to insure that his conceit will not pass unnoticed. Suppose, for example, you have thought of something to say that is pretty damn good if you say so yourself. The device, in effect, is to say so yourself. If you want to devastate a certain work as "a study of vulgarity in high places," don't say this flat out. Earlier in the sentence prepare the reader for the drollery ahead with something like "what I am tempted to call" or "what could best be described as" or "If it had to be defined in a sentence, it might well be called. . . ."

Every writer his own claque.

(5) *Deciphered Notes Device; or Cute-Things-I-Have-Said.*

In this one you are your own stooge as well. You feed yourself lines. By means of the slender fiction that you have written something on the back of an envelope or the margin of a program, you catch yourself good-humoredly trying to decipher these shrewd, if cryptic, little jottings. *Viz.*: "Their diagnoses are not nearly as crisp as those I find in my notes"; " . . . sounds like an inadequate description, but it's all I have on my notes, and it may conceivably be a very high compliment."

(6) *The Kicker.* An echo effect. "My reactions [included] an irritable feeling that eleven o'clock was past Miss Keim's bedtime,"—and now the Kicker—"*not to mention my own.*" This type of thing practically writes itself. "She returns home. She should never have left home in the first place. ———."

(7) *Wit of Omission.* By calling attention to the fact that you are not going to say it, you suggest that there is something very funny you could say if only you wanted to. "A thought occured to me at this point," you may say, when otherwise stymied, "but I think we had better not go into *that.*"

(8) *The Planned Colloquialism.* The casual writer savors colloquialisms. This is not ordinary colloquial talk—nobody is more quickly provoked than the casual writer by ordinary usage. It is, rather, a playful descent into the vulgate. Phrases like "darn," awfully," "as all getout," "mighty," and other folksy idioms are ideal. The less you would be likely to use the word normally yourself the more pointed the effect. Contrast is what you are after, for it is the facetious interplay of language levels—a blending, as it were, of the East Fifties and the Sticks—that gives the Casual Style its off-hand charm.

(9) *Feigned Forgetfulness.* Conversation gropes; it is full of "what I really meant was" and "maybe I should have added," backings and fillings and second thoughts of one kind or another. Writing is different; theoretically, ironing out second thoughts beforehand is one of the things writers are paid to do. In the Casual Style, however, it is exactly this exposure of the writer composing in public that makes it so casual. For the professional touch, then, ramble, rebuke yourself in print ("what I really meant, I guess"), and if you have something you feel you should have said earlier, don't say it earlier, but say later that you guess you should have said it earlier.

(10) *The Subject-Apologizer, or Pardon-Me-for-Living.* The Casual Stylist must always allow for the possibility that his subject is just as boring to the reader as it is to him. He may forestall this by seeming to have stumbled on it by accident, or by using phrases like: "If this is as much news to you as it is to me," or "This, in case you've been living in a cave lately, is. . . ."

(11) *The Omitted Word.* This all began modestly enough the day a *New Yorker* writer dropped the articles "the" and "a" from the initial sentence of an anecdote (*e.g.,* "Man we know told us"; "Fellow name of Brown"). Now even such resolutely lowbrow writers as Robert Ruark affect it, and they are applying it to any part of speech anywhere in the sentence. You can drop a pronoun ("Says they're shaped like pyramids"; verb ("You been away

from soap opera the last couple of weeks?"); or preposition ("Far as glamour goes . . . ").

(12) *The Right Word.* In the lexicon of the casual writer there are a dozen or so adjectives which in any context have, to borrow a phrase, a guaranteed charm. Attrition is high—"brittle," "febrile," "confected," for example, are at the end of the run. Ten, however, defy obsolescence: *antic, arch, blurred, chaste, chill, crisp, churlish, disheveled, dim, disembodied.*

They are good singly, but they are even better when used in tandem; *c.f.,* "In an arch, antic sort of way"; "In an arch, blurred sort of way;" "In an arch, crisp sort of way." And so on.

Finally, the most multi-purpose word of them all: "altogether." Frequently it is the companion of "charming" and "delightful," and in this coupling is indispensable to any kind of drama criticism. It can also modify the writer himself (*e.g.,* "Altogether, I think . . ."). Used best, however, it just floats, unbeholden to any other part of the sentence.

Once you have mastered these twelve devices, you too should be able to write as casually as all getout. At least it seems to me, though I may be wrong, that they convey an elusive archness which the crisp literary craftsman, in his own dim sort of way, should altogether cultivate these days. Come to think of it, the charm of the Casual Style is something less than clear to me, but we needn't go into *that.* Fellow I know from another magazine says this point of view best described as churlish. Not, of course, that it matters.

Dwight Macdonald

SOURCE: "Laugh and Lie Down," in *Partisan Review,* Vol. IV, No. 1, December, 1937, pp. 44-53.

[*An American essayist and critic, Macdonald was a noted proponent of various radical causes from the mid-1930s until his death in 1982. In the following excerpt, he criticizes the attitudes and editorial style that he considers representative of the* New Yorker.]

More persistently than any other American magazine the *New Yorker* has exploited a distinctive attitude towards modern life. The typical *New Yorker* writer has given up the struggle to make sense out of a world which daily grows more complicated. His stock of data is strictly limited to the inconsequential. His *Weltanschauung*—a term which would greatly irritate him—is the crudest sort of philistine "common sense." But unlike most exponents of "common sense," the *New Yorker* type is spectacularly incompetent in the practical affairs of everyday life. He is abashed by machines, easily dominated by extraverts, incapable of making out an income tax return, in constant difficulties with the gas company, his landlord, and The State. Out of these limitations the *New Yorker* extracts its peculiar kind of humor: the humor of the inadequate.

It hardly needs to be pointed out that the *New Yorker*'s contributors are by no means as feckless as, for literary purposes, they choose to appear. Their ignorance is no more to be taken seriously than the ironic humility with which Socrates treats his opponents. Quite deliberately, they prune their talents into a certain shape, and if this means extensive intellectual amputations, so much the worse for the intellect. The magazine has its tone, to which its contributors keep with faithful ear. It is the tone of a cocktail party at which the guests are intelligent but well-bred. No subjects are taboo, so long as they are "amusing." But, as any experienced hostess knows, too earnest handling rubs off the bloom. Moderation in all things, including humor. The *New Yorker* has been known to reject contributions because they were too funny. Its editors would have considered Mark Twain too crude and Heine too high-brow for their purposes. Between reality and its readers the *New Yorker* interposes a decent veil, which would be rent by any immoderate inspiration on its writers' part.

If there is an octopus-like humor trust, twining its tentacles around the nation's best wit, the *New Yorker* is it. There are no competitors. *Life* is no longer humorous, *Judge* has no prestige, and the rest are at or below the *College Humor* level. Current publishers' lists contain no less than seven volumes of *New Yorker* material. In thirteen years the *New Yorker* has become an institution comparable to *Punch.*

The *New Yorker* owes its present dominance to the fact that it is the only important vehicle for the humor of the urban intelligentsia. From the Civil War to the World War, the dominant school of humor based itself on the small-town culture of the hinterland. Humorists like Artemus Ward and Bill Nye attacked the big bourgeoisie of the East in their cultural outworks at the same time as their political allies, the populists, attacked the East in its economic citadel: Wall Street. The War destroyed the populist position in humor as in politics, and it laid the economic foundation for the triumph of Big Business in the twenties. In the post-war *Kulturkampf* the provinces steadily lost ground to the intelligentsia of the big cities. Populist humor gave way to sophisticated humor: Petroleum V. Nasby yielded to Robert Benchley.

The new humor was of two schools: Menckenian satire and the dissociative, or dada, humor introduced by Benchley and Frank Sullivan. Most humorists were influenced by both schools. Ring Lardner, for example, practiced Menckenian satire in his short stories, and also produced dada work like his autobiography (*The Story of a Wonder Man*). Lardner began his career in the *Saturday Evening Post* and ended it in the *New Yorker.* This shift of allegiance was probably not a conscious strategem. Even in his earliest stories there is an undertone of satire, not enough to interfere with their success in the popular press but quite definitely there. The shift in humor merely allowed Lardner to say directly what he had always thought about the provinces.

The *New Yorker* will be thirteen years old next February. Since 1925 it has changed little in form, much in its point of view. "The Talk of the Town" and "Profiles," still its most important departments, were established under those names in the first issue. From the first, also, headings were set in the distinctive angular type-face used today. By

1927 the *New Yorker* had differentiated itself from the other humorous weeklies. The scraps of verse and prose conventional to such journals had been replaced by a few long contributions. The first number contained a pioneer one-line joke, and within two years the *New Yorker* had made this form of humor peculiarly its own. But if externals have changed little, editorial policies have been revolutionized.

The *New Yorker* was established to exploit commercially two groups of sophisticated readers: those who followed Mencken and Nathan and those who looked to the Manhattan wits centering around the Algonquin Hotel. Its keynote was: "Not edited for the Old Lady from Dubuque." It had been appearing only a few months when the Scopes evolution trial in Tennessee took place. Here was the perfect, foolproof issue: the clash of cultures in its crudest form. No literate reader but was with Darrow and Darwin against Bryan and the Bible. Furthermore, Bryan was the personal symbol of all that was most hateful and absurd to the East. The editors of the *New Yorker* sensed complete reader-support. Week after week they printed cartoons lampooning Bryan, cartoons of a brutality unique in its history. They ran editorials, articles, eyewitness accounts of the trial. For a time it almost seemed that the *New Yorker* had been founded specially to report on the Scopes affair. It was an extraordinary but hardly an incomprehensible outburst.

On its first birthday the *New Yorker* editorialized: "We declared a year ago that it was not the *New Yorker*'s intention to tap the North American steppe region by offering the natives mirrors and colored beads in the form of the recognized brands of hokum": 'The North American steppe region,' 'the Old Lady from Dubuque,' 'the Pickle Princes of Peoria'—such phrases are literary wild oats. The present editors would deplore alike their sound and their sense. Their sense because whereas at the end of its first year the *New Yorker* announced that its 40,000 circulation was "almost all of it in the city and suburbs," today exactly half its 125,000 readers live outside New York. And their sound, because exuberance is no longer the *New Yorker*'s "line." The brash Menckenians and the aggressively sophisticated Algonquins have been superseded by the timorous and bewildered Thurber. The *New Yorker* as well as the National City Bank bears the marks of 1929.

The *New Yorker*'s immediate reaction to the market crash was to set a distance between itself and the business community. That week it editorialized: "The collapse of the market, over and above the pain, couldn't help but be amusing. It is amusing to see a fat land quivering in panicky fright. The quake, furthermore, verified our suspicions that our wise and talky friends hadn't known for months what they were talking about when they were discussing stocks." This detachment from "our wise and talky friends" was something new. It grew with the depression. But such protestations should not be taken too seriously. All that had really happened was that the *New Yorker*'s honeymoon with the oligarchy was over and it had begun to look on its consort more critically. But the marriage has not been dissolved.

The transition from the self-confident, magisterial satire

of the Scopes trial period to the gentle humor of a Thurber, self-confessed ninny and know-nothing, simply reflects a similar change in the position of the ruling class. The present *New Yorker* formula for pathos and humor is an expression of a deep-rooted uncertainty about itself which this class has come to feel because of its impotence in the late economic crisis.

The clearest way to define the "tone" of the *New Yorker* of today is to contrast it with the old *American Mercury*, which in its time had very much the same relation to the intelligentsia. The antithesis holds at almost every point. The *Mercury* gloried in its lack of inhibitions. Its language was violent, bombastic, direct, impatient of restraint and a stranger to nuance. Its humor was explosive and shrill. Its realism was raw, crude, uncompromisingly frank about sex. The *Mercury* would print almost anything *pour épater le (petit) bourgeois*. The *New Yorker*, on the contrary, is anxious to avoid shocking any one. Its literary style is subtle, oblique, its humor subdued to the point of monotony.

What the *New Yorker* has done to the realistic tradition of the twenties is especially interesting. Superficially, its fiction remains within the tradition. It is realism with a difference however: deodorized, deloused, reminiscent of William Dean Howells rather than of Dreiser. The sad, deftly unaccented, dullish little tales of Robert M. Coates are the type examples of *New Yorker* "realism." Coates, John O'Hara, Kay Boyle, and other contributors have developed a pseudo-realism which has all the advantages and none of the drawbacks of the real thing. (In their extra-*New Yorker* writing, these authors are less inhibited.) The reader, that is to say, enjoys the illusion of "seeing life" without suffering the embarrassment of actually doing so. These writers admit the existence of sex, but they are at considerable pains to protect the reader from its grosser aspects. They frequently describe the life of the submerged classes, and always with sensibility. Here, too, they are careful not to shock the bourgeois reader. Poverty is suggested rather than bluntly described, and their underdogs are drawn, not from the proletariat, whose sufferings are meaningful and hence tragic, but rather from the ranks of the declassed. They write of minor actors, of provincials drifting rootless in the jungle of the city, of boxers and alcoholics and prostitutes. From these futile lives they extract a facile pathos. The *New Yorker* has formularized the pathos as well as the humor of the inadequate. Treated subjectively, inadequacy may be comic. Presented objectively, it yields a mild kind of pathos, verging towards— but skillfully kept just this side of the sentimental.

The *New Yorker* is the last of the great family journals. Its inhibitions stretch from sex to the class struggle. It can be read aloud in mixed company without calling a blush to the cheek of the most virtuous banker. The subjects of its profiles, especially if they are wealthy and powerful, are treated deferentially. This summer President Gifford of the American Telephone & Telegraph Company was presented to the readers of the *New Yorker* in three instalments quivering with sympathy. The muck raked up last winter by Congressional investigators is delicately ignored, and Mr. Gifford is depicted as an intelligent, modest, rather pathetic person, distressed by his eminence and anxious only to live democratically among his fellow citizens. In the deodorized pages of the *New Yorker,* the 1917 revolution becomes "this violent phase of Russian experience," and diabetics are "those dieters who can't abide sugar." The magazine's inhibitions may have a neurotic as well as a social basis. According to *Fortune,* Harold Ross, who founded the *New Yorker* and has always dominated its editorial policies, lives in constant terror of earthquakes, crossing streets, and physical assault. His editorial prudishness is legendary. Arno's once-famous Whoops Sisters had to be sobered up because they shocked him. The other editors are also interesting psychoanalytically. One is a hypochondriac, another can't bring himself to open his morning mail, and so on. One editor suffered from amnesia and ulcers of the stomach until his salary was raised. The Freudian approach would also have something to say about Thurber and Sullivan, both of whom find in humor an escape from neurotic symptoms.

Bergson calls laughter "a social gesture." Considered thus, it is a response to the contrast between the comic object and a generally accepted norm. In societies that are flourishing and hence united—such as produced Aristophanes, Molière, and the other classic humorists—the validity of the social norm is unchallenged. It is enough merely to point out a departure from it to get a humorous effect. Laughter is thus a defense of the social order, like the police force, and humor tends to be satirical. But in decadent societies, when all values are called into question, a more complex procedure is necessary. The *New Yorker*'s humor is a criticism of the social norm as well as of the comic object. Typically, it establishes a relationship between a rational observer and an irrational person or phenomenon—so far the classic formula. But the observer is ineffectual, and the comic object is not only irrational but also overpowering, so that for all his perception, the observer is unable to cope with the object. Thus the humorist also becomes a source of amusement, and humor is drawn as much from the insufficiency of the norm as from its violation.

This is not to say that the one type of humor is, in itself, superior to the other. Each is "right" for its particular stage of social development. That the "prosperity" of the twenties was unhealthy might have been demonstrated by the social historian, quite without benefit of statistics, simply by the inferior quality of Menckenian satire. For this humor was of the "classic" type: aggressive satire based on the social values of the big bourgeoisie. But since this class was economically superfluous, the Menckenian humor had a false base and hence today seems forced and artificial. The *New Yorker*'s humor is superior because it is an accurate expression of a decaying social order.

The object with which the *New Yorker* humorist so disastrously collides may be almost anything. Common categories are: a personality; The Machine; a series of deplorable but apparently inevitable occurrences; some form of "Theory." Towards these, and indeed all other phenomena the humorist's reaction is a mixture of awe and condescension. He is awed by the vitality of the person, the efficiency of The Machine, the inscrutable hand of Nemesis, and the abstruse complexity of the theory. At the same time, he cannot but feel a certain superiority toward the illogical mental processes of the person, the humdrum, unimaginative practicality of The Machine, the pointlessness of the disasters, and the esoteric pretensions of the theory. Such reactions may be expected of observers who are extremely intelligent but also a bit neurotic. For none of these humorists are precisely Rabelaisian. In fact, Rabelais would probably appeal to them more as a comic theme himself than as a master to be imitated.

The most common of these categories is the first. Two recent successful series belong to it: Clarence Day's *Life with Father* and Leonard Q. Ross's *The Education of Hyman Kaplan.* In social background Mr. Day (the elder) and Mr. Kaplan are polar opposites, but temperamentally they are similar: overbearing, quite without doubt or even consciousness of themselves, bursting with will and vitality, and, above all, masterfully, irresistibly unreasonable. Thurber's splendidly vigorous grandfather (who also happens to be violently insane) in *My Life and Hard Times* is another such creation. Of the three, Thurber's is much the most freely imaginative creation. In general, his treatment of the classic *New Yorker* comic theme (which he, more than any one else, originated) often transcends realistic observation to reach an absolute, personal fantasy. In my opinion, Thurber is the *New Yorker*'s most important writer, and his *My Life and Hard Times* (1933) contains the best humor of the entire post-war period.

In the class war the *New Yorker* is ostentatiously neutral. It makes fun of subway guards and of men-about-town, of dowagers and laundresses, of shop-girls and debutantes. It refuses, officially, to recognize the existence of wars, strikes, and revolution, just as it doesn't mention the more unpleasant diseases or the grosser aspects of sexual passion. Deliberately—for these gentlemen know very well what they are about—its editors confine their attention to trivia. This is not to say they oppose change, since that too would commit them. They affect a gentle bewilderment toward the social system, as if it were some labyrinthine, and potentially dangerous, piece of machinery. With shrewdly calculated vagueness, they pronounce that it is all very complicated, that only experts can understand it, and that they are not, Thank God, experts.

The *New Yorker*'s position in the class war, however, is not so simple as its editors would have us believe. Its neutrality is itself a form of upper class display, since only the economically secure can afford such Jovian aloofness from the common struggle. In times like these there is something monstrously inhuman in the deliberate cultivation of the trivial. "Jeanette MacDonald marries Gene Raymond in a church, of all places. Hay-fever people can have their nostrils ionized. Seventy shop-girls swoon en masse in France. The midsummer ice season starts in the Adirondacks. A new purge in Russia. A Fascist gain in Spain. Will Hays authorizes a six-foot kiss." Only a neurotic, a well-fed neurotic, could thus desensitize himself.

But even the *New Yorker* cannot pass over certain crying social injustices. Even the *New Yorker* has its moments—March 13, 1937, and July 10, 1937, to be specific. On the first date it boldly denounced President Roosevelt for his infamous Court Plan, and on the second it gave its support to the newspaper publishers in their conflict with the Newspaper Guild. It is good to know that when the foundations of society are imperilled, the *New Yorker* may be depended on to quit fooling around and get down to business. Among the thousands of editorials which the *New Yorker* has printed in its thirteen years of existence, these are unique on several counts. For one thing, they are almost painfully in earnest, with only the most perfunctory touches of humor. For another, they are quite badly written—perhaps because it is hard to maintain the elegant-trifler pose when one's deepest emotions are involved. And for still another, in them the *New Yorker,* with not a trace of its customary fastidious horror of the banal, bases its argument on the same old slogans already worn threadbare in the Republican press. The Court Plan is an assault on "liberty," and the Newspaper Guild threatens the "freedom of the press."

There are humorous magazines which attempt no more than to be "funny" in a miscellaneous way. *Punch* and the old *Life* were such, and so is *Judge.* There are also those with a consistent class viewpoint, and these are likely to be both more profitable and longer-lived. Such are *Punch* and the *New Yorker.* The *New Yorker* is comparatively infantile, but already it has struck roots deep into the American scene. *Punch* gives the English ruling class a sense of the continuity of their tradition. The *New Yorker* gives our ruling class the even more satisfactory sensation of establishing a tradition in a landscape notably barren of such ornaments.

It is worth while spending a few words on the *New Yorker*'s criticism of art and letters as an instance of what might be called the Park Avenue attitude toward the arts. The chief quality of *New Yorker* criticism is its amiability. Since to Park Avenue, art is important chiefly as a means of killing time, what is required is not critics but tipsters. Park Avenue wants tips on the really amusing books and plays just as it wants tips on the really amusing night clubs. And it wants them delivered as painlessly as possible. So the *New Yorker*'s criticism is, above all, "sprightly." Mr. Robert A. Simon is able to talk about music in the same breezy, casually well-bred accents as the colleague who signs "Foot-Fault" to his comments on tennis. "The Vivaldi concerto had a poetic slow movement, surrounded by a couple of bouncing divisions of a sort which Vivaldi could probably write while you waited." Or: "Mr. Rachmaninoff's second piano concerto . . . was a five star finale." Or: "Miss Andreva was a snappy Musetta, but she gave in to a temptation to whoop things up, and Puccini's music hits back when it's whooped." (Music criticism also hits back when it's whooped.) The least bad of the critics is Clifton P. Fadiman. But he, too, is a master of the "easy" (to say the least) style. Thus: " . . . lovely as it is, *The Years* is just the merest mite dull." Or his summary of Osborn's *Freud and Marx*: "Mr. Osborn takes the first step toward bringing the boys together." The most amiable of the critics is Lewis Mumford, who "does" art. For catholicity of taste he is second only to the lady who does dresses and hats, and in mastery of the *cliché* he is her superior. In a single issue last winter, Mr. Mumford (1) called John Singleton Copley "the first great American

artist," (2) pointed out "the strength and delicacy of Arnold Friedman's paintings," (3) spoke of Burliuk as "a painter who invests the commonplace with a very personal fantasy," (4) called Karl Hofer "probably the best-rounded German painter of his generation" and found in his work "a mixture of beauty and terror, of grace and agony that makes it curiously representative of his whole generation," (5) saluted John Carroll as "a diabolically good painter" and observed of one of his nudes: "The modelling of the trunk and the beauty of its outline takes the breath away."

The clearest evidence of the class nature of the *New Yorker* is, of course, its advertising. Its readers are expected to buy Paris gowns, airplanes, vintage wines, movie cameras, Tiffany jewelry, air conditioning, round-the-world trips, et cetera. Interlarded with the advertisements are various "departments," devoted to practical advice on the great problem of upper class life: how to get through the day without dying of boredom. Here the class character of the *New Yorker* emerges with brutal effect. After reading Mr. Coates' tender little stories, after the drolleries of Thurber or White—so fine and free, so independent of sordid commerce—it is somehow shocking to come upon a two column discussion of imported olive oil. From the cloudland of fantasy one drops abruptly to the dollars-and-cents earth of luxurious living. One lands with a bump. It would almost seem that the people for whom Messers. White and Thurber write must be an altogether different set from those to whom Messers. Saks and Tiffany address their advertisements.

Judging from the *New Yorker*'s "departments," its readers travel a good deal, are fussy about restaurants and clothes, and follow closely the more fashionable sports, namely: golf, polo, football, squash raquets, tennis, yachting, and horse-racing. They take a well-bred interest in books, music, art, the cinema and the theatre. Their standard of living includes custom-made shoes at $50 and boots at $100 (trees: $30), satin curtains at $120 a pair (not including the labor), jaguar hunting in Brazil at $1250 per month per person, fireside seats covered in saddle leather ("with hand-colored decorations celebrating the chase") at $45, and visits to Baron Pantz's Austrian castle ("The entrance fee of $1,000 entitles you to go to Mittersill at any time . . . at a flat rate of $10 a day.")

But even such celestial creatures, like all the rest of us, have their problems. Really quite odd problems. Nature, the incorrigible, is usually involved. Sometimes the question is how to get closer to her. They buy, at $5 each, painted metal trumpet-vine blossoms, which they fill with sweetened water and thus attract humming birds. Or they install beehives ($21 each) in their windows and watch the bees through a glass panel. More often, the problem is how to thwart nature. They solve the dog-vs.-rug problem with Dog Tex, "a pure, almond-scented liquid." To keep from being awakened too early—in the city by street noises; in the country, by starlings—they buy small pink instruments called Flents, "the magical ear stopples." For night motoring, to shut out the glare of approaching headlights, they buy eyeglasses with the upper half smoked. ("Ground to your own prescription and mounted in white gold, they cost from $18 up.") For daytime motoring they have the Sunair Auto Top Co. put sliding roofs on their cars at $250 each. Their women have many special problems, with appropriate solutions. A recent technological advance is the "windshield-wiper" powder compact, which has an arm that automatically wipes clean the mirror when the compact is opened ($6.50 up).

It would be rash to assume that most of the 120,444 people who read the *New Yorker* every week are plutocratic enough to buy $50 shoes and $120 curtains. A survey of the financial status of the average reader might reveal score interesting things. It is quite possible that most readers of the *New Yorker,* like most movie-goers, are comparatively humble folk who are willing to pay a small admission fee for a peep into the *haut monde.* Such people might well enjoy reading tips on expensive living with not the slightest thought of making use of the information. For all one knows, the center of gravity of the *New Yorker*'s circulation may be closer to Lexington Avenue than to Park Avenue. In this country, of all countries, the class war is complicated by the persistence of the old American custom of keeping up with the Joneses.

Anthony Harrigan

SOURCE: "*The New Yorker*: A Profile," in *The Catholic World,* Vol. CLXXIV, No. 1044, 1952, pp. 444-47.

[*An American journalist, Harrigan has had a distinguished career as a foreign correspondent covering assignments in Vietnam, Cuba, South Africa, and other countries. In the following essay, he offers a critical evaluation of the* New Yorker *as a magazine whose editorial attitudes betray a complacent ignorance of the social and political realities of American life.*]

Visiting Englishmen frequently ask the name of the American equivalent of the great English humor magazine *Punch.* This question, which is perfectly reasonable, discloses a situation completely unreasonable; there is no equivalent in this country. That is, there is no comic magazine that is also a serious magazine in the sense that high comedy is always serious. Certainly, *The New Yorker* does not fill the bill.

The New Yorker is the first of a new American species and, one may hope, the last of the line. There cannot be genuine comedy where there is no real tragedy, loss, happiness or despair. None of these come alive in the pages of the smug, self-satisfied court gazette of the merchants of our celebrity culture, which is published in mid-town Manhattan. The pleasures and pains of *The New Yorker* are synthetic, not a proud shoot springing out of the soil of native humor—the case with *Punch.*

In these United States there is ample scope for editorial wit. Indeed laughter has frequently proven itself the best reformer. To laugh, and by laughter to reform, is admirable. But *The New Yorker* regales its readers with stories and articles that imply a complete lack of respect for people. In its pages, individuality is treated with stylized derision.

Once upon a time *The New Yorker* may have struck some

good blows at social superstition. Nowadays it is stereotyped, does not challenge any of the sacred cows of the *status quo.* The comedy displayed in the magazine misses the pathos and virtues of essential American life. The openhandedness and simplicity, directness and kindness, and what Mary McCarthy has termed "a certain gentle timidity" of the American character—is ridiculed.

No doubt a part of the trouble lies in the fact that the magazine has no roots in place. It is *The New Yorker* in name only. It has no especially significant place in the life of intelligent New Yorkers as does the *Times* in the newspaper field. Reading the magazine, one might easily think that Manhattan was built one fine day in the nineteen twenties. The magazine's memory is a blank beyond that point.

The New York of the past, the New York of the Grand Army of the Republic parades, the old downtown theater district, Hudson River day boats, shanty settlements on the upper East Side—all that might be part of the history of Cincinnati or St. Louis. Sundered from New York's fascinating, turbulent, uproarious past, the magazine has a meager and mean sense of the present. The collective editorial sneer extends to the entire Brownstone era and Mrs. Astor's pet horse.

Its roots are not in a place but in a sensibility. Like an unfortunately large number of present-day American magazines, it is essentially a woman's magazine written by men. There is to be found in its pages a simpering tone, a passion for cuteness, a fondness for precious little designs in linoleum. Art and high thought are given the lap-robe treatment. The proper set of liberal opinions are as socially important as a silver fox neckpiece.

The very language in which the articles are written is indicative of this quality. Witness the mincing tone of this little bit of advice in the Night Life department: "Café Society—Maxine Sullivan's still, small voice and Jack Prince's big, rumpus-room one." Or perhaps the item from the same department on the El Morocco: "Life in the stately homes of England was never more baronial than the activities here."

It is obvious that the editors of *The New Yorker* do not appreciate the fact that the character of humbug changes from generation to generation. It may be that the magazine was refreshing in tone and effect in its early days; but the corn-belt sophisticates have multiplied rapidly since the twenties, and Mr. Babbitt would not recognize the country club where in the reading room the members are enjoying *The New Yorker.*

The New Yorker is so fascinated with the contemplation of its navel that it is blind to all the changes in the country since the magazine's heyday. One wonders by what device the editors keep faith in the imaginary sparkling qualities of *The New Yorker* humor. Perhaps they have learned a lesson from the moguls of Hollywood, and keep their eyes fixed on the take at the box office.

The old formulas continue to woo and win readers. The endless array of stale cartoons with overstuffed garden club ladies and chorus girls who understand daddy and bank accounts, and the seemingly machine-made profiles of television magnates and brush company owners—these to draw the crowd. But one would imagine that this fact would do little to quiet the conscience of the editors, inasmuch as *True Romances* and all its breed thrive by adding machine standards.

To be sure, the magazine is not without talent. One encounters sensitive, erudite book reviews prepared by Edmund Wilson, Alfred Kazin, and Lionel Trilling; a bit of Richard Wilbur's excellent formalist poetry, the mannered stories of Peter Taylor and Mary McCarthy, the gothic cartoons of Charles Addams. However, virtually every magazine prints good writing now and again. The bulk of the magazine, however, is loaded with dull, trivial stories about uninteresting children in suburban towns, news of feminine fashions, letters from Paris and London which are uniform in style and approach, and vacant gossip concerning celebrities observed on the Manhattan night club circuit.

The profiles have no discernible significance. The Talk of the Town department customarily launches a fair-sized puff in each issue, reminds readers that the advertisement of luxury items does not prevent the editors from being just as liberal and *avant-garde* as the next fellow.

Naturally, the whole thing smacks of affectation and lust after the fashionable utterance. Apparently the editors consider the United Nations something to be coy about with one's fashionable friends, as though it were a shop where one could buy frightfully good alligator belts or specially made mayonnaise.

As regards the race problem, they are very chummy; but simple, natural treatment of the Negro race is as about as common a thing as a photograph of a Negro bride in the society section of the *Times* or *Tribune*. All these things are part of an artificial folksy relationship with the fortunate sophisticates who are "in the know" as regards the "right thing."

The editors of *The New Yorker* have a precise idea of their typical readers. There is the suburban wife who wishes her mate would display an interest in Picasso reproductions and French films instead of stud poker and "shoot-em-up" westerns. There is the young reporter on an Atlanta newspaper who aspires to work on one of the Luce publications.

Alas, there are many thousands, of newly-rich Americans without traditional standards and a great anxiety that the simple life is deficient in objects of virtue. There are enough of this type of reader to make *The New Yorker* very big business indeed.

Obviously, the editors are of the opinion that the country is not divided into good and bad people but fashionable Big people and unsophisticated Little people. They fail to grasp the truth that in America today the struggle to do the right and brave thing is a mute drama, but very real none the less. The opportunity for tender comedy is great, and it is completely absent from *The New Yorker*.

As the house organ of the middle-brow, *The New Yorker*'s role is the opposite of what the early readers conceived it to be. Instead of being the voice of literate and witty writers who expose human follies, it is a publishing business operated on the principle that America is a spectacle and the majority of the people queer sights to be exploited for the benefit of the upper-bracket celebrity-worshiping society.

Consequently, the folkways of outlanders, the people who live in ignorance of the Stork Club and "21," are placed in a class with Zulu war dances and the marriage customs of Malayans. *The New Yorker* has created so weird an image of America that the editors themselves seem to believe that the country at large is a backwoodsy page from the book for *Oklahoma*.

The living culture of Americans, whether on Hester Street or Beacon Hill, is described as something quaint. The spiritually defunct existence of native sophisticates of *The New Yorker* variety is presented as the pinnacle of civilization on this side of the Atlantic.

The character of the advertising carried in *The New Yorker* is an index of the magazine's place and significance. Bergdorf Goodman; Merrill, Lynch, Pierce, Fenner & Beane; Prince Matchabelli perfume; H. Dubois & Co., makers of Sea Island voile shirtings; the Copacabana; The Homestead are, for example, advertisers.

There is nothing wrong with these firms or their desire to advertise in *The New Yorker*; but it is evident that the vaunted awareness of the magazine is on no higher plane than the gold cuff-link smartness of the luxury enterprises advertised.

The truth which emerges from a consideration of *The New Yorker* is that the editors cannot make any criticism in a comic vein so long as they are identified with the fashionable interests of Manhattan pseudo-society. Indeed if one thinks about the magazine's notion of the "smart" life and relates it to the glittering articles displayed in its pages, one soon understands that the humor is neither particularly arresting nor very humane. The magazine seems to envision New York and the country through the eyes of a supercilious young fashion reporter who goes about in search of quaint taxicab drivers and elevator operators with philosophical ideas.

The basic assumption made in this type of story is that the ordinary man or woman is devoid of a soul and moral sensitivity, that it is a superb teasing surprise when the ordinary human being utters a thought about God or mankind, the hereafter or social justice. *The New Yorker* is essentially contemptuous of values; it doesn't give a continental about the fitness of fashionable society's mode of life, whether night club celebrities or nature's noblemen is what the American system breeds. The magazine is only interested in the fact that a moneyed class exists and that in suburbia there is a widespread mania to ape "smart" New York ways and be puffed up with the pride of sophisticates.

Hilton Kramer

SOURCE: "Harold Ross's 'New Yorker': Life as a Drawing-Room Comedy," in *Commentary*, Vol. 28, No. 2, August, 1959, pp. 122-27.

[*An American critic, Kramer is best known for his books and essays on modern art. In the following review of James Thurber's* The Years with Ross, *Kramer characterizes the work published in the* New Yorker *as essentially trivial and bland.*]

A few years ago when the art critic for the *New Yorker* went abroad to report on current art activities in London, Paris, and other European centers, I began receiving regular telephone calls, often several a week, from a zealous young man in that magazine's Checking Department. I confess that the first time the fellow introduced himself, I thought the Checking Department must be something like the Accounting Office and I couldn't imagine why he wanted to talk to me. When he made it clear that he was a kind of researcher, I was, as I suppose many people are the first time around, rather flattered to think I could help out such an august body in its scrutiny of the facts, and I cheerfully volunteered a considerable amount of information on the question at hand, namely, the relationship of certain French critics to schools and styles of painting. In the course of the first week's telephone conversations, I found myself giving a little lecture on the ideological positions of some of the major critics on the Paris art scene. It was the kind of information which anyone following the international art scene with more than passing interest would pick up in the course of his reading and observation. I hadn't, at that date, even been to Paris myself.

Naturally, after this personal contribution to upholding the *New Yorker*'s famous standard of accuracy, I was curious to see what the articles had to say. As they began appearing in the magazine, I was astonished to find myself reading the same old stuff one always found in the *New Yorker* wherever art was the subject under discussion. There were the same tired phrases and the same bored attitudes, as if the writer had only just managed to shake loose of his ennui long enough to take note here and there of what was going on. If one took the phrasing of the article literally, it seemed that the writer had only just happened to "drop in" to this or that exhibition, that he merely chanced to "catch" a certain artist's work or to note a certain critic's position. The phraseology fairly slouched in its attitude of repose, and no doubt acted as a balm to those readers who might be worried lest the subject get too serious.

Yet, behind this air of relaxation, one could not help detecting the terrifying relentlessness with which a serious subject—and a subject, moreover, in which the writer's vital personal response counts for a great deal—had been parodied, trimmed, ridiculed, and finally made boring and absurd by the author's attempt to make it seem completely effortless, utterly common-sensical, and open to the most easygoing attention. But I was struck all the more at the absurdity of this feigned ease when I realized that it wasn't the author's work—my conversations with the young man from the Checking Department made it clear that the author himself had sweated over his reports and, even at that, hadn't got matters quite straight—but that of the rewrite man. I marveled at the discrepancy between the pains taken to get the facts of the matter as accurate as possible, and the quite different effort that had gone into making the subject seem easy and almost inconsequential to the reader.

Anyone who ponders this discrepancy will sooner or later want to come up with some explanation of its necessity. For myself, I don't see how we can avoid concluding that the principal reason for the *New Yorker*'s method is ignorance: the ignorance of writers first of all, and ultimately the ignorance of readers. In a society which could assume a certain level of education and sophistication in its writers and journalists—which could make the assumption because it shared in that education and sophistication—there would be more of a public faith that writers knew more or less what they are talking about. A few inaccuracies of fact here and there would be of little consequence, and indeed might even be welcome. (Half of the most enjoyable letters-to-the-editor in the English weeklies would never be written if that country's most cultivated journalists and men of letters were not always overstepping the bounds of factuality on some point or other.) Only where there is a deep-seated ignorance, abetted by a phony desire to appear completely knowledgeable, is factual error or some minor fault of usage an unforgivable sin.

The *New Yorker*'s editorial method strikes me as a peculiarly American phenomenon, and it is instructive to compare it to the method of *Time,* which most *New Yorker* men regard with contempt and disdain (having graduated, many of them, from the Luce academy themselves). In some ways the method is remarkably similar. For just as *Time* aspires to turn every political story or book review into a middlebrow soap opera, the *New Yorker* attempts to make every encounter with culture and politics a drawing-room comedy. Where it succeeds in this endeavor, it commands the greatest loyalty from its readers. The cartoons, I suppose, are the most sustained example, but some of the magazine's celebrated writers have also become famous through this endeavor. The role of smug drawing-room comedian was the specialty of the late Wolcott Gibbs during his long tenure as drama critic, and it is still the special—one often thinks, the only—talent of the present incumbents in the movie, art, and music departments.

What I could not have realized before reading James Thurber's memoir of the late Harold Ross [*The Years with Ross*], the founder and first editor of the *New Yorker,* is the degree to which the *New Yorker*'s method was the direct outgrowth of the ignorance of the man who founded it, a man who was in many ways such a key figure in the history of American journalism and manners for over a quarter of a century. Thurber provides a warm, affectionate, mildly humorous account of Ross. If, as a book, *The Years with Ross* is also prolix, sentimental, and filled with something dangerously close to self-love, it only resembles the kind of family reminiscences which have become a stock feature of the *New Yorker* itself. Since Thurber's connections with Ross and the *New Yorker* go back to the 20's, his memoir also has some of the elements of an informal company history—a company history written by a humorist who is placed in the difficult position of having to repeat many well-known company jokes. *The Years with Ross* is written with all the love, honesty, and inside information which one has a right to expect from an old friend and colleague, but to anyone who didn't know Ross personally—and for all I know, perhaps to many who did—the figure who emerges from its pages is not a very attractive man. He is ignorant and vain, often cruel and stupid, and in the grip of a dream which is always—in this country anyway—supposed to forgive all the sins which ignorance, vanity, and cruelty inspire: the dream of technical perfection.

Harold Ross was born in Aspen, Colorado, in 1892. He went to work as a reporter on the Salt Lake City *Tribune* when he was fourteen, and later worked for papers in California and in the South. During the First World War he was editor of the *Stars and Stripes* in Paris. When he came to New York after the war, he worked for the *American Legion Weekly* and *Judge,* and began making plans for the weekly magazine that would become the *New Yorker.* The magazine was founded in 1925—"the outstanding flop of 1925," Thurber calls it. Its beginnings were slow and not very distinguished. Its initial printing was 15,000 copies, and its literary contributions were not, as Thurber admits, exactly brilliant. Gradually, the magazine gained momentum as it gathered around itself the journalists, humorists, and cartoonists who were eventually responsible for its success: Dorothy Parker, E. B. White, Wolcott Gibbs, Robert Benchley, Alexander Woollcott, Marc Connelly, Gluyas Williams, Helen Hokinson, Peter Arno, and of course, Thurber himself.

What these contributors brought to the magazine was an air of big-town sophistication. They aspired to a style which would be jovial, deadpan, and slightly bored. Above all, it was to be a style, which, for all its knowingness, was to be terribly, terribly innocent. Altogether, it was a concept of sophistication which at the very start was stilted and phony. It was to be sophistication without any talk of sex, politics, or religion—which is to say, sophistication with the guts removed. It had to rely on personalities in entertainment, business, and café society for its comic as well as its reportorial sustenance. In the original prospectus for the *New Yorker,* Ross indicated that "There will be a personal mention column—a jotting down in the small-town newspaper style of the comings, goings, and doings in the village of New York." This bizarre idea that the ultimate in sophistication was to regard New York as a "village" whose most trivial comings, goings, and doings had to be checked and rechecked by a staff of zealous researchers before the most ephemeral item of reportage could be committed to print, underscores the phoniness of the whole enterprise.

The *New Yorker* was in its beginnings very much a newspaperman's idea of a magazine, and a small-town newspaperman at that. One soon discovers in reading Thurber's memoir that most of the contributions which earn one's respect in the magazine nowadays—say, the occasional literary pieces by Edmund Wilson, the poems by Theodore Roethke, Howard Nemerov, and others, the architectural criticism of Lewis Mumford, and, this past year, the drama criticism of Kenneth Tynan—would have been beyond Ross's ken and outside his interest. He apparently regarded Clifton Fadiman, during his term as the *New*

Yorker's book critic, as too much of a highbrow to be completely understood by himself. His opinion of Edmund Wilson, who succeeded Fadiman, is unreported.

Thurber does not refrain from reporting the celebrated examples of Ross's ignorance. He was a man on whom the most common literary reference was lost. Everyone will have his favorite story on this subject, but I think one of the most illuminating is Thurber's account of an evening spent with Ross, Mencken, and Nathan. Ross is often thought to be a kind of Menckenesque figure, and Thurber's anecdote shows how mistaken this view is:

> . . . Mencken and I began talking about Willa Cather. We were still discussing "the old girl" when Ross caught the name, turned it over in his mind a couple of times, and then said, "Willa Cather. Willa Cather—did he writer *The Private Life of Helen of Troy?*" I couldn't see Mencken's face, but I felt the puzzled quality of his silence, and hastily came to the rescue of a situation hopelessly snarled by Ross's incomprehensible confusion of Willa Cather and John Erskine. "Ross hasn't read a novel since *When Knighthood Was in Flower,*" I said, "or *Riders of the Purple Sage.* He doesn't read anything except what goes into his magazine."

> "I haven't got time to read novels," Ross admitted.

Far from resembling Mencken, Ross was distinctly the kind of unlettered provincial who, had he held any position other than the one he did hold on the *New Yorker,* would have been the perfect target for Mencken's jibes about the ignornace of the American businessman.

Without a fuller and less sentimental history of the *New Yorker*'s first decade, we cannot know to what degree Ross himself was actually responsible for its success. Reading between the lines in Thurber's book, one has a sense that E. B. White, Katharine Angell, Wolcott Gibbs, and Thurber himself gave the magazine its distinctive character. In any case, one thing is clear enough: Ross was primarily responsible for the fanatical devotion to clarity and accuracy which has come to characterize the *New Yorker*'s editorial style. In a way, I suppose, only someone like Ross, unread and without curiosity on any literary or intellectual subject, could have brought the *New Yorker*'s editorial method to such an advanced state of refinement. Only someone who could regard language as a purely technical medium, as open as any other technique to mechanical scrutiny, could have pushed this method to its final triumph over expression itself. A mind less barren would have been sidetracked by some distracting intellectual substance.

Yet it was not only its editorial method Ross perfected, but also the magazine's peculiar outlook on the world of sophisticated culture. The Irish critic Donat O'Donnell, writing about Thurber's book in the London *Spectator,* has recently given the best account of the nature of this outlook and Ross's role in it: "An important source of the *New Yorker*'s financial strength today is that great class which thinks itself entitled not merely to appear but actually to *feel* cultured, without undergoing any dull and painful preparation, such as being educated. The conquest of this class was Ross's achievement."

By the time of Ross's death, in 1951, the task of keeping up the appearance of sophisticated culture was already far more complex than it had been in the early days, and for that reason there was already a great deal in the magazine which was beyond the interest or comprehension of Ross himself. Since his death, the task has grown even more complicated and the magazine itself rather less certain about its exact domain of interest.

Still, the divided, slightly schizophrenic outlook which has characterized the *New Yorker* all along, and which necessarily characterizes any publication or individual who feigns an interest in cultural matters without the curiosity or capacity to face them squarely on their own terms, continues to mark the tone and substance of the *New Yorker* today. That is Ross's legacy to his heirs. It turns up in many small ways, and occasionally in rather blunt and unequivocal terms. I think this is immediately evident if we consider what has happened to the drama criticism in the *New Yorker* since the death of Wolcott Gibbs.

Gibbs's successor has been not one man, but two—and a neater demonstration of the schizoid mentality of the *New Yorker's* present editorship would be hard to find. On the one hand, there is Kenneth Tynan, the brilliant and witty critic of the London *Observer,* who was invited over to cover the Broadway season. On the other hand, there is a young company man named Donald Malcolm, who was assigned to the off-Broadway theater. Now Tynan is not only a witty and literate critic with a talent for the stylish phrase; he is also hard-headed in matters of dramatic art, and he has recently demonstrated the kind of concern for the social and political significance of the theater which would have been extremely distasteful (if indeed comprehensible) to Harold Ross. Inevitably, perhaps, because of his interest in both the aesthetics of the theater and the social crisis of our time, Tynan has become something of a Brechtian in his critical views. A Brechtian writing about the Broadway theater for the *New Yorker:* what could be more unlikely? Yet, confined to Broadway, Tynan is not in a position to offend *New Yorker* taste. He can blast away, if he likes, against Broadway offerings, and his writing still falls into the category of critical snobbery that regular addicts of the magazine expect from Gibbs's successor.

The off-Broadway theater, however, is out of bounds to Tynan. The task of reporting on this sphere of dramatic art, where occasionally a play of some literary, avantgarde interest shows up, has been given to Mr. Malcolm, who must represent some kind of biological mutation in being an earnest, educated, articulate spokesman for all the philistine values so dearly beloved by Ross himself. His review last season of Chekhov's *Ivanov* made history (of a kind) even in the annals of a magazine noted for this kind of thing. Written as a colloquy between the critic and a cab driver and ostensibly a parody of the Chekhovian style, Malcolm's "review" managed very neatly to bypass the entire substance of the play. The editors are right in thinking they have a real "find" in this young man; his employment pays in full their debt to Ross's memory no matter how far they may have to go in offending it in other directions.

There are a lot of laughs as well as some tiresome and irrelevant anecdotes in Thurber's memoir, but there is one chapter which remains unassimilated to the neat image of Ross and his times. I found it memorable and shocking, but scarcely understandable in the bland terms of Thurber's prose. It is the chapter called "The Secret Life of Harold Winney," and in this case Thurber's glib reference to his own Walter Mitty story only serves to betray his incapacity to deal with a subject which, in truth, might have been a challenge to Dostoevsky.

Harold Winney was Ross's private secretary from 1935 to 1941. "In his years with Ross," Thurber writes, "the pallid, silent young man steadily swindled the editor out of a total of seventy-one thousand dollars." Thurber himself regarded Winney with extreme distaste: "I remember [him] mainly for his cold small voice, his pale nimble fingers, and his way of moving about the corridors and offices like a shadow." Apparently Ross did not take sufficient notice of him to have any feelings at all. "I do not believe that Harold Ross ever looked at the man closely enough to have been able to describe him accurately," Thurber writes. "He was what Ross once irritably described as a 'worm'—that is, an unimportant cog in the *New Yorker* wheel, a noncreative person."

Winney came to work for Ross at a time when the magazine was expanding and Ross's work was growing more burdensome. He delegated fantastic powers to his anonymous secretary, including complete control over his bank accounts and financial securities. During a trip to Europe in 1938, Ross gave Winney power of attorney over his financial holdings, and never revoked the privilege when he returned to New York. Moreover, what made it easy for Winney to draw more and more easily on Ross's fortune was his boss's gambling habits; Ross was a steady and heavy loser at cards, and Winney took advantage of the situation to make each loss greater than it actually was. After seventy-one thousand dollars had been swindled and the chaotic state of his financial affairs was finally brought to Ross's attention, Winney committed suicide.

"When investigators examined his apartment," Thurber writes, "they found, among other things, a hundred and three suits of clothes which he had bought with the money stolen from Ross." Winney had also carried on correspondence with a real estate firm in Tahiti, with a view to settling there on his small fortune, but the war prevented him from realizing this ambition. Meanwhile, Winney seems to have spent a good deal of the money at the race track, and on gifts to men friends of sports cars, skiing equipment, and other sundries of this order. He had given an election night champagne party at the Astor in November 1940.

For myself, I find something apposite and meaningful in Harold Winney's mulcting his boss on such a grand scale and for such seemingly trivial ends. He was clearly living out the fantasy life of ease and comfort—the life of sports cars, the race track, champagne parties, and expensive vacations—which the *New Yorker* works so hard to inspire in its readers. In his working hours he conformed to that hardworking demeanor, the whole laborious regimen, which Ross imposed on the magazine, and in his leisure hours he conformed to the life which the *New Yorker* advertisements and editorial departments have held up for a generation as an ideal: the life of languid, expensive, effete pleasures. Reading Thurber's bare and rather superior account of Harold Winney, it occurred to me that this wretched man was probably the only person who ever truly lived his life entirely in terms of the values espoused in the pages of the *New Yorker*. It seems more than just that he did so at the expense of the man who was most responsible for what remains, after all, an image of life that is provincial, adolescent, and at several removes from reality.

Richard Brookhiser

SOURCE: "The Evil of Banality," in *National Review,* New York, Vol. XXXVII, October 4, 1985, pp. 47-9.

[*An American author, Brookhiser has written several books on American politics and was a speech writer for George Bush. From 1979 to 1987 he worked as a senior editor and later managing editor of the* National Review. *In the following essay, he offers an attack on the features, contributors, and editorial policies of the* New Yorker *under the editorship of William Shawn.*]

The New Yorker has been with us for sixty years, 34 of them under the direction of Mr. William Shawn. That makes Mr. Shawn (who never appears in print without his honorific) America's longest-tenured editor-in-chief. He is also America's most-respected editor-in-chief, for reasons that are widely known, even legendary. When Mr. Shawn receives a manuscript, he is back to his writer, with his comments, the next day. He is thorough, solicitous, unfailingly polite. Mr. Shawn's writers don't produce stories, as if they were factories; they are encouraged to nurture them, as if they were ewes. Why then does his magazine stink?

The stories that greeted *The New Yorker*'s recent change of ownership covered every other aspect of the magazine—industry gossip on details of the sale; the fears and anxieties of the employees; the eccentricities of the magazine's operation. Everything, except the central fact that confronts the reader, week after week: the boring, annoying, impenetrable waste of time *The New Yorker* has become. Not a total waste (nothing ever is). That, no doubt, is what keeps us going; charmed by a caption, or a filler, or the fussy look of the thing, we continue to hope, against all the evidence of experience, that it will get better. It never does. Its dullness has moral, as well as aesthetic consequences. This is a reader's cry of pain.

The single feature of *The New Yorker* that gives consistent pleasure is its cartoons. (That makes *The New Yorker* one of the two major magazines in America, along with *Playboy,* that is read for its illustrations.) The talking dogs and cats, the cocktail parties, the businessmen at their big desks, the same businessmen newly arrived in Heaven or (more often) Hell—the cartoons are like *Honeymooners* reruns, always the same, always hilarious. Ten years ago,

William Hamilton was the funniest cartoonist in America. He caught a type—young people of the upper middle class, formerly rebellious, but returning, in the mid-Seventies, to their roots—years before the *Official Preppie Handbook* was published. My favorite Hamilton showed a smiling group of four at a cocktail party. "Did I meet you," said one—he was still wearing a mustache and modest sideburns—"at the March on the Pentagon, or at the Essex hunt?" The up-to-the-minute cartoonist nowadays seems to be Edward Koren, whose Upper West Side/academic types, indistinguishable from the monstrous furry animals they keep, are slightly less well-off, slightly less sold-out, and much wackier. Look for someone to label them about 1991.

There may be a formal reason for the cartoons' excellence. A cartoon usually consists of a single panel, occasionally subdivided, no larger than a page. The longest captions never go longer than a short paragraph. As a result, the cartoon must be a hit-and-run form—terse, lively, typical.

Beyond the cartoon's four corners, things quickly disintegrate. Starting at the back of the book (let us save the worst for last), one finds the book reviews of John Updike. Updike the critic gives the safe opinion, sanely expressed. Of him it may be said, by way of both blame and praise, that he is not Ezra Pound; he won't discover the next T. S. Eliot; but he also won't fall for Social Credit.

What can be said of Pauline Kael? The most ferocious attack on her movie reviewing appeared several years ago in *The New York Review of Books,* by Renata Adler, another *New Yorker* contributor. It was, in some ways, an ideal *New Yorker* piece, for Miss Adler made her point by assembling a list of a few hundred of Miss Kael's favorite adjectives and adverbs—"trashy," "campy," "garbagey," etc., etc. Since these words are inherently meaningless, Miss Adler argued, Miss Kael must be meaningless as well. *Q. non E. D.* Miss Kael's writing *is* vulgar; on the other hand, that makes it about the liveliest in the magazine.

Andrew Porter, the music reviewer, takes us closer to the alkaline springs of *The New Yorker*'s sterility. There are three kinds of bad music criticism: enthusiasm; archaeology; and theory. The first reduces Chopin to Poland and moonlight; the second concentrates on the thickness of his piano strings; while the third analyzes the G double sharp in measure 25 that is recalled five pages later by the enharmonic A natural. Porter practices the second form, with excursions into the third. He knows everything about the history of music, and he repeats it in every issue. He is remorseless, implacable. Sometimes the flow of his pedantry coalesces into a coherent argument: A few years ago, for instance, he asked the nagging question, Suppose Beethoven's metronome markings were taken seriously? Mostly, though, we get the excitement of regurgitated performances: This *Don Carlo* was like last year's, though unlike renditions I heard in 1972 and 1957 (three years from now, the current performance will have been added to the backfile). It is like thumbing through a scrapbook of old Met programs.

The true wasteland of minutiae is the middle of the book.

A portion of *The New Yorker*'s core is devoted to fiction, and a small portion of that is the work of good, if repetitive, writers: Isaac Bashevis Singer's thousandth story about Polish cabalists, Laurie Colwin's hundredth story about adultery (I wonder sometimes about *Mr.* Colwin. "Great story, dear . . . ah, is there something you want to talk about?") The bulk of the fiction belongs to the genre of Epiphanies of Sensitive Young Women; in Josh Gilder's words, small stories that get smaller and smaller as they go along. Something has to be small, to leave room for the nonfiction. In these novel-length think-pieces, these dictionary-length articles, these encyclopediac series—four pieces on asbestos; Ved Mehta on all his cousins, or the population of India, whichever lasts longest—detail takes over. They are the Gobi, the Sahara. Boundless and bare, the lone and level sands of information stretch far away.

Not all of this information is necessarily uninteresting, and all of it is guaranteed to be factual. Accuracy is *The New Yorker*'s proudest boast. The magazine maintains a paddockful of fact checkers whose duty it is to comb every story for imprecisions. If you report that someone ran up a flight of a dozen steps, they will visit the building and advise that the steps number 13. If you describe a character buying American cigarettes in Paris in such and such a year, they will investigate and discover that there was a strike among the French distributors of that particular brand, which made it unavailable at that time. (I have both stories on the authority of the authors involved; anyone with journalistic connections can add two or three of his own.) What is lost in the hoarding of facts is proportion. With proportion go a number of other things—good writing, primarily; also common sense, and truth.

Consider the magazine's coverage of the last election.

> [The candidate] wore a jacket, shirt, and tie, a pattern of statesmanlike conventionality on a night when everybody off the platform was coatless and tieless. The tie itself was a quiet pattern of inkblots against an olive and pearl background. . . . "We got a wonderful climate," he said, and paused to wipe the sweat from his face with a handkerchief soaked in Coca-Cola, which he poured from a bottle out of a bucket of ice handed to him by one of the lesser candidates on his ticket. The bugs soaring up at the edge of the lighted area and converging on the floodlights formed a haze as thick as a beaded curtain.

That is a specimen of *The New Yorker*'s political reporting. Unfortunately, it comes from the coverage of the 1960 Louisiana gubernatorial race by A. J. Liebling. The 1984 presidential race was handled by Elizabeth Drew.

> Little Rock, Arkansas. The chartered DC-9 in which we have been travelling—carrying 13 Mondale staff members as well as the candidate, 33 reporters, and 11 still photographers, members of television crews, and television producers—arrived here early this evening. Mondale also has Zell Miller, the Lieutenant Governor of Georgia, and Ned McWherter, the Speaker of the House of Tennessee, traveling with him, and he introduces them at his various stops.

The process of creation is as plain as a fileted fish. From the reporter's notes, to her word processor, to the fact checkers—does Zell have two l's? McWherter two e's? count the reporters (how did they manage to overlook the TV crewmen?)—and so to the exquisitely printed page. And if anyone involved in the process had had any thoughts or feelings about Miller, McWherter, Arkansas, airplanes, or Mondale, the result might even have been readable. *Facts on File* would have done it better; a court reporter could have done as well. Mrs. Drew's plane flight may be a trivial passage, as trivial as Liebling's swarm of insects. But the trouble with Mrs. Drew's kind of writing is that it makes everything trivial. Her candidate and Liebling's both go on to give speeches. But we care about what Liebling's will say; Mrs. Drew's gets a yawn. (To think that Mr. Shawn was once Liebling's editor.)

Facts were not the only things being retailed in Elizabeth Drew's stories. Her own politics are liberal, and she inserted them into her featureless accounts in ways that were both sly and stupid.

> "Grenada [she quoted George Bush at the Dallas convention] was a turning point for democracy in this hemisphere and a proud moment in the history of this country." (This morning's *Dallas Times-Herald* had a banner story headlined GRENADA VOTERS MAY UNDO U.S. INVASION. The story says, "As the unelected interim government that has ruled Grenada since October moves toward setting a date for elections to replace the Marxist regime deposed by the invasion, Grenadians and U.S. officials fear that the balloting may merely reinstate one of the extremist parties associated with the political turmoil of the past decade." It says that the Grenadian Hotel Association, among others, has asked for a postponement of the election.) Bush ends on an upbeat note.

This is sly, because Mrs. Drew smuggles in an argument as a quotation (don't look at me, I'm just reading the *Times-Herald*). It's stupid, because the argument—that Grenada was a flop, and Bush won't admit it—rests on such diddley-squat evidence. (Are we supposed to change foreign policies every time a story appears in the Dallas papers? Has anyone, even *The New Yorker*'s fact checkers, heard a peep out of the Grenadian Hotel Association recently?)

The fact is, facts prove nothing. The relations of facts, and their relations to what we want, prove everything. But in order for those relations to be calibrated, writers must employ the tools of discrimination, and expression. This is the evil of banality: In *The New Yorker*'s columns nothing can be distinguished; neither desires nor principles can honestly raise their heads.

That is why the thoughts of *New Yorker* writers, when they occur, are so confused, wrongheaded, or irrelevant. When they are detached from accompanying masses of fact, as in "The Talk of the Town," they rise off the page in flatulent weightlessness. In three successive issues this February, we were told: that the Bahais of Iran were being persecuted (true), a situation that might be remedied by Senate ratification of the Genocide Convention (silly); that the Jaruzelski regime, trying the murderers of Father Popieluszko (its own minions), "faced a version of the dilemma that President Nixon and his aides faced when the Watergate burglars were first brought to trial" ("the Polish crime," *The New Yorker* noted, in passing, "was, of course, more serious . . . "); finally, that the Bhopal chemical explosion "was Three Mile Island all over again" (give or take a few thousand corpses). The Bhopal leader went on to say that "what truly grips us" in accounts of disaster "is not so much the numbers as the spectacle of suddenly vanishing competence." I decided that the only vanishing competence I could see was *The New Yorker*'s; I haven't read "The Talk of the Town" since.

If it improves, let me know. I'll be flipping through the cartoons.

FICTION, JOURNALISM, AND HUMOR AT THE *NEW YORKER*

Lionel Trilling

SOURCE: " 'New Yorker' Fiction," in *The Nation*, New York, Vol. 154, No. 15, April 11, 1942, pp. 425-26.

[*Trilling was one of the twentieth century's most significant and influential American literary and social critics, and he is often called the single most important American critic to apply Freudian psychological theories to literature. In the following excerpt, Trilling discusses short stories published by the* New Yorker *as works of "great moral intensity."*]

Recently, reading Fielding and Dickens again, I was struck by the change that our time has brought about in the relation of writer and reader. The old literary relation was a "polite" one—literature was assumed to be a means of social intercourse, the reader and writer were supposed to be aware of each other as friends engaged in a matter of common interest. But since the end of the nineteenth century there has grown up a competing—and by now largely victorious—assumption according to which literature is thought to be not so much a social as a scientific or religious activity; the reader, though permitted to be present at the research or ritual, is naturally not to be noticed.

One of the indications of the changed attitude is the decrease in lightness and humor in work which pretends to seriousness. The contrivance of a comic incident and the turning of a witty phrase are in effect a kind of flattery; they suggest direct notice of the reader, an avowed social effort on the part of the writer. Shaw was perhaps the last great mind to think with laughter and to invite his public to join him. American literature of the past three decades is largely solemn, even lugubrious, and its prose seems to be consciously at war with wit. The scientific and religious assumption has made the social one seem almost frivolous; for example, the important novels of E. M. Forster have never received adequate recognition because their polite, colloquial relation with the reader casts doubt on their se-

riousness, and a few years ago the pleasant small talent of S. N. Behrman had to advance specious reasons why there is always time for comedy.

It is one of the admirable things about the *New Yorker* magazine that it insists on continuing the old polite tradition of literature. The *New Yorker* is always aware of its readers and knows just who they are—the intelligent, comfortably-fixed, urbane, moral people who dress in good taste, enjoy all the arts but also all the sports, and in their politics are liberal but not rash. This, at any rate, is what we become as we read the *New Yorker,* and if the magazine flatters us by supposing that we are better off or more genteel than in fact we are, it also supposes that we are literate, intelligent, and quietly public-spirited.

And just as Dickens, having established a perfect social communion with his public, introduced into his novels the most withering indictments of the ideas and institutions by which his public lived, the *New Yorker* publishes along with its more genial contents, with its anecdotes, its comic drawings, and its excellent journalism, a kind of short story the main characteristic of which is its great moral intensity. Every week, at the barber's or the dentist's or on the commuting train, a representative part of the middle class learns about the horrors of snobbery, ignorance, and insensitivity and about the sufferings of children, servants, the superannuated, and the subordinate, weak people of all sorts. From these weekly stories sixty-eight were recently selected for the volume *Short Stories from the "New Yorker"*; they make one of the most "socially conscious" and one of the most grimly moral books lately published.

There can be no question about the talent of all these stories or about the brilliance of many of them, and their impulse to serious moral judgment is so urgent that to the future historian of the middle class they will inevitably seem documents of prime importance. But perhaps the first thing one remarks when these stories are taken out of their polite setting and brought together in a single volume is that, by some editorial anomaly, they deny the polite tradition the rest of the *New Yorker* maintains. Almost all the authors subscribe to the myth of their personal non-existence or of their merely corporate existence; they are all the same anonymous person, and you feel about them that, just as any scientist might take over another's research or any priest take over another's ritual duty, almost any one of these writers might write another's story in the same cool, remote prose. They all stand at about the same distance from their subject—perhaps Irwin Shaw a little closer than most or John O'Hara a little farther away—and all make similar sharp, sad observations about people with about the same degree of silent objectivity. And somehow, despite their admirable technical skill and despite their high earnestness, their stories have a mortuary quality; they are bright, beautiful, but dead. They all have point, but on that point they seem to impale not only the specimen to be observed but themselves as well.

In some part, perhaps, this effect may be attributed to the length of these stories; they have just room enough to make the sharp perception but not room enough for a play of emotion around it. The perception, to be adequately dramatic within this confining space, must be uncompromising and unmodulated; and because finality is always moving, these stories like to bring life, through some triviality, to a crisis and then a full stop. Even when we have such fine sensibilities as those of Kay Boyle or Louise Bogan, and even when they declare themselves in the service of affirmation, we feel that they have embalmed life for our inspection.

And behind the urgent morality of many of these stories I cannot help suspecting something very like cruelty. It is a peculiarly modern cruelty, unconsciously allied with the humanitarian sentiments and exercising itself by subtle moral perceptions. It is inherent in these stories in varying degrees of complexity, but it appears with a naive simplicity in Dorothy Parker's "Arrangement in Black and White," of which the intended point is that a young woman's expressions of liberal "tolerance" for a Negro singer are actually the expressions of her intense snobbery; but certainly the further and concealed point of the story is the great pleasure Miss Parker gets from her pursuit of this easy victim, the moral grandeur she offers her readers at small emotional expense. Surely the clue to the value of these emotions lies in Miss Parker's other story in the collection, in which, comparing herself with a group of Spanish Loyalists, she indulges in the luxury of self-contempt.

All satire has, of course, the pleasure of attack; what keeps the great satirists from cruelty is their open expression of anger, their clear avowal of their pleasure in the attack. But in many of the *New Yorker* stories—for example, in all three of Sally Benson's, in Mark Connolly's, in Marjorie Kinnan Rawlings's, in Mark Schorer's, in Tess Slesinger's, in Benedict Thielen's, even in Sherwood Anderson's (it is significantly unlike his characteristic work)—the authors avow nothing; indeed, in their defense of virtue they do not condescend to attack at all, they merely lay traps of situation into which the doomed characters must inevitably fall. In these stories immorality is exposed not by the author's aggression but by the character's unwariness; the author allows us to view the result but disclaims all responsibility, having made clear by his style that he is not really a person at all.

Most of the stories in *Short Stories from the "New Yorker"* are serious; but something of the same effect appears in the comic stories too. Arthur Kober, for example, writes his Bronx chronicles—they are collected in *My Dear Bella*—with a detachment so great as to be almost an animus. For a writer to withdraw so much of his feeling from his characters is to leave them shivering and naked; for Kober to record without comment and with so little expressed emotion the turns of speech and the tricks of behavior of his people is not to refrain from judgment but to make a judgment of contempt. And in Kober's case it results in a kind of inaccuracy; his method seems to accommodate nothing but the pettiness and ill-temper of his Jews, and Daniel Fuchs and Jerome Weidman surpass him in telling the literal truth about a similar group. I find the same unexplained animus in Benedict Thielen's *Stevie* stories. In a rather foolish preface in which he assures us that he has higher interests than Stevie, Thielen explains that his ill-

natured vulgarian deserves to be written about simply because he exists; but it is not convincing—we want to know why. We do know why Flaubert pursued Bouvard and Pecuchet, and the reasons were large and good. But it is hard to see in Thielen's pursuit of Stevie any other motive than the pure pleasure of mousing.

Three collections of *New Yorker* stories avoid the quality of cruelty which I have referred to. John Collier's *Presenting Moonshine* is full of the most ingenious sadism which addresses itself in open and friendly terms to the Perfect Murderer in each of us; it seems to me considerably less fierce than the literature of ingenious moral traps. Sally Benson's *Junior Miss* does not give me the pleasure it gives so many, but I prefer these slight stories to her weightier three in the *New Yorker* anthology; her adolescent girl cannot be written about without some affectionate responsibility. And James Reid Parker's *Attorneys at Law* is so very explicit in its animus and speaks with so much contemptuous gusto of a world in which immorality is so taken for granted that it is quite without moral ambiguity.

But of the *New Yorker* writers certainly the most gifted and morally the soundest is Ludwig Bemelmans. His *Hotel Splendide* contains much of his best work and one of the most successful stories I know, "The Magician Entertains the Ballet." Bemelmans is wholly in the old polite tradition. He courts the reader with the wit of his surprising prose, and of all the writers I have mentioned he is the only one who has an affection for his characters. Out of some humility or courage he has no need to speak with the authoritative voice of anonymity; he consents to exist as no more than a person and to admit that it is he, Bemelmans, who is at work.

The result is that his moral judgments are far less intense than his colleagues' but far more just; they are never bleak and desperate; even when they are adverse they are warm and forgiving. It is, I feel, an important aspect of his peculiar moral tone that he alone of the *New Yorker* writers creates a world that is colored, palpable, and full of smells; the others, for all their remarkable sensibility, are not aware of the senses; their perception is ascetic, and their characters, conceived in a kind of wordly puritanism, have no real bodies. But Bemelmans thinks with his senses and allows even his disagreeable characters the privileges of bodily existence, the magician with his stale cakes and passions quite as much as the ballet girls with the lemon slices between their toes and their adoration of Pavlowa.

Bemelmans is, in the good sense of the word, a modest talent, possibly not much more than a quaint one. It can scarcely benefit such a talent to inflate it beyond its true proportions, and yet it seems to me that his work is important because in these days its characteristic quality is so rare. Bemelmans, without ever descending to loose emotion and without ever losing his worldliness and his satiric eye, has a kind of healthy contentment with human nature; and in a world in which literary sensibility seems almost to depend upon the frustration of high hopes and to find its easiest expression in bleakness, his work, with its bright humanism, stands as both protest and affirmation.

Roger Angell

SOURCE: "Storyville," in *The New Yorker,* Vol. LXX, No. 19, June 27-July 4, 1994, pp. 104-09.

[Angell is an American author who has written several books about baseball and was the fiction editor of the New Yorker from 1956 to 1994. In the following essay, he reflects on the criteria for accepting works of fiction submitted to the New Yorker.]

Do anything long enough, and you hang up a record. Just go to bed every night, and before you know it you've passed Sleeping Beauty. Set down the dog's dinner, day by day, and pretty soon he's put away enough Alpo to feed the Dallas Cowboys on Thanksgiving. "Hey," said a colleague of mine, sticking his head in my office door the other day. "Did you know that you've rejected fifteen thousand stories here? I just figured it out. Fifteen thousand, easy."

Well, thanks. I got out a pencil and did some figuring, and decided that eighteen thousand was probably more like it. I tried to envision that many manuscripts trudging back home again in the rain, and to imagine the reception they got there when they rang the bell—"Oh. You again"—and, wincing, I heard the mumbled apologies and explanations. Then I added on all the other mournful regiments of rejected fiction sent back from this salient, down the years, by fellow-editors of mine in the same line of work: a much larger body of the defeated and the shot-down—a whole bloody Caporetto. "We regret . . . ," I murmured unhappily to myself. "Thank you for . . . " I sounded like a field marshal.

The regret is real, though it may vary in depth from one manuscript to the next. What is certain is that no one can read fiction for thirty-eight years, or thirty-eight *weeks,* and go on taking any pleasure in saying no. It works the other way around. You pick up the next manuscript, from a long-term contributor or an absolute stranger ("Prize in Undergraduate Composition; two summers at Pineaway under Guy de Maupassant; stories in *Yurì, Springboard,* and *Yclept;* semifinalist in . . . "), and set sail down the page in search of life, or signs of life; your eye is caught and you flip eagerly to the next page and the one after that. Can it be? Mostly, almost always, it is not—or not quite. You read on to the end (well, not always to the end) and then make a note to yourself about what you will say to your old friend who hasn't sold a story here in two years, or what to put, in some lines scribbled at the end of the printed form, to the young or not so young author who has laid his or her soul out on these eighteen pages but somehow not in a way that makes you want to slow down and enter this particular bar in company with Jay and Hugo and Lynn, or hear more of what was said on the back porch on a particular night of recriminations and fireflies. Sometimes there is a little descriptive passage or some paragraphs of dialogue, or the tone or tinge of a page or two, to single out for praise or encouragement, but even these responses, let it be said, may go into a return letter as much to make yourself feel better, a bit less of a monster, as in any great hopes of getting a socko manuscript from this same author in a month's time.

There seems to be a lot of misunderstanding about fiction. "How do you get a story published in *The New Yorker?*" somebody asks. "Send it in, and if we like it we'll publish it," I reply, and my interlocutor shoots me a knowing look and says, "No, *seriously—*"

"Are you looking for the typical *New Yorker* story?" someone else asks. "Sure, lady," I want to answer back. "The one that's exactly like Borges and Brodkey and Edna O'Brien and John O'Hara and Susan Minot and Eudora Welty and Niccolò Tucci and Isaac Singer. That's the one, except with more Keillor and Nabokov in it. Whenever we find one of those, we snap it right up."

A distinguished reporter here, the author of long, ferociously researched articles, stopped by to see me one day in great excitement, to say he was giving up all this drudgery and would write only fiction from now on. "Fiction writers never have to leave their desks, do they?" he said.

"Well, no," I said. "Except for one thing."

"What's that?"

"They have to get up to vomit," I said.

A visiting reporter from a media journal once asked, "What are you people looking for in the fiction line? What are your standards?"

I stalled for time. "I don't know what they are," I mumbled at last. "We've never decided. We want something good—you know, something we like."

"No, *seriously,*" she said, but when she saw that we were serious (I had cunningly laid on some colleagues) she closed her notebook. Her piece never appeared.

The writers are the main players, which means that we can hurry past such esoterica as the opinion sheet, on which two or three or more fiction editors weigh in helpfully or warily or stubbornly ("Hate to disagree, but—") on an incoming manuscript; often the process turns up some structural flaws, and the work is shipped back to its creator for minor or major repairs. Or rejected. No contributor is spared this blunt possibility, which may explain why certain celebrated authors have attempted to negotiate an acceptance before a story of theirs is sent along, or have stopped submitting altogether. Lack of unanimity on an opinion sheet is not uncommon, nor is the brave or truculent silence of a dissenting editor in the face of a story that has been taken in spite of his or her fervent objections: a turn of events that brings brief, rushing doubts about the future of Western civilization, or about the sanity of the Editor, who has had the last word. This is a weekly, thank God, and a few days later we fiction people are out in the hall exclaiming over a new manuscript, by an old standby or a total unknown, that has just gone the rounds: "Have you *read* it? Isn't that terrific!" Some writer has made our day, and we are collegial once again, gleaming in reflected brilliance.

Just as there is no one way to write a story, there is no one way to edit it for publication, or to deal with its author over an extended period of time. What is being set down here, I mean, is one editor's experiences and recollections of these semi-private matters—a selective history that cannot give proper honor to my departmental colleagues, past and present, or to writers whose work did not happen to come my way. What I noticed about bygone fellow fiction editors at the magazine—among them, Robert Henderson, William Maxwell, Robert Hemenway, Rachel MacKenzie, Frances Kiernan, Patricia Strachan, and Veronica Geng—was how much alike they were in their passion for their work, and how different in the ways they went about it. The same holds true for my present friends and everyday companions here, whose devoted attentions continue the long line of *New Yorker* stories—over six thousand of them so far—while properly encouraging its alteration, almost issue by issue, in directions unforeseen. Fiction is special, of course, for its text must retain the whorls and brush-splashes of the author: the touch of the artist. At the same time, the editor should not feel much compunction about asking the writer the same questions he would put to himself about a swatch of his own prose: Is it clear? Does it say what I wanted it to say? Is it too long? Does it *sound* right—does it carry the tone that I want the reader to pick up right here? Is it, just possibly, too short? And so on. (It's no coincidence, by the way, that so many *New Yorker* fiction editors have also been writers.)

Some distinguished editors here have forsworn most such meddling, particularly with young contributors, on the theory that the writer almost always knows best. My own instincts lean the other way, for the obligation to preserve the sanctity of a neophyte's script is counterbalanced by my hope that he will, by life habit, come to ask himself those short, tough questions as he writes along, never omitting the big question at the end: Is it good enough? Is it any good at all? Lifelong practitioners—the best ones, I've noticed—ask themselves this every day: that's why they look the way they do (hunched over their word processors, or at the bar next door), which is like morticians.

That new story we exclaimed about will be brilliant, but perhaps not right away. A week has gone by, and its author—a young man in his twenties, let's say, not previously published in *The New Yorker* or anywhere else—is in my office. We are sitting side by side at the desk, with his manuscript between us, and on its top page he finds some light pencillings and question marks. What's this? The joyful, sunstruck expression he has worn ever since he got the good news fades a fraction; middle age, one could say, has just begun. They *edit* fiction here? "Don't worry," I say. "Let's take a look. Down here, do you want these three whole lines about the dog, who doesn't turn up again in the story until . . . until over here on page 11? Do you want to say something quicker about the dog? Up to you . . . But before this, up here at the top of the paragraph, I'm not sure why the father seems so bitter. Do you need to explain that, or have you made him seem angrier than you meant to? Well, let's mark that and move on . . . Over here on page 4, just after Lucinda goes off in the truck, you've used this same construction for the third time in a row—you've got awfully fond of those dashes. Want to do it some other way? And then here's your 'dirgelike darkness,' right in the middle of this wonderful scene. Can darkness have a *sound*? What should we do about that?"

I pause and look at him. He is trying to decide whether I'm simply a bully or someone out to steal his writer's soul. Perhaps it's neither. How can he be persuaded that these are the same wireworms and dust balls that every writer discovers in the corners of his beautiful prose, no matter how carefully he has woven it and laid it down? The young man looks pale, and who can blame him? He feels himself at a brink. He wants to be an artist, but he also wants to be a pro. His words, which once looked so secure, so right, are beginning to let him down. Why is this all so hard? Why has the language suddenly turned balky? He needs time to think it over.

"Never mind the dashes," I offer now. "I think they'll work fine. And you can look at that 'dirgelike' later on, when this is all in type."

We go on to the next page, and I have a passing brief memory of other writers, sitting just here to my left, as we bend over a manuscript or a proof together. William Maxwell, cheerfully x-ing out a proposed line change (marked "for clarity" at the margin of the galley), smiles and says, "I don't want to be *too* clear." Donald Barthelme, encountering a short paragraph with my "Omit?" at its flank, sighs and reddens. He is the cleanest of writers, and proud. "Well, yes, goddam it, if you say so," he mutters at last. "I count on you to get the hay out." And then it is my turn to wonder if I'm right. Later on, I may recall some words of William Shawn's—the only advice about editing I ever heard him put forward. "It's very easy to make somebody's manuscript into the best story ever written," he said. "The trick is to help the writer make it into the best story he can write on that particular day."

If I could do it, I would invite the first-time author to come back on a day when I am sitting here with John Updike, going over the galley proofs of a story of his, or discussing them with him on the telephone. Updike has rewritten (in his angling pencilled handwriting) some lines of his, up on top of a long paragraph, and we are trying to decide about a word in the middle of one sentence. "Well, you may be right," he says in his soft, musing way. "Which do you think *sounds* better?" He says the phrase with the word in it over to himself once or twice and makes a decision. The following day, after this and a dozen other burning trifling matters have been resolved, I overnight the revised page proofs to him at his home in Massachusetts, and two days later—on the morning the story must go to press—the proofs come back to me with the word and the whole section we discussed crossed out. The top of the paragraph has been redone in pencil, done differently: the content is the same, but the tone, the feeling, of the passage has shifted. Elsewhere on the proofs, Updike has altered some bits of punctuation, crossed out things, reworded something else. This is the way the story will appear in the magazine, and, later on, the way it will read in the next collection of Updike's stories. The book will go into libraries, and into some school and college curricula, I imagine. The way the story reads—the words that students will find in the book and will believe were put down that way from the beginning, cut in stone—is only another stage in the struggle to get the writing to do its work: the version that the author and the editor had to let go of in the end.

The young writer's own galleys (with some of the queries and suggestions taken, others not) will be finished up, too, one day, and he and I will shake hands, out by the elevators. The story will appear next week—a great moment for us both. He is launched, and his tippy little canoe will soon disappear round the bend, on a journey whose duration no one can tell. I don't think he knows how short it may turn out to be, or how unimaginably long. "Let us hear from you," I say.

Reading short-fiction manuscripts can be wearing and wearisome from day to day and week to week. Every human situation, every sort of meeting or conversation, is something you have read before or know by heart. But then here comes a story—maybe only a couple of paragraphs in that story—and you are knocked over. Your morning has been changed; *you* are changed. A young woman and her sister, a nun, are talking in the back yard in the evening, and Sister Mary Clare says that she is going to take a vow of silence. "Do you think it's a bad idea?" she asks, and her sister says no, it's a good idea.

> "If you care, I'm not very happy," Sister said.
>
> "You were never happy," Melissa said. "The last time I saw you laughing was the day that swing broke. Remember that day?"

Spare and pure, the story murmurs along to its ending. It is intimate and painful and then it stops, and these particular lives go on. It is Mary Robison's "Sisters," her first acceptance here—though not, I believe, her first submission. It was written in 1977 and now feels like part of its time, but what I felt when I came to those lines is still fresh and strong. Every fiction editor here has had such an experience, and eagerly waits for the next one.

That same era brought a freshet of striking fiction from Ann Beattie: along with the painful, sensual feelings of loss in those stories came assemblages of characters apparently insatiable for company but increasingly alone— young men and women talking and cooking, arriving from somewhere, telling stories, picking up on ironic details, patting the dog, getting drunk, changing the music, driving to town for pizza, waking up in the night, waiting for something else to happen. The titles—"Vermont," "Tuesday Night," "Shifting," "Downhill," "A Vintage Thunderbird," "Colorado," and the rest—are a generational montage now, but the stories remain vital news for anyone who read them when they were just written and just out.

"Epiphanies" became the chic, dismissing word for scenes of this kind, but other forms of the short story, arriving here in due course, seemed only to reach the same ends by a different route. Bobbie Ann Mason's scrupulously detailed accounts of a younger K mart generation of Southerners, living in mobile homes and shabby condos and making do with the remnants of their parents' lost rural America, brought characters less inclined to linger on what was happening around them but perhaps no less aware that something had been going wrong in their world. Mason is such a sharp noticer of down-home detail—her people make Star Trek needlepoint pillows, own cats named Moon Pie, unexpectedly find the name "Navratilova" floating in their heads, and know that

"Radar Love" is a great driving song—that we sometimes don't give her her full due as a chronicler of American loss. I remember once asking whether her men and women felt emotion without always finding ways to show it, and she said, "I don't understand. I thought these stories were nothing but emotion." Then, a year or two later, while she was finishing her poignant post-Vietnam novel, *In Country,* a section of which ran here in 1985, she called me and said, "The emotion has turned up. I don't think I can *stand* much more of this."

We editors wait for whatever it is that the writers are trying to discover, and sometimes it arrives here in surprising forms. Once, it arrived in a flash—a gas explosion in a parking lot, where some kids were listening to Bruce Springsteen over their radios and had flicked their lighters during "Born in the U.S.A." That 1988 story, Alan Sternberg's "Blazer," was the first of his gritty, eloquent panoramas of southern Connecticut mechanics and builders and carpenters and cops and landfill inspectors toughing out hard times and industrial decline, along with their wives—who, all in all, were handling it a lot better than they were.

Stories and groups of stories work differently, and may require editors and readers to learn their particular tone and language before they can reach us, sometimes while an author is also struggling to find a direction or an opening that is not yet clear. Now and then, a writer stakes out an entire region of the imagination and of the countryside— one thinks of Cheever, Salinger, Donald Barthelme, and Raymond Carver, and now Alice Munro and William Trevor—which becomes theirs alone, marked in our minds by unique inhabitants and terrain. Writers at this level seem to breathe the thin, high air of fiction without effort, and we readers, visiting on excursion, feel a different thrumming in our chests as we look about at a clearer, more acute world than the one we have briefly departed. Reading Alice Munro's tales (the old word fits here) brings back for me, every time, the mood of thrilling expectancy with which I read the entrancing events in all those variously tinted fairy-story collections of my childhood—"The Blue Fairy Book," "The Yellow Fairy Book," "The Grey Fairy Book," and the rest. Trevor's stories, by contrast, are quieting, but with the awful calm of acceptance: his precise, deadly stitchings of country or family circumstances and cruelties leave their victims, for the most part, silent or almost decorously murmurous in resignation.

Ruth Prawer Jhabvala's stories, arriving here (on crinkly, tightly typed airmail paper) from India in a steady stream through the sixties and seventies, moved at a pace that sometimes made me fidget or sigh impatiently for more action and swifter developments—but only while I was still in the early pages. Reading along, I would find myself slowing, and listening to the sounds and hours of a different continent, as I grew aware of the grinding societal weight with which lives were being fixed, in comical or gruesome or affecting fashion, in the multilayered modern India she knew so well. Mrs. Jhabvala, who is Polish but is married to an Indian architect, wrote, in the introduction to her last collection, *Out of India,* of her deep discomfort with the hypocrisies and ironies of her second country. "I have no heart for these things here," she said, and, "All the time I know myself to be on the back of this great animal of poverty and backwardness." Almost in self-defense, it appears, she watched and wrote. Her stories can be satirical (a wealthy, Anglicized young Indian, making out with a similarly modernized girl on a date, thinks, I am kissing a Parsee), or simultaneously touching and tough-minded (an old woman attempts to explain the lifelong passion that keeps her close to the elderly, Dutch-born sahib who has been her careless lover), or scarifying (in a similar situation, a police superintendent sexually mounts his Muslim mistress while encouraging her to pray out loud, after her fashion, on her knees). Jhabvala's fiction runs more to novels these days, and since leaving India she has given most of her attention to screenwriting, as her Oscar-winning screenplays for the long-established Merchant-Ivory production company attest. It would be ungrateful to complain.

The movies have also snatched away a different but no less valued contributor, Woody Allen. Most of his work for this magazine, to be sure, came in the form of wild parodies and casuals, which isn't quite what we're talking about here, but at least one submission, "The Kugelmass Episode," is a dazzling short story, a Koh-i-noor of the form—not the first attribute that would come to mind while one is wheezing or pounding one's thigh in happiness over the C.C.N.Y. humanities professor Sidney Kugelmass, who, through the ministrations of a magician, is able to bring the live Emma Bovary to New York (he stashes her at the Plaza) and, conversely, to visit her at Yonville. Allen's modest early submissions here so resembled the work of his literary hero S. J. Perelman that I had to remind him that we already had the original on hand; he saw the point and came up with the remedy, almost overnight. Those first casuals also seemed to carry a joke, or sometimes two or three jokes, in every sentence— something that didn't work as well on the page as it did when one heard the same stuff during one of Woody's standup routines at the Bitter End. "*Fewer* laughs?" he said doubtfully, and, horrified at the thought, I nodded yes—yes, please.

"Whatever Works" should be the sampler that a fiction editor keeps affixed to his wall, or up over the water cooler. Mary Robison's story "Yours" seemed to have some missing manuscript pages when it turned up in the mail in 1980, but after I'd read its seven hundred and ninety words it was plain that a single line more would be much less. "We" was the title of Mary Grimm's 1988 story about a Midwestern working-class neighborhood of young newly married women friends, and the pronoun was repeated through multiple scenes, in paragraph after paragraph, as the group became less obsessed with sex and more with children, tried out recipes and new jobs, and grew older and more private together. The "we" was an impossibility, a trick, but one that became more pleasing and useful and right as the story moved to its terrific conclusion.

You never know. Edith Templeton's engaging first-person stories of her childhood in the grand-monde nurseries and castles of Czechoslovakia in the nineteen-twenties, which ran here thirty years ago and more, offered no preparation for "The Darts of Cupid," in 1968, a rending erotic love story about a married British woman working in the United States War Office outside London during the Second World War: a novella of power and perfection. Twenty-three years passed, and then here came her "Nymph & Faun," a twisted tale about money and wills and antique silver and marital cruelty that unfolds, at length, in a writhingly intimate conversation between an art dealer and a reclusive older woman, a widow, who understand each other because each can speak the drawling, edged, deadly language of the British upper crust. Mrs. Templeton, who lives in Bordighera, on the Italian Riviera, readily admits that most of her stories are true stories, but this time the mining and extraction of a clear line of events from her many pages of manuscript, and then her early and late galley proofs (on which her interpolations, done in green ink, ran to dogs and artists, British naval parlance, psychiatry, Mayfair scandals, quotations from Dante and Isaac Singer and Thomas Mann, visits to a Maharaja and the King of Nepal, Hemingway's suicide, and the workings of international art dealerships), produced from each of us long letters filled with questions and explanations but set down in tones of trust and mutual pleasure over the work we were engaged in together. It almost made me wish I'd been an antiquarian, so that I could concentrate on keeping hold of things instead of taking them out. We parted at last (we have never met), after exchanging a final thick set of airmailed galleys and agreeing that it was time to push this child out the door to fend for itself. I have at hand a page of her correspondence, discussing point 14, on galley 20, where she describes a figure of Dürer's, in the story. "I'd like it to stand—hood, scythe, hourglass . . . death being alone, and not wanting to be had up for speeding." And she adds, "As Goethe said of a painter, 'He doesn't paint red velvet, but the idea of it.'" Her stories, she wrote to me farther along in this letter, were "outside facts underpainted with subjective feelings"—a definition of fiction that will do as well as any other.

What becomes clear is that we can't sum up this tough, shifting, indefinable medium with these samplings, or talk about a few *New Yorker* story writers while excluding the vital many, including those scores of contributors who gave us one or two or three wonderful works of fiction and then, for one reason or another, or for no apparent reason, could not or did not write more. To convey some idea of the long flow of fiction here, I can do no more than list a handful of splendid contributors, whose names and work will have to stand for the rest: Eudora Welty, Mavis Gallant, Gabriel Garcìa Márquez, Nancy Hale, Brian Friel, Jean Stafford, Jean Rhys, Edward Newhouse, Robert M. Coates, Peter Handke, Roald Dahl, Deborah Eisenberg, Milan Kundera, Mark Helprin, Michael Chabon, Tom Drury, Doris Lessing, Shirley Hazzard, Frederick Barthelme, Peter Taylor, Laurie Colwin, Jamaica Kincaid, Alice Adams, Cynthia Ozick, Nicholson Baker, Thom Jones.

There have been stories in this magazine that felt like nothing in the language that had come before, and there is great pleasure for me in thinking back to some of our predecessor fiction editors—among them Katharine White and Gus Lobrano and William Maxwell—and imagining what they must have felt when they first read John Cheever's "The Enormous Radio" (or "Goodbye, My Brother" or "The Country Husband"); Frank O'Connor's "My Da"; Shirley Jackson's "The Lottery"; J. D. Salinger's "A Perfect Day for Bananafish" and "For Esmé—with Love and Squalor"; Vladimir Nabokov's "Lance"; Harold Brodkey's "Sentimental Education"; Muriel Spark's "The Prime of Miss Jean Brodie"; and many others.

It's funny, too, to look back at myself, thirty years ago, opening the stories from Donald Barthelme (with his name typed at the top left corner of the manila envelope) that first brought us his pasteups and headlines, the falling dog, the pitched street battles with bands of Comanches, the lost fathers, Eugénie Grandet and Montezuma and Hokie Mokie, and the seven men—Bill, Hubert, Kevin, and the others—living with Snow White while she dreams of princes and pushes her shopping cart. "What *is* this?" subscribers asked indignantly, and though it wasn't always easy to frame an answer, what we all knew for certain, editors and readers (most of them) alike, was that we were lucky.

The new is alluring, but not always what matters most. What is more pleasing to a long-term editor or a loyal subscriber than to watch a master of fiction—a Prospero or a Jefferson of the form—as he walks his thematic acres and then, once again, falls to work? John Updike, unfailingly curious and spirited and reflective, circles back to the Maples, or to his native Pennsylvania small town, or to his mother and her death, reopening and revisiting lives and connections he has been setting down in these pages for forty years; and some of the late stories—"A Sandstone Farmhouse," "His Mother Inside Him," "Playing with Dynamite"—carry a grave power not touched by him before. William Maxwell goes home to his boyhood in Lincoln, Illinois, still again, to bring back a shocking sixty-year-old murder (that novel, *So Long, See You Tomorrow,* ran here in 1979), or to tell about his brother's terrible accident, or to reconsider the complex, silent lives of the black servants in his family's house and in other houses then, and, if we think at first that we have been there before, the story, without fail, will show us why this trip was essential for him and for us.

Weeks and stories go by, and one of the records that are being run up, one realizes, is a life's work. V. S. Pritchett is as old as the century, and, while there is little about him that feels monumental, he is England's grand master of the short story and our language's presiding man of letters. He has been a contributor to this magazine for forty-five years, and, if he has at last laid aside his pen, the total of his published pieces here (stories and incomparable reviews and critical works), which stands at a pausing hundred and four, will always suggest that the next one may turn up in tomorrow's mail. Reading the stories once again, we see the freedom he has felt with strangers and odd ducks, and hear his avidity for dialogue. Children and elders, clubmen and decorators, hairdressers and anti-

quarians and bullying menservants, cranky or sensual widows, and gardeners and shopkeepers and artists are on hand, in story after story, all crammed together, misunderstanding and mystifying each other, giving themselves away in noble or squalid fashion, startling themselves with life.

Sir Victor has always insisted that he is more craftsman than artist, and claims that plots are almost beyond him, but he is too modest. The three interconnected Noisy Brackett stories, which begin with "The Key to My Heart," are made up of car chases, crooked business dealings, drunkenness, gossip, class snobbery, and comic invention: the ingredients of a Feydeau farce, one might say, except that they are also stuffed with heartbreak and sexual suffering. Rereading them, you relish the craftsmanship, but then your eye is caught, once again, by something else. Birds, for instance. I had remembered " . . . and the rooks came out of the elms like bits of black paper," in "The Key to My Heart," but not "A soft owl flew over the lane." The short adjective, instead of the expected adverb, is art itself, and makes a place and a mood and a time of day, an entire scene, out of seven words.

Call back the interviewer. This is what we're looking for in the fiction line: We want that owl.

John E. Drewry

SOURCE: "A Study of *New Yorker* Profiles of Famous Journalists," in *Journalism Quarterly,* Vol. 23, No. 4, December, 1946, pp. 370-80.

[*An American educator and journalist, Drewry wrote on communications and American media. In the following excerpt, he surveys* New Yorker *profiles of famous journalists, including cartoonists, press agents, and radio commentators, that appeared during the magazine's first twenty years of publication.*]

When my *Post Biographies of Famous Journalists* appeared in 1942, Professor R. E. Wolseley, then of the Medill School of Journalism, Northwestern University, and now of Syracuse University, wrote, "I hope you will bring together the *New Yorker's* Profiles that deal with journalists . . . for that would make a good companion volume."

This suggestion, seconded by several other reviewers of the *Post* book, led to an examination of the *New Yorker* file and the preparation of this study of the Profiles of newspapermen, authors, publishers, cartoonists, press agents, playwrights, and radio commentators which appeared in this periodical during its first twenty years (1925-45).

. . . [One hundred and twelve] Profiles of journalists (using the term in the general sense to cover all types of writers) were published by the *New Yorker* during its first twenty years, or an average of five a year. The sketches of journalists appeared more frequently during the early years, but were longer in later years.

To read the names of those who were treated during this

twenty-year period is to know those who in the judgment of *New Yorker* editors were sufficiently in the limelight or of such stature as to warrant attention by a periodical which quickly became a kind of sociological barometer for the sophisticates and intellectuals. To be recognized by the *New Yorker,* even for castigation, satire, or ridicule, is in the nature of an achievement. Who, then, were the big names in journalism and literature from 1925 to 1945? . . .

Most of those in [the Profiles] are definitely "big names." With a few exceptions, they are persons whose identities are household words among both the literati and the working press. The fame of some of them has crossed professional boundaries, and they are as well known by the laity as movie actresses or men of military achievement. Clare Luce or the late Alexander Woollcott are examples.

More than being in the limelight, however, these are men and women of achievement, some of whom have made significant contributions to the particular phase of journalism or literature they happen to serve. The New York *Times* of today, for example, is in a sense a memorial to or the lengthened shadow of the late Adolph S. Ochs and Carr V. Van Anda. Again, although no longer published as a separate magazine, *Vanity Fair* was during its heydey but the journalistic counterpart of Frank Crowninshield, and as such earned for itself a permanent niche in the halls of American periodical history. Clare Luce (then Clare Boothe) also made her contribution to the success of *Vanity Fair* and, moreover, before there was a *Life,* or she had become Clare Luce, she tried to sell a then uninterested *Time* editor on the idea of a pictorial periodical. "I hear that you're getting out a picture magazine," she is reported by Margaret Case Harriman as having said to Mr. Luce when they first met in 1933. "Luce considered this remark, and replied, 'No. I don't think it would work.' 'But why not?' cried Clare. She had been one of the leaders in a futile campaign to turn the expiring *Vanity Fair* into a picture magazine, and the subject was dear to her . . . " Exactly how much credit she deserves for the picture magazine idea would be difficult to determine. She and Mr. Luce were married in 1935 and the new *Life* appeared in 1936.

If a difference may be made between literary journalism and the daily press, it should be pointed out that *New Yorker* Profiles lean somewhat in the direction of the former. Some of the subjects are associated in the public mind more with magazines and books than with newspapers— George Jean Nathan, Frank Crowninshield, Robert E. Sherwood, and Clare and Henry Luce, for example. Others, the working newspapermen, are not what *Time* calls newshawks, but rather they belong to the literati or executive class—persons like Alexander Woollcott, Heywood Broun, and Carr V. Van Anda. This distinction means that these *New Yorker* Profiles have a flavor somewhat different from that of the *Post Biographies.* In a word, each has something of the tone and spirit of the magazine. If the *Post* may be regarded as the roast beef and Irish potatoes of periodical journalism, the *New Yorker* is the champagne of the magazine world—a sparkling wine which provides much stimulation and some nourishment.

Of those treated in journalistic Profiles during the first twenty years of the *New Yorker,* three have been written about twice. Carr V. Van Anda, the celebrated managing editor of the New York *Times,* was the subject of an unsigned sketch March 7, 1925 (entitled simply "V. A."), and was again the subject of a Profile by Alva Johnston in 1935. The first piece on Mr. Van Anda was the first sketch of a newspaperman to appear in the *New Yorker* and came out when the magazine was less than a month old. The other two who have twice been written about in Profiles are Sinclair Lewis and Hendrik Willem van Loon. The first article on Mr. Lewis came early in the magazine's history. Entitled "In America's Image," it was published July 18, 1925, the year of the publication of *Arrowsmith,* and at the time of the great discussion of *Main Street* (1920) and *Babbitt* (1922). The other Profile of Mr. Lewis came a decade later (1934), and was by another equally eminent student of American mores—W. E. Woodward. The first sketch of Mr. van Loon was during the second year of the *New Yorker,* was signed by "Search-light," a pen-name which was often used with the early Profiles— probably an office device to mark the work of one or several staff members. The second van Loon biography came much later (1943), was much longer, and was written by Richard O. Boyer.

Only two of the writers of these Profiles have themselves been the subjects of such articles—Heywood Broun and Alexander Woollcott. Mr. Broun was written about in the October 1, 1927, issue by "R. A.," and himself did the piece on Charles Townsend Copeland ("The Passionate Professor") the following January 21. Mr. Woollcott, who had Profiled such worthies as Edwin L. James, George S. Kaufman, and Noel Coward, was treated by Wolcott Gibbs.

The longest Profiles have been those of Walter Winchell (six installments), William Randolph Hearst (five installments), Russell Birdwell (four installments), Roy Howard (four installments), Alexander Woollcott (three installments), Robert L. Simon and M. Lincoln Schuster (three installments), Hendrik Willem van Loon (three installments), Joseph Medill Patterson (three installments), Christy Walsh (three installments), and Nicholas Murray Butler (three installments).

Originally a short form of biography, the Profile during the years has evolved into a much longer and more detailed approach to personality delineation, with the result that the two-installment Profile is now fairly common. Many of the titles which appear subsequently in this article were in two parts—those, for example, of Walter B. Pitkin, Lucius Beebe, Dorothy Thompson, Robert S. Ripley, Ralph Ingersoll, and Somerset Maugham. (Some will wonder why reference is not made in this paragraph to the series on *Reader's Digest* by John Bainbridge. This series and several other journalistic Profiles do not fall within the first twenty-year period of the *New Yorker.*)

The 112 Profiles of journalists which were published 1925-45 are the work of sixty-five writers, who are both staff members and free-lance contributors. Geoffrey T. Hellman leads with eight, followed by Alva Johnston, seven; Alexander Woollcott, six; and Margaret Case Harriman and Wolcott Gibbs, five each. The unknown "Searchlight" also has five to his or her credit. Several Nobel and Pulitzer prize winners are among the writers and subjects of these Profiles.

What is more significant, however, than the statistical facts is an appraisal of the Profile as a literary form—its development and a comparison of it with biography as handled by other periodicals. "The interesting story to me," wrote Wolcott Gibbs in a letter (October 15, 1943) to the writer, "is the gradual development of the Profile from its very feeble beginning (*vide* your Nathan selection) to its present remarkably thorough form. . . . In essence, it is the story of Ross's ferocious curiosity about people—struggling against the mechanical limitations of a fifteen cent magazine and the lethargy of authors generally. . . . "

Although biography has always been a stock item with most magazines, only a few have so perfected their own patterns that they have come to be associated in the public mind with these periodicals. The *American Magazine,* under the editorship of John M. Siddall, featured inspirational biography—a kind of factual, up-to-the-minute Horatio Alger treatment of the lives of the successful. The *American Mercury,* under H. L. Mencken, stressed debunking biography. *Life,* with what it calls the "Close-up," uses a great many pictures. *Look* introduced the plan of paralleling its biographical articles with marginal notes by the subjects themselves. Other periodicals, from time to time, have tried various schemes for individualizing their handling of biography, but the fact remains that the *New Yorker* Profile is the most distinctive of magazine personality patterns and the best known, especially among the intelligentsia.

The Profile, as Clifton Fadiman once wrote, "is not a short biography. It's not a personality sketch. It's not an exercise in the apt arrangement of anecdote. It's not a *chronique scandalouse.* It's not an evaluation of character. It's all of these and none. It is—a Profile. . . . It is possible to make out a case for the Profile as a form of composition no less specific than the familiar essay, the sonnet, the one-act play. The Profile obeys certain rules. . . . An interesting profile can be made only of a person whose features are decided. In fact, mere regularity of outline does not lend itself to profiling." Subjects of Profiles, by and large, according to Mr. Fadiman, "some admirable, some (I think) hateful, some useful, some frivolous—all have a common quality. They jut out. They are literally outstanding."

These "outstanding" persons are usually not without their eccentricities. Some feel that the more eccentric an individual is, the better subject he is for a Profile. Such a person has more of what H. L. Mencken calls the "human juices," and is on that account a better specimen for the literary operating table and the "chaste, dispassionate manner of the clinic." Or, as Mr. Fadiman cleverly puts it, "Profiles are happiest when their subjects are wackiest."

Not only do Profile subjects have their share of eccentricities, but they are not always in sympathy with the mores of the herd. "The *New Yorker,*" writes Mr. Fadiman, "is read, by and large, by respectable people. Its Profiles, by and large, are about people who laugh at respectability. The connection is obvious."

From a literary and journalistic standpoint, the Profile (a term which was suggested during pre-publication days of the *New Yorker* by James Kevin McGinnis) is neither simple biography nor the superficial human interest story. It combines both—biographical facts and emotional appeal—but it goes much further. It is, in a sense, what Gamaliel Bradford liked to call "psychography"—a term of his own creation intended especially as a label for his own work.

"Psychography," wrote Mr. Bradford, "is the condensed, essential, artistic presentation of character. . . . Out of the perpetual flux of actions and circumstances that constitutes a man's whole life, it seeks to extract what is essential, what is permanent and vitally characteristic." Psychography, Mr. Bradford explained, often makes much of little and apparently trivial happenings, and so do these *New Yorker* Profiles, "A word spoken carelessly, a brief look or gesture, will sometimes tell us more of the history of a soul than elaborate pages of psychological analysis, and persons who are not at all trained in such analysis may interpret the word or the gesture with unerring skill," the American Lytton Strachey wrote. As an example, he cited Theodore Roosevelt as the kind of man to whom fishing was unattractive because it was too slow. Roosevelt's delight in rocking chairs revealed the restlessness of the man. "He killed mosquitoes as if they were lions, and lions as if they were mosquitoes."

There are many parallel instances in these Profiles. Henry Luce's impatience with trivial conversation is a case in point. "Prone he," writes Wolcott Gibbs, "to wave aside pleasantries, social preliminaries, to get at once to the matter in hand. . . . To ladies full of gentle misinformation he is brusque, contradictory, hostile; says that his only hobby is 'conversing with somebody who knows something.' "

The Profile has much informational value. Increasingly through the years thoroughness has been stressed, with the result that today some Profiles compare favorably with a master's thesis or a doctor's dissertation for adequacy of detail, balance, proportion, and other qualities associated with sound scholarship. But there is nothing pedantic about these Profiles. They have an incisive quality, a charm, and a flavor that few academic treatises ever attain. The *New Yorker* has long been famous for its wit and satire, and nowhere are these qualities more to be enjoyed than in the Profiles section.

Definitely "not . . . for the old lady in Dubuque" (Editor Harold Ross's original slogan for the periodical), the basic editorial conception of the *New Yorker* "was of caviar—to publish a weekly magazine of . . . delicate humor and satire, written *up* to the highest standard"—to quote from *Fortune*'s exhaustive study (August, 1934). "Anchor to the windward has been . . . (the) 'Profile' department. . . . "

Just as the Profile stands apart from other magazine biography, so is its preparation a literary process all its own.

It is much more than ordinary article-writing. Although only one name ordinarily appears as the author, such a piece represents the tedious and involved efforts and the considered judgment of many persons, including several editors. An article on Harold Ross and the *New Yorker* by Dale Kramer and George R. Clark in *Harper's* Magazine provides an inner sanctum picture of the production of a Profile, thus:

> When a writer is assigned to a Profile he sets carefully to work, turning over a vast amount of ground. He talks at length with the friends and enemies of the man he is writing about. He picks up gossip and weighs and checks it for possible truth. In effect, the writer acts as detective, prosecuting attorney, defense attorney, and lower-court judge. Ross himself sits in the high court.

> William Shawn, the "fact" editor-in-chief, is a frail-looking man blessed with great diplomatic ability. If he considers the Profile fairly complete he has it put into type before sending it to Ross for a final fixing. At the same time a staff of meticulous researchers headed by Frederick Packard are set to work checking the writer's facts and sources. Ross is usually in a towering rage before passing the third paragraph. He pencils such outbursts as "What mean?" and "Oh, my God" furiously into the margins, and upon coming across a piece of slang with which he is not familiar he is likely to accuse the writer of making it up. If a piece of pertinent information, such as the subject's birth date, is omitted, his indignation is boundless. Once he spent several happily profane hours when, by mistake, he read the second installment of a two-part Profile, thinking it was the first; about eighty important details had been covered in the first section and were therefore lacking in the part he was reading.

> Ross's comments are passed back to Shawn, who usually deletes the harsher terms before showing them to the writer. When the first proofs of Geoffrey Hellman's three-part piece on the Metropolitan Museum (for example) went back to the author there were one hundred and forty-seven numbered queries by Ross on them, and Hellman doesn't think this is a record. Sometimes Ross suggests shifting of emphasis, the switching of paragraphs; or he may order the whole sent to the writer for another trial. Being anything but nice, the writers send sharp criticism of Ross's editing back to him through diplomatic channels, and they often succeed in driving him from a strongly held point. Finally, when the author's job is done, Ross and the editors go to work with tiny hammers, pliers, and micrometers, pounding and twisting and testing sentences until the smooth, apparently effortless prose style of the *New Yorker* is achieved. No Lucely-written phrase finds its way into the magazine, unless with malice prepense.

Substantiating and supplementing what Messrs. Kramer and Clark have written, Mrs. Margaret Case Harriman in the foreword of her *Take Them Up Tenderly* gives a behind-the-scenes picture of how Profiles came into being—the persons who write them ("writers of Profiles . . . are a race apart"), how the facts are obtained ("Profile-writers interview their subjects . . . long and thoroughly . . . also . . . a number of (a) people who have long known and loved the subjects, and (b) people who have long known and hated the subjects"), and how the subjects of "Profiles" react (they "complain very little, considering the thoroughness of our reports").

Mrs. Harriman also tells how carefully Profiles are checked by the editors before publication. "The first version of a Profile comes back to its author with numbers pencilled in the margins corresponding to the numbers of notes and queries from editors, which are typed on separate pages and attached to the manuscript," she writes. "A good Profile-writer gets from twenty to thirty editors' queries. Practically perfect writers like Wolcott Gibbs and St. Clair McKelway seldom get more than five or six."

In the selection of journalists for Profile treatment, the *New Yorker*—possibly unintentionally—has anticipated a broadening of the meaning of the word *journalist* which has been the subject of comment recently among educators. Was Hendrik van Loon, for example, a journalist? What about Messrs. Simon and Schuster—to take two more from among the many who have been written about in the past twenty years? Certainly these and others in the list which follows are not journalists in the narrow dictionary meaning of the term. But, as Dr. Ralph D. Casey of the University of Minnesota has written, "the dictionary definition is inadequate. Journalism makes use of any . . . medium for the transmission of symbols which convey ideas, information, counsel and guidance, advertising, emotional attitudes." Journalism, in the broad sense, includes not only newspapers—small town dailies and weeklies as well as the great metropolitan journals—but also press associations and syndicates, certain phases of the radio, specialized magazines and trade journals, general magazines, various aspects of book publishing, advertising, publicity, much of the production and promotion work in motion pictures and the theater, and much editorial, instructional, and research work for schools, colleges, and social agencies. And by the same token, the term *journalist* includes all those who give responsible and creative direction to the multifarious agencies for the diffusion of intelligence.

Even this broad definition of journalism cannot be stretched, however, to include a few of those in the following list. Such persons as Franklin D. Roosevelt, Dr. Nicholas Murray Butler, Dr. John Dewey, Dr. Harry Emerson Fosdick, Dr. Newnan Leander Hoopingarner, Dr. A. S. W. Rosenback, Dr. John B. Watson, and Mae West are clearly on the periphery of journalism. But they are all authors, some have written for newspapers and magazines, and a few (notably Dr. Butler, President Roosevelt, and Miss West) are as much masters of the theory and practice of public opinion and its motivations as any teacher of journalism or newspaperman in the country. A psychologist could make much of the kinship of newspaper, magazine, and radio writers, artists, actors, educators, and ministers through *motivation*. All are stirred and propelled by a strong creative urge. All are articulate—much more so than workers in other businesses and professions. All derive their greatest satisfaction through the conception, gestation, and birth of brain children. . . .

As for the reaction of those who have been Profiled, Geoffrey T. Hellman . . . reports that "although some of my Profile subjects have threatened to sue me for libel or to molest me physically, [some] remained friendly, even after publication. Frank Crowninshield went so far as to present me with the gold pencil which Jimmy Speyer gave *him,* and which I mention in the Profile; I would like to emphasize the fact that this gift was made *after* publication, and that Mr. Crowninshield gave me no inkling of such an attention during my many interviews with him. Dick Simon and Max Schuster seemed a little hurt during the first few weeks after the articles on them appeared, but they brightened up after the *Reader's Digest* published extracts from the pieces, retaining only the more innocent passages, and our relations are now cordial, or seem so to me. Apart from the Crowninshield pencil, the only gift I recall from a subject was an imitation fried egg, which the Imitation Food Products Company of Brooklyn sent me after I wrote a 'Talk of the Town' piece about them. I gave this to my maternal grandmother."

Mr. Hellman says that all his profiles have "been improved, before publication, by editing in the office, notably at the hands of H. W. Ross, the editor of the magazine, and William Shawn, the managing editor"—a sentiment which undoubtedly is shared by other Profile writers.

Matthew Arnold has written that "journalism is literature in a hurry." Lawrence Martin has said that "literature . . . is simply journalism that has showed lasting interest—journalism with staying powers." Both these statements are applicable to the Profiles. . . . They may have been hastily done—there is almost as much pressure in the preparation of the content of a weekly such as the *New Yorker* as in the city rooms of some metropolitan dailies. But however much of a hurry may have marked their preparation and publication, they have "staying powers." Professor Martin has said that "the literature of today was the journalism of yesterday; and the best of journalism of today will be the literature of tomorrow." This statement, too, is largely applicable here. One cannot read dozens of Profiles . . . without a growing admiration for Harold Ross and his associates, who have in two decades developed the Profile into a form of literature which is as distinctive as biography itself and which may now be regarded as the hallmark of personality delineation at its best.

M. Thomas Inge

SOURCE: "*The New Yorker* Cartoon and Modern Graphic Humor," in *Studies in American Humor,* n.s. Vol. 3, No. 1, Spring, 1984, pp. 61-73.

[*Inge is an American critic and educator who has described himself as "a literary and cultural historian with strong interests in editing, bibliography, and criticism," as well as "nineteenth- and twentieth-century American literature and culture, with specific focuses on American humor, Southern ethnic writing, twentieth-century fiction, American literature abroad, popular culture, comic art, biography, and intellectual history." In the following excerpt, Inge examines the influence of* New Yorker *cartoons on American pictorial humor.*]

When Harold Ross issued his often quoted prospectus for his new magazine in 1925, he noted in the first sentence, "The *New Yorker* will be a reflection in the word and picture of metropolitan life." Thus the graphics were to share equal importance with the text. And if the *New Yorker* has, as one historian of modern magazines claims, "changed the character of American humor, introduced a new approach to magazine biography, set high standards of reporting, and thereby influenced the course of American journalism" [Theodore Peterson, *Magazines in the Twentieth Century,* 1964], it has also profoundly influenced the development of the American gag cartoon and established the standards against which the works of all modern practicing cartoonists are measured.

When American readers picked up the premier issue of February 21, 1925 from their newsstands, the first thing they saw was a cartoon on the cover. This was a drawing in watercolor of a Regency figure of aristocratic bearing dressed in top hat and a riding habit with a monocle in his gloved hand. (A similar figure had appeared in 1894 on the cover of the first issue of the Chicago literary magazine *The Chap-Book,* whose high literary standards served to inspire many American magazines who sought a sophisticated audience.) There is some suggestion of a pastoral setting by way of an abstract butterfly and a cloud. The figure, as rendered by artist Rea Irvin, eventually was given a name by writer Corey Ford—Eustace Tilley—and it came to symbolize *The New Yorker* itself and its reputation for urbane wit and commentary. The cover is reprinted each anniversary issue. From the beginning, then, graphic and verbal humor went hand in hand.

It was under Ross's eccentric but superb editorship from the beginning until his death in 1951 that the *New Yorker* cartoon was formulated and achieved its definitive and influential form. As was true with the entire premise for the magazine, what was wanted was vaguely somewhere in Ross's mind, so discovering the right artists and styles was a hit or miss proposition and usually frustrating for those around him. At the beginning Ross saw a possible model in the durable British humor magazine *Punch,* and he would leaf through recent issues with Rea Irvin, his first art editor, and point out examples of the kind of thing he thought suitable. While the *Punch* artists satirized contemporary fads, fashions, and social mores, they did so with all the stilted style of magazine illustrators more interested in gracing the page with an attractive drawing than in creating a comic image. While a few Punch cartoons inspired direct imitations in the early issue of *The New Yorker,* it was soon clear to everyone that a more original approach had to be found, some distinctive concept that would establish a modern comic art for the modern sophisticated reader.

In the first place, Ross asked of the cartoon the question literary critics were asking of a modern piece of fiction, which by then was distinguished by its consistent use of point of view. As the reader, he wanted to know "Where am *I* in this picture?" That is, he felt that the reader's vantage point should be one that reasonably would allow him

William Shawn.

or her to eavesdrop, observe the action, or even be a part of the proceedings being humorously treated. This was a question seldom considered by most cartoonists of the time. His second question was more subtle than it sounded: "Who's talking?" Ross believed that there should be no confusion in the reader's mind about who is talking to whom, as was often the case in contemporary cartoons which required captions identifying the speakers, as in the style of a play script.

These concerns over point of view and dialogue not only made contributing artists more conscious craftsmen, but they lead gradually to a major innovation in comic art and made *The New Yorker* the most influential force in the evolution of the single panel gag cartoon of this century. Cartoons in other humorous publications of the time, such as *Punch* or the American *Life,* where Rea had worked as an art editor before joining the staff of *The New Yorker,* had at least two lines of dialogue, usually introduced by the names of the speakers, more often than not simply identified by *he* and *she.* In a 1904 *Life* cartoon by Charles Dana Gibson, for example, a gentleman caller inquires, "You might ask your mistress if she is at home." The maid responds, "It's no use, sir. She saw you coming."

Sometimes the captions are lengthy and insufferably tedious, as in the following for a drawing by a *Life* artist named Foster:

Mrs. Pileitton (To her coachman): "James, I

trust that you are an attendant at religious exercises?"

"Oh, yes, mem. I goes as often as I has the chance, mem."

"And I trust that you feel it your duty to lead such a life here as will assure you a place among the good in the next world?"

"Oh, yes, mem, I tries to. Thank you kindly, mem."

"I am glad of it James. I have been so much pleased with your services that it is a real comfort to me to know that if we are permitted to have coachmen in Heaven, I may continue to employ you there."

Whatever humor resides in these two examples is hopelessly lost in a social decorum and a class structure that no longer exist, but what is useful for our purposes is to note that in neither case does the drawing add anything to the effect. Basically magazine cartoons before Ross were merely illustrated dialogues with punchlines that carried the full freight of the comedy. The single line caption was the exception rather than the rule. Ross was personally irritated by the classic two-line joke to the extent that he published one he particularly detested in each anniversary issue of *The New Yorker* but with its lines transposed:

Pop: A man who thinks he can make it in par.

Johnny: What is an optimist, pop?

In his drive for originality and distinction, Ross initiated a trend towards simplicity in dialogue, clarity in the identity of the speaker, and integrity in the relationship between pictures and text. This resulted in the development of the successful *The New Yorker* style one-line cartoon. All of the earlier humor magazines, European and American, had used the one-line cartoon from time to time, but not with a systematic eye toward developing its full comic potential. If the one-liner was to work best, there had to be no doubt about who was speaking because it was the picture that came first in the eye of the viewer and the speaker afterwards. Either a clear verbal gesture had to be evident in the drawing or the caption had to infer the speaker unmistakably, principle which in the application would immediately distinguish the poorly thought out and carelessly executed cartoons from the thoughtful ones. Finally, both picture and caption had to work together simultaneously to achieve a total effect which neither would have alone. This last transition rendered most of the contemporary humor magazines old-fashioned and quaintly irrelevant. In sum, Ross's standards marked a singular new development in the history of graphic humor here and abroad. The practice of effective cartooning would never be the same.

The change Ross had accomplished was viewed by some as a natural kind of evolutionary process, at least according to one report of a luncheon conversation between *New Yorker* staff writer James Kevin McGuinness, British cartoonist and writer Oliver Herford, and famed artist and then publisher of *Life* Charles Dana Gibson:

Gibson remarked to Herford and McGinness that he did not think the *New Yorker* would last. Herford disagreed. *Punch,* he said, had succeeded with the long narrative joke below the cartoons. *Life* had succeeded by condensing the joke to the he-she formula. *The New Yorker* had condensed it further to the one-line joke and so, he thought, could not fail.

Ross's interest in simplicity and direct impact on the reader was so intense, in fact, that he would have been happy to abandon the caption altogether, had that been possible. A cartoon which told its own story without recourse to punchline seemed to him the ultimate form of graphic humor. But cartoonists who could achieve pure pantomime and yet maintain humor of a complex or sophisticated nature were very rare. The closest Ross could come was a cartoonist named Otto Soglow who specialized in very simple line drawings without benefit of shading or complicating detail. One of his creations for *The New Yorker,* a mute ruler of a fantasy kingdom simply called *The Little King,* made the transition to the pages of the color Sunday funny papers as a popular character, but most of his work, while it seemed to delight Ross, was oddly naive and unsophisticated for the pages of the magazine, particularly when compared with the highly talented work that was emerging under Ross's tutelage.

One by one Ross discovered and brought into his fold of regular contributors some of America's finest cartooning talents. In the first year of publication Ross used a drawing submitted by a fashion illustrator named Helen Hokinson. It featured a plump woman hanging over a rail to wave bon voyage to a departing ship at the pier. She was the first of the soon to be famous Hokinson Girls, a collection of chubby, ample-bosomed, society women who carried out their responsibilities as club-woman in a befuddled, vague, but amiable way. Although her cartoons constituted one of *The New Yorker*'s most popular features until her death in an air accident in 1949, and she had no more avid a set of followers than the actual matrons she satirized, her humor today would be considered antifeminist and demeaning.

One day a carelessly dressed but handsome young man of aristocratic appearance dropped off at the office some drawings for consideration. The son of a prominent New York family, Curtis Arnoux Peters was then living the bohemian life of a musician in jazz age speakeasies until Ross signed him up under the name of Peter Arno. His early cartoons featured two tipsy slap-stick women called the Whoops Sisters, but he abandoned them despite their popularity for a more worldy-wise series featuring chorus girls, kept women, and businessmen in pursuit of hedonistic pleasures. His lecherous gentlemen and young women established a genre which such publications as *Esquire* and *Playboy* would later imitate with endless variation.

Also among these early contributors were George Price, distinguished by a clean but expressive line used to portray the eccentricities of mean-tempered old men and working-class couples (the only member of that original group still drawing today in his eighties with over 3,000 cartoons published); Gluyas Williams, who specialized in neatly outlined and stylized depictions of the life and times of the

American businessman and suburbanite (well-known also for his splendid illustrations for the books and essays of Robert Benchley); Alan Dunn, who mastered the use of charcoal and grease pencil in his broad satires of urban living and was one of the most prolific of the *New Yorker* cartoonists (over 1,900 cartoons and 9 covers published between 1926 and 1974); Gardner Rea, whose strong sense of design and balance resulted in pleasing patterns; and last but not least James Thurber, a very special case.

Through his friendship with E. B. White, with whom he would collaborate on a book, *Is Sex Necessary?,* in 1929, Thurber was hired as a member of the editorial staff (even though his writings had been rejected 20 times before a submission was accepted). White and Thurber established, through their "Talk of the Town" columns, the *New Yorker* style of humorous comment, but Thurber also wanted to do cartoons. His drawing style was so naive and undisciplined, his ideas were so absurd and whimsical, and the end products so eccentric and individual, however, that Ross resisted using them. When he yielded, it was these very idiosyncrasies that won over the readers, and Thurber's irresistible sketches of the seal in the bedroom, the battle between the sexes (including the seventeen-part series "The War Between Men and Women"), implausible dogs and other creatures, and bewildered little men overcome by the complexities of existence—these became inextricably associated with the entire *New Yorker* school of humor. When critics complained to Ross that Thurber was a "fifth-rate" artist, Ross whimsically defended him by asserting that he was at least "third-rate." The truth is that Thurber as a cartoonist was delightfully sui generis and without equal in American humor.

In addition to Al Frueh, Mary Petty, and Carl Rose, who were on the list of regular contributors at the start, the 1930s witnessed the addition of a number of brilliant wielders of pen and ink, including Charles Addams, Perry Barlow, Whitney Darrow, Jr., Robert Day, Richard Decker, Syd Hoff, C. E. Martin, Garrett Price, Barbara Shermund, William Steig, and Richard Taylor. In the 1940s, these would be joined by another talented generation, including Sam Cobean, Joseph Farris, Dana Fradon, Frank Modell, Mischa Richter, Saul Steinberg, and Barney Tobey.

Perhaps one of the things that accounted for the success of *The New Yorker* in its golden years from 1925 to Ross's death in 1951 was the fact that it had steady unbroken editorial leadership, and the same has largely been true in the cartoon department with Rea Irvin serving as art director from 1925 to 1939 and James Geraghty succeeding him until 1973. While Ross always made the final decision, he liked for the weeding out to be a group process, with selected members of the staff sitting in on the selection of finalists after an initial selection by the art director. Thus a group sensibility was brought to bear in achieving the *New Yorker* style of comic art.

Also, the cartoons themselves were often the products of a staff effort rather than the works of individual artists. Sometimes the artist was supplied with an idea for a cartoon, other times the caption would be changed after the cartoon was submitted, or even the cartoon alone might be purchased with the staff providing the punchline. One of the best known cartoons to appear in the magazine was the result of such collaborative effort in 1928. Carl Rose had submitted a cartoon featuring a young mother at the dinner table with her daughter, but none found his caption, now forgotten, suitable. E. B. White saw the drawing and suggested a caption which would become famous: "It's broccoli, dear," says the mother, and the daughter replies, "I say it's spinach, and I say the hell with it." The shocking sophistication of the child is the incongruity at the heart of the comedy here, but so appropriate was the cartoon's depiction of a response to a common situation that "spinach" entered the language as a term of disparagement and the girl's retort came to signify "Don't confuse me with the facts when I want to indulge my prejudices." Ironically, this sort of two-line caption was the very thing Ross was working away from in his insistence on the single-line caption.

Other *New Yorker* cartoons have made lasting contributions to the American language. In 1941 a cartoon by Peter Arno appeared which featured an aircraft designer with plans under his arm walking away from a plane crash to which the military, ground crew, and ambulance are racing (the pilot, fortunately, we see at a distance has bailed out with a parachute). The caption, "Well, back to the old drawing board," has become a standard response to a situation which has failed to develop as planned. A 1950 cartoon by Alex Graham, in which a flying saucer has landed in a field and its two extraterrestrial occupants are talking to a horse, has the punchline "Take me to your president." Slightly transposed to "Take me to your leader," this phrase was repeated to humorous effect in thousands of other cartoons, films, and visual media.

Three of what are probably the best known cartoons in the world appeared in *The New Yorker,* two of them by James Thurber from the early 1930s. In one, a seal is leaning over the headboard of a bed while the wife complains to the husband: "All right, have it your way—you heard a seal bark!" In the second, a fencer has neatly decapitated his opponent with the exclamation "Touche!" The third by Charles Addams, a specialist in macabre humor, is from 1940 and has no caption. It features a mysterious skier who has somehow maneuvered a tree so that one ski track appears on each side. In all three it is the inexplicable, the surprise, and the mystery of the event which intrigue the reader.

Just as there is really no such thing as a *New Yorker* short story, general belief to the contrary, there is no such thing as a *New Yorker* cartoon. As British cartoonist William Hewison facetiously put the argument, the *New Yorker* artists "produced four drawings: a sugar daddy and dewy blonde; two hoboes sitting on a park bench in Central Park; a drunk te/te-a'-te/te with a barman; a man and wife getting into a car after a dinner party." Such a summary points up the problem of attempting to identify a typical cartoon from the magazine. Each of these scenes serves to remind us of individual cartoonists, and the truth is that *The New Yorker* has served primarily as a vehicle for major comic talents to develop their individual styles and distinctive visions.

If there is any single thread that connects the thousands of cartoons to appear in *The New Yorker,* it is the demands they place on the reader. One must be well-read, in touch with culture of the past and present, sensitive to the eccentricities of human nature, and familiar with the latest trends in society, politics, and the mass media, to understand and appreciate them. Along with other developments in film, television, and the graphic arts, the *New Yorker* cartoon has served to create a visually literate society, but one which must also be literate in traditional ways to respond to the sophisticated humor of the subject or situation.

Under the editorial direction of William Shawn, who succeeded Harold Ross in 1951, and art director James Geraghty, *The New Yorker* continued to seek out and use the work of each decade's best cartoonists in the 1950s and 1960s. Eldon Dedini, Lee Lorenz, Henry Martin, Charles Saxon, and James Stevenson became contributors in the 1950s, and in the 1960s were added George Booth, Mort Gerberg, William Hamilton, Bernard Handelsman, Edward Koren, Warren Miller, Ronald Searle, and Robert Weber. Lee Lorenz succeeded Geraghty as art director in 1973 and has added to this stellar list such artists as Sam Gross, Arnie Levin, Robert Mankoff, Lou Myers, Bill Woodman, and Jack Ziegler. Clearly there has been no let down in effort to maintain the quality of the *New Yorker* tradition in comic art.

Some, however, feel that the first 25 years were the best and that now the magazine has settled into a comfortable routine that is all too predictable and only smugly humorous. William Hewison, one of the best commentators on the art of the cartoon, has put it this way:

> Ross's boys shook the old cartoon formula to pieces and kicked most of the bits away—where formerly it was static, congested and ponderously naturalistic they went after simplicity, directness and movement. They were after a humor that was essentially quick and visual. One would guess that every cartoon produced today—in Britain or Europe or anywhere else—is in direct descent from *The New Yorker* humor drawings of that period.

One would not argue with this conclusion, yet *The New Yorker* is the one publication to which readers still turn for America's best graphic comedy. The editors receive today over 2,500 submissions a week from which approximately 20 are selected for publication, and most of these come from the 40 to 50 artists on whose work they have first option. *The New Yorker* remains for cartoonists the most prestigious place to publish and for readers the most consistently entertaining source of that form of humor it has itself revitalized and transformed for the twentieth century—the cartoon.

George Woodcock

SOURCE: "In the Beginning There Was Ross . . . ," in *Commonweal,* Vol. CII, No. 8, July 4, 1978, pp. 247-48.

[*Woodcock is a Canadian educator, editor, and critic best known for his biographies of George Orwell and Thomas*

Merton. He also founded Canada's most important literary journal, Canadian Literature, *and has written extensively on the literature of Canada. In the following excerpt, he offers an analysis of the influence of the* New Yorker *on American journalism and literature.*]

It is hard to think of an internationally read and celebrated magazine that, in many of its aspects, is more localized than *The New Yorker*. From the beginning it has been an intimate voice—though not of course the only one—of a great city. But that great city happened, during the most important years of the magazine that bore its name, to become for a while the leading center of world culture. In the far away days of the Twenties, when Harold Ross emerged as a bear of letters out of rustic fastnesses to found—almost out of a hatred of sophistication—one of the age's most sophisticated periodicals, New York was still a relatively humble third in comparison with Paris and London. By no means all American writers then recognized it as their cultural center, and the great postwar trek to Europe (which Wilde had anticipated years before with his quip that all good Americans go to Paris when they die) had emphasized its unattractiveness at that time in comparison with the major European capitals. Better, then, to imagine one was starving in the Quartier Latin than to know one was prospering in Manhattan!

But by the peak age of *The New Yorker*—Ross's last decade and Shawn's first—the situation had changed; between the end of World War II and the mid-sixties, the lights of La Ville Lumière had notably dimmed and London was finding that Angry Young Men were also Dull Young Men; then the most dazzling work in literature, in painting, in the theater, seemed to radiate from a New York that had gathered to itself an astonishing number of the surviving talents of the shattered Old World.

In such a setting *The New Yorker* burnt with a brilliant if not exactly a gem-like flame, and it became one of the vehicles by which native-born Americans demonstrated that the great war renaissance on the western shore of the Atlantic was not merely a matter of acquired émigré talent, for surprisingly few of the important writers and artists who created and sustained the journal were born beyond American boundaries. Indeed it was an important role of *The New Yorker* to sustain American writers—like Edmund Wilson and James Thurber, John Updike and John Cheever, Truman Capote and E. B. White, Dorothy Parker and John O'Hara—who became respected figures in world literary estimation.

There are less dramatic but equally striking ways in which, remaining firmly rooted in its local soil, *The New Yorker* laid its mark not merely on North American journalism, but also on the whole North American middlebrow way of thinking (and here I am including Canada as well as the United States). Two months ago, when a staff writer from a Toronto magazine proposed to write a kind of long critical-personal piece on me, he called it "a Profile," and I remembered that Ross at *The New Yorker* was the originator of that special kind of interim biography which fills the space between the interview article and the book-length life. And a month before that, when one of my books received a favorable short notice in *The New*

Yorker, I was astonished, by the number of phone calls I received, to realize that even among Canadian academics such an accolade was worth more than—for example—the two-page review in the London *Times Educational Supplement,* which aroused perhaps one-tenth of the attention of three column inches in *The New Yorker*.

The balance of the local and the universal, the evanescent and the timeless; perhaps that is the true model not only for good journalism (to which *The New Yorker* has always remained dedicated) but also for those excursions into fields of wider interest (so notably exemplified in, say, Edmund Wilson's essays and Shirley Jackson's stories and Theodore Roethke's poems) that have brought *The New Yorker* a sustained readership not only outside the metropolis but even outside the country. In this direction, with its in-depth investigations and its many-parted profiles as well as with its fiction and poetry, *The New Yorker* has carried on admirably the tradition of journalism for more than the passing day that began with the great English and Scottish quarterlies more than a century and a half ago. Yet this magazine in which Hazlitt and Lamb might have found a congenial place has still remained a useful weekly journal of events and affairs for culturally-minded Americans of New York and the seaboard states.

How has it all been done? How has this journal of conservative appearance, whose outdated and obstructive layout often exasperate one to the point of almost—but never finally—cancelling one's subscription, carried on so well for so long? The two books I am reviewing, both written by men who have spent years in *The New Yorker* office as staff writers, are interesting principally for the insight they give into the actual creative mechanisms that have sustained *The New Yorker*.

What Brendan Gill reveals in *Here at The New Yorker* is likely to tell writers on the outside much about why they have never been on the inside. For it becomes clear that, under both Ross and the more literarily inclined Shawn, *The New Yorker* was always run like a modified newspaper office. Most of the work, even by writers we consider figures in their own right, has been done in the shabby little cubicles on the spot, and the journal has been sustained—despite internal feuds and jealousies—by the kind of *esprit de corps* that comes from habitual association in the same place. One realizes, reading this often appealing account of people whose names have become familiar over the years, how deeply *The New Yorker* is set in the physical landscape of hotels and bars and streets where its writers have lived and drunk and worked together. In some ways it reminds one of the small, physically tight literary worlds of Johnson's London and Baudelaire's Paris, and certainly it has resulted in a magazine cohesive in form, idiosyncratic in character and unexpectedly sustained in its level of journalism.

At the same time, it is surprising how few *New Yorker* stars have turned out good book writers. *The New Yorker* profile tends to take on a relaxed, unstructured form which rambles sympathetically through the advertisement-broken pages of the magazine, but which seems limp and unurgent within the covers of a book. There is the same kind of limpness about Brendan Gill's book, which is really a series of anecdotes and personal sketches loosely connected by a running account of the two editors, Ross and Shawn. Anyone wanting to mine it for a history of American literary manners or New York journalism will find it useful, but in general it is marred not only by prolixity but also by the irritatingly self-complacent persona that Brendan Gill projects.

Thurber's persona, as projected by Gill, is unpleasant, and it is hardly more attractive in Burton Bernstein's biography, *Thurber.* Bernstein also was a staff writer at *The New Yorker,* but his prose suggests that little rubbed off. "Thurber had just simply forgot about it." "Maybe he was just starting to wise up." "It was all a barrel of laughs for a while." Typical sentences, these, in a book that is never more than plodding and trivial. Bernstein has little idea of the biographer's craft and pads his book tediously by letting his subject ramble for page after page of uninteresting and self-pitying letters.

The real fact is that Thurber, as pathetic as he was unattractive, was one of those artists who were interesting mainly for their work and whose lives make poor reading even in the best circumstances. The final effect of Bernstein's book is not to enhance one's esteem of Thurber, but to deepen one's doubts of his ultimate significance. When a rival artist once complained to Ross that his work had been put aside for drawings by that "fifth-rater" Thurber, Ross replied judiciously, "No, third-rater!" One might amend this upwards, for the whole of Thurber's work, to second-rater. His was the fate of the humorist who pushes his special faculty too far. Like the spiritualist medium who has to fake when the psychic gift fails to work, the professional humorist has to make bogus jokes when the real ones will not come, and for this reason writers who try to sustain a reputation for being funny over a long period usually produce work of declining quality. With the one exception of Twain (and even he grew shaky towards the end), the great humorists have been those, like Lewis Carroll and Edward Lear, whose output has been small but choice. Even Wilde was completely successful in only one of his plays, and Thurber was no Wilde. Perhaps he can best be compared with Stephen Leacock, who filled the gaps between his genuinely inspired passages of wit with a complacent facetiousness which he standardized and could fit in like prefabricated units. There is much of Thurber that today seems prefabricated and given a little cosmetic treatment to make it seem individual.

Thurber had to endure many blows of fate, and, posthumously, not the least will be Bernstein's *Thurber.* One can question whether a biography by another hand is necessary in view of the fanciful biography Thurber provided for himself, which was a great deal more interesting than his real life. But one can also exclaim over the bitter chance that provides a humorist, even of the second class, with a biographer who writes as if he had never laughed.

THE NEW *NEW YORKER*

William Shawn

SOURCE: "The Talk of the Town: Notes and Comment," in *The New Yorker,* Vol. LXI, No. 9, April 22, 1985, pp. 35-6.

[*An American editor, Shawn joined the staff of the* New Yorker *in 1933 as a reporter for the magazine's "Talk of the Town" section. In 1952 he succeeded Harold Ross as editor of the magazine. In the following excerpt, which appeared as an unsigned "Talk of the Town" feature in anticipation of a merger between the New Yorker Magazine, Inc., and Advance Publications, Inc., the editors of the* New Yorker *reaffirm the magazine's long-standing policy of "editorial independence."*]

In 1925, when the magazine was founded, by Harold Ross (its first editor-in-chief) and Raoul Fleischmann (its first publisher), *The New Yorker,* like any new publication, had to fumble its way toward its natural character. We, the editorial people, knew by instinct that to be able to make *The New Yorker* the magazine we wanted it to be we had to separate ourselves from the business side of the venture. We felt that editorial independence was total or was nothing, that the line had to be drawn firmly and with finality. We therefore asserted our editorial independence. We did not write anything down; we just made the point in the course of a number of brief conversations. In this impromptu manner we claimed our independence, and, since we realized that it was a privilege, we determined not to take it for granted but to guard it carefully. Raoul Fleischmann, obeying some happy instinct of his own, acknowledged it and scrupulously respected it as long as he lived. When he died, in 1969, he was succeeded by his son, Peter Fleischmann, who, with wisdom and courage, followed his father's example to the letter. In sixty years, neither man ever made an editorial suggestion, ever commented favorably or unfavorably on anything we published or on any editorial direction the magazine was taking, ever permitted the advertising or circulation or accounting people to bring any pressure to bear on us. The Fleischmanns seemed to find satisfaction enough in providing a business framework within which we could get out the best magazine that we were capable of creating. There may have been occasions when both men were displeased or perplexed by what they found in the magazine, but, if so, they acted with restraint and self-discipline: they said nothing. The result was an absolute editorial independence rare in publishing history.

In a week or two, the stockholders of The New Yorker Magazine, Inc., will be asked to vote on a merger with Advance Publications, Inc. Advance belongs to S. I. Newhouse, Jr., and Donald Newhouse, who are brothers. Their company is a conglomerate that owns nine Condé Nast magazines, twenty-nine newspapers, a cable-television network, and a book-publishing company, Random House. Donald Newhouse mainly looks after the newspapers and the cable system, and S. I. Newhouse mainly looks after the magazines and the book publishing, but the brothers make all major decisions together. In the merger agreement between The New Yorker Magazine, Inc., and Advance Publications, Inc., we have been assured that *The New Yorker* "will be operated on a stand-alone basis as a separate company." In addition, Advance has said in the agreement that it wishes to maintain *The New Yorker*'s "personnel and their operating practices and traditions, including the tradition of complete editorial independence: the editors having total control of the magazine's editorial character, policies, procedures, and content." As we approach the beginning of a new phase, we reassert our editorial independence. We reassert it with these few formal words. We feel certain that the Newhouses will respect it as rigorously as the Fleischmanns did.

But what does this editorial independence mean? What is it, actually? It is simply freedom. It frees us to say what we believe to be true, to report what we believe to be true, to write what we want to write, to draw what we want to draw—to publish what we want to publish—with no outside intervention, without fear, without constraints, in defiance of commercial pressures or any other pressures beyond those of our own conscience and sense of responsibility. It also frees us to be open to experiment and innovation, to new forms and styles, whether journalistic or literary. The freedom that the editorial office enjoys includes the freedom of every staff writer and every staff artist and every editor (and every non-staff contributor) to follow his or her own impulses, inclinations, aspirations, passionate interests. No writer or artist or editor is ever given an order. When a journalistic writer undertakes a new project, it is always done in full agreement with the editor; the two have to bring to it the same enthusiasm. And no editing is ever imposed on a writer; every editorial suggestion is presented in the form of a question, and is settled by agreement between writer and editor. The artists are similarly free. And our editors edit only what they are willing to edit.

We edit *The New Yorker* as a magazine for readers, not as an advertising medium. We regard our readers as readers, not as consumers or as a "market." Just as advertising is an essential part of our country's life, it is an essential part of *The New Yorker*'s life. But it must not be linked to the editorial content of the magazine. They belong in separate realms, and the two realms must remain separate, must remain cordially apart. In this atmosphere of freedom, we have never published anything in order to sell magazines, to cause a sensation, to be controversial, to be popular or fashionable, to be "successful." We have published only what we thought had merit of one kind or another.

The business ownership of *The New Yorker* may change hands, but the idea of *The New Yorker*—the tradition of *The New Yorker,* the spirit of *The New Yorker*—has never been owned by anyone and never will be owned by anyone. It cannot be bought or sold. It exists in the minds of a group of writers, artists, editors, and editorial assistants who have been drawn together by literary, journalistic, aesthetic, and ethical principles they share, and by a shared outlook on the world. Whatever else may happen, it will endure. We need not name or define our principles

or standards, for they are implicit in what we publish in our pages each week. Yet this may be the moment to say that if *The New Yorker* could be everything we want it to be it would unfailingly combine thorough, accurate, fresh, inspired reporting with fiction that runs deep and says something that hasn't been said before; it would be funny as frequently as possible; it would contribute something of worth to the national discourse; it would cast light; it would be well-wishing; and it would be human. In an age when television screens are too often bright with nothing, we value substance. Amid a chaos of images, we value coherence. We believe in the printed word. And we believe in clarity. And in immaculate syntax. And in the beauty of the English language. We believe that the truth can turn up in a cartoon, in one of the magazine's covers, in a poem, in a short story, in an essay, in an editorial comment, in a humor piece, in a critical piece, in a reporting piece. And if any single principle transcends all the others and informs all the others it is to try to tell the truth. *The New Yorker* will continue to change, as it has changed through the years, but our basic principles and standards will remain exactly what they have been. With that knowledge, and with the assurances that we freely asked our prospective publishers to give us and that they freely gave, we are confident that we will preserve *The New Yorker*—not merely a magazine that bears its name but *this* magazine: *The New Yorker* itself.

Edwin Diamond

SOURCE: "The Talk of 'The New Yorker'," in *New York* Magazine, Vol. XVIII, No. 12, March 25, 1985, pp. 14, 16, 18.

[*An American journalist, Diamond has worked as an editor for several prominent American publications, including* New York *magazine and* Esquire. *He has also written several book-length studies of American television and* Jimmy Carter: A Character Portrait *(1980). In the following essay, he reflects on the editorial character of the* New Yorker *under William Shawn and speculates on the changes pending in the magazine's policy following its purchase by Advance Publications.*]

The men and women of *The New Yorker* have long existed on a plane apart from workers at other magazines. The intellectual standing of their magazine, the generous pay, the university-like tenure, the absence of deadlines for many staffers, the respect accorded their work (it's always "the artists" at the magazine, never "the cartoonists"), and above all, the magnanimous, moral, nurturing figure of the editor, William Shawn, *Mister* Shawn—all this makes *The New Yorker* a self-enclosed universe unique in American journalism.

Over the years, people at the magazine have offered various metaphors to convey to outsiders the rarefied quality of life on the inside. One of the more vivid images came last week from Hendrik Hertzberg, a *New Yorker* staff writer for seven years and, until recently, editor of *The New Republic*. "Under the cold sea of the world is this warm flow of water with its own ecology," he says. "That's *The New Yorker,* where strange creatures develop and flourish. The source of that warmth, the sustaining jet, is, of course, Mr. Shawn."

With the announcement that S. I. Newhouse Jr., whose family already owns the Condé Nast magazine group and Random House, among other properties, was buying *The New Yorker,* the clever images have taken on a certain pained reality. The magazine's delicate ecology is about to change.

The New Yorker, which a few weeks ago marked its sixtieth anniversary, has had but one family owner and two editors, Harold Ross from 1925 to 1951, and William Shawn since then. If the stock-holders accept Newhouse's offer (already approved by the board of directors) when it is presented to them formally this month, then the Fleischmann family—Peter Fleischmann, son of founder Raoul, and Peter's son Stephen—will be gone, replaced by strangers. More to the point, the way many of the men and women of *The New Yorker* tell it, William Shawn, the nourishing source of the magazine, will himself be at risk, and with him *The New Yorker*'s special place in magazine journalism.

Naturally, not everyone at the magazine thinks in such apocalyptic terms. The reactions to the sale, says the writer Calvin Trillin, "depend on your feelings about the Fleischmanns, about Newhouse, and about *The New Yorker.*" Trillin reports a spectrum of opinions, ranging from "Good, now we're in the hands of people who know how to publish magazines" to "The Huns are at the gates."

The Fleischmanns, as a family, stir no real animosity among the staff. They and the board of directors behaved as good capitalists are supposed to, taking $200 a share for stock that sold at $130 before Newhouse put his money on the table. Peter Fleischmann, 63 and not in good health, had to be thinking of his own retirement, while Stephen, 31, who works for the magazine's president, has shown little interest in running the business side. "We've had a benign ownership for 60 years," says Trillin. "Perhaps Ross insisted on it, perhaps the Fleischmanns didn't want to know what went on. Whatever the reason, they left us alone, which is what writers and artists want." If anyone asked the staff today who it would like as owner, Trillin adds, "the answer would be 'the Fleischmanns in perpetuity.' "

Si Newhouse, as an individual, doesn't agitate the staff very much, either. Rather, the *New Yorker* people seem upset at the idea of their magazine's even being associated with the Condé Nast magazines, a group made up of *Vogue, Glamour, Mademoiselle, Gentlemen's Quarterly, Gourmet, House & Garden, Self, Bride's,* and *Vanity Fair.* "If you surveyed the *New Yorker* staff with one of those word-reaction tests," says Trillin, "and the choices were 'Newhouse' and 'Condé Nast,' then 'Newhouse' would come out way ahead." In the eyes of *The New Yorker*'s artists and writers, Condé Nast represents flash, fashion, and, in the case of *Vanity Fair,* the faltering of a less than grand ambition. "Those magazines are in every way opposite to the image of *The New Yorker,*" says one staff writer at *The New Yorker.*

Whatever Si Newhouse may think of such hauteur, he has moved quickly to offer his assurances that, as a statement issued by *The New Yorker*'s board put it, the magazine will be allowed to "operate on a stand-alone basis as a separate company." The statement also pledged that no changes would be made in the staff or in the "practices and traditions" of the magazine.

That, of course, is pure acquisition-ese. The fact is, changes in people and practices are inevitable at *The New Yorker.* That's what much of the apprehension is about, on the part of people at the magazine and readers who value the at times maddening ways of *The New Yorker.* It can be, at once, important, boring, provocative, stale, original, and repetitive. Like the game of baseball, the magazine often manages to cram twenty minutes of excitement into three hours.

The talk of the *New Yorker* staff is about change, and specifically about the Succession Question—who will be the next editor? William Shawn is 77 years old, a reality that many people in the ecosystem try to shut out. With a childlike faith that defies actuarial tables, staff people marvel at how vigorous Shawn appears. "Oh yes, he looks tired from all this business," one writer told me last week. "But he's still so bright, so effective, so *sane.* . . . He looks like a man in his fifties." Like others in the *New Yorker* family, this writer wants everything to stay the same: "Our hopes seem to be that Mr. Newhouse and Mr. Shawn will hit it off." It's as if the revered editor will live forever, and the designation of a new editor for the post-Shawn era will be postponed forever.

Shawn himself has intermittently struggled to loosen the filial cords that bind him and his staff-family. In 1977-78, *The New Yorker* endured its first Great Succession Crisis. Back then, it appeared that Shawn had designated Jonathan Schell, a staff writer, as the next editor of *The New Yorker.* Various staff people at various times let Shawn know of their objections to Schell—that he wasn't a good pencil man; that he lacked humor, breadth, and the other skills of a Great Editor; that he wasn't, in short, William Shawn. So ended the first Schell game; Schell relinquished the editing duties he had been given and returned to his writer's work. In 1982, the same thing happened again: Schell probe, staff reaction, Shawn retreat.

Nothing much else was said about succession until last year. In November, Shawn appointed two staff editors, John Bennet and Charles McGrath, as co-managing editors, Bennet for nonfiction, McGrath for fiction. Neither man is regarded as a serious heir to the Great Editor tradition of Ross or Shawn, but the fact that both men are under 40 suggests a certain managerial shrewdness: Lacking the qualities to take charge themselves, Bennet and McGrath are presumably young and malleable enough to carry on the *New Yorker* traditions under non-Shawn leadership.

Shawn, it seems, has been more willing to look unblinkingly into the future than have some of his staff. When Newhouse initially said he would acquire 17 percent of the *New Yorker* stock last November, Shawn started meeting with small, ad hoc groups of his staff. Writers who attended these meetings recall them as part informational and part therapeutic—"Shawn let people have their say, and then he had his say." Next, Shawn appointed a group of twelve staff people to go beyond free-form group sessions. Like Youngstown steel unionists or any other blue-collar stiffs about to be merged or purged or conglomeratized, the artists and writers formed a workers' committee (variously known as Mr. Shawn's Council or the Editorial Group). The committee is chaired by Shawn and includes John Bennet and such *New Yorker* staff people as Paul Brodeur, John Brooks, and Thomas Whiteside.

One committee member, who spoke only on the condition that he not be identified, said the committee's goal was a "meeting of the minds with Mr. Newhouse" in order to get "guarantees of editorial independence with legal standing." To do that, Shawn and the committee have engaged lawyer Peter Ryan of Fried, Frank, Harris, Shriver & Jacobson. But since this committee member acknowledges the group is powerless to prevent the sale even if it wanted to, and since Newhouse has already pledged corporate independence from Condé Nast for *The New Yorker,* there can be only one guarantee on anyone's mind: the "right" to continue the *New Yorker* traditions, and the "right," reserved either for Shawn or for some other editorial entity, to name the next editor.

But whether Newhouse will surrender that basic prerogative of ownership seems problematic at best—at least to an outsider. Shawn himself told the *Times* last week that he didn't think a legal document was needed—though he acknowledged that some staff people wanted one. Instead, he said, he would try "man to man . . . [to] work things out" with Newhouse. Some of the staff put a Pangloss on events—in the best of all worlds, all that's required is for Shawn and Newhouse to get together—following Shawn's lead. Others maintain that they need a written document. And still others regard the committee as posturing. "Do you think people will actually walk out of here?" one star writer asks.

Already a couple of Outsider names have been floated as possible successors to Shawn. One is Robert Silvers, 55, who just sold his interest in *The New York Review of Books* but is continuing as editor. Another is Robert Gottlieb, 53, editor-in-chief at Knopf. Gottlieb last week gave out a statement of the kind we have come to recognize as a nondenial denial. ("It's very flattering . . . [but] I have a great job. . . . *The New Yorker* has a great editor.") Both men have proven intellectual records. Gottlieb, in addition, has enough stuff-of-legends eccentricities to qualify him for Great Editor.

The *New Yorker* staff's reactions to these reports range from hard-line ("If Newhouse doesn't give the guarantees, then there will be mass resignations") to ambivalent ("We don't know Newhouse's character," says another member of the committee, "so we shouldn't assume that he won't do everything we want, but we also don't know that he will do what we want").

At times, though, it seems that the *New Yorker* staff is not so much hawkish or dovish as ostrichlike. Last week, one of the magazine's bigger stars worried that any imminent appointment of someone like Gottlieb would be too great a leap for *The New Yorker* to take. But, the writer said, if Si Newhouse left the magazine's editorial side completely alone, and if Shawn continued in charge into the midfuture—another five to eight years, say—and if the editor designate were to hang around quietly and observe, then maybe there would be no problems of succession.

A strange world, indeed. But perhaps only *The New Yorker,* yes, *The New Yorker,* could make it work.

The *New Yorker*'s advertising policy:

From the founding of the *New Yorker,* its editor, Harold Ross, insisted on an editorial department free from any domination by the business office; and he was fortunate in having as a major financial backer Raoul Fleischmann, who believed in a separation of the editorial and business functions. "Great advertising mediums are operated for the reader first, for profits afterwards," the magazine observed in its code of publishing practice in 1933, and that attitude was reflected in an intraoffice memorandum by the advertising director more than thirty years later: "We must all bear in mind always that our first obligation is to our readers and our second obligation is to our present and past advertisers." Ross insisted on the right to veto all advertising copy; after his death, the editorial and advertising staffs cooperated in turning down thousands of dollars worth of advertising each year. Reasons for rejection varied. Among them were that the product or the advertisement itself was in poor taste, that the product would not appeal to readers of the magazine, that copy and layout were below its standards of quality, and that space was not available. The editorial staff complained that the magazine carried too much advertising; it could not, it said, obtain enough editorial content of quality to balance the advertising. For that reason, the magazine in 1960 limited its number of advertising pages. The *New Yorker*'s treatment of advertisers struck some as cavalier; one correspondent complained in the letters column of *Advertising Age* in 1960: "Their salesmen do not see you, they grant you an audience; their advertising departments do not sell advertising, they accept it."

Theodore Peterson, in his Magazines in the Twentieth Century, *University of Illinois Press, 1964.*

Eric Utne

SOURCE: "Tina's *New Yorker,*" in *Columbia Journalism Review,* Vol. XXXI, No. 6, March-April, 1993, pp. 31-6.

[*In the following essay, Utne reports on changes in the* New Yorker *under the editorship of Tina Brown.*]

In a speech to current and prospective *New Yorker* advertisers at the Rainbow Room late last year, Tina Brown proclaimed that "substance is back in style. . . . In the era we enter I sense that politics and process will be intensely interesting to people again. Seriousness will be sexy again."

She went on to describe some of the changes she has wrought at *The New Yorker,* which she said were to "preserve the identity of the magazine while recognizing that too many good pieces were going unread." Among the changes: she has reduced the frequency of the "daunting big read" (her phrase for 20,000-or-so word articles); added a number of shorter columns between "Talk of the Town" and the features well; increased the paper weight by 20 percent "to showcase the artwork and the advertising"; restored the original Caslon body typeface; introduced an expanded table of contents, running folio heads, and bylines at the top of articles; added loads of color illustrations and more color cartoons; dropped in the occasional black-and-white photo, including regular portraits by Richard Avedon; and begun running many more ads for the kinds of things that rarely, if ever, appeared in the pre-Newhouse *New Yorker,* like blue jean and underwear ads featuring half-nude models, and scratch-and-sniff perfume inserts (since dropped).

She also introduced a host of new contributors, including executive editor Rick Hertzberg, who edited *The New Republic* for seven of the last twelve years. Hertzberg presides over and sometimes writes the newly positioned lead-off political think piece, "Comment." Other new blood includes Harvard's Afro-American Studies chairman Henry Louis Gates, Jr.; cartoonists Jules Feiffer (who'd never been in *The New Yorker* before) and Art Spiegelman (creator of *Maus*); author Ken Auletta, whose first offering in his new column called "Annals of Communications" covered the David Letterman and Jay Leno flap; *Den of Thieves* author James Stewart; and Washington correspondent and former *New Republic* writer Sidney Blumenthal, who replaces Elizabeth Drew.

Although Brown told her audience that "the culture our readers are interested in now is international. Our horizon today ought to be global," she failed to mention that she wasn't renewing the contracts of longtime foreign correspondents Raymond Bonner and Stan Sesser, and has reportedly told colleagues that she wants to reduce the number of "situationers" (longish profiles of foreign countries).

Brown concluded her remarks by promising her advertisers that the new *New Yorker* would be "more relevant and more timely without being a slave to the week's headlines or the culture hype." This approach, she said, would "capture a new era and a new generation," which the advertisers no doubt heard to mean that Brown would deliver them thirtysomething readers instead of the fortysomething median age of the current readership.

When invited to write a review of the new *New Yorker,* I inquired, "Why me?" "You're the perfect person to do it," I was assured. "No," I pressed. "Why *really*?" The response: "Because no one else will touch it."

I must confess I'm not one of the faithful who read every issue of the old *New Yorker*. Though I'm a magazine junkie, and started *Utne Reader* to indulge my habit, *The New Yorker* has never been on my must-read list. The way I read the old *New Yorker* was to let the issues pile up (at my father's house) until someone told me there was some-thing I just had to read—usually by Paul Brodeur, Bill McKibben, Pauline Kael, or John McPhee. I was content to wait for that happy confluence of truly stunning, important ideas and brilliant exposition, like Jonathan Schell's *Fate of the Earth.* I'd pass on the five-part series on grain or the articles about "somebody's childhood in Pakistan," as Dorothy Parker once quipped about William Shawn's *New Yorker* of the '60s.

So while I was surprised to be asked to write the review, I was too curious, or perhaps foolhardy, to decline. What is it about Queen Tina that commands such underwhelming public loquacity among the usually quick-to-shoot pundits of American journalism? Is it the long shadow that the Newhouse media empire (Knopf, Random House, twenty-nine newspapers, fourteen magazines, cable TV, etc.) casts over the publishing landscape? Or is there something about Herself? To find out, I visited *The New Yorker*'s offices at 20 West 43rd Street.

Arriving for a 5 P.M. appointment with executive editor Rick Hertzberg, I was told to wait in the reception area, which is a stark space much like any other New York reception area, except this one was devoid of reading material. There wasn't even a copy of *The New Yorker*. The receptionist offered me a cup of coffee, then directed me down the corridor to the lunchroom to retrieve it. Like the rest of *The New Yorker*'s office space, the lunchroom-kitchen area has off-white walls and linoleum floors. It, too, was without reading matter, except for a wall rack that carried dozens of copies of the last three issues of a newsletter titled *Work and Family Life: Balancing Job and Personal Responsibilities.*

At 5:22 P.M. the clickity click of two-inch pumps caught my attention. Looking up, I recognized Herself, led by a little woman hurrying backwards, just ahead of Tina Brown, talking non-stop. Brown looked surprisingly tall (or was the talking woman exceedingly short?). Brown's camel-colored wrap was shapeless and limp. She gripped three bags: a big, black, Gucci-like handbag with an oversized gold chain-link shoulder strap, and two big shopping bags. The little woman, who turned out to be *The New Yorker*'s first-ever director of public relations, Maurie Perl, never stopped talking until the elevator door closed between them. Brown had not said a word.

Hertzberg arrived a few minutes later, returning from the funeral of the abstract impressionist painter Richard Pousette-Dart, who was his childhood neighbor in Westchester. Hertzberg's mood was somber but cordial. He smoked Salems. He wore a pin-striped, gray-flannel suit, blue shirt, and conservative tie. Throughout the nearly hour-and-a-half tour that followed, every person we visited or met in the halls, including writers David Remnick and Veronica Geng, considered his attire worthy of comment.

The New Yorker's offices, designed under the regime of Tina Brown's predecessor, Robert Gottlieb, are not laid out to encourage intra-office schmoozing. The hallways are so stark that I expected a pair of the endless closed doors to burst open at any moment, orderlies rushing by with a patient on a stretcher. The one space that invites conviviality is the open stairway between the 16th and 17th floors and the nearby library tables.

My tour mostly consisted of a visit to Perl's office, where, at 6:30 P.M. Hertzberg's watch began beeping to let him know it was time to catch the evening news. Hertzberg channel-jumped on Perl's TV for a few minutes, then settled on Peter Jennings's report. After watching for ten minutes or so he switched off the set. "Slow news day." He and Perl then took a call from a freelance copywriter, whom they congratulated profusely for "terrific" recent publicity releases.

The tour ended in Hertzberg's tiny office, which at that time was next door to Brown's, adjacent to the long library tables used for page make-up and fact-checking. Passing by the hallowed, legendary fact-checking area reminded me of something I had noticed on the first page of the first issue I saw after Brown took over—two glaring typos. Almost apologetically, I asked Hertzberg if he had seen them, since they were in the "Comment" column that he edits. "Typos," he replied. "What typos?"

I mentioned that the column with the offending errors had something to do with the press's post-election mistreatment of Clinton. Hertzberg produced the November 23rd issue. I just happened to have a yellow highlighter in my pocket, so I marked the little intruders for him.

Hertzberg summoned his assistant, Josh, and we were quickly flanked by a half dozen proofreaders, fact-checkers, and interns, waving earlier versions of galley proofs that had escaped the typos. "This is awful," Josh moaned. "It must have been a computer glitch."

Brown met me the next day in her corner office. Pulling her chair around to my side of the desk, she leaned forward and graciously made me feel that I could take as much of her time as I wanted, so I did.

We talked about editorial philosophy: "I edit for what interests me basically, and I think it is the only way to edit. I don't think about who is going to be angered. I feel that if it interests me it interests the readership." Reader surveys: "No, I have never done that." *The New Yorker* legend: "I feel the weight of the mystique. . . . I want to try things, experiment with things, have a license to fail. I could do that when I was at *The Tatler* and *Vanity Fair*. Here we are in a strange situation where the mystique is really enormous but the commercial reality was very dire. But I'm not complaining. You have to get on and do a lively magazine. It's about today and you know our readers are about today."

Midway through our interview she got up and asked one of her assistants to dig out a copy of a scathing critique of William Shawn's *New Yorker* written some twenty-three years ago by one-time *New Yorker* contributor Seymour Krim. I later found it to include such lines as "The virility, adventurousness, (and) connection with the living tissue of your audience can only be restored by rebirth. This is not about to happen in the near future and could only occur after the present *New Yorker* trust fades away and twenty years hence stirs the fires of someone who buys

the title and is then animated, directed, by the legend of a memorable past joined with a love of the living present."

She must have liked those lines.

I told her it didn't seem right that a magazine edited by Tina Brown would not carry photos by Annie Leibovitz and Helmut Newton. She replied by asking if I liked the Avedon photos, then went on to say, "I will use a photograph where it is appropriate. . . . I think that it's really working in the magazine. It doesn't feel like a violation of the magazine's traditions. I have had very positive feedback on that."

The negative feedback I heard most often, I told her, is that the magazine has become insistently, overwhelmingly topical. Even her friends, like *Village Voice* editor Jonathan Larsen, say she's gone too far. "The magazine needed to become more topical, but she's made it relentlessly so at the expense of the serendipitous, leisurely pace of her predecessors. You can find the topical any where, but not the timeless."

"I want to be both topical *and* timeless," she said. "Timeless takes longer to create. Still, I don't think that it's become overwhelmingly topical. . . . My goal is to have one piece that really is of the moment and one piece that could be offbeat—a whole other rhythm. I wouldn't want to see the magazine ever won by one or the other strand. . . . You have to create a certain urgency in a magazine to compel people to buy it and read it. I think the decline in ads was brought about by people feeling that the magazine didn't really matter anymore. It was just, 'Oh well, I'll just get to it.' "

When I asked what would be her version of Saul Steinberg's famous *New Yorker* cover of Manhattan looking west, she said, "I think the whole idea of being a New Yorker is up for grabs. . . . The city is increasingly balkanized. What it's really about is race warfare and conflict. And that's one of the subjects the magazine will address very powerfully: What is it to be a New Yorker?. . . . This is an area that I think has been rather neglected in the magazine. Some of the foreign coverage has been great but some of the domestic coverage has been wanting—there hasn't been enough of it. I've tried to redress that. I've got Jane Kramer, who normally writes about Europe, writing an extraordinary piece about places in the Bronx. It's wonderful to see her eye turned to another area. And we have Susan Sheehan doing a fantastic two-part series about what it's like to live in welfare projects."

We talked about some of her favorite *New Yorker* profiles (Kenneth Tynan on Johnny Carson, George Trow on Ahmet Ertegun), and about readership. I asked if she sees her fortysomething readership getting younger. "Yes, I do," she said. "And I think, to put it bluntly, it could not get any older. . . . That's not to say that I want to lose the old readers, but . . . the magazine basically skipped a generation and we have to get that generation back."

She talked about improved newsstand sales. "They were down to 6,000 copies sold on the New York newsstands. Now we're selling in New York what the magazine was selling nationally and internationally earlier in the year."

The New Yorker's president and c.e.o., Steven Florio, later told me that the magazine's newsstand sales, which averaged 20,000 per issue worldwide last year, have increased to 20,000 in New York City alone, and are up to 40,000 worldwide on average and as many as 60,000 on some issues. He attributes the increase to "all the press" the magazine has been getting and the fact that "we're so much more topical now." He said the fact that the magazine's draw (number of copies put out on the newsstand) has gone from 65,000 copies per issue last year to as many as 120,000 does not mean the company has "flooded the marketplace with copies to artificially inflate the newsstand sale. That has not happened. Si Newhouse would never let us do that. First and foremost, this guy's a businessman."

According to a current staff writer, Brown's "unflagging preoccupation with being hot, snappy, and of-the-moment" has led to a precipitous increase in typos and to the recent charges that some "Talk of the Town" pieces have been inaccurate because Brown puts off decisions until the last moment, which means the pieces cannot be adequately fact-checked. She has killed a number of stories as late as Thursday night (the magazine prints on Saturday). A recent profile of Al Sharpton was rushed into print on short notice to beat a similar, and some say richer, story in *The New York Times Magazine*. The beleaguered proofreaders and fact-checkers have been known to resist Brown's capriciousness directly, but to no avail.

When I asked Brown if there had been any uprisings by current or former writers, I was unaware that she was in the midst of asking at least a dozen staff writers and editors from previous regimes to move out of their offices (which many have interpreted as dismissals, even though some may still have contracts in place). Among them were Michael Arlen, Burton Bernstein, Naomi Bliven and Bruce Bliven, Jr., Jane Boutwell, William Wertenbaker, Wallace White, and Cynthia Zarin. At least two, Henry S. F. Cooper and Ved Mehta, refused to go.

Brown claimed the transition was going smoothly. "They've been very supportive," she said. "What about Garrison Keillor's departure?" I asked. She said Keillor left because she hired James Wolcott, who had written a column about him in *Vanity Fair* that Keillor found very, very offensive. "I wrote saying that I'm sorry you went before we had a chance to meet. And he wrote back that he hopes to publish something one day. I don't think there's any particular acrimony. He's a good writer."

When I later asked Keillor if Brown's account of his departure was accurate, he told me, "Tina Brown has a lot of nerve explaining why I left *The New Yorker* when she never bothered to ask me in the first place. I left because I love *The New Yorker* and because she is the wrong person to edit it. I didn't want to be on the premises to watch it suffer under her hand."

Keillor says the magazine he wanted to write for "is gone now, bought by a billionaire . . . who has ended the long tradition of editorial independence there.

"*The New Yorker* is a glorious and dear American institution," Keillor said, "but Ms. Brown, like so many Brits, seems most fascinated by the passing carnival and celebri-ty show in America. Fiction, serious reporting, the personal essay, criticism, all that made *The New Yorker* great, do not engage her interest apparently. She has redesigned it into a magazine that looks and reads an awful lot like a hundred other magazines. The best writing to appear in Ms. Brown's *New Yorker*, in fact, was the section of tributes to William Shawn, which read like an obituary for *The New Yorker*."

No one can accuse Brown of not paying her writers well. At *Vanity Fair* Brown paid her favorites upwards of $100,000 to write four or five pieces a year. One media source says that Alexander Chancellor, the former editor of the London *Spectator* whom Brown imported to edit "Talk of the Town," makes $140,000 a year and was given an apartment and a "no receipts" expense account. Since Brown has brought on many more people than she's let go, and still pays writers what Gottlieb did (about $30,000 for a 20,000 word piece), insiders at the magazine speculate that her budget must have increased dramatically.

But Brown said, "No, it's the same budget. It's a very complex thing. . . . Shawn hired everyone with different arrangements. . . . It's been very difficult to get inside of and understand how it works. . . . It *doesn't* work. I'm just proceeding in my own cautious way."

She cited similar factors when I asked if she'd considered running a masthead listing the magazine's approximately 140-person editorial staff. "That is one tradition I am very happy to be without," she replied. "This magazine is sort of a mare's-nest of strong hierarchies, yet it's non-hierarchical. Once you do a masthead you put one over another who never saw himself as over or under another. It's too complex, too weird. It would be a nightmare. It would only encourage the management to halve the staff, so I prefer not to do it."

Back in 1970, Krim complained that *The New Yorker* had lost its "subtle, enormous influence" on American culture as soon as it began to "scoop in sweet advertising money." Now Brown's mandate is to rescue the magazine from its current "dire commercial reality" by scooping in more advertising money. (*The New Yorker* reached its peak of 6,143 ad pages in 1966. In 1981 it sold 4,304 pages. By 1991 it had fallen to just 2,002 pages. For 1992, pages stayed flat, at 2,007.)

Under Brown, according to Jerry Brennan, a former research analyst in *The New Yorker*'s marketing department who now sells ads for *New York* magazine, advertising has won the war with editorial. The evidence, he says, is at the front of the book, where many more fractional ads are now "braided into the editorial copy, and full-page ads get the preferred right-hand position opposite the new 'Comment.'" At the old *New Yorker*, the entire "Talk of the Town" section was kept free of ads.

Though the clustering of ads in the front may make the magazine appear to be fairly bursting with ads, perception is not reality. According to Steven Cohn, editor of the trade journal *min* (Media Industry Newsletter), which carries a running "box score" on weekly magazines' ad sales, advertising at *The New Yorker* was up only 2 percent for the three months under Brown in 1992. (Florio expects total ad pages to increase 5 percent in 1993.) When asked if he knew of any special efforts *The New Yorker* is now making to increase ad sales, Cohn replied, "I guess they're selling Tina, just as they did when she was at *Vanity Fair.*"

And Brown seems a willing participant, co-hosting with Florio regular "roundtables" for advertisers, including a recent special luncheon, attended by Elton John and Lauren Hutton, to celebrate the unveiling of a new ten-page Gianni Versace ad spread in the February 8 issue. The ads feature fashion photographs by none other than staff photographer Richard Avedon. Brown's willingness to mix editorial with advertising would have been considered unseemly by Mr. Shawn, who took great pains to keep the editorial side independent from the business side.

Indeed, Brown seems to have become *The New Yorker's* primary selling point. The magazine's new direct mail subscription promotion is a two-panel postcard that offers subscriptions for just $16 per year. The card is similar to one the magazine used before Brown took over, only now Tina Brown's name is emblazoned all over it, with lines like, "First offer with Tina Brown as editor," and "For only 32¢ an issue, *The New Yorker* brings you the best cartoons, humor, fiction, reporting, and Tina Brown . . . the best magazine editor in the country." Florio has been trumpeting the mailing to trade journals, saying that the two-million-piece campaign, which was mailed in the last week of December, got more responses after ten days than previous mailings did after twenty-five days. (Industry experts point out that the Tina Brown-as-product-benefit mailing was sent out via first class postage, whereas previous mailings always went out via third class, which delays delivery and therefore response rates.)

Patti Hagan, a fact-checker at *The New Yorker* under Shawn for fifteen years and now the gardening columnist for *The Wall Street Journal,* says, "I'm most turned off by Marky Mark having sex in Calvin Klein's ads at the front of the book, followed a few weeks later by a signed [Susan Orlean] 'Talk of the Town' interview with Marky Mark about his underwear ads. This would never happen at the old *New Yorker.*"

Although William Shawn adamantly resisted public relations in all its forms, Brown is the reigning master-stoker of the star-hyping machine, and Maurie Perl, who flacked for Barbara Walters at ABC, is no slouch either.

But Brown may not be happy about all the ink she got recently for her very public tiff with authors John Le Carré and William Shawcross. She published a blistering review of Shawcross's new biography of media baron Rupert Murdoch, who had long ago hired and then fired Brown's husband, Harold Evans. She was then accused by Le Carré, who is a friend of Shawcross, of publishing "one of the ugliest pieces of partisan journalism that I have witnessed, [intended to] assure your readers that the unflattering portrait of Harold Evans provided in the book is mere Murdoch propaganda." Brown dismissed Le Carré's charge as "sexist." Le Carré responded that "the ethics of the great magazine of which you are now editor [are at stake]. God protect *The New Yorker* from the English."

Brown seems to be using the "Talk of the Town" section in particular to ruffle feathers and gain attention. In the January 11 issue she ran an unsigned piece defending East German dictator Erich Honecker, written by Irene Dische, the wife of Honecker's defense lawyer. The next week she ran an unsigned piece by new staff writer Jeffrey Toobin that was critical of his ex-boss, Iran-contra special counsel Lawrence Walsh. Toobin had been taken to court by Walsh in an attempt to block his book about the Iran-contra investigation.

"Now," says a New York media critic, " 'Talk of the Town' reads like a media gossip column." Until Brown imported Chancellor, whose ruddy complexion and jovial personality inspired staffers to call him Admiral Stockdale, the section was edited by Chip McGrath, who maintained the magazine's traditional aversion to public relations hype in favor of the obscure, the odd, the eccentric, and the *un*controversial. As Shawn liked to say, "We avoid topicality at all costs."

At the old *New Yorker,* "Talk" pieces were never assigned. Writers proposed stories, and if they were approved, they pursued them. Now, in search of the right "mix," Brown and Chancellor regularly assign "hot and snappy" pieces to their staff writers, many of which the writers simply but politely reject. So concerned were some staffers about the new direction of "Talk of the Town" that at a rare *New Yorker* meeting some senior staff members pressed their concerns to Chancellor. Chancellor was "very open and agreeable," says one staff writer who attended the meeting, "but since then 'Talk of the Town' has gone on as before, driven primarily by public relations considerations."

Faced with similar financial realities, most reasonable people would probably do just as Brown has done, if they had the talent. Though nearly everyone I talked to has some quibble about the new *New Yorker* (to some of the old guard, any change, no matter how minor, would be a sacrilege), most people admitted that they're reading it more now. This, for a magazine that had become America's most-admired and least-read publication, is something of a turnaround.

So far, Brown seems to be accomplishing the goals she set for herself. She has made *The New Yorker* the most-talked-about magazine in America. She has given it a face lift without changing it beyond recognition. And, perhaps most important to her and her boss, she has raised newsstand and ad sales.

But she has attained these goals at a cost—the loss of the magazine's special role as the torchbearer for a uniquely American (and very unBritish) brand of civility and decency.

The New Yorker of old always seemed to me an exercise in defining and refining the ideas deemed permissible for admission to civilized discourse. It had the courage to disagree with the conventional wisdom even as it defined it, through genuine soul-searching rather than through politically correct polemic. In its coverage of the United States' involvement in Nicaragua, Grenada, and the Persian Gulf, the magazine asked tough questions that few other mainstream publications dared to ask, just as it had earlier about McCarthyism, civil rights, and the Vietnam War.

By allowing such radicals as Michael Harrington, James Baldwin, and Barry Commoner to fling their incendiary ideas from its pages, *The New Yorker* served notice to the American establishment that these untitled and unfamous authors deserved a hearing.

It's too early to tell whether Brown's *New Yorker* is congenial to new and challenging ideas. If her editing of *Vanity Fair* is any indication, it may actually become hostile to them, not because Brown isn't interested in ideas, but because, as critic Geoffrey Stokes, sees it, she fears that "anything difficult or complex, and especially anything ambiguous," would be "boring" to her readers.

To her credit, Brown has published a number of powerful pieces that are certainly worthy of the old *New Yorker*, such as Richard Preston's article on rainforest viruses, Marshall Frady's profile of Malcolm X, and the memorial tribute to William Shawn.

Nonetheless, Brown has transformed *The New Yorker* and especially "Talk of the Town" into a kind of weekly epistle for America's new orthodoxy—the cult of personality. She rules as its high priestess. She's the one who decides whom to bless and whom to shun.

Will she allow *The New Yorker* to provide safe haven for America's heretofore silenced rebels and unseen minorities? (I'd like to see her use more writing by women, like Barbara Ehrenreich, Louise Erdrich, and Winona LaDuke.) Will she give voice to the blasphemies of its infidels? (How about working with some of *Spy* magazine's best writers, like Bruce Handy, Paul Rudnick, and Kurt Andersen? They are the true wits of our day.) Will she give a hearing to America's heretical visionaries and prophetic poets (Gary Snyder and Stephen Mitchell)?

Just how serious is Tina Brown when she says, "Seriousness will be sexy again"? Will it be sexy enough to survive in the new *New Yorker*? Or will seriousness prove too boring?

FURTHER READING

Anthologies

Harriman, Margaret Case. *Take Them up Tenderly: A Collection of Profiles.* New York: Alfred A. Knopf, 1945, 266 p.
    Collection of biographical sketches first published in the *New Yorker*.

Ho Hum: Newsbreaks from the "New Yorker." New York: Farrar & Rinehart, 1931, 116 p.
    Collection of humorous news items originally excerpted and published in the *New Yorker*; includes an introduction by E. B. White and illustrations by longtime *New Yorker* artist Otto Soglow.

Secondary Sources

Bernstein, Burton. *Thurber.* New York: Dodd, Mead, 1975, 532 p.
    Biography of James Thurber that contains chapters doc-

umenting the *New Yorker*'s early years and his involvement with the magazine.

Davies, Russell. "Just a Smile at Twilight." *The Times Literary Supplement* (24 September 1976): 1203.
    Review of two collections of *New Yorker* cartoons that discusses characteristics typical of drawings published in the magazine.

Ingersoll, Ralph McAllister. *Points of Departure: An Adventure in Autobiography.* New York: Harcourt, Brace, & World, 1961, 247 p.
    Autobiography by the first managing editor of the *New Yorker* contains sections on Harold W. Ross and the founding of the magazine.

Johnson, Robert Owen. *An Index to Literature in the "New Yorker,"* 3 vols. Metuchen, N. J.: The Scarecrow Press, 1969-1976, 1741 p.
    Indexes fiction, poetry, reviews, and nonfiction published in the *New Yorker* through Volume L (17 February 1975).

Kramer, Dale. *Ross and the "New Yorker."* Garden City, N. Y.: Doubleday, 1951, 306 p.
    Noncritical biography of Harold W. Ross that documents the founding and early years of the *New Yorker*.

Kunkel, Thomas. *Genius in Disguise: Harold Ross of the "New Yorker."* New York: Random House, 1995, 497 p.
    Biography of *New Yorker* founder Harold Ross that argues against the common perception of him as a crude personality and an unschooled editor, instead portraying him as having a "keen native intellect, a searching curiosity, and a droll humor—qualities Ross imprinted onto his magazine."

McGrath, Charles. "The Ross Years." *The New Yorker* (20-27 February 1995): 180-95.
    Profile of Harold Ross. Included with the essay are letters by Ross selected and edited by Thomas Kunkel, author of *Genius in Disguise: Harold Ross of the "New Yorker."*

Pinck, Dan. "Paging Mr. Ross: Old Days at the 'New Yorker'."
    Encounter LXIX, No. 1 (June 1987): 5-11.
    Personal memoir of Ross by a former *New Yorker* officeboy.

Seelye, John. "Black on White." *The New Republic* 147, No. 26 (29 December 1962): 21-3.
    Meditation on the effect of the appearance of James Baldwin's "Letter from a Region in My Mind," a work about the racial oppression experienced by African-Americans, amid numerous advertisements for luxuries in the pages of the *New Yorker*.

Thurber, James. *The Years with Ross.* Boston: Little, Brown, 1957, 310 p.
    Memoir of Harold Ross and the *New Yorker* by a close friend to Ross and major figure in the magazine's development.

Weber, Ronald. "Letting Subjects Grow: Literary Nonfiction from the *New Yorker*." *The Antioch Review* 36, No. 4 (Fall 1978): 486-99.
    Describes the characteristics of *New Yorker* "art-

journalism" through close examination of Jane Kramer's *The Last Cowboy* and John McPhee's *Coming into the Country*.

Twentieth-Century
Literary Criticism

Cumulative Indexes
Volumes 1-58

How to Use This Index

The main references

Calvino, Italo
1923-1985.....CLC 5, 8, 11, 22, 33, 39,
73; SSC 3

list all author entries in the following Gale Literary Criticism series:

BLC = *Black Literature Criticism*
CLC = *Contemporary Literary Criticism*
CLR = *Children's Literature Review*
CMLC = *Classical and Medieval Literature Criticism*
DA = *DISCovering Authors*
DC = *Drama Criticism*
HLC = *Hispanic Literature Criticism*
LC = *Literature Criticism from 1400 to 1800*
NCLC = *Nineteenth-Century Literature Criticism*
PC = *Poetry Criticism*
SSC = *Short Story Criticism*
TCLC = *Twentieth-Century Literary Criticism*
WLC = *World Literature Criticism, 1500 to the Present*

The cross-references

See also CANR 23; CA 85-88;
obituary CA 116

list all author entries in the following Gale biographical and literary sources:

AAYA = *Authors & Artists for Young Adults*
AITN = *Authors in the News*
BEST = *Bestsellers*
BW = *Black Writers*
CA = *Contemporary Authors*
CAAS = *Contemporary Authors Autobiography Series*
CABS = *Contemporary Authors Bibliographical Series*
CANR = *Contemporary Authors New Revision Series*
CAP = *Contemporary Authors Permanent Series*
CDALB = *Concise Dictionary of American Literary Biography*
CDBLB = *Concise Dictionary of British Literary Biography*
DLB = *Dictionary of Literary Biography*
DLBD = *Dictionary of Literary Biography Documentary Series*
DLBY = *Dictionary of Literary Biography Yearbook*
HW = *Hispanic Writers*
JRDA = *Junior DISCovering Authors*
MAICYA = *Major Authors and Illustrators for Children and Young Adults*
MTCW = *Major 20th-Century Writers*
NNAL = *Native North American Literature*
SAAS = *Something about the Author Autobiography Series*
SATA = *Something about the Author*
YABC = *Yesterday's Authors of Books for Children*

Literary Criticism Series
Cumulative Author Index

Anthony, Peter
See Shaffer, Anthony (Joshua); Shaffer, Peter (Levin)

Anthony, Piers 1934- . . . . **CLC 35**
See also AAYA 11; CA 21-24R; CANR 28; DLB 8; MTCW

Antoine, Marc
See Proust, (Valentin-Louis-George-Eugene-) Marcel

Antoninus, Brother
See Everson, William (Oliver)

Antonioni, Michelangelo 1912- . . . . . **CLC 20**
See also CA 73-76; CANR 45

Antschel, Paul 1920-1970
See Celan, Paul
See also CA 85-88; CANR 33; MTCW

Anwar, Chairil 1922-1949 . . . . **TCLC 22**
See also CA 121

Apollinaire, Guillaume . . **TCLC 3, 8, 51; PC 7**
See also Kostrowitzki, Wilhelm Apollinaris de

Appelfeld, Aharon 1932- . . . . **CLC 23, 47**
See also CA 112; 133

Apple, Max (Isaac) 1941- . . . . **CLC 9, 33**
See also CA 81-84; CANR 19; DLB 130

Appleman, Philip (Dean) 1926- . . . . . **CLC 51**
See also CA 13-16R; CAAS 18; CANR 6, 29

Appleton, Lawrence
See Lovecraft, H(oward) P(hillips)

Apteryx
See Eliot, T(homas) S(tearns)

Apuleius, (Lucius Madaurensis)
125(?)-175(?) . . . . **CMLC 1**

Aquin, Hubert 1929-1977 . . . . **CLC 15**
See also CA 105; DLB 53

Aragon, Louis 1897-1982 . . . . **CLC 3, 22**
See also CA 69-72; 108; CANR 28; DLB 72; MTCW

Arany, Janos 1817-1882 . . . . **NCLC 34**

Arbuthnot, John 1667-1735 . . . . **LC 1**
See also DLB 101

Archer, Herbert Winslow
See Mencken, H(enry) L(ouis)

Archer, Jeffrey (Howard) 1940- . . . . **CLC 28**
See also BEST 89:3; CA 77-80; CANR 22

Archer, Jules 1915- . . . . **CLC 12**
See also CA 9-12R; CANR 6; SAAS 5; SATA 4

Archer, Lee
See Ellison, Harlan (Jay)

Arden, John 1930- . . . . **CLC 6, 13, 15**
See also CA 13-16R; CAAS 4; CANR 31; DLB 13; MTCW

Arenas, Reinaldo
1943-1990 . . . . **CLC 41; HLC**
See also CA 124; 128; 133; DLB 145; HW

Arendt, Hannah 1906-1975 . . . . **CLC 66**
See also CA 17-20R; 61-64; CANR 26; MTCW

Aretino, Pietro 1492-1556 . . . . **LC 12**

Arghezi, Tudor . . . . **CLC 80**
See also Theodorescu, Ion N.

Arguedas, Jose Maria
1911-1969 . . . . **CLC 10, 18**
See also CA 89-92; DLB 113; HW

Argueta, Manlio 1936- . . . . **CLC 31**
See also CA 131; DLB 145; HW

Ariosto, Ludovico 1474-1533 . . . . **LC 6**

Aristides
See Epstein, Joseph

Aristophanes
450B.C.-385B.C. . . . . **CMLC 4; DA; DC 2**

Arlt, Roberto (Godofredo Christophersen)
1900-1942 . . . . **TCLC 29; HLC**
See also CA 123; 131; HW

Armah, Ayi Kwei 1939- . . . . **CLC 5, 33; BLC**
See also BW 1; CA 61-64; CANR 21; DLB 117; MTCW

Armatrading, Joan 1950- . . . . **CLC 17**
See also CA 114

Arnette, Robert
See Silverberg, Robert

Arnim, Achim von (Ludwig Joachim von Arnim) 1781-1831 . . . . **NCLC 5**
See also DLB 90

Arnim, Bettina von 1785-1859 . . . . **NCLC 38**
See also DLB 90

Arnold, Matthew
1822-1888 . . . . . **NCLC 6, 29; DA; PC 5; WLC**
See also CDBLB 1832-1890; DLB 32, 57

Arnold, Thomas 1795-1842 . . . . . . **NCLC 18**
See also DLB 55

Arnow, Harriette (Louisa) Simpson
1908-1986 . . . . **CLC 2, 7, 18**
See also CA 9-12R; 118; CANR 14; DLB 6; MTCW; SATA 42; SATA-Obit 47

Arp, Hans
See Arp, Jean

Arp, Jean 1887-1966 . . . . **CLC 5**
See also CA 81-84; 25-28R; CANR 42

Arrabal
See Arrabal, Fernando

Arrabal, Fernando 1932- . . . **CLC 2, 9, 18, 58**
See also CA 9-12R; CANR 15

Arrick, Fran . . . . **CLC 30**

Artaud, Antonin 1896-1948 . . . . . **TCLC 3, 36**
See also CA 104

Arthur, Ruth M(abel) 1905-1979 . . . . **CLC 12**
See also CA 9-12R; 85-88; CANR 4; SATA 7, 26

Artsybashev, Mikhail (Petrovich)
1878-1927 . . . . **TCLC 31**

Arundel, Honor (Morfydd)
1919-1973 . . . . **CLC 17**
See also CA 21-22; 41-44R; CAP 2; CLR 35; SATA 4; SATA-Obit 24

Asch, Sholem 1880-1957 . . . . **TCLC 3**
See also CA 105

Ash, Shalom
See Asch, Sholem

Ashbery, John (Lawrence)
1927- . . . . . . **CLC 2, 3, 4, 6, 9, 13, 15, 25, 41, 77**
See also CA 5-8R; CANR 9, 37; DLB 5; DLBY 81; MTCW

Ashdown, Clifford
See Freeman, R(ichard) Austin

Ashe, Gordon
See Creasey, John

Ashton-Warner, Sylvia (Constance)
1908-1984 . . . . **CLC 19**
See also CA 69-72; 112; CANR 29; MTCW

Asimov, Isaac
1920-1992 . . . . . . **CLC 1, 3, 9, 19, 26, 76**
See also AAYA 13; BEST 90:2; CA 1-4R; 137; CANR 2, 19, 36; CLR 12; DLB 8; DLBY 92; JRDA; MAICYA; MTCW; SATA 1, 26, 74

Astley, Thea (Beatrice May)
1925- . . . . **CLC 41**
See also CA 65-68; CANR 11, 43

Aston, James
See White, T(erence) H(anbury)

Asturias, Miguel Angel
1899-1974 . . . . **CLC 3, 8, 13; HLC**
See also CA 25-28; 49-52; CANR 32; CAP 2; DLB 113; HW; MTCW

Atares, Carlos Saura
See Saura (Atares), Carlos

Atheling, William
See Pound, Ezra (Weston Loomis)

Atheling, William, Jr.
See Blish, James (Benjamin)

Atherton, Gertrude (Franklin Horn)
1857-1948 . . . . **TCLC 2**
See also CA 104; DLB 9, 78

Atherton, Lucius
See Masters, Edgar Lee

Atkins, Jack
See Harris, Mark

Atticus
See Fleming, Ian (Lancaster)

Atwood, Margaret (Eleanor)
1939- . . . . . **CLC 2, 3, 4, 8, 13, 15, 25, 44, 84; DA; PC 8; SSC 2; WLC**
See also AAYA 12; BEST 89:2; CA 49-52; CANR 3, 24, 33; DLB 53; MTCW; SATA 50

Aubigny, Pierre d'
See Mencken, H(enry) L(ouis)

Aubin, Penelope 1685-1731(?) . . . . **LC 9**
See also DLB 39

Auchincloss, Louis (Stanton)
1917- . . . . **CLC 4, 6, 9, 18, 45**
See also CA 1-4R; CANR 6, 29; DLB 2; DLBY 80; MTCW

Auden, W(ystan) H(ugh)
1907-1973 . . . . . **CLC 1, 2, 3, 4, 6, 9, 11, 14, 43; DA; PC 1; WLC**
See also CA 9-12R; 45-48; CANR 5; CDBLB 1914-1945; DLB 10, 20; MTCW

Audiberti, Jacques 1900-1965 . . . . . . **CLC 38**
See also CA 25-28R

Audubon, John James
1785-1851 . . . . **NCLC 47**

Auel, Jean M(arie) 1936- . . . . **CLC 31**
See also AAYA 7; BEST 90:4; CA 103; CANR 21

Auerbach, Erich 1892-1957 . . . . **TCLC 43**
See also CA 118

Bertolucci, Bernardo   1940- .... **CLC 16**
See also CA 106

Bertrand, Aloysius   1807-1841 .... **NCLC 31**

Bertran de Born   c. 1140-1215 ..... **CMLC 5**

Besant, Annie (Wood)   1847-1933 ... **TCLC 9**
See also CA 105

Bessie, Alvah   1904-1985.......... **CLC 23**
See also CA 5-8R; 116; CANR 2; DLB 26

Bethlen, T. D.
See Silverberg, Robert

Beti, Mongo................. **CLC 27; BLC**
See also Biyidi, Alexandre

Betjeman, John
1906-1984 .... **CLC 2, 6, 10, 34, 43**
See also CA 9-12R; 112; CANR 33;
CDBLB 1945-1960; DLB 20; DLBY 84;
MTCW

Bettelheim, Bruno   1903-1990 ...... **CLC 79**
See also CA 81-84; 131; CANR 23; MTCW

Betti, Ugo   1892-1953 .... **TCLC 5**
See also CA 104

Betts, Doris (Waugh)   1932-.... **CLC 3, 6, 28**
See also CA 13-16R; CANR 9; DLBY 82

Bevan, Alistair
See Roberts, Keith (John Kingston)

Bialik, Chaim Nachman
1873-1934 .... **TCLC 25**

Bickerstaff, Isaac
See Swift, Jonathan

Bidart, Frank   1939- .... **CLC 33**
See also CA 140

Bienek, Horst   1930-............ **CLC 7, 11**
See also CA 73-76; DLB 75

Bierce, Ambrose (Gwinett)
1842-1914(?) .... **TCLC 1, 7, 44; DA;**
                                      SSC 9; WLC
See also CA 104; 139; CDALB 1865-1917;
DLB 11, 12, 23, 71, 74

Billings, Josh
See Shaw, Henry Wheeler

Billington, (Lady) Rachel (Mary)
1942- .... **CLC 43**
See also AITN 2; CA 33-36R; CANR 44

Binyon, T(imothy) J(ohn)   1936- .... **CLC 34**
See also CA 111; CANR 28

Bioy Casares, Adolfo
1914- ...... **CLC 4, 8, 13; HLC; SSC 17**
See also CA 29-32R; CANR 19, 43;
DLB 113; HW; MTCW

Bird, Cordwainer
See Ellison, Harlan (Jay)

Bird, Robert Montgomery
1806-1854 .... **NCLC 1**

Birney, (Alfred) Earle
1904- .... **CLC 1, 4, 6, 11**
See also CA 1-4R; CANR 5, 20; DLB 88;
MTCW

Bishop, Elizabeth
1911-1979 ...... **CLC 1, 4, 9, 13, 15, 32;**
                                      DA; PC 3
See also CA 5-8R; 89-92; CABS 2;
CANR 26; CDALB 1968-1988; DLB 5;
MTCW; SATA-Obit 24

Bishop, John   1935-............... **CLC 10**
See also CA 105

Bissett, Bill   1939-............... **CLC 18**
See also CA 69-72; CAAS 19; CANR 15;
DLB 53; MTCW

Bitov, Andrei (Georgievich)   1937-... **CLC 57**
See also CA 142

Biyidi, Alexandre   1932-
See Beti, Mongo
See also BW 1; CA 114; 124; MTCW

Bjarme, Brynjolf
See Ibsen, Henrik (Johan)

Bjornson, Bjornstjerne (Martinius)
1832-1910 .... **TCLC 7, 37**
See also CA 104

Black, Robert
See Holdstock, Robert P.

Blackburn, Paul   1926-1971 ...... **CLC 9, 43**
See also CA 81-84; 33-36R; CANR 34;
DLB 16; DLBY 81

Black Elk   1863-1950 .... **TCLC 33**
See also CA 144; NNAL

Black Hobart
See Sanders, (James) Ed(ward)

Blacklin, Malcolm
See Chambers, Aidan

Blackmore, R(ichard) D(oddridge)
1825-1900 .... **TCLC 27**
See also CA 120; DLB 18

Blackmur, R(ichard) P(almer)
1904-1965 .... **CLC 2, 24**
See also CA 11-12; 25-28R; CAP 1; DLB 63

Black Tarantula, The
See Acker, Kathy

Blackwood, Algernon (Henry)
1869-1951 .... **TCLC 5**
See also CA 105

Blackwood, Caroline   1931- .... **CLC 6, 9**
See also CA 85-88; CANR 32; DLB 14;
MTCW

Blade, Alexander
See Hamilton, Edmond; Silverberg, Robert

Blaga, Lucian   1895-1961 .... **CLC 75**

Blair, Eric (Arthur)   1903-1950
See Orwell, George
See also CA 104; 132; DA; MTCW;
SATA 29

Blais, Marie-Claire
1939- .... **CLC 2, 4, 6, 13, 22**
See also CA 21-24R; CAAS 4; CANR 38;
DLB 53; MTCW

Blaise, Clark   1940-............... **CLC 29**
See also AITN 2; CA 53-56; CAAS 3;
CANR 5; DLB 53

Blake, Nicholas
See Day Lewis, C(ecil)
See also DLB 77

Blake, William
1757-1827 ..... **NCLC 13, 37; DA; WLC**
See also CDBLB 1789-1832; DLB 93;
MAICYA; SATA 30

Blasco Ibanez, Vicente
1867-1928 .... **TCLC 12**
See also CA 110; 131; HW; MTCW

Blatty, William Peter   1928-........ **CLC 2**
See also CA 5-8R; CANR 9

Bleeck, Oliver
See Thomas, Ross (Elmore)

Blessing, Lee   1949-............... **CLC 54**

Blish, James (Benjamin)
1921-1975 .... **CLC 14**
See also CA 1-4R; 57-60; CANR 3; DLB 8;
MTCW; SATA 66

Bliss, Reginald
See Wells, H(erbert) G(eorge)

Blixen, Karen (Christentze Dinesen)
1885-1962
See Dinesen, Isak
See also CA 25-28; CANR 22; CAP 2;
MTCW; SATA 44

Bloch, Robert (Albert)   1917-1994... **CLC 33**
See also CA 5-8R; 146; CAAS 20; CANR 5;
DLB 44; SATA 12

Blok, Alexander (Alexandrovich)
1880-1921 .... **TCLC 5**
See also CA 104

Blom, Jan
See Breytenbach, Breyten

Bloom, Harold   1930- .... **CLC 24**
See also CA 13-16R; CANR 39; DLB 67

Bloomfield, Aurelius
See Bourne, Randolph S(illiman)

Blount, Roy (Alton), Jr.   1941- ..... **CLC 38**
See also CA 53-56; CANR 10, 28; MTCW

Bloy, Leon   1846-1917............ **TCLC 22**
See also CA 121; DLB 123

Blume, Judy (Sussman)   1938-... **CLC 12, 30**
See also AAYA 3; CA 29-32R; CANR 13,
37; CLR 2, 15; DLB 52; JRDA;
MAICYA; MTCW; SATA 2, 31, 79

Blunden, Edmund (Charles)
1896-1974 .... **CLC 2, 56**
See also CA 17-18; 45-48; CAP 2; DLB 20,
100; MTCW

Bly, Robert (Elwood)
1926- .... **CLC 1, 2, 5, 10, 15, 38**
See also CA 5-8R; CANR 41; DLB 5;
MTCW

Boas, Franz   1858-1942.......... **TCLC 56**
See also CA 115

Bobette
See Simenon, Georges (Jacques Christian)

Boccaccio, Giovanni
1313-1375 .... **CMLC 13; SSC 10**

Bochco, Steven   1943-............. **CLC 35**
See also AAYA 11; CA 124; 138

Bodenheim, Maxwell   1892-1954 ... **TCLC 44**
See also CA 110; DLB 9, 45

Bodker, Cecil   1927- .... **CLC 21**
See also CA 73-76; CANR 13, 44; CLR 23;
MAICYA; SATA 14

Boell, Heinrich (Theodor)
1917-1985 .... **CLC 2, 3, 6, 9, 11, 15, 27,**
                                      32, 72; DA; WLC
See also CA 21-24R; 116; CANR 24;
DLB 69; DLBY 85; MTCW

Boerne, Alfred
See Doeblin, Alfred

Bogan, Louise 1897-1970..... CLC 4, 39, 46
See also CA 73-76; 25-28R; CANR 33;
DLB 45; MTCW

Bogarde, Dirk .... CLC 19
See also Van Den Bogarde, Derek Jules
Gaspard Ulric Niven
See also DLB 14

Bogosian, Eric 1953- .... CLC 45
See also CA 138

Bograd, Larry 1953-.............. CLC 35
See also CA 93-96; SATA 33

Boiardo, Matteo Maria 1441-1494 .... LC 6

Boileau-Despreaux, Nicolas
1636-1711 .... LC 3

Boland, Eavan (Aisling) 1944-... CLC 40, 67
See also CA 143; DLB 40

Bolt, Lee
See Faust, Frederick (Schiller)

Bolt, Robert (Oxton) 1924-........ CLC 14
See also CA 17-20R; CANR 35; DLB 13;
MTCW

Bombet, Louis-Alexandre-Cesar
See Stendhal

Bomkauf
See Kaufman, Bob (Garnell)

Bonaventura.................... NCLC 35
See also DLB 90

Bond, Edward 1934-...... CLC 4, 6, 13, 23
See also CA 25-28R; CANR 38; DLB 13;
MTCW

Bonham, Frank 1914-1989......... CLC 12
See also AAYA 1; CA 9-12R; CANR 4, 36;
JRDA; MAICYA; SAAS 3; SATA 1, 49;
SATA-Obit 62

Bonnefoy, Yves 1923-........ CLC 9, 15, 58
See also CA 85-88; CANR 33; MTCW

Bontemps, Arna(ud Wendell)
1902-1973 .... CLC 1, 18; BLC
See also BW 1; CA 1-4R; 41-44R; CANR 4,
35; CLR 6; DLB 48, 51; JRDA;
MAICYA; MTCW; SATA 2, 44;
SATA-Obit 24

Booth, Martin 1944-.............. CLC 13
See also CA 93-96; CAAS 2

Booth, Philip 1925-.............. CLC 23
See also CA 5-8R; CANR 5; DLBY 82

Booth, Wayne C(layson) 1921- ..... CLC 24
See also CA 1-4R; CAAS 5; CANR 3, 43;
DLB 67

Borchert, Wolfgang 1921-1947 ..... TCLC 5
See also CA 104; DLB 69, 124

Borel, Petrus 1809-1859........ NCLC 41

Borges, Jorge Luis
1899-1986 ... CLC 1, 2, 3, 4, 6, 8, 9, 10,
13, 19, 44, 48, 83; DA; HLC; SSC 4;
WLC
See also CA 21-24R; CANR 19, 33;
DLB 113; DLBY 86; HW; MTCW

Borowski, Tadeusz 1922-1951 ...... TCLC 9
See also CA 106

Borrow, George (Henry)
1803-1881 .... NCLC 9
See also DLB 21, 55

Bosman, Herman Charles
1905-1951 .... TCLC 49

Bosschere, Jean de 1878(?)-1953... TCLC 19
See also CA 115

Boswell, James
1740-1795 .... LC 4; DA; WLC
See also CDBLB 1660-1789; DLB 104, 142

Bottoms, David 1949-............. CLC 53
See also CA 105; CANR 22; DLB 120;
DLBY 83

Boucicault, Dion 1820-1890...... NCLC 41

Boucolon, Maryse 1937-
See Conde, Maryse
See also CA 110; CANR 30

Bourget, Paul (Charles Joseph)
1852-1935 .... TCLC 12
See also CA 107; DLB 123

Bourjaily, Vance (Nye) 1922- .... CLC 8, 62
See also CA 1-4R; CAAS 1; CANR 2;
DLB 2, 143

Bourne, Randolph S(illiman)
1886-1918 .... TCLC 16
See also CA 117; DLB 63

Bova, Ben(jamin William) 1932-.... CLC 45
See also CA 5-8R; CAAS 18; CANR 11;
CLR 3; DLBY 81; MAICYA; MTCW;
SATA 6, 68

Bowen, Elizabeth (Dorothea Cole)
1899-1973 ...... CLC 1, 3, 6, 11, 15, 22;
SSC 3
See also CA 17-18; 41-44R; CANR 35;
CAP 2; CDBLB 1945-1960; DLB 15;
MTCW

Bowering, George 1935-........ CLC 15, 47
See also CA 21-24R; CAAS 16; CANR 10;
DLB 53

Bowering, Marilyn R(uthe) 1949-... CLC 32
See also CA 101

Bowers, Edgar 1924- .... CLC 9
See also CA 5-8R; CANR 24; DLB 5

Bowie, David .... CLC 17
See also Jones, David Robert

Bowles, Jane (Sydney)
1917-1973 .... CLC 3, 68
See also CA 19-20; 41-44R; CAP 2

Bowles, Paul (Frederick)
1910- .... CLC 1, 2, 19, 53; SSC 3
See also CA 1-4R; CAAS 1; CANR 1, 19;
DLB 5, 6; MTCW

Box, Edgar
See Vidal, Gore

Boyd, Nancy
See Millay, Edna St. Vincent

Boyd, William 1952-....... CLC 28, 53, 70
See also CA 114; 120

Boyle, Kay
1902-1992 ..... CLC 1, 5, 19, 58; SSC 5
See also CA 13-16R; 140; CAAS 1;
CANR 29; DLB 4, 9, 48, 86; DLBY 93;
MTCW

Boyle, Mark
See Kienzle, William X(avier)

Boyle, Patrick 1905-1982......... CLC 19
See also CA 127

Boyle, T. C.
See Boyle, T(homas) Coraghessan

Boyle, T(homas) Coraghessan
1948- .... CLC 36, 55; SSC 16
See also BEST 90:4; CA 120; CANR 44;
DLBY 86

Boz
See Dickens, Charles (John Huffam)

Brackenridge, Hugh Henry
1748-1816 .... NCLC 7
See also DLB 11, 37

Bradbury, Edward P.
See Moorcock, Michael (John)

Bradbury, Malcolm (Stanley)
1932- .... CLC 32, 61
See also CA 1-4R; CANR 1, 33; DLB 14;
MTCW

Bradbury, Ray (Douglas)
1920- ... CLC 1, 3, 10, 15, 42; DA; WLC
See also AITN 1, 2; CA 1-4R; CANR 2, 30;
CDALB 1968-1988; DLB 2, 8; MTCW;
SATA 11, 64

Bradford, Gamaliel 1863-1932..... TCLC 36
See also DLB 17

Bradley, David (Henry, Jr.)
1950- .... CLC 23; BLC
See also BW 1; CA 104; CANR 26; DLB 33

Bradley, John Ed(mund, Jr.)
1958- .... CLC 55
See also CA 139

Bradley, Marion Zimmer 1930-..... CLC 30
See also AAYA 9; CA 57-60; CAAS 10;
CANR 7, 31; DLB 8; MTCW

Bradstreet, Anne
1612(?)-1672 .... LC 4; DA; PC 10
See also CDALB 1640-1865; DLB 24

Brady, Joan 1939- .... CLC 86
See also CA 141

Bragg, Melvyn 1939- .... CLC 10
See also BEST 89:3; CA 57-60; CANR 10;
DLB 14

Braine, John (Gerard)
1922-1986 .... CLC 1, 3, 41
See also CA 1-4R; 120; CANR 1, 33;
CDBLB 1945-1960; DLB 15; DLBY 86;
MTCW

Brammer, William 1930(?)-1978 .... CLC 31
See also CA 77-80

Brancati, Vitaliano 1907-1954..... TCLC 12
See also CA 109

Brancato, Robin F(idler) 1936-..... CLC 35
See also AAYA 9; CA 69-72; CANR 11,
45; CLR 32; JRDA; SAAS 9; SATA 23

Brand, Max
See Faust, Frederick (Schiller)

Brand, Millen 1906-1980.......... CLC 7
See also CA 21-24R; 97-100

Branden, Barbara .... CLC 44

Brandes, Georg (Morris Cohen)
1842-1927 .... TCLC 10
See also CA 105

Brandys, Kazimierz 1916- .... CLC 62

Branley, Franklyn M(ansfield)
1915- .... **CLC 21**
See also CA 33-36R; CANR 14, 39;
CLR 13; MAICYA; SAAS 16; SATA 4,
68

Brathwaite, Edward Kamau 1930-... **CLC 11**
See also BW 2; CA 25-28R; CANR 11, 26,
47; DLB 125

Brautigan, Richard (Gary)
1935-1984 .... **CLC 1, 3, 5, 9, 12, 34, 42**
See also CA 53-56; 113; CANR 34; DLB 2,
5; DLBY 80, 84; MTCW; SATA 56

Braverman, Kate 1950- .... **CLC 67**
See also CA 89-92

Brecht, Bertolt
1898-1956 ...... **TCLC 1, 6, 13, 35; DA;**
DC 3; WLC
See also CA 104; 133; DLB 56, 124; MTCW

Brecht, Eugen Berthold Friedrich
See Brecht, Bertolt

Bremer, Fredrika 1801-1865 ..... **NCLC 11**

Brennan, Christopher John
1870-1932 .... **TCLC 17**
See also CA 117

Brennan, Maeve 1917- .... **CLC 5**
See also CA 81-84

Brentano, Clemens (Maria)
1778-1842 .... **NCLC 1**
See also DLB 90

Brent of Bin Bin
See Franklin, (Stella Maraia Sarah) Miles

Brenton, Howard 1942- .... **CLC 31**
See also CA 69-72; CANR 33; DLB 13;
MTCW

Breslin, James 1930-
See Breslin, Jimmy
See also CA 73-76; CANR 31; MTCW

Breslin, Jimmy .... **CLC 4, 43**
See also Breslin, James
See also AITN 1

Bresson, Robert 1907- .... **CLC 16**
See also CA 110

Breton, Andre 1896-1966... **CLC 2, 9, 15, 54**
See also CA 19-20; 25-28R; CANR 40;
CAP 2; DLB 65; MTCW

Breytenbach, Breyten 1939(?)- .. **CLC 23, 37**
See also CA 113; 129

Bridgers, Sue Ellen 1942- .... **CLC 26**
See also AAYA 8; CA 65-68; CANR 11,
36; CLR 18; DLB 52; JRDA; MAICYA;
SAAS 1; SATA 22

Bridges, Robert (Seymour)
1844-1930 .... **TCLC 1**
See also CA 104; CDBLB 1890-1914;
DLB 19, 98

Bridie, James .... **TCLC 3**
See also Mavor, Osborne Henry
See also DLB 10

Brin, David 1950-................ **CLC 34**
See also CA 102; CANR 24; SATA 65

Brink, Andre (Philippus)
1935- .... **CLC 18, 36**
See also CA 104; CANR 39; MTCW

Brinsmead, H(esba) F(ay) 1922- .... **CLC 21**
See also CA 21-24R; CANR 10; MAICYA;
SAAS 5; SATA 18, 78

Brittain, Vera (Mary)
1893(?)-1970 .... **CLC 23**
See also CA 13-16; 25-28R; CAP 1; MTCW

Broch, Hermann 1886-1951....... **TCLC 20**
See also CA 117; DLB 85, 124

Brock, Rose
See Hansen, Joseph

Brodkey, Harold 1930-........... **CLC 56**
See also CA 111; DLB 130

Brodsky, Iosif Alexandrovich 1940-
See Brodsky, Joseph
See also AITN 1; CA 41-44R; CANR 37;
MTCW

Brodsky, Joseph .. **CLC 4, 6, 13, 36, 50; PC 9**
See also Brodsky, Iosif Alexandrovich

Brodsky, Michael Mark 1948- ..... **CLC 19**
See also CA 102; CANR 18, 41

Bromell, Henry 1947-.............. **CLC 5**
See also CA 53-56; CANR 9

Bromfield, Louis (Brucker)
1896-1956 .... **TCLC 11**
See also CA 107; DLB 4, 9, 86

Broner, E(sther) M(asserman)
1930- .... **CLC 19**
See also CA 17-20R; CANR 8, 25; DLB 28

Bronk, William 1918-............. **CLC 10**
See also CA 89-92; CANR 23

Bronstein, Lev Davidovich
See Trotsky, Leon

Bronte, Anne 1820-1849......... **NCLC 4**
See also DLB 21

Bronte, Charlotte
1816-1855 ... **NCLC 3, 8, 33; DA; WLC**
See also CDBLB 1832-1890; DLB 21

Bronte, (Jane) Emily
1818-1848 .... **NCLC 16, 35; DA; PC 8;**
WLC
See also CDBLB 1832-1890; DLB 21, 32

Brooke, Frances 1724-1789 .... **LC 6**
See also DLB 39, 99

Brooke, Henry 1703(?)-1783 .... **LC 1**
See also DLB 39

Brooke, Rupert (Chawner)
1887-1915 .... **TCLC 2, 7; DA; WLC**
See also CA 104; 132; CDBLB 1914-1945;
DLB 19; MTCW

Brooke-Haven, P.
See Wodehouse, P(elham) G(renville)

Brooke-Rose, Christine 1926- ...... **CLC 40**
See also CA 13-16R; DLB 14

Brookner, Anita 1928-...... **CLC 32, 34, 51**
See also CA 114; 120; CANR 37; DLBY 87;
MTCW

Brooks, Cleanth 1906-1994 ..... **CLC 24, 86**
See also CA 17-20R; 145; CANR 33, 35;
DLB 63; MTCW

Brooks, George
See Baum, L(yman) Frank

Brooks, Gwendolyn
1917- ...... **CLC 1, 2, 4, 5, 15, 49; BLC;**
DA; PC 7; WLC
See also AITN 1; BW 2; CA 1-4R;
CANR 1, 27; CDALB 1941-1968;
CLR 27; DLB 5, 76; MTCW; SATA 6

Brooks, Mel...................... **CLC 12**
See also Kaminsky, Melvin
See also AAYA 13; DLB 26

Brooks, Peter 1938-.............. **CLC 34**
See also CA 45-48; CANR 1

Brooks, Van Wyck 1886-1963...... **CLC 29**
See also CA 1-4R; CANR 6; DLB 45, 63,
103

Brophy, Brigid (Antonia)
1929- .... **CLC 6, 11, 29**
See also CA 5-8R; CAAS 4; CANR 25;
DLB 14; MTCW

Brosman, Catharine Savage 1934-.... **CLC 9**
See also CA 61-64; CANR 21, 46, 46

Brother Antoninus
See Everson, William (Oliver)

Broughton, T(homas) Alan 1936- ... **CLC 19**
See also CA 45-48; CANR 2, 23

Broumas, Olga 1949- .... **CLC 10, 73**
See also CA 85-88; CANR 20

Brown, Charles Brockden
1771-1810 .... **NCLC 22**
See also CDALB 1640-1865; DLB 37, 59,
73

Brown, Christy 1932-1981........ **CLC 63**
See also CA 105; 104; DLB 14

Brown, Claude 1937- .... **CLC 30; BLC**
See also AAYA 7; BW 1; CA 73-76

Brown, Dee (Alexander) 1908-.. **CLC 18, 47**
See also CA 13-16R; CAAS 6; CANR 11,
45; DLBY 80; MTCW; SATA 5

Brown, George
See Wertmueller, Lina

Brown, George Douglas
1869-1902 .... **TCLC 28**

Brown, George Mackay 1921-.... **CLC 5, 48**
See also CA 21-24R; CAAS 6; CANR 12,
37; DLB 14, 27, 139; MTCW; SATA 35

Brown, (William) Larry 1951-...... **CLC 73**
See also CA 130; 134

Brown, Moses
See Barrett, William (Christopher)

Brown, Rita Mae 1944-..... **CLC 18, 43, 79**
See also CA 45-48; CANR 2, 11, 35;
MTCW

Brown, Roderick (Langmere) Haig-
See Haig-Brown, Roderick (Langmere)

Brown, Rosellen 1939-............ **CLC 32**
See also CA 77-80; CAAS 10; CANR 14, 44

Brown, Sterling Allen
1901-1989 .... **CLC 1, 23, 59; BLC**
See also BW 1; CA 85-88; 127; CANR 26;
DLB 48, 51, 63; MTCW

Brown, Will
See Ainsworth, William Harrison

Brown, William Wells
1813-1884 .... **NCLC 2; BLC; DC 1**
See also DLB 3, 50

Browne, (Clyde) Jackson 1948(?)-... CLC 21
See also CA 120

Browning, Elizabeth Barrett
1806-1861 ..... NCLC 1, 16; DA; PC 6;
WLC
See also CDBLB 1832-1890; DLB 32

Browning, Robert
1812-1889 .... NCLC 19; DA; PC 2
See also CDBLB 1832-1890; DLB 32;
YABC 1

Browning, Tod 1882-1962 .... CLC 16
See also CA 141; 117

Bruccoli, Matthew J(oseph) 1931- .. CLC 34
See also CA 9-12R; CANR 7; DLB 103

Bruce, Lenny .... CLC 21
See also Schneider, Leonard Alfred

Bruin, John
See Brutus, Dennis

Brulard, Henri
See Stendhal

Brulls, Christian
See Simenon, Georges (Jacques Christian)

Brunner, John (Kilian Houston)
1934- .... CLC 8, 10
See also CA 1-4R; CAAS 8; CANR 2, 37;
MTCW

Bruno, Giordano 1548-1600........ LC 27

Brutus, Dennis 1924- .... CLC 43; BLC
See also BW 2; CA 49-52; CAAS 14;
CANR 2, 27, 42; DLB 117

Bryan, C(ourtlandt) D(ixon) B(arnes)
1936- .... CLC 29
See also CA 73-76; CANR 13

Bryan, Michael
See Moore, Brian

Bryant, William Cullen
1794-1878 .... NCLC 6, 46; DA
See also CDALB 1640-1865; DLB 3, 43, 59

Bryusov, Valery Yakovlevich
1873-1924 .... TCLC 10
See also CA 107

Buchan, John 1875-1940 .... TCLC 41
See also CA 108; 145; DLB 34, 70; YABC 2

Buchanan, George 1506-1582 .... LC 4

Buchheim, Lothar-Guenther 1918- ... CLC 6
See also CA 85-88

Buchner, (Karl) Georg
1813-1837 .... NCLC 26

Buchwald, Art(hur) 1925-.......... CLC 33
See also AITN 1; CA 5-8R; CANR 21;
MTCW; SATA 10

Buck, Pearl S(ydenstricker)
1892-1973 .... CLC 7, 11, 18; DA
See also AITN 1; CA 1-4R; 41-44R;
CANR 1, 34; DLB 9, 102; MTCW;
SATA 1, 25

Buckler, Ernest 1908-1984........ CLC 13
See also CA 11-12; 114; CAP 1; DLB 68;
SATA 47

Buckley, Vincent (Thomas)
1925-1988 .... CLC 57
See also CA 101

Buckley, William F(rank), Jr.
1925- .... CLC 7, 18, 37
See also AITN 1; CA 1-4R; CANR 1, 24;
DLB 137; DLBY 80; MTCW

Buechner, (Carl) Frederick
1926- .... CLC 2, 4, 6, 9
See also CA 13-16R; CANR 11, 39;
DLBY 80; MTCW

Buell, John (Edward) 1927-........ CLC 10
See also CA 1-4R; DLB 53

Buero Vallejo, Antonio 1916- ... CLC 15, 46
See also CA 106; CANR 24; HW; MTCW

Bufalino, Gesualdo 1920(?)-........ CLC 74

Bugayev, Boris Nikolayevich 1880-1934
See Bely, Andrey
See also CA 104

Bukowski, Charles
1920-1994 .... CLC 2, 5, 9, 41, 82
See also CA 17-20R; 144; CANR 40;
DLB 5, 130; MTCW

Bulgakov, Mikhail (Afanas'evich)
1891-1940 .... TCLC 2, 16; SSC 18
See also CA 105

Bulgya, Alexander Alexandrovich
1901-1956 .... TCLC 53
See also Fadeyev, Alexander
See also CA 117

Bullins, Ed 1935- .... CLC 1, 5, 7; BLC
See also BW 2; CA 49-52; CAAS 16;
CANR 24, 46, 46; DLB 7, 38; MTCW

Bulwer-Lytton, Edward (George Earle Lytton)
1803-1873 .... NCLC 1, 45
See also DLB 21

Bunin, Ivan Alexeyevich
1870-1953 .... TCLC 6; SSC 5
See also CA 104

Bunting, Basil 1900-1985.... CLC 10, 39, 47
See also CA 53-56; 115; CANR 7; DLB 20

Bunuel, Luis 1900-1983 .. CLC 16, 80; HLC
See also CA 101; 110; CANR 32; HW

Bunyan, John 1628-1688 .. LC 4; DA; WLC
See also CDBLB 1660-1789; DLB 39

Burford, Eleanor
See Hibbert, Eleanor Alice Burford

Burgess, Anthony
. CLC 1, 2, 4, 5, 8, 10, 13, 15, 22, 40, 62,
81
See also Wilson, John (Anthony) Burgess
See also AITN 1; CDBLB 1960 to Present;
DLB 14

Burke, Edmund
1729(?)-1797 .... LC 7; DA; WLC
See also DLB 104

Burke, Kenneth (Duva)
1897-1993 .... CLC 2, 24
See also CA 5-8R; 143; CANR 39; DLB 45,
63; MTCW

Burke, Leda
See Garnett, David

Burke, Ralph
See Silverberg, Robert

Burney, Fanny 1752-1840 .... NCLC 12
See also DLB 39

Burns, Robert
1759-1796 ...... LC 3; DA; PC 6; WLC
See also CDBLB 1789-1832; DLB 109

Burns, Tex
See L'Amour, Louis (Dearborn)

Burnshaw, Stanley 1906-..... CLC 3, 13, 44
See also CA 9-12R; DLB 48

Burr, Anne 1937-................. CLC 6
See also CA 25-28R

Burroughs, Edgar Rice
1875-1950 .... TCLC 2, 32
See also AAYA 11; CA 104; 132; DLB 8;
MTCW; SATA 41

Burroughs, William S(eward)
1914- .... CLC 1, 2, 5, 15, 22, 42, 75;
DA; WLC
See also AITN 2; CA 9-12R; CANR 20;
DLB 2, 8, 16; DLBY 81; MTCW

Burton, Richard F. 1821-1890.... NCLC 42
See also DLB 55

Busch, Frederick 1941- ... CLC 7, 10, 18, 47
See also CA 33-36R; CAAS 1; CANR 45;
DLB 6

Bush, Ronald 1946- .... CLC 34
See also CA 136

Bustos, F(rancisco)
See Borges, Jorge Luis

Bustos Domecq, H(onorio)
See Bioy Casares, Adolfo; Borges, Jorge
Luis

Butler, Octavia E(stelle) 1947-..... CLC 38
See also BW 2; CA 73-76; CANR 12, 24,
38; DLB 33; MTCW

Butler, Robert Olen (Jr.) 1945-..... CLC 81
See also CA 112

Butler, Samuel 1612-1680 .... LC 16
See also DLB 101, 126

Butler, Samuel
1835-1902 ...... TCLC 1, 33; DA; WLC
See also CA 143; CDBLB 1890-1914;
DLB 18, 57

Butler, Walter C.
See Faust, Frederick (Schiller)

Butor, Michel (Marie Francois)
1926- .... CLC 1, 3, 8, 11, 15
See also CA 9-12R; CANR 33; DLB 83;
MTCW

Buzo, Alexander (John) 1944-...... CLC 61
See also CA 97-100; CANR 17, 39

Buzzati, Dino 1906-1972 .... CLC 36
See also CA 33-36R

Byars, Betsy (Cromer) 1928-....... CLC 35
See also CA 33-36R; CANR 18, 36; CLR 1,
16; DLB 52; JRDA; MAICYA; MTCW;
SAAS 1; SATA 4, 46, 80

Byatt, A(ntonia) S(usan Drabble)
1936- .... CLC 19, 65
See also CA 13-16R; CANR 13, 33;
DLB 14; MTCW

Byrne, David 1952-.............. CLC 26
See also CA 127

Byrne, John Keyes 1926-
See Leonard, Hugh
See also CA 102

Byron, George Gordon (Noel)
    1788-1824 ...... **NCLC 2, 12; DA; WLC**
    See also CDBLB 1789-1832; DLB 96, 110

C. 3. 3.
    See Wilde, Oscar (Fingal O'Flahertie Wills)

Caballero, Fernan 1796-1877..... **NCLC 10**

Cabell, James Branch 1879-1958 ... **TCLC 6**
    See also CA 105; DLB 9, 78

Cable, George Washington
    1844-1925 .... **TCLC 4; SSC 4**
    See also CA 104; DLB 12, 74

Cabral de Melo Neto, Joao 1920-... **CLC 76**

Cabrera Infante, G(uillermo)
    1929- .... **CLC 5, 25, 45; HLC**
    See also CA 85-88; CANR 29; DLB 113;
    HW; MTCW

Cade, Toni
    See Bambara, Toni Cade

Cadmus and Harmonia
    See Buchan, John

Caedmon fl. 658-680............. **CMLC 7**
    See also DLB 146

Caeiro, Alberto
    See Pessoa, Fernando (Antonio Nogueira)

Cage, John (Milton, Jr.) 1912- ..... **CLC 41**
    See also CA 13-16R; CANR 9

Cain, G.
    See Cabrera Infante, G(uillermo)

Cain, Guillermo
    See Cabrera Infante, G(uillermo)

Cain, James M(allahan)
    1892-1977 .... **CLC 3, 11, 28**
    See also AITN 1; CA 17-20R; 73-76;
    CANR 8, 34; MTCW

Caine, Mark
    See Raphael, Frederic (Michael)

Calasso, Roberto 1941- .... **CLC 81**
    See also CA 143

Calderon de la Barca, Pedro
    1600-1681 .... **LC 23; DC 3**

Caldwell, Erskine (Preston)
    1903-1987 .... **CLC 1, 8, 14, 50, 60**
    See also AITN 1; CA 1-4R; 121; CAAS 1;
    CANR 2, 33; DLB 9, 86; MTCW

Caldwell, (Janet Miriam) Taylor (Holland)
    1900-1985 .... **CLC 2, 28, 39**
    See also CA 5-8R; 116; CANR 5

Calhoun, John Caldwell
    1782-1850 .... **NCLC 15**
    See also DLB 3

Calisher, Hortense
    1911- .... **CLC 2, 4, 8, 38; SSC 15**
    See also CA 1-4R; CANR 1, 22; DLB 2;
    MTCW

Callaghan, Morley Edward
    1903-1990 .... **CLC 3, 14, 41, 65**
    See also CA 9-12R; 132; CANR 33;
    DLB 68; MTCW

Calvino, Italo
    1923-1985 ..... **CLC 5, 8, 11, 22, 33, 39,
                              73; SSC 3**
    See also CA 85-88; 116; CANR 23; MTCW

Cameron, Carey 1952- .... **CLC 59**
    See also CA 135

Cameron, Peter 1959-............ **CLC 44**
    See also CA 125

Campana, Dino 1885-1932....... **TCLC 20**
    See also CA 117; DLB 114

Campbell, John W(ood, Jr.)
    1910-1971 .... **CLC 32**
    See also CA 21-22; 29-32R; CANR 34;
    CAP 2; DLB 8; MTCW

Campbell, Joseph 1904-1987 .... **CLC 69**
    See also AAYA 3; BEST 89:2; CA 1-4R;
    124; CANR 3, 28; MTCW

Campbell, Maria 1940-........... **CLC 85**
    See also CA 102; NNAL

Campbell, (John) Ramsey 1946- .... **CLC 42**
    See also CA 57-60; CANR 7

Campbell, (Ignatius) Roy (Dunnachie)
    1901-1957 .... **TCLC 5**
    See also CA 104; DLB 20

Campbell, Thomas 1777-1844 .... **NCLC 19**
    See also DLB 93; 144

Campbell, Wilfred .... **TCLC 9**
    See also Campbell, William

Campbell, William 1858(?)-1918
    See Campbell, Wilfred
    See also CA 106; DLB 92

Campos, Alvaro de
    See Pessoa, Fernando (Antonio Nogueira)

Camus, Albert
    1913-1960 .... **CLC 1, 2, 4, 9, 11, 14, 32,
                         63, 69; DA; DC 2; SSC 9; WLC**
    See also CA 89-92; DLB 72; MTCW

Canby, Vincent 1924-............ **CLC 13**
    See also CA 81-84

Cancale
    See Desnos, Robert

Canetti, Elias
    1905-1994 .... **CLC 3, 14, 25, 75, 86**
    See also CA 21-24R; 146; CANR 23;
    DLB 85, 124; MTCW

Canin, Ethan 1960-............... **CLC 55**
    See also CA 131; 135

Cannon, Curt
    See Hunter, Evan

Cape, Judith
    See Page, P(atricia) K(athleen)

Capek, Karel
    1890-1938 ..... **TCLC 6, 37; DA; DC 1;
                                        WLC**
    See also CA 104; 140

Capote, Truman
    1924-1984 ...... **CLC 1, 3, 8, 13, 19, 34,
                             38, 58; DA; SSC 2; WLC**
    See also CA 5-8R; 113; CANR 18;
    CDALB 1941-1968; DLB 2; DLBY 80,
    84; MTCW

Capra, Frank 1897-1991........... **CLC 16**
    See also CA 61-64; 135

Caputo, Philip 1941-.............. **CLC 32**
    See also CA 73-76; CANR 40

Card, Orson Scott 1951- .... **CLC 44, 47, 50**
    See also AAYA 11; CA 102; CANR 27, 47;
    MTCW

Cardenal (Martinez), Ernesto
    1925- .... **CLC 31; HLC**
    See also CA 49-52; CANR 2, 32; HW;
    MTCW

Carducci, Giosue 1835-1907...... **TCLC 32**

Carew, Thomas 1595(?)-1640........ **LC 13**
    See also DLB 126

Carey, Ernestine Gilbreth 1908-.... **CLC 17**
    See also CA 5-8R; SATA 2

Carey, Peter 1943-............. **CLC 40, 55**
    See also CA 123; 127; MTCW

Carleton, William 1794-1869...... **NCLC 3**

Carlisle, Henry (Coffin) 1926-...... **CLC 33**
    See also CA 13-16R; CANR 15

Carlsen, Chris
    See Holdstock, Robert P.

Carlson, Ron(ald F.) 1947-........ **CLC 54**
    See also CA 105; CANR 27

Carlyle, Thomas 1795-1881 .. **NCLC 22; DA**
    See also CDBLB 1789-1832; DLB 55; 144

Carman, (William) Bliss
    1861-1929 .... **TCLC 7**
    See also CA 104; DLB 92

Carnegie, Dale 1888-1955 .... **TCLC 53**

Carossa, Hans 1878-1956........ **TCLC 48**
    See also DLB 66

Carpenter, Don(ald Richard)
    1931- .... **CLC 41**
    See also CA 45-48; CANR 1

Carpentier (y Valmont), Alejo
    1904-1980 .... **CLC 8, 11, 38; HLC**
    See also CA 65-68; 97-100; CANR 11;
    DLB 113; HW

Carr, Caleb 1955(?)-.............. **CLC 86**

Carr, Emily 1871-1945........... **TCLC 32**
    See also DLB 68

Carr, John Dickson 1906-1977 ...... **CLC 3**
    See also CA 49-52; 69-72; CANR 3, 33;
    MTCW

Carr, Philippa
    See Hibbert, Eleanor Alice Burford

Carr, Virginia Spencer 1929-....... **CLC 34**
    See also CA 61-64; DLB 111

Carrier, Roch 1937-........... **CLC 13, 78**
    See also CA 130; DLB 53

Carroll, James P. 1943(?)-........ **CLC 38**
    See also CA 81-84

Carroll, Jim 1951- .... **CLC 35**
    See also CA 45-48; CANR 42

Carroll, Lewis .... **NCLC 2; WLC**
    See also Dodgson, Charles Lutwidge
    See also CDBLB 1832-1890; CLR 2, 18;
    DLB 18; JRDA

Carroll, Paul Vincent 1900-1968.... **CLC 10**
    See also CA 9-12R; 25-28R; DLB 10

Carruth, Hayden
    1921- ...... **CLC 4, 7, 10, 18, 84; PC 10**
    See also CA 9-12R; CANR 4, 38; DLB 5;
    MTCW; SATA 47

Carson, Rachel Louise 1907-1964... **CLC 71**
    See also CA 77-80; CANR 35; MTCW;
    SATA 23

Cleaver, (Leroy) Eldridge
1935- . . . . CLC 30; BLC
See also BW 1; CA 21-24R; CANR 16

Cleese, John (Marwood) 1939- . . . . . CLC 21
See also Monty Python
See also CA 112; 116; CANR 35; MTCW

Cleishbotham, Jebediah
See Scott, Walter

Cleland, John 1710-1789 . . . . LC 2
See also DLB 39

Clemens, Samuel Langhorne 1835-1910
See Twain, Mark
See also CA 104; 135; CDALB 1865-1917;
DA; DLB 11, 12, 23, 64, 74; JRDA;
MAICYA; YABC 2

Cleophil
See Congreve, William

Clerihew, E.
See Bentley, E(dmund) C(lerihew)

Clerk, N. W.
See Lewis, C(live) S(taples)

Cliff, Jimmy. . . . . CLC 21
See also Chambers, James

Clifton, (Thelma) Lucille
1936- . . . . CLC 19, 66; BLC
See also BW 2; CA 49-52; CANR 2, 24, 42;
CLR 5; DLB 5, 41; MAICYA; MTCW;
SATA 20, 69

Clinton, Dirk
See Silverberg, Robert

Clough, Arthur Hugh 1819-1861 . . NCLC 27
See also DLB 32

Clutha, Janet Paterson Frame 1924-
See Frame, Janet
See also CA 1-4R; CANR 2, 36; MTCW

Clyne, Terence
See Blatty, William Peter

Cobalt, Martin
See Mayne, William (James Carter)

Coburn, D(onald) L(ee) 1938- . . . . . . CLC 10
See also CA 89-92

Cocteau, Jean (Maurice Eugene Clement)
1889-1963 . . . . CLC 1, 8, 15, 16, 43; DA;
                                           WLC
See also CA 25-28; CANR 40; CAP 2;
DLB 65; MTCW

Codrescu, Andrei 1946- . . . . CLC 46
See also CA 33-36R; CAAS 19; CANR 13,
34

Coe, Max
See Bourne, Randolph S(illiman)

Coe, Tucker
See Westlake, Donald E(dwin)

Coetzee, J(ohn) M(ichael)
1940- . . . . CLC 23, 33, 66
See also CA 77-80; CANR 41; MTCW

Coffey, Brian
See Koontz, Dean R(ay)

Cohen, Arthur A(llen)
1928-1986 . . . . CLC 7, 31
See also CA 1-4R; 120; CANR 1, 17, 42;
DLB 28

Cohen, Leonard (Norman)
1934- . . . . CLC 3, 38
See also CA 21-24R; CANR 14; DLB 53;
MTCW

Cohen, Matt 1942- . . . . CLC 19
See also CA 61-64; CAAS 18; CANR 40;
DLB 53

Cohen-Solal, Annie 19(?)- . . . . CLC 50

Colegate, Isabel 1931- . . . . CLC 36
See also CA 17-20R; CANR 8, 22; DLB 14;
MTCW

Coleman, Emmett
See Reed, Ishmael

Coleridge, Samuel Taylor
1772-1834 . . NCLC 9; DA; PC 11; WLC
See also CDBLB 1789-1832; DLB 93, 107

Coleridge, Sara 1802-1852 . . . . . . NCLC 31

Coles, Don 1928- . . . . CLC 46
See also CA 115; CANR 38

Colette, (Sidonie-Gabrielle)
1873-1954 . . . . . . TCLC 1, 5, 16; SSC 10
See also CA 104; 131; DLB 65; MTCW

Collett, (Jacobine) Camilla (Wergeland)
1813-1895 . . . . NCLC 22

Collier, Christopher 1930- . . . . CLC 30
See also AAYA 13; CA 33-36R; CANR 13,
33; JRDA; MAICYA; SATA 16, 70

Collier, James L(incoln) 1928- . . . . . CLC 30
See also AAYA 13; CA 9-12R; CANR 4,
33; CLR 3; JRDA; MAICYA; SATA 8,
70

Collier, Jeremy 1650-1726 . . . . LC 6

Collins, Hunt
See Hunter, Evan

Collins, Linda 1931- . . . . CLC 44
See also CA 125

Collins, (William) Wilkie
1824-1889 . . . . NCLC 1, 18
See also CDBLB 1832-1890; DLB 18, 70

Collins, William 1721-1759 . . . . LC 4
See also DLB 109

Colman, George
See Glassco, John

Colt, Winchester Remington
See Hubbard, L(afayette) Ron(ald)

Colter, Cyrus 1910- . . . . CLC 58
See also BW 1; CA 65-68; CANR 10;
DLB 33

Colton, James
See Hansen, Joseph

Colum, Padraic 1881-1972 . . . . CLC 28
See also CA 73-76; 33-36R; CANR 35;
CLR 36; MAICYA; MTCW; SATA 15

Colvin, James
See Moorcock, Michael (John)

Colwin, Laurie (E.)
1944-1992 . . . . CLC 5, 13, 23, 84
See also CA 89-92; 139; CANR 20, 46, 46;
DLBY 80; MTCW

Comfort, Alex(ander) 1920- . . . . CLC 7
See also CA 1-4R; CANR 1, 45

Comfort, Montgomery
See Campbell, (John) Ramsey

Compton-Burnett, I(vy)
1884(?)-1969 . . . . . . CLC 1, 3, 10, 15, 34
See also CA 1-4R; 25-28R; CANR 4;
DLB 36; MTCW

Comstock, Anthony 1844-1915 . . . . TCLC 13
See also CA 110

Conan Doyle, Arthur
See Doyle, Arthur Conan

Conde, Maryse 1937- . . . . CLC 52
See also Boucolon, Maryse
See also BW 2

Condillac, Etienne Bonnot de
1714-1780 . . . . LC 26

Condon, Richard (Thomas)
1915- . . . . CLC 4, 6, 8, 10, 45
See also BEST 90:3; CA 1-4R; CAAS 1;
CANR 2, 23; MTCW

Congreve, William
1670-1729 . . . LC 5, 21; DA; DC 2; WLC
See also CDBLB 1660-1789; DLB 39, 84

Connell, Evan S(helby), Jr.
1924- . . . . CLC 4, 6, 45
See also AAYA 7; CA 1-4R; CAAS 2;
CANR 2, 39; DLB 2; DLBY 81; MTCW

Connelly, Marc(us Cook)
1890-1980 . . . . CLC 7
See also CA 85-88; 102; CANR 30; DLB 7;
DLBY 80; SATA-Obit 25

Connor, Ralph . . . . TCLC 31
See also Gordon, Charles William
See also DLB 92

Conrad, Joseph
1857-1924 . . . . TCLC 1, 6, 13, 25, 43, 57;
                                     DA; SSC 9; WLC
See also CA 104; 131; CDBLB 1890-1914;
DLB 10, 34, 98; MTCW; SATA 27

Conrad, Robert Arnold
See Hart, Moss

Conroy, Pat 1945- . . . . CLC 30, 74
See also AAYA 8; AITN 1; CA 85-88;
CANR 24; DLB 6; MTCW

Constant (de Rebecque), (Henri) Benjamin
1767-1830 . . . . NCLC 6
See also DLB 119

Conybeare, Charles Augustus
See Eliot, T(homas) S(tearns)

Cook, Michael 1933- . . . . CLC 58
See also CA 93-96; DLB 53

Cook, Robin 1940- . . . . CLC 14
See also BEST 90:2; CA 108; 111;
CANR 41

Cook, Roy
See Silverberg, Robert

Cooke, Elizabeth 1948- . . . . CLC 55
See also CA 129

Cooke, John Esten 1830-1886 . . . . . NCLC 5
See also DLB 3

Cooke, John Estes
See Baum, L(yman) Frank

Cooke, M. E.
See Creasey, John

Cooke, Margaret
See Creasey, John

Cooney, Ray . . . . CLC 62

Davison, Peter (Hubert) 1928- ..... **CLC 28**
See also CA 9-12R; CAAS 4; CANR 3, 43;
DLB 5

Davys, Mary 1674-1732............ **LC 1**
See also DLB 39

Dawson, Fielding 1930- .... **CLC 6**
See also CA 85-88; DLB 130

Dawson, Peter
See Faust, Frederick (Schiller)

Day, Clarence (Shepard, Jr.)
1874-1935 .... **TCLC 25**
See also CA 108; DLB 11

Day, Thomas 1748-1789............. **LC 1**
See also DLB 39; YABC 1

Day Lewis, C(ecil)
1904-1972 .... **CLC 1, 6, 10; PC 11**
See also Blake, Nicholas
See also CA 13-16; 33-36R; CANR 34;
CAP 1; DLB 15, 20; MTCW

Dazai, Osamu .... **TCLC 11**
See also Tsushima, Shuji

de Andrade, Carlos Drummond
See Drummond de Andrade, Carlos

Deane, Norman
See Creasey, John

**de Beauvoir, Simone (Lucie Ernestine Marie
Bertrand)**
See Beauvoir, Simone (Lucie Ernestine
Marie Bertrand) de

de Brissac, Malcolm
See Dickinson, Peter (Malcolm)

de Chardin, Pierre Teilhard
See Teilhard de Chardin, (Marie Joseph)
Pierre

Dee, John 1527-1608 .... **LC 20**

Deer, Sandra 1940-............... **CLC 45**

De Ferrari, Gabriella .... **CLC 65**

Defoe, Daniel
1660(?)-1731 .... **LC 1; DA; WLC**
See also CDBLB 1660-1789; DLB 39, 95,
101; JRDA; MAICYA; SATA 22

de Gourmont, Remy
See Gourmont, Remy de

de Hartog, Jan 1914-............. **CLC 19**
See also CA 1-4R; CANR 1

de Hostos, E. M.
See Hostos (y Bonilla), Eugenio Maria de

de Hostos, Eugenio M.
See Hostos (y Bonilla), Eugenio Maria de

Deighton, Len .... **CLC 4, 7, 22, 46**
See also Deighton, Leonard Cyril
See also AAYA 6; BEST 89:2;
CDBLB 1960 to Present; DLB 87

Deighton, Leonard Cyril 1929-
See Deighton, Len
See also CA 9-12R; CANR 19, 33; MTCW

Dekker, Thomas 1572(?)-1632....... **LC 22**
See also CDBLB Before 1660; DLB 62

de la Mare, Walter (John)
1873-1956 .. **TCLC 4, 53; SSC 14; WLC**
See also CDBLB 1914-1945; CLR 23;
DLB 19; SATA 16

Delaney, Franey
See O'Hara, John (Henry)

Delaney, Shelagh 1939-........... **CLC 29**
See also CA 17-20R; CANR 30;
CDBLB 1960 to Present; DLB 13;
MTCW

Delany, Mary (Granville Pendarves)
1700-1788 .... **LC 12**

Delany, Samuel R(ay, Jr.)
1942- .... **CLC 8, 14, 38; BLC**
See also BW 2; CA 81-84; CANR 27, 43;
DLB 8, 33; MTCW

De La Ramee, (Marie) Louise 1839-1908
See Ouida
See also SATA 20

de la Roche, Mazo 1879-1961...... **CLC 14**
See also CA 85-88; CANR 30; DLB 68;
SATA 64

Delbanco, Nicholas (Franklin)
1942- .... **CLC 6, 13**
See also CA 17-20R; CAAS 2; CANR 29;
DLB 6

del Castillo, Michel 1933- .... **CLC 38**
See also CA 109

Deledda, Grazia (Cosima)
1875(?)-1936 .... **TCLC 23**
See also CA 123

Delibes, Miguel .... **CLC 8, 18**
See also Delibes Setien, Miguel

Delibes Setien, Miguel 1920-
See Delibes, Miguel
See also CA 45-48; CANR 1, 32; HW;
MTCW

DeLillo, Don
1936- ..... **CLC 8, 10, 13, 27, 39, 54, 76**
See also BEST 89:1; CA 81-84; CANR 21;
DLB 6; MTCW

de Lisser, H. G.
See De Lisser, Herbert George
See also DLB 117

De Lisser, Herbert George
1878-1944 .... **TCLC 12**
See also de Lisser, H. G.
See also BW 2; CA 109

Deloria, Vine (Victor), Jr. 1933-.... **CLC 21**
See also CA 53-56; CANR 5, 20; MTCW;
NNAL; SATA 21

Del Vecchio, John M(ichael)
1947- .... **CLC 29**
See also CA 110; DLBD 9

de Man, Paul (Adolph Michel)
1919-1983 .... **CLC 55**
See also CA 128; 111; DLB 67; MTCW

De Marinis, Rick 1934-........... **CLC 54**
See also CA 57-60; CANR 9, 25

Demby, William 1922-....... **CLC 53; BLC**
See also BW 1; CA 81-84; DLB 33

Demijohn, Thom
See Disch, Thomas M(ichael)

de Montherlant, Henry (Milon)
See Montherlant, Henry (Milon) de

Demosthenes 384B.C.-322B.C. ... **CMLC 13**

de Natale, Francine
See Malzberg, Barry N(athaniel)

Denby, Edwin (Orr) 1903-1983 ..... **CLC 48**
See also CA 138; 110

Denis, Julio
See Cortazar, Julio

Denmark, Harrison
See Zelazny, Roger (Joseph)

Dennis, John 1658-1734............ **LC 11**
See also DLB 101

Dennis, Nigel (Forbes) 1912-1989.... **CLC 8**
See also CA 25-28R; 129; DLB 13, 15;
MTCW

De Palma, Brian (Russell) 1940-.... **CLC 20**
See also CA 109

De Quincey, Thomas 1785-1859 ... **NCLC 4**
See also CDBLB 1789-1832; DLB 110; 144

Deren, Eleanora 1908(?)-1961
See Deren, Maya
See also CA 111

Deren, Maya .... **CLC 16**
See also Deren, Eleanora

Derleth, August (William)
1909-1971 .... **CLC 31**
See also CA 1-4R; 29-32R; CANR 4;
DLB 9; SATA 5

Der Nister 1884-1950............ **TCLC 56**

de Routisie, Albert
See Aragon, Louis

Derrida, Jacques 1930-............ **CLC 24**
See also CA 124; 127

Derry Down Derry
See Lear, Edward

Dersonnes, Jacques
See Simenon, Georges (Jacques Christian)

Desai, Anita 1937-............. **CLC 19, 37**
See also CA 81-84; CANR 33; MTCW;
SATA 63

de Saint-Luc, Jean
See Glassco, John

de Saint Roman, Arnaud
See Aragon, Louis

Descartes, Rene 1596-1650 .... **LC 20**

De Sica, Vittorio 1901(?)-1974 ..... **CLC 20**
See also CA 117

Desnos, Robert 1900-1945........ **TCLC 22**
See also CA 121

Destouches, Louis-Ferdinand
1894-1961 .... **CLC 9, 15**
See also Celine, Louis-Ferdinand
See also CA 85-88; CANR 28; MTCW

Deutsch, Babette 1895-1982 .... **CLC 18**
See also CA 1-4R; 108; CANR 4; DLB 45;
SATA 1; SATA-Obit 33

Devenant, William 1606-1649 ...... **LC 13**

Devkota, Laxmiprasad
1909-1959 .... **TCLC 23**
See also CA 123

De Voto, Bernard (Augustine)
1897-1955 .... **TCLC 29**
See also CA 113; DLB 9

De Vries, Peter
1910-1993 .... **CLC 1, 2, 3, 7, 10, 28, 46**
See also CA 17-20R; 142; CANR 41;
DLB 6; DLBY 82; MTCW

Dexter, Martin
See Faust, Frederick (Schiller)

Dowson, Ernest Christopher
1867-1900 .... **TCLC 4**
See also CA 105; DLB 19, 135

Doyle, A. Conan
See Doyle, Arthur Conan

Doyle, Arthur Conan
1859-1930 ...... **TCLC 7; DA; SSC 12; WLC**
See also AAYA 14; CA 104; 122;
CDBLB 1890-1914; DLB 18, 70; MTCW;
SATA 24

Doyle, Conan
See Doyle, Arthur Conan

Doyle, John
See Graves, Robert (von Ranke)

Doyle, Roddy 1958(?)- .... **CLC 81**
See also AAYA 14; CA 143

Doyle, Sir A. Conan
See Doyle, Arthur Conan

Doyle, Sir Arthur Conan
See Doyle, Arthur Conan

Dr. A
See Asimov, Isaac; Silverstein, Alvin

Drabble, Margaret
1939- .... **CLC 2, 3, 5, 8, 10, 22, 53**
See also CA 13-16R; CANR 18, 35;
CDBLB 1960 to Present; DLB 14;
MTCW; SATA 48

Drapier, M. B.
See Swift, Jonathan

Drayham, James
See Mencken, H(enry) L(ouis)

Drayton, Michael 1563-1631 .... **LC 8**

Dreadstone, Carl
See Campbell, (John) Ramsey

Dreiser, Theodore (Herman Albert)
1871-1945 ...... **TCLC 10, 18, 35; DA; WLC**
See also CA 106; 132; CDALB 1865-1917;
DLB 9, 12, 102, 137; DLBD 1; MTCW

Drexler, Rosalyn 1926- .... **CLC 2, 6**
See also CA 81-84

Dreyer, Carl Theodor 1889-1968.... **CLC 16**
See also CA 116

Drieu la Rochelle, Pierre(-Eugene)
1893-1945 .... **TCLC 21**
See also CA 117; DLB 72

Drinkwater, John 1882-1937 ...... **TCLC 57**
See also CA 109; DLB 10, 19

Drop Shot
See Cable, George Washington

Droste-Hulshoff, Annette Freiin von
1797-1848 .... **NCLC 3**
See also DLB 133

Drummond, Walter
See Silverberg, Robert

Drummond, William Henry
1854-1907 .... **TCLC 25**
See also DLB 92

Drummond de Andrade, Carlos
1902-1987 .... **CLC 18**
See also Andrade, Carlos Drummond de
See also CA 132; 123

Drury, Allen (Stuart) 1918- .... **CLC 37**
See also CA 57-60; CANR 18

Dryden, John
1631-1700 ... **LC 3, 21; DA; DC 3; WLC**
See also CDBLB 1660-1789; DLB 80, 101,
131

Duberman, Martin 1930- .... **CLC 8**
See also CA 1-4R; CANR 2

Dubie, Norman (Evans) 1945- ...... **CLC 36**
See also CA 69-72; CANR 12; DLB 120

Du Bois, W(illiam) E(dward) B(urghardt)
1868-1963 ...... **CLC 1, 2, 13, 64; BLC; DA; WLC**
See also BW 1; CA 85-88; CANR 34;
CDALB 1865-1917; DLB 47, 50, 91;
MTCW; SATA 42

Dubus, Andre 1936- ... **CLC 13, 36; SSC 15**
See also CA 21-24R; CANR 17; DLB 130

Duca Minimo
See D'Annunzio, Gabriele

Ducharme, Rejean 1941- .... **CLC 74**
See also DLB 60

Duclos, Charles Pinot 1704-1772 ..... **LC 1**

Dudek, Louis 1918- .... **CLC 11, 19**
See also CA 45-48; CAAS 14; CANR 1;
DLB 88

Duerrenmatt, Friedrich
1921-1990 ...... **CLC 1, 4, 8, 11, 15, 43**
See also CA 17-20R; CANR 33; DLB 69,
124; MTCW

Duffy, Bruce (?)- .... **CLC 50**

Duffy, Maureen 1933- .... **CLC 37**
See also CA 25-28R; CANR 33; DLB 14;
MTCW

Dugan, Alan 1923- .... **CLC 2, 6**
See also CA 81-84; DLB 5

du Gard, Roger Martin
See Martin du Gard, Roger

Duhamel, Georges 1884-1966 .... **CLC 8**
See also CA 81-84; 25-28R; CANR 35;
DLB 65; MTCW

Dujardin, Edouard (Emile Louis)
1861-1949 .... **TCLC 13**
See also CA 109; DLB 123

Dumas, Alexandre (Davy de la Pailleterie)
1802-1870 .... **NCLC 11; DA; WLC**
See also DLB 119; SATA 18

Dumas, Alexandre
1824-1895 .... **NCLC 9; DC 1**

Dumas, Claudine
See Malzberg, Barry N(athaniel)

Dumas, Henry L. 1934-1968 ..... **CLC 6, 62**
See also BW 1; CA 85-88; DLB 41

du Maurier, Daphne
1907-1989 ...... **CLC 6, 11, 59; SSC 18**
See also CA 5-8R; 128; CANR 6; MTCW;
SATA 27; SATA-Obit 60

Dunbar, Paul Laurence
1872-1906 ...... **TCLC 2, 12; BLC; DA; PC 5; SSC 8; WLC**
See also BW 1; CA 104; 124;
CDALB 1865-1917; DLB 50, 54, 78;
SATA 34

Dunbar, William 1460(?)-1530(?) .... **LC 20**
See also DLB 132, 146

Duncan, Lois 1934-. .... **CLC 26**
See also AAYA 4; CA 1-4R; CANR 2, 23,
36; CLR 29; JRDA; MAICYA; SAAS 2;
SATA 1, 36, 75

Duncan, Robert (Edward)
1919-1988 .... **CLC 1, 2, 4, 7, 15, 41, 55; PC 2**
See also CA 9-12R; 124; CANR 28; DLB 5,
16; MTCW

Dunlap, William 1766-1839 .... **NCLC 2**
See also DLB 30, 37, 59

Dunn, Douglas (Eaglesham)
1942- .... **CLC 6, 40**
See also CA 45-48; CANR 2, 33; DLB 40;
MTCW

Dunn, Katherine (Karen) 1945-..... **CLC 71**
See also CA 33-36R

Dunn, Stephen 1939- .... **CLC 36**
See also CA 33-36R; CANR 12; DLB 105

Dunne, Finley Peter 1867-1936.... **TCLC 28**
See also CA 108; DLB 11, 23

Dunne, John Gregory 1932-........ **CLC 28**
See also CA 25-28R; CANR 14; DLBY 80

Dunsany, Edward John Moreton Drax
Plunkett 1878-1957
See Dunsany, Lord
See also CA 104; DLB 10

Dunsany, Lord.................... **TCLC 2**
See also Dunsany, Edward John Moreton
Drax Plunkett
See also DLB 77

du Perry, Jean
See Simenon, Georges (Jacques Christian)

Durang, Christopher (Ferdinand)
1949- .... **CLC 27, 38**
See also CA 105

Duras, Marguerite
1914- ...... **CLC 3, 6, 11, 20, 34, 40, 68**
See also CA 25-28R; DLB 83; MTCW

Durban, (Rosa) Pam 1947-........ **CLC 39**
See also CA 123

Durcan, Paul 1944-............. **CLC 43, 70**
See also CA 134

Durkheim, Emile 1858-1917 ...... **TCLC 55**

Durrell, Lawrence (George)
1912-1990 .... **CLC 1, 4, 6, 8, 13, 27, 41**
See also CA 9-12R; 132; CANR 40;
CDBLB 1945-1960; DLB 15, 27;
DLBY 90; MTCW

Durrenmatt, Friedrich
See Duerrenmatt, Friedrich

Dutt, Toru 1856-1877........... **NCLC 29**

Dwight, Timothy 1752-1817...... **NCLC 13**
See also DLB 37

Dworkin, Andrea 1946- .... **CLC 43**
See also CA 77-80; CANR 16, 39; MTCW

Dwyer, Deanna
See Koontz, Dean R(ay)

Dwyer, K. R.
See Koontz, Dean R(ay)

Dylan, Bob 1941- ...... **CLC 3, 4, 6, 12, 77**
See also CA 41-44R; DLB 16

Eagleton, Terence (Francis)   1943-
  See Eagleton, Terry
  See also CA 57-60; CANR 7, 23; MTCW

Eagleton, Terry .... **CLC 63**
  See also Eagleton, Terence (Francis)

Early, Jack
  See Scoppettone, Sandra

East, Michael
  See West, Morris L(anglo)

Eastaway, Edward
  See Thomas, (Philip) Edward

Eastlake, William (Derry)   1917- ..... **CLC 8**
  See also CA 5-8R; CAAS 1; CANR 5;
  DLB 6

Eastman, Charles A(lexander)
  1858-1939 .... **TCLC 55**
  See also NNAL; YABC 1

Eberhart, Richard (Ghormley)
  1904- .... **CLC 3, 11, 19, 56**
  See also CA 1-4R; CANR 2;
  CDALB 1941-1968; DLB 48; MTCW

Eberstadt, Fernanda   1960- .... **CLC 39**
  See also CA 136

Echegaray (y Eizaguirre), Jose (Maria Waldo)
  1832-1916 .... **TCLC 4**
  See also CA 104; CANR 32; HW; MTCW

Echeverria, (Jose) Esteban (Antonino)
  1805-1851 .... **NCLC 18**

Echo
  See Proust, (Valentin-Louis-George-Eugene-)
  Marcel

Eckert, Allan W.   1931- .... **CLC 17**
  See also CA 13-16R; CANR 14, 45;
  SATA 27, 29

Eckhart, Meister   1260(?)-1328(?) .. **CMLC 9**
  See also DLB 115

Eckmar, F. R.
  See de Hartog, Jan

Eco, Umberto   1932- .... **CLC 28, 60**
  See also BEST 90:1; CA 77-80; CANR 12,
  33; MTCW

Eddison, E(ric) R(ucker)
  1882-1945 .... **TCLC 15**
  See also CA 109

Edel, (Joseph) Leon   1907- ...... **CLC 29, 34**
  See also CA 1-4R; CANR 1, 22; DLB 103

Eden, Emily   1797-1869 .... **NCLC 10**

Edgar, David   1948- .... **CLC 42**
  See also CA 57-60; CANR 12; DLB 13;
  MTCW

Edgerton, Clyde (Carlyle)   1944- .... **CLC 39**
  See also CA 118; 134

Edgeworth, Maria   1767-1849 ...... **NCLC 1**
  See also DLB 116; SATA 21

Edmonds, Paul
  See Kuttner, Henry

Edmonds, Walter D(umaux)   1903- .. **CLC 35**
  See also CA 5-8R; CANR 2; DLB 9;
  MAICYA; SAAS 4; SATA 1, 27

Edmondson, Wallace
  See Ellison, Harlan (Jay)

Edson, Russell .... **CLC 13**
  See also CA 33-36R

Edwards, Bronwen Elizabeth
  See Rose, Wendy

Edwards, G(erald) B(asil)
  1899-1976 .... **CLC 25**
  See also CA 110

Edwards, Gus   1939- .... **CLC 43**
  See also CA 108

Edwards, Jonathan   1703-1758 .... **LC 7; DA**
  See also DLB 24

Efron, Marina Ivanovna Tsvetaeva
  See Tsvetaeva (Efron), Marina (Ivanovna)

Ehle, John (Marsden, Jr.)   1925- .... **CLC 27**
  See also CA 9-12R

Ehrenbourg, Ilya (Grigoryevich)
  See Ehrenburg, Ilya (Grigoryevich)

Ehrenburg, Ilya (Grigoryevich)
  1891-1967 .... **CLC 18, 34, 62**
  See also CA 102; 25-28R

Ehrenburg, Ilyo (Grigoryevich)
  See Ehrenburg, Ilya (Grigoryevich)

Eich, Guenter   1907-1972 .... **CLC 15**
  See also CA 111; 93-96; DLB 69, 124

Eichendorff, Joseph Freiherr von
  1788-1857 .... **NCLC 8**
  See also DLB 90

Eigner, Larry .... **CLC 9**
  See also Eigner, Laurence (Joel)
  See also DLB 5

Eigner, Laurence (Joel)   1927-
  See Eigner, Larry
  See also CA 9-12R; CANR 6

Eiseley, Loren Corey   1907-1977 ..... **CLC 7**
  See also AAYA 5; CA 1-4R; 73-76;
  CANR 6

Eisenstadt, Jill   1963- .... **CLC 50**
  See also CA 140

Eisenstein, Sergei (Mikhailovich)
  1898-1948 .... **TCLC 57**
  See also CA 114

Eisner, Simon
  See Kornbluth, C(yril) M.

Ekeloef, (Bengt) Gunnar
  1907-1968 .... **CLC 27**
  See also CA 123; 25-28R

Ekelof, (Bengt) Gunnar
  See Ekeloef, (Bengt) Gunnar

Ekwensi, C. O. D.
  See Ekwensi, Cyprian (Odiatu Duaka)

Ekwensi, Cyprian (Odiatu Duaka)
  1921- .... **CLC 4; BLC**
  See also BW 2; CA 29-32R; CANR 18, 42;
  DLB 117; MTCW; SATA 66

Elaine .... **TCLC 18**
  See also Leverson, Ada

El Crummo
  See Crumb, R(obert)

Elia
  See Lamb, Charles

Eliade, Mircea   1907-1986 .... **CLC 19**
  See also CA 65-68; 119; CANR 30; MTCW

Eliot, A. D.
  See Jewett, (Theodora) Sarah Orne

Eliot, Alice
  See Jewett, (Theodora) Sarah Orne

Eliot, Dan
  See Silverberg, Robert

Eliot, George
  1819-1880 .... **NCLC 4, 13, 23, 41; DA;
                                        WLC**
  See also CDBLB 1832-1890; DLB 21, 35, 55

Eliot, John   1604-1690 .... **LC 5**
  See also DLB 24

Eliot, T(homas) S(tearns)
  1888-1965 ..... **CLC 1, 2, 3, 6, 9, 10, 13,
     15, 24, 34, 41, 55, 57; DA; PC 5; WLC 2**
  See also CA 5-8R; 25-28R; CANR 41;
  CDALB 1929-1941; DLB 7, 10, 45, 63;
  DLBY 88; MTCW

Elizabeth   1866-1941 .... **TCLC 41**

Elkin, Stanley L(awrence)
  1930- ... **CLC 4, 6, 9, 14, 27, 51; SSC 12**
  See also CA 9-12R; CANR 8, 46, 46;
  DLB 2, 28; DLBY 80; MTCW

Elledge, Scott .... **CLC 34**

Elliott, Don
  See Silverberg, Robert

Elliott, George P(aul)   1918-1980 ..... **CLC 2**
  See also CA 1-4R; 97-100; CANR 2

Elliott, Janice   1931- .... **CLC 47**
  See also CA 13-16R; CANR 8, 29; DLB 14

Elliott, Sumner Locke   1917-1991 ... **CLC 38**
  See also CA 5-8R; 134; CANR 2, 21

Elliott, William
  See Bradbury, Ray (Douglas)

Ellis, A. E. .... **CLC 7**

Ellis, Alice Thomas .... **CLC 40**
  See also Haycraft, Anna

Ellis, Bret Easton   1964- .... **CLC 39, 71**
  See also AAYA 2; CA 118; 123

Ellis, (Henry) Havelock
  1859-1939 .... **TCLC 14**
  See also CA 109

Ellis, Landon
  See Ellison, Harlan (Jay)

Ellis, Trey   1962- .... **CLC 55**

Ellison, Harlan (Jay)
  1934- .... **CLC 1, 13, 42; SSC 14**
  See also CA 5-8R; CANR 5, 46, 46; DLB 8;
  MTCW

Ellison, Ralph (Waldo)
  1914-1994 .... **CLC 1, 3, 11, 54, 86;
                                        BLC; DA; WLC**
  See also BW 1; CA 9-12R; 145; CANR 24;
  CDALB 1941-1968; DLB 2, 76; MTCW

Ellmann, Lucy (Elizabeth)   1956- .... **CLC 61**
  See also CA 128

Ellmann, Richard (David)
  1918-1987 .... **CLC 50**
  See also BEST 89:2; CA 1-4R; 122;
  CANR 2, 28; DLB 103; DLBY 87;
  MTCW

Elman, Richard   1934- .... **CLC 19**
  See also CA 17-20R; CAAS 3; CANR 47

Elron
  See Hubbard, L(afayette) Ron(ald)

Eluard, Paul .... **TCLC 7, 41**
  See also Grindel, Eugene

Elyot, Sir Thomas   1490(?)-1546 ..... **LC 11**

Elytis, Odysseus 1911-......... **CLC 15, 49**
See also CA 102; MTCW

Emecheta, (Florence Onye) Buchi
1944-............... **CLC 14, 48; BLC**
See also BW 2; CA 81-84; CANR 27;
DLB 117; MTCW; SATA 66

Emerson, Ralph Waldo
1803-1882 ...... **NCLC 1, 38; DA; WLC**
See also CDALB 1640-1865; DLB 1, 59, 73

Eminescu, Mihail 1850-1889 ..... **NCLC 33**

Empson, William
1906-1984 .... **CLC 3, 8, 19, 33, 34**
See also CA 17-20R; 112; CANR 31;
DLB 20; MTCW

Enchi Fumiko (Ueda) 1905-1986.... **CLC 31**
See also CA 129; 121

Ende, Michael (Andreas Helmuth)
1929-...................... **CLC 31**
See also CA 118; 124; CANR 36; CLR 14;
DLB 75; MAICYA; SATA 42, 61

Endo, Shusaku 1923-..... **CLC 7, 14, 19, 54**
See also CA 29-32R; CANR 21; MTCW

Engel, Marian 1933-1985.......... **CLC 36**
See also CA 25-28R; CANR 12; DLB 53

Engelhardt, Frederick
See Hubbard, L(afayette) Ron(ald)

Enright, D(ennis) J(oseph)
1920-................... **CLC 4, 8, 31**
See also CA 1-4R; CANR 1, 42; DLB 27;
SATA 25

Enzensberger, Hans Magnus
1929-...................... **CLC 43**
See also CA 116; 119

Ephron, Nora 1941-.......... **CLC 17, 31**
See also AITN 2; CA 65-68; CANR 12, 39

Epsilon
See Betjeman, John

Epstein, Daniel Mark 1948- .... **CLC 7**
See also CA 49-52; CANR 2

Epstein, Jacob 1956- .... **CLC 19**
See also CA 114

Epstein, Joseph 1937-............ **CLC 39**
See also CA 112; 119

Epstein, Leslie 1938- .... **CLC 27**
See also CA 73-76; CAAS 12; CANR 23

Equiano, Olaudah
1745(?)-1797 .... **LC 16; BLC**
See also DLB 37, 50

Erasmus, Desiderius 1469(?)-1536.... **LC 16**

Erdman, Paul E(mil) 1932- .... **CLC 25**
See also AITN 1; CA 61-64; CANR 13, 43

Erdrich, Louise 1954-......... **CLC 39, 54**
See also AAYA 10; BEST 89:1; CA 114;
CANR 41; MTCW; NNAL

Erenburg, Ilya (Grigoryevich)
See Ehrenburg, Ilya (Grigoryevich)

Erickson, Stephen Michael 1950-
See Erickson, Steve
See also CA 129

Erickson, Steve .... **CLC 64**
See also Erickson, Stephen Michael

Ericson, Walter
See Fast, Howard (Melvin)

Eriksson, Buntel
See Bergman, (Ernst) Ingmar

Eschenbach, Wolfram von
See Wolfram von Eschenbach

Eseki, Bruno
See Mphahlele, Ezekiel

Esenin, Sergei (Alexandrovich)
1895-1925 .... **TCLC 4**
See also CA 104

Eshleman, Clayton 1935-........... **CLC 7**
See also CA 33-36R; CAAS 6; DLB 5

Espriella, Don Manuel Alvarez
See Southey, Robert

Espriu, Salvador 1913-1985........ **CLC 9**
See also CA 115; DLB 134

Espronceda, Jose de 1808-1842... **NCLC 39**

Esse, James
See Stephens, James

Esterbrook, Tom
See Hubbard, L(afayette) Ron(ald)

Estleman, Loren D. 1952-......... **CLC 48**
See also CA 85-88; CANR 27; MTCW

Eugenides, Jeffrey 1960(?)-........ **CLC 81**
See also CA 144

Euripides c. 485B.C.-406B.C. .... **DC 4**
See also DA

Evan, Evin
See Faust, Frederick (Schiller)

Evans, Evan
See Faust, Frederick (Schiller)

Evans, Marian
See Eliot, George

Evans, Mary Ann
See Eliot, George

Evarts, Esther
See Benson, Sally

Everett, Percival L. 1956-......... **CLC 57**
See also BW 2; CA 129

Everson, R(onald) G(ilmour)
1903-...................... **CLC 27**
See also CA 17-20R; DLB 88

Everson, William (Oliver)
1912-1994 .... **CLC 1, 5, 14**
See also CA 9-12R; 145; CANR 20; DLB 5,
16; MTCW

Evtushenko, Evgenii Aleksandrovich
See Yevtushenko, Yevgeny (Alexandrovich)

Ewart, Gavin (Buchanan)
1916-.................... **CLC 13, 46**
See also CA 89-92; CANR 17, 46, 46;
DLB 40; MTCW

Ewers, Hanns Heinz 1871-1943 ... **TCLC 12**
See also CA 109

Ewing, Frederick R.
See Sturgeon, Theodore (Hamilton)

Exley, Frederick (Earl)
1929-1992 .... **CLC 6, 11**
See also AITN 2; CA 81-84; 138; DLB 143;
DLBY 81

Eynhardt, Guillermo
See Quiroga, Horacio (Sylvestre)

Ezekiel, Nissim 1924-............. **CLC 61**
See also CA 61-64

Ezekiel, Tish O'Dowd 1943-....... **CLC 34**
See also CA 129

Fadeyev, A.
See Bulgya, Alexander Alexandrovich

Fadeyev, Alexander............... **TCLC 53**
See also Bulgya, Alexander Alexandrovich

Fagen, Donald 1948-.............. **CLC 26**

Fainzilberg, Ilya Arnoldovich 1897-1937
See Ilf, Ilya
See also CA 120

Fair, Ronald L. 1932-............. **CLC 18**
See also BW 1; CA 69-72; CANR 25;
DLB 33

Fairbairns, Zoe (Ann) 1948- .... **CLC 32**
See also CA 103; CANR 21

Falco, Gian
See Papini, Giovanni

Falconer, James
See Kirkup, James

Falconer, Kenneth
See Kornbluth, C(yril) M.

Falkland, Samuel
See Heijermans, Herman

Fallaci, Oriana 1930-............. **CLC 11**
See also CA 77-80; CANR 15; MTCW

Faludy, George 1913-............. **CLC 42**
See also CA 21-24R

Faludy, Gyoergy
See Faludy, George

Fanon, Frantz 1925-1961..... **CLC 74; BLC**
See also BW 1; CA 116; 89-92

Fanshawe, Ann 1625-1680 .... **LC 11**

Fante, John (Thomas) 1911-1983 ... **CLC 60**
See also CA 69-72; 109; CANR 23;
DLB 130; DLBY 83

Farah, Nuruddin 1945-....... **CLC 53; BLC**
See also BW 2; CA 106; DLB 125

Fargue, Leon-Paul 1876(?)-1947 ... **TCLC 11**
See also CA 109

Farigoule, Louis
See Romains, Jules

Farina, Richard 1936(?)-1966 .... **CLC 9**
See also CA 81-84; 25-28R

Farley, Walter (Lorimer)
1915-1989 .... **CLC 17**
See also CA 17-20R; CANR 8, 29; DLB 22;
JRDA; MAICYA; SATA 2, 43

Farmer, Philip Jose 1918-....... **CLC 1, 19**
See also CA 1-4R; CANR 4, 35; DLB 8;
MTCW

Farquhar, George 1677-1707 .... **LC 21**
See also DLB 84

Farrell, J(ames) G(ordon)
1935-1979 .... **CLC 6**
See also CA 73-76; 89-92; CANR 36;
DLB 14; MTCW

Farrell, James T(homas)
1904-1979 ...... **CLC 1, 4, 8, 11, 66**
See also CA 5-8R; 89-92; CANR 9; DLB 4,
9, 86; DLBD 2; MTCW

Farren, Richard J.
See Betjeman, John

Farren, Richard M.
See Betjeman, John

Fassbinder, Rainer Werner
1946-1982 .... CLC 20
See also CA 93-96; 106; CANR 31

Fast, Howard (Melvin) 1914- ...... CLC 23
See also CA 1-4R; CAAS 18; CANR 1, 33;
DLB 9; SATA 7

Faulcon, Robert
See Holdstock, Robert P.

Faulkner, William (Cuthbert)
1897-1962 ..... CLC 1, 3, 6, 8, 9, 11, 14,
18, 28, 52, 68; DA; SSC 1; WLC
See also AAYA 7; CA 81-84; CANR 33;
CDALB 1929-1941; DLB 9, 11, 44, 102;
DLBD 2; DLBY 86; MTCW

Fauset, Jessie Redmon
1884(?)-1961 .... CLC 19, 54; BLC
See also BW 1; CA 109; DLB 51

Faust, Frederick (Schiller)
1892-1944(?) .... TCLC 49
See also CA 108

Faust, Irvin 1924- .... CLC 8
See also CA 33-36R; CANR 28; DLB 2, 28;
DLBY 80

Fawkes, Guy
See Benchley, Robert (Charles)

Fearing, Kenneth (Flexner)
1902-1961 .... CLC 51
See also CA 93-96; DLB 9

Fecamps, Elise
See Creasey, John

Federman, Raymond 1928- ...... CLC 6, 47
See also CA 17-20R; CAAS 8; CANR 10,
43; DLBY 80

Federspiel, J(uerg) F. 1931- .... CLC 42

Feiffer, Jules (Ralph) 1929- .... CLC 2, 8, 64
See also AAYA 3; CA 17-20R; CANR 30;
DLB 7, 44; MTCW; SATA 8, 61

Feige, Hermann Albert Otto Maximilian
See Traven, B.

Feinberg, David B. 1956- .... CLC 59
See also CA 135

Feinstein, Elaine 1930- .... CLC 36
See also CA 69-72; CAAS 1; CANR 31;
DLB 14, 40; MTCW

Feldman, Irving (Mordecai) 1928- .... CLC 7
See also CA 1-4R; CANR 1

Fellini, Federico 1920-1993 ..... CLC 16, 85
See also CA 65-68; 143; CANR 33

Felsen, Henry Gregor 1916- .... CLC 17
See also CA 1-4R; CANR 1; SAAS 2;
SATA 1

Fenton, James Martin 1949- .... CLC 32
See also CA 102; DLB 40

Ferber, Edna 1887-1968 .... CLC 18
See also AITN 1; CA 5-8R; 25-28R; DLB 9,
28, 86; MTCW; SATA 7

Ferguson, Helen
See Kavan, Anna

Ferguson, Samuel 1810-1886 ..... NCLC 33
See also DLB 32

Ferling, Lawrence
See Ferlinghetti, Lawrence (Monsanto)

Ferlinghetti, Lawrence (Monsanto)
1919(?)- .... CLC 2, 6, 10, 27; PC 1
See also CA 5-8R; CANR 3, 41;
CDALB 1941-1968; DLB 5, 16; MTCW

Fernandez, Vicente Garcia Huidobro
See Huidobro Fernandez, Vicente Garcia

Ferrer, Gabriel (Francisco Victor) Miro
See Miro (Ferrer), Gabriel (Francisco
Victor)

Ferrier, Susan (Edmonstone)
1782-1854 .... NCLC 8
See also DLB 116

Ferrigno, Robert 1948(?)- .... CLC 65
See also CA 140

Feuchtwanger, Lion 1884-1958 ..... TCLC 3
See also CA 104; DLB 66

Feuillet, Octave 1821-1890 ...... NCLC 45

Feydeau, Georges (Leon Jules Marie)
1862-1921 .... TCLC 22
See also CA 113

Ficino, Marsilio 1433-1499 .... LC 12

Fiedeler, Hans
See Doeblin, Alfred

Fiedler, Leslie A(aron)
1917- .... CLC 4, 13, 24
See also CA 9-12R; CANR 7; DLB 28, 67;
MTCW

Field, Andrew 1938- .... CLC 44
See also CA 97-100; CANR 25

Field, Eugene 1850-1895 .... NCLC 3
See also DLB 23, 42, 140; MAICYA;
SATA 16

Field, Gans T.
See Wellman, Manly Wade

Field, Michael .... TCLC 43

Field, Peter
See Hobson, Laura Z(ametkin)

Fielding, Henry
1707-1754 .... LC 1; DA; WLC
See also CDBLB 1660-1789; DLB 39, 84,
101

Fielding, Sarah 1710-1768 .... LC 1
See also DLB 39

Fierstein, Harvey (Forbes) 1954- ... CLC 33
See also CA 123; 129

Figes, Eva 1932- .... CLC 31
See also CA 53-56; CANR 4, 44; DLB 14

Finch, Robert (Duer Claydon)
1900- .... CLC 18
See also CA 57-60; CANR 9, 24; DLB 88

Findley, Timothy 1930- .... CLC 27
See also CA 25-28R; CANR 12, 42;
DLB 53

Fink, William
See Mencken, H(enry) L(ouis)

Firbank, Louis 1942-
See Reed, Lou
See also CA 117

Firbank, (Arthur Annesley) Ronald
1886-1926 .... TCLC 1
See also CA 104; DLB 36

Fisher, M(ary) F(rances) K(ennedy)
1908-1992 .... CLC 76
See also CA 77-80; 138; CANR 44

Fisher, Roy 1930- .... CLC 25
See also CA 81-84; CAAS 10; CANR 16;
DLB 40

Fisher, Rudolph
1897-1934 .... TCLC 11; BLC
See also BW 1; CA 107; 124; DLB 51, 102

Fisher, Vardis (Alvero) 1895-1968.... CLC 7
See also CA 5-8R; 25-28R; DLB 9

Fiske, Tarleton
See Bloch, Robert (Albert)

Fitch, Clarke
See Sinclair, Upton (Beall)

Fitch, John IV
See Cormier, Robert (Edmund)

Fitzgerald, Captain Hugh
See Baum, L(yman) Frank

FitzGerald, Edward 1809-1883 .... NCLC 9
See also DLB 32

Fitzgerald, F(rancis) Scott (Key)
1896-1940 .... TCLC 1, 6, 14, 28, 55;
DA; SSC 6; WLC
See also AITN 1; CA 110; 123;
CDALB 1917-1929; DLB 4, 9, 86;
DLBD 1; DLBY 81; MTCW

Fitzgerald, Penelope 1916-... CLC 19, 51, 61
See also CA 85-88; CAAS 10; DLB 14

Fitzgerald, Robert (Stuart)
1910-1985 .... CLC 39
See also CA 1-4R; 114; CANR 1; DLBY 80

FitzGerald, Robert D(avid)
1902-1987 .... CLC 19
See also CA 17-20R

Fitzgerald, Zelda (Sayre)
1900-1948 .... TCLC 52
See also CA 117; 126; DLBY 84

Flanagan, Thomas (James Bonner)
1923- .... CLC 25, 52
See also CA 108; DLBY 80; MTCW

Flaubert, Gustave
1821-1880 .... NCLC 2, 10, 19; DA;
SSC 11; WLC
See also DLB 119

Flecker, (Herman) James Elroy
1884-1915 .... TCLC 43
See also CA 109; DLB 10, 19

Fleming, Ian (Lancaster)
1908-1964 .... CLC 3, 30
See also CA 5-8R; CDBLB 1945-1960;
DLB 87; MTCW; SATA 9

Fleming, Thomas (James) 1927- .... CLC 37
See also CA 5-8R; CANR 10; SATA 8

Fletcher, John Gould 1886-1950 ... TCLC 35
See also CA 107; DLB 4, 45

Fleur, Paul
See Pohl, Frederik

Flooglebuckle, Al
See Spiegelman, Art

Flying Officer X
See Bates, H(erbert) E(rnest)

Fo, Dario 1926- .... CLC 32
See also CA 116; 128; MTCW

Fogarty, Jonathan Titulescu Esq.
See Farrell, James T(homas)

Folke, Will
See Bloch, Robert (Albert)

Follett, Ken(neth Martin) 1949- .... **CLC 18**
See also AAYA 6; BEST 89:4; CA 81-84;
CANR 13, 33; DLB 87; DLBY 81;
MTCW

Fontane, Theodor 1819-1898 ..... **NCLC 26**
See also DLB 129

Foote, Horton 1916- .... **CLC 51**
See also CA 73-76; CANR 34; DLB 26

Foote, Shelby 1916- .... **CLC 75**
See also CA 5-8R; CANR 3, 45; DLB 2, 17

Forbes, Esther 1891-1967 .... **CLC 12**
See also CA 13-14; 25-28R; CAP 1;
CLR 27; DLB 22; JRDA; MAICYA;
SATA 2

Forche, Carolyn (Louise)
1950- .... **CLC 25, 83, 86; PC 10**
See also CA 109; 117; DLB 5

Ford, Elbur
See Hibbert, Eleanor Alice Burford

Ford, Ford Madox
1873-1939 .... **TCLC 1, 15, 39, 57**
See also CA 104; 132; CDBLB 1914-1945;
DLB 34, 98; MTCW

Ford, John 1895-1973 .... **CLC 16**
See also CA 45-48

Ford, Richard 1944- .... **CLC 46**
See also CA 69-72; CANR 11, 47

Ford, Webster
See Masters, Edgar Lee

Foreman, Richard 1937- .... **CLC 50**
See also CA 65-68; CANR 32

Forester, C(ecil) S(cott)
1899-1966 .... **CLC 35**
See also CA 73-76; 25-28R; SATA 13

Forez
See Mauriac, Francois (Charles)

Forman, James Douglas 1932- ...... **CLC 21**
See also CA 9-12R; CANR 4, 19, 42;
JRDA; MAICYA; SATA 8, 70

Fornes, Maria Irene 1930- ...... **CLC 39, 61**
See also CA 25-28R; CANR 28; DLB 7;
HW; MTCW

Forrest, Leon 1937- .... **CLC 4**
See also BW 2; CA 89-92; CAAS 7;
CANR 25; DLB 33

Forster, E(dward) M(organ)
1879-1970 ..... **CLC 1, 2, 3, 4, 9, 10, 13,
15, 22, 45, 77; DA; WLC**
See also AAYA 2; CA 13-14; 25-28R;
CANR 45; CAP 1; CDBLB 1914-1945;
DLB 34, 98; DLBD 10; MTCW;
SATA 57

Forster, John 1812-1876 .... **NCLC 11**
See also DLB 144

Forsyth, Frederick 1938- ...... **CLC 2, 5, 36**
See also BEST 89:4; CA 85-88; CANR 38;
DLB 87; MTCW

Forten, Charlotte L. .... **TCLC 16; BLC**
See also Grimke, Charlotte L(ottie) Forten
See also DLB 50

Foscolo, Ugo 1778-1827 .... **NCLC 8**

Fosse, Bob .... **CLC 20**
See also Fosse, Robert Louis

Fosse, Robert Louis 1927-1987
See Fosse, Bob
See also CA 110; 123

Foster, Stephen Collins
1826-1864 .... **NCLC 26**

Foucault, Michel
1926-1984 .... **CLC 31, 34, 69**
See also CA 105; 113; CANR 34; MTCW

Fouque, Friedrich (Heinrich Karl) de la Motte
1777-1843 .... **NCLC 2**
See also DLB 90

Fournier, Henri Alban 1886-1914
See Alain-Fournier
See also CA 104

Fournier, Pierre 1916- .... **CLC 11**
See also Gascar, Pierre
See also CA 89-92; CANR 16, 40

Fowles, John
1926- .... **CLC 1, 2, 3, 4, 6, 9, 10, 15, 33**
See also CA 5-8R; CANR 25; CDBLB 1960
to Present; DLB 14, 139; MTCW;
SATA 22

Fox, Paula 1923- .... **CLC 2, 8**
See also AAYA 3; CA 73-76; CANR 20,
36; CLR 1; DLB 52; JRDA; MAICYA;
MTCW; SATA 17, 60

Fox, William Price (Jr.) 1926- ..... **CLC 22**
See also CA 17-20R; CAAS 19; CANR 11;
DLB 2; DLBY 81

Foxe, John 1516(?)-1587 .... **LC 14**

Frame, Janet .... **CLC 2, 3, 6, 22, 66**
See also Clutha, Janet Paterson Frame

France, Anatole .... **TCLC 9**
See also Thibault, Jacques Anatole Francois
See also DLB 123

Francis, Claude 19(?)- .... **CLC 50**

Francis, Dick 1920- .... **CLC 2, 22, 42**
See also AAYA 5; BEST 89:3; CA 5-8R;
CANR 9, 42; CDBLB 1960 to Present;
DLB 87; MTCW

Francis, Robert (Churchill)
1901-1987 .... **CLC 15**
See also CA 1-4R; 123; CANR 1

Frank, Anne(lies Marie)
1929-1945 .... **TCLC 17; DA; WLC**
See also AAYA 12; CA 113; 133; MTCW;
SATA 42

Frank, Elizabeth 1945- .... **CLC 39**
See also CA 121; 126

Franklin, Benjamin
See Hasek, Jaroslav (Matej Frantisek)

Franklin, Benjamin 1706-1790 ... **LC 25; DA**
See also CDALB 1640-1865; DLB 24, 43,
73

Franklin, (Stella Maraia Sarah) Miles
1879-1954 .... **TCLC 7**
See also CA 104

Fraser, (Lady) Antonia (Pakenham)
1932- .... **CLC 32**
See also CA 85-88; CANR 44; MTCW;
SATA 32

Fraser, George MacDonald 1925- .... **CLC 7**
See also CA 45-48; CANR 2

Fraser, Sylvia 1935- .... **CLC 64**
See also CA 45-48; CANR 1, 16

Frayn, Michael 1933- ...... **CLC 3, 7, 31, 47**
See also CA 5-8R; CANR 30; DLB 13, 14;
MTCW

Fraze, Candida (Merrill) 1945- ..... **CLC 50**
See also CA 126

Frazer, J(ames) G(eorge)
1854-1941 .... **TCLC 32**
See also CA 118

Frazer, Robert Caine
See Creasey, John

Frazer, Sir James George
See Frazer, J(ames) G(eorge)

Frazier, Ian 1951- .... **CLC 46**
See also CA 130

Frederic, Harold 1856-1898 ...... **NCLC 10**
See also DLB 12, 23

Frederick, John
See Faust, Frederick (Schiller)

Frederick the Great 1712-1786 ...... **LC 14**

Fredro, Aleksander 1793-1876 ..... **NCLC 8**

Freeling, Nicolas 1927- .... **CLC 38**
See also CA 49-52; CAAS 12; CANR 1, 17;
DLB 87

Freeman, Douglas Southall
1886-1953 .... **TCLC 11**
See also CA 109; DLB 17

Freeman, Judith 1946- .... **CLC 55**

Freeman, Mary Eleanor Wilkins
1852-1930 .... **TCLC 9; SSC 1**
See also CA 106; DLB 12, 78

Freeman, R(ichard) Austin
1862-1943 .... **TCLC 21**
See also CA 113; DLB 70

French, Albert 1944(?)- .... **CLC 86**

French, Marilyn 1929- ...... **CLC 10, 18, 60**
See also CA 69-72; CANR 3, 31; MTCW

French, Paul
See Asimov, Isaac

Freneau, Philip Morin 1752-1832 .. **NCLC 1**
See also DLB 37, 43

Freud, Sigmund 1856-1939 .... **TCLC 52**
See also CA 115; 133; MTCW

Friedan, Betty (Naomi) 1921- ...... **CLC 74**
See also CA 65-68; CANR 18, 45; MTCW

Friedman, B(ernard) H(arper)
1926- .... **CLC 7**
See also CA 1-4R; CANR 3

Friedman, Bruce Jay 1930- .... **CLC 3, 5, 56**
See also CA 9-12R; CANR 25; DLB 2, 28

Friel, Brian 1929- .... **CLC 5, 42, 59**
See also CA 21-24R; CANR 33; DLB 13;
MTCW

Friis-Baastad, Babbis Ellinor
1921-1970 .... **CLC 12**
See also CA 17-20R; 134; SATA 7

Frisch, Max (Rudolf)
1911-1991 ..... **CLC 3, 9, 14, 18, 32, 44**
See also CA 85-88; 134; CANR 32;
DLB 69, 124; MTCW

Fromentin, Eugene (Samuel Auguste)
1820-1876 .... **NCLC 10**
See also DLB 123

Gates, Henry Louis, Jr. 1950-...... **CLC 65**
See also BW 2; CA 109; CANR 25; DLB 67

Gautier, Theophile 1811-1872 ..... **NCLC 1**
See also DLB 119

Gawsworth, John
See Bates, H(erbert) E(rnest)

Gaye, Marvin (Penze) 1939-1984 ... **CLC 26**
See also CA 112

Gebler, Carlo (Ernest) 1954-....... **CLC 39**
See also CA 119; 133

Gee, Maggie (Mary) 1948-........ **CLC 57**
See also CA 130

Gee, Maurice (Gough) 1931-....... **CLC 29**
See also CA 97-100; SATA 46

Gelbart, Larry (Simon) 1923- ... **CLC 21, 61**
See also CA 73-76; CANR 45

Gelber, Jack 1932-........ **CLC 1, 6, 14, 79**
See also CA 1-4R; CANR 2; DLB 7

Gellhorn, Martha (Ellis) 1908- .. **CLC 14, 60**
See also CA 77-80; CANR 44; DLBY 82

Genet, Jean
1910-1986 ... **CLC 1, 2, 5, 10, 14, 44, 46**
See also CA 13-16R; CANR 18; DLB 72;
DLBY 86; MTCW

Gent, Peter 1942-................ **CLC 29**
See also AITN 1; CA 89-92; DLBY 82

Gentlewoman in New England, A
See Bradstreet, Anne

Gentlewoman in Those Parts, A
See Bradstreet, Anne

George, Jean Craighead 1919-...... **CLC 35**
See also AAYA 8; CA 5-8R; CANR 25;
CLR 1; DLB 52; JRDA; MAICYA;
SATA 2, 68

George, Stefan (Anton)
1868-1933 .... **TCLC 2, 14**
See also CA 104

Georges, Georges Martin
See Simenon, Georges (Jacques Christian)

Gerhardi, William Alexander
See Gerhardie, William Alexander

Gerhardie, William Alexander
1895-1977 .... **CLC 5**
See also CA 25-28R; 73-76; CANR 18;
DLB 36

Gerstler, Amy 1956-.............. **CLC 70**

Gertler, T. .... **CLC 34**
See also CA 116; 121

Ghalib 1797-1869 .... **NCLC 39**

Ghelderode, Michel de
1898-1962 .... **CLC 6, 11**
See also CA 85-88; CANR 40

Ghiselin, Brewster 1903- .... **CLC 23**
See also CA 13-16R; CAAS 10; CANR 13

Ghose, Zulfikar 1935-............ **CLC 42**
See also CA 65-68

Ghosh, Amitav 1956- .... **CLC 44**

Giacosa, Giuseppe 1847-1906 ...... **TCLC 7**
See also CA 104

Gibb, Lee
See Waterhouse, Keith (Spencer)

Gibbon, Lewis Grassic .... **TCLC 4**
See also Mitchell, James Leslie

Gibbons, Kaye 1960- .... **CLC 50**

Gibran, Kahlil
1883-1931 .... **TCLC 1, 9; PC 9**
See also CA 104

Gibson, William 1914-........ **CLC 23; DA**
See also CA 9-12R; CANR 9, 42; DLB 7;
SATA 66

Gibson, William (Ford) 1948- ... **CLC 39, 63**
See also AAYA 12; CA 126; 133

Gide, Andre (Paul Guillaume)
1869-1951 .... **TCLC 5, 12, 36; DA;
SSC 13; WLC**
See also CA 104; 124; DLB 65; MTCW

Gifford, Barry (Colby) 1946-....... **CLC 34**
See also CA 65-68; CANR 9, 30, 40

Gilbert, W(illiam) S(chwenck)
1836-1911 .... **TCLC 3**
See also CA 104; SATA 36

Gilbreth, Frank B., Jr. 1911-....... **CLC 17**
See also CA 9-12R; SATA 2

Gilchrist, Ellen 1935-.. **CLC 34, 48; SSC 14**
See also CA 113; 116; CANR 41; DLB 130;
MTCW

Giles, Molly 1942-.............. **CLC 39**
See also CA 126

Gill, Patrick
See Creasey, John

Gilliam, Terry (Vance) 1940-....... **CLC 21**
See also Monty Python
See also CA 108; 113; CANR 35

Gillian, Jerry
See Gilliam, Terry (Vance)

Gilliatt, Penelope (Ann Douglass)
1932-1993 .... **CLC 2, 10, 13, 53**
See also AITN 2; CA 13-16R; 141; DLB 14

Gilman, Charlotte (Anna) Perkins (Stetson)
1860-1935 .... **TCLC 9, 37; SSC 13**
See also CA 106

Gilmour, David 1949-............. **CLC 35**
See also CA 138

Gilpin, William 1724-1804....... **NCLC 30**

Gilray, J. D.
See Mencken, H(enry) L(ouis)

Gilroy, Frank D(aniel) 1925-........ **CLC 2**
See also CA 81-84; CANR 32; DLB 7

Ginsberg, Allen
1926- ...... **CLC 1, 2, 3, 4, 6, 13, 36, 69;
DA; PC 4; WLC 3**
See also AITN 1; CA 1-4R; CANR 2, 41;
CDALB 1941-1968; DLB 5, 16; MTCW

Ginzburg, Natalia
1916-1991 .... **CLC 5, 11, 54, 70**
See also CA 85-88; 135; CANR 33; MTCW

Giono, Jean 1895-1970......... **CLC 4, 11**
See also CA 45-48; 29-32R; CANR 2, 35;
DLB 72; MTCW

Giovanni, Nikki
1943- ...... **CLC 2, 4, 19, 64; BLC; DA**
See also AITN 1; BW 2; CA 29-32R;
CAAS 6; CANR 18, 41; CLR 6; DLB 5,
41; MAICYA; MTCW; SATA 24

Giovene, Andrea 1904-............. **CLC 7**
See also CA 85-88

Gippius, Zinaida (Nikolayevna) 1869-1945
See Hippius, Zinaida
See also CA 106

Giraudoux, (Hippolyte) Jean
1882-1944 .... **TCLC 2, 7**
See also CA 104; DLB 65

Gironella, Jose Maria 1917-....... **CLC 11**
See also CA 101

Gissing, George (Robert)
1857-1903 .... **TCLC 3, 24, 47**
See also CA 105; DLB 18, 135

Giurlani, Aldo
See Palazzeschi, Aldo

Gladkov, Fyodor (Vasilyevich)
1883-1958 .... **TCLC 27**

Glanville, Brian (Lester) 1931-...... **CLC 6**
See also CA 5-8R; CAAS 9; CANR 3;
DLB 15, 139; SATA 42

Glasgow, Ellen (Anderson Gholson)
1873(?)-1945 .... **TCLC 2, 7**
See also CA 104; DLB 9, 12

Glaspell, Susan (Keating)
1882(?)-1948 .... **TCLC 55**
See also CA 110; DLB 7, 9, 78; YABC 2

Glassco, John 1909-1981 .... **CLC 9**
See also CA 13-16R; 102; CANR 15;
DLB 68

Glasscock, Amnesia
See Steinbeck, John (Ernst)

Glasser, Ronald J. 1940(?)- .... **CLC 37**

Glassman, Joyce
See Johnson, Joyce

Glendinning, Victoria 1937-........ **CLC 50**
See also CA 120; 127

Glissant, Edouard 1928-........ **CLC 10, 68**

Gloag, Julian 1930- .... **CLC 40**
See also AITN 1; CA 65-68; CANR 10

Glowacki, Aleksander
See Prus, Boleslaw

Glueck, Louise (Elisabeth)
1943- .... **CLC 7, 22, 44, 81**
See also CA 33-36R; CANR 40; DLB 5

Gobineau, Joseph Arthur (Comte) de
1816-1882 .... **NCLC 17**
See also DLB 123

Godard, Jean-Luc 1930-........... **CLC 20**
See also CA 93-96

Godden, (Margaret) Rumer 1907-.... **CLC 53**
See also AAYA 6; CA 5-8R; CANR 4, 27,
36; CLR 20; MAICYA; SAAS 12;
SATA 3, 36

Godoy Alcayaga, Lucila 1889-1957
See Mistral, Gabriela
See also BW 2; CA 104; 131; HW; MTCW

Godwin, Gail (Kathleen)
1937- .... **CLC 5, 8, 22, 31, 69**
See also CA 29-32R; CANR 15, 43; DLB 6;
MTCW

Godwin, William 1756-1836...... **NCLC 14**
See also CDBLB 1789-1832; DLB 39, 104,
142

Goethe, Johann Wolfgang von
1749-1832 .... NCLC 4, 22, 34; DA;
PC 5; WLC 3
See also DLB 94

Gogarty, Oliver St. John
1878-1957 .... TCLC 15
See also CA 109; DLB 15, 19

Gogol, Nikolai (Vasilyevich)
1809-1852 .... NCLC 5, 15, 31; DA;
DC 1; SSC 4; WLC
See also DLB 83

Goines, Donald
1937(?)-1974 .... CLC 80; BLC
See also AITN 1; BW 1; CA 124; 114;
DLB 33

Gold, Herbert 1924-....... CLC 4, 7, 14, 42
See also CA 9-12R; CANR 17, 45; DLB 2;
DLBY 81

Goldbarth, Albert 1948-......... CLC 5, 38
See also CA 53-56; CANR 6, 40; DLB 120

Goldberg, Anatol 1910-1982 .... CLC 34
See also CA 131; 117

Goldemberg, Isaac 1945- .... CLC 52
See also CA 69-72; CAAS 12; CANR 11,
32; HW

Golding, William (Gerald)
1911-1993 .... CLC 1, 2, 3, 8, 10, 17, 27,
58, 81; DA; WLC
See also AAYA 5; CA 5-8R; 141;
CANR 13, 33; CDBLB 1945-1960;
DLB 15, 100; MTCW

Goldman, Emma 1869-1940 ...... TCLC 13
See also CA 110

Goldman, Francisco 1955- .... CLC 76

Goldman, William (W.) 1931-.... CLC 1, 48
See also CA 9-12R; CANR 29; DLB 44

Goldmann, Lucien 1913-1970 ...... CLC 24
See also CA 25-28; CAP 2

Goldoni, Carlo 1707-1793 .... LC 4

Goldsberry, Steven 1949-......... CLC 34
See also CA 131

Goldsmith, Oliver
1728-1774 .... LC 2; DA; WLC
See also CDBLB 1660-1789; DLB 39, 89,
104, 109, 142; SATA 26

Goldsmith, Peter
See Priestley, J(ohn) B(oynton)

Gombrowicz, Witold
1904-1969 .... CLC 4, 7, 11, 49
See also CA 19-20; 25-28R; CAP 2

Gomez de la Serna, Ramon
1888-1963 .... CLC 9
See also CA 116; HW

Goncharov, Ivan Alexandrovich
1812-1891 .... NCLC 1

Goncourt, Edmond (Louis Antoine Huot) de
1822-1896 .... NCLC 7
See also DLB 123

Goncourt, Jules (Alfred Huot) de
1830-1870 .... NCLC 7
See also DLB 123

Gontier, Fernande 19(?)- .... CLC 50

Goodman, Paul 1911-1972.... CLC 1, 2, 4, 7
See also CA 19-20; 37-40R; CANR 34;
CAP 2; DLB 130; MTCW

Gordimer, Nadine
1923- .... CLC 3, 5, 7, 10, 18, 33, 51, 70;
DA; SSC 17
See also CA 5-8R; CANR 3, 28; MTCW

Gordon, Adam Lindsay
1833-1870 .... NCLC 21

Gordon, Caroline
1895-1981 ... CLC 6, 13, 29, 83; SSC 15
See also CA 11-12; 103; CANR 36; CAP 1;
DLB 4, 9, 102; DLBY 81; MTCW

Gordon, Charles William 1860-1937
See Connor, Ralph
See also CA 109

Gordon, Mary (Catherine)
1949- .... CLC 13, 22
See also CA 102; CANR 44; DLB 6;
DLBY 81; MTCW

Gordon, Sol 1923-................. CLC 26
See also CA 53-56; CANR 4; SATA 11

Gordone, Charles 1925-.......... CLC 1, 4
See also BW 1; CA 93-96; DLB 7; MTCW

Gorenko, Anna Andreevna
See Akhmatova, Anna

Gorky, Maxim.............. TCLC 8; WLC
See also Peshkov, Alexei Maximovich

Goryan, Sirak
See Saroyan, William

Gosse, Edmund (William)
1849-1928 .... TCLC 28
See also CA 117; DLB 57, 144

Gotlieb, Phyllis Fay (Bloom)
1926- .... CLC 18
See also CA 13-16R; CANR 7; DLB 88

Gottesman, S. D.
See Kornbluth, C(yril) M.; Pohl, Frederik

Gottfried von Strassburg
fl. c. 1210-................. CMLC 10
See also DLB 138

Gould, Lois .... CLC 4, 10
See also CA 77-80; CANR 29; MTCW

Gourmont, Remy de 1858-1915.... TCLC 17
See also CA 109

Govier, Katherine 1948-.......... CLC 51
See also CA 101; CANR 18, 40

Goyen, (Charles) William
1915-1983.........CLC 5, 8, 14, 40
See also AITN 2; CA 5-8R; 110; CANR 6;
DLB 2; DLBY 83

Goytisolo, Juan
1931- .... CLC 5, 10, 23; HLC
See also CA 85-88; CANR 32; HW; MTCW

Gozzano, Guido 1883-1916 .... PC 10
See also DLB 114

Gozzi, (Conte) Carlo 1720-1806 .. NCLC 23

Grabbe, Christian Dietrich
1801-1836 .... NCLC 2
See also DLB 133

Grace, Patricia 1937-............. CLC 56

Gracian y Morales, Baltasar
1601-1658 .... LC 15

Gracq, Julien................. CLC 11, 48
See also Poirier, Louis
See also DLB 83

Grade, Chaim 1910-1982 .... CLC 10
See also CA 93-96; 107

Graduate of Oxford, A
See Ruskin, John

Graham, John
See Phillips, David Graham

Graham, Jorie 1951-.............. CLC 48
See also CA 111; DLB 120

Graham, R(obert) B(ontine) Cunninghame
See Cunninghame Graham, R(obert)
B(ontine)
See also DLB 98, 135

Graham, Robert
See Haldeman, Joe (William)

Graham, Tom
See Lewis, (Harry) Sinclair

Graham, W(illiam) S(ydney)
1918-1986 .... CLC 29
See also CA 73-76; 118; DLB 20

Graham, Winston (Mawdsley)
1910- .... CLC 23
See also CA 49-52; CANR 2, 22, 45;
DLB 77

Grant, Skeeter
See Spiegelman, Art

Granville-Barker, Harley
1877-1946 .... TCLC 2
See also Barker, Harley Granville
See also CA 104

Grass, Guenter (Wilhelm)
1927- ..... CLC 1, 2, 4, 6, 11, 15, 22, 32,
49; DA; WLC
See also CA 13-16R; CANR 20; DLB 75,
124; MTCW

Gratton, Thomas
See Hulme, T(homas) E(rnest)

Grau, Shirley Ann
1929- .... CLC 4, 9; SSC 15
See also CA 89-92; CANR 22; DLB 2;
MTCW

Gravel, Fern
See Hall, James Norman

Graver, Elizabeth 1964-.......... CLC 70
See also CA 135

Graves, Richard Perceval 1945- .... CLC 44
See also CA 65-68; CANR 9, 26

Graves, Robert (von Ranke)
1895-1985 ...... CLC 1, 2, 6, 11, 39, 44,
45; PC 6
See also CA 5-8R; 117; CANR 5, 36;
CDBLB 1914-1945; DLB 20, 100;
DLBY 85; MTCW; SATA 45

Gray, Alasdair (James) 1934- ...... CLC 41
See also CA 126; CANR 47; MTCW

Gray, Amlin 1946- .... CLC 29
See also CA 138

Gray, Francine du Plessix 1930-.... CLC 22
See also BEST 90:3; CA 61-64; CAAS 2;
CANR 11, 33; MTCW

Gray, John (Henry) 1866-1934 .... TCLC 19
See also CA 119

Gray, Simon (James Holliday)
1936- .... CLC 9, 14, 36
See also AITN 1; CA 21-24R; CAAS 3;
CANR 32; DLB 13; MTCW

Gray, Spalding 1941- . . . . **CLC 49**
See also CA 128

Gray, Thomas
1716-1771 . . . . . . **LC 4; DA; PC 2; WLC**
See also CDBLB 1660-1789; DLB 109

Grayson, David
See Baker, Ray Stannard

Grayson, Richard (A.) 1951- . . . . **CLC 38**
See also CA 85-88; CANR 14, 31

Greeley, Andrew M(oran) 1928- . . . . **CLC 28**
See also CA 5-8R; CAAS 7; CANR 7, 43;
MTCW

Green, Brian
See Card, Orson Scott

Green, Hannah
See Greenberg, Joanne (Goldenberg)

Green, Hannah . . . . **CLC 3**
See also CA 73-76

Green, Henry . . . . **CLC 2, 13**
See also Yorke, Henry Vincent
See also DLB 15

Green, Julian (Hartridge) 1900-
See Green, Julien
See also CA 21-24R; CANR 33; DLB 4, 72;
MTCW

Green, Julien . . . . **CLC 3, 11, 77**
See also Green, Julian (Hartridge)

Green, Paul (Eliot) 1894-1981 . . . . . . **CLC 25**
See also AITN 1; CA 5-8R; 103; CANR 3;
DLB 7, 9; DLBY 81

Greenberg, Ivan 1908-1973
See Rahv, Philip
See also CA 85-88

Greenberg, Joanne (Goldenberg)
1932- . . . . **CLC 7, 30**
See also AAYA 12; CA 5-8R; CANR 14,
32; SATA 25

Greenberg, Richard 1959(?)- . . . . **CLC 57**
See also CA 138

Greene, Bette 1934- . . . . **CLC 30**
See also AAYA 7; CA 53-56; CANR 4;
CLR 2; JRDA; MAICYA; SAAS 16;
SATA 8

Greene, Gael . . . . **CLC 8**
See also CA 13-16R; CANR 10

Greene, Graham
1904-1991 . . . . **CLC 1, 3, 6, 9, 14, 18, 27,
37, 70, 72; DA; WLC**
See also AITN 2; CA 13-16R; 133;
CANR 35; CDBLB 1945-1960; DLB 13,
15, 77, 100; DLBY 91; MTCW; SATA 20

Greer, Richard
See Silverberg, Robert

Greer, Richard
See Silverberg, Robert

Gregor, Arthur 1923- . . . . **CLC 9**
See also CA 25-28R; CAAS 10; CANR 11;
SATA 36

Gregor, Lee
See Pohl, Frederik

Gregory, Isabella Augusta (Persse)
1852-1932 . . . . **TCLC 1**
See also CA 104; DLB 10

Gregory, J. Dennis
See Williams, John A(lfred)

Grendon, Stephen
See Derleth, August (William)

Grenville, Kate 1950- . . . . **CLC 61**
See also CA 118

Grenville, Pelham
See Wodehouse, P(elham) G(renville)

Greve, Felix Paul (Berthold Friedrich)
1879-1948
See Grove, Frederick Philip
See also CA 104; 141

Grey, Zane 1872-1939 . . . . **TCLC 6**
See also CA 104; 132; DLB 9; MTCW

Grieg, (Johan) Nordahl (Brun)
1902-1943 . . . . **TCLC 10**
See also CA 107

Grieve, C(hristopher) M(urray)
1892-1978 . . . . **CLC 11, 19**
See also MacDiarmid, Hugh
See also CA 5-8R; 85-88; CANR 33;
MTCW

Griffin, Gerald 1803-1840 . . . . **NCLC 7**

Griffin, John Howard 1920-1980 . . . . **CLC 68**
See also AITN 1; CA 1-4R; 101; CANR 2

Griffin, Peter 1942- . . . . **CLC 39**
See also CA 136

Griffiths, Trevor 1935- . . . . **CLC 13, 52**
See also CA 97-100; CANR 45; DLB 13

Grigson, Geoffrey (Edward Harvey)
1905-1985 . . . . **CLC 7, 39**
See also CA 25-28R; 118; CANR 20, 33;
DLB 27; MTCW

Grillparzer, Franz 1791-1872 . . . . . . **NCLC 1**
See also DLB 133

Grimble, Reverend Charles James
See Eliot, T(homas) S(tearns)

Grimke, Charlotte L(ottie) Forten
1837(?)-1914
See Forten, Charlotte L.
See also BW 1; CA 117; 124

Grimm, Jacob Ludwig Karl
1785-1863 . . . . **NCLC 3**
See also DLB 90; MAICYA; SATA 22

Grimm, Wilhelm Karl 1786-1859 . . **NCLC 3**
See also DLB 90; MAICYA; SATA 22

Grimmelshausen, Johann Jakob Christoffel
von 1621-1676 . . . . **LC 6**

Grindel, Eugene 1895-1952
See Eluard, Paul
See also CA 104

Grisham, John 1955- . . . . **CLC 84**
See also AAYA 14; CA 138; CANR 47

Grossman, David 1954- . . . . **CLC 67**
See also CA 138

Grossman, Vasily (Semenovich)
1905-1964 . . . . **CLC 41**
See also CA 124; 130; MTCW

Grove, Frederick Philip . . . . **TCLC 4**
See also Greve, Felix Paul (Berthold
Friedrich)
See also DLB 92

Grubb
See Crumb, R(obert)

Grumbach, Doris (Isaac)
1918- . . . . **CLC 13, 22, 64**
See also CA 5-8R; CAAS 2; CANR 9, 42

Grundtvig, Nicolai Frederik Severin
1783-1872 . . . . **NCLC 1**

Grunge
See Crumb, R(obert)

Grunwald, Lisa 1959- . . . . **CLC 44**
See also CA 120

Guare, John 1938- . . . . **CLC 8, 14, 29, 67**
See also CA 73-76; CANR 21; DLB 7;
MTCW

Gudjonsson, Halldor Kiljan 1902-
See Laxness, Halldor
See also CA 103

Guenter, Erich
See Eich, Guenter

Guest, Barbara 1920- . . . . **CLC 34**
See also CA 25-28R; CANR 11, 44; DLB 5

Guest, Judith (Ann) 1936- . . . . **CLC 8, 30**
See also AAYA 7; CA 77-80; CANR 15;
MTCW

Guild, Nicholas M. 1944- . . . . **CLC 33**
See also CA 93-96

Guillemin, Jacques
See Sartre, Jean-Paul

Guillen, Jorge 1893-1984 . . . . **CLC 11**
See also CA 89-92; 112; DLB 108; HW

Guillen (y Batista), Nicolas (Cristobal)
1902-1989 . . . . . **CLC 48, 79; BLC; HLC**
See also BW 2; CA 116; 125; 129; HW

Guillevic, (Eugene) 1907- . . . . **CLC 33**
See also CA 93-96

Guillois
See Desnos, Robert

Guiney, Louise Imogen
1861-1920 . . . . **TCLC 41**
See also DLB 54

Guiraldes, Ricardo (Guillermo)
1886-1927 . . . . **TCLC 39**
See also CA 131; HW; MTCW

Gunn, Bill . . . . **CLC 5**
See also Gunn, William Harrison
See also DLB 38

Gunn, Thom(son William)
1929- . . . . **CLC 3, 6, 18, 32, 81**
See also CA 17-20R; CANR 9, 33;
CDBLB 1960 to Present; DLB 27;
MTCW

Gunn, William Harrison 1934(?)-1989
See Gunn, Bill
See also AITN 1; BW 1; CA 13-16R; 128;
CANR 12, 25

Gunnars, Kristjana 1948- . . . . **CLC 69**
See also CA 113; DLB 60

Gurganus, Allan 1947- . . . . **CLC 70**
See also BEST 90:1; CA 135

Gurney, A(lbert) R(amsdell), Jr.
1930- . . . . **CLC 32, 50, 54**
See also CA 77-80; CANR 32

Gurney, Ivor (Bertie) 1890-1937 . . . **TCLC 33**

Gurney, Peter
See Gurney, A(lbert) R(amsdell), Jr.

Guro, Elena 1877-1913 . . . . **TCLC 56**

Gustafson, Ralph (Barker) 1909-.... **CLC 36**
See also CA 21-24R; CANR 8, 45; DLB 88

Gut, Gom
See Simenon, Georges (Jacques Christian)

Guthrie, A(lfred) B(ertram), Jr.
1901-1991 .... **CLC 23**
See also CA 57-60; 134; CANR 24; DLB 6;
SATA 62; SATA-Obit 67

Guthrie, Isobel
See Grieve, C(hristopher) M(urray)

Guthrie, Woodrow Wilson 1912-1967
See Guthrie, Woody
See also CA 113; 93-96

Guthrie, Woody .... **CLC 35**
See also Guthrie, Woodrow Wilson

Guy, Rosa (Cuthbert) 1928-........ **CLC 26**
See also AAYA 4; BW 2; CA 17-20R;
CANR 14, 34; CLR 13; DLB 33; JRDA;
MAICYA; SATA 14, 62

Gwendolyn
See Bennett, (Enoch) Arnold

H. D. .... **CLC 3, 8, 14, 31, 34, 73; PC 5**
See also Doolittle, Hilda

H. de V.
See Buchan, John

Haavikko, Paavo Juhani
1931- .... **CLC 18, 34**
See also CA 106

Habbema, Koos
See Heijermans, Herman

Hacker, Marilyn 1942- .... **CLC 5, 9, 23, 72**
See also CA 77-80; DLB 120

Haggard, H(enry) Rider
1856-1925 .... **TCLC 11**
See also CA 108; DLB 70; SATA 16

Haig, Fenil
See Ford, Ford Madox

Haig-Brown, Roderick (Langmere)
1908-1976 .... **CLC 21**
See also CA 5-8R; 69-72; CANR 4, 38;
CLR 31; DLB 88; MAICYA; SATA 12

Hailey, Arthur 1920- .... **CLC 5**
See also AITN 2; BEST 90:3; CA 1-4R;
CANR 2, 36; DLB 88; DLBY 82; MTCW

Hailey, Elizabeth Forsythe 1938-... **CLC 40**
See also CA 93-96; CAAS 1; CANR 15

Haines, John (Meade) 1924-....... **CLC 58**
See also CA 17-20R; CANR 13, 34; DLB 5

Haldeman, Joe (William) 1943-..... **CLC 61**
See also CA 53-56; CANR 6; DLB 8

Haley, Alex(ander Murray Palmer)
1921-1992 .... **CLC 8, 12, 76; BLC; DA**
See also BW 2; CA 77-80; 136; DLB 38;
MTCW

Haliburton, Thomas Chandler
1796-1865 .... **NCLC 15**
See also DLB 11, 99

Hall, Donald (Andrew, Jr.)
1928- .... **CLC 1, 13, 37, 59**
See also CA 5-8R; CAAS 7; CANR 2, 44;
DLB 5; SATA 23

Hall, Frederic Sauser
See Sauser-Hall, Frederic

Hall, James
See Kuttner, Henry

Hall, James Norman 1887-1951 ... **TCLC 23**
See also CA 123; SATA 21

Hall, (Marguerite) Radclyffe
1886(?)-1943 .... **TCLC 12**
See also CA 110

Hall, Rodney 1935- .... **CLC 51**
See also CA 109

Halleck, Fitz-Greene 1790-1867 .. **NCLC 47**
See also DLB 3

Halliday, Michael
See Creasey, John

Halpern, Daniel 1945- .... **CLC 14**
See also CA 33-36R

Hamburger, Michael (Peter Leopold)
1924- .... **CLC 5, 14**
See also CA 5-8R; CAAS 4; CANR 2, 47;
DLB 27

Hamill, Pete 1935- .... **CLC 10**
See also CA 25-28R; CANR 18

Hamilton, Clive
See Lewis, C(live) S(taples)

Hamilton, Edmond 1904-1977...... **CLC 1**
See also CA 1-4R; CANR 3; DLB 8

Hamilton, Eugene (Jacob) Lee
See Lee-Hamilton, Eugene (Jacob)

Hamilton, Franklin
See Silverberg, Robert

Hamilton, Gail
See Corcoran, Barbara

Hamilton, Mollie
See Kaye, M(ary) M(argaret)

Hamilton, (Anthony Walter) Patrick
1904-1962 .... **CLC 51**
See also CA 113; DLB 10

Hamilton, Virginia 1936-.......... **CLC 26**
See also AAYA 2; BW 2; CA 25-28R;
CANR 20, 37; CLR 1, 11; DLB 33, 52;
JRDA; MAICYA; MTCW; SATA 4, 56,
79

Hammett, (Samuel) Dashiell
1894-1961 .... **CLC 3, 5, 10, 19, 47;
SSC 17**
See also AITN 1; CA 81-84; CANR 42;
CDALB 1929-1941; DLBD 6; MTCW

Hammon, Jupiter
1711(?)-1800(?) .... **NCLC 5; BLC**
See also DLB 31, 50

Hammond, Keith
See Kuttner, Henry

Hamner, Earl (Henry), Jr. 1923- ... **CLC 12**
See also AITN 2; CA 73-76; DLB 6

Hampton, Christopher (James)
1946- .... **CLC 4**
See also CA 25-28R; DLB 13; MTCW

Hamsun, Knut .... **TCLC 2, 14, 49**
See also Pedersen, Knut

Handke, Peter 1942- .. **CLC 5, 8, 10, 15, 38**
See also CA 77-80; CANR 33; DLB 85,
124; MTCW

Hanley, James 1901-1985 ... **CLC 3, 5, 8, 13**
See also CA 73-76; 117; CANR 36; MTCW

Hannah, Barry 1942- .... **CLC 23, 38**
See also CA 108; 110; CANR 43; DLB 6;
MTCW

Hannon, Ezra
See Hunter, Evan

Hansberry, Lorraine (Vivian)
1930-1965 ...... **CLC 17, 62; BLC; DA;
DC 2**
See also BW 1; CA 109; 25-28R; CABS 3;
CDALB 1941-1968; DLB 7, 38; MTCW

Hansen, Joseph 1923-............. **CLC 38**
See also CA 29-32R; CAAS 17; CANR 16,
44

Hansen, Martin A. 1909-1955..... **TCLC 32**

Hanson, Kenneth O(stlin) 1922-.... **CLC 13**
See also CA 53-56; CANR 7

Hardwick, Elizabeth 1916- .... **CLC 13**
See also CA 5-8R; CANR 3, 32; DLB 6;
MTCW

Hardy, Thomas
1840-1928 ...... **TCLC 4, 10, 18, 32, 48,
53; DA; PC 8; SSC 2; WLC**
See also CA 104; 123; CDBLB 1890-1914;
DLB 18, 19, 135; MTCW

Hare, David 1947- .... **CLC 29, 58**
See also CA 97-100; CANR 39; DLB 13;
MTCW

Harford, Henry
See Hudson, W(illiam) H(enry)

Hargrave, Leonie
See Disch, Thomas M(ichael)

Harjo, Joy 1951- .... **CLC 83**
See also CA 114; CANR 35; DLB 120;
NNAL

Harlan, Louis R(udolph) 1922- ..... **CLC 34**
See also CA 21-24R; CANR 25

Harling, Robert 1951(?)- .... **CLC 53**

Harmon, William (Ruth) 1938-..... **CLC 38**
See also CA 33-36R; CANR 14, 32, 35;
SATA 65

Harper, F. E. W.
See Harper, Frances Ellen Watkins

Harper, Frances E. W.
See Harper, Frances Ellen Watkins

Harper, Frances E. Watkins
See Harper, Frances Ellen Watkins

Harper, Frances Ellen
See Harper, Frances Ellen Watkins

Harper, Frances Ellen Watkins
1825-1911 .... **TCLC 14; BLC**
See also BW 1; CA 111; 125; DLB 50

Harper, Michael S(teven) 1938- .. **CLC 7, 22**
See also BW 1; CA 33-36R; CANR 24;
DLB 41

Harper, Mrs. F. E. W.
See Harper, Frances Ellen Watkins

Harris, Christie (Lucy) Irwin
1907- .... **CLC 12**
See also CA 5-8R; CANR 6; DLB 88;
JRDA; MAICYA; SAAS 10; SATA 6, 74

Harris, Frank 1856(?)-1931 .... **TCLC 24**
See also CA 109

Harris, George Washington
1814-1869 . . . . **NCLC 23**
See also DLB 3, 11

Harris, Joel Chandler 1848-1908 . . . **TCLC 2**
See also CA 104; 137; DLB 11, 23, 42, 78, 91; MAICYA; YABC 1

Harris, John (Wyndham Parkes Lucas) Beynon 1903-1969
See Wyndham, John
See also CA 102; 89-92

Harris, MacDonald . . . . **CLC 9**
See also Heiney, Donald (William)

Harris, Mark 1922- . . . . **CLC 19**
See also CA 5-8R; CAAS 3; CANR 2; DLB 2; DLBY 80

Harris, (Theodore) Wilson 1921-. . . . **CLC 25**
See also BW 2; CA 65-68; CAAS 16; CANR 11, 27; DLB 117; MTCW

Harrison, Elizabeth Cavanna 1909-
See Cavanna, Betty
See also CA 9-12R; CANR 6, 27

Harrison, Harry (Max) 1925- . . . . . . **CLC 42**
See also CA 1-4R; CANR 5, 21; DLB 8; SATA 4

Harrison, James (Thomas)
1937- . . . . **CLC 6, 14, 33, 66**
See also CA 13-16R; CANR 8; DLBY 82

Harrison, Jim
See Harrison, James (Thomas)

Harrison, Kathryn 1961- . . . . **CLC 70**
See also CA 144

Harrison, Tony 1937-. . . . . **CLC 43**
See also CA 65-68; CANR 44; DLB 40; MTCW

Harriss, Will(ard Irvin) 1922- . . . . . . **CLC 34**
See also CA 111

Harson, Sley
See Ellison, Harlan (Jay)

Hart, Ellis
See Ellison, Harlan (Jay)

Hart, Josephine 1942(?)- . . . . **CLC 70**
See also CA 138

Hart, Moss 1904-1961 . . . . **CLC 66**
See also CA 109; 89-92; DLB 7

Harte, (Francis) Bret(t)
1836(?)-1902 . . . . **TCLC 1, 25; DA; SSC 8; WLC**
See also CA 104; 140; CDALB 1865-1917; DLB 12, 64, 74, 79; SATA 26

Hartley, L(eslie) P(oles)
1895-1972 . . . . **CLC 2, 22**
See also CA 45-48; 37-40R; CANR 33; DLB 15, 139; MTCW

Hartman, Geoffrey H. 1929-. . . . . . . **CLC 27**
See also CA 117; 125; DLB 67

Haruf, Kent 19(?)- . . . . **CLC 34**

Harwood, Ronald 1934-. . . . . **CLC 32**
See also CA 1-4R; CANR 4; DLB 13

Hasek, Jaroslav (Matej Frantisek)
1883-1923 . . . . **TCLC 4**
See also CA 104; 129; MTCW

Hass, Robert 1941-. . . . . **CLC 18, 39**
See also CA 111; CANR 30; DLB 105

Hastings, Hudson
See Kuttner, Henry

Hastings, Selina. . . . . **CLC 44**

Hatteras, Amelia
See Mencken, H(enry) L(ouis)

Hatteras, Owen. . . . . **TCLC 18**
See also Mencken, H(enry) L(ouis); Nathan, George Jean

Hauptmann, Gerhart (Johann Robert)
1862-1946 . . . . **TCLC 4**
See also CA 104; DLB 66, 118

Havel, Vaclav 1936-. . . . . **CLC 25, 58, 65**
See also CA 104; CANR 36; MTCW

Haviaras, Stratis. . . . . **CLC 33**
See also Chaviaras, Strates

Hawes, Stephen 1475(?)-1523(?) . . . . . **LC 17**

Hawkes, John (Clendennin Burne, Jr.)
1925- . . . . . . **CLC 1, 2, 3, 4, 7, 9, 14, 15, 27, 49**
See also CA 1-4R; CANR 2, 47; DLB 2, 7; DLBY 80; MTCW

Hawking, S. W.
See Hawking, Stephen W(illiam)

Hawking, Stephen W(illiam)
1942- . . . . **CLC 63**
See also AAYA 13; BEST 89:1; CA 126; 129

Hawthorne, Julian 1846-1934 . . . . . **TCLC 25**

Hawthorne, Nathaniel
1804-1864 . . . . . . **NCLC 39; DA; SSC 3; WLC**
See also CDALB 1640-1865; DLB 1, 74; YABC 2

Haxton, Josephine Ayres 1921-
See Douglas, Ellen
See also CA 115; CANR 41

Hayaseca y Eizaguirre, Jorge
See Echegaray (y Eizaguirre), Jose (Maria Waldo)

Hayashi Fumiko 1904-1951. . . . . . . **TCLC 27**

Haycraft, Anna
See Ellis, Alice Thomas
See also CA 122

Hayden, Robert E(arl)
1913-1980 . . . . . . **CLC 5, 9, 14, 37; BLC; DA; PC 6**
See also BW 1; CA 69-72; 97-100; CABS 2; CANR 24; CDALB 1941-1968; DLB 5, 76; MTCW; SATA 19; SATA-Obit 26

Hayford, J(oseph) E(phraim) Casely
See Casely-Hayford, J(oseph) E(phraim)

Hayman, Ronald 1932-. . . . . **CLC 44**
See also CA 25-28R; CANR 18

Haywood, Eliza (Fowler)
1693(?)-1756 . . . . **LC 1**

Hazlitt, William 1778-1830 . . . . . . **NCLC 29**
See also DLB 110

Hazzard, Shirley 1931- . . . . **CLC 18**
See also CA 9-12R; CANR 4; DLBY 82; MTCW

Head, Bessie 1937-1986. . . **CLC 25, 67; BLC**
See also BW 2; CA 29-32R; 119; CANR 25; DLB 117; MTCW

Headon, (Nicky) Topper 1956(?)- . . . **CLC 30**

Heaney, Seamus (Justin)
1939- . . . . **CLC 5, 7, 14, 25, 37, 74**
See also CA 85-88; CANR 25; CDBLB 1960 to Present; DLB 40; MTCW

Hearn, (Patricio) Lafcadio (Tessima Carlos)
1850-1904. . . . . **TCLC 9**
See also CA 105; DLB 12, 78

Hearne, Vicki 1946-. . . . . **CLC 56**
See also CA 139

Hearon, Shelby 1931-. . . . . **CLC 63**
See also AITN 2; CA 25-28R; CANR 18

Heat-Moon, William Least. . . . . **CLC 29**
See also Trogdon, William (Lewis)
See also AAYA 9

Hebbel, Friedrich 1813-1863. . . . . . **NCLC 43**
See also DLB 129

Hebert, Anne 1916- . . . . **CLC 4, 13, 29**
See also CA 85-88; DLB 68; MTCW

Hecht, Anthony (Evan)
1923- . . . . **CLC 8, 13, 19**
See also CA 9-12R; CANR 6; DLB 5

Hecht, Ben 1894-1964 . . . . **CLC 8**
See also CA 85-88; DLB 7, 9, 25, 26, 28, 86

Hedayat, Sadeq 1903-1951. . . . . . . **TCLC 21**
See also CA 120

Hegel, Georg Wilhelm Friedrich
1770-1831 . . . . **NCLC 46**
See also DLB 90

Heidegger, Martin 1889-1976 . . . . . . **CLC 24**
See also CA 81-84; 65-68; CANR 34; MTCW

Heidenstam, (Carl Gustaf) Verner von
1859-1940 . . . . **TCLC 5**
See also CA 104

Heifner, Jack 1946-. . . . . **CLC 11**
See also CA 105; CANR 47

Heijermans, Herman 1864-1924 . . . **TCLC 24**
See also CA 123

Heilbrun, Carolyn G(old) 1926-. . . . . **CLC 25**
See also CA 45-48; CANR 1, 28

Heine, Heinrich 1797-1856 . . . . **NCLC 4**
See also DLB 90

Heinemann, Larry (Curtiss) 1944- . . **CLC 50**
See also CA 110; CANR 31; DLBD 9

Heiney, Donald (William) 1921-1993
See Harris, MacDonald
See also CA 1-4R; 142; CANR 3

Heinlein, Robert A(nson)
1907-1988 . . . . . . **CLC 1, 3, 8, 14, 26, 55**
See also CA 1-4R; 125; CANR 1, 20; DLB 8; JRDA; MAICYA; MTCW; SATA 9, 69; SATA-Obit 56

Helforth, John
See Doolittle, Hilda

Hellenhofferu, Vojtech Kapristian z
See Hasek, Jaroslav (Matej Frantisek)

Heller, Joseph
1923- . . . . **CLC 1, 3, 5, 8, 11, 36, 63; DA; WLC**
See also AITN 1; CA 5-8R; CABS 1; CANR 8, 42; DLB 2, 28; DLBY 80; MTCW

Hirsch, E(ric) D(onald), Jr. 1928-... **CLC 79**
See also CA 25-28R; CANR 27; DLB 67;
MTCW

Hirsch, Edward 1950- .... **CLC 31, 50**
See also CA 104; CANR 20, 42; DLB 120

Hitchcock, Alfred (Joseph)
1899-1980 .... **CLC 16**
See also CA 97-100; SATA 27;
SATA-Obit 24

Hitler, Adolf 1889-1945.......... **TCLC 53**
See also CA 117

Hoagland, Edward 1932- .... **CLC 28**
See also CA 1-4R; CANR 2, 31; DLB 6;
SATA 51

Hoban, Russell (Conwell) 1925-... **CLC 7, 25**
See also CA 5-8R; CANR 23, 37; CLR 3;
DLB 52; MAICYA; MTCW; SATA 1,
40, 78

Hobbs, Perry
See Blackmur, R(ichard) P(almer)

Hobson, Laura Z(ametkin)
1900-1986 .... **CLC 7, 25**
See also CA 17-20R; 118; DLB 28;
SATA 52

Hochhuth, Rolf 1931-........ **CLC 4, 11, 18**
See also CA 5-8R; CANR 33; DLB 124;
MTCW

Hochman, Sandra 1936-.......... **CLC 3, 8**
See also CA 5-8R; DLB 5

Hochwaelder, Fritz 1911-1986...... **CLC 36**
See also CA 29-32R; 120; CANR 42;
MTCW

Hochwalder, Fritz
See Hochwaelder, Fritz

Hocking, Mary (Eunice) 1921- ..... **CLC 13**
See also CA 101; CANR 18, 40

Hodgins, Jack 1938-.............. **CLC 23**
See also CA 93-96; DLB 60

Hodgson, William Hope
1877(?)-1918 .... **TCLC 13**
See also CA 111; DLB 70

Hoffman, Alice 1952-............. **CLC 51**
See also CA 77-80; CANR 34; MTCW

Hoffman, Daniel (Gerard)
1923- .... **CLC 6, 13, 23**
See also CA 1-4R; CANR 4; DLB 5

Hoffman, Stanley 1944-............ **CLC 5**
See also CA 77-80

Hoffman, William M(oses) 1939- ... **CLC 40**
See also CA 57-60; CANR 11

Hoffmann, E(rnst) T(heodor) A(madeus)
1776-1822 .... **NCLC 2; SSC 13**
See also DLB 90; SATA 27

Hofmann, Gert 1931-............. **CLC 54**
See also CA 128

Hofmannsthal, Hugo von
1874-1929 .... **TCLC 11; DC 4**
See also CA 106; DLB 81, 118

Hogan, Linda 1947-.............. **CLC 73**
See also CA 120; CANR 45; NNAL

Hogarth, Charles
See Creasey, John

Hogg, James 1770-1835.......... **NCLC 4**
See also DLB 93, 116

Holbach, Paul Henri Thiry Baron
1723-1789 .... **LC 14**

Holberg, Ludvig 1684-1754.......... **LC 6**

Holden, Ursula 1921-............ **CLC 18**
See also CA 101; CAAS 8; CANR 22

Holderlin, (Johann Christian) Friedrich
1770-1843 .... **NCLC 16; PC 4**

Holdstock, Robert
See Holdstock, Robert P.

Holdstock, Robert P. 1948-........ **CLC 39**
See also CA 131

Holland, Isabelle 1920- .... **CLC 21**
See also AAYA 11; CA 21-24R; CANR 10,
25, 47; JRDA; MAICYA; SATA 8, 70

Holland, Marcus
See Caldwell, (Janet Miriam) Taylor
(Holland)

Hollander, John 1929-...... **CLC 2, 5, 8, 14**
See also CA 1-4R; CANR 1; DLB 5;
SATA 13

Hollander, Paul
See Silverberg, Robert

Holleran, Andrew 1943(?)-......... **CLC 38**
See also CA 144

Hollinghurst, Alan 1954-.......... **CLC 55**
See also CA 114

Hollis, Jim
See Summers, Hollis (Spurgeon, Jr.)

Holmes, John
See Souster, (Holmes) Raymond

Holmes, John Clellon 1926-1988.... **CLC 56**
See also CA 9-12R; 125; CANR 4; DLB 16

Holmes, Oliver Wendell
1809-1894 .... **NCLC 14**
See also CDALB 1640-1865; DLB 1;
SATA 34

Holmes, Raymond
See Souster, (Holmes) Raymond

Holt, Victoria
See Hibbert, Eleanor Alice Burford

Holub, Miroslav 1923-............. **CLC 4**
See also CA 21-24R; CANR 10

Homer c. 8th cent. B.C.- ..... **CMLC 1; DA**

Honig, Edwin 1919-............... **CLC 33**
See also CA 5-8R; CAAS 8; CANR 4, 45;
DLB 5

Hood, Hugh (John Blagdon)
1928- .... **CLC 15, 28**
See also CA 49-52; CAAS 17; CANR 1, 33;
DLB 53

Hood, Thomas 1799-1845........ **NCLC 16**
See also DLB 96

Hooker, (Peter) Jeremy 1941-...... **CLC 43**
See also CA 77-80; CANR 22; DLB 40

Hope, A(lec) D(erwent) 1907- .... **CLC 3, 51**
See also CA 21-24R; CANR 33; MTCW

Hope, Brian
See Creasey, John

Hope, Christopher (David Tully)
1944- .... **CLC 52**
See also CA 106; CANR 47; SATA 62

Hopkins, Gerard Manley
1844-1889 .... **NCLC 17; DA; WLC**
See also CDBLB 1890-1914; DLB 35, 57

Hopkins, John (Richard) 1931-...... **CLC 4**
See also CA 85-88

Hopkins, Pauline Elizabeth
1859-1930 .... **TCLC 28; BLC**
See also BW 2; CA 141; DLB 50

Hopkinson, Francis 1737-1791 ...... **LC 25**
See also DLB 31

Hopley-Woolrich, Cornell George 1903-1968
See Woolrich, Cornell
See also CA 13-14; CAP 1

Horatio
See Proust, (Valentin-Louis-George-Eugene-)
Marcel

Horgan, Paul 1903- .... **CLC 9, 53**
See also CA 13-16R; CANR 9, 35;
DLB 102; DLBY 85; MTCW; SATA 13

Horn, Peter
See Kuttner, Henry

Hornem, Horace Esq.
See Byron, George Gordon (Noel)

Horovitz, Israel (Arthur) 1939-..... **CLC 56**
See also CA 33-36R; CANR 46; DLB 7

Horvath, Odon von
See Horvath, Oedoen von
See also DLB 85, 124

Horvath, Oedoen von 1901-1938... **TCLC 45**
See also Horvath, Odon von
See also CA 118

Horwitz, Julius 1920-1986......... **CLC 14**
See also CA 9-12R; 119; CANR 12

Hospital, Janette Turner 1942-..... **CLC 42**
See also CA 108

Hostos, E. M. de
See Hostos (y Bonilla), Eugenio Maria de

Hostos, Eugenio M. de
See Hostos (y Bonilla), Eugenio Maria de

Hostos, Eugenio Maria
See Hostos (y Bonilla), Eugenio Maria de

Hostos (y Bonilla), Eugenio Maria de
1839-1903 .... **TCLC 24**
See also CA 123; 131; HW

Houdini
See Lovecraft, H(oward) P(hillips)

Hougan, Carolyn 1943- .... **CLC 34**
See also CA 139

Household, Geoffrey (Edward West)
1900-1988 .... **CLC 11**
See also CA 77-80; 126; DLB 87; SATA 14;
SATA-Obit 59

Housman, A(lfred) E(dward)
1859-1936 ...... **TCLC 1, 10; DA; PC 2**
See also CA 104; 125; DLB 19; MTCW

Housman, Laurence 1865-1959..... **TCLC 7**
See also CA 106; DLB 10; SATA 25

Howard, Elizabeth Jane 1923- ... **CLC 7, 29**
See also CA 5-8R; CANR 8

Howard, Maureen 1930- ..... **CLC 5, 14, 46**
See also CA 53-56; CANR 31; DLBY 83;
MTCW

Howard, Richard 1929- ...... **CLC 7, 10, 47**
See also AITN 1; CA 85-88; CANR 25;
DLB 5

Howard, Robert Ervin 1906-1936... **TCLC 8**
See also CA 105

Howard, Warren F.
See Pohl, Frederik

Howe, Fanny 1940- .... **CLC 47**
See also CA 117; SATA 52

Howe, Irving 1920-1993........... **CLC 85**
See also CA 9-12R; 141; CANR 21;
DLB 67; MTCW

Howe, Julia Ward 1819-1910 ..... **TCLC 21**
See also CA 117; DLB 1

Howe, Susan 1937-............... **CLC 72**
See also DLB 120

Howe, Tina 1937-............... **CLC 48**
See also CA 109

Howell, James 1594(?)-1666 .... **LC 13**

Howells, W. D.
See Howells, William Dean

Howells, William D.
See Howells, William Dean

Howells, William Dean
1837-1920 .... **TCLC 7, 17, 41**
See also CA 104; 134; CDALB 1865-1917;
DLB 12, 64, 74, 79

Howes, Barbara 1914- .... **CLC 15**
See also CA 9-12R; CAAS 3; SATA 5

Hrabal, Bohumil 1914-........ **CLC 13, 67**
See also CA 106; CAAS 12

Hsun, Lu .... **TCLC 3**
See also Shu-Jen, Chou

Hubbard, L(afayette) Ron(ald)
1911-1986 .... **CLC 43**
See also CA 77-80; 118; CANR 22

Huch, Ricarda (Octavia)
1864-1947 .... **TCLC 13**
See also CA 111; DLB 66

Huddle, David 1942- .... **CLC 49**
See also CA 57-60; CAAS 20; DLB 130

Hudson, Jeffrey
See Crichton, (John) Michael

Hudson, W(illiam) H(enry)
1841-1922 .... **TCLC 29**
See also CA 115; DLB 98; SATA 35

Hueffer, Ford Madox
See Ford, Ford Madox

Hughart, Barry 1934-............. **CLC 39**
See also CA 137

Hughes, Colin
See Creasey, John

Hughes, David (John) 1930- .... **CLC 48**
See also CA 116; 129; DLB 14

Hughes, (James) Langston
1902-1967 ..... **CLC 1, 5, 10, 15, 35, 44;**
BLC; DA; DC 3; PC 1; SSC 6; WLC
See also AAYA 12; BW 1; CA 1-4R;
25-28R; CANR 1, 34; CDALB 1929-1941;
CLR 17; DLB 4, 7, 48, 51, 86; JRDA;
MAICYA; MTCW; SATA 4, 33

Hughes, Richard (Arthur Warren)
1900-1976 .... **CLC 1, 11**
See also CA 5-8R; 65-68; CANR 4;
DLB 15; MTCW; SATA 8;
SATA-Obit 25

Hughes, Ted
1930- .... **CLC 2, 4, 9, 14, 37; PC 7**
See also CA 1-4R; CANR 1, 33; CLR 3;
DLB 40; MAICYA; MTCW; SATA 27,
49

Hugo, Richard F(ranklin)
1923-1982 .... **CLC 6, 18, 32**
See also CA 49-52; 108; CANR 3; DLB 5

Hugo, Victor (Marie)
1802-1885 .. **NCLC 3, 10, 21; DA; WLC**
See also DLB 119; SATA 47

Huidobro, Vicente
See Huidobro Fernandez, Vicente Garcia

Huidobro Fernandez, Vicente Garcia
1893-1948 .... **TCLC 31**
See also CA 131; HW

Hulme, Keri 1947- .... **CLC 39**
See also CA 125

Hulme, T(homas) E(rnest)
1883-1917 .... **TCLC 21**
See also CA 117; DLB 19

Hume, David 1711-1776............. **LC 7**
See also DLB 104

Humphrey, William 1924-......... **CLC 45**
See also CA 77-80; DLB 6

Humphreys, Emyr Owen 1919-..... **CLC 47**
See also CA 5-8R; CANR 3, 24; DLB 15

Humphreys, Josephine 1945-.... **CLC 34, 57**
See also CA 121; 127

Hungerford, Pixie
See Brinsmead, H(esba) F(ay)

Hunt, E(verette) Howard, (Jr.)
1918- .... **CLC 3**
See also AITN 1; CA 45-48; CANR 2, 47

Hunt, Kyle
See Creasey, John

Hunt, (James Henry) Leigh
1784-1859 .... **NCLC 1**

Hunt, Marsha 1946-.............. **CLC 70**
See also BW 2; CA 143

Hunt, Violet 1866-1942 .... **TCLC 53**

Hunter, E. Waldo
See Sturgeon, Theodore (Hamilton)

Hunter, Evan 1926- .... **CLC 11, 31**
See also CA 5-8R; CANR 5, 38; DLBY 82;
MTCW; SATA 25

Hunter, Kristin (Eggleston) 1931-... **CLC 35**
See also AITN 1; BW 1; CA 13-16R;
CANR 13; CLR 3; DLB 33; MAICYA;
SAAS 10; SATA 12

Hunter, Mollie 1922-............. **CLC 21**
See also McIlwraith, Maureen Mollie
Hunter
See also AAYA 13; CANR 37; CLR 25;
JRDA; MAICYA; SAAS 7; SATA 54

Hunter, Robert (?)-1734............ **LC 7**

Hurston, Zora Neale
1903-1960 .... **CLC 7, 30, 61; BLC; DA;**
SSC 4
See also BW 1; CA 85-88; DLB 51, 86;
MTCW

Huston, John (Marcellus)
1906-1987 .... **CLC 20**
See also CA 73-76; 123; CANR 34; DLB 26

Hustvedt, Siri 1955-.............. **CLC 76**
See also CA 137

Hutten, Ulrich von 1488-1523...... **LC 16**

Huxley, Aldous (Leonard)
1894-1963 ..... **CLC 1, 3, 4, 5, 8, 11, 18,**
35, 79; DA; WLC
See also AAYA 11; CA 85-88; CANR 44;
CDBLB 1914-1945; DLB 36, 100;
MTCW; SATA 63

Huysmans, Charles Marie Georges
1848-1907
See Huysmans, Joris-Karl
See also CA 104

Huysmans, Joris-Karl.............. TCLC 7
See also Huysmans, Charles Marie Georges
See also DLB 123

Hwang, David Henry
1957- .... **CLC 55; DC 4**
See also CA 127; 132

Hyde, Anthony 1946-............ **CLC 42**
See also CA 136

Hyde, Margaret O(ldroyd) 1917- ... **CLC 21**
See also CA 1-4R; CANR 1, 36; CLR 23;
JRDA; MAICYA; SAAS 8; SATA 1, 42,
76

Hynes, James 1956(?)-............ **CLC 65**

Ian, Janis 1951- .... **CLC 21**
See also CA 105

Ibanez, Vicente Blasco
See Blasco Ibanez, Vicente

Ibarguengoitia, Jorge 1928-1983.... **CLC 37**
See also CA 124; 113; HW

Ibsen, Henrik (Johan)
1828-1906 .... **TCLC 2, 8, 16, 37, 52;**
DA; DC 2; WLC
See also CA 104; 141

Ibuse Masuji 1898-1993.......... **CLC 22**
See also CA 127; 141

Ichikawa, Kon 1915-............. **CLC 20**
See also CA 121

Idle, Eric 1943-................. **CLC 21**
See also Monty Python
See also CA 116; CANR 35

Ignatow, David 1914-...... **CLC 4, 7, 14, 40**
See also CA 9-12R; CAAS 3; CANR 31;
DLB 5

Ihimaera, Witi 1944- .... **CLC 46**
See also CA 77-80

Ilf, Ilya....................... TCLC 21
See also Fainzilberg, Ilya Arnoldovich

Immermann, Karl (Lebrecht)
1796-1840 .... **NCLC 4**
See also DLB 133

Inclan, Ramon (Maria) del Valle
See Valle-Inclan, Ramon (Maria) del

Infante, G(uillermo) Cabrera
See Cabrera Infante, G(uillermo)

Kallman, Chester (Simon)
1921-1975 .... **CLC 2**
See also CA 45-48; 53-56; CANR 3

Kaminsky, Melvin 1926-
See Brooks, Mel
See also CA 65-68; CANR 16

Kaminsky, Stuart M(elvin) 1934- ... **CLC 59**
See also CA 73-76; CANR 29

Kane, Paul
See Simon, Paul

Kane, Wilson
See Bloch, Robert (Albert)

Kanin, Garson 1912-.............. **CLC 22**
See also AITN 1; CA 5-8R; CANR 7;
DLB 7

Kaniuk, Yoram 1930-............. **CLC 19**
See also CA 134

Kant, Immanuel 1724-1804 ...... **NCLC 27**
See also DLB 94

Kantor, MacKinlay 1904-1977 ...... **CLC 7**
See also CA 61-64; 73-76; DLB 9, 102

Kaplan, David Michael 1946- ...... **CLC 50**

Kaplan, James 1951- .... **CLC 59**
See also CA 135

Karageorge, Michael
See Anderson, Poul (William)

Karamzin, Nikolai Mikhailovich
1766-1826 .... **NCLC 3**

Karapanou, Margarita 1946-....... **CLC 13**
See also CA 101

Karinthy, Frigyes 1887-1938 ...... **TCLC 47**

Karl, Frederick R(obert) 1927-..... **CLC 34**
See also CA 5-8R; CANR 3, 44

Kastel, Warren
See Silverberg, Robert

Kataev, Evgeny Petrovich 1903-1942
See Petrov, Evgeny
See also CA 120

Kataphusin
See Ruskin, John

Katz, Steve 1935-................. **CLC 47**
See also CA 25-28R; CAAS 14; CANR 12;
DLBY 83

Kauffman, Janet 1945-............. **CLC 42**
See also CA 117; CANR 43; DLBY 86

Kaufman, Bob (Garnell)
1925-1986 .... **CLC 49**
See also BW 1; CA 41-44R; 118; CANR 22;
DLB 16, 41

Kaufman, George S. 1889-1961..... **CLC 38**
See also CA 108; 93-96; DLB 7

Kaufman, Sue .... **CLC 3, 8**
See also Barondess, Sue K(aufman)

Kavafis, Konstantinos Petrou 1863-1933
See Cavafy, C(onstantine) P(eter)
See also CA 104

Kavan, Anna 1901-1968...... **CLC 5, 13, 82**
See also CA 5-8R; CANR 6; MTCW

Kavanagh, Dan
See Barnes, Julian

Kavanagh, Patrick (Joseph)
1904-1967 .... **CLC 22**
See also CA 123; 25-28R; DLB 15, 20;
MTCW

Kawabata, Yasunari
1899-1972 ..... **CLC 2, 5, 9, 18; SSC 17**
See also CA 93-96; 33-36R

Kaye, M(ary) M(argaret) 1909-..... **CLC 28**
See also CA 89-92; CANR 24; MTCW;
SATA 62

Kaye, Mollie
See Kaye, M(ary) M(argaret)

Kaye-Smith, Sheila 1887-1956..... **TCLC 20**
See also CA 118; DLB 36

Kaymor, Patrice Maguilene
See Senghor, Leopold Sedar

Kazan, Elia 1909-.......... **CLC 6, 16, 63**
See also CA 21-24R; CANR 32

Kazantzakis, Nikos
1883(?)-1957 .... **TCLC 2, 5, 33**
See also CA 105; 132; MTCW

Kazin, Alfred 1915- .... **CLC 34, 38**
See also CA 1-4R; CAAS 7; CANR 1, 45;
DLB 67

Keane, Mary Nesta (Skrine) 1904-
See Keane, Molly
See also CA 108; 114

Keane, Molly.................... **CLC 31**
See also Keane, Mary Nesta (Skrine)

Keates, Jonathan 19(?)-........... **CLC 34**

Keaton, Buster 1895-1966 .... **CLC 20**

Keats, John
1795-1821 ... **NCLC 8; DA; PC 1; WLC**
See also CDBLB 1789-1832; DLB 96, 110

Keene, Donald 1922- .... **CLC 34**
See also CA 1-4R; CANR 5

Keillor, Garrison................... **CLC 40**
See also Keillor, Gary (Edward)
See also AAYA 2; BEST 89:3; DLBY 87;
SATA 58

Keillor, Gary (Edward) 1942-
See Keillor, Garrison
See also CA 111; 117; CANR 36; MTCW

Keith, Michael
See Hubbard, L(afayette) Ron(ald)

Keller, Gottfried 1819-1890....... **NCLC 2**
See also DLB 129

Kellerman, Jonathan 1949- .... **CLC 44**
See also BEST 90:1; CA 106; CANR 29

Kelley, William Melvin 1937-...... **CLC 22**
See also BW 1; CA 77-80; CANR 27;
DLB 33

Kellogg, Marjorie 1922-............ **CLC 2**
See also CA 81-84

Kellow, Kathleen
See Hibbert, Eleanor Alice Burford

Kelly, M(ilton) T(erry) 1947-....... **CLC 55**
See also CA 97-100; CANR 19, 43

Kelman, James 1946-.......... **CLC 58, 86**

Kemal, Yashar 1923- .... **CLC 14, 29**
See also CA 89-92; CANR 44

Kemble, Fanny 1809-1893 .... **NCLC 18**
See also DLB 32

Kemelman, Harry 1908-........... **CLC 2**
See also AITN 1; CA 9-12R; CANR 6;
DLB 28

Kempe, Margery 1373(?)-1440(?) ..... **LC 6**
See also DLB 146

Kempis, Thomas a 1380-1471 ...... **LC 11**

Kendall, Henry 1839-1882....... **NCLC 12**

Keneally, Thomas (Michael)
1935-...... **CLC 5, 8, 10, 14, 19, 27, 43**
See also CA 85-88; CANR 10; MTCW

Kennedy, Adrienne (Lita)
1931- .... **CLC 66; BLC; DC 5**
See also BW 2; CA 103; CAAS 20; CABS 3;
CANR 26; DLB 38

Kennedy, John Pendleton
1795-1870 .... **NCLC 2**
See also DLB 3

Kennedy, Joseph Charles 1929-
See Kennedy, X. J.
See also CA 1-4R; CANR 4, 30, 40;
SATA 14

Kennedy, William 1928-... **CLC 6, 28, 34, 53**
See also AAYA 1; CA 85-88; CANR 14,
31; DLB 143; DLBY 85; MTCW;
SATA 57

Kennedy, X. J.................... **CLC 8, 42**
See also Kennedy, Joseph Charles
See also CAAS 9; CLR 27; DLB 5

Kent, Kelvin
See Kuttner, Henry

Kenton, Maxwell
See Southern, Terry

Kenyon, Robert O.
See Kuttner, Henry

Kerouac, Jack ..... **CLC 1, 2, 3, 5, 14, 29, 61**
See also Kerouac, Jean-Louis Lebris de
See also CDALB 1941-1968; DLB 2, 16;
DLBD 3

Kerouac, Jean-Louis Lebris de 1922-1969
See Kerouac, Jack
See also AITN 1; CA 5-8R; 25-28R;
CANR 26; DA; MTCW; WLC

Kerr, Jean 1923-................. **CLC 22**
See also CA 5-8R; CANR 7

Kerr, M. E. .... **CLC 12, 35**
See also Meaker, Marijane (Agnes)
See also AAYA 2; CLR 29; SAAS 1

Kerr, Robert .... **CLC 55**

Kerrigan, (Thomas) Anthony
1918- .... **CLC 4, 6**
See also CA 49-52; CAAS 11; CANR 4

Kerry, Lois
See Duncan, Lois

Kesey, Ken (Elton)
1935- ...... **CLC 1, 3, 6, 11, 46, 64; DA;
WLC**
See also CA 1-4R; CANR 22, 38;
CDALB 1968-1988; DLB 2, 16; MTCW;
SATA 66

Kesselring, Joseph (Otto)
1902-1967 .... **CLC 45**

Kessler, Jascha (Frederick) 1929-.... **CLC 4**
See also CA 17-20R; CANR 8

Kornbluth, C(yril) M.   1923-1958. . . . TCLC 8
  See also CA 105; DLB 8

Korolenko, V. G.
  See Korolenko, Vladimir Galaktionovich

Korolenko, Vladimir
  See Korolenko, Vladimir Galaktionovich

Korolenko, Vladimir G.
  See Korolenko, Vladimir Galaktionovich

Korolenko, Vladimir Galaktionovich
    1853-1921 . . . . TCLC 22
  See also CA 121

Kosinski, Jerzy (Nikodem)
    1933-1991 . . . . CLC 1, 2, 3, 6, 10, 15, 53,
                                               70
  See also CA 17-20R; 134; CANR 9, 46, 46;
    DLB 2; DLBY 82; MTCW

Kostelanetz, Richard (Cory)   1940- . . CLC 28
  See also CA 13-16R; CAAS 8; CANR 38

Kostrowitzki, Wilhelm Apollinaris de
    1880-1918
  See Apollinaire, Guillaume
  See also CA 104

Kotlowitz, Robert   1924- . . . . CLC 4
  See also CA 33-36R; CANR 36

Kotzebue, August (Friedrich Ferdinand) von
    1761-1819 . . . . NCLC 25
  See also DLB 94

Kotzwinkle, William   1938- . . . CLC 5, 14, 35
  See also CA 45-48; CANR 3, 44; CLR 6;
    MAICYA; SATA 24, 70

Kozol, Jonathan   1936- . . . . CLC 17
  See also CA 61-64; CANR 16, 45

Kozoll, Michael   1940(?)- . . . . CLC 35

Kramer, Kathryn   19(?)- . . . . CLC 34

Kramer, Larry   1935- . . . . CLC 42
  See also CA 124; 126

Krasicki, Ignacy   1735-1801 . . . . . . NCLC 8

Krasinski, Zygmunt   1812-1859 . . . . NCLC 4

Kraus, Karl   1874-1936 . . . . TCLC 5
  See also CA 104; DLB 118

Kreve (Mickevicius), Vincas
    1882-1954 . . . . TCLC 27

Kristeva, Julia   1941- . . . . CLC 77

Kristofferson, Kris   1936- . . . . CLC 26
  See also CA 104

Krizanc, John   1956- . . . . CLC 57

Krleza, Miroslav   1893-1981 . . . . CLC 8
  See also CA 97-100; 105; DLB 147

Kroetsch, Robert   1927- . . . . . . CLC 5, 23, 57
  See also CA 17-20R; CANR 8, 38; DLB 53;
    MTCW

Kroetz, Franz
  See Kroetz, Franz Xaver

Kroetz, Franz Xaver   1946- . . . . CLC 41
  See also CA 130

Kroker, Arthur   1945- . . . . CLC 77

Kropotkin, Peter (Aleksieevich)
    1842-1921 . . . . TCLC 36
  See also CA 119

Krotkov, Yuri   1917- . . . . CLC 19
  See also CA 102

Krumb
  See Crumb, R(obert)

Krumgold, Joseph (Quincy)
    1908-1980 . . . . CLC 12
  See also CA 9-12R; 101; CANR 7;
    MAICYA; SATA 1, 48; SATA-Obit 23

Krumwitz
  See Crumb, R(obert)

Krutch, Joseph Wood   1893-1970. . . . CLC 24
  See also CA 1-4R; 25-28R; CANR 4;
    DLB 63

Krutzch, Gus
  See Eliot, T(homas) S(tearns)

Krylov, Ivan Andreevich
    1768(?)-1844 . . . . NCLC 1

Kubin, Alfred   1877-1959 . . . . TCLC 23
  See also CA 112; DLB 81

Kubrick, Stanley   1928- . . . . CLC 16
  See also CA 81-84; CANR 33; DLB 26

Kumin, Maxine (Winokur)
    1925- . . . . CLC 5, 13, 28
  See also AITN 2; CA 1-4R; CAAS 8;
    CANR 1, 21; DLB 5; MTCW; SATA 12

Kundera, Milan
    1929- . . . . CLC 4, 9, 19, 32, 68
  See also AAYA 2; CA 85-88; CANR 19;
    MTCW

Kunene, Mazisi (Raymond)   1930- . . . CLC 85
  See also BW 1; CA 125; DLB 117

Kunitz, Stanley (Jasspon)
    1905- . . . . CLC 6, 11, 14
  See also CA 41-44R; CANR 26; DLB 48;
    MTCW

Kunze, Reiner   1933- . . . . CLC 10
  See also CA 93-96; DLB 75

Kuprin, Aleksandr Ivanovich
    1870-1938 . . . . TCLC 5
  See also CA 104

Kureishi, Hanif   1954(?)- . . . . CLC 64
  See also CA 139

Kurosawa, Akira   1910- . . . . CLC 16
  See also AAYA 11; CA 101; CANR 46, 46

Kushner, Tony   1957(?)- . . . . CLC 81
  See also CA 144

Kuttner, Henry   1915-1958 . . . . TCLC 10
  See also CA 107; DLB 8

Kuzma, Greg   1944- . . . . CLC 7
  See also CA 33-36R

Kuzmin, Mikhail   1872(?)-1936 . . . . TCLC 40

Kyd, Thomas   1558-1594 . . . . . . LC 22; DC 3
  See also DLB 62

Kyprianos, Iossif
  See Samarakis, Antonis

La Bruyere, Jean de   1645-1696 . . . . . . LC 17

Lacan, Jacques (Marie Emile)
    1901-1981 . . . . CLC 75
  See also CA 121; 104

Laclos, Pierre Ambroise Francois Choderlos
    de   1741-1803 . . . . NCLC 4

Lacolere, Francois
  See Aragon, Louis

La Colere, Francois
  See Aragon, Louis

La Deshabilleuse
  See Simenon, Georges (Jacques Christian)

Lady Gregory
  See Gregory, Isabella Augusta (Persse)

Lady of Quality, A
  See Bagnold, Enid

La Fayette, Marie (Madelaine Pioche de la
    Vergne Comtes   1634-1693 . . . . . . LC 2

Lafayette, Rene
  See Hubbard, L(afayette) Ron(ald)

Laforgue, Jules   1860-1887 . . . . NCLC 5

Lagerkvist, Paer (Fabian)
    1891-1974 . . . . CLC 7, 10, 13, 54
  See also Lagerkvist, Par
  See also CA 85-88; 49-52; MTCW

Lagerkvist, Par
  See Lagerkvist, Paer (Fabian)
  See also SSC 12

Lagerloef, Selma (Ottiliana Lovisa)
    1858-1940 . . . . TCLC 4, 36
  See also Lagerlof, Selma (Ottiliana Lovisa)
  See also CA 108; SATA 15

Lagerlof, Selma (Ottiliana Lovisa)
  See Lagerloef, Selma (Ottiliana Lovisa)
  See also CLR 7; SATA 15

La Guma, (Justin) Alex(ander)
    1925-1985 . . . . CLC 19
  See also BW 1; CA 49-52; 118; CANR 25;
    DLB 117; MTCW

Laidlaw, A. K.
  See Grieve, C(hristopher) M(urray)

Lainez, Manuel Mujica
  See Mujica Lainez, Manuel
  See also HW

Lamartine, Alphonse (Marie Louis Prat) de
    1790-1869 . . . . NCLC 11

Lamb, Charles
    1775-1834 . . . . NCLC 10; DA; WLC
  See also CDBLB 1789-1832; DLB 93, 107;
    SATA 17

Lamb, Lady Caroline   1785-1828 . . NCLC 38
  See also DLB 116

Lamming, George (William)
    1927- . . . . CLC 2, 4, 66; BLC
  See also BW 2; CA 85-88; CANR 26;
    DLB 125; MTCW

L'Amour, Louis (Dearborn)
    1908-1988 . . . . CLC 25, 55
  See also AITN 2; BEST 89:2; CA 1-4R;
    125; CANR 3, 25, 40; DLBY 80; MTCW

Lampedusa, Giuseppe (Tomasi) di . . . TCLC 13
  See also Tomasi di Lampedusa, Giuseppe

Lampman, Archibald   1861-1899 . . NCLC 25
  See also DLB 92

Lancaster, Bruce   1896-1963 . . . . CLC 36
  See also CA 9-10; CAP 1; SATA 9

Landau, Mark Alexandrovich
  See Aldanov, Mark (Alexandrovich)

Landau-Aldanov, Mark Alexandrovich
  See Aldanov, Mark (Alexandrovich)

Landis, John   1950- . . . . CLC 26
  See also CA 112; 122

Landolfi, Tommaso   1908-1979 . . . CLC 11, 49
  See also CA 127; 117

Landon, Letitia Elizabeth
1802-1838 .... **NCLC 15**
See also DLB 96

Landor, Walter Savage
1775-1864 .... **NCLC 14**
See also DLB 93, 107

Landwirth, Heinz 1927-
See Lind, Jakov
See also CA 9-12R; CANR 7

Lane, Patrick 1939- .... **CLC 25**
See also CA 97-100; DLB 53

Lang, Andrew 1844-1912 .... **TCLC 16**
See also CA 114; 137; DLB 98, 141;
MAICYA; SATA 16

Lang, Fritz 1890-1976 .... **CLC 20**
See also CA 77-80; 69-72; CANR 30

Lange, John
See Crichton, (John) Michael

Langer, Elinor 1939- .... **CLC 34**
See also CA 121

Langland, William
1330(?)-1400(?) .... **LC 19; DA**
See also DLB 146

Langstaff, Launcelot
See Irving, Washington

Lanier, Sidney 1842-1881 .... **NCLC 6**
See also DLB 64; MAICYA; SATA 18

Lanyer, Aemilia 1569-1645 .... **LC 10**

Lao Tzu .... **CMLC 7**

Lapine, James (Elliot) 1949- .... **CLC 39**
See also CA 123; 130

Larbaud, Valery (Nicolas)
1881-1957 .... **TCLC 9**
See also CA 106

Lardner, Ring
See Lardner, Ring(gold) W(ilmer)

Lardner, Ring W., Jr.
See Lardner, Ring(gold) W(ilmer)

Lardner, Ring(gold) W(ilmer)
1885-1933 .... **TCLC 2, 14**
See also CA 104; 131; CDALB 1917-1929;
DLB 11, 25, 86; MTCW

Laredo, Betty
See Codrescu, Andrei

Larkin, Maia
See Wojciechowska, Maia (Teresa)

Larkin, Philip (Arthur)
1922-1985 .... **CLC 3, 5, 8, 9, 13, 18, 33,
39, 64**
See also CA 5-8R; 117; CANR 24;
CDBLB 1960 to Present; DLB 27;
MTCW

Larra (y Sanchez de Castro), Mariano Jose de
1809-1837 .... **NCLC 17**

Larsen, Eric 1941- .... **CLC 55**
See also CA 132

Larsen, Nella 1891-1964 ..... **CLC 37; BLC**
See also BW 1; CA 125; DLB 51

Larson, Charles R(aymond) 1938-... **CLC 31**
See also CA 53-56; CANR 4

Lasker-Schueler, Else 1869-1945 .. **TCLC 57**
See also DLB 66, 124

Latham, Jean Lee 1902-.......... **CLC 12**
See also AITN 1; CA 5-8R; CANR 7;
MAICYA; SATA 2, 68

Latham, Mavis
See Clark, Mavis Thorpe

Lathen, Emma .... **CLC 2**
See also Hennissart, Martha; Latsis, Mary
J(ane)

Lathrop, Francis
See Leiber, Fritz (Reuter, Jr.)

Latsis, Mary J(ane)
See Lathen, Emma
See also CA 85-88

Lattimore, Richmond (Alexander)
1906-1984 .... **CLC 3**
See also CA 1-4R; 112; CANR 1

Laughlin, James 1914-............ **CLC 49**
See also CA 21-24R; CANR 9, 45; DLB 48

Laurence, (Jean) Margaret (Wemyss)
1926-1987 .. **CLC 3, 6, 13, 50, 62; SSC 7**
See also CA 5-8R; 121; CANR 33; DLB 53;
MTCW; SATA-Obit 50

Laurent, Antoine 1952- .... **CLC 50**

Lauscher, Hermann
See Hesse, Hermann

Lautreamont, Comte de
1846-1870 .... **NCLC 12; SSC 14**

Laverty, Donald
See Blish, James (Benjamin)

Lavin, Mary 1912- ...... **CLC 4, 18; SSC 4**
See also CA 9-12R; CANR 33; DLB 15;
MTCW

Lavond, Paul Dennis
See Kornbluth, C(yril) M.; Pohl, Frederik

Lawler, Raymond Evenor 1922- .... **CLC 58**
See also CA 103

Lawrence, D(avid) H(erbert Richards)
1885-1930 .... **TCLC 2, 9, 16, 33, 48;
DA; SSC 4; WLC**
See also CA 104; 121; CDBLB 1914-1945;
DLB 10, 19, 36, 98; MTCW

Lawrence, T(homas) E(dward)
1888-1935 .... **TCLC 18**
See Dale, Colin
See also CA 115

Lawrence of Arabia
See Lawrence, T(homas) E(dward)

Lawson, Henry (Archibald Hertzberg)
1867-1922 .... **TCLC 27; SSC 18**
See also CA 120

Lawton, Dennis
See Faust, Frederick (Schiller)

Laxness, Halldor .... **CLC 25**
See also Gudjonsson, Halldor Kiljan

Layamon fl. c. 1200-............ **CMLC 10**
See also DLB 146

Laye, Camara 1928-1980 ... **CLC 4, 38; BLC**
See also BW 1; CA 85-88; 97-100;
CANR 25; MTCW

Layton, Irving (Peter) 1912- ..... **CLC 2, 15**
See also CA 1-4R; CANR 2, 33, 43;
DLB 88; MTCW

Lazarus, Emma 1849-1887........ **NCLC 8**

Lazarus, Felix
See Cable, George Washington

Lazarus, Henry
See Slavitt, David R(ytman)

Lea, Joan
See Neufeld, John (Arthur)

Leacock, Stephen (Butler)
1869-1944 .... **TCLC 2**
See also CA 104; 141; DLB 92

Lear, Edward 1812-1888 .... **NCLC 3**
See also CLR 1; DLB 32; MAICYA;
SATA 18

Lear, Norman (Milton) 1922- ...... **CLC 12**
See also CA 73-76

Leavis, F(rank) R(aymond)
1895-1978 .... **CLC 24**
See also CA 21-24R; 77-80; CANR 44;
MTCW

Leavitt, David 1961-............. **CLC 34**
See also CA 116; 122; DLB 130

Leblanc, Maurice (Marie Emile)
1864-1941 .... **TCLC 49**
See also CA 110

Lebowitz, Fran(ces Ann)
1951(?)-................. **CLC 11, 36**
See also CA 81-84; CANR 14; MTCW

Lebrecht, Peter
See Tieck, (Johann) Ludwig

le Carre, John .... **CLC 3, 5, 9, 15, 28**
See also Cornwell, David (John Moore)
See also BEST 89:4; CDBLB 1960 to
Present; DLB 87

Le Clezio, J(ean) M(arie) G(ustave)
1940- .... **CLC 31**
See also CA 116; 128; DLB 83

Leconte de Lisle, Charles-Marie-Rene
1818-1894 .... **NCLC 29**

Le Coq, Monsieur
See Simenon, Georges (Jacques Christian)

Leduc, Violette 1907-1972......... **CLC 22**
See also CA 13-14; 33-36R; CAP 1

Ledwidge, Francis 1887(?)-1917 ... **TCLC 23**
See also CA 123; DLB 20

Lee, Andrea 1953- .... **CLC 36; BLC**
See also BW 1; CA 125

Lee, Andrew
See Auchincloss, Louis (Stanton)

Lee, Don L. .... **CLC 2**
See also Madhubuti, Haki R.

Lee, George W(ashington)
1894-1976 .... **CLC 52; BLC**
See also BW 1; CA 125; DLB 51

Lee, (Nelle) Harper
1926- .... **CLC 12, 60; DA; WLC**
See also AAYA 13; CA 13-16R;
CDALB 1941-1968; DLB 6; MTCW;
SATA 11

Lee, Helen Elaine 1959(?)- .... **CLC 86**

Lee, Julian
See Latham, Jean Lee

Lee, Larry
See Lee, Lawrence

Lee, Lawrence 1941-1990.......... **CLC 34**
See also CA 131; CANR 43

Loti, Pierre .... **TCLC 11**
See also Viaud, (Louis Marie) Julien
See also DLB 123

Louie, David Wong 1954- .... **CLC 70**
See also CA 139

Louis, Father M.
See Merton, Thomas

Lovecraft, H(oward) P(hillips)
1890-1937 .... **TCLC 4, 22; SSC 3**
See also AAYA 14; CA 104; 133; MTCW

Lovelace, Earl 1935- .... **CLC 51**
See also BW 2; CA 77-80; CANR 41;
DLB 125; MTCW

Lovelace, Richard 1618-1657....... **LC 24**
See also DLB 131

Lowell, Amy 1874-1925 .... **TCLC 1, 8**
See also CA 104; DLB 54, 140

Lowell, James Russell 1819-1891 .. **NCLC 2**
See also CDALB 1640-1865; DLB 1, 11, 64, 79

Lowell, Robert (Traill Spence, Jr.)
1917-1977 ... **CLC 1, 2, 3, 4, 5, 8, 9, 11, 15, 37; DA; PC 3; WLC**
See also CA 9-12R; 73-76; CABS 2;
CANR 26; DLB 5; MTCW

Lowndes, Marie Adelaide (Belloc)
1868-1947 .... **TCLC 12**
See also CA 107; DLB 70

Lowry, (Clarence) Malcolm
1909-1957 .... **TCLC 6, 40**
See also CA 105; 131; CDBLB 1945-1960;
DLB 15; MTCW

Lowry, Mina Gertrude 1882-1966
See Loy, Mina
See also CA 113

Loxsmith, John
See Brunner, John (Kilian Houston)

Loy, Mina .... **CLC 28**
See also Lowry, Mina Gertrude
See also DLB 4, 54

Loyson-Bridet
See Schwob, (Mayer Andre) Marcel

Lucas, Craig 1951- .... **CLC 64**
See also CA 137

Lucas, George 1944- .... **CLC 16**
See also AAYA 1; CA 77-80; CANR 30;
SATA 56

Lucas, Hans
See Godard, Jean-Luc

Lucas, Victoria
See Plath, Sylvia

Ludlam, Charles 1943-1987 ..... **CLC 46, 50**
See also CA 85-88; 122

Ludlum, Robert 1927- .... **CLC 22, 43**
See also AAYA 10; BEST 89:1, 90:3;
CA 33-36R; CANR 25, 41; DLBY 82;
MTCW

Ludwig, Ken...................... **CLC 60**

Ludwig, Otto 1813-1865.......... **NCLC 4**
See also DLB 129

Lugones, Leopoldo 1874-1938 ..... **TCLC 15**
See also CA 116; 131; HW

Lu Hsun 1881-1936 .... **TCLC 3**

Lukacs, George .... **CLC 24**
See also Lukacs, Gyorgy (Szegeny von)

Lukacs, Gyorgy (Szegeny von) 1885-1971
See Lukacs, George
See also CA 101; 29-32R

Luke, Peter (Ambrose Cyprian)
1919- .... **CLC 38**
See also CA 81-84; DLB 13

Lunar, Dennis
See Mungo, Raymond

Lurie, Alison 1926-........ **CLC 4, 5, 18, 39**
See also CA 1-4R; CANR 2, 17; DLB 2;
MTCW; SATA 46

Lustig, Arnost 1926-.............. **CLC 56**
See also AAYA 3; CA 69-72; CANR 47;
SATA 56

Luther, Martin 1483-1546.......... **LC 9**

Luzi, Mario 1914-................ **CLC 13**
See also CA 61-64; CANR 9; DLB 128

Lynch, B. Suarez
See Bioy Casares, Adolfo; Borges, Jorge
Luis

Lynch, David (K.) 1946-.......... **CLC 66**
See also CA 124; 129

Lynch, James
See Andreyev, Leonid (Nikolaevich)

Lynch Davis, B.
See Bioy Casares, Adolfo; Borges, Jorge
Luis

Lyndsay, Sir David 1490-1555 ...... **LC 20**

Lynn, Kenneth S(chuyler) 1923-.... **CLC 50**
See also CA 1-4R; CANR 3, 27

Lynx
See West, Rebecca

Lyons, Marcus
See Blish, James (Benjamin)

Lyre, Pinchbeck
See Sassoon, Siegfried (Lorraine)

Lytle, Andrew (Nelson) 1902-...... **CLC 22**
See also CA 9-12R; DLB 6

Lyttelton, George 1709-1773........ **LC 10**

Maas, Peter 1929- .... **CLC 29**
See also CA 93-96

Macaulay, Rose 1881-1958 ..... **TCLC 7, 44**
See also CA 104; DLB 36

Macaulay, Thomas Babington
1800-1859 .... **NCLC 42**
See also CDBLB 1832-1890; DLB 32, 55

MacBeth, George (Mann)
1932-1992 .... **CLC 2, 5, 9**
See also CA 25-28R; 136; DLB 40; MTCW;
SATA 4; SATA-Obit 70

MacCaig, Norman (Alexander)
1910-..................... **CLC 36**
See also CA 9-12R; CANR 3, 34; DLB 27

MacCarthy, (Sir Charles Otto) Desmond
1877-1952 .... **TCLC 36**

MacDiarmid, Hugh
.... **CLC 2, 4, 11, 19, 63; PC 9**
See also Grieve, C(hristopher) M(urray)
See also CDBLB 1945-1960; DLB 20

MacDonald, Anson
See Heinlein, Robert A(nson)

Macdonald, Cynthia 1928-...... **CLC 13, 19**
See also CA 49-52; CANR 4, 44; DLB 105

MacDonald, George 1824-1905..... **TCLC 9**
See also CA 106; 137; DLB 18; MAICYA;
SATA 33

Macdonald, John
See Millar, Kenneth

MacDonald, John D(ann)
1916-1986 .... **CLC 3, 27, 44**
See also CA 1-4R; 121; CANR 1, 19;
DLB 8; DLBY 86; MTCW

Macdonald, John Ross
See Millar, Kenneth

Macdonald, Ross..... **CLC 1, 2, 3, 14, 34, 41**
See also Millar, Kenneth
See also DLBD 6

MacDougal, John
See Blish, James (Benjamin)

MacEwen, Gwendolyn (Margaret)
1941-1987 .... **CLC 13, 55**
See also CA 9-12R; 124; CANR 7, 22;
DLB 53; SATA 50; SATA-Obit 55

Macha, Karel Hynek 1810-1846.. **NCLC 46**

Machado (y Ruiz), Antonio
1875-1939 .... **TCLC 3**
See also CA 104; DLB 108

Machado de Assis, Joaquim Maria
1839-1908 .... **TCLC 10; BLC**
See also CA 107

Machen, Arthur................... **TCLC 4**
See also Jones, Arthur Llewellyn
See also DLB 36

Machiavelli, Niccolo 1469-1527 .. **LC 8; DA**

MacInnes, Colin 1914-1976...... **CLC 4, 23**
See also CA 69-72; 65-68; CANR 21;
DLB 14; MTCW

MacInnes, Helen (Clark)
1907-1985 .... **CLC 27, 39**
See also CA 1-4R; 117; CANR 1, 28;
DLB 87; MTCW; SATA 22;
SATA-Obit 44

Mackay, Mary 1855-1924
See Corelli, Marie
See also CA 118

Mackenzie, Compton (Edward Montague)
1883-1972 .... **CLC 18**
See also CA 21-22; 37-40R; CAP 2;
DLB 34, 100

Mackenzie, Henry 1745-1831 .... **NCLC 41**
See also DLB 39

Mackintosh, Elizabeth 1896(?)-1952
See Tey, Josephine
See also CA 110

MacLaren, James
See Grieve, C(hristopher) M(urray)

Mac Laverty, Bernard 1942-....... **CLC 31**
See also CA 116; 118; CANR 43

MacLean, Alistair (Stuart)
1922-1987 .... **CLC 3, 13, 50, 63**
See also CA 57-60; 121; CANR 28; MTCW;
SATA 23; SATA-Obit 50

Maclean, Norman (Fitzroy)
1902-1990 .... **CLC 78; SSC 13**
See also CA 102; 132

Maxwell, William (Keepers, Jr.)
1908- . . . . **CLC 19**
See also CA 93-96; DLBY 80

May, Elaine 1932- . . . . **CLC 16**
See also CA 124; 142; DLB 44

Mayakovski, Vladimir (Vladimirovich)
1893-1930 . . . . **TCLC 4, 18**
See also CA 104

Mayhew, Henry 1812-1887 . . . . . . **NCLC 31**
See also DLB 18, 55

Maynard, Joyce 1953- . . . . **CLC 23**
See also CA 111; 129

Mayne, William (James Carter)
1928- . . . . **CLC 12**
See also CA 9-12R; CANR 37; CLR 25;
JRDA; MAICYA; SAAS 11; SATA 6, 68

Mayo, Jim
See L'Amour, Louis (Dearborn)

Maysles, Albert 1926- . . . . **CLC 16**
See also CA 29-32R

Maysles, David 1932- . . . . **CLC 16**

Mazer, Norma Fox 1931- . . . . **CLC 26**
See also AAYA 5; CA 69-72; CANR 12,
32; CLR 23; JRDA; MAICYA; SAAS 1;
SATA 24, 67

Mazzini, Guiseppe 1805-1872 . . . . **NCLC 34**

McAuley, James Phillip
1917-1976 . . . . **CLC 45**
See also CA 97-100

McBain, Ed
See Hunter, Evan

McBrien, William Augustine
1930- . . . . **CLC 44**
See also CA 107

McCaffrey, Anne (Inez) 1926- . . . . . . **CLC 17**
See also AAYA 6; AITN 2; BEST 89:2;
CA 25-28R; CANR 15, 35; DLB 8;
JRDA; MAICYA; MTCW; SAAS 11;
SATA 8, 70

McCall, Nathan 1955(?)- . . . . **CLC 86**
See also CA 146

McCann, Arthur
See Campbell, John W(ood, Jr.)

McCann, Edson
See Pohl, Frederik

McCarthy, Charles, Jr. 1933-
See McCarthy, Cormac
See also CANR 42

McCarthy, Cormac 1933- . . . . . **CLC 4, 57, 59**
See also McCarthy, Charles, Jr.
See also DLB 6, 143

McCarthy, Mary (Therese)
1912-1989 . . . **CLC 1, 3, 5, 14, 24, 39, 59**
See also CA 5-8R; 129; CANR 16; DLB 2;
DLBY 81; MTCW

McCartney, (James) Paul
1942- . . . . **CLC 12, 35**

McCauley, Stephen (D.) 1955- . . . . . **CLC 50**
See also CA 141

McClure, Michael (Thomas)
1932- . . . . **CLC 6, 10**
See also CA 21-24R; CANR 17, 46, 46;
DLB 16

McCorkle, Jill (Collins) 1958- . . . . . . **CLC 51**
See also CA 121; DLBY 87

McCourt, James 1941- . . . . **CLC 5**
See also CA 57-60

McCoy, Horace (Stanley)
1897-1955 . . . . **TCLC 28**
See also CA 108; DLB 9

McCrae, John 1872-1918 . . . . **TCLC 12**
See also CA 109; DLB 92

McCreigh, James
See Pohl, Frederik

McCullers, (Lula) Carson (Smith)
1917-1967 . . . . **CLC 1, 4, 10, 12, 48; DA;
SSC 9; WLC**
See also CA 5-8R; 25-28R; CABS 1, 3;
CANR 18; CDALB 1941-1968; DLB 2, 7;
MTCW; SATA 27

McCulloch, John Tyler
See Burroughs, Edgar Rice

McCullough, Colleen 1938(?)- . . . . . . **CLC 27**
See also CA 81-84; CANR 17, 46, 46;
MTCW

McElroy, Joseph 1930- . . . . **CLC 5, 47**
See also CA 17-20R

McEwan, Ian (Russell) 1948- . . . **CLC 13, 66**
See also BEST 90:4; CA 61-64; CANR 14,
41; DLB 14; MTCW

McFadden, David 1940- . . . . **CLC 48**
See also CA 104; DLB 60

McFarland, Dennis 1950- . . . . **CLC 65**

McGahern, John
1934- . . . . **CLC 5, 9, 48; SSC 17**
See also CA 17-20R; CANR 29; DLB 14;
MTCW

McGinley, Patrick (Anthony)
1937- . . . . **CLC 41**
See also CA 120; 127

McGinley, Phyllis 1905-1978 . . . . . . **CLC 14**
See also CA 9-12R; 77-80; CANR 19;
DLB 11, 48; SATA 2, 44; SATA-Obit 24

McGinniss, Joe 1942- . . . . **CLC 32**
See also AITN 2; BEST 89:2; CA 25-28R;
CANR 26

McGivern, Maureen Daly
See Daly, Maureen

McGrath, Patrick 1950- . . . . **CLC 55**
See also CA 136

McGrath, Thomas (Matthew)
1916-1990 . . . . **CLC 28, 59**
See also CA 9-12R; 132; CANR 6, 33;
MTCW; SATA 41; SATA-Obit 66

McGuane, Thomas (Francis III)
1939- . . . . **CLC 3, 7, 18, 45**
See also AITN 2; CA 49-52; CANR 5, 24;
DLB 2; DLBY 80; MTCW

McGuckian, Medbh 1950- . . . . **CLC 48**
See also CA 143; DLB 40

McHale, Tom 1942(?)-1982 . . . . . . **CLC 3, 5**
See also AITN 1; CA 77-80; 106

McIlvanney, William 1936- . . . . **CLC 42**
See also CA 25-28R; DLB 14

McIlwraith, Maureen Mollie Hunter
See Hunter, Mollie
See also SATA 2

McInerney, Jay 1955- . . . . **CLC 34**
See also CA 116; 123

McIntyre, Vonda N(eel) 1948- . . . . . **CLC 18**
See also CA 81-84; CANR 17, 34; MTCW

McKay, Claude . . . . . **TCLC 7, 41; BLC; PC 2**
See also McKay, Festus Claudius
See also DLB 4, 45, 51, 117

McKay, Festus Claudius 1889-1948
See McKay, Claude
See also BW 1; CA 104; 124; DA; MTCW;
WLC

McKuen, Rod 1933- . . . . **CLC 1, 3**
See also AITN 1; CA 41-44R; CANR 40

McLoughlin, R. B.
See Mencken, H(enry) L(ouis)

McLuhan, (Herbert) Marshall
1911-1980 . . . . **CLC 37, 83**
See also CA 9-12R; 102; CANR 12, 34;
DLB 88; MTCW

McMillan, Terry (L.) 1951- . . . . . **CLC 50, 61**
See also BW 2; CA 140

McMurtry, Larry (Jeff)
1936- . . . . **CLC 2, 3, 7, 11, 27, 44**
See also AITN 2; BEST 89:2; CA 5-8R;
CANR 19, 43; CDALB 1968-1988;
DLB 2, 143; DLBY 80, 87; MTCW

McNally, T. M. 1961- . . . . **CLC 82**

McNally, Terrence 1939- . . . . . . **CLC 4, 7, 41**
See also CA 45-48; CANR 2; DLB 7

McNamer, Deirdre 1950- . . . . **CLC 70**

McNeile, Herman Cyril 1888-1937
See Sapper
See also DLB 77

McPhee, John (Angus) 1931- . . . . . . **CLC 36**
See also BEST 90:1; CA 65-68; CANR 20,
46, 46; MTCW

McPherson, James Alan
1943- . . . . **CLC 19, 77**
See also BW 1; CA 25-28R; CAAS 17;
CANR 24; DLB 38; MTCW

McPherson, William (Alexander)
1933- . . . . **CLC 34**
See also CA 69-72; CANR 28

Mead, Margaret 1901-1978 . . . . **CLC 37**
See also AITN 1; CA 1-4R; 81-84;
CANR 4; MTCW; SATA-Obit 20

Meaker, Marijane (Agnes) 1927-
See Kerr, M. E.
See also CA 107; CANR 37; JRDA;
MAICYA; MTCW; SATA 20, 61

Medoff, Mark (Howard) 1940- . . . **CLC 6, 23**
See also AITN 1; CA 53-56; CANR 5;
DLB 7

Medvedev, P. N.
See Bakhtin, Mikhail Mikhailovich

Meged, Aharon
See Megged, Aharon

Meged, Aron
See Megged, Aharon

Megged, Aharon 1920- . . . . **CLC 9**
See also CA 49-52; CAAS 13; CANR 1

Mehta, Ved (Parkash) 1934- . . . . **CLC 37**
See also CA 1-4R; CANR 2, 23; MTCW

Melanter
See Blackmore, R(ichard) D(oddridge)

Melikow, Loris
See Hofmannsthal, Hugo von

Melmoth, Sebastian
See Wilde, Oscar (Fingal O'Flahertie Wills)

Meltzer, Milton 1915- . . . . **CLC 26**
See also AAYA 8; CA 13-16R; CANR 38;
CLR 13; DLB 61; JRDA; MAICYA;
SAAS 1; SATA 1, 50, 80

Melville, Herman
1819-1891 . . . . **NCLC 3, 12, 29, 45; DA;
SSC 1, 17; WLC**
See also CDALB 1640-1865; DLB 3, 74;
SATA 59

Menander
c. 342B.C.-c. 292B.C. . . . . **CMLC 9; DC 3**

Mencken, H(enry) L(ouis)
1880-1956 . . . . **TCLC 13**
See also CA 105; 125; CDALB 1917-1929;
DLB 11, 29, 63, 137; MTCW

Mercer, David 1928-1980 . . . . **CLC 5**
See also CA 9-12R; 102; CANR 23;
DLB 13; MTCW

Merchant, Paul
See Ellison, Harlan (Jay)

Meredith, George 1828-1909 . . . **TCLC 17, 43**
See also CA 117; CDBLB 1832-1890;
DLB 18, 35, 57

Meredith, William (Morris)
1919- . . . . **CLC 4, 13, 22, 55**
See also CA 9-12R; CAAS 14; CANR 6, 40;
DLB 5

Merezhkovsky, Dmitry Sergeyevich
1865-1941 . . . . **TCLC 29**

Merimee, Prosper
1803-1870 . . . . **NCLC 6; SSC 7**
See also DLB 119

Merkin, Daphne 1954- . . . . **CLC 44**
See also CA 123

Merlin, Arthur
See Blish, James (Benjamin)

Merrill, James (Ingram)
1926- . . . . **CLC 2, 3, 6, 8, 13, 18, 34**
See also CA 13-16R; CANR 10; DLB 5;
DLBY 85; MTCW

Merriman, Alex
See Silverberg, Robert

Merritt, E. B.
See Waddington, Miriam

Merton, Thomas
1915-1968 . . **CLC 1, 3, 11, 34, 83; PC 10**
See also CA 5-8R; 25-28R; CANR 22;
DLB 48; DLBY 81; MTCW

Merwin, W(illiam) S(tanley)
1927- . . . **CLC 1, 2, 3, 5, 8, 13, 18, 45, 86**
See also CA 13-16R; CANR 15; DLB 5;
MTCW

Metcalf, John 1938- . . . . **CLC 37**
See also CA 113; DLB 60

Metcalf, Suzanne
See Baum, L(yman) Frank

Mew, Charlotte (Mary)
1870-1928 . . . . **TCLC 8**
See also CA 105; DLB 19, 135

Mewshaw, Michael 1943- . . . . **CLC 9**
See also CA 53-56; CANR 7, 47; DLBY 80

Meyer, June
See Jordan, June

Meyer, Lynn
See Slavitt, David R(ytman)

Meyer-Meyrink, Gustav 1868-1932
See Meyrink, Gustav
See also CA 117

Meyers, Jeffrey 1939- . . . . **CLC 39**
See also CA 73-76; DLB 111

Meynell, Alice (Christina Gertrude Thompson)
1847-1922 . . . . **TCLC 6**
See also CA 104; DLB 19, 98

Meyrink, Gustav . . . . **TCLC 21**
See also Meyer-Meyrink, Gustav
See also DLB 81

Michaels, Leonard
1933- . . . . **CLC 6, 25; SSC 16**
See also CA 61-64; CANR 21; DLB 130;
MTCW

Michaux, Henri 1899-1984 . . . . . **CLC 8, 19**
See also CA 85-88; 114

Michelangelo 1475-1564 . . . . **LC 12**

Michelet, Jules 1798-1874 . . . . **NCLC 31**

Michener, James A(lbert)
1907(?)- . . . . **CLC 1, 5, 11, 29, 60**
See also AITN 1; BEST 90:1; CA 5-8R;
CANR 21, 45; DLB 6; MTCW

Mickiewicz, Adam 1798-1855 . . . . . **NCLC 3**

Middleton, Christopher 1926- . . . . . . **CLC 13**
See also CA 13-16R; CANR 29; DLB 40

Middleton, Richard (Barham)
1882-1911 . . . . **TCLC 56**

Middleton, Stanley 1919- . . . . **CLC 7, 38**
See also CA 25-28R; CANR 21, 46, 46;
DLB 14

Middleton, Thomas 1580-1627 . . . . **DC 5**
See also DLB 58

Migueis, Jose Rodrigues 1901- . . . . . **CLC 10**

Mikszath, Kalman 1847-1910 . . . . . **TCLC 31**

Miles, Josephine
1911-1985 . . . . **CLC 1, 2, 14, 34, 39**
See also CA 1-4R; 116; CANR 2; DLB 48

Militant
See Sandburg, Carl (August)

Mill, John Stuart 1806-1873 . . . . . **NCLC 11**
See also CDBLB 1832-1890; DLB 55

Millar, Kenneth 1915-1983 . . . . **CLC 14**
See also Macdonald, Ross
See also CA 9-12R; 110; CANR 16; DLB 2;
DLBD 6; DLBY 83; MTCW

Millay, E. Vincent
See Millay, Edna St. Vincent

Millay, Edna St. Vincent
1892-1950 . . . . . . **TCLC 4, 49; DA; PC 6**
See also CA 104; 130; CDALB 1917-1929;
DLB 45; MTCW

Miller, Arthur
1915- . . . . **CLC 1, 2, 6, 10, 15, 26, 47, 78;
DA; DC 1; WLC**
See also AITN 1; CA 1-4R; CABS 3;
CANR 2, 30; CDALB 1941-1968; DLB 7;
MTCW

Miller, Henry (Valentine)
1891-1980 . . . . **CLC 1, 2, 4, 9, 14, 43, 84;
DA; WLC**
See also CA 9-12R; 97-100; CANR 33;
CDALB 1929-1941; DLB 4, 9; DLBY 80;
MTCW

Miller, Jason 1939(?)- . . . . **CLC 2**
See also AITN 1; CA 73-76; DLB 7

Miller, Sue 1943- . . . . **CLC 44**
See also BEST 90:3; CA 139; DLB 143

Miller, Walter M(ichael, Jr.)
1923- . . . . **CLC 4, 30**
See also CA 85-88; DLB 8

Millett, Kate 1934- . . . . **CLC 67**
See also AITN 1; CA 73-76; CANR 32;
MTCW

Millhauser, Steven 1943- . . . . **CLC 21, 54**
See also CA 110; 111; DLB 2

Millin, Sarah Gertrude 1889-1968 . . **CLC 49**
See also CA 102; 93-96

Milne, A(lan) A(lexander)
1882-1956 . . . . **TCLC 6**
See also CA 104; 133; CLR 1, 26; DLB 10,
77, 100; MAICYA; MTCW; YABC 1

Milner, Ron(ald) 1938- . . . . **CLC 56; BLC**
See also AITN 1; BW 1; CA 73-76;
CANR 24; DLB 38; MTCW

Milosz, Czeslaw
1911- . . . **CLC 5, 11, 22, 31, 56, 82; PC 8**
See also CA 81-84; CANR 23; MTCW

Milton, John 1608-1674 . . . **LC 9; DA; WLC**
See also CDBLB 1660-1789; DLB 131

Min, Anchee 1957- . . . . **CLC 86**

Minehaha, Cornelius
See Wedekind, (Benjamin) Frank(lin)

Miner, Valerie 1947- . . . . **CLC 40**
See also CA 97-100

Minimo, Duca
See D'Annunzio, Gabriele

Minot, Susan 1956- . . . . **CLC 44**
See also CA 134

Minus, Ed 1938- . . . . **CLC 39**

Miranda, Javier
See Bioy Casares, Adolfo

Mirbeau, Octave 1848-1917 . . . . **TCLC 55**
See also DLB 123

Miro (Ferrer), Gabriel (Francisco Victor)
1879-1930 . . . . **TCLC 5**
See also CA 104

Mishima, Yukio
. . . . **CLC 2, 4, 6, 9, 27; DC 1; SSC 4**
See also Hiraoka, Kimitake

Mistral, Frederic 1830-1914 . . . . . . **TCLC 51**
See also CA 122

Mistral, Gabriela . . . . **TCLC 2; HLC**
See also Godoy Alcayaga, Lucila

Mistry, Rohinton 1952- . . . . **CLC 71**
See also CA 141

Mitchell, Clyde
See Ellison, Harlan (Jay); Silverberg, Robert

Mitchell, James Leslie 1901-1935
See Gibbon, Lewis Grassic
See also CA 104; DLB 15

Mitchell, Joni 1943- . . . . CLC 12
See also CA 112

Mitchell, Margaret (Munnerlyn)
1900-1949 . . . . TCLC 11
See also CA 109; 125; DLB 9; MTCW

Mitchell, Peggy
See Mitchell, Margaret (Munnerlyn)

Mitchell, S(ilas) Weir 1829-1914 . . TCLC 36

Mitchell, W(illiam) O(rmond)
1914- . . . . CLC 25
See also CA 77-80; CANR 15, 43; DLB 88

Mitford, Mary Russell 1787-1855. . NCLC 4
See also DLB 110, 116

Mitford, Nancy 1904-1973. . . . . CLC 44
See also CA 9-12R

Miyamoto, Yuriko 1899-1951 . . . . . TCLC 37

Mo, Timothy (Peter) 1950(?)- . . . . . . CLC 46
See also CA 117; MTCW

Modarressi, Taghi (M.) 1931- . . . . . CLC 44
See also CA 121; 134

Modiano, Patrick (Jean) 1945- . . . . . CLC 18
See also CA 85-88; CANR 17, 40; DLB 83

Moerck, Paal
See Roelvaag, O(le) E(dvart)

Mofolo, Thomas (Mokopu)
1875(?)-1948 . . . . TCLC 22; BLC
See also CA 121

Mohr, Nicholasa 1935- . . . . . . CLC 12; HLC
See also AAYA 8; CA 49-52; CANR 1, 32;
CLR 22; DLB 145; HW; JRDA; SAAS 8;
SATA 8

Mojtabai, A(nn) G(race)
1938- . . . . CLC 5, 9, 15, 29
See also CA 85-88

Moliere 1622-1673 . . . . LC 10; DA; WLC

Molin, Charles
See Mayne, William (James Carter)

Molnar, Ferenc 1878-1952. . . . . . . TCLC 20
See also CA 109

Momaday, N(avarre) Scott
1934- . . . . CLC 2, 19, 85; DA
See also AAYA 11; CA 25-28R; CANR 14,
34; DLB 143; MTCW; NNAL; SATA 30,
48

Monette, Paul 1945- . . . . CLC 82
See also CA 139

Monroe, Harriet 1860-1936. . . . . . . TCLC 12
See also CA 109; DLB 54, 91

Monroe, Lyle
See Heinlein, Robert A(nson)

Montagu, Elizabeth 1917- . . . . NCLC 7
See also CA 9-12R

Montagu, Mary (Pierrepont) Wortley
1689-1762 . . . . LC 9
See also DLB 95, 101

Montagu, W. H.
See Coleridge, Samuel Taylor

Montague, John (Patrick)
1929- . . . . CLC 13, 46
See also CA 9-12R; CANR 9; DLB 40;
MTCW

Montaigne, Michel (Eyquem) de
1533-1592 . . . . LC 8; DA; WLC

Montale, Eugenio 1896-1981. . . CLC 7, 9, 18
See also CA 17-20R; 104; CANR 30;
DLB 114; MTCW

Montesquieu, Charles-Louis de Secondat
1689-1755 . . . . LC 7

Montgomery, (Robert) Bruce 1921-1978
See Crispin, Edmund
See also CA 104

Montgomery, L(ucy) M(aud)
1874-1942 . . . . TCLC 51
See also AAYA 12; CA 108; 137; CLR 8;
DLB 92; JRDA; MAICYA; YABC 1

Montgomery, Marion H., Jr. 1925- . . CLC 7
See also AITN 1; CA 1-4R; CANR 3;
DLB 6

Montgomery, Max
See Davenport, Guy (Mattison, Jr.)

Montherlant, Henry (Milon) de
1896-1972 . . . . CLC 8, 19
See also CA 85-88; 37-40R; DLB 72;
MTCW

Monty Python
See Chapman, Graham; Cleese, John
(Marwood); Gilliam, Terry (Vance); Idle,
Eric; Jones, Terence Graham Parry; Palin,
Michael (Edward)
See also AAYA 7

Moodie, Susanna (Strickland)
1803-1885 . . . . NCLC 14
See also DLB 99

Mooney, Edward 1951-
See Mooney, Ted
See also CA 130

Mooney, Ted . . . . CLC 25
See also Mooney, Edward

Moorcock, Michael (John)
1939- . . . . CLC 5, 27, 58
See also CA 45-48; CAAS 5; CANR 2, 17,
38; DLB 14; MTCW

Moore, Brian
1921- . . . . CLC 1, 3, 5, 7, 8, 19, 32
See also CA 1-4R; CANR 1, 25, 42; MTCW

Moore, Edward
See Muir, Edwin

Moore, George Augustus
1852-1933 . . . . TCLC 7
See also CA 104; DLB 10, 18, 57, 135

Moore, Lorrie . . . . CLC 39, 45, 68
See also Moore, Marie Lorena

Moore, Marianne (Craig)
1887-1972 . . . . CLC 1, 2, 4, 8, 10, 13, 19,
                                     47; DA; PC 4
See also CA 1-4R; 33-36R; CANR 3;
CDALB 1929-1941; DLB 45; DLBD 7;
MTCW; SATA 20

Moore, Marie Lorena 1957-
See Moore, Lorrie
See also CA 116; CANR 39

Moore, Thomas 1779-1852. . . . . . . NCLC 6
See also DLB 96, 144

Morand, Paul 1888-1976 . . . . CLC 41
See also CA 69-72; DLB 65

Morante, Elsa 1918-1985. . . . . . . CLC 8, 47
See also CA 85-88; 117; CANR 35; MTCW

Moravia, Alberto. . . . . . . CLC 2, 7, 11, 27, 46
See also Pincherle, Alberto

More, Hannah 1745-1833 . . . . NCLC 27
See also DLB 107, 109, 116

More, Henry 1614-1687. . . . . LC 9
See also DLB 126

More, Sir Thomas 1478-1535 . . . . . . LC 10

Moreas, Jean. . . . . TCLC 18
See also Papadiamantopoulos, Johannes

Morgan, Berry 1919- . . . . CLC 6
See also CA 49-52; DLB 6

Morgan, Claire
See Highsmith, (Mary) Patricia

Morgan, Edwin (George) 1920- . . . . . CLC 31
See also CA 5-8R; CANR 3, 43; DLB 27

Morgan, (George) Frederick
1922- . . . . CLC 23
See also CA 17-20R; CANR 21

Morgan, Harriet
See Mencken, H(enry) L(ouis)

Morgan, Jane
See Cooper, James Fenimore

Morgan, Janet 1945- . . . . CLC 39
See also CA 65-68

Morgan, Lady 1776(?)-1859. . . . . . NCLC 29
See also DLB 116

Morgan, Robin 1941- . . . . CLC 2
See also CA 69-72; CANR 29; MTCW;
SATA 80

Morgan, Scott
See Kuttner, Henry

Morgan, Seth 1949(?)-1990 . . . . CLC 65
See also CA 132

Morgenstern, Christian
1871-1914 . . . . TCLC 8
See also CA 105

Morgenstern, S.
See Goldman, William (W.)

Moricz, Zsigmond 1879-1942 . . . . . TCLC 33

Morike, Eduard (Friedrich)
1804-1875 . . . . NCLC 10
See also DLB 133

Mori Ogai . . . . TCLC 14
See also Mori Rintaro

Mori Rintaro 1862-1922
See Mori Ogai
See also CA 110

Moritz, Karl Philipp 1756-1793 . . . . . . LC 2
See also DLB 94

Morland, Peter Henry
See Faust, Frederick (Schiller)

Morren, Theophil
See Hofmannsthal, Hugo von

Morris, Bill 1952- . . . . CLC 76

Morris, Julian
See West, Morris L(anglo)

Morris, Steveland Judkins 1950(?)-
See Wonder, Stevie
See also CA 111

Morris, William 1834-1896 . . . . NCLC 4
See also CDBLB 1832-1890; DLB 18, 35, 57

Neihardt, John Gneisenau
1881-1973 . . . . CLC 32
See also CA 13-14; CAP 1; DLB 9, 54

Nekrasov, Nikolai Alekseevich
1821-1878 . . . . NCLC 11

Nelligan, Emile 1879-1941. . . . . . . TCLC 14
See also CA 114; DLB 92

Nelson, Willie 1933- . . . . CLC 17
See also CA 107

Nemerov, Howard (Stanley)
1920-1991 . . . . CLC 2, 6, 9, 36
See also CA 1-4R; 134; CABS 2; CANR 1,
27; DLB 6; DLBY 83; MTCW

Neruda, Pablo
1904-1973 . . . . . CLC 1, 2, 5, 7, 9, 28, 62;
DA; HLC; PC 4; WLC
See also CA 19-20; 45-48; CAP 2; HW;
MTCW

Nerval, Gerard de
1808-1855 . . . . NCLC 1; SSC 18

Nervo, (Jose) Amado (Ruiz de)
1870-1919 . . . . TCLC 11
See also CA 109; 131; HW

Nessi, Pio Baroja y
See Baroja (y Nessi), Pio

Nestroy, Johann 1801-1862 . . . . . . NCLC 42
See also DLB 133

Neufeld, John (Arthur) 1938- . . . . . . CLC 17
See also AAYA 11; CA 25-28R; CANR 11,
37; MAICYA; SAAS 3; SATA 6, 81

Neville, Emily Cheney 1919- . . . . CLC 12
See also CA 5-8R; CANR 3, 37; JRDA;
MAICYA; SAAS 2; SATA 1

Newbound, Bernard Slade 1930-
See Slade, Bernard
See also CA 81-84

Newby, P(ercy) H(oward)
1918- . . . . CLC 2, 13
See also CA 5-8R; CANR 32; DLB 15;
MTCW

Newlove, Donald 1928- . . . . CLC 6
See also CA 29-32R; CANR 25

Newlove, John (Herbert) 1938- . . . . . CLC 14
See also CA 21-24R; CANR 9, 25

Newman, Charles 1938- . . . . CLC 2, 8
See also CA 21-24R

Newman, Edwin (Harold) 1919- . . . . CLC 14
See also AITN 1; CA 69-72; CANR 5

Newman, John Henry
1801-1890 . . . . NCLC 38
See also DLB 18, 32, 55

Newton, Suzanne 1936- . . . . CLC 35
See also CA 41-44R; CANR 14; JRDA;
SATA 5, 77

Nexo, Martin Andersen
1869-1954 . . . . TCLC 43

Nezval, Vitezslav 1900-1958 . . . . . . TCLC 44
See also CA 123

Ng, Fae Myenne 1957(?)- . . . . CLC 81

Ngema, Mbongeni 1955- . . . . CLC 57
See also BW 2; CA 143

Ngugi, James T(hiong'o) . . . . CLC 3, 7, 13
See also Ngugi wa Thiong'o

Ngugi wa Thiong'o 1938- . . . . . CLC 36; BLC
See also Ngugi, James T(hiong'o)
See also BW 2; CA 81-84; CANR 27;
DLB 125; MTCW

Nichol, B(arrie) P(hillip)
1944-1988 . . . . CLC 18
See also CA 53-56; DLB 53; SATA 66

Nichols, John (Treadwell) 1940- . . . . CLC 38
See also CA 9-12R; CAAS 2; CANR 6;
DLBY 82

Nichols, Leigh
See Koontz, Dean R(ay)

Nichols, Peter (Richard)
1927- . . . . CLC 5, 36, 65
See also CA 104; CANR 33; DLB 13;
MTCW

Nicolas, F. R. E.
See Freeling, Nicolas

Niedecker, Lorine 1903-1970. . . . CLC 10, 42
See also CA 25-28; CAP 2; DLB 48

Nietzsche, Friedrich (Wilhelm)
1844-1900 . . . . TCLC 10, 18, 55
See also CA 107; 121; DLB 129

Nievo, Ippolito 1831-1861 . . . . NCLC 22

Nightingale, Anne Redmon 1943-
See Redmon, Anne
See also CA 103

Nik. T. O.
See Annensky, Innokenty Fyodorovich

Nin, Anais
1903-1977 . . . . . . CLC 1, 4, 8, 11, 14, 60;
SSC 10
See also AITN 2; CA 13-16R; 69-72;
CANR 22; DLB 2, 4; MTCW

Nissenson, Hugh 1933- . . . . CLC 4, 9
See also CA 17-20R; CANR 27; DLB 28

Niven, Larry . . . . CLC 8
See also Niven, Laurence Van Cott
See also DLB 8

Niven, Laurence Van Cott 1938-
See Niven, Larry
See also CA 21-24R; CAAS 12; CANR 14,
44; MTCW

Nixon, Agnes Eckhardt 1927- . . . . . . CLC 21
See also CA 110

Nizan, Paul 1905-1940. . . . . TCLC 40
See also DLB 72

Nkosi, Lewis 1936- . . . . CLC 45; BLC
See also BW 1; CA 65-68; CANR 27

Nodier, (Jean) Charles (Emmanuel)
1780-1844 . . . . NCLC 19
See also DLB 119

Nolan, Christopher 1965- . . . . CLC 58
See also CA 111

Norden, Charles
See Durrell, Lawrence (George)

Nordhoff, Charles (Bernard)
1887-1947 . . . . TCLC 23
See also CA 108; DLB 9; SATA 23

Norfolk, Lawrence 1963- . . . . CLC 76
See also CA 144

Norman, Marsha 1947- . . . . CLC 28
See also CA 105; CABS 3; CANR 41;
DLBY 84

Norris, Benjamin Franklin, Jr.
1870-1902 . . . . TCLC 24
See also Norris, Frank
See also CA 110

Norris, Frank
See Norris, Benjamin Franklin, Jr.
See also CDALB 1865-1917; DLB 12, 71

Norris, Leslie 1921- . . . . CLC 14
See also CA 11-12; CANR 14; CAP 1;
DLB 27

North, Andrew
See Norton, Andre

North, Anthony
See Koontz, Dean R(ay)

North, Captain George
See Stevenson, Robert Louis (Balfour)

North, Milou
See Erdrich, Louise

Northrup, B. A.
See Hubbard, L(afayette) Ron(ald)

North Staffs
See Hulme, T(homas) E(rnest)

Norton, Alice Mary
See Norton, Andre
See also MAICYA; SATA 1, 43

Norton, Andre 1912- . . . . CLC 12
See also Norton, Alice Mary
See also AAYA 14; CA 1-4R; CANR 2, 31;
DLB 8, 52; JRDA; MTCW

Norton, Caroline 1808-1877 . . . . . . NCLC 47
See also DLB 21

Norway, Nevil Shute 1899-1960
See Shute, Nevil
See also CA 102; 93-96

Norwid, Cyprian Kamil
1821-1883 . . . . NCLC 17

Nosille, Nabrah
See Ellison, Harlan (Jay)

Nossack, Hans Erich 1901-1978 . . . . . CLC 6
See also CA 93-96; 85-88; DLB 69

Nostradamus 1503-1566. . . . . LC 27

Nosu, Chuji
See Ozu, Yasujiro

Notenburg, Eleanora (Genrikhovna) von
See Guro, Elena

Nova, Craig 1945- . . . . CLC 7, 31
See also CA 45-48; CANR 2

Novak, Joseph
See Kosinski, Jerzy (Nikodem)

Novalis 1772-1801 . . . . NCLC 13
See also DLB 90

Nowlan, Alden (Albert) 1933-1983 . . CLC 15
See also CA 9-12R; CANR 5; DLB 53

Noyes, Alfred 1880-1958 . . . . TCLC 7
See also CA 104; DLB 20

Nunn, Kem 19(?)- . . . . CLC 34

Nye, Robert 1939- . . . . CLC 13, 42
See also CA 33-36R; CANR 29; DLB 14;
MTCW; SATA 6

Nyro, Laura 1947- . . . . CLC 17

Oates, Joyce Carol
1938- ...... CLC 1, 2, 3, 6, 9, 11, 15, 19,
33, 52; DA; SSC 6; WLC
See also AITN 1; BEST 89:2; CA 5-8R;
CANR 25, 45; CDALB 1968-1988;
DLB 2, 5, 130; DLBY 81; MTCW

O'Brien, Darcy 1939-............ CLC 11
See also CA 21-24R; CANR 8

O'Brien, E. G.
See Clarke, Arthur C(harles)

O'Brien, Edna
1936- ... CLC 3, 5, 8, 13, 36, 65; SSC 10
See also CA 1-4R; CANR 6, 41;
CDBLB 1960 to Present; DLB 14;
MTCW

O'Brien, Fitz-James 1828-1862... NCLC 21
See also DLB 74

O'Brien, Flann....... CLC 1, 4, 5, 7, 10, 47
See also O Nuallain, Brian

O'Brien, Richard 1942- .... CLC 17
See also CA 124

O'Brien, Tim 1946-.......... CLC 7, 19, 40
See also CA 85-88; CANR 40; DLBD 9;
DLBY 80

Obstfelder, Sigbjoern 1866-1900... TCLC 23
See also CA 123

O'Casey, Sean
1880-1964 .... CLC 1, 5, 9, 11, 15
See also CA 89-92; CDBLB 1914-1945;
DLB 10; MTCW

O'Cathasaigh, Sean
See O'Casey, Sean

Ochs, Phil 1940-1976............. CLC 17
See also CA 65-68

O'Connor, Edwin (Greene)
1918-1968 .... CLC 14
See also CA 93-96; 25-28R

O'Connor, (Mary) Flannery
1925-1964 .... CLC 1, 2, 3, 6, 10, 13, 15,
21, 66; DA; SSC 1; WLC
See also AAYA 7; CA 1-4R; CANR 3, 41;
CDALB 1941-1968; DLB 2; DLBD 12;
DLBY 80; MTCW

O'Connor, Frank.......... CLC 23; SSC 5
See also O'Donovan, Michael John

O'Dell, Scott 1898-1989........... CLC 30
See also AAYA 3; CA 61-64; 129;
CANR 12, 30; CLR 1, 16; DLB 52;
JRDA; MAICYA; SATA 12, 60

Odets, Clifford 1906-1963 .... CLC 2, 28
See also CA 85-88; DLB 7, 26; MTCW

O'Doherty, Brian 1934-........... CLC 76
See also CA 105

O'Donnell, K. M.
See Malzberg, Barry N(athaniel)

O'Donnell, Lawrence
See Kuttner, Henry

O'Donovan, Michael John
1903-1966 .... CLC 14
See O'Connor, Frank
See also CA 93-96

Oe, Kenzaburo 1935-........ CLC 10, 36, 86
See also CA 97-100; CANR 36; MTCW

O'Faolain, Julia 1932-....... CLC 6, 19, 47
See also CA 81-84; CAAS 2; CANR 12;
DLB 14; MTCW

O'Faolain, Sean
1900-1991 .... CLC 1, 7, 14, 32, 70;
SSC 13
See also CA 61-64; 134; CANR 12;
DLB 15; MTCW

O'Flaherty, Liam
1896-1984 .... CLC 5, 34; SSC 6
See also CA 101; 113; CANR 35; DLB 36;
DLBY 84; MTCW

Ogilvy, Gavin
See Barrie, J(ames) M(atthew)

O'Grady, Standish James
1846-1928 .... TCLC 5
See also CA 104

O'Grady, Timothy 1951- .... CLC 59
See also CA 138

O'Hara, Frank
1926-1966 .... CLC 2, 5, 13, 78
See also CA 9-12R; 25-28R; CANR 33;
DLB 5, 16; MTCW

O'Hara, John (Henry)
1905-1970 .... CLC 1, 2, 3, 6, 11, 42;
SSC 15
See also CA 5-8R; 25-28R; CANR 31;
CDALB 1929-1941; DLB 9, 86; DLBD 2;
MTCW

O Hehir, Diana 1922- .... CLC 41
See also CA 93-96

Okigbo, Christopher (Ifenayichukwu)
1932-1967 ..... CLC 25, 84; BLC; PC 7
See also BW 1; CA 77-80; DLB 125;
MTCW

Olds, Sharon 1942-........ CLC 32, 39, 85
See also CA 101; CANR 18, 41; DLB 120

Oldstyle, Jonathan
See Irving, Washington

Olesha, Yuri (Karlovich)
1899-1960 .... CLC 8
See also CA 85-88

Oliphant, Laurence
1829(?)-1888 .... NCLC 47
See also DLB 18

Oliphant, Margaret (Oliphant Wilson)
1828-1897 .... NCLC 11
See also DLB 18

Oliver, Mary 1935-........... CLC 19, 34
See also CA 21-24R; CANR 9, 43; DLB 5

Olivier, Laurence (Kerr)
1907-1989 .... CLC 20
See also CA 111; 129

Olsen, Tillie
1913- .... CLC 4, 13; DA; SSC 11
See also CA 1-4R; CANR 1, 43; DLB 28;
DLBY 80; MTCW

Olson, Charles (John)
1910-1970 ..... CLC 1, 2, 5, 6, 9, 11, 29
See also CA 13-16; 25-28R; CABS 2;
CANR 35; CAP 1; DLB 5, 16; MTCW

Olson, Toby 1937- .... CLC 28
See also CA 65-68; CANR 9, 31

Olyesha, Yuri
See Olesha, Yuri (Karlovich)

Ondaatje, (Philip) Michael
1943- .... CLC 14, 29, 51, 76
See also CA 77-80; CANR 42; DLB 60

Oneal, Elizabeth 1934-
See Oneal, Zibby
See also CA 106; CANR 28; MAICYA;
SATA 30

Oneal, Zibby .... CLC 30
See also Oneal, Elizabeth
See also AAYA 5; CLR 13; JRDA

O'Neill, Eugene (Gladstone)
1888-1953 ...... TCLC 1, 6, 27, 49; DA;
WLC
See also AITN 1; CA 110; 132;
CDALB 1929-1941; DLB 7; MTCW

Onetti, Juan Carlos 1909-1994 ... CLC 7, 10
See also CA 85-88; 145; CANR 32;
DLB 113; HW; MTCW

O Nuallain, Brian 1911-1966
See O'Brien, Flann
See also CA 21-22; 25-28R; CAP 2

Oppen, George 1908-1984 .... CLC 7, 13, 34
See also CA 13-16R; 113; CANR 8; DLB 5

Oppenheim, E(dward) Phillips
1866-1946 .... TCLC 45
See also CA 111; DLB 70

Orlovitz, Gil 1918-1973 .... CLC 22
See also CA 77-80; 45-48; DLB 2, 5

Orris
See Ingelow, Jean

Ortega y Gasset, Jose
1883-1955 .... TCLC 9; HLC
See also CA 106; 130; HW; MTCW

Ortiz, Simon J(oseph) 1941-....... CLC 45
See also CA 134; DLB 120; NNAL

Orton, Joe .... CLC 4, 13, 43; DC 3
See also Orton, John Kingsley
See also CDBLB 1960 to Present; DLB 13

Orton, John Kingsley 1933-1967
See Orton, Joe
See also CA 85-88; CANR 35; MTCW

Orwell, George
.... TCLC 2, 6, 15, 31, 51; WLC
See also Blair, Eric (Arthur)
See also CDBLB 1945-1960; DLB 15, 98

Osborne, David
See Silverberg, Robert

Osborne, George
See Silverberg, Robert

Osborne, John (James)
1929- .... CLC 1, 2, 5, 11, 45; DA; WLC
See also CA 13-16R; CANR 21;
CDBLB 1945-1960; DLB 13; MTCW

Osborne, Lawrence 1958- .... CLC 50

Oshima, Nagisa 1932- .... CLC 20
See also CA 116; 121

Oskison, John Milton
1874-1947 .... TCLC 35
See also CA 144; NNAL

Ossoli, Sarah Margaret (Fuller marchesa d')
1810-1850
See Fuller, Margaret
See also SATA 25

Ostrovsky, Alexander
1823-1886 .... NCLC 30

Otero, Blas de 1916-1979.......... CLC 11
See also CA 89-92; DLB 134

Otto, Whitney 1955-.............. CLC 70
See also CA 140

Ouida........................ TCLC 43
See also De La Ramee, (Marie) Louise
See also DLB 18

Ousmane, Sembene 1923- .... CLC 66; BLC
See also BW 1; CA 117; 125; MTCW

Ovid 43B.C.-18(?).......... CMLC 7; PC 2

Owen, Hugh
See Faust, Frederick (Schiller)

Owen, Wilfred (Edward Salter)
1893-1918 ...... TCLC 5, 27; DA; WLC
See also CA 104; 141; CDBLB 1914-1945;
DLB 20

Owens, Rochelle 1936-............. CLC 8
See also CA 17-20R; CAAS 2; CANR 39

Oz, Amos 1939- ... CLC 5, 8, 11, 27, 33, 54
See also CA 53-56; CANR 27, 47; MTCW

Ozick, Cynthia
1928-........ CLC 3, 7, 28, 62; SSC 15
See also BEST 90:1; CA 17-20R; CANR 23;
DLB 28; DLBY 82; MTCW

Ozu, Yasujiro 1903-1963.......... CLC 16
See also CA 112

Pacheco, C.
See Pessoa, Fernando (Antonio Nogueira)

Pa Chin........................ CLC 18
See also Li Fei-kan

Pack, Robert 1929-.............. CLC 13
See also CA 1-4R; CANR 3, 44; DLB 5

Padgett, Lewis
See Kuttner, Henry

Padilla (Lorenzo), Heberto 1932-... CLC 38
See also AITN 1; CA 123; 131; HW

Page, Jimmy 1944-.............. CLC 12

Page, Louise 1955-.............. CLC 40
See also CA 140

Page, P(atricia) K(athleen)
1916-.................... CLC 7, 18
See also CA 53-56; CANR 4, 22; DLB 68;
MTCW

Paget, Violet 1856-1935
See Lee, Vernon
See also CA 104

Paget-Lowe, Henry
See Lovecraft, H(oward) P(hillips)

Paglia, Camille (Anna) 1947-....... CLC 68
See also CA 140

Paige, Richard
See Koontz, Dean R(ay)

Pakenham, Antonia
See Fraser, (Lady) Antonia (Pakenham)

Palamas, Kostes 1859-1943........ TCLC 5
See also CA 105

Palazzeschi, Aldo 1885-1974...... CLC 11
See also CA 89-92; 53-56; DLB 114

Paley, Grace 1922-.... CLC 4, 6, 37; SSC 8
See also CA 25-28R; CANR 13, 46, 46;
DLB 28; MTCW

Palin, Michael (Edward) 1943-..... CLC 21
See also Monty Python
See also CA 107; CANR 35; SATA 67

Palliser, Charles 1947-............ CLC 65
See also CA 136

Palma, Ricardo 1833-1919........ TCLC 29

Pancake, Breece Dexter 1952-1979
See Pancake, Breece D'J
See also CA 123; 109

Pancake, Breece D'J............... CLC 29
See also Pancake, Breece Dexter
See also DLB 130

Panko, Rudy
See Gogol, Nikolai (Vasilyevich)

Papadiamantis, Alexandros
1851-1911 .... TCLC 29

Papadiamantopoulos, Johannes 1856-1910
See Moreas, Jean
See also CA 117

Papini, Giovanni 1881-1956...... TCLC 22
See also CA 121

Paracelsus 1493-1541.............. LC 14

Parasol, Peter
See Stevens, Wallace

Parfenie, Maria
See Codrescu, Andrei

Parini, Jay (Lee) 1948- .... CLC 54
See also CA 97-100; CAAS 16; CANR 32

Park, Jordan
See Kornbluth, C(yril) M.; Pohl, Frederik

Parker, Bert
See Ellison, Harlan (Jay)

Parker, Dorothy (Rothschild)
1893-1967 .... CLC 15, 68; SSC 2
See also CA 19-20; 25-28R; CAP 2;
DLB 11, 45, 86; MTCW

Parker, Robert B(rown) 1932-...... CLC 27
See also BEST 89:4; CA 49-52; CANR 1,
26; MTCW

Parkin, Frank 1940-.............. CLC 43

Parkman, Francis, Jr.
1823-1893 .... NCLC 12
See also DLB 1, 30

Parks, Gordon (Alexander Buchanan)
1912-................ CLC 1, 16; BLC
See also AITN 2; BW 2; CA 41-44R;
CANR 26; DLB 33; SATA 8

Parnell, Thomas 1679-1718.......... LC 3
See also DLB 94

Parra, Nicanor 1914-........ CLC 2; HLC
See also CA 85-88; CANR 32; HW; MTCW

Parrish, Mary Frances
See Fisher, M(ary) F(rances) K(ennedy)

Parson
See Coleridge, Samuel Taylor

Parson Lot
See Kingsley, Charles

Partridge, Anthony
See Oppenheim, E(dward) Phillips

Pascoli, Giovanni 1855-1912 ...... TCLC 45

Pasolini, Pier Paolo
1922-1975 .... CLC 20, 37
See also CA 93-96; 61-64; DLB 128;
MTCW

Pasquini
See Silone, Ignazio

Pastan, Linda (Olenik) 1932- ...... CLC 27
See also CA 61-64; CANR 18, 40; DLB 5

Pasternak, Boris (Leonidovich)
1890-1960 ...... CLC 7, 10, 18, 63; DA;
PC 6; WLC
See also CA 127; 116; MTCW

Patchen, Kenneth 1911-1972... CLC 1, 2, 18
See also CA 1-4R; 33-36R; CANR 3, 35;
DLB 16, 48; MTCW

Pater, Walter (Horatio)
1839-1894 .... NCLC 7
See also CDBLB 1832-1890; DLB 57

Paterson, A(ndrew) B(arton)
1864-1941 .... TCLC 32

Paterson, Katherine (Womeldorf)
1932-.................... CLC 12, 30
See also AAYA 1; CA 21-24R; CANR 28;
CLR 7; DLB 52; JRDA; MAICYA;
MTCW; SATA 13, 53

Patmore, Coventry Kersey Dighton
1823-1896 .... NCLC 9
See also DLB 35, 98

Paton, Alan (Stewart)
1903-1988 ...... CLC 4, 10, 25, 55; DA;
WLC
See also CA 13-16; 125; CANR 22; CAP 1;
MTCW; SATA 11; SATA-Obit 56

Paton Walsh, Gillian 1937-
See Walsh, Jill Paton
See also CANR 38; JRDA; MAICYA;
SAAS 3; SATA 4, 72

Paulding, James Kirke 1778-1860.. NCLC 2
See also DLB 3, 59, 74

Paulin, Thomas Neilson 1949-
See Paulin, Tom
See also CA 123; 128

Paulin, Tom.................... CLC 37
See also Paulin, Thomas Neilson
See also DLB 40

Paustovsky, Konstantin (Georgievich)
1892-1968 .... CLC 40
See also CA 93-96; 25-28R

Pavese, Cesare 1908-1950 .... TCLC 3
See also CA 104; DLB 128

Pavic, Milorad 1929-............. CLC 60
See also CA 136

Payne, Alan
See Jakes, John (William)

Paz, Gil
See Lugones, Leopoldo

Paz, Octavio
1914-........ CLC 3, 4, 6, 10, 19, 51, 65;
DA; HLC; PC 1; WLC
See also CA 73-76; CANR 32; DLBY 90;
HW; MTCW

Peacock, Molly 1947-............. CLC 60
See also CA 103; DLB 120

Ray, Satyajit 1921-1992....... **CLC 16, 76**
See also CA 114; 137

Read, Herbert Edward 1893-1968.... **CLC 4**
See also CA 85-88; 25-28R; DLB 20

Read, Piers Paul 1941- ...... **CLC 4, 10, 25**
See also CA 21-24R; CANR 38; DLB 14;
SATA 21

Reade, Charles 1814-1884 .... **NCLC 2**
See also DLB 21

Reade, Hamish
See Gray, Simon (James Holliday)

Reading, Peter 1946- .... **CLC 47**
See also CA 103; CANR 46, 46; DLB 40

Reaney, James 1926- .... **CLC 13**
See also CA 41-44R; CAAS 15; CANR 42;
DLB 68; SATA 43

Rebreanu, Liviu 1885-1944 .... **TCLC 28**

Rechy, John (Francisco)
1934- .... **CLC 1, 7, 14, 18; HLC**
See also CA 5-8R; CAAS 4; CANR 6, 32;
DLB 122; DLBY 82; HW

Redcam, Tom 1870-1933 .... **TCLC 25**

Reddin, Keith..................... **CLC 67**

Redgrove, Peter (William)
1932-..................... **CLC 6, 41**
See also CA 1-4R; CANR 3, 39; DLB 40

Redmon, Anne.................... **CLC 22**
See also Nightingale, Anne Redmon
See also DLBY 86

Reed, Eliot
See Ambler, Eric

Reed, Ishmael
1938- ... **CLC 2, 3, 5, 6, 13, 32, 60; BLC**
See also BW 2; CA 21-24R; CANR 25;
DLB 2, 5, 33; DLBD 8; MTCW

Reed, John (Silas) 1887-1920 ...... **TCLC 9**
See also CA 106

Reed, Lou........................ **CLC 21**
See also Firbank, Louis

Reeve, Clara 1729-1807 .... **NCLC 19**
See also DLB 39

Reich, Wilhelm 1897-1957........ **TCLC 57**

Reid, Christopher (John) 1949-..... **CLC 33**
See also CA 140; DLB 40

Reid, Desmond
See Moorcock, Michael (John)

Reid Banks, Lynne 1929-
See Banks, Lynne Reid
See also CA 1-4R; CANR 6, 22, 38;
CLR 24; JRDA; MAICYA; SATA 22, 75

Reilly, William K.
See Creasey, John

Reiner, Max
See Caldwell, (Janet Miriam) Taylor
(Holland)

Reis, Ricardo
See Pessoa, Fernando (Antonio Nogueira)

Remarque, Erich Maria
1898-1970 .... **CLC 21; DA**
See also CA 77-80; 29-32R; DLB 56;
MTCW

Remizov, A.
See Remizov, Aleksei (Mikhailovich)

Remizov, A. M.
See Remizov, Aleksei (Mikhailovich)

Remizov, Aleksei (Mikhailovich)
1877-1957 .... **TCLC 27**
See also CA 125; 133

Renan, Joseph Ernest
1823-1892 .... **NCLC 26**

Renard, Jules 1864-1910 .... **TCLC 17**
See also CA 117

Renault, Mary.............. **CLC 3, 11, 17**
See also Challans, Mary
See also DLBY 83

Rendell, Ruth (Barbara) 1930- .. **CLC 28, 48**
See also Vine, Barbara
See also CA 109; CANR 32; DLB 87;
MTCW

Renoir, Jean 1894-1979 .... **CLC 20**
See also CA 129; 85-88

Resnais, Alain 1922-............. **CLC 16**

Reverdy, Pierre 1889-1960 .... **CLC 53**
See also CA 97-100; 89-92

Rexroth, Kenneth
1905-1982 ...... **CLC 1, 2, 6, 11, 22, 49**
See also CA 5-8R; 107; CANR 14, 34;
CDALB 1941-1968; DLB 16, 48;
DLBY 82; MTCW

Reyes, Alfonso 1889-1959 .... **TCLC 33**
See also CA 131; HW

Reyes y Basoalto, Ricardo Eliecer Neftali
See Neruda, Pablo

Reymont, Wladyslaw (Stanislaw)
1868(?)-1925 .... **TCLC 5**
See also CA 104

Reynolds, Jonathan 1942-....... **CLC 6, 38**
See also CA 65-68; CANR 28

Reynolds, Joshua 1723-1792 .... **LC 15**
See also DLB 104

Reynolds, Michael Shane 1937- .... **CLC 44**
See also CA 65-68; CANR 9

Reznikoff, Charles 1894-1976 .... **CLC 9**
See also CA 33-36; 61-64; CAP 2; DLB 28,
45

Rezzori (d'Arezzo), Gregor von
1914- .... **CLC 25**
See also CA 122; 136

Rhine, Richard
See Silverstein, Alvin

Rhodes, Eugene Manlove
1869-1934 .... **TCLC 53**

R'hoone
See Balzac, Honore de

Rhys, Jean
1890(?)-1979 .... **CLC 2, 4, 6, 14, 19, 51**
See also CA 25-28R; 85-88; CANR 35;
CDBLB 1945-1960; DLB 36, 117; MTCW

Ribeiro, Darcy 1922- .... **CLC 34**
See also CA 33-36R

Ribeiro, Joao Ubaldo (Osorio Pimentel)
1941-.................... **CLC 10, 67**
See also CA 81-84

Ribman, Ronald (Burt) 1932- .... **CLC 7**
See also CA 21-24R; CANR 46, 46

Ricci, Nino 1959-................ **CLC 70**
See also CA 137

Rice, Anne 1941- .... **CLC 41**
See also AAYA 9; BEST 89:2; CA 65-68;
CANR 12, 36

Rice, Elmer (Leopold)
1892-1967 .... **CLC 7, 49**
See also CA 21-22; 25-28R; CAP 2; DLB 4,
7; MTCW

Rice, Tim(othy Miles Bindon)
1944-...................... **CLC 21**
See also CA 103; CANR 46

Rich, Adrienne (Cecile)
1929- .... **CLC 3, 6, 7, 11, 18, 36, 73, 76;
PC 5**
See also CA 9-12R; CANR 20; DLB 5, 67;
MTCW

Rich, Barbara
See Graves, Robert (von Ranke)

Rich, Robert
See Trumbo, Dalton

Richards, David Adams 1950-...... **CLC 59**
See also CA 93-96; DLB 53

Richards, I(vor) A(rmstrong)
1893-1979............. **CLC 14, 24**
See also CA 41-44R; 89-92; CANR 34;
DLB 27

Richardson, Anne
See Roiphe, Anne (Richardson)

Richardson, Dorothy Miller
1873-1957 .... **TCLC 3**
See also CA 104; DLB 36

Richardson, Ethel Florence (Lindesay)
1870-1946
See Richardson, Henry Handel
See also CA 105

Richardson, Henry Handel.......... **TCLC 4**
See also Richardson, Ethel Florence
(Lindesay)

Richardson, Samuel
1689-1761 .... **LC 1; DA; WLC**
See also CDBLB 1660-1789; DLB 39

Richler, Mordecai
1931-....... **CLC 3, 5, 9, 13, 18, 46, 70**
See also AITN 1; CA 65-68; CANR 31;
CLR 17; DLB 53; MAICYA; MTCW;
SATA 27, 44

Richter, Conrad (Michael)
1890-1968 .... **CLC 30**
See also CA 5-8R; 25-28R; CANR 23;
DLB 9; MTCW; SATA 3

Riddell, J. H. 1832-1906 .... **TCLC 40**

Riding, Laura.................... **CLC 3, 7**
See also Jackson, Laura (Riding)

Riefenstahl, Berta Helene Amalia 1902-
See Riefenstahl, Leni
See also CA 108

Riefenstahl, Leni.................. **CLC 16**
See also Riefenstahl, Berta Helene Amalia

Riffe, Ernest
See Bergman, (Ernst) Ingmar

Riggs, (Rolla) Lynn 1899-1954 .... **TCLC 56**
See also CA 144; NNAL

Riley, James Whitcomb
1849-1916 .... **TCLC 51**
See also CA 118; 137; MAICYA; SATA 17

Riley, Tex
See Creasey, John

Rilke, Rainer Maria
1875-1926 .... **TCLC 1, 6, 19; PC 2**
See also CA 104; 132; DLB 81; MTCW

Rimbaud, (Jean Nicolas) Arthur
1854-1891 ..... **NCLC 4, 35; DA; PC 3;**
WLC

Rinehart, Mary Roberts
1876-1958 .... **TCLC 52**
See also CA 108

Ringmaster, The
See Mencken, H(enry) L(ouis)

Ringwood, Gwen(dolyn Margaret) Pharis
1910-1984 .... **CLC 48**
See also CA 112; DLB 88

Rio, Michel 19(?)-................. **CLC 43**

Ritsos, Giannes
See Ritsos, Yannis

Ritsos, Yannis 1909-1990..... **CLC 6, 13, 31**
See also CA 77-80; 133; CANR 39; MTCW

Ritter, Erika 1948(?)-............. **CLC 52**

Rivera, Jose Eustasio 1889-1928... **TCLC 35**
See also HW

Rivers, Conrad Kent 1933-1968...... **CLC 1**
See also BW 1; CA 85-88; DLB 41

Rivers, Elfrida
See Bradley, Marion Zimmer

Riverside, John
See Heinlein, Robert A(nson)

Rizal, Jose 1861-1896........... **NCLC 27**

Roa Bastos, Augusto (Antonio)
1917- .... **CLC 45; HLC**
See also CA 131; DLB 113; HW

Robbe-Grillet, Alain
1922- ..... **CLC 1, 2, 4, 6, 8, 10, 14, 43**
See also CA 9-12R; CANR 33; DLB 83;
MTCW

Robbins, Harold 1916-............. **CLC 5**
See also CA 73-76; CANR 26; MTCW

Robbins, Thomas Eugene 1936-
See Robbins, Tom
See also CA 81-84; CANR 29; MTCW

Robbins, Tom............... **CLC 9, 32, 64**
See also Robbins, Thomas Eugene
See also BEST 90:3; DLBY 80

Robbins, Trina 1938- .... **CLC 21**
See also CA 128

Roberts, Charles G(eorge) D(ouglas)
1860-1943 .... **TCLC 8**
See also CA 105; CLR 33; DLB 92;
SATA 29

Roberts, Kate 1891-1985 .... **CLC 15**
See also CA 107; 116

Roberts, Keith (John Kingston)
1935- .... **CLC 14**
See also CA 25-28R; CANR 46, 46

Roberts, Kenneth (Lewis)
1885-1957 .... **TCLC 23**
See also CA 109; DLB 9

Roberts, Michele (B.) 1949-........ **CLC 48**
See also CA 115

Robertson, Ellis
See Ellison, Harlan (Jay); Silverberg, Robert

Robertson, Thomas William
1829-1871 .... **NCLC 35**

Robinson, Edwin Arlington
1869-1935 .... **TCLC 5; DA; PC 1**
See also CA 104; 133; CDALB 1865-1917;
DLB 54; MTCW

Robinson, Henry Crabb
1775-1867 .... **NCLC 15**
See also DLB 107

Robinson, Jill 1936-............... **CLC 10**
See also CA 102

Robinson, Kim Stanley 1952- ...... **CLC 34**
See also CA 126

Robinson, Lloyd
See Silverberg, Robert

Robinson, Marilynne 1944-........ **CLC 25**
See also CA 116

Robinson, Smokey................. **CLC 21**
See also Robinson, William, Jr.

Robinson, William, Jr. 1940-
See Robinson, Smokey
See also CA 116

Robison, Mary 1949-............. **CLC 42**
See also CA 113; 116; DLB 130

Rod, Edouard 1857-1910 .... **TCLC 52**

Roddenberry, Eugene Wesley 1921-1991
See Roddenberry, Gene
See also CA 110; 135; CANR 37; SATA 45;
SATA-Obit 69

Roddenberry, Gene .... **CLC 17**
See also Roddenberry, Eugene Wesley
See also AAYA 5; SATA-Obit 69

Rodgers, Mary 1931-............. **CLC 12**
See also CA 49-52; CANR 8; CLR 20;
JRDA; MAICYA; SATA 8

Rodgers, W(illiam) R(obert)
1909-1969 .... **CLC 7**
See also CA 85-88; DLB 20

Rodman, Eric
See Silverberg, Robert

Rodman, Howard 1920(?)-1985..... **CLC 65**
See also CA 118

Rodman, Maia
See Wojciechowska, Maia (Teresa)

Rodriguez, Claudio 1934-......... **CLC 10**
See also DLB 134

Roelvaag, O(le) E(dvart)
1876-1931 .... **TCLC 17**
See also CA 117; DLB 9

Roethke, Theodore (Huebner)
1908-1963 ...... **CLC 1, 3, 8, 11, 19, 46**
See also CA 81-84; CABS 2;
CDALB 1941-1968; DLB 5; MTCW

Rogers, Thomas Hunton 1927- ..... **CLC 57**
See also CA 89-92

Rogers, Will(iam Penn Adair)
1879-1935 .... **TCLC 8**
See also CA 105; 144; DLB 11; NNAL

Rogin, Gilbert 1929-............. **CLC 18**
See also CA 65-68; CANR 15

Rohan, Koda .... **TCLC 22**
See also Koda Shigeyuki

Rohmer, Eric.................... **CLC 16**
See also Scherer, Jean-Marie Maurice

Rohmer, Sax .... **TCLC 28**
See also Ward, Arthur Henry Sarsfield
See also DLB 70

Roiphe, Anne (Richardson)
1935- .... **CLC 3, 9**
See also CA 89-92; CANR 45; DLBY 80

Rojas, Fernando de 1465-1541 ..... **LC 23**

Rolfe, Frederick (William Serafino Austin
Lewis Mary) 1860-1913...... **TCLC 12**
See also CA 107; DLB 34

Rolland, Romain 1866-1944....... **TCLC 23**
See also CA 118; DLB 65

Rolvaag, O(le) E(dvart)
See Roelvaag, O(le) E(dvart)

Romain Arnaud, Saint
See Aragon, Louis

Romains, Jules 1885-1972 .... **CLC 7**
See also CA 85-88; CANR 34; DLB 65;
MTCW

Romero, Jose Ruben 1890-1952 ... **TCLC 14**
See also CA 114; 131; HW

Ronsard, Pierre de
1524-1585 .... **LC 6; PC 11**

Rooke, Leon 1934-............ **CLC 25, 34**
See also CA 25-28R; CANR 23

Roper, William 1498-1578.......... **LC 10**

Roquelaure, A. N.
See Rice, Anne

Rosa, Joao Guimaraes 1908-1967... **CLC 23**
See also CA 89-92; DLB 113

Rose, Wendy 1948-............... **CLC 85**
See also CA 53-56; CANR 5; NNAL;
SATA 12

Rosen, Richard (Dean) 1949-....... **CLC 39**
See also CA 77-80

Rosenberg, Isaac 1890-1918....... **TCLC 12**
See also CA 107; DLB 20

Rosenblatt, Joe .... **CLC 15**
See also Rosenblatt, Joseph

Rosenblatt, Joseph 1933-
See Rosenblatt, Joe
See also CA 89-92

Rosenfeld, Samuel 1896-1963
See Tzara, Tristan
See also CA 89-92

Rosenthal, M(acha) L(ouis) 1917-... **CLC 28**
See also CA 1-4R; CAAS 6; CANR 4;
DLB 5; SATA 59

Ross, Barnaby
See Dannay, Frederic

Ross, Bernard L.
See Follett, Ken(neth Martin)

Ross, J. H.
See Lawrence, T(homas) E(dward)

Ross, Martin
See Martin, Violet Florence
See also DLB 135

Ross, (James) Sinclair 1908-....... **CLC 13**
See also CA 73-76; DLB 88

Rossetti, Christina (Georgina)
1830-1894 ... **NCLC 2; DA; PC 7; WLC**
See also DLB 35; MAICYA; SATA 20

Rossetti, Dante Gabriel
1828-1882 . . . . **NCLC 4; DA; WLC**
See also CDBLB 1832-1890; DLB 35

Rossner, Judith (Perelman)
1935- . . . . **CLC 6, 9, 29**
See also AITN 2; BEST 90:3; CA 17-20R;
CANR 18; DLB 6; MTCW

Rostand, Edmond (Eugene Alexis)
1868-1918 . . . . **TCLC 6, 37; DA**
See also CA 104; 126; MTCW

Roth, Henry 1906- . . . . **CLC 2, 6, 11**
See also CA 11-12; CANR 38; CAP 1;
DLB 28; MTCW

Roth, Joseph 1894-1939 . . . . **TCLC 33**
See also DLB 85

Roth, Philip (Milton)
1933- . . . . . . **CLC 1, 2, 3, 4, 6, 9, 15, 22,
31, 47, 66, 86; DA; WLC**
See also BEST 90:3; CA 1-4R; CANR 1, 22,
36; CDALB 1968-1988; DLB 2, 28;
DLBY 82; MTCW

Rothenberg, Jerome 1931- . . . . **CLC 6, 57**
See also CA 45-48; CANR 1; DLB 5

Roumain, Jacques (Jean Baptiste)
1907-1944 . . . . **TCLC 19; BLC**
See also BW 1; CA 117; 125

Rourke, Constance (Mayfield)
1885-1941 . . . . **TCLC 12**
See also CA 107; YABC 1

Rousseau, Jean-Baptiste 1671-1741 . . . **LC 9**

Rousseau, Jean-Jacques
1712-1778 . . . . **LC 14; DA; WLC**

Roussel, Raymond 1877-1933 . . . . . **TCLC 20**
See also CA 117

Rovit, Earl (Herbert) 1927- . . . . **CLC 7**
See also CA 5-8R; CANR 12

Rowe, Nicholas 1674-1718 . . . . **LC 8**
See also DLB 84

Rowley, Ames Dorrance
See Lovecraft, H(oward) P(hillips)

Rowson, Susanna Haswell
1762(?)-1824 . . . . **NCLC 5**
See also DLB 37

Roy, Gabrielle 1909-1983 . . . . **CLC 10, 14**
See also CA 53-56; 110; CANR 5; DLB 68;
MTCW

Rozewicz, Tadeusz 1921- . . . . **CLC 9, 23**
See also CA 108; CANR 36; MTCW

Ruark, Gibbons 1941- . . . . **CLC 3**
See also CA 33-36R; CANR 14, 31;
DLB 120

Rubens, Bernice (Ruth) 1923- . . . **CLC 19, 31**
See also CA 25-28R; CANR 33; DLB 14;
MTCW

Rudkin, (James) David 1936- . . . . . . **CLC 14**
See also CA 89-92; DLB 13

Rudnik, Raphael 1933- . . . . **CLC 7**
See also CA 29-32R

Ruffian, M.
See Hasek, Jaroslav (Matej Frantisek)

Ruiz, Jose Martinez . . . . **CLC 11**
See also Martinez Ruiz, Jose

Rukeyser, Muriel
1913-1980 . . . . **CLC 6, 10, 15, 27**
See also CA 5-8R; 93-96; CANR 26;
DLB 48; MTCW; SATA-Obit 22

Rule, Jane (Vance) 1931- . . . . **CLC 27**
See also CA 25-28R; CAAS 18; CANR 12;
DLB 60

Rulfo, Juan 1918-1986 . . . . **CLC 8, 80; HLC**
See also CA 85-88; 118; CANR 26;
DLB 113; HW; MTCW

Runeberg, Johan 1804-1877 . . . . . . **NCLC 41**

Runyon, (Alfred) Damon
1884(?)-1946 . . . . **TCLC 10**
See also CA 107; DLB 11, 86

Rush, Norman 1933- . . . . **CLC 44**
See also CA 121; 126

Rushdie, (Ahmed) Salman
1947- . . . . **CLC 23, 31, 55**
See also BEST 89:3; CA 108; 111;
CANR 33; MTCW

Rushforth, Peter (Scott) 1945- . . . . . **CLC 19**
See also CA 101

Ruskin, John 1819-1900 . . . . **TCLC 20**
See also CA 114; 129; CDBLB 1832-1890;
DLB 55; SATA 24

Russ, Joanna 1937- . . . . **CLC 15**
See also CA 25-28R; CANR 11, 31; DLB 8;
MTCW

Russell, (Henry) Ken(neth Alfred)
1927- . . . . **CLC 16**
See also CA 105

Russell, Willy 1947- . . . . **CLC 60**

Rutherford, Mark . . . . **TCLC 25**
See also White, William Hale
See also DLB 18

Ryan, Cornelius (John) 1920-1974 . . . **CLC 7**
See also CA 69-72; 53-56; CANR 38

Ryan, Michael 1946- . . . . **CLC 65**
See also CA 49-52; DLBY 82

Rybakov, Anatoli (Naumovich)
1911- . . . . **CLC 23, 53**
See also CA 126; 135; SATA 79

Ryder, Jonathan
See Ludlum, Robert

Ryga, George 1932-1987 . . . . **CLC 14**
See also CA 101; 124; CANR 43; DLB 60

S. S.
See Sassoon, Siegfried (Lorraine)

Saba, Umberto 1883-1957 . . . . **TCLC 33**
See also CA 144; DLB 114

Sabatini, Rafael 1875-1950 . . . . . . **TCLC 47**

Sabato, Ernesto (R.)
1911- . . . . **CLC 10, 23; HLC**
See also CA 97-100; CANR 32; DLB 145;
HW; MTCW

Sacastru, Martin
See Bioy Casares, Adolfo

Sacher-Masoch, Leopold von
1836(?)-1895 . . . . **NCLC 31**

Sachs, Marilyn (Stickle) 1927- . . . . . **CLC 35**
See also AAYA 2; CA 17-20R; CANR 13,
47; CLR 2; JRDA; MAICYA; SAAS 2;
SATA 3, 68

Sachs, Nelly 1891-1970 . . . . **CLC 14**
See also CA 17-18; 25-28R; CAP 2

Sackler, Howard (Oliver)
1929-1982 . . . . **CLC 14**
See also CA 61-64; 108; CANR 30; DLB 7

Sacks, Oliver (Wolf) 1933- . . . . **CLC 67**
See also CA 53-56; CANR 28; MTCW

Sade, Donatien Alphonse Francois Comte
1740-1814 . . . . **NCLC 47**

Sadoff, Ira 1945- . . . . **CLC 9**
See also CA 53-56; CANR 5, 21; DLB 120

Saetone
See Camus, Albert

Safire, William 1929- . . . . **CLC 10**
See also CA 17-20R; CANR 31

Sagan, Carl (Edward) 1934- . . . . **CLC 30**
See also AAYA 2; CA 25-28R; CANR 11,
36; MTCW; SATA 58

Sagan, Francoise . . . . **CLC 3, 6, 9, 17, 36**
See also Quoirez, Francoise
See also DLB 83

Sahgal, Nayantara (Pandit) 1927- . . . **CLC 41**
See also CA 9-12R; CANR 11

Saint, H(arry) F. 1941- . . . . **CLC 50**
See also CA 127

St. Aubin de Teran, Lisa 1953-
See Teran, Lisa St. Aubin de
See also CA 118; 126

Sainte-Beuve, Charles Augustin
1804-1869 . . . . **NCLC 5**

**Saint-Exupery, Antoine (Jean Baptiste Marie
Roger) de**
1900-1944 . . . . **TCLC 2, 56; WLC**
See also CA 108; 132; CLR 10; DLB 72;
MAICYA; MTCW; SATA 20

St. John, David
See Hunt, E(verette) Howard, (Jr.)

Saint-John Perse
See Leger, (Marie-Rene Auguste) Alexis
Saint-Leger

Saintsbury, George (Edward Bateman)
1845-1933 . . . . **TCLC 31**
See also DLB 57

Sait Faik . . . . **TCLC 23**
See also Abasiyanik, Sait Faik

Saki . . . . **TCLC 3; SSC 12**
See also Munro, H(ector) H(ugh)

Sala, George Augustus . . . . **NCLC 46**

Salama, Hannu 1936- . . . . **CLC 18**

Salamanca, J(ack) R(ichard)
1922- . . . . **CLC 4, 15**
See also CA 25-28R

Sale, J. Kirkpatrick
See Sale, Kirkpatrick

Sale, Kirkpatrick 1937- . . . . **CLC 68**
See also CA 13-16R; CANR 10

Salinas (y Serrano), Pedro
1891(?)-1951 . . . . **TCLC 17**
See also CA 117; DLB 134

Salinger, J(erome) D(avid)
1919- ...... **CLC 1, 3, 8, 12, 55, 56; DA;
SSC 2; WLC**
See also AAYA 2; CA 5-8R; CANR 39;
CDALB 1941-1968; CLR 18; DLB 2, 102;
MAICYA; MTCW; SATA 67

Salisbury, John
See Caute, David

Salter, James 1925- .... **CLC 7, 52, 59**
See also CA 73-76; DLB 130

Saltus, Edgar (Everton)
1855-1921 .... **TCLC 8**
See also CA 105

Saltykov, Mikhail Evgrafovich
1826-1889 .... **NCLC 16**

Samarakis, Antonis 1919- .... **CLC 5**
See also CA 25-28R; CAAS 16; CANR 36

Sanchez, Florencio 1875-1910 ..... **TCLC 37**
See also HW

Sanchez, Luis Rafael 1936- .... **CLC 23**
See also CA 128; DLB 145; HW

Sanchez, Sonia 1934- ... **CLC 5; BLC; PC 9**
See also BW 2; CA 33-36R; CANR 24;
CLR 18; DLB 41; DLBD 8; MAICYA;
MTCW; SATA 22

Sand, George
1804-1876 ...... **NCLC 2, 42; DA; WLC**
See also DLB 119

Sandburg, Carl (August)
1878-1967 .... **CLC 1, 4, 10, 15, 35; DA;
PC 2; WLC**
See also CA 5-8R; 25-28R; CANR 35;
CDALB 1865-1917; DLB 17, 54;
MAICYA; MTCW; SATA 8

Sandburg, Charles
See Sandburg, Carl (August)

Sandburg, Charles A.
See Sandburg, Carl (August)

Sanders, (James) Ed(ward) 1939- ... **CLC 53**
See also CA 13-16R; CANR 13, 44;
DLB 16

Sanders, Lawrence 1920- .... **CLC 41**
See also BEST 89:4; CA 81-84; CANR 33;
MTCW

Sanders, Noah
See Blount, Roy (Alton), Jr.

Sanders, Winston P.
See Anderson, Poul (William)

Sandoz, Mari(e Susette)
1896-1966 .... **CLC 28**
See also CA 1-4R; 25-28R; CANR 17;
DLB 9; MTCW; SATA 5

Saner, Reg(inald Anthony) 1931- .... **CLC 9**
See also CA 65-68

Sannazaro, Jacopo 1456(?)-1530 ...... **LC 8**

Sansom, William 1912-1976....... **CLC 2, 6**
See also CA 5-8R; 65-68; CANR 42;
DLB 139; MTCW

Santayana, George 1863-1952 ..... **TCLC 40**
See also CA 115; DLB 54, 71

Santiago, Danny .... **CLC 33**
See also James, Daniel (Lewis); James,
Daniel (Lewis)
See also DLB 122

Santmyer, Helen Hoover
1895-1986 .... **CLC 33**
See also CA 1-4R; 118; CANR 15, 33;
DLBY 84; MTCW

Santos, Bienvenido N(uqui) 1911-... **CLC 22**
See also CA 101; CANR 19, 46, 46

Sapper .... **TCLC 44**
See also McNeile, Herman Cyril

Sappho fl. 6th cent. B.C.-.... **CMLC 3; PC 5**

Sarduy, Severo 1937-1993 .... **CLC 6**
See also CA 89-92; 142; DLB 113; HW

Sargeson, Frank 1903-1982 .... **CLC 31**
See also CA 25-28R; 106; CANR 38

Sarmiento, Felix Ruben Garcia
See Dario, Ruben

Saroyan, William
1908-1981 ..... **CLC 1, 8, 10, 29, 34, 56;
DA; WLC**
See also CA 5-8R; 103; CANR 30; DLB 7,
9, 86; DLBY 81; MTCW; SATA 23;
SATA-Obit 24

Sarraute, Nathalie
1900- .... **CLC 1, 2, 4, 8, 10, 31, 80**
See also CA 9-12R; CANR 23; DLB 83;
MTCW

Sarton, (Eleanor) May
1912- .... **CLC 4, 14, 49**
See also CA 1-4R; CANR 1, 34; DLB 48;
DLBY 81; MTCW; SATA 36

Sartre, Jean-Paul
1905-1980 .... **CLC 1, 4, 7, 9, 13, 18, 24,
44, 50, 52; DA; DC 3; WLC**
See also CA 9-12R; 97-100; CANR 21;
DLB 72; MTCW

Sassoon, Siegfried (Lorraine)
1886-1967 .... **CLC 36**
See also CA 104; 25-28R; CANR 36;
DLB 20; MTCW

Satterfield, Charles
See Pohl, Frederik

Saul, John (W. III) 1942- .... **CLC 46**
See also AAYA 10; BEST 90:4; CA 81-84;
CANR 16, 40

Saunders, Caleb
See Heinlein, Robert A(nson)

Saura (Atares), Carlos 1932-....... **CLC 20**
See also CA 114; 131; HW

Sauser-Hall, Frederic 1887-1961.... **CLC 18**
See also CA 102; 93-96; CANR 36; MTCW

Saussure, Ferdinand de
1857-1913 .... **TCLC 49**

Savage, Catharine
See Brosman, Catharine Savage

Savage, Thomas 1915- .... **CLC 40**
See also CA 126; 132; CAAS 15

Savan, Glenn 19(?)- .... **CLC 50**

Sayers, Dorothy L(eigh)
1893-1957 .... **TCLC 2, 15**
See also CA 104; 119; CDBLB 1914-1945;
DLB 10, 36, 77, 100; MTCW

Sayers, Valerie 1952- .... **CLC 50**
See also CA 134

Sayles, John (Thomas)
1950- .... **CLC 7, 10, 14**
See also CA 57-60; CANR 41; DLB 44

Scammell, Michael .... **CLC 34**

Scannell, Vernon 1922- .... **CLC 49**
See also CA 5-8R; CANR 8, 24; DLB 27;
SATA 59

Scarlett, Susan
See Streatfeild, (Mary) Noel

Schaeffer, Susan Fromberg
1941- .... **CLC 6, 11, 22**
See also CA 49-52; CANR 18; DLB 28;
MTCW; SATA 22

Schary, Jill
See Robinson, Jill

Schell, Jonathan 1943-........... **CLC 35**
See also CA 73-76; CANR 12

Schelling, Friedrich Wilhelm Joseph von
1775-1854 .... **NCLC 30**
See also DLB 90

Schendel, Arthur van 1874-1946 ... **TCLC 56**

Scherer, Jean-Marie Maurice 1920-
See Rohmer, Eric
See also CA 110

Schevill, James (Erwin) 1920-....... **CLC 7**
See also CA 5-8R; CAAS 12

Schiller, Friedrich 1759-1805 .... **NCLC 39**
See also DLB 94

Schisgal, Murray (Joseph) 1926-..... **CLC 6**
See also CA 21-24R

Schlee, Ann 1934-................ **CLC 35**
See also CA 101; CANR 29; SATA 36, 44

Schlegel, August Wilhelm von
1767-1845 .... **NCLC 15**
See also DLB 94

Schlegel, Friedrich 1772-1829 .... **NCLC 45**
See also DLB 90

Schlegel, Johann Elias (von)
1719(?)-1749 .... **LC 5**

Schlesinger, Arthur M(eier), Jr.
1917- .... **CLC 84**
See also AITN 1; CA 1-4R; CANR 1, 28;
DLB 17; MTCW; SATA 61

Schmidt, Arno (Otto) 1914-1979.... **CLC 56**
See also CA 128; 109; DLB 69

Schmitz, Aron Hector 1861-1928
See Svevo, Italo
See also CA 104; 122; MTCW

Schnackenberg, Gjertrud 1953-..... **CLC 40**
See also CA 116; DLB 120

Schneider, Leonard Alfred 1925-1966
See Bruce, Lenny
See also CA 89-92

Schnitzler, Arthur
1862-1931 .... **TCLC 4; SSC 15**
See also CA 104; DLB 81, 118

Schor, Sandra (M.) 1932(?)-1990 ... **CLC 65**
See also CA 132

Schorer, Mark 1908-1977 .... **CLC 9**
See also CA 5-8R; 73-76; CANR 7;
DLB 103

Schrader, Paul (Joseph) 1946-...... **CLC 26**
See also CA 37-40R; CANR 41; DLB 44

Schreiner, Olive (Emilie Albertina)
1855-1920 .... **TCLC 9**
See also CA 105; DLB 18

Shammas, Anton 1951-............ CLC 55

Shange, Ntozake
1948- .... CLC 8, 25, 38, 74; BLC; DC 3
See also AAYA 9; BW 2; CA 85-88;
CABS 3; CANR 27; DLB 38; MTCW

Shanley, John Patrick 1950-....... CLC 75
See also CA 128; 133

Shapcott, Thomas William 1935- ... CLC 38
See also CA 69-72

Shapiro, Jane.................... CLC 76

Shapiro, Karl (Jay) 1913- .. CLC 4, 8, 15, 53
See also CA 1-4R; CAAS 6; CANR 1, 36;
DLB 48; MTCW

Sharp, William 1855-1905 .... TCLC 39

Sharpe, Thomas Ridley 1928-
See Sharpe, Tom
See also CA 114; 122

Sharpe, Tom.................... CLC 36
See also Sharpe, Thomas Ridley
See also DLB 14

Shaw, Bernard.................. TCLC 45
See also Shaw, George Bernard
See also BW 1

Shaw, G. Bernard
See Shaw, George Bernard

Shaw, George Bernard
1856-1950 .... TCLC 3, 9, 21; DA; WLC
See also Shaw, Bernard
See also CA 104; 128; CDBLB 1914-1945;
DLB 10, 57; MTCW

Shaw, Henry Wheeler
1818-1885 .... NCLC 15
See also DLB 11

Shaw, Irwin 1913-1984....... CLC 7, 23, 34
See also AITN 1; CA 13-16R; 112;
CANR 21; CDALB 1941-1968; DLB 6,
102; DLBY 84; MTCW

Shaw, Robert 1927-1978 .... CLC 5
See also AITN 1; CA 1-4R; 81-84;
CANR 4; DLB 13, 14

Shaw, T. E.
See Lawrence, T(homas) E(dward)

Shawn, Wallace 1943- .... CLC 41
See also CA 112

Shea, Lisa 1953-................. CLC 86

Sheed, Wilfrid (John Joseph)
1930- .... CLC 2, 4, 10, 53
See also CA 65-68; CANR 30; DLB 6;
MTCW

Sheldon, Alice Hastings Bradley
1915(?)-1987
See Tiptree, James, Jr.
See also CA 108; 122; CANR 34; MTCW

Sheldon, John
See Bloch, Robert (Albert)

Shelley, Mary Wollstonecraft (Godwin)
1797-1851 .... NCLC 14; DA; WLC
See also CDBLB 1789-1832; DLB 110, 116;
SATA 29

Shelley, Percy Bysshe
1792-1822 .... NCLC 18; DA; WLC
See also CDBLB 1789-1832; DLB 96, 110

Shepard, Jim 1956-............... CLC 36
See also CA 137

Shepard, Lucius 1947- .... CLC 34
See also CA 128; 141

Shepard, Sam
1943- .... CLC 4, 6, 17, 34, 41, 44; DC 5
See also AAYA 1; CA 69-72; CABS 3;
CANR 22; DLB 7; MTCW

Shepherd, Michael
See Ludlum, Robert

Sherburne, Zoa (Morin) 1912-...... CLC 30
See also AAYA 13; CA 1-4R; CANR 3, 37;
MAICYA; SAAS 18; SATA 3

Sheridan, Frances 1724-1766........ LC 7
See also DLB 39, 84

Sheridan, Richard Brinsley
1751-1816 ... NCLC 5; DA; DC 1; WLC
See also CDBLB 1660-1789; DLB 89

Sherman, Jonathan Marc.......... CLC 55

Sherman, Martin 1941(?)-......... CLC 19
See also CA 116; 123

Sherwin, Judith Johnson 1936-... CLC 7, 15
See also CA 25-28R; CANR 34

Sherwood, Frances 1940-.......... CLC 81

Sherwood, Robert E(mmet)
1896-1955 .... TCLC 3
See also CA 104; DLB 7, 26

Shestov, Lev 1866-1938 .... TCLC 56

Shiel, M(atthew) P(hipps)
1865-1947 .... TCLC 8
See also CA 106

Shiga, Naoya 1883-1971.......... CLC 33
See also CA 101; 33-36R

Shilts, Randy 1951-1994 .... CLC 85
See also CA 115; 127; 144; CANR 45

Shimazaki Haruki 1872-1943
See Shimazaki Toson
See also CA 105; 134

Shimazaki Toson.................. TCLC 5
See also Shimazaki Haruki

Sholokhov, Mikhail (Aleksandrovich)
1905-1984 .... CLC 7, 15
See also CA 101; 112; MTCW;
SATA-Obit 36

Shone, Patric
See Hanley, James

Shreve, Susan Richards 1939-...... CLC 23
See also CA 49-52; CAAS 5; CANR 5, 38;
MAICYA; SATA 41, 46

Shue, Larry 1946-1985............ CLC 52
See also CA 145; 117

Shu-Jen, Chou 1881-1936
See Hsun, Lu
See also CA 104

Shulman, Alix Kates 1932- ...... CLC 2, 10
See also CA 29-32R; CANR 43; SATA 7

Shuster, Joe 1914- .... CLC 21

Shute, Nevil.................... CLC 30
See also Norway, Nevil Shute

Shuttle, Penelope (Diane) 1947- ..... CLC 7
See also CA 93-96; CANR 39; DLB 14, 40

Sidney, Mary 1561-1621 .... LC 19

Sidney, Sir Philip 1554-1586.... LC 19; DA
See also CDBLB Before 1660

Siegel, Jerome 1914- .....
See also CA 116

Siegel, Jerry
See Siegel, Jerome

Sienkiewicz, Henryk (Adam A
1846-1916 ....
See also CA 104; 134

Sierra, Gregorio Martinez
See Martinez Sierra, Gregor

Sierra, Maria (de la O'LeJarra
See Martinez Sierra, Maria (
O'LeJarraga)

Sigal, Clancy 1926-.........
See also CA 1-4R

Sigourney, Lydia Howard (Hu
1791-1865 ....
See also DLB 1, 42, 73

Siguenza y Gongora, Carlos de
1645-1700 ....

Sigurjonsson, Johann 1880-19

Sikelianos, Angelos 1884-1951

Silkin, Jon 1930- ....
See also CA 5-8R; CAAS 5;

Silko, Leslie (Marmon)
1948-................
See also AAYA 14; CA 115;
CANR 45; DLB 143; NNA

Sillanpaa, Frans Eemil 1888-1
See also CA 129; 93-96; MT

Sillitoe, Alan
1928-.......... CLC 1,
See also AITN 1; CA 9-12R;
CANR 8, 26; CDBLB 196C
DLB 14, 139; MTCW; SAT

Silone, Ignazio 1900-1978 ....
See also CA 25-28; 81-84; CA
CAP 2; MTCW

Silver, Joan Micklin 1935- ...
See also CA 114; 121

Silver, Nicholas
See Faust, Frederick (Schiller)

Silverberg, Robert 1935- .....
See also CA 1-4R; CAAS 3; C
36; DLB 8; MAICYA; MT(

Silverstein, Alvin 1933-......
See also CA 49-52; CANR 2;
JRDA; MAICYA; SATA 8,

Silverstein, Virginia B(arbara Op
1937-..................
See also CA 49-52; CANR 2;
JRDA; MAICYA; SATA 8,

Sim, Georges
See Simenon, Georges (Jacques

Simak, Clifford D(onald)
1904-1988 ....
See also CA 1-4R; 125; CANR
DLB 8; MTCW; SATA-Obit

Simenon, Georges (Jacques Christ
1903-1989 .... CLC 1,
See also CA 85-88; 129; CANR
DLB 72; DLBY 89; MTCW

Simic, Charles 1938-... CLC 6,
See also CA 29-32R; CAAS 4;
33; DLB 105

Snow, Frances Compton
See Adams, Henry (Brooks)

Snyder, Gary (Sherman)
1930- . . . . **CLC 1, 2, 5, 9, 32**
See also CA 17-20R; CANR 30; DLB 5, 16

Snyder, Zilpha Keatley 1927- . . . . . . **CLC 17**
See also CA 9-12R; CANR 38; CLR 31;
JRDA; MAICYA; SAAS 2; SATA 1, 28,
75

Soares, Bernardo
See Pessoa, Fernando (Antonio Nogueira)

Sobh, A.
See Shamlu, Ahmad

Sobol, Joshua. . . . . **CLC 60**

Soderberg, Hjalmar 1869-1941 . . . . **TCLC 39**

Sodergran, Edith (Irene)
See Soedergran, Edith (Irene)

Soedergran, Edith (Irene)
1892-1923 . . . . **TCLC 31**

Softly, Edgar
See Lovecraft, H(oward) P(hillips)

Softly, Edward
See Lovecraft, H(oward) P(hillips)

Sokolov, Raymond 1941- . . . . **CLC 7**
See also CA 85-88

Solo, Jay
See Ellison, Harlan (Jay)

Sologub, Fyodor . . . . **TCLC 9**
See also Teternikov, Fyodor Kuzmich

Solomons, Ikey Esquir
See Thackeray, William Makepeace

Solomos, Dionysios 1798-1857 . . . **NCLC 15**

Solwoska, Mara
See French, Marilyn

Solzhenitsyn, Aleksandr I(sayevich)
1918- . . . . . . **CLC 1, 2, 4, 7, 9, 10, 18, 26,**
34, 78; DA; WLC
See also AITN 1; CA 69-72; CANR 40;
MTCW

Somers, Jane
See Lessing, Doris (May)

Somerville, Edith 1858-1949 . . . . . . **TCLC 51**
See also DLB 135

Somerville & Ross
See Martin, Violet Florence; Somerville,
Edith

Sommer, Scott 1951- . . . . **CLC 25**
See also CA 106

Sondheim, Stephen (Joshua)
1930- . . . . **CLC 30, 39**
See also AAYA 11; CA 103; CANR 47

Sontag, Susan 1933- . . . **CLC 1, 2, 10, 13, 31**
See also CA 17-20R; CANR 25; DLB 2, 67;
MTCW

Sophocles
496(?)B.C.-406(?)B.C. . . . . . **CMLC 2; DA;**
DC 1

Sorel, Julia
See Drexler, Rosalyn

Sorrentino, Gilbert
1929- . . . . **CLC 3, 7, 14, 22, 40**
See also CA 77-80; CANR 14, 33; DLB 5;
DLBY 80

Soto, Gary 1952- . . . . **CLC 32, 80; HLC**
See also AAYA 10; CA 119; 125; DLB 82;
HW; JRDA; SATA 80

Soupault, Philippe 1897-1990 . . . . . **CLC 68**
See also CA 116; 131

Souster, (Holmes) Raymond
1921- . . . . **CLC 5, 14**
See also CA 13-16R; CAAS 14; CANR 13,
29; DLB 88; SATA 63

Southern, Terry 1926- . . . . **CLC 7**
See also CA 1-4R; CANR 1; DLB 2

Southey, Robert 1774-1843 . . . . **NCLC 8**
See also DLB 93, 107, 142; SATA 54

Southworth, Emma Dorothy Eliza Nevitte
1819-1899 . . . . **NCLC 26**

Souza, Ernest
See Scott, Evelyn

Soyinka, Wole
1934- . . . . **CLC 3, 5, 14, 36, 44; BLC;**
DA; DC 2; WLC
See also BW 2; CA 13-16R; CANR 27, 39;
DLB 125; MTCW

Spackman, W(illiam) M(ode)
1905-1990 . . . . **CLC 46**
See also CA 81-84; 132

Spacks, Barry 1931- . . . . **CLC 14**
See also CA 29-32R; CANR 33; DLB 105

Spanidou, Irini 1946- . . . . **CLC 44**

Spark, Muriel (Sarah)
1918- . . . . **CLC 2, 3, 5, 8, 13, 18, 40;**
SSC 10
See also CA 5-8R; CANR 12, 36;
CDBLB 1945-1960; DLB 15, 139; MTCW

Spaulding, Douglas
See Bradbury, Ray (Douglas)

Spaulding, Leonard
See Bradbury, Ray (Douglas)

Spence, J. A. D.
See Eliot, T(homas) S(tearns)

Spencer, Elizabeth 1921- . . . . **CLC 22**
See also CA 13-16R; CANR 32; DLB 6;
MTCW; SATA 14

Spencer, Leonard G.
See Silverberg, Robert

Spencer, Scott 1945- . . . . **CLC 30**
See also CA 113; DLBY 86

Spender, Stephen (Harold)
1909- . . . . **CLC 1, 2; 5, 10, 41**
See also CA 9-12R; CANR 31;
CDBLB 1945-1960; DLB 20; MTCW

Spengler, Oswald (Arnold Gottfried)
1880-1936 . . . . **TCLC 25**
See also CA 118

Spenser, Edmund
1552(?)-1599 . . . . **LC 5; DA; PC 8; WLC**
See also CDBLB Before 1660

Spicer, Jack 1925-1965 . . . . . . **CLC 8, 18, 72**
See also CA 85-88; DLB 5, 16

Spiegelman, Art 1948- . . . . **CLC 76**
See also AAYA 10; CA 125; CANR 41

Spielberg, Peter 1929- . . . . **CLC 6**
See also CA 5-8R; CANR 4; DLBY 81

Spielberg, Steven 1947- . . . . **CLC 20**
See also AAYA 8; CA 77-80; CANR 32;
SATA 32

Spillane, Frank Morrison 1918-
See Spillane, Mickey
See also CA 25-28R; CANR 28; MTCW;
SATA 66

Spillane, Mickey . . . . **CLC 3, 13**
See also Spillane, Frank Morrison

Spinoza, Benedictus de 1632-1677 . . . . **LC 9**

Spinrad, Norman (Richard) 1940- . . . **CLC 46**
See also CA 37-40R; CAAS 19; CANR 20;
DLB 8

Spitteler, Carl (Friedrich Georg)
1845-1924 . . . . **TCLC 12**
See also CA 109; DLB 129

Spivack, Kathleen (Romola Drucker)
1938- . . . . **CLC 6**
See also CA 49-52

Spoto, Donald 1941- . . . . **CLC 39**
See also CA 65-68; CANR 11

Springsteen, Bruce (F.) 1949- . . . . . . **CLC 17**
See also CA 111

Spurling, Hilary 1940- . . . . **CLC 34**
See also CA 104; CANR 25

Spyker, John Howland
See Elman, Richard

Squires, (James) Radcliffe
1917-1993 . . . . **CLC 51**
See also CA 1-4R; 140; CANR 6, 21

Srivastava, Dhanpat Rai 1880(?)-1936
See Premchand
See also CA 118

Stacy, Donald
See Pohl, Frederik

Stael, Germaine de
See Stael-Holstein, Anne Louise Germaine
Necker Baronn
See also DLB 119

Stael-Holstein, Anne Louise Germaine Necker
Baronn 1766-1817 . . . . **NCLC 3**
See also Stael, Germaine de

Stafford, Jean 1915-1979 . . . **CLC 4, 7, 19, 68**
See also CA 1-4R; 85-88; CANR 3; DLB 2;
MTCW; SATA-Obit 22

Stafford, William (Edgar)
1914-1993 . . . . **CLC 4, 7, 29**
See also CA 5-8R; 142; CAAS 3; CANR 5,
22; DLB 5

Staines, Trevor
See Brunner, John (Kilian Houston)

Stairs, Gordon
See Austin, Mary (Hunter)

Stannard, Martin 1947- . . . . **CLC 44**
See also CA 142

Stanton, Maura 1946- . . . . **CLC 9**
See also CA 89-92; CANR 15; DLB 120

Stanton, Schuyler
See Baum, L(yman) Frank

Stapledon, (William) Olaf
1886-1950 . . . . **TCLC 22**
See also CA 111; DLB 15

Starbuck, George (Edwin) 1931- . . . . **CLC 53**
See also CA 21-24R; CANR 23

Stark, Richard
See Westlake, Donald E(dwin)

Staunton, Schuyler
See Baum, L(yman) Frank

Stead, Christina (Ellen)
1902-1983 . . . . CLC 2, 5, 8, 32, 80
See also CA 13-16R; 109; CANR 33, 40;
MTCW

Stead, William Thomas
1849-1912 . . . . TCLC 48

Steele, Richard 1672-1729 . . . . LC 18
See also CDBLB 1660-1789; DLB 84, 101

Steele, Timothy (Reid) 1948- . . . . CLC 45
See also CA 93-96; CANR 16; DLB 120

Steffens, (Joseph) Lincoln
1866-1936 . . . . TCLC 20
See also CA 117

Stegner, Wallace (Earle)
1909-1993 . . . . CLC 9, 49, 81
See also AITN 1; BEST 90:3; CA 1-4R;
141; CAAS 9; CANR 1, 21, 46, 46;
DLB 9; DLBY 93; MTCW

Stein, Gertrude
1874-1946 . . . . . . TCLC 1, 6, 28, 48; DA;
WLC
See also CA 104; 132; CDALB 1917-1929;
DLB 4, 54, 86; MTCW

Steinbeck, John (Ernst)
1902-1968 . . . . . . CLC 1, 5, 9, 13, 21, 34,
45, 75; DA; SSC 11; WLC
See also AAYA 12; CA 1-4R; 25-28R;
CANR 1, 35; CDALB 1929-1941; DLB 7,
9; DLBD 2; MTCW; SATA 9

Steinem, Gloria 1934- . . . . CLC 63
See also CA 53-56; CANR 28; MTCW

Steiner, George 1929- . . . . CLC 24
See also CA 73-76; CANR 31; DLB 67;
MTCW; SATA 62

Steiner, K. Leslie
See Delany, Samuel R(ay, Jr.)

Steiner, Rudolf 1861-1925 . . . . TCLC 13
See also CA 107

Stendhal
1783-1842 . . . . . NCLC 23, 46; DA; WLC
See also DLB 119

Stephen, Leslie 1832-1904 . . . . TCLC 23
See also CA 123; DLB 57, 144

Stephen, Sir Leslie
See Stephen, Leslie

Stephen, Virginia
See Woolf, (Adeline) Virginia

Stephens, James 1882(?)-1950 . . . . . . TCLC 4
See also CA 104; DLB 19

Stephens, Reed
See Donaldson, Stephen R.

Steptoe, Lydia
See Barnes, Djuna

Sterchi, Beat 1949- . . . . CLC 65

Sterling, Brett
See Bradbury, Ray (Douglas); Hamilton,
Edmond

Sterling, Bruce 1954- . . . . CLC 72
See also CA 119; CANR 44

Sterling, George 1869-1926 . . . . . . TCLC 20
See also CA 117; DLB 54

Stern, Gerald 1925- . . . . CLC 40
See also CA 81-84; CANR 28; DLB 105

Stern, Richard (Gustave) 1928- . . . CLC 4, 39
See also CA 1-4R; CANR 1, 25; DLBY 87

Sternberg, Josef von 1894-1969 . . . . . CLC 20
See also CA 81-84

Sterne, Laurence
1713-1768 . . . . LC 2; DA; WLC
See also CDBLB 1660-1789; DLB 39

Sternheim, (William Adolf) Carl
1878-1942 . . . . TCLC 8
See also CA 105; DLB 56, 118

Stevens, Mark 1951- . . . . CLC 34
See also CA 122

Stevens, Wallace
1879-1955 . . . . TCLC 3, 12, 45; DA;
PC 6; WLC
See also CA 104; 124; CDALB 1929-1941;
DLB 54; MTCW

Stevenson, Anne (Katharine)
1933- . . . . CLC 7, 33
See also CA 17-20R; CAAS 9; CANR 9, 33;
DLB 40; MTCW

Stevenson, Robert Louis (Balfour)
1850-1894 . . . . NCLC 5, 14; DA;
SSC 11; WLC
See also CDBLB 1890-1914; CLR 10, 11;
DLB 18, 57, 141; JRDA; MAICYA;
YABC 2

Stewart, J(ohn) I(nnes) M(ackintosh)
1906- . . . . CLC 7, 14, 32
See also CA 85-88; CAAS 3; CANR 47;
MTCW

Stewart, Mary (Florence Elinor)
1916- . . . . CLC 7, 35
See also CA 1-4R; CANR 1; SATA 12

Stewart, Mary Rainbow
See Stewart, Mary (Florence Elinor)

Stifle, June
See Campbell, Maria

Stifter, Adalbert 1805-1868 . . . . . . NCLC 41
See also DLB 133

Still, James 1906- . . . . CLC 49
See also CA 65-68; CAAS 17; CANR 10,
26; DLB 9; SATA 29

Sting
See Sumner, Gordon Matthew

Stirling, Arthur
See Sinclair, Upton (Beall)

Stitt, Milan 1941- . . . . CLC 29
See also CA 69-72

Stockton, Francis Richard 1834-1902
See Stockton, Frank R.
See also CA 108; 137; MAICYA; SATA 44

Stockton, Frank R. . . . . TCLC 47
See also Stockton, Francis Richard
See also DLB 42, 74; SATA 32

Stoddard, Charles
See Kuttner, Henry

Stoker, Abraham 1847-1912
See Stoker, Bram
See also CA 105; DA; SATA 29

Stoker, Bram . . . . TCLC 8; WLC
See also Stoker, Abraham
See also CDBLB 1890-1914; DLB 36, 70

Stolz, Mary (Slattery) 1920- . . . . CLC 12
See also AAYA 8; AITN 1; CA 5-8R;
CANR 13, 41; JRDA; MAICYA;
SAAS 3; SATA 10, 71

Stone, Irving 1903-1989 . . . . CLC 7
See also AITN 1; CA 1-4R; 129; CAAS 3;
CANR 1, 23; MTCW; SATA 3;
SATA-Obit 64

Stone, Oliver 1946- . . . . CLC 73
See also CA 110

Stone, Robert (Anthony)
1937- . . . . CLC 5, 23, 42
See also CA 85-88; CANR 23; MTCW

Stone, Zachary
See Follett, Ken(neth Martin)

Stoppard, Tom
1937- . . . . . . CLC 1, 3, 4, 5, 8, 15, 29, 34,
63; DA; WLC
See also CA 81-84; CANR 39;
CDBLB 1960 to Present; DLB 13;
DLBY 85; MTCW

Storey, David (Malcolm)
1933- . . . . CLC 2, 4, 5, 8
See also CA 81-84; CANR 36; DLB 13, 14;
MTCW

Storm, Hyemeyohsts 1935- . . . . CLC 3
See also CA 81-84; CANR 45; NNAL

Storm, (Hans) Theodor (Woldsen)
1817-1888 . . . . NCLC 1

Storni, Alfonsina
1892-1938 . . . . TCLC 5; HLC
See also CA 104; 131; HW

Stout, Rex (Todhunter) 1886-1975 . . . CLC 3
See also AITN 2; CA 61-64

Stow, (Julian) Randolph 1935- . . CLC 23, 48
See also CA 13-16R; CANR 33; MTCW

Stowe, Harriet (Elizabeth) Beecher
1811-1896 . . . . NCLC 3; DA; WLC
See also CDALB 1865-1917; DLB 1, 12, 42,
74; JRDA; MAICYA; YABC 1

Strachey, (Giles) Lytton
1880-1932 . . . . TCLC 12
See also CA 110; DLBD 10

Strand, Mark 1934- . . . . . . CLC 6, 18, 41, 71
See also CA 21-24R; CANR 40; DLB 5;
SATA 41

Straub, Peter (Francis) 1943- . . . . . . CLC 28
See also BEST 89:1; CA 85-88; CANR 28;
DLBY 84; MTCW

Strauss, Botho 1944- . . . . CLC 22
See also DLB 124

Streatfeild, (Mary) Noel
1895(?)-1986 . . . . CLC 21
See also CA 81-84; 120; CANR 31;
CLR 17; MAICYA; SATA 20;
SATA-Obit 48

Stribling, T(homas) S(igismund)
1881-1965 . . . . CLC 23
See also CA 107; DLB 9

Strindberg, (Johan) August
1849-1912 . . . . . . TCLC 1, 8, 21, 47; DA;
WLC
See also CA 104; 135

Stringer, Arthur 1874-1950 . . . . **TCLC 37**
See also DLB 92

Stringer, David
See Roberts, Keith (John Kingston)

Strugatskii, Arkadii (Natanovich)
1925-1991 . . . . **CLC 27**
See also CA 106; 135

Strugatskii, Boris (Natanovich)
1933- . . . . **CLC 27**
See also CA 106

Strummer, Joe 1953(?)- . . . . **CLC 30**

Stuart, Don A.
See Campbell, John W(ood, Jr.)

Stuart, Ian
See MacLean, Alistair (Stuart)

Stuart, Jesse (Hilton)
1906-1984 . . . . **CLC 1, 8, 11, 14, 34**
See also CA 5-8R; 112; CANR 31; DLB 9,
48, 102; DLBY 84; SATA 2;
SATA-Obit 36

Sturgeon, Theodore (Hamilton)
1918-1985 . . . . **CLC 22, 39**
See also Queen, Ellery
See also CA 81-84; 116; CANR 32; DLB 8;
DLBY 85; MTCW

Sturges, Preston 1898-1959 . . . . **TCLC 48**
See also CA 114; DLB 26

Styron, William
1925- . . . . **CLC 1, 3, 5, 11, 15, 60**
See also BEST 90:4; CA 5-8R; CANR 6, 33;
CDALB 1968-1988; DLB 2, 143;
DLBY 80; MTCW

Suarez Lynch, B.
See Bioy Casares, Adolfo; Borges, Jorge
Luis

Su Chien 1884-1918
See Su Man-shu
See also CA 123

Suckow, Ruth 1892-1960
See also CA 113; DLB 9, 102; SSC 18

Sudermann, Hermann 1857-1928 . . **TCLC 15**
See also CA 107; DLB 118

Sue, Eugene 1804-1857 . . . . **NCLC 1**
See also DLB 119

Sueskind, Patrick 1949- . . . . **CLC 44**
See also Suskind, Patrick

Sukenick, Ronald 1932- . . . . . **CLC 3, 4, 6, 48**
See also CA 25-28R; CAAS 8; CANR 32;
DLBY 81

Suknaski, Andrew 1942- . . . . **CLC 19**
See also CA 101; DLB 53

Sullivan, Vernon
See Vian, Boris

Sully Prudhomme 1839-1907 . . . . . . **TCLC 31**

Su Man-shu . . . . **TCLC 24**
See also Su Chien

Summerforest, Ivy B.
See Kirkup, James

Summers, Andrew James 1942- . . . . . **CLC 26**

Summers, Andy
See Summers, Andrew James

Summers, Hollis (Spurgeon, Jr.)
1916- . . . . **CLC 10**
See also CA 5-8R; CANR 3; DLB 6

Summers, (Alphonsus Joseph-Mary Augustus)
Montague 1880-1948 . . . . **TCLC 16**
See also CA 118

Sumner, Gordon Matthew 1951- . . . . **CLC 26**

Surtees, Robert Smith
1803-1864 . . . . **NCLC 14**
See also DLB 21

Susann, Jacqueline 1921-1974 . . . . . . **CLC 3**
See also AITN 1; CA 65-68; 53-56; MTCW

Suskind, Patrick
See Sueskind, Patrick
See also CA 145

Sutcliff, Rosemary 1920-1992 . . . . . . **CLC 26**
See also AAYA 10; CA 5-8R; 139;
CANR 37; CLR 1; JRDA; MAICYA;
SATA 6, 44, 78; SATA-Obit 73

Sutro, Alfred 1863-1933 . . . . **TCLC 6**
See also CA 105; DLB 10

Sutton, Henry
See Slavitt, David R(ytman)

Svevo, Italo . . . . **TCLC 2, 35**
See also Schmitz, Aron Hector

Swados, Elizabeth 1951- . . . . **CLC 12**
See also CA 97-100

Swados, Harvey 1920-1972 . . . . **CLC 5**
See also CA 5-8R; 37-40R; CANR 6;
DLB 2

Swan, Gladys 1934- . . . . **CLC 69**
See also CA 101; CANR 17, 39

Swarthout, Glendon (Fred)
1918-1992 . . . . **CLC 35**
See also CA 1-4R; 139; CANR 1, 47;
SATA 26

Sweet, Sarah C.
See Jewett, (Theodora) Sarah Orne

Swenson, May
1919-1989 . . . . **CLC 4, 14, 61; DA**
See also CA 5-8R; 130; CANR 36; DLB 5;
MTCW; SATA 15

Swift, Augustus
See Lovecraft, H(oward) P(hillips)

Swift, Graham (Colin) 1949- . . . . **CLC 41**
See also CA 117; 122; CANR 46, 46

Swift, Jonathan
1667-1745 . . . . . . **LC 1; DA; PC 9; WLC**
See also CDBLB 1660-1789; DLB 39, 95,
101; SATA 19

Swinburne, Algernon Charles
1837-1909 . . . . . . **TCLC 8, 36; DA; WLC**
See also CA 105; 140; CDBLB 1832-1890;
DLB 35, 57

Swinfen, Ann . . . . **CLC 34**

Swinnerton, Frank Arthur
1884-1982 . . . . **CLC 31**
See also CA 108; DLB 34

Swithen, John
See King, Stephen (Edwin)

Sylvia
See Ashton-Warner, Sylvia (Constance)

Symmes, Robert Edward
See Duncan, Robert (Edward)

Symonds, John Addington
1840-1893 . . . . **NCLC 34**
See also DLB 57, 144

Symons, Arthur 1865-1945 . . . . **TCLC 11**
See also CA 107; DLB 19, 57

Symons, Julian (Gustave)
1912- . . . . **CLC 2, 14, 32**
See also CA 49-52; CAAS 3; CANR 3, 33;
DLB 87; DLBY 92; MTCW

Synge, (Edmund) J(ohn) M(illington)
1871-1909 . . . . **TCLC 6, 37; DC 2**
See also CA 104; 141; CDBLB 1890-1914;
DLB 10, 19

Syruc, J.
See Milosz, Czeslaw

Szirtes, George 1948- . . . . **CLC 46**
See also CA 109; CANR 27

Tabori, George 1914- . . . . **CLC 19**
See also CA 49-52; CANR 4

Tagore, Rabindranath
1861-1941 . . . . **TCLC 3, 53; PC 8**
See also CA 104; 120; MTCW

Taine, Hippolyte Adolphe
1828-1893 . . . . **NCLC 15**

Talese, Gay 1932- . . . . **CLC 37**
See also AITN 1; CA 1-4R; CANR 9;
MTCW

Tallent, Elizabeth (Ann) 1954- . . . . . **CLC 45**
See also CA 117; DLB 130

Tally, Ted 1952- . . . . **CLC 42**
See also CA 120; 124

Tamayo y Baus, Manuel
1829-1898 . . . . **NCLC 1**

Tammsaare, A(nton) H(ansen)
1878-1940 . . . . **TCLC 27**

Tan, Amy 1952- . . . . **CLC 59**
See also AAYA 9; BEST 89:3; CA 136;
SATA 75

Tandem, Felix
See Spitteler, Carl (Friedrich Georg)

Tanizaki, Jun'ichiro
1886-1965 . . . . **CLC 8, 14, 28**
See also CA 93-96; 25-28R

Tanner, William
See Amis, Kingsley (William)

Tao Lao
See Storni, Alfonsina

Tarassoff, Lev
See Troyat, Henri

Tarbell, Ida M(inerva)
1857-1944 . . . . **TCLC 40**
See also CA 122; DLB 47

Tarkington, (Newton) Booth
1869-1946 . . . . **TCLC 9**
See also CA 110; 143; DLB 9, 102;
SATA 17

Tarkovsky, Andrei (Arsenyevich)
1932-1986 . . . . **CLC 75**
See also CA 127

Tartt, Donna 1964(?)- . . . . **CLC 76**
See also CA 142

Tasso, Torquato 1544-1595 . . . . **LC 5**

Tate, (John Orley) Allen
1899-1979 . . . . **CLC 2, 4, 6, 9, 11, 14, 24**
See also CA 5-8R; 85-88; CANR 32;
DLB 4, 45, 63; MTCW

Tate, Ellalice
See Hibbert, Eleanor Alice Burford

Tate, James (Vincent) 1943- ... **CLC 2, 6, 25**
See also CA 21-24R; CANR 29; DLB 5

Tavel, Ronald 1940-.............. **CLC 6**
See also CA 21-24R; CANR 33

Taylor, C(ecil) P(hilip) 1929-1981... **CLC 27**
See also CA 25-28R; 105; CANR 47

Taylor, Edward 1642(?)-1729.... **LC 11; DA**
See also DLB 24

Taylor, Eleanor Ross 1920-......... **CLC 5**
See also CA 81-84

Taylor, Elizabeth 1912-1975 ... **CLC 2, 4, 29**
See also CA 13-16R; CANR 9; DLB 139;
MTCW; SATA 13

Taylor, Henry (Splawn) 1942-...... **CLC 44**
See also CA 33-36R; CAAS 7; CANR 31;
DLB 5

Taylor, Kamala (Purnaiya) 1924-
See Markandaya, Kamala
See also CA 77-80

Taylor, Mildred D.................. **CLC 21**
See also AAYA 10; BW 1; CA 85-88;
CANR 25; CLR 9; DLB 52; JRDA;
MAICYA; SAAS 5; SATA 15, 70

Taylor, Peter (Hillsman)
1917-...... **CLC 1, 4, 18, 37, 44, 50, 71;
SSC 10**
See also CA 13-16R; CANR 9; DLBY 81;
MTCW

Taylor, Robert Lewis 1912-........ **CLC 14**
See also CA 1-4R; CANR 3; SATA 10

Tchekhov, Anton
See Chekhov, Anton (Pavlovich)

Teasdale, Sara 1884-1933......... **TCLC 4**
See also CA 104; DLB 45; SATA 32

Tegner, Esaias 1782-1846........ **NCLC 2**

Teilhard de Chardin, (Marie Joseph) Pierre
1881-1955 .... **TCLC 9**
See also CA 105

Temple, Ann
See Mortimer, Penelope (Ruth)

Tennant, Emma (Christina)
1937-.................... **CLC 13, 52**
See also CA 65-68; CAAS 9; CANR 10, 38;
DLB 14

Tenneshaw, S. M.
See Silverberg, Robert

Tennyson, Alfred
1809-1892 .. **NCLC 30; DA; PC 6; WLC**
See also CDBLB 1832-1890; DLB 32

Teran, Lisa St. Aubin de .... **CLC 36**
See also St. Aubin de Teran, Lisa

Terence 195(?)B.C.-159B.C....... **CMLC 14**

Teresa de Jesus, St. 1515-1582 ...... **LC 18**

Terkel, Louis 1912-
See Terkel, Studs
See also CA 57-60; CANR 18, 45; MTCW

Terkel, Studs.................... **CLC 38**
See also Terkel, Louis
See also AITN 1

Terry, C. V.
See Slaughter, Frank G(ill)

Terry, Megan 1932-.............. **CLC 19**
See also CA 77-80; CABS 3; CANR 43;
DLB 7

Tertz, Abram
See Sinyavsky, Andrei (Donatevich)

Tesich, Steve 1943(?)-......... **CLC 40, 69**
See also CA 105; DLBY 83

Teternikov, Fyodor Kuzmich 1863-1927
See Sologub, Fyodor
See also CA 104

Tevis, Walter 1928-1984 .... **CLC 42**
See also CA 113

Tey, Josephine................... **TCLC 14**
See also Mackintosh, Elizabeth
See also DLB 77

Thackeray, William Makepeace
1811-1863 .... **NCLC 5, 14, 22, 43; DA;
WLC**
See also CDBLB 1832-1890; DLB 21, 55;
SATA 23

Thakura, Ravindranatha
See Tagore, Rabindranath

Tharoor, Shashi 1956-............. **CLC 70**
See also CA 141

Thelwell, Michael Miles 1939-..... **CLC 22**
See also BW 2; CA 101

Theobald, Lewis, Jr.
See Lovecraft, H(oward) P(hillips)

Theodorescu, Ion N. 1880-1967
See Arghezi, Tudor
See also CA 116

Theriault, Yves 1915-1983........ **CLC 79**
See also CA 102; DLB 88

Theroux, Alexander (Louis)
1939-..................... **CLC 2, 25**
See also CA 85-88; CANR 20

Theroux, Paul (Edward)
1941-......... **CLC 5, 8, 11, 15, 28, 46**
See also BEST 89:4; CA 33-36R; CANR 20,
45; DLB 2; MTCW; SATA 44

Thesen, Sharon 1946-............. **CLC 56**

Thevenin, Denis
See Duhamel, Georges

Thibault, Jacques Anatole Francois
1844-1924
See France, Anatole
See also CA 106; 127; MTCW

Thiele, Colin (Milton) 1920- .... **CLC 17**
See also CA 29-32R; CANR 12, 28;
CLR 27; MAICYA; SAAS 2; SATA 14,
72

Thomas, Audrey (Callahan)
1935-.................. **CLC 7, 13, 37**
See also AITN 2; CA 21-24R; CAAS 19;
CANR 36; DLB 60; MTCW

Thomas, D(onald) M(ichael)
1935-.................. **CLC 13, 22, 31**
See also CA 61-64; CAAS 11; CANR 17,
45; CDBLB 1960 to Present; DLB 40;
MTCW

Thomas, Dylan (Marlais)
1914-1953 ... **TCLC 1, 8, 45; DA; PC 2;
SSC 3; WLC**
See also CA 104; 120; CDBLB 1945-1960;
DLB 13, 20, 139; MTCW; SATA 60

Thomas, (Philip) Edward
1878-1917 .... **TCLC 10**
See also CA 106; DLB 19

Thomas, Joyce Carol 1938-........ **CLC 35**
See also AAYA 12; BW 2; CA 113; 116;
CLR 19; DLB 33; JRDA; MAICYA;
MTCW; SAAS 7; SATA 40, 78

Thomas, Lewis 1913-1993 .... **CLC 35**
See also CA 85-88; 143; CANR 38; MTCW

Thomas, Paul
See Mann, (Paul) Thomas

Thomas, Piri 1928-.............. **CLC 17**
See also CA 73-76; HW

Thomas, R(onald) S(tuart)
1913-................. **CLC 6, 13, 48**
See also CA 89-92; CAAS 4; CANR 30;
CDBLB 1960 to Present; DLB 27;
MTCW

Thomas, Ross (Elmore) 1926-...... **CLC 39**
See also CA 33-36R; CANR 22

Thompson, Francis Clegg
See Mencken, H(enry) L(ouis)

Thompson, Francis Joseph
1859-1907 .... **TCLC 4**
See also CA 104; CDBLB 1890-1914;
DLB 19

Thompson, Hunter S(tockton)
1939-................. **CLC 9, 17, 40**
See also BEST 89:1; CA 17-20R; CANR 23,
46, 46; MTCW

Thompson, James Myers
See Thompson, Jim (Myers)

Thompson, Jim (Myers)
1906-1977(?) .... **CLC 69**
See also CA 140

Thompson, Judith .... **CLC 39**

Thomson, James 1700-1748........ **LC 16**

Thomson, James 1834-1882...... **NCLC 18**

Thoreau, Henry David
1817-1862 ...... **NCLC 7, 21; DA; WLC**
See also CDALB 1640-1865; DLB 1

Thornton, Hall
See Silverberg, Robert

Thurber, James (Grover)
1894-1961 ... **CLC 5, 11, 25; DA; SSC 1**
See also CA 73-76; CANR 17, 39;
CDALB 1929-1941; DLB 4, 11, 22, 102;
MAICYA; MTCW; SATA 13

Thurman, Wallace (Henry)
1902-1934 .... **TCLC 6; BLC**
See also BW 1; CA 104; 124; DLB 51

Ticheburn, Cheviot
See Ainsworth, William Harrison

Tieck, (Johann) Ludwig
1773-1853 .... **NCLC 5, 46**
See also DLB 90

Tiger, Derry
See Ellison, Harlan (Jay)

Tilghman, Christopher 1948(?)-..... **CLC 65**

Tillinghast, Richard (Williford)
1940-..................... **CLC 29**
See also CA 29-32R; CANR 26

Timrod, Henry 1828-1867 .... **NCLC 25**
See also DLB 3

Tindall, Gillian 1938-.............. **CLC 7**
See also CA 21-24R; CANR 11

Tiptree, James, Jr. .... **CLC 48, 50**
See also Sheldon, Alice Hastings Bradley
See also DLB 8

Titmarsh, Michael Angelo
See Thackeray, William Makepeace

Tocqueville, Alexis (Charles Henri Maurice Clerel Comte) 1805-1859..... **NCLC 7**

Tolkien, J(ohn) R(onald) R(euel)
1892-1973 ...... **CLC 1, 2, 3, 8, 12, 38; DA; WLC**
See also AAYA 10; AITN 1; CA 17-18;
45-48; CANR 36; CAP 2;
CDBLB 1914-1945; DLB 15; JRDA;
MAICYA; MTCW; SATA 2, 32;
SATA-Obit 24

Toller, Ernst 1893-1939......... **TCLC 10**
See also CA 107; DLB 124

Tolson, M. B.
See Tolson, Melvin B(eaunorus)

Tolson, Melvin B(eaunorus)
1898(?)-1966 .... **CLC 36; BLC**
See also BW 1; CA 124; 89-92; DLB 48, 76

Tolstoi, Aleksei Nikolaevich
See Tolstoy, Alexey Nikolaevich

Tolstoy, Alexey Nikolaevich
1882-1945 .... **TCLC 18**
See also CA 107

Tolstoy, Count Leo
See Tolstoy, Leo (Nikolaevich)

Tolstoy, Leo (Nikolaevich)
1828-1910 ...... **TCLC 4, 11, 17, 28, 44; DA; SSC 9; WLC**
See also CA 104; 123; SATA 26

Tomasi di Lampedusa, Giuseppe 1896-1957
See Lampedusa, Giuseppe (Tomasi) di
See also CA 111

Tomlin, Lily.................... **CLC 17**
See also Tomlin, Mary Jean

Tomlin, Mary Jean 1939(?)-
See Tomlin, Lily
See also CA 117

Tomlinson, (Alfred) Charles
1927-............ **CLC 2, 4, 6, 13, 45**
See also CA 5-8R; CANR 33; DLB 40

Tonson, Jacob
See Bennett, (Enoch) Arnold

Toole, John Kennedy
1937-1969 .... **CLC 19, 64**
See also CA 104; DLBY 81

Toomer, Jean
1894-1967 ...... **CLC 1, 4, 13, 22; BLC; PC 7; SSC 1**
See also BW 1; CA 85-88;
CDALB 1917-1929; DLB 45, 51; MTCW

Torley, Luke
See Blish, James (Benjamin)

Tornimparte, Alessandra
See Ginzburg, Natalia

Torre, Raoul della
See Mencken, H(enry) L(ouis)

Torrey, E(dwin) Fuller 1937-....... **CLC 34**
See also CA 119

Torsvan, Ben Traven
See Traven, B.

Torsvan, Benno Traven
See Traven, B.

Torsvan, Berick Traven
See Traven, B.

Torsvan, Berwick Traven
See Traven, B.

Torsvan, Bruno Traven
See Traven, B.

Torsvan, Traven
See Traven, B.

Tournier, Michel (Edouard)
1924-.................. **CLC 6, 23, 36**
See also CA 49-52; CANR 3, 36; DLB 83;
MTCW; SATA 23

Tournimparte, Alessandra
See Ginzburg, Natalia

Towers, Ivar
See Kornbluth, C(yril) M.

Townsend, Sue 1946-.............. **CLC 61**
See also CA 119; 127; MTCW; SATA 48, 55

Townshend, Peter (Dennis Blandford)
1945-.................... **CLC 17, 42**
See also CA 107

Tozzi, Federigo 1883-1920........ **TCLC 31**

Traill, Catharine Parr
1802-1899 .... **NCLC 31**
See also DLB 99

Trakl, Georg 1887-1914........... **TCLC 5**
See also CA 104

Transtroemer, Tomas (Goesta)
1931-................... **CLC 52, 65**
See also CA 117; 129; CAAS 17

Transtromer, Tomas Gosta
See Transtroemer, Tomas (Goesta)

Traven, B. (?)-1969............. **CLC 8, 11**
See also CA 19-20; 25-28R; CAP 2; DLB 9,
56; MTCW

Treitel, Jonathan 1959-........... **CLC 70**

Tremain, Rose 1943-.............. **CLC 42**
See also CA 97-100; CANR 44; DLB 14

Tremblay, Michel 1942-........... **CLC 29**
See also CA 116; 128; DLB 60; MTCW

Trevanian...................... **CLC 29**
See also Whitaker, Rod(ney)

Trevor, Glen
See Hilton, James

Trevor, William
1928-............ **CLC 7, 9, 14, 25, 71**
See also Cox, William Trevor
See also DLB 14, 139

Trifonov, Yuri (Valentinovich)
1925-1981 .... **CLC 45**
See also CA 126; 103; MTCW

Trilling, Lionel 1905-1975.... **CLC 9, 11, 24**
See also CA 9-12R; 61-64; CANR 10;
DLB 28, 63; MTCW

Trimball, W. H.
See Mencken, H(enry) L(ouis)

Tristan
See Gomez de la Serna, Ramon

Tristram
See Housman, A(lfred) E(dward)

Trogdon, William (Lewis) 1939-
See Heat-Moon, William Least
See also CA 115; 119; CANR 47

Trollope, Anthony
1815-1882 ...... **NCLC 6, 33; DA; WLC**
See also CDBLB 1832-1890; DLB 21, 57;
SATA 22

Trollope, Frances 1779-1863..... **NCLC 30**
See also DLB 21

Trotsky, Leon 1879-1940........ **TCLC 22**
See also CA 118

Trotter (Cockburn), Catharine
1679-1749 .... **LC 8**
See also DLB 84

Trout, Kilgore
See Farmer, Philip Jose

Trow, George W. S. 1943-........ **CLC 52**
See also CA 126

Troyat, Henri 1911-.............. **CLC 23**
See also CA 45-48; CANR 2, 33; MTCW

Trudeau, G(arretson) B(eekman) 1948-
See Trudeau, Garry B.
See also CA 81-84; CANR 31; SATA 35

Trudeau, Garry B................. **CLC 12**
See also Trudeau, G(arretson) B(eekman)
See also AAYA 10; AITN 2

Truffaut, Francois 1932-1984...... **CLC 20**
See also CA 81-84; 113; CANR 34

Trumbo, Dalton 1905-1976 .... **CLC 19**
See also CA 21-24R; 69-72; CANR 10;
DLB 26

Trumbull, John 1750-1831....... **NCLC 30**
See also DLB 31

Trundlett, Helen B.
See Eliot, T(homas) S(tearns)

Tryon, Thomas 1926-1991 .... **CLC 3, 11**
See also AITN 1; CA 29-32R; 135;
CANR 32; MTCW

Tryon, Tom
See Tryon, Thomas

Ts'ao Hsueh-ch'in 1715(?)-1763....... **LC 1**

Tsushima, Shuji 1909-1948
See Dazai, Osamu
See also CA 107

Tsvetaeva (Efron), Marina (Ivanovna)
1892-1941 .... **TCLC 7, 35**
See also CA 104; 128; MTCW

Tuck, Lily 1938-................ **CLC 70**
See also CA 139

Tu Fu 712-770.................... **PC 9**

Tunis, John R(oberts) 1889-1975 ... **CLC 12**
See also CA 61-64; DLB 22; JRDA;
MAICYA; SATA 30, 37

Tuohy, Frank.................... **CLC 37**
See also Tuohy, John Francis
See also DLB 14, 139

Tuohy, John Francis 1925-
See Tuohy, Frank
See also CA 5-8R; CANR 3, 47

Turco, Lewis (Putnam) 1934- ... **CLC 11, 63**
See also CA 13-16R; CANR 24; DLBY 84

Wallace, Irving 1916-1990....... **CLC 7, 13**
See also AITN 1; CA 1-4R; 132; CAAS 1;
CANR 1, 27; MTCW

Wallant, Edward Lewis
1926-1962.................. **CLC 5, 10**
See also CA 1-4R; CANR 22; DLB 2, 28,
143; MTCW

Walpole, Horace 1717-1797......... **LC 2**
See also DLB 39, 104

Walpole, Hugh (Seymour)
1884-1941.................. **TCLC 5**
See also CA 104; DLB 34

Walser, Martin 1927-............. **CLC 27**
See also CA 57-60; CANR 8, 46, 46;
DLB 75, 124

Walser, Robert 1878-1956....... **TCLC 18**
See also CA 118; DLB 66

Walsh, Jill Paton................. **CLC 35**
See also Paton Walsh, Gillian
See also AAYA 11; CLR 2; SAAS 3

Walter, Villiam Christian
See Andersen, Hans Christian

Wambaugh, Joseph (Aloysius, Jr.)
1937-..................... **CLC 3, 18**
See also AITN 1; BEST 89:3; CA 33-36R;
CANR 42; DLB 6; DLBY 83; MTCW

Ward, Arthur Henry Sarsfield 1883-1959
See Rohmer, Sax
See also CA 108

Ward, Douglas Turner 1930-....... **CLC 19**
See also BW 1; CA 81-84; CANR 27;
DLB 7, 38

Ward, Mary Augusta
See Ward, Mrs. Humphry

Ward, Mrs. Humphry
1851-1920.................. **TCLC 55**
See also DLB 18

Ward, Peter
See Faust, Frederick (Schiller)

Warhol, Andy 1928(?)-1987........ **CLC 20**
See also AAYA 12; BEST 89:4; CA 89-92;
121; CANR 34

Warner, Francis (Robert le Plastrier)
1937-..................... **CLC 14**
See also CA 53-56; CANR 11

Warner, Marina 1946-............. **CLC 59**
See also CA 65-68; CANR 21

Warner, Rex (Ernest) 1905-1986.... **CLC 45**
See also CA 89-92; 119; DLB 15

Warner, Susan (Bogert)
1819-1885................. **NCLC 31**
See also DLB 3, 42

Warner, Sylvia (Constance) Ashton
See Ashton-Warner, Sylvia (Constance)

Warner, Sylvia Townsend
1893-1978.................. **CLC 7, 19**
See also CA 61-64; 77-80; CANR 16;
DLB 34, 139; MTCW

Warren, Mercy Otis 1728-1814... **NCLC 13**
See also DLB 31

Warren, Robert Penn
1905-1989.... **CLC 1, 4, 6, 8, 10, 13, 18,
39, 53, 59; DA; SSC 4; WLC**
See also AITN 1; CA 13-16R; 129;
CANR 10, 47; CDALB 1968-1988;
DLB 2, 48; DLBY 80, 89; MTCW;
SATA 46; SATA-Obit 63

Warshofsky, Isaac
See Singer, Isaac Bashevis

Warton, Thomas 1728-1790........ **LC 15**
See also DLB 104, 109

Waruk, Kona
See Harris, (Theodore) Wilson

Warung, Price 1855-1911........ **TCLC 45**

Warwick, Jarvis
See Garner, Hugh

Washington, Alex
See Harris, Mark

Washington, Booker T(aliaferro)
1856-1915............. **TCLC 10; BLC**
See also BW 1; CA 114; 125; SATA 28

Washington, George 1732-1799...... **LC 25**
See also DLB 31

Wassermann, (Karl) Jakob
1873-1934.................. **TCLC 6**
See also CA 104; DLB 66

Wasserstein, Wendy
1950-............. **CLC 32, 59; DC 4**
See also CA 121; 129; CABS 3

Waterhouse, Keith (Spencer)
1929-..................... **CLC 47**
See also CA 5-8R; CANR 38; DLB 13, 15;
MTCW

Waters, Roger 1944-............. **CLC 35**

Watkins, Frances Ellen
See Harper, Frances Ellen Watkins

Watkins, Gerrold
See Malzberg, Barry N(athaniel)

Watkins, Paul 1964-............. **CLC 55**
See also CA 132

Watkins, Vernon Phillips
1906-1967.................. **CLC 43**
See also CA 9-10; 25-28R; CAP 1; DLB 20

Watson, Irving S.
See Mencken, H(enry) L(ouis)

Watson, John H.
See Farmer, Philip Jose

Watson, Richard F.
See Silverberg, Robert

Waugh, Auberon (Alexander) 1939-.. **CLC 7**
See also CA 45-48; CANR 6, 22; DLB 14

Waugh, Evelyn (Arthur St. John)
1903-1966...... **CLC 1, 3, 8, 13, 19, 27,
44; DA; WLC**
See also CA 85-88; 25-28R; CANR 22;
CDBLB 1914-1945; DLB 15; MTCW

Waugh, Harriet 1944- .... **CLC 6**
See also CA 85-88; CANR 22

Ways, C. R.
See Blount, Roy (Alton), Jr.

Waystaff, Simon
See Swift, Jonathan

Webb, (Martha) Beatrice (Potter)
1858-1943.................. **TCLC 22**
See also Potter, Beatrice
See also CA 117

Webb, Charles (Richard) 1939-...... **CLC 7**
See also CA 25-28R

Webb, James H(enry), Jr. 1946-.... **CLC 22**
See also CA 81-84

Webb, Mary (Gladys Meredith)
1881-1927.................. **TCLC 24**
See also CA 123; DLB 34

Webb, Mrs. Sidney
See Webb, (Martha) Beatrice (Potter)

Webb, Phyllis 1927-............. **CLC 18**
See also CA 104; CANR 23; DLB 53

Webb, Sidney (James)
1859-1947.................. **TCLC 22**
See also CA 117

Webber, Andrew Lloyd............. **CLC 21**
See also Lloyd Webber, Andrew

Weber, Lenora Mattingly
1895-1971.................. **CLC 12**
See also CA 19-20; 29-32R; CAP 1;
SATA 2; SATA-Obit 26

Webster, John 1579(?)-1634(?)....... **DC 2**
See also CDBLB Before 1660; DA; DLB 58;
WLC

Webster, Noah 1758-1843....... **NCLC 30**

Wedekind, (Benjamin) Frank(lin)
1864-1918.................. **TCLC 7**
See also CA 104; DLB 118

Weidman, Jerome 1913-............ **CLC 7**
See also AITN 2; CA 1-4R; CANR 1;
DLB 28

Weil, Simone (Adolphine)
1909-1943.................. **TCLC 23**
See also CA 117

Weinstein, Nathan
See West, Nathanael

Weinstein, Nathan von Wallenstein
See West, Nathanael

Weir, Peter (Lindsay) 1944-....... **CLC 20**
See also CA 113; 123

Weiss, Peter (Ulrich)
1916-1982.............. **CLC 3, 15, 51**
See also CA 45-48; 106; CANR 3; DLB 69,
124

Weiss, Theodore (Russell)
1916-................... **CLC 3, 8, 14**
See also CA 9-12R; CAAS 2; CANR 46, 46;
DLB 5

Welch, (Maurice) Denton
1915-1948.................. **TCLC 22**
See also CA 121

Welch, James 1940-......... **CLC 6, 14, 52**
See also CA 85-88; CANR 42; NNAL

Weldon, Fay
1933-........ **CLC 6, 9, 11, 19, 36, 59**
See also CA 21-24R; CANR 16, 46, 46;
CDBLB 1960 to Present; DLB 14;
MTCW

Wellek, Rene 1903- .... **CLC 28**
See also CA 5-8R; CAAS 7; CANR 8;
DLB 63

Literary Criticism Series
Cumulative Topic Index

This index lists all topic entries in Gale's *Classical and Medieval Literature Criticism, Contemporary Literary Criticism, Literature Criticism from 1400 to 1800, Nineteenth-Century Literature Criticism,* and *Twentieth-Century Literary Criticism.*

Topic Index

TCLC Cumulative Nationality Index

Nationality Index

Miro (Ferrer), Gabriel (Francisco Victor) **5**
Ortega y Gasset, Jose **9**
Pereda (y Sanchez de Porrua), Jose Maria de
 16
Perez Galdos, Benito **27**
Salinas (y Serrano), Pedro **17**
Unamuno (y Jugo), Miguel de **2, 9**
Valera y Alcala-Galiano, Juan **10**
Valle-Inclan, Ramon (Maria) del **5**

SWEDISH
Bengtsson, Frans (Gunnar) **48**
Dagerman, Stig (Halvard) **17**
Heidenstam, (Carl Gustaf) Verner von **5**
Lagerloef, Selma (Ottiliana Lovisa) **4, 36**
Soderberg, Hjalmar **39**
Strindberg, (Johan) August **1, 8, 21, 47**

SWISS
Ramuz, Charles-Ferdinand **33**
Rod, Edouard **52**
Saussure, Ferdinand de **49**
Spitteler, Carl (Friedrich Georg) **12**
Walser, Robert **18**

SYRIAN
Gibran, Kahlil **1, 9**

TURKISH
Sait Faik **23**

UKRAINIAN
Aleichem, Sholom **1, 35**
Bialik, Chaim Nachman **25**

URUGUAYAN
Quiroga, Horacio (Sylvestre) **20**
Sanchez, Florencio **37**

WELSH
Davies, W(illiam) H(enry) **5**
Lewis, Alun **3**
Machen, Arthur **4**
Thomas, Dylan (Marlais) **1, 8, 45**

Nationality Index